Yearbook on
International
Communist Affairs
1983

Yearbook on International Communist Affairs

1983

Parties and Revolutionary Movements

EDITOR: Robert Wesson

ASSISTANT EDITOR: Margit N. Grigory

AREA EDITORS

Thomas H. Henriksen	•	Africa and the Middle East
Robert Wesson	•	The Americas
Ramon H. Myers	•	Asia and the Pacific
Milorad M. Drachkovitch	•	Eastern Europe and the Soviet Union
Dennis L. Bark	•	Western Europe

HOOVER INSTITUTION PRESS
Stanford University, Stanford, California

Hoover Press Publication 286

International Standard Book Number 0-8179-7861-5
International Standard Serial Number 0084-4101
Library of Congress Catalog Card Number 67-31024

Manufactured in the United States of America

Contents

ASIA AND THE PACIFIC

EASTERN EUROPE AND THE SOVIET UNION

WESTERN EUROPE

Preface

This seventeenth edition of the *Yearbook on International Communist Affairs* continues generally in the line of its predecessors. There have been some changes of personnel. Margit N. Grigory, who has cooperated in the preparation of the *Yearbook* for several years, has become assistant editor. The area editorship for Asia and the Pacific has been resumed by Ramon H. Myers, who filled this position for the 1980 and previous *Yearbooks*. Profiles were prepared by 74 scholars, some of whom wrote more than one; their names and affiliations appear at the end of the individual essays. John Ziemer, in addition to copy editing the entire volume in a brief period, prepared a subject index to supplement the customary name index, prepared by Margit Grigory. Area curators of the Hoover Institution Library, especially Joseph W. Bingaman, contributed generously to the preparation of the bibliography.

It is the purpose of this *Yearbook* to provide data on the condition, organization, policies, activities, and international relations of communist or Marxist-Leninist parties throughout the world during 1982. It is the policy of the *Yearbook* to cover communist parties and communist-aligned movements as completely as possible. Information is derived primarily from published sources, including local papers and broadcasts as reported by the U.S. Foreign Broadcast Information Service. This edition includes information on seven countries or colonies not covered by the 1982 *Yearbook*; namely, Saudi Arabia, Bahrain, Zimbabwe, Nigeria, Trinidad and Tobago, Guadeloupe, and Martinique. Thus, this edition presents 106 profiles.

The question of inclusion or exclusion of various parties or groups that espouse a quasi Marxist-Leninist ideology but are not officially "communist" is difficult. This difficulty applies to "national liberation" movements and, more important, to ruling parties. In considering the latter, the following aspects have been taken into account: rhetoric, socialization of the economy, party organization, participation in communist meetings and organizations, and adherence to the foreign policy line of the strongest communist state, the Soviet Union. It seems realistic to consider the present governments of Nicaragua and Grenada in the same category as that of Cuba, while Algeria and Libya, despite their radicalism, are evidently less aligned. Mozambique, Angola, and Ethiopia, called "vanguard" states by the Soviet party, seem rather clearly affiliated with the "world communist movement"; Benin and the Congo Republic are somewhat less clear-cut cases and have not been included in the *Yearbook*. However, the identification of the ruling organizations of Nicaragua, Grenada, Angola, Mozambique, and Ethiopia with the communist movement hardly seemed sufficiently firm to justify their inclusion in the Register of Communist Parties.

While the format of the previous editions has been retained with only minor changes, an effort has been made to systematize coverage of individual countries somewhat more than in the past. This is particularly true of the profiles on ruling parties and the well-organized parties of Western Europe, which present basic information in schematic fashion.

Robert Wesson

* * *

The following abbreviations are used for frequently cited publications and news agencies:

CSM	*Christian Science Monitor*
FBIS	*Foreign Broadcast Information Service*
IB	*Information Bulletin* (of the *WMR*)
JPRS	*Joint Publications Research Service*

NYT	*New York Times*
WMR	*World Marxist Review*
WP	*Washington Post*
YICA	*Yearbook on International Communist Affairs*
ACAN	Agencia Centro Americano Noticias
ADN	Allgemeiner Deutscher Nachrichtendienst
AFP	Agence France-Presse
ANSA	Agenzia Nazionale Stampa Associata
AP	Associated Press
BTA	Bulgarska telegrafna agentsiya
ČETEKA	Československá tisková kancelár
DPA	Deutsche Presse Agentur
KPL	Khaosan Pathet Lao
MENA	Middle East News Agency
MIT	Magyar Távirati Iroda
NCNA	New China News Agency
PAP	Polska Agencja Prasowa
UPI	United Press International
VNA	Vietnam News Agency

REGISTER OF
COMMUNIST PARTIES

Register of Communist Parties[1]

Orientation:	B—pro-Beijing M—pro-Moscow	IM—Independent Moderate IR—Independent Radical		**Status:**	* ruling + legal	# unrecognized 0 proscribed

AFRICA AND THE MIDDLE EAST (18)

Party/Date Founded	Mid-1982 Population (est.)	Communist Party Membership	Party Leader	Orient./ Status	Congress (if any)	Percentage of Vote; Seats in Legislature
Algeria Socialist Vanguard Party (PAGS) 1920	20,000,000	400–500 est.	Sadig Hadjeres	M/#	—	—
Bahrain National Liberation Front of Bahrain (NFL/B) 1955	380,000	negligible	Yusuf al-Hassan	M/0	—	—
Egypt Egyptian Communist Party (ECP) 1921	44,740,000	500 est.	—	M/0	—	—
Iran Communist Party of Iran (Tudeh Party) 1941	41,203,000	n.a.	Nureddin Kianuri	M/+	—	3.0 (1980); —
Iraq Iraqi Communist Party (ICP) 1934	14,034,000	2,000 est.	Aziz Muhammad	M/0	—	—
Israel Communist Party of Israel (CPI, "Rakah") 1948	4,000,000 (1,300,000 in occupied terr.)	1,500 est.	Meir Vilner	M/+	—	—

Country / Party (founded)	Population	Party membership	Leader	Status		Last election
Jordan Communist Party of Jordan (CPJ) 1951	3,300,000		Fayig Muhammad	M/0	—	—
Lebanon Lebanese Communist Party (LCP) 1924	3,000,000	under 1,000	George Hawi	M/+	—	—
Morocco Party of Progress and Socialism (PPS) 1943	21,000,000	14–16,000 est.	'Ali Yata	M/+	—	—(1977); 1 of 264
Nigeria Socialist Working People's Party of Nigeria (SWPP) 1978	82,396,000	1,500–4,000 est.	Chiake Anozie	M/#	—	
Réunion Réunion Communist Party (PCR) 1959	500,000	n.a.	Paul Vergès	M/+	—	
Saudi Arabia Communist Party of Saudi Arabia (CPSA) 1975	9,795,000	10,000 claim	Abd-al-Rahim Salih	M/0	—	
Senegal Independence and Labor Party (PIT)	5,991,000	negligible	Seydou Cissoko	M/+	—	
South Africa South African Communist Party (SACP) 1953	30,021,000	n.a.	Yusef Dadoo	M/0	—	
Sudan Sudanese Communist Party (SCP) 1946	19,868,000	n.a.	Muhammad Ibrahim Nugud	M/0	—	
Syria Syrian Communist Party (SCP) 1944	9,423,000	5,000 est.	Khalid Bakhdash	M/+	—	—(1982);—
Tunisia Tunisian Communist Party (PCT) 1920	7,000,000	100 est.	Muhammad Harmel	M/+	—	

Party/Date Founded	Mid-1982 Population (est.)	Communist Party Membership	Party Leader	Orient./ Status	Congress (if any)	Percentage of Vote; Seats in Legislature
Yemen (Aden) Yemen Socialist Party (YSP)	2,022,000	n.a.	Ali Nasir Muhammad al-Hasani	M/*	—	—

THE AMERICAS

Party/Date Founded	Mid-1982 Population (est.)	Communist Party Membership	Party Leader	Orient./ Status	Congress (if any)	Percentage of Vote; Seats in Legislature
Argentina Communist Party of Argentina (CPA) 1918	28,593,000	65,000 est.	Athos Fava	M/+	—	—
Bolivia[2] Communist Party of Bolivia (PCB) 1940	5,633,000	300 est.	Jorge Kolle Cueto	M/+	—	—(1980);—
Brazil[3] Brazilian Communist Party (PCB) 1960	127,734,000	6,000 est.	Giocondo Gervasi Dias	M/#	Seventh 13 Dec.	—(1982);—
Canada Communist Party of Canada (CPC) 1921	24,469,000	2,500 est.	William Kashtan	M/+	Twenty-Fifth 13–15 Feb.	.05(1980);—
Chile[4] Communist Party of Chile (CPC) 1922	11,323,000	20,000 est.	Luís Corvalán	M/0	—	—
Colombia Communist Party of Colombia (PCC) 1930	26,631,000	12,000 est.	Gilberto Vieira	M/+	—	1.2 (1982); 4 of 313

Country / Party (Year)	Population	Party membership	Leader		Congress	Election
Costa Rica[5] Popular Vanguard Party (PVP) 1931	2,396,000	3,500 est.	Manuel Mora Valverde	M/+	—	3.2 (1982); —
Cuba Cuban Communist Party (PCC) 1965	9,771,000	434,143 claim	Fidel Castro	M/*	—	—(1981); all 499
Dominican Republic Dominican Communist Party (PCD)	6,013,000	5,000 est. (combined)	Narciso Isa Conde	M/+	—	7.1 (1982); —
Ecuador Communist Party of Ecuador (PCE)	8,537,000	500 est.	René Mauge	M/+	—	—
El Salvador[6] Popular Revolutionary Bloc (BPR)	4,617,000	60,000 est.	Facundo Guardado y Guardado	M/0	—	—(1982);—
Guadeloupe Guadeloupe Communist Party (PCG)	305,000	3,000 est.	Guy Daninthe	M/+	—	38.6 (1981); 1 of 36
Guatemala Guatemalan Party of Labor (PGT) 1950	7,537,000	750 est.	Carlos González	M/0	—	—
Guyana People's Progressive Party (PPP) 1950	870,000	n.a.	Cheddi Jagan	M/+	Twenty-First 31 July–2 Aug.	20.4 (1980); 10 of 65
Haiti Unified Party of Haitian Communists (PUCH) 1968	6,054,000	350 est.	René Theodore	M/0	—	—
Honduras Honduran Communist Party (PCH) 1927	4,103,000	1,500 est.	Rigoberto Padilla Rush	M/#	—	—(1981);—

Party/Date Founded	Mid-1982 Population (est.)	Communist Party Membership	Party Leader	Orient./ Status	Congress (if any)	Percentage of Vote; Seats in Legislature
Jamaica[7] Workers' Party of Jamaica (WPJ) 1978	2,295,000	n.a.	Trevor Munroe	M/+	—	—
Martinique Martinique Communist Party (PCM) 1957	302,000	1,000 est.	Armand Nicolas	M/+	—	6.4 (1981); —
Mexico[8] United Socialist Party of Mexico (PSUM) 1919	71,330,000	201,000 claim 121,000 est.	Pablo Gómez	IM/+	—	5.8 (1982); 17 of 400
Nicaragua[9] Nicaraguan Socialist Party (PSN) 1937	2,643,000	250 est.	Luís Sánchez	M/+	—	—
Panama People's Party of Panama (PPP) 1930	2,011,000	5-600 est.	Rubén Darío Souza	M/+	—	— (1978); —
Paraguay Paraguayan Communist Party (PCP) 1928	3,347,000	3,500 est.	Antonio Maidana (if alive)	M/0	—	—
Peru Communist Party of Peru (PCP-U)	18,631,000	10,000 claim	Jorge del Prado	M/+	Eighth 27–31 Jan.	2.8 (1980); 2 of 60
Puerto Rico[10] Puerto Rican Socialist Party (PSP)	3,187,566	150 est.	Juan Marí Bras	M/+	—	0.3 (1980); —

Country / Party	Population	Membership	Leader	Status	Congress	Election
Suriname	400,000					
Communist Party of Suriname (CPS) 1981		50 est.	Bram Mehr	IR/+	—	—
Trinidad & Tobago	1,203,000					
People's Popular Movement (PPM) 1981		100 est.	Michael Als	M/+	—	—
United States	232,195,000					
Communist Party, USA (CPUSA) 1919		20,000 claim	Gus Hall	M/+	—	—(1980); —
Uruguay	2,961,000					
Uruguayan Communist Party (PCU)		5–10,000 est.	Rodney Arismendi	M/0	—	—(1971);-
Venezuela	18,427,000					
Venezuelan Communist Party (PCV) 1931		3–5,000 est.	Radamés Larrazábal	M/+	—	—(1982); —

ASIA AND THE PACIFIC (21)

Country / Party	Population	Membership	Leader	Status	Congress	Election
Afghanistan	12,500,000					
People's Democratic Party of Afghanistan (PDPA) 1965		11,000 est. 80,000 claim	Babrak Karmal	M/*	—	—
Australia	15,001,000					
Communist Party of Australia (CPA) 1920		2,000 est.	Judy Mundey		Twenty-Seventh 12–14 June	—(1980); —
Socialist Party of Australia (SPA) 1971		1,500 est.	Pat Clancy	M/+	—	—(1980); —
Bangladesh	93,040,000					
Communist Party of Bangladesh (CPB)		2,500 est.	Mohammed Farhad	M/0	—	—
Burma	36,166,000					
Burmese Communist Party (BCP) 1939		3,000 claim	Thakin Ba Thein Tin	B/0	—	—

Party/Date Founded	Mid-1982 Population (est.)	Communist Party Membership	Party Leader	Orient./ Status	Congress (if any)	Percentage of Vote; Seats in Legislature
China	1,008,175,000					
Chinese Communist Party (CCP)1921		39,000,000 claim	Hu Yaobang	B/*	Twelfth 1–7 September	—
India	723,762,000					
Communist Party of India (CPI)		585,000 claim	Rajeswara Rao	M/+	Twelfth 21–28 March	2.6 (1980); 12 of 544
Communist Party Marxist (CPM) 1964		270,000 claim	E.M.S. Namboodiripad	IM/+	Eleventh 26–31 Jan.	6.2 (1980); 37 of 544
Indonesia	157,595,000					
Indonesian Communist Party (PKI)		under 400 est.	Jusuf Adjitorop	B/0	—	—(1982);—
Japan	118,600,000					
Japan Communist Party (JCP) 1922		400,000 est.	Tetsuzo Fuwa	IM/+	Sixteenth 27–31 July	10.4 (1980); 29 of 511
Kampuchea	5,900,000					
People's Revolutionary Party (KPRP) 1951		n.a.	Heng Samrin	M/*	—	99.0 (1981); all 117
Democratic Kampuchea (DK)		n.a.	Pol Pot	B/0	—	—
Korea (North)	18,500,000					
Korean Workers' Party (KWP) 1949		3,000,000 claim	Kim Il-song	IR/*	—	100 (1982); all 615
Laos	3,800,000					
Lao People's Revolutionary Party (LPRP) 1945		35,000 claim	Kaysone Phomvihan	M/*	Third 27–30 April	—

Country / Party	Population	Membership	Leader	Status	Vote % (year); seats
Malaysia					
Communist Party of Malaya (CPM)	14,661,000 (1,421,000 in Sarawak)	3,000 est.	—	B/0	—
North Kalimantan Communist Party (NKCP)		under 200 in Sarawak	—	B/0	—
Mongolia	1,759,000				
Mongolian People's Revolutionary Party (MPRP) 1921		76,240 claim	Yumjaagyin Tsedenbal	M/*	99.0 (1977); all 354
Nepal					
Communist Party of Nepal-pro Beijing (CPN-B) 1949	15,020,000	4,000 est.	Man Mohan Adhikari	B/0	—
New Zealand	3,120,000				
Communist Party of New Zealand (CPNZ) 1921		under 100 est.	—	IM/+	—
Socialist Unity Party (SUP) 1965		300 est.	Gordon Harold "Bill" Andersen	M/+	—
Pakistan[11]					
Communist Party of Pakistan (CPP)	93,106,000	under 200 est.	Azaz Nasir	M/0	—
Philippines	51,574,000				
Communist Party of the Philippines, Marxist-Leninist (CPP-ML) 1968		5,000 est.	Rodolfo Salazar	B/0	—
Philippine Communist Party (PKP)		200 est.	F. Macapagal	M/0	—
Singapore	2,472,000				
Communist Party of Malaya, branch (CPM) 1930		200 est.	—	B/0	—
Sri Lanka	15,000,000				
Communist Party of Sri Lanka (CPSL) 1943		5,000 est.	Kattorge P. Silva	M/+	1.9 (1977); 1 of 168

Party/Date Founded	Mid-1982 Population (est.)	Communist Party Membership	Party Leader	Orient./ Status	Congress (if any)	Percentage of Vote; Seats in Legislature
Thailand Communist Party of Thailand (CPT) 1942	49,823,000	1,200 est.	Pracha Tanyapaibul[12]	B/0	Fourth March/April	—
Vietnam Vietnamese Communist Party (VCP) 1930	52,000,000	1,727,784 claim	Le Duan	M/*	Fifth 27–31 March	97.9 (1981); all 538

EASTERN EUROPE AND THE SOVIET UNION (9)

Party/Date Founded	Mid-1982 Population (est.)	Communist Party Membership	Party Leader	Orient./ Status	Congress (if any)	Percentage of Vote; Seats in Legislature
Albania Albanian Party of Labor (APL) 1941	2,752,300	146,363 claim	Enver Hoxha	IR/*	—	99.9 (1979); all 250 Democratic Front
Bulgaria Bulgarian Communist Party (BCP) 1903	8,903,000	825,876 claim	Todor Zhivkov	M/*	—	99.99 (1981); all 400 Fatherland Front
Czechoslovakia Communist Party of Czechoslovakia (KSČ) 1921	15,345,000	1,584,011 claim	Gustáv Husák	M/*	—	99.0 (1981); all 350 National Front
Germany: German Democratic Republic Socialist Unity Party (SED) 1946	16,700,000	2,202,277 claim	Erich Honecker	M/*	—	99.9 (1981); all 500 National Front
Hungary Hungarian Socialist Workers' Party (HSWP) 1918	10,700,000	811,833 claim	János Kádár	M/*	—	99.3 (1980); all 352 Patriotic People's Front

Country / Party	Population	Membership	Leader		Congress	Election / Vote
Poland Polish United Workers' Party (PUWP) 1948	36,200,000	2,488,000 claim	Wojciech Jaruzelski	M/*	—	99.5 (1980); all 460 National Unity Front
Romania Romanian Communist Party (PCR) 1921	22,550,000	3,150,000 claim	Nicolae Ceauşescu	M/*	—	98.5 (1980); all 369 Front of Socialist Democracy and Unity
USSR Communist Party of the Soviet Union (CPSU) 1898	269,000,000	17,800,000 claim	Yuri Andropov	M/*	—	99.9 (1979); all 1500 CPSU approved
Yugoslavia League of Communists of Yugoslavia (LCY) 1920	22,500,000	2,200,000 claim	Mitja Ribičič	1M/*	Twelfth 26–29 June	— (1978); all 308 Socialist Alliance

WESTERN EUROPE (23)

Country / Party	Population	Membership	Leader		Congress	Election / Vote
Austria Communist Party of Austria (KPO) 1918	7,555,000	15,000 est.	Franz Muhri	M/+	Extraordinary 30 January	0.96 (1979); —
Belgium Belgian Communist Party (PCB:KPB) 1921	9,920,000	14,000 est.	Louis van Geyt	1M/+	Twenty-Fourth 26–28 March	2.13 (1981); 2 of 212
Cyprus Progressive Party of the Working People (AKEL)[13] 1922	642,000	12,000 est.	Ezekias Papaioannou	M/+	Fifteenth 13-15 May	32.8 (1981); 12 of 35
Denmark Communist Party of Denmark (DKP) 1919	5,118,000	10,900 claim 7,000 est.	Jorgen Jensen	M/+	—	1.1 (1981); —

Party/Date Founded	Mid-1982 Population (est.)	Communist Party Membership	Party Leader	Orient./ Status	Congress (if any)	Percentage of Vote; Seats in Legislature
Finland Finnish Communist Party (SKP) 1918	4,800,000	50,000 claim	Jouko Kajanoja	M/ +	Extraordinary May 14–15	17.9 (1979); 35 of 200 People's Democratic League
France French Communist Party (PCF) 1920	54,200,000	710,000 claim	Georges Marchais	M/ +	Twenty-Fourth 3–7 February	16.2 (1981); 44 of 491
Germany: Federal Republic of German Communist Party (DKP) 1968	61,560,000	48,856 claim	Herbert Mies	M/ +	—	0.2 (1980); —
Great Britain Communist Party of Great Britain (CPGB) 1920	56,000,000	18,500 est.	Gordon McLennan	M/ +	—	0.5 (1979); —
Greece Communist Party of Greece (KKE) 1921	9,740,000	73,000 claim	Kharilaos Florakis	M/ +	Eleventh 15–18 Dec.	10.9 (1981); 13 of 300
Iceland People's Alliance (AB) 1968	229,000	2,200 est.	Svavar Gestsson	IM/ +	—	19.7 (1979); 11 of 60
Ireland Communist Party of Ireland (CPI) 1921	3,500,000	500 est.	Andrew Barr	M/ +	Eighteenth 14–16 May	— (1982); —

Country / Party	Population	Party Membership	Leader	Status	Congress	Election
Italy						
Italian Communist Party (CPI) 1921	57,353,000	1,720,000 claim	Enrico Berlinguer	IM/+	—	30.4 (1979); 201 of 630
Luxembourg						
Communist Party of Luxembourg (CPL) 1921	365,000	600 est.	René Urbany	M/+	—	5.0 (1979); 2 of 59
Malta						
Communist Party of Malta (CPM) 1969	330,262	150 est.	Anthony Baldacchino	M/+	—	— (1981); —
Netherlands						
Communist Party of the Netherlands (CPN) 1909	14,349,000	15,000 est.	Elli Izeboud	IM/+	Twenty-Eighth 26–28 Nov.	1.79 (1982); 3 of 150
Norway						
Norwegian Communist Party (NKP) 1923	4,100,000	500 est.	Hans I. Kleven	M/+	—	0.3 (1981); —
Workers' Communist Party (AKP) 1973		under 1,000 est.	Paal Steigan	B/+	—	0.7 (1981); —
Portugal						
Portuguese Communist Party (PCP) 1921	9,964,000	187,000 claim	Alvaro Cunhal	M/+	—	16.7 (1980); 41 of 250
San Marino						
Communist Party of San Marino (PCS) 1941	22,000	300 est.	Ermenegildo Gasperoni	IM/+	—	25.0 (1978); 16 of 60
Spain						
Spanish Communist Party (PCE) 1920	39,000,000	less than 100,000 est.	Gerardo Iglesias	IM/+	—	3.8 (1982); 4 of 350
Sweden						
Party of the Left—Communists (VPK) 1921	8,323,000	17,800	Lars Werner	IM/+	—	5.6 (1982); 20 of 349
Switzerland						
Swiss Labor Party (PdA) 1921	6,343,000	5,000 est.	Armand Magnin	M/+	—	1.5 (1979); 3 of 200

Party/Date Founded	Mid-1982 Population (est.)	Communist Party Membership	Party Leader	Orient./ Status	Congress (if any)	Percentage of Vote; Seats in Legislature
Turkey	48,105,000					
Communist Party of Turkey (TKP) 1920		negligible	Ismail Bilen	M/0	—	—
West Berlin	1,900,000					
Socialist Unity Party of West Berlin (SEW)[14] 1949		7,000 est.	Horst Schmitt	M/+	—	0.7 (1981): —

1. In the large majority of the countries not ruled by communist parties, there are two or more competing Marxist-Leninist communist parties. The Register includes only the party deemed the strongest regardless of affiliation, except for a few cases, such as India, where two important rival parties are listed. In some cases, footnotes refer to secondary communist parties.

2. A radical party under the leadership of Oscar Zamora is also active.

3. The Maoist Communist Party of Brazil (PCdoB) also has some importance.

4. The radical Movement of the Revolutionary Left (MIR), may have more adherents but is hardly organized as communist party.

5. The Communist Party of Costa Rica took the name of Popular Vanguard in 1943.

6. The Communist Party of El Salvador, headed by Shafik Handal, has a relatively small following.

7. The Jamaican Communist Party, also pro-Soviet, is less important.

8. The Communist Party of Mexico, originally founded in 1919, joined in a coalition with several leftist splinters to form the United Socialist Party.

9. The effective quasi-communist party of Nicaragua is the Sandinista National Liberal Front (FSLN).

10. The Puerto Rican Communist Party (PCP), also pro-Soviet, is somewhat smaller.

11. Now part of the National Progressive Party (NPP).

12. Possibly a nom de guerre for Thong Chaemsi.

13. AKEL descended from the Communist Party of Cyprus (KKK), founded in 1922.

14. The SEW is considered a subsidiary of the ruling movement in East Germany.

Introduction
The Communist World, 1982

The communist movement in the world gradually seems to be becoming more ambiguous and amorphous. As may be observed from the Register of Communist Parties, many parties, even those closely affiliated with the Soviet Union, use a designation other than "communist," the appellation that Lenin considered important for his party and the member-parties of the Comintern. In many countries the chief pro-Soviet party calls itself a "socialist" or a "workers' party," while the party or parties bearing the name of "communist" are independent or anti-Soviet.

Lenin attached great importance to the Third International, or Comintern, which regarded itself as the future government of the world and the visible manifestation of proletarian unity. Now the only consequential world communist political organization is the directorate of the magazine *Problems of Peace and Socialism*, or as published in English, *World Marxist Review*, headquartered in Prague. Since 1960, it has been impossible to assemble a world communist conclave, and the Soviet party seems long since to have given up trying. Even international front organizations prosper only by pretending, in the manner of the World Peace Council, to have nothing to do with world revolution.

Doctrinal unity has also vanished. Communist leaders in Western Europe and the Third World routinely denounce Soviet actions, such as repression in Afghanistan or Poland. In a large majority of non-communist-ruled countries, there are rival parties claiming to represent the workers and to stand for true Marxism-Leninism; in many countries there are several such, one looking for guidance to the Soviet Union, others to China, Albania, the memories of Trotsky's Fourth International, or other sources of socialistic or anti-Western inspiration. An odd example is the relatively successful Peruvian terrorist organization known as the Shining Path, said to mix Marxism with nostalgia for the Incas. When communist parties attach "M-L" (Marxist-Leninist) to their names, as they do in dozens of countries, this signifies rejection of the Soviet Union as insufficiently revolutionary.

The Marxist-Leninist thinking that still unites these various parties even as they quarrel among themselves is more an attitude than a doctrine. Very little is said anywhere outside the Soviet sphere about the "dictatorship of the proletariat." Even within the sphere of Soviet domination, there are marked differences of policy and temper, as between Hungary and Bulgaria. The Soviet Union has much leverage only where it has a military presence: if it attempts to compel strong parties to acknowledge its leadership, they usually rebel; if it allows parties to follow their own inclinations, they diverge endlessly. Little is heard of "proletarian internationalism," the code phrase for Soviet hegemony.

Yet there remains sufficient unity to justify treating the movement as a reality. The Soviet Union continues to pretend that world communism is powerful and basically unified, and Andropov has followed his predecessors in stressing the importance of its unity. The Soviet state maintains a certain leadership, as was demonstrated when high-ranking Communists from all around the world (Albania excepted) came to Brezhnev's funeral. Significantly, party figures were favored over mere state personalities; U.S. party secretary Gus Hall outranked Vice-President Bush, at least to the extent of being received first by Andropov. There are many visits and delegations from "fraternal parties" to the Mecca of world communism, and congresses of both ruling and nonruling parties are dignified by the presence of guests representing as many approved parties as possible. There is also regional travel and communication. Numerous Latin American party leaders, for example, go to Cuba for guidance or assistance. From time to time, moreover, parties affirm their community by conferences, such as the gathering of ten Arab communist parties in April 1982.

Communist parties around the world communicate easily, using much the same vocabulary. They also ordinarily have roughly the same structure, with a general or first secretary, a small executive committee commonly called a "politburo," and a larger coordinating central committee. At the inception of the communist movement, shortly after the Russian Revolution, leftists were inspired to subordinate themselves to Lenin's organization by the image of the new society of social justice. This has long since faded; but they remain attached by the image of power and the assistance that a great power can give its friends. Under former police chief Andropov, perhaps even more than under party boss Brezhnev, the Soviet Union has become a model not of revolutionary change but of modernized authoritarianism, a strongly governed and disciplined society. Lenin is still an icon for all the parties, even those of China and Albania, not because he stood for the masses but because he taught how to organize a communist party to grasp and wield power.

The essential unity of the Marxist-Leninist movement is not pro-Sovietism but anti-Westernism, especially anti-Americanism. Various radical parties may fight against one another and criticize the Soviet or other leading parties, but almost all dislike the United States most of all. They may have little concern for what Marx actually theorized about the factory proletariat, and the "dictatorship of the proletariat" is an outmoded slogan, but they agree on anticapitalism, dislike for the "bourgeoisie," and the "world capitalist system." They stand above all for "anti-imperialism," which in practice is almost equivalent to anti-Americanism.

In contrast to the 1920s, world communism now rests not on admiration for the Soviet Union and its policies but on dislike for the economic and to some extent political domination of the Western powers, especially the United States. In Western Europe, the chief attraction of the communist movement is the fear of nuclear war and distrust of U.S. strategic policy, emotions that draw many noncommunists to the side of the few Moscow-faithful. In the Near East, the chief attraction is resentment against Israel and its principal protector. In southern Africa, the main issue for communism is the alleged association of the United States with South African apartheid. In Central America it is the support, present and past, of the United States for conservative military-dominated regimes. Throughout the Third World, Marxist-Leninists (and many others) are convinced that capitalists manipulate world markets to lower prices of their raw material exports and raise costs to them of importing manufactures, technology, and capital. Multinational corporations, the largest sector of which are based in the United States, are the chief villains in the communist world view, along with the CIA that should serve them; and communism sometimes seems, or presents itself, as little more than extreme nationalism.

World communism is the spearhead of the resentment of those who feel more or less deprived or pushed around by the advanced industrial world, a drive sharpened and mounted but not made or controlled by the Soviet Union. As such, it prospers to a considerable extent with the failures and misfortunes of the Western world, especially the United States. The past year has not been a good one for the Western sphere, with the severest recession since the 1930s bringing grievous debt, financial, and trade problems. Although the Soviet sphere also had a poor economic year, the balance was against the West, and accordingly one might expect that the Marxist-Leninist cause prospered in 1982. Rather remarkably, it has hardly done so.

The outstanding event of the year, however, was probably the replacement of Leonid Brezhnev by Yuri Andropov as head of the Soviet state. It soon became apparent that Andropov, as might be expected of the longtime chief of the KGB, promised more discipline at home and a dynamic foreign policy. It was to be assumed that he would put his mark, probably more decisively than Brezhnev, on the Soviet sphere in Eastern Europe and the Soviet-led movement around the world. The accession to the throne of Lenin by the chief of the semimilitary police represented, however, another step away from the original meaning of the Russian Revolution.

Another potentially important development was the cooling of relations between the United States and China and the reopening of dialogue, although not yet friendship, between the two giants of communism. Their rapprochement was hindered, however, by the ongoing conflicts in Afghanistan and Kampuchea, both of which seriously damaged the communist position in Asia.

In the Middle East, communist prestige suffered from the defeat of the Palestine Liberation Organization in Lebanon, the apparent inferiority of Soviet arms used by Syria, and the inability of the Soviet Union to play a significant role in the entire crisis or to influence moves toward Israeli-Arab negotiations. In sub-Saharan

Africa, concurrently, Soviet influence appeared weakened chiefly by inability to fill material needs, and various Marxist-Leninist-oriented states turned to the West in compensation.

In the Americas, political and economic problems made opportunities for radicals of all brands, but the Communists in most countries continued to be a minor political force, awaiting worse times. In Bolivia, however, they emerged to play an important part in the redemocratized state. In El Salvador, communist-led guerrillas strengthened their hold on large parts of the countryside. The dictator of Suriname turned to Castro for help in holding power and apparently added one to the trio of Marxist or quasi-Marxist states in the Caribbean area. An offsetting reversal for the Marxist-Leninists was the apparent success of the Rios Montt government of Guatemala in reducing the long-standing insurgency.

Hoover Institution   Robert Wesson

AFRICA AND THE MIDDLE EAST

Introduction

A troika of conflicts in the Middle East has continued to keep the region high on the Soviet Union's priority list of foreign policy concerns. The deep troubles in southern Lebanon, Afghanistan, and Iran earlier seemed to offer ample opportunity for replacing Western influence or filling a political vacuum, but 1982 appeared to represent a diminution of these prospects. Seen from the current vantage point, the ongoing battle between Arab and Israeli, especially in the lower third of Lebanon, at the beginning of 1982 portended a continuation of a leverage point for Soviet designs. In February, it was reported that the Soviet Union had recently supplied the Palestine Liberation Organization (PLO) with $50 million worth of sophisticated weapons, including surface-to-air missiles, rapid detection radar, and heavy artillery (Kuwaiti News Agency, *FBIS*, 6 February). A month earlier at a banquet in Lebanon with the International Relations Committee of the Communist Party of the Soviet Union, Yassir Arafat, head of the PLO, stated "that our relations with the Soviet Union are strategic and reflect that we are in the same trench" (Voice of Palestine, 27 January; *FBIS*, 28 January). Moscow additionally supplied more Soviet military hardware to Syria under an agreement signed in March (Voice of Lebanon, 10 March; *FBIS*, 11 March). The Syrian Communist Party's Central Committee, moreover, praised the government's "steadfast stand in the face of the U.S. imperialist, Zionist and reactionary plots" (Damascus domestic service, 11 March; *FBIS*, 12 March).

Despite appearances, Soviet gains were not secure, for at nearly the same time some one hundred Russian military experts repatriated their families from Syria because of threats from the Muslim Brotherhood (Voice of Lebanon, 25 January; *FBIS*, 26 February). Yet an undermining, at least temporarily, of Soviet fortunes in the eastern Mediterranean crescent came not from a fundamentalist Islamic organization but from the blitzkrieg Israeli invasion of Lebanon during the summer. Israel's attack not only destroyed or captured huge amounts of Moscow's armaments given to Syria and the Palestinians but also cast doubt on the weaponry's quality, which contributed to a certain loss of prestige in the region (Karen Dawisha, "The U.S.S.R. in the Middle East: Superpower in Eclipse?" *Foreign Affairs*, 61, no. 2, p. 39). In the wake of the Israeli onslaught, Moscow resumed and stepped up its military assistance to Syria so as to replace the equipment lost in Lebanon's Bekaa Valley (Radio Free Lebanon, 19 November; *FBIS*, 22 November). But Moscow refrained from mentioning support from Syria or from citing the Syrian-Soviet treaty of friendship and cooperation signed in 1980.

To the east in Iran, the relationship between the revolutionary regime of Ayatollah Ruhollah Khomeini and Moscow cooled. In spite of its anti-Western credentials, the ayatollah's militant theocracy manifested antagonistic policies toward the Soviet Union. For example, there were Iranian demonstrations at the Soviet Embassy in Tehran, a steady propaganda blast directed at its northern neighbor (as well as material support for the Afghan rebel resistance to the Soviet occupation), an unwillingness to increase economic ties, and a ruthless liquidation of hundreds of leftist opponents such as the Mojahedin-e Khalq and socialists. Even the Iranian communist party, the Tudeh, which survived other purges, was subject to increasingly restrictive measures. The Tehran regime's efforts to export its brand of revolution to the Persian Gulf states is perceived by some analysts as running counter to Soviet policy by inviting a further U.S. presence in the region (Youssef M. Ibrahim, "Soviet-Iranian Relationship Cooling," *WSJ*, 19 July).

While the Iran-Iraq war dragged on (with the new dimension of Iran's invasion into the territory of its foe in July), the Iraqi Communist Party announced "courageous attacks against the institutions and mercenaries of the fascist regime" (Voice of Iraqi People, 1 September; *FBIS*, 2 September). Its Central Military Bureau issued a communiqué describing the use of booby traps and mines as new methods to escalate operations and diversify targets and objectives.

Elsewhere in the Middle East, the Palestinian Communist Party (PCP) was founded in February. This party brought together members of the Communist Party of Jordan from the West Bank, Gaza, and areas beyond the borders of Jordan as well as members of the Palestinian Communist Organization in Lebanon (*WMR*, April). This new party regarded the PLO as the sole and exclusive representative of the Palestinian people. The announcement on the formation of the PCP noted that the decision was taken "in view of the expansion of the international recognition of the demand for the establishment of the independent Palestinian state" (*al-Hamishmar*, Tel Aviv, 14 February; *FBIS*, 17 February). For its part, the PLO cooperated with Latin American revolutionaries. Regarding this assistance, Arafat stated that the PLO's policy is "to cooperate with all our strength with the Sandinist revolution as well as with the Salvadoran revolutionaries in their struggle against Napoleon Duarte's dictatorship" (EFE, Madrid, 8 February; *FBIS*, 9 February).

In early April, there was a meeting of representatives of communist and workers' parties of Arab countries, including the National Liberation Front of Bahrain and the communist parties of Jordan, Tunisia, Algeria, Saudi Arabia, the Sudan, Syria, Palestine, Lebanon, and Egypt. They adopted a statement condemning Israel and the United States for occupying the West Bank, the Gaza Strip, and the Golan Heights and criticizing the Israeli dissolution of municipal councils in Nablus, El Bir, and Ramallah and the reclosing of Bir-Zeit University. The statement called on "the Arab peoples, upon their progressive patriotic forces to strengthen solidarity with our brothers and sisters in the occupied territories and step up the struggle against the interests and influence of U.S. imperialism in the region." (*IB*, June.)

The same parties, except the Tunisian, Algerian, and Sudanese groups, met in Damascus in late May. The statement produced was similar in tone to the previous one, except that the delegates widened their condemnation of the United States and its allies beyond the Palestinian issue to include "crimes against progressive Arab regimes." It went on to declare that "the USA encourages the crimes of the Moslem Brotherhood in Syria, launches armed provocations against Libya, puts pressure on Algeria, and carries on subversive activity against democratic Yemen" (ibid., July). This pronouncement also mentioned the paramount importance of a solid alliance with the USSR.

To the south, on the Horn of Africa, the regional conflicts sputtered on into 1982. Neither Soviet arms and advisers nor Cuban troops could extinguish the smoldering Eritrean struggle for secession from Ethiopia, an ally of the Eastern bloc. The fortunes of the two Eritrean movements declined greatly this year, but the Eritrean rebels were still capable of inflicting casualties on their opponents. According to one report, some 70 Soviet and Cuban experts together with 60 Ethiopian officers were killed when Eritrean forces shot down a plane on its way to a military base in Asmara (Cairo domestic service, 9 February; *FBIS*, 10 February). Despite urgings from Moscow, the Commission to Organize the Party of the Working People of Ethiopia, the ruling movement, made little progress in its efforts to form a vanguard political party with cells in the countryside. Ethiopia, however, still remains aligned with Moscow.

Opponents of Libyan leader Moammar Khadafy formed a Somalia-based movement, the Organization for the Liberation of Libya, which called for "a just and democratic government in Libya" (Sudanese News Agency, Khartoum, 22 April; *FBIS*, 23 April). Libya itself served as headquarters for the Sudanese Socialist Popular Front, which called on the Sudanese armed forces "to consolidate themselves with the popular masses in one front, with the aim of destroying the regime of" President Jafar Numayri (Jamahiriya News Agency, 7 January; *FBIS*, 8 January). Further to the west and along the Atlantic seaboard of northwest Africa, the war for control over the Western Sahara (formerly Spanish Sahara) persisted between Morocco and the Polisario (Popular Front for the Liberation of Saguia el-Hamra and Rio de Oro). Backed by Algeria, the Polisario kept up its harassing tactics to gain a hold over the arid land. It declared a Saharan Arab Democratic Republic, which has been recognized by some fifty countries.

Down the east African coast, the People's Republic of Mozambique experienced another year of economic troubles and a spreading antigovernment insurgency. These concerns prompted the government to pass out arms to the rural population in certain areas and to continue to search for financial aid and investment from the West while maintaining its Marxist-Leninist orientation and its prominent alliances with the Warsaw Pact countries. Across the Mozambique Channel on the island of Madagascar, the leader of the left-wing Monima-Kamivombio Nationalist Party, Monja Jaona, charged that the November presidential elections had been rigged to ensure the re-election of President Didier Ratsiraka, who won with 80 percent of the vote (*NYT*, 15 December). Leftists fared much better on Mauritius by winning all 60 directly elected seats in June. Aneerood Jugnauth, chairman of the Mauritian Militant Movement, replaced the incumbent, Seewoosagur Ramgoolam, as prime minister when the Labor Party went down to defeat after holding power since 1968.

The state of Zimbabwe continued to experience bloody squabbles between the ruling Zimbabwe African National Union and the opposition Zimbabwe African People's Union. Prime Minister Robert Mugabe's goal of moving toward a one-party state accounts for some of the violence in this ethnically divided land (BBC, London, 1 March; *FBIS*, 3 March). At a May Day rally in Harare, Mugabe set forth ten tasks to be accomplished to create a socialist society. These included the participation of workers in lawful unions and the support of workers for the government's policies. (Harare domestic service, 1 May; *FBIS*, 4 May.)

In nearby Lesotho, tranquility was punctuated occasionally by attacks on police posts and military barracks by the Lesotho Liberation Army, the military branch of the external faction of Ntsu Mokhele's Basutoland Congress Party (AFP, Paris, 25 March; *FBIS*, 25 March). The Communist Party of Lesotho marked its twentieth anniversary with an article written by Jacob Mosoto and published in *Pravda*. Mosoto wrote that the party "is still working under cover" and that "enemy number one of the Basuto people still is the racist regime of the Republic of South Africa" (Tass, 4 May; *FBIS*, 10 May).

South Africa, which surrounds the enclave of Lesotho, saw an increase in sabotage raids from the African National Congress, which is closely associated with the Communist Party of South Africa, the oldest party on the continent. Many of the raids on its eastern flank were staged originally from Zimbabwe and Mozambique. On the western side of the republic, attention remained concentrated on the continuing antiguerrilla campaign being waged for Namibia by South African forces. As part of its counterinsurgency effort, Pretoria mounted several attacks into southern Angola to disrupt the preparations of the leftist-oriented South-West African People's Organization (SWAPO), which is contesting South Africa's control of Namibia.

Reports surfaced in Western newspapers that Marxist Angola purged nationalist leaders because they favored the removal of Cuban troops—a South African precondition for its withdrawal from Namibia—to facilitate a settlement of the conflict in Angola's southern neighbor. According to these stories, the dismissal of officials was followed by the installation of Marxists loyal to the Moscow line ("Angola Quietly Purges Its 'Nationalist' Leaders," *Guardian*, London, 16 July).

In other developments, the Central Committee of the ruling Congolese Labor Party in the People's Republic of the Congo decided to postpone the "elections for the renewal of the people's power" until 1984 (AFP, Paris, 2 September; *FBIS*, 3 September). The thin veneer of actual socialism implemented in the Congo has led French journalists to label the Congolese leadership "Marxist-capitalist" (Leon Dash, "Socialist Congo Prospers Through Mix of Capitalism and Oil," *WP*, 20 June).

Ghana's coup on 31 December 1981 continued to draw attention. Flight Lieutenant Jerry Rawlings ousted freely elected President Hilla Limann, instituted a draconian campaign against corruption, and turned to Libya for aid and inspiration (*NYT*, 7 January). The ruling Provisional National Defense Council (PNDC) also turned to the Soviet bloc for economic development while not closing its doors to the West. One member of the PNDC stated that "the socialist countries are the true friends of Africa" (Accra domestic service, 3 April; *FBIS*, 7 April). In October, the PNDC announced the launching of "the second phase of the revolution" and the formation of Workers' and People's Defense Committees because "counterrevolutionaries have increased their activities" (Accra domestic service, 6 October; *FBIS*, 7 October).

In Benin, Pope John Paul, while on a tour of various countries on the continent, heard a polemical speech delivered by the president, Mathieu Kerekou. The Beninese leader extolled the perfection of his Marxist regime and denounced "foreign domination" of Africa (Don A. Schanche, "Pope Gets Marxist

Lecture on Visit to Benin," *Los Angeles Times*, 18 February). Later in the year, the Central Committee of the People's Revolutionary Party of Benin ordered a restructuring of state bodies to reduce their number from fifteen to four to improve efficiency (AFP, Paris, 24 April; *FBIS*, 27 April).

Elsewhere in West Africa, the People's Revolutionary Republic of Guinea continued its flirtation with capitalism. After 24 years of Marxist-styled totalitarian government, Guinea's economy is a virtual shambles. Long a close ally of the Soviet Union's in Africa, President Ahmed Sékou Touré insisted this year that a World Bank-backed contract for operating an ambitious new billion-dollar iron ore complex be awarded to a U.S. steel company because of its superior management. In July, the onetime Father of African Socialism traveled to New York to appeal to Wall Street for increased private investment (*WSJ*, 21 September). In neighboring Senegal, which has fourteen political parties, the congress of the ruling Socialist Party stood behind its own candidate, Abdou Diouf, who is the current Senegalese head of state, for the presidential and parliamentary elections scheduled for February 1983. The congress, however, declared that it seeks to form a national union government with other parties in order to unify the nation (AFP, Paris, 12 December; *FBIS*, 14 December). (Despite the official announcement of the implementation of a confederation between Senegal and Gambia on 1 February, to be known as Senegambia, the *Yearbook* will, as last year, keep Senegal distinct because the coverage of communist and left-wing movements belongs to Senegal alone.)

The West African country of Upper Volta underwent a military coup in November. The new president, Maj. Jean-Baptiste Ouedraogo, announced as one of the government's six objectives the "establishing of true social justice" (AFP, Paris, 27 November; *FBIS*, 1 December). But at year's end, the exact nature of the military government's ideological orientation was unclear.

It remains to mention briefly a few activities of foreign communist states in Africa. The Soviet Union's efforts to establish an influence in Namibia through SWAPO prompted concern among U.S. congressmen visiting the southwest African country (*WP*, 29 March). The Soviet Union and its allies dispatched a number of delegations to many African states and received several African visitors. Agreements were also signed with some sub-Saharan states. For example, Togo entered into a protocol agreement for cultural and scientific cooperation with the USSR (Lome domestic service, 11 February; *FBIS*, 18 February), and Angola signed a cooperation protocol with Czechoslovakia (ANGOP, Luanda, 3 March; *FBIS*, 4 March).

The People's Republic of China's actions were still modest. Since China backed the losers in the Angolan civil war in 1975, it has assumed a much lower profile (for more information, see Warren Weinstein and Thomas H. Henriksen, eds., *Soviet and Chinese Aid to African States*, New York: Praeger, 1980). Among other signs of a gradual return to a more active policy in African affairs, China agreed to recognize Angola and to start talks in Paris to establish diplomatic relations (*WP*, 28 September). China donated medicine and medical equipment to Mali (Bamako domestic service, 3 August; *FBIS*, 5 August). Beijing also signed an agreement of military cooperation with the Sudan (Sudanese News Agency, Khartoum, 25 January; *FBIS*, 28 January). These Chinese actions do not point to a return of the sharp Sino-Soviet rivalry of an earlier period (for background, see Thomas H. Henriksen, ed., *Communist Powers and Sub-Saharan Africa*, Stanford: Hoover Institution Press, 1981). China's limited activities imply an un-willingness to surrender all initiative in Africa to the Soviet Union.

Hoover Institution   Thomas H. Henriksen

Algeria

The Algerian Communist Party (Parti communiste algerien; PCA) was founded in 1920 as an extension of the French Communist Party. It has existed independently since 1936. Following Algerian independence in 1962, dissident left-wing elements of the legal National Liberation Front (NLF) joined with Communists from the outlawed PCA to form the Popular Resistance Organization. In January 1966, this group was renamed the Socialist Vanguard Party (Parti de l'avant-garde socialiste; PAGS), which is recognized in the communist world as the official Algerian communist party. Membership is now estimated to be 400 to 500. The population of Algeria is just under twenty million.

Leadership and Party Affairs. Sadiq Hadjeres is first secretary of the party. Other prominent members of the party in recent years are believed to include former PCA Secretary General Larbi Bukhali, Bashir Hadj 'Ali, Ahmad Karim, and 'Ali Malki. Both Hadjeres and Malki have contributed to the *World Marxist Review* and the *Information Bulletin* on behalf of the PAGS.

Political Situation. During its fourth year in power, the government of President Chadli Benjedid continued the process begun in 1980 of consolidating its position (see *YICA*, 1982, p. 6). A large number of key technocrats from the previous regime of Houari Boumediene (1965–1978) were replaced by the Benjedid regime. The loss of these highly competent technocrats has contributed to a decline in economic efficiency and most factories now run at only 25 to 50 percent of capacity. Other, longer-term economic problems include agricultural shortages and unemployment. Algeria imports 50 percent of its cereals and 70 percent of its food, accounting for half of government expenditures. Algeria has a million unemployed workers, plus another million employed abroad. Although the government creates 100,000–150,000 new jobs a year, this number is insufficient to absorb entrants into the labor force.

Popular reactions to economic hardships have taken two forms. Many of the disadvantaged have expressed their discontent by espousing Islamic fundamentalism. A large number of private mosques constructed in modest surroundings serve as the platform for critical attacks against corruption and the "arrogance" of Algeria's newly rich. Attempts by the government to influence religious thought by the construction of public mosques and the appointment of imams have been only marginally successful. In 1982, the resurgence of Islamic fundamentalist feeling in Algeria manifested itself in commando raids against tourist hotels in the southern part of the country, attacks against young women in Western dress, and clashes between Muslim activists and militant Marxists in the universities. The regime moved in December to assert its authority by arresting 23 Muslim fundamentalists, whom it accused of belonging to "subversive organizations" (*Le Monde*, Paris, 15 December). The other major expression of popular discontent surfaced among Algeria's large Berber minority, which comprises about 25 percent of the population. Although the specific Berber grievances expressed in the past three years have dealt with freedom of expression and university curricula, the underlying issue is Arabization of the educational system, which threatens the economic well-being of the Berber community by limiting entrée to public-sector jobs to those with an Arabic education.

Activities of the PAGS. The PAGS has generally viewed the Benjedid regime as opportunist and reformist compared with the more militant Boumediene regime, and in late 1981 it accused the current government of having made a "swing to the right" (ibid., 27–28 September 1981). Operating in a hostile political climate and without legal standing, the PAGS prudently opted to maintain a low profile during

1982. The party did not take any public positions of note on either domestic or international issues. Instead, the PAGS focused its energies on the mass organizations of the ruling NLF, Algeria's only government-approved political party. Thus, PAGS members moved to take over the leadership of the National Union of Algerian Youth, and the party continued to place cells in factories to compete with the units of the General Union of Algerian Workers, the government-sanctioned labor union. In November 1981, a PAGS delegation attended a four-day meeting in Prague to consider the work from 1977 to 1981 of the international journal of communist and workers' parties, the *World Marxist Review* (*IB*, January).

Foreign Policy. Algeria stressed its adherence to genuine nonalignment in 1982 and generally tried to pursue a more balanced position between the two superpowers. The Benjedid government continued Algeria's traditional support for national liberation movements, including the Palestine Liberation Organization, the South-West African People's Organization, and the Polisario Front. Algeria's strong support for the admission of the Polisario's government-in-exile, the Saharan Arab Democratic Republic (SADR), to the Organization of African Unity (OAU) caused tensions with Libya, which tried unsuccessfully to host an OAU summit in Tripoli in August and then again in November. Halting moves toward an Algerian-Libyan union occurred earlier in the year when a joint Algerian-Libyan ministerial council began meeting in Algiers in April. Relations with another radical Arab state, the People's Democratic Republic of (South) Yemen developed with visits to Algiers by Yemeni leaders in February and April. In May, Algeria hosted a four-day Mediterranean conference of some 30 left-wing political parties and organizations, which called on the people of the region to condemn "imperialism's strategic redeployment in the Middle East and the Maghreb" (AFP, 8 May; *FBIS*, 14 May).

In 1982, Algeria continued its pattern of receiving official visits of Soviet dignitaries, including Soviet Minister of Justice Vladimir I. Terebilov in February and a delegation of the Supreme Soviet in August; the latter visit was the occasion of Algerian-Soviet parliamentary talks (Algiers domestic service, 24 February, 28 August; *FBIS*, 1 March, 30 August). In December, Algeria again abstained on the U.N. General Assembly resolution calling for the withdrawal of foreign (Soviet) troops from Afghanistan. At the same time, however, Algeria took concrete steps in 1982 to broaden its relations with the United States. These actions included the purchase of eight Lockheed C-130 transport planes and spare parts worth $146 million and a visit to Algiers in December by U.S. Secretary of Commerce Malcolm Baldrige, who led a trade and investment mission of over 30 members. The Baldrige mission marked the first visit to Algeria by a cabinet member of the Reagan administration.

Publications. At infrequent intervals, the PAGS issued the clandestine journal *Sawt al-Sha'b* (Voice of the people).

Portland State University   John Damis

Angola

The ruling Marxist-Leninist political party of Angola, the Popular Movement for the Liberation of Angola–Labor Party (Movimento Popular de Libertação de Angola–Partido do Trabalho; MPLA-PT), was founded as the MPLA in 1956. The party, a secret movement to resist the Portuguese dictatorship, was led for the most part by urban-based *mestiços* and intellectuals. Only when they were forced into exile and guerrilla warfare in the 1959–1961 period did a concerted effort begin to recruit among the predominantly rurál population of Angola. The initial leaders of the MPLA were known for being poets as much as politicians and included Viriato da Cruz, Mario de Andrade, and Agostinho Neto. The MPLA drew its non-African support primarily from the Portuguese Communist Party. From that base, it obtained continuing support, both moral and material, from leftist groups in Western Europe and governments in Eastern Europe.

The base of the MPLA prior to the 1974 revolution in Portugal was never solid, however, as disputes over ideological rigor caused the defection of various factions, most notably those headed by Gentil Viana, Joaquim Pinto de Andrade, and Daniel Chipenda. The MPLA had difficulties, too, in finding a secure exile base; it was forced out of Zaire by the presence of Holden Roberto's National Front for the Liberation of Angola (Frente Naçional de Libertação de Angola; FNLA) and out of Congo (Brazzaville) by aligning itself with the wrong domestic political faction. It found an uneasy base in Lusaka, Zambia, from which it never conducted particularly effective guerrilla warfare against the Portuguese colonial authorities. In the 1974–1975 period, however, the MPLA was catapulted into power in Luanda by virtue of being favored by significant factions in the ruling military junta in Lisbon, and by virtue of receiving massive external support from Cuba and the Soviet Union in the military showdown with the two other major factions in Angolan politics, the FNLA and Jonas Savimbi's National Union for the Total Independence of Angola (União Nacional para e Independência Total de Angola; UNITA).

The MPLA was renamed the MPLA-PT in December 1977 at the first major post-independence party congress. The party's chief ideologist, Lucio Lara, considered the move necessary to enhance the role of workers in the governing party (allocated at least 20 percent of the congress's seats by statute) and to encourage the development of Angola in a Marxist direction.

Organization and Leadership.   The MPLA and its Central Committee monopolize political power in the areas of the country under the control of the central government. Day-to-day control is exercised by a much smaller group, the Political Bureau, headed by the president, currently José Eduardo dos Santos, who replaced Agostinho Neto on the latter's death in late 1979. In the period since 1980, a vast political infrastructure has been created on paper, consisting of a People's Assembly, provincial assemblies, and a number of electoral colleges meant to represent the various constituencies appropriate to a Marxist-Leninist state. Dos Santos not only holds the position of president of the country, but is also chairman of the MPLA-PT and presides over the People's Assembly.

The Central Committee held its tenth session on 16–22 June, and the final communiqué described the long-term challenge for the MPLA-PT: "To ensure effective progress in strengthening discipline and party leadership and prestige—the sole guarantee of close links with the popular masses and the most effective means of guidance and control within the state and society." Past problems identified as still prevalent included: "Carelessness, indiscipline, lack of coordination in various state bodies as a result of individualism, the excessive autonomies of the ministries." (Luanda domestic service, 23 June; *FBIS*, 24 June.) Immediately following the Central Committee session, dos Santos launched a major national campaign to recruit new members into the party, specifically focusing on "the most politically-aware members of the working class and peasantry and those intellectuals who identify fully with the interests of those two classes" (Luanda domestic service, 29 June; *FBIS*, 30 June).

The frequent bickering between various factions of the party in recent years (dividing sometimes on racial issues and on other occasions over policies toward the Soviet Union) was not particularly prominent in 1982. The purging of Manuel Pedro Pacavira, secretary for productivity in the MPLA-PT Central Committee, gave rise to speculation on factional interplay owing to his clear role in the "black power" and anti-Soviet faction. Others countered, however, that he was a likely person to be relieved of responsibilities, in view of the massive economic problems faced by the party and consequent loss of government credibility with the population. (AFP, 15 July; *FBIS*, 15 July; *NYT*, 1 August.)

Mass Organizations.   The MPLA-PT took the lead in organizing mass support groups for the regime even before creating constitutional instruments and representative assemblies. Among the most important sectors organized thus far are youth, women, trade unionists, and various militia groups.

The National Union of Angolan Workers (UNTA) plays a powerful role in the political affairs of Angola, owing partly to the support given by UNTA members to the MPLA during the struggles of 1974–1975. On paper, 90 percent of the country's workers belong to the unions, including those in the countryside. The union leadership does not believe that "free, independent, and autonomous unions are viable" (*Intercontinental Press,* 9 November 1981). UNTA participates very actively in international activities of the Soviet-front World Federation of Trade Unions, with frequent exchanges occurring with Cuban trade unionists.

The youth movement, frequently called the Angolan Pioneers, is given major emphasis by the MPLA-PT as a recruiting tool for bringing young people into the party. The youth wing of the party has relatively lax standards for admission of people under 25, but provides for a re-examination of their political credentials when they reach that age. The Organization of Angolan Women also fulfills a major mobilization role for the regime, and all three elements (youth, women, and labor) are invariably cited in speeches by the country's president as he exhorts greater production, mobilization, and revolutionary consciousness (Launda domestic service, 30 January, 5 February; *FBIS,* 2 and 9 January).

Domestic Affairs.   The domestic realities of Angola since obtaining independence in the mid-1970s have been chaos and war. Economic and social conditions have suffered greatly as a result, and the most draconian kinds of control mechanisms have not tamed a situation considered out of control by many observers.

The sociopolitical problems stem from a combination of deeply ingrained ethnic divisions among the Angolan people and the continuing war between the government and opposition forces in the east and south of the country. The thorough alienation of the Ovimbundu people from the Luanda regime, first through the defection of Daniel Chipenda from the MPLA and more recently through the organization of UNITA by Jonas Savimbi, has resulted in a loss of government control over about one-third of the country. Various other parts of the country are simply beyond the administrative reach of the ineffecive bureaucracy, particularly in the north near the Zairian border. These tensions have resulted in the steady use of the death penalty for a range of crimes, from sedition to murder and stealing: six men were condemned to death in April in Luanda, as were five more in Lobito, three in Cabinda in May, and several more in Cabinda in June (ANGOP, 10 April; *FBIS,* 12 and 25 April, 17 May, 29 June). Amid this disorder, UNITA forces continued to overrun government-held towns from time to time, thereby replenishing their arms supplies (*FBIS,* 2 June; *NYT,* 11 November).

The economic scene has been bright only on the issue of oil production, undertaken through a management contract with Gulf Oil Company. At the end of 1981, Gulf and Angola announced plans to raise oil production from the current 93,000 barrels a day to 200,000 by 1985 (*Qil and Gas Journal,* 16 November 1981). With the most valuable oil-producing acreage just offshore, there is little danger from military insurgencies such as UNITA or the Front for the Liberation of Cabinda. The rest of the economy, however, remained in a shambles. Planning Minister Lopo do Nascimento said early in 1982 that Angola could not hope to be spared "a food crisis that was getting worse all over Africa." Dos Santos complained that privately produced food available in Angolan markets had dropped by more than 25 percent in 1981. (*Guardian,* 7 January.) Travelers got into the habit of taking food with them to Luanda in 1982, and the system of food production and distribution clearly regressed in 1982; the country was said to import 90 percent of the national food requirements (*African Index,* 15 April). The MPLA-PT failed to find a way to revive the export-earning coffee plantations abandoned by Portuguese owners; not only did indigenous managerial skills not exist, but more important, labor indiscipline meant that workers could not be kept on the plantations with incentives to work. For income, then, the MPLA-PT Marxists became overwhelmingly dependent on the capitalist world of oil markets.

International Relations.   The foreign policy of Angola is entirely colored by the dependence of the MPLA-PT on the Soviet Union and Cuba. The historical relationship is a solid one, including arms supplies to the MPLA as an anticolonial force and training for MPLA cadres in the Soviet Union during the Angolan revolutionary period. The October 1976 treaty of friendship and cooperation between Moscow and Luanda, valid for twenty years and committing both sides to the closest cooperation between political parties, is the axis around which Angola constructs its foreign relations. The MPLA's claims to be an authentic Marxist-

Leninist party were confirmed by that agreement, even more so than by the cooperation agreements with Cuba signed in July 1976. Of course, the Cuban agreements—and several more are signed on the occasion of each high-level visit from one country to the other—have constituted more important steps in terms of concrete cooperation. Recent estimates suggest that nearly 20,000 Cuban military advisers and support personnel are in Angola, along with nearly 5,000 civilian advisers and technicians in such areas as agriculture, industrial planning, and political cadre organization.

The maintenance of those ties with other communist states and parties results in a constant exchange of high-level visits. A representative sample would include visits by Lucio Lara to Moscow in January (Tass, 20 January; *FBIS*, 21 January), Dr. Dieter Albrecht, vice-chairman of the East German State Committee for Planning in Luanda in late January (ANGOP, 27 January; *FBIS*, 29 January), and Cuban Politburo member Jorge Risquet in Luanda in February (Luanda domestic service, 9 February; *FBIS*, 10 February)—a pace kept up throughout 1982. No major agreements were signed by Angola during the year, although various forms of past cooperation were continued or expanded into new technical areas. In January, a new ten-year economic agreement was signed with the Soviet Union (Luanda domestic service, 26 January; *FBIS*, 27 January; *WP*, 22 January; Tass, 20 January). A new three-year economic cooperation agreement was signed with Bulgaria in May (Luanda domestic service, 4 May; *FBIS*, 6 May). An agreement on "naval repairs" with the Soviet Union was signed in May by the respective fisheries ministers (ANGOP, 27 May; *FBIS*, 1 June). Also characteristic was a five-year cooperation agreement signed in July by the Angolan League for Friendship and Solidarity with Peoples and the Cuban Institute for Friendship with Peoples (ANGOP, 29 July; *FBIS*, 30 July).

Ties with non-Marxist states continued to vacillate throughout the year, with intermittent fighting occurring with South African troops in the south, negotiations with the United States as the proponent of a plan to settle the Namibian conflict, and gradual exploration of renewed ties with Portugal. In the last case, the highlight of the year was the visit of Portuguese President Gen. Antonio dos Santos Ramalho Eanes, in April (ANGOP, 15 April; *FBIS*, 20 April). Following that state visit, cooperation was stepped up, and Portuguese-run schools for dependents of Portuguese citizens residing in Angola were reopened. Relations with the United States remained very cool, although the frequent negotiations over Namibia resulted in one major prisoner exchange at the end of the year, with UNITA releasing a Soviet prisoner and the MPLA-PT releasing three U.S. citizens charged with illegally piloting aircraft in Angolan airspace.

Publications and Information.   The MPLA Central Committee has consistently reaffirmed the crucial importance of the control of information in Angola and has devoted major resources to maintaining strict ties. The Central Committee resolution of 23 June on the media stressed the roles of the national radio and of ANGOP (the official Angolan news agency) which are clearly "linked with the very consolidation of national awareness in the struggle against international imperialism and its lackeys" (ANGOP, 23 June; *FBIS*, 24 June). Staff journalists must be MPLA-PT members. The two daily newspapers, *A Jornal de Angola* and *Diario de Luanda*, are used primarily for domestic mobilization. During 1982, the newspapers were moving toward increasing revolutionary puritanism; the Central Committee directed editors "to do away with sensationalism and the cult of the sports personality."

School of Advanced International Studies   Richard E. Bissel
Johns Hopkins University

Biography. *José Eduardo dos Santos.* In September 1979, the Central Committee of the MPLA elected José Eduardo dos Santos its president. At the same time, in accordance with the constitution, he became chief of state and commander of the armed forces. Born in 1942, dos Santos earned a degree in petroleum engineering in the Soviet Union in the early 1960s. He joined the MPLA in 1961 and took an active part in the liberation struggle against the Portuguese. He served during 1961–1962 as vice-president of the MPLA youth wing in Leopoldville (now Kinshasa) and later became the first MPLA representative in Brazzaville.

Dos Santos has been a member of the party's Central Committee and Political Bureau since September 1974. When Angola gained independence in November 1975, dos Santos became foreign minister. In 1976, he was appointed first deputy prime minister. One year later, he became Central Committee secretary for economic development and planning. In December 1978, he was named minister of planning, a post he held until becoming president on the death of Agostinho Neto. Sources: *Pravda,* 19 December 1979; *Africa Who's Who,* 1973.

Alexandria, Virginia   Joyce Myrick

Bahrain

The illegal National Liberation Front of Bahrain (NLF/B), formed in 1955, is often the only organization not bearing the communist party title participating in meetings of Arab Communists, for example, most recently in May and July (*WMR,* April 1981; *al-Safir,* Beirut, 26 May; Tass, Moscow, 12 July). A recent Soviet account suggests that this organization is a "revolutionary democratic" party moving toward "vanguard" status on its way to becoming a full-fledged communist party (*Voprosy istorii,* April), although a year earlier, on 6 March 1981, an NLF/B spokesman, over Radio Moscow, spoke of at least some if not all of his organizational cohorts as "Communists."

The reluctance of the NLF/B to proclaim itself a communist party may be related to its alleged policy of trying to form a united front of "national forces," enunciated at the Twenty-Sixth Congress of the Communist Party of the Soviet Union (1981) and resulting in an agreement with the country's Popular Front before the month was out (Radio Moscow, 6 and 16 March 1981). Besides this, little is known about the Popular Front. This non-communist-party status is also suited to the NLF/B's proclaimed gradualism—instead of revolution it calls for freedom from "imperialist" domination from abroad and for the establishment of democratic freedoms at home (*WMR,* April 1981). It also lends credibility to what appears to be, in the absence of any observable activity to the contrary, the main function of this organization—the enunciation of Soviet foreign policy objectives (even to the extent of lauding the Afghanistan invasion—Radio Peace and Progress, Moscow, 16 February 1980).

For such a shadowy organization, the NLF/B has a well-published leadership. It has a directing body variously labeled the "leading," "executive," "steering" or "governing" committee. Its chairman is Yusuf al-Hassan. Its most frequent spokesman, however, is its "international relations responsible," Abdallah Ali al-Rashid; it was al-Rashid, for example, who represented the NLF/B at the CPSU congress in 1981 and the July 1982 Dimitrov anniversary celebrations in Sofia (Radio Moscow, 6 March 1981; *Rabotnichesko delo,* 20 June). Other members of the Leading Committee are Jasim Muhammad, Mukhtar Abd-al-Latif, Aziz Mahmud, and, possibly, Ahmad Ibrahim Muhammad al-Thawadi (*WMR,* February 1981, January 1982; *L'Humanité,* 4 February; World Peace Council, *List of Members, 1980–1983*).

In keeping with its Soviet-line propaganda function, the NLF/B and its affiliated organizations are quite active in the international fronts. The Bahrain Peace and Solidarity Organization is affiliated with both the World Peace Council (WPC) and the Afro-Asian Peoples' Solidarity Organization (AAPSO). Abdallah al-Rashid was one of fifteen Bahrainis elected to the WPC in September 1980 as well as one of two Bahrainis attending the November 1981 AAPSO Presidium meeting in Kabul. NLF/B Chairman al-Hassan and al-Thawadi are also WPC members. The Bahrain Union of Democratic Youth and the National Union of Bahraini Students are affiliated with the World Federation of Democratic Youth and International Union of Students, respectively. The country also has an affiliate (name unknown) of the Women's International Democratic Federation. In the absence of any further information on the subject, however, we can only assume that the Bahraini youth, student, and women's fronts bear the same relationship to the NLF/B as does the Peace and Solidarity Organization. These fronts have not been noted as active inside Bahrain.

McLean, Virginia   Wallace H. Spaulding

Egypt

The small Egyptian Communist Party was founded in 1921 but has been illegal almost continuously since that time, although it reportedly held its First Congress on Egyptian territory in September 1980 (see *YICA*, 1982, p. 12). Communism in Egypt has consistently been manifested more as a general movement of factional groups than as a well-coordinated party. Leftist activity continues to center around the National Progressive Unionist Grouping or Party (NPUG/NPUP) under the leadership of Khalid Muhyi al-Din, one of the original Free Officers of the 1952 revolution and long identified with Marxist elements in the country.

Domestic Developments. The assassination of President Anwar Sadat in October 1981 continued to affect developments in Egypt and in Egyptian foreign policy. President Mohammad Hosni Mubarak sought to consolidate his position at home and abroad and to develop his own particular political style and policy. As part of this effort, he released many of the dissidents of the right and left imprisoned by Sadat and sought to improve the regime's relations with them. He also sought to portray his regime as aware of Egypt's problems and active in solving them. In a speech delivered on 8 November 1981 to the People's Assembly and the Consultative Council and broadcast on Radio Cairo, Mubarak stressed that the primary policy of the government was to put the economy on a firm footing in order to ensure social justice as a basis for stability. On 2 January Mubarak replaced the government he inherited from Sadat and made Fu'ad Muhyi al-Din prime minister. Despite changes in personnel, no alterations were anticipated in foreign policy, particularly in relation to Egypt's commitment to the Camp David accords or the peace treaty process with Israel (*WP*, 3 January).

Much of the year was one of consolidation at home for Mubarak, although this effort was interrupted by the war in Lebanon and associated developments. In the spring, the terms of the Egyptian-Israeli peace treaty were met as Israel completed its withdrawal from the Sinai Peninsula and normalization between Egypt and Israel was implemented. But the negotiation process was interrupted on 14 June when Egypt informed the United States that it had suspended talks with Israel on Palestinian self-rule because of the Israeli invasion of Lebanon; the peace process, however, would continue (*NYT*, 15 June). President Mubarak repeatedly condemned Israel's invasion of Lebanon (particularly the actions in Beirut) and continued to insist on Palestinian rights to a homeland (ibid., 4 August). The government-controlled press also condemned both Israel and the United States for the developments in Lebanon. Despite this often sharp criticism, no suggestion of severing relations with Israel or abrogating the Camp David accords was proffered. Opposition political parties were more vocal than the government and declared a "national campaign against all Zionist and United States presence in Egypt." They formed an Egyptian Nationalist Committee in Solidarity with the Palestinian and Lebanese Peoples and called for a boycott of Israel and the United States. (Ibid., 1 July.)

No real movement was possible throughout the summer, and the bilateral effort was overshadowed by the Reagan initiative announced at the beginning of September. The Egyptian government said that the Reagan peace initiative contained "positive aspects" and could provide some momentum for the Middle East peace process.

Domestic Dissent and Opposition. Opposition to the Egyptian government continued to come from both left and right. At issue were domestic economic and social policies and foreign policies focusing on the peace process with Israel. The leftist groups also sought improved relations with the socialist states.

Members of two communist organizations working to propagate communist principles in Egypt were arrested. They had recently increased their activities in Egypt—including the preparation of inflammatory leaflets. These elements belonged to the Egyptian Communist Party (ECP) and the Egyptian Workers' Communist Party (EWCP). Sixty-five members of the two communist organizations were arrested on 4–5 November 1981. It was noted that members of the ECP tried to rebuild the party's organizational structure following the release of its members and to resume its activities. They have been escalating their antiregime activities and sought to establish a national democratic front to overthrow the existing regime, annul the Camp David agreements, and establish a communist society in the country. The EWCP has escalated its activities in order to overthrow the regime and establish a communist society in the country. It called for boycotting normalization with Israel, advocated instigating the masses against the regime, and called for rapprochement with the Soviet Union. (MENA, 8 November 1981; *FBIS,* 9 November 1981.)

A spokesman for the ECP's Central Committee condemned the Egyptian regime's stand at the U.N. General Assembly, where it abstained from condemning Israel's aggressive and expansionist policy. It also noted that Mubarak's visit to Washington further confirmed that he was following the old scheme. (Damascus, Saudi Arabia News Agency, 6 February; *FBIS,* 9 February.)

The public prosecutor's office announced on 11 February that 31 persons, constituting an illegal party organization called the Egyptian Communist Party–8 January, had been seized on 8 February. The organization was identified as aiming at instituting a communist system in the country. Those arrested were accused of incitement and instigation through printing and circulating opposition leaflets containing attacks on the domestic and foreign policies of the regime. (MENA, 11 February; *FBIS,* 12 February.) A branch of the organization had also been established abroad (MENA, 5 April; *FBIS,* 7 April). *Pravda* (8 April) reported that those arrested were accused of "distributing printed publications propagandizing Marxist teaching" (*FBIS,* 15 April).

The ECP described the Israeli withdrawal from Sinai as a cheap comedy performed according to a scenario prepared by Washington and called on the people to oppose the new U.S. occupation of Egyptian territory. A statement issued by Michael Kamil, a member of the ECP Political Bureau, said that a U.S. occupation had replaced the Israeli occupation. It called on the Arab peoples to struggle against the U.S. occupation of Sinai and against U.S. military bases in the Middle East and the facilities offered to the Pentagon by reactionary Arab regimes. (Radio Moscow, 27 April; *FBIS,* 28 April.)

In late May, the ECP joined the Bahraini National Liberation Front and the Jordanian, Saudi, Syrian, Iraqi, Palestinian, and Lebanese communist parties in issuing a statement attacking Camp David and the Egyptian-Israeli peace treaty. The statement noted that the process was a cover-up for the reoccupation of Sinai by the United States and its NATO allies. it also noted that "U.S. imperialism, Israel, the Arab reaction and secessionist forces allied with Israel and its agents in the area are all cooperating in order to heighten tension in Lebanon and create ideological and communal disputes with the aim of dividing the national ranks and pushing Lebanon to the Camp David path in order to include it in the capitulationist group." It attacked other aspects of Egyptian foreign policy and noted that "democracy for the popular masses and the nationalist and progressive forces and parties and the organizations of workers, peasants and all the toilers is a natural right and a condition for their triumph." Further, "hostility to communism is effectively being exploited by the imperialist, Zionist and reactionary quarters in order to carry out their criminal plans . . . Hostility to communism as a political system and revolutionary ideology is hostility to democracy and the popular masses and opens a breach in the wall of the general national struggle." (*Al-Safir,* 26 May; *FBIS,* 2 June.)

A mass meeting on the sixth anniversary of the formation of the NPUG was held in Cairo. 'Abd al-Ghaffar Shukri, a member of the NPUG Secretariat, demanded the speediest liberation of all people arrested for political reasons in September–October 1981 and called for early parliamentary elections since the present composition of the National Assembly fails to reflect the real political situation in Egypt (*Pravda*, 13 April; *FBIS*, 19 April).

The second political session of the NPUG's general congress revealed continued opposition to Camp David and the Egyptian-Israeli peace treaty because of the high cost that was paid in return for Israeli withdrawal. The declaration noted: "We believe the major danger facing the Arab nation is the danger of the escalating Israeli aggression and threats." It called for increased democratization at home and abandonment of the "so-called open-door economic policy." (*Al-Ahali*,19 May; *FBIS*, 25 May.) In an interview published in February, NPUG leader Khalid Muhyi ad-Din noted that the regime in Egypt had remained the same despite a change at the top but that there was a new style in politics. This included "the nonindulgence of abuse against certain foreign superpowers, such as the Soviet Union." A commitment to see changes in Egyptian domestic and foreign policies remained. (*Al-Bayan*, Dubai, 16 February; *FBIS*, 19 February.)

Ibrahim Shukri, leader of the Socialist Labor Party, stated that relations between Egypt and the Arabs should be improved and that trade and diplomatic relations between Egypt and the Soviet Union at the ambassadorial level should be resumed (MENA, 29 May; *FBIS*, 2 June).

Tass (13 June), reporting from Cairo, noted that the First Congress of the Socialist Labor Party had completed its work. The congress favored the democratization of the country's political and social life and demanded that the Egyptian government pursue a policy of nonalignment and neutrality. It also called for real confrontation to repel Israeli attacks on the Lebanese and Palestinian people and to support the legitimate struggle of the Palestinian people to return to their homeland, their right to self-determination, and the right to set up an independent national state. It called for striking at U.S. interests in the region and consolidating relations with the Soviet Union, the loyal friend of the Arab people's just struggle. (*Pravda*, 14 June; *FBIS*, 16 June.)

Members of the congress sent a telegram to Yassir Arafat hailing "the Palestinian Revolution's struggle against blatant Israeli aggression." Shukri called for ending the state of emergency and the immediate release of all detainees. The congress issued a number of recommendations at its conclusion. It sought to rally the Arabs to confront the Zionist danger and appealed to Iraq and Iran to stop fighting and to direct their forces toward repelling Israeli aggression. It called for strict adherence to the policy of nonalignment, restoration of the balance in Egypt's relations with the superpowers, and the exchange of ambassadors again between Egypt and the Soviet Union. It also called for suspension of diplomatic relations, a halt to the normalization measures with Israel, and an end to the autonomy talks. It renewed its demands for an end to the state of emergency, the abolition of all laws restricting public and individual freedoms, and the lifting of restrictions on political parties. (*Al-Ahali*, 19 June; *FBIS*, 23 June.)

In an interview published in February, Lt. Gen. Sa'd al-Din al-Shadhili, secretary general of the Egyptian National Front, noted: "Our disagreement with President Sadat was not over personal matters. We opposed his foreign, economic and domestic policies. President Mubarak's declaration that he will pursue Sadat's line means that the same policy will continue and, this being the case, we will oppose Hosni Mubarak just as we opposed Sadat . . . Opposition in Egypt is growing daily, but it needs more organization." The goal is to change the domestic and foreign policy of Egypt. (*Al-Jazirah*, Riyadh, 17 February; *FBIS*, 3 March.)

Attention in Egypt focused more on the opposition from the right than the left. The state security agency arrested 140 persons for investigation in connection with their membership in two extremist religious organizations that want to forcibly impose Islamic law and seek to incite the masses (*Al-Ahram*, 5 April; *FBIS*, 12 April).

Another indictment accused an underground group called Jihad of trying to overthrow the government; 302 persons were charged with being ringleaders or activist members of this secret Muslim organization dedicated to transforming Egypt into an Islamic state through violence. The state prosecutor said that 1,225 people had been arrested and that more indictments would be handed down. The bulk of the 302 defendants are men in their mid-twenties from middle-class backgrounds, and many are students. (*NYT*, 10 May.) In early June, the interior minister announced that the total number of people arrested so far under the emergency law had not exceeded 3,000 (excluding the defendants in the Jihad case). All those arrested were accused of being members of secret organizations that believe in violence and terrorism; the government said that their arrest was necessary to ensure that 44 million Egyptians would make progress. (MENA, 4 June; *FBIS*, 4 June.)

On 16 September, MENA announced that an undisclosed number of Muslim fundamentalist extremists had been arrested on charges of planning to overthrow the government of President Mubarak. The plotters were accused of belonging to Jihad; some unidentified Arabs and Egyptians living abroad were also said to be involved in the conspiracy. The government claimed that the group had planned to attack prisons where Muslim extremists were jailed in connection with the assassination of President Sadat and that the plotters planned a series of terrorist activities, including acts of sabotage aimed at creating public panic. Arms and propaganda materials were seized. Those in prison included some holdovers from the Sadat era and some new religious extremists arrested under Mubarak. (*NYT*, 17 September; MENA, 15 and 16 September; *FBIS*, 17 September.) Fifty-eight members of a terrorist organization were arrested, and a search continued for a number of fugitives (MENA, 17 September; *FBIS*, 21 September). On 14 November, 84 defendants detained as members of extremist religious organizations were released (MENA, 14 November; *FBIS*, 16 November). On 18 November, it was announced that the trial of 302 members of Jihad would begin on 4 December. This group included nineteen men already found guilty for the assassination of President Sadat. (AFP, 18 November; *FBIS*, 19 November.) On 4 December, a group of 280 people, mostly associated with Jihad went on trial in Cairo on charges of conspiring to overthrow the government after the assassination of Sadat. Many were linked with the violence in Asyut after Sadat was killed in which 66 people were reported killed. Officials have charged that the plot was to establish a fundamentalist Islamic government patterned on that of Khomeini's in Iran. The principal defendants include Sheikh Omar Abdul Rhaman and Col. Aboud al-Zomor. (*NYT*, 5 December.) The prosecutor in charge of the trial demanded that the death penalty be imposed and noted that many of the defendants represented an ideology that "regarded the president of the republic [Anwar Sadat] and his aides as heretics who should be killed" (*WP*, 26 December).

Relations with the Socialist Bloc.   In January, Foreign Minister Kamal Hassan 'Ali said that "Egypt has requested the assistance of 66 [previously expelled] Soviet experts in the sphere of cooperation between the two countries in the major projects" (ibid., 25 January). 'Ali emphasized that the improvement of Egyptian relations with Moscow would not affect relations with Washington. Commenting on published reports concerning the Soviet experts, 'Ali noted that their stay would be for a specified period to install equipment contracted for before their expulsion. (MENA, 26 January; *FBIS*, 27 January.) *Al-Ahram* noted that the decision to bring the Soviet experts back to Egypt was made for economic reasons and that there had been no political contacts at any level between Egypt and the Soviet Union. It noted, however, that this did not mean that Egypt was not prepared to make such contacts. (MENA, 28 January; *FBIS*, 29 January.) President Mubarak subsequently asserted that there were no secret contacts with the Soviet Union (MENA, 9 February; *FBIS*, 10 February). *Al-Akhbar* commented editorially that there was no reason to sever relations with any friendly or unfriendly state. The Soviet Union had been Egypt's ally and had provided arms and aid when it was not readily available from other sources. Now "we welcome a new form of cooperation with the Soviet Union." Normal relations were possible, and the two countries should cooperate. (Radio Cairo, 6 February; *FBIS*, 8 February.)

As Mubarak noted, "The Soviet Union has an embassy here and it lacks only an ambassador. it is natural to have diplomatic relations with the Soviet Union because it is one of the two superpowers and not a small country that can be disregarded . . . The existence of diplomatic relations and the exchange of ambassadors between us and the Soviet Union does not necessarily mean our relations with the United States will deteriorate." (MENA, 18 November; *FBIS*, 19 November.)

Deputy Chinese Foreign Trade Minister Zhang Genghe arrived in Cairo on 12 March, heading a delegation for an eight-day visit. His delegation participated in meetings to renew the trade and payment protocol between the two countries for 1982. A special Chinese envoy, He Ying, arrived in Cairo on 23 May for meetings with President Mubarak and senior Egyptian officials. They discussed international events and joint cooperation in the technical, economic and trade fields (MENA, 24 May; *FBIS*, 25 May). He Ying described the meetings as "important and useful" and noted that they had been held in a friendly atmosphere (Radio Cairo, 24 May; *FBIS*, 25 May). Chinese Prime Minister Zhao Ziyang arrived in Egypt in late December at the start of a ten-nation visit to Africa. "The purpose of my visit is to promote understanding and friendship, strengthen solidarity and cooperation and learn from the African people." He is the highest-ranking official to visit since Zhou Enlai came to Cairo in 1964. He met with President Mubarak and other senior officials. (*NYT,* 21 December.) It was subsequently announced that President Mubarak will probably visit China early in April 1983 (MENA, 21 December; *FBIS,* 23 December). It was reported that the two sides reviewed issues of common concern, including foreign policy matters involving the Middle East, Southeast Asia, Africa, and the Third World (MENA, 22 December; *FBIS,* 23 December). It was also reported that China had agreed to supply Egypt with 60 to 80 F-7 fighter planes built on a Soviet MiG-21 design, to be assembled in Egypt. The two sides also discussed other areas of military and economic cooperation. (AFP, Paris, 22 December; *FBIS,* 23 December.)

George Washington University   Bernard Reich

Ethiopia

The Commission to Organize the Party of the Working People of Ethiopia (COPWE), established in December 1979, has made little progress in its efforts to form a vanguard political party. COPWE, however, is gradually replacing the Provisional Military Administrative Council, or Dergue, as the supreme governmental institution. At the moment the two are virtually interchangeable. Mengistu Haile Mariam is chairman of COPWE and of the Dergue; the seven members of COPWE's Executive Committee, headed by Mengistu, are all members of the Dergue; 79 of the 123 full and candidate members of COPWE's Central Committee are members of the armed forces or police; all ten members of the Dergue's Standing Committee and all of the estimated 32 members of the Dergue's Central Committee are on COPWE's Central Committee; all fourteen of COPWE's provincial committees are led by Dergue members. Established initially to create a workers' party on the Soviet model, COPWE is a highly centralized organization that has established nine political/governmental committees to organize the functioning of the party and state. Almost all decisions, however, are made by the Executive Committee. The establishment of a genuine workers' party seems a long way off, as the military, under the guise of COPWE, still controls Ethiopia.

In addition to Mengistu, the leading figures of COPWE are Fikre-Selassie Wogderess (head of ideological affairs), Felleki Gedli-Giorgis (foreign minister), Amanuel Ande Mikael (secretary general of the political/military campaign against the Eritrean rebels), Tesfaye Gebre Kidan (minister of defense), Berhanu Bayih (responsible for foreign relations), Dawit Wolde Ghiorghis (member of the Central Committee), Legessie Asfaw (in charge of political organizations), and Teka Tulu (director of security). Mengistu, however, is the most powerful of all.

Auxiliary organizations include the Revolutionary Ethiopia's Women's Association (established 1980); the All-Ethiopian Trade Union (1977); the All-Ethiopian Peasant Association (1977), which coordinates the activities of peasant associations in the interior (total membership over seven million farmers); and the kebelles (1975), or urban dwellers' associations, which act as judicial, political, and administrative authorities in urban neighborhoods, each kebelle overseeing 200–500 households. Elections or appointments to all these organizations are supervised by COPWE's Central Committee.

Figures on COPWE membership are unobtainable or unreliable. However, some 1,500–2,000 COPWE representatives usually attend plenary sessions. COPWE usually meets twice yearly in plenary session. Major publications are *Serto Ader* (Working people), the *Ethopian Herald* (English–language newspaper), and the *Negarit Gazetta* (official government organ, which publishes all laws).

Party Affairs. The Dergue announced on 10 March that farmers' and workers' unions would be strengthened to create "unity and solidarity . . . in promoting the revolutionary struggle" (Addis Ababa domestic service, 10 March). COPWE was put in charge of union reorganization.

The fourth plenary session of COPWE met in June. In addressing the session, Mengistu called on the workers of Ethiopia to increase agricultural production, whose shortcomings he called "the most worrying of our major economic problems" (ibid., 18 June). He also claimed that the Red Star revolutionary campaign in Eritrea, initiated in January, had the twin objectives of crushing the secessionist rebellion and carrying out a massive reconstruction of the Eritrean economy.

Domestic Affairs. The seventh full-scale offensive against the Eritrean secessionist movements (see YICA, 1982, p. 17), the Red Star campaign, was labeled a success after one month by the Ethiopian government (AFP, 22 February). Although Ethiopia's claims were disputed by the Eritrean People's Liberation Front (EPLF), it was clear that by midyear the forces of the EPLF and the Eritrean Liberation Front were in some disarray. Already in March "a serious effort [was] under way to rebuild the [economy] . . . reactivate social institutions, and shore up the confidence of the local population" (ibid., 11 March). The two-pronged military/economic attack was characterized a major success by Mengistu (Addis Ababa domestic service, 18 June). There is little doubt that the secessionists have continued to fare badly against Ethiopia, and their struggle for independence has been severely curtailed by continued military losses.

The first cases in Ethiopia's anticorruption campaign were initiated early in the year. A number of former government and COPWE officials were charged with embezzlement, bribery, and breach of trust. The offenders were charged with violating the Anticorruption Law promulgated in September 1981.

Sweden and Norway maintained early in the year that the Ethiopian Evangelical church had been seized by the government and that 600 Lutheran churches had been closed. At the same time, the Canadian Association for Ethiopian Jews accused Ethiopia of arresting and torturing Ethiopian Jews (Falashas). In late 1981, the *Frankfurter Allgemeine Zeitung* (14 November 1981), quoting a Dergue document, reported that a crackdown on religion in Ethiopia would occur in 1982 "to exploit the historic conflicts between Christians and Muslims and to produce tensions between these two reactionary systems" so as to strengthen the position of Marxism-Leninism in Ethiopia. Ethiopia denied the validity of the document. Still, suppression of religious activity did occur in late 1981 and in 1982.

Foreign Policy. Soviet-Ethiopian relations were reported to be under some strain even though the USSR has sent some U.S. $2 billion in military aid to Ethiopia and stationed some 1,500 military advisers in the country. According to numerous reports, the main complaint of the Soviet Union "concerns Ethiopia's reluctance to introduce Soviet-style party rule . . . that would ensure Ethiopia's continued pro-Soviet orientation in the long run" (*Free Press Journal*, New Delhi, 24 March). Unhappy with the slow progress of COPWE in forming a regular vanguard party, the USSR has been pressuring Mengistu to move more rapidly in this area. Still, the ties between Ethiopia and the Soviet Union and Eastern bloc countries are strong, even though Mengistu has sent high-level delegations to Western Europe to improve relations. The dispute over the establishment of a party (with Mengistu claiming that more time is needed) has brought to light some of the contradictions in Ethiopia's international affairs.

In late 1981, Mengistu praised Secretary General Leonid Brezhnev and stated that "relations between our two countries have reached a high level of cooperation and mutual understanding" (*Pravda*, 9 November 1981). In January 1982, a Soviet Peace Committee delegation visiting Addis Ababa noted "the long-standing friendship between the two countries" (Addis Ababa domestic service, 20 January). At about the same time, "relations were strengthened" between the Revolutionary Ethiopia's Women's Association and the Committee of Soviet Women. At the end of January, COPWE and the Communist Party of Cuba signed a pact strengthening cooperation between them. In 1982, a COPWE delegation attended the Fifth Congress of the Vietnamese Communist Party, and Ethiopia signed a protocol strengthening cultural and scientific cooperation between Ethiopia and the USSR and put into effect an agreement with the German Democratic Republic that recognized the common duty "of a Marxist-Leninist party in socialist construction" (ADN, 28 November 1981). An agreement was also signed with South Yemen and Libya in May initiating the coordination of their mass media.

It would be making too much of an issue to overdramatize the dispute between the USSR and Ethiopia over the progress of COPWE in establishing a vanguard party. Ethiopia is still very much aligned with Soviet foreign policy, almost always votes with the Soviet Union in the United Nations, and is very much beholden to the Soviet Union for its military aid. Its advances to the West notwithstanding, Ethiopia remains a solid ally of the USSR.

Despite Ethiopia's blistering attack on U.S. foreign policy in February (Addis Ababa domestic service, 18 February), U.S. and West German firms were looking into the feasibility of constructing tourist hotels in Addis Ababa, the World Bank was asked to consider a $10 million loan, part of which would be used to prepare documents for Western bidding on oil exploration concessions, and Ethiopia requested Western countries to increase their economic aid (*Arabia*, March). In March, the French embassy in Addis Ababa was ordered to reduce its staff by half because of French criticism of Ethiopia's offensive in Eritrea.

In early July, 7,000 Ethiopian troops supporting the Somali Democratic Salvation Front invaded and occupied two Somali villages along the border east of the Ethiopian-controlled Ogaden desert. The Ethiopian air force bombed Somali troop positions in frontier villages. (*NYT*, 25 July, 8 October.) The Ethiopian attack was in response to Somali support for the Western Somali Liberation Front's continued attempt to wrest the Ogaden from Ethiopia. Sporadic fighting in the Ogaden took place throughout the first part of 1982, and 250 Ethiopian soldiers were reported killed. In late July, the United States announced it was airlifting $5.5 million in military equipment to Somalia. By November, it was reported that Ethiopia had withdrawn its forces from one of the Somali villages. Although Moscow (Tass, 13 July) and Addis Ababa (*CSM*, 15 July) derided the reports of Ethiopia's occupation, it seemed clear from the multiple number of news reports that Ethiopa had indeed struck directly at Somalia.

State University of New York   Peter Schwab
College at Purchase

Iran

The year under review saw a continuation and even a worsening of the chaotic situation rampant in Iran since the fall of the shah in 1978. The Islamic Republican Party (IRP) and its leader, Ayatollah Ruhollah Khomeini, are struggling against numerous challenges to their regime, both from the right and the left and from inside and outside the country. Separatist movements abound in Azerbaijan, Baluchistan, and especially Kurdistan, where the Kurdish Democratic Party of Abdorrahman Qasemlu (presently in exile in Paris) has an army of 12,000 regular and 60,000 reserve troops fighting pitched battles against the *pasdaran* (Islamic Revolutionary Guard Corps). The opposition Mojahedin-e Khalq is also allied to the Kurds. The economy is characterized by high unemployment, rising inflation, declining food supplies, and pervasive fear (*Los Angeles Times*, 10 February). Despite hatred of the "arch-satan," in 1981 Iran purchased more than $300 million worth of U.S. farm products. The two-year-old Iran-Iraq war shows no signs of ending soon. Iranian forces made significant progress and by mid-1982 were able to push the Iraqis back across the border in some areas. The decision to send Iranian troops into Iraq after them, however, has led to a complete standstill of the Iranians in the salt marshes east of Basra. Iraqis still occupy border areas of Iran further north. In the midst of all these troubles stand many opposition groups, from the large Kurdish national rebellion to tribal risings, such as that of the Qashqai around Shiraz. There continue to be Marxist groups as well, of various shades—the Maoist Marxists (the Peykar and the Razmandegan groups), the

Islamic Marxists (the Mojahedin-e Khalq and the minority faction of the Fedayin-e Khalq, and many others), and the Moscow Marxists (the Tudeh Party and the majority faction of the Fedayin-e Khalq).

The roots of communism in Iran date to the Red Army's invasion of parts of the Caspian littoral in 1917–1918 and the short-lived Gilan Republic of 1920–1921 in the same area. Throughout the 1930s, the illegal Communist Party of Iran (Hezb-e Komunist-e Iran) operated clandestinely. Following the Soviet occupation of northern Iran in 1941, the movement reappeared as the Tudeh Party (Hezb-e Tudeh-ye Iran), or the "party of the masses." This regenerated group increased in strength until in 1944 the party claimed a membership of 25,000. Under Soviet aegis, independent and pro-Soviet republics were created in Azerbaijan and Kurdistan. At this time, the Tudeh Party was represented by three cabinet members in the Tehran government. With the pullout of Soviet troops in 1946 and the collapse of these republics, the power of the Tudeh party began to decline. In February 1949, the Pahlavi government formally outlawed the Tudeh Party. During the oil crisis of 1951–1953, the party's strength again rose, and it supported Prime Minister Mohammad Mossadegh's National Front government. The pro-royalist coup of August 1953 ended not only the Mossadegh regime, but also the growing influence of the Tudeh Party. From 1953 until 1979, the Tudeh Party was centered in East Germany. Its leaders there consisted of exiled party figures, such as Dr. Iraj Eskandari, longtime party secretary.

The events of late 1978 and early 1979 that deposed the Pahlavi dynasty also led to the Tudeh Party's return to Iran. After 26 years in exile, the party returned as the only communist organization recognized and allowed to operate openly by the new Islamic Republic.

From 1980 on, the party, under the leadership of a new general secretary, Nureddin Kianuri, has consistently supported the Islamic revolution and Ayatollah Khomeini, but has, nevertheless, run a gauntlet of political ups and downs. The organization was legal, but its operations remained semiclandestine. Its Tehran headquarters were occupied by Hezbollahi religious extremists, and the party held no rallies or demonstrations. It seemed hesitant to anger the Islamic masses, who were anticommunist and anti-Russian for religious and historical reasons. Rather, it preferred to gain strength by infiltrating the ruling IRP. In July 1981, Ayatollah Mohammad Beheshti supposedly negotiated with the Tudehis and promised to appoint three pro-communist ministers in return for Soviet support. By August, there were said to be three communist ministers in the cabinet: the defense minister, the executive minister, and the minister for planning and budget. The Tudeh Party also had its problems. Khomeini said that communism was as bad as Western capitalism, prevented a Tudeh delegation from attending a party congress in Moscow, banned publication of Tudeh's newspaper from June until September 1981, and declared Tudeh officials ineligible as candidates for the Majles. In spite of this, the Tudeh Party was in the strongest position it had known since the early 1950s.

The year turned out to be one of serious reverses for the Tudeh Party. Already in November 1981, Prime Minister Mir Hossein Musavi had declared that members of the Tudeh Party and its ally, the majority faction of the Fedayin-e Khalq, had infiltrated the Revolutionary Guards and other fundamentalist organizations. He warned that all infiltrators would be executed (*NYT*, 23 November 1981). At the end of November 1981, the Tudeh publication *Payam-e Mardom* was again banned (*FBIS*, 1 December 1981). In early 1982, there was much speculation on the strength of the Tudeh, especially over the clandestine radio stations of various opposition groups. Finally, at the beginning of March, the official Iranian newspaper, *Ettela'at*, implied that the Tudeh Party was among those working against the interests of the Islamic republic (ibid., 30 March). The Tudehis, of course, protested. In an open letter to the East German publication *Horizont*, they complained that their party had practically been deprived of all possibilities for political work and that its members had been thrown into prisons solely for being committed to the party (ibid., 15 July). Soon thereafter, another Tudeh organ, *Ettehad-e Mardom*, was also banned. In the 16 July issue of the leftist Viennese paper *Volksstimme*, Kianuri again complained of harassment (ibid., 21 July). The month of August saw the Islamic government turn against a small group called the Union of Communists in Iran (Tashkilat-e Ettehadiye-ye Komunistha-ye Iran) with a vengeance. The group supposedly attacked a small city in Mazanderan. Revolutionary Guards counterattacked and arrested or killed more than a hundred members, including the entire leadership, and seized all equipment (ibid., 18 August). This breakaway group no longer has any connection with the Tudeh Party; the fact that they called themselves communists, however, was bound to have repercussions for the Tudehis. At about the same time, Khomeini learned that the Communists were planning to foment several peasant revolts. The ayatollah moved immediately, banning Tudeh's publications and replacing Islamic government officials with communist leanings. *L'Ex-*

press (Paris, 20 August) reported that "It was a hard blow for the Tudeh. While a number of its influential members were arrested, others immediately went underground, and a small group fled abroad, specifically to the Soviet Union. In order to maintain its legitimacy, the Tudeh has made changes in its organization. Thus, the leader of Iranian Communist Party, Nurredin Kianuri, had yielded his place to a 'pro-Khomeinist' personality, Babak Amir Khosravi. Despite this, the break between the Tudeh and the regime seems final. As one of his associates said, 'The imam wants to be finished once and for all with these *moshreks* [heathen].'"

On 23 August, the Tehran paper *Jomhuri-ye Eslami* criticized the position of the Tudeh Party and its allies on the war with Iraq. The Tudeh position was that Iran should not invade Iraq but should seek a diplomatic settlement. This position turned out to be identical to that of the Soviet Union (*FBIS*, 25 August). Finally, on 7 November, the clandestine radio station, Free Voice of Iran (Seda-ye Azad-e Iran) reported: "Nureddin Kianuri, former general secretary of the Iranian Tudeh Party, has escaped to the GDR [German Democratic Republic]. There have been no reports available on the details of his escape from Iran. However, rumors say that he escaped with the help and cooperation of one of the regime's influential mullahs. Ehsan Tabari also has been arrested in Rasht. He is a member of the Tudeh Party's Political Bureau and one of the Soviet Union's fifth column agents in Iran. Tabari, who holds the title of the theoretician of the Tudeh Party of Iran, which is affiliated with Moscow, is one of those people who played an active role together with Kianuri in bringing Khomeini to power in Iran. According to our correspondent, following the escape of Vladimir Kuzichkin, the Soviet diplomat, from Iran to London, the names of the leaders of leftist groups affiliated with the Soviet Union have been passed to Western intelligence officials who, in turn, passed these names and other information to the so-called Islamic regime. According to the same report by our correspondent in Tehran, Khomeini's regime is currently in possession of the names of 400 Tudeh Party activists who have infiltrated the armed forces, the Foreign Ministry, the Revolution[ary] Guards Corps, the police, the gendarmerie and some so-called revolutionary organizations of the regime. The regime gradually is arresting them. Some already have been arrested; others are still being sought. The regime's agents are trying to identify other activists of the Tudeh Party and leftist groups affiliated with Moscow in the government's administrative organizations." (Ibid., 10 November.)

Organization and Leadership.   The leadership of the Tudeh organization is presently in a state of flux. First Secretary Nureddin Kianuri is reported to have fled to East Germany, as have many other leaders. Currently acting in Kianuri's place in Iran is Babak Amir Khosravi. Ehsan Tabari, chief theoretician, and many others have been imprisoned by the government.

The exact membership of the Tudeh Party is unknown. In the legislative elections of March 1980, it received some 60,000 votes in Tehran, barely 3 percent of the electorate (*L'Express*, 18–24 September 1981). In mid-1981, its newspaper *Mardom* (when allowed to publish) had a circulation of 45,000 copies (*Le Matin*, Paris, 27 August 1981). Currently most regular members are in hiding, in exile, or in prison.

Domestic Issues.   Since the ayatollah assumed power, the Soviet Union's basic policy toward Iran has consisted of three major goals: (1) to gain influence in the country by supporting Khomeini; (2) to foster anti-American and anti-Western sentiment in Iran; and (3) to bolster the position of its surrogate in Iran, the Tudeh Party. Except for the recent destruction of the Tudeh organization, these policies are still in effect. Until late 1982, the Tudehis' domestic policy closely followed this line. The party resolutely supported Khomeini and the Islamic revolution, stating that the regime's "decisive political trend is Iman Khomeini's anti-imperialist policy uniting the people" (*IB*, September 1981).

The Tudeh has also been staunchly opposed to Bani Sadr and went so far as to ask that all powers be transferred from the president to the parliament (ibid.). The party has shown an equal dislike for other leftist groups, especially the Kurdish Democratic Party and the Mojahedin-e Khalq. Of the latter they declared that: "the leadership of the Organization of People's Mujahedin and other left-extremist groupings, whose spokesmen used to talk about freedom for the masses, about the need to break the chains of national and class oppression, have in effect joined the hated camp of champions of freedom who are in fact the gravediggers of freedom, have turned their misled supporters into an instrument of the conspiracies being woven by the counterrevolution's united front" (ibid., March).

The party stands for destruction of internal and external enemies of the Iranian revolution, strengthening national defense, economic self-sufficiency (especially in agriculture), social justice for the working class, and social justice and national rights for non-Persian peoples, including cultural and administrative "self-determination" or "autonomy" (ibid.).

Foreign Policy. The Tudeh Party's foreign policy has continued to feature three main tenets—anti-Americanism, anti-imperialism, and anti-Zionism. This trinity is still blamed for most of Iran's problems, external and internal, as well as for attacks on the Tudeh Party by other Iranian groups and political parties.

Generally speaking, the foreign policy of the Iranian Islamic Republic toward the countries of the Eastern bloc has been less than satisfactory to the Soviet Union (*Pravda*, 9 March). Economic relations were brisk in 1982, with Iran purchasing weapons and industrial and strategic goods from the USSR, North Korea, East Germany, Czechoslovakia, and Bulgaria and selling petroleum to them in return. The only Western nations trading with Iran seem to be Japan and Turkey (*WP*, 26 November). Political relations between Iran and the East, however, have steadily worsened. The country abounded with rumors of Soviet infiltrators, North Korean and Cuban troops within the borders, a Soviet surveillance station just outside Iran's borders, and Tudeh members receiving military training at Soviet bases in Afghanistan (*Daily Telegraph*, London, 24 May; *FBIS*, 12 March). In April, an Iranian-Soviet gas pipeline was blown up near Rasht for "unknown reasons" (AFP, Paris, 6 April). The *Wall Street Journal* (19 July) said that British diplomats noted that over the past few months Iran had ended its honeymoon with the Tudeh Party and that a Tehran government spokesman claimed that Iran had shot down a Russian helicopter pursuing Afghan rebels near the Iranian border. In November, a senior Iranian official said that the Soviet invasion of Afghanistan was a "cynical action, just what you would expect from atheists." Another said that Iran was the best protection the West could have in the area against a Soviet takeover. (*NYT*, 14 November.) The severe crackdown on the Tudeh Party in late 1982 would seem to corroborate the demise of Iranian-Soviet friendship.

Other Marxist Organizations. During the past year, Marxist organizations of various shades in Iran have continued to proliferate. Presently there are more than a dozen in addition to the Tudeh. They include the Communist Union of Iran (Tashkilat-e Ettehadiye-ye Iran), the Socialist Workers' Party (Hezb-e Kargaran-e Sosialist; HKS), the Revolutionary Workers' Party (Hezb-e Kargaran-e Enqelabi; HKE), the Workers' Unity Party (Hezb-e Vahdat-e Kargaran; HVK), the Mojahedin-e Khalq, two factions of the Fedayin-e Khalq, the two Maoist groups (Peykar and Razmandegan), and several others. Most of these are small, relatively impotent groupings. (For more detailed descriptions, see *YICA*, 1982, pp. 22–23.)

Khomeini's government and the Revolutionary Guards have lumped all of them together under one convenient title, *monafeqin* (hypocrites), and waged a vicious campaign in 1982 to rid Iran of them. It is true that these groups have been responsible for the assassinations of dozens of members of Khomeini's clerical government, but on the other hand, the Revolutionary Guards killed in battle or arrested and executed several hundreds of these groups' adherents in 1982, causing most of the organizations to virtually collapse. Although the actual number is unknown, it has been estimated by some sources that during Khomeini's regime more than 30,000 persons have been executed officially.

Publications. Iran's Marxist factions used to publish a number of newspapers. The Tudeh Party issued the daily *Mardom* (The people) and the weekly *Donya* (The world). The HKE put out the weekly *Kargar* (The worker), the HKS the fortnightly *Che Bayad Kard?* (What is to be done?), and the HVK the weekly *Hemmat* (Aspiration). The Maoist group, Peykar, published a paper called *Edalat* (Justice). All of these appeared more or less regularly in Tehran, except for periods when the Iranian government temporarily suspended publication of one or another of them. The Mojahedin distribute many pamphlets, and their vendors are frequently attacked and their stocks destroyed by fundamentalist Muslims. The Fedayin-e Khalq has no regular publication, but issues occasional tracts and handbills. Gradually, however, the Islamic revolutionary government has been silencing these voices of the opposition. At present it is not known which of them still appear.

Hoover Institution   Joseph D. Dwyer

Iraq

The Iraqi Communist Party (ICP) has experienced many ups and downs since its founding over 40 years ago. Its greatest strength came in the mid-1940s and for two years after the fall of the monarchy in 1958. There is bitter enmity between the ICP and Iraq's ruling Baath Party stemming from the Communists' attacks on Baathists in 1959 and the latter's bloody reprisals in 1963 when 8 of 26 ICP Central Committee members were killed. During the fifteen years of the current Baath regime, ICP fortunes have on the whole been poor. From 1973 to 1979, the ICP participated in the Baath-controlled National Progressive Front. In 1979, ICP representatives were ousted from the cabinet, and the party was, in practice, denied any freedom to act; it was legal but repressed.

General Political Situation. The war with Iran, to which the ICP is opposed, dominated Iraqi life in 1982 to a far greater extent than in 1981. Iraqi forces, which had penetrated swiftly into Iranian territory in the first weeks of the war, were pushed back close to their borders in 1982. When Iraq called for negotiations, Iran refused. Its leaders asserted that they had no intention of conquering Iraq. "The only condition" for ending the war, said Khomeini, "is that the regime in Baghdad must fall and must be replaced by an Islamic republic" (*al-Majallah*, London, 20–26 November; *FBIS*, 23 November). Redeployed Iraqi forces have held off Iranian offensives for several months, and at year's end, the two armies continued to face each other along the international border.

The Baath regime has been politically damaged by military setbacks and by the humiliation of having the nonaligned conference scheduled to be held in Baghdad shifted to India because of the war. (President Saddam Husayn had put great store in hosting the conference and having a leading role in the movement.) The regime responded with a vigorous campaign, employing both propaganda and job/status sanctions; its theme is that true Iraqis willingly fight and sacrifice for their country. It has also made overtures for support to some erstwhile domestic enemies, allowing some displaced Kurds to return to their homes and releasing some Communists jailed for antiregime activites.

Communist Activities. The ICP, however, has continued the policy of opposition to the Baath government in Iraq, which it adopted in 1979 (see *YICA*, 1982, p. 24). In mid-1982, it condemned "the ruling regime in Baghdad and . . . [held] it responsible for all the serious political consequences, disasters and grave human losses caused by this [Iraq-Iran] war" (statement of eight Arab communist parties, *al-Safir*, Beirut, 26 May; *FBIS*, 2 June). Its opposition activity has been confined to the Kurdish regions of Iraq. A combination of very tight government security controls and fairly strong support—for the war, if not for the regime and its leaders—by the populace has virtually eliminated any significant communist activity in the major cities and towns, where two-thirds of Iraqis live. An ICP Central Committee member admitted that antiregime disturbances in Baghdad's working-class quarters were not the work of Communists. His assertion that the Democratic National Front "can only be pleased if Khomeini facilitates the fall of the Ba'thist regime" makes the ICP not just antiregime but also unpatriotic in the eyes of many Iraqis. (Interview with Fahri Karim, *L'Espresso*, Rome, 13 June; *FBIS*, 18 June.)

The ICP has continued its participation with the Democratic Party of Kurdistan/Iraq and the Socialist Party of Kurdistan in the Democratic National Front and has made some progress toward its goal of a comprehensive front of opposition forces. ICP and Patriotic Union of Kurdistan representatives met in July and issued a statement calling for unity among "nationalist forces" (Voice of the Iraqi Revolution, 7 July;

FBIS, 9 July). This agreement has led to a limited measure of joint antiregime activity by Patriotic Union and Democratic National Front elements.

Guerrilla activity against the central government continues in the Kurdish areas, although it is hampered by hostility and occasional fighting among the several Kurdish groups. ICP Central Committee member Fahri Karim claimed that "over a thousand Kurdish and Arab partisans" were in the field (*L'Espresso*, 13 June; *FBIS*, 18 June).

Around the beginning of 1982, the Kurd Aziz Muhammad was re-elected first secretary of the ICP's Central Committee (Voice of Iraqi Kurdistan, 8 February, citing the "latest issue" of *Tariq al-Sha'b*, the ICP paper; *FBIS*, 10 February). The place and circumstances of Aziz Muhammad's re-election were not specified, but he and other party leaders live outside Iraq. Aziz Muhammad was received twice by senior Syrian officials during the year. The party's dependence on Syrian goodwill became more noticeable in 1982; Syria helps opposition forces in Iraq and several times has permitted ICP statements to be aired over Syrian broadcast facilities. This is in part a function of Syria's close association with Iran and of its bitter hostility to the Baghdad regime.

The release of Communists from detention in Iraq (Radio Monte Carlo, 20 July; *FBIS*, 21 July) has been cited by one source as the reason for the USSR's willingness to improve relations and to be more forthcoming about arms supplies (MENA, Cairo, citing *al-Majallah*, 23 September; *FBIS*, 28 September). There are indications of strong differences of view within the ICP over responding to this move by Baghdad (*al-Majallah*, 16–22 October; *FBIS*, 20 October).

Government-to-government relations between Iraq and the USSR improved during the year. In April, celebrations of the tenth anniversary of the treaty of friendship and cooperation were restrained. In early June, the Soviets accorded Iraqi Deputy Prime Minister Tariq Aziz an unusually cool reception when he visited Moscow, apparently looking for military and political aid (*WP*, 5 and 6 June). A few days later, Iraq announced that it was withdrawing its forces in Iran to the international border. By autumn, the USSR had become more forthcoming with arms (Drew Middleton, *NYT*, 14 November). The year ended with relations at a respectable, but not close, level.

The exiled ICP leadership took an active part in inter-Arab communist affairs. It joined the Bahrain National Liberation Front and the Saudi, Jordanian, Syrian, Lebanese, Egyptian, and Palestinian communist parties in a statement on the situation in the Middle East. It opposed the Gulf Cooperation Council, the Camp David accords, and the imperialist, Zionist, reactionary alliance. It supported the Steadfastness and Confrontation Front of Syria, the People's Democratic Republic of Yemen, Libya, Algeria, and the Palestine Liberation Organization. By joining in this statement, the ICP gave its approval to the newly created Palestine Communist Party. (*Al-Safir*, 26 May; *FBIS*, 2 June.)

Swarthmore, Pennsylvania   John F. Devlin

Israel

Israel (population, four million, not including occupied territories) has a parliamentary form of government and a competitive multiparty system. Since the establishment of the state, communist parties have always been legal and have participated openly in political life; although regularly getting only a small minority of the vote, the parties' representation in the Knesset (parliament) is enhanced by the system of proportional representation. The Democratic Front for Peace and Equality (DFPE), which is dominated by the Communist Party of Israel (CPI), has had four seats (including three members of the CPI itself) in the Knesset since the last elections (1981). A poll conducted in October shows that the same level of electoral support continues (*Jerusalem Post*, International Edition, 7–13 November). The DFPE dominates politics in Arab towns but otherwise is peripheral to the political system and totally isolated from both the now dominant coalition led by the rightist Likud Bloc and the opposition Labor Alignment. No Communist has ever participated in any Israeli government.

Communist activity is illegal in the occupied territories, including the Palestinian-inhabited Gaza Strip and West Bank, with their population of over 1.3 million. Procommunist newspapers are banned in these territories, and possession of communist posters sometimes results in imprisonment. Some members of the Druze sect in the occupied Golan Heights (in effect annexed with the extension of Israeli law to the area in 1981) have apparently joined the CPI.

History. The New Communist List (Reshima Kommunistit Hadasha; RAKAH), mainly Arab in membership, broke away from the Israeli Communist Party (Miflaga Kommunistit Isra'elit; MAKI) in 1965. The disappearance of MAKI during the 1970s left RAKAH (as it is still widely called, although it is known internationally simply as the CPI) as Israel's only communist party. (For details, see *YICA*, 1982, p. 26.)

Membership. The CPI's membership is estimated at about 1,500, about 80 percent of whom are Arabs. But many of the party's leaders (including a majority on top party organs) are Jewish.

Leaders. The general secretary is Meir Vilner (a Jew). Tawfiq Toubi (an Arab) is deputy general secretary. Wolf Erlich and R. Khuri are chairman and deputy chairman, respectively, of the Central Control Commission. The Nineteenth Congress met in 1981, and another congress is scheduled for 1985. Plenary sessions of the Central Committee are normally held several times each year. There is a Politburo of nine members and four alternates and a seven-member Secretariat. The three CPI members of the Knesset are Tawfiq Zayyad (who is also mayor of Nazareth, Israel's largest Arab town), Vilner, and Toubi. Other prominent figures (all of whom are members of the Politburo) include Ruth Lubich, David Khenin, and Emile Habibi. No new developments in leadership or organization were reported during 1982.

Auxiliary Organizations and Principal Publications.   See *YICA*, 1982, pp. 27, 29.

Activities.   As usual, the CPI played a leading role in the celebration of the Day of the Land, celebrated by Arabs in Israel (and now also in the occupied territories) every 30 March to protest Israeli policies. Zayyad and Vilner were among the main speakers in the town of Sakhnin at a rally attended by 10,000 people. A general strike, which (according to Zayyad, quoted in *NYT*, 31 March) was run by the DFPE, was widely observed by Arabs, including noncommunists. Zayyad's wife and seven others were detained by police in Nazareth. Demonstrators flew Palestinian flags in several places, and youths stoned the police station in the town of Arrabe. Anticommunists led rival anti-Israeli protests in some places. The CPI organized rallies in Nazareth and other Arab towns on May Day (1 May).

According to the *Jerusalem Post* (International Edition, 4–10 July), the CPI maintained a "low profile in the villages" in the immediate aftermath of the Israeli invasion of Lebanon in June, with "the only activity reported" being "a conference on the virtues of the Soviet Union" in one town. However, there were violent protests lasting for several days in Arab towns—and incited by the CPI, according to Israeli officials—in the wake of the massacre of Palestinians in Lebanon during September. One Arab woman was killed, and police shot several people. Others, including Zayyad's eleven-year-old son, were beaten. (*NYT*, 23 September; *Jerusalem Post*, International Edition, 26 September–2 October, 3–9 October, 31 October–6 November.)

Policies.   On the domestic front, the CPI continues to emphasize its opposition to discrimination against the Arabs. Also, it calls for "a substantial reduction of the military budget, which would make it possible to bring nearer the solution of pressing economic problems, such as inflation." Only vague calls were made for "reshaping of the economic and social policy in the interest of the working people and middle strata." (Vilner, in *IB*, August 1981.)

As regards the broader aspects of the Arab-Israeli conflict, the CPI demands complete Israeli withdrawal from the occupied territories and acceptance of the Palestinians' right to self-determination and their own state. It also supports the continued existence of Israel within its pre-1967 frontiers. It accepts the right of Palestinian refugees to return. (Sammy Smooha and Don Peretz, "The Arabs in Israel," *Journal of Conflict Resolution*, September, p. 462.)

In November 1981, the ninth plenary meeting of the Central Committee "resolutely condemned the brutal measures of oppression . . . against the Palestinian people in the occupied territories." The policy of "finding new 'quislings' who would collaborate with the occupation authorities, at imposing 'administrative self-government' Camp David–style in order to perpetuate the occupation and pursue a colonialist policy" was singled out, as were "mass reprisals," curfews, "destruction of houses, the closing of [Bir Zeit University], the banning of the newspaper *Al-Fajr* (Dawn), mass arrests of prominent activists . . . and the brutal treatment of demonstrators." (*IB*, January, p. 30.) Pointing to the establishment of "civilian administration" in the occupied territories as a step toward annexation, the DFPE introduced a motion of no confidence in the Knesset in March (*World Affairs Report*, 12, no. 2, p. 244). The CPI was allegedly the "moving force" behind the Druze opposition to Israeli policies in the Golan Heights (Jersalem domestic service, 6 April; *FBIS*, 7 April). Vilner called "abolishing the colonial settlements in the Arab territories . . . the future government's top priority task" (*IB*, August 1981).

Erlich "condemned in the strongest terms the latest aggression" in Lebanon and demanded "an immediate cease-fire" and "unconditional withdrawal" (ADN, East Berlin, 25 June; *FBIS*, 30 June). Lubich said she was "ashamed that the sons of the Jewish people . . . are now bombing towns and killing innocent people in Lebanon" (BTA, Sofia, 3 July; *FBIS*, 6 July). Toubi declared that "the Israeli Government . . . bears responsibility for the mass murders of Palestinians in Beirut" and called for "a commission to expose those involved in the monstrous crimes." He also condemned the Reagan plan of 1 September for its rejection of Palestinian self-determination and for being "a further development of the Camp David agreements which cleared the way for aggression against Lebanon." (*Pravda*, 2 October; *FBIS*, 8 October.)

On broader international issues, the CPI strongly echoed Soviet positions. Lubich condemned the United States for "trying to create in the Middle East an aggressive pact with Israeli help" and of aiming at "toppling of the progressive anti-imperialist regimes of the region" (BTA, Sofia, 3 July; *FBIS*, 6 July). Khenin condemned "the new destructive weapons being developed, the decision of the Reagan administration on the production of the neutron weapon and the NATO decision on stationing new medium-range missiles in Western Europe" and praised "the initiatives of the Soviet Union, aimed at calming tension, disarmament and cutting down on the proliferation of the production of nuclear weapons and other mass destructive weapons to the point of destroying them." More broadly, he expressed "appreciation for the important role the Soviet Union plays and for how its policy benefits all nations" and condemned "incitement by the extremist, imperialist circles who are committing slander about the Soviet threat." (Radio Peace and Progress, Moscow, 26 December 1981; *FBIS*, 4 January.)

Foreign Contacts. Vilner led a delegation to a meeting in Athens of communist parties of fourteen countries in the Middle East and Red Sea and eastern Mediterranean regions in October 1981. Representatives of 90 communist parties (including the CPI) met in Prague in November 1981 to consider the work of the *World Marxist Review*. An Israeli delegation, including Khenin, Salim Jubran (a member of the Central Committee), and some noncommunists, visited the Soviet Union in December 1981 and met with Soviet representatives in plants, higher-education institutions, and other organizations on the invitation of the Soviet Peace Committee.

In May, Toubi was awarded the Order of Friendship of Peoples on the occasion of his sixtieth birthday. Khenin met with Polish party leaders in Warsaw in June. In the same month, Erlich met with East German party leaders in Berlin. Vilner headed a CPI delegation to Prague for an official visit in July at the invitation of the Czechoslovak Central Committee.

Erlich, Habibi, Felicia Langer (a lawyer known for her defense of accused Arabs), Lubich, and Toubi are listed among the thirteen Israeli members of the World Peace Council for 1980–1983.

Other Marxist Groups.   For information on the Israeli Socialist Organization (Matzpen) and breakaway organizations and on the Israeli New Left (SIAH), see *YICA*, 1982, p. 29.

With the formal approval of the Communist Party of Jordan (CPJ) in December 1981, a Palestinian Communist Party (PCP) was formed in February by the Palestinian Communist Organization in the West Bank and Gaza Strip (formerly part of the CPJ), Palestinian Communists in Lebanon, and Palestinian members of the CPJ outside Jordan (Voice of Palestine, 13 February; *FBIS*, 17 February). It is designed to operate in the Gaza Strip and West Bank and among other Palestinians without Jordanian citizenship living outside Jordan (the East Bank), presumably not including Arabs in Israel proper. According to one account, the PCP was already established in Gaza in December 1981 by people with close ties to George Habash, leader of the Popular Front for the Liberation of Palestine (Jerusalem domestic service, 28 January; *FBIS*, 29 January).

A founding congress was held, and a general secretary and a Politburo and Central Committee were chosen. (The date and location of the congress and the names of those chosen to fill the positions were not announced.) According to one report (Jerusalem domestic service, 12 February; *FBIS*, 12 February), the establishment of this party lacked Soviet approval and was a protest against improved relations between Amman and Moscow (Jerusalem domestic service, 8 December 1981; *FBIS*, 9 December 1981). But later it was reported that the Soviet Union supported the formation of the PCP, although it had opposed such a development in the past (*al-Hamishmar*, Tel Aviv, 14 February; *FBIS*, 17 February). The party newspaper, *al-Watan* (The homeland) is distributed clandestinely in the occupied territories. Dhamin Awdah, a member of the Central Committee, said a military wing will be organized to struggle against Israeli occupation (Kuwaiti News Agency, 13 February; *FBIS*, 17 February).

The PCP is said to hope to gain representation in the Palestine National Council and other organs of the Palestine Liberation Organization (PLO). A party communiqué announced acceptance of the PLO as the sole legitimate representative of the Palestinian people and of the PLO's call for establishment of an independent Palestinian state and for Israeli withdrawal and return of Palestinian refugees. It declared a willingness to work with other groups against Zionism and imperialism while retaining its ultimate commitment to communism. It condemned the Camp David agreements and Israeli settlements in occupied territories and supported the late Soviet President Leonid Brezhnev's call for an international conference to settle the Arab-Israeli conflict. (*al-Hamishmar*, 14 February; *FBIS*, 17 February.)

Vilner described the formation of the PCP as "the right step at the right time" and as "an historic shift as far as the communist movement in the Middle East is concerned" (ibid.). The PLO "withheld comment," at least initially (Kuwaiti News Agency, 13 February; *FBIS*, 17 February).

Conditions and Problems.   A general commitment to the functioning system of free elections and parliamentary government and the maintenance of a relatively high standard of living (severe economic problems, including the world's highest inflation rate, often exceeding 130 percent, notwithstanding), as well as Soviet and communist opposition to Israeli policies, make major communist support among the Jewish population unimaginable under foreseeable conditions. Even the economically disadvantaged, underrepresented Oriental Jews (those of Middle Eastern origin) have been attracted to a right-wing rather than to a left-wing stance and have been largely responsible for the recent predominance of the Likud. The Oriental Jewish splinter group known as the Black Panthers, which is allied with the CPI in the DFPE (and whose leader, Charlie Biton, is the only non-CPI member of the DFPE in the Knesset), represents a minor countercurrent.

Electoral support for the DFPE comes almost entirely from the Arab population, which is heavily concentrated in Galilee (northern Israel) and forms nearly 17 percent of the country's population (*Jerusalem Post*, International Edition, 7–13 November). Despite their Israeli citizenship, members of this minority increasingly identify with their fellow Palestinian Arabs and their cause. They are also embittered over various kinds of discrimination against them, particularly the gradual process of expropriating Arab land. With Arab nationalist parties banned, the Communists provide the only outlet for Arab grievances. For the most part, Arabs vote communist despite rather than because of the CPI's ideology. Also, some elements of the Arab population reject the CPI as being too soft in its espousal of Arab rights and acceptance of the legitimacy of Israel as a state. The CPI's appeal to the Arab population, on the other hand, seems to bar major success with the Jewish majority. General support for noncommunist factions of the PLO makes major support for a communist party unlikely in the occupied territories.

Foreign Policies.   Israel's foreign policy has always been dominated by its conflict with the Arab world. With the USSR and radical Third World movements supporting the Arabs, Israel has come to be at increasing odds with them. Thus Israel's invasion of Lebanon in 1982 is sometimes seen as a defeat of Soviet clients and as proof of the hollowness of Moscow's support for the Arabs; on the other hand, such actions—particularly the refusal so far to withdraw from occupied territories and to permit Palestinian self-determination—are thought by many as likely to result ultimately in the radicalization of the region.

Indiana State University

Glenn E. Perry

Jordan

The Communist Party of Jordan (al-Hizb al-Shuyu'i al-Urdunni; CPJ) was officially established in June 1951 and has operated under the guise of various popular front organizations since that time. Its work has centered on the West Bank, where it has drawn support from students, teachers, professional workers, and the lower middle class.

The CPJ has been illegal since 1957, although the government's normally repressive measures have been relaxed on occasion. At present, communist party membership is punishable by jail sentences of from three to fifteen years. Israeli sources report that Jordan has promised the Soviet Union that it will permit the CPJ to operate openly, although not under its own name, within the framework of the Jordanian-USSR Friendship Committee (*FBIS*, 2 July 1981). Few other radical organizations are active in Jordan; however, various Palestinian groups, such as the Marxist-oriented Popular Front for the Liberation of Palestine (embittered by "repression" of the Palestinians during 1970–1971), urge the overthrow of King Hussein. They appear to have little overt influence in Jordan. Beginning in 1982, Israel clamped down on the party in the West Bank because it had engaged in terrorist activities.

In late December 1981, the CPJ's Central Committee agreed to authorize the leaders of the Palestine Communist Organization, based on the West Bank and the Gaza Strip, to conduct preparatory work for establishing an independent Palestinian Communist Party (PCP) (*IB*, March). It was reported in early 1982 that the PCP, grouping Palestinian Communists in Lebanon, the West Bank, and the Gaza Strip as well as expatriate members of the CPJ, had been formed (*FBIS*, 11 February). The PCP held a founding congress and elected a secretary general and a Politburo. According to a communiqué published in *al-Nida'*, the Lebanese Communist Party daily, the PCP was established with the CPJ's blessing, but no date or place for the congress was cited (ibid.).

The CPJ probably has no more than a few hundred members; PCP membership is unknown. Jordan's population of about 3.3 million includes roughly 850,000 in Israeli-occupied East Jerusalem and the West Bank.

Leadership and Organization.   The CPJ is said to be a tightly organized, well-disciplined network of small cells. (For details regarding party leaders, see *YICA*, 1979, p. 413.) Jordanian members of the World Peace Council, a principal Soviet front, several of them previously identified as CPJ members, include Marwan al-Hussain, Omar Banna, Izz al-Din Tell, Samir Haddad, Marwan Hamoud (member of the Jordanian Senate); Mazen Husseini (secretary of the WPC); Ahmed Ireikat, Munther Karain, Dr. Hassan Khreis, Dr. Issa Koussous (member of the Jordanian Senate); Da ad Madh (president of the Jordanian Women's Union); Issa Mdanat (general secretary of the Peace and Solidarity Committee); Zuhair Mubaideen, Faris Nabulsi (president of the Peace and Solidarity Committee, Salem Nahas, Abdul Rahman Yaqhi (professor and president of the Writers' Union); Yacoub Ziyadin (vice-president of the Peace and Solidarity Committee) (Information Centre of the WPC, Helsinki, n.d.).

Until recently, there were several West Bank communist factions, including the Palestine Communist Organization (PCO), an establishment group headed by Bashir Barghuti, and the smaller Palestine Communist Party. Evidence is lacking as to whether both factions or only the PCO were reconstituted as the new Palestinian Communist Party, which was to include Palestinians living outside Jordan but not those who are citizens of Jordan. The latter were to be the exclusive responsibility of the CPJ, while Palestinian members of the CPJ living abroad would automatically join the PCP. (*IB*, March.) Prior to the Lebanese war, the Communists were said to have become increasingly active in the occupied territories, and many mayors of West Bank Palestinian towns were considered to be "procommunist" (AFP, Paris, 11 February; *FBIS*, 11 February).

Auxiliary and Mass Organizations. The Palestine National Front (PNF) is composed of professional and labor union representatives and "patriotic personalities." It was established in August 1973 on the West Bank, evidently on CPJ initiative, by Muhammad Abu Mayzar. A small organization with an estimated strength of 100–500 men, it is a resistance group reportedly containing communist exiles from Jordan, Syria, Iraq, and Lebanon. The PNF follows the Palestine Liberation Organization (PLO) line and advocates an independent Palestinian state comprising the West Bank and the Gaza Strip. Its program includes mass political struggle and armed resistance in the occupied territories. The PNF's precise relation to the CPJ or to the new PCP is unknown.

Party Internal Affairs. The CPJ has been described officially as the working-class party of two fraternal peoples—Jordanian and Palestinian. Despite its support of Palestinian statehood, the CPJ traditionally has been somewhat suspicious of the PLO.

The aim of the new PCP is the "establishment of an independent Palestinian state and the consolidation of the unity of the Palestinian people," according to a party communiqué (*FBIS*, 11 February). The party accepts the proposition that the Palestinian state should be created "in territories to be evacuated by Israel" (ibid.). The PCP is to be "guided in its activity by the doctrine of Marxism-Leninism, the principles of proletarian internationalism, and the documents of the international meetings of communist workers' parties, and is structured in accordance with the principles of democratic centralism" (*WMR*, April). Although the PCP accepts the PLO as the sole legitimate representative of the Palestinian people, it asserts the right to be represented in the PLO (ibid.).

Domestic Attitudes and Activities. The CPJ's leaders have consistently denounced the "reactionary regime" in Amman and its links with "imperialism." The CPJ's 1980 Central Committee report analyzes in some detail the party's attitudes toward the Jordanian government, the Palestinian revolution, and the PLO. (For further elaboration, see *YICA*, 1982, pp. 31–32.)

International Activities and Attitudes. In a statement published in the Beirut newspaper *al-Safir* on 26 May (*FBIS*, 2 June), the CPJ and the PCP joined six other Arab communist parties in denouncing "U.S. imperialism, Israel and the Arab reaction" for attempting to achieve a "complete imperialist hegemony" in the Middle East. The statement condemned the efforts of some Arab states to reconcile themselves to the Egyptian regime, criticized Iraq for starting the war with Iran, and deplored the U.S. "blockade" of Libya as well as the threats against the People's Democratic Republic of Yemen and the buildup of reactionary forces in the Persian Gulf region. In particular, it was noted, "U.S. imperialism openly sides with Israel," a "strategic ally" that provides the United States an "imperialist base." Israeli threats against Lebanon were described as "part of the imperialist-Zionist-reactionary plan" to liquidate the Palestinian revolution's armed presence, "thus ending its political role as the sole legitimate representative of the Palestinian Arab people," and to implement Israel's autonomy plan for the occupied territories. The statement concluded that the USSR is the "foremost" of the "trusted allies" of the Arab national liberation movement. Moreover, Arab-Soviet friendship is the "basic guarantee" for success in the masses' struggle for national and social liberation. (Ibid.)

Naim Ashhab, a member of the PCP Politburo and a former CPJ official, elaborated on similar themes in "The People's Will Is Unbroken—The Struggle Goes On," an analysis of the Palestinian situation as a result of the Lebanese war (*WMR*, October). Ashhab termed the Lebanese war "a stage in the process of stepping up world tensions begun by the Reagan Administration, the most reactionary and aggressive US administration of the recent period." The war underlined the new level of U.S.-Israeli coordination in implementing the "strategic cooperation" agreement signed in the fall of 1981, at the same time that it emphasized the "low efficiency" of the Arabs' Steadfastness and Resistance Front. The article denounced President Reagan for his supposed support of Israel while the "Israel butchers [were] perpetrating genocide in Lebanon." The U.S. aim, in Ashhab's view, was to achieve domination of the region and obtain "monopoly control" of the Middle East's energy resources through support of Israel. Ashhab asserted that Arab opinion was especially angered that Saudi Arabia had failed to use the oil weapon and its foreign-exchange reserves to pressure the West to halt the Israeli aggression.

Despite Israel's military might, its plans for a blitzkrieg miscarried, according to Ashhab, and the myth of Israeli superiority was "exploded." Israeli casualties were higher than in all previous wars. Beirut under siege was said to resemble the 1871 Paris Commune. The Palestinian resistance helped to stimulate an antiwar movement in Israel and, along with world opinion and U.N. debates and an international commission investigating Israeli crimes, played a part in thwarting the objectives of the U.S.-Israeli alliance. Ashhab described a U.S.-Israeli effort—apparently unsuccessful—to blackmail Jordan into entering the Camp David peace process and "ultimately becoming an accomplice in the liquidation of the rights of the Palestinian people."

The Ashhab article predicted that if Israel annexed the West Bank and Gaza, it would try to force a majority of Arabs to leave by using terrorist tactics. Ashhab opposed the formation of a Palestinian government-in-exile, which might injure Palestinian unity and weaken the PLO. The Soviet Union was thanked for "the necessary moral and material aid and support" to the Palestinian and Lebanese victims, as evidenced by President Brezhnev's messages to Reagan and Arafat. (Ibid.).

Publications. The CPJ publishes *al-Jamahir* (Masses) and an underground newspaper, *al-Watan* (Homeland); both appear once or twice a month, the former in Jordan and latter on the West Bank. The party also has issued a political and theoretical magazine *al-Haqiqah* (Truth), distributed in Jordan and the West Bank. These publications have been circulated clandestinely on both sides of the Jordan River, except for *al-Watan*, which has been restricted mainly to the West Bank. The PNF also publishes is own newspaper, *Filastin* (Palestine). News of the CPJ activities, as well as those of the new PCP, frequently appears in the organs of the Lebanese Communist Party, *al-Akhbar* and *al-Nida'*.

U.S. Department of State   Norman F. Howard
Washington D.C.

(Note: Views expressed in this article are the author's own and do not represent those of the State Department.)

Lebanon

The roots of the Lebanese Communist Party (al-Hizb al-Shuyu'i al-Lubnani; LCP) are traceable to the establishment of the Lebanese People's Party in October 1924 by intellectuals and workers. The LCP's First Congress was held in December 1943–January 1944. Initially unresponsive to Arab nationalism, the party adopted a more sympathetic stance at its Second Congress in July 1968. According to LCP Secretary General George Hawi, the party's membership remained stable at about 2,000 in the late 1960s but has increased seven to eight times since then (*Monday Morning*, 8–14 June, 1981; *FBIS*, 17 June 1981). The greatest influx of new members took place in 1974 when the membership allegedly increased more than 60 percent—all of them under age 25. Membership doubled during the 1975–1976 civil war, when the party was said to have about 5,000 volunteers under arms. The Communists traditionally have drawn much of their support from the Greek Orthodox community, although Shia Muslims are increasingly active in the party. The population of Lebanon is about three million (the demographic impact of the civil war and subsequent internal strife cannot be determined accurately).

Leadership and Organization. The congress, which is supposed to be convened every four years, is the supreme LCP organ. Owing to the instability in Lebanon, the Fourth Congress was not held until 1979 and was characterized by complete secrecy. During the congress, Niqula al-Shawi was elected to the new post of party president, an honorary position created for the longtime LCP leader. George Hawi, the effective leader of the party, was elected secretary general. (For a listing of Central Committee members, see *YICA*, 1981, p. 14.) Members of the World Peace Council in Lebanon, some of them Communists, are reported to include Sheikh Abdallah Aleili, George Abou-Chaar, George Batal (member of the LCP Politburo), Fouad Chabaklo, Marie Edde-Tabet, Albert Farhat (secretary of the Lebanese Peace Movement), Elias Habre (president of the National Trade Union Federation), Dr. Hachem Husseini (member of parliament), El-Sayed Ali Mahdi Ibrahim, Farid Joubrane, (member of parliament), Walid Jumblat (president of the Progressive Socialist Party), Msgr. Paul Khoury (archbishop of the Greek Orthodox Church of Southern Lebanon), Dr. Albert Mansour (member of parliament), Farouk Massarani, Dr. Hussein Mroueh, Nadim 'Abd al-Samad (member of the LCP Politburo and secretary of its Central Committee) (Information Centre of the WCP, Helsinki, n.d.). 'Abduh Dib al-Laqqis, a communist official from Baalbek, was reportedly a defendant in a murder trial in Beirut (Voice of Lebanon, 29 April; *FBIS*, 30 April). Rafic Samhoun, a member of the LCP Politburo, noted that the Secretariat has evolved into "a purely executive body" and that LCP administrative work has become more efficient. According to Samhoun, since the Second Congress in 1962, LCP "party life has been placed on the foundation of the Leninist principles of democratic centralism"; party committees were enlarged both to reinvigorate them and to improve leadership; party work in "large" factories, among agricultural workers, and poor peasants was intensified in order to increase the LCP's working-class component; and the party assigned members to work in trade unions, young people's associations, and student, intellectual, professional, and sports groups. (*WMR*, February.)

Domestic Views and Activities. The LCP has taken an active role in Lebanese affairs. It belongs to the National Movement, a coalition of leftist parties, and its secretary general has been described variously as "vice-president" of the National Movement or simply "member" of the Executive Office of the movement's Politboro (*FBIS*, 27 February, 17 June 1981). According to Rafic Samhoun, the LCP has "begun to play the leading role in the class struggle." It is "the main contingent of the Lebanese national-patriotic movement" and is active in the movement's central political council and regional councils. During the civil war, beginning in 1975, "armed struggle became the basic form of our [LCP] activity." Since 1979, significant progress has been registered toward the Fourth Congress goal of turning the LCP into a "mass fighting party." In "fascist"-controlled territory (that dominated by the Phalange), the party operated in very small groups, and the LCP "had to go over entirely to an illegal status." In "Israeli-occupied" Lebanon, presumably the region controlled by dissident Maj. Saad Haddad prior to the Israeli invasion, the LCP combined illegal work with guerrilla operations against Israeli forces and their accomplices, while in the so-called national-patriotic areas, the LCP joined military activities with work in the social sector and protecting the security of the population. Samhoun says that the party believes in establishing "people's security committees" in every district and neighborhood to protect the inhabitants against subversion. (WMR, February.)

In a statement shortly before the Israeli invasion, the LCP urged support for the Palestinian revolution and the Lebanese National Movement, confronted as they both were by Israeli aggression; establishment of the broadest possible Lebanese national front; and resistance to efforts to "drag Lebanon into a capitulationist settlement with Israel" (al-Safir, 26 May; FBIS, 2 June).

The year 1982 witnessed the continuation of battles between communist groups and Amal, the Shia militia. For example, Amal-communist clashes took place in the Baalbek district in December 1981 and again in January 1982; in Beirut, involving the Organization of Communist Action, in January; and in southern Lebanon in January. In mid-April, communist militiamen reportedly killed a local Amal leader at a checkpoint in southern Lebanon, setting off six days of fighting in the south as well as clashes in Beirut and its suburbs. A confrontation between communist forces and the "Tripoli popular resistance" occurred in the Tripoli area in late July (Voice of Lebanon, 31 July; FBIS, 4 August).

Rafic Samhoun analyzed the Lebanese situation following the Israeli invasion in an article entitled "When Masks Are Discarded: Roots of the New Israeli Act of Aggression in the Middle East" (WMR, August). He noted the basic conditions leading to the Israeli action: Arab reaction, assisted by Saudi Arabia, was becoming more active; imperialism, Zionism, and reaction were attempting to destroy the alliance among the Palestinian resistance, the Lebanese national patriotic forces, and Syria; and Israel was concerned about the growing resistance in the West Bank and Gaza led by the Palestine Liberation Organization (PLO). Israel's war aim, according to Samhoun, was to destroy the PLO's military and political influence in the Middle East and put an end to the Palestinian resistance. Israel also wanted to make Syria more "pliable" and to encourage the establishment of a compliant, reactionary regime in Lebanon that would cooperate with Israel. The article denounced Israel's use of barbarous weapons and scorched-earth tactics. Israel "had recourse to undisguised genocide, aiming at the physical extermination of the Palestinians" resident in Lebanon. Samhoun alleged that the Israeli invasion was started with "the knowledge and approval of Washington" and continued with U.S. support.

According to Tass, the LCP issued a statement in October in Nabatiyah and other southern towns urging more vigorous resistance to the Israeli invaders (Tass, Moscow, 20 October; FBIS, 21 October). The statement asserted that Israel's occupation of Lebanon was part of a U.S.-Israeli plan to dominate the Middle East, in which Israel played the role of political, economic, and cultural policeman. Israel's attempt to plunge Lebanon into civil war was being resisted by the Lebanese masses' desire for national unity. In particular, the LCP called for a general patriotic congress—to be attended by all political forces—that would develop a plan to liberate occupied Lebanon and secure the release of all detainees from Israeli jails.

International Views and Activities. The LCP has maintained a consistently pro-Soviet posture, as revealed in its statements and activities over the years. According to Rafic Samhoun, fraternal cooperation with the USSR and other socialist countries is the only route to a just peace in the Middle East (WMR, August). In January, Karen Brutents, deputy chief of the Soviet party's International Department, visited Beirut and met with George Hawi and other LCP officials "within the framework of cooperation and exchange of visits" between the Soviet party and "the friendly Lebanese Communist Party." Brutents also met with the Lebanese president and prime minister. An LCP communiqué following the visit noted that both sides shared identical views on the dangers of imperialist policies, particularly those of the United States. The LCP thanked the USSR for its "principled policies" in defense of world peace and a just Middle East settlement, including the right of the Palestinians to their own state under PLO leadership. (Al-Safir, 26

January; *FBIS*, 29 January.) In a statement published in *al-Safir* on 26 May, the LCP along with seven other Arab communist parties declared that Arab-Soviet friendship was essential for success in the popular struggle for liberation (*FBIS*, 2 June; for further elaboration of the viewpoint expressed in this article, see the profile on Jordan). In June, Central Committee Secretary Nadim 'Abd al-Samad met with his Soviet counterpart, Boris Ponomarev, and Karen Brutents in Moscow. They discussed the Lebanese situation, and Samad thanked the Soviet party and the Soviet Union for their "aid and support" to the Lebanese and the Palestinians. Both parties demanded an immediate end to the Israeli blockade of Beirut and Israel's withdrawal from Lebanon. (Tass, 25 June; *FBIS*, 28 June.) In October, a delegation of the All-Arab People's Congress, including LCP Politburo member George Batal, met in Moscow with officials of the Supreme Soviet and the International Department. The two sides, purporting to represent the Soviet and Arab publics, demanded immediate, total Israeli withdrawal from Lebanon, supported Lebanon's quest for territorial integrity and sovereignty, condemned Israel's "barbarous aggression," and criticized U.S. connivance with Israeli crimes in Lebanon (Tass, Moscow, 20 October; *FBIS*, 21 October).

In other international activities, Bulgaria's State Council awarded the Order of Georgi Dimitrov to LCP President al-Shawi for contributing to the struggle against imperialism, strengthening the unity between the workers' movement and international communism, and promoting Bulgarian-Lebanese ties (BTA, Sofia, 18 June; *FBIS*, 21 June). George Hawi received the East German ambassador to Lebanon in July and praised the solidarity of the German people with the Lebanese and Palestinians in their struggle against Israel. Hawi stated that the LCP's aim at present was to achieve the unity of all Lebanese parties and forces in their opposition to Israeli occupation. He thanked the USSR for its support of the Arabs and its opposition to "imperialist-Zionist occupation" (*Neues Deutschland*, East Berlin, 26 July; *FBIS*, 28 July).

LCP Politburo member Karim Ruwwah visited South Yemen in August (Aden domestic service, 20 August; *FBIS*, 24 August). In a late 1981 statement in Beirut, Hawi called for greater solidarity with the Libyan people, who were said to be threatened by imperialism, Zionism, and reaction. He asserted that an Israeli-Egyptian plan of aggression against Libya was being implemented with direct U.S. participation. (*IB*, September 1981.)

Publications.   The party publishes a daily newspaper, *al-Nida'* (The call), which celebrated its twentieth anniversary in 1979. Other LCP publications, distributed with varying degrees of regularity during the Lebanese crisis, are the weekly magazine *al-Akhbar* (The news) and the literary and ideological monthly *al-Tariq* (The road). These organs also serve as general information media for illegal communist parties in the Middle East.

The Organization of Communist Action (OCAL).   The OCAL, composed mostly of students, was formed in May 1970 and held its First Congress in 1971. Like the LCP, it has drawn recruits from Shia migrants in Beirut. Its secretary general is Muhsin Ibrahim, who is also secretary general of the National Movement. The OCAL has consistently supported the Palestinian resistance and has maintained close ties with the Democratic Front for the Liberation of Palestine. Since its First Congress, the OCAL has moderated its strong support for China in the Sino-Soviet conflict; at present it rejects loyalty either to Moscow or Beijing. In recent years, the OCAL and the LCP have drawn closer.

Following a meeting of its Politburo, reported in *al-Nahar* (16 May; *FBIS*, 21 May), OCAL called for the containment of the "fascist" Phalangist regime. It criticized U.S. attempts to attract Arab states to its side under Egyptian leadership and to polarize Arab governments by relying on Saudi Arabia and the reactionaries in the Persian Gulf region. According to the OCAL, the aim of the U.S.-Arab reactionary plot, led by President Hosni Mubarak of Egypt, is to liquidate the Palestinian revolution, encircle Syria and Libya, liquidate South Yemen's "progressive posture," isolate Algeria, and "cancel out" the Lebanese National Movement and the Syrian role in Lebanon in order to force a peace with Israel. The OCAL called for "an Arab national counteroffensive against U.S. interests and for a real and decisive confrontation with the imperialist-Zionist-reactionary alliance." Although OCAL supports Iran's Islamic revolution, is asserts that Iran has been unable "to promote real revolutionary solutions to the problems of democracy, social progress and the national rights of the Iranian peoples."

Following the Lebanese war, Muhsin Ibrahim warned against transgressions by the Christian militias and the Lebanese army. In a press interview on 11 October, he urged the multinational force in Lebanon to intervene to protect citizens, nationalists, and refugees in the camps. In the light of security plans for Beirut, he called for removal of barriers still being erected by the militias. (Clandestine Voice of Arab Lebanon, 12 October; *FBIS*, 13 October.) In May, an OCAL delegation led by Politburo member Fawaz al-Tarabulsi visited South Yemen and stressed OCAL's full support for the Palestinian cause, solidarity with South Yemen, and support of the Soviet initiative to limit the arms race (Aden domestic service, 2 May; *FBIS*, 6 May).

U.S. Department of State   Norman F. Howard
Washington, D.C.

(Note: Views expressed in this article are the author's own and do not represent those of the State Department.)

Morocco

The Moroccan Communist Party (Parti communiste marocain), founded in 1943 as a branch of the French Communist Party, was banned by the French protectorate in 1952. After three years of open operations in independent Morocco, it was banned in 1959. Renamed the Party of Progress and Socialism (Parti du progrès et du socialisme; PPS), it was granted legal status in 1974. In the 1976 municipal elections, the party secured a modest representation on the city council of Casablanca. The PPS participated in the Moroccan national elections in the spring of 1977 and won one seat in parliament. The PPS has about 800 active cell members, and estimates of total party membership range from 1,500 to 4,000. Morocco's population is just over 21 million.

Leadership and Party Affairs. The PPS's Second Congress (February 1979) re-elected 'Ali Yata as secretary general and elected a seven-member Secretariat (see *YICA*, 1980, p. 425).

Political Situation. Political unrest was muted in Morocco during 1982, although a variety of tensions continued just below the surface. King Hassan used the continuation of the seven-year war over the Western Sahara as a rationale for delaying a long-promised liberalization of the political system. Economic strains continued to result from a sluggish performance in the agricultural sector, although the grain harvest showed a marked improvement over the disastrous drought of 1981. Disturbances occurred on university campuses, where students demanded the withdrawal of security guards. In December 1981, police arrested about a hundred students from Mohammed V University in Rabat following violent clashes with security guards recently placed on the campus (AFP, 10 December 1981; *FBIS*, 17 December 1981).

Activities of the PPS. The view of the PPS toward the country's economic crisis and social tensions remains substantially unchanged (see *YICA*, 1981, p. 18). The PPS's short-term goals are more efficient management of the existing economic system to strengthen the internal front against neighboring Algeria and more equitable distribution of the benefits of the economic system. The party favors the replacement of the present government coalition by a broad national front government that includes the Moroccan left, that is, the PPS and the Socialist Union of Popular Forces, the country's major left-wing opposition party. In

November 1981, the PPS sent a delegation to Prague to attend a four-day meeting to consider the work from 1977 to 1981 of the international journal of communist and workers' parties, the *World Marxist Review* (*IB*, January).

Foreign Policy. The PPS remains a solid supporter of the Moroccan government in the campaign to "recover" the Western Sahara, a former Spanish colony claimed by Morocco. This support includes harsh criticism of socialist Algeria, which is blamed by the Moroccan government for the continuation of the costly conflict. On Middle East issues, the party condemns Israeli aggression and criticizes U.S. "interference" in the Arab world. These views were stated by PPS Secretary General 'Ali Yata, the party's sole member of parliament and editor of the PPS daily journal *al-Bayane*, during an August 1981 visit to Bulgaria (Sofia domestic service, 28 August 1981; *FBIS*, 1 September 1981).

Morocco received a series of visits during 1982 from high-level Soviet officials. Among the visitors were Education Minister Georgy Veselov in March (Rabat domestic service, 23 March; *FBIS*, 24 March); a delegation headed by the first deputy minister of health, which attended the Istiqlal Party congress in April (*Pravda*, 24 April; *FBIS*, 28 April); a Soviet party delegation led by the deputy chief of the Central Committee's International Department, which went to Casablanca in May at the invitation of the PPS (Moscow Arabic service, 13 May; *FBIS*, 19 May); a parliamentary delegation led by the deputy chairman of the Supreme Soviet Presidium, which made a three-day working visit in August (Maghreb Arabe Presse, Rabat, 12 August; *FBIS*, 13 August); and a high official of the Foreign Ministry, who visited that same month (Rabat domestic service, 18 August; *FBIS*, 19 August). These visits did not deter the semiofficial Moroccan press from complaining bitterly about the use of sophisticated Soviet-made weapons against Moroccan forces in the Western Sahara and questioning Moscow's professed neutrality in the Saharan dispute (*Le Matin*, Paris, 23 January; *FBIS*, 3 February).

While maintaining a broad range of working relations with the Soviet Union, Morocco strengthened its military relationship with the United States in 1982, leading some foreign observers to describe a new "strategic axis" between Washington and Rabat (see *Le Monde diplomatique*, July, pp. 6–7). Between October 1981 and February 1982, a stream of high-level U.S. officials visited Morocco, including Secretary of Defense Caspar Weinberger, Secretary of Commerce Malcolm Baldrige, and Secretary of State Alexander Haig. In November 1981, the United States agreed to provide Morocco with various measures to counter Soviet-made SA-6 missile systems recently introduced into battle against Moroccan forces in the Sahara. During Haig's visit in February, the United States and Morocco agreed to establish a joint military commission. Haig also expressed interest in obtaining transit rights at former U.S. military installations in Morocco for use by U.S. aircraft as part of the Rapid Deployment Force being planned for the Middle East. These transit rights could permit U.S. planes to land and refuel at Moroccan air bases during periods of military emergency in the Middle East. The question of U.S. transit rights in Morocco was a major topic of interest during King Hassan's official state visit to Washington from 18 to 20 May. Within a week, the United States and Morocco signed a military agreement in Washington. This accord, in force for six years and renewable, provides U.S. forces transit rights at two Moroccan air bases during times of crisis in the Middle East. (*NYT*, 28 May.)

Publications. The PPS publishes two daily newspapers, *al-Bayane* in French and *al-Makafih* (The fighter) in Arabic.

Portland State University   John Damis

Mozambique

The Front for the Liberation of Mozambique (Frente de Libertação de Moçambique; FRELIMO), "a Marxist-Leninist vanguard party," has been in power in Mozambique since 1975. This year saw mounting threats from guerrilla forces in the countryside and from a deteriorating economy. Yet the political structure and longevity of FRELIMO have allowed it to survive downturns in its fortunes in the past.

FRELIMO, formed from three small parties, held its First Congress in September 1962. Afterwards, it waged a guerrilla war against Portuguese colonial rule from 1964 to 1974. (For more background, see *YICA*, 1982, p. 37.) An independent People's Republic of Mozambique was proclaimed on 25 June 1975.

Organization and Leadership. In the course of FRELIMO's "struggle for liberation" against Lisbon's rule, the guerrilla front moved leftward. FRELIMO's Second Congress in 1968 adopted many features of standard communist organization, including cell structure, democratic centralism, self-criticism, and pervasive Marxian terminology. This radicalization process helped to generate internal feuds, resulting in several assassinations among the leadership. The most prominent death was that of FRELIMO President Eduardo Mondlane in 1969. After a six-month rule by a troika, Samora Moises Machel, who commanded the military forces, became president as well.

On 25 June, during a celebration marking the twentieth anniversary of the founding of FRELIMO, President Machel was awarded the honorary title "hero of the People's Republic of Mozambique" (Maputo domestic service, 25 June; *FBIS*, 29 June). In August, the FRELIMO Central Committee awarded Machel a medal of internationalism for the liberation of Zimbabwe (Maputo domestic service, 22 August; *FBIS*, 24 August).

The Third Congress in 1977 approved the Central Committee's recommendation for the transformation of FRELIMO into a "Marxist-Leninist vanguard party" (Mozambique, Angola and Guinea Information Centre, *Central Committee Report of the Third Congress of FRELIMO*, p. 33; for additional background, see *YICA*, 1982, p. 40).

Since independence FRELIMO has sought to erect the conventional structures of a communist party in power. At the apex of FRELIMO's organizational scheme is the Congress; three have been convened since the formation of FRELIMO, and one is planned for 1983. Official figures state that at the Third Party Congress, 40 percent of the delegates were classified as working class, 27 percent as peasants, and 33 percent as belonging to the white-collar sector, the army, and so on. The Third Congress expanded the membership of the Central Committee, which is to implement the policy adopted by the congresses, to 67 members. Central Committee meetings are called to maintain continuity.

In 1982, the tenth session of the Central Committee expelled one of its members, João Facitela Pelembe, for his political, moral, and social behavior (Maputo domestic service, 22 August; *FBIS*, 24 August). During the same session, it was announced that the economy and the guerrilla situation within the country will be the main topics at the Fourth Congress (Maputo domestic service, 17 August; *FBIS*, 19 August).

Between meetings, the Central Committee depends on the Permanent Political Committee, a type of political bureau, whose ten-member composition was determined by the last congress. This committee has wide powers because it is the policymaking body of FRELIMO. Most of the committee's members also hold ministerial positions in the government and sit on the Council of Ministers, the cabinet of the government. The Permanent Political Committee constitutes Mozambique's supreme political authority. Its members are

Samora Moises Machel, Marcelino dos Santos, Joaquim Alberto Chissano, Alberto Joaquim Chipande, Armando Emilio Guebuza, Jorge Rebelo, Mariano Matsinha, Sebastião João Marcos Mabote, Jacinto Soares Veloso, and Mário de Graça Machungo. All except Machungo have been members of FRELIMO since its inception. As yet, no exact figures on the size of the party have been reported. A campaign to widen the party's base among the population in 1978 stated that it entailed the "admission of tens of thousands of new members to the party" (People's Power, no. 12, p. 41).

Mozambique's constitution, which was approved by the Central Committee in 1977, accorded FRELIMO the status of a state institution since the "People's Republic of Mozambique is guided by the political line laid down by FRELIMO" (Art. 3). On 18 and 19 March, the first party national conference, convened by the ninth session of the Central Committee, was held in Maputo. Its objectives were (1) to draft topics for the Fourth Congress; (2) to launch a broad party and mass movement in support of the Fourth Congress; and (3) to study possible alterations in the status and program of FRELIMO (Maputo domestic service, 20 March; Facts and Reports, 12, no. G, p. 12).

In Mozambique, as in long-established communist states, the most prominent party members hold important posts in the government. The constitution provides that the president has the power to make many appointments. President Samora Machel, who is also president of FRELIMO, is empowered to appoint provincial governors and members of the Council of Ministers, among others. His power reaches to annulling decisions of the provincial assemblies. The congress abolished the office of vice-president.

When FRELIMO reorganized its guerrilla army along conventional lines in 1980, it formed a customary officer corps and conferred high military rank on leading party officials. President Machel received the title of field marshal. (For other appointments, see YICA, 1982, p. 39.) The constitution regards the People's National Assembly as the highest legislative organ. The National Assembly is made up of delegates from throughout the country chosen by an elaborate election process. (For details, see ibid.) Members of the Council of Ministers and the ten provincial governors also sit in the National Assembly.

Mass Organizations.   During the guerrilla war for independence, FRELIMO, like other political movements, made special appeals to various groups in the population. Women, for example, received much attention in the course of the war. This trend continued into the independence era. The Organização da Mulher Moçambicana (Organization of Mozambican Women), according to its pronouncements, seeks to liberate women from their traditional standing and increase their economic and political opportunities, in addition to publicizing and implementing the party line. FRELIMO has also established a Mozambique Youth Organization and formed hundreds of production councils for factories, mills, and foundries (People's Power, no. 10, p. 21; for additional background, see YICA, 1982, p. 39). Much less well established are national organizations for artists and journalists.

The People's Forces for the Liberation of Mozambique (FPLM).   Mozambique's army developed from a guerrilla force in the independence war. It is still in the process of being remolded as a conventional army with heavy weapons and military vehicles. The government uses the 15,000-man FPLM as both a defense force and a mobilizing cadre to spread the party message. The widening presence of the Resistencia Nacional Moçambicana (Mozambique National Resistance; MNR)—an antigovernment guerrilla force, which in the last year has spread sabotage operations over much of the countryside—has necessitated that the FPLM concentrate on internal security ("Havoc in the Bush," Africa Confidential, 21 July). The MNR, for example, struck at power lines in the central zone, leaving the city of Beira without electricity and water for days, and cut the oil pipeline to Beira from Zimbabwe. It also abducted numerous foreign technicians working on projects within the country. Some have been released.

Led by Afonso Dhlakama, the MNR is reputed to receive support from the Republic of South Africa. Yet it remains a truism of insurgent wars that guerrilla forces cannot operate without some popular endorsement or, at least, the tacit support of those disaffected with their opponents. (NYT, 1 November.) To counter the MNR's raids, the FPLM stepped up its arming and training of select elements of the population in areas under attack, such as Chimoro district, Tete province, and Maputo province. Increasing concerns for security partially explain the issuing of identity cards to Maputo's population. Another part of this registration drive is seen as a means to cope with the heavy population drift to the capital city. Maputo's population in April was reported to be 850,000, a rise of 100,000 since the national census in August 1980. (*People's Power*, no. 20, p. 38.)

Domestic Affairs. In 1982, the Mozambican economy continued to deteriorate, and the Maputo government moved to seek Western economic assistance. Only tea production appeared to exceed preindependence output, according to official Mozambican sources (*Notícias*, 15 July). One explanation of the poor economy is the disruptions caused by the MNR. Worsening economic conditions, in turn, create conditions favorable to the MNR. The serious military situation required the government to appoint military commanders to all ten provinces (Maputo domestic service, 5 March; *FBIS*, 10 March).

Another explanation for Mozambique's economic plight stems from its policies of implementing Marxist-Leninist doctrines. The nationalization of much private property and indeed the services of doctors, lawyers, and morticians contributed to the flight of Portuguese settlers who possessed the skills and capital necessary for sustained development. In 1981 Machel announced a change in policy allowing for more private, small-scale initiatives (see *YICA*, 1982, p. 41). This year Mozambique sought closer ties with the European Economic Community (ECC) by entering negotiations with the Lomé Convention, which links the ECC with African, Caribbean, and Pacific states (*Times*, London, 11 October). To deal with a flourishing black market, the government opened special, high-priced shops in major cities. These shops are state-owned and stocked with imported foodstuffs, electronics equipment, and consumer items (*African Business*, February).

Mozambique faced several defections this year. Jorge Costa, national security director, fled to South Africa. Soon after, Zulfikar Tricamegy, of the financial department in the Presidency, and Antonio Rocha, from the Mozambican embassy in Zimbabwe, fled. Later, João Ataide, Mozambique's ambassador to Portugal, abandoned his post. (*People's Power*, no. 20, p. 37.)

International Affairs. At independence the People's Republic of Mozambique theoretically adopted a policy of nonalignment. As with many Third World nations, professed nonalignment means a search for diverse international relations so as to attract aid and trade. At the Third Congress, President Machel, however, stated that Mozambique considers "the socialist countries and the Marxist-Leninist Parties" its "natural allies" (*Africa Contemporary Record*, 1976–77, p. B297). This compatibility with socialist states and Marxist-Leninist parties stems from the political orientation of the ruling FRELIMO party.

During the war, FRELIMO relied almost totally on communist countries for military aid. Nonmilitary assistance came from international organizations and some Western countries. Because FRELIMO received sustained aid from both the Soviet Union and the People's Republic of China, it generally kept aloof from the Sino-Soviet controversy. Many observers concluded that FRELIMO stood closer to Beijing than to Moscow since Chinese cadres in southern Tanzania trained Mozambican recruits in Mao Zedong's politics as well as in military tactics. After independence Mozambique moved closer to the Soviet camp and has remained closer to Moscow than to Beijing. (For additional background, see *YICA*, 1982, p. 40.) Once again, Mozambique this year voted against a resolution demanding that the Soviet Union withdraw its troops from Afghanistan (*NYT*, 11 November).

Beginning in 1981, Mozambique began to reach out to noncommunist countries for assistance in dealing with its faltering economy and rising guerrilla opposition. The most salient example of Mozambique's turning to the West was its first agreement with West Germany. In the agreement, Maputo accepted the West German view of Berlin—disputed by the Warsaw Pact countries, which refuse to see Berlin as a state of the Federal Republic (*Guardian*, 10 August). Consequently, Bonn withdrew its veto of EEC aid to Mozambique, and a $10 million EEC loan has been agreed in principle. Maputo also sought out and received Portuguese military support to combat the MNR. Lisbon dispatched a military attaché to Maputo to facilitate training and support in Mozambique, and Mozambican officers are scheduled to receive military training in Portugal in 1983 (*CSM*, 17 November). Soviet naval vessels continued to anchor in Mozambican ports during the year.

In May, FRELIMO signed a five-year cooperation agreement with Tanzania's ruling party, Chama Cha Mapinduzi, aimed at fostering closer ties between the two parties and "at synchronizing their respective national development strategies" (Radio Dar es Salaam to east, central, and southern Africa, 6 May; *FBIS*, 7 May).

Approaches to the West have not diminished Mozambique's economic as well as political and social orientation toward the communist world. Soviet-Mozambican trade reportedly tripled between 1980 and 1981 and is expected to increase further in the future (*World Affairs Report*, 12, no. 1, p. 119). Cuba, Bulgaria, and East Germany continued to furnish aid. In 1982, 2,000 Mozambicans reportedly departed for Bulgaria for training and education (*African Business*, September). North Korea and Mozambique signed a protocol of cooperation in agriculture, construction, industry, and trade. Mozambique also signed an agreement with Libya for economic and technical cooperation (Maputo domestic service, 10 March; *FBIS*, 11 March).

FRELIMO's chief international concern remained South Africa. Although Pretoria provides economic assistance to Mozambique's railways and Maputo's harbor, it backs the MNR, which disrupts Mozambican development. Concern in South Africa about Mozambique revolves around its support for guerrilla forces opposed to white rule from Pretoria. FRELIMO's support led South African Defense Minister Magnus Malan to warn that his country might find it necessary to initiate a "Lebanese-type invasion" of Mozambique (*Southern Africa*, December, p. 10). Mozambican officials also stated that the government of Malawi has allowed MNR forces to set up bases on Malawian territory for attacks into Zambezia province in central Mozambique (Johannesburg domestic service, 6 October; *FBIS*, 7 October).

Publications. The government controls all media. Since independence, FRELIMO has relied on two main publications to carry its messages to the populace: the daily paper *Notícias* and the weekly magazine *O Tempo*. In 1981, the government launched two more national-circulation newspapers to improve the popular appeal of the media. *Diario de Moçambique* appears in Beira, Mozambique's second city, and *Domingo* is distributed on Sundays. (For additional background, see *YICA*, 1982, p. 41.) *Voz da Revolução*, an organ of the Central Committee, focuses on developing theoretical studies of Marxism and FRELIMO policies for Mozambique.

Hoover Institution   Thomas H. Henriksen

Nigeria

The return to civilian rule in Nigeria in December 1979 also marked the emergence of a new communist party, the Socialist Working People's Party of Nigeria (SWPP). The SWPP is the lineal descendant of the Socialist Workers and Farmers Party, which was banned by the military government in 1966. The SWPP held its first congress in November 1978, and delegates from fourteen of the nineteen states attended. The SWPP hoped to contest the November 1979 elections but was unable to meet the conditions set down by the Federal Electoral Commission. These conditions included the establishment of party offices in at least thirteen states and a provision opening the party to all citizens. By December the SWPP had not received a certificate of recognition, and it appears unlikely that it will do so in time for the November 1983 elections.

The SWPP continues its activities as an "association." Its declared aim is "to organize the working people of Nigeria towards winning political power and building a socialist state founded on the ideas of Scientific Socialism, that is, on the impregnable alliance of the working class, the farmers, progressive intelligentsia, the masses of the toiling people of our country and on proletarian internationalism" (*African Communist*, no. 79, p. 99). The party publishes a journal, *New Horizon*, and works actively in the new labor organization, the Nigerian Labour Congress (*WMR*, October 1981, p. 53).

Many SWPP leaders are veterans of left-wing and communist activities in Nigeria. Chairman Chiake Anozie led the Nigerian delegation to the East German party congress in April 1981 (ADN, 8 April 1981). Wahab Goodluck, the deputy chairman of the SWPP, attended the Bulgarian party congress in March 1981 and the Czech congress in April 1981 (*Rudé Právo*, 8 April 1981). Dapo Fatogun is secretary general of SWPP and chief editor of *New Horizon,* the Nigerian edition of the *World Marxist Review.* Fatogun attended the Soviet party congress in February–March 1981 (*Pravda,* 7 March 1981) and was present at the French party congress (*L'Humanité*, 4 February). Dr. Lasisi A. Osunde is secretary of *New Horizon* (*WMR*, January 1978, p. 77) and deputy secretary general of the Nigerian Labour Congress.

One of the last acts of the military government in 1978 was to pass a trade union law that set up only one recognized trade union body, the Nigerian Labour Congress. Prominent communist labor leaders such as S. Imoudu, Wahab Goodluck, and S. U. Bassey were banned from any further trade union activity. However, a number of communist trade union leaders who had been active in the Nigerian Trade Union Congress hold senior positions in the new union. The SWPP, although an unregistered association, is putting most of its efforts into the Nigerian Labour Congress. Given the volatile nature of the Nigerian economy and the Nigerian labor movement, the SWPP feels its message will fall on willing ears (ibid., October 1981, p. 53).

Washington, D.C.   Jack H. Mower

Réunion

The island of Réunion is a French overseas department with a population of approximately 500,000. The Réunion Communist Party (Parti communiste réunionnaise; PCR), a legal political party, was organized in 1959 when the Réunion federation of the French Communist Party became autonomous. Réunion, like other French overseas departments, is administered by a Paris-appointed prefect and an elected general council. Réunion is represented by three deputies and two senators in the French parliament.

Since the election of François Mitterrand in May 1981, the PCR has focused on the economic development of Réunion (*Indian Ocean Newsletter*, 3 July). The traditional question of the island's status has now been shifted aside by a political debate on the future of the department's economy, which is based primarily on sugarcane production (ibid., 30 October).

In a 2 December session, the French Constitutional Council vetoed a bill calling for a proportionally elected unicameral assembly on Réunion. The council ruled that the bill, which had been approved earlier by the French National Assembly, exceeded the adaptive measures regarding overseas departments in the French constitution (ibid., 11 December). Regional council elections are to be held on 20 February 1983, the date originally scheduled for the election of the aborted single assembly (ibid.). The verdict of the Constitutional Council represents a major victory for opposition forces on the island. Following Mitterrand's election, the PCR, without officially discarding its demands for autonomy, considered the president's program calling for the creation of a proportionally elected council at the department level, "in charge of local matters in each department," an acceptable one (ibid.). The PCR could have modified its position after the Constitutional Council reversed the Assembly's decision, but, inexplicably, it did not do so.

Party Organization and Leadership.   The PCR's conventional communist party organizational base of cells is grouped into nineteen sections. The Central Committee has 32 members, the Politburo 12, and the Secretariat 5. The party claimed 10,000 members as of September 1981. Names of party officers were not released under the previous government.

Paul Vergès, a member of the European Parliament since 1979, is secretary general of the PCR. He is also mayor of Le Port. Central Committee member Bruny Payet is head of the General Federation of Réunion Workers and a member of the World Peace Council and the General Council of the World Federation of Trade Unions. Other prominent members of the PCR are Elie Hoarau, Jean-Baptiste Ponama, Julien Ramin, Ary Yee Chong Tchi-kan, Gervais Barret, Roger Hoarau, Hippolite Piot, Laurence Vergès, Daniel Lallemand, and Lucet Langenier.

The PCR also coordinates the activites of allied groups of the communist left on the island: the Réunion Front of Autonomous Youth, the General Federation of Réunion Workers, the General Federation of Réunion Farmers and Cattlemen, the Union of Réunion Women, and the Christian Witness Union. The Anticolonialist Front for Réunion Autonomy was created in 1979 to incorporate a united force of these organizations in their struggle for the island's autonomy.

Domestic Policies and Activities. The major goal of the PCR, self-determination through democratic and popular autonomy, is the foundation of the party's domestic and international policies. The PCR contends that the neocolonial status of Réunion is the cause of the island's social and economic problems. The party continues to strive for a more balanced economy and a means of redressing the inequalities between social benefits in France and on the island.

An extraordinary party congress that was scheduled for 1982 was not held. (Information concerning rescheduling of the congress is currently unavailable.) In preparation for the 1983 municipal elections, the PCR has announced plans to hold a special conference to adopt a comprehensive economic program (ibid., 15 May, 3 July).

International Activities. The PCR continues to maintain close links with the communist parties of other French overseas departments. In addition, members of the PCR participate regularly in various international conferences and communist party activities. The PCR supports the liberation struggles of South Africa and Namibia, endorses the Palestine Liberation Organization, and approves the Soviet occupation of Afghanistan. The party favors the creation of a zone of peace in the Indian Ocean and has repeatedly called for the removal of military forces in the region.

Publications. *Témoignages,* the PCR's 24-page daily newspaper, has a circulation of about 10,000. The General Confederation of Réunion Workers publishes the semimonthly *Travailleur réunionnais.*

Alexandria, Virginia   Joyce Myrick

Saudi Arabia

What is now the illegal and underground Communist Party of Saudi Arabia (CPSA) existed as the National Reform Front during 1954–1958 and the Saudi National Liberation Front (SNLF) during 1958–1975 (*WMR*, November 1974, p. 122). It adopted its present name at a joint conference with the National Liberation Front of Bahrain and the Iraqi Communist Party in Baghdad in or prior to October 1975 (AFP, Beirut, 26 October

1975; *Neues Deutschland*, 11 November 1975).

The top CPSA leader appears never to have been publicly identified, although certain spokesmen have been noted. Abdallah Muhammad was cited as an SNLF Executive Committee member in his article in the November 1974 *World Marxist Review*. Abd-al-Rahim Salih and Salim Hamid represented the CPSA at the "international scientific conference" cosponsored by the *World Marxist Review* and the East German party in East Berlin in October 1980 (*Neues Deutschland*, 21 and 23 October 1980). And one Hamad Mubarak was the CPSA's representative at the March 1982 Indian Communist Party Congress (*New Age*, 4 April 1982).

The unidentified CPSA representative to the 1981 Bulgarian party congress stated: "Our party has directed its efforts toward establishing a broad fatherland front, including all national and opposition forces in Saudi Arabia and abroad, with the purpose of toppling the king's regime and liquidating the influence of U.S. imperialism and the international monopolies that control our national resources" (*Rabotnichesko delo*, 9 April 1981). This statement made more specific the CPSA's general policy outline produced at its March 1980 Central Committee meeting. The latter had also applauded the temporary seizure of the mosque at Mecca and the Shia rioting in the country's Eastern province in November 1979 as "popular action against the ruling power" (*al-Nida*, 13 April 1980), even though each had been religiously motivated. On the second anniversary of these events, the CPSA reiterated its call for a united front (Radio Moscow, 28 December 1981).

Just who the CPSA has succeeded in getting as allies in such a united front is not known. Two possibilities would be the non-CPSA members included in the Saudi National Peace Committee and the Democratic Youth Organization, affiliates of the World Peace Council and World Federation of Democratic Youth, respectively. It is assumed that most of the CPSA front activity takes place abroad, just as the party's own leadership was stated to have been located in Aden as of late 1976 (Radio Moscow, 1 October 1976).

Since the October 1980 East Berlin conference, the CPSA has been notably active internationally, however. It sent representatives to the congresses of the Bulgarian and East German parties in April 1981 and to meetings of Arab communist parties in May 1981, May 1982, and July 1982. It also participated in the preparatory and regular meetings of the communist parties of "the Eastern Mediterranean, Middle Eastern, and Red Sea regions" in July and September 1981, respectively (*Rizospastis*, 8 July 1981; *Jerusalem Post*, 16 October 1981). Finally, it participated in the conference on the work of the *World Marxist Review* held in Prague in November 1981 (*Pravda*, 28 November 1981). There is no indication in all these activities that the CPSA is anything but pro-Soviet, and the support it gets from pro-Soviet media would seem to substantiate this.

McLean, Virginia   Wallace H. Spaulding

Senegal

On 24 April 1981, the National Assembly adopted a bill lifting restrictions on the number of political parties. In the following year, eleven parties were registered. Seven of these call themselves Marxist; one more Marxist party is awaiting action on its application. In an interview in *Le Monde* (6 November 1981), President Abdou Diouf said, "The multiparty system in Senegal is irreversible." The result has been the growth of a number of small political parties calling themselves Marxist and/or socialist, but only a few of them have any international standing.

The major effect of the deregulation of parties has been a loss of influence by the African Independence Party (Parti africain de l'indépendance; PAI), led by Majmout Diop. The PAI, estimated to have had about 2,000 members, had been the only legally registered communist party. The pro-Soviet clandestine wing of the PAI renamed itself the Independence and Labor Party (Parti de l'indépendance et du travail; PIT).

Although the PIT lost several of its leading members, including former prime minister Mamadou Dia, it has emerged as the most relevant communist party internationally. Semy Pathe Gueye set forth the PIT's goals in an article entitled "Loyalty to Leninist Principles" in the January 1982 issue of the *World Marxist Review*. Gueye attended the 1982 conference of the French Communist Party (*L'Humanité,* 4 February). The PIT has a representative on the *World Marxist Review* Editorial Council in Prague and publishes a local French-language edition in Dakar. Amadou Dansoko is first deputy secretary general and frequently acts as PIT spokesman. Seydou Cissoko is secretary general of the PIT (for an interview, see *African Communist,* no. 84). Maguette Thiam is reported as assistant general secretary of the PIT and chief editor of the party's publication, *Ande Sopi*. The PIT is clearly the favorite party of the international communist movement.

Another party that espouses a brand of socialism is the Democratic League–Labor Party Movement (Ligue démocratique–Mouvement pour le parti du travail), which has close ties with several trade unions. The pro-Chinese party is the And-Jëf Revolutionary Movement for the New Democracy (And-Jëf mouvement revolutionnaire pour la démocratie nouvelle). One of its leading members is a former government minister, Abdoulaye Ly. The Union for People's Democracy (Union pour la démocratie populaire) is headed by Hamedine Racine Guisse and takes a pro-Albanian position. A new party, the Workers Socialist Organization (Organization de travail et socialisme; OST) has requested recognition (AFP, 22 January). The OST follows the principles of the Fourth International Socialist Movement. Mamadou Dia is now associated with the Popular Democratic Movement (Mouvement démocratique populaire), which has as its major plank something called self-management socialism.

The current Abdou Diouf government appears more concerned about possible Libyan subversion than it does about the activities of the several Marxist parties. Senegalese ties with France remain close, and U.S. Vice-President George Bush visited Dakar during November 1982.

Washington, D.C.   Jack H. Mower

South Africa

In its twenty-ninth year as an illegal party, the South African Communist Party (SACP) continued to follow long-established policies forged in the crucible of its underground existence.

At the time of its clandestine establishment in 1953, the SACP was struggling to readjust from the relatively open style of politics that had characterized its predecessor, the Communist Party of South Africa, the continent's first Marxist-Leninist party, established in 1921 and dissolved in 1950 on the eve of its proscription by the Nationalist government under the Suppression of Communism Act. In its 29 years of legal, but often harassed, existence, the Communist Party of South Africa never had more than several thousand members, but as South Africa's first nonracial political party, it had moved from an overwhelmingly white membership based among English-speaking workers and professionals to a multiracial membership including Afrikaners and representatives of all the country's black racial groups. From the 1930s, its members played increasingly prominent roles in emerging trade unions for black and white workers and actively participated in the major political organizations demanding full rights for Africans, Coloureds, and Asians.

Initially unprepared for underground activities, the majority of the Central Committee voted to disband the party, but in 1953 at a secret national conference a core of leading party members reconstituted the organization as the South African Communist Party. Throughout the 1950s, party members worked to establish new forms of party activities under unrelenting government persecution while simultaneously participating vigorously in the barely tolerated, but growing legal extraparliamentary movement that brought together the long-established African National Congress (ANC) and the South African Indian Congress together with the post-1950 organizations, including the Coloured Peoples' Congress, the Congress of Democrats (for whites), and the multiracial South African Congress of Trade Unions. In the wake of Sharpeville and the banning of the ANC in 1960, the SACP revealed its existence publicly for the first time; shortly thereafter it joined with leaders of the ANC in establishing Umkhonto we Sizwe as a separate organization to conduct sabotage (commenced in December 1961) and ultimately to undertake guerrilla warfare. The shift away from the nonviolent tactics thitherto practiced by both organizations spurred tough new government legislation and security measures in the early 1960s, "a ferocity of reprisal which almost decimated the movement, which smashed the Party headquarters and penetrated deeply into its membership cells; and which finally made the retreat of the Party and the ANC leadership into temporary exile abroad essential if anything was to be saved for rebuilding" (*African Communist*, no. 86, p. 44). Longtime party activists who escaped imprisonment and found sanctuary in sympathetic African countries and Europe worked intimately with exiled ANC leaders to create new machinery for both operation in exile and repenetration of South Africa. Surmounting internal squabbles and unevenly circumventing ever-harsher government measures to thwart all radical opposition, the SACP and its allies were able clandestinely to rebuild a rudimentary organization within South Africa. In the late 1970s and early 1980s, trained militants and their supporters have dramatically increased armed attacks on selected military and industrial installations to complement expanded campaigns in support of trade union activity and political mobilization among all racial groups in the country.

Neither membership figures nor the racial composition of the SACP can be estimated, given the current situation. Unquestionably the SACP has attracted new and younger members from among those who participated in the Soweto demonstrations and the political upsurge that followed. It would seem that most senior party leaders as well as many party members work primarily outside the country in the dispersed African and European centers where exiles are concentrated; other focal points of party membership are most likely in larger South African cities.

Organization and Leadership. For ten years, the chairman of the SACP has been Dr. Yusef Dadoo, a 73-year-old Indian medical practitioner. The other visible high party official is the general secretary, Moses Mabhida, a 59-year-old African trade unionist who was engaged in full-time work in Umkhonto we Sizwe prior to his assumption of the party post in 1981. Both men are longtime party members from the pre-1950 legal period who went into exile in the early 1960s. The SACP has not publicly listed other members of the Political Bureau and the Central Committee; in the party press almost all contributors sign with assumed names.

The SACP maintains its close alliance with the ANC. Since its establishment in 1912, the ANC has, with the exception of a brief period in the 1930s, welcomed Communists, as well as all other Africans, into its ranks. Common struggles against the Nationalist government in the 1950s blurred differences that had surfaced in the late 1940s between the Communist Party of South Africa and the ANC; the breakaway of the Pan-African Congress in 1959, in part over the unwillingness of ANC leaders to reject cooperation with Communists as well as non-Africans, strengthened those within the organization who were willing to work closely with Communists. Heightened persecution in the wake of the outlawing of the ANC in 1960, together with shared hardships underground and in exile, brought the ANC and the SACP even closer in the 1960s. With the opening of ANC membership to South Africans of all races in 1969, previous barriers barring non-Africans (communist and noncommunist) from the ANC were eliminated; prominent non-

African Communists were immediately given posts on important ANC bodies. In the present situation, according to ANC President Oliver Tambo,. "the relationship between the ANC and the SACP is not an accident of history, nor is it a natural and inevitable development. For, as we can see, similar relationships have not emerged in the course of liberation struggles in other parts of Africa . . . our alliance is a living organism that has grown out of struggle. We have built it out of our separate and common experiences . . . Our organizations have been able to agree on fundamental strategies and tactical positions while retaining our separate identities . . . Within our revolutionary alliance, each organization has a distinct and vital role to play. A correct understanding of these roles and respect for their boundaries has ensured the survival and consolidation of our cooperation and unity." (*Sechaba*, September 1981, pp. 4–5.) In the perspective of a SACP spokesman, "African nationalists can[not] be at the same time proletarian internationalists, but . . . African nationalists can develop to become proletarian internationalists. This is the general trend in progressive Africa and the ANC is not out of step." (*African Communist*, no. 88, p. 30.)

Domestic Activities and Attitudes. The SACP remains committed to its twenty-year-old party program, adopted at an underground national conference in 1962 and elaborated at an augmented meeting of the Central Committee held in exile in 1979, with further statements by the Political Bureau and Central Committee in 1980 and 1981. On the occasion of the sixtieth anniversary of the founding of the Communist Party of South Africa in 1921, the Central Committee of the SACP characterized itself as "a vital part of the liberation forces headed by the African National Congress," which aim "to unite all sections and classes amongst the oppressed and other truly democratic forces for a revolution . . . whose main content is the national liberation of African and other black oppressed groups, [and which] must put an end to race discrimination in all its forms, restore the land and wealth of our country to the people and guarantee democracy, freedom and equality of rights and opportunities to all." This immediate struggle for a national democratic revolution is intimately linked with the struggle for a future socialist South Africa in which "the key force has always been, and will continue to be, the black working class in alliance with the masses of the landless working people. It is this class which finds its most staunch champions in our South African Communist Party." (Ibid., no. 86, pp. 7–8.)

Invoking Lenin's concept of a vanguard party as elaborated in *What Is to Be Done?*, a party spokesman asserted, "We must not view the two struggles (the national democratic and socialist) as absolutely compartmentalized. Revolution is an uninterrupted process, and the socialist revolution advances immediately from the democratic in a single continuum. These are the positions which the South African Communist Party advances." (Ibid., no. 90, pp. 33–34.) In this context another spokesman called on the SACP to fulfill its basic function "to pursue the path of socialism, to win adherents to our struggle for socialism and to raise the level of understanding of socialism among our workers, peasants and intellectuals and all population groups." But the "main emphasis and focus" must be on the working class. "We cannot ignore and delay organizing and leading our working class. We must recruit new personnel and give them an understanding of our role as set out by Lenin in *What is to Be Done?*" (Ibid., no. 89, p. 28.)

Considerations of the potential for a transition to socialism and the imperative for the SACP to organize the working class reflect an apparent conviction that prospects for further expansion of revolutionary struggle are good. The SACP is heartened by splits within Nationalist ranks and views Nationalist efforts at "reforms" and "power sharing" as signs of a crisis from which "there is no way out within the limits of white supremacy." The response of the SACP "must be to step up our offensive on all fronts, to win and organize support from wider and wider sections of the people, of all races and colours, until final victory is won. The present confusion and pessimism in enemy ranks is proof that the labour and the wounds are not in vain. The end is in sight." (Ibid., no. 90, pp. 18–19.)

International Views and Activities. The beleaguered position of the South African government coincides, in the view of the SACP, with "the new offensive of imperialism under the aegis of the Reagan administration. In the name of anti-Sovietism their aim is not only to destroy the socialist community, but also to destabilize the national liberation movements and stem the tide towards social progress and democracy everywhere." In the eyes of SACP Chairman Dadoo, "the paramount need of the present time is for the unity in action of the international communist movement and the consolidation and strengthening of the three vital forces of our time—the socialist community, the national liberation movements and the working class of the capitalist countries." (Ibid., no. 91, p. 90.)

The SACP continues to make clear that these goals can best be achieved by full identification with the Communist Party of the Soviet Union and policies supported by it. A statement of the SACP Central Committee gave full support to the declaration of martial law in Poland (ibid., no. 89, pp. 96–97), while the reprinting of a speech by Gus Hall, chairman of the Communist Party, USA, attacking both the Spanish and Italian communist parties for their "opportunism" and criticism of the Polish government served to reiterate the stance of the SACP against the Eurocommunism of both parties (ibid., no. 90, pp. 35–60).

Party leaders undoubtedly maintained contact, as in previous years, with the ruling parties of the Soviet Union and its East European allies, although there were no extensive reports of official visits by SACP delegations to these countries. Most likely the SACP also continued to reach out to African radical and socialist parties—both the ruling parties in Angola and Mozambique, characterized by one SACP spokesman as "functioning vanguard parties," and other parties, characterized as "revolutionary democratic movements [that] have consciously opted for socialist orientation of society" and "base their foundation on a number of key Marxist-Leninist propositions" and thus "can be regarded as transitional vanguard parties" (ibid., p. 33).

Publications. "In the interest of African solidarity, and as a forum for Marxist-Leninist thought throughout our Continent," the SACP since 1959 has published the quarterly *African Communist*, utilizing printers in the German Democratic Republic and a distribution office in London, which also sells other public party documents. The SACP's major ally, the ANC, also utilizes the same arrangement to publish its major journal, the monthly *Sechaba,* aimed at both members and external sympathizers.

Within South Africa, *The African Communist* is circulated underground along with internally produced party documents and Marxist-Leninist classics. The ANC also distributes literature clandestinely within South Africa.

Through the cooperation of the state radio stations of Angola, Madagascar, Tanzania, and Zambia, Radio Freedom, Voice of the African National Congress and the People's Army, Umkhonto we Sizwe, makes daily short- and medium-wave broadcasts in the morning and in the evening.

Duke University   Sheridan Johns

Sudan

The Sudanese Communist Party (al-Hizbal Shuyui al-Sudani; SCP) traces its origins to 1946. After being implicated in a coup in 1971, the party was banned. It continues to operate illegally; its leaders are in exile. According to the party's own figures, the trade union leaders arrested by the government include about 200 functionaries of the SCP (*IB*, no. 6, p. 67). As the head of Sudan's security services put it, the SCP has attempted to "rally" its organization within Sudan (*FBIS*, 15 June). This task has been eased by the country's ongoing economic crisis and by the presence within Sudan of between two and three million refugees, many of them destitute. The SCP was at one time the largest communist party on the African continent. Its present membership is unknown. Such support as it enjoys derives from intellectuals, students, certain sympathizers within the armed forces, selected railway workers, tenant farmers, and some Sudanese refugees in Ethiopia.

Leadership and Organization. The party's secretary general in Muhammad Ibrahim Nugud. Other prominent functionaries include the following Secretariat members: Ali al-Tijani al-Tayyib, secretary of the SCP Khartoum Provincial Committee (arrested in 1980 as the party's reported second-in-command); Abu al-Qasim Amin; Dr. Izz-al Din Ali Amir, also reportedly a Politburo member, head of the SCP International Department, and a Central Committee member; Sulayman Hamid, a Politburo member; Al-Gazuli Said, member of the Politburo and the Central Committee; and Muhammad Ahmad Sulayman, a Politburo member. Additional Central Committee members reportedly include Sudi Darag, Khadr Nasr, Abd-al-Majid Shakak, Hassan Gassim al-Sid (a member of the World Peace Council's Presidential Committee and a staff member of the World Federation of Trade Unions), and Ibrahim Zakariya, acting secretary general of the World Federation of Trade Unions.

Domestic Issues. The SCP calls for a coalition of all political parties and movements, including trade union organizations, peasant and student associations, and women and the young, to save the country from the ongoing economic crisis. The SCP "does not profess that its political influence spreads to all strata of the people or that it has some magic wand for saving the country." The SCP looks to influencing "the leadership of the trade unions, of peasant and student organizations, and all the working people." According to the SCP, "neglect of painstaking everyday work among the masses in expectation of a spontaneous powerful upsurge in their activity" must lead to inertia among the masses. (*IB*, no. 6, pp. 63–69.) The SCP strongly opposes ill-prepared coups launched by individuals and lacking a mass basis, like that recently carried out by Col. Saad Bahaar. Only an alliance of all democratic and revolutionary forces can save the country. (*African Communist*, no. 86, pp. 79–80.) This union must be shaped into a broad Front of Struggle for Democracy and Salvation of the Country open to all those opposed to the existing dictatorship. The new front should not serve "as a screen for adventurist putschist aspirations," but should involve both the people at large and the armed forces in effecting the revolution. (*WMR*, June, pp. 80–85.)

According to the SCP, Sudan's basic troubles spring from the machinations of foreign monopolies and the International Monetary Fund. Foreign investors and the Sudanese bourgeoisie have amassed riches, but Sudan is drifting into bankruptcy. Sudan now labors under a huge foreign debt; President Jafar Numayri has deprived the masses of democratic liberties and trade union rights; emigration has reached catastrophic proportions; agricultural output has declined; and the prices of staple goods have skyrocketed. Unemployment is an ever-present threat, and the workers' living standard has dropped as a result of the government's wage freeze and political persecution. The government's program for economic revival is bound to fail. The irrigation projects planned by the authorities will have deleterious consequences, since they will increase the scope of private business, and will serve only the interests of rich farmers, big capitalists, and wholesalers.

The SCP's immediate objectives include the restoration of trade union rights, reopening of enterprises that have shut down, repeal of legislation dealing with state security, and the convocation of a national congress composed of all political parties, trade unionists, qualified scholars, and businessmen to examine the root causes of the country's malaise. The congress should elaborate a minimum program designed to rally the people and preserve them from "arbitrary rule and impending anarchy." (*IB*, no. 6, pp. 63–69.)

International Policy. The SCP condemns what it calls the "mounting aggressiveness of U.S. imperialist circles" and deplores the machinations of Arab leaders who have "cast their lot with imperialism." The party particularly opposes "imperialist threats" made against Libya, U.S. arms sales to Sudan, and the activities of "Zionist aggressors" in the Middle East. The party supports what it calls the peaceful policy of the Soviet Union, especially the constructive proposals made with regard to a Middle Eastern peace settlement at the 1981 Soviet party congress and subsequently elaborated by Leonid Brezhnev. The United States, the SCP charges, has used its influence in the Middle East to make direct threats against other states, to build up its naval power in the Mediterranean, and to use Egypt as a base for pre-emptive strikes against other countries. The Arab nations must therefore resist Zionist aggression, reject "capitulationist deals," and oppose U.S. subversion. The supreme object of the SCP should be to prevent a U.S.-inspired diktat designed to increase the danger of war and to suppress the popular forces within the Arab world as a whole. (*WMR*, January, pp. 92–93.)

The SCP participated at the end of 1981 in an international conference in Prague, where 90 communist parties discussed the policy of the *World Marxist Review* (*IB*, 7 January, p. 7).

Hoover Institution   L. H. Gann

Syria

The Syrian Communist Party (al-Hizb al-Shuyu'i al-Suri; SCP) is an offshoot of the Lebanese Communist Party, which was founded in 1924. Cooperation between the SCP and the Syrian government began shortly after the Baath coup of 8 March 1963. In March 1972, the party gained de facto legality through its participation in the Baathist-led National Progressive Front (NFP), composed of the Baath Party, the SCP, and other nationalist forces. There are at least two dissident SCP factions, one led by Riyad al-Turki, who left the party in 1973, and another created in 1980 by expelled Central Committee member Murad Yusuf. Membership in the SCP is estimated at less than 5,000, with a possible 10,000 sympathizers.

Leadership and Organization. Khalid Bakhdash, a 70-year-old Kurd, was re-elected secretary general of the SCP at its Fifth Congress (May 1980). In May, the Central Committee organized a celebration to mark the seventieth birthday of Bakhdash. Addressing the meeting, Bakhdash stated that he had given 52 years of his life to the party. He called for further strengthening "cooperation with the socialist community of states headed by the Soviet Union." (*Pravda*, 21 November; *FBIS*, 8 December.) Yusuf Faisal is deputy secretary general. The Politburo consists of Bakhdash, Ibrahim Bakr, Khalid Hammami, Maurice Salibi, 'Umar Sibai, and Daniel Ni'mah. Bakhdash is the SCP representative in the NFP. In the general elections of 1977, six SCP members were elected to the 195-seat Syrian legislature. The November 1981 parliamentary elections resulted in a loss of all SCP seats.

Domestic Activities. In obedience to Soviet directives, the SCP is a strong advocate of and participant in the NFP, which is dominated by the Baath Party led by President Hafiz al-Asad. In a speech at the Fifth SCP Congress, Bakhdash advocated the strengthening of the state sector of the economy and support of the Baath in its struggle against the reactionary Muslim Brotherhood, as well as the general goals of the Baath Party. He went on to lend SCP support to the regime in its efforts to improve the economy and living standards of the Syrian people. The SCP backs the regime's opposition to the Camp David peace settlement between Egypt and Israel, characterizing it as an attempt by the United States to "impose its will on the Arab peoples and to draw them into the orbit of reactionary policy." (*FBIS*, 9 July 1980.) Furthermore, the SCP supports Syria's Lebanese policy, which is viewed as advocating national concord founded on Lebanon's independence, territorial integrity, preservation of its unity, and of course, evacuation of Israeli forces from Lebanon. The SCP also has attacked "bankrupt" Eurocommunism.

International Views. The SCP regards the Egyptian-Israeli treaty as a "capitulationist" peace with an aggressor (Israel) and a betrayal of the true interests of the Egyptian people and the Arabs in general. Egyptian-U.S. cooperation is viewed as a plot to weaken the influence of the Soviet Union in the Arab world. The SCP attacked Egyptian President Anwar Sadat personally, alleging that he had little support among the Egyptian people. The SCP, along with the rest of the Syrian regime, gloated over Sadat's assassination. The Baathist regime in Iraq is criticized by the SCP for its bloody repression of Communists and its effort to eliminate Kurdish autonomy.

In 1982 Bakhdash visited Bulgaria and Hungary; other party leaders traveled to the Soviet Union. During 1981–1982, Bakhdash met communist party leaders from the Soviet Union, Bulgaria, Egypt, Romania, and East Germany. The SCP fully backs the Soviet intervention in Afghanistan and the pro-Soviet regimes in Kampuchea, Vietnam, and Laos; it condemns "imperialist" interference in Poland.

The Syrian Baathist regime closely parallels the SCP in its support of Moscow's goals, especially those in the Middle East. This past year, the SCP's Central Committee praised the government's "steadfast stand in the face of the U.S. imperialist, Zionist and reactionary plots" (Damascus domestic service, 11 March; *FBIS*, 12 March). Baath leaders regularly visit Eastern bloc countries, and delegations from them are sent to Damascus periodically. In an unusual step in the fall of 1980, Asad visited Moscow and signed a twenty-year friendship treaty with the Soviet Union, after years of refusing to do so. The Soviet Union is Syria's main arms supplier, and it has received some of Moscow's most up-to-date arms; consequently there is a feeling of deep gratitude to the Soviet Union among Syrians. There are over 3,500 Soviet and Eastern bloc military advisers in the country, and Moscow has on more than one occasion seriously threatened to intervene militarily in support of Syria against Israel. The Soviets quickly resupplied the Syrian armed forces with planes and antiaircraft missiles after Syria suffered severe losses of equipment at the hands of the Israelis in June 1982. However, Moscow has been reluctant to be drawn into increasing its commitment to Syria despite Syrian calls for a "military alliance." Despite Moscow's heavy investment in the country, Syria cannot be considered a Soviet puppet.

The SCP calls for a comprehensive Middle East settlement based on Israel's total withdrawal from the occupied territories and the securing of the legitimate rights of the Palestinians, including an independent national state. As for the European socialist parties, Bakhdash has accused them of a lack of concern for the welfare of the peoples of the developing countries and has stated that the Socialist International is being used by imperialism to deradicalize and "pacify" progressive forces.

The SCP together with other Arab communist parties met in April and adopted a statement condemning Israel and the United States for occupying the West Bank, the Gaza Strip, and the Golan Heights (*IB*, June, pp. 37–38). The SCP also met with seven regional communist workers' parties in Damascus in late May. The declaration issued by the Damascus meeting was similar in tone to the earlier one; but it went on to condemn the United States and its allies for "crimes against progressive Arab regimes" (ibid., July, p. 33). The statement also held the United States responsible for encouraging the "crimes of the Muslim Brotherhood"—a particular concern to the SCP since the zealous Islamic sect opposes both local Communists and the Soviet Union.

Bethesda, Maryland   Gordon Torrey

Tunisia

The Tunisian Communist Party (Parti communiste tunisien; PCT) was founded in 1920 as a branch of the French Communist Party and became independent in 1937. The banning of the PCT in 1963 formalized a single-party state under the direction of the Destourian Socialist Party (PSD). In July 1981, the government lifted the ban on the PCT, ending the party's eighteen-year period of clandestine existence. Membership in the PCT is estimated to be about one hundred. The population of Tunisia is just under seven million.

Leadership and Party Affairs. The PCT's Eighth Congress (February 1981) re-elected Muhammad Harmel as secretary general and elected a three-member Secretariat—Harmel, Muhammad al-Nafa'a, and 'Abd al-Hamid ben Mustafa; a six-member Politboro—Harmel, al-Nafa'a, ben Mustafa, Hisham Sakik, 'Abd al-Majid Tariki, and Salah Hajji; and a twelve-member Central Committee (*Le Maghreb*, 12 September 1981).

Political Situation. The political climate in Tunisia during 1982 was marked by a mood of defiance throughout the country. Many Tunisians had anticipated the National Assembly elections of November 1981 as the culmination of President Habib Bourguiba's promised inauguration of a new era of liberal domestic politics. When the coalition of the ruling PSD and the powerful General Union of Tunisian Workers (UGTT) won all 136 assembly seats, however, members of the political opposition and foreign observers declared that the PSD had rigged the voting. Cooperation between the PSD and the UGTT broke down shortly after the election. One reward for the UGTT's support in the election was the release from prison of union leader Habib Achour, who soon demanded that the government double the minimum wage. Increased social tensions were evident in a series of strikes by transport workers, bank and insurance company employees, and schoolteachers in February. These strikes—intended to secure higher wages and better working conditions—were a protest against the government's economic policies of removing subsidies on many basic commodities while freezing wages. The tense situation eased somewhat in the spring following a wage agreement between the government and the UGTT.

Activities of the PCT. The PCT limited its participation in the National Assembly elections to a symbolic effort because the government did not guarantee equal participation for party candidates in all constituencies. The PCT fielded only six candidates but used the election campaign as an opportunity to air its views to a wider segment of the Tunisian public. The party's election program supported progressive reforms while condemning such government policies as political trials and repression of the opposition (for details of the PCT's participation in the National Assembly elections, see the interview with Muhammad Harmel, *WMR,* March, pp. 38–39).

PCT Secretary General Muhammad Harmel described the elections as a "colossal farce" and the results as "unabashedly rigged." Harmel claimed that the party received from 15 to 25 percent of the votes cast in Tunis, plus a majority in Gafsa and a large number in Gabes. Other opposition parties were required to poll 5 percent of the vote in order to gain legal status. Since the PCT was exempt from this requirement, its legal status was not affected by the official results of the elections (94.6 percent of the votes for the PSD-UGTT coalition). Enjoying the status of a legal party, the PCT opted in 1982 to operate as a loyal opposition. While protesting the government's manipulation of the elections, Harmel stated that the PCT "abides by its constructive stand and intends doing all in its power to help gradually surmount the obstacles to a democratic process consistent with national interests and the aspirations of the people" (ibid., p. 39). During a meeting with Prime Minister Muhammad M'zali in July, Harmel raised a variety of problems concerning human rights in Tunisia, a multiparty political system, and the country's economic and social orientation (*Le Temps,* Paris, 4 July).

Foreign Policy. The PCT moved quickly to try to exploit the public reaction in Tunisia to the Israeli invasion of Lebanon. In late June, the party issued a communiqué (published in *La Presse,* 29 June) condemning apparent U.S. complicity in Israel's aggression. The communiqué singled out Washington's veto of a U.N. Security Council resolution requesting that Israel not attack Beirut and blamed the United States in advance for the destruction of the Lebanese capital. Citing hostile U.S. intentions toward the Palestinians and progressive Lebanese forces, the PCT communiqué called on all Arab governments to adjust their relations with Washington and on the Tunisian government in particular to freeze its relations with the United States and to dissolve the U.S.-Tunisian Joint Military Commission.

In November 1981, the PCT sent a delegation to Prague to attend a four-day meeting to consider the work from 1977 to 1981 of the international journal of communist and workers' parties, the *World Marxist Review* (*IB,* January).

In the late summer, the more moderate wing of the Palestine Liberation Organization (PLO), al-Fatah, chose Tunis as its new headquarters following the agreement to evacuate Beirut. The Tunisian government agreed to receive 970 Palestinian guerrillas. In an effort to isolate the PLO fighters from the Tunisian population, the government established a special settlement for the guerrillas in a remote area of the country. In the fall, PLO Chairman Yassir Arafat arrived in Tunis to set up residence there.

Tunisia focused much of its foreign policy energies on relations with neighboring Libya. In late 1981, these relations deteriorated badly when Libya vetoed Tunisia's bid to join the Organization of Arab Petroleum Exporting Countries and then expelled several thousand Tunisian workers whose papers it claimed were not in order. In early 1982, Libyan leader Moammar Khadafy made two visits to Tunis in an effort to improve relations and promote a political union between the two countries. During his second visit in late February, Tunisia and Libya signed an agreement providing for coordination of the two countries' foreign policies, plus coordination of plans for agricultural, industrial, and electrical production and the linking of road, rail, and communication networks (*NYT*, 1 March). Khadafy took a concrete step toward better relations by offering to invite an additional 20,000–30,000 Tunisian workers to Libya.

Aware of the unpredictability of Libyan foreign policy, Tunisian leaders have been anxious for several years to improve the defensive capabilities of Tunisia's 28,000-man military force. In this context Tunisia increased its military purchases from the United States from $15 million in 1981 to $90 million in 1982. These purchases include M-60 tanks, a squadron of F-5 fighters, ground-to-air missiles, a radar system, coastal patrol boats, helicopters, and armored personnel carriers (*Los Angeles Times,* 26 November).

Publications. In the fall of 1981, the PCT resumed publication of its weekly newspaper, *al-Tarik al-Jadid* (The new path).

Portland State University   John Damis

Yemen:
People's Democratic Republic
of Yemen

The People's Democratic Republic of Yemen (PDRY) has been governed by a militant, Marxist-oriented regime since June 1969. Although a local communist party, the People's Democratic Union (PDU), has existed for two decades, the party has never been the dominant power in South Yemeni (PDRY) politics. Throughout the 1970s, the PDU's status and role in national affairs have been highly circumscribed by the practical necessity, both legal and political, for it to operate in close association with a substantially larger organization.

In 1982, the PDU enjoyed official status in the prevailing, larger organization, the Yemen Socialist Party (YSP). PDU members held one of five posts in the YSP's Politburo—both the YSP's and the government's highest policymaking body—and several seats on the YSP's 47-member Central Committee. In addition, PDU representatives sat in the nonparty 111-member Supreme People's Council, which served as a consultative body and debating forum for the government. These positions, in addition to other, less formal ones within the national power structure, have accorded the PDU a degree of influence in PDRY politics far beyond what its limited membership (estimated at less than 500) would suggest. (For a history of the PDU, YSP, and PDRY, see *YICA*, 1982, pp. 56–59.)

Whether the PDU would be able to maintain, let alone increase, its previous position of influence on national policy questions had by 1983 come to depend on whether changes occurring in the country's external environment would necessitate a diminution in its influence generally. Certainly a less visibly prominent role was regarded as a sine qua non if the regime's efforts to improve relations with Saudi Arabia and the Gulf states—and, toward that end, with North Yemen and Oman—were to succeed.

During 1982, the regime's efforts to effect a rapprochement with Sana'a and Muscat—its neighbors to the northwest and northeast—were at once more numerous and successful than any since the short-lived reconciliation with Saudi Arabia in 1976. An agreement between the PDRY and Oman concluded on 27 October signaled an end to nearly fifteen years of mutual enmity. A joint draft constitution calling for unity between the two Yemens, which pointedly made no reference either to "socialism" or to the kind of economic system that might be adopted, was completed and submitted to their respective governments for discussion, debate, and amendment prior to a referendum in each of the countries. And the YSP, during its sixth annual meeting in May, went to greater lengths than in previous years to stress peaceful coexistence with the PDRY's neighbors.

The more pragmatic tone to YSP and PDRY government policy that these initiatives implied was evidence of a national need for financial assistance from the country's more economically endowed neighbors to the north. It was indicative as well of the force of two other factors: (1) an awareness, even among YSP and PDU stalwarts, of the relatively limited political and diplomatic dividends produced by their more doctrinaire approach to international relations during the previous half-decade; and (2) Soviet encouragement of such overtures to the PDRY's wealthier Arab neighbors. Behind the latter phenomenon was Moscow's preference for avoiding the necessity of providing the level of additional financial assistance needed from its own funds and, also, a hope that USSR–Gulf states relations might improve as a consequence.

In the PDRY's relationships with countries outside the Arabian peninsula, however, a substantially different foreign policy tactic was pursued. Both the YSP and the PDU, as cases in point, not only retained but broadened and deepened their links with a dozen or more Arab, African, and Asian communist parties as well as European and Latin American parties. During the course of the year, YSP Chairman Ali Nasir Muhammad al-Hasani completed an extensive tour of the Soviet Union and several other Eastern bloc countries, signing new bilateral agreements and solidifying bilateral party and governmental links at each stop along the way. He devoted special personal attention to intensifying YSP cooperation with kindred political groupings in Syria, Lebanon, Algeria, Ethiopia, France, and Cuba. In February, on behalf of the World Peace Council, he hosted a major international conference in Aden devoted to "the Middle East and the dangers of the imperialist military buildup."

At the interregional level, the nucleus around which many of these activities revolved, was the alliance, established in August 1981, which grouped the PDRY, Libya, and Ethiopia as joint signatories to a treaty of friendship and cooperation. The first meeting of the Tripartite Supreme Council, the highest organ of the alliance, was held in Aden in May and presided over by Ali Nasir Muhammad. In the discussions that ensued, the parties reiterated the essentially strategic nature of the alliance, signifying that its specific purposes remained their joint opposition to the Camp David agreements, imperialism, reactionary regimes, and Zionist designs on Arab lands, on the one hand, and, on the other, the more general goal of making it difficult for their adversaries to attack or undermine them in isolation.

The YSP and PDU, as in previous years, were simultaneously active in developing bilateral relations with the Communist Party of the Soviet Union. The frequency of visits between the two countries' party officials, functionaries of their supreme organs of state power, and representatives of their respective parliamentary bodies reached an all-time high. At a less visible level, there occurred an equally impressive exchange of working visits between their respective youth groups, World Marxist Review journalists, and officials of their Ministries of Interior, Planning, and Justice.

The event of most tangible relevance to the PDRY's pressing economic needs, however, was the third annual meeting in Aden on 6 April of the Soviet-PDRY Standing Committee on Economic Cooperation. The committee, established at the time of the 1979 Treaty of Friendship and Cooperation, reached an agreement on launching a range of new activities aimed at strengthening industrial and agricultural development in the PDRY as well as planning and technical training. The level of mutual interest and involvement that these visits manifested demonstrated how little in the PDRY's general foreign policy orientation had changed in terms of its relationship with Moscow. Some 1,500 Soviet military and technical personnel remained in the country alongside a similar number of East Germans in the state security apparatus and a comparable contingent of Cubans working as advisers in the popular militias and as physicians and paramedics at health centers throughout the country. The nature and extent of such a foreign presence provided ample testimony to the Eastern bloc's continuing stake in the PDRY's stability, security, and development. It was an indication as well that the interests at stake for the bloc remained as strategic and ideological as before and—notwithstanding the changes in the PDRY's relationships with neighboring countries—of how minimal were the immediate prospects for their lessening in any fundamental way.

American Educational Trust   John Duke Anthony
Washington, D.C.

Zimbabwe

The Zimbabwe African National Union (ZANU) is the ruling party of the republic of Zimbabwe. Though not an avowedly communist party, it professes to be Marxist in ideology. It was formed in 1963 by the African nationalist Ndabaningi Sithole after he split from Joshua Nkomo's Zimbabwe African Peoples' Union (ZAPU). Robert Mugabe, a Marxist, became ZANU secretary general under Sithole's presidency. In the late 1960s, ZANU launched a guerrilla war against the white-dominated Rhodesian government under Prime Minister Ian Smith. Much of ZANU's logistical and training support came from the People's Republic of China. After a bitter power struggle in 1974, Mugabe was elected to replace Sithole as party president. Internal leadership struggles continued, but by the time of the Geneva conference in 1976, Mugabe had gained almost complete control. At the Geneva conference, the front-line states forced Moscow-supported Nkomo and his ZAPU into a Patriotic Front (PF) alliance with Mugabe and ZANU in order to present a stronger, more united opposition to the Rhodesian regime.

This fragile fabric of unity began to unravel in February 1980 when Nkomo-led ZAPU contested the pre-independence elections as a separate party. ZANU won a stunning landslide, gaining 57 of the 100 parliamentary seats to ZAPU's 20. Mugabe emerged as prime minister when Zimbabwe achieved independence from Britain in April 1980. ZANU's strength derives mainly from the majority Shona people, while ZAPU's support comes overwhelmingly from the Ndebele, who comprise only 18 percent of the population.

After independence, the two parties formed a coalition government but this collapsed in early 1982 after Nkomo spurned Mugabe's call for a merger into a single party. In February, Mugabe sacked Nkomo from his cabinet post, along with other ZAPU ministers, accusing them of stockpiling arms in preparation for a coup. ZAPU/PF and ZANU have since been in an adversarial relationship.

Organization and Leadership. ZANU is directed by a 58-member Central Committee, under the presidency of Robert Mugabe. Simon Muzenda is vice-president. No secretary general has been named since the purging of Edgar Tekere in 1981. No party congress has been convened since 1963, and none is planned for fear it might lead to party factionalization. ZANU has not yet established a framework of auxiliary mass organizations or an ideological institute.

Nearly 80 percent of the Central Committee members have been elected to parliament, and the majority of cabinet portfolios are held by committee members. The committee meets occasionally, usually at least five times annually. Leadership is collective, and decisions are by consensus. Alongside the Central

Committee is the National Executive, which rarely meets. Both organs are overwhelmingly Shona in ethnic composition but are divided ideologically. ZANU's professed Marxism has been substantially diluted since the end of the liberation struggle and its elevation as the ruling party. Mugabe has become more cautious and pragmatic in his policies. He is committed to a mixed economy, has refrained from expropriating private property, and pays fair market prices for all government acquisitions. ZANU tolerates the white-dominated private sector because it is so vital to the economy. However, it seeks greater state control and the progressive expansion of the state in economic development. Toward that end, the government has purchased the major newspapers, a large bank, and a pharmaceutical company and is in the process of establishing a state-owned minerals-marketing board. Over the next three years, it aims to resettle 165,000 families on two-thirds of the commercial land presently under white ownership. In the area of social services and education, the government has introduced free health care for people earning less than Z$150 a month and free education at the primary-school level. State agricultural, industrial, and trading schemes have been delayed because of high capital costs. (*African Business,* August.)

Many radical members of ZANU feel Mugabe is moving too slowly in introducing Marxian socialism. Several militant members of the Central Committee have been purged, notably Edgar Tekere, the former secretary general. Marxist rhetoric continues, although most committee members are more Marxist in name than in practice. The leading and most ideological party members include Enos Nkala, minister of national supply; Herbert Ushewokunze, home minister; Emmerson Munangagwa, director of Central Intelligence; and Eddison Zvobgo, minister of legal and parliamentary affairs. Other party militants include Major General Tungamirayi and Lt. Gen. Rex Nhongo of the National Army. The moderates coalesce around Minister for Economic Development Bernard Chidzero, who is a close confidant of Mugabe's.

Considerable tension over national policies exists between radicals and moderates within the party's Central Committee and the cabinet. There is also a subtle power struggle between the cabinet and the Central Committee over their respective roles in administrative decision-making. ZANU's major publication, *Moto* magazine, tends to reflect the more militant, Marxist wing. The government-owned radio and television services have recently come under ZANU party domination. The country's major dailies, once privately held by a South African–based conglomerate, are also falling under strong ZANU editorial influence.

Domestic Affairs. Zimbabwe's population is deeply and bitterly divided over fundamental questions of power and of national purpose and direction. The whites, numbering approximately 160,000, are generally opposed to ZANU's socialistic policies but grudgingly cooperate. Most of the Ndebele resent Shona political domination and remain in ZAPU as an implacable opposition. Both groups staunchly oppose the creation of a one-party state. In response, Mugabe has pledged that such a move will not occur before the 1985 elections. Nevertheless, mutual suspicions and recriminations run deep and tend to impair the functioning of parliament. As a result, Zimbabwe has become a de facto one-party state.

Anti-ZANU activity has greatly escalated since Nkomo's removal from the cabinet in February. Nearly 7 percent (mostly ZAPU supporters) of the 49,000-strong National Army have deserted and returned to bush guerrilla warfare. Military armories have been attacked, farms have been burned, Mugabe's residence was shot at, six foreign tourists were abducted, and nearly a quarter of the air force was destroyed by a guerrilla raid on a major air base. (*NYT,* 7 August.) There were also firefights just inside Zimbabwe's borders with Mozambique and South Africa, involving former white Rhodesian soldiers allegedly in South African employ.

Mugabe has responded to these internal and external threats by using emergency powers instituted by the former white Rhodesian government. Over 425 dissidents, mainly Ndebele, were arrested, including two top ZAPU military commanders and two white air force officers. Much of Matabeleland, the center of antigovernment activity, was placed under dusk-to-dawn curfew. (*WP,* 6 July, 13 October.) But throughout 1982, the security situation in the western provinces deteriorated steadily. All this came at a time of economic decline and food shortages caused by the global recession and the country's worst drought in 36 years.

International Positions. ZANU and the Zimbabwe government officially adhere to a policy of nonalignment. The government actively seeks loans from such multinational agencies as the World Bank.

Mugabe is personally interested in attracting foreign investment, and in 1982 he led a mission to countries in the European Economic Community (*Africa Report,* August). Vice-President George Bush was given a warm welcome in Harare, as was David Rockefeller, former chairman of Chase Manhattan Bank and a leading advocate of international capitalism (*Africa News,* 15 November). The country has received more than $162 million in U.S. aid and entered into a joint corporate venture with the U.S. food-processing firm of H. J. Heinz, allowing the company an unprecedented 51 percent controlling interest (*African Business,* December). On the other hand, the government has refused to adopt an investment code or to give ironclad assurances against future expropriations. Consequently, Zimbabwe has failed to attract anticipated new foreign investment.

Relations with the People's Republic of China have been extremely warm since ZANU's inception. Chinese Prime Minister Zhao Ziyang was scheduled to visit Zimbabwe early in January 1983 to strengthen those historic ties. To date, bilateral trade has been minuscule. The North Koreans have trained Zimbabwe's Fifth Brigade and will return soon to train the Sixth. Parliamentary delegations have recently visited Romania, Bulgaria, Hungary, and Yugoslavia. East Germany's foreign minister was warmly received in Harare (*Moto,* October), and the two countries signed a radio agreement providing for the exchange of programs (*African Business,* October). Relations with the Soviet Union, a former Nkomo supporter, have begun to improve, and in January, Mugabe hosted a delegation of Soviet party workers. However, Zimbabwe-Soviet trade has not grown significantly since the achievement of black majority rule. By force of historical circumstances, South Africa remains Zimbabwe's major trade partner. In an effort to reduce that dependence and to diversify its regional trade, Zimbabwe has played a major role in the establishment of the Southern African Development Coordination Conference and the Preferential Trade Agreement with central and eastern African countries. Zimbabwe is a member of the Organization of African Unity and supports the liberation of Namibia and the overthrow of the present regime in South Africa.

New York University   Richard W. Hull

THE AMERICAS

Introduction

Although Latin America lost salience as a focus of East-West contest in 1982, there were significant developments, and the ideologues of the Kremlin could take more satisfaction in the overall picture there than in Africa, the Middle East, or Asia.

Most of the gain was potential rather than realized as continuing recession, unemployment, inflation, trade imbalances, and looming debt crises by year's end promised to generate radicalism and anti-U.S. agitation, from which communist and quasi-communist parties could hardly fail to profit. Further belt tightening was called for to meet external obligations, but it could be expected to cause political turbulence, if not the predicted "crisis of capitalism." The largest countries of Latin America—Mexico, Brazil, and Argentina—were particularly overshadowed by an excessive burden of debt.

In many countries of Latin America, communist parties gained influence and respectability during 1982. In Brazil, the first open elections in eighteen years gave a number of Communists places in federal and state legislatures, although the party remained unrecognized. The arrest of many communist leaders soon after the 15 November elections probably was a sign of fear of growing communist influence. In Argentina, the communist party was an active participant in discussions for the promotion of a transfer of power to a civilian government. Its status was dependent in large part on the varying warmth of relations between the Soviet Union and the Argentine military government.

In a number of other countries, communist parties gained in influence and respectability during 1982. Disorders in newly democratic Ecuador and Peru gave the Communists opportunities for leadership. The fall of the Bolivian military dictatorship placed a leftist, Hernán Siles Suazo, in the presidency; he named Communists as ministers of labor and mines, the first ever to participate in the Bolivian government at this level. Siles also reopened and expanded relations with Cuba, the Soviet Union, and other communist countries. In Colombia, the official communist party continued to work within the legal political framework, and several guerrilla movements continued their nonpacific campaigns, while the new conservative president moved his country's foreign policy toward neutrality. The Venezuelan Communist Party improved its position among the contending leftist parties, while Venezuela also shifted toward the "nonaligned" group, of which Fidel Castro is currently president.

Suriname turned to apparently close affiliation with Cuba, Nicaragua, and Grenada. The National Military Council, headed by Lt. Col. Desi Bouterse, had followed an irregularly socialistic course after taking power in February 1980. During 1982, the opposition attempted several times to mobilize against the dictatorship, but it was repressed violently, especially bloodily in December, when some Cubans were said to be involved. Economic aid from the Netherlands and the United States was cut off, and Bouterse turned to Cuba for support. The communist party was insignificant, but Bouterse seemed to rely heavily on Castro to stay in power, and the realignment of the Suriname dictatorship had potential strategic importance.

In Central America, the balance was mixed. The Sandinista government of Nicaragua came under increased external pressure, especially from guerrillas operating near or from Honduras. On the other hand, it moved away from the pluralist and nearer the Cuban model. The government of El Salvador was strengthened by the very large turnout in March elections, and presumably for this reason the guerrillas were rather inactive for several months. By the end of the year, however, they had advanced from terroristic sabotage to trying to control territory and were perhaps stronger than ever, although still incapable of holding major centers. The government continued to suffer from deep rifts between rightists and moderates while the leftists were apparently more unified than ever. In Honduras, leading Communists were arrested. President Luís Monge of Costa Rica attacked the party as pro-Nicaragua subversives, while President Reagan was warmly applauded. Most significantly, the new government of Efraín Ríos Montt in Guatemala claimed by late 1982 to have brought to an end the guerrilla struggle that had been going on for twenty years. This was optimistic, but the level of violence had certainly diminished and the authority of the government had been restored in many formerly guerrilla-held villages. The policy of "rifles and beans," of mobilizing peasants to hold off guerrillas and rewarding their loyalty to the government, appeared to be successful.

Castro, not the Soviet general secretary, continued to be the chief figure of Latin America communism, and Cuba continued in 1982 to pursue "revolutionary internationalism," maintaining military forces in Angola, Ethiopia, and several other African countries. The U.S. government closed most of the few remaining channels between the two countries, but Cuban prestige in the hemisphere recovered from the setbacks of 1981. This was largely a result of the Falkland/Malvinas war, in which Cuba strongly supported Argentina, which gratefully reversed its anti-Castro stance, praised Cuba, and signed a trade agreement. The Argentines also expressed strong solidarity with the Sandinista government of Nicaragua (which they had been helping to harass) in return for the latter's backing in the Malvinas issue.

Soviet policy toward Latin America continued dual, cheering radical movements so far as they were not clearly anti-Soviet while trying to weave closer commercial and other ties with governments, however anticommunist, such as Argentina and Brazil. The Soviet Union made little progress, however, except in Bolivia. Most notable was its failure to profit from the Falklands/Malvinas war. It seemed conceivable that Argentina might turn to the Soviet Union for support, possibly becoming a Soviet ally. However, the failure of the Soviet Union to provide the Argentines with more than verbal backing caused disillusionment.

In North America, the Communist Party, U.S.A. played on fears of nuclear war; unhappiness with U.S. foreign policy, especially in Central America; opposition to increased defense spending and reductions in social programs; and unemployment. It consequently was able to increase somewhat its membership and influence through a network of organizations. The same general issues plus U.S.-Canadian trade frictions helped the several Canadian Marxist-Leninist parties, although they were divided between the Communist Party of Canada in English Canada and rival parties of separatist inclinations in Quebec.

Hoover Institution   Robert Wesson

Argentina

Illegal but not strongly repressed, the Communist Party of Argentina (Partido Comunista de la Argentina; PCA) has to operate under a rightist military government. It is the successor to a wing of the Socialist Party that joined the Comintern in 1918. It is and always has been conspicuously loyal to the Soviet Union, which has caused something of a problem for it in a country so self-consciously nationalistic and traditionally independent in its general international posture.

Although forced to operate underground in the 1930s, by World War II the PCA had acquired a very significant following in the industrial labor force, a position of strength that it lost with the coming of

President Juan D. Perón (1946–1955), who sponsored a massive trade union movement of his own. To some degree, the PCA has never recovered from this blow, and its continuing (and vastly unequal) rivalry with Peronism for the allegiance of the Argentine working class explains both its relative lack of political importance and also its somewhat ambivalent attitude toward the various right-wing military regimes that have, among other things, attempted to suppress or eradicate Peronism during the past 25 years.

Party membership may be estimated at around 65,000. The secretary general is Athos Fava, who took over the Central Committee in June 1980. Other leaders include Roldolfo Ghioldi, Irene Rodríguez, Jorge Pereyra, and Pedro Tadioli. Veteran leader Orestes Ghioldi died on 12 April.

The principal party publication, the newspaper *Qué Pasa*, was suppressed in 1982.

PCA Activities.   Although political parties were illegal from the military coup of 1976 to the sudden lifting of the ban in July 1982, the Communists suffered fewer restrictions than other movements on the left, which were banned outright. The PCA was merely "suspended"; its headquarters remained open; and as recently as 1981, *Qué Pasa* was readily available. It is natural to assume, as did the *New York Times,* that "the junta tolerates the party largely because it is handy for maintaining relations with the Soviet Union"— with whom Argentina sustains an intense commercial relationship; "Argentine Communists are often the middlemen in trade." On the other hand, party leaders themselves have complained of persecution and harassment and have claimed their share in the army of persons who have disappeared since 1976 (*YICA*, 1981, p. 33). In the final days of 1981, three party buildings in Buenos Aires were raided by the federal police, who arrested 30 leaders, among them Fernando Nadra, Roberto Vallarino, and Central Committee member Fanny Edelman. In January 1982, a federal judge sentenced PCA militant Carlos Enrique Taboada to preventive custody for engaging in political activities, and on 10 April *Pravda* complained that the first secretary of the Paraguayan Communist Party, Antonio Maidana, kidnapped in Buenos Aires in 1980 along with another "comrade in struggle," had been handed over by Argentine authorities to Gen. Alfredo Stroessner's police (*FBIS*, 14 April).

The sudden tightening of restrictions on party activities in early 1982 may be interpreted as a reflection of the new Argentine relationship with the Reagan administration and a consequent desire to impose some measure of coherence on Argentine domestic and foreign policies. Nonetheless, by mid-1982 the Communists were resurfacing in the context of a war with Great Britain in the South Atlantic. Taking full advantage of Soviet support for the Argentine position, PCA militants were conspicuous in street demonstrations and in the pronouncements of the opposition parties (the so-called Multiparty Group). In September, the party held its first rally since 1976, attracting 20,000 persons to the Luna Park Stadium in Buenos Aires; an additional 3,000 who could not be accommodated had to follow events from outside.

Party View and International Contacts.   The curious Argentine-Soviet relationship (of which more below) has created certain ideological difficulties for PCA leaders. While unreservedly critical of right-wing military governments elsewhere in Latin America, they carefully qualify their views on the Argentine junta. Thus, Central Committee member Rubens Escaro told a Cuban journalist in November 1981 that although the PCA had not—as often alleged—granted "critical support" to the regime, there were in fact different strains within it. The main enemy was "Pinochetism," against which "we had to concentrate the fight . . . to keep it from achieving total power. It was necessary not to mix [these different currents] but unmix them and establish a broad range of allies . . . The danger of a fascist dictatorship cannot be ignored." However, he added, "so far, fascism has been unsuccessful." (*Bohemia*, 20 November 1981.)

The accession of Gen. Leopoldo F. Galtieri to the presidency at the end of 1981 and a new Argentine assertiveness in hemispheric security issues led party spokesmen to drop their equivocal tone momentarily. The new president's "rightism," according to PCA Secretary General Athos Fava, originated in the United States, "a country that demands alignment with Reagan and with imperialism . . . and the closure of paths leading to an authentic democratic opening" (Noticias Argentinas, 31 January; *FBIS*, 10 February).

In the interview cited above, Escaro reiterated a constant party theme: the need for an entente between communist and Peronist workers, so that the labor movement could ensure "its complete independence from the state, the bosses, and the political parties." He hoped that the unions would "renounce exclusive sectarianism, ideological discrimination, and compromises with the factions in power," which is another way of saying that he hoped Peronism would cease to be the main current of labor politics in Argentina.

Although the party maintains fraternal contacts with the Cuban party, its main lines run to Eastern Europe. In 1982, for example, a study delegation led by Oscar Arévalo, member of the Political Commission of the Central Committee, visited the German Democratic Republic.

Membership and Front Organizations.   Before the 1976 coup the party claimed 125,000 members, although other sources suggest that the real figure is slightly more than half that number. There is no reason to assume that, given the political environment since then, there has been a notable increase (*YICA*, 1981, p. 33). While a majority of members are manual workers, the leadership is decidedly middle class.

The PCA youth movement, the Federación Juvenil Comunista, claimed 40,000 members before the coup; since then, it has been subjected to considerable harassment. As noted, the labor wing of the party has made few inroads into the Peronist-controlled unions. The Communists control the Argentine Permanent Assembly on Human Rights, whose data on jailings and disappearances are considered to be among the most complete. The Argentine branch of the World Peace Council includes two dozen figures prominent in political, religious, and cultural life.

Other Leftist Groups.   Other communist parties in Argentina include the Revolutionary Communist Party (Partido Comunista Revolucionario), the Communist Vanguard (Vanguardia Comunista), and the Marxist-Leninist Communist Party (Partido Comunista Marxista-Leninista de la Argentina), all of which are anti-Soviet. Trotskyism is represented by various contending groups, all of which claim to be Peronist in some fashion or other. One engaged in guerrilla activities in the early 1970s and was largely liquidated by the military after the coup. Another, the Popular Front of the Left (Frente de la Izquierda Popular), led by historian Jorge Abelardo Ramos, is conspicuously opposed to political violence and operates with greater freedom than its rivals.

Scattered remnants of the more violence-prone Trotskyist groups continue to exist—in a fragile clandestineness within the country and with some notoriety in Mexico and Western Europe. These include the Montoneros and the Revolutionary Army of the People (Ejército Revolucionario del Pueblo; ERP). While Mexican President José López Portillo received Montonero leader Mario Firmenich with full honors in April, there do seem to be limits to Mexican hospitality. Thus, in October 1981, Mexican police arrested four Argentines purportedly affiliated with the ERP, one of whom was the brother of Ernesto "Che" Guevara. They were charged subsequently with kidnapping the niece of the opposition party's presidential candidate for a U.S. $1.7 million ransom.

The Domestic and International Framework.   It is impossible to understand the role and attitudes of the PCA without some reference to the larger picture of Argentine relations with the USSR. In the last five or six years, Argentina has become a major supplier of cereals and other agricultural products to the Soviet Union, to the point that the USSR accounts for between 75 and 80 percent of Argentina's total cereal exports (30 percent of all sales abroad). This makes Argentina Moscow's leading trading partner in the developing world, a situation unlikely to change soon. In July 1980, the two countries signed a five-year agreement for the annual delivery of at least four million tons of corn and sorghum and 500,000 tons of soya beans; in April 1981, a further agreement arranged for the annual export of 60,000–100,000 tons of frozen beef. (Great Britain, Foreign and Commonwealth Office, *Background Brief*, April 1982.)

In addition to hard currency, Argentina receives for its agricultural exports some Soviet machinery and equipment, as well as nuclear fuel. An existing trade agreement, due to have expired in early 1982, was extended for three more years in August. Under another arrangement, the Soviets undertook to provide enriched uranium for the Atucha II reactor. To some degree the Argentine-Soviet entente is reflected in dealings with other nations of the Eastern bloc. Thus, in 1982 Argentina was visited by trade missions and/ or signed new commercial agreements with Cuba, Czechoslovakia, the German Democratic Republic, and Bulgaria.

The relationship has had some rather curious political consequences: on one hand, Soviet media have been notably restrained in their comments on the military governments that have ruled Argentina since 1976, and Soviet representatives have generally abstained in international forums from blanket condemnations of political repression in Argentina. President Galtieri even received a warm telegram of congratulations from Leonid Brezhnev in January 1982, shortly after seizing the presidency from ailing Gen. Roberto Viola. For its part, the Argentine government, piqued at sanctions imposed by the Carter administration for human rights violations, was the only major grain-exporting country to reject the U.S. call in 1980 for an embargo on the Soviet Union after the invasion of Afghanistan. (Argentina, however, did boycott the Moscow Olympics.)

There have, however, been strict geographical limits to this ideological agnosticism: the Argentine military continues to be strongly concerned over Marxist subversion in Central America and, particularly after the change of governments in the United States in early 1981, sought to assist the Reagan administration in that region. Its exact contribution is not fully known, but there have been persistent reports of Argentine military training missions in El Salvador and Honduras, which in turn have provoked heated criticism, not only by the PCA, but by other, more mainstream political forces. The most spectacular allegation made in 1982 was that Argentina was promoting a plan to create an inter-American force to intervene in El Salvador; this was heatedly denied by the Foreign Ministry. The government also brusquely dismissed charges by the Sandinista regime in Nicaragua of having financed counterrevolutionaries in that country.

At the moment when the Argentine role in Central America was approaching the point of acute controversy at home, the armed forces chose to forcibly reincorporate into the national domain an archipelago off the country's Atlantic coast seized in 1833 by the British and occupied since then as the Falkland Islands (the Malvinas on Argentine maps). This sudden act was greeted with an unprecedented outburst of applause and national euphoria, to which all political forces—the PCA included—wholeheartedly subscribed. When mediation efforts under U.S. Secretary of State Alexander Haig failed to fashion a compromise that would avoid war, the U.S. publicly sided with Great Britain, which retook the islands with a hastily assembled but brilliantly led task force of soldiers and marines.

The U.S. failure to remain neutral led to a sudden, drastic shift in official mood in Buenos Aires. There were periodic threats that Argentina would, if necessary, turn to the Soviets for military aid (*NYT*, 30 May), and there were reports—quickly denied by the Air Ministry—of Argentine plans to acquire MiGs in exchange for grain shipments (*Buenos Aires Herald*, 17 June; Noticias Argentinas, 17 June; *FBIS*, 18 June). Although the Soviets did not, as apparently was expected, veto a U.N. Security Council resolution calling for an Argentine withdrawal from the islands, Moscow generally supported the Argentine claim and used the opportunity to attack the Thatcher government and the Reagan administration.

The most significant diplomatic consequence of the war was a dramatic reorientation of Argentina's posture in Central America and in the forums of the Third World. Seventy military advisers were reportedly withdrawn from Central America, and there were indications that new ambassadors would be named to both Cuba and Nicaragua; fully accredited representatives had previously been withdrawn with the suggestion that they would not be replaced. Foreign Minister Nicanor Costa Méndez even journeyed to Havana in June for a meeting of the nonaligned movement, chaired by Cuban President Fidel Castro. On that occasion, the foreign minister signed a $100 million trade agreement with the Cubans, the first since 1876, and characterized relations with the regime there as "excellent." For their part, many Asian and African delegates to the conference were reportedly surprised "at the unusually radical stance [Costa Méndez] adopted . . . on numerous Third World issues" during the deliberations (*NYT*, 5 June).

The surrender of the Argentine expeditionary force in June led to the replacement of President Galtieri by a provisional military regime, which on 19 July lifted the six-year ban on political parties. Elections were announced for some time in late 1983, with a new civilian government to take office early in 1984. Major General Reynaldo Bignone, the new chief executive, immediately drew Argentina back from partnership with the Cubans in the nonaligned movement, but insisted that the close relationship with the United States would not be resumed. As one correspondent characterized the posture of the new government, it would be "fiercely anticommunist, non-aligned, pro-Western, and anti-Yankee, all at once" (*WP*, 7 July). The prospect of a new civilian government did not significantly alter this evaluation.

American Enterprise Institute   Mark Falcoff

Bolivia

A dramatic change in national politics late in 1982 completely altered the situation of the Bolivian far left and all of the country's civilian parties. General Guido Vildoso, the third military president since the coup of 1980 and the second to hold office in 1982, suddenly decided to allow the congress elected in July 1980 to meet and elect a new president, an action that had been thwarted by the coup of Gen. Luís García Meza two years earlier. The congress chose Hernán Siles Suazo, an ex-president and the clear front-runner in the 1980 election. The reasons for Vildoso's action included the severest economic and foreign-exchange crisis since the Great Depression, the absolute discrediting of the military regime because of its bloodthirsty repression and the participation of its leaders in the international cocaine trade, and persistent and massive resistance by civilian parties and the labor movement.

Virtually all far-left parties and tendencies in Bolivia originated in one of five original groups: (1) the pro-Stalinist Party of the Revolutionary Left (Partido de Izquierda Revolucionaria), established in 1940, whose heirs include the pro-Moscow Communist Party of Bolivia (Partido Comunista de Bolivia; PCB) and the pro-Beijing Marxist-Leninist Communist Party of Bolivia (Partido Comunista de Bolivia Marxista-Leninista); (2) the Trotskyist Revolutionary Workers' Party (Partido Obrero Revolucionario; POR), also organized in 1940, the ancestor of many other parties, most still using the same name; (3) the National Liberation Army (Ejército de Liberación Nacional), a guerrilla group organized by Ernesto "Che" Guevara in 1966, which in 1975 established the Revolutionary Party of Bolivian Workers (Partido Revolucionario de los Trabajadores de Bolivia); (4) the middle-of-the-road Christian Democratic Party, which gave birth to the Movement of the Revolutionary Left (Movimiento de Izquierda Revolucionaria; MIR) in 1971; and (5) the center-left Nationalist Revolutionary Movement (MNR), which gave rise to a dissident left-wing group that formed the Socialist Party (Partido Socialista de Bolivia) in the early 1970s. The total membership of these factions probably does not exceed 5,000.

The spearhead of the civilian resistance that precipitated the downfall of the military regime was the central labor organization, the Central Obrera Boliviana (COB). This is led by Juan Lechín Oquendo, its executive secretary for 30 years and head of the Miners Federation (FSTMB) for 40 years and also of the Revolutionary Party of the Nationalist Left (Partido Revolucionario de la Izquierda Nacionalista), which split from the MNR in 1963. Also influential within the COB are the pro-Moscow and pro-Beijing Communists and the Trotskyite POR faction headed by Guillermo Lora.

In August, the FSTMB, which had been relegalized along with the COB earlier in the year, held a national convention, which demanded a return to constitutional civilian rule, nationalization of the banks and foreign trade, and a moratorium on payments on the foreign debt. Soon afterwards, on 26 August, it called a 48-hour general strike. This was followed in September by a spreading strike movement throughout urban and mining centers, culminating in a protest march of 100,000 people through La Paz on 15 September and a general strike call by the COB on 16 September. (*Intercontinental Press*, 1 November.)

In the face of this situation, President Vildoso decided to allow the 1980 congress to meet and choose his successor. It did so on 5 October, electing Hernán Siles president and Jaime Paz Zamora of the MIR as vice-president. They had been the candidates in 1980 of the Popular Democratic Union (Union Democratica Popular; UDP) coalition, composed of Siles's Left National Revolutionary Movement (Movimiento Nacionalista Revolucionaria de Izquierda; MNRI), the MIR, and the pro-Moscow PCB.

On taking office on 10 October, President Siles appointed a cabinet composed of seven members of the

MNRI, six of the MIR, two members of the PCB, and two independents. The PCB received the portfolios of Labor and Mines. This was the first time that the PCB had ever participated in a cabinet.

Throughout the early part of the year, the PCB supported the policy advocated by Hernán Siles of carrying on underground work while seeking to take advantage of whatever opportunities there were for legal activities. David García, a member of the PCB Politburo, said in an April interview that the PCB "had to give battle to the Trotskyites and Maoists and various other groups of leftists who sought to confine the whole of the struggle to action deep in the underground" (*WMR*, April).

On 6 July, Ramiro Barrenechea, another Politburo member, issued a demand in the name of the PCB for immediate elections to choose a civilian president and a new congress (*FBIS*, 7 July). However, along with the rest of the UDP, the pro-Moscow Communists accepted the reconvening of the congress elected in 1980 and its choosing of Siles and Paz Zamora.

Subsequent to Siles's inauguration, Jorge Kolle Cueto, PCB first secretary and a senator, denounced the congress, which is controlled by non-UDP elements, as "unrepresentative of the social sectors." He announced that the PCB would seek "a referendum and municipal elections to allow this new correlation of social forces to stand out more clearly." (AFP, 27 October.)

The other far-left factions were aligned with the opposition throughout the year. The "Combate" POR faction, headed by Hugo González Moscoso and affiliated with the United Secretariat of the Fourth International, had indicated its support of Siles before he assumed power (*Intercontinental Press*, 17 November 1980). However, subsequent to Siles's inauguration, it supported the COB in its unwillingness to accept posts in the Siles government unless it had a majority in the cabinet and determined the government's policies (ibid., 1 November).

Economic and diplomatic relations between Bolivia and communist-ruled countries grew during the year, under both the military regime and the Siles government. In January, a delegation from the Soviet Nonferrous Metallurgy Ministry visited the country to study difficulties at a tin volatilization plant at La Palca, which had been built with Soviet technical help (Radio Illimani, 7, 16, and 29 January). In March, Soviet Ambassador Sergei Kovalev "promised technical, cultural, scientific and industrial aid" to Bolivia (*FBIS*, 9 March). During the next month, the Bolivian steel firm SIDERSA conferred with visiting Soviet authorities on the possibility of receiving financial and technical aid from the USSR (ibid., 20 April).

A Cuban delegation headed by Vice-President Carlos Rafael Rodríguez attended the inauguration of President Siles. Rodríguez addressed a joint session of the Bolivian congress and during his speech defended Che Guevara's guerrilla effort in Bolivia during the 1960s. Sergio Ramírez Mercado, a member of the ruling Sandinista junta in Nicaragua, also attended, and the Siles government took advantage of his presence to announce a resumption of diplomatic relations with Nicaragua. (Ibid., 13 October.)

Rutgers University   Robert J. Alexander

Brazil

The *abertura* (political opening) of the military government of President João Baptista Figueiredo, which reached a culmination in the congressional and state elections of 15 November, gave an opportunity for the country's various far-left groups to campaign more or less openly, although none was legalized by the government. However, there were threats early in the year to prosecute a number of the Brazilian

Communist Party leaders in Sao Paulo, and in mid-December Secretary General Giocondo Gervasi Dias and six other members of the Central Committee were detained by federal authorities, along with 77 others attending what some called the "seventh congress" and others a "seminar" (*FBIS*, 15 December). The semilegal status of the party was thus thrown into doubt.

The original Communist Party of Brazil (Partido Comunista do Brasil; PCdoB), founded in March 1922, remains the most important Marxist-Leninist organization in the nation. Several small groups that broke away or were expelled from the party in its first decade formed a Trotskyist movement that subsequently split into several factions, a number of which still remain. In 1960, the original pro-Soviet party changed its name to Brazilian Communist Party (Partido Comunista Brasileiro; PCB). A pro-Chinese element broke away the following year, and in February 1962 adopted the original party name, PCdoB. This group has since abandoned allegiance to China and become pro-Albanian. After the establishment of the military dictatorship in 1964, several new far-left groups were formed, most of them by PCB dissidents, which advocated and practiced for several years various kinds of guerrilla warfare. The only one that seems to have survived is MR-8, originally established by a communist ex-deputy, Carlos Marighella.

Organization and Leadership. For the first time since the military coup, the PCB has been able since 1980 to establish an organizational structure at virtually all levels. At its pinnacle, the party has a so-called leadership collective, or Central Committee, led by Secretary General Giocondo Gervasi Dias, with Salomão Malina, Teodoro Mello, Luiz Tenório de Lima, Geraldo Rodrigues dos Santos, and Givaldo Siqueira among its other members. In most states the party was able to reorganize state committees, as well as municipal committees in many cities and towns. It publishes a national weekly, *Voz da Unidade*, and has also put out a number of pamphlets and other publications.

Domestic Activities. Early in the year, the federal police brought charges under the National Security Law against Lindolfo Silva and Regis Fratte, members of the Central Committee of the PCB and nominal proprietors of the Jurua Publishing House, which puts out *Voz da Unidade*. The specific charge was that they had brought out a "subversive" publication, a booklet entitled *Novos Rumos*, in commemoration of the sixtieth anniversary of the establishment of the Communist Party. (*O Estado de São Paulo*, 15 January.) However, there was no indication that these charges were pushed to conclusion.

Much of the PCB's activity during the year was taken up with election efforts. It continued to urge the theme of national unity among the scattered parties opposed to the military regime. As early as October 1981, Giocondo Dias had argued that "the Communists believe the opposition forces should be able to unite and formulate a common platform . . . As one of the opposition forces, and in keeping with our traditional behavior, we are ready to exercise the greatest effort and collaboration for the unity of opposition forces and negotiations leading to democratization of the nation and reorientation of the economy." (*Voz da Unidade*, 25 September–2 October 1981.)

The PCB was not a legal party and therefore could not run candidates of its own. Generally, it supported the nominees of the Brazilian Democratic Movement Party (Partido Movimento Democrático Brasileiro; PMDB), the largest of the opposition groups. Geraldo Rodrigues dos Santos, a member of the PCB Central Committee, noted "the decision by the Central Committee to support PMDB . . . candidates. Our election tactics call for defeating the authoritarian regime, and the most viable candidate for the democratic forces in Rio de Janeiro is the PMDB candidate."

However, in Rio de Janeiro the PCB policy put the party in an equivocal position. The PMDB candidate for governor was Deputy Miro Teixeira, who was also supported by the outgoing governor, a strong supporter of the military government, but principal opposition nominee was Leonel Brizola, ex-governor of Rio Grande do Sul state and a federal deputy from Rio de Janeiro during the early 1960s. Geraldo Rodrigues dos Santos claimed that Brizola did "not represent conditions of unity" (*Folha de São Paulo*, 3 June). Brizola ultimately won the election.

It was particularly striking that the PCB offered no support to the Workers' Party (Partido dos Trabalhadores; PT), organized by Luis Inacio da Silva ("Lula"), the most outstanding trade union leader to appear in the 1970s and head of the metal workers of São Paulo. Hercules Correa, a member of the PCB Central Committee, explained the PCB attitude by saying that the policy of the PT "disunites, divides. So it benefits the central power and assists President Figueiredo's authoritarian plans." (*Jornal do Brasil*, 10 June.)

Factional Struggle with Luiz Carlos Prestes.   The struggle between the leadership of the PCB and its former longtime (37 years) secretary general, Luiz Carlos Prestes, continued during the year. In June, Central Committee member Geraldo Rodrigues dos Santos announced that Prestes had been expelled from the party. He commented that the break with Prestes "is permanent, and its major lesson is that the party must honor its leaders, but it must not deify them or transform them into myths." He accused Prestes of breaking with the party when he did not get his way within its top leadership.

Dos Santos said that Prestes's dissidence resulted because "he advocates immediate struggle for the socialist revolution, and that limits the scope for alliances. On the pretext of anticapitalist struggle, a number of alliances with sectors of the national bourgeoisie participating in the single front are excluded. We, on the contrary, feel that . . . first it is necessary to defeat the regime and clear the way for the formation of a government of democratic forces that will permit the exercise of freedoms, the organization of the working class, and the struggle for socialism." (*Folha de São Paulo*, 3 June.)

Prestes announced that he regarded his expulsion as "perfectly natural." He added that "I am very happy that the Brazilian people will know that I have nothing to do with the right-wing opportunistic orientation decided on by Geraldo and his comrades on the Central Committee." (Ibid., 4 June.) Prestes broke with the PCB with regard to the election in Rio de Janeiro. He was reported to be supporting Leonel Brizola (ibid., 3 June).

Principles and Program of the PCB.   The most complete statement of the current position of the PCB was a document submitted for discussion in connection with the forthcoming Seventh Congress. It started by proclaiming that "considering the current situation in Brazil and in the world, the revolution has real possibilities of reaching its objectives through means that may exclude armed struggle, insurrection, and civil war . . . The working classes are struggling for their deepest interest; namely, the conquest of political democracy . . . as a condition that will favor, among other essential aspects of their struggle, revolutionary changes through nonviolent means." The party also claimed that "within the framework of a democratic society, military participation in the political life of a country is a positive fact."

As for the future of the PCB itself, the document foresaw its becoming "a democratic party of the masses that will be capable of absorbing every type of class and social level struggling for democratic freedom . . . as a path toward achieving socialism in Brazil." It will be "profoundly nationalist, democratic, and internationalist . . . a party that, in view of the type of its relations with other political organizations within and without our national borders, is autonomous and independent. In sum, a party that adopts Marxism-Leninism as an instrument for the analysis of reality."

PCB Secretary General Giocondo Dias provoked considerable comment by observing in February that "increasing intervention by the state in the economy helps the process of socializing the nation." He continued by saying that the military government's economic policy "is taking long strides toward socialism," but that "its triumph in Brazil will be brought about by a law of history: every capitalist country is heading toward socialism, just as feudalism was replaced by capitalism." He added that two things were necessary for the success of socialism: "establishment of a regime of complete freedom and organization of the working class and masses of the people. In this respect, Brazil today is certainly much closer to socialism than, for example, in 1940." (*O Estado de São Paulo*, 6 February.)

International Views and Contacts.   The PCB maintained its alignment with the Soviet Union, the Soviet party, and other parties aligned with it. This was most clearly demonstrated after the suppression of Solidarity by the Polish government. Secretary General Dias argued on the occasion of the declaration of martial law in Poland in December 1981 that "General Wojciech Jaruzelski did not climb to power in Poland through a military coup." He added "everything that has been done . . . in Warsaw complies with Polish constitutional principles." He denounced the ten million members of Solidarity because "they united to fight against the regime" and claimed that "Poland will come out of this crisis stronger and closer to socialism." (TELAM, 7 February.)

In March, on its sixtieth anniversary, the PCB received a number of congratulatory greetings from other communist parties. Among these were messages from the Bulgarian and Italian parties. (*FBIS*, 30 March; *L'Unità*, Rome, 27 March.)

Communist Party of Brazil. Like the PCB, the PCdoB continued during the year to restructure its organization on a more or less open basis. It continued to be the strongest of the groups to the left of the PCB. It publishes the periodical *Tribuna da Luta Operaria*. It also continued to be aligned internationally with the Albanian party. On the occasion of the sixtieth anniversary of the establishment of Brazilian communism, the PCdoB received a message of congratulations from Enver Hoxha, first secretary of the Albanian Party of Labor. The message claimed that "the Communist Party of Brazil is the heir of the best traditions of the Brazilian working class and people, the defender and applicant of the ideology of Marxism-Leninism in the concrete conditions of Brazil." It added that the Albanian Party of Labor will stand side by side with the sister Communist Party of Brazil in the common struggle for the triumph of Marxism-Leninism and the cause of socialism and the liberation of the peoples." (*FBIS*, 26 March.)

Other Organizations. Other far-left groups continued to be active during the year. These include the Revolutionary Communist Party and the MR-8, which broke from the PCB during the late 1960s, and at least three Trotskyist groups. The MR-8 took an active part in the election campaign in some states.

At least three of the Trotskyist international factions have followers in Brazil. Until 1980 the Convergencia Socialista group, publishing a newspaper with the same name, was aligned with the United Secretariat. However, a majority of the group aligned with the Argentine Trotskyist leader Nahuel Moreno, when he broke with the United Secretariat. The minority withdrew to form a new group, publishing the fortnightly *El Tempo*. A third group, the International Socialist Organization, is aligned with the international faction headed by the French leader Pierre Lambert.

In June, Jose Maria de Almeida, a leader of the Convergencia Socialista participated in a roundtable discussion in which he expounded the positions of the group. When asked whether "intellectuals, university students, wives of workers" would have the vote in the socialist regime that Convergencia Socialista advocated, he replied: "No. There would be elections for workers' councils, and all the working population would vote. Now, if you want to know whether the bourgeoisie will participate in this process, they will not. We advocate freedom or organization for all socialist parties of the working class, but there will not be room for any bourgeois parties. Absolutely none. In my conception, there are two classes in society: the proletariat and the bourgeoisie. There is no third class." (*O Estado de São Paulo*, 20 June.)

All three Trotskyist groups worked more or less closely with the Partido dos Trabalhadores of trade union leader Lula.

Economic and Diplomatic Relations with Communist Countries. Economic relations between Brazil and the Soviet Union and East European countries, which have been growing in recent years, intensified during 1982 as a consequence of a series of bilateral negotiations. In August, a meeting of the Brazil–USSR joint trade commission reached an accord extending an existing agreement for exchange of Soviet machinery and equipment for Brazilian manufactured goods and primary products. This accord increased the proportion of Brazilian manufactured goods from 30 percent of all shipments to the USSR to 50 percent. (*Jornal do Brasil*, 1 August.) Subsequently, Soviet technical and financial help was agreed to for a project for extracting alcohol from wood and for a land reclamation program (ibid., 3 October; *FBIS*, 6 October). At the end of October, the two countries renewed a maritime agreement (*O Globo*, 28 October).

Late in March, a trade agreement was signed with Hungary, covering a three-year period and providing for Brazil to sell Hungary U.S. $435 million worth of goods, including soybean meal, cocoa, coffee, textiles, and a wide range of manufactured goods. Hungary pledged to sell Brazil about $145 million worth of goods in the same period. In April, it was announced that Brazil was the most important Third World trading partner of Poland, the two-way commerce amounting to about $700 million (*FBIS*, 20 April).

Rutgers University   Robert J. Alexander

Canada

Several Marxist-Leninist parties and groups operate legally in Canada. The oldest and largest is the Communist Party of Canada (CPC). Since its founding in 1921, the CPC has been consistently pro-Moscow in alignment. The Workers Communist Party (Marxist-Leninist) (WCP), founded in 1979, is pro–Beijing. The Communist Party of Canada (Marxist-Leninist) (CPC-ML), founded in 1970, is pro-Albanian. The Marxist-Leninist Organization of Canada–In Struggle (MLOC), founded in 1972, has no formal international affiliation. Several Trotskyist groups exist, including the Revolutionary Workers League (RWL), Group socialiste des travailleurs (GST), Trotskyist League (TL), and Forward Readers Group (FRG).

In the last federal election (1980), the combined vote for all communist parties was less than 0.2 percent of the total. Communist candidates ran in the 1982 provincial elections in New Brunswick, Saskatchewan, and Alberta. No candidates were elected. The parties have been increasingly active in municipal elections, notably in Vancouver, Winnipeg, and Toronto, and several members have won election.

The Canadian economy, mired in its worst recession in the postwar period, has a record 1.5 million unemployed (12.8 percent of the labor force). In an effort to control inflation and the deficit, the federal government, along with most provincial governments, legislated limits on salary increases for public employees. The right to strike was also abolished for the affected workers. There has been, as a result, discussion within the labor movement, particularly in Quebec, of the need for a general strike. Increased dissatisfaction with the Parti Quebecois (PQ), has fostered new proposals among the Quebec left for an alternate organization that could better pursue the twin goals of independence and socialism. Much of the attention has focused on the newly formed Mouvement Socialiste, a loose alliance of Marxists.

In foreign affairs one of the most controversial measures has been the agreement with the United States to test Cruise missiles in Canada. This has acted as a catalyst for the peace movement. At least 126 Canadian cities held municipal referenda, and an average 77 percent of the voters called for disarmament. The most jarring event was the 14 October bombing of the Litton factory in Toronto, where crucial Cruise components are constructed. Seven persons were injured. The group Direct Action claimed responsibility.

Communist Party of Canada. Headquartered in Toronto, with an estimated 2,500 members, the CPC ran one candidate in the Saskatchewan and eight in the Alberta provincial elections. William Tuomi, the Alberta leader, died, and Gordon Massie moved from Saskatchewan to become the acting leader in Ontario. Celebrating its sixtieth year of existence, the CPC held its Twenty-Fifth Party Convention on 13–15 February in Toronto. Among the highlights were the publication of the long-awaited *Canada's Party of Socialism: History of the Communist Party of Canada, 1921–1976* and a call to update the party program, "The Road to Socialism in Canada" (*Canadian Tribune [CT]*, 22 February). The convention was described as being "united," "young," and with a high percentage of women (30 percent) and unionists (45 percent) (ibid., 22 February, 1 March). Nevertheless a call was made for "rejuvenating . . . the democratic women's movement" and bringing more women and immigrants into the party (*A New Course For Canada*, pp. 15, 47). While noting a certain "fracturing" of some "ultra-left groupings," delegates were warned that "the ultra-left is striving to establish a firm foothold in the trade union movement" (ibid., pp. 14, 31). Members were advised to distinguish Maoists and Trotskyists from young persons temporarily succumbing to "pseudo-left" doctrines. Accordingly the party should strive to "overcome its isolation" and avoid "sectarian aloofness." Good policies alone were not enough; they must be taken to the people (*CT*, 1

March). The party was also criticized for lagging behind the workers' militant upsurge (*New Course*, p. 11). A call was also made for a new quality in party work and for placing "ourselves on an emergency footing" (*CT*, 1 November). It was reported that the Young Communist League, reborn in 1970, has augmented its membership by 30 percent (ibid., 20 September). Increasingly, municipal politics is stressed as fertile territory since "anti-communism is not as divisive as elsewhere, and where the hegemony of social democracy in the progressive movement is weaker" (*Communist Viewpoint* [*CV*], Spring). Communists ran under the label of the Committee of Progressive Electors in Toronto and Vancouver and the Labour Election Committee in Winnipeg. Some have been successful in the last two cities. Claiming that "capitalism is now in a chronic crisis," the CPC sought to distribute a million copies of the pamphlet *Take Canada out of the Crisis* (*CT*, 29 March, 26 April). The CPC asserts that employment is the key problem and calls on governments to end their restraint policies (ibid., 11 January, 6 September). The CPC opposes all wage controls and restrictions on the right to strike (ibid., 5 April, 3 May). Legislation prohibiting plant closures and mass layoffs is proposed, and a moratorium on foreclosures of home and farm mortgages is demanded (ibid., 11 January, 5 July). The party is urged to organize the unemployed (ibid., 1 November). While favoring job creation through increased government expenditure, the CPC rejects "massive giveaways" to large multinational corporations (ibid., 26 April, 6 September). Instead "nationalization under democratic control" is posited (ibid., 8 February).

The CPC is critical of the new Canadian constitution for its failure to give Quebec a veto (ibid., 13 December). Since the PQ government is now seen as biased against the workers, the CPC believes conditions are ripe for a new federated left in Quebec (*CV*, Spring, August, October).

The CPC, striving to lessen U.S. control over Canadian affairs (*New Course*, p. 6), criticizes increased U.S. pressures on Canada designed to change the Foreign Investment Review Agency and the National Energy Programme (*CT*, 18 January, 22 February). The CPC points out that Canadian economic woes are part of the price for being so dependent on the United States (ibid., 25 January, 1 November). Greater trade with the communist states is offered as a solution (ibid., 3 May). Increasingly concerned over Reagan's cold war stance, arms race escalations, and advocacy of the doctrine of a winnable nuclear war, the CPC warns that "the main question today is the growing danger of war" (ibid., 22 February). As a result, there has been a "birth of a mass peace movement" (*CV*, October) composed of a coalition of many forces including the Canadian Peace Congress led by its newly elected secretary, Gordon Flowers. Some 150,000 persons signed the congress's petition "Peace Is Everybody's Business."

The CPC urged Canadians to refuse permission for the testing of the Cruise missile in Canada and to demand a cessation of Litton's manufacturing of the Cruise guidance system, withdrawal from NATO, NORAD, and the Defense Production Sharing Agreement, a ban on all U.S. military flights over Canada, and a declaration of Canada as a nuclear-free zone (*CT*, 8 March, 19 April, 5 July, 1 November, 13 December). The CPC also rejected the government's suggestion that Canada should join the Organization of American States and called instead for a Canadian foreign policy independent of the United States (ibid., 3 May, 1 November). The CPC continues to echo Soviet positions in foreign affairs.

Workers Communist Party. Headquartered in Montreal, with an estimated membership of 1,500, the WCP ran one candidate in the New Brunswick provincial election (*Forge*, 15 October). Party membership is 80 percent Quebeckers and 51 percent women (ibid., 12 November, December). Observing that the widespread crisis of socialism has engendered "skepticism" and "cynicism," the WCP acknowledges that it is "gripped by a profound crisis" and "re-evaluation" of its past work (ibid., 17 September, 12 November, December). In the past year, it has been increasingly buffeted by membership losses, including about a third of the Quebec members, mostly women and workers. The $150,000 fund-raising drive collected only $55,000 (ibid., 10 September, 19 November), necessitating cutbacks in the size and frequency of the party newspaper and the closing of both the Toronto and Montreal bookstores (ibid., 5 and 12 November, December). As the WCP prepared for its Second Congress, 300 activists convened the key Quebec district conference. Significant internal disagreements and criticisms were revealed. The party leadership was "increasingly discredited," and the party was criticized for its chauvinism against women, Quebecois, and proletarians. It was also rebuked for its sectarian "closed-minded approach to progressives." Organizationally, the WCP was criticized for being "bureaucratic" and "Stalinist." Proposals were also heard to re-evaluate "democratic centralism" and "vanguard" status and to remove leaders "at any time." Full autonomy for the Quebec nation and all women's organizations was also advocated. Even the continued need for the party was questioned. The Quebec district leaders were suspended and replaced by temporary leaders. (Ibid., December.)

Observing that since the Quebec referendum, Canadian capitalists and federalists have launched an "unprecedented attack" on Quebec (ibid., 11 June; *October*, Summer), the WCP sees the new constitution, which was imposed without the Quebec people's consent, as the "biggest setback since Confederation" (*Forge*, 5 March, 2 April). It notes that Quebec is not recognized as a nation, has lost its traditional veto and right to self-determination, and has not been granted a right to secede (ibid., 2 and 9 April). While opposing Quebec's independence, the WCP demands a radical transformation of the confederation and considerable autonomy for Quebec (ibid., 5 March, 2 April, 11 June). The PQ's essentially pro-capitalist orientation remains under attack as does the new Mouvement Socialiste (*October*, December 1981). The WCP challenges both groups' assertion that independence and socialism can be pursued simultaneously (ibid., Summer). They are also seen as being inconsistent in their lack of full support for the rights of native peoples (*Forge*, 11 June; *October*, Summer). The WPC was criticized for its tactics in Quebec. It was felt that the leadership, in employing a mechanical definition of the primary and secondary contradictions, had "underestimated and ignored the stepped up chauvinist attacks against Quebec and has been contemptuous of the Quebec national movement." (*Forge*, 12 and 19 November). Particular criticism was directed at the WCP call for members to spoil their ballots in the referendum (ibid., December). The urgent task now posed was to "strengthen the national movement in Quebec" (*October*, Summer).

Believing that "today the labour movement is clearly on the defensive," the WCP calls for a fight against wage freezes (*Forge*, 12 February, 3 September). Critical of trade union leaders' "defeatism," the WCP rejects all labor-management cooperation such as tripartism and employee participation in management (ibid., 23 and 30 April, 3 September; *October*, Summer); it calls instead for a general strike (*Forge*, 18 June). In this regard, the WCP was active as part of the Open Rank and File Caucus within the Canadian Labour Congress. The WCP believes that workers' power can come only through "violent revolution," "nationalization without compensation," and the dictatorship of the proletariat (*October*, December 1981; *Forge*, 23 April). It portrays the New Democratic Party (NDP) as a class-collaborationist party that seeks only to transform capitalism and will attack workers' rights (*Forge*, 19 March, 3 September).

With regard to the peace movement, the WCP warns, however, that "peace activists . . . must distinguish real friends from phony allies" (*October*, December 1981). It calls for Canada to become a weapons-free zone and to ban all Cruise missile testing in Canada (*Forge*, 19 March, 4 June). Canada should get out of NATO and NORAD and pursue a nonaligned foreign policy (*October*, December 1981). Critical of Canada's integration into the U.S. "war machine" (*Forge*, 19 March), the WCP characterizes Canada as "one of the world's leading merchants of death." Workers are urged to stop weapons from coming off Canadian assembly lines (ibid., 4 June). The WCP calls for disarmament of both superpowers (ibid., 30 April) and demands that they both pull their troops out of Europe (*October*, December 1981). While Reagan's stress on U.S. military might is noted, the WCP suggests there is now a significant gap between the United States, imperialist ambitions and its real power (*Forge*, 14 May). The USSR, having ceased to be socialist, has degenerated into "fascist" "state monopoly capitalism" that increasingly is exhibiting qualities that are "aggressive" and reflect a "drive for world domination" (*Forge*, 26 February, 16 April, 28 May; *October*, Summer). The USSR has become the "main troublemaker in the world" (*Forge*, 26 February). The WCP concedes that in the past it has been insufficiently critical of China and too quick to accept ready-made answers, but nevertheless is concerned that current Chinese leaders are too prone to write off the Cultural Revolution and to pursue economic policies that will only exacerbate corruption and bureaucracy (ibid., 12 March, 18 June, 19 November). The WCP warns that the danger of degeneration of socialist revolutions is "paramount" (*October*, December 1981) and expresses concern that socialism and working-class power have been so fragile. It speculates that a key factor is that Marxist-Leninist theory has lagged (*Forge*, 19 November).

Communist Party of Canada (Marxist-Leninist). The CPC-ML is headquartered in Montreal and has membership estimated at 500 to 1,000. In July, its Fourth Congress in Montreal culminated in an international rally attended by 1,500 persons, including a five-member delegation from Albania headed by Enver Halili of the Central Committee of the Albanian Labor Party (*People's Canada Daily News* [*PCDN*],

19 July). Just prior to the congress, Hardial Bains, first secretary of the party, published his new book, *The Necessity For Revolution*. According to the CPC-ML, developments are occurring rapidly in the objective sphere, and this necessitates an improvement in the quality of party work and work tempo (ibid., 20 December).

The party has established at least 25 different front organizations, the most significant being the People's Front Against Racist and Fascist Violence, the Revolutionary Trade Union Opposition, the Democratic Women's Union of Canada, the East Indian Defence Committee, the West Indian People's Organization, and the Communist Youth Union of Canada (M-L).

Perceiving that the bourgeoisie has launched an all-out ideological attack against the workers, the CPC-ML believes that although objective conditions are ripe for revolution, subjective conditions lag (ibid., 6 January, 2 April, 26 August). Accordingly, the party calls on workers to reject the "class collaborationist" schemes of union "bigwigs" and to reject all demands for cutbacks in salaries and services (ibid., 29 March, 8 September). Efforts should be made to resist the shifting of the burden of the crisis onto the backs of the working class. The CPC-ML rejects pressure to unite with revisionists (ibid., 3 August). Accordingly, the new Mouvement Socialiste is condemned for opposing democratic centralism and embracing ideological pluralism (ibid., 1 July). Similarly the NDP is portrayed as a bourgeois party with a "socialist mask" that, when in power, fosters "state monopoly capitalism" (ibid., 30 March). The PQ is characterized as seeking to split people by "reactionary narrow nationalism and chauvinism" (ibid., 8 October). Policies of "genocide" against native peoples and "super-exploitation" of immigrants provide evidence, according to the CPC-ML, that there is a growing tendency toward fascism and state-fostered racism (ibid., 3 March, 24 April). The bourgeois state, portrayed as composed of the "biggest murderers, assassins and terrorists," necessitates that the people militantly defend themselves against such assaults (ibid., 21 August). The CPC-ML asserts that fascists and racists have no right to speak or organize and has blocked several pro-Israeli speaking engagements and Defence Department recruitment meetings at several universities (ibid., 25 and 27 February, 14, 19 and 20 October, 11 December). CPC-ML militancy has frequently led to scuffles, arrests, and fines (*Voice of the People*, September).

On the international situation, the danger of war is seen as increasing because the United States and the Soviet Union are preparing to redivide the world (*PCDN*, 31 March, 28 September, 30 October). Disarmament talks are dismissed as "fraudulent" and will not lessen the arms race (ibid., 17 July, 30 October). The USSR is described as a "fascist dictatorship of the bourgeoisie" and China as "the most reactionary war mongering socialist-imperialist power" (ibid., 3 March, 1 April, 7 October). Canada's withdrawal from NATO and NORAD and refusal to test Cruise missiles are advocated (ibid., 17 July). Albania is the only state seen to be pursuing a proper course of action.

Marxist-Leninist Organization of Canada–In Struggle.   The MLOC, with an estimated core membership of 400, eschewed electoral politics and called on its members to spoil their ballots.

Domestically, while conceding Quebec's right to self-determination, the MLOC called for unity between Quebec and Canadian workers to defeat the Canadian imperialist bourgeoisie (*In Struggle*, 6 and 21 April). Some Quebec members questioned the MLOC's stand on the referendum and suggested that it had displayed an erroneous attitude toward Quebec nationalism (ibid., 9 March).

Internationally, the MLOC observed with dismay the degeneration of socialist states (ibid., 18 May) and the crisis in Marxist-Leninist movements. Noting the attacks on Polish workers and the Afghan people, the MLOC condemned efforts by some parties to seek a reconciliation with the imperialist USSR (*International Forum*, August 1981). Communists were advised to resist the "romantic myth" of "one big happy socialist camp."

Organizationally, the MLOC conceded that it "is in the midst of a deep crisis" (*In Struggle*, 18 May). Following the Quebec referendum, a split emerged in the Central Committee. Increasingly, the MLOC has broken into several distinct groupings. Of the two main tendencies, the Collective of 30, guided by MLOC Secretary General Charles Gagnon, sought to reaffirm Leninist features, while dropping Stalinist excesses (ibid., 22 June). The group Building a Majority Consensus sought to find a revolutionary alternative between Leninism and social democracy. Accordingly, it rejected the old party program and sought a more pluralist, open-ended perspective that would permit unity among groups on the left and a decentralized organizational structure that would permit greater rank-and-file participation by women, workers, and other groups. (Ibid., 6 April.)

In Struggle, the organization's newspaper, became the forum for a lively and wide-ranging debate leading up to the Fourth Congress, held 21–24 May in Montreal. Members conceded that the crisis of Marxism-Leninism was "deep" and that the period of "certitude" and "dogma" had passed (ibid., 23 March, 4 May). In the words of one activist, "Who can say where the socialist countries are?" (ibid., 6 April). Observing that the MLOC program was based on a model "developed in isolated, economically backward countries," some members disturbed by events in Poland began to question whether Marxism-Leninism was not the "ideological basis for totalitarianism" and sought to remove such "blinders" (ibid., 23 March, 18 May, 22 June.) The failure of workers to "rally" to the communist movement despite deteriorating economic conditions led many to suggest Marxism-Leninism was "ossified" and "sterile." Particularly weak was the analysis of the USSR. (Ibid., 6 April, 22 June.) Increasingly voices were raised for the MLOC to become more active in "reform" struggles such as women's problems, ecology, and nuclear warfare (ibid., 6 April, 18 May).

The compatibility of Marxism and feminism was repeatedly raised (*Proletarian Unity*, March), and past practices within the MLOC of subordinating women's issues were criticized. Women, along with gays and lesbians, successfully lobbied for the right to form their own caucuses (ibid., March; *In Struggle*, 23 March). As ideological diversity and caucus groups increased, the MLOC's capacity for "united action" diminished dramatically (*In Struggle*, 18 May). Members could no longer agree on MLOC organizational principles such as a single vanguard party, democratic centralism, or tactics such as alliances with other leftists and participation in elections (ibid., 23 March, 6 April, 18 May). The Fourth Congress rejected the old constitution and methods but could not agree on a new minimal basis for unity. Accordingly, the paralysis was ended by a vote of 187 to 25 in favor of disbanding (ibid., 22 June). Some groupings indicated a desire to rebuild a revolutionary organization.

Revolutionary Workers League.   The RWL belongs to the Trotskyist Fourth International and has several hundred members. It unsuccessfully ran candidates for mayor in four cities. The Young Socialist Organizing Committee is its youth wing. While on the whole supporting the union-based reformist NDP, the RWL is nevertheless critical of the NDP leadership and calls for the NDP to take a more socialist and pro-Quebec position (*Socialist Voice*, 22 February). Recently several RWL members were expelled from the NDP (ibid., 6 December). The RWL criticizes the PQ for its antilabor orientation but does concede some positive role for the PQ as a nationalist party (ibid., 11 January, 8 February, 27 September). The RWL admits its abstention in the referendum was an error (*The Struggle for Socialism Today*). The Mouvement Socialiste is criticized for its reformism. The RWL portrays the United States as imperialist and fostering war. While critical of the USSR's bureaucratic system, it believes the Soviet Union nevertheless has abolished capitalism (*Socialist Voice*, 7 June). Only Cuba is seen to have avoided bureaucratic rule (ibid., 11 January).

Groupe Socialiste de Travailleurs.   The GST, affiliated with the Fourth International (International Committee), is estimated to be the second-largest Trotskyist organization. The GST favors Quebec independence and the creation of a workers' party in Quebec.

Trotskyist League.   The TL denies that the RWL is revolutionary, noting that the RWL is unwilling to use violence and supports the reformist NDP. While critical of the Stalinist degeneration of the USSR caused by a parasitic leadership caste, the TL claims that the USSR and Cuba, nevertheless, should be defended from attacks. It calls for a military victory in El Salvador.

Forward Readers Group.   The FRG chooses to operate within the NDP. Despite the deficiencies of that party, the FRG sees the NDP as the only mass labor vehicle capable of coming to power. Attempting to follow the example of the left-wing shift in the British Labour Party, the FRG suggests that the growing malaise in the NDP is an indication of rank-and-file discontent with NDP leaders' attempts to push the party into a rightist electoral stance. The FRG calls on the NDP to become bolder in its commitment to socialism, its program of class struggle (*Forward*, January), and opposition to Canada's military treaties.

Publications.   Among CPC publications are the weekly *Canadian Tribune* (Toronto) and *Pacific Tribune* (Vancouver); the semimonthly French-language *Combat*; the new quarterly *Communist Viewpoint*; the irregular *Le Communist*; and the bimonthly youth magazines *New Horizons* and *Jeunesse militante*. The CPC publishes the North American editions of the Prague-based *World Marxist Review* and *Information Bulletin* in Toronto. A French-language version of the former entitled *Nouvelle Revue internationale* also appears. The CPC-ML publishes daily and weekly versions of *People's Canada Daily News* and *Le Quotidien du Canada populaire*. A number of front organizations issue publications, some of which are *Voice of the Youth, Voice of the People, West Indian, Etincelle, Bulletin de nouvelles, Femmes démocratiques, Non aux coupures,* and *Revolutionary Trade Union Opposition of Canada*. The WCP publishes the weekly newspapers *Forge* and *La Forge*, as well as the theoretical journals *October* and *Octobre*. Until its demise, the MLOC published the bilingual weekly newspaper *In Struggle/En Lutte*, the quarterly theoretical journal *Proletarian Unity*, and the trilingual *International Forum*. With the cessation of the MLOC, several offshoot publications are anticipated. *Cahiers brouillons* has already appeared. *Socialist Voice* and *Lutte ouvrière* are the two sister bimonthly publications of the RWL. Following the split in the RWL, *Combat socialiste* is now published by a splinter group, the Socialist Challenge Organization. The GST publishes *Tribune ouvrière*. The TL publishes the monthly *Sparticist Canada*. Other revolutionary left-wing publications include *Forward* (FRG), *Left-words* (Marxist Socialist Organizing Committee), and *Workers Action* (International Socialists).

Royal Military College of Canada   Alan Whitehorn

Chile

The Communist Party of Chile, although outlawed and persecuted, still functions clandestinely in Chile. It is the oldest and strongest communist party in Latin America, tracing its roots to the Workers' Socialist Party founded in 1912 by Luís Emilio Recabarren. In 1919, Recabarren affiliated his Workers' Federation with the Moscow-oriented World Labor Organization, and in 1922 the present communist party was founded, drawing its support mainly from workers and intellectuals. It played an important part in the establishment of the Popular Front in Chile in 1938, and in 1946 the Communists joined in the cabinet of President Gabriel González Videla. A year later, however, the party was banned, after the Chilean congress passed the Law for the Permanent Defense of Democracy, which outlawed the party. In 1956, the law was repealed, and a year later the Communists entered into an electoral alliance with the Chilean Socialist Party—the Popular Action Front. The party now endorsed the *via pacifica* to socialism. In elections between 1958 and 1973, it normally received 10–15 percent of the popular vote.

In 1969 and 1970, the communist party took the lead in the formation of the six-party Popular Unity Alliance that led to the narrow victory in September of the Socialist candidate, Salvador Allende, with 36 percent of the vote in a three-way presidential race. After a military coup overthrew Allende in September 1973, the party was outlawed, its headquarters burned, and its leaders placed in detention camps. Most of them were later permitted to go into exile, but they left behind them a clandestine organization that claims 10,000–25,000 members and sympathizers, organized in 5,000 cells.

Since its founding, the party has been pro-Moscow in its international policies. Today its exiled leaders are supported by the Soviet Union and regularly broadcast over Radio Moscow. Within Chile it continues to be influential among trade unionists, and it dominates the illegal but active National Trade Union Coordinating Committee (Coordinadora Nacional Sindical), founded in 1980. Between 1973 and 1980, the Communists attempted to maintain the Popular Unity Alliance in exile and to develop a cooperative relationship with the centrist Christian Democratic Party. Despite the party's continuing rhetoric about the need for cooperation and unity of action, that policy was effectively abandoned in the 1980s. In 1981 Luís Corvalán, the party's secretary general, endorsed the *lucha armada*, and the Communists began to collaborate more closely with the Movement of the Revolutionary Left (MIR), which they had opposed during the Allende period, when the party line favored the *via pacifica*. In 1981 and 1982, the Communists seemed to have adopted the Nicaraguan revolution as their model and to have given up hope for the return of democracy to Chile by other than violent means.

Meanwhile, exile Socialist groups in Western Europe and Latin America were attempting to unite all groups committed to democratic socialism. Following a meeting of the Popular Unity parties in Mexico in early June where the split between those committed to violence and the others became evident, the principal Socialist leaders in exile other than Clodomiro Almeyda issued the Declaration of Rome, signed by former senator and Socialist Party Secretary General Carlos Altamirano (who had abandoned his earlier violent rhetoric in favor of support for democratic socialism); Aniceto Rodríguez, an earlier secretary general of the party; and Raúl Ampuero of the Popular Socialists, who had left the main body of the Socialist Party in 1967. The statement endorsed Marxism "as a framework of historical analysis" but denounced Soviet intervention in Afghanistan and Poland and supported democracy, pluralism, and human rights. This was followed in July by a broad call for Socialist Convergence, issued in Milan, and signed by 88 exile leaders of the Socialist, Christian Left, and United Popular Action parties currently living in Western Europe, Mexico, and Venezuela. It stated that "the essential characteristic of a renovated socialism does not consist exclusively in the critical vision of Marxism but in the capacity to understand and carry out a policy which is a process of development of the people" and that among its signers were those "inspired by Marxism, by Christianity, and by secular humanism" who were working for "a new national consensus which is broader than those of the past." (*Chile America*, July–September, pp. 77–79.)

The same process of unification of the left that excluded the Communists and the MIR was also taking place in Chile. There the Convergencia Socialista did not consist of more than a few leaders and intellectuals since open organization was forbidden. But those leaders were active in publishing the popular journal *APSI* until it was suppressed in September and the economic review *Vector*, which critically analyzed the regime's current policies. Besides suppressing *APSI*, the government also attempted to expel the leaders of the Christian left for violating the political recess, but late in 1982 their court sentence was overruled on appeal. (The Radical Party did not participate in the Convergencia, and its leadership was divided since its former secretary general, Anselmo Sule, in exile in Mexico had supported the Communists, the MIR, and the Almeyda Socialists—a move that the Radicals within Chile repudiated).

The result of these new alignments was to leave the communist party relatively isolated on the left with the MIR (whose leader, Andrés Pascal Allende, in an interview in *Newsweek* in January, once again endorsed armed revolution), while the socialist and Catholic left prepared for a possible political opening as a result of the failure of the Friedmanite laissez-faire policies of "the Chicago boys" under Pinochet. A further step in their isolation took place at the end of the year when a press conference was held in Santiago announcing the formation of the Project for National Development, a multisectoral group including leaders from all former political parties except for the communist party and the MIR. Its aim was to develop a national consensus and establish a timetable for the transition to democracy and civilian rule.

Despite their isolation, the Communists were still a political force to be reckoned with. In the last part of the year, they were able to exploit the generalized dissatisfaction with the Pinochet regime, fueled by a deepening economic crisis that produced 25 percent unemployment, a 13 percent drop in gross national product, and factory closings and bankruptcies in the hundreds, to organize the first large-scale antigovernment demonstrations in Santiago since the 1973 coup.

The Pinochet government continued to have no diplomatic relations with the Soviet Union and to denounce the opposition as communist-inspired. It maintained low-level relations with Romania and had extensive trade with China, a major market for its copper and lumber. The two groups on the left also disagree on foreign policy; the Convergencia favors nonalignment, while the Communists continue to support the Soviet Union and to an increasing degree Cuba—the latter a shift from their stance in the 1960s.

The Soviet intervention in Afghanistan and suppression of worker organizations in Poland had much to do with the split. So did the success of democratic socialists under Felipe González in Spain, who won the 1982 elections after a period of transition from a regime that bore many resemblances to that of Pinochet. But the most important consideration must have been the realization by the left that violence does not solve anything and that it is only in a regime of freedom and human rights that reform and social progress are possible. If that lesson has been learned from the suffering of the past decade, there is hope for the political future of Chile.

Princeton University   Paul E. Sigmund

Colombia

The communist movement in Colombia has undergone various transformations in both name and organization since the party's initial formation in December 1926. The Communist Party of Colombia (Partido Comunista de Colombia; PCC) was publicly proclaimed on 17 July 1930. In July 1965, a schism within the PCC between pro-Soviet and pro-Chinese factions resulted in the latter's becoming the Communist Party of Colombia, Marxist-Leninist (PCC-ML). Only the PCC has legal status. It has been allowed to participate in elections under its own banner since 1972. In 1982, the PCC participated in the March legislative elections as the leading member of a leftist coalition, receiving approximately 1 percent of the vote. The coalition elected one member to the 114-seat Senate and three members to the 199-seat Chamber of Representatives. In the May presidential elections, the coalition's candidate, Gerardo Molina Ramírez, received 82,856 (1.2 percent) votes.

According to U.S. intelligence sources, the PCC has 12,000 members. Although the party contends that its ranks have increased in recent years, the 1982 elections suggest that the party's growth has been less than its leaders had hoped, especially in the larger cities. The PCC exercises only marginal influence in national affairs.

The party is headed by a fourteen-member Executive Committee and a 54-member Central Committee. The highest party authority is the Congress, convened at four-year intervals. The Thirteenth Congress was held in November 1980. The general secretary of the PCC is Gilberto Vieira. Other important members of the Central Committee are Jesús Villegas, Alvaro Vásquez, Manuel Cepeda, Teofilo Forero, Roso Osorio, Pástor Pérez, Carlos Romero, Jaime Caycedo, Hernando Hurtado, José Cardona Hoyos, Mario Upegui, and Alvaro Mosquera. A major source of the party's influence is its control of the Trade Union Confederation of Workers of Colombia (CSTC), which claims a membership of 300,000 and is a member of the Soviet-front World Federation of Trade Unions. The PCC attempts to influence the CSTC through the National Federation of Agrarian Syndicates, which functions as a part of the CSTC.

The PCC's youth organization, the Communist Youth of Colombia (JUCO), has an estimated membership of 2,000. The JUCO operates through the National Youth Coordinating Committee, where it plays an active role in promoting party policy among university and secondary school students.

Guerrilla Warfare. Although not a serious threat to the government, guerrilla warfare has been a feature of Colombian life since the late 1940s; the current wave began in 1964. The four main guerrilla organizations are the Revolutionary Armed Forces of Colombia (FARC), long controlled by the PCC; the M-19, a guerrilla organization that claims to be the armed hand of the National Popular Alliance (ANAPO);

the pro-Chinese People's Liberation Army (EPL), which is the guerrilla arm of the PCC-ML; and the Castroite National Liberation Army (ELN). A fifth group, the Trotskyist-oriented Workers' Self-Defense Movement, was reportedly dismantled in June with the capture of its principal leaders in Bogotá (*El Espectador*, 2 June).

According to intelligence estimates, the FARC has expanded its areas of influence in recent years to include portions of the departments of Huila, Caquetá, Tolima, Cauca, Boyacá, Santander, Antioquia, Valle, Meta, Cundinamarca, and the intendancy of Arauca. According to the FARC's principal leader, Manuel Marulanda Vélez, the movement has 3,000 combatants operating on 23 fronts. In addition to Marulanda, other important leaders of the FARC's 22-member high command are Jacobo Arenas, Martín Villa, and Jaime Guaracas (ibid., 29 November). The FARC's general headquarters is located somewhere in the border zone between Caquetá and Huila. Each FARC unit (or squad) consists of a minimum of twelve members. Two units constitute a guerrilla cell. Four units, with an equal number of replacements, make up a column. Each of the FARC's rural fronts is composed of two columns, numbering about 200 men. The leadership mechanisms and general policy of the FARC are determined by the PCC's bylaws and political resolutions emitted at various congresses and plenums and presumably transmitted to the various fronts through Marulanda's directives.

In January, the FARC announced a six-month recess in its military operations in order to permit normal congressional and presidential elections (AFP, 7 January). While the FARC's direct military actions declined, government sources accused the movement of intensifying its kidnapping of wealthy landowners and ranchers for ransom. According to the military, seventeen civilians were kidnapped by guerrillas during the first three weeks of January (*El Tiempo*, 22 January). Of some 28 kidnap victims held by guerrilla organizations and criminal gangs in June, 15 were attributed to the FARC, 3 to the M-19, and 2 to the ELN (*El Espectador*, 9 June).

On 15 June, the FARC's general staff announced an end to the electoral truce and renewed military actions in the department of Caquetá. The army reported seven soldiers and one officer killed in a FARC ambush in the jurisdiction of San Vicente del Caguán (*El Tiempo*, 16 June). On 20 June, the government decreed an end to the state of siege and terminated the security statute imposed in September 1978. General Francisco Naranjo Granco, director of the National Police, claimed that military forces had "neutralized subversive action" and reduced the guerrilla movements' capacity to disrupt order (Caracol, 28 June; *FBIS*, 29 June). Army sources disclosed that "serious conflicts of interest" arose between FARC and EPL units operating in southern Colombia. According to military intelligence, FARC and EPL columns clashed in the Meta and Caquetá areas in a dispute over their respective zones of operation (*El Siglo*, 16 June). Previously, military sources confirmed that the FARC had "executed" four EPL members in a disagreement over the collection of extortion money from ranchers in Antioquia and Córdoba (*El Tiempo*, 22 March).

In late July, Marulanda said the FARC was prepared to initiate a peace dialogue with President-elect Belisario Betancur (EFE, 28 July). In a communiqué circulated to local news media, the FARC asked Betancur to arrange for talks before the army undertook any new antiguerrilla offensive (*El Tiempo*, 1 September). Jacobo Arenas stressed that the FARC was ready to initate a dialogue "on behalf of peace." However, he implied that talks were also under way with ELN and M-19 leaders to discuss joint guerrilla action (*El Espectador*, 20 September). Colombia's defense minister, Gen. Fernando Landazábal Reyes, cited a resurgence of guerrilla activity in rural areas during a meeting in September with regional military commanders. Although Landazábal claimed that guerrillas were conducting operations "on a daily basis," he added that their actions were not a serious threat to democratic institutions (AFP, 12 September).

At a secret meeting with government and church officials in October, the FARC reiterated its support for amnesty, but warned the president that any peace initiative would require major changes in the country's socioeconomic structure (LATIN, 13 October; *FBIS*, 14 October). The FARC continued its guerrilla actions in October and November while the Colombian congress debated a general amnesty proposal. The army reported fourteen FARC guerrillas killed in skirmishes in the mountains of eastern Colombia. Andrés Sarmiento, second-in-command of the FARC's 9th Front, was killed during a shoot-out on the outskirts of Puerto Berrio (EFE, 19 and 23 October). FARC units kidnapped ranch owners in Santander, Valle and El César departments during the last week in October and assaulted towns in Antioquia and Santander in early November (AFP, 29 October; *El Espectador*, 10 November).

In late November, the FARC conditioned its acceptance of the government's amnesty law on the withdrawal of army troops from areas considered combat zones. In a major statement of policy, the FARC requested a meeting with President Betancur or his Peace Commission to seek agreement on fundamental economic and social reforms for the country. In addition to the demilitarization of war zones, the FARC demanded that the Death to Kidnappers squad (Muerte a Secuestradores; MAS) be dismantled and that protection be provided for guerrillas who accepted the amnesty. According to Marulanda, none of the FARC's fronts had been authorized to accept amnesty at this time. He told a reporter that the FARC would resist "just a little" to see what happened to its proposals (*El Espectador*, 29 November). On 30 November, the chairman of the Peace Commission, Otto Morales, committed himself to discussing with Marulanda and other guerrilla leaders measures complementary to the amnesty law. Specifically, the government proposed a four-year, $800 million investment plan to provide land, housing, education, health care, and jobs to those who accepted the amnesty (*El Tiempo*, 1 December).

The military emphatically rejected the Peace Commission's suggestion that active guerrilla zones be demilitarized to expedite the country's pacification. In an appearance before the Chamber of Representatives, General Landazábal denied allegations that the army was opposed to the amnesty proposal. He described the offer as a "magnanimous gesture" since "the guerrillas are not strong enough to threaten the country's democratic stability" (ibid., 3 and 14 November).

Domestic Attitudes and Activities.   The PCC recognizes the experience of the Communist Party of the Soviet Union as an ideological source, but it also takes "maximum account of the national characteristics and revolutionary and democratic traditions of the Colombian people." This has enabled the party to devise its own tactics, which combine diverse forms of mass struggle ranging from electoral campaigns to guerrilla warfare.

The Thirteenth Congress (1980) reaffirmed the party's commitment to the creation of a broad antimonopoly and anti-imperialist front. As a basis for forming this front, the party approved a program aimed at combating inflation, increasing wages, nationalizing oil and coal resources, and providing free health, education, and social assistance programs.

The PCC took part in the organization of a national popular front with various socialist groups and the independent left movement of FIRMES for the March elections. According to military sources, documents confiscated from FARC guerrillas indicated that the PCC financed the political campaign of some of its members with money received through extortion and kidnapping (ibid., 22 March). The PCC supported the presidential candidacy of Gerardo Molina, former National University rector and founder of the FIRMES movement.

According to Gilberto Vieira, in recent years the PCC has pursued a policy of fostering unity between urban workers and the peasantry. In a number of regions, peasant struggles take the form of guerrilla warfare, which the PCC maintains is firmly connected with the issue of agrarian reform and opposition to the military forces that protect the interests of large landowners. The party is actively engaged in efforts to organize peasant unions, including the organization of the Indian population in Cauca, where the PCC supports the Regional Indian Council (*Voz Proletaria*, 17 June).

On 6 September, the PCC's Executive Committee met with President Betancur and cabinet officials as part of the government's plan to approach various public opinion sectors in an effort to achieve peace. According to Vieira, the president was receptive toward the party's proposals to establish an immediate dialogue with guerrilla leaders. However, he described as "unrealistic" the defense minister's proposal that guerrillas turn in their weapons as a demonstration of "good intentions" (ibid., 9 September).

In October, the PCC asked the army to stop pursuing its militants as a contribution to "real peace." Alberto Rojas, the party's representative to the Peace Commission, stressed that the military must "cease its undeclared war" against communism if the country is to achieve a true climate of peace. Rojas accused the military of "unacceptable interference" in Colombia's political life (AFP, 9 October). In a harsh exchange with General Landazábal, Vieira charged that in the past 30 years the army has killed some 2,000 peasants. He accused the defense minister of "protecting" the terrorist group MAS, which, according to the Colombian Human Rights Committee, has killed 112 people and has kidnapped twenty more since its creation at the end of 1981 (Havana international service, 20 October). For his part, General Landazábal claimed that through the operations of FARC, the PCC has been responsible for the murder of over 30,000 peasants in the past 34 years (AFP, 7 October).

International Views and Positions. The PCC faithfully follows the Soviet line in its international positions. In a report to the Thirteenth Congress, Vieira described the international situation as "complicated and dangerous" due to the "more belligerent policy of imperialism." He accused the United States of opposing détente and creating a policy of confrontation with the USSR (*Voz Proletaria*, 13 November 1980). According to Vieira, the party is engaged primarily in the struggle for the emancipation of the Colombian people. However, the PCC insists that it is impossible to remain neutral in the "great international struggle" between socialism and capitalism. The party therefore stands in solidarity with the socialist countries and with the Soviet Union, which is "an inspiring example for the working people of the bourgeois countries." As "patriots and internationalists," Colombian Communists unreservedly support the Soviets' achievements. (Ibid., 20 June.)

In the Western Hemisphere, the PCC charged that Washington's current policy is directed at destabilizing the revolutionary governments of Cuba and Nicaragua and at strengthening reactionary regimes in El Salvador and Guatemala. Party officials hailed the unity declaration announced by Guatemala's guerrilla movements in February 1982 and reiterated their support for the "heroic struggle" of the Salvadoran people. (Ibid., 8 April.)

Party statements have been highly supportive of the change that President Betancur has brought to Colombia's international policy by seeking entry into the nonaligned movement and moving away from Colombia's close identification with the United States during the latter years of the preceding administration. Party leaders endorsed Betancur's candid recommendations to President Reagan in December calling for new economic and social policies that "respect the rights and needs of Latin American nations" and the elimination of "exclusions in the inter-American system," an apparent reference to Cuba's exclusion from the Organization of American States. (Ibid., 9 December.)

Publications. The PCC publishes the weekly newspaper *Voz Proletaria* (reported circulation 45,000), which completed its twenty-fifth year of publication on 20 July; the theoretical journal *Documentos Políticos* (5,000); and the Colombian edition of *World Marxist Review* (7,500). The JUCO publishes a monthly supplement to the *Voz Proletaria*. The FARC publishes the clandestine bulletin *Resistencia*.

The Maoists. The PCC-ML is firmly pro-Chinese. Its present leadership hierarchy is not clearly known. The PCC-ML has an estimated membership of one thousand. Unlike the PCC, it has not attempted to obtain legal status, and its impact in terms of national life is insignificant. Its official news organ is *Revolución*. The Marxist-Leninist League of Colombia publishes the monthly *Nueva Democracia*. PCC-ML statements are sometimes found in Chinese publications and those of pro-Chinese parties in Europe and Latin America.

The PCC-ML's guerrilla arm, the EPL, was the first to attempt a revolutionary "people's war" in Latin America. The EPL has conducted only limited operations since 1975, although several rural attacks were attributed to the group in 1982. In a November communiqué, the EPL announced its rejection of the government's amnesty plan and called on other revolutionary sectors to "battle opportunism in their leaderships" (*El Tiempo*, 4 November). EPL guerrillas killed four peasants near Turbo in Antioquia, after accusing them of being army informers (AFP, 9 November). An EPL unit occupied the town of Frontino in Antioquia in late November, killing two policemen and fleeing with ammunition and supplies (*El Espectador*, 28 November).

The independent Revolutionary Workers' Movement (MOIR) has aspired since 1971 to become the first mass-based Maoist party in Latin America. Its leadership and organization are independent of those of the PCC-ML. The MOIR has no military branch and has been unable to strengthen its political position since its poor showing in the 1978 elections. According to one of its principal leaders, Marcelo Torres, six MOIR militants have been killed in the past two years as the result of political violence. Torres accuses the PCC of being the "principal cause" for the abandonment by the Colombian left of its revolutionary path for a "reformist position" (ibid., 28 November).

The M-19. The M-19, which first appeared in January 1974 as the self-proclaimed armed branch of ANAPO, takes its name from the contested presidential election of 19 April 1970. Since 1976, the M-19 has been actively involved in Colombia's guerrilla movement, pursuing "a popular revolution of national liberation aimed toward socialism." Intelligence sources have identified former law student and ex-JUCO member Jaime Bateman Cayón as the M-19's top leader, with ex-ANAPO congressman Carlos Toledo Plata, Iván Marino Ospina, Alvaro Fayad Delgado, Rosemberg Pabón Pabón, Germán Rojas Niño, Marcos Chalista, and Ramiro Lucio Escobar among the more prominent members of the movement's political and military commands. Army campaigns have severely weakened the M-19's capacity to sustain military operations in recent years. The movement has an estimated 500 to 1,000 members (*WP*, 11 November).

Ideologically, the M-19 is a heterogeneous group embracing revolutionary principles ranging from Castroism to Trotskyism. Differences of opinion exist among the movement's leaders regarding operational tactics and future strategy. According to documents confiscated from an alleged M-19 defector, for much of 1982 the movement "struggled without a unified command" and "suffered from poor operational organization, a lack of means of communications, and a shortage of weapons and ammunition" (*El Tiempo*, 29 May). A division within the M-19 surfaced in late October when a hard-line faction rejected the amnesty and advocated the continuation of armed struggle (AFP, 31 October).

Since the M-19's abortive "invasion" of Putumayo in March 1981 in which several hundred militants were captured, the M-19 has shown itself increasingly disposed to seek a "peace dialogue" with the government. Although the M-19 threatened to sabotage the presidential elections, security forces registered a succession of military successes against the movement's forces operating in southern Colombia and in Bogotá (*El Tiempo*, 9 March, 29 May).

In May, approximately 150 rank-and-file members and several prominent leaders of the M-19 were convicted of various crimes and given sentences of up to twenty years, ending a trial that lasted more than two years (*El Espectador*, 27 May). In June, the M-19 announced a truce in its guerrilla activities "to facilitate" the government's suspension of the state of siege. The movement's leaders asked President-elect Betancur for a general amnesty for all political prisoners and proposed a patriotic dialogue to create "a mass movement for democracy and the consolidation of peace." (*El Tiempo*, 24 June.) Following the Eighth National Guerrilla Conference in Caquetá in August, the M-19 high command formally advised the Betancur government of its desire to achieve complete pacification of the country. In September, M-19 spokesman Ramiro Lucio joined representatives from the traditional Liberal and Conservative parties and the PCC in the first of a series of meetings to discuss national problems (AFP, 15 September). Jaime Bateman met secretly with Congressman Bula Hoyos, who submitted the government's amnesty plan. In a communiqué released in Panama on 16 October, the M-19 credited the Betancur government with "creating a favorable climate for a democratic debate" and reiterated its support for the amnesty law. However, the document stipulated that the guerrillas' full acceptance would depend upon "a demilitarization of the peasant regions, elimination of paramilitary groups, and an end to the persecution of the labor, civic, student, and peasant leaders, and of our militants" (ACAN, 16 October).

At a guerrilla summit in southern Santander, the M-19's political command denied that its forces had particpated in recent guerrilla attacks and claimed that it was not holding any kidnap victims (EFE, 2 November). The M-19 reiterated its "total support" for the amnesty law, but noted that it would "continue to wield its arms because the situations that led the popular classes to armed struggle still prevail" (*El Espectador*, 3 November). The movement subsequently indicated its willingness to surrender its weapons, conditional on the success of a national dialogue with the country's major political and social sectors. The movement reiterated that internal military action will not cease in order to demonstrate that the M-19 is "an active organization that can use its weapons to press for true social change" (AFP, 17 November).

At the end of November, the M-19 insisted that a six-month truce be declared to permit an analysis of the nation's fundamental problems. The government tacitly rejected the idea of a truce, claiming that it had decreed an amnesty on 22 November, not an armistice. Civilian authorities reported in early December that a hundred guerrillas (of an estimated 4,000) had accepted the amnesty benefits during the first ten days since their promulgation (*El Espectador*, 30 November).

In late December, the intendant of Putumayo, Jorge Fuerbringer, met with key M-19 leaders somewhere in the Putumayo jungle. According to Fuerbringer, the leaders with whom he talked (Iván Marino Ospina, second-in-command of the organization; Germán Rojas Niño, commander of the southern front; and Marcos Chalista, chief of the column operating in Caquetá) "do not share Marxist ideals, much less Leninist ideals." He described them as "staunchly nationalistic" with "a Colombian nationalist ideology, which distinguishes them from other guerrilla groups" (*El Tiempo*, 28 December).

The National Liberation Army.   The ELN was formed in Santander in 1964 under the inspiration of the Cuban revolution. It undertook its first military action in January 1965. Once recognized as the largest and most militant of the guerrilla forces operating in Colombia, the ELN has never recovered from the toll exacted on its leadership and urban network in recent years by government forces, including the defection in 1976 of its principal founder and maximum leader, Fabio Vásquez Castaño. Twelve of the ELN's top leaders have been killed in its eighteen years of existence, resulting in the dismemberment of the movement into viciously feuding local groups.

Since late 1979, ELN operations have been limited to the middle Magdalena region and infrequent urban activities in Bogotá and Medellín. In October, the ELN confirmed the death of Diego Uribe Escobar, a Franciscan priest who was one of the movement's highest-ranking leaders (EFE, 30 October). The ELN published a clandestine bulletin in November announcing it would continue the armed struggle. Officials in Caldas subsequently announced that 25 ELN members had accepted the government's amnesty (*El Espectador*, 17 and 21 November). Like the EPL, the ELN no longer appears to be relevant to the future course of guerrilla activity in Colombia.

Guerrilla Prospects.   At year's end, M-19 guerrillas continued under attack by army units in the south, while members of the high command denounced death threats from the MAS. Despite recent incidents involving the FARC and M-19, guerrilla leaders were meeting relatively openly with senior government officials. Some confusion surrounds the attitude of the different groups. The EPL and the ELN declared they have no intention of accepting the amnesty. The FARC and M-19 are prepared to lay down their weapons, but not to surrender them. As Jaime Bateman said, the M-19 might stop firing its weapons but will never turn them in because "that would be like surrendering, and we have not been defeated" (ibid., 17 September).

Few doubt that President Betancur is sincere in seeking a settlement, but there are others, on both sides, who see little to be gained by making peace. Thus far the government has met guerrilla demands to lift the state of siege, remove the security statute, initiate peace talks, and obtain congressional backing for an unconditional amnesty, including an ambitious investment plan to provide generous amnesty benefits.

According to most observers, the ultimate solution and durability of any peace settlement depends on the cooperation of the military. General Landazábal has given no indication that the armed forces are prepared to accept guerrilla demands for the demilitarization of the countryside, which would seriously impinge on the military's self-perceived role as a national institution. In the absence of legislation that provides for the disarming of the guerrillas, military authorities are unlikely to accept a truce with armed groups responsible for attacks on military and police personnel and property, civilian kidnappings, and extortion.

Washington College   Daniel L. Premo

Costa Rica

The communist party in Costa Rica competes actively but not very successfully in the democratic political process. Founded in 1931 by Manuel Mora Valverde, it changed its name in 1943 to Popular Vanguard Party (Partido Vanguardia Popular; PVP), which it still uses today. The pro-Soviet party, still under the leadership of Secretary General Manuel Mora, 72, is a fairly well disciplined party with a strong organizational base in several labor unions; some of its ideas, presented in its weekly newspaper, *Libertad*, have fairly broad appeal across party boundaries. Other prominent PVP members are Deputy Secretary General Eduardo Mora Valverde, Luís Orlando Corrales, Manuel Delgado, and Humberto Vargas Carbonell. The party has approximately 3,500 members. Delgado told an international symposium at midyear that the PVP realized it had to become a "numerically large party functioning in close unity with the masses, the trade unions, public and peasant organizations, the students, and young working people. In order to do this it would have to maintain its basic guidelines while adopting flexible tactics." For this reason, at its Thirteenth Congress in 1980, the party had introduced the status of probationary member. (*WMR*, August.)

The PVP has reaffirmed its stated belief in applying flexible tactics to hasten the formation of the broadest possible democratic alliance. Along this line, the party remained the dominant member of the United People (Pueblo Unido; PU) coalition, which also includes the Revolutionary Movement of the People (Movimiento Revolucionario del Pueblo; MRP) and the Costa Rican Socialist Party (Partido Socialista Costarricense; PSC). The PU is headed by another PVP septuagenarian, Arnoldo Ferreto, a founding member of the Soviet-front World Peace Council. The PU won four congressional seats in the February elections, three of them going to PVP members (Ferreto, Eduardo Mora Valverde, and Freddy Menéndez) and one to the MRP (Sergio Erick Ardón). In November Mora resigned and turned his seat over to PSC member Alvaro Montero Mejía. This made it possible for each party of the PU coalition to have at least one congressional seat, complying with a pre-election agreement among the coalition members. Conflict arose during the year between the PVP and the MRP, the latter charging that the former was dogmatic and refused to allow any decision-making participation by other members of the coalition; the PVP denied everything (*La Nación*, San Jose, 6 and 12 September). Ardón gained worldwide publicity by attacking the United States at a ceremony honoring President Reagan during his December visit.

Costa Rican politics and the activities of the PVP were dominated by three issues during 1982: the 7 February presidential and congressional elections and their aftermath, problems of the debt-ridden economy, and national security in the highly unstable Central American region.

In the February elections, the National Liberation Party (NLP) and its presidential candidate, Luís Alberto Monge, won 57.3 percent of the vote; the incumbent party, the Unity coalition, and its presidential candidate, won 32.7 percent. The PU and its presidential candidate, Rodrigo Roberto Gutiérrez, took 3.2 percent, up from 2.7 in 1978. The Central Committee of the PVP, in its evaluation of the elections, stated that participation had "enhanced the coalition's influence in the nation's political life" and that, above all, it had given its members "extensive experience of mobilizing the people" (*WMR*, September).

The Costa Rican economy began a critical downward spiral about two years ago when energy prices increased, income from coffee exports fell, and payments on heavy international borrowing became excessive. Economic activity decreased by 4.6 percent in 1981 and by about 5.9 percent in 1982. Inflation in 1982 was about 100 percent. (*NYT*, 21 November.) At a plenary meeting in March, the PVP concluded that "vacillating social sectors, most members of the middle strata and the working class, which were sympathetic to the PU coalition, sided at the decisive moment with the NLP, hoping that this party would be able to carry out a program of reforms intended to cope with the crisis without provoking political and social upheavals likely to lead to violence" (*IB*, June). Since then, the party has condemned President Monge's austerity measures and played an active role in encouraging economically disruptive labor unrest. "In Costa Rica the masses are not yet enlightened and organized enough," Political Commission Chairman Corrales wrote. "However, a worsening economic situation combines with other factors to create the prerequisites of a notable expansion of the people's struggle." (*WMR*, September.)

The security issue dominated PVP relations with the government and the public throughout the year. The government is concerned about PVP activities (see below) and by the PVP's description of the Latin American revolution as "a single process encompassing the whole area" (ibid., May). Typical of the conflict was an exchange at the end of July. Monge charged that the Communists were taking advantage of the nation's problems to try to destabilize the country's democratic system and that a communist fifth column was working against Costa Rican interests by conducting strikes and other disturbances around the country (Radio Reloj, San Jose, 30 July; *FBIS*, 2 August). In a paid advertisement in *La Nación* (31 July), Manuel Mora wrote the president that in reality "the Costa Rican Communists are more interested in defending the democratic government than are the dark forces you have begun to represent." He continued that the "asphyxiation" of the national economy came from Washington, not Moscow or Havana. Finally he charged that while the Communists were not trying to destabilize the Costa Rican government, the president was lending his support to "imperialists" who planned to invade Nicaragua and "set fire to the whole Central American isthmus, including our own country." The communist weekly *Libertad* editorialized at the end of November, on the occasion of President Ronald Reagan's visit to Costa Rica, that his presence would be a "historic shame to the country" (*FBIS*, 29 November).

PVP devotion to the causes of the Soviet Union is unlimited, and this has heightened government concern over the party's international contacts. On the sixty-fifth anniversary of the Bolshevik victory in Russia, for example, the PVP not only published a long editorial in *Libertad* on the Soviet Union entitled "The Bastion of World Peace," but reprinted the editorial as a paid advertisement on a full page of *La Nación* (8 November). On the same day, the Soviet embassy bought another page in *La Nación* to advertise its accomplishments.

At various times during the year, the government alleged that Costa Rican Marxists received arms and other support from Cuba and Nicaragua, that young Communists were being sent to Libya for six months of training in terrorism, and that groups from the Palestine Liberation Organization and Libya were in Costa Rica and in position to "blow us up at any moment" (*La Nación*, 27 March, 2 April, 6 August). The government also attacked the PVP for promoting strikes among banana workers and others from September to November through the communist-dominated Unitary Confederation of Workers and its affiliates, among them the banana pickers' union.

Domestic terrorism, sometimes conducted against foreign nationals, increased markedly during the year. Concern over these domestic threats to national security, as well as ongoing border problems with Nicaragua and the influx of a thousand Salvadoran refugees each month, led the Monge government to improve its security system. Since the country has no army, this has meant enlarging and rearming the 4,300-man Civil Guard, the 3,000-man Rural Guard, and the 500-man Police Force and the setting up of a 10,000-member Police Reserve in November.

The Costa Rican government scheduled some talks with Nicaraguan leaders during the year as border skirmishes became a regular concern. The Nicaraguan government objected that the last two Costa Rican administrations allowed dissident Sandinista leader Edén Pastora (and other anti-Sandinista forces) to live in Costa Rica, though Pastora was temporarily expelled from the country at one time. Costa Ricans countered that Nicaraguans—and Salvadoran guerrillas—were involved in its domestic affairs. In July, three Nicaraguan diplomats were expelled from the country. By the end of the year, the Costa Ricans had granted residency to Pastora for as long as he remains apolitical, the Salvadoran guerrillas had assured Monge that they had not and would not become involved in Costa Rican affairs, and political leaders in San José and Managua were seriously discussing a noninterference understanding. Also, the Costa Rican government ordered the Soviet Union to reduce its embassy personnel from 28 to 8.

Hoover Institution   William E. Ratliff

Cuba

The Communist Party of Cuba (PCC) has been, under several names, the ruling and sole legal party since the early days of Castro's rule. It more than doubled its membership from 100,000 to 202,807 between 1970 and December 1975, when the party held its First Congress. As 1982 began, the PCC had more than doubled again, reaching 434,143 members and candidates for membership (*WMR*, July 1981). This recent increase in party membership is associated with a widened coalition of technical elites within the Political Bureau, Secretariat, and Central Committee, which were established by the 1975 Party Congress. The addition of these new agencies remodeled the party along traditional Leninist lines.

These significant changes are explained by the early history of the PCC. Following its inauguration in 1965, the PCC experienced a period when its committees rarely met and its membership remained limited. During this era, effective control of the party and government was centralized under Fidel Castro's direct leadership. He was backed by loyal followers drawn from the July 26th Movement, whose members fought with Castro in the revolution. While the PCC played a vanguard role in directing other mass organizations, the latter were the principal instruments for mobilizing Cuba's population. They included the Committees for the Defense of the Revolution (CDRs), the Confederation of Cuban Workers, the Confederation of Cuban Women (FMC), and the Communist Youth League (UJC).

This *fidelista* system produced high political mobilization, but ineffective economic management. It resulted in the dramatic failure of the 1970 sugar harvest and growing pressure to revise the party and government. The result was an expanded PCC with more qualified individuals and a party restructured along Leninist lines, legitimizing it as Cuba's major governing institution—all of which occurred at the 1975 party congress. These changes produced greater political institutionalization, although Fidel and Raúl Castro and their followers still dominate the major organs of the PCC, state, and government.

Party and Government Leadership. Cuba's leadership during 1982 reflected the earlier process of institutionalization and a broadened diversity of elites in the upper echelons of power. Yet it also demonstrated the continuation of Castro's power base. Fidel remained in multiple leadership positions: first secretary of the PCC, president of both the Council of State and Council of Ministers, and commander in chief. His brother, Raúl, retained the position of minister of the Revolutionary Armed Forces (FAR), in addition to being first vice-president of the Councils of State and Ministers. Meanwhile, other July 26th followers remained in high positions. (For a list of party leaders, see *YICA*, 1981, p. 62.)

The background to Castro's continued predominance in the context of a new organizational setting dates back to the mid-1970s. Institution-building after the 1970 sugar harvest failure led to the formation of a Soviet-style government system, complete with a National Assembly of People's Power, Council of State, and Council of Ministers, implemented through the constitution of February 1976. The National Assembly is composed of 499 deputies elected for five years by municipal assemblies. The Council of State, the highest representative body of the state, consists of 31 members elected by the National Assembly. Its president, Fidel Castro, is both head of state and head of government. The Council of Ministers is named by the president of the Council of State.

Party Internal Affairs. In December 1981, the National Assembly met in Havana to elect and approve its supreme bodies and to hold the first session of its second legislature. It elected Fidel Castro president of the Council of State and Raúl Castro first vice-president, along with three July 26th members (Juan Almeida, Ramiro Valdés, and Guillermo García) and two "old Communists" (Carlos Rafael Rodríguez and Blas Roca) as vice-presidents. "Old Communists" are those whose ties extend back to the Popular Socialist Party (Partido Socialista Popular), the party that predated Castro's revolution. Thus, four of the six vice-presidents are former members of Castro's guerrilla army. As president of the Council of State, Fidel Castro then nominated the Council of Ministers. His list included Raúl Castro as first vice-president and a number of July 26th followers as vice-presidents, including Ramiro Valdés, Guillermo García, Osvaldo Dorticós, Osmany Cienfuegos, and Diocles Torralba. (*Granma*, 10 January.) Flavio Bravo Pardo, a friend of President Castro from university days, head of the UJC, and a former captain in the rebel army against Batista, left the Council of State to become National Assembly president, replacing the ailing Blas Roca.

Mass Organizations and Congresses. Among Cuba's mass organizations, the most significant growth occurred within the recently formed Territorial Militia Troops (MTT). In his annual speech commemorating the anniversary of the abortive assault on the Moncada Barracks on 26 July 1953, Castro reported that more than 500,000 citizens, male and female, had been enrolled, trained, and armed during the previous months (*FBIS*, 27 July). This development reflected Cuba's growing concern over a potential war with the United States following the entry of the new administration in Washington.

Castro subsequently reported that the Pioneers (an affiliate of the UJC) had enrolled two million members. In all, four million children and adolescents have passed through Pioneer ranks. (*Granma*, 18 April.) Castro noted that the UJC continued to work closely with the Federation of Students in Intermediate Education and the Federation of University Students and cooperated closely with other mass organizations, such as the FMC, the CDRs, unions, and peasant organizations. Through these UJC efforts, 95 percent of all students in urban areas take part in productive work, as well as academic studies, during their training years. The UJC meanwhile remains strong in both the FAR and the Ministry of the Interior, working to create a "communist consciousness."

The National Association of Small Farmers (ANAP) held its Sixth Congress in May. Fidel Castro's speech to this gathering showed increased attention to the farm sector by Cuba's communist leaders. ANAP membership in the PCC and the UJC in 1982 increased over earlier years. A number of ANAP staff members have studied in East Germany, the Soviet Union, and Bulgaria.

Domestic Affairs. *Cuba's Military Buildup.* Following a trend established in 1981, Cuba's deepening emphasis on national security and fear of potential war with the United States continued in policy statements, citizenship training in the MTT, and a strengthened FAR. Castro used the occasion of the Tenth World Trade Union Congress, held in Havana on 10 February, to emphasize Cuba's concern with the arms race, including its implications for Third World economic development and Cuban security. "Cuba," he said, "is a country struggling for development in the midst of constant threats, slanderous campaigns, and a rigid economic blockade." He specifically focused on the "threats of direct military intervention" and the "danger of new imperialist aggression." He said that Cuba would not acknowledge any constraint on its "sovereign prerogative to purchase the weapons it keeps necessary for its defense . . . our enemies do not frighten us by rattling their weapons." (Ibid., 21 February.)

By 1982, Cuba had the largest and best-equipped armed forces in Latin America, with the exception of Brazil. While the average percentage of population in military service in Latin America was 0.4, in Cuba the figure reached 2.29. In 1982, the army numbered approximately 200,000, the navy 11,000, and the air force 16,000 (*Europa Year Book*, 1982). Army reserves numbered another 130,000, while paramilitary forces included 15,000 State Security Forces, 3,000 border guards, and a Youth Labor Army of about 100,000. Conscription is for a three-year period, and conscripts perform nonmilitary functions, such as working on the land.

In 1981, the Soviet Union supplied Cuba with 62,000 tons of equipment, the largest amount since the Cuban missile crisis of 1962. In early 1982, a second squadron of MiG-23 fighter planes arrived in Cuba to complement the twenty MiG-23 fighter-bombers received from Moscow in 1977–1978 (*Radio Free Europe–Radio Liberty Research*, no. 63). These recent deliveries are intended to upgrade and replace previous equipment, to support the MTT, which is projected to reach one million people; to stockpile weapons that can be transshipped to regional clients in Central America; and to demonstrate Moscow's support for Havana, while lowering the risk that Moscow would be directly involved in a conflict between Cuba and the United States (ibid., no. 347).

A special report on Cuban-Soviet relations, released by the U.S. government in 1982, raised significant concerns about the implications of increased Cuban military capabilities in 1982. While the 200 MiG-23 fighters stationed in Cuba can conduct round-trip missions to a limited area in Central America, staging from Nicaragua or Grenada would expand their combat radius to include all of Central America and the northern tier of South America (ibid.). Meanwhile, the Soviet presence in Cuba included a ground-force brigade of about 2,600 men, a military advisory group of 2,000, and an intelligence-collection facility. Cuba is the base for an additional estimated 6,000 to 8,000 Soviet civilian advisers. This Soviet operation is the largest intelligence-collection facility outside the USSR, and it monitors U.S. military and civilian communications. (Ibid.)

Economic Conditions. Conditions in the sugar and other sectors improved during 1982, but there was continuing evidence of both internally and externally caused difficulties. The sugar harvest of 1981–1982, completed by July 1982, was the second largest ever recorded, reaching 8.21 million tons. This much-improved sugar yield may indicate that problems with disease have been overcome, thanks to planting of disease-resistant strains. (*Latin America Commodity Report*, 30 July.) This success allowed Cuba to meet plans to expand its sales to the communist bloc. Much of Cuba's sugar exports go to Eastern Europe and the USSR; during the first three months of 1982, the Soviet Union had already taken approximately 75 percent of Cuba's sugar. The Castro government reported other achievements during 1982—37 power plants installed in the mountains since 1980, new irrigation and drainage facilities, increased coffee and rice production, and new investments in electric plants, oil, nickel, sugar, citrus, textiles, and machinery, all with the help of the Soviet Union (*FBIS*, 27 July).

Yet economic problems continued to plague Cuba. Castro warned the 100,000 people gathered for the 26 July anniversary celebrations that a "capitalist crisis" now affected them. He stressed that some people faced shorter workweeks and lower salaries due to the worldwide economic recession. "We are going to have difficulties in the coming years," he told the crowd, and "the difficulties could be major." (*NYT*, 28 July.) Castro cited declining prices for sugar and coffee, coupled with high interest rates and import quotas, which made trade difficult. Castro also pointed to declining world demand for nickel, the country's second largest export (*Latin America Commodity Report*, 13 August).

Cuba's hard-currency earnings come from the Western countries, with whom Cuba conducts about 20 percent of its trade. Indebtedness to the West is increasing; it reached $3.5 billion during 1982, with the interest payment estimated at $800 million. The remaining portion of Cuba's export earnings from Western trade went to the purchase of medicine and food, diverting scarce capital from investment in industry and construction. "It could be," Castro said, "that our economy in the coming years could grow only a little or not at all," noting that growth in the past year had been only 3 percent (*NYT*, 28 July).

Among Cuba's economic difficulties remained the human element. Speaking before the ANAP congress in May, Castro referred repeatedly and openly to "thieves" engaged in fraud in the administration of state enterprises (*Latin America Regional Report*, 11 June). Overall productivity continued to lag as the government cracked down on free-market entrepreneurs—salesmen hawking a variety of articles, such as footwear, textiles, and other items, from which they derived "enormous profits" (*Granma*, 1 April). Hundreds of arrests were made in early 1982 as part of a major crackdown on corruption, a campaign that extended to Cuba's most popular sport, baseball. A number of school administrators were arrested in April on charges of corruption and theft involving school supplies. (*Latin America Weekly Report*, 2 April, 7 May.)

In light of these difficulties, it is not surprising that a March report of the Joint Economic Committee of the U.S. Congress assessed Cuba's economic problems as "systemic and generally deteriorating" ("Cuba Faces the Economic Realities of the 1980s").

In an effort to address the difficult economic situation, the Cuban government began to try to secure foreign cooperation. In February, the government promulgated the country's first foreign investment law, which included a search for joint ventures with Western and developing countries in agriculture, tourism, shipping, export, and service industries (*Latin America Weekly Report*, 18 February). The effects of these efforts remained to be seen by year's end, although Mexico has expressed interest in helping Cuba develop a holiday resort. Cuba's tourist industry remained somewhat depressed by Washington's restoration of a ban on business and pleasure travel to Cuba by U.S. citizens after May and by lack of private incentives normally associated with the tourist industry. Cuban tourism suffers from limited and isolated facilities, coupled with poor food.

Cuban-Soviet Economic Ties. Cuba's internal economic conditions cannot be isolated from the Soviet Union, for without Moscow's economic aid the Cuban economy would collapse. During 1982, the Soviet Union provided approximately $4 billion, about $11 million per day or over $1.00 per capita. These economic transfers consist of soft loans, inexpensive oil supplies, and high prices for Cuba's sugar and nickel exports. It is estimated that Havana owed Moscow approximately $9 billion by 1982, an amount scheduled for repayment in 1986 (*NYT*, 17 June). During 1982, the USSR paid approximately four times the world price for Cuban sugar and supplied 95 percent of Cuba's oil needs at less than half the price charged by the Organization of Petroleum Exporting Countries. Cuba and the USSR signed a trade protocol for 1982 in February, based on the trade agreement in effect for the 1981–1982 period (*FBIS*, 11 February).

Moscow's subsidized oil trade with Cuba represents substantial hard currency it might otherwise earn by selling on the open market. Moscow's purchase of Cuban sugar at well over the market price is especially important from the Cuban perspective; sugar accounted for 83 percent of Cuba's exports in 1982, compared with 80 percent in 1957 before the Cuban revolution. Additional Soviet support in the energy field includes work on the country's first nuclear power plant, to be built in Cienfuegos. This project is an 880 Mw operation, based on conventional water-cooled Soviet reactors (ibid., 7 May). Cuba announced in July that Soviet collaboration in the nickel, textile, electrical, and building industries would increase and that the Cubans and Soviets had approved a plan to accelerate scientific and technical development in Cuba (*Latin America Weekly Report*, 16 July). In July, Carlos Rafael Rodríguez said that the "Soviet Union is the basic element in Cuba's economic development" (*Granma*, 2 July). A factor behind this Cuban-Soviet relationship is the U.S. trade embargo against Cuba. In early 1982, for example, the study of the Cuban economy prepared by the Joint Economic Committee concluded that the twenty-year-old trade embargo was forcing Cuba deeper into the Soviet camp (*NYT*, 4 April).

Foreign Policy.   Carlos Rafael Rodríguez wrote in December 1981, "Cuba will always carry out revolutionary internationalism" (*Cuba Socialista*, no. 1; *Intercontinental Press*, 7 June). Cuba continued its traditional dedication to "internationalism" during 1982. Castro reported that 120,000 Cuban servicemen had served outside the country by 1982, paralleled by an additional 30,000 doctors, teachers, engineers, and technicians who had worked abroad, primarily in Africa, but also in the Middle East, Nicaragua, and Grenada (*NYT*, 23 June). In some of these countries, notably Angola and Iraq, the Cuban government receives payment in hard currencies for its services, but this is exceptional. As part of its internationalist posture, Cuba provides scholarships for foreign students to study on the island. Cuba's Social Welfare Ministry announced that 400 scholarships were made available in 1982, while some 1,200 Nicaraguan and 2,300 Mozambican students attended Cuban schools during the year, under previous arrangements.

Cuba's wide-ranging foreign policy led to a stream of high-level delegations to Cuba as well as travel abroad by Cuban foreign policy leaders. Foreign visitors included delegations from Afghanistan, Canada, East Germany, France, Iraq, Hungary, Japan, Mexico, Mongolia, Nicaragua, the Soviet Union, and Yugoslavia. Cuban Foreign Minister Isidro Malmierca Peoli toured several Middle Eastern capitals; he met with and expressed support for Palestine Liberation Organization leader Yassir Arafat and Syrian President Hafiz al-Asad (*FBIS*, 28 June).

The presence of 15,000 to 20,000 Cubans in Angola blocked negotiations over independence for Namibia. The United States endorsed South Africa's demands that independence for Namibia be linked to a prior or simultaneous withdrawal of Cuban troops from Angola, while Castro stated that Cubans would be withdrawn only after South African troops departed from Namibia (ibid., 8 February). Castro insisted that Cuban forces remained in Angola at the request of the Angolan government to help train the People's Armed Forces for the Liberation of Angola and to help them defend the sovereignty of the People's Republic of Angola. Cuba's military presence in Angola is paralleled by a trade and economic agreement, signed in December 1981, which called for increased bilateral cooperation in agriculture, livestock, sugar, public health, construction, education, and sports (ibid., 18 December 1981). Cuba and the People's Republic of the Congo issued a joint declaration in July, blaming the United States for worsening international conditions, while earlier in February, a high-level Cuban delegation headed by Jorge Risquet, a member of the PCC Politburo and Secretariat, visited Mozambique, Tanzania, Ethiopia, Zambia, and Zimbabwe (ibid., 4 February). In Libya, 3,000 Cuban "internationalists" worked in construction, industry, and agriculture (ibid., 10 September).

In Latin America, the major focus of Cuban activity centered in Central America. The success of the Sandinista revolution in Nicaragua (July 1979) had led to an upgrading of both Cuban and Soviet ideological emphasis on "armed struggle" as a major factor in the noncapitalist path to development in the Caribbean Basin, the rehabilitation of "Che" Guevara's theories on guerrilla actions, and a Castroite stress on the unity of communist parties with insurrectional forces in "political-military fronts" as agents of change (*America Latina*, no 3, 1980). By 1982, there were some 2,000 Cuban military advisers in Nicaragua in addition to an estimated 4,000 Cuban civilian advisers and 70 Soviet military advisers (*NYT*, 10 March).

Other features of Cuban policy in Central America suggested a growing fear in Havana of a direct military threat from the United States and a desire to negotiate a number of issues in Central America.

Castro denied that Cuba had supplied arms aid to guerrillas in El Salvador and Guatemala through Nicaragua after early 1981 (ibid., 9 September). The Cuban government endorsed Mexican President José López Portillo's peace initiative for the Caribbean Basin, announced in February (ibid., 24 February). In April, a high-ranking Cuban foreign policy spokesman told a visiting delegation of U.S. newsmen and foreign policy specialists that Cuba would like to see tensions in the region reduced through negotiations with the United States and that neither Cuba nor the Soviet Union was capable of bailing Nicaragua out of its long-term economic difficulties (*Chicago Sun Times*, 6 April). Yet Cuba continued its posture as the chief Latin American critic of U.S. "capitalism and imperialism," provided propaganda support to guerrillas in El Salvador and Guatemala, and strongly supported the new leftist government in Grenada.

The Falklands/Malvinas crisis provided an opportunity for Cuba to improve its relations with a number of Central and South American countries (*WP*, 21 June). Before the British-Argentine conflict, Cuba's relations with Latin America had slipped in many respects—strained relations with Panama and Costa Rica over Havana's previous interventions in the Caribbean Basin, severe tensions with Argentina, and difficulties with Colombia and Venezuela, which also resented Cuban intervention in the Caribbean Basin and Cuba's growing military presence in Nicaragua. Cuba strongly supported the Argentine position against U.S. and British "imperialism" and "colonialism," as did Cuban-supported Nicaragua (ibid., 6 June). President Castro judged that the crisis had produced the "most nationalist Latin American sentiments that I have ever known." He placed Havana side by side with Costa Rica, Mexico, Panama, Venezuela, Peru, and other countries that denounced U.S. support of British military force against Argentina. (*NYT*, 7 June.)

As leader of the Third World nonaligned movement, Castro called a conference in Havana in June, which assailed British actions (*WP*, 6 June). Argentina's foreign minister, Nicanor Costa Méndez, spoke at the plenary meeting of the conference and expressed his gratitude to Cuba as the "pride of the Caribbean," a major departure from Argentina's earlier statements about Cuba (*FBIS*, 5 June). Argentina subsequently signed a $100 million trade agreement with Havana and offered to send 7,000 tons of wheat to help Nicaragua overcome food shortages (*NYT*, 4 June). Cuba and Venezuela held cordial meetings in June, leading to speculation about a possible restoration of diplomatic relations (*FBIS*, 2 July). At year's end, however, relations were strained with Guatemala, Costa Rica, Honduras, and Panama over Cuba's role in the deteriorating Central American setting, including its expanding role in Nicaragua (ibid., 2 and 12 October). Nor did the Falklands crisis produce much-needed trade relations with Brazil, which were reportedly blocked by conservative members of Brazil's armed forces (*WP*, 21 August).

Cuba continued to perceive the United States as the principal source of "international tension" with the socialist community of states, the main cause of an arms race with the USSR, and an increased military threat to Cuba and its socialist-oriented allies in the Caribbean Basin (*FBIS*, 12 February). Specific reasons for this Cuban posture included the U.S. arms buildup vis-à-vis the Soviet Union (ibid.), continuing U.S. operations in the Honduran-Nicaraguan border area directed against Nicaragua (*Latin American Times*, 9 November), and veiled U.S. threats about military action against Cuba early in the year (*WP*, 17 June). Cuba argued that its own military increases were provoked by these threats to its national security (ibid.). Washington's backing of Great Britain in the Falklands/Malvinas crisis heightened the Cuban-U.S. adversarial relationship. At the opening of a meeting of foreign ministers of the nonaligned countries, held in Havana in June, Foreign Minister Malmierco denounced the United States and Great Britain for their "colonial aggression" (*NYT*, 3 June). The United States also closed down the Florida firm that flies Cuban exiles and others from Cuba—cutting off the only direct link between the United States and Cuba—and blocked U.S. travelers to Cuba in an effort to reduce Cuba's hard-currency earnings from U.S. tourism (*CSM*, 12 April).

Havana argued during 1982 that the United States misrepresented its actions in El Salvador and displayed little interest in opening a true dialogue with Cuba. Carlos Rafael Rodríguez insisted that Cuba had not shipped any arms to the Salvadoran guerrillas for more than a year and said that a high-level dialogue with Cuba begun during 1981 had come to an end due to lack of U.S. interest (*WP*, 21 June). He saw clear evidence of this in Washington's tightening of its long-standing trade embargo. Any move toward negotiation with the United States based on Cuba's prior separation from the Soviet Union, as suggested by the United States in January, was completely ruled out by Havana. President Castro viewed such offers with "deep contempt" (*Latin America Weekly Report*, 23 May).

Publications. The official organ of the Cuban Communist Party, *Granma*, is published six days a week and has a circulation of approximately 600,000. *Granma* is also published in Spanish, English, and French international weekly editions and distributed free of charge abroad to about 100,000 readers. Other major Cuban publications include the Havana daily *Juventud Rebelde*, organ of the UJC, with a circulation of 200,000; *Bohemia*, a general weekly newsmagazine of about 300,000 copies; and *Verde Olivo*, the FAR publication. Prensa Latina, the Cuban news agency, has an estimated 34 offices abroad and access to two satellite communications channels to Moscow. The United States' efforts to launch a new radio station, Radio Martí, to broadcast to Cuba from Florida, led Cuba to step up transmissions to block commercial broadcasts within the U.S. (*WP*, 18 August). Cuba has 40 radio stations of high power and twenty television stations. Havana broadcasts in eight languages on several shortwave frequencies for up to a total of 50 hours weekly, a substantial broadcasting effort that in part lay behind Radio Martí.

State University of New York   W. Raymond Duncan
College at Brockport

Dominican Republic

The Dominican Republic has long had a diverse but marginally influential collection of Marxist-Leninist organizations. The fifteen largest, even taken together, are small in comparison to the country's major parties. The communist groups are thought to have a combined membership of approximately 5,000 persons, although many more Dominicans are drawn in varying degrees to their policy recommendations. None of the communist candidates won seats in the national congress. The main Marxist-Leninist party, with close ties to the Soviet Union and Cuba, is the Dominican Communist Party (Partido Comunista Dominicano; PCD). Its longtime secretary general is Narciso Isa Conde. An active international spokesman for the party during 1982 was Central Committee member César Pérez.

Dominican politics during 1982 revolved around the campaign for president, elections on 16 May, the suicide of the outgoing president just before the 16 August inauguration of his successor, and the programs launched by the new chief executive. More than a dozen parties participated in the election. Many of the small ones were Marxist-Leninist, but three non-Marxist parties won 92.9 percent of the vote—most important were the Dominican Revolutionary Party (46.6 percent) and the runner-up Reformist Party (36.5 percent). At his inauguration, the new president, Salvador Jorge Blanco, stated that the country was "financially bankrupt." The primary reasons, he said, were rising energy costs and falling income from exports, particularly sugar. He stated that "for severe illnesses severe remedies" were necessary and immediately announced a one-year freeze on wages as well as salary cuts for himself and other state employees, tax increases, measures to conserve foreign exchange and increase local production, and other similar policies.

The PCD condemns the United States for the restrictive economic policies that "cause tremendous social tensions" and "give rise to repressive tendencies in the state sector" (Radio Havana, 14 November; *FBIS*, 16 November). In September, the PCD was the most prominent of ten communist parties and groups to reject the economic measures of the new Dominican government as "an offensive against the living standard of the workers and the popular masses" (EFE, Madrid, 11 September). Three months after the inauguration, Isa Conde charged that "deterioration and the erosion of credibility has begun. We are moving toward harder struggles and worsening social tensions," he added. (Radio Havana, 14 November.)

In November, Isa Conde stated, "It is up to the Dominican left to take an important step in its political existence, and that step is unification" (ibid.). In fact, long before the May elections, the PCD had called for leftist unity, stating that a formula for "unity in the conditions of a functioning representative bourgeois democracy is the most important and complicated problem we have to face" (*IB*, May). In March, the party worked out a unity agreement with the Movement for Socialism and the Movement for Socialist Unity. Isa Conde ran as presidential candidate of the three parties. The group conducted an active campaign, although the PCD national electoral board charged that there was systematic harassment of its members (Santo Domingo Radio Mil, 31 March).

Six other leftist organizations formed the United Left (IU) in February to contest the May elections. The parties involved were the Anti-imperialist Patriotic Union (UPA), the Dominican Workers' Party (PTD), the Communist Workers' Nucleus, the Workers' Socialist Movement, the Socialist Party, and the Dominican People's Movement. Their presidential and vice-presidential candidates—Franklin Franco of the UPA and Juan B. Mejía of the PTD, respectively—came from the Marxist-Leninist nucleus of the front. Prior to the election, Franco, a professor at the Autonomous University of Santo Domingo, stated that members of the IU "categorically reject all types of terrorist, anarchist, or speculative actions that alienate the revolutionary masses." He noted that while the rightist parties are "facing divisions that shake their foundations," the left is "drawing together, expanding perspectives, pooling experiences, and moving toward unity." (*El Caribe*, Santo Domingo, 11 February.) Nonetheless, when their program was offered to the PCD and its allies, no broader agreement could be worked out.

Hoover Institution   William E. Ratliff

Ecuador

The Communist Party of Ecuador (PCE) continued to play an active role in the agitated politics of Ecuador during 1982. The new leadership chosen in November 1981, headed by Secretary General René Mauge and Secretary of the Central Committee Milton Jijón Saavedra, emphasized the building of closer relationships with the working class and tactical alliance with leftist forces during a time of heightened social tension and expanding class struggle. They also expressed their solidarity with the people of Cuba, Nicaragua, and Grenada and the patriotic struggle in El Salvador and Guatemala, as well as their support for Soviet policies against imperialism. (*FBIS*, 4 and 25 March; *World Affairs Report*, 12, no. 2, p. 214.) Party membership, estimated at 500, continued small, but the party had a growing number of followers, estimated around 3,000. The party acquired considerable prestige from its role in two successful general strikes.

Prospects for class struggle were enhanced by a number of crises during the year. A bitter personal feud in January and February between President Osvaldo Hurtado Larrea and his congressionally imposed vice-president, León Roldós Aguilera, threatened for a time to involve the military (*Los Angeles Times*, 7 March). In March and May, the sucre was devalued, provoking cries of protest from unions, farmers, and producers (*Latin America Regional Report*, 2 April; *Latin America Weekly Report*, 21 May). The sluggish world demand for oil, Ecuador's major export, forced continued downward revisions in economic growth estimates, from 3.2 percent early in the year to negative growth rates by the year's end (*FBIS*, 12 August; *El Comercio*, 29 September). In August and September, the fragile political coalition by which the Hurtado administration retained some capacity to influence legislation broke apart with the congress's censure of Oil

Minister Eduardo Ortega and the withdrawal of the Concentration of Popular Forces from participation in the government (*FBIS*, 7 September). This was followed by the withdrawal of the Democratic Left and the Democratic Party later in the year (*Visión*, 6 December). As a result, President Hurtado was forced to turn to political independents for his cabinet. By far the most serious challenge came in October, when a strike led by the transport sector and the United Labor Front (FUT) provoked substantial violence and the invocation of a week-long state of emergency (*NYT*, 26 October). Although President Hurtado was able to defuse the crisis by allowing substantial increases in bus fares and wages, subsequent strikes temporarily disrupted the universities and paralyzed production in the oil fields (*FBIS*, 2 and 16 November, 10 December). The Marxist-Leninist parties and popular organizations remained divided, but showed a growing capacity to take advantage of the political and economic difficulties the government was experiencing (*Latinamerica Press*, Lima, 18 November, pp. 5–6).

The PCE-controlled Confederation of Ecuadorean Workers (CTE) continued to form part of the coalition of four workers' confederations, the FUT, which called two general strikes during the year. The 23–24 September strike, which demanded, among other things, wage increases and a price freeze, was only partially successful. While supported by the CTE, the Maoist-oriented Federation of Ecuadorean University Students and the National Union of Teachers, and several small groups, it was opposed by other FUT members, including the Christian Democratic Ecuadorean Federation of Catholic Workers, because of its political objective of "destabilizing the administration" rather than "furthering class interests." (*Latin America Weekly Review*, 1 October; *FBIS*, 27 September.) However, the powerful independent transport union, the National Federation of Professional Drivers of Ecuador, kept up the pressure with a fairly successful five-day strike between 27 September and 2 October, in which the government was forced to use official and military vehicles to provide some public transportation services (*FBIS*, 28 September, 4 October). The most serious challenge to the government occurred as a result of the FUT's second general strike on 20–22 October, which most other unions joined, including the transport workers. This was in response to the government's mid-October decision to increase gasoline prices by 120 percent (to about $1.00 per gallon) and flour by 100 percent (to about $0.16 per pound) (*Los Angeles Times*, 21 October). Demonstrations and riots occurred in major cities throughout the country, prompting the government to declare a state of emergency between 21 and 27 October. By the time things calmed down, at least five deaths and several hundred arrests were reported (*NYT*, 26 October; *FBIS*, 21–28 October). The government responded to this dramatic show of labor strength, if not unity, by meeting with FUT leaders, lifting the state of emergency, and declaring a 50 percent increase in bus fares and a 35 percent wage increase for workers nationwide (*FBIS*, 2 November). The FUT responded by withdrawing its call for yet another general strike in November (ibid., 8 November). The FUT's conciliatory gesture may have been one of the motives behind the creation in late November of a new Marxist labor federation, the Ecuadorean General Workers' Union (UGTE). Its leader, metalworker Patricio Aldaz, said that the UGTE would try to recover for the workers and peasants the labor leadership that "until now has been in the hands of a bureaucracy of lawyers" (ibid., 29 November).

Although the National Federation of Chambers of Industry called for the resignation of the leading civilian political figures in December in the midst of continuing strike activity, economic difficulties, and a few isolated terrorist incidents, President Hurtado weathered the storm by his ability to work out creative, if short-term, solutions to legitimate grievances (ibid., 20 November, 29 December; *El Comercio*, 28 November; *Visión*, 6 December). Furthermore, he continued to count on the military to support constitutional solutions to Ecuador's problems (*FBIS*, 20 November).

Foreign Service Institute   David Scott Palmer

El Salvador

During 1982, El Salvador suffered through the third year of its sanguinary civil war between U.S.-backed government forces and Marxist-Leninist rebels guided by several radical leftist parties. The war has had a devastating effect on the country. Many factories have closed, important bridges have been destroyed, and 20 percent of the country is without electric power at any one time. There are some 200,000 internal refugees, while an estimated half-million persons have fled the country. (*This Week Central America and Panama*, 6 September.) Almost half the labor force is unemployed. The change from a governing revolutionary junta to an elected constituent assembly, headed by ultra-rightist Roberto D'Aubuisson, and the appointment of the pro-military Alvaro Magaña as provisional president of the republic following elections on 28 March did not improve the government's position in the civil war significantly. The land reform program decreed by the junta in March 1980 was at a standstill. The U.S. ambassador estimated that rightist death squads had killed about 30,000 persons in the last three years (ibid., 8 November).

Marxist Movements. The oldest, though by no means largest, of the Marxist movements is the Communist Party of El Salvador (Partido Comunista de El Salvador; PCES), founded in 1925. Since 1972, its secretary general has been Shafik Jorge Handal. After having been committed for several decades to peaceful change, the PCES announced its rebirth as a guerrilla movement in January 1980. The political arm of the PCES is the National Democratic Union (Unión Nacional Democratica; UDN), headed by Mario Aguiñada, which still enjoys legal status although its leadership is now in exile. The PCES-UDN enjoys close ties with the Soviet Union. Taking advantage of the weakness of the PCES and the existence of widespread discontent among the peasants, workers, and students, three very large Marxist organizations came into existence in the mid-1970s: the Popular Revolutionary Bloc (Bloque Popular Revolucionario; BPR), led by Facundo Guardado y Guardado; the Unified Popular Action Front (Frente Acción Popular Unificada; FAPU), under Alberto Ramos; and the Popular Leagues of 28 February (Ligas Populares 28 de Febrero; LP-28), under José Leoncio Pichinte. The BPR has much the largest following, perhaps 60,000. There is also a small Marxist group called the Popular Liberation Movement (Movimiento de Liberación Popular; MLP), whose secretary general is Dr. Fabio Castillo Figueroa.

In the same manner in which the PCES became the guerrilla arm of the UDN, so each of the other Marxist movements in the late 1970s adopted an armed group already in existence. The BPR became linked to Salvador Cayetano Carpio's Popular Liberation Forces (Fuerzas Populares de Liberación; FPL); FAPU joined forces with Fermán Cienfuegos's Armed Forces of National Resistance (Fuerzas Armadas de Resistencia Nacional; FARN); LP-28 adopted the Trotskyite People's Revolutionary Army (Ejército Popular Revolucionario; ERP), of Joaquín Villalobos; and the MPL united with Roberto Roca's Central American Revolutionary Workers' Party (Partido Revolucionario de Trabajadores Centroamericanos; PRTC). The five armed groups united in November 1980 to form the Unified Revolutionary Directorate (Directorio Revolucionario Unificada; DRU), with each of their respective chiefs participating. The DRU, whose coordinator is Salvador Cayetano Carpio, controls the military activities of the rebel armed forces, which are collectively known as the Farabundo Martí National Liberation Front (Frente Farabundo Martí de Liberación Nacional; FMLN), named in honor of the martyred founder of the PCES.

The five Marxist political organizations, UDN, BPR, FAPU, LP-28, and MLP, are represented by their secretaries general on the Revolutionary Coordination of the Masses (Coordinadora Revolucionario de Masas; CRM), which meets in exile. The CRM parties are also represented in the umbrella political group of the rebellion, the Democratic Revolutionary Front (Frente Democrático Revolucionario; FDR), whose president is Dr. Guillermo Manuel Ungo of the small democratic socialist party known as the National Revolutionary Movement (Movimiento Nacional Revolucionario; MNR). Also adhering to the FDR is a splinter group from the Christian Democratic Party, known as Popular Social Christian Movement (Movimiento Popular Social Cristiano); whose leader is Rubén Ignacio Zamora Rivas. Several major unions are also represented on the executive committee of the FDR. The FDR's Political Diplomatic Commission serves as a virtual government in exile in Mexico City. The commission is chaired by Dr. Ungo, with Rubén Zamora, Fabio Castillo, José Napoleón Rodríguez Ruiz (FAPU), Ana Guadalupe Martínez (LP-28), and Salvador Samayoa (BPR) as members. During 1982, the FDR continued to seek support abroad. In January, Dr. Ungo met with French Foreign Minister Claude Cheysson, whose country along with Mexico had recognized the political status of the FMLN-FDR in 1981. A joint communiqué said that the forthcoming elections would not solve El Salvador's problems. A permanent FMLN diplomatic mission for the Caribbean was also established under Ramón Cardona, with headquarters on Grenada. Shafik Handal continued his frequent trips to Eastern European capitals.

Although the five armed movements are gathered together under the DRU of the FMLN, they vary greatly in size and power. The FPL is by far the largest of the armed movements, while the PCES and the PRTC are "without significant armed forces" (*WP*, 22 February). There are also profound differences in ideology, with the FPL favoring a prolonged popular war of attrition and the ERP calling for a massive uprising to bring a quick end to the struggle. However, the facts of the military situation tend to favor the FPL view. The FMLN is estimated to have some 4,000 regular troops, with a militia drawn from those in rebel-held territory numbering about 15,000 (*NYT*, 26 September). Numerous guerrillas also operate behind government lines.

The Civil War. Official Salvadoran government casualty figures for the period 1 July 1981 to 30 June 1982 listed 1,073 troops killed in action, 2,584 wounded, and 144 missing in action. Five colonels were among those killed. The total casualties, which do not include desertions, rumored to be numerous, are 20 percent of the entire armed forces of El Salvador. (*This Week Central America and Panama*, 6 September.) These figures do not include those who fell in the heaviest fighting of the war, which raged from June to December of this year. Rebel casualties may be presumed to be proportionately high. The addition of three special battalions, the Atlacatl and Atonatl, trained by U.S. advisers, and the Ramón Belloso, trained in the United States, seeemed to improve the army only marginally. The character of the war changed in 1982, becoming increasingly a war of position rather than one of hit-and-run operations on the part of the rebels. By February, it was estimated, possibly with some exaggeration, that about one-fourth of the country had fallen into FMLN hands (*WP*, 21 February). The principal areas of rebel control were the northern two-thirds of the department of Morazán down to the Cordillera Nahuacaterique, except for the city of Perquín, which changed hands a half-dozen times; the northern one-third of Chalatenango down to about La Reina; and an area of northern Cabañas department along the Honduran border. In addition, the FMLN held a 300 sq. km. area of Guazapa volcano and its surroundings, centering on the village of Palo Grande in Cuscatlán department; a smaller region from San Pedro hill to Siguatepeque Hill north of the Panamerican highway in San Vincente; and a region south of the city of Usulatán stretching to the Pacific. The Guazapa encampment was particularly vexing to the government as it lay only 25 km. from San Salvador. Within the northern territories under FMLN control, the rebels have organized schools, hospitals, and local governments for about twenty villages in the so-called "arc of liberty" south of the Honduran border. An estimated 60,000 peasants live in the FMLN-held zones. (*NYT*, 26 January.)

The FMLN has divided the entire country into four fronts, which are in turn subdivided into sections. Each front is named for a fallen hero of earlier revolts. The Western Feliciano Ama Front comprises Ahuachapán, Santa Ana, and Sonsonate departments and is the least active. The Central Modesto Ramírez Front covers La Libertad, San Salvador, Chalatenango, and Cuscatlán departments and was commanded by Alejandro Montenegro of the ERP until his capture in Honduras on 22 August. The Near Central Anastasio Aquino Front consists of Cabañas, San Vicente, and La Paz, while the Eastern Francisco Sánchez Front covers Usulután, San Miguel, Morazán and La Unión departments and is headed by Joaquín Villalobos of the ERP. An important subunit of the Eastern Front is called the North Eastern Front, which is located in Morazán and commanded by Jorge Meléndez, known as "Comandante Jonas."

In December 1981, the Salvadoran army launched a major drive into Morazán, called "Operation Hammer and Sickle," with the newly formed Atlacatl battalion leading the way. Rebel strongholds north of San Francisco de Gotera were overrun and an estimated thousand civilians killed, but the FMLN counterattacked before Christmas and retook most of the lost territory. United States Ambassador Deane Hinton characterized the government drive as the biggest ever mounted, "and with some of the fewest results, too" (*WP*, 31 January). The FMLN then went over to the offensive during January and February of the current year. FMLN guerrillas seized the Ilopango military airbase on the outskirts of San Salvador on 27 January. Before withdrawing, they destroyed 70 percent of the government air force, including twelve jets and six helicopters. Although the equipment was soon replaced by the United States, government prestige was badly shaken. (*This Week Central America and Panama*, 1 February.) To offset this, the government launched two U.S.-trained battalions against Guazapa volcano in late February, but the drive stalled against the well-entrenched FMLN positions and ended by mid-March.

Despite government predictions to the contrary, the FMLN made no concerted effort to disrupt the elections of 28 March. There were raids into San Antonio Abad and Apopa, just north of the capital, but the only full-scale assault was against the city of Usulután. This city was largely overrun by rebel troops on 25 March, and it was held until 30 March, making elections impossible in that region. The FMLN also blew up an important bridge on the coastal highway. In April, the government responded with an all-out drive into Usulután and another large offensive in Morazán. The results of these drives were slight.

The tempo of the fighting picked up considerably after 1 June. First the government launched a major drive into Chalatenango using the Atlacatl and Ramón Belloso battalions. Three thousand Honduran troops crossed over into Chalatenango to aid in this operation. But the center of attention soon shifted to Morazán, where yet again the FMLN overran Perquín. This occasioned the "fiercest combat of the war" (*NYT*, 15 June), and it was not until 21 June that the rebels withdrew from what was left of Perquín after aerial bombardment. During the Morazán operation, a helicopter containing the government's front commander, Col. Salvador Beltrán Luna, and the deputy defense minister, Col. Francisco Adolfo Castillo, was shot down. The former was killed and the latter captured by the FMLN. Colonel Castillo was made to appear on the rebels' Radio Venceremos in another propaganda victory for the FMLN. These operations produced heavy government casualties and left the rebels stronger (ibid., 10 July). Nevertheless, Assembly President D'Aubuisson declared that the FMLN had "played its last card" and was declining (*El Salvador News Gazette*, 11 July). In mid-July, the government launched a drive into Chalatenango, which was supposedly the largest yet (*La Prensa Gráfica*, 16 July), but it took more punishing casualties. In August, all three U.S.-trained battalions moved against FMLN positions in San Vicente and Usulután.

Some success in these operations during August and September led Defense Minister Gen. José Guillermo García to declare in early October that the FMLN was "on the run." On 10 October, however, the FMLN launched its "October offensive," seizing Las Vueltas and El Jícaro in Chalatenango on that day, killing 116 soldiers and capturing 58. Perquín, San Fernando, and Torola in Morazán fell on 13 October after heavy fighting, and an attack was launched toward San Salvador from Guazapa on 17 October. (*This Week Central America and Panama*, 18 October.) Although Perquín was later retaken by the government, the government forces did not, as in the past, move to retake much of the territory seized by the rebels. General García declared that the army would not fall "into the trap of the subversives" and have its forces chewed up in frontal assaults. As a result, the FMLN was left "in control of a broad swath of land" (*Boston Globe*, 15 November). This seemed to suggest that some advantage had been gained by the FMLN, but through December the war stagnated, and no victory by either side seemed likely in the immediate future.

Biographies. *Salvador Cayetano Carpio.* Carpio was born about 1920 in San Salvador to a working-class family. He joined the PCES at the age of 28 and rose to be its secretary general. He was dissatisfied with the inactivity that Moscow had imposed on the party and broke with the PCES in 1970, forming the FPL. In 1972, his new organization began a series of terrorist activities including assassinations, kidnappings for ransom, and robbery. The BPR affiliated itself with his movement in 1979, giving him a large base for recruits. Despite his years, Carpio, who is known as Comandante Marcial, has taken an active role in the civil war, being coordinator of the DRU and a frequent visitor to the front lines. It was reported that he was almost captured by government forces near Guazapa in July and eighteen of his bodyguard were killed

(*Diario de Hoy*, 2 July). A later report held that he had been killed in a firefight near that same location (*This Week Central America and Panama*, 22 November). This report has not been confirmed.

Shafik Jorge Handal.   His name is also given as Jorge Shafik and Jorge Shafick Handal. He was born about 1931 in Usulután to a Palestinian Christian family from Bethlehem. He studied law at the national university and joined the PCES at the age of twenty. Jailed and exiled on various occasions, he eventually succeeded Salvador Cayetano Carpio as secretary general of the PCES and, through its front group, the UDN, combined with the Christian Democrats and the MNR in offering presidential candidates in 1972 and 1977. Until August 1979, when he endorsed the revolutionary struggle, he followed the line that El Salvador could be transformed through peaceful, democratic means. The next January, he announced that the PCES would become a guerrilla band. The actual fighting strength of the PCES remains small, and Handal himself, who has a sedentary disposition, is not a battlefield commander. His chief value to the FMLN is as a contact man with the Eastern bloc countries, where he is a frequent visitor, and with the Palestinians and other Arab groups because of his ancestry.

Eastern Connecticut State University   Thomas P. Anderson

Grenada

Grenada is led by the New Jewel Movement (NJM), headed by its 37-year-old socialist prime minister, Maurice Bishop. The NJM assumed power in March 1979, when Bishop engineered the overthrow of Sir Eric Gairy, the dominant political leader in Grenada for much of the post-World War II period. The Gairy era led to Grenada's independence in 1974, but it produced centralized political control, initially through Gairy's Grenada United Labor Party (formed in 1952) and later through strong-arm tactics, patronage, and personalist politics. Resistance to Gairy evolved at first spontaneously, but it eventually became more organized in the 1970s through trade unions, public organizations, and the press. Growing discontent led to the formation of two leftist political organizations—the Joint Effort for Welfare, Education and Liberation (JEWEL), led by Unison Whiteman, and the Movement for the Assemblies of the People (MAP), headed by Bishop and Kendrick Radix. The merger of these two groups in 1973 became known as the NJM, which its leaders describe as "the vanguard capable of directing the actions of the people" (*WMR*, September 1980).

Bishop describes the NJM's March 1979 revolution as a reaction against 25 years of Gairyism. During this period, according to Bishop, Gairyism "had devasted the social and economic fabric of our society" and "destroyed our country's international standing—Grenada was reduced to the laughingstock of the international community, land of a tin-pot dictator lost in extraterrestrial dreams, preoccupied with UFO's, obsessed with his divinity, but brutal and ruthless in the exercise of power" (*Intercontinental Press*, 21 December 1981). In many respects, Bishop was correct. Gairy was compared by his opponents to "Papa Doc" Duvalier of Haiti for his ruthlessness and his efforts to terrorize the opposition. Critics of Bishop, however, argue that the Grenadian people have lost many basic rights under the NJM's revolution because the NJM substituted a "dictatorship of the left (Bishop) for the old dictatorship of the right (Gairy)," through its "clear Marxist-Leninist orientation" (*Clat Newsletter*, July).

NJM leaders, in fact, stress the party's adherence to the ideas of "scientific socialism" and the "principles of democratic centralism," where the NJM "is the sole organized force with real influence over the masses" (*WMR*, September 1980). The NJM is a member of the Socialist International, and its leaders make no secret of their Marxist views, friendship with Cuba and Nicaragua, and desire to promote relations with all socialist countries. As Bishop recently stated, Grenada is "at an anti-imperialist, national democratic, socialist-oriented stage of development" (ibid., April).

The NJM's Statement of Principles, formulated in June 1974, is both nationalist and socialist. This document sets forth the fundamental objectives of Bishop's movement: the striving for economic reconstruction and democratization of the society through a distinctly socialist economic and political process. The statement includes: "(1) People's participation, people's politics, people's democracy; (2) People's cooperatives for the collective development of the people; (3) Health care based on need; (4) Full development of the people's talents, abilities, and culture; and (5) Full control, as a people, of our natural resources" (*Intercontinental Press*, 21 December 1981). As Whiteman, Grenada's minister of foreign affairs, stated in October 1981, "Since the triumph of the revolution on March 13, 1979, we have proceeded to put the country on the path of a socialist orientation" (ibid., 26 October 1981).

Party and Government Organization. The 1979 revolution produced a new political system, the People's Revolutionary Government (PRG), whose leaders came from the previous merger of JEWEL and MAP. Bishop assumed the premiership of the PRG and has remained in that position. By 1982, Bishop also headed the offices of Information, Health, Defense, and Interior. Bernard Coard, formerly a university lecturer, rose to the positions of deputy prime minister and minister of finance, trade, industry, and planning. Whiteman now heads the Ministry of Foreign Affairs, formerly held by Bishop, as well as the Ministry of Tourism. Radix controls Legal Affairs, Agro-Industry, and Fisheries. George Louison is minister of agriculture, rural development, and cooperatives; Hudson Austin of communications, works, and labor; and Norris Bain of housing. Jacqueline Creft is minister of education, youth, and social affairs. Selwyn Strachman, formerly the minister of communications, works, and labor, is now the minister of national mobilization. This office oversees efforts to mobilize people into militias for the defense of the country. The PRG also created a new Ministry of Women's Affairs in 1982, headed by Jacqueline Creft.

Grenada's NJM and government organizations continue to be patterned after Cuba's. This trend is not surprising in view of Grenada's extremely close ties with Cuba following the establishment of diplomatic relations between the two countries in April 1979. The NJM now includes a Political Bureau and Central Committee, consisting of high government officials, such as Bishop and Coard (ibid., 8 March, 5 April). And like Cuba, Grenada's party and government systems are supported by mass organizations. By 1982, their membership amounted to approximately 30,000 people, or about 60 percent of Grenada's adult population. Grenada's mass organizations incorporate the country's ten trade unions (10,000 members), the National Youth Organization (7,000), the National Women's Organization (7,000), a Peasant's Organization (1,000), and the Young Pioneers (6,000) for children age 5 to 14. In addition, a number of parish and workers' parish councils have been formed; they meet monthly to express opinions and "to join in decision-making" (*WMR*, April). Finally, in the Cuban tradition, people's militias have been formed all over the country, in addition to the People's Revolutionary Army, to give the country a sense of security. The people's militias consist of about 25,000 volunteers.

Party and Government Internal Affairs. A number of national meetings, rallies, and militia activities occurred during 1982. These reflected the PRG's emphasis on the need to extend mass organization and to increase revolutionary awareness among the island's workers. Approximately a thousand Grenadians gathered in St. George's in January to attend the first National Conference of Delegates of Mass Organizations on the Economy. Through meetings of this type, the PRG sought to raise the consciousness of Grenadians about their economy, to cut waste and corruption, and to increase efficiency in production— all problems plaguing Grenada, somewhat akin to similar conditions in Cuba (*Intercontinental Press*, 22 February). This conference led to two months of discussions involving thousands of Grenadians in parish councils and other mass organizations, all of which contributed to the formulation of the 1982 budget, presented at a mass meeting in March by the Minister of Finance Bernard Coard (*Latin America Regional Report*, 26 March).

Other party and government internal affairs suggest the increasing mobilization of Grenada's population along a Cuban model. The PRG marked the third anniversary of the 1979 revolution during celebrations held in March, which attracted over 500 foreign participants representing 33 countries and political delegates from all over the Caribbean (ibid.). Following the Cuban fashion of identifying each year of the revolution with a specific slogan, the March PRG celebrations designated 1982 as the "year of economic reconstruction." The March celebrations also produced the Third Julian Fedon National Maneuver, which included all the island's armed forces—the army, police, and militia. Julian Fedon, a planter who led a rebellion against the British in 1795, is considered by the PRG to be Grenada's first revolutionary leader. This type of maneuver reflected the PRG's concern about possible direct U.S. action against the island, a cause for concern that began to develop in 1981. In July 1982, Maurice Bishop, in his role as commander in chief of the armed forces, called for stepped-up recruitment of Grenadians into the People's Revolutionary Militia (*FBIS*, 14 July).

Domestic Affairs.   While 1981 was devoted to developing mass organizations, 1982 centered on the economy. The reasons for this concern were no light matter, with unemployment running at 25 percent, food imports estimated at $22 million, a falloff in tourism, and declining export income measured against spiraling import costs due to worldwide inflation.

Grenada's economy continued to be plagued by obstacles to development. The price of cocoa, one of Grenada's main exports, fell by 55 percent. The country had more nutmeg in storage than it could sell, and the price of bananas was very low. Prime Minister Bishop blamed these and other economic problems on the recession affecting the industrial capitalist countries and the persistent imbalance of trade between "imperialist" industrialized countries and poor underdeveloped countries like Grenada. Bishop told the audience gathered to mark the third anniversary of Grenada's revolution (13 March) that the PRG was squeezed by the "imperialist countries," which controlled the prices paid for Grenada's bananas, cocoa, and nutmeg and the prices charged for goods imported by Grenada to stimulate its own development (*Intercontinental Press*, 19 August). Bishop stressed the need to diversify production and told the people that they must "work harder, produce more, and build Grenada" (*FBIS*, 14 March). The state sector has extended its control over areas such as road building, water supplies, telephone, electric power, port facilities, and other infrastructure projects in the quest for rapid economic growth. Agricultural development occupies much attention; diversified production is a major goal. Agricultural planning is guided in part by the new Industrial Development Ministry and the National Cooperative Development Agency. Agriculture Minister Louison stated in April that agriculture is "the main basis for the industrialisation of our country" (*Bridgetown Advocate-News*, 17 April). Help in expanding the state sector comes from Cuba, Iraq, Algeria, Syria, Libya, other countries in the Organization of Petroleum Exporting Countries, Korea, Tanzania, Nigeria, Mexico, Venezuela, Kenya, the European Economic Community, Canada, and the socialist countries.

Grenada's new international airport, estimated to cost well over $75 million, is 40 percent complete. Cuban efforts on this project are noteworthy, given the approximately 300 Cuban construction workers involved on the project. Venezuela, meanwhile, has provided about 10,000 gallons of oil worth $800,000 for the project, with additional help coming from Libya, Syria, Algeria, Iraq, and the European Development Fund. (*Nation*, Bridgetown, 12 May.) Grenada claims that the international airport is strictly for domestic purposes, such as expanded tourism, and not for military use, as might easily be inferred.

Grenada's private sector also plays a role in the PRG's economic development. In mid-1982, the government published an investment code expressing readiness to support and encourage the private sector and to ensure the security of investors' interests. The private sector is, as might be expected, excluded from ownership and control of areas such as public utilities, national transport, communications, infrastructure, and trade in certain sectors (*Latin America Weekly Report*, 27 September). The PRG, for example, bought out the Commonwealth Development Corporation's 49 percent share holding in Grenada's Electricity Services in April, which made the company fully state owned (ibid., 27 August). Yet the government returned the local Coca-Cola bottling plant (seized in September, 1979) to its private operators in March. Minister of Finance and Trade Bernard Coard emphasized that there is developing in Grenada a "small, but growing and dynamic 'stratum' of the private sector which is engaged in direct production in the area of manufacturing" (*Bridgetown Advocate-News*, 28 May). Yet all is by no means stable between the PRG and the private sector. Chamber of Commerce President David Minors complains that the PRG is using the businessmen's group as window-dressing. The Chamber of Commerce is especially critical of new licensing regulations on exports and imports, increased company taxes, and the inability to publish its monthly bulletin because of the law banning newspapers for one year, which went into effect in June 1981. (*Trinidad Guardian*, 9 April.)

Foreign Policy. Grenada's foreign policy follows a distinctly leftward course and is increasingly tied to the Soviet Union and Cuba. Bishop led a delegation to Moscow in July, which produced new aid and trade agreements. The Soviets extended to the PRG a $7.7 million line of credit, repayable over ten years at 3 percent interest, with provision for a grace period in repayment, to finance construction of a satellite earth station, feasibility studies for an east coast port, and purchase of equipment for an improved water supply and sewage disposal system. The USSR also agreed to give Grenada a gift of $1.4 million to cover the purchase of a spray plane for agriculture use, 400 tons of flour, clothing, and steel. Moscow agreed to purchase quantities of Grenadian cocoa and nutmeg over a five-year period (*FBIS*, 29 July). These agreements may be interpreted as resulting from the Falklands/Malvinas crisis, which has led the Soviets to give a higher priority to Latin America (*Times*, London, 29 July). Before the Moscow trip, Bishop and a delegation visited Bulgaria, East Germany, and Libya. This trip produced a $14 million line of credit from East Germany to purchase agricultural equipment, help from Bulgaria in buying ice-making machinery, and a $4 million interest-free loan from Libya—in addition to Libyan assistance in construction of the international airport (*FBIS*, 23 June). Minister of Health Christopher de Wiggs Brother visited Yugoslavia in June to attend the Twelfth Congress of the League of Communists of Yugoslavia.

Grenada's ties with Cuba remain strong. Cuban aid covers a wide range of activities, including help in constructing the international airport, health care, culture, housing, sports facilities, advisers on planning and collection of statistics, agro-industries, the construction of a new radio station, transportation, and the maintenance and development of the island's electricity network. The presence of about 300 construction workers on the international airport is the most prominent feature of Cuban assistance, but help in the agricultural sector is pronounced. An agreement signed in 1981 led to progress in a number of agricultural areas, such as fruit production, irrigation, and exchange of agricultural information. The total number of Cubans in Grenada is approximately 400, with all salaries paid for by the Cubans. (*Intercontinental Press*, 3 May.) Cuban aid also included twelve doctors and three dentists. Over 250 Grenadian youths currently study on scholarships in Cuba. Cuba granted a total of 84 scholarships to Grenada for academic year 1982-83. These awards involve study in the fields of animal husbandry, agronomy, agricultural economics, pest control, and nursing (*FBIS*, 2 August). In September, Cuba and the PRG signed an air traffic cooperation act regarding air service between the two countries (ibid., 15 September). Cuba, moreover, periodically extends gifts to the PRG, for example, 40 tractors in June and ten fishing trawlers between 1979 and 1982.

Cuba's influence on Grenada is both direct and indirect. Grenada has adopted one foreign assistance aspect of Cuban foreign policy. It has sent youths to help in Nicaragua's literacy campaign in the English-speaking areas of Bluefields on the Atlantic coast and to assist Cuban teachers in that effort. When the president of Mozambique, Samora Machel, visited Cuba in May, he stopped over in Georgetown, Grenada. Machel said that he welcomed Grenada's "anticolonialist stand as well as its nonaligned foreign policy." In return, Bishop said, "Mozambique and Grenada shared the same victories and were united in struggle against one common enemy—United States imperialism." (Ibid., 25 May.) In August, Bishop visited Fidel Castro in Cuba, and the two leaders discussed the close fraternal links between the two countries (*Granma*, 9 August).

Grenada's relations with the United States remained unimproved during 1982. Bishop complained of U.S. military harassment, took a decidedly dim view of Washington's Caribbean Basin Initiative, and argued that the United States pursued a Monroe Doctrine posture aimed at "perpetuating hegemonism, interventionism, or backyardism in this region of ours." Bishop chastised the U.S. Caribbean Basin Initiative for excluding small socialist islands like Grenada, its insufficient funding, its support for "fascist dictatorships and oligarchies as represented by El Salvador," and its apparent goal of dealing with "narrow military, security, and strategic considerations of the U.S." rather than demonstrating a genuine concern with "economic and social development of the people of this region." (*Intercontinental Press*, 19 April.) As for the turmoil in Central America, such as guerrilla action in El Salvador, frictions between Nicaragua and Honduras, conflict between Cuba and the United States, Grenada favors the Mexican-French proposal of February, which calls for negotiated political settlements. The PRG wishes to see relations between the United States and Grenada improved, but it blames the United States for not showing interest in bettering these conditions. Prime Minister Bishop visited France in September and spoke with President François Mitterrand about securing French political and economic help in the PRG's struggle against U.S. pressures. The chances of improved U.S.-Grenadian affairs were distinctly poor by year's end.

In November, in Ocho Rios, Jamaica, the Caribbean Community (Caricom), which includes the leaders of the English-speaking Caribbean, held its first meeting in seven years. A major issue at this meeting was the lack of elections, political imprisonments, and the closing of the free press in Grenada (*NYT*, 19 November). At the final session of the four-day meeting, Prime Minister Bishop vowed to institute at least limited democratic reforms on his island, and he reportedly offered to allow Caricom nations to place observers in Grenada to ensure that leftist guerrillas were not training on the island or using it to travel to and from Cuba (*WP*, 19 November). Bishop, however, also declared the issue of elections a "red herring" and argued that the people of Grenada were participating fully in the government. "This revolution did not take place for the calling of elections, but for food, for bread, for justice, for housing—to insure that the people for the first time would have the right to participate." Bishop stated that elections would eventually be held, when the population was adequately prepared and a new constitution developed, but that no outside pressure would force Grenada "to advance its agenda." (*NYT*, 17 November.)

Publications.   Press activities are strictly limited in Grenada. The PRG closed down the privately owned *Torchlight* (an independent weekly) in 1979 on the charge that it threatened national security. In June 1981, the PRG vilified 26 Grenadians who launched a mimeographed weekly entitled the *Grenadian Voice* as CIA accomplices and closed it down after the first printing. The principal newspaper is the weekly *Free West Indian*, with a circulation of about 6,000. The *New Jewel Movement Weekly* reaches an estimated 5,000 readers. In July, Havana's news agency, Prensa Latina, opened an office in Grenada to cover the eastern Caribbean.

In March, the PRG officially opened a new 50-kw transmitter, a gift from Cuba to the government-owned and operated Radio Free Grenada (*FBIS*, 11 March). Some observers believe this increase in power for Radio Free Grenada, larger than that required for a 136,000 sq. mi. island, will be utilized as an outlet for Cuban news programs. The PRG's Television Free Grenada complements the PRG's broadcasting capabilities and makes weekly broadcasts concerning the revolutionary movement. One program, for example, is conducted by the Young Pioneers (ibid., 4 November 1981).

State University of New York   W. Raymond Duncan
College at Brockport

Guadeloupe

The Guadeloupe Communist Party (Parti communiste guadeloupeen; PCG) continued to be one of the most important political forces in the French overseas department of Guadeloupe. The PCG is led by its longtime secretary general, Guy Daninthe. Among the members of the twelve-person Political Bureau are Daniel Genies, A. Louber, Pierre Tarer, Christian Celeste, Henri Bangou, and Serge Pierre-Justin. The PCG is thought to have about 3,000 members. Party member Ernest Moutoussamy holds one of three Guadeloupan seats in the French Chamber of Deputies. The two main PCG auxiliary organizations are the Union of Guadeloupan Communist Youth, whose secretary general is Jean-Claude Lombion, and the Union of Guadeloupan Women. The PCG plays a leading role in the General Confederation of Labor of Guadeloupe (CGTG). The PCG's weekly organ is *L'Etincelle*, which celebrated its thirty-eighth anniversary at midyear.

The Seventh Congress of the PCG, held in May 1980, formulated the strategy followed by the party during 1982. This strategy was expanded on at the Second National Conference of the PCG in January (*L'Etincelle*, 9 and 16 January) and as the year progressed. A resolution passed at the conference said that party branches should be expanded, become more active, and be reinforced at enterprises around the country. As social and political changes occur, it is necessary to devote more time to educational work, with particular attention given to the youth of the nation. Also, the party must enforce greater discipline, the "strict observance of the principles of inner-party democracy." (*WMR*, July; *L'Etincelle*, 16 January.) The PCG maintained contacts with fraternal communist parties through visits to Guadeloupe by officials from the Soviet bloc and by trips to Europe by PCG leaders. The PCG deputy in the French parliament maintained contacts with European political leaders.

The PCG found it easier to work with the French government of François Mitterrand than with that of his predecessor, Valéry Giscard d'Estaing. However, it was as hard as ever to make headway with local officials in Guadeloupe itself, and thus frustration and failure marked the year for the Communists. The party proposed a greater degree of cooperation by leftist forces and advocated revitalization of the sagging economy, in part through the expansion of tourism, as well as improved health, education, and transportation programs (*L'Etincelle*, 26 June). In 1981, the PCG took particular aim at sugar industry owners, who were cutting back on production and causing high unemployment; through the CGTG, the party participated in strikes and rallies that scored some successes. During 1982, particular emphasis was put on the need for modernizing the sugar industry and diversifying agriculture (ibid., 17 July, 2 October).

At the same time, the party devoted extensive time and space to the longer-term problems of the best eventual political structure for the island. It called for decentralization, for an autonomous democratic and popular government that would support the people's right to self-determination (*WMR*, February; *L'Etinceelle*, 2 October). It also supported the formation of a much-discussed Single Assembly (Assemblée unique), with proportional representation, to govern the French overseas departments. When the decentralization program suffered a setback in December, the PCG remarked on the amazing durability of the colonial mentality.

The PCG adopted standard Soviet-line positions on international affairs, ranging from condemnations of U.S. policies in the Caribbean to opposition to the development by the United States of a neutron bomb (*L'Etincelle*, 16 January).

Hoover Institution   William E. Ratliff

Guatemala

The communist party in Guatemala, renamed the Guatemalan Party of Labor (Partido Guatemalteco del Trabajo; PGT) in 1950, originated in the predominantly communist-controlled Socialist Labor Unification founded in 1921. The PGT operated legally between 1951 and 1954, playing an active role in the administration of President Jacobo Arbenz. Outlawed in 1954 following the overthrow of Arbenz, it has since operated underground. Although the party has some influence among students, intellectuals, and workers, its role in national affairs is insignificant. According to U.S. intelligence sources, the PGT has about 750 members.

The Guatemalan political scene was dominated in 1982 by the continuing struggle between various Marxist-led guerrilla movements and counterinsurgency operations by the military. An army offensive in late 1981 was countered in February by "an alliance and intensification of the revolutionary struggle" by the country's four main guerrilla groups. Backed by a coalition of governing parties, a former defense minister Gen. Angel Aníbal Guevara, predictably won the 7 March presidential elections. Less predictably, a group of young, dissatisfied army officers carried out a coup d'etat on 23 March, which nullifed the general elections and elevated to power former general Efraín Ríos Montt, the defeated candidate in the fraudulent 1974 elections. Successively, the Ríos Montt regime announced a 30-day amnesty decree on 1 June, a state of siege on 1 July, and the start of a "final war" ("Victory '82") against the guerrillas. The military's "pacification" policy of "rifles and beans" was denounced by guerrilla and civilian opponents as a scorched-earth policy of massive dislocation and genocide directed against Indians and peasants located in the heavily populated areas of northern and western Guatemala. In December, Ríos Montt met with President Ronald Reagan in Honduras and affirmed that armed conflict in Guatemala "has ended." He announced the Triple T plan to provide "a roof, a job, and something to eat" to the 70 percent of the population forgotten by previous administrations. He also pledged to return the country to a constitutional form of government by 1984.

Guerrilla and General Violence.   As part of its counterinsurgency campaign, the Guatemalan army "asked" the news media in May to downplay the importance of guerrilla and communist operations (AFP, 8 May). Since the imposition of press censorship on 1 July, the only news about the guerrilla situation available beyond that provided by official army communiqués is occasional clandestine bulletins and political manifestos issued by the various guerrilla organizations and opposition movements and infrequent statements by church and human rights groups.

Four guerrilla groups have been active in Guatemala in recent years. The Revolutionary Armed Forces is the military arm of the PGT (see below). The Rebel Armed Forces (Fuerzas Armadas Rebeldes; FAR) was originally a military commission of the PGT when it was formed in the early 1960s. In the late 1970s, FAR developed considerable influence in the trade union movement, and its activists played a key role in the formation of the Central Nacional de Trabajadores and the broad-based National Committee for Labor Unity, both of which have been subjected to heavy repression since 1978. FAR was active in 1982 primarily in Guatemala City, Chimaltenango and the remote Petén region. It is believed to have fewer than a hundred members, plus several hundred sympathizers. In July, FAR claimed responsibility for bombing the Guatemalan offices of the Honduran airline SAHSA to protest Washington's interventionist role in Honduras (Cadena de Emisoras Unidas, 27 July; FBIS, 29 July). A FAR communiqué in August claimed that its forces had inflicted more than 50 casualties on the Guatemalan army and carried out numerous acts of sabotage and propaganda in the previous four months (Havana international service, 10 August). FAR also reported that members of the new Tecum-Umán guerrilla front operating in the central highlands inflicted some one hundred casualties on army troops during clashes in Chimaltenango in August and September (ibid., 1 October).

A third guerrilla organization is the Armed People's Organization (Organización del Pueblo en Armas; ORPA), whose founders were originally part of FAR. ORPA prepared for eight years before launching its first military actions in September 1979. Little is known of the ORPA's leaders, membership, or political orientation, although according to Guatemalan intelligence sources, its principal leader is Gaspar Ilón. Unlike the Guerrilla Army of the Poor (EGP), ORPA has no mass organizations and operates primarily as a military entity. Other guerrilla leaders have criticized ORPA's lack of political organization, which they claim has reduced its overall effectiveness. A good portion of ORPA's organization in Guatemala City was destroyed in 1981 due to security leaks (see YICA, 1982, p. 111). ORPA reported in June that it had temporarily occupied towns in Huehuetenango and San Marcos departments. Guerrilla units also occupied 35 farms and set fire to another five, prompting landowners in Huehuetenango to protest that guerrillas had taken over control of land in the region (Prensa Libre, 4 May). ORPA rejected the government's amnesty offer as "an act of cynicism" and continued to conduct guerrilla actions, mainly in the departments of San

Marcos, Quezaltenango, Suchitepéquez, and Escuintla. During three years of military operations, ORPA claims to have carried out 905 military actions and 66 ambushes of army patrols, inflicting over two thousand casualties on government forces (*El Nuevo Diario*, Managua, 3 October). In late December, ORPA reported a total of 392 actions for 1982, including 38 ambushes and the occupation of "dozens" of villages. The communiqué claimed that 700 casualties had been inflicted on government troops, attesting to the alleged failure of the regime's operation "Victory '82." (Havana international service, 31 December.)

The largest and most active of Guatemala's guerrilla organizations is the Guerrilla Army of the Poor (Ejército Guerrillero de los Pobres; EGP). The EGP's founders broke from FAR in the 1960s mainly because of differences over policy toward the Indian populaton. The EGP proper was formed in 1972 and now operates on seven fronts. It is the only guerrilla group to have a truly national organization (*Latin America Regional Report*, 24 September). The EGP has an estimated 1,500 combatants, although some of its leaders claim as many as 3,000. The EGP has organized massive popular support in the Indian highland departments of Quiché, Huehuetenango, Chimaltenango, and Alta and Baja Verapaz. The EGP's major activities in 1982 are discussed below.

Although not a guerrilla organization, the 31 January People's Front (FP-31) was created in 1981 "to combat the government at the political level." Taking its name from the occupation of the Spanish Embassy in 1980, the FP-31 is composed of student, worker, and peasant organizations, including the Robín García Student Front, the Felipe Antonio García Revolutionary Workers nuclei, and the Committee for Peasant Unity (CUC), which works closely with the EGP. Members of the CUC seized the Brazilian Embassy on 12 May to denounce the repression of Indian communities. In an advertisement exacted as part of the ransom exchange, the FP-31 charged that since the March coup, "more than 3,000 persons have been killed and thousands of peasants from the departments of Huehuetenango, Quiché, Petén, Izabal, and Chiquimula have been forced to seek refuge in Mexico or Honduras" (*La Nación*, San José, 15 May).

In February, Guatemala's four major guerrilla groups proclaimed an alliance, the Guatemalan National Revolutionary Unity (Unidad Revolucionaria Nacional Guatemalteca; URNG). The URNG's political platform promised to end repression, racial discrimination, and economic domination by the rich; guaranteed the establishment of a truly representative government; and adopted a nonaligned foreign policy (LATIN, 9 February; *FBIS*, 10 February). The URNG declared that the only path open to the Guatemalan people was a "revolutionary people's war." To this end, they called for the formation of "a great front of patriotic unity." In response to the URNG's request, Guatemalan exiles in Mexico City organized the Committee of Patriotic Unity (Comité Guatemalteco de Unidad Patriótica; CGUP). The CGUP is composed of the primary opposition political forces in Guatemala, including units of the United Revolutionary Front, the Democratic Front Against Repression, and the Directorate of the National Committee of Labor Unity (AFP, 17 February).

From January through June, the URNG claims to have carried out 250 harassment attacks on military positions, hundreds of sabotage actions, 203 occupations of municipalities, and 1,302 guerrilla actions of various kinds, inflicting 1,592 casualties on army troops (Havana international service, 5 September). In May, the URNG accused the Ríos Montt government of launching a genocidal campaign to exterminate the population in extensive sectors of western and northern Guatemala (Managua domestic service, 6 May; *FBIS*, 10 May). Government Minister Gen. Horacio Maldonado Schaad denied any responsibility for the massacres. He suggested they were being committed by guerrillas in reprisal against peasants who no longer cooperated with them (*Prensa Libre*, 22 May). Guerrilla leaders subsequently claimed to have defeated the army's counteroffensive in Quiché, leaving the military with "no alternative but to implement a 'scorched-earth' policy in which they massacre defenseless residents and then claim that these are military successes" (Havana international service, 5 September).

Coincident with implementation of the state of siege on 1 July, Ríos Montt announced a general offensive against guerrillas in the Quiché region, the beginning of a "rifles and beans" campaign intended to eradicate "subversives" from those departments of greatest guerrilla activity and, eventually, from the country as a whole (AFP, 5 July). Official sources reported frequent clashes in Quiché and Huehuetenango during July and August, with over 200 "subversive outlaws" killed during the first month of the "final war" against leftist insurgents (*Prensa Libre*, 9, 15, and 17 July, 4 August). The intensification of the military's counterinsurgency campaign produced a propaganda war of accusations and denials between the government and its opponents over responsibility for the massive dislocation and killing of Indian peasants.

According to Mexican and U.N. officials, thousands of Guatemalan refugees entered southern Mexico following the July offensive, most of them Indian peasants whose villages were attacked and, at times, burned by army patrols or destroyed by guerrillas who have resorted to increasingly brutal intimidation. Estimates of the number of new refugees range upward from 9,000, with more than 35,000 Guatemalans now believed to be living in border areas inside Mexico, and perhaps an additional 70,000 more in the interior (*NYT*, 18 August; *WP*, 3 January 1983).

In October, Amnesty International charged that in its first four months of government, the Ríos Montt regime massacred more than 2,600 Indians and peasants in carrying out its counterinsurgency programs. According to Amnesty International, between March and July military and "civil defense" forces perpetrated "mass executions" on at least 112 occasions (press release, 11 October). The government dismissed the charges as "totally false" and stated that no massacres or murders that could be attributed to public security forces had occurred since Ríos Montt came to power. At a press conference in Mexico City, CGUP spokesmen charged that more than 8,000 persons, 90 percent of them Indians, were killed in a three-month period between August and October (*Granma*, Havana, 14 November). For its part, the URNG announced on 8 November that guerrilla groups had killed 166 soldiers and members of paramilitary organizations and wounded 144 in operations carried out between 1 July and 27 September. During the same period, guerrillas also killed 21 persons described as informers or collaborators with the armed forces. (LATIN, 8 November; *FBIS*, 10 November.)

During military operations in November, the army dismantled six guerrilla camps and located arms and ammunition depots in northwestern Guatemala. It reported that the camps were probably used to keep thousands of peasants captive (Guatemalan domestic service, 26 November; *FBIS*, 3 December). Meeting with the international press in December, Ríos Montt affirmed that armed conflict in Guatemala "has ended." Asked to comment on reports that the Guatemalan army was pursuing a scorched-earth policy by destroying villages suspected of harboring guerrillas, Ríos Montt stated: "We have no scorched-earth policy; we have a policy of scorched Communists" (*NYT*, 6 December).

Army and other government officials now emphasize their efforts to meet the economic and social needs of the long-neglected Indian peasants they claim to have "rescued" from the guerrillas. The army has established a plan for operational support in areas of conflict based on rigid control of the rural population and extensive civil action programs. In 850 villages where there is no military presence, some 300,000 Indians have been organized into civilian self-defense units (*Prensa Libre*, 5 December). Patrols of civilian militia, armed primarily with sticks and machetes, are assigned to protect peasants who have returned to resettle their communities (ibid., 20 December). Guatemala's Committee of National Reconstruction claims to have overseen the reorganization of municipal government in 90 villages in departments heavily affected by violence (ibid., 7 December). In areas now tightly regimented and controlled by the government, the death toll has reportedly declined dramatically (*WP*, 3 January 1983).

After nine months of systematic counterinsurgency operations, the Ríos Montt government appears to have "pacified" major portions of Quiché, Huehuetenango, Sololá, and Chimaltenango. However, it would be premature to accept the general's claim that armed struggle in Guatemala has ended. According to a recent issue of *El Informador Guerrillero*, the press organ of Guatemala's insurgent forces, combatants of the URNG inflicted 42 casualties on the army in actions carried out in 7 of the country's 22 departments during December. According to the URNG, guerrillas carried out 39 military operations in Huehuetenango, Quiché, San Marcos, and in the capital (Havana international service, 19 December). In a final discordant note at year's end, guerrillas identifying themselves as members of the People's Revolutionary Movement (Movimiento Revolucionario del Pueblo) kidnapped the daughter of Honduran President Roberto Suazo Córdoba in Guatemala City on 14 December. They negotiated her release on 23 December in return for the broadcast in Guatemala of a political manifesto and its publication throughout Central America and Mexico in leading newspapers (AFP, 24 December).

Politically motivated killings involving leftist groups and right-wing paramilitary organizations have been a common feature of Guatemalan life since the mid-1960s. Political life became increasingly violent after Gen. Romeo Lucas García assumed the presidency in 1978. The systematic assassination of people in opinion-making positions by self-proclaimed death squads, such as the Secret Anticommunist Army, has decimated university faculties, student associations, rural cooperatives, trade unions, peasant leagues, and the leadership of moderate and left-of-center political organizations. Assassinations and "disappearances" continued in early 1982. However, urban death squad activity, which church and human rights organizations have charged is directly controlled by the government, declined somewhat in the first months after Ríos Montt came to power. The degree to which this impression is the result of government censorship imposed under the state of siege is difficult to ascertain. The Guatemalan Human Rights Commission reported that 83 civilians were killed, 33 were kidnapped, and 13 others "disappeared" in September and October (LATIN, 8 November). Although Ríos Montt is believed to exercise a moderating influence, the evidence suggests that kidnappings and disappearances are again occurring regularly, especially at the National University of San Carlos, where more than 40 students, professors, and university workers disappeared in the last two months of the year.

What does appear certain is that the Reagan administration is more favorably disposed toward recommending the resumption of economic and military aid to the Guatemalan government. Although the U.S. State Department's official position in December was that the administration did not have enough information about Guatemala's progress toward democracy to make a final decision, President Reagan characterized Ríos Montt as a man "totally dedicated to democracy" who is getting a "bum rap" from critics in the United States (WP, 2 January 1983).

At a news conference following his talks with President Reagan, Ríos Montt pledged to issue new laws on the formation of political parties and the electoral process by 23 March 1983. He promised to "open up the political process to a degree unprecedented in Guatemala" by guaranteeing the participation of self-proclaimed socialist parties in the electoral process (NYT, 6 December). He reiterated that a constituent assembly would be created in late 1983 or early 1984. Referring to a return to constitutionality, the Guatemalan leader said that "now that the 'subversive communists' have come to an end, the 'intellectual communists' can go to the polls and win by means of votes, rather than bullets" (ACAN, 9 December).

Guatemalan authorities have consistently charged that Cuba and Nicaragua are the "main causes of subversion in Guatemala and Central America" (Prensa Libre, 15 January). Defense Minister Gen. Oscar Mejía Victores affirmed that documents captured in September confirmed allegations that Cuba and Nicaragua are training Guatemalan guerrillas. He stressed that most of the weapons the guerrillas receive come from Cuba by way of Mexico or Nicaragua. (AFP, 13 September.) The Reagan administration appeared to concur with this judgment by intensifying its efforts to portray Ríos Montt as "a man of great integrity faced with a challenge from guerrillas armed and supported from outside Guatemala" (NYT, 7 December). The feeling in Washington is that without a show of support from the United States, specifically approval of the long-delayed sale of helicopter spare parts, Ríos Montt is in danger of being ousted by hard-line elements within Guatemala's military. After some initial doubts, the United States now seems determined to back Ríos Montt in the interests of promoting stability in the region.

Leadership and Organization. Little information is available on PGT leaders or structure. Since 1972, two general secretaries and nineteen ranking members of the Central Committee have "disappeared," apparently the victims of assassination. The current general secretary is Carlos González. Other prominent members of the Central Committee are Antonio Castro, Daniel Ríos, José Cardoza Aguilar, Otto Sánchez, Jorge Muñoz, A. Bauer País, Antonio Fuentes, Pedro González Torres, and Pablo Hernández.

The PGT has a youth auxiliary, the Patriotic Youth of Labor (Juventud Patriótica del Trabajo; JPT). Student agitators are active at the secondary and university levels but disclaim direct affiliation with the PGT. Student leaders supported by the PGT have been unsuccessful in recent years in gaining control of the influential Association of University Students (AEU), although the AEU's statements on domestic issues tend to be strongly critical of the government and its inability to control right-wing extremists. Members of the JPT are believed to be active in the Robín García Student Front and other student organizations involved with the FP-31.

The PGT also controls the clandestine Guatemalan Autonomous Federation of Trade Unions, a small and relatively unimportant labor organization. The federation affiliated with the communist-front World Federation of Trade Unions in October 1974. The National Committee for Labor Unity, which includes some 70 unions, has become the most important voice for organized labor in Guatemala. Some observers believe that its militant activities in recent years have resulted from increasing PGT influence within its ranks.

Domestic Attitudes and Activities.   It is difficult to determine whether the PGT's Central Committee met on a regular basis during 1982. Similarly, there are few sources that reveal the content of any political resolutions that may have been adopted. In order to characterize the PGT's attitudes on domestic and foreign issues, it is necessary to rely on statements of party leaders made in foreign publications or in occasional interviews. Clandestine bulletins attributed to the PGT appear occasionally in Guatemala, but their authenticity is questionable.

For over 25 of the party's 32 years of existence, it has been forced to work underground and subjected to varying levels of persecution. Despite such adverse conditions, the party claims a steady increase in influence among the masses, especially among workers, peasants, and other sectors of the population that it says are "suffering from capitalist oppression and exploitation."

Since its Fourth Congress in 1969, the PGT has adhered to the position that the revolution can triumph only through the use of force. Until May 1981, however, the party did not commit itself fully to armed struggle. The Political Commission of the Central Committee viewed as an important step the formation of the URNG and declared that "every effort must be made to overcome weaknesses due to disunity." According to the party, no political-military organization on its own can achieve a revolutionary war of the people as a whole against the military. (*IB*, May.)

In Carlos González's view, the experience of the past three years has shown clearly that the best way to produce a reactivation of mass movements is by stepping up the armed struggle. The PGT is so convinced of this that it no longer proposes the creation of political, ideological, and organizational conditions to carry out armed actions. According to González, the PGT now suggests that "it is only through military work" that they can advance "in areas where there are difficulties" for mass organization. González admits that the party's views have been influenced recently by the unification process involving political-military organizations such as the EGP, ORPA, and FAR. The PGT has not abandoned entirely its traditional forms of struggle through mass fronts. However, its leadership now more openly admits that "the possibilities for legal work have decreased." (*El Nuevo Diario*, Managua, 4 October.) Recurrent tensions between the political and military commissions of the party have resulted in a number of splits. No faction is strong militarily, although the PGT maintains strong international links and residual influence in the trade union and student movements.

The PGT dismissed the March coup as a maneuver "inspired by imperialism" to give the military a different image. With no large clandestine press, the PGT has turned increasingly to the kidnapping and ransom of public figures to secure publicity and publication of its political views. In commenting on the spectacular kidnappings of the director of *Prensa Libre* and the son of Guatemala's government minister, a PGT spokesman explained that the party resorts to such activity "only when we have no other means to publicly express ourselves" (Havana international service, 7 August). In one such manifesto, the PGT accused the government of misleading local and international public opinion by attributing the mass murders of Indian peasants to the revolutionary movement. The party charged the army with committing massacres in Quiché, Huehuetenango, Alta Verapaz, and other departments with "as much or more cruelty and cynicism than during previous governments." It accused the army of pursuing a scorched-earth policy of genocide "with the objectives of subduing the peasant villages through terror and depopulating settlements of Indian origin." (*FBIS*, 18 August.)

International Positions and Contacts.   The PGT's positions on international issues follow those of the USSR closely. According to Otto Sánchez, Guatemalan Communists view strengthening the party's solidarity with the Soviet Union and other socialist countries as their primary international duty. The party maintains that by steadfastly supporting the USSR, the international working class "strengthens its solidarity with all the peoples fighting for political emancipation, economic independence, democracy, peace and socialism" (*WMR*, April 1979).

The party's Central Committee declared in August that the "reactionary sector" in Guatemala is "supported and counselled by the armies of the United States, Israel and South Africa." It denounced Washington's efforts to use Guatemala in the regionalization of the conflict in Central America, describing Ríos Montt as "an imperialist puppet and well-known anticommunist who has turned over his country's government to the United States." PGT leader Simón Sánchez denounced Guatemala's membership in the Central American Democratic Community (CDC), criticizing the CDC as "a means to finance an aggressive plan aimed at the siege against Nicaragua." He accused the United States of converting Honduras into the rearguard of an imperialist invasion of Central America and warned that if the United States risks launching an intervention in the region, "it may encounter an anti-imperialist response . . . worse than a Vietnam." (Havana international service, 7 and 20 August.)

Guerrilla Army of the Poor. The EGP undertook its initial military operations in November 1975. Its membership is believed to have increased from an initial 300 to an estimated 1,500 in 1982. Five independent commands operate in the countryside and one in Guatemala City. The formation of a sixth guerrilla front was announced in May to operate in Izabal and Chiquimula departments (ibid., 31 May). The movement's rural fronts were most active in the mountainous regions of Quiché and Huehuetenango in northwestern Guatemala; in Chimaltenango, Sololá, and Alta and Baja Verapaz in the central highlands; near Escuintla, along the tropical Pacific coast; and to a lesser extent, in the department of Zacapa, where the guerrillas had their strongest support in the late 1960s. The EGP's principal leader is César Montes, a member of the Revolutionary Armed Forces until that group was crushed with U.S. assistance during the civilian administration of Julio Méndez Montenegro (1966-1970).

The EGP's principal thesis is that the revolutionary war in Guatemala cannot be conceived without the mass participation of the people. In the absence of legal means for change, EGP leaders believe that securing the support and active participation of Guatemala's Indian population is decisive. The incorporation of the Indians into the people's war and the promotion of guerrilla methods of struggle by Indians in an effort to achieve their liberation is viewed by EGP theorists as Guatemala's fundamental contribution to revolution in Latin America. (Havana international service, 19 January.)

According to EGP leader Carmelo Díaz, the EGP does not have separate political and military organizations. The movement consists of groups that conduct political work and also serve as combat units. According to Díaz, guerrillas operate in urban areas in commando-type combat groups in detachments of 20 to 30 men. For attacks on military barracks and rural operations, the EGP has specially trained groups numbering about 80 men. The EGP's rural fronts rely heavily on peasants to supply food and provide information concerning troop movements and actions taken by local authorities. (*Latinskaia Amerika*, May.)

During February and March, EGP units occupied several towns in the western highlands and carried out acts of sabotage in the capital. In a communiqué sent to news media in May, the EGP termed the government amnesty a "farce" and claimed that it would become "a legal way to attack towns that do not yield to security forces." The communiqué added that "massacres will now be turned into military victories over alleged guerrilla groups that operate in what will be areas under the state of emergency." (ACAN, 31 May.) A former EGP guerrilla who accepted the amnesty claimed that the organization is recruiting young people, especially students, to be sent to Cuba for training. According to the informant, the EGP plans to carry out its final assault in two years when the recruits return from Cuba. (*Prensa Libre*, 1 July.) In July, the EGP charged that the military was using bacteriological warfare in its attempts to massacre the civilian population. Guerrilla leaders called on international organizations to investigate the charges in various municipalities in Quiché, where they claim "thousands" of peasants were killed during the first three months of the army's offensive. (Havana international service, 6 July, 26 August.)

The EGP issued a communiqué in September reporting 47 attacks and harassment operations against army units, the occupation of four villages, and the obstruction of highway traffic. The EGP inflicted 183 casualties on government troops, including 90 killed. In various military operations in Huehuetenango during November and December, EGP forces claim to have killed 160 soldiers and wounded a hundred more (ibid., 29 December).

After nine months in power, the Ríos Montt regime has developed a more systematic approach to counterinsurgency than its immediate predecessors. Military intelligence now provides the army with more accurate data on guerrilla strength, tactics, and movements, enabling special forces to select their targets with much more precision. In areas where military intelligence points to a guerrilla offensive, "preventive terror" has been used effectively. Army and civil defense units masquerading as guerrillas have visited villages, killed indiscriminately, and then returned later in uniform to "rescue the survivors" and organize them into civil defense units (*Latin America Regional Report*, 24 September).

The military's overall policy has had some success, but, despite Ríos Montt's optimism in December, the guerrillas are not yet on the point of defeat. The URNG forces are experienced and still enjoy the advantages of favorable terrain and supply routes through Mexico that are almost impossible to detect. While the guerrillas retain considerable popular support, their leaders are seriously worried about their inability to protect friendly villages from army reprisals and the emphemeral nature of their support in areas where the army has announced grandiose development schemes. Plans to establish liberated zones in areas of long-standing guerrilla strength, such as the Ixil triangle in Quiché, are now seen as premature. Guerrilla organizations have been forced to rethink their strategy, exposing the fragility of the unity agreement reached in February. Fundamental differences still exist between the FAR and the EGP over the best means of using such political organizations as the FP-31 and the Democratic Front Against Repression. Within the PGT, several factions have begun to argue that the limited "freedoms" offered by the government are sufficient to redirect the party's energies away from the armed struggle and toward a revitalization of the trade union movement. There is now general agreement that the revolutionary war will prove much longer than was envisaged earlier in the year.

Washington College   Daniel L. Premo

Guyana

The People's Progressive Party (PPP), the principal opposition party in Guyana, was founded in 1950. In 1969, party leader Cheddi Jagan aligned the PPP unequivocally with the Soviet Union, and in turn, Soviet leaders recognized the PPP as a communist party. Party leaders say that the transformation of the PPP into a Leninist organization began in 1969.

The PPP, which represents mainly Guyanese of East Indian background, is a legal organization in opposition to the ruling People's National Congress (PNC), which represents mostly Guyanese of African background. The PNC is led by Forbes Burnham, onetime PPP member and third-term Guyanese president. Jagan repeatedly charges that the Burnham government represses the Guyanese people and the PPP by violations of basic human rights and specific policies such as obstructing, through indirect press censorship, PPP contacts with the Guyanese people.

The only other revolutionary organization of any consequence in Guyana is the small Working People's Alliance (WPA), led by Clive Thomas, which publishes the paper *Dayclean*. This Marxist-Leninist group disclaims any international affiliation, but maintains close ties to Cuba and many revolutionary parties and governments in the Caribbean.

The PPP is thought to have approximately 500 active and influential members. In the past few years, some blacks have joined the party, while some East Indians have drifted into the PNC, thus diluting the racial orientation slightly. The PPP's Twentieth Congress in August 1979 elected a Politburo, Secretariat, and a 32-member Central Committee. The Politburo (Executive Committee) consists of Cheddi Jagan (general secretary), his wife, Janet Jagan (secretary for international affairs), Ram Karran (labor), Feroze Mohamed (education), Pariag Sukhai (mass organizations), Clinton Collymore (propaganda), Narbada Persaud (finance), Isahak Basir, Rohit Persaud, Cyril Belgrave, Reepu Daman Persaud, and Harry Persaud Nokta. The nine PPP leaders elected to the Guyanese parliament in 1980 were Cheddi Jagan, Janet Jagan, Collymore, Mohamed, Basir, Belgrave, Rohit Persaud, Ram Karran, and Narbada Persaud. The PPP publications are the four-page weekly party organ, *Mirror*, and an irregular quarterly theoretical journal, *Thunder*.

The PPP held its Twenty-First Congress during the first week of August. The congress was attended by 504 delegates and 150 observers, including 29 visitors from the communist parties of the Soviet Union, Cuba, and eighteen other countries. The average age of the delegates was 30 years, the youngest ever. Distinguished service awards were given to Janet Jagan and Ram Karran. (*Mirror*, 8 August.)

At a symposium entitled "The Art of Being the Vanguard," sponsored by the *World Marxist Review*, PPP delegate Clément Rohee stated that "numerical strength is not the sole nor even the most important" factor determining a party's influence and leadership. The PPP is "in the process of transformation from a mass but organizationally loose party into a Leninist party of the new type." Change has been difficult due to limited resources and a lack of trained cadres. The last Central Committee meeting deprived many people of their party membership because they had failed to take an active role in party activities. Patience and correct orientation are needed to overcome the objective obstacles of capitalist relations, traditions, and religions. After the PPP congress, Janet Jagan pointed out that political work is often carried out in working places and from door to door. A top-level Action Committee was set up after the congress to oversee the organizational and ideological strengthening of the party.

Throughout the year, PPP leaders traveled to Soviet-bloc and other countries. Cheddi Jagan was denied entrance to the United States in June when Washington refused to grant visas to Jagan and several hundred other foreigners who wanted to visit the United States as delegates to a meeting of the Soviet-front World Peace Council.

The most important PPP mass organizations are the Progressive Youth Organization (PYO) and the Women's Progressive Organization (WPO). The PYO, traditionally a strong source of personal support for Cheddi Jagan, is headed by First Secretary Navin Chandarpal, a member of the PPP Central Committee. Among its members are Rohit Persaud and Isahak Basir. The PYO, originally called the Pioneer Youth League, celebrated its thirtieth anniversary in September. This "training ground for young Communists" (ibid., 17 June) focuses on the problems of employment, education, equality, and socialism (ibid., 12 September). The WPO is headed by Janet Jagan, Gail Teixeira, and Indra Chandarpal and also concentrates on employment and socialism.

The party exercises considerable influence in the labor movement, particularly through the Guyana Agricultural and General Workers' Union (GAWU), headed by Ram Karran. The GAWU, based in the sugar industry, is the largest union in the country and claims some 20,000 members. In most instances the GAWU cooperates with three other militant unions—the Clerical and Commercial Workers' Union, headed by Gordon Todd; the National Association of Agricultural, Commercial and Industrial Employees, headed by N. K. Gopaul; and the University of Guyana Staff Association, led by WPA leader Clive Thomas. Together they claim to represent 40 percent of Guyana's workers (ibid., 27 September 1981). The four unions are frequently at odds with the Guyana Trades Union Congress and its general secretary, Joseph Pollydore, charging that the congress often collaborates with the state (the largest employer). The GAWU held its Tenth Congress in February (ibid., 7 and 28 February).

The PPP charged in September that "Guyana has now joined Haiti and the Dominican Republic to form the most corrupt, pauperised and bankrupt unholy trinity in Latin America (ibid., 19 September). Guyana is described as a "country of shortages," ranging from food and medicine to jobs and human and political rights (ibid., 17 October); the PPP is particularly critical of government suppression of the press by withholding newsprint (ibid., 31 January, 12 December; *Thunder*, April-June). A study by the WPO stated that three-quarters of Guyanese children under the age of five are suffering from malnutrition and face the danger of mental retardation or an early death (*Mirror*, 12 September). Sixteen years after independence, *Mirror* editorialized (30 May), Guyana is in a "head-long plunge into total disaster!" The congress in August called for the removal of the PNC government and the "establishment of a people's revolutionary democratic government as a necessary step to our socialist goal." This is to be sought by unifying the Guyanese people on several levels: the working class; the workers and peasants; and finally, "the revolutionary alliance of the working class, the peasant farmers, the revolutionary intellectuals and progressive businessmen and middle strata." (Ibid., 8 August.) In October, Cheddi Jagan told the West Indies News Service, "If violence is used against the people, then the people sometimes have to resort to revolutionary violence to remove the government" (*FBIS*, October). In a speech to the Trades Union Congress, Burnham remarked that there was no room in Guyana for subversion (AFP, 30 October; *FBIS*, 3 November).

Specific PPP development proposals include restoration of political and industrial democracy; a shift in trade patterns toward the socialist bloc; a large-scale agro-industrial drive; incentives to farmers and other producers; a freeze on military and police expenditures; a strengthening of the state sector; more exports and job opportunities; assistance to the cooperative sector in productive fields; and workers' control in industry and agriculture (*Mirror*, 5 December).

The PPP joined the PNC in affirming Guyana's sovereignty over the Essequibo territory—some two-thirds of the nation—which is claimed by Venezuela (ibid., 11 July). Otherwise, the PPP criticized Guyana's stand in favor of Great Britain on the Falklands/Malvinas dispute with Argentina and rejected the United States' Caribbean Basin Initiative as simply another ploy of "U.S. imperialism" (ibid., 11 April, 14 November). The PPP hosted a meeting of eleven Caribbean revolutionary parties in August after the conclusion of the PPP congress (ibid., 8 August).

Revolutionary radicalism in Guyana is fostered by the virtual bankruptcy of the national economy, tensions between ethnic and political groups, the political domination of Burnham's PNC, and the ideological objectives of the revolutionary forces.

Hoover Institution   William E. Ratliff

Haiti

Two communist parties were formed in Haiti during the mid-1960s, when two existing Marxist-Leninist parties broke up and a realignment of members occurred. An April 1969 Haitian law declared all forms of communist activity crimes against the state, punishable by confiscation of property and death.

The pro-Soviet Unified Party of Haitian Communists (Parti unifié des communistes Haitiens; PUCH) was formed in 1968. Membership in the PUCH during 1982 was estimated at approximately 350 persons, all of whom were in jail, working underground in Haiti, or active among exiles in Europe, the Soviet Union, and the Americas, particularly Cuba. Primary spokesmen for the party during the year were its secretary general, Réné Theodore, and Secretariat member Max Bourgolly. Gerard Pierre-Charles was the main PUCH representative on the Soviet-front World Peace Council. Other members of the PUCH include party spokesman Frank Hypolitte and Secretariat member Rock Derose, who was arrested at the end of 1981 and held in prison throughout the year despite an extensive campaign conducted for his release by communist parties around the world.

The Haitian Workers' Party (PTH) was founded in 1966 and considered itself Maoist until 1976, when party leaders concluded the Chinese had adopted a revisionist position. The PTH claims to be more influential than the PUCH, and it is thought to have roughly the same number of members. A PTH leader stated in early 1982 that two newer communist organizations had been set up outside the country, namely the 18 May and the Forward groups (*Intercontinental Press*, 22 March).

Haiti is the only American nation on the United Nation's list of the world's 32 least-developed countries. It is estimated that from 40 to 50 percent of Haiti's six million people are unemployed or underemployed. The country has been under the repressive control of the Duvalier family since 1957, when Francois "Papa Doc" Duvalier seized control. When Papa Doc died in 1971, he was succeeded by his son, Jean-Claude "Baby Doc," who then became president-for-life. The Haitian military routed a small invasion force, launched from south Florida, which landed in January on the islands of Tortuga and Turks and intended to go from there to overthrow the government. Police arrested many Haitians during 1982 for questioning (as in the case of friends of short-term finance minister Marc Bazin), generally on the suspicion of subversive activities. In September, Duvalier unexpectedly gave a presidential pardon to the most celebrated prisoners in the country, 22 members of the Christian Democratic Party who had been convicted of sedition and sentenced to fifteen (later reduced to six) years in prison. He also announced that all exiles could get visas to return home. Although not many Haitians returned, hundreds fled the country during 1982, as in years past, generally by boat, often landing in Florida, creating immigration problems with the U.S. government. The Haitian government expressed its enthusiasm for President Ronald Reagan's Caribbean Basin Initiative.

The PUCH, which is part of the so-called Haitian Democratic Union, condemned Duvalier's "liberalization measures," charging that they were simply a ploy to "attempt to split the opposition in exile." A document drawn up by the PUCH Secretariat in May declared that repression continues against unions, the media, and individuals. Repeating a call issued on many occasions, the party stated, "What is needed now more than ever is the unity of action of the democratic forces. The PUCH has always manifested its active support for the establishment of a people's unity front." But, the party noted at midyear, some "forces of the opposition" have turned to armed struggle to replace the dictator. (*Horizont*, East Berlin, no. 27; *FBIS*, 8 July.)

In the area of international affairs, Secretary General Theodore stated in February, shortly after the U.S. government presented the Caribbean Basin Initiative, that the United States had become frightened by the socialist victories in Grenada and Nicaragua and had created the Caribbean program simply to assure its continued dominance in the region (Radio Peace and Progress, Moscow, 24 February; *FBIS*, 26 February). The PUCH maintains close ties to the Soviet Union. It looks on Cuba as the guiding light for revolutionaries in the Caribbean, as Pierre-Charles brings out in his new book, *El Caribe a la hora de Cuba*, published in Havana.

The PTH is part of the Union of Haitian Patriotic and Democratic Forces. According to a leader of the PTH, interviewed in the Trotskyist *Intercontinental Press* (22 March), his is an "anticapitalist party that is carrying out an anti-imperialist, antifeudal and antidictatorial struggle." In order to accomplish its mission, he added, "we feel that it is necessary to prepare for armed struggle." The PTH objects that the PUCH, which supported armed struggle until the "liberalization" announced in 1978, has not reverted to its earlier position despite several subsequent waves of repression.

Hoover Institution   William E. Ratliff

Honduras

The year 1982 may well have been the most important in recent decades for the Honduran Communist Party (PCH) and for the Honduran left in general. The government accused the party of widespread involvement in terrorist activities, and Rigoberto Padilla Rush, the party's general secretary, was forced to flee the country with the security forces in hot pursuit. Padilla Rush's departure in turn apparently led to a struggle within the party to determine his replacement.

Continuing tensions within the region and increasing political-economic tensions in Honduras itself led to a proliferation of leftist groups, most of which included an armed guerrilla component. The rapid growth of such groups during 1982 dramatically increased the number of terrorist incidents in Honduras and infighting among the left's various new factions. This infighting spawned an effort to form a united front among the five major guerrilla groups as had been done previously in Nicaragua, El Salvador, and Guatemala.

The Honduran Communist Party has a history of sporadic persecution and factionalism that generally parallels that of other communist parties in the region. It was organized in 1927 and then disbanded in 1932 during the dictatorship of Tiburcio Carías Andino. In 1957, the party was declared illegal but has managed to function since that time with varying degrees of openness depending on the government in power and the general political situation. In 1971, the broadening rift between the Soviet Union and Communist China led to a split within the party and formation of the Communist Party of Honduras/Marxist-Leninist (PCH-ML). This pro-Chinese faction was relatively inactive during the 1970s but was associated with formation of the Revolutionary People's Front (FPR) and its armed wing, the Lorenzo Zelaya Command, in 1981.

Due to its illegal status, the PCH's size is not known. It may contain as many as 1,500 members, although rapid changes during recent years in the structure of the left may have reduced this number while expanding membership in other left-wing organizations. Most observers doubt that the party was large or influential enough to meet the requirement of 10,000 signatures necessary to register as a legal party under the 1978 electoral law. The party has remained influential within secondary schools and universities as well as within the organized labor movement. It continues to sponsor the Federation of Secondary Students and the Socialist Student Front, which participate in a variety of mass demonstrations and meetings in support of party political goals.

Important changes occurred during 1982 in the leadership of the PCH. Two days after a guerrilla attack on power plants in Tegucigalpa on 4 July, the police attempted to arrest Rigoberto Padilla Rush, PCH general secretary since 1978. Thinking that he had fled his house by car, the police gave chase, only to find that he had slipped out the back door. Padilla Rush's flight into exile apparently led to a struggle over succession with competition for the general secretary's position taking place between Herminio Deras, Héctor Hernández, Mario Turcios, and Miguel Carías (*La Tribuna*, 12 August). This infighting was compounded by the party leaders' continued disagreement over the extent to which violent means should be used to attain revolutionary ends within the current Central American and domestic context. The "conservative" element had at one point included Dionisio Ramos, who left the party in 1980 after failing to convince the leadership that the party should limit itself to encouraging intellectual change. In 1982, Mario Sosa Navarro, who had served as a bridge to other political parties, left for similar reasons. Perhaps due to these increasing problems within the party (and/or government repression), the PCH weekly, *Patria*, ceased publication in the spring.

These developments within the PCH leadership took place within an atmosphere of increasing terrorist activities and acts of political repression by Honduran security forces. In July, the government accused the party of engaging in a broad pattern of terrorist activities designed to destroy power plants, bridges, and highways and of attempting to pollute Tegucigalpa's water supply in some unspecified manner (*FBIS*, 27 July). Party leaders in exile raised their level of rhetoric with regard to the existing domestic situation. In August, the Central Committee issued an appeal to the Honduran working people that noted that the country's problems could not be solved simply by a return to constitutional order. Nor were they directly attributable to the regional crisis or "communist agitators." Rather, Honduran difficulties were due to the exhaustion of the possibilities for economic progress found in the model of dependent capitalism. The Central Committee suggested that the left unite to overthrow the existing government, the government improve the lot of the working class through wage increases and other measures, an agrarian reform program be implemented, and the government end its repressive policies and actions against the left. (Ibid., 4 August.) Rigoberto Padilla Rush later stated the reasons behind the party's new confrontational attitude toward the Honduran government: "No one can accuse the PCH of having adopted an attitude of confrontation with the government because . . . it recognized the validity of the results of the election of November 1981. Despite this, the government has launched a campaign of repression against the people. It is the Liberal government that has institutionalized repression. It began to oppress our people and to violate its promises to the Honduran electorate the very moment it entered into an alliance with the most intransigent and reactionary sectors of the Honduran army." (Ibid., 10 August.) By late September, Padilla Rush was arguing that increased guerrilla activity demonstrated that the people were not afraid of the army and that President Roberto Suazo Córdova's continued kowtowing to the army would probably lead to a military coup (ibid., 28 September).

Other Left-Wing Movements and Activities.   Developments within the PCH during 1982 were partly a result of the proliferation of left-wing groups, some of which had roots in the party itself. As such groups expanded in number and scope of activity, questions concerning ideology and tactics fragmented the party and forced it to attempt to define its role more clearly. What follows is a list of these groups and what is known from scattered sources about their origins, ideology, and activities.

The People's Revolutionary Union (URP) was formed in 1978 as an offshoot of the PCH (*Latin America Weekly Report*, 24 September). It was initially led by PCH member Professor Tomás Nativí,who taught at the National Autonomous University. During the fall of 1981, Honduran security forces seized a number of left-wing leaders including Nativí, and URP General Secretary Fidel Martínez was killed. After these losses, it was assumed that the movement had suffered a fatal blow. (*WP*, 13 December 1981.) However, developments in 1982 suggest that the URP has remained intact and capable of sustained action.

In January, Honduran security forces arrested fourteen youths who they claimed had been recruited by URP member Professor Ramón Amilcar Cerna González. The youths were mostly peasants from the departments of Olancho, Colón, and Copán who were being taken to Nicaragua to receive guerrilla training. The security forces claimed that two other such groups had already received training in Cuba, Nicaragua, and Libya. Their goal was to form a viable party of Central American workers at the regional level.

The most important organization affiliated with the URP is the Movement of Popular Liberation "Cinchonero" (MLP). The MLP was apparently formed in 1978 at the same time as the URP and appears to be the armed wing of this political-military organization. Several accounts of the origin of the name have been given. One suggests that it is named after Serapio "Cinchonero" Romero, who was executed in 1869 after participating in a movement to stop the seizure of peasant lands (*Intercontinental Press*, 4 October). Another traces its roots to an attempt by mine workers in 1886 to retain their jobs with the foreign-controlled Rosario Mining Company (*FBIS*, 27 September). The Cinchoneros first gained international attention when they hijacked a Honduran airliner in March 1981.

On 17 September, twelve Cinchoneros seized the Chamber of Commerce headquarters in San Pedro Sula and took hostage 80 prominent Honduran businessmen and several high government officials who were holding a meeting to discuss the state of the national economy. The guerrillas' demands called for (1) freeing Honduran and Salvadoran political prisoners, (2) ending incursions by the Honduran military into El Salvador, (3) expulsion of foreign military advisers, (4) expulsion of the followers of Anastasio Somoza, (5) repeal of the new antiterrorist law, and (6) Honduran withdrawal from the Central American Democratic Community (*Intercontinental Press*, 4 October). After eight days of negotiations, the guerrillas released the remaining hostages at the San Pedro Sula airport and flew to Cuba by way of Panama.

The Morazan Front of Honduran Liberation (FMLH) has had a sporadic existence since it was initially founded in 1960 as a Castroite splinter group within the PCH. It was restructured in 1969 as a result of differences over tactics that resulted from changing Cuban perspectives on revolution in Latin America. On 16 September, 1979, the FMLH was refounded, apparently as a direct result of the fall of Anastasio Somoza in Nicaragua and the new opportunities that were perceived to exist for revolutionary activity within the region. It is named after Francisco Morazan, a Honduran national hero and liberal active during the early nineteenth century in the movement for Central American unification. Morazan was considered an appropriate ideological symbol because of his fight against foreign domination (British) and against the Honduran oligarchy. The FMLH claims to have two main objectives: seizure of political power in order to change the antiquated structure of dependent capitalism and establishment of a broadly-based mass democracy in Honduras on the basis of a large-scale agrarian reform (*Dialogo Social*, Panama, July). This group has been sporadically active in terrorist activities since 1980 and claims to have gained sufficient strength for a more active guerrilla war phase. Little is known about its leadership and internal structure.

The Revolutionary People's Front (FPR) was founded in 1981 as an offshoot of the PCH/ML. Its armed wing is the Lorenzo Zelaya Revolutionary Command, which takes its name from a peasant leader of the National Federation of Peasants who was killed by security forces in 1965 (*Latin America Weekly Report*, 24 September). The government claims that the Lorenzo Zelaya Command has no separate identity but rather serves as a Honduran adjunct of Nicaragua's Sandinista National Liberation Front. The FPR and Lorenzo Zelaya Command have been active in publicizing the presence of right-wing followers of Anastasio Somoza on Honduran soil.

In January, Honduran security forces claim to have discovered a safe house in Tegucigalpa used by members of the FPR that contained a large stock of small arms and other military equipment (*CSM*, 6 August). In early August, the Lorenzo Zelaya Command claimed responsibility for the bombing in Tegucigalpa of several embassies and the Pan American Life Insurance Building. It has also been active in the city of San Pedro Sula. (*FBIS*, 31 August.)

The Froylan Turcios Revolutionary Command is a new revolutionary group named after a Honduran minister of education who adopted a nationalist and anti-imperialist posture during the 1920s. It claimed responsibility for the bombing of two power plants in Tegucigalpa on 4 July. Six people were killed and $10 million worth of damage done in a display of force that the guerrillas claimed was aimed at getting Honduran troops to leave Salvadoran soil. The Honduran army claimed that there was no Froylan Turcios Command and said that the bombings were the work of Salvadoran commandos associated with the Farabundo Martí Front for National Liberation. The army suggested that the precision and timing with which the operation was conducted were highly reminiscent of the front's operations in El Salvador. (*Los Angeles Times*, 16 July.)

Developments Influencing the Honduran Left. The growth and evolution of the Honduran left (including the communist party) has been heavily influenced by a number of internal and external developments. Internally, Honduras continues to experience mounting inflation, unemployment, and national debt. These economic circumstances have made it difficult for President Roberto Suazo Córdova and the Liberal Party to establish the legitimacy of new civilian institutions. Factionalism continues within both the Liberal and National parties, and political corruption persists. In addition, the new civilian government has chosen to support the armed forces openly in their policy of repressing dissidents through detention and arrest and has allowed the military an increasing role in both political and military decisionmaking.

The Central American crisis impacted Honduras heavily during 1982. Thirty to forty thousand refugees (primarily from Nicaragua and El Salvador) now live in the country. There have been numerous border skirmishes between refugee followers of Anastasio Somoza and Sandinista forces. One indication of the extent to which Honduras has been drawn into the broader regional crisis was the kidnapping of President Suazo Córdova's daughter in December by guerrillas in Guatemala.

To a considerable extent, the growth of the left in Honduras is a function of the convergence of such external developments with existing indigenous movements. Honduras has become a small part of the regional (and international) battleground between left and right and is used by outside groups as a transit route to supply arms to Salvadoran guerrillas. The vastly increased U.S. military and economic role in Honduras during 1982 added to pressure on the existing political system.

New Mexico State University   Steve C. Ropp

Jamaica

Jamaica has essentially a two-party system, consisting of the conservative Jamaica Labor Party (JLP), in power since 1980, and the democratic socialist People's National Party (PNP), which ruled Jamaica between 1972 and 1980. Prime Minister Edward Seaga heads the JLP and is militantly anticommunist. Michael Manley is leader of the PNP, a party known for its rapport with Cuba and the broadly leftist ideological spectrum of its membership. Within this setting, Marxism finds outlets through some of the members of the PNP and in the members of Jamaica's two small communist parties: the Jamaican Communist Party (JCP) and the Workers' Party of Jamaica (WPJ). The JCP was founded in 1975 and is headed by its general secretary, Chris Lawrence. The WPJ was established in 1978 and is led by Trevor Munroe.

Of the two communist parties, the WPJ is the more influential, in part because it is the successor of a previous Jamaican opposition organization, the Workers' Liberation League. The latter was founded in 1974 by a number of small groups who were discontented with the prevailing two-party system and undoubtedly inspired by the then strong leftist political currents at work elsewhere in the Caribbean Basin, notably Cuba. Both the WPJ and the JCP supported Michael Manley in the hotly contested general elections of 1980.

Party Membership and Auxiliary Organizations. The WPJ is a pro-Moscow party, estimated to control 1 to 3 percent of Jamaica's popular vote (*Bridgetown Advocate-News*, 9 March). Key WPJ members include Barry Chevannes, Tony Harriott, Percy Thompson, and Robert Lewis (editor of the WJP newspaper, *Struggle*). Although membership figures in the WPJ have not been published, the party claims that two of every five poor youths and two of every ten workers support communism (*Struggle*, 11 September 1981). Principal WPJ-led mass organizations are the Young Communist League (YCL), the Committee of Women for Progress (CWP), the University and Allied Workers Union (UAWU), and the National Union of Democratic Teachers. The YCL is dedicated to education for unemployed young people (ibid., 19 January, 8 May, 28 August 1981), while the CWP seeks to strengthen the consciousness of women and to lead them in struggles for their rights (ibid., 9 October). The UAWU, founded in 1971, appears to be active in about thirty plants (ibid., 23 October). The general secretary of the UAWU is WPJ leader Trevor Munroe.

Party Internal Affairs. Relations between the WPJ and the PNP, relatively friendly during the Manley years (1972-1980), began to sour following the 1980 general elections. Trevor Munroe reported in 1981 that the relationship between the two parties had "taken a dip," but that cooperation continued "at all levels" (*Marxism Today*, May 1981). By late December 1981, the PNP had distanced itself even more from the WPJ and actually fingered the Marxist party as one of the reasons why it lost the 1980 elections (Caribbean News Agency [CANA], Bridgetown, 17 December 1981). On the eve of the WPJ's Second Congress, held in December 1981, Munroe sought to de-emphasize these differences: "There is a common point in our position to imperialism, but the PNP's relationship with ourself is problematic. In no country in the world where there is a socialist and communist party does it not create problems at different times." He said the WPJ would continue to forge a unity of purpose among the "progressive forces" in the "anti-imperialist struggle," but that the WPJ would at all times maintain its "identity as a worker party." (Ibid.)

The JLP, in attempting to strengthen its own position on the Jamaican political stage, tries to encourage a popular perception of close association between the WPJ and PNP and a predilection for violent activities on their part, despite the obvious friction between the WPJ and PNP. National Security Minister Winston Spaulding alleged in September 1981 that the PNP was in league with the WPJ to carry out "subversive activities," including guerrilla training. The PNP general secretary, D. K. Duncan, rejected these allegations as "dangerous." The bodyguard of Trevor Munroe was arrested during this period on charges of illegal possession of firearms and forged driver's licenses, and the police claimed that "subversive" literature dealing with explosives had been found in Munroe's car, leading them to believe that armed subversive groups using forged documents were active throughout Jamaica. (*Latin America Weekly Report*, 11 and 30 September 1981.) In December 1981, Seaga suggested that there were links between guns found in Jamaica and those used by guerrillas in El Salvador, which could be linked to the PNP (the *Daily Gleaner*, 24 December 1981). These allegations of PNP and WPJ orientations toward armed violence took another form in early 1982. As the rate of violent crime escalated in this period, pro-government journalists and publications, such as the afternoon *Star* (published by the conservative *Gleaner* company), claimed that "many of Jamaica's gun murders were the work of Communists" (*Latin America Weekly Report*, 7 May).

Frictions within the PNP over the question of communist members of the party emerged in late 1982. Dudley Thompson, a high-ranking PNP leader, signaled the start of party infighting by saying that all Communists within the PNP should leave. This position raised questions as to whether D. K. Duncan, the acknowledged leader of the left, would be able to retain his position as general secretary. But the party's National Executive Committee returned Duncan to this position in October, in part because Manley strongly praised his work. The re-election of Duncan, however, did not change the standoff between the PNP and the WPJ, which continued to be fueled by statements from Manley that the PNP intended to fight the WPJ as resolutely as it would the JLP (ibid., 15 October).

Domestic Affairs. Thanks to U.S. backing of the Seaga government, the Jamaican economy experienced its first real economic growth in seven years. The Reagan administration has provided approximately $230 million in loans and direct aid since Seaga took office and has encouraged U.S. businessmen to invest in Jamaica. When President Reagan unveiled the Caribbean Basin Initiative in March, he hailed Prime Minister Seaga's market-oriented government as a model for the Caribbean. During President Reagan's visit to Jamaica in April, Seaga praised the Caribbean Basin Initiative and thanked the United States for its aid and investment (*NYT*, 7 April). But by mid-1982, a number of problems had emerged in the Jamaican economy, which became targets for WPJ and PNP criticism.

Jamaica's economic difficulties took various forms. Demand for Jamaica's bauxite began to plummet, the foreign debt began to soar, and U.S. investment proved sluggish. The foreign debt rose to $2.1 billion, nearly as large as Mexico's debt on a per capita basis, and unemployment reached 26 percent. Many workers were laid off as over 30 Jamaican factories shut down during 1982. Perhaps the biggest problem was the drastic drop in world demand for bauxite, largely because the U.S. aluminum industry—Jamaica's key client for bauxite and alumina—was operating at only 58 percent of capacity during 1982 (*Business Week*, 18 October). Jamaica's economic situation has not been helped by periodic strikes, such as the island-wide sugar strike in April, which affected all eleven sugar factories (*FBIS*, 21 April).

These conditions brought sharp criticism from both the PNP and the WPJ. WPJ leader Trevor Munroe argued that discontent was growing among all social classes in Jamaica, except the very rich, and that discontent was now becoming combined with fear. "The people," he said, "will discover that sooner or later it is impossible to live and that they will need to resist and to remove this government." (CANA, Bridgetown, 30 April.) The WPJ also accused the Seaga government of human rights abuses. Monroe claimed that figures compiled by the Jamaica Council for Human Rights from press reports and police releases demonstrated that 322 persons were killed and 21 wounded by Jamaica's police forces in 1981—an increase of 36 percent over 1980 (*FBIS*, 8 November).

Manley, meanwhile, accused the Seaga government of falsifying unemployment figures. PNP leaders stressed that hardly any of the JLP goals had been accomplished (ibid., 5 November). On this point, the PNP and WJP were united.

Foreign Policy. Prime Minister Seaga broke relations with Cuba in October 1981, an act that brought sharp reactions from the PNP and the WPJ. The PNP's cordial relations with Cuba had led to substantial Cuban participation in school and mini-dam construction, medical programs, and agricultural projects. The PNP stated that a large number of patients in several Jamaican hospitals had come to depend on Cuban doctors; the PNP estimated that Cuban doctors had seen an average of 22,000 patients each month since

1976. The party also said that Cuba had provided construction aid worth more than JCA $40 million (U.S. $22.4), food aid, and programs of joint cooperation between both countries. (Ibid., 2 November 1981.)

The PNP alleged that the break in Jamaica's relations was due either to the direct instructions from the United States or to the JLP's wish to divert attention from the "economic miracle" that was supposed to be occurring (ibid., 13 November 1981). Jamaica's break in relations with Cuba led the PNP to send a delegation to Cuba, headed by former foreign minister and chairman of the PNP, Percival James Patterson, who condemned the action of the JLP government (ibid., 12 November 1981). The WJP also condemned the Seaga government for the break in relations, stating that the JLP sought to win favors from the United States through an undeclared war against Cuba (ibid., 31 October).

The Seaga government defended its decision, stating that it had information that Jamaican students in Cuba were trained in "revolutionary tactics and techniques" with a view to returning Michael Manley and the PNP to power (ibid., 18 November 1981). The Seaga government subsequently denied visas to the Cuban delegation to the Second Congress of the WPJ (*Latin America Weekly Report*, 1 January).

The WPJ articulated a number of foreign policy positions during 1982. It advocated forging an anti-interventionist movement in the Caribbean Basin, accused the Seaga government of pursuing an economic policy dictated by the International Monetary Fund and the World Bank, and severely criticized the U.S. Caribbean Basin Initiative (CANA, Bridgetown, 30 April). As might be expected, the WPJ attacked the United States' foreign policy, accusing it of anticommunist "hysteria" as demonstrated by "mounting U.S. aggressions against Cuba, Nicaragua, and Grenada." The WPJ saw its internationalist duties as rendering moral and political support to these countries and expanding contacts with the communist, workers', and other progressive parties of the region. (*FBIS*, 20 December 1981.) Given the PNP's opposition to the WPJ throughout 1982, however, the range of political options open to Jamaica's key communist party, in foreign as well as domestic policies, was considerably narrower than it had been during the days of the PNP government.

State University of New York   W. Raymond Duncan
College at Brockport

Martinique

The Martinique Communist Party (Parti communiste martiniquais; PCM), founded in September 1957, continued to be an important political force during 1982 in the French overseas department of Martinique. The PCM is led by its longtime secretary general, Armand Nicolas. Among the members of the thirteen-member Political Bureau are Philibert Dufeal, André Constant, G. Lordinot, and Pierre Zobda-Quitman. The Central Committee has 33 members and the Secretariat four. The party is thought to have approximately a thousand members. In December, Political Bureau member Dufeal was re-elected secretary general of the powerful General Confederation of Martiniquan Workers. The PCM held its Seventh Congress in April 1980. Since then, the party claims to have increased its contacts with peasants and young people, telling them how socialism can solve problems the colonial government has failed to eliminate (*WMR*, May). The party's weekly organ is *Justice*.

The PCM has found it easier to work with the French government of François Mitterrand than with that of his predecessor, Valéry Giscard d'Estaing. However, the party claimed it was as hard as ever to get the local officials in Martinique to accept any significant reforms. In order to overcome the strengths of the island's entrenched political leaders, and to overcome a weak economy and sagging buying power for the people, the party has repeatedly called on the leftist organizations of the country to unite. Little unity has been achieved. (*Justice*, 3 June, 11 November.) Unity was needed more by the PCM than by the neighboring Guadeloupe Communist Party since the former is not as strong on its own as the latter. One of the main impediments to PCM expansion was the need to compete for popular support with the famous poet and intellectual Aimé Césaire, head of the Martinique Progressive Party.

The PCM has turned its attention to both immediate and long-term domestic problems, ranging from education (ibid., 30 September) to national self-determination. No party in the French overseas departments was more outspoken in its support for the concept of the Single Assembly (Assemblée unique), which would provide proportional representation in a single legislative body governing the French overseas departments. When the proposal suffered a legislative setback in December, the PCM Political Bureau reacted sharply, noting that the colonial interests of French monopolists and Martiniquan capitalists had triumphed once again (ibid., 16 December).

The PCM did not devote much attention to international affairs, but when it did it took standard Soviet-line positions on all major issues, from criticism of U.S. policies in Central America to the arms race. Some of its leaders visited Soviet-bloc countries and hosted visitors in return. Although the PCM advocates independence through nonviolent means, the party held much-heralded memorial sessions on the twenty-second anniversary of the death of political theorist Franz Fanon. Fanon, a native of Martinique, concluded "the wretched of the earth" could seize their independence only by violent revolution (ibid., 25 March, 1 and 8 April).

The Trotskyist Socialist Revolution Group, led by Gilberto Pago, Philippe Pierre-Charles, and others, is believed to have about a hundred active members. It was founded in 1971 after a split in the PCM. (See *Intercontinental Press*, 18 January.)

Hoover Institution   William E. Ratliff

Mexico

The Mexican Communist Party (Partido Comunista Mexicano; PCM), founded in 1919, is one of the oldest in the world. It used the PCM name from 1920 until late 1981, when it merged with four smaller parties and took the name United Socialist Party of Mexico (Partido Socialista Unificado de Mexico; PSUM). The party was denied official registration from 1946 to 1979, when a new election law stated that any party receiving at least 1.5 percent of the vote in a trial election would be legal and could hold seats in the legislature.

The PSUM—incorporating the former PCM, the Revolutionary Socialist Party (Partido Socialista Revolucionario), the Mexican People's Party (Partido Popular Mexicano), the Socialist Action and Unity Movement (Movimiento de Acción y Unidad Socialista), and the Popular Action Movement (Movimiento de Acción Popular)—has an estimated membership of 120,000. At its First Congress, held in Mexico City in March, PSUM delegates differed over both program and leadership questions. It was concluded that the 75-member Central Committee, 35 of whom came from the old PCM, would select the highest officers, which it did on 16 March when it elected a 21-member Political Commission and a seven-member Secretariat. The latter body included Pablo Gómez (secretary general), Salvador Castañeda (elections), Rolando Cordera (agrarian), Eduardo Montes (information and propaganda), César Navarro (party development), Marcos Leonel (international), and Jesús Sosa (finance and administration). The PSUM weekly paper is *Así Es* (*That is how it is*).

The PSUM campaigned actively in the 1982 elections. Its presidential candidate, longtime PCM Secretary General Arnoldo Martínez Verdugo, secured 3.65 percent of the votes. Miguel de la Madrid, the victorious candidate of the Institutional Revolutionary Party (PRI), took 71.63 percent and the runner-up, Pablo Emilio Madero of the National Action Party, won 16.41 percent. The Trotskyist Revolutionary Workers' Party (PRT) won 1.85 percent and the Socialist Workers' Party (PST) 1.52 percent. The PSUM won eighteen of the proportionally distributed congressional seats, and the PST won nine. (Información Sistemática, Mexico City, 15 August.) (The PCM had won eighteen seats in the midterm congressional elections in 1979, and the PST had taken eleven.) The PSUM was one of several parties to charge irregularities; it claimed it should have had 350,000 more votes than the electoral commission recognized. The PSUM subsequently said that it had really won 5.81 percent of the vote (*WMR*, October).

The primary internal party concern of the PCM in 1981 and of the PSUM after that was achieving the broadest possible unity of leftist forces in Mexico for electoral and other purposes. This unity of the left became increasingly important toward the end of 1982 when the full magnitude of Mexico's economic crisis shook international confidence in the government. As Martínez Verdugo told the *Los Angeles Times* (5 February), "The problem of the left in Mexico is that it has been fragmented. This is the sickness of the left throughout Latin America." The formation of the PSUM had been dictated by the needs of the revolutionary movement, according to an article entitled "How and Why Unification Took Place" (*WMR*, February). But a more broadly based unity remained impossible. Efforts to unite with the Mexican Workers' Party (Partido Mexicano de los Trabajadores) and its popular leader, Herberto Castillo, failed to materialize in 1981 (see *Proceso*, Mexico City, 19 July) or in 1982. The PSUM and the PRT announced an interest in forming an alliance in October (Notimex, 4 October; *FBIS*, 6 October), although there was reason to believe that PRT members are divided on the possibility. On a different level, nine political parties and organizations, including the PSUM, the PST, the PRT, and others, agreed in August to form the National Committee for the Defense of the People's Economy in order to fight for common economic objectives (*Excelsior*, 30 August).

The PSUM does not have a strong position in the labor movement, although party leaders hope that their critiques of the economic failures of the PRI government, including its excessive dependence on Western loans, will change that. Pablo Gómez commented just before the July elections that the left in general was weak in the universities: "There are barely any important student struggles anywhere with well-defined programs and organizations. The university movement is at a low ebb." (Ibid., 2 May.)

Over the decades, many Mexican Communists have been reluctant to adhere strictly to a Soviet (or any other) political line. After 1968, when the PCM condemned the Soviet bloc invasion of Czechoslovakia, it leaned strongly toward an independent—Eurocommunist—position. The PSUM maintained that independence of international pressures in 1982, typical as well of Mexican governments over the decades, although ties existed with the communist parties of the Soviet Union and Cuba. In general the PSUM approved of Mexican government criticism of the elections in El Salvador and of U.S. policy toward Nicaragua, of trade and other accords with Cuba, and other policies. At the same time, it was highly critical of government dependence on the United States and Western Europe for trade and aid.

The PSUM found few occasions to comment on the Latin American guerrillas—particularly from the Southern Cone countries and Central America—who assembled in Mexico to plot the overthrow of governments in Chile, Argentina, Guatemala, and other countries. The party did condemn terrorist killings of Mexicans, including a PST deputy in Veracruz in November.

Hoover Institution   William E. Ratliff

Nicaragua

The ruling party of Nicaragua is the Sandinista Front of National Liberation (Frente Sandinista de Liberación Nacional; FSLN). The FSLN was formed in 1961 by the late Carlos Fonseca Amador as a guerrilla movement. It remained small and divided for years, but in 1968 it challenged the government of Anastasio Somoza Debayle in a civil war and took Managua on 19 July 1979. All the prominent leaders of the FSLN profess to be Marxists, and one of the chief leaders of the movement, Humberto Ortega, declared on 15 November 1981, that "Marxism-Leninism is the scientific doctrine that guides our revolution" (*NYT*, 17 November 1981). After visiting Nicaragua a year later, Carlos Andres Pérez, head of the Latin American section of the Socialist International and former president of Venezuela, stated that "to say that Nicaragua at this moment has a Marxist-Leninist government is an undoubted exaggeration" (ibid., 8 December). Nicaragua does, however, maintain very close relations with Cuba and the Soviet Union and is treated by them as a Marxist-Leninist revolutionary state. There are some 4,000 Cuban advisers in Nicaragua, about half of them military personnel, and a small number of Russian advisers.

Nicaragua maintains the parallel structure of party and state common to Eastern bloc countries, with a loose formal membership (roughly estimated at 40,000) and local and regional organizations. The ruling group within the FSLN, and the actual governing body of the country, is the nine-member National Directorate: Daniel and Humberto Ortega Saavedra, Jaime Wheelock Román, Tomás Borge Martínez, Henry Ruiz Hernández, Bayardo Arce Castaño, Carlos Núñez, Luís Carrión Cruz, and the Mexican-born Víctor Manuel Tirado López. The official governing body of Nicaragua is the three-member National Junta of Government, composed of Sergio Ramírez Mercado, Rafael Córdova Rivas (the only non-Sandinista), and Daniel Ortega, who is the coordinator of the Junta. Some members of the directorate also serve in the cabinet. Humberto Ortega is minister of defense, Tomás Borge is minister of the interior, Jaime Wheelock is minister of agrarian development, Henry Ruiz is minister of planning, and Luís Carrión is vice-minister of interior. Other important ministers of state are Father Miguel D'Escoto Brockman (foreign relations), Virgilio Godoy (labor), Alejandro Martínez Cuenca (foreign trade), Carlos Timmerman (education), and Joaquín Cuadra Chamorro (finance). There is also a Council of State, with largely advisory powers, which is composed of representatives of the FSLN, its various mass organizations, some other political parties, and other interest groups. Sandinista leader Carlos Núñez chairs the council.

Within the FSLN, Bayardo Arce heads the Political Commission, while Dora María Téllez heads the most important of the Sandinista mass organizations, the Sandinista Defense Committees (Comités de Defensa Sandinista), which are organized from the neighborhood to the national level and are supposed to work on various local improvement projects, assist in government campaigns, and maintain vigilance against counterrevolutionary activity. Other mass organizations include the Sandinista Youth 19 July (Juventud Sandinista 19 de Julio) and the Association of Nicaraguan Women (Asociacion de Mujeres Nicaraguenses).

Other parties generally favorable to the Sandinista revolution are the Nicaraguan Socialist Party (Partido Socialista Nicaraguense), a Moscow-oriented communist party founded in 1937, the Independent Liberal Party (Partido Liberal Independiente), and the Popular Christian Social Party (Partido Popular Social Cristiano). These combine with the FSLN to form the Revolutionary Front. There is also a small group called the Communist Party of Nicaragua (Partido Comunista Nicaraguense), which is Trotskyite and generally hostile to the Sandinistas. Twenty-one leaders of this group, including party chief Eli Altamirano, were jailed in October 1981 and released in March 1982. Opposition parties that still functioned at the end of

1982 included the Social Christian Party, the Democratic Conservative Party, and the Social Democratic Party. By a law passed in November 1982, all parties must participate in the Council of State and any party may be outlawed, without any further appeal, by the Supreme Court of Justice. Assets of outlawed parties become state property. The most important opposition movement had been Alfonso Robelo's Nicaraguan Democratic Movement, but its leaders fled abroad in May and suspended all operations in June, charging government persecution.

The Armed Forces.   The role of the military, whose chief is Humberto Ortega, continued to be prominent, given the increasing threats both external and internal that the FSLN government faced. In March, the United States charged that high-altitude aerial photographs revealed that the People's Sandinista Army (Ejército Popular Sandinista; EPS) was making a major military buildup, including lengthening runways to accommodate MiG-21 fighters, which Nicaraguan pilots were alleged to be learning to fly in Eastern Europe. It was also pointed out that many Russian tanks had been delivered. The EPS numbers some 20,000 to 25,000 persons, with about 80,000 more in the Popular Sandinista Militia, which is ill-armed and of dubious fighting quality. The air force consisted in September of three helicopters and an equal number of old training planes. (Ibid., 10 September.) In January, Nicaragua concluded a $17 million agreement with France to purchase two additional helicopters, two patrol boats, and a fleet of trucks (*This Week Central America and Panama*, 11 January). Despite rumors throughout the year that the MiG-21 fighters were coming, they never appeared. In November, the Foreign Ministry announced that the purchase had been called off as a goodwill gesture toward the United States (ibid., 29 November).

Internal Problems.   Due to fears of counterrevolutionaries at home and abroad, the government imposed a state of emergency on 15 March, which was periodically extended throughout the year, giving the government the right to take over means of communication or disband organizations. The government's trouble with the business community and organized labor continued, even though three prominent business leaders arrested in October 1981 were released in March and pardoned by the Council of State in September. The Superior Council of Private Enterprise continued to accuse the government of being unwilling to promote a role for the private sector. The major independent union in Nicaragua, the Nicaraguan Confederation of Workers (Confederación Nicaraguense de Trabajadores; CNT) also had problems with the government, which favored its own union, the Sandinista Workers Central (Central Sandinista de Traba-jadores). Jaime Wheelock warned in January that the CNT "will not be given a chance to prosper" and accused it of treason (Radio Sandino, 27 January; *FBIS*, 1 February). In an apparent government coup against the union, it was announced in September that the "rank and file" had expelled the leadership of the CNT for "political deviation" and placed a pro-Sandinista, Antonio Joaquín Rodríguez, in charge (Radio Sandino, 8 September; *FBIS*, 10 September).

The opposition political parties in the Nicaraguan Democratic Coordination also had frequent difficulties with the government. In October, they called for advancing the elections scheduled for 1985 to 1984, but Daniel Ortega declared the elections of 1985 might be postponed if Nicaragua were at war at that time (*NYT*, 11 October). Humberto Ortega had already warned that the elections would not be a "lottery" to determine who would hold power but would serve to strengthen the revolution. Tomás Borge predicted that "the Sandinistas will last as long as the British monarchy." (*San Francisco Daily Telegraph*, 12 March.)

The government continued to pressure independent news sources. When the state of emergency was declared, all radio stations were put into a "chain" that could broadcast only the government's own news reports. The stations were not allowed to resume independent newscasts until June. Currently, the government owns 17 of the 51 stations in the country (*Los Angeles Times*, 17 September). There are three newspapers in the country, the government's own *Barricada*, the pro-government *El Nuevo Diario*, and the more hostile *La Prensa*, which has been the target of considerable government pressure. It was closed down for the fifth time since the FSLN came to power when, on 14 January, employees allegedly fired on a crowd from the mass organizations of the FSLN protesting outside the building. The paper was allowed to resume operations three days later. Under the state of emergency, *La Prensa*, like the rest of the press, was subject to prior censorship. Despite this it was suspended five more times during the year.

The Sandinista government and both Catholic and Protestant religious groups also locked horns during the year. Although the Catholic church strongly supported the overthrow of Somoza, relations between church and state soon deteriorated. The episcopal conference, comprising all of Nicaragua's bishops and presided over by Msgr. Miguel Obando y Bravo, the archbishop of Managua, frequently condemned the growing authoritarianism of the FSLN. The state responded with verbal abuse, Tomás Borge labeling the bishops "theologians of death" (*This Week Central America and Panama*, 7 June). To counteract the influence of the bishops, the Sandinistas attempted to create a "people's church," a body of Catholic clergy who would work closely with the government and ignore the bishops. Pope John Paul II condemned this as a "grave deviation." The text of his condemnation was not allowed to run in *La Prensa*, though the progovernment papers published it on a back page, along with the government's rebuttal. The strangest incident of the year took place in Masaya on 11 August when a Salesian priest was stripped naked in a house he was visiting and tossed into a waiting crowd of government supporters outside. This led to antigovernment demonstrations in Masaya in which three persons were killed. (*NYT*, 21 August.) The government then seized the Salesian academy in Masaya and held it for a month. Demonstrating a curious evenhandedness, the government also launched a campaign against Protestant evangelical sects and the Mormons, all of whom it labeled "counterrevolutionaries." Twenty churches and other buildings belonging to the Jehovah's Witnesses, the Seventh Day Adventists, and the Mormons were seized in August; many missionaries of these groups, and the Baptists as well, were exiled.

Another problem was the slow pace of agrarian reform during the year. Jaime Wheelock declared in June that he had distributed 45,000 *manzanas* (26,500 acres) of land to peasants, but admitted that at that rate it would take 50 years to distribute the land. He added, however, that the pace would be speeded up and that all the land would be distributed in ten years. (ACAN, Panama City, 28 June; *FBIS*, 30 June.)

The Economy. Nicaragua's economic situation continued to be desperate, with unemployment running at 10 percent and underemployment much higher, an inflation rate of about 25 percent, and a foreign debt that had grown from $1.4 billion when the Sandinistas seized power to a staggering $2.5 billion (*Los Angeles Times*, 25 December 1981). The Nicaraguan government blamed its economic problems on the United States, which Central Bank President Alfredo César Aguirre accused of "economic agression" (*This Week Central America and Panama*, 25 January). But when, following a disastrous series of floods in June, the United States offered aid, Nicaragua refused to accept it. Jaime Wheelock declared that Nicaragua could not accept aid from a country "that wants to destroy Nicaragua and its people" (Managua domestic service, 11 June; *FBIS*, 14 June). Similarly, in August, Managua rejected a U.S. aid package of $5.1 million in loans to the private sector, Deputy Foreign Minister Víctor Hugo Tinaco calling it "a direct interference in our internal affairs" (*Boston Globe*, 31 August).

Loans were forthcoming from other sources, however. During the first half of the year, Nicaragua received $150 million in loans from Western European countries and members of the Organization of Petroleum Exporting Countries (*This Week Central America and Panama*, 31 May). Cuba also supplied $130 million of financial and technical aid (*WP*, 7 April). During 1981, the Soviet Union had provided only 3 percent of Nicaragua's foreign assistance, but in May, Moscow agreed to a $100 million loan with a five-year grace period and $50 million dollars for technical assistance, both at 4 percent interest (*Intercontinental Press*, 24 May). That same month, however, the country was rocked by the resignation of Alfredo César as head of the Central Bank. He had been attempting to aid the private sector, which still accounts for 60 percent of the Nicaraguan economy, and this caused him to feud with Planning Minister Henry Ruiz. Luís Figueroa, said to be loyal to Ruiz, succeeded César. Another blow was the decision of Standard Fruit in October to terminate all operations in Nicaragua. Standard cited heavy losses, but Managua believed that the move was political.

The Contras. Those Nicaraguans who actively oppose the Sandinista revolution by illegal means, either in the country or in exile, are known as *contras*, and they were extremely active during the year. The *contras* include former Somocistas, disillusioned Sandinistas, Indians, and other persons generally opposed to socialism. The umbrella group representing the majority of the contras is the Nicaraguan Democratic Force (Fuerza Democrática Nicaraguense), which includes the 15 September Legion (Somocistas), the Nicaraguan Democratic Union (mostly ex-Sandinistas), and the Indian group known as MISURATA. Contra guerrilla bands are active in such regions as the Matagalpa Mountains and throughout the department of Zelaya. Many others are based in neighboring Honduras and make frequent incursions into

Nicaragua, blowing up bridges, ambushing government patrols, and murdering local officials. This activity was the basis of the state of emergency imposed in March. EPS forces have chased contra bands into Honduras, and this occasioned a strong protest from that country in January. Nicaragua believes the Honduran government is deeply involved in contra activity and Foreign Minister D'Escoto accused Gen. Gustavo Alvarez, the head of the Honduran army, of direct complicity (ACAN, Panama City, 25 July; *FBIS*, 27 July). In July, after heavy border raids, Interior Minister Borge warned that some 5,000 contras were poised to attack from Honduras (*CSM*, 16 July). Evidence of U.S. involvement in the activities of the contras surfaced in 1982, first in the *Washington Post* (10 March), and then in *Newsweek* (8 November). Both said that the CIA had been allocated $19 million for its efforts to train and equip contras in the border camps. Neither report was denied by Washington; a CIA spokesman offered the clarification that "we are trying to keep Managua off balance and apply steady pressure to stop providing military aid to the insurgents in El Salvador" (*This Week Central America and Panama*, 8 November). How much aid Nicaragua was supplying to the Salvadoran rebels was a matter for speculation, but Washington plainly felt that this aid justified the covert operation in Honduras, even though these acts give the Sandinistas an excuse to curtail liberties and create widespread popular support for the FSLN among the nationalistic Nicaraguan people.

One person whom the contras of the FDN had counted on to join them apparently decided to go his own way. Edén Pastora, one of the FSLN's top battlefield commanders, left Nicaragua on 7 July 1981. He surfaced in Costa Rica on 15 April, denouncing the Nicaraguan government for betraying the revolution and for lacking respect for political pluralism and human rights (*NYT*, 16 April). He subsequently formed an independent contra group, the Sandinista Revolutionary Front. Costa Rica, however, expelled him, and he was forced to go to Mexico. He then dissolved his organization on 27 July and sought asylum in Costa Rica. His plans from that point on remained in doubt. However, his fellow exile, Alfonso Robelo, announced in June that he was joining the armed contra movement.

The Miskito Problem.   Closely related to the problem of the contras is that of the Miskito, Sumo, and Rama Indians in the Atlantic coast department of Zelaya. Tribal peoples, but by no means primitives, they are an admixture of Indian, Caribbean black, and some European stock and speak English as well as their Indian languages. Most are Protestants belonging to the Moravian sect. Left alone by Somoza, they deeply resent the attempts of the Sandinistas to impose the Spanish language on them through their literacy program and to substitute government cooperatives for the Indians' traditional communal farming patterns. As many as 10,000 have fled to Honduras, and of these many have taken up arms in contra groups. The government of Nicaragua decided on the forced resettlement of those communities near the Honduran border and marched an estimated 85,000 Indians to camps in the interior, where they were reported in September to be short of supplies (ibid., 5 September). Seventy-one Indians were sentenced to prison for counterrevolutionary activity in March.

Foreign Affairs.   Government leaders continued to scurry abroad seeking loans, supplies, and arms. Daniel Ortega, Henry Ruiz, and Miguel D'Escoto went to Moscow in May and obtained considerable aid. At the same time, Sergio Ramírez toured Western European capitals, Carlos Timmerman visited the Vatican in an attempt to improve relations, and Víctor Manuel Tirado went to Eastern European capitals and then to Vietnam. Daniel Ortega was in France in July to confirm the arms deal and met with President François Mitterrand, who remains a firm supporter of the FSLN. Foreign Minister D'Escoto was at the United Nations in August, condemning the "Zionist regime" of Israel for its activities in Lebanon. He also went to Mexico to press for a revival of the Mexican initiative for talks with the United States.

The deep hostility between the United States and Nicaragua continued to dominate the foreign affairs of the FSLN. Repeated efforts from Managua to open a dialogue went nowhere. Ambassador to the United States Francisco Fiallos Navarro informed Washington in March that Managua was ready to begin talks on the basis of a plan by which Nicaragua would cease to supply the Salvadoran rebels in return for a U.S. pledge to restrain the contras, but Washington did not accept the proposal (*CSM*, 16 April). President José López Portillo of Mexico advanced a plan by which Nicaragua would reduce its military forces in return for a curtailment of contra activity, but Washington did not regard this as a serious offer (*This Week Central America and Panama*, 26 April). Nicaragua strenuously renewed its call for talks in July, and a State

Department spokesman conceded that "the ball is in our court" (*NYT*, 8 July). By then, it was evident that talks were unlikely as long as the Salvadoran civil war continued. Despite intense lobbying by the United States, Nicaragua easily won a seat on the United Nations Security Council in October.

The Sandinistas' foreign policy suffered a severe propaganda blow when Ambassador Fiallos in an interview with the opposition *La Prensa*, roundly criticized his own government, calling it a leftist dictatorship, urged drastic changes in the direction of participatory democracy, and called for a dialogue between the FSLN and Edén Pastora. He was promptly dismissed on 19 December. (Ibid., 22 December.)

Eastern Connecticut State University   Thomas P. Anderson

Panama

The year under review found the communist People's Party of Panama (PPP) continuing to adjust to its new legal status and to the national struggle for political power that followed the death of Gen. Omar Torrijos on 31 July 1981.

The PPP was founded in 1930 by José María Blasquez de Pedro, a Spanish émigré. It is now under the leadership of Rubén Darío Souza, who was re-elected to the position of general secretary at the extraordinary legalization congress held in July 1981. Because of the government's desire to have a number of political parties supporting it and the PPP's miraculous ability to produce needed signatures, it is difficult to determine the real extent of the PPP's support. Party membership is estimated at around 500–600.

Party Affairs. The PPP was banned from 1953 to 1968 but continued to operate with varying degrees of openness depending on existing government policy. Following the 1968 coup that brought Torrijos to power, the PPP gave its support to the government, and individual party members were recruited to serve in some ministries. Although the party was denied formal recognition along with all of the other traditional parties, it was given special status as an important element in Torrijos's political coalition.

After promulgation of a new constitution in 1978, the PPP moved toward the achievement of legal recognition along with other parties. It was finally granted full legal status on 13 August 1981 after having obtained the 30,000 signatures required by law.

After legalization, the party sought to expand its traditionally narrow organizational base by developing a new experimental outreach program. The Political Bureau made the decision to launch an ideological education campaign that was to last for four months and to include not only party members but potential supporters among the masses. (*WMR*, February.) Recognition as a legal political organization required that the party adopt new tactics and techniques aimed at broadening its electoral support base. The struggle for political power created problems for the Communists as some aspirants for leadership within the National Guard and within the larger political parties sought approval and support from the United States by verbally demonstrating their anticommunist credentials. At the same time, the attempt by such aspiring leaders to construct a broad base of national support meant that the Communists were sometimes courted and continued to hold influential government positions.

Since the death of Torrijos, the party leadership has attempted to maintain its ties to groups within the governing coalition that remain sympathetic to the left, but at the same time divorce itself from conservative elements. Political Bureau member Miguel Porcel stated: "Our attitude to the government could be described as one of critical support with the important specification that we consider ourselves active participants in the democratic process. The nation's present leadership represents diverse forces. The Communists, while supporting the government's progressive measures, firmly resist the anti-popular and anti-labor activity of rightists who have wormed their way into the highest echelons of power." (Ibid.)

At the cabinet level, the party lost some of its strongest allies in the shuffling of positions that followed the July retirement for health reasons of President Arístides Royo. However, Raúl Rodríguez, a member of the PPP Central Committee, was appointed minister of housing (*Dialogo Social*, September). According to one report, he had been expelled from the party shortly before his appointment (*FBIS*, 5 August).

International Relations.   The party continued its strong support for the policies of the Soviet Union. In late December 1981, a party communiqué suggested that the measures taken by Gen. Wojciech Jaruzelski in Poland were timely and would serve to guarantee the survival of socialist democracy in that country (ibid., 21 December 1981). Two months later, the party vigorously protested to the Panamanian minister of foreign affairs when two Soviet scientists were granted asylum in the U.S. Embassy (ibid., 11 February). Perhaps the most important development internationally was a meeting between Costa Rican and Panamanian Communists in October. A joint communiqué on Central America noted that the regional crisis was the project of dependent capitalist economies. It further suggested that Central American peoples should have the right to self-determination and that the Farabundo Martí National Liberation Front be recognized as representing the true interests of the Salvadoran people. (Ibid., 3 November.)

Marxist Party.   During 1982, the pro-Chinese faction of the Panamanian Communists (Communist Party/Marxist-Leninist; PC-ML) launched a virulent attack against the leadership and policies of the orthodox pro-Soviet faction. Rodrigo Morales, a member of the PC-ML Reconstruction Bureau and Central Committee accused Rubén Darío Souza and other key PPP figures of being neo-Solanists who had perpetuated themselves in power since the early 1950s when Celso Solano led the party. Morales further claimed that the PPP had turned into a collaborationist and right-wing fascist party that did not serve the interests of the people. The PC-ML would continue, he said, to struggle as it had since 1973 to return Panamanian communism to a truly revolutionary course. (Ibid., 19 April.)

Developments Influencing the Left.   Developments on the left have been influenced by the increasingly open struggle for power that has taken place in the wake of Torrijos's death. Liberal and conservative factions existed within the official Democratic Revolutionary Party, the National Assembly, and the National Guard. President Arístides Royo pursued policies both domestically and internationally that were more appealing to the liberals, including a call for expanded diplomatic relations with communist countries. In January, Foreign Minister Jorge Illueca suggested that Panama's lack of formal diplomatic relations with Communist China and the Soviet Union was increasingly anachronistic. It is widely believed that it was the administration's pursuit of improved diplomatic relations with such countries, coupled with criticism of the policies of the United States, that led to President Royo's removal by the National Guard in July. The fact that conservative businessman Juan José Amado replaced Illueca as foreign minister supported such an interpretation.

General Rubén Darío Paredes emerged as a leading contender to replace Omar Torrijos and to run for the presidency in the 1984 election. Paredes is relatively conservative and has stated that communism will not be allowed to enter Panama. In September, he issued a warning to Havana with regard to the continued Cuban military presence in Nicaragua, arguing that this presence threatened Panama's vital interests since the United States would not be inclined to return the canal to Panamanians in the year 2000 (*La Nación Internacional*, 7-13 October). However, in spite of considerable right-wing posturing and rhetoric, there were few signs that General Paredes or the government led by President Ricardo de la Espriella intended to sever ties to the left either domestically or internationally. Domestically, the left (broadly defined) remained a critical base of political support that Paredes could not relinquish to his rivals within the National Guard. In August, he met with PPP leaders including Rubén Darío Souza, indicating that he intended to deal with and represent all political sectors (*La República*, 22 August). Internationally, Ricardo de la Espriella's visit in November to Nicaragua and Mexico defined the limits of Panama's drift to the right. De la Espriella supported Cuban membership in the Organization of American States, criticized the United States for intervening militarily against the Nicaraguan Sandinistas through Honduras, and backed the Mexican-Venezuelan peace proposals for Central America (*FBIS*, 12 November).

New Mexico State University   Steve C. Ropp

Paraguay

The Paraguayan Communist Party (Partido Comunista Paraguayo; PCP), founded in 1928, has been illegal during most of its history, and today the majority of its estimated 3,500 members are in exile. Nevertheless, periodic arrests of Communists inside Paraguay serve as reminders that an underground movement persists there. The PCP was weakened in the early 1960s when it split into pro-Soviet and pro-Chinese factions. Each faction was headed by one of the party's two original founders. Obdulio Barthe became a rallying symbol for those Communists remaining loyal to Moscow, while Oscar Creydt led those who broke away to find inspiration in the more radical approach to revolution represented by Beijing. The latter group had become increasingly critical of Moscow's advocacy of peaceful, gradualist tactics. Rather than working through broad, popular coalitions that included bourgeois reformers—as, for instance, Communists in Chile have—Creydt's pro-Chinese Communists preferred to proceed toward mass insurrection by working closely with peasants and proletarians, urging them to organize.

The pro-Chinese faction received a severe setback in March when the Paraguayan police discovered one of its rural cells. Thirty Communists were arrested; nine others who escaped were being hunted in nearby forests. Some of the guerrillas later made public confessions in which they told how they had been trained in China and then set to foment revolution in the Paraguayan interior. They had been particularly active in the provinces of Caaguazú and Caazapá, where some violent incidents had recently occurred. In addition to capturing the guerrillas, the police reportedly discovered a printing press, a large amount of revolutionary literature, and a "people's prison" for hiding kidnapped persons while ransom was being arranged. (Asunción Teledifusora, 15 and 16 March; *FBIS*, 16 and 19 March.)

The pro-Soviet faction of the PCP also had its problems. Its titular leader, Barthe, died in December 1981, and its first secretary, Antonio Maidana, has been missing since his arrest on 17 August 1980 in Buenos Aires. He, along with Emilio Roa, a labor organizer and member of the PCP Central Committee, had been picked up by the Argentine military. Neither man has been heard from since. Some people thought they had been killed, but in a January radio broadcast from Moscow, Ananias Maidana, the missing leader's brother, claimed that the two men had been turned over to Paraguayan authorities. He said that they had been held at a prison about 40 km outside Asunción, but had recently been transferred to an island prison camp deep in the northern jungles. Later, in April, he reported that his brother and Roa were at a military fort near the Bolivian border. (*World Affairs Report* 12, no. 2, p. 216.)

Meanwhile, the pro-Soviet Communists were still trying to gain admittance to the National Accord, Paraguay's four-party opposition coalition. Like almost everyone else in Paraguay, the PCP senses the approaching end of the Stroessner era and wants to be in a position to make the most of any opportunities that arise during the transition. There have been persistent rumors from many quarters that Gen. Alfredo Stroessner's health is failing. For example, National Accord spokesman Luís Resck of the Christian Democratic Party recently claimed that he had been reliably informed that Stroessner had a severe heart condition and was having difficulty moving his right arm. Such assertions ought to be taken with some skepticism. Earlier in the year, some members of the opposition predicted that Stroessner's health would keep him from running for another presidential term. He later accepted the Colorado Party's nomination. Nevertheless, the general was 70 in November, and it is clear that his departure cannot be very far off. There are signs of his loosening grip in the government's inability to keep the economy under control: inflation is rising, the currency recently had to be devalued, and businessmen—in a rare show of defiance—are demanding relief from the government's tight-money policy. Even in the normally docile Paraguayan Labor Confederation, Stroessner's control is being challenged by an antigovernment Group of Nine. It is questionable whether the PCP or the National Accord can take advantage of these problems, however. Leaderless and isolated, the Communists are not likely to be a serious threat. The parties composing the National Accord are said to be squabbling among themselves, as personal and doctrinal differences undermine their quest for unity. (Ibid., 12, no. 1, pp. 70-71; *Quarterly Economic Review*, 1st Quarter, 1982, pp. 3, 11-12; *New Times*, January, pp. 12-13.)

Newcomb College   Paul H. Lewis
Tulane University

Peru

The Communist Party of Peru (PCP-U) continued to function as a legal opposition movement during 1982. Pushed by the growing militancy of the main communist labor federation, the General Confederation of Peruvian Workers (CGTP), it moved toward a harder pro-Soviet line, however, in the midst of growing economic difficulties and political turmoil.

There was a major shakeup at the party convention of 27-31 January. After 25 preliminary regional meetings, 230 delegates met in Lima for the PCP-U's Eighth Extraordinary Party Congress, with the slogan, "For a more Leninist and Mariáteguist [after José Carlos Mariátegui, founder of the PCP] party" (*Oiga*, 25 January, p 37). Representing the party's 10,000 members (ibid., p. 39), the delegates agreed unanimously to boycott any effort to establish a social pact, to reject the National Labor Council (CNT— the Belaúnde administration's effort to bring labor, management, and the government together to work out labor problems), to adopt forms of struggle other than the strike as circumstances require, and to recognize that the electoral path is not the route to seizing power. They also agreed to enter, as needed, "circumstantial alliances" with the centrist American Popular Revolutionary Alliance (APRA) party and supported the military authorities in Poland (ibid., 8 February, p. 28.) The results of the congress signaled the defeat of more moderate factions seeking some independence from Moscow and their replacement by supporters of a much harder political line.

This was reflected in the substantial changes in the composition of the Central Committee of the PCP-U. Longtime Secretary General Jorge del Prado escaped being deposed by only a few votes. Others were not as fortunate. Among those expelled were financial official Mario Ugarte Hurtado (dishonorably), 25-year-veteran Under Secretary General Raúl Acosta Salas, economist José Martínez, ex-*Unidad* editor Alfredo Abarca, ex-bank union leader Antonio Zúñiga, trade union leader Pedro Mayta, Ivan Méndez, Raúl Núñez, Ernesto Rojas, and Manuel de Priego. The new committee is expected to be controlled by Gustavo Espinoza Montesinos, Guillermo Herrera, Asunción Caballero Méndez, Jorge del Prado, Olivera Vila, and Isidoro Gamarra. It also includes Roberto Rojas, Valentín Pacho, Julián Serra, Jaime Figueroa, Víctor

Checa, Antonio Torres Andrade, César Alva, and Carlos Bonino, along with the president of the United Left (IU), Alfonso Barrantes Lingan. (Ibid.; *Opinión Libre*, 4 February, p. 7; *Unidad*, February.)

Party leaders felt that major internal adminstrative problems had been resolved as a result of the congress and that the party was entering a new stage and now was prepared to meet new challenges in Peru much more advantageously. The election of Alán García as head of APRA signaled a victory for that party's more progressive elements. This increased the possibility of some "tactical alliance" between APRA and the IU, though probably not until after each party or grouping tested its strength in the November 1983 municipal elections. Midyear opinion polls showed popular support for the IU and the rest of the Marxist-Leninist left at 9 percent and for APRA at 16.9 percent. The ruling Popular Action Party had 16.8 percent and the conservative Popular Christian Party 13.1 percent. (*Caretas*, 5 July, p. 15.) With a worsening of the economic situation, increased strikes, and terrorism as the year progressed, PCP-U Secretary General Jorge del Prado appeared to take a public position more sympathetic to the radical left than had previously been the case. He opposed the establishment of states of emergency and noted that "the people's struggle grows more intense every day and is on a good path" (*FBIS*, 3 September).

In the international arena, a delegation led by IU leader Barrantes visited China and Cuba at the end of 1981, and PCP-U Secretary General del Prado traveled to Eastern Europe in mid-1982. In statements to the East German and Hungarian media, del Prado emphasized the themes of the anti-imperialist strategy, the importance of a united left in Peru with a joint action program, and the working-class backgrounds of the new Central Committee members (*Horizont*, East Berlin, no. 15, p. 12; *Népszabadság*, Budapest, 13 July, p. 3). In addition, the IU followed up on proposals made in Mexico City in October 1981 to establish a continental secretariat for South American leftist parties by holding a three-day meeting in Lima in August. Delegations from Argentina, Bolivia, Brazil, Chile, Ecuador, Paraguay, Peru, and Uruguay attended. In their Declaration of Lima, they expressed their solidarity with Cuba, Grenada, and Nicaragua against threats from the United States and their support for guerrilla and popular front groups in El Salvador to hold talks to try to find a political settlement. They also denounced the pro-colonialist stand of the United States in the Malvinas/Falklands crisis and established a standing commission to study the major problems of South America. (Tass, 17 August.)

Domestic Affairs. Of great concern to the more moderate Marxist-Leninist left, as well as to the government and the population at large, was the dramatic increase in terrorist incidents attributed to or claimed by Shining Path (Sendero Luminoso; PCP-SL). The most radical of all 24 Marxist-Leninist parties operating in Peru, the PCP-SL announced in March the unleasing of a popular war in Peru (*La República*, 12 March). For the first time, the clandestine organization claimed responsibility for a terrorist action, the dramatic assault by some 150 armed militants on Ayacucho Prison, in which 16 died and 247 prisoners were freed (of whom 54 were subsequently identified as terrorists (*FBIS*, 9 March; *Latin America Weekly Report*, 12 March, p. 7). The Ayacucho jailbreak marked the beginning of a series of direct confrontations by terrorists, as the government prefers to call them, with police and public officials. They occurred in various parts of the country with mounting frequency and loss of life, centered primarily in Ayacucho, Apurímac, Huancavelica, and Lima. Minister of the Interior Gen. (ret.) José Gigliardi, reported to the Peruvian congress that between January and the end of August there had been 263 terrorist incidents in Lima and 147 in Ayacucho alone, with 42 deaths (eighteen policemen, one soldier, and 23 terrorists) (*Latin America Weekly Report*, 10 September, p. 6). Other reports noted over 3,000 raids on government offices, foreign embassies, private businesses, and public utilities during the Belaúnde government's two years in office (*Los Angeles Times*, 29 August).

There were new spates of incidents in September and again in December. In symbolic acts of supreme defiance of authorities, PCP-SL activists caused almost total blackouts simultaneously in both Lima and Ayacucho to ring out the year and to celebrate PCP-SL leader Abimael Guzmán's birthday, with lighted hammers and sickles on hills overlooking both cities (*Latin America Weekly Report*, 10 December, p. 4). With the escalation of violence and the apparent inability of police forces to deal effectively with it, at year's end the Belaúnde government and the armed forces officer corps ended their long reluctance to get the military directly involved in operations against Shining Path. On 29 December, President Fernando Belaúnde Terry signed a decree declaring a 60-day state of emergency in five provinces of Ayacucho (Huanta, La Mar, Cangallo, Víctor Fajardo, and Huamanga), the province of Andahuaylas in Apurímac, and Angaraes in Huancavelica, which placed the military in charge of internal order in those isolated Indian highland areas (*FBIS*, 3 January 1983). It remained to be seen whether the military would be able to repeat its rapid success in 1965 against three guerrilla fronts in the highlands.

The progression of violent activity by PCP-SL follows the phases of the armed struggle set forth by the organization's maximum leader, Comrade Gonzalo (Abimael Guzmán). With the Ayacucho jailbreak, the third phase, "generalization of violence and development of guerrilla war," began. The period beginning after the March 1980 decision to "attack the symbols of the bourgeoisie state and of revisionist elements" had been the second stage. The seventeen years of preparation before that, primarily in Ayacucho, was the period of the first stage, "converting the backward areas into advanced and solid bases of revolutionary support." Those still to come are "the conquest and expansion of the bases of support" and "the seige of the cities and the total collapse of the state." (*Caretas*, 20 September, pp. 20–23, 64, 65; *Latin America Regional Report*, 8 October, p. 2.)

Amid considerable strike activity early in the year, the Belaúnde administration announced formation of a new National Labor Council and Social Pact (CNT), which was designed to mediate labor disputes through the participation of labor, management, and the government (*El Comercio*, 21 February). In spite of the best efforts of popular Minister of Labor Alfonso Grados Bertorini, successful on several past occasions in securing communist union involvement, the CGTP refused to participate from the start. However, the other major federations did, including the velasquista (after President Juan Velasco Alvarado, 1968–1975) Confederation of Workers of the Peruvian Revolution and the APRA-led General Confederation of Workers. By October, nevertheless, the noncommunist labor representatives had followed the CGTP's lead, adducing that, because of government economic policy, the CNT had failed to promote concerted social action (*FBIS*, 14 October).

As inflation rose back to 1981 levels of over 70 percent, strike activity increased, involving for the first time on a national level the leading peasant organizations, the Marxist-Leninist Peruvian Peasant Federation and the velasquista National Agrarian Confederation. In late November, they were joined by the north coast sugar cooperative labor groups, Fendecap and Fetap, in a two-day strike protesting low farm prices. Their tactics included blocking major highways to prevent produce from reaching Lima (*Latin America Weekly Report*, 3 December, p. 3).

The 3,000-odd industrial communities dating from the Velasco administration voted in December by a four-to-one margin to keep the communities intact. The government had proposed a substantial increase in profit sharing (from 10 to 17 percent), and the repurchase by companies of labor shares, in exchange for the elimination of the industrial communities, a move favored by industrialists (*Latin America Regional Report*, 17 December, p. 3).

Foreign Service Institute   David Scott Palmer

Puerto Rico

The main Puerto Rican revolutionary organization is the Puerto Rican Socialist Party (Partido Socialista Puertorriqueño; PSP). The PSP is headed by Secretary General Juan Marí Bras, a close friend of Fidel Castro's, who has often visited Cuba with much fanfare over the years, and President Carlos Gallisa, also a frequent visitor in Havana. The party, with an estimated membership of about 150, held a congress in 1979 and elected a Secretariat, Political Bureau, and Central Committee. In the November 1980 elections for governor, the highest elective office in Puerto Rico, PSP candidate Luís Lansell Hernández received 0.3 percent of the vote. The PSP publishes the paper *Claridad*. The chief issue in PSP politics is its conviction that "the first necessary step towards socialism in Puerto Rico is the winning of independence and the establishment of a state guided by our people's national and social interests" (*WMR*, September). The PSP is thought to have insisted (through Cuba) that a vote on independence be taken in the U.N. General Assembly even when it was clear the loss would be humiliating, if instructive (*Latin American Weekly Report*, 1 October).

The Puerto Rican Communist Party (Partido Comunista Puertorriqueño), with an estimated 125 members, is a pro-Soviet party with close ties to the Communist Party, USA. Two small parties of Trotskyist orientation are the International Workers' League and the Puerto Rican Socialist League (LSP). The LSP was founded in 1964 and is led by Juan Antonio Corretjei; it reportedly has ties to the Progressive Labor Party of the United States.

The main terrorist groups associated with Puerto Rico are (1) the Armed Forces of Puerto Rican National Liberation (Fuerzas Armadas de Liberación Nacional Puertorriqueña), which specializes in bombings in the United States and whose actions have ranged from the deadly bombing at a tavern in Manhattan in 1975 to a series of bombs exploded at government buildings in Manhattan and Brooklyn on 31 December; (2) the Boricua Popular Army, the Macheteros ("machete wielders"), who bombed a number of power installations in Puerto Rico in November 1981; and (3) the Armed Forces of Popular Resistance.

Several political, social, and economic factors encourage the growth of revolutionary, even terrorist, groups in the United States' commonwealth of Puerto Rico. One is the depressed state of the economy. Existing economic problems, such as high unemployment, have been exacerbated by some policies of the Reagan administration. According to commonwealth leaders, the Caribbean Basin Initiative, which was before the U.S. Congress for the last eleven months of 1982 and which is intended to boost sagging economies in the region, would further cripple the Puerto Rican economy (ibid., 19 February; *WP*, 3 August).

The nature of the special relationship between the Spanish-speaking island and the United States, in a region that is particularly sensitive to real or imagined colonialism, virtually invites criticism from some quarters. (This is so even though as recently as 1980 the political parties supporting commonwealth and statehood each won 47 percent of the vote in an island-wide election, while the pro-independence forces got only 6 percent.) Even though the United Nations recognized the noncolonial character of the commonwealth status in 1953, pro-independence groups in Puerto Rico, generally with strong backing and even encouragement from Cuba, have repeatedly pressed the U.N. General Assembly to discuss the "colonial" status of the island. The Cuban press called the 1981 decision to discuss the issue in the General Assembly during 1982 the most important contribution to the Puerto Rican self-determination effort of the year (*Granma*, English edition, 3 January). But when the vote came before the Assembly on 24 September, the effort to declare Puerto Rico a colony was defeated by a vote of 70 to 30, with 43 abstentions. When President Reagan announced in January that he would support statehood for Puerto Rico if the people there expressed a preference for this in a free and democratic election, Cuba responded that this was more "gunboat diplomacy." According to Cuba, Reagan's proposal "is based on an extremely dangerous concept of US imperialism, which denies so-called small nations the right to establish their sovereign states and shape their destiny on their own." (*WMR*, April.)

Hoover Institution   William E. Ratliff

Suriname

The Communist Party of Suriname (CPS) is a tiny dissident organization in a country ruled by one of the Caribbean's most turbulent revolutionary forces, the Revolutionary Front of Suriname (RFS) under the leadership of Lt. Col. Desi Bouterse. The pro-Albanian CPS was founded in July 1981 and is led by Bram Mehr. Its membership may be around 50. As editor of the party paper, *Modro*, Mehr has accused Bouterse and the RFS of political vacillation, and on at least one occasion, the government responded by putting the CPS head in jail for a week (*Latin America Regional Report*, 7 May).

Bouterse and the RFS found Mehr a mere skirmish in a much broader battle to achieve political supremacy in the former Dutch colony. (Suriname, with its current population of approximately 400,000, became independent in 1975.) The leftist officers of the Suriname National Military Council seized power and set up a government in February 1980. Bouterse soon became the dominant power—his RFS was formally founded in December 1981—and instituted policies threatening to the traditional political, social, and economic forces in the country. Thus began a series of attempted coups against the military leaders, including two major efforts in 1982, which have resulted in the elimination of many opposition leaders, ever tighter government control of all aspects of the nation, and increasing support from Cuba and Soviet-bloc countries generally. The Cuban Communist Party paper *Granma* (16 May, English edition) called Suriname "a country in revolution," and pro-Soviet Communist Cheddi Jagan in neighboring Guyana remarked that Suriname "has joined the other shining outposts of revolution in the Caribbean—Cuba, Nicaragua and Grenada" (*Mirror*, Georgetown, 7 February). The Soviet Union, which established diplomatic relations with Suriname in 1978, opened an embassy in Paramaribo in early 1982.

Major showdowns during 1982, in the midst of a stagnating economy and a generally unsettled political scene, came in March and December. Bouterse dismissed the Suriname president and other government officers in February. An armed uprising on 11 March was put down with several deaths and the execution of the rebel leader. In April, an army-led Policy Center was set up to make decisions during the transitional phase to a new democratic order. Late in the year, the RFS and its international supporters charged that exiles in Holland, the so-called Committee to Restore Democracy in Suriname, were planning a counterrevolutionary invasion of the country. Some alleged that the U.S. Central Intelligence Agency was behind it all (ibid., 7 November). The Moederbond (Mother Union—the largest trade union in the country, with 36 affiliates—launched a major strike in early November to coincide with the visit to Suriname of Grenada's prime minister, Maurice Bishop. Then in early December, the government announced that it had uncovered a coup plot planned for Christmas Day. The government admitted that more than a dozen prominent political and other leaders, among them Moederbond's chairman, Cyril Daal, were shot during a cleanup campaign, which included the burning of two radio stations, a newspaper office, and the Moederbond headquarters (*Latin America Weekly Report*, 17 December). The RFS said the dissidents were killed "trying to escape," while the opposition—which claims there were two to three times as many casualties—said they were executed. According to an Agence France-Presse report on 11 December (*FBIS*, 12 December), the Suriname government was considering calling for Soviet or Cuban troops if the opposition resorted to foreign assistance. However, a number of news items from Suriname during December reported that Cuban forces already were in Suriname and had masterminded the countercoup activities.

Hoover Institution   William E. Ratliff

Trinidad and Tobago

There are several small Marxist-Leninist parties or groups in Trinidad and Tobago. The most important is probably the People's Popular Movement (PPM), founded in 1981 and led by Chairman Michael Als, with a membership of about a hundred. Other pro-Soviet parties are the February Eighteenth Movement, led by James Millette, set up in 1972; the Workers Revolutionary Committee, led by James Poon, dating from 1980; and the United Revolutionary Organization, established in 1971 and currently leaderless. In addition, a Maoist organization, the National Movement for the True Independence of Trinago, is tied to the Oil Fields Workers Trade Union; founded in 1974, it is led by Teddy Belgrave. Two revolutionary Trotskyist organizations, the New Beginning Movement and the Workers Revolutionary League have also emerged. There is a Communist Party of Trinidad and Tobago, which follows an Albanian line and dates from August 1979. The radical non-Marxist left continues to be represented by the National Joint Action Committee, a black nationalist movement dating from 1968 with a marked anti-imperialist ideology, under the leadership of Makandal Daaga.

Still dominated by the heritage of Eric Williams, who died in 1981, and his People's National Movement, the oil-rich, twin-island nation of Trinidad and Tobago plays a key role in the Caribbean. At present its communist groupings are totally fragmented and out of power. However, the highly vocal PPM did accuse the United States of "acts of aggression, destabilization, and intimidation (in an unclassified letter to the U.S. embassy, 9 September). President Reagan's Caribbean Basin Initiative came under hostile criticism from James Millette, who is also chairman of the Trinidad and Tobago Peace Council, an affiliate of the Soviet-front World Peace Council. He called the initiative "a new model of imperialist aggression" (*Tribune: A Journal of Socialist Thought*, Saint Lucia, June). Michael Aberdeen, of the PPM, also attacked the Reagan plan as "a strategy for U.S. domination and plunder," whose major preoccupation "is to reverse the revolutionary gains made by the progressive forces" (*Trinidad Guardian*, 11 August).

Trinidad's current minister of national security, John Donaldson, submitted information on persons with communist connections "involved in an alleged plot to overthrow the government" (Caribbean News Agency, Bridgetown, 15 July). These charges were denied by all parties.

Relations worsened between the more numerous and wealthier Trinidadians, who are of both black and East Indian origin, and the Tobagonians, who are predominantly black. The leader of the leftist-nationalist Democratic Action Congress and chairman of the Tobago House of Assembly, A. N. R. Robinson, issued renewed claims for Tobago's independence, saying, "We should call it quits peacefully rather than waste time and get on one another's nerves" (*Trinidad Guardian*, 16 July).

Early in the year, Janko Lazarevski, Yugoslav ambassador for the English-speaking Caribbean, presented his credentials and called on the two nonaligned countries to increase "cooperation, both bilateral and in the wider international arena" (*Borba*, Belgrade, 12 March).

Gordon College   Theodore R. Malloch

United States

The largest communist organization in the United States, formed in 1919, is the Communist Party, USA (CPUSA). Party General Secretary Gus Hall claimed 20,000 members for the party in 1981. In January 1981, he estimated that 300,000 others "consider themselves communists" but are afraid to join the party (*NYT*, 6 January 1981). By September 1982, Hall, on a membership drive around the country, claimed that 500,000 people who were not CPUSA members sympathized with party goals (*San Jose Mercury*, 12 September). The CPUSA made a major effort to increase its membership during 1982, and according to Hall, communist influence "is growing faster than anytime in the last 30 years" (ibid.). Jack West, a member of the CPUSA Political Bureau, explained the need for a "mass party," by which he means "a party of sufficient size to be rooted strongly among the working class, the oppressed sections, the farmers, and the professionals-intellectuals; a party able to contest and win elections, beginning at the local level; a party able to participate in a broad anti-monopoly, all people's coalition and make a decisive contribution to it; and, lastly, a party which is steadfast in its class and revolutionary principles, and does not forsake them in order to enlist more supporters." The builders of this party, he added, must be "competent and steeled cadres" so that they will develop what Hall called "organized, active and militant rank-and-file movements." (*WMR*, August; *Political Affairs*, June.) On another occasion, West added that whenever possible the rank-and-file "should work as a force within the mainstream majority and less as an anti-establishment minority" (*Political Affairs*, September).

Prominent CPUSA leaders, besides Hall, are Henry Winston (national chairman), Arnold Bechetti (national secretary), James Jackson (education director), Victor Perlo (economics), and Michael Zagarell, who is editor of the CPUSA organ, *Daily World*, which appears five times a week. Hall is editor of the party's monthly theoretical journal, *Political Affairs*. Winston received the Georgi Dimitrov Prize in Bulgaria in June.

Much of the CPUSA's limited influence in the United States comes from a network of organizations that are dominated by, though not officially tied to, the party. These include the Young Workers Liberation League (YWLL), which serves as the party's youth wing. The national chairman of the YWLL is James Steele; its paper is *Young Worker*. Other CPUSA national fronts include the National Alliance Against Racist and Political Repression, whose membership includes onetime CPUSA presidential candidate Charlene Mitchell, who serves as chairman, and Angela Davis; the Committee for Trade Union Action and Democracy; the National Council on American-Soviet Friendship; the Chile Solidarity Committee; the National Anti-imperialist Movement in Solidarity with African Liberation; the Committee for a Just Peace in the Middle East; and Women for Racial and Economic Equality.

The CPUSA held its Second Extraordinary Conference on 23–25 April—the first extraordinary conference since 1933—in Milwaukee, Wisconsin. It was attended by a thousand representatives of the party hierarchy and of the "primary party organizations"—the shops and communities throughout the country. The meeting was devoted to analyzing what a *Political Affairs* editorial in September, on the sixty-third anniversary of the party, called "the most devastating, all-round crisis to strike the capitalist system since World War II." The objective was to develop what Hall called "The All-People's Fightback Front" (ibid., June). There were some problems: some unions were compromising, while grass-roots movements were not yet sufficiently coordinated. However, in most respects party leaders were pleased and optimistic over what they saw in small towns, cities, universities, and unions. They noted and supported what they saw as a rising anti-Reagan tide, activities ranging from the "no-nuke" and nuclear freeze movements to opposition to U.S. involvement in El Salvador and campaigns against Reaganomics and racist, antipeople politicians. These activities are "harbingers of a great wave of struggle" to come. The elections of 1982, the September editorial concluded, "offer an opportunity to deal the Reaganites the first telling blow." And in the judgment of the CPUSA, the November elections did strike that blow.

The CPUSA describes the world in terms virtually indistinguishable from those used by the Communist Party of the Soviet Union, at times simply reprinting articles by Soviet writers in CPUSA publications. Confrontations with the U.S. government became major issues, whether they are over the State Department's refusal to grant visas to members of the Soviet-front World Peace Council or over the temporary confiscation of publications from Cuba by the postal service.

There are several Trotskyist parties in the United States. The most important is the Socialist Workers' Party (SWP), founded in 1938, which claims 2,000 members. It is a member of the United Secretariat of the Fourth (Trotskyist) International, although since 1940 it has claimed to be legally disaffiliated from that organization because of the requirements of the Voorhis Act. The SWP publishes the weekly *Militant* and, for the United Secretariat of the Fourth International, the weekly *Intercontinental Press*.

The SWP is led by National Secretary Jack Barnes and National Cochairperson Mary-Alice Waters. The SWP and its youth support group, the Young Socialist Alliance, threw their annual convention in Oberlin, Ohio, from 31 July to 5 August. Some 1,200 people from all over the United States and abroad attended. Half were workers; half were under 30; 73 were Afro-Americans, and 66 were Latinos. Party leaders reported great success in the program begun several years ago of "concentrating their members in large industries." Barnes explained the SWP program for spreading its influence in the labor movement as a three-step affair: explaining problems, popularizing a program of demands for workers' welfare, and taking an active role in the "skirmishes and battles that are already breaking out." (*Militant*, 3 September.)

The SWP emphasizes the same issues as CPUSA: unemployment, racism, militarism, imperialism, and—the favorite term of the year—fightback. However, it often adopts more militant positions on domestic and international affairs than does the CPUSA, as is evident in a random comparison of issues of the *Daily World* and the *Militant*. For example, *Militant* (26 February) advocated more forceful union responses to workers' problems than the CPUSA would condone. And the SWP highlighted what it sees as the critical interrelation between domestic and international protests. On domestic affairs, the SWP sometimes defines its position by attacking the CPUSA, noting, for example, that the extraordinary conference was simply "to mobilize ranks of the Communist Party and its youth organization . . . for all-out participation in the 1982 Democratic Party primaries and the November elections" (ibid., 5 March, 4 June). On international affairs, the SWP supported the Solidarity movement in Poland and devoted considerable attention to revolutionary warfare in Central America and the Caribbean.

Among the other numerous Marxist-Leninist organizations in the United States are two Trotskyist groups: the Workers World Party, under chairman Sam Marcy, and the Sparticist League. Other parties include the Communist Workers' Party, under Jerry Tung, which has fractured into the Line of March and the Theoretical Review groups; the unstable Communist Party (Marxist-Leninist); and the Revolutionary Communist Party.

Hoover Institution   William E. Ratliff

Uruguay

The continued repression of the Uruguayan Communist Party (Partido Comunista del Uruguay; PCU) left the movement with little option but to pursue its activities in exile. The first secretary of the PCU, Rodney Arismendi, continued to call for a return to constitutional government and a general amnesty for all political prisoners, many of whom were active members of the party. As a member of the Broad Front (Frente Amplio), the PCU officially supported the call for casting blank ballots in the internal party elections. However, party pronouncements made it clear that the PCU was not preventing its adherents from voting for antimilitary candidates in the two traditional parties.

On international matters, the PCU issued a joint communiqué with the Communist Party of Argentina denouncing U.S. and British imperialism in the Falklands war. Arismendi, traveling widely in Europe, frequently denounced U.S. policy in Central America.

In Uruguay, the military government continued its repression of the left, especially the Communists. During January, the government announced it had broken a communist cell whose members were engaged in infiltration of a newly organized trade union. In March, more detailed information on this affair was released. The government offered the activities of the Union Group (Fracción Sindical) as proof of continued communist subversion. Nevertheless, a high-ranking Soviet trade delegation did visit Montevideo in April.

In November, Héctor Rodríguez, one of the PCU's most important labor leaders, was released from prison after serving a nine-year term. Several other PCU members were also freed, although many more remained incarcerated even after their sentences had expired. This situation has made the issue of a general amnesty of the utmost priority for the PCU.

The Opposition and Prospects for Redemocratization. The military regime, attempting to recover from the overwhelming rejection in November 1980 of the constitution they had presented to the Uruguayan people, promulgated a Law of Political Parties permitting the resumption of activity by Uruguay's two traditional parties, the Blancos (Partido Nacional) and Colorados (Partido Colorado), and an insignificant conservative group, the Unión Cívica. The Communist, Socialist, and Christian Democratic parties, as well as all groups that had participated in the 1971 elections under the banner of the Broad Front, continued to be outlawed. According to the new law, no political party composed of individuals who belonged to organizations now declared illegal will be recognized. In addition, "no political party following the ends, ideology, principles, party name, or type of actions that evidence indirect or direct connection with foreign political parties, institutions, or organizations, or with another state will be recognized." (*Desde Uruguay*, no. 15.) As Gen. Julio C. Rapela, chairman of the Armed Forces Political Affairs Commission, commented, Marxist parties would remain proscribed because Uruguay "cannot afford to put a worm into the apple that will eventually destroy it" (Reuters, 1 November; *FBIS*, 3 November).

The regime permitted the legalized groups to hold internal party elections on 29 November. Voters went to the polls to elect 500 members to each party's convention. Under the military's transition plan, during 1983 these conventions would choose the executive leadership of their respective party. This leadership would then work with the armed forces to draft a new constitution and select presidential candidates for the promised November 1984 elections.

The party elections, even more dramatically than the 1980 plebiscite, resulted in a disastrous political defeat for the military. Antimilitary candidates took some 91 percent of the Blanco vote and 72 percent of the Colorado vote. With a protest blank ballot of 7 percent, the opposition vote totaled 82 percent of all votes cast. The Blanco slate of candidates associated with exiled Senator Wilson Ferreira Aldunate received about 75 percent of its party's vote. In the Colorado Party, the principal pro-government candidate, ex-President Jorge Pacheco Areco, received less than 28 percent of his party's vote and less than 12 percent of the overall vote. This latest rejection of the military by Uruguay's citizens raises the possibility that democratic rule may return to Uruguay earlier than the March 1985 military timetable, and perhaps without the restrictive conditions the military would like to impose.

The commander of the army, Gen. Boscan Hontou, a hard-liner, reminded everyone that the elections were a first step and that the armed forces were still intent on obtaining a constitution that would presumably still include their pet project—a national security council. The military would dominate this body and thereby exercise a veto power over virtually all aspects of government policy.

The military's ability to stick to its timetable and constitutional priorities is made even more questionable by the economic situation. The worldwide recession hit the country hard. The gross domestic product fell 8 percent, and unemployment rose to 13 percent in 1982. In late November, the government announced it would let the peso float and would remove all export subsidies. Economics Minister Valentín Arismendi subsequently resigned the post he had held since 1976.

The military still rule in Uruguay, but economic conditions and the defeat they suffered in the party elections place them in an increasingly isolated position. The initiative is now with the opposition at home and abroad. They must stand together in insisting on a speedy return to civilian government, the rule of law, and the full restoration of civil liberties. As the big winner in the party elections, Wilson Ferreira Aldunate, expressed it: "We have the destiny of the country in our hands. If we do not take it, the fault will be our own." (*El Día*, Mexico City, 21 December.)

The exile community and the internal opposition were greatly encouraged by the results of the party elections. Such exile groups as the Convergencia Democrática Uruguaya and the Broad Front could take much encouragement from the cooperation and calls for unity extended to each other by the victorious slates of antimilitary candidates.

But the military's initial reaction to its renewed rejection by the people was not encouraging. On 17 December, Gen. Yamandu Trinidad, minister of the interior, pointedly remarked that "in this country a timetable has been fixed and the armed forces are going to carry it out regardless of pressure or urgency from anyone" (*Desde Uruguay*, no. 1, 1983). Presumably, this includes 82 percent of the citizenry.

William Patterson College of New Jersey   Martin Weinstein

Venezuela

Founded in 1931, the Venezuelan Communist Party (PCV) has reason to feel satisfied with the results of its 1982 pre-election maneuvering within the archipelago of parties that constitute Venezuela's political left. It has become a member in good standing of the multiparty coalition, the New Alternative, that supports the candidacy of José Vicente Rangel. By 1982, all efforts to seek a broad-based leftist unity candidate by means of an unprecedented primary to be run by the multiparty National Coordinating Entity of the Left ceased. The PCV succeeded in preventing the anti-Soviet, Eurocommunist candidacy of Teodoro Petkoff of the Movement Toward Socialism (MAS) from gaining control of the left. As late as April, the PCV was busily engaged in mobilizing to secure a victory for Rangel in the multiparty left-wing primary (*Tribuna Popular*, 1 April).

The Falklands war also enabled the party to join the rhetorical anticolonial support given to Argentina for its "occupation" of the Falklands (*FBIS*, 13 April) and to pressure the government not to purchase British Hawk airplanes. PCV leader Radamés Larrazábal attacked the U.S. mediation effort in the Falklands dispute as "merely" a device "to give the British time to prepare better to attack Argentina" (Caracas Radio Continente, 3 May; *FBIS*, 6 May).

The PCV also publicly denounced the decision of the Venezuelan armed forces to participate in the Ocean Venture military maneuvers with the U.S. navy, calling these exercises "a threat to the Central American and Caribbean peoples" (*FBIS*, 17 March). The PCV found much encouragement in Venezuela's movement toward "a position . . . just adopted by Mexico" in order to prevent war in Central America and to "oppose the invasion of Nicaragua that is being prepared by the North Americans," according to a radio interview with Jesús Faria, secretary general of the party (Havana international service, 13 October; *FBIS*, 15 October). Faria was also pleased with Venezuela's seeking full membership in the nonaligned movement.

Movement Toward Socialism.   Teodoro Petkoff, presidential candidate of MAS, retained his celebrity status in the U.S. press (see *YICA*, 1982, p. 149). In a *Washington Post* interview (16 August), Petkoff insisted that not even a smashing electoral failure would send him back to the hills as a guerrilla. "Democracy now is a value in itself," according to Petkoff, "it existed long before capitalism came about." Another MAS spokesman, Bayardo Sardi, was also reported to have stated that the MAS version of socialism is not hostile to the role the United States has in the hemisphere (ibid.).

Despite its becoming the dominant force on the left and Venezuela's third strongest party in the 1979 municipal election results, MAS and the Petkoff candidacy were in trouble in 1982. Petkoff had earned the enmity of the PCV, Cuba's Fidel Castro, and such leftist competitors as José Vicente Rangel because of his moderate, anti-Soviet stance.

Opposition to Petkoff's candidacy emerged within MAS in August. Tirso Pinto, deputy secretary general, denounced the "Teodorist faction" for its break with the left and its refusal to accept a José Vicente–MAS team as the basis of unity of the left. The pro–José Vicente Rangel faction in MAS was especially furious at Petkoff's "convergence" with the "oligarchic sectors," his ambition to make MAS a "third leg of the system," and his anticommunist positions. (*El Nacional*, 7 August.) Other than Tirso Pinto, none of MAS's top leaders were among the hundred or so signatories to the Pinto statement.

Late 1981 and early 1982 opinion polls showed that José Vicente Rangel was clearly in the lead on the left, but these same polls also indicated that Petkoff was gaining (*Resumen*, 1 November 1981). In March, MAS Secretary General Pompeyo Márquez was unequivocal in his support of Petkoff as the only viable candidate for the left and was equally adamant that there was "no possibility of reconciliation between PCV and MAS" (*El Nacional*, 25 March). Pompeyo Marquez also seemed to have downgraded the importance of the multiparty primary because of the opposition to the PCV.

José Vicente Rangel, the candidate of the New Alternative coalition, differed from Petkoff in his willingness to praise the Cuban regime. In an interview on Cuban radio, Rangel stated that the complete normalization of Venezuelan-Cuban relations is one of his goals and that "Cuba is not an aggressor" (Havana international service, 4 November; *FBIS*, 8 November). Rangel also felt that divisions in the left may prevent it from realizing its 1983 electoral potential.

Other Parties and Personalities.   On 25 November, the various parties supporting Vicente Rangel proclaimed his candidacy in a massive outdoor rally in downtown Caracas. The slogan of the rally was "The people [supporting Rangel] won't fit in the Poliedro" (a popular enclosed sports arena). This slogan was designed as an invidious comparison to the 27 October rally that proclaimed the candidacy of Petkoff in the Poliedro. (*SIC–Centro Gumilla*, no. 450, December.)

The Supreme Court of Justice ended the dispute between the two factions of the Movement of the Revolutionary Left (MIR), which split in 1980 (see *YICA*, 1981, pp. 115–16). The court decided that the faction headed by Moisés Moleiro should retain the name because it appeared to better represent the "orthodox" MIR position advocating a "dictatorship of the proletariat" (AFP, Paris, 12 August; *FBIS*, 16

August). In the fall, Moleiro, secretary general of MIR, announced his support of Petkoff. The party's 1978 presidential candidate, Americo Martín, has favored José Vicente Rangel.

As the left formally abandoned its efforts to achieve a unity candidate in August, the People's Electoral Movement (MEP), the party on the left with the strongest labor sector, decided to support José Vicente Rangel. MEP Secretary General Jesús Paz Galarraga stated that the left should consider the December 1983 elections as its "primary" in order to judge whether Rangel or Petkoff obtains the greater share of the vote. Galarraga indicated that the left might gain 12–16 percent of the vote (AFP, Paris, 11 August; *FBIS*, 13 August).

The independent-minded leaders of the Radical Cause (Causa R) stayed aloof from the Petkoff-Rangel struggle and nominated Jorge Olivarria, editor of *Resumen* magazine, as their presidential candidate.

Douglas Bravo, leader of the Venezuelan Revolutionary Party, had "rebuffed" the offer for an electoral "teaming up" advanced by Gen. (ret.) Arnaldo Castro Hurtado (*Economist* Intelligence Unit, *Quarterly Economic Review on Venezuela*, 3rd Quarter 1982). Bravo had denied that any talks were going on with Castro Hurtado (see *YICA*, 1982, p. 151). According to the *Economist*'s report, Castro Hurtado "has acquired a reputation for eccentricity" for his effort to team up with Douglas Bravo.

Guerrilla Communism.   Starting with the spectacular hijacking of three Venezuelan airliners on 7 December 1981 and twin attacks on small rural communities near the Orinoco oil belt in eastern Venezuela in late November and December 1981, the year 1982 witnessed a guerrilla resurgence. Guerrilla activity seemed to have been exclusively the work of the Red Flag (BR) organization.

BR leader Gabriel Puerta Aponte had reportedly claimed that he considered himself a Venezuelan version of Yugoslavia's Tito and Albania's Hoxha. Some also saw a Libyan connection. In March, Puerta Aponte and an "entire cell" of the BR were captured in Caracas. About four guerrillas were killed in antiguerrilla operations during March and April.

In early October, the army and police attacked a BR guerrilla camp near the town of Anaco in eastern Venezuela. About 23 of the estimated 40 to 60 guerrillas and two government troops were reported killed in three days of fighting (AFP, Paris, 5 October; *FBIS*, 7 October; *Latin America Weekly Report*, 15 October).

Accounts of the clash stated that "the dying Venezuelan guerrilla movement was dealt one of the harshest blows in its history"; a later account reported that some of the guerrillas "evaded" the military siege (Latin Radio, Buenos Aires, 7 October; *FBIS*, 8 October). Two BR leaders, Roberto Rincon and Esperatriz Guzmán, were reported killed. Puerta Aponte also reported from his prison cell that his group had been dealt a "harsh blow."

There was no indication that sabotage was involved in the tragic December fire that destroyed one of Caracas's principal sources of electric power.

Possible links between Colombia's M-19 guerrillas and the BR were being investigated. Security police director Roberto Uzcategui also stated that Cuban agents may have been involved in the coordinated December 1981 triple hijacking (*WP*, 15 April). Uzcategui was quoted as saying that the hijacking was organized by "a Caribbean tropical power."

Domestic Politics.   The forthcoming December 1983 presidential and legislative elections dominated the political news of 1982. As of late December 1982, eight prospective candidates had been nominated. Both the left and the right had apparently failed to achieve a credible unity candidate to challenge the electoral dominance of the two centrist parties: the Democratic Action and the Social (or Christian) Democrats.

This failure to unite should prevent the left from fully exploiting the grave economic situation Venezuela is presently facing. Unemployment as of late 1982 may have reached one-half million, out of a labor force estimated at 4.2 million persons (*El Nacional*, 28 December). An indication of the troubled times came in late September when a former finance minister, Luís Ugueto, requested in New York that the international banking community agree to allow Venezuela to convert its short-term debt into long-term credits and to convert debts owed by autonomous government agencies and public corporations (estimated at about $18.5 billion) to a central government debt (*NYT*, "Business Day," 30 September). Rumors also persist that Venezuela's currency will soon be devalued.

The turmoil wrought by the present economic situation is illustrated by the fall 1982 decision both to repatriate the international reserves of the state-owned Venezuelan Petroleum Company (PDVSA) and to place these funds under the control of the Central Bank. Some of these repatriated funds had been used in November 1982 to prevent the collapse of the nation's principal bank, the Banco de los Trabajadores (BTV), whose largest shareholder had been the labor confederation. The BTV reportedly held about 10 percent of the total deposits in private banks. (*NYT*, 30 November; *Latin America Weekly Report*, 3 December.)

Perhaps reflecting the economic hard times, coming elections, and the continuing violence in Central America, Venezuela's foreign policy seemed to have shifted from one emphasizing a "coincidence" with the United States to one of greater Third World militancy. Venezuela joined Mexico in mid-1982 in encouraging a peaceful resolution to the ongoing Central American tragedy. In July, President Luís Herrera Campins attended the third anniversary celebration of the Sandinista victory in Managua, Nicaragua (*FBIS*, 15 July). During his stay, President Herrera Campins called for greater pluralism in Nicaragua and for peace between Nicaragua and Honduras (*WP*, 12 July).

There were also moves toward a new détente with Cuba (*FBIS*, 7 July). A key adviser to President Herrera Campins, Gonzalo García Bustillos, met with Cuban Vice-President Carlos Rafael Rodríguez. Venezuelan Foreign Minister Alberto Zambrano Velasco publicly indicated Venezuela's willingness to cooperate with Cuba to defend "strictly Latin American interests," perhaps a reference to the Falklands war (ibid., 12 July). Anticolonialism and Latin American solidarity were the reasons given for Venezuela's support of Argentina (*NYT*, 5 May). The Falklands war may also have been the cover under which the PDVSA reserves in British banks were withdrawn. The move toward détente with Cuba may have been strained by reports that Venezuelan guerrillas who became active in late 1981 may have received training in Cuba (*El Tiempo*, Bogotá, 7 January).

Venezuela's shift toward a Third World identity was further illustrated by its vote to place the issue of the alleged colonial status of Puerto Rico on the agenda of the U.S. General Assembly (*NYT*, 23 September). Venezuela also formally joined the nonaligned movement by upgrading its representation from observer to full member (ibid., 28 September).

The continuing territorial dispute with Guayana remained rhetorical (ibid., 21 June). Economic ties between Venezuela and Guayana were strengthened in 1982. The moratorium on formally presenting territorial claims signed in 1970 ended this year (*Los Angeles Times*, 11 February; *NYT*, 21 June).

Interviewed on Argentina radio (Noticias Argentina, Buenos Aires, 13 August; *FBIS*, 13 August), Foreign Minister Zambrano Velasco suggested that the headquarters of the Organization of American States be moved from the United States to Panama.

University of Louisville   David Eugene Blank

ASIA AND THE PACIFIC

Introduction

The communist parties of North Korea, China, Vietnam, Laos, Kampuchea, Mongolia, and Afghanistan control populations of around 1.2 billion people, or roughly half of the population in the Asia and Pacific region. In Japan, India, Nepal, and Sri Lanka, the communist parties have been legally active and opposed to the major parties in power. Yet their political influence has not increased in recent years, and all efforts to form coalitions with other left-wing parties have been unsuccessful. The Indian, Nepali, and Sri Lankan parties have splintered into pro-Moscow and pro-Beijing factions. Only in Japan has the communist party opted for an independent line, preferring to model its policies after those of the Eurocommunist parties. In Australia and New Zealand, the communist parties are legal, but their members are split over policy debates and the parties have not provided any serious opposition to the governing parties or exerted any real influence on public opinion. However, party leaders serve as officers in labor unions that often exert very great influence over public affairs.

Although the communist party is legal in Bangladesh, it was inactive in 1982 because the government-imposed martial law forbade all political activities. Burma, Indonesia, Singapore, the Philippines, Thailand, and Pakistan have banned communist activities. Because of favorable environmental conditions for guerrilla operations, however, the communist parties of these states have managed to survive underground and wage a campaign of violence and propaganda from the jungles of Malaysia, Burma, Thailand, and the Philippines.

States with Ruling Communist Parties. It was in the seven countries ruled by communist parties that certain key events took place in 1982. War continued to rage in Afghanistan and Kampuchea. Vietnam struggled to prop up its client states of Laos and Kampuchea. China's leaders struggled to modernize an apathetic, cynical society. North Korea's party and army remained divided over the likely successor to Kim Il-song as that aging autocrat tried to legitimize his son Chong-il as his successor. Mongolia continued to criticize China and declare its enduring friendship for the Soviet Union.

Without Soviet military backing and economic aid, the Babrak Karmal regime in Afghanistan could not survive. European observers recently estimated current Soviet strength at 152,000, a figure said to include 90,000 infantrymen in divisions with another 50,000 in support. Since the Soviet intervention began in December 1979, some 12,000 to 15,000 Soviet troops have been killed or wounded. In 1982, the Soviets increased their use of helicopters, now thought to number between 500 and 600. Soviet strategy now is to select an area of guerrilla activity and attack with troops carried by helicopters and supported, once on the ground, by MI-24 attack helicopters. These improved Soviet tactics have been accompanied by a slower improvement in guerrilla tactics. Smaller guerrilla units under a single command now do much of the fighting, instead of the large, unorganized bands that first attacked Soviet troops and thus suffered heavy losses. Newer weapons are also entering the country in greater quantities to improve the Afghan resistance's strike force capabilities.

Babrak Karmal has applied much of his energy to recruiting for the communist party and the ever-dwindling army. Party standards for entry have deteriorated, with newer members coming from the illiterate and poor. Once very young and old men—the only ones left—are pressed into military service, they are subjected to intense indoctrination in isolation from the population. No major leadership changes have occurred in the party except that in late 1982 two new Central Committee members were named. The government has tried to decentralize its authority by allowing local leaders more control in the provinces, but this tactic often backfires with communities' withdrawing their support for the state and party. As Soviet troops continue to destroy crops and villages, farmers flee to towns and cities or into bordering Pakistan, which has received nearly three million refugees since the Soviet invasion. The Soviet Union responded by providing 80,000 tons of wheat, 10,000 tons of flour, and 20 million rubles worth of textiles to the country in 1982 alone.

In Kampuchea, the People's Revolutionary Party (KPRP), backed by Hanoi and Moscow, continued to rule much of the country but still waged war with pro-Chinese forces led by Pol Pot, which call themselves Democratic Kampuchea. In 1982, the KPRP announced that former party leader Pen Sovan was receiving treatment for "mental illness." Vietnam transferred more military responsibility to the regime's fledgling army, and during the dry season (November to May), sporadic fighting continued in the jungles. Meanwhile, Pol Pot's forces joined a coalition of smaller noncommunist groups led by Prince Norodom Sihanouk and former premier Son Sann. The KPRP continued its attempt to rally public support through its extensive grass-roots auxiliary organizations made up of youth, women, and labor groups.

In Laos, the party's Third Congress elected a Central Committee of 49 with six alternates—producing an average age of 55 and four female members. General Secretary Kaysone Phomvihan reported moderate economic gains and an end to the food shortages, but he admitted that the country depended heavily on technicians from Vietnam, the USSR, and other countries. Party leaders lavished praise and expressed profuse gratitude for Vietnam. Laos continued to be Vietnam's client state. A cabinet minister who defected to China in 1981 said that a Working Committee for the West comprising 140 Vietnam cadres made all important decisions for the Laotian communist party and government.

Vietnam's 1.7 million-member party is still controlled by a Politburo of thirteen members, of whom the top five have an average age of 74. The Fifth Party Congress convened in late March 1982 in an atmosphere of gloom and self-condemnation. Party leaders lashed out at declining party morale, poor organization, and cadres' inefficiency. Politburo member Pham Van Dong told the congress that the country faced serious economic difficulties, a message repeated for many years now, and Secretary General Le Duan's political report presented a candid series of party failings. When the congress ended, no policy changes were announced.

Vietnam's leaders continued to vilify China, blaming that country for Hanoi's economic difficulties. References to Moscow were effusive. Plans were announced for realizing higher economic targets. The Central Committee underwent some change, as 67 new members were added and the total rose from 133 to 152. So far, however, the aging leadership has managed to stifle and forestall any serious party factionalism.

In China, the Twelfth Party Congress convened in early September 1982, with the top leaders reporting and setting new tasks for the party and the country. The congress adopted a new constitution, supposedly expunged of leftist errors. Hua Guofeng was removed from the Politburo but retained his seat on the Central Committee. Hu Yaobang was elected general secretary. A new Central Advisory Commission was founded, with Deng Xiaoping as its chairman. The party has tried to streamline both the bureaucracy and its own ranks, but so far, with very limited success.

At the Fifth National People's Congress in November–December, Premier Zhao Ziyang presented the Sixth Five-Year Plan, and Finance Minister Wang Bingqian reported on the state budget. The new plan calls for greater investments in energy and transport as well as for urban housing, education, science, and culture. Wang announced that the state expected to tap local administrative units for more funding to expand its spending for construction on the key projects cited in the new five-year plan. He also targeted a reduction in defense spending from 16.5 to 14.5 percent of the 1983 budget.

China's foreign policy underwent gradual but important changes. China mended its fences with the French Communist Party and responded favorably to Moscow's calls for negotiations to resolve long-standing difficulties. China's premier visited a number of African states in December, indicating China's efforts to strengthen ties with Third World countries. This new posturing suggests a new strategy of distancing China from the two superpowers and projecting it as a leader of Third World states.

On the domestic front, the Beijing leadership called for a renewed effort to fight economic crimes, admitting the seriousness of the problem and citing these as now rampant. Party factionalism at the provincial level remains a serious problem. Throughout 1982, countless reports surfaced in the media of party leaders in various provinces being arrested, tried, and imprisoned for various crimes, often committed during the Cultural Revolution. The party organ *Red Flag* made repeated appeals for members to cultivate a "socialist spiritual civilization" and to seek out model socialists for the populace to imitate.

North Korea's three million–member party tightly controls a population of nearly nineteen million people. The party continues to foster loyalty to Kim Il-song and his ideology of *chuch'e*, a strange corpus of ideas stressing national identity and self-reliance. Kim's son Chong-il enjoyed considerable public exposure and received warm adulation in the press, but there are indications within the ranks of both the party and the army of unhappiness about his replacing his father. The government held rallies in November to pledge popular support to fulfill the goals set forth in the current seven-year plan. Soviet publications in late 1982 contained articles stating that large segments of North Korea's heavy industry and even some of its light industry had been built with extensive Soviet financial and technical aid. In fact, one account mentioned that up to 40 percent of the growth in output of major industrial products during the 1970s came from Soviet-financed plants. According to recent financial statements, Pyongyang's Western debt came to U.S. $840 million. North Korea defaulted on its interest payments in 1974, 1978, and 1981. In international affairs, Pyongyang's leaders continued to play the Soviet Union off against China, but a slight tilt toward Beijing seemed evident, with top leaders from both countries exchanging several visits.

Mongolia's small party of 76,240 rules a population of around 1,759,000. Some personnel shake-ups occurred in the Ministries of Defense, Justice, and Public Security, and an extensive purge of the Academy of Sciences led to that body's complete reorganization. In spite of these and other changes and replacements, overall continuity of party policy remained. On the domestic scene, Mongolia continues to increase its output and export to the USSR of copper and molybdenum. Mongolia warmly backs the foreign policy line of the Soviet Union and, in spite of the recent Sino-Soviet thaw, accused China of militarizing Inner Mongolia as a "launching pad of struggle against the Mongolian People's Republic" and repeatedly attacked China for its treatment of ethnic minorities.

Clearly, this huge communist-dominated portion of Asia is not unified except in the intent of each state's communist party to achieve and realize total control over its citizenry. National and domestic interests combine to pit China against Vietnam and its client states and to make for serious tensions between China and the Soviet Union and to a lesser extent between North Korea and the USSR. Nor have these communist-ruled states shown any real capacity to modernize their economies. The economic system in all of these states is beset with very serious problems, but the political and ideological capabilities of these communist parties to control their population remain awesome.

States with Legal Communist Party Opposition.   In six Asian and Pacific states, communist parties legally operate as opposition groups. Even so, party influence in these states has dwindled rather than expanded in recent years. Oddly enough, in Japan, New Zealand, and Australia, which enjoy the highest per capita income in the region, the communist party enjoys support primarily from the urban intelligentsia and professional classes, whereas in India, Sri Lanka, and Nepal, some party members come from the urban and rural working poor.

In all of these states, there seems to be enough central government stability to guarantee middle-of-the-road political governance. Furthermore, the cultures of these countries contain a dimension of tolerance for differences of opinion and behavior, and the communist party is not perceived as a force threatening the polity. At the same time, however, party members seem to abide by the law wherever possible. All this is not to argue that should economic retrogression take place and political instability beset these countries, the communist party could not and would not extend its influence over grass-roots organizations and try to expand political control and power.

Of these states, Japan has the highest communist party membership (over 400,000), and the party's newspaper, *Red Flag*, is said to have over 3.5 million readers, which is probably an exaggeration. In July, the party held its Sixteenth Congress and voted in a younger slate of Central Committee members, including more women. The party still has 29 members in the House of Representatives out of a total number of 511 seats, making it the fifth-largest party in the country. A recent poll showed about 2.4 percent of the public supporting the party. Party leaders publicly criticized Soviet policies in Poland and

Afghanistan. Rumors circulated of a possible rapprochement between the Japanese and Chinese communist parties, but so far this has not occurred.

In India party members are concentrated primarily in the states of West Bengal and Kerala, but remain split, with an independent faction much better organized and publicly backed than the pro-Moscow faction. The independent faction held its Eleventh Congress in late January but made no significant changes in the ranks of its aging leaders, who average around 65. The pro-Moscow party held its Twelfth Congress in the spring and adopted a more critical line against Indira Gandhi's leadership. Both factions registered modest gains in adding new members to party rolls.

Sri Lanka's communist party of only 6,000 members is pro-Moscow; there is also a Trotskyist faction. The former has tried to ally itself with other leftist parties but so far without success. The pro-Moscow group has criticized the government for making agreements with U.S. firms.

In Australia a leader of the pro-Beijing faction of the communist party, Norm Gallagher, is president of a labor union. In 1982, the government charged him with receiving illegal commissions. All factions of the communist party continued to promote leftist international causes such as supporting a ban on handling cargo for Israeli vessels and protesting visitations of U.S. nuclear-powered warships. Membership in the independent Communist Party of Australia is around 2,000. Its congress in June condemned Soviet interference in Poland and passed a resolution that each country should pursue its own road toward socialism.

The communist party of New Zealand still remains splintered, the largest faction supporting the Moscow line. That group, the Socialist Unity Party, is governed by a ten-member National Committee, and its president, Gordon Harold "Bill" Anderson, also serves as a high-ranking officer in several key labor unions. The party remained quiet during 1982 because of events in Poland. A Maoist faction operates underground and continues to have some appeal to radical students and intellectuals.

In Bangladesh the communist party, like all other political parties, became inactive when martial law was declared in March 1982. The military government has been trying to encourage private enterprise, especially family farmers, and throughout the year relative calm prevailed.

Communists in Nepal are still divided into pro-Chinese and pro-Soviet factions. During 1982, communist leaders remained quiet, although there was widespread public criticism of Prime Minister Surya Bahadur Thapa for his government's failure to end the food crisis and for mounting corruption.

States with Banned Communist Parties. For many years, Burma, Pakistan, and the members of the Association of Southeast Asian Nations have tried to suppress all vestiges of organized communist activity, most particularly, the party-led guerrilla forces that melt away into the jungles and resort to armed violence. With varying success, these states have managed to stamp out most forms of violence organized by the Communists. Yet the danger remains especially great in the Philippines, where the economy has suffered greatly from the international recession and criticism of President Marcos's regime continues to mount. Many rural poor might be driven by desperation to join the ranks of the communist guerrillas. If political instability erupts and military and security forces cannot continue their effective policing actions, communist guerrilla activities could become extremely disruptive.

The communist parties in all of these states have primarily been pro-Beijing, and many actually have received material and spiritual support from the PRC in the past. In 1981, the PRC foreign policy line began to change to one of urging these communist parties to seek some kind of rapprochement with the ruling government parties. In the case of Thailand, this switch has proved to be rather successful, with many Communists surrendering to government forces, but in the Philippines and Malaysia the party continues to pursue its guerrilla activities on an independent basis.

In early 1983, a group of 466 communist insurgents surrendered in northern Thailand, bringing to more than 1,800 the number that had defected since December. This large-scale defection comes after the government reported in May 1982 that two major groups have been fighting for control over the Politburo. By early September, some members began to defect, led first by Udom Srisuwan, a founding member of the party, who told officials he had become disillusioned with pro-Chinese influence over the party. Other defections followed, so that the party's armed wing now might number as low as 750 guerrillas compared with 2,000–3,000 about three years ago. The group still fighting in the jungles and hills apparently is following the Maoist strategy of using armed struggle to develop "liberated" base areas. This would mean that its leaders are oblivious to the tactical shifts in Beijing, and armed struggle from these small units can be expected to continue into the future.

In Singapore and Pakistan, communist activity is absent. The Singapore government has successfully eradicated communist activity in the island-state, although several hundred members of the Malaysian party may still operate underground. In Pakistan the communist party and its organizations have been banned since 1954, but communist sympathizers have supported other political parties and exerted some influence on public opinion. In 1982, the government of President Zia continued to ban political activities and to arrest people it considered "antisocial and subversive." Pakistan continues to worry about Soviet troops in Afghanistan and has allowed the United States to train Afghan insurgents within its borders. Pakistan continues to have cordial relations with the PRC, and Zia traveled to China on 17–22 October 1982.

Malaysia's security forces continued to seek out and kill communist guerrillas and to maintain strict vigilance in the cities against any signs of communist propaganda. Communist guerrillas continued their tactics of probing and inciting violence where government strength was weakest.

In Indonesia the government has successfully eliminated all communist efforts to organize, and party leaders live in either Moscow, Prague, or Beijing. State security forces keep close surveillance over the thousands of political prisoners arrested in 1965 who have been released in recent years.

Burma's communist party is currently led by 73-year-old Thakin Ba Thein Tin, now believed to be living in Beijing. Little is known about the Central Committee members, and party membership has probably decreased from the 3,000 claimed in 1979. The party has units in different parts of the country organized around military base areas; its strength is largest in areas bordering China and Laos. Guerrilla forces number higher than party membership, but a figure of 30,000 cited in 1982 was probably on the high side. The party continues to call on the Rangoon government to resume peace negotiations broken off in 1981, and the civil war still continues, with government forces attacking insurgent base areas during the dry season. In late 1982, the government was preparing for a large-scale offensive against communist base areas.

In the Philippines the Beijing-oriented communist party has a guerrilla force called the New People's Army (NPA), which uses selective terror to undermine the government's authority. In 1982, the NPA was very active in the southern provinces, especially in the Samar region, attacking small government forces, killing or kidnapping local leaders, and trying to win popular support. The scale and frequency of such violence appear to follow that of previous years.

So far the NPA has not successfully linked up with the Moro National Liberation Front, a group of Muslim insurgents. Should that happen, the government would have a very serious problem on its hands. Further, as domestic opposition groups increasingly criticize President Marcos and his administration, the government incessantly watches for any signs of an alliance between those forces and the communist party.

Soviet Imperialism in Asia. The Soviet imperial threat in Asia and the Pacific continues with ever greater naval activity taking place between Soviet Far Eastern ports, Camrahn Bay in Vietnam, and the Indian Ocean. The Soviet Union also dispatched a group of some 21 MiG fighters to the much disputed Kurile islands, which the Soviets control. The Soviet Union also warned Japan in January 1983 that any further military buildup within Japan could lead to an attack more destructive than the nuclear destruction of Hiroshima and Nagasaki in World War II.

The Soviet military presence in Afghanistan continued but at a slightly increased level over 1981, and Soviet military and economic aid still flowed into Vietnam, Laos, and Kampuchea. The most significant development, perhaps, was the beginning of a Sino-Soviet thaw, with firm prospects for renewed negotiations in 1983 to resolve the military confrontation along the 3,000-mile border.

Hoover Institution   Ramon H. Myers

Afghanistan

In 1967, two years after its founding, the People's Democratic Party of Afghanistan (PDPA) split into opposing Parcham and Khalq wings. Both kept the PDPA name and both were loyal to Moscow, but each maintained a separate organization and recruitment program. Khalq, led by Nur Mohammed Taraki, the PDPA's founder, depended for support on the relatively poor rural intelligentsia and recruited almost solely among Pushtuns, the dominant (55 percent) Afghan ethnic group. Parcham, less numerous but more broadly representative ethnically, was urban oriented and appealed to a wealthier group of educated Afghans. It was led by Babrak Karmal, son of an Afghan general. Both groups focused their initial recruitment efforts on intellectuals, media employees, and especially teachers. When President Mohammed Daoud overthrew the Afghan monarchy in 1973, the Parchamis at first collaborated with him, but the Khalqis remained in opposition and began an intensive clandestine recruitment effort among the military in preparation for the PDPA coup that was to follow five years later.

Under Soviet pressure, Parcham and Khalq formally reunited in mid-1977, and their combined strength was enough to overthrow Daoud and inaugurate the Democratic Republic of Afghanistan (DRA) in April 1978. They almost immediately fissioned again, however, with Taraki sending the most prominent Parchamis into diplomatic exile as ambassadors and jailing or demoting most of those who remained in Afghanistan. When a Parchami plot to unseat Taraki was uncovered in the summer of 1978, the ambassadors were recalled but disobeyed the order and fled into exile in Eastern Europe.

Meanwhile, popular resistance to Khalq's rigidly Marxist-Leninist rule grew rapidly and soon threatened to topple the new regime in spite of massive Soviet military aid. In September 1979, the Soviets attempted to force another artificial reconciliation between Parcham and Khalq, but their plan to place all blame for the schism on Taraki's deputy, Hafizullah Amin, backfired when Amin himself seized power and murdered Taraki. Amin, however, could not pacify his rebellious people, and on 27 December 1979, Soviet troops invaded, shot Amin, and restored the Parchamis to power. Babrak (he affects the surname Karmal, "friend of labor" or "Kremlin," for political purposes) became the new leader and tried to heal the breach with the Khalqis on the one side and the Afghan population on the other. In neither effort was he successful, and the regime in 1982 maintained a tenuous hold on power only in a few main Afghan towns and only thanks to 105,000 Soviet combat troops protecting them.

Population. 12–13 million in 1982 (no census ever taken; over 3 million Afghans have fled the country since 1978)

Party. People's Democratic Party of Afghanistan (Jamiyat-e-Demokratiki Khalq-e-Afghanistan; PDPA)

Founded. 1965

Membership. Officially, more than 80,000 in "over 2,000 primary party organizations" of whom "nearly half" are candidates (*Kabul New Times*, 18 December). These figures are almost certainly inflated. Western estimates range down to 11,000 full members, including 3,000 Parchamis and 8,000 Khalqis (*NYT*, 18 March).

Secretary General. Babrak Karmal

Politburo. 9 members: Babrak Karmal, Sultan Ali Keshtmand (prime minister), Dr. Najibullah (chief of the State Information [security] Service, KHAD), Nur Ahmad Nur (member, Revolutionary Council Presidium), Ghulam Dastigir Panjsheri, Brig. Gen. Mohammed Rafiee (deputy prime minister), Dr. Anahita Ratebzad (Presidium member and head of the Democratic Women's Organization of Afghanistan), Lt. Col. Mohammed Aslam Watanjar (minister of communications), Dr. Saleh Mohammed Zeary (Presidium member); 4 alternate members: Gen. Abdul Qader (minister of defense), Abdul Zahoor Razmjo (secretary, Kabul city committee), Mahmoud Baryalai, Mohammed Ismail Danesh

Secretariat. 7 members: Mahmoud Baryalai, Babrak Karmal, Dr. Niaz Mohammed Momand, Nur Ahmad Nur, Dr. Saleh Mohammed Zeary, Gen. Mohammed Yaseen Sadeqi (army chief of political affairs), Mir Saheb Karwal (administrator of Central Zone)

Central Committee. 41 identified full members, 16 identified alternates

Last Congress. First, 1 January 1965, Kabul. (A second congress allegedly was scheduled for spring 1982 but was downgraded to a party conference because of Parcham-Khalq disagreements.) (Of those mentioned above, only Danesh, Watanjar, and Zeary are believed to have been associated with the Khalq faction at one time or another. All appear to have downplayed their Khalqi affiliation since the Parchamis took over. All others listed appear to be Parchamis.)

Auxiliary Organizations. National Fatherland Front (NFF, membership unknown), Saleh Mohammed Zeary, chairman; Central Council of Trade Unions (claims 94,000 members), Abdus Sattar Purdeli, president; Democratic Youth Organization of Afghanistan (DYOA, claims 90,000 members), Burhan Ghiyasi, secretary; Democratic Women's Organization of Afghanistan (DWOA, claims 50,000 members), Anahita Ratebzad, chairman

Publications. *Haqiqat-e-Enqelabe Saur* (The truth about the saur revolution), Central Committee daily organ; *Haqiqat-e-Sarbaz* (The soldier's truth); *Dehqan* (Peasant); *Darafshe Djavanan* (The banner of youth), a weekly in Pashtu and Dari; *Kar* (Labor), began publication May 1982; *Kabul New Times*, English-language daily; the official news agency is Bakhtar.

Party Developments. During 1982, the combination of a drive to recruit new PDPA members and a purge of some of the old guard (probably recalcitrant Khalqis for the most part) succeeded in altering the makeup of the party without, however, improving its quality. New membership cards were distributed on 10 January in an effort to "cleanse and purify" the party (U.K. Foreign and Commonwealth Office, *Background Brief*, May). "The youth and new members form more than half [the PDPA] strength," said Babrak (*Kabul New Times*, 20 March; *FBIS*, 8 April), but it was a different youth from that which the PDPA had attracted previously. Whereas in earlier years the party had been made up almost entirely of intellectuals and academics (in 1978, Taraki had claimed that most PDPA members were teachers), by March 1982 the middle levels of the party—as reflected in the 836 who attended the party conference in Kabul—showed only about half with higher education and about 15 percent with incomplete secondary education or none at all. The "higher intelligentsia," including teachers, constituted less than 5 percent of the delegates (*Afghanistan Newsletter*, October). The ratio of intellectuals to the semi-educated and illiterate was doubtless even lower among the newest recruits, the majority of whom, according to party claims, were peasants, workers, or soldiers of peasant or worker background. Entry requirements for such persons were eased in early 1982: only two, not three, party members were needed as sponsors; the sponsors needed to have been full members for only two, not three, years; and the candidate himself had to spend only six months, not one year, as a probationer before achieving full membership (Radio Kabul, 23 March; *FBIS*, 30 March).

The most intense recruiting effort seems to have occurred in the armed forces, where a captive audience of young officers and conscripts could be subjected to indoctrination and forceful persuasion in isolation from the anticommunist influences of the population at large. Over 75 percent of army officers were members or candidate members of the PDPA or DYOA (Radio Kabul, 23 October; *FBIS*, 27 October), and the army claimed more than 20,000 permanent and probationary members (*Kabul New Times*, 24 August). For the rest, recruitment could have had little success in the 90 percent of the country over which the DRA had at best only nominal control. Presumably it was limited to the population of the few government-controlled towns. According to Babrak, the "several thousand" party members and probationary members in Kabul made up the "biggest part" of the PDPA, an indication not only of the membership's concentration in the capital but also of its smaller than claimed size (Bakhtar, 24 February; *FBIS*, 26 February).

Lowering the educational level, however, in no way solved the PDPA's fundamental internal problem, the Parcham-Khalq internecine rivalry. Throughout the year, repeated calls for unity and complaints that the "previous diseases of fractionism and factionalism are still being noticed" were mixed with comments about the "weaknesses, deficiencies, and shortcomings" in the training of party cadres (Bakhtar, 24 February; *FBIS*, 26 February). The clearest sign of the depth of the schism came when the March PDPA conference was abruptly terminated after only 30 hours. Originally expected to include about 1,700 elected delegates, the conference mustered only 841 party appointees, of whom five could not attend "for good reason." (*Afghanistan Newsletter*, October.) (Five deaths attributed to intraparty shoot-outs on 11 March may be behind their failure to appear [*NYT*, 17 March].) Apparently Parchami efforts to rig the election of delegates to a full-fledged party congress had been unsuccessful, and the elections were curtailed to keep the Khalqis from obtaining a majority. By arbitrarily appointing delegates to the conference—a maneuver permitted for conferences but not for congresses under the old party rules—the Parchamis were able to secure a 60–40 majority but at the price of such bitterness that no formal vote counts were released (ibid.). New party rules (a constitution) were later published as a document of the conference, but they differed from those in effect since 1965 only in their removal of references to Marxism-Leninism and socialism, considered inappropriate for a country in the national-democratic stage of development. An "action program" to consolidate all security forces under the party was also adopted at the conference but appeared to have little practical effect either organizationally or operationally (U.S. Department of State, Special Report no. 106, December).

Reports of Khalqi cooperation with the resistance, a logical consequence of the feud with the Parchamis, continued in 1982. According to one defector, "at least three quarters of the 800 persons responsible to the prime minister were aiding the resistance in one form or another," either by providing information or actually participating in nighttime raids against government targets in Kabul. The same source claimed that Gen. Abdul Wodood, a Khalqi, had been shot by the Soviets on suspicion of having collaborated with the resistance. (AFP, 9 November; *FBIS*, 10 November.) Collaboration may not have been as massive as this source claimed—another defector estimated that 40–45 percent of the senior officials were sympathetic to the resistance (AFP, 30 March; *FBIS*, 31 March)—but it was clearly a serious security factor for the PDPA and the Soviets.

The Central Committee held its seventh plenum on 6 December 1981. The key problems, as outlined by Babrak, were the struggles against the resistance, factionalism, and "lack of initiative." Apparently in reference to the last, he said, "Some of the party leaders stubbornly do not want to go among the people," presumably a reflection of PDPA officials' legitimate concern that they might be assassinated if they left Kabul. Perhaps as a substitute for the personal approach, it was decided to increase propaganda output and raise the Bakhtar news agency to ministerial status. (Radio Kabul, 17 December 1981; *FBIS*, 21 December 1981.)

At the eighth plenum, held on 11 March, the issues were again intraparty solidarity (now in first place) and presentation of a draft action program for the PDPA. This, it was stated, would be placed before the upcoming PDPA conference. (Radio Kabul, 11 March; *FBIS*, 12 March.) Although the plenum took place only 72 hours before the conference, no mention was made of the conference's time or place, which remained secret until after it had closed; the first formal problem before the plenum may have been party unity, but security obviously remained a dominant concern.

The ninth plenum finished its work in late July. Its messages again were unity and the fight against the resistance ("counterrevolution"), but it also called for greater party appreciation of the Afghan people's devotion to Islam as well as respect for local customs (Radio Kabul, 31 July; *FBIS*, 2 August). Perhaps the most significant aspect of the ninth plenum was the fact that broadcast of Babrak's keynote speech, traditionally made from tape recordings immediately after each plenum, was delayed this time for several days. When it finally appeared on the radio, it was read by an announcer. It may be that the Soviets disapproved of the secretary general's choice of words on local customs and religion, both highly sensitive subjects in the adjacent Soviet Central Asian republics, and insisted on some changes.

In November, before an audience of middle-level DRA and PDPA executives, security officers, and military officers gathered from all over the country for a joint seminar of organizational departments, Babrak gave a revealing speech on the problems facing the party. Even in the abbreviated summary broadcast over Radio Kabul, it was clear that ideological, organizational, and party unity (mentioned no fewer than eleven times in the six paragraphs covering the first half of the speech) was a key element still eluding the party management. It was termed a "crucial issue in the destiny of the party, revolution, people, and our . . . homeland," as well as a prerequisite for dealing with the resistance. As corollaries, iron discipline in party affairs, selection and promotion of personnel on merit, not personal connections, and the inculcation of the party's ideology, first into its own rank and file and then into the population at large, were all emphasized. The party's "international responsibility" was also underscored, but without reference to specific tasks or expectations. Finally, almost as an afterthought, Babrak noted that his audience should work to enhance the national economy and raise the Afghan standard of living. (Radio Kabul, 3 November; *FBIS*, 5 November.)

The tenth plenum, held on 12 December, was devoted almost entirely to the problems of recruiting, training, organizing, unifying, and promoting new cadres. Babrak's marathon speech (*Kabul New Times*, 15–20 December) hailed some achievements, including the alleged recruitment of over 15,000 new candidate members between March and September, but for each compliment there was a corresponding criticism that indicated where the most serious weaknesses in the party lay. He emphasized the need for more members (especially youth and women) and for a better ethnic cross section. More fundamentally, he warned against careerists, "alien elements," "unwilling" personnel (perhaps an indication of recruitment under duress), opportunists, conspirators, "even enemies," and he urged that these be removed from the party even as new members were being recruited. He demanded that new members be eager, efficient, and prepared to propagandize the masses. In this regard he faulted older members for not training the new recruits, for failing to utilize their talents in party work while they were still only candidates, and for not promoting them to positions of more responsibility when they became full members. He was especially critical of the vacuum in the middle levels of the party organization and the fact that Afghans trained in the USSR and Eastern Europe were not being moved ahead to fill these slots. Even in provinces where the resistance was not disrupting the government, he said, political and organizational work was unsatisfactory. At the end of his speech, he again traced the root cause of the party's problems to a lack of unity.

Reading between the lines of Babrak's speeches, it appeared that the PDPA's experiment in opening the party to the masses it was supposed to represent had neither solved the Parcham-Khalq controversy nor made the party more palatable to the Afghan population.

The PDPA was no more successful in promoting its fronts. During the year, individual groups like the DYOA and the DWOA received regular publicity in the Kabul press but mostly in connection with their leaders' greeting delegations from sister organizations abroad. There were few if any propaganda extravaganzas. The umbrella NFF held its second plenum only in June 1982, a year after its founding. Its purpose remained the melding of diverse Afghan elements into a cohesive bedrock of popular support for the party. Despite a minimum age requirement of only fifteen years and steady propaganda promoting membership, however, the NFF commanded little respect or popularity and remained moribund for most of the year. Its total membership has not been revealed.

There were no leadership changes in the party until the end of the year, when two new Central Committee secretaries and two new alternate Politburo members were named. General Mohammed Yaseen Sadeqi, who had replaced Gul Aqa as chief of political affairs in the army, and Mir Saheb Karwal, the administrator of the Central Zone, were named secretaries at the tenth plenum. At the same time, Minister of Defense Abdul Qader and Abdul Zahoor Razmjo, secretary of the Kabul city committee, were appointed alternates on the Politburo. (*Kabul New Times*, 13 December.)

Domestic Affairs. The dominant problem affecting all aspects of life in Afghanistan in 1982 was the continuation and strengthening of opposition, nonviolent as well as violent, to the DRA and the Soviet occupation. The flow of refugees into Pakistan, and to a lesser extent Iran, continued, and at year's end there were estimated to be more than three million Afghan exiles, about a fifth of the pre-1978 population (U.K. Foreign and Commonwealth Office, *Background Brief*, November). Noteworthy defectors included Afghanistan's former ambassador to the United Nations for eighteen years, the deputy chief of KHAD, the chief of the KHAD academy's Iran and Pakistan section, the military attaché to New Delhi, the ambassador to Bangladesh, and a top codes expert.

In the DRA army, the annual desertion (10,000) and casualty (5,000) rates continued to match the ever more draconian conscription efforts of the authorities, and the weakened military establishment was estimated at 30,000–40,000 (U.S. Department of State, Special Bulletin no. 106, December). The deserters not only swelled the guerrilla (mujahidin) ranks, but provided a continuous resupply of arms and ammunition. Badly demoralized, the army often warned the resistance of impending joint Soviet-DRA operations against them and occasionally opened their lines to let the mujahidin escape encirclement (*FEER*, 19 March). Other security forces, including KHAD, Sarandoy (Ministry of Interior security police), and the volunteer militia (called "soldiers of the revolution" in PDPA parlance), were believed to total no more than 20,000 at the start of 1982. A captured communication from the Sarandoy commander in Afghanistan's second largest city, Kandahar, to the minister of interior reported that his forces had shrunk by over 75 percent and that only about half of his 617 remaining privates were fit for action. His losses were due not only to casualties suffered in antiresistance operations (and presumably to desertions) but to official transfers to Kabul that he had not approved. He also noted that the security situation could improve if "progressives" could be persuaded to stay in the province instead of leaving for Kabul. (AFP, 19 February; *FBIS*, 22 February.) Babrak himself voiced complaints that the lower ranks of Sarandoy officers were inadequately aware of the severity of the "class struggle," and he urged more active political work to "noticeably improve" their combat capabilities (Radio Kabul, 20 October; *FBIS*, 22 October). Meanwhile, a defector from the police academy reported that training had been reduced from three years to three months to make up for desertions (Radio Karachi, 20 November; *FBIS*, 26 November). Even KHAD, which was being coached by both East German and Soviet security agencies, came in for muted accusations of deviation (Radio Kabul, 23 May; *FBIS*, 25 May).

Meanwhile, morale in the resistance continued high, boosted in part by the operation of three clandestine FM radio stations within 50 kilometers of Kabul itself that provided up-to-date information on resistance operations (*CSM*, 2 July).

The DRA response to the deteriorating security situation was efforts, often self-canceling, both to woo and to bludgeon its citizens into obedience. In a move to gain support in the countryside, the regime announced a plan to decentralize the government, promising to leave local affairs in the hands of local leaders.Villages were supposed to defend themselves with their own volunteer militia, and the central government would pay the equivalent of up to $60 for volunteers to this force. The Shinwari tribe that controls much of the border region near Jalalabad was reported to have accepted the offer, imperiling transit routes for the mujahidin to and from their sanctuaries in Pakistan. (*Los Angeles Times*, 10 February.) At the same time, the regime continued with its 1981 de-emphasis on land reform in early 1982. In both of these moves, it was in effect acknowledging that it could not control the countryside and hoped that it could enlist the political support it could not achieve by force.

Far from having the desired effect, the move appears to have caused an almost immediate backlash, probably from the more rigidly Marxist-Leninist Khalqis. By the time of the party conference in March, there was a renewed emphasis on land reform, and Babrak's speech called for the central organs to carry the struggle to the provinces, not for the provinces to handle matters on their own (Radio Kabul, 15 March; *FBIS*, 30 March).

To attract new recruits into the army, the regime promised twelfth-grade certificates to tenth-grade dropouts who served for two years, and it guaranteed entrance into higher education without examination to eleventh-grade volunteers (*CSM*, 2 July). Those servicemen who re-enlisted were promised a host of benefits, including choice of post, higher pay, weekly passes to visit families, higher salaries, acceptance into military academies, and (for five-year veterans) an allotment of land for their families (Radio Kabul, 24 December 1981; *FBIS*, 29 December 1981).

Other blandishments offered the armed forces included promotions (10,000) and lavish dispensation of medals and orders (*Kabul New Times*, 24 August). For the civilians, penalties connected wth peasant tax arrears over the past three years were annulled (Bakhtar, 21 March; *FBIS*, 23 March). A regular program of broadcasts to Pakistan was designed to entice refugees home, as was propaganda about a DRA amnesty for all who heeded the call (*Kabul New Times*, 11 September).

These measures, however, were accompanied or succeeded by harsher policies that undid whatever success they may have enjoyed. The draft age was expanded from its old 21–35-year-old range to 19–39, and press gangs roamed Kabul streets to snatch persons both older and younger for service (U.S. Department of State, Special Report no. 106, December). On 2 August, Kabul announced the extension of compulsory military service from two and a half years to three (ibid.). The Shinwaris, whom the DRA had tried to win over with promises of autonomy, became liable for the draft, despite a fifty-year tradition exempting them from military service. A three-day peaceful demonstration in Kabul finally won for them a revocation of this policy, and the government demobilized the Shinwaris it had already drafted. (AFP, 10 November; *FBIS*, 12 November.) The confrontation (including a threat by the demonstrators to kill a government spokesman) cannot have helped the DRA's relations with the tribe. Reports of torture and beatings of dissidents by the government continued (*CSM*, 2 July).

In the economic sphere, the country continued to suffer drastically from the fighting, impoverished by an estimated $2 billion per year in lost gross national product. During July, rationing of bread, flour, chicken, and meat was instituted to control the runaway inflation that continued from 1981, when prices of staples jumped 200–500 percent. (*Current History*, May.) The USSR provided 80,000 tons of wheat, 10,000 tons of flour, and 20 million rubles worth of textiles and other consumer goods gratis. Still more was needed, however, and was supplied on a barter basis to cover the DRA's import needs of 150,000–200,000 tons of wheat, 30,000 tons of rice, 17,000 tons of vegetable oil, and 70,000 tons of sugar, as well as thousands of tons of dairy products. (Radio Kabul, 15 October; *FBIS*, 19 October.) The need for these imports was due in part to Soviet policies of destroying crops and driving farmers into exile or the cities in order to deny food and support to the resistance.

Foreign trade reportedly increased, although the inflation factor probably skewed the figures. According to Minister of Commerce Mohammed Khan Jalalar, Afghan exports were expected to increase slightly to $600 million in 1982, with natural gas exports constituting over $300 million and crude oil (a new product) $45 million. The USSR was to be the major importer, absorbing 59 percent of Afghan exports, while trade with capitalist countries would shrink. (*Pravda*, Bratislava, 22 July; *FBIS*, 28 July.) Other close links with the USSR included the opening of the Termez-Hairatan road and rail bridge over the Amu Darya (Oxus River) and the planned extension of a 220 kv power line into Afghanistan (*Kabul New Times*, 7 October). Afghanistan also signed aid and trade agreements with members of the Council for Mutual Economic Assistance, including Bulgaria and Czechoslovakia. Bulgarian trade was to increase fifteen times in the period 1982–1987. The agreement called for Bulgaria to supply vehicles, buses, tank trucks, and clothing in exchange for Afghan oil, cotton, leather, and wool. The Bulgarians would also provide factories for processing Afghan agricultural products. (Ibid., 9 October.)

Within Afghanistan, Babrak reiterated his dedication to a mixed economy, one that would tolerate and even promote some private enterprise in light industry and trade, while retaining the basic levers of economic power in the hands of the state. The land reform measures he promoted starting in March combined both land and irrigation reform, and he pledged that the party and state would help in developing production and marketing cooperatives for the peasants. On the other hand, he emphasized that "the principle of voluntary membership in the cooperatives will be strictly observed and no coercion [on peasants to join] will be permitted." (Ibid., 1–8 and 20 March; *FBIS*, 8 April.)

Leadership changes in the DRA were relatively minor. Two men left their posts on the Presidium of the Revolutionary Council. Dr. Abdul Ghaffar Lakanwal, a Parchami, became minister of agriculture and land reform instead, replacing Fazl Rahim Momand, a nonparty man. Major General Abdul Qader, named acting minister of defense in January in the absence of Maj. Gen. Mohammed Rafiee, who was studying in the USSR, finally took over as minister and left the Presidium. Two others were relieved of their ministries but remained deputy prime ministers; Guldad, a Khalqi, was replaced as minister of higher education by Sarwar Mangal, a Parchami; Abdul Majid Sarbiland, a Parchami, was dropped as minister of information and culture, but no replacement was named. Two additional deputy prime ministers named during the year were Khalil Ahmad Abawi, head of planning, and Rafiee, former minister of defense, both Parchamis.

Some additional influential individuals were given ministerial rank: president of the central bank Mehrabuddin Paktiawal; head of the State Planning Committee Khalil Ahmad Abawi; Minister of Irrigation Ahmad Shah Sorkhabi, whose apparat had been split off from the Ministry of Water and Power; president of local organs and state power Abdul Majid Qayumi; president of the administrative department of the

Council of Ministers Dr. Najibullah Masir; and president of the central statistical organization Fazl Rahim Momand, the former minister of agriculture (*Kabul New Times*, 29 August).

Given the military, political, and economic crisis that enveloped the country, perhaps the most unusual feature of the leaders' lives was the frequency and duration of their travel abroad. For example, Babrak spent nearly six weeks in East Germany and the USSR in May and June. Rafiee, commander of the air force and air defense Col. Nazar Mohammed, and commander of the Central Army corps Col. Khalilullah spent a year in training in the USSR. Other leaders traveled for extended periods all over the world. With Soviet domination over decision making in all parts of the Afghan government, their presence was apparently unneeded and perhaps unwanted.

In the military field there were constant skirmishes between the resistance and Soviet-DRA forces, plus some pitched battles. Resistance strongholds in Paghman, just 12 miles from Kabul, and the Panjshir Valley, close to the Soviet airbase at Bagram, 60 miles to the north, were overrun several times by large-scale government operations, and Soviet forces continued to use lethal chemical warfare agents against selected, remote resistance targets (U.S. Department of State, Special Report no. 106, December). When at a disadvantage, however, the mujahidin would simply melt into the hills, snipe at the occupation troops, and eventually effect their withdrawal. Even when on the defensive, the mujahidin scored heavily: a convoy of young PDPA activists recruited to join the Soviet-DRA assault on the Panjshir in June was attacked, and hundreds were killed (*NYT*, 30 June). The resistance scored doubly in this operation because the victims were Khalqis and their leaders were enraged that equally suitable Parchami youth had been exempted from duty or were conveniently absent when the call to arms came (*FEER*, 9 July).

Whereas in 1981 Kabul was relatively secure for the DRA and the Soviets, in 1982 partisan attacks on government buildings, the Soviet Embassy, Soviet living compounds, and individual PDPA officials became more and more frequent in the capital. By the end of the year, they even included daylight raids. The airfields at Jalalabad and Bagram were attacked repeatedly and a number of Soviet aircraft destroyed (*NYT*, 31 December). The mujahidin captured a number of communist officials, took them to liberated areas, and put them to death after summary trials. Others were hanged publicly in their own towns and left as examples.

There was one deliberate kidnaping of a Soviet hostage, the geologist E.R. Okrimyuk, who was unwise enough to claim personal connections with Soviet President Leonid Brezhnev and Premier Nikolai Tikhonov. The mujahidin tried to exchange him for 50 prisoners held by the DRA, but were unsuccessful in negotiating the trade and eventually killed him. (*FEER*, 23 April.) Three Soviet POWs captured in 1981 were sent to Switzerland where they were held incommunicado by the Swiss in accordance with an unpublicized agreement with the USSR (*Possev*, Frankfurt, October). Four others joined them in November (U.S. Department of State, Special Report no. 106, December). Others were held in Afghanistan, and a few even converted to Islam and joined the resistance (*FEER*, 27 August).

Mujahidin losses were relatively light because they retained the initiative and avoided direct confrontation with superior government or Soviet forces. They lost one charismatic leader, Abdul Halim, who led the resistance inside Kabul, but vigorous partisan activities inside the capital continued after his death (*WP*, 15 October).

The increasing frequency of accounts of mujahidin rocket attacks on surface targets and success in shooting down armored helicopters seemed to indicate that more sophisticated weapons than those captured from Soviet and DRA troops were finding their way into resistance hands. Despite reprisals by DRA and Soviet forces against villages suspected of aiding the partisans, the resistance seemed stronger and more confident than ever as 1982 drew to a close.

Foreign Affairs.   With its very existence resting entirely on Soviet support, the DRA has no native foreign policy. Even on such regional issues as Pushtunistan (the promotion of separatist nationalism among the Pushtuns in Pakistan, a long-standing Afghan policy that predates the 1978 communist coup), the Afghan party and state have no choice but to follow Moscow's instructions. Although it may have been the USSR's original intention to use its Afghan surrogates to inflame Pushtun nationalism and thus to destabilize Pakistan, any efforts they may have made in this direction were more than offset by the overwhelming anti-Soviet and anti-DRA reaction of the Pushtun tribes to the Soviet invasion and occupation. During the first half of the year, there were some pro forma Pushtunistan releases from Kabul (Radio Kabul, 16 April; *FBIS*, 20 April), but they lacked conviction and had no perceptible effect in Pakistan. By a wide margin in 1982, Afghanistan was a net importer of revolution, not an exporter.

Afghanistan's credentials as a nonaligned state are recognized by other members of that movement, but can scarcely be taken very seriously by those nations that again in 1982 voted with the overwhelming U.N. majority (114–21) for the removal of "all foreign troops" from the country (*Afghan Realities*, October/ November). Afghanistan's delegates to Soviet international fronts like the World Peace Council and the Afro-Asian Peoples' Solidarity Organization (AAPSO) provided marginal additional support for Soviet initiatives, but again could not have been very convincing as independent ballots. A mujahidin rocket attack on the hotel in Kabul where AAPSO delegates were holding a meeting in November 1981 was an embarrassing episode for both the Afghans and AAPSO's Soviet sponsors.

The DRA's friendly relations with other members of Moscow's international entourage were as predictable as its hostile relations with the United States and its allies. Regionally, Afghan propaganda focused primarily on anti-Pakistan and anti-Zionist themes.

Although the USSR showed no signs of any immediate intention of removing its forces, the pressures to do so appeared to be mounting, and the signals from Moscow were mixed. On the one hand, there was an increase in the Soviet garrison from 85,000 to 105,000 (*NYT*, 27 December). As in previous years, the construction of permanent barracks and supply depots was interpreted by some analysts as a sign of a Soviet intent to remain indefinitely. The process of Sovietization was also marked. Soviet textbooks and the Russian language became standard in Afghan schools, and the majority of the faculty at Kabul University were reported to be Soviet (*Afghan Realities*, September). At least 1,200 Afghan children were sent to Soviet Pioneer camps during the summer (*Kabul New Times*, 5 September), and the Soviet scholarship program for 6,000–10,000 older students continued. In February, a satellite communications and television link was established. (U.S. Department of State, Special Report no. 106, December.) More ominous, Lt. Gen. Ghulam Siddiq Miraki, the deputy chief of KHAD who defected to Pakistan, claimed to have access to information on a Soviet plan to annex all of Afghanistan. The plan was allegedly abandoned after Babrak failed to achieve a PDPA consensus that would have allowed him to petition for more Soviet troops and admission into the USSR, but an alternative plan for the Soviet Union to annex at least the nine northern Afghan provinces was supposedly still under consideration as of Brezhnev's death in November. (AP, 16 December.) Later articles in the official press extolling the benefits of union republic membership in the USSR may have been connected in some way with this allegation (*Kabul New Times*, 25 December). Meanwhile, there were continued reports that the USSR had all but annexed the Wakhan Corridor, the finger of Afghan territory extending to the Chinese border in the northeast (*NYT*, 8 December).

Nevertheless, there were incentives for Moscow to withdraw and some signals that it was considering such a move. The continued erosion of the USSR's prestige all over the world, not only for the fact of its aggression but (perhaps even more significant) for its failure to deal with the resistance, continued to affect Soviet policies elsewhere. In March, India, traditionally an apologist for Soviet actions and heretofore ambivalent on the Afghanistan issue, called for a Soviet withdrawal (BBC, 2 April). (The Afghan reactivation of the joint Indo-Afghan Commission on Economic and Technological Cooperation that followed this Indian move may have been an attempt to influence India away from its stand [Bakhtar, 16 May; *FBIS*, 17 May].) Eurocommunists and left-wing socialists called for a Soviet withdrawal, and the Bertrand Russell Tribunal protested the Soviet incineration of Afghan civilians who had taken refuge in an underground cistern (*Times*, London, 8 December).

Another factor affecting Soviet willingness to remain must have been the threat of a revolutionary spillover into the USSR itself. One Afghan resistance organization (Jamiat-e-Islami) claimed to have 2,500 card-carrying members in Soviet Tadzhikistan, and another claimed to have made three raids into Soviet Central Asia (*CSM*, 26 July; AFP, 29 October; *FBIS*, 1 November). The success of the Afghan resistance has led to a sharp increase in anti-Islamic activities by the USSR in its Muslim republics (BBC, 22 September). Even in traditionally Catholic Lithuania, revulsion against the Soviet intervention led to a protest by an underground civil rights journal (*Times*, London, 26 August).

An indirect indicator that the USSR was concerned about the spillover effect was a change in its willingness to portray the occupation in detail. Whereas in early 1982, *Red Star* had conceded that the life of Soviet soldiers in Afghanistan was "hard . . . sometimes very, very hard" (*Krasnaia zvezda*, 23

February; *FBIS*, 26 February), by autumn it had reverted to an earlier posture of concealing from its readers the fact that recipients of military decorations had received them for valor in combat there. Instead, the outstanding performances were supposed to have come "during maneuvers" (*Krasnaia zvezda*, 6 October). Part of the Soviet concern doubtless came from the desertion of some individual soldiers to the Afghan side. By year's end, there was a report that Uzbek troops guarding Bagram airbase had led resistance fighters through minefields around the base, enabling them to destroy a number of helicopters and other aircraft (*NYT*, 31 December).

The hints emanating from Kabul and Moscow concerning a negotiated settlement and Soviet withdrawal gathered strength in the course of the year. Although there was no explicit change in the Soviet position that Soviet troops would be withdrawn "only after an end to the outside military interference in Afghanistan" (that is, after the resistance had been crushed), the DRA welcomed the April visit of Diego Cordovez, dispatched by the U.N. secretary general to seek a peaceful solution (Radio Kabul, 13 April; *FBIS*, 14 April). Later, the Pakistani and Afghan foreign ministers met in Geneva to discuss a four-point program involving the withdrawal of foreign troops, nonintervention in the internal affairs of Afghanistan, guarantees of noninterference, and the voluntary return of Afghan refugees now in Pakistan. Cordovez reported that "broad agreement" had been reached (*NYT*, 6 June), and Moscow also signaled its official blessing of these talks (Radio Moscow, 14 June; *FBIS*, 15 June).

While the Geneva talks were under way, the United States and the USSR were also discussing the same matter bilaterally and privately in Moscow. Although there was no sign of change in the basic Soviet position, the willingness to negotiate was taken as an encouraging sign (*NYT*, 24 July). By the end of the year, the Soviets appeared to have agreed in principle to a return of Afghanistan to its status quo ante of a truly nonaligned buffer state, but were still insisting on some tangible sign of U.S. and Chinese goodwill as a prerequisite for concessions. No movement on withdrawal was anticipated before 1984. (*CSM*, 28 October.) A later report indicated that Pakistan's president, General Zia ul Haq, might agree to cut off all aid to the resistance in return for the promise of a phased withdrawal of Soviet troops over an 18 to 24 month period (*Times*, London, 18 November), although this would leave the resistance dangerously vulnerable in the interim. The death of Leonid Brezhnev in November and the assumption of Soviet leadership by Yuri Andropov presumably affected all Soviet policies to some degree, but the specific effect on the Kremlin's position on Afghanistan was not clear as the year drew to a close.

Even if all outside parties could agree on a program to restore Afghanistan's independence, the resistance's inability to unite in a consensus exile government would remain a stumbling block to meaningful negotiations. In the best of circumstances, Afghans have traditionally found it hard to unify beyond the framework of family and tribe, and efforts to create an effective umbrella organization of exiles in Pakistan (actively discouraged by Soviet agents as well as by Afghan proclivities [*San Francisco Chronicle*, 9 June]), have been largely unsuccessful. At some point this problem must be addressed by the Afghans themselves if they do not wish to cede their country to the USSR by default.

Novato, California   Ruth L. and Anthony Arnold

Australia

Several communist parties function legally within Australia's parliamentary democracy. None has significant electoral support. In the last national election, held in October 1980, the most successful communist candidate, Judy Mundey of the Communist Party of Australia (CPA), polled only 4 percent of the vote in her district. Moreover, the growth prospects of Australia's communist parties are not good. Australia is an affluent society in which middle-class values predominate, and there is widespread distrust of communism and the Soviet Union. Nevertheless, communist parties have been able to exert somewhat more influence than their minuscule size would suggest, largely because some of their leaders occupy key positions in the trade union movement.

The largest and oldest faction of Australia's communist movement is the CPA, founded in 1920. During the early 1960s, the CPA was wracked by an internal debate that echoed the Sino-Soviet ideological dispute, and in 1964 the pro-Beijing faction broke away to form the Communist Party of Australia/Marxist-Leninist (CPA/ML). A second split occurred in 1971 between CPA members who had grown dissatisfied with Soviet policies and those who remained loyal to Moscow. The latter group split away to form the Socialist Party of Australia (SPA), leaving the CPA in the hands of members who favored an independent, Eurocommunist orientation.

The CPA's membership has been estimated at about 2,000 but this figure is probably too high. Only 200 delegates and observers attended the party's Twenty-Seventh Congress in June (*Tribune*, 23 June). The CPA continues to follow a Eurocommunist line, attempting to exploit nationalist, isolationist sentiment. The CPA was quick to condemn Soviet interference in Poland, and a resolution passed by the congress called for socialism without the imposition of a universal model.

Between congresses, which are held every three years, the CPA is run by an eight-member Executive Committee and a 30-member National Committee. The Twenty-Seventh Congress elected several new faces to the national committee, but the inner circle of leaders, which includes Judy Mundey, Bernard Taft, Mark Taft, Robert Durbridge, Brian Aarons, and Laurie Carmichael, remained essentially unchanged. The CPA publishes a weekly newspaper, the *Tribune*, and a theoretical journal, the *Australian Leftist Review*.

The second largest communist party, the SPA, remains strongly pro-Moscow. It accuses the CPA of being "a petty bourgeois party, anti-Marxist-Leninist, and anti-Soviet" (*Socialist*, 2 December 1981). The SPA supported the imposition of martial law in Poland, attributing Poland's problems to CIA and Zionist machinations. SPA members of the Waterside Workers Federation (WWF) fought an attempt by the union's national leaders to impose a ban on loading and unloading Polish ships in response to the suppression of the Polish labor movement. When the WWF, after much debate, finally resolved to impose a one-week ban on Polish ships in January, the SPA-influenced Sydney branch of the WWF undercut the decision by issuing a public statement supporting the Polish government.

The SPA is led by Pat Clancy, who is secretary of the Building Workers Industrial Union. Clancy was re-elected president of the SPA at the party's Fourth Congress in October 1981. Other key leaders are Peter Symon, general secretary; Jack McPhillips, Central Committee chairman and secretary; and Alan Miller, Central Committee secretary. The SPA's newspaper is the *Socialist*.

The pro-Beijing CPA/ML is led by Edward Hill. It publishes a weekly newspaper, *Vanguard*, and a theoretical journal, *Australian Communist*. One of its leading members, Norm Gallagher, is president of the Builders' Laborers' Federation. Gallagher was much in the news during late 1982 because of charges brought against him by the government for allegedly receiving illegal commissions in his capacity as union leader.

Australia's principal Trotskyite group is the tiny Socialist Workers Party, which is associated with the Fourth International in Brussels. Its newspaper is *Direct Action*.

All of Australia's communist parties compete for influence within the trade union movement and, to a lesser extent, among students and intellectuals. They have tried to capitalize on Australia's current economic problems by criticizing the economic policies of the Liberal–National Party coalition government headed by Prime Minister Malcolm Fraser. In particular, they have espoused alternate policies that might appeal to a labor sector concerned about rising unemployment and stagnating real wages. The CPA, for example, pledged to resist restructuring the economy (which it assumes will cost jobs), to fight for "social control" over economic policy, and to push for a massive transfer of economic resources to the working class (*Tribune,* 23 June).

The communist parties also continued to be active in promoting various leftist international causes, sometimes in cooperation with noncommunist antinuclear or peace organizations. The Israeli invasion of Lebanon evoked considerable strident protests from the CPA and SPA, and in August the WWF and other maritime unions placed a ban on handling cargo for Israeli vessels. The communist parties also participated in protests of port visits by U.S. nuclear-powered warships (in April and August), of uranium mining, and of abridgement of aboriginal land rights. They also espoused the causes of a nuclear-free Pacific and nuclear disarmament.

The Fraser government's relations with the Soviet Union cooled further during 1982, largely as a result of events in Poland. In January, the Australian government announced its full support for Western sanctions designed to bring about the end of martial law in Poland. It also announced that Australia would keep in place the measures it had taken two years earlier in response to the Soviet invasion of Afghanistan. These measures included termination of fisheries cooperation; denial of landing rights to the Soviet national airline, Aeroflot; and suspension of all scientific exchange programs. The ban on scientific exchange developed into a public controversy in August when some Australian scientists protested the denial of visas to two Soviet scientists invited to attend the International Congress of Biochemistry in Perth. The Australian government subsequently announced new guidelines that would allow Soviet scientists to visit Australia for international conferences but not for bilateral exchanges.

Prime Minister Fraser has been in the forefront of those advocating a strong Western defense posture against the Soviets. In March, he accused the Soviet ambassador of making a "grave threat" against Australia in telling the press that Fraser's decision to allow U.S. B-52 flights to operate through Darwin could make Australia a nuclear target (Reuters, 5 March). At the Third Commonwealth Heads of Government Regional Meeting, held in Fiji in October, Fraser urged Pacific island governments to take steps to prevent the extension of Soviet influence into their region.

In contrast, Australia's relations with the People's Republic of China continued to improve in 1982. Fraser paid a well-publicized visit to Beijing in August, during which he announced that Australia would provide $16 million in bilateral aid to China over the next five years (*FBIS,* 5 August).

Arlington, Virginia   Ralph L. Braibanti

Bangladesh

The Communists have very little influence in Bangladesh. The small Communist Party of Bangladesh is wracked by factionalism, the military leadership of the country is generally pro-Western and conservative, and political activities have been prohibited since the establishment of martial law rule in March 1982. In addition, radicalism in Bangladesh tends to find expression in various forms of populism rather than communism.

Lieutenant General Hossain Mohammed Ershad, army chief of staff, assumed power as chief martial law administrator on 24 March following several months of tension between the military and political leaders. The assassination of President Ziaur Rahman in May 1981 led to the unraveling of the dominant Bangladesh Nationalist Party (BNP), a loose umbrella organization composed of many factions that Ziaur Rahman had pieced together. His vice-president, former Supreme Court Justice Abdus Sattar, was not able to establish cohesion among the competitive BNP groups. Sattar's assumption of the presidency in the November 1981 elections did not stabilize the situation within the BNP. The jockeying for power among its factions gave the impression of disorder, which concerned the country's military leaders.

Even before the November presidential elections, Ershad had expressed his support for some undefined type of military role in the decision-making process. In response, Sattar created the National Security Council in early 1982, consisting of the president, the vice-president, and the three military service chiefs, to advise the government on policy questions. The military, apparently not satisfied with this arrangement and concerned with the continuing squabbling within the BNP, moved on 24 March to replace the civilian government. It dismissed the president and the prime minister, dissolved parliament, and suspended the constitution. Martial law regulations prohibited political activities and dissolved student unions.

Ershad, in his announcement of martial law government, noted that a major reason for the military action was widespread political corruption. Besides the drive against corruption, he has taken steps designed to bring government administration closer to the people. He has reduced the number of ministries, established benches of the High Court in each of the country's four administrative divisions, and established the *thana* (county) as the basic administrative unit of government. He has promised elections to the *thana parishads* (committees) on a nonparty basis as the first step in restoring democracy nationally. (*FEER*, 24 December.) Soon after assuming power, Ershad told reporters that he envisaged a two-year time frame for national elections, to be held "as soon as the situation turns favorable to public interest" (AFP, Hong Kong, 18 April). The military government has also encouraged the private sector and stressed free-market incentives to stimulate agricultural production. So far, the country has remained relatively calm. There is no evidence of communist political activity.

On the foreign policy front, Ershad has emphasized continuity. Relations with China, already very good, were reaffirmed by Ershad's 27 November–2 December visit to the PRC. China, for its part, sent several trade and cultural delegations to Bangladesh during the year. Relations with the USSR have remained proper, if not particularly warm. Ershad told reporters in June that he had talked to Soviet Foreign Minister Andrei Gromkyo in New York and that the talks would "resolve the little misunderstanding" in Soviet-Bangladeshi relations (ibid., 23 June). His government has moved to give more substance to the bilateral relationship with the USSR. It negotiated a cultural exchange agreement with the USSR for 1982–1983, concluded a barter trade protocol, and worked out an agreement for Soviet credits to the large Ghorashal thermal power plant. In addition, the USSR set up a program providing academic grants over the next five years for Bangladeshi students in the Soviet Union. The Bangladeshi government sent an official representative to Brezhnev's funeral. Nonetheless, there remains considerable suspicion of the Soviet Union because of its continued presence in Afghanistan and its close relations with India. Shortly before Ershad's November visit to China, Bangladesh recognized the Democratic Kampuchea government.

The various pro-communist parties and their student and labor fronts remained moribund during the year, in part because of the imposition of martial law rules against political activities (*Bangkok Post*, 2 May). Besides the pro-Soviet Communist Party of Bangladesh, there are pro-Soviet factions within the National Awami Party. Among the pro-Chinese groups are the Sammyabad Dal (Marxist/Leninist), the United People's Party, the Jatiya Ganomukti Union, and some factions of the National Awami Party. However, all of these groups lack a grass-roots organizational structure. There are also pro-Soviet and pro-Chinese factions in the Awami League, probably the only organized political party in the country. However, the moderate elements of the Awami League are in firm control of the party.

Arlington, Virginia   Walter K. Andersen

Burma

The Burmese Communist Party (BCP), founded on 15 August 1939, was a leading part of the nationalist coalition that directed the struggle for Burmese independence. The BCP has been plagued by ideological schisms from its inception. A Trotskyite group broke with the party mainstream in 1947. This split was followed by a major break with the noncommunist nationalists. In March 1948, three months after Burma gained independence, the BCP split with the new nationalist government. Outlawed, the party has been in insurrection ever since. Some of the early Burmese Communists defected from the party and eventually became influential figures in the military-socialist government that has ruled Burma since 1962. Since the early 1960s, the BCP has been avowedly pro-Chinese, characterizing itself as a party guided by Marxism-Leninism–Mao Zedong Thought. Pro-Soviet Communists were purged from the party in a paroxysm of ideological infighting that nearly destroyed the BCP itself in the mid-1960s.

Leadership and Organization.   The party is led by Central Committee Chairman Thakin Ba Thein Tin, a 73-year-old veteran of the communist movement, who is believed to reside in Beijing. The Central Committee, reconstituted in 1975, is composed of at least twenty members, of whom two were mentioned in commentaries during 1982: First Vice-President Pe Tint and Central Committee and Politburo member Myo Myint (*FEER*, 2 April). Nothing is known of their background. Like other Central Committee members, they may be part of the BCP leadership that exiled itself to Beijing in 1953 and returned to party leadership following the mid-1960 factional purges.

In 1979, the BCP claimed some 3,000 members, including candidate members. The party is organized in military-administrative regions, the largest of which is the Northeast Military Region along the Chinese border in Burma's Shan state. Also important is the 815th Military Region, south of the Northeast Military Region along Burma's border with China and Laos. There are reportedly two smaller areas of operation, identified as the 101st and 202d military regions in the Shan state. These are both unlocated, but probably west of the Salween River. Another small area is believed to exist along the Chinese border in Burma's Kachin state. The least active party units are apparently those in Arakan state, Tenasserim division, and the "Northwest division" (probably coincident with the government's Magwe division). Estimates of the size of the BCP's guerrilla force, a loose organization of units up to battalion-size, range from 8,000 to 15,000 men operating generally east of the Salween River in the mountainous area of northeastern Burma bordering China's Yunnan province. Reports of a 30,000-man BCP militia were mentioned in U.S. Department of State testimony before the Senate Committee on Foreign Relations on 6 May (*Southeast Asian Drug Trade*, Washington, D.C., 1982, p. 9). This figure should be regarded with some caution as it included both the armed main forces and the local militias that Burmese insurgent practice indicates would be largely unarmed and with minimal training.

Since 1971, the BCP has broadcast its propaganda over the Voice of the People of Burma (VOPB), a clandestine radio station transmitting out of China's Yunnan province.

Party Internal Affairs.   The dominant themes in BCP broadcasts were the call for the Rangoon government to resume peace negotiations broken off in 1981 (see *YICA*, 1982, pp. 169–171, for a discussion of the peace talks and their subsequent collapse) and explanations and justifications of the BCP position on the peace talks. Party statements attempted to pressure Rangoon to resume negotiations by enlisting support from noncommunist elements in Burmese society. The appeals apparently have had little effect, however, on improving the poor reputation of the BCP among most of the population. The BCP's forty-third anniversary statement described the difficulties the party has encountered: "From the time our party was founded until now, it has advanced along a path strewn with self-sacrifices and hardships" (VOPB, 6 September; *FBIS*, 8 September). The "tortuous path" followed by the BCP was put in the context of a "more tense and complicated" international situation dominated by imperialism and Soviet and U.S. hegemonism, particularly Soviet hegemonism. In this geopolitical situation, according to the BCP, some countries have been forced to wage national wars to oppose imperialist expansion, and the BCP believes that Burma could face a similar threat. (VOPB, 24 January; *FBIS*, 27 January.) With this in mind, the BCP claimed it took a step toward terminating the Burmese civil war, pursuing negotiations "after taking the time to discuss, consult and educate the party, the army, and the local people" (VOPB, 30 December 1981; *FBIS*, 15 January). The BCP challenged Rangoon's own peace initiatives and stated that the government's Burma Socialist Programme Party (BSPP) clamored for an intensification of the war and that the "military government" has included an "unprecedented amount for military spending" in its budget. In spite of this, the BCP reaffirmed its interest in reconvening the peace talks. "As long as the military government continues to resort to military means, the BCP will mobilize the people, firmly join hands with its allies and continue to wage the just war to defend itself and struggle through to final victory. At the same time, it will continue to struggle for the sake of ending the civil war, building peace and promoting national unity." (VOPB, 24 January; *FBIS*, 27 January.) "The BCP is prepared to hold another round of talks whenever the opportunity arises" (VOPB, 28 March; *FBIS*, 1 April). The BCP program was summarized as the "six struggles": (1) to end the civil war and build peace in the country; (2) to win full democratic rights for the people; (3) to build national unity; (4) to raise the people's standard of living; (5) to oppose the two superpowers, particularly Soviet social imperialism; and (6) to preserve world peace (VOPB, 21 March; *FBIS*, 26 March).

While continuing to reaffirm its willingness to rejoin peace discussions, the BCP maintained its long-standing critique of the government's Burmese Way to Socialism. BCP commentary on Rangoon's economic policies reflected the party's need to differentiate its own "socialism" from that of the government. "However hard one may claim Burma is a socialist country, the fact is that Burma under the Ne Win–San Yu military government remains within the clutch of the capitalist world and its economy is reliant on all stripes of imperialism" (VOPB, 21 March; *FBIS*, 26 March).

With the BCP's preoccupation with the peace-talk theme, other ideological concerns were given little stress. Whether these other ideological considerations were simply set aside by party commentators or whether changes in the party's internal situation and its relations with its Chinese mentors have provoked a significant ideological shift remain problematic. The paucity of published VOPB propaganda makes it difficult to address the questions, but there were some tantalizing hints of the extent to which the BCP leadership was trying to keep pace with the vicissitudes of ideological change in Beijing. The once frequent characterization of the BCP ideological orientation as Marxism-Leninism–Mao Zedong Thought all but disappeared in VOPB broadcasts, the single exception being the reference in the party's anniversary statement. The VOPB apparently shut down for a period in August just prior to the Twelfth Congress of the

Chinese Communist Party. While there was no announcement or explanation of the shutdown, its effect was evident in a three-week delay of the party's anniversary statement, due 15 August, but not transmitted until 6 September.

Domestic Activities. The VOPB provided little information on party activities during the year. On the domestic front, broadcasts primarily carried commentary challenging government policies. As noted above, the central propaganda theme focused on the break in peace talks and Rangoon's alleged unwillingness to return to negotiations. The BCP accused the government of "squandering away" Burma's resources in "waging a reactionary civil war" (VOPB, 5 June; *FBIS*, 10 June). While the BCP asserted its readiness to reopen talks, it charged the BSPP with intensifying the civil war. A BCP statement concluded that "the Ne Win–San Yu military clique's party will . . . be noted for its infamy and will go down as a blotch on the history of Burma" (VOPB, 6 September; *FBIS*, 8 September).

BCP criticism of the government's economic policies was also sharp and demonstrated a sophistication increasingly common over the past few years. "Everyone—including babies and the aged—had to pay about 38.5 kyat each for the war budget which came to one-third of the total," according to one party commentary (VOPB, 30 December 1981; *FBIS*, 15 January). Another broadcast claimed that 10–11 percent of each person's income is now taken in taxes, of which 34.73 percent "is wasted in waging civil war" (VOPB, 5 June; *FBIS*, 10 June). A 23 May broadcast attacked the government's assertion that Burma must be part of an interdependent world economic system and stated that this disguised Burma's unilateral dependence on capitalist countries. The BCP said that the government is using loans to develop raw materials subject to foreign price manipulation in the attempt to buy foreign industrial goods. "Although the big shots of the military clique are vociferously calling for self-reliance . . . the apparent fact is that they themselves . . . are sinking in a quagmire of debts" (VOPB, 23 May; *FBIS*, 4 June). "Because of the various reactionary policies laid down by successive reactionary governments, including the military government, Burmese people have to beg for a living [that is, depend on foreign loans] although they live on a throne." Despite resources and the diligence of its people, "the country is thirsting for water while on a raft in mid-stream." (VOPB, 11 January; *FBIS*, 15 January.) The government's response to the BCP propaganda campaign was typified in a 5 July *Working People's Daily* editorial: "Insurgency is obstructing our efforts for a better life. Insurgents stop at nothing to destroy what the people have been trying to build."

The government's draft citizenship bill was also a target for criticism. The BCP called it "the military clique's manifesto declaring its bourgeois, racial bigotry." The BCP said that the government was preying on internal minority groups to divert attention from other problems. Government leaders, "once groomed by Japanese fascists and later . . . loyalists of the British expansionists, have always practiced racial bigotry towards citizens as well as foreigners." (VOPB, 14 June; *FBIS*, 17 June.)

The VOPB renewed its attack on the citizenship law in October when it broadcast a rejoinder to BSPP Chairman U Ne Win's speech marking the approval of the law by the Pyithu Hluttaw (national assembly). While the BCP seemed to share the government's sentiments in denying citizenship status to Indians who had emigrated to Burma during the colonial period, the BCP was steadfastly critical of Ne Win because he did not distinguish between these Indians and those "people who have naturally crossed borders frequently because they reside in densely forested and hilly border areas." (VOPB, 25 October; *FBIS*, 29 October.) In this case, the VOPB criticism appears to acknowledge, albeit indirectly, the government's past allegations that BCP insurgents have been recruited on both sides of the Sino-Burmese border. BCP propaganda also charged that Ne Win's defense of the citizenship law neglected the real culprits—the "Kuomintang bandits" who continue to live in Burma's Shan state.

While the insurgency continued unabated, information on the fighting was sporadic on both sides. Battle reports were spotty, seldom acknowledging more than a clash. The BCP claimed that government military operations, probably a dry season offensive (Rangoon gives little publicity to anti-BCP operations), were mounted against the insurgents' base areas following the breakdown of peace talks. These engagements, however, do not seem to have reached the same levels of intensity as those in the late 1970s. (*FEER*, 1 October.) A 21 January statement from BCP headquarters denounced the government's "frenzied preparations for an offensive" and stated that the Burmese military would be effectively smashed by BCP determination to defend its "wealthy and pleasant base area, built with the sweat and blood of thousands of martyrs as well as the lives, property and farms of our elders, brothers and sisters." The BCP warned that

Rangoon's soldiers risked "being drowned in the sea of people's war," losing their lives "only to preserve the power and luxuries of the military clique." (VOPB, 24 January; *FBIS*, 27 January.)

Consistent with the military line laid down at the 1979–1980 party meetings (see *YICA*, 1981, pp. 130–31), BCP military units seemed to have refrained from any significant large-scale battles. The reduction in Chinese military assistance to the insurgents and chronic problems of communications and logistics have kept BCP attacks on government forces small, if not persistent. The VOPB carried a number of battle reports of insurgent raids in northern and eastern Shan state and in Kachin state, but in all cases the engagements appeared to involve company-size or smaller units. The guerrillas kept up pressure on government communications lines with ambushes and frequent minings. In each reported clash or ambush, the BCP claimed a few government casualties and captured a few weapons. (See, for instance, *FBIS*, 20, 23, and 29 July, 17 and 24 September.) Unlike previous years, there were no reports in 1982 of the capture of larger weapons. Nor did the BCP claim the downing of any government aircraft. In addition, the VOPB did not broadcast a cumulative battle summary as it has in the past, although it did present a report summarizing eight months of military action by a combined BCP–Shan State Nationalities Liberation Organization (SSNLO) force (see below). (VOPB, 3 October; *FBIS*, 8 October.)

Government attempts to persuade BCP insurgents to break ranks and rally to Rangoon continued to meet with some success. A government statement in June noted that 67 insurgents including the deputy regional commander of the 4047 Brigade had surrendered between 1 April and 15 June and had brought with them 69 assorted weapons (Rangoon domestic service, 15 June; *FBIS*, 17 June). A photograph accompanying the story of the defections in the government's *Working People's Daily* (16 June) displayed a number of Chinese-made weapons surrendered by the insurgents. In the past Rangoon has rarely publicized the capture or seizure of Chinese-made weapons out of a reluctance to point an accusing finger at China, with which it tries to maintain good relations. Publication of this photograph and a subsequent story on one of the defectors detailing his training and residence in China (*Working People's Daily*, 30 June) were a significant departure from past practice in treating the BCP's China connection. In a curious way, publication of the China link by Rangoon suggests the extent to which Beijing's changing relations with the BCP have defused the political sensitivity of the issue.

There were signs that as the rainy season ended in October, Rangoon was preparing for a new, large-scale offensive against BCP base areas. In late October, senior military commanders, including the vice-chiefs of staff, the intelligence director, and the artillery commander, traveled to northeastern Shan state for an inspection of the tactical commands and a review of the military situation in the Sino-Burmese border area (Rangoon domestic service, 27 October; *FBIS*, 29 October). In recent years, such "inspection tours" have presaged major government offensives.

Hard pressed by Rangoon's forces, the BCP's efforts to enlist allies among Burma's ethnic minorities continued, but the Communists had little noticeable success in forging new alliances; relations with erstwhile past allies remained troubled. A "joint statement" broadcast by VOPB on 1 September accused the government of "destroying peace, democracy, unity and genuine equality for national groups" and of not practicing a correct policy of active nonalignment and independence. The statement was signed by the Central Committee of the Kachin Independence Organization (KIO), the Kayah New Land Revolutionary Council, the Karenni State Nationalities Liberation Front, and the SSNLO, as well as the BCP. (*FBIS*, 2 September.) The only militarily significant BCP ally among the signatories is the KIO, led by Brang Seng. It has an estimated strength of 4,500–5,000 armed men and generally operates in eastern and northern Kachin state. With the possible exception of the SSNLO, the other groups are fairly recent creations about which little is known. They are probably splinter groups that broke away from larger, noncommunist ethnic insurgent organizations. The KIO's relatively large military force and its own direct links to Chinese supporters in Yunnan province give the KIO considerable independence from the BCP (an article in *Asiaweek*, 16 April, reported that the KIO receives material support, including some weapons, from the Chinese and that KIO trading with the Chinese finances some of the Kachin insurgent activity). The alliance with the Communists dates to 1976. While it has its benefits for both sides, the alliance is not without its serious strains. Furthermore, rumors of splits within the KIO continue (ibid.), reportedly generated by opposition within KIO ranks to the BCP alliance.

The significance of the ties with other groups is difficult to gauge. On 15 December 1981, the VOPB broadcast a congratulatory message to the SSNLO on the thirty-third anniversary of its armed revolution (the 11 December 1949 uprising of the Pa-O National Organization, the leading ethnic group in the military arm of the SSNLO). As noted earlier, reports of SSNLO military cooperation were broadcast in a joint battle report, but the actions themselves were of little military significance. Relations with other ethnic insurgent groups were mentioned during the year, but their importance remains questionable. For instance, on 1 October the VOPB broadcast a joint battle report of the BCP and the Shan State Army (SSA), the military arm of the Shan State Progress Party (SSPP), and this was followed two days later by the broadcast of a separate SSA battle report (*FBIS*, 8 October). As with so much of politics in the Golden Triangle, however, these reports seemed anomalous. It was reported in 1981 that the SSPP had formally abrogated its 1976 alliance with the BCP (see *Focus*, Bangkok, October 1981). Furthermore, the SSPP was among the participants in a midyear meeting of the National Democratic Front (other participants included the Karen National Union and the Karenni National Progress Party), which issued a statement characterizing the BCP as a tool of foreign interests and condemning BCP leaders as ruthless oppressors of the people in areas of communist control (*Bangkok Post*, 8 August). The Democratic Front was reportedly trying to set up a common military front, including the SSA, to challenge the BCP.

The BCP's opium-trading activities, a mix of politics and economics for the BCP (see *YICA*, 1981, p. 131, 1982, p. 173) continued, although the BCP's major narcotics contact, the Shan United Army (SUA), was the target of three Thai military attacks in January, May, and December against its Thai-based headquarters. The disruption of the SUA's sanctuaries and its heroin-refining facilities in the Thai-Burma border area may have affected the SUA-BCP connection. There were indications that the BCP may be trying to forge new drug-trading links with a splinter group of the Lahu State Army, led by A Pi. The A Pi group, once allied with the BCP but believed to be operating as part of the SSA since 1978–1979, attempted to take over Doi Lang, Burma, a key narcotics center on the Thai-Burma border, in early 1982. It was forced out of Doi Lang by the SUA in July, which publicly announced that its actions were motivated by a desire to rid the border area of communist groups (*Bangkok Post*, 28 July). The situation in the border area remains very confusing, and it is difficult to determine the extent to which the BCP has gained a foothold, directly or indirectly, in this region. The Thai government believes that the BCP has sought to open a conduit through which support can be provided to Thai communist insurgents (Reuters, 24 July; *NYT*, 25 July; *Bangkok Post*, 27 July) but the evidence of such a conduit is circumstantial.

The drug-trading activities of the insurgents were vilified in Rangoon. A 28 June *Working People's Daily* editorial condemned the activity, saying it exposed "the utter bankruptcy of their principles—ideological or otherwise." Subsequent to a Burmese army operation against A Pi's refineries in the Doi Lang area, another editorial (7 July) singled out "BCP insurgents and their lackeys who have been openly engaged in the production and smuggling of opium and its more sinister derivatives to support their unwelcome existence in the frontier jungles."

BCP attempts to win support in other restive quarters have been no more successful than the party's efforts with the ethnic insurgents and warlord narcotics-trafficking organizations. A 30 June broadcast on the VOPB appealed for student support of the people's revolution and commented, "May the glorious tradition of students' struggle shine forever" (*FBIS*, 1 July). Although many Burmese students reportedly are alienated from the government, there was little evidence this year to suggest that students were joining the BCP. Some might be attracted to the clarion call of the party, but most remain culturally as well as physically isolated from BCP centers.

International Views and Contacts.   The VOPB offered up little on the BCP's international line. For the first time, there were no reports of BCP greetings to fraternal parties. (The absence of such familiar greetings, however, may be more a reflection of gaps in monitoring by the Foreign Broadcast Information Service or reductions in VOPB broadcast time than a significant change in party policy.) What little was broadcast indicates that the BCP continues to follow basically the Chinese lead on international developments. The New Year's statement of the BCP Central Committee essentially toed the Chinese line. It noted that none of the problems commented on in the previous year had been solved and many were becoming worse: "These are some of the problems that remained: The Soviet occupation and aggression in Afghanistan; the Vietnamese aggression and occupation in Kampuchea; the intensifying war between Iran and Iraq. The problems and crisis in Poland remain unresolved during 1981, and martial law has been declared. The situation is beyond control, and the prospect of Soviet military intervention looms.

"New problems and events emerged continuously during 1981. Angola was invaded by the racist South Africa, the nuclear reactor in Iraq was bombed and attacked by Israel, a Soviet spy submarine equipped with nuclear weapons was caught redhanded in Swedish territory, two Libyan planes were shot down by US planes for alleged provocation during a military exercise by US military forces, the Egyptian president was assassinated, Israel blatantly annexed Syria's Golan Heights, and the nuclear rivalry between the Soviet Union and US—which started with the deployment of Soviet medium range nuclear missiles in Europe during 1977—became more intensified. On the whole, the old problems remained unsolved and new problems emerged continuously. Thus, 1981 was marked by more turmoil and unrest." (VOPB, 30 December 1981; *FBIS*, 31 December 1981.)

This accounting is remarkably matter of fact and free of cant. To the extent a villain is singled out, it is, not unexpectedly, the Soviet Union. But the frequent references to "Soviet hegemonism" and "little hegemonism of the Vietnamese" that appeared in previous VOPB broadcasts disappeared in 1982. A strong Soviet endorsement of the BSPP carried over Radio Moscow's Burmese service (*FBIS*, 7 July) apparently went unchallenged by the VOPB. This all may, in fact, represent a softening of the BCP's hard line on the Soviets, which in turn could reflect China's modest moves toward resolving long-standing differences with Moscow.

In the circumstances, the state of the BCP's relations remains a vexing question. There is little doubt that China has reduced its assistance to the BCP, although some supplies still trickle in. Beijing still supports the party in principle, but China evidently places a higher premium on continuing to improve its relations with Rangoon and other Southeast Asian countries. Material support to the insurgents works against this goal. The BCP has firmly wedded itself to Maoist revolutionary doctrine, and the changing status of this doctrine in Beijing has undoubtedly created ideological problems within BCP ranks, further complicating the difficulties ensuing from the reduction of military aid. Since the ideological ruptures in the BCP in the mid-1960s, there has been scant evidence of either ideological development or contact with other communist movements independent of the Chinese. Given this situation, the BCP appears to have few options other than adjusting to China's changes.

Publications. Burmese communist propaganda is disseminated over the VOPB, which has broadcast since 1971 from a facility in Yunnan province in China. It is monitored by the Foreign Broadcast Information Service, which publishes selected commentary from the VOPB on an irregular basis.

U.S. Department of State   Charles B. Smith, Jr.
Washington, D.C.   Jon A. Wiant

(Note: Views expressed in this article are the authors' own and do not necessarily represent those of the U.S. Department of State.)

China

The Chinese Communist Party is the largest communist party in the world. It has ruled China since 1949. Since the death of longtime leader Mao Zedong in 1976, the party has increasingly come under the domination of pragmatists, led by Deng Xiaoping.

Population. 1,008,175,288

Party. Chinese Communist Party (Zhongguo gongchan dang; CCP)

Founded. 1921

Membership. Over 39 million

General Secretary. Hu Yaobang

Standing Committee of the Politburo. 6 members: Hu Yaobang, Ye Jianying (chairman, National People's Congress [NPC]), Deng Xiaoping, Zhao Ziyang (premier), Li Xiannian, Chen Yun (vice-chairman, NPC)

Politburo. 25 full members (listed in order of number of strokes in their surname): Wan Li (vice-premier), Xi Zhongxun (vice-chairman, NPC), Wang Zhen, Wei Guoqing (vice-chairman, NPC), Ulanfu (vice-chairman, NPC), Fang Yi (state councillor), Deng Xiaoping, Deng Yingchao (vice-chairman, NPC), Ye Jianying, Li Xiannian, Li Desheng, Yang Shangkun (vice-chairman, NPC), Yang Dezhi, Yu Qiuli (state councillor), Song Renqiong, Zhang Tingfa, Chen Yun, Zhao Ziyang, Hu Qiaomu, Hu Yaobang, Nie Rongzhen, Ni Zhifu, Xu Xiangqian, Peng Zhen (vice-chairman, NPC), Liao Chengzhi (vice-chairman, NPC); 3 alternate members (listed in order of number of votes): Yao Yilin (vice-premier), Qin Jiwei, Chen Muhua

Secretariat. 9 full members: Wan Li, Xi Zhongxun, Deng Liqun, Yang Yong, Yu Qiuli, Gu Mu (state councillor), Chen Pixian, Hu Qili, Yao Yilin; 2 alternate members: Qiao Shi, Hao Jianxiu

Military Commission. Chairman: Deng Xiaoping; 4 vice-chairmen: Ye Jianying, Xu Xiangqian, Nie Rongzhen, Yang Shangkun (permanent vice-chairman)

Central Advisory Commission. Chairman: Deng Xiaoping; 4 vice-chairmen: Bo Yibo (state councillor), Xu Shiyou, Tan Zhenlin (vice-chairman, NPC), Li Weihan

Central Commission for Discipline Inspection. First secretary: Chen Yun; second secretary: Wang Heshou; 5 secretaries: Wang Congwu, Han Guang, Li Chang, Ma Guorui, Han Tianshi

Central Committee. 348 full and alternate members

Last Congress. Twelfth, 1–11 September, in Beijing

Auxiliary Organizations. All-China Women's Federation; Communist Youth League of China (50 million members), led by First Secretary Wang Zhaoguo (elected 1982); All-China Federation of Trade Unions, led by Ni Zhifu

Publications. The official and most authoritative publication of the CCP is the newspaper *Renmin Ribao* (People's daily), published in Beijing. The theoretical journal of the Central Committee, *Hongqi* (Red flag) is published approximately once a month. The daily paper of the People's Liberation Army (PLA) is *Jiefangjunbao* (Liberation Army daily). The weekly *Beijing Review* (BR), published in English and several other languages, carries translations of important articles, editorials, and documents from the three aforementioned publications and from other sources. *China Daily,* the first English-language national newspaper in the PRC, began official publication in Beijing (and Hong Kong) on 1 June 1981. The official news agency of the party and government is the New China News Agency (Xinhua; NCNA).

Organization and Leadership. According to the party constitution, the National Congress of the party is the "highest leading body" of the CCP. Normally, the National Congress is held once every five years. However, except for the most recent congress, the twelfth, which met in September 1982, all previous ones have been convened early or postponed. The congress elects a Central Committee, which leads when the congress is not in session. The Central Committee elects the Political Bureau (Politburo), the Standing Committee of the Politburo, the Secretariat, and the general secretary of the Central Committee. The Politburo and its Standing Committee act for the Central Committee when it is not in session. The Secretariat handles the day-to-day work of the Central Committee under the direction of the Politburo and its Standing Committee. The general secretary of the Central Committee convenes the meetings of the Politburo and presides over the work of the Secretariat. In September 1982, the CCP abolished the post of chairman. The Central Committee also decides on the members of the Military Commission of the Central

Committee, whose chairman is a member of the Standing Committee of the Politburo. There is also a Central Advisory Commission, created in September 1982, which "acts as political assistant and consultant to the Central Committee." Members of this commission must be party members of at least 40-years' standing who have rendered considerable service. Finally, there is a Central Commission for Discipline Inspection, which functions under the Central Committee.

The Twelfth Party Congress, which met 1–11 September, elected the Twelfth Central Committee. Of its 348 full and alternate members, 211, or more than 60 percent, were elected to the Central Committee for the first time, and two-thirds of these new members are under 60, the youngest being 38. As many as 59 of the 211 are professional and technological cadres, so that 17 percent of the Twelfth Central Committee have such expertise as compared with only 2.7 percent of the Eleventh Central Committee. (*BR*, 20 September.)

Primary party organizations are found in factories, shops, schools, offices, city neighborhoods, people's communes, cooperatives, farms, townships, towns, companies of the People's Liberation Army (PLA), and other basic units where there are three or more party members. The PLA's General Political Department is the political-work organ of the Military Commission, and it directs party and political work in the armed forces. According to the newly revised party constitution (Article 23), the organizational system and organs of the party in the PLA are to be prescribed by the Military Commission.

The highest organ of state power in the PRC is the National People's Congress (NPC). The NPC is elected for a term of five years and holds one session each year, although both of these stipulations are subject to alteration. The fifth session of the Fifth NPC was held 26 November to 10 December.

The NPC elects a Standing Committee composed of a chairman, vice-chairman, the secretary general, and other members. The officers and members of the Fifth NPC Standing Committee were elected on 5 March 1978. Two have since died; four new vice-chairmen were added on 1 July 1979; five were added in September 1980; one resigned in April 1980; five resigned in September 1980 (for a complete list, see *YICA*, 1981, p. 135).

The 1982 Fourth PRC Constitution restored the post of president (previously translated as chairman) of the PRC. The president represents the state in its domestic affairs and its relations with foreign states. A vice-president assists him in his tasks. Both are elected for five-year terms and may not serve more than two consecutive terms. The president, pursuant to the decisions of the NPC and its Standing Committee, promulgates statutes; appoints and removes the premier, vice-premiers, state councillors, ministers in charge of ministries or commissions, auditor-general, and secretary general of the State Council; confers state orders, medals, and titles of honor; grants special pardons; proclaims martial law; proclaims a state of war; and orders mobilization. He receives foreign diplomatic representatives and appoints and recalls plenipotentiary representatives stationed abroad, as well as ratifies and abrogates treaties and important agreements concluded with foreign states pursuant to the decisions of the NPC Standing Committee. (Articles 79–81.)

The State Council is the Central People's Government of the PRC and as such is the executive body of the NPC and the NPC's Standing Committee; it is the highest organ of state administration. The State Council was extensively reorganized in 1982. It is composed of the premier, vice-premiers, the state councillors, the ministers in charge of ministries and of commissions, the auditor-general, and the secretary general. (For a list of members, see *BR*, 10 May.) On 19 November, Wu Xueqian replaced Huang Hua as foreign minister and Zhang Aiping replaced Geng Biao as defense minister.

The People's Political Consultative Conference (CPPCC) is the official organization of the PRC's united front policy. The CPPCC is organized into a National Committee, which holds plenary sessions and elects the CPPCC's Standing Committee. The current Fifth National Committee, at its fifth session in November–December, had 1,997 members (NCNA, Beijing, 24 November; *FBIS*, 26 November). Deng Xiaoping is chairman of the CPPCC's National Committee. The CPPCC also has local committees at the provincial, autonomous region, municipal, and other levels.

The People's Liberation Army (PLA) includes the Chinese navy and air force. It recently had about 4.5 million men, but appears to be cutting back (David Bonavia, *FEER*, 23 April). The 1982 constitution established a Central Military Commission, which is to direct the armed forces of the country. Since 1978, the chairman of the CCP, a post now abolished, had been commander in chief of the armed forces. The new state constitution says little of the specific responsibilities of the Central Military Commission or of its relationship to the CCP Central Committee's Military Commission. Deng Xiaoping is chairman of the latter commission.

Domestic Party Affairs.   The year under review was marked by major meetings that sanctioned some significant developments. The most important of these meetings were the Twelfth Party Congress in September and the fifth session of the Fifth NPC in late November and early December. Both meetings brought forth newly revised constitutions. Deng Xiaoping dominated most of these developments, although he continued to encounter some, if not serious, resistance during the year. Concern for economic development continued to overshadow ideology, but the socialist road was repeatedly reaffirmed amid expressions of concern over inroads of bourgeois liberalism. A prominent feature of the year was the latest concerted effort to reform the entire cadre system. Among the measures employed to this end, with varying success, was the abolishment of life tenure for leading cadres, the streamlining of government organizations, arrangements for the retirement of veteran cadres, and the promotion to leading posts of larger numbers of middle-aged and younger cadres.

Dealing firmly with "economic crimes" was also regarded as one of the most important government tasks of 1982, and a particular effort was made to crack down on smuggling rings in Guangdong, Fujian, and Zhejiang (*BR,* 22 February). Among those caught in the roundup was Yang Yibang, vice-minister of chemical industry, who was removed from all posts because of infractions that included entering into a fraudulent agreement with a Hong Kong businessman (ibid., 9 August).

The year began somewhat incongruously with discussion of a Central Committee circular on reaffirming the Daqing experience, thus resurrecting an issue reminiscent of the radical era. However, although the possibility of intended ambiguity in the exercise cannot be discounted, earlier radical interpretation of the slogan was specifically criticized (ibid., 11 January). Aside from this curious early note, most of the year's activities saw Deng Xiaoping–inspired policies and programs being briskly implemented.

The twenty-second session of the Standing Committee of the Fifth NPC was held 22 February–8 March. The session approved a plan put forward by Premier Zhao Ziyang on 2 March for restructuring the State Council. The plan anticipated the reduction of the number of vice-premiers from thirteen to two and the merging and reducing of the 98 ministries, commissions, and agencies under the State Council to 52. The staff of this central bureaucracy was to be cut from 49,000 to 32,000. A new standing committee of the State Council—consisting of the premier, vice-premiers, state councillors, and secretary general—was to be set up. The newly designated position of state councillor was to be equal to that of vice-premier. The streamlining was to be carried out in stages, beginning with twelve ministries. The session approved a resolution for severely punishing criminals who damage the state economy. It approved a Law of Civil Procedure, the trial implementation of which was to begin on 1 October. The session also passed a resolution pardoning and releasing all former Nationalist party, government, and military personnel and special agents below the county and regimental levels who were still in custody. (Ibid., 15 March.) This complemented the similar decision made in March 1975 that pardoned and released former Nationalist personnel above the county and regimental levels. No rationale was provided as to why the lower-ranking personnel were given seven additional years of punishment.

The twenty-third session of the Standing Committee of the Fifth NPC was held 22 April–4 May. The session announced that Wan Li and Yao Yilin would remain vice-premiers and the other eleven would be removed from their posts. Yu Qiuli, Geng Biao, and eight others were appointed state councillors. The meeting approved the progress of the State Council restructuring program. Premier Zhao Ziyang reported that the planned 52 ministries and commissions would be further reduced to 41. He said that the number of ministers and vice-ministers, apart from those concurrently holding the posts of ministers, had been reduced from 505 to 167, a cut of 67 percent. The session appointed 23 new ministers; 11 others retained their posts. It approved the 1982 economic and social development plan. The session considered the arrangements for the 1982 state budget as feasible, pointing out that it allowed for a deficit of 3.0 billion yuan. The session approved the Regulations Concerning the Requisition of Land for Capital Construction and decided other personnel matters.

The twenty-third session also adopted the draft of the revised constitution of the PRC, after considering explanations on the draft given by Peng Zhen, vice-chairman of the Constitution Revision Committee, on 22 April. The draft constitution was then made public for discussion throughout the country, to be further revised in time for submission to the fifth session of the Fifth NPC later in the year. (Ibid., 10 May.)

Reporting on the draft 1982 economic and social development plan at the session, Vice-Premier Yao Yilin outlined seven tasks and targets for the year: (1) a better harvest in agriculture and overall development of agriculture, forestry, animal husbandry, sideline occupations, and fisheries; (2) a faster rate of development in light industry and further readjustments toward a service orientation for heavy industry; (3) efforts to increase revenue and limit expenditure in order to maintain a basic balance between the two; (4) control over the scale of capital construction and rational utilization of investment; (5) a good balance between supply and demand on the market, stable prices, and expansion of foreign trade; (6) strengthening of scientific and technological research and development of cultural, educational, and public health undertakings; and (7) on the basis of expanded production ensuring the stability of the people's livelihood and continuing to improve it (ibid., 24 May).

One of the principal contradictions confronting Chinese leaders as they attempt to promote modernization is "bourgeois liberalization." In April, Hu Qiaomu, then president of the Academy of Social Sciences, further refined comments he had made at a forum on ideological questions in 1981. Hu said that the present tendency toward bourgeois liberalization was characterized by "calling for the adoption of the bourgeois parliamentarism, including the two-party system, campaigning for office, bourgeois freedoms of speech, press, assembly and association, bourgeois individualism and even anarchism." Advocates of such bourgeois freedoms "promote bourgeois profit-seeking mentality and behaviour, the bourgeois way of life, vulgar tastes and its standards of morality and the arts." The "essence of this bourgeois ideological tendency lies in consciously or unconsciously demanding China forsake the socialist road and install the so-called capitalist liberal system." While acknowledging the need for certain freedoms, Hu maintained that "we do not hesitate to wage resolute struggle against anyone who negates, opposes or undermines China's socialist cause and the leadership of the Chinese Communist Party." (Ibid., June.) Hu's remarks were part of a concerted crackdown that had continued from the previous year on manifestations of liberalism and suspected criticism of Marxism or the party. Hence, much press attention was given to alleged examples of bourgeois behavior. The anticorruption campaign was closely related to the renewed vigilance against undue foreign influence. A trade magazine editor, Li Guangyi, was given a five-year prison term for "betraying state secrets" (ibid., 17 May), and an American teacher, Lisa Wichser, was expelled from China in June for allegedly "stealing China's secret information" (ibid., 14 June). In general, foreigners felt, and complained about being, quarantined from Chinese friends and associates.

Over a ten-day period in early June, China undertook the most ambitious census in the history of mankind, employing a thousand computer technicians, 4,000 data-entry workers, 100,000 coders, a million census supervisors, and four million census enumerators (*Asian Wall Street Journal*, 9 July). Preliminary tabulations were released in October, revealing a mainland population of 1,008,175,288 as of 1 July. This represents an increase of more than 313 million in eighteen years and an average annual increase of 17,421,863, or 2.1 percent. An overall figure of 1,031,882,511, which includes the populations of Taiwan, Quemoy, Matsu, Hong Kong, and Macao, was also given. (Ibid., 28 October.)

The seventh plenary session of the Eleventh Central Committee was held on 6 August, following a six-day preparatory meeting. The plenary session was attended by 185 members and 112 alternate members of the Central Committee and 21 observers. Presiding were Politburo Standing Committee members Hu Yaobang, Ye Jianying, Deng Xiaoping, Zhao Ziyang, Li Xiannian, Chen Yun, and Hua Guofeng. The plenary session examined and adopted a report of the Central Committee to the Twelfth Party Congress and the revised draft of the CCP constitution. The session paid respects to retired leaders Liu Bocheng and Cai Chang. It decided to convene the Twelfth Party Congress on 1 September. (*BR*, 16 August.)

The twenty-fourth plenary session of the Fifth NPC Standing Committee completed its meetings on 23 August. The session resolved to convene the fifth session of the Fifth NPC in November. It heard a report by Minister of Foreign Affairs Huang Hua and passed resolutions approving the final state accounts for 1981; adopting laws on marine environmental protection, trademarks, and China's participation in the Convention Relating to the Status of Refugees; approving a consular treaty with Yugoslavia; adopting the latest plan of restructuring institutions under the State Council; making the New China News Agency a component of the State Council and appointing Mu Qing as its director-general; and merging several bodies into a Commission in Charge of Science, Technology, and Industry for National Defense, with Chen Bin as minister in charge. Also, it appointed Lu Jiaxi president of the Academy of Sciences, relieving Fang Yi, and Ma Hong president of the Academy of Social Sciences, replacing Hu Qiaomu. (*FBIS*, 24 August.)

The Twelfth Party Congress was held in the Great Hall of the People in Beijing, 1–11 September. In attendance were 1,545 delegates and 145 alternate delegates. In the opening speech, Deng Xiaoping restated the three major tasks for the 1980s: "to intensify socialist modernization, to strive for reunification and particularly for the return of Taiwan to the motherland, and to combat hegemonism and safeguard world peace." At the core of these tasks, he said, was economic construction. (*BR*, 6 September.) Chairman (at the time) Hu Yaobang then gave the main report to the congress, entitled "Create a New Situation in All Fields of Socialist Modernization" (full text in ibid., 13 September). The report, which was subsequently approved, was divided into six parts: "1. A historic change and the great new tasks; 2. Bring about an all-round upsurge of the socialist economy; 3. Strive to attain a high level of socialist spiritual civilization; 4. Strive to attain a high level of socialist democracy; 5. Adhere to an independent foreign policy; and 6. Build the Party into a firm leading core for the cause of socialist modernization." Hu pointed out that in the next five years efforts will be made to bring about a fundamental turn for the better in China's financial and economic situation, in the standards of public conduct, and in the party's style of work. He also said that in the twenty years from 1981 to the end of the century, the general objective of China's economic construction is to quadruple the gross annual value of industrial and agricultural production.

The congress adopted a new constitution. According to Hu Qiaomu, newly elected member of the Politburo, the new constitution discarded the "left" errors of the previous charter while retaining the "merits" of the constitutions produced at the Seventh and Eighth party congresses. Hu Qiaomu reduced the revisions to three major points: (1) stricter requirements for party members, especially cadres; (2) new provisions with regard to the party's organization, including the addition of the Advisory and Discipline Inspection commissions and elimination of the posts of party chairman and vice-chairmen; and (3) more detailed and concrete provisions regarding democratic centralism and party discipline. Here, Hu Qiaomu noted that the new stipulation is that party committees at all levels function on the principle of combining collective leadership with individual responsibility based on the division of labor. Furthermore, all forms of personality cult are forbidden. (Ibid., 27 September.) The new constitution eschews the radical rhetoric of the 1977 version and defines the party's tasks in terms of economic modernization. It plays down the role of class struggle.

The Twelfth Congress also endorsed a report by the Central Commission for Discipline Inspection and elected the Twelfth Central Committee. Li Xiannian gave the closing speech on 11 September.

The first plenary session of the Twelfth Central Committee was held 11–13 September. The session elected the members and alternate members of the Politburo, the members of the Politburo's Standing Committee, the general secretary, the members and alternate members of the Secretariat, and the chairman and vice-chairmen of the Military Commission. On the second day, the session approved the leading members of the Central Advisory Commission and the Central Commission for Discipline Inspection. (Ibid., 20 September.) Removed from the Politburo was Hua Guofeng, Mao Zedong's handpicked successor, who had already been removed from the party chairmanship in 1981. The other members of the Politburo's Standing Committee remained unchanged. Hu Yaobang, who was party chairman until the post was abolished, was elected general secretary. Deng Xiaoping was the only member of the Standing Committee to become a member of the new Central Advisory Commission, of which he was elected chairman. There had been some expectation that Ye Jianying, and perhaps Li Xiannian and Chen Yun as well, would also be elected to this commission. Deng also remained chairman of the party's Military Affairs Commission. Others removed from the Politburo in addition to Hua Guofeng were Liu Bocheng, Geng Biao, Peng Chong, and Xu Shiyou. Geng Biao and Xu Shiyou both became members of the Central Advisory Commission. Liu Bocheng is aged and infirm. Hua Guofeng and Peng Chong retain membership on the Central Committee. The new members of the Politburo are Wan Li, Xi Zhongxun, Song Renqiong, Hu Qiaomu, Liao Chengzhi, Yang Shangkun, and Yang Dezhi. Saifudin was removed as an alternate member of the Politburo, while Yao Yilin and Qin Jiwei joined Chen Muhua as alternate members. Previously disgraced leaders, including Wu De and Chen Xilian, were elected to the Central Advisory Commission, and Wang Dongxing became an alternate member of the Central Committee. Overall, the changes in the top leadership suggest a balance shifting in favor of Deng Xiaoping's moderates, with a trend toward younger, more technocratically minded cadres assuming important positions. Nevertheless, military representation is still much in evidence, and it is speculated that this may be a reason that Deng Xiaoping remains in control of the Military Affairs Commission (*Asian Wall Street Journal,* 13 September).

General Secretary Hu Yaobang spoke at the first plenum on 13 September on tasks for 1983. He said that the Central Committee was not prepared to hold any plenary sessions or work conferences during the coming winter or next spring. First, he advised that party members study the documents of the Twelfth Party Congress. Second, he noted that the streamlining of central party and government organs had been basically completed, but recommended that these reforms be continued at the provincial, municipal, and autonomous regional levels and then at the prefectural and city levels "sooner rather than later," so that they can be completed by the spring of 1984. He said that the Sixth NPC is scheduled for May or June of 1983. Third, Hu noted the call by the Twelfth Party Congress for consolidation of the party. He said that the Secretariat believes there should be meticulous preparation, guidance, and organization of this new party consolidation scheduled to start in 1983. Some pilot projects, he said, should be taken at the central level, as well as in the provinces, municipalities, and autonomous regions, this winter or next spring. On this basis, an improved document on party consolidation will be drafted after the conclusion of the Sixth NPC in May or June 1983 or by autumn of 1983 at the latest. He said that this will be one of the central items on the agenda of the second plenary session of the Twelfth Central Committee. The plan is to finish party consolidation throughout the country over a period of three years beginning in the fall of 1983. Fourth, Hu admonished his comrades never to slacken efforts in economic work, in order to approach the target of achieving a fundamental turn for the better in the financial and economic situation, in social morality, and in the party's style by 1986. Finally, Hu emphasized that the future of the party and the state in the next five years "hinges on us who collectively form the new central leadership and the new combat headquarters." (*BR,* 1 November.)

On 27 September, the *Liberation Army Daily* published an interesting editorial acknowledging that an article it had published on 28 August by Zhao Yiya entitled "Communist Ideology Is the Core of Socialist Spiritual Civilization" had "serious theoretical and political mistakes" and its publication was a "dereliction of duty and a grave political and organizational mistake on our part." The article reaffirmed the paper's need to "obey the party's absolute leadership." The offending article, it appears, had propagated a "left" viewpoint in the name of opposing bourgeois liberalization. It was pointed out that publication of the erroneous article revealed that "among a very small number of comrades in the party and the army there indeed remains the pernicious influence of "left" ideas." (*FBIS,* 29 September.)

On 3 October, the Central Committee and the State Council decided that staff members of the central party and government organizations are to undergo a six-month, full-time course of educational training every three years. This program is to assure that after five years of rotating studies with regular pay, these cadres will attain a cultural and professional level equivalent to that of secondary school graduates. (*BR,* 25 October.)

The twenty-fifth session of the Fifth NPC Standing Committee met 12–19 November. The session set the agenda for the fifth session of the Fifth NPC. The Standing Committee session approved the appointment of Wu Xueqian as minister of foreign affairs and Zhang Aiping as state councillor and minister of national defense. The session adopted a law on the protection of cultural relics and another on food hygiene. It also approved a decision to open two inland ports on the Yangtze River to foreign ships: Nantong and Zhangjia, 51 and 78 nautical miles, respectively, from Wusong at the mouth of the river. The session also discussed the Organic Law of the NPC, the Organic Law of the State Council, and the organic laws of the local people's congresses and people's governments at all levels. (Ibid., 29 November.)

The fifth session of the Fifth NPC, 26 November–10 December, was attended by 3,155 delegates (*FBIS,* 26 November). Ye Jianying, aged 85, opened the session. NPC Vice-Chairman Peng Zhen reported on the revised draft of the constitution, Premier Zhao Ziyang presented the Sixth Five-Year Plan, and Minister of Finance Wang Bingqian reported on implementation of the 1982 state budget and on the draft budget for 1983.

Premier Zhao unveiled the Sixth Five-Year Plan on 30 November (the full text was made available two weeks later). This was the first five-year plan to be made public since the first plan in 1953 and the only one to be approved by the NPC. This latest plan should have been published in 1980 but was delayed because of the three-year adjustment period and the difficulty in setting specific targets for the whole five-year-plan period. The plan concentrates investment in energy and transport since shortages in both areas obstruct efforts to modernize the economy. The plan also accelerates the pace of urban housing construction and increases expenditures on education, science, and culture. This contrasts with previous plans, which emphasized heavy industry at the expense of housing and consumer needs. Zhao promised a rise in income averaging 6 percent per year. Among the many obstacles is the population increase, which must be held to 13.0 per 1,000 per year so that the 1985 total population will be around 1.060 billion (the 1982 census revealed a current growth rate of 14.55 per 1,000). In order to meet agricultural targets, the growth in output will have to average 4 to 5 percent a year, compared to an average of 3.4 percent per year during the 28 years from 1953 to 1980. (In 1982, with a bumper crop, output grew by more than 5 percent.) As for industry, Zhao said the economic results of the previous 28 years had been very poor. Total investment in fixed assets during the five-year-plan period will be U.S. $180 million. (*CSM*, 1 December.)

The Sixth Five-Year Plan revealed that China is to develop two major economic zones, one on the Yangtze River delta centered on Shanghai, the other in north China centered on Shanxi province and including part of Inner Mongolia, Shaanxi, Ningxia, and Henan provinces. The plan indicated that coastal areas will focus on high-grade, precision, advanced, and new industrial products and promote foreign trade. Inland areas will concentrate on the development of energy resources, transportation, and raw materials and increase consumer-goods production and agricultural output. A special fund of $250 million will be used for underdeveloped areas. The Shanghai zone is to comprise a network of cities with relatively high levels of technology. The most advanced cities will produce for export, while less advanced cities will handle the domestic market. The second zone will emphasize heavy industries, including coal and chemicals. Interregional economic cooperation is called for. All cities are to map out urban development plans by the end of 1983. Large cities will be strictly controlled, while medium-sized cities will develop "appropriately" and small cities will be actively developed. Satellite towns are to be developed for the largest cities. In contrast to previous policy, individuals will be encouraged to own houses. A number of cities are to be selected to experiment with the sale of houses. Defense spending is to fall as a percentage of the total budget, being targeted at 14.5 percent of the budget or two percentage points lower than the 16.5 percent it had under the last five-year plan. Defense Minister Zhang supported this cutback in defense spending and said it was essential to retrench on defense expenditures in order to ensure a rapid development of the economy, which is the basis for strengthening defense capabilities. (*Asian Wall Street Journal*, 13 December.)

In his report on 1 December, Minister of Finance Wang Bingqian said that China will raise $10.25 billion for a construction fund to build key energy and transport projects in the next three years. A sizable proportion of these funds is to come from the "extra-budgetary funds of various localities, departments and units and from after-tax profits of big collectively owned economic enterprises." The effect of this measure will be to tap the resources of local governments and big enterprises, which have benefited from the decentralization policy of recent years. The measure represents a growing tendency toward recentralization. (Ibid., 14 December.)

The NPC adopted the newly revised state constitution, the fourth since the founding of the PRC. The Fourth PRC Constitution, consisting of a preamble and 138 articles in four chapters, is the most comprehensive charter thus far and appears to be a serious attempt to provide a legal framework for the country. The constitution emphasizes individual rights and circumscribes the powers of the government and the party, proclaiming that "all state organs, the armed forces, all political parties and public organizations and all enterprises and undertakings must abide by the constitution and the law." On the other hand, Peng Zhen explained that the "four cardinal principles—adherence to the socialist road, to the people's democratic dictatorship, to leadership by the Communist Party of China, and to Marxism-Leninism and Mao Zedong Thought—constituted the overall guidelines for drafting the constitution." (*FBIS*, 26 November.) The Fourth PRC Constitution does restore an earlier provision that "all citizens are equal before the law" deleted from the 1975 and 1978 documents. Other articles provide for the inviolability of the personal dignity of citizens, freedom of religious belief, inviolability of the home, and freedom and privacy of correspondence. Taken away, however, is the right of workers to strike, which had been a prominent feature of the previous constitution. Like the new party constitution, the new state charter clearly reflects a shift in emphasis from class struggle to economic development. The preamble affirms that "the basic task of the nation in the years to come is to concentrate its efforts on socialist modernization." The document reaffirms that the state-owned sector is the leading force in the national economy, but also provides for collective ownership and even for individual ownership of enterprises. It also specifically allows foreign investment in China and permits economic cooperation between foreign and Chinese organizations, with the "lawful rights and interests" of foreigners being protected by law. Nevertheless, it also declares that the state "combats capitalist, feudalist and other decadent ideas." The "strategic policy" of economic development, according to Peng, is to be implemented unswervingly, "unless there should be a massive invasion by the enemy." The Fourth Constitution also underscores the role of intellectuals, who have often been the target of political campaigns: "In building socialism, it is imperative to rely on the workers, peasants and intellectuals and to unite with all the forces that can be united." Previous versions referred only to workers and peasants.

The new constitution makes some significant changes in the state structure. In a move to separate the executive and legislative branches, it prohibits members of the NPC's Standing Committee from holding posts in any of the administrative, judicial, or procuratorial organs of the state. It restores the position of chief of state, which had been abolished during the Cultural Revolution. It ends the system of lifelong tenure by stipulating that several top officials cannot serve more than two consecutive five-year terms. These officials include the president and vice-president, the chairman and vice-chairman of the NPC, and the premier and vice-premiers. The Fourth Constitution also establishes a State Central Military Commission to lead the armed forces. The previous constitution had named the chairman of the party as the commander in chief of the PLA. The constitution placed overall responsibility for the State Council on the premier. It strengthened the system of people's congresses and local organs of state power "under the unified leadership of the central authorities." It changed the system of the rural people's commune, divesting it of governmental responsibilities by establishing organs of political power at the township level. Henceforth, the people's commune is to be only an organizational form of the rural collective economy. The constitution also provides for setting up special administrative regions when necessary, presumably to accommodate Taiwan, Hong Kong, and Macao at some future points.

The fifth session of the Fifth NPC also restored the original words of China's national anthem, "The March of the Volunteers," by deleting a sentence exalting Mao Zedong's banner that had been inserted in 1978 (*Asian Wall Street Journal*, 6 December).

The fifth session of the Fifth National Committee of the CPPCC began on 24 November, two days before the NPC session. Deng Xiaoping, as chairman of the National Committee, declared the session open. Liu Lantao, vice-chairman of the CPPCC National Committee and of the Committee for the Revision of the CPPCC Constitution, explained the draft of the revised document. The CPPCC has had two constitutions before this third document; the first was adopted in 1954 and the second in 1978. Liu said that the third plenary session of the Fifth National Committee in September 1980 had decided to revise the second constitution because the work of the united front and the CPPCC had entered a new historical period as a result of the great progress in the country's political, economic, and cultural fields since the third plenary session of the Eleventh Central Committee of the CCP in December 1978. The third constitution, according to Liu, "reflected the party's principles and policies set by the 3rd Plenary Session of the 11th CPC Central Committee, eliminated the erroneous left theory and wording in the 1978 constitution, summed up the CPPCC's basic experiences gained from its work of over 30 years, and reflected the requirements for the united front and the CPPCC during the new historical stage of development." (NCNA, Beijing, 24 November; *FBIS*, 26 November.) As customary, the delegates to the CPPCC National Committee meeting subsequently attended the meetings of the NPC as observers.

International Views and Positions. There were significant developments in China's foreign relations in 1982, highlighted by a new assertion of "independence" and a renewed orientation to the Third World— a line sanctioned at the Twelfth Party Congress in September. The new line has strong nationalistic overtones, perhaps as a response to the waning of ideology in China. Much attention was given to Taiwan and to Hong Kong, with an eye to ultimate unification. Nevertheless, the dominant interest in economic development was reflected in the continuation of a vigorous foreign trade, in further efforts to attract foreign economic cooperation, and in the continuing program of sending students abroad. This dominant theme meshed uneasily with nationalistic and ideological attempts to keep foreigners quarantined from other than business relationships with Chinese and concern about the rise in defections to the West (which included some highly publicized cases). Premier Zhao Ziyang visited North Korea on 20–24 December 1981 (in addition to four earlier foreign trips in 1981). He made two more trips abroad in 1982, visiting Japan on 31 May–5 June and departing from China in mid-December for a month-long visit to Africa. Relations with the Soviet Union took a turn for the better with the resumption of formal talks, which had been suspended for three years because of the Soviet invasion of Afghanistan. Political relations with Washington were strained over the U.S. sale of arms to Taiwan, until this issue was resolved for the time being with another historic communiqué on 17 August. Relations with Japan were similarly strained over the issue of revisions in Japanese textbooks (concerning Japanese military expansionism earlier in the century), but this was largely resolved during Japanese Prime Minister Zenko Suzuki's visit to China in September. Relations with Vietnam remained tense, as the Vietnamese occupation of Kampuchea continued.

Among the prominent visitors to China during the year were Zairian President Mobutu Sese Seko, U.S. Vice-President George Bush and Senate Majority Leader Howard Baker, Japanese Prime Minister Zenko Suzuki, British Prime Minister Margaret Thatcher, U.N. Secretary General Javier Pérez de Cuellar, North Korean President Kim Il-Song, Peruvian Prime Minister Manuel Ulloa Elias, West German President Karl Carstens, French Communist Party General Secretary Georges Marchais, Pakistani President Moham-mad Zia ul Haq, Libyan Colonel Moammar Khadafy, Democratic Kampuchean President Norodom Sihanouk, Prime Minister Son Sann, and Vice-President Khieu Samphan (each separately), Philippine President Ferdinand Marcos's wife, Mme. Imelda Marcos, Maltese Prime Minister Dom Mintoff, Nepalese King Birendra (visiting Gansu and Tibet), French Foreign Minister Claude Cheysson, Australian Prime Minister Malcolm Fraser, Cape Verde President Aristides Pereira, Thai Prime Minister Prem Tinsulanond and (earlier) Foreign Minister Siddhi Savetsila, Algerian President Chadli Benjedid, Liberian Head of State Samuel Kanyon Doe, Guinea-Bissaun Head of State João Bernardo Vieira, Romanian President Nicolae Ceauşescu, Brazilian Foreign Minister Ramiro Saraiva Guerreiro, Upper Volta Foreign Minister Félix Tiemtaraboum, Moroccan Prime Minister Maati Bouabid, and Jordanian King Hussein.

China continued its creation since 1979 of a structure of law in order to facilitate and order commercial transactions and to provide assurances to potential foreign investors and business associates. In 1982, there were promulgated, for example, offshore petroleum regulations and implementing regulations for the Foreign Enterprise Income Tax Law (*BR*, 30 January, 5 April). There still remain numerous legal gaps to be filled and the question of how faithfully the new laws will be implemented. Despite such problems, it is expected that new laws and further refinements will be made, and the authorities are trying to develop "law consciousness" (see, for example, Timothy A. Gelatt, "Chinese Advances in Foreign Business Law," *Asian Wall Street Journal*, 8 September). The new PRC constitution specifically protects the lawful interests of foreigners. But cautious foreigners have preferred thus far to invest in low-risk, quick-return projects (see, for example, ibid., 27 May). Senior Chinese officials gave assurances at a business-promotion seminar in Canton in June. About 400 foreign businessmen and 600 Chinese officials attended the initial ceremony of the five-day meeting, which aimed at attracting about $900 million in foreign investments for 121 projects. Wei Yuming, vice-minister for foreign economic relations and trade, told participants that in coming years China hopes to attract investment in the following areas: (1) energy development; (2) light industry, textiles, foods, pharmaceuticals, telecommunications, and electronics; (3) building materials, machinery, iron and steel, and chemicals; (4) agriculture, animal husbandry, and breeding projects; and (5) tourism. A Chinese banking official at the meeting said that China's use of commercial bank loans has dropped since 1980, noting that most of its borrowings in 1978 and 1979 from foreign commercial banks have been repaid. In the three years ending in 1981, China had attracted about $2.9 billion in pledged foreign investments (ibid., 8 June). In 1981, foreign loans to China totaled $8.78 billion (ibid., 26 May).

The China National Offshore Oil Corporation began during the year to let contracts for the exploration and development of China's continental shelf. Forty-six companies, half of them American, have already put $200 million into seismic surveys, and all but six of them are bidding on parcels being offered in the South China Sea. (*NYT*, 5 September.)

Interestingly enough, China has become a dollar-rich Third World country that currently is lending more than it borrows, a fact that seems to contradict the image generally projected. Retrenchments caused by recent economic adjustments have slowed domestic Chinese investment at the same time that dollar earnings continue to accumulate. Meanwhile, China invests abroad in order to take advantage of high interest rates. It is expected that once the Chinese development program is fully on track, following the temporary period of adjustment, this situation will change. (*Asian Wall Street Journal*, 24 November.)

The decentralization of China's foreign trading activities has been highly successful. Between 1979 and 1981, the years of the policy, exports rose by 29 percent annually, compared with an annual growth of 17 percent in the previous three years. These policies are expected to continue despite some recent measures by Beijing to monitor provincial trading corporations more closely (ibid., 24 November). In December, Chinese government figures revealed an unexpected drop in overall trade figures for 1982; although exports were expected to rise 0.5 percent over 1981, imports were expected to fall 1.9 percent (ibid., 20 December).

The September visit of Prime Minister Margaret Thatcher to China provided the occasion for the initiation of serious deliberations regarding the future of Hong Kong. This was necessary since the lease on the Crown Colony's New Territories is due to lapse in 1997, and uncertainty is clearly beginning to affect mortgages and long-term planning. Deng Xiaoping and Thatcher issued a joint statement following their talk, asserting that each side had made its position clear and that both agreed to continue negotiations through diplomatic channels with the common aim of maintaining the stability and prosperity of Hong Kong. The New China News Agency, however, added a further significant paragraph in its release of the statement: "The Chinese Government's position on the recovery of the sovereignty of the whole region in Hong Kong is unequivocal and known to all" (*NYT*, 25 September). In November, Hu Yaobang told Thai Prime Minister Prem Tinsulanond that the recovery of Hong Kong and Taiwan was part of China's national policy along with modernization and opposition to hegemonism (*Asian Wall Street Journal*, 22 November).

China and Vanuatu established diplomatic relations on 26 March (*BR*, 5 April). China and Angola decided to recognize each other, with representatives contacting each other in Paris on 27 September to discuss normalization of relations and the establishment of diplomatic relations (ibid., 4 October). The French Communist Party (pro-Soviet) and China restored formal relations, after a suspension of seventeen years, during the visit of Georges Marchais in October (ibid., 25 October).

Foreign Minister Huang Hua addressed the U.N. General Assembly on 4 October, giving an overview of China's position on current world issues (text in ibid., 11 October).

China launched its twelfth earth satellite (since the first in 1970) on 9 September; it returned to earth successfully on 14 September (ibid., 20 September). It carried out a submarine-based carrier rocket launching test from under water to a designated target area between 7 and 16 October (ibid., 25 October).

Relations with the USSR. The year saw a concerted effort, particularly from the Soviet side, to improve relations, and by year's end it appeared that progress had indeed been made. The 20 October 1981 initiative from the Soviet Union, which had been "under study" by the Chinese, was renewed dramatically by President Leonid Brezhnev in a speech on 24 March in Tashkent. The Chinese response was negative, but the Soviets persisted. On 20 May, Igor Aleksandrov (a pen name used for authoritative statements) published a conciliatory article in *Pravda* expanding on the Brezhnev proposal. This article appeared during the 14–21 May visit to Beijing of the leading Soviet China specialist, Mikhail Kapitsa, head of the First Far Eastern Department of the USSR Ministry of Foreign Affairs. Another prominent Soviet Asia specialist, S. L. Tikhvinsky, had spent the second half of January in Beijing.

Further signs of the thaw came during the year. A session of the joint Sino-Soviet Commission for Navigation on Border Rivers was held in Heihe, Heilongjiang province, from 10 February to 16 March. Agreement was reached on most of the questions discussed, and a protocol was signed. (*FBIS*, 17 March.) Three Chinese economists visited the Soviet Union in late winter to study the Soviet economic structure, planning and management system, and other subjects (ibid., 19 March). A Chinese gymnastic team competed in tournaments in Moscow and Riga in March and April (ibid., 22 March). On 16 April, the two countries signed a trade and payments agreement for 1982 (ibid., 16 April). On 29 June, the Union of Soviet Societies for Friendship and Cultural Relations with Foreign Countries and the Soviet-Chinese Friendship Society held a soiree in Moscow commemorating the fifty-fifth anniversary of the Guangzhou Commune (ibid., 1 July). A Soviet athletic delegation participated, for the first time in seventeen years, in a sports event in China—the 1982 Beijing Track and Field International Tournament (*WP*, 16 June). Also of relevance was a meeting of the joint Boundary Inspection Commission, which met in Ulan Bator 18 February to 3 April, the first such meeting since China and Mongolia agreed in 1964 to discussions on border problems (*NYT*, 7 April).

On 26 September, Brezhnev, speaking in Azerbaijan, again underscored the importance he ascribed to improving relations with China (ibid., 27 September). The following day, Premier Zhao Ziyang was quoted as saying that China's attitude toward the Soviet Union had not changed, despite expectations of renewed contacts (ibid., 28 September). Nevertheless, high-level talks were soon resumed, the first time since their suspension following the 1979 round of talks. The talks were held in Beijing, 5 to 21 October, between delegations headed by Deputy Foreign Minister Leonid Ilyichev and Vice–Foreign Minister Qian Qichen. During and after the talks, the Chinese maintained that Sino-Soviet relations could not improve markedly as long as Vietnam was intervening in Kampuchea, more than a million Soviet troops were massed on the Sino-Soviet frontier and in Outer Mongolia, and the Soviet army was intervening in Afghanistan. The most pressing issue, it was stressed, was Kampuchea because of the fighting in progress. (AFP, 1 November; *FBIS,* 2 November.) The talks did not result in any change in any of these three areas. However, the two sides did agree to exchange sports teams, five from each side in 1983 (*WP,* 27 October). The Chinese also agreed to send a special envoy to Moscow during the winter for a second round of consultations that was expected to expand commercial and cultural ties between the two countries (ibid., 2 November).

Foreign Minister Huang Hua attended the funeral of Leonid Brezhnev in Moscow and on 16 November had a 90-minute discussion with Soviet Foreign Minister Andrei Gromyko. It was the highest-level encounter between officials of the two countries since 1969. On his return to Beijing, Minister Huang said that he was optimistic about the next round of Sino-Soviet talks (*NYT,* 19 November). Huang Hua's optimism was matched by Viktor Afanasyev, editor in chief of *Pravda,* who on 19 November said that he saw brighter prospects for improved Sino-Soviet relations than he did for those between the United States and the Soviet Union. Afanasyev thought that the most promising area for substantive progress was on the Soviet-Chinese border, inasmuch as this was, he said, a "bilateral question" (meaning that the other two issues emphasized by the Chinese were not). Afanasyev thought that it was quite possible that the two sides could agree to a mutual troop reduction. (*CSM,* 22 November.)

In order to allay apprehensions over the implications of improvements in Sino-Soviet relations, Deng Xiaoping reassured Thai Prime Minister Prem Tinsulanond that the process of normalization with Moscow did not mean a diminution of China's resolve to oppose Soviet "hegemonism" or to remove Vietnamese troops from Kampuchea (ibid., 22 November).

The replacement of Huang Hua by Wu Xueqian on 19 November, on Huang's return from Moscow, was not taken to mean that a major shift in China's foreign policy was in the offing. This personnel shift, along with the replacement of Defense Minister Geng Biao by Zhang Aiping on the same date, had long been expected.

Relations with the United States.   Political relations were considerably strained over arms sales to Taiwan, an issue that had already become prominent in 1981. Assistant Secretary for East Asian Affairs John Holdridge visited Beijing in January to notify the Chinese that President Reagan had decided not to sell the FX fighter to Taiwan, but rather to continue to coproduce the F-5E beyond the 1983 termination date. Also initiated during this visit was a search for mutually acceptable principles to deal with arms sales. (Michel Oksenberg, "A Decade of Sino-American Relations," *Foreign Affairs,* Fall, p. 193.) On 5 April, Reagan sent letters to Zhao Ziyang and Deng Xiaoping; a third Reagan letter was hand-delivered in May by Vice-President George Bush to Hu Yaobang. (Senator Barry Goldwater, during a visit to Taiwan in June, revealed that Reagan had sent a "top secret" letter of reassurance a few days earlier to Republic of China President Chiang Ching-kuo [*Asian Wall Street Journal,* 8 June].) Senator Howard Baker, during a visit to China in June, conveyed to Deng Xiaoping Reagan's commitment to a one-China policy and to the building of a stronger relationship. Baker also reported that Deng wanted the U.S. Congress to amend the Taiwan Relations Act, but Baker added that he himself did not favor a revision at this point. (Ibid., 3 June.)

On 17 August, a carefully worded compromise joint communiqué on the Taiwan arms sale issue was announced. For their part, the Chinese reiterated their policy of seeking a peaceful reunification of Taiwan. The United States conceded that it did not seek to carry out a long-term policy of arms sales to Taiwan. Specifically, "its arms sales to Taiwan will not exceed, either in qualitative or in quantitative terms, the level of those supplied in recent years since the establishment of diplomatic relations . . . and . . . it intends gradually to reduce its sale of arms to Taiwan, leading, over a period of time, to a final resolution." (Text in *BR,* 23 August.) The communiqué was not a full resolution of the issue. It did not allay Chinese suspicions of U.S. intentions, and in the weeks that followed, there were many articles in the Chinese media and comments by Chinese leaders insisting on forthright and sincere U.S. compliance. On the other hand, there also was criticism that further U.S. concessions had been made needlessly, including the charge that the communiqué was "appeasement" (see Robert Wesson, *Asian Wall Street Journal,* 17 September).

Apart from the strain in relations occasioned by the arms sales issue, the relationship was altered somewhat by China's shift to a more independent posture, aiming toward achieving some sort of equidistance between the superpowers, a reorientation that came to be sanctioned at the Twelfth Party Congress in September and that was underscored by the renewal of formal Sino-Soviet talks in October. Despite this trend, however, it appears that the Chinese—or at least Deng Xiaoping and his adherents— favor a continued tilt toward the United States and even a loose form of strategic cooperation. Nevertheless, the warming Sino-Soviet relationship began to raise concern among some Americans by the end of the year.

On the other hand, economic relations continued to prosper, especially with continued grain sales and improving prospects for energy development projects. However, China's trade deficit with the United States narrowed in the January–October period to less than half of what it had been in the same period in 1981 (ibid., 16 December). Also, there was the possibility of untoward consequences for economic relations if a satisfactory new agreement on textiles was not reached by 31 December, when a three-year agreement was to expire (ibid., 21 December).

Similarly, in cultural relations, while there was considerable activity and traffic, there were also strains. Chinese authorities were concerned at the increasing number of defections; they unsuccessfully sought to have the United States deny asylum to their leading woman tennis player (*NYT,* 4 August). Conversely, many Americans continued to take umbrage at unreciprocal features in relations with China. The American fascination with China that had characterized so much of the 1970s was clearly on the wane, and in 1982, in particular, increasing numbers of American publications were critical—perhaps best exemplified by an April article in *Harper's,* written by an American recently returned from a teaching stint in China, entitled "China Stinks." Yet there seemed to be no diminution of tourist travel to China, and there remained much other evidence of continuing American interest in China.

University of Hawaii   Stephen Uhalley, Jr.

Biography. *Deng Xiaoping.* On 7 September, at the end of the Twelfth CCP Congress, former CCP Vice-Chairman Deng Xiaoping emerged a man clearly in control of the party and the country, even though, according to pre-congress speculations, not all of his political maneuvers were realized. The 78-year-old power behind the CPC ("no matter where he is," noted a Western diplomat [*NYT,* 6 September]) has been gradually consolidating power into his hands and into those of his protégés since the Eleventh CCP Congress in 1977 and grooming younger cadres (*FBIS,* 18 September) for the task of running the party according to his policies. These policies are to eradicate the vestiges of the personality cult and individual- ism instilled by Mao Zedong and his Cultural Revolution, tighten party membership, loyalty, and discipline, control the armed forces, eliminate bureaucratic corruption, introduce a pragmatic approach to the country's chaotic and inefficient economy, and then transfer these gains and the established order to his handpicked successors.

Deng has no notion of giving up leadership. With Hu Yaobang, his longtime protégé, fellow-sufferer during Deng's periods of disgrace, and faithful bridge partner as general secretary, with Zhao Ziyang as premier, and with other supporters firmly in place, Deng can run the party even in semiretirement. This power and control at age 78 represent the culmination of an active, ambitious political life for the well- educated (a French school in Chongqing, Far Eastern University in Moscow) son of one of the richest families in Sichuan province. He was born on 22 August 1904 in Guangan, Sichuan, and after completing his education and spending six years in France, he rose steadily in the party: dean of education of the Military Academy in Shaanxi in 1926; first chief of staff in 1930 and then director of the Propaganda Department in 1932 of the Red Army; political commissar of the PLA, 1948–1954; minister of finance in 1953; vice–chairman of National Defense Council, 1954–1967; vice-premier of the State Council in 1954; member of the Politburo, 1955–1957; and secretary of the Eighth Central Committee. Deng's rise was abruptly halted by the Cultural Revolution in 1967, when he disappeared from public view until 1973. At that time, he emerged as a member of the Tenth Central Committee. A year later he became a member of the Politburo, chief of the general staff of the PLA, vice-director of the Military Affairs Committee, and vice-premier of State Council. In 1976, he was once again attacked, this time as an "unrepentant capitalist roader" by Mao's heirs and dropped from view for nearly a year. In 1977, he was reinstated as a Politburo member and chief of staff of the PLA. He served as vice-chairman of the party from 1977 to 1980 and became chairman of the party's Military Affairs Commission in 1981. That he was "rehabilitated" twice within a decade testifies to the vagaries of political power within the party and the sinewy resistance of this bright, energetic, calculating politician.

This pragmatic power broker recognizes political and economic expediency and compromise as survival techniques. He knew how to trade off the retention of his Politburo seat for his chairmanship of military affairs within the Central Committee and the expansion of Politburo membership. The same flexible attitude permits him to probe possibilities of rapprochement with the Soviets for savings on reduced border forces, to offer Taiwan economic autonomy for reunification with the Mainland, to euphemistically avoid capitalism by calling the farmers' endeavors to sell produce from their private plots "individual responsibility," and to entertain Western notions, goods, and trade in exchange for technological modernization. This last trade-off is being reduced and modified greatly, however. Deng's concern with corruption of Chinese ethics and the reintroduction of the personality cult by the free flow of Western goods and ideas has shrunk the East-West trade and dialogue. According to Western calculations, his policy can work only if his economic program succeeds in satisfying all of the provinces, and for that, he must pacify the intellectuals, whose skills he needs to translate his economic plans into reality. Without economic success, the army will remain a significant pocket of resistance because military modernization is not at the top of Deng's list of economic projects. (Sources: *1982–1983 International Who's Who; Boston Globe,* 6 July; *FEER,* 12 and 26 February, 2 April; *The Sun,* 28 March; *Daily Telegraph,* 23 March; *NYT,* 5, 6, 7, and 13 September, 3 October; *Asian Wall Street Journal,* 8 July; *WP,* 14 August, 20 November; *Los Angeles Times,* 30 August, 3, 4, 6 September; *CSM,* 2, 13 September; *FBIS,* 18 September; *Miami Herald,* 21 August; *Newsweek,* 20 September.)

Hoover Institution   Margit N. Grigory

India

The major Indian communist parties—the pro-Soviet Communist Party of India (CPI) and the more independent Communist Party Marxist (CPM)—cooperated more closely with each other during 1982 than at any time since the split of the Indian communist movement in 1964. The two parties, however, are still far from a merger.

The CPI and CPM each held a national congress during the year, and both congresses reaffirmed support for the "left and democratic" unity line adopted at their previous congress. At the CPM congress, the strong backing of the foreign policy of the USSR removed a major hurdle that stood in the way of cooperation between the two communist parties. They still differed, however, on which political parties to include in a "legitimate" front against Indira Gandhi's Congress (I) Party. There were also significant internal differences within the CPM on its new foreign policy line and within the CPI on its approach to Gandhi.

The Congress (I) continued to dominate the Indian political scene during the year. It controls over two-thirds of the seats in parliament (the next general election comes in 1985) and it dominates 15 of the country's 22 state assemblies. (The Communists control two state governments—West Bengal and

Tripura—and have 37 of the 526 sitting members of parliament.) However, important state elections during the year demonstrated that the Congress (I) is losing popular support all over the country. This development has encouraged the opposition parties to cooperate more closely with each other as they detect a potential victory in the 1985 election. The Communists for the first time since the 1964 party split worked together in the state elections. However, they were successful only in traditional party strongholds.

On the foreign policy front, Gandhi moved to improve relations with the United States and thus to establish more balance in India's foreign policy. She also took steps to normalize relations with Pakistan and the PRC, besides strengthening Indian ties with the states of Western Europe and with the moderate states of West Asia. The Communists, while generally supportive of Gandhi's foreign policy, expressed concern at these developments. On the other hand, they vigorously attacked her domestic policies. During the year, she took additional steps to reduce bureaucratic controls over the economy and to ease regulations that impede foreign investment in India. Her government also continued to seek concessional loans from multilateral lending agencies.

Communist Party Marxist.   The CPM is better organized and electorally more successful than the CPI. The CPM controls the governments of the large state of West Bengal and the smaller northeastern state of Tripura. Its front organizations have also grown more rapidly than CPI-affiliated groups. The CPM claims some eleven million members in its various front groups, the CPI only about five million.

The CPM held its Eleventh Congress at Vijayawada from 26 to 31 January. The most dramatic decision of the congress was the virtual abandonment of the party's long-standing policy of equidistance between USSR and the PRC. Reversing the stand taken at the 1978 Tenth Congress, which charged the USSR with "revisionism," the delegates supported a political draft praising the USSR for "taking a forthright stand against US imperialism." The delegates backed Soviet actions in Afghanistan and the presence of Vietnamese troops in Kampuchea and opposed Eurocommunism and the Solidarity movement in Poland. The delegates also supported a resolution criticizing the PRC for "collaborating" with the United States. (See discussion in *Indian Express*, 31 January.) However, the strong West Bengal unit tried unsuccessfully to get the delegates to amend the political draft with language reaffirming the more traditional policy of equidistance between the USSR and the PRC. The defeat of this effort was a significant victory for the leadership of General Secretary E.M.S Namboodiripad, who champions the position favoring support of the USSR's foreign policy. Nonetheless, only two weeks before the start of the congress the West Bengal leaders had demonstrated their more favorable view of the PRC by feting a three-person Chinese trade union delegation, thus providing the first opportunity in India for direct contact between the CPM and the Chinese Communist Party. Pramode Das Gupta, the powerful organizational secretary of the West Bengal unit, also accepted an invitation to visit China. Das Gupta, a Politburo member, led the fight at Vijayawada to tone down the CPM's criticism of China.

The CPM delegates again entrusted the party's top positions to its aging leadership. Namboodiripad was re-elected general secretary and the 40 sitting members of the Central Committee were also returned. Two new members brought its strength to 42, three short of the mandated 45. (The average age of the Central Committee is 65.) The nine-person Politburo was also re-elected; the average age of its members is 70. (The youngest member is 60.)

The party leadership announced its success in carrying out the Tenth Congress's decision to expand party membership (*Times of India*, 26 January). The West Bengal unit added 39,000 members for a new total of 82,000, while the Kerala unit grew from 62,000 to 104,000. These two states, traditional party bastions, still constitute over 60 percent of the total party membership of 270,000, although only four of the nine Politburo members are from these two states. Nonetheless, the party was able to double the number of activists since its 1978 congress.

The leadership, nevertheless, engaged in self-criticism about the sluggish expansion of CPM front groups (ibid., 30 January). They argued that there is no basis for widespread fears that the rapid growth of the front groups will result in a dilution of the CPM's class character. (Some party members also expressed concern about the drive to expand the party membership itself.) The party's major front organizations are its agricultural front, the All-India Kisan Sabha (5.7 million); the student affiliate, Students' Federation (714,000); and the labor front, the Centre for Indian Trade Unions (1.5 million). (*Statesman*, 19 July.)

Tactics.   The Vijayawada congress established a two-track strategy: (1) a broad front in cooperation with "bourgeois" parties against Gandhi and (2) a united front of "left" parties. There were differing views on where the emphasis should be placed. Party leaders in traditional areas of strength (for example, West Bengal) tend to place greater emphasis on the former. The powerful West Bengal unit, along with a few other state units, indirectly criticized the central leadership for focusing on left unity by attacking its decision to help bring down the Janata government of Morarji Desai in 1979, which paved the way for Indira Gandhi's return to power in January 1980. The central leadership, for its part, criticized the CPI for underplaying the "growing authoritarian dictatorship" of Gandhi. Politburo member M. Basuvapunaiah underscored a basic tactical difference with the CPI, noting that the right-of-center Bharatiya Janata Party (BJP), which many in the CPI consider politically untouchable because of its strongly anti-Soviet stance, is too powerful a political force to overlook in any realistic struggle against Mrs. Gandhi's government. (Ibid., 23 February.)

The leadership of the smaller CPI pushed hard to speed up the pace of cooperation. However, CPM General Secretary Namboodiripad, shortly before the CPI congress, cautioned CPI leaders that there was no chance for a merger of the two parties in the near future (ibid., 4 March). The CPI tried unsuccessfully to get the CPM to duplicate the CPI-CPM national coordination committee at the state level. When the Karnataka state units of the two parties held a joint conference in June, Namboodiripad publicly chastised the Karnataka CPM. He reminded his comrades that the CPM stood for "left" *and* "democratic" unity and not "left" unity alone (*Hindu*, 28 July). He noted that the CPM would cooperate with the CPI and other parties on specific issues, but merger was now out of the question. The major joint action of the two parties was a September mass rally for peace held at New Delhi. The two parties also worked together on 19 January to support the country's first nationwide strike, which protested passage of legislation prohibiting strikes in a set of industries defined as "essential." They also supported the August police strike in Bombay.

Communist Party of India.   The pro-Soviet CPI held its Twelfth Congress in Varanasi on 21–28 March. Despite considerable speculation that the party would soften its stance on Gandhi, the congress again took a harsh line toward her government, especially its domestic policies. Indeed, the political report charged that she was "undermining democracy itself." The congress, however, generally approved of her foreign policy, although it detected such "vacillations" as equating the Soviet and U.S. naval buildups in the Indian Ocean, loans from multilateral lending agencies, and normalization moves with China.

Nonetheless, a significant minority (some one-quarter according to press estimates) advocated a more "positive" approach to the prime minister and a more cautious approach to the CPM. They unsuccessfully proposed diluting the powers of General Secretary Rajeswara Rao, who is closely associated with the "left" unity line. Central Executive Committee member Yogendra Sharma, a leading advocate of the minority viewpoint, wrote Rao that his efforts to cooperate more closely with the CPM were "suicidal" and that the Communist Party of the Soviet Union (CPSU) for its part also considers Rao's critical approach toward Mrs. Gandhi "incorrect" (*Indian Express*, 30 September). He claimed that the CPSU finds three positive features in Gandhi—her foreign policy, her capacity to maintain national unity, and her will to fight "right reaction." In effect, Sharma was asking the party to revert to its pre-1977 policy of backing Gandhi (and hinting that the CPSU supports this move). Perhaps bowing to dissident pressures, the central leadership pointed to the BJP as a greater "threat" to democracy than is Gandhi.

The dissidents did succeed in getting the central leadership to demarcate the CPI more clearly from the CPM. The key amendment on this point reads: "The CPI firmly upholds the invincible banner of Marxism-Leninism and proletarian internationalism. It pledges anew its unflinching adherence to the commonly agreed conclusions of international meetings of Communist and workers parties . . . The CPI fights against Maoism, Euro-Communism and similar other alien ideas. The CPI fights against anti-Communism and all slanders against the Soviet Union . . . It spares no effort for defending and strengthening the unity of the world Communist movement, of which the CPSU is the vanguard." (*Times of India*, 29 March.) This effort reflected widespread fear within CPI ranks that the more disciplined CPM cadres will overawe their CPI counterparts. The leader of the Bihar delegation publicly observed that General Secretary Rao's emphasis on "left" cooperation was "ideologically disarming" the CPI cadres of his state (*Indian Express*, 21 March).

Rao sought to dampen such criticism by stating in his inaugural address to the congress that the CPI had neglected the task of building "the broadest anti-imperialist front," which would include the Congress (I). He assured the delegates that the CPI "will not hesitate to join hands" with Gandhi "to unite all the anti-imperialist forces to defend our country's foreign policy against US imperialism and its allies." (*Times of India*, 21 March.) Nonetheless, Rao in the concluding speech to the congress stated that two of the party's four major tasks are a struggle against "the anti-people and anti-democratic policies" of Gandhi's government and the construction of a "left and democratic unity" front to oppose Gandhi (*Indian Express*, 29 March).

Despite the criticism of Rao, he was re-elected unopposed to the party's most powerful office. All of the party's top leaders were retained on the 125-member National Council, and Rao's supporters continued to dominate the eleven-person Central Executive Committee. In addition, the delegates strengthened his position by dropping the post of chairman, which had been created in 1962 for S. A. Dange, who left the CPI in 1981 because of its critical approach toward Gandhi.

The CPI claims to have more members than the CPM, although it was able to add only 20,000 new members in 1982. The party total is now some 585,000. The increase tended to occur in those states where the CPI is already relatively strong: Bihar (131,000), Andhra Pradesh (93,000), Kerala (56,000), and Tamil Nadu (49,000).

The CPI and the CPSU.   Signs of some disagreement between the majority CPI leadership's position on Gandhi and that of the CPSU appeared during the year. The official Soviet position is to establish even closer ties with Gandhi's government, yet the pro-Soviet CPI continues to oppose her. Gandhi openly complained about the CPI's stand to Brezhnev when he visited India in December 1980. She did so again during a September 1982 visit to Moscow. She was particularly angry about the CPI's cooperation with the Hindu nationalist BJP during the July presidential election. In the August no-confidence debate in parliament, Gandhi stated that the CPI did not even have the backing of its "mentors." (*Hindu International Edition*, 28 August.)

Rao responded to Gandhi's attacks by noting that her "vituperative attacks" would not deter the CPI from fighting the "anti-people and anti-democratic policies of her government." "We are," he stated, "for building a left democratic national alternative to the ruling party." (AFP, Hong Kong, 25 September.) He had earlier told newsmen that "we do not seek advice of any Communist Party, not even the Communist Party of the Soviet Union" (ibid., 28 July). He made this statement soon after returning from the USSR, where, according to *Pravda* (27 June), he had met Yuri Andropov. According to leaked Indian reports of this meeting, CPSU leaders suggested to Rao that the CPI tone down its criticism of Gandhi and that it avoid any kind of cooperation with the anti-Soviet BJP (*Indian Express*, 18 July). In July, the CPI's National Council discussed Rao's stand favoring a broad "anti-authoritarian front" (that is, anti-Gandhi), including even the BJP under special circumstances. Despite the reported opposition of the CPSU and the severe criticism of some national leaders, the National Council backed Rao by a vote of 76 to 20. (Ibid., 28 July.)

Because of the embarrassing stand of the CPI toward Gandhi, the CPSU may have purposely downgraded the delegation it sent to the Twelfth Congress. The four-person delegation was led by Eduard A. Shevardnadze, first secretary of the Georgian unit of the CPSU and a nonvoting alternate member of the Politburo. At previous congresses, the CPSU delegation was led by an important central leader. (In 1969, for example, the Soviet group was led by Mikhail Suslov.) Shevardnadze, for his part, restricted his comments to foreign policy issues and the positive role of India in furthering world peace. He later paid a courtesy call on Gandhi.

The CPSU may have tried to send a message to the CPI in a lengthy article by CPSU Central Committee member Rostislav A. Ulyanovsky, a leading Soviet India-watcher, in a pro-Soviet Indian publication (*Link*, 26 December). His principal theme was that "the right-wing reactionary forces represent a dangerous alternative" to Gandhi. He justified a concentration of power in Gandhi's hands with the observation that leadership plays a critical role in a "classic eastern country" like India and that Indira Gandhi deserves mass support because of "her own qualities of an outstanding stateswoman of Asia, her dynamism, energy, resolution, will power and skill" in entering into "contact with the masses both on holidays and in times of trouble." He concluded with an indirect call for closer ties between the CPI and Gandhi: "The liquidation of disunity between the democratic movement and the forces of social progress, their alliance with similar forces acting in the same direction against the right-wing danger are objectively becoming a task of primary importance for the further development and renewal of Indian society."

A major fear of Soviet India-watchers, as reflected in the Ulyanovsky article, is that a successor to Gandhi might take a negative foreign policy line toward the USSR. The question then is whether General Secretary Rao's hard line toward Gandhi indicates deep fissures between the CPI and the CPSU. Rao himself argues publicly that the CPI is independent of Moscow, although one prominent Indian political commentator notes that his protests are "too good to be true" (Ravindra Nath in *Indian Express*, 9 April). Rather, the USSR may want the CPI both to reduce its public criticism of Gandhi (for the sake of better state-to-state relations) and to encourage left unity (in the event Gandhi's grip on power loosens). A communist reunion in India under exclusive Soviet auspices would be a major gain for the USSR. Numerous Indian press reports have noted Soviet efforts to bring about closer CPM-CPI cooperation and generous Soviet financial support of both parties (*Amrita Bazar Patrika*, 27 December 1981). A stronger communist party would play a more important role in the political process should Mrs. Gandhi's popular standing plummet, and the USSR apparently wants Indian Communists well-positioned to do so. But a merger of the two communist parties would be impeded if the CPI suddenly reversed its position on Gandhi because of the CPM's unrelenting hostility toward her. The more likely explanation of the apparent difference between the CPI and the CPSU is the latter's dilemma about how to balance its concern for good state-to-state relations with its desire for a united and pro-Soviet Indian communist movement. The differences within the CPI give the CPSU leverage to apply pressure one way or the other as circumstances change.

Elections.   There were two sets of important state assembly elections during the year. The results underscore the erosion of Gandhi's popular support. The CPI and CPM did well in traditional strongholds, but poorly elsewhere. In May, new legislatures were elected in Himachal Pradesh, Haryana, West Bengal, and Kerala. A left front dominated by the CPM retained control of the West Bengal government and a left alliance in Kerala came close to forming a government there. These two states have been traditional centers of communist strength. However, the Communists, as expected, did not win a single seat in the two Hindi-speaking states of Himachal Pradesh and Haryana. The left-front alliance in West Bengal, which included the CPM and the CPI as well as several small leftist parties, won 238 of 294 seats, 8 more than in 1977. The CPM for its part dropped slightly from 178 to 174, although it still held an absolute majority in the state assembly. The CPI with 7 seats was a relatively minor junior partner. The CPM, which has focused on building up its rural base, proved that it had managed to construct a rural organization able to deliver votes. The Kerala election pitted the eleven-party Congress (I)–led United Democratic Front (UDF) against the six-party communist-led Left Democratic Front (LDF). The UDF emerged with 77 of the 140 seats and the LDF the rest. The CPM and CPI each lost substantially in a campaign in which they were blamed for the escalating political violence in the state. The CPM dropped from 34 to 26 seats, still the largest single party in the state, and the CPI dropped from 17 to 12.

The next set of state elections occurred on 5 January 1983. New legislatures were chosen in the two large southern states of Andhra Pradesh and Karnataka, two traditional Congress (I) strongholds. Elections were also held in the small northeastern state of Tripura, which had a CPM-dominated ministry. Major upsets occurred in the two southern states. Middle-of-the-road regional parties outpolled Gandhi's Congress (I) Party in both. The Communists worked together in both states, although they generally performed less well this time than in the last state elections in 1977. In Andhra Pradesh, the CPI dropped from six to three seats and the CPM from eight to four in the 294-member assembly. In Karnataka, the CPI won three seats, as it had in 1977, while the CPM moved from zero to four in the 224-member assembly. The CPM again won a majority in Tripura. However, it lost substantial support in the tribal areas of the state to the Congress (I) Party.

The formation of a left-front government in West Bengal led to some tensions among the coalition partners. The CPM demanded the division of two important ministries—health and agriculture—held by its small allies in the outgoing government. The CPM would take control of one part of each of the divided ministries. Pramode Das Gupta, who represented the CPM in the talks, was unwilling to compromise and the small left-front partners reluctantly agreed to the CPM's unilateral step. Das Gupta's death in November in a Beijing hospital deprived the West Bengal unit of its key organizational leader and the CPM of its most articulate spokesman among those advocating a return to the policy of equidistance between the PRC and the USSR. Das Gupta was replaced by 72-year-old Saroj Mukherjee.

Smaller Communist Parties. A multitude of small communist groups have split off from the parent CPI and the CPM over the past fifteen years. None has gained significant popular support, and none won in any of the various elections during the year.

The All-India Communist Party of India (AICP), founded by CPI Chairman S.A. Dange in 1980 to protest General Secretary Rao's anti-Gandhi line, held a three-day plenum in a Bombay suburb in late January that was attended by some 350 delegates. The delegates praised Prime Minister Gandhi's leadership and called for the unity of all "patriotic" and "democratic" forces in the country to fight against "international imperialism." The party, in an obvious inflation of its size, claimed that its membership had expanded from 10,000 in 1981 to 70,000 in 1982. Dange, a Lenin Peace Prize winner, was snubbed by the USSR, which turned down his request for a transit visa to stop over in Moscow on the way to the Havana session of the World Federation of Trade Unions. This move may have been a Soviet signal of its opposition to any further exodus from the CPI to the AICP.

A growing number of violent incidents occurred between the police and the various revolutionary groups associated with the Marxist-Leninist movement. Some four dozen groups have split off from the CPM because of its insufficiently revolutionary program. Some estimates claim that they have about 30,000 activists. The major revolutionary communist groups are the Provincial Central Committee of the Communist Party of India–Marxist/Leninist (CPI-M/L), the Communist Party of India–Marxist/Leninist (Reddy) group, the Anti–Lin Biao group of the CPI-M/L, the Unity Committee of the Communist Revolutionaries of India, and the CPI-M/L Peoples War group. Recently, these associations have stepped up activities among students and workers. Their center of activity remains West Bengal and Kerala, two states with strong communist roots. The Marxist-Leninists (referred to in the Indian Press as Naxalites) made some moves to establish closer links, but with little success. In late 1982, several groups met to analyze the Naxalite failure to generate mass support over the past decade. A Central Reorganization Committee produced a lengthy document, "Towards a New Phase of the Spring Thunder," which analyzed past mistakes. (*Statesman*, 27 December.) The document suggested that the Marxist-Leninists have placed too much emphasis on an "annihilation of class enemies" line and too little on establishing a concrete political-economic program.

Arlington, Virginia   Walter K. Andersen

Indonesia

Indonesia's leaders continue to perceive communism as having little influence in the island-state, and they now have begun to worry about preventing violent crime. Yet the government continues to keep a close eye on the thousands of political prisoners, or *tapol* (arrested in 1965 in connection with the Indonesian communist coup attempt), who have been released in recent years.

General elections for the Indonesian parliament were held in the spring without incident. The two very small, pro-Beijing and pro-Moscow communist parties have neither been able to expand their numbers nor to have any influence on political activities. The leader of the Moscow faction, Satiajaya Sudiman, who allegedly lives abroad, either in Moscow or Prague, was quoted in the pro-Soviet journal *World Marxist Review* (June, pp. 13–14) as saying that the Indonesian Communist Party (Parti Komunis Indonesia; PKI) can still influence Indonesian public opinion, but there were no tangible manifestations of this influence throughout 1982.

The General Political Situation.   In early August 1982, Admiral Sudomo of the chief domestic security service (Kopkamtib) declared that his agency now was concerned mainly with industrial strikes, urban crime, student demonstrations, and the new problems that had arisen from economic development, chiefly overcrowded cities with their poverty and human frustration (*NYT,* 5 August).

President Suharto, in his state address to the Indonesian parliament on the occasion of Indonesia's national day celebration on 16 August made no mention of the actual or latent danger of communism but emphasized that "our security situation has been satisfactorily stable." Suharto did note, however, the government had to pay "more serious attention" to eliminating violent crimes, including robberies and hijackings, and other "disorders which have been a source of public restlessness." (*FBIS,* 17 August.)

But other Indonesian officials still raise the specter of domestic communist subversion. In July, Maj. Gen. Norman Sasono, head of the Greater Djakarta Security Command, inaugurated an Anti-Latent Communist Danger Assistance Board in the Indonesian capital. This board is supposed to provide "increased supervision and guidance" for the more than 5,500 released *tapol* in the Djakarta area. Because other local government agencies were not supervising the *tapol,* Sasono pointed out, this new board would register and monitor all released *tapol* to prevent them from forming networks, changing their name or profession, establishing cadres, implementing communist ideology, or providing means for traveling in secret, agitating, or spreading propaganda and subversion. Sasono argued that "communist doctrines are always a threat" and therefore the government would watch the *tapol* to ensure that they did not take advantage of "social problems to spread communism." (*Asia Record,* August, p. 11.)

The government identification cards given to tapol have special markings on them to denote their former political status. In some areas the tapol must report regularly to the authorities. Tapol are still barred from certain forms of employment, such as the civil and armed services and "essential industries." The unemployment rate among the tapol is certainly higher than among the rest of the population. (U.S. Department of State, *Country Reports on Human Rights Practices for 1981,* p. 595.) Many tapol are often rearrested and released without trial or explanation, and some tapol have reported that they have been warned not to attend any public meeting without receiving approval from the authorities (*FEER,* 19, March pp. 26–27).

It is not known how many tapol were permitted to vote in the 4 May general elections. But in December 1981, Home Affairs Minister Amir Mahmud said that after a "study and evaluation" of the tapol, there were more than 1.5 million persons "whose voting rights in the 1982 election cannot be considered" (*FBIS,* 8 December 1981). In September 1982, Mahmud warned Achehnese provincial leaders that although national development had progressed, the national struggle against "contradictory ideologies" was not yet over. "We must not get ourselves trapped by and drawn into" such creeds as "Communism," "liberalism," "social democratic groups" and "extreme theocracy." (Ibid., 23 September.)

In the 4 May general elections for the 364 contested seats in the Indonesian parliament, the government party, Golkar, won 246 seats (a gain of 14 over the 1977 elections), while the two opposition parties, the predominantly Muslim United Development Party and the Democratic Party of Indonesia, won 94 and 24 seats respectively (a loss of 5 seats for each). More than 75 million Indonesians, or 91.4 percent of all registered voters, allegedly cast ballots. As the election campaign became more tense, some violence erupted in Djakarta on 18 March and rapidly spread to other areas. The final death toll came to 58; 204 people were arrested, and at least 38 were to be tried for having committed criminal offenses. (*NYT,* 11 May; *FBIS,* 19 March, 16 June; *Asia Record,* July; *Asia Research Bulletin,* 30 June, p. 932.)

During the election campaign, Home Affairs Minister Mahmud warned that the Indonesian people did not want political stability disrupted and were "strongly opposed to Communism," "the capitalist system," the "social democratic system," and Islamic theocracy. But in responding to the election violence, the Suharto government seemed to want to restrict political ideologies that opposed the officially endorsed ideology of *Pantjasila* (the Five Pillars of the Indonesian State, which include a belief in God, nationalism, democracy, socialism, and justice and humanitarianism). In his 16 August national day address, President Suharto warned of the extreme dangers and "fanaticism" coming from the "presence of other principles" in opposition political parties. Although his remarks appeared to be addressed mainly toward the Muslim United Development Party, which stresses Islamic principles, Suharto's warning underscored the ideological commitment of the government to oppose any left-oriented group. (*FBIS,* 5 March; *FEER,* 27 August, p. 20.)

Meanwhile many prominent Indonesians have begun to criticize the government. Army Gen. (ret.) A. H. Nasution, a former defense minister and chairman of the People's Congress, sent a letter on 5 March to Indonesian parliamentary leaders sharply criticizing alleged violations of the Indonesian constitution in sixteen years that Suharto has been in power. Nasution charged that the government had violated human rights, abused its power through such extraconstitutional bodies as the security agency Kopkamtib, and still had not ended the "virtual state of emergency" first announced by Suharto on 3 October 1965 (*Sarawak Tribune,* 10 March). Again on 18 August former Governor of Djakarta Gen. Ali Sadikin, speaking for the prominent Indonesian government critics known as Petition 50 Group, attacked the Suharto regime in a "statement of concern" before parliament. He charged that the May general elections had no real democratic basis because the government had the power to appoint persons to both parliament and the People's Congress. The parliament was merely a rubber stamp of the government. (*FBIS,* 20 August.)

Foreign Affairs. The Suharto government still has not resumed diplomatic relations with the People's Republic of China. In mid-May, Indonesian Foreign Minister Mochtar Kusumaatmadja declared that while relations were "improving," the Suharto government wanted "more reassurance" that Beijing had really changed its attitude toward supporting communist insurgents. Kusumaatmadja said that "Beijing's refusal" to give such assurances was the main stumbling block preventing diplomatic normalization. (*Straits Times,* Singapore, 25 May.) A few months earlier, the Indonesian foreign minister had said that diplomatic normalization would be "based solely" on a consideration of Indonesia's national interest. In June, Indonesian Vice-President Adam Malik declared that the Djakarta government did not as yet think the time "ripe" for normalization. Malik added that the Suharto government was afraid of "being cheated" if relations were "restored." The Indonesian vice-president admitted, however, that a Chinese delegation had visited Indonesia to participate in the Sixth Asian Table Tennis World Championship. He also said that Indonesia was sending another trade delegation to Beijing to promote the sale of 20,000 tons of Indonesian rubber. When asked whether an official Chinese trade delegation would visit Djakarta in the future, Malik answered that if a delegation comes, "it will be private businessmen from China." (*FBIS,* 30 December 1981, 8 June.)

Meanwhile, the Djarkarta daily *Indonesian Observer* (27 July) urged the United States not to ignore the continuing Chinese threat to Asia, and the Djakarta daily *Indonesia Times* (20 September) noted that China was still assisting "Chinese underground movements in Southeast Asia" and that "PKI leaders are still being maintained in Beijing" (*FBIS,* 28 July, 23 September).

A new difficulty between Djakarta and Beijing developed at the close of August, when China reportedly lodged a claim to part of the mineral-rich Natuna island group in the southern reaches of the South China Sea. Now claimed and occupied by Indonesia, these islands are also being claimed by the Socialist Republic of Vietnam. On 23 June, a group of 56 armed and uniformed Vietnamese dissidents, led by a Vietnamese army lieutenant who said that fear of the communist regime had prompted their escape, landed on the Natuna islands (ibid., 23 June). Control over the territorial waters of the mineral-rich islands has been a long-standing source of dispute between Djakarta and Hanoi. It has not yet been determined if these were genuine Vietnamese refugees.

Indonesian-Soviet relations worsened during the year. On 19 December 1981, Radio Moscow reported that the Central Committee of the PKI (Soviet wing) had sent a brief congratulatory message to Leonid Brezhnev on his seventy-fifth birthday (*Berita Buana,* Djakarta, 6 January). Chalid Mawardi, chairman of the Indonesian parliament's Defense and Foreign Affairs Committee, sharply criticized Radio Moscow on 9 January for having carried the PKI message. Mawardi said that the broadcast had been "purposely made" to influence the Indonesian people. This incident demonstrated that the PKI was still a "latent threat" to Indonesia. (*FBIS,* 9 January.) Reportedly, the Indonesian ambassador in Moscow also protested the broadcast. In subsequent days there were anti-Soviet demonstrations, one of them by the Indonesian

National Youth Committee, in front of the Soviet Embassy in Djakarta. The youths handed a protest note to an embassy official. (*Nation Review,* Bangkok, 28 January.)

On 8 February, the Indonesian Foreign Ministry declared persona non grata and ordered expelled within 24 hours the assistant Soviet military attaché, Lt. Col. S. P. Igorov, charging him with "spying activities which endangered the security of the state." It was further announced that a "regrettable" incident had taken place on 9 February at Djakarta's Halim Perdanakusumah Airport. A party of embassy staff members had accompanied Igorov to see him off. Among them was Aleksandr Finenko, head of the Aeroflot office in Djakarta. According to an Indonesian Foreign Ministry statement, Indonesian authorities were seeking Finenko because of his involvement with Igorov in spying activities. When Finenko was detained by Indonesian security officials at the airport, Soviet embassy personnel attempted to prevent his arrest, and a struggle ensued. Finenko ultimately was arrested at the airport. Another Soviet diplomat, who also had been apprehended because of his involvement in the melee surrounding Finenko's arrest, was set free after Soviet Ambassador Ivan Shpedko personally went to the Djakarta military command to protest. (*FBIS*, 9 February.)

Igorov's downfall apparently came on 4 February, when he was observed meeting an Indonesian officer from the Walil (Compulsory Training Command) and receiving a camera and roll of film. The Indonesian officer, Lt. Col. Sudaryanto, subsequently admitted that he had been working for the USSR for the past five years. According to Djakarta Military Commander Norman Sasono, both Finenko and Sudaryanto would stand trial on charges of subversion. On 15 February, Security Chief Sudomo said that the Suharto government had requested the Soviet embassy to send Finenko out of the country because he was in "poor health" following a hunger strike (ibid., 12 and 16).

The Indonesian press then published angry anti-Soviet editorials and reports on the "spy network," and the Indonesian government closed the Soviet consulate in the Borneo town of Bandjermassin. On 10 February, Indonesian youths staged a demonstration in front of the Soviet consulate in Medan, North Sumatra. Vice-President Malik warned foreign nations with diplomatic missions in Indonesia "to refrain from interfering in the internal affairs" of the country.

In the area of trade Indonesia remains interested in furthering good relations with the Soviet bloc. In March, the chiefs of Indonesian diplomatic missions in Europe met in Djakarta to explore ways of increasing trade with Eastern Europe. Indonesian Foreign Minister Mochtar Kusumaatmadja said that Indonesia expected to intensify its direct trade with Eastern Europe, even though exports from Eastern Europe had "traditionally been conducted" through Western Europe (ibid., 3 March). On 2 July, Indonesian-Romanian economic discussions were concluded in Bucharest, following a visit by Romanian Foreign Minister Stefan Andrei to Djakarta. The two countries agreed to expand their trade. The Bucharest government wants to import some two million tons of crude oil from Indonesia in 1982 and five million tons by early 1983. No formal Indonesian undertaking to supply Romania with this amount of oil was given because of disagreements between the two countries over payment procedures. Indonesian oil exports to Romania presumably will increase. Indonesia also agreed to consider the Romanian offer of facilities at the free zone in the Romanian port of Sulina and a Romanian bid to provide some 1300 freight wagons for the Indonesian state railway. (Ibid., 2 and 13 July.)

In mid-May, Mochtar declared that while Vietnam was not an enemy, Indonesia still opposed certain Vietnamese policies. Earlier he had stressed that Indonesia opposed the idea that the Association of Southeast Nations (ASEAN) supply arms to the anti-Vietnamese resistance in Kampuchea on the grounds that ASEAN should not take a "confrontative attitude" toward Hanoi (ibid., 17 December 1981, 18 May). On another occasion, Mochtar was at pains to dissociate ASEAN's policy toward the Kampuchean problem from the Sino-Vietnamese conflict. He contended that ASEAN should not be completely identified with China because that was not in "ASEAN's interests" (*Asian Wall Street Journal,* 17 May). An independent Vietnam, acting as a buffer to Chinese expansionism, has been the reason for Djakarta's moderate attitude toward Hanoi in the Kampuchean crisis. Indonesian spokesmen have repeatedly stressed that direct talks with Vietnam on the issue are necessary. (*FBIS*, 22 June.)

However, Djakarta still distrusts any Vietnamese policy that tries to placate ASEAN opinion and falls short of a Vietnamese withdrawal from Kampuchea. Mochtar dismissed a Vietnamese offer in February to open border negotiations with Thailand if some Vietnamese forces withdrew from Kampuchea. The

Indonesian foreign minister described this Vietnamese bid as an attempt to "isolate Thailand and to cut it off from the other ASEAN Nations" (ibid., 24 March).

Djakarta also pressed the various anti-Vietnamese Kampuchean factions to form a coalition against Hanoi. Late in February, the Suharto government endorsed Malaysia's warning to the Democratic Kampuchea underground regime of Khieu Samphan and Pol Pot that it could not take continued ASEAN support in the United Nations for granted if such a coalition failed. When the anti-Vietnamese Kampuchean coalition headed by Prince Norodom Sihanouk was formed on 22 June, state-owned Radio Djakarta declared that this coalition "at least reflects the will of the Kampuchean resistance movements against the Vietnamese military occupation which has already lasted more than three years," adding that majority support for the coalition in the United Nations probably could be maintained (ibid., 24 June). The *Indonesia Times* (24 June), which often reflects government opinion, was more cautious, warning that the coalition should avoid giving the impression that it was heavily supported by China, for this would heighten Vietnam's "sensitivity." After the formation of the Sihanouk-led coalition government, other Indonesian papers praised a new Vietnamese willingness to "find a way out of the 'quagmire'" of its Kampuchean involvement (*FBIS*, 27 July). At the United Nations, Indonesia continued to oppose the seating of the Hanoi-backed government of the People's Republic of Kampuchea led by President Heng Samrin.

On 28 October, Vietnamese Foreign Minister Nguyen Co Thach arrived in Djakarta for a three-day visit. Thach reportedly expressed Vietnam's desire to import Indonesian urea fertilizer and textiles. Indonesian Foreign Minister Mochtar Kusumaatmadja declined to comment. In a press interview in Djakarta, Thach rejected the recent U.N. action to give Kampuchea's seat in the world body to the new anti-Vietnamese coalition headed by Prince Sihanouk. Thach also said the objectives of his Djakarta visit had been realized. These objectives were a "continuation of talks and bilateral relations." (Ibid., 1 November.) According to a comment from Moscow on Thach's visit, Indonesia and Vietnam had common goals of national development, and Hanoi's Vietnam News Agency reported that Thach's discussions had taken place "in an atmosphere of frankness and friendship" (ibid., 10 November).

University of Bridgeport   *Justus M. van der Kroef*

Japan

The Japan Communist Party (JCP) was founded on 15 July 1922. Before World War II, the JCP was an illegal party, and its membership never exceeded a thousand. During the U.S. occupation of Japan after the war, the JCP became a legitimate and active party and immediately grew in membership and political influence. This lasted until the early 1950s, when it suffered a loss of support and official suppression as a result of the Korean War and the JCP's advocacy of violent means to attain political goals.

The JCP learned a lesson, and by the end of the decade it began to advocate the "peaceful road" to political power. The party platform adopted at the Eighth Congress in 1961, which advocated the "parliamentary road" to power made the JCP a Eurocommunist party. The JCP line or program has remained basically unchanged since 1961.

The JCP's success in elections has varied considerably, reflecting ups and downs that result from the JCP's position as a protest party. When it experiences victories, many voters immediately abandon the party for fear that it will gain control of the government. The JCP's vacillating fortunes at the polls also result from party campaign practices, which are based more on principles than on realism, and its tendency to field too many candidates, some only for the purpose of educating the public. In the 1974 national elections, the JCP won 6.4 million votes (12 percent), which translated into 20 seats out of 252 in the upper house. In the 1975 local elections, the party won 3,165 of 76,216 seats in prefectural, municipal, town, and village assemblies. This was a peak, however, and in 1976 the party lost half of its seats in the more powerful lower house, a performance repeated the next year in the upper house election. In 1979, the JCP regained the seats it had lost in the House of Representatives, or lower house, through better planning and electioneering and a slight increase in popular support for the party. In the last national election in 1980, the JCP lost again in elections to both houses of the Diet, although its 10.4 percent vote share was down only a fraction of a percent over the 1979 elections.

The JCP is one of the largest nonruling communist parties in the world. There seems little hope, however, that the party, either alone or in coalition with other leftist parties, will win control of the Diet. In fact, the JCP's relations with other leftist parties are poor and have worsened in recent years.

The JCP regards itself an independent communist party and, since the 1960s, has been on good terms with neither the Soviet Union nor the People's Republic of China. The party's closest allies are European communist parties. The JCP has long condemned radical and terrorist groups in Japan, such as the Red Army, and maintains no ties with such organizations.

Party Internal Affairs.   The JCP has a membership of something over 400,000 in a population of 118.6 million *(Asia 1983 Yearbook,* p. 6). The National Police Agency put the membership of the JCP at 400,000 in December 1981 *(KDK Information,* 1 February). In July, Chairman Kenji Miyamoto stated that membership was 480,000 *(FBIS,* 27 July). Miyamoto put the number of subscriptions to *Akahata* (Red flag), the party's newspaper, at over 3.5 million, although this figure may be exaggerated somewhat and is clearly short of the goal of four or five million mentioned by party leaders throughout the year. In his New Year's speech, Miyamoto declared that the party had grown by 20,000 in 1981 and subscriptions to *Akahata* had shown a net gain of 110,000. Even if this figure is correct, the party is behind in collecting for subscriptions to the paper, suggesting that there is, in fact, little or no real growth in readership.

The JCP held its Sixteenth Congress in July, commemorating the sixtieth anniversary of the founding of the party. At the end of the meeting, a new Central Committee consisting of 189 regular and 22 candidate or alternate members was elected. The new Central Committee was considerably younger. Female membership increased from 12 to 27.

The JCP has 29 representatives in the House of Representatives out of a total of 511. This made the party the fifth largest in the lower house. In the House of Councillors, the JCP held 12 seats out of 252, making it the fourth largest party there. Overall the JCP ranks fifth among the parties. (*Liberal Star,* December.) The JCP had only one seat less than the Democratic Socialist Party and only 20 less than the Komei Party. However, its strength was less than one-third that of the Japanese Socialist Party and less than one-tenth that of the ruling Liberal Democratic Party.

The next election is scheduled for mid-1983 and will be for seats in the House of Councillors. A poll taken in the fall showed 2.4 percent of the public supporting the JCP—giving it a rating of fifth among Japanese political parties and indicating little change from a year or two ago *(FBIS,* 2 September).

In local elections in 1982, the JCP did not fare particularly well. In April, the candidate supported by the JCP and the Japan Socialist Party lost in the race for governorship of Niigata prefecture. The JCP candidate (also supported by other leftist parties) also lost the gubernatorial race in Kyoto prefecture. The JCP candidate for the Yokohama mayorship lost. JCP victories in other races did not offset these defeats.

The biggest event for the JCP during the year were several changes in the top leadership of the party. Kenji Miyamoto, who is 73 and was hospitalized a year ago, stepped down as party chairman. He was replaced by Tetsuzo Fuwa (see biographical sketch at the end of this profile). Miyamoto's health and the need for a younger, more energetic person at the party's helm prompted the change, which had been anticipated for some time. The party's elder statesman, "godfather" Sanzo Nosaka, also retired from the position of chairman of the Central Committee. Nosaka is 90 years old. He is one of the original founders of the party and was its leader for a number of years. Nosaka became honorary chairman.

Miyamoto became the new chairman of the Central Committee and will no doubt remain active in party decision making as long as his health remains reasonably good. Deputy Secretary General Kaneko

Mitsuhiro assumed the post of secretary general, which was vacant after Fuwa's promotion to the top position.

These changes were made at the close of the Sixteenth Congress in July. However, neither these leadership changes nor the speeches and decisions made at the congress indicated any important change in direction. An "international symposium" held at the same time as the party congress was attended by leaders of ten communist parties, mostly from Europe. This reaffirmed the JCP's Eurocommunist stance and emphasized its perception that its most important friends are European parties.

Relations with the communist parties of both the Soviet Union and China remained cool, as has been the case for nearly twenty years. Early in the year, Chairman Miyamoto condemned the leadership of Poland, saying that it was the first case among socialist countries where this sort of military rule had been in force. He asserted that the Military Council for National Salvation in Poland is unconstitutional and that Poland's decision to establish martial law had been influenced by the Soviet Union. (Ibid., 15 January.) He went on to say that the Soviet "military bloc" restricts the sovereign rights of member-countries.

Subsequently *Akahata* assailed Soviet policy in both Poland and Afghanistan, asserting that it is unrealistic to regard the Soviet Union as a "bulwark of peace" or a "vanguard." *Akahata* referred to the Soviet presence in Afghanistan as "armed intervention." (BBC, 27 April.) During the year, the JCP also criticized the Soviet Union for its global military buildup and for its "occupation" of several islands claimed by Japan north of Hokkaido.

The JCP was also at odds during the year with the Prague-based *World Marxist Review,* which claims to represent the world communist movement. *Akahata* condemned the journal's position that it is the first task of communist parties to combat anti-Sovietism, saying that this line is a "fundamental mistake" since it assumes that the Communist Party of the Soviet Union (CPSU) is a "leading party or leading center standing above all other communist parties." (Ibid.) JCP spokesmen went on to say that the *Review* had become little more than a propaganda organ for the Kremlin.

Moscow reacted with anger, criticizing the JCP in various official statements and in the magazine *Kommunist.* Soviet leaders seemed especially sensitive to JCP criticism in the context of efforts to picture the USSR as having peaceful intentions worldwide and while trying to exert greater influence on the antiwar movement in Western Europe and elsewhere. Moscow was also jockeying for position with the United States on arms control.

In November, the JCP made public letters received in April and May from the CPSU asking the JCP to make a united effort on the global antiwar campaign. Tomio Nishizawa, the JCP's spokesman on international issues, stated that the letters had been sent in an effort to build a common front to influence the Reagan administration. He noted that the letters were made public because of Brezhnev's death, but did not hint that this would be the occasion for seeking a new relationship with the CPSU. (*FBIS,* 23 November.)

Early in the year, there were rumors of a rapprochement between the JCP and the Chinese Communist Party (CCP). Several JCP members reportedly visited the Chinese Embassy in Tokyo early in the year, and *Akahata* ceased carrying advertisements for anti-Chinese books. Meanwhile an official Chinese journal reprinted an *Akahata* article written by Tetsuzo Fuwa. A Chinese newspaper also carried the memoirs of late JCP leader Sen Katayama. (See ibid., 5 May.)

Hiroshi Tachiki, an official spokesman for the JCP, however, denied that relations between the two parties would be normalized (ibid.). Subsequently, in response to Chinese overtures that the two parties should talk, the JCP replied that there was only one condition: "Stop interventionist activities toward the JCP adopted since the Cultural Revolution in 1965" (*KDK Information,* 1 March).

Hope of a rapprochement seemed to be dashed completely in June. The JCP accused China of "maintaining an alliance with the U.S.—an imperialist power." This was described in a draft resolution for the June congress as one of the "big errors" committed by the CCP. Another "error" cited was China's intervention in the affairs of other countries. (*FBIS,* 11 June.)

Party Policies. The year brought no significant changes in JCP policies. In fact, the installation of a new leadership was noticeably not accompanied by new policy pronouncements.

The JCP leadership gave new stress to its antiwar stance during the year, in response to the growing influence of the antinuclear movement in a number of countries, including Japan. At the congress, Miyamoto called on the Japanese people to launch a grass-roots movement against nuclear weapons.

Miyamoto noted that 82 million Japanese had signed antinuclear petitions aimed at influencing the U.N. disarmament session, which he called a "historic and epochal achievement" (ibid., 27 July). He went on to say that opposition to limited nuclear war and the Japan-U.S. security treaty were incompatible. Elsewhere, the JCP continued its attack on the security treaty, even though the other leftist parties have endorsed it and opinion polls indicate a growing majority sense the need for the treaty.

Miyamoto also criticized the government for what he called policies "promoting militarism" by increasing defense spending (ibid.). Thus the JCP remained adamantly opposed to an increase in the military budget or a change in the status of the military in Japan. On this issue the JCP's stance was unique among the political parties in Japan but consistent with its past positions on this issue.

JCP leaders also remained harsh in their criticism of corruption in government and "money politics." In June, a JCP Diet member called for the resignation of a Diet member convicted of taking bribes in the Lockheed scandal—the first such resolution made in the Diet in the post–World War II period (ibid., 9 June).

When the Liberal Democratic Party picked its new leader in November, who subsequently became prime minister, the JCP was unabashed in its criticisms. Miyamoto called newly installed Prime Minister Yasuhiro Nakasone a "supporter of right-wing ideology and an advocate of constitutional revision"— referring to Article 9 of the constitution, which prohibits war as a policy and does not allow Japan to rearm. He and other JCP leaders warned that Nakasone would pave the way for a defense buildup under the Japan-U.S. security alliance. Party spokesmen also noted that Nakasone was a protégé of former Prime Minister Kakuei Tanaka, who is still under indictment in the Lockheed scandal for receiving bribes, and that Nakasone's cabinet appointments "disgracefully" reflected Tanaka's influence. (Ibid., 26 November.)

The JCP also attacked the Liberal Democratic Party–sponsored election bill that passed the Diet in August. This bill, which establishes a proportional system and forces candidates to run as party representatives instead of as individuals, will favor the Liberal Democratic Party. Although the JCP publicly opposed the bill, there is reason to believe that it, in fact, favored the bill, inasmuch as the JCP's superior organization will actually help it in the 1983 election under the new election rules (*Asia 1983 Yearbook*, p. 169).

Relations between the JCP and Japan's other political parties remained generally less than cordial. Miyamoto described as "doomed to failure" the so-called "moderate alliance" of the Komei Party and the Japan Socialist Party and called for "progressive unity" between the JCP and the Japan Socialist Party (*NYT*, 4 July). There seemed little prospect, however, that this would come about, and the next month JCP leaders denounced the Socialists for collusion with the Liberal Democratic Party on the election bill (*Japan Times*, 22 August). At about the same time, JCP leaders declared publicly that the so-called centrist-leftist coalition between the Komei Party and the Japan Socialist Party was helping conservative forces and said that they hoped that the Japan Socialist Party would stop its "descent into the rightist camp" (*FBIS*, 11 June).

The JCP was pleased, however, with the decision of the Japan Teachers Union to support the "progressive alliance" instead of the "center coalition" (*NYT*, 4 July). Otherwise, the JCP's relationship with various unions, auxiliary organizations, and support groups remained unchanged.

Political-Economic Relations in Japan.   Despite a drop-off in economic growth and large (by Japanese standards) unemployment, plus concern by the public about economic problems, jobs, and welfare, the JCP was unable to take advantage of any of these issues effectively. Its long-standing positions on economic growth, unemployment, and welfare won little attention, and the JCP was unable or unwilling to make any changes to adjust. Given the conservative trend in Japanese politics, it may be impossible for the JCP to make a better or broader appeal to the masses than it is now. Clearly, most public opinion polls reflected greater support for conservative solutions to economic and social problems.

The one trend that seemed to favor the JCP was the renewed concern about nuclear war and the antiwar protest movement. In May, the Diet passed a resolution proposing the abolition of nuclear weapons. At almost the same time, a large rally in Tokyo was attended by between 200,000 and 400,000 people (*CSM*, 25 May). It is uncertain, however, how effectively the JCP can use the antiwar movement in Japan or elsewhere. So far the party has won some attention and sympathy for its positions on the issue, but it can hardly translate this into increased voter support or political influence.

Another hot political issue in Japan during 1982 was the problem of budget deficits. The JCP strongly criticized the government for its incompetence on fiscal matters and even called on Prime Minister Zenko Suzuki to resign. On the other hand, the JCP was unable to benefit from the government's problems. Suzuki, in fact, proposed added spending to stimulate the economy. The JCP applauded this, but the proposal was criticized from other quarters as adding to the budget deficit. The government cut pay increases to government workers and broached the idea of turning over the Japanese National Railways to private ownership. But on neither of these issues could the JCP ride the tide of mass opinion.

Likewise, criticism of the government's handling of the economy was muted by comparisons Liberal Democratic Party leaders made with other countries—which made Japan look good. Problems in most communist countries also weakened the public's willingness to accept JCP suggestions for curing the economic malaise. Social problems in contrast seemed unimportant. In any case, there was no overriding or even critically important social issue that the JCP could focus on and translate into a political issue with which it might make electoral gains.

Foreign Policy Issues. Japan's bad relations with the Soviet Union, which have worsened in recent years, have been a factor that has hurt the JCP despite its anti-Soviet stance on various foreign policy issues and its lack of contacts with the Soviet Union. The JCP has taken a stronger stance on the Northern Territories issue than have the other political parties, yet this has not helped the party. In fact, the issue itself seems to have alienated voters from the JCP since many in Japan still associate it with the Soviet Union. The same is true of Japan's policies toward Poland, Afghanistan, and Indochina. Tokyo has taken an anti-Soviet stance on all three of these issues, as has the JCP, but this has not been to the JCP's advantage in terms of its public appeal.

Japan's foreign policy has favored better relations with China. But the JCP has not been able to exploit this relationship because of its strained relations with the CCP and its reluctance to seek a new relationship with the CCP because of its stand as an independent communist party. Improving relations with China would also conflict with the JCP's anti-U.S. stance.

The JCP remains alone among the Japanese parties in its stand against the Japan-U.S. defense treaty. This may give the JCP added public support in the future, especially from the left. On the other hand, the issue is declining in importance, and a larger segment of the population accepts the treaty as necessary. Likewise, although U.S.-Japan relations contain some serious problems, the most sensitive issue is the trade relationship, which is not something the JCP can make much of. Another issue is U.S. pressure on Japan to spend more on defense and take on added defense responsibilities. This is potentially an issue the JCP can capitalize on, but so far it has not done so successfully. Recent polls indicate that there is strong reluctance among the Japanese public to spend more on defense, notwithstanding U.S. pressure, a reluctance that should help the JCP. On the other hand, the polls also reflect a growing understanding of the problems by both Americans and Japanese (*Liberal Star,* 10 May, 10 July).

Japan's relations with a number of other countries were clouded during 1982 by the textbook controversy. When the Ministry of Education tried to tone down descriptions of Japan's behavior and policies during World War II, relations with China, Korea, and Taiwan were affected, as were relations with almost all Southeast Asian countries. The JCP's antiwar stance put it in a position to exploit the problem, at least in terms of taking the ruling Liberal Democratic Party to task. Yet the JCP was not effective in terms of increasing its popularity at home by taking up the issue.

Biography. *Tetsuzo Fuwa.* Fuwa was born on 26 January 1930 in Tokyo. He joined the JCP in 1947 while a student at Tokyo's prestigious First High School. Subsequently he attended Tokyo University, Japan's premier institution of higher learning, graduating with a degree in physics in 1953. After graduation, he made labor and union work his career until 1964, when he was invited to work at party headquarters in the areas of Marxist-Leninist theory and international problems. At the same time, he was promoted to alternate membership on the Central Committee. Two years later, he was advanced to full membership. In July 1970, Fuwa was elected to the seven-member Permanent Presidium of the JCP and appointed chief of the party Secretariat. In July 1982, he was elected chairman of the JCP.

Fuwa has been a prolific writer and is one of the members of the JCP whose works have been published in book form for general public consumption. Fuwa is associated with the "parliamentary path" to power and the respectable nature of the JCP in recent years. He is sometimes referred to as "the prince" because of his outstanding educational background, good looks, and youthful accomplishments. Fuwa was for some time the only member of the JCP Presidium to hold a seat in the Diet.

Southwestern at Memphis   John F. Copper

Kampuchea

There are two competing communist organizations in Kampuchea. The ruling Kampuchea People's Revolutionary Party (KPRP) is pro-Hanoi and pro-Moscow. The pro-Chinese resistance group led by Pol Pot is known as the DK (for Democratic Kampuchea, the name of their short-lived republic). Both groups can be regarded as offshoots of Ho Chi Minh's Indochina Communist Party (ICP), although the DK became strongly anti-Vietnamese during the 1970s.

In 1945, the ICP was nominally disbanded, but in Kampuchea the Pracheachon Party was widely regarded as its Hanoi-controlled successor. During the 1950s and early 1960s, the Pracheachon was allowed to contest elections, but it achieved only token success at the polls. Meanwhile, at the end of the first Indochina war in 1954, a number of Cambodians, including some born in South Vietnam, were taken to North Vietnam for political and military training. After the outbreak of war in Kampuchea in 1970, perhaps as many as several hundred of these were sent back to Kampuchea by the Vietnamese government. Most of them are believed to have been killed in action during the 1970–1975 war or purged by Pol Pot's DK organization.

The leaders of the DK had gone underground in 1962 (when Sihanouk cracked down on their activities), but most of them apparently remained in Kampuchea. During the 1970–1975 war, they accepted aid from Hanoi, but carefully prevented Hanoi from taking over their movement. From 1975 to 1979, they controlled Kampuchea. China was virtually their only foreign supporter.

Population. 5.9 million (1982 est.)

Party. Kampuchea People's Revolutionary Party (KPRK)

Founded. 1951 (Communist Party of Cambodia)

Secretary General. Heng Samrin

Politburo. 7 members: Heng Samrin (chairman, Council of State), Chan Si (premier), Say Phuthang (vice-chairman, Council of State), Chea Sim (chairman, National Assembly), Bou Thang (defense minister), Hun Sen (vice-chairman, Council of Ministers; foreign minister), Chea Soth (minister of planning)

Secretariat. 7 members: Heng Samrin, Say Phuthang, Chan Si, Bou Thang, Hun Sen, Chea Soth, Chan Phin

Central Committee. 18 full and 2 alternate members

Last Congress. Fourth, 26–29 May, in Phnom Penh

Auxiliary Organizations. Kampuchea Front for National Construction, Kampuchea Women's Association, Kampuchea Youth Association

Publications. *Kampuchea; Kaset Kantoap Padivoat* (Revolutionary army)

In December 1978 and January 1979, Vietnamese forces invaded Kampuchea, pushed Pol Pot's group out of Phnom Penh, and installed a regime led by the KPRP. With a few exceptions, the KPRP leaders, who continued in power through 1982, were among the survivors of the group of Cambodians trained in North Vietnam during the 1950s and 1960s. The main exception was Heng Samrin, the head of the regime, who defected from Pol Pot's group in the mid-1970s. Heng Samrin has spent little time in Vietnam, but he appears to be fully responsive to Hanoi's directives. Thousands of Vietnamese and hundreds of Soviet advisers continued to guide Kampuchea's policies.

Internal Party Affairs.   During 1982, the only official comment (on the government-controlled radio) concerning Pen Sovan's ouster as leader of the party and government in December 1981 was that he was receiving treatment for "mental illness." There was no suggestion that he might return to a role in running the country or party.

Domestic Affairs.   Perhaps the main development in 1982, as far as the Phnom Penh regime was concerned, was Vietnam's transfer of more military responsibilities to the regime's fledgling army. Radio reports of battles during the dry season (November to May) and wet season (June to October) suggested that Khmer forces, probably combined with Vietnamese units, were seeing an increasing amount of action. On the opposing side, Pol Pot's organization formed a coalition with the small noncommunist resistance groups led by Prince Norodom Sihanouk and former premier Son Sann. The same radio reports indicated that the noncommunist resistance was bearing a large share of the Vietnamese attacks.

The government continued to try to rally public support among the Khmer people through a full range of auxiliary organizations—including youth groups, women's groups, and labor organizations. Few data are available to measure their success. Visiting journalists usually see only what the regime wants them to see, and their reports of a general return to normalcy must be read with caution. However, there were signs of some improvement in the food situation, although Kampuchea had not regained its role as a net food exporter. The numbers of refugees fleeing the country also appears to have declined in 1982, no doubt in part because of a well-publicized harsher policy by the Thai government, which feared being permanently burdened with a large number of Indochinese refugees.

Foreign Affairs.   The diplomatic struggle over Kampuchea grew even more intense in 1982. Vietnam and the Soviet Union and their KPRP clients sought to persuade as many nations as possible that it would be futile to try to reverse the results of Vietnam's invasion. The members of the Association of Southeast Asian Nations (ASEAN) and China supported the resistance coalition. The leaders of the resistance made an effective bid for international support at the 1982 U.N. General Assembly, gaining over 90 votes to retain the Khmer seat at the United Nations. An ASEAN resolution calling for the withdrawal of "foreign troops" gained over a hundred votes.

China's policy toward Kampuchea seemed to undergo some change during 1982. Early in the year, Beijing appeared to have little interest in forming a coalition of the three Khmer resistance groups. In May, the Thai foreign minister failed to gain China's support for a coalition agreement. Yet in June, agreement on a coalition was reached in time for the annual meeting of ASEAN foreign ministers. Later, the Chinese seemed to be moving toward full support for the ASEAN position of seeking a neutral, noncommunist Kampuchea. Beijing proposed a plan to the Soviets in October by which China would begin talks with Vietnam if the latter began to pull its troops out of Kampuchea and announced a timetable for the withdrawal (Hong Kong, AFP, 1 January 1983; *FBIS*, 4 January 1983).

Marlboro, Maryland   William Scharf

Korea

The Korean Communist Party (KCP) was formed in Seoul in 1925, but ceased to function in 1928 because of Japanese suppression. Shortly after World War II, a revived KCP appeared briefly in Seoul, but the communist movement suddenly shifted to the Soviet-occupied northern zone, where the North Korean Central Bureau of the KCP was formed in October 1945 under Soviet auspices. Three major factions of Korean Communists who had been in China, the Soviet Union, and Korea merged and on 23 June 1949 formed the Korean Workers' Party (KWP). The KWP, under longtime leader Kim Il-song, now rules the Democratic People's Republic of Korea (DPRK).

Population. 18.5 million

Party. Korean Workers' Party (Choson Nodong-dang; KWP)

Founded. 1949

Membership. 3 million

General Secretary. Kim Il-song

Presidium. 5 members: Kim Il-song (PDRK president), Kim Il (PDRK vice-president), O Chin-u (minister of the People's Armed Forces), Kim Chong-il (Kim Il-song's son and designated successor), Yi Chong-ok (premier)

Politburo. 19 full members: Kim Il-song, Kim Il, O Chin-u, Kim Chong-il, Yi Chong-ok, Pak Song-chol (DPRK vice-president), Yim Chun-chu, So Chol, O Paek-yong, Kim Chung-nin, Kim Yong-nam, Chon Mun-sop, Kim Hwan, Yon Hyong-muk, O Kuk-yol, Kang Song-san (DPRK first deputy premier), Paek Hak-im, Choe Yong-nim, So yun-sok; 17 alternate members: Ho Tam (DPRK deputy premier, foreign minister), Yun Ki-pok, Choe Kwang (deputy premier), Cho Se-ung, Choe Chae-u (DPRK deputy premier), Kong Chin-tae (DPRK deputy premier), Chong Chun-ki (DPRK deputy premier), Chong Kyong-hui, Yi Kun-mo, Hyon Mu-kwang, Kim Kang-hwan, Ye Son-sil, Kye Ung-tae (DPRK deputy premier), Kang Hi-won, Hong Song-nam, Chon Pyong-ho, Kim Tu-man

Secretariat. 11 members: Kim Il-song, Kim Chong-il, Kim Chung-nin, Kim Yong-nam, Kim Hwan, Yon Hyong-muk, Yun Ki-pok, Hwang Chang-yop (chairman, Supreme People's Assembly), Hyon Mu-kwang, Ho Chong-suk (vice-chairman, Supreme People's Assembly), So Kwang-hui

Central Committee. 145 full and 103 alternate members

Last Congress. Sixth, 10–15 October 1980, in Pyongyang

Auxiliary Organizations. General Federation of Trade Unions of Korea (2 million members), League of Socialist Working Youth of Korea (2.7 million), Union of Agricultural Working People of Korea, Korean Democratic Women's Union, General Federation of the Unions of Literature and Arts of Korea, Korean Committee for Solidarity with the World People, and the united front organization, the United Democratic Fatherland Front.

Publications. *Nodong Sinmun* (Workers' daily), the KWP daily; *Kulloja* (Workers), the KWP monthly journal; *Minchu Choson* (Democratic Korea), the organ of the Supreme People's Assembly and the cabinet; *Choson Inminkun Sinmun* (Korean People's Army news); English-language publications are the *Pyongyang Times, People's Korea,* and *Korea Today,* all weeklies; the Korean Central News Agency (KCNA) is the official news agency.

Leadership and Organization.   The KWP Presidium of the Politburo, the Politburo, and Secretariat decide policy in the DPRK and dominate the Central Committee. The present central government structure consists of three pillars: the Central People's Committee, a policymaking and supervisory body under KWP guidance; the State Administration Council, an organ to execute policies already decided by the Central People's Committee; and the Standing Committee of the Supreme People's Assembly, a symbolic, honorific body that allegedly functions as the legislative branch.

The seventh Supreme People's Assembly, elected on 28 February, had 615 members or 36 more than the sixth assembly elected in 1977. The first session of the seventh Supreme People's Assembly was held in Pyongyang on 5 April. The one-day session unanimously re-elected Kim Il-song as president of the DPRK for a four-year term and elected the officers of the assembly and the ministers of state. (For a list of those elected and details of the session, see *FBIS*, 6 and 7 April.)

The cult of the North Korean dictator and his family members continued unabated in 1982. DPRK mass media constantly stressed that loyalty to Kim Il-song and his ideology of *chuch'e* (self-identity or national identity) should continue from generation to generation, and the program of making his son Kim Chong-il political successor was further implemented. The DPRK regime marked its thirty-fourth anniversary in a ceremony held on 8 September in Pyongyang, accenting the "wise" leadership of President Kim and his successor-designate/son, Chong-il. During 1982, *Nodong Sinmun,* never ceased demanding party members' loyalty to the junior Kim.

On 15 April, the DPRK celebrated the seventieth birthday of Kim Il-song with great fanfare throughout the country. North Korea invited as many as 209 delegations from 118 countries to join the celebration. On 14 April, North Korea dedicated a 60-meter-high triumphal arch constructed at the entrance to Kim Il-song Stadium in the capital of the DPRK in memory of "General Kim Il-song's march of triumph into Pyongyang to liberate the Korean people from Japanese colonial rule in 1945." Also dedicated were a 170-meter-high tower celebrating the *chuch'e* idea, the Grand People's Study Hall, and the First Pyongyang Department Store. A congratualtory message written in the name of the KWP Central Committee, the Central People's Committee, and the State Administration Council called Kim a "great theoretician and outstanding leader of revolution who made imperishable achievements for the Korean and world revolution." The North Korean leader was also decorated with the title "Hero of the DPRK." On 16 April, a public rally was held at Kim Il-song Stadium to deliver to Kim "letters of loyalty" from every corner of North Korea. The letters pledged loyalty to Kim Il-song and Kim Chong-il.

In mid-August, the publishing house of the KWP brought out *Forty Years of Creation and Construction Under Red Sunrays* (5 vols.), on the history of Kim's revolutionary struggles after his return to North Korea in 1945. The authors of these reminiscences included senior party and governmental figures.

All North Koreans were urged to study a treatise on the *chuch'e* ideology recently written by Kim Chong-il. According to *Nodong Sinmun* (1 April), the junior Kim's treatise, sent to the national forum on the *chuch'e* ideology held on 25–31 March to mark Kim Il-song's birthday, was a guideline for the party and state. The treatise has been translated and brought out by the DPRK's Foreign Languages Publishing House for foreign audiences. In late 1982, North Korea launched an international propaganda campaign lauding the "greatness of dear leader Comrade Kim Chong-il" and advertising his treatise on *chuch'e* in foreign newspapers. Earlier in mid-February, the DPRK regime had decorated Kim Chong-il with the title "Hero of the DPRK" on his fortieth birthday. He was also awarded a gold star medal and the National Order, First Degree. A commentary aired by Radio Pyongyang (14 February) called Kim Chong-il, the "beloved leader." The commentary, entitled the "Great Leadership of Beloved Leader Comrade Kim Chong-il Characterized by His Bold Operation and Extraordinary Propulsion," said, "Victory and glory will always go to the people who follow beloved leader Comrade Kim Chong-il." On 28 February, Kim Chong-il was elected to the Supreme People's Assembly. But in the new DPRK government, formed on 5 April, his name was excluded from the new administrative leadership lineup. During 1982, Kim Chong-il made numerous public appearances and also embarked on a series of inspection and guidance tours similar to those undertaken by his father for many years to inspire the people or explain new policy directives.

Chon Chang-chol, 77-year-old secretary of the Standing Committee of the Supreme People's Assembly from December 1972 to April 1982, who ranked fifty-third on the Sixth KWP Central Committee, died on 12 March. Choe Hyon, concurrently a member of the KWP Politburo, vice-chairman of the National Defense Commission, member of both the Central People's Committee and the Military Commission of the KWP, died on 9 April at the age of 75.

Since the Sixth KWP Congress in October 1980, one full member of the Politburo has been demoted to alternate membership, one alternate member of the Politburo has been purged, two party secretaries have been demoted, and three new members have been named to the Secretariat. Demoted to alternate membership on the Politburo was Kye Ung-tae. Newly appointed to the Secretariat were Hyon Mu-kwang, So Kwang-hi, and Ho Chong-suk. Meanwhile, Hong Si-hak and Pak Su-tong were dropped from the Secretariat. Kim Chol-man, who ranked twenty-sixth and won candidate membership on the Politburo at the Sixth KWP Congress, was purged.

Kang Hi-won and Hong Song-nam were named alternative members of the Politburo after the Sixth KWP Congress. They seemed to have filled vacancies created by Kim Chol-man's purge and Choe Hyon's death.

At the sixth plenum of the sixth KWP Central Committee held 29–31 August in Hamhung, the committee elected two full members and two alternate members to the Politburo, thereby increasing the number of Politburo seats to 36. The two new full members were Choe Yong-nim and So Yun-sok. They had been elected candidate members of the Politburo at the Sixth KWP Congress. The two new candidate members of the Politburo were Chon Pyong-ho, who ranked 109th on the roster of the Sixth Central Committee elected at the Sixth KWP Congress, and Kim Tu-nam, whose ranking was 124th. Kang Song-san, one of the thirteen deputy premiers, was appointed first deputy premier by a decree of the Central People's Committee on August 31.

Domestic Attitudes and Activities.   The DPRK government's budget for fiscal 1982, adopted at the session of the Supreme People's Assembly on 5 April, totaled 22,546 million *won* (U.S. $11.1 billion). This represented a 9 percent increase in revenues and a 10.9 percent rise in spending over fiscal 1981. Of the expenditures, 61.6 percent ($6.8 billion) was allocated to the economic sector, 20.8 percent ($2.3 billion) to social welfare, and 14.5 percent ($1.6 billion) to the military. The actual defense expenditure is no doubt higher because Pyongyang hides defense expenditures in other sectors.

A joint session of the KWP Central Committee and the Supreme People's Assembly convened on 14 April to hear President Kim Il-song speak on policy. The meeting, the first of its kind in North Korea's political history, came nine days after the one-day session of the Supreme People's Assembly and one day before Kim's birthday, which was declared a "most festive national holiday and a grand political festival." Kim's speech mentioned governmental affairs, economic matters, the unification question, and diplomacy, but he failed to present any new policy and simply confirmed the party line he had set at the Sixth KWP Congress.

During 1982, the North Korean people were exhorted to complete this year's portion of the current Seven-Year Economic Plan (1978–1984) ahead of schedule. During the latter half of 1982, the DPRK regime launched a "speed in the 1980s" campaign to implement President Kim Il-song's 5 June call for completing the ten-point economic target plan during this decade. (The ten economic goals for completion in the 1980s are to reclaim 300,000 *jongbo* (735,000 acres) of land and to produce 100 billion kwh of electricity, 120 million tons of coal, 15 million tons of steel, 1.5 million tons of nonferrous metals, 20 millions tons of cement, 7 million tons of chemical fertilizer, 1.5 billion meters of cloth, 5 million tons of marine products, and 15 million tons of grain.)

Workers at major workshops and factories throughout North Korea held rallies on 22–23 November to pledge their utmost efforts to realize the current Seven-Year Economic Plan presented by the KWP. These rallies further supported the resolution of the "Chollima pioneers," who on 12 November in Pyongyang promised to promote the production campaign in every sector of the economy.

North Korea was once again unable to pay the interest on the U.S. $840 million it owed to Western countries (*FEER,* 3 December). North Korea has been insolvent since May, and the president of the DPRK's Trade Bank visited London in July to ask creditors not to impose sanctions against his country.

South Korea. North Korea's relations with South Korea remained hostile. North Korea stepped up its harsh propaganda attacks on the Seoul government under President Chun Doo-hwan, calling him the head of a "mangy fascist clique." On 26 January, the DPRK rejected South Korea's renewed proposals for a summit meeting to deal with unification and its formula calling for a reunified state based on a unified constitution. On 17 August, the DPRK rejected the South's 15 August call for a Seoul-Pyongyang summit meeting.

International Views and Positions. During 1982, Pyongyang mounted an intensive diplomatic offensive against South Korea to undermine the international position of the Seoul regime and to develop world support for its own unification policy. Parliamentary, trade, and goodwill missions were dispatched abroad or invited to North Korea. Numerous friendly diplomatic gestures were made, especially to Third World countries, which increasingly dominate the United Nations. In particular, the DPRK sought to prevent recognition of the "two Koreas" concept by the world community; to isolate South Korea from the Third World, the communist bloc, and even the Western world; and to drum up diplomatic support for its demand to remove U.S. forces from South Korea. During 1982, the DPRK established diplomatic ties with Naura (25 February), Malawi (25 June), and Suriname (11 October). These actions brought to 105 the number of countries with which North Korea had diplomatic ties.

During 1982, the following heads of Third World countries visited North Korea: Prince Norodom Sihanouk, former Cambodian head of state and currently the head of the Anti-Vietnamese Kampuchean United Front (March, June, July, and November); President Aristides Pereiera of Cape Verde (May); Maltese Premier Dom Mintoff (June); President Manuel Pinto da Costa of São Tomé and Principe (October); Pakistani President Mohammad Zia ul Haq (October); Col. Moammar Khadafy of Libya (October); and André Kolingba, chairman of the Military Committee for National Redressing and head of state of the Central African Republic (November).

The DPRK dispatched a number of party and government leaders (Vice-President Pak Song-chol, Premier Yi Chong-ok, Foreign Minister Ho Tam, and Hwang Chang-yop, chairman of the Standing Committee of the Supreme People's Assembly) to the following Third World countries during 1982 in an effort to strengthen ties with nonaligned countries: Algeria, Cuba, Grenada, Guyana, Iran, Malaysia, Mozambique, Nicaragua, Thailand, Upper Volta, Zambia, and Zimbabwe.

Kim Chong-il visited Malta in early December to learn English, the pro-government newspaper *L'Orizzont* in Valletta reported on 2 December. The newspaper, quoting informed sources, said that the junior Kim came to Malta at the invitation of Prime Minister Dom Mintoff.

On 11 June, North Korea harshly castigated President Mobutu Sese Seko of Zaire, who made a four-day visit to South Korea in June, calling him an "errand boy of the United States."

On 8 June, the DPRK issued a statement condemning the Israeli invasion of Lebanon and expressing its support of the Palestine Liberation Organization. North Korea promised to dispatch troops to Lebanon, if requested, to aid the Palestinian and Arab people fighting the invading Israelis, a Pyongyang government statement said on 29 June.

North Korea provided almost 40 percent of the estimated U.S. $2 billion in arms Iran acquired from foreign countries during 1982 (*NYT*, 19 December). In addition, Pyongyang sent 300 military instructors to Iran.

In midsummer, the DPRK donated U.S. $10,000 to Kampuchean refugees in Thailand through Prince Norodom Sihanouk.

North Korea and Libya signed a friendship and cooperation pact on 2 November at the end of the Libyan head of state's five-day visit to Pyongyang, which began on 29 October. The twelve-article pact, signed by President Kim and Colonel Khadafy, commits Pyongyang and Tripoli to military cooperation in case of war by providing military materiel and experts. The pact is for ten years and will be extended for five years automatically if both parties agree. North Korea and Libya also signed an agreement on economic, scientific, technical, and cultural cooperation.

On 10 December, the DPRK Central News Agency issued a protest to Panama for expelling a four-man North Korean parliamentary mission from Panama City on 4 December. The Panamanian government gave no reasons for its action.

The Soviet Union and China.   During 1982, Pyongyang continued to maintain its middle-of-the-road position in the Sino-Soviet rift, although it moved slightly closer to China. Moscow and Beijing competed with verbal assurances and material support for North Korea's friendship. Both countries urged the prompt withdrawal of U.S. troops from South Korea and supported Pyongyang's demand for direct U.S.-DPRK contacts to settle the Korean problem and the DPRK's proposal for reunification.

A number of Soviet publications in 1982 reported the Kremlin's previous economic aid to North Korea, giving surprisingly detailed evidence of DPRK dependency on foreign economic aid (see Ron Richardson, "Big Brother Barks," *FEER,* 3 December, pp. 96–98). These reports clearly contradict Pyongyang's assertion that its economic progress since the mid-1960s has come largely from its own efforts. This revelation came as the DPRK appeared to be moving away from Moscow and tilting closer toward Beijing.

Hwang Chang-yop, chairman of the Standing Committee of the Supreme People's Assembly, visited Moscow in mid-August and met with the chairman of the Supreme Soviet. North Korea declared 15 November, the day of Leonid Brezhnev's funeral, a day of national mourning. Pyongyang sent Vice-President Pak Song-chol to Moscow for Brezhnev's funeral. President Kim il-song sent a congratulatory message to Yuri Andropov upon his election to the office of general secretary of the Communist Party of the Soviet Union.

A party-government delegation led by Premier Yi Chong-ok, left Pyongyang for Moscow on 19 December to attend a ceremony marking the sixtieth anniversary of the founding of the Soviet Union. While in Moscow, the delegation held talks with Soviet leaders about the Korean peninsula, Soviet economic aid to North Korea, and other matters of mutual concern.

There were, however, indications of closer ties with Beijing. For example, a banquet hosted on 9 July by the acting Chinese ambassador to Pyongyang was attended by such top North Korean leaders as People's Armed Forces Minister O Chin-u and Foreign Affairs Minister Ho Tam, while that hosted on 5 July by the Soviet ambassador to North Korea was attended by such lesser dignitaries as Chairman Kong Chin-tae of the Trade Commission and Deputy Foreign Affairs Minister Kil Chae-kyong.

Another sign of Pyongyang's closer relations with Beijing came in June when Chinese Defense Minister Geng Biao and a Chinese military mission made a nine-day visit to North Korea to promote military cooperation between the two countries. The Chinese and North Korean military delegations met just hours after the Chinese arrived in Pyongyang on 14 June. The DPRK regime did not disclose what was discussed at the meeting, simply saying that the two sides were in accord on all issues. O Chin-u, People's Armed Forces minister, said on 21 June that North Korea was the front line of China. His remarks came at a banquet hosted by the visiting Chinese defense minister for North Korean military and party leaders. Geng Biao also spoke of closer Beijing-Pyongyang military cooperation.

North Korean watchers in Seoul speculated that Pyongyang was likely to receive fighters, missiles, and warships from China. China supplied North Korea with 40 Chinese-made MiG-21 jet fighters in early 1982. The transfer of the jets was confirmed by U.S. spy satellites. (*Asahi Shimbun,* 12 October.)

For the first time since 1976, Kim Il-song made a visit to Beijing (16–25 September). The DPRK leader was accompanied by People's Armed Forces Minister O Chin-u, Foreign Affairs Minister Ho Tam, and other key government officials. In a banquet hosted by the Chinese party and government, Chinese Communist Party General Secretary Hu Yaobang further confirmed China's close ties with Pyongyang by disclosing that he, with Deng Xiaoping (the top Chinese leader), had visited North Korea in April. Their secret visit to Pyongyang had been to congratulate Kim on his birthday. While in China, Kim Il-song met with Deng Xiaoping, Hu Yaobang, and Premier Zhao Ziyang. The DPRK Central Broadcasting Station reported these meetings but did not disclose what was discussed.

North Korean watchers in Seoul speculated that Kim wants Beijing's recognition of Pyongyang's hereditary political succession, needs China's continued military assistance, and seeks to establish a common diplomatic strategy.

No joint communiqué was issued at the end of Kim Il-song's visit to China. Also, no Chinese leader overtly praised the leadership of Kim Chong-il, although Chinese Defense Minister Geng Biao mentioned the junior Kim's leading role when he visited North Korea in June.

On 28 October, China and North Korea concluded a long-term trade agreement and on 11 November renewed an agreement on "science cooperation projects."

The DPRK Central People's Committee decorated some forty Chinese civil engineers in a ceremony held in Pyongyang on 29 November (Radio Beijing, 30 November). The Chinese engineers were taking part in North Korean construction work of an undisclosed nature.

Europe. On 17 April, Romanian President Nicolae Ceauşescu flew into Pyongyang on an official visit to North Korea. A mission of the French Communist Party led by Secretary General Georges Marchais made a four-day visit to North Korea in late October and held three rounds of talks with a delegation of the KWP headed by Kim Il-song. A statement issued by the French communist leader at the end of his Pyongyang visit on 28 October made clear that there were differences between the French Communist Party and the KWP over some issues.

At the invitation of the DPRK regime, François de Grossourve made a nine-day visit to Pyongyang starting on 22 November as a special envoy of President François Mitterrand. In his meeting with President Kim Il-song on 27 November, the French envoy delivered President Mitterrand's personal message to Kim (DPRK Central Broadcasting Station, 28 November). In the message, President Mitterrand confirmed the promise he had made to President Kim when he visited Pyongyang in February 1981 as leader of the French Socialist Party. Pyongyang did not mention the contents of the promise.

Japan. Relations between the DPRK and Japan have never been cordial. In Pyongyang's views, Japan is excessively partial to Seoul, pursues a policy of "two Koreas," and is hostile toward North Korea, as exemplified by the Japanese government's strong opposition to a drastic reduction of U.S. ground forces in South Korea. North Korean media continued to denounce growing Japanese "imperialism" in South Korea and the alleged collusion between Tokyo and Washington to preserve their mutual "colonial interest" in the Korean peninsula.

The Japanese government has never had political or diplomatic ties with the DPRK regime, limiting itself to cultural, athletic, and economic exchanges. Due to combined pressures from Japan's business and trade interests and left-wing political and labor groups, nongovernmental contacts are expected to continue to increase during the early 1980s, although official exchanges between Pyongyang and Tokyo do not appear likely.

Trade officials of Japan and China agreed to use the port of Chongjin on the east coast of North Korea as the harbor for bilateral trade between Japan and two northeastern provinces of China (*Dong-A Ilbo*, 22 October). Under the plan, commodities produced in Jilin and Heilongjiang provinces will be sent to Chongjin by train for subsequent reshipment to Japan. Japanese trade and maritime industry sources said that the DPRK had approved the proposal, first made by the Chinese.

Tokyo rejected the proposed visit to Japan in February of a North Korean mission led by Hyon Chun-kuk, deputy chief of the DPRK Committee for Cultural Relations with Foreign Countries and a member of the KWP Central Committee, because the North Korean group might engage in political activities during their tour. Pyongyang countered by refusing to permit a Japanese mission's visit to North Korea in May and by seizing several Japanese fishing boats for violating the 50-mile North Korean Military Security Zone in the Sea of Japan. In response, the Japanese foreign minister said on 26 June that Tokyo would admit Pyongyang's mission if it contained no politicians.

In summer of 1982, the DPRK government severely denounced the revision of textbooks to show a more favorable view of Japan's behavior in World War II. On 30 November, the DPRK Central Broadcasting Station called Prime Minister Yasuhiro Nakasone "a ringleader" of Japanese military expansionism and a proponent of revision of the no-war constitution.

The United States. During 1982, the DPRK increased its hostility toward the United States. Pyongyang condemned the United States for supporting Chun Doo-hwan's "fascist" regime in Seoul and repeatedly urged Washington to withdraw all U.S. troops and lethal weapons from South Korea.

On 20 May, North Korea called the United States "an archenemy of the Korean people" and launched a campaign denouncing the centennial anniversary of the establishment of relations between Korea and the United States.

In late October, Washington strongly denied a *Far Eastern Economic Review* report of 22 October that Washington and Pyongyang had had direct trade links since 1979.

The United States served notice on 9 December that it might shut down the DPRK observer mission to the United Nations in New York City unless North Korea surrendered for trial a diplomat charged with the attempted rape of an American woman.

United Nations. As in the preceding years, the Korean question was absent from the agenda of the annual session of the U.N. General Assembly.

Biography. *Kim Il-song.* Kim has been the leader of North Korea since its independence in 1948. He is today the undisputed supreme leader of his country.

Kim Il-song (his name at birth was Kim Song-chu) was born on 15 April 1912 in Mankyungdae, a village near Pyongyang. After his family emigrated to southern Manchuria in 1919, he gradually began to participate in anti-Japanese nationalist activities there. In the early 1930s, he became the leader of a tiny band of Korean partisans within a Chinese communist guerrilla army in Manchuria. Failing to cope with the Japanese army's deadly siege tactics, he and his surviving Korean guerrilla colleagues escaped in 1940 to the Soviet far eastern provinces, where they stayed until 1945.

Kim Il-song returned to North Korea shortly after the country was occupied by the Soviet army in August 1945. With the backing of the Soviet occupation authorities, he began to establish a communist state in the northern half of the Korean peninsula. He gradually consolidated his one-man rule by eliminating rival factions, and today his Manchurian guerrilla faction dominates the DPRK power structure. As state president, party chief, and commander in chief of the armed forces, Kim Il-song holds all of the strings of power.

Since the mid-1950s, Kim Il-song has pursued an increasingly nationalistic, independent, and self-reliant policy by successfully playing off the Soviet Union against China. In the process, he has managed to shake off his old image as a puppet of either China or the Soviet Union.

Kim Il-song's first wife, Kim Chong-suk, whom he met in 1936 in a Manchurian guerrilla camp, died of tuberculosis in 1949 at the age of 31. She bore him two sons (one of them is Kim Chong-il) and a daughter. In 1950, Kim married his present wife, Kim Song-ae. He has five children (two sons and three daughters) by his second marriage.

Washington College   Tai Sung An

Laos

Communist activity in Laos has always been closely linked to the communist movement in Vietnam. After many years of fighting with other political forces and occasional periods of participation in the government, the Communists assumed full control of the country in 1975, establishing the Lao People's Democratic Republic (LPDR).

Population. 3.8 million (estimated)

Party. Lao People's Revolutionary Party (Phak Pasason Lao; LPRP)

Founded.   1945

Membership.   35,000

General Secretary.   Kaysone Phomvihan (LPDR premier)

Political Bureau.   7 members: Kaysone Phomvihan, Nouhak Phoumsavan, Souphanouvong (LPDR president), Phoumi Vongvichit, Khamtai Siphandon, Phoun Sipsaseut, Sisomphon Lovansai

Secretariat.   9 members: Kaysone Phomvihan, Nouhak Phoumsavan, Khamtai Siphandon, Phoun Sipaseut, Sisomphon Lovansai, Sali Vongkhamsao, Sisavat Keobounphan, Samon Vi-gnaket, Maichantan Sengmani

Central Committee.   49 full members, 6 alternate members (for names, see *FBIS*, 30 April)

Last Congress.   Third, 27–30 April, in Vientiane

Auxiliary Organizations.   Lao Front for National Construction (relatively inactive in 1982)

Publications.   *Siang Pasason* (Voice of the people), LPRP central organ, published in Vientiane; Pathet Lao News Agency (Khaoson Pathet Lao; KPL)

Leadership and Organization.   The LPRP held its Third Congress from 27 to 30 April in Vientiane. Previous party congresses were held in 1955 and 1972. The congress elected a Central Committee of 49 full and six alternate members, a considerable enlargement from the previous 22 full members and six alternates. The first plenary meeting of the new Central Committee elected a seven-member Political Bureau identical with the previous one. The Secretariat, however, was enlarged from four to nine members.

According to information given out at the congress, the average age of the new Central Committee was 55, with the youngest being 38 and the oldest 74. There were four female members. Ethnic composition of the new committee was 79 percent lowland Lao, a noticeable increase over the previous one and a result of heavy recruiting of new party members in the provinces along the Mekong Valley after the takeover in 1975; 15 percent Lao Theung; and 6 percent Lao Soung (mainly Hmong, Yao, and Man). Of the 55 members, 15 had been members of the Indochinese Communist Party. (Radio Vientiane, 30 April; *FBIS*, 4 May.)

Prior to the convening of the party congress in the capital, provincial party congresses were held in the sixteen provinces. These congresses, usually attended by at least one Political Bureau member, served as occasions to evoke achievements in various fields and the Chinese threat or the bonds of solidarity linking this or that province with its neighboring province in Vietnam or Kampuchea, as the geographical situation warranted.

Domestic Attitudes and Activities.   In his report to the LPRP congress, Kaysone Phomvihan claimed that national revenue per capita had increased by 40 percent in the past six years. In this time period, he said, agricultural and forestry output had increased 1.5 times, while rice production had risen from 700,000 tons in 1976 to 1,145,000 tons in 1981. Numbers of cattle increased from 900,000 to 1,300,000. Over the past six years, acreage under cultivation increased by 33.5 percent and the area of irrigated rice fields doubled, he said. The number of machines used in agricultural work increased fivefold. Since 1980, he claimed, Laos had basically solved the problem of food shortages. (Radio Vientiane, 27 April; *FBIS*, 5 May.)

Four provinces had basically completed the setting up of agricultural cooperatives in rice-growing areas, Kaysone said. The state managed 188 state-owned industrial factories, having a total of 15,000 workers. Throughout the country there were a total of 180 state-owned shops, 346 cooperative stores, and 150 service bases. Nevertheless, he added, enormous difficulties remained in the economic area. (Ibid.)

Over the past six years, Kaysone said, the number of leading party cadres from the district level upwards had increased threefold, that of professional and technical cadres fivefold, and the number of party members overall by 50 percent. Laos still depends in many areas of special expertise on technicians from Vietnam, the Soviet Union, and other countries. It was also clear from Kaysone's remarks that the activities of various antigovernment groups, which have been reported to be active in both northern and southern Laos, have been a serious impediment to economic reconstruction and progress.

By the terms of a decree from the president's office on 16 July, the name of the Laotian army was officially changed from Lao People's Liberation Army to Lao People's Army.

International Views and Policies. The LPDR continued to follow Hanoi's line in international affairs. At the conference of Indochinese foreign ministers held in Vientiane in February, for instance, the Lao foreign minister echoed Vietnam's views on the Kampuchean problem and supported Vietnamese proposals for talks with China on Sino-Vietnamese differences (VNA, Hanoi, 17 February; *FBIS*, 18 February). In its direct relations with China, however, the LPDR respected the formalities, exchanging messages with Chinese leaders and seeming to wish to avoid a rupture of diplomatic relations (Radio Vientiane, 2 October; *FBIS*, 4 October). Tensions along borders with China and Thailand, whether real or imagined, continued at a high pitch during the year.

The "special relationship" Laos shares with Vietnam, however, continued to be the dominant factor in Laos's international relations. On 18 July, the fifth anniversary of the signing of the Treaty of Friendship and Cooperation gave rise to an outpouring of expressions of praise and gratitude for Vietnam. It was reported that the two countries had "fulfilled the task of demarcating the border line between the two countries." (Radio Vientiane, 18 July; *FBIS*, 20 July.)

On numerous other occasions, LPDR leaders referred to the past history of Vietnam's intervention in Laos, which gave rise to the legal enshrining of the "special relationship." Kaysone Phomvihan, for instance, in his speech to the Savannakhet provincial party committee conference in March, declared that the people of this area of Laos had had the "honor to score achievements contributing to the defense and building of the historic trail—the trail under the name of great Comrade Ho Chi Minh, the trail which led our three Indochinese nations to march forward to the achievement of complete victory over the U.S. imperialist aggressors." He went on to urge his listeners to "pay attention to further enhancing and strengthening the combat coordination between the Lao armed forces and the Vietnamese volunteer forces." (Radio Vientiane, 19 March; *FBIS*, 12 April.) Billeting on its soil the thousands of Vietnamese troops still in the country is one of the prices Laos must pay as the smaller of the two in their "special relationship."

A rare glimpse of the actual mechanism by which Hanoi exercises complete control over what happens in the LPDR was given by a former bureau director of the LPDR Ministry of Health, Khamsengkeo Sengsthith, who defected to China in 1981. In an interview, he said that all decisions are taken by a special body of 140 Vietnamese cadres called the Working Committee for the West, or CP-38. This committee, he said, is headed by Nguyen Xuan (not the Vietnamese ambassador in Vientiane of the same name) (*FEER*, 26 March). A report of a similar decision-making group of Vietnamese cadres in Kampuchea, called the "B-68 unit," was recently brought to Bangkok by two defectors (*NYT*, 9 October).

International Activities and Contacts. Kaysone, as in previous years, was a frequent visitor to Moscow during the year. He made a "friendly visit" in March, during which he conferred the LPDR's highest decoration, the Gold Order of the State, on Leonid Brezhnev (Radio Vientiane, 21 March; *FBIS*, 22 March). In August and September, Kaysone made a further, more prolonged, visit to Moscow, possibly because of poor health; he again had a meeting with Brezhnev (Radio Vientiane, 1 October; *FBIS*, 1 October). (Kaysone observed his sixty-second birthday on 12 December.) Kaysone also led the LPRP delegation to the Fifth Congress of the Vietnam Communist Party in March (Radio Vientiane, 1 April; *FBIS*, 1 April). For Brezhnev's funeral in November, however, Souphanouvong led the Lao delegation (Radio Vientiane, 19 November; *FBIS*, 19 November). Souphanouvong had been on a visit to Cuba only a few days previously (VNA, Hanoi, 9 November; *FBIS*, 9 November).

Bethesda, Maryland   Arthur J. Dommen

Malaysia

Malaysian security forces, often in cooperation with the Thai military, have continued their efforts to eradicate all remnants of the Communist Party of Malaya (CPM) and a small, radical breakaway faction that calls itself the Communist Party of Malaya, Marxist-Leninist (CPM-ML). In 1982 government forces killed a small number of communist guerrillas (estimates vary), and there were no major incidents of violence or civic disruption caused by communist insurgents.

Domestic Developments.   The familiar pattern of government announcements describing progress in its anticommunist struggle, combined with warnings of new CPM threats and tactics, continued throughout 1982. In late October 1981, the Malaysian deputy inspector general of police, Tan Sri Mohamad Amin Osman, announced that 63 communist "terrorists" had been "eliminated" in 1981 and that there were now "only about 230 terrorists" still operating in the "jungles of Pahang, Perak and Kelantan" (*FBIS*, 30 October 1981). This appears to have been an overestimate because in late March 1982, Osman's superior, the inspector general of police, Tan Sri Haniff Omar, declared that in all of south Thailand, peninsular Malaysia, and Sarawak during 1981 a total of only 57 communist terrorists had been killed compared with 51 in 1980 (Bernama, Kuala Lumpur, 25 March; *Sarawak Tribune*, 26 March). In mid-January, Malaysian army sources disclosed that since August of the previous year 20 communist terrorists had been killed and six others wounded by security forces in border operations along Bukit Merapit in Perak alone *(FBIS,* 19 January). Toward the close of 1981, three new anti-insurgent operations were announced by the Malaysian army in the Thai-Malaysian border area and along the east-west highway. Military sources claim that the highway continues to be a major CPM target because the area where the highway was constructed previously had been used by the CPM to penetrate into Kelantan and Perak.

At the same time, Malaysian police warned that the CPM was launching a new propaganda campaign to win supporters among Malays (ibid., 2 December 1981). The Malaysian government's Criminal Investigation Department accused the CPM of attempting to infiltrate various legal and "open" organizations like trade unions and political parties. Datuk Abdul Aziz Bin Ahmad, managing director of the prominent Malay-language biweekly paper *Watan*, was arrested on 17 October 1981 under the Internal Security Act (ISA) for publishing "Communist propaganda articles" in several issues of his paper (ibid., 20 and 22 October 1981). In mid-December 1981, the Home Affairs Ministry announced that "poison pen letters" designed to play on "government weaknesses in a subtle way" had been discovered in the Malacca area. The letters presumably were written by unnamed "Communist elements and racial and religious extremists." (Bernama, Malacca, 19 December 1981.)

Despite claims of government vigilance and internal fissures in the CPM, the Malaysian communist movement's insurgency persisted. In early December 1981, military spokesmen claimed to know the names of all 160 members of a faction of the CPM active along the Malaysian-Thai border. These insurgents, "armed with automatic weapons," had been operating both in Sadao on the Thai side and in Padang Besar on the Malaysian side and since 1972 had been extorting donations from villagers in these areas. *(Straits Times,* 4 December 1981.) In early January, communist terrorists belonging to the CPM-ML were reported by Malaysian military spokesmen to be "stepping up" their attacks along the frontier area, in an effort to "cripple the economy of the border towns" and to deter tourists from visiting the border region. In Kota Baru quantities of weapons and ammunition were seized. (Ibid., 5 January.) In early February, the government reported that twenty communist guerrillas had been killed in military operations along the Bukit Berapit from August through December of the previous year (*Sarawak Tribune*, 2 February).

The Perak state secretary reported that the bodies of sixteen communist terrorists had been discovered near Kampung Katib in Betong, and police authorities in Pahang state declared that the communist threat in Pahang had been "curbed," although they admitted that at one point in the 1970s, there had been up to 200 communist insurgents in the state (*FBIS*, 5 January). By March, the prime minister of Perak state was warning the population "to be on guard" against the Communists' threats that they would persist in attempts to seize the government. The minister emphasized that the struggle against the Communists had to be waged not only by the security forces but also by people "loyal to the country." The Communists would not be able to operate at all, according to the minister, if people did not cooperate with them by giving them food. (*Sarawak Tribune*, 11 March.)

Early in April, there were new warnings about an ongoing communist recruitment campaign. Datuk Rais Yatim, the chief minister of the state of Negri Sembilan, declared that there appeared to be a communist attempt to win recruits among villagers in the border areas of the states of Selanggor and Negri Sembilan. Village heads were warned to contact security authorities immediately in the event any insurgents appeared in their areas. (Bernama, Jelebu, 3 April.) In the state of Pahang, the Malaysian deputy defense minister, Abang Abu Bakar Mustaffa, announced that some rubber tappers in the Mengkarak region of that state had been establishing ties with the communist guerrillas. A CPM ammunition dump had been discovered in Mengkarak, he said, along with communist propaganda materials and women's garments, suggesting that some of the local insurgents were female. A rubber tapper had been arrested after a guerrilla ambush of security forces, and other rubber tappers were suspected of having given warnings of the approach of government forces to the insurgents. (*Straits Times*, 18 March.)

Intermittent clashes with communist guerrillas continued during the year. In May, the military commander of peninsular Malaysia, Gen. Datuk Hashim Mohamed, said that at least six communist terrorists may have been killed between the end of 1981 and the close of February 1982. In mid-June, Thai security forces in Yala reported killing three CPM guerrillas in an ambush near the Malaysian frontier. These deaths brought to seven the number of insurgents killed in the area during the preceding week alone. The insurgents had been ambushed by the Thai military as the guerrillas were returning from a food-collecting mission in the interior of Yala province. Thai forces earlier had been mobilized for anti-insurgent action after some CPM units had attacked two rubber estates in Yala. (Ibid., 21 June.)

Meanwhile, in Sarawak, North Kalimantan Communist Party (NKCP) activity declined during the year. The NKCP continues to suffer defections because of the government's amnesty program, and no clashes with NKCP units were reported. Nevertheless, the Sarawak director of internal security, Datuk Mahmud Nasir, warned the public that communist insurgents were a threat to the state's security, despite their greatly reduced numbers. He estimated that some 120 NKCP "remnants" still were "lurking in the jungle" of the Rajang Security Command (Rascom) and in the state's First Division. He said, however, that there was no evidence of any new recruitment into the insurgent organization. It remained difficult for security forces to wipe out the last of the guerrillas, Nasir added, because of the vast jungle in which they were clustered. In March, Rascom's chief executive officer, William Tang, said that in his area, which covers portions of Sarawak's Third, Sixth, and Seventh Divisions, the number of insurgents had been reduced from 500 in 1972 to "fewer than 90" at present. The reduction of the insurgents had been made possible, according to Tang, because of the systematic elimination of the guerrillas' food and ammunition dumps and hideouts. But, he added, the task had now become more difficult because the NKCP had broken up into small units in order to "wage terrorism against the people." Six land development projects had been opened in the Rascom area to "resettle families harassed by Communist terrorists." (*Sarawak Tribune*, 9 September 1981, 28 March.)

Public criticism still continued over the government's policy toward suspected subversives. The ISA and related legislation have permitted the jailing of people, without trial, on suspicion of subversive activity. It is not known how many are held under the ISA or the condition of their imprisonment. In November 1981, the Malaysian government announced that since the ISA began in 1969, a total of 3,101 persons had been detained and 2,613 released, leaving 488 still incarcerated (U.S. Department of State, *Country Reports on Human Rights Practices for 1981*, February, p. 642). In November 1981, Malaysian Deputy Premier Datuk Musa Hitam announced, however, that 513 persons were being held under the ISA.

He added that the Malaysian government would continue to use the provisions of the ISA against anyone or any group that threatened the nation's security. (*FBIS*, 4 November 1981.)

In May, Hitam defended his government by saying that Malaysia "does not have any political prisoners" (*Malaysian Digest*, 30 June, p. 2). "Only persons who are committed to the violent overthrow of the government" were being detained. "We do not detain people who oppose us politically." Musa said that "certain international organizations" were "deliberately attempting" to put Malaysia in a bad light because of the detainees issue. He reiterated an offer first made by the Malaysian government in February 1982 that those being detained without trial "for security reasons" were qualified for "adoption" by any foreign person, organization, or country; the consent of the detainee had to be obtained, however, before he could be taken out of the country (*FBIS*, 4 June). In August, Malaysian Premier Datuk Mahathir Mohamed declared that the ISA continued to remain essential for the security of the nation. He added that the government saw no reason for modifying the security act. (Ibid., 5 August.)

When a visiting team of seven lawyers, representing such organizations as the International Federation of Civil Rights in Paris and the Civil Liberties Union of Japan, made "representations" to Malaysian officials regarding the ISA, a commentary over the government-owned Radio Kuala Lumpur declared that the Malaysian government had no intention of being "apologetic" to the lawyers. The lawyers had been told that in the last 30 years, 2,045 policemen and soldiers and 2,543 civilians had been killed because of terrorist actions and that hundreds of others had been maimed or injured. The government was aware that the ISA was "harsh"—"it is deliberately intended to be so." (Ibid., 10 August.) Foreign observers who have interviewed present or former ISA detainees have described the cramped and unhealthy conditions in which the detainees were kept (*Frankfurter Allgemeine Zeitung*, 20 July). According to Premier Mahathir Mohamed, the Malaysian government cannot afford to relax the provisions of the ISA, "as chances are, those who are guilty would get away" (*Malaysian Digest*, 31 August, p. 1).

The Malaysian government has been prepared to use leniency in suppressing subversion. Freedom continues to be granted to detainees. Although unauthorized possession of firearms carries a mandatory death sentence under the ISA, on 27 July the Malaysian High Court granted an indefinite stay of execution to four ethnic Chinese Malaysians convicted of owning weapons illegally (*Asiaweek*, 6 August, p. 15). However, the Malaysian Federal Court has ruled that the death penalty is constitutional, and in 1978 the right of criminal appeals to the Privy Council in London was nullified by Malaysian legislation. In October, a prominent Malaysian criminal lawyer and opposition member of parliament estimated that since 1980, 31 persons had been executed under the ISA (*Asia Record*, November, p. 16). A total of 50 other persons condemned for violation of the Narcotics Act section of the ISA are said to be awaiting execution (*Amnesty International Report*, 1982, p. 220).

Meanwhile, the Interior Affairs Ministry of Thailand reportedly has agreed in principle to grant Thai citizenship to CPM members as an incentive for Communists to surrender to the authorities. The proposal was said to be part of a "political offensive" being considered by the Thai government against CPM insurgents operating from Thai bases. (*FBIS*, 8 September.) There has been no official Malaysian reaction to the proposal, but privately Malaysian security officials have expressed reservations to this author.

The Thai citizenship proposal underscores the sensitive nature of Thai-Malaysian collaboration in combating CPM operations. In May, after a meeting of the Thai-Malaysian border committee established to facilitate joint operations against communist guerrillas, a Thai spokesman admitted that "there are times when the two countries' priorities" in the anticommunist drive "don't always go hand in hand." Malaysia is concerned more with the CPM, and the Thais are preoccupied with extremist Muslim secessionists operating in the border area. (Ibid., 25 May.) At a 26 August meeting between Malaysia Deputy Premier Musa Hitam and Thai Interior Minister Sitthi Jirarote in Kuala Lumpur to analyze the persistent border guerrilla problem, Musa reportedly questioned whether the Thai–Malaysian border committee meetings "had been truly successful or otherwise." Musa seemed to be challenging the Thai government to improve its performance. (*Asiaweek*, 17 September, p. 18.) Musa's blunt statement underscored the skepticism among Malaysian observers that the Thais are less interested in destroying the CPM than Kuala Lumpur is because the CPM in southern Thailand is seen to serve as a useful counterweight to the Muslim extremist and secessionist elements. Earlier, a Malaysian military spokesman had declared that his government was "ready to cooperate with Thailand" in suppressing Muslim extremist and Muslim separatist insurgents (*FBIS*, 4 August).

Meanwhile, Thai military spokesmen have voiced their own frustration over anti-CPM operations. The commander of one Thai special counterinsurgency task force in Betong declared that it was the CPM that had been "causing misunderstandings between Thai and Malaysian soldiers" by firing on Malaysian troops from Thai territory, leading the Malaysians to think they were under attack from the Thais. The intermittent clashes between Muslim extremists, some of whom are said to have adopted "a socialist ideology," and CPM elements in Thailand's Yala province, have endangered the lives of the people living there. In the Than To district of Yala, according to one Thai official, "We never know when it will be our turn" and "we can't trust any checkpoints even if they are set up by government authorities" (ibid., 7 and 13). Combined Thai-Malaysian military action has continued, however, and in early April, a joint Thai-Malaysian helicopter gunship attack, combined with assaults by ground forces, took place. The operation destroyed a CPM camp in the Betong area, which reportedly housed "several hundred guerrillas." (*Straits Times*, 10 April.) A Thai-Malaysian joint land boundary committee conference in early September officially demarcated about 335.6 kilometers of the frequently disputed frontier between the two countries—about 60 percent of the entire border line (*FBIS*, 13 September).

Despite the CPM's tactic of "protracted insurgency," it has not affected Malaysia's political establishment. Following the warnings by Home Affairs Ministry spokesmen to refrain from aiding the Communists and not to raise "sensitive issues" (*Sarawak Tribune*, 5 and 7 April), the 22 April general and state assembly elections in Malaysia produced an overwhelming victory for the ruling Barisan Nasional (National Front; BN) coalition of parties. The BN won 132 of the 154 parliamentary seats (compared with 130 in the 1978 elections) and retained control of all eleven state assemblies in peninsular Malaysia. Those in the Borneo states of Sarawak and Sabah also remain under BN control. In most cases the BN won increased majorities in the state assemblies, and the main left-wing opposition party, the Democratic Action Party, lost nine of its sixteen national parliamentary seats. (*Malaysian Digest*, 15 May, p. 1; *Asia Research Bulletin*, 30 June, p. 936.) The incumbent Malaysian premier, Datuk Mahathir Mohamed, heads a somewhat revamped cabinet, which is likely to remain in office for the next five years.

Party Tactics and Programs. In June, attempts made during the preceding months by CPM leaders to close ranks with the rival and growing CPM-ML failed, and according to Thai intelligence, bloody clashes erupted between them in and around the Betong salient of Thailand's southern Yala province, which juts out into the Malaysian state of Perak. As the CPM-ML, claiming to be more genuinely "revolutionary" and "communist," sought to expand its influence among the Betong population, the CPM at first appeared to try and heal the rift with its rival, but ultimately it resorted to a campaign of internecine fighting. Graves were discovered in Betong of dead guerrillas, with one grave bearing the sign "CPM-ML victory" (*Asia Record*, August, p. 10). The CPM also appears to have beaten back efforts by Muslim secessionist groups in Southern Thailand, such as the Pattani United Liberation Organization (PULO), to challenge CPM control in the Betong salient. In the process, the CPM's Twelfth Regiment of about 500 armed and uniformed guerrillas usually stationed in and near the salient had to be expanded to 700. The new troops were drawn from the mostly Muslim Tenth Regiment in the Waeng district of Thailand's Narathiwat province. The Tenth Regiment's manpower had to be reduced from about 600 to 380. (*Bangkok Post*, 20 May; *FBIS*, 26 May.)

Other estimates of the Twelfth Regiment's location have in the past generally placed it outside Betong (and Thailand) and just north of Baling in Malaysia's Kedah state. Other smaller CPM "assault units" and "independent platoons," ranging from 50 to 150 men, operate in other peninsular Malaysian states, such as Perak, Pahang, and Kelantan (see map, *Asia Research Bulletin*, 31 January, p. 886).

On 1 January, longtime CPM Chairman Chin Peng and his Central Committee issued a New Year's message, urging both the party and the Malayan National Liberation Army (MNLA), the CPM's main guerrilla force, to move ahead "heroically to score new victories" (*FBIS*, 13 January). The message's main significance lay in its attribution to Chin Peng. According to unconfirmed reports from recent CPM defectors and Thai intelligence sources, Chin Peng died from natural causes about two years ago "somewhere in the border area of the Malaysian States of Perak and Pahang" (*FEER*, 24 September, p. 15). If Chin Peng in fact was dead, it would be a severe blow to the CPM, for he had been both leader and principal strategist for more than thirty years.

The newest CPM front, the Malay Nationalist Revolutionary Party of Malaya (PKMRM), founded in May 1981 (see *YICA*, 1982, p. 208), also issued a New Year's message in the name of its chairman, C. D.

Abdullah. The PKMRM, organized to appeal particularly to dissident Muslim and ethnic Malay sentiments, stated in this message that "the struggle to defend the sacredness and freedom of religious activities
continued to develop." The message added that "religious groups in various places" in the country had
launched all manner of "struggles" against oppression and were condemning the United Malay National
Organization (UMNO), the main ethnic Malay party in the ruling government coalition, "for not adhering
to Islamic teachings." (FBIS, 13 January.)

In its thirty-third anniversary message on 1 February, the MNLA charged that both the "Kuala Lumpur
and Singapore cliques" (presumably the governments) had over the past few years been intensifying their
"reactionary" repression of "democratic rights," including "torturing political detainees," conspiring
with foreign capitalists, and "undermining small and medium-sized" indigenous entrepreneurs. The "main
contradiction" in Malayan society, according to this message, was between the Kuala Lumpur and
Singapore "cliques" and "the people of all nationalities and various strata." However, another "contradiction," said to be "on the rise" and extremely important, was the "contradiction" between "Soviet-
Vietnamese hegemonism and its running dogs" and the "people" of all nationalities and strata in Malaysia.
The statement concluded that not only general action for "democratic rights" had to be undertaken, but also
a "resolute struggle against the infiltration and subversion of our country by Soviet-Vietnamese hegemonism" had to be waged. (Ibid., 10 February.)

This MNLA statement reflects the CPM's continuing policy that the separate existence of Malaysia and
Singapore is still illegal. The CPM continues to speak for Malayan and Singapore Communists and is trying
to establish a Republic of Malaya composed of both peninsular Malaysia and Singapore. Noteworthy in the
MNLA statement was the reference to "Soviet-Vietnamese hegemonism" and its "running dogs." This
reference may reflect the Beijing-oriented CPM's concern over the Malaysian government's persistent
attempt to seek a political modus vivendi with Vietnam.

In a 24 May message from the CPM's clandestine transmitter in South China, the Voice of Malayan
Democracy, the PKMRM commemorated its first anniversary. During the year, no message was issued by
the Islamic Unity Party (Paperi), which had supported CPM appeals to ethnic Malays and Muslims. Paperi
statements have been declining in frequency, and its functions probably have been absorbed by the
PKMRM. In the anniversary message, familar CPM themes, previously articulated in Paperi statements,
were heard—for example, the poverty of the "Malay masses," the failure of the Malaysian government's
New Economic Policy, the widening gap between rich and poor, the intrigues and diversionary tactics of the
UMNO, and its political "exploitation" of Malay rights and of Islam (ibid., 2 June).

On 20 June, the CPM's Central Committee and the MNLA issued a joint statement marking the thirty-
fourth anniversary of the outbreak of the Malaysian struggle against the "British imperialists." After
reviewing the CPM–MNLA struggle since then, the statement asserted that "the task of the war now" was
to oppose the "reactionaries" and "imperialism" in the interests of safeguarding the "people's interest"
and to resist "Soviet-Vietnamese hegemonism." The CPM must hold aloft "the three red banners" of
"party development, armed struggle and united front." The rural areas must come first in launching
"protracted guerrilla warfare," while in the cities secret organizations and "underground work" should be
intensified. The "broadest democratic national united front" must be developed, and the ideology of the
"Marxism–Leninism–Mao Zedong Thought" remains the CPM's guide. (Ibid., 29 June.) In a congratulatory message over its clandestine transmitter on 30 September, the CPM commemorated the thirty-third
anniversary of the People's Republic of China. The message criticized those in the Association of Southeast
Asian Nations (ASEAN) who ignored the dangers posed by the USSR and Vietnam in Southeast Asia and
who tried to portray People's China as a "threat" (ibid., 5 October).

There is some indication that the membership composition of the CPM may be changing. In late
August, Malaysian Deputy Premier Datuk Musa Hitam voiced concern that a "growing number of Thai
Communists" were replacing the aging Malay members of the CPM. Hitam also noted "the many instances
of cooperation" between the CPM and the Communist Party of Thailand. (Straits Times, 27 August.)

International Aspects. A trade delegation from the People's Republic of China visited Kuala Lumpur
in August following a visit by a Malaysian delegation to Beijing in May. In early 1982, the Chinese had
signed contracts worth an estimated $7.85 milion for the purchase of 61,400 cubic meters of Malaysian
timber and timber products. (FBIS, 26 August.) The official Malaysian radio hailed what was perceived to

be a PRC policy change toward Communists in Southeast Asia, noting that at the Twelfth Congress of the Chinese Communist Party (CCP) in September, the CCP announced that it would no longer support communist insurgencies in other countries. The commentary also noted that although Beijing had closed the radio station in Yunnan that broadcast Thai communist propaganda, "for Malaysia the picture will not be that bright if current trends continue." The commentary charged that China still appears to be supporting the CPM with broadcast facilities, that "the umbilical cord between the CPM and the CCP is still there for all to see," and that "better evidence is needed for the air of suspicion to clear." (Ibid., 17 September.)

The Voice of Malayan Democracy broadcast the text of a 31 August congratulatory telegram sent by the CPM Central Committee to the Twelfth CCP Congress. The telegram noted that the Chinese party had made a "correct evaluation of the historical position of the great teacher, Comrade Mao Zedong," and that the peoples and parties of Malaya and China "have a very close revolutionary friendship and strong militant unity." It closed with the words "Long live Marxism–Leninism–Mao Zedong Thought." (Ibid., 3 September.)

On 11 February, North Korean Premier Yi Chong-ok arrived in Kuala Lumpur for an official visit. An air transport agreement was signed, and expanded trade possibilities and joint venture efforts in construction and transportation between the two countries were discussed. Premier Yi endorsed the Malaysian-initiated ASEAN concept of a "zone of peace, freedom, and neutrality" in Southeast Asia, adding that "the neutrality of the Nonaligned Movement should also be maintained." A North Korean technical mission will visit Malaysia in the near future to study the usages of palm oil. (Ibid., 16 February.)

The Kampuchean problem and relations with the Socialist Republic of Vietnam remained major Malaysian concerns. Radio Kuala Lumpur stressed that after three years of occupying Kampuchea, Vietnam remained "bogged down" in an "unwinnable" Kampuchean guerrilla war and that Hanoi had become "isolated internationally as it never has been before." Vietnam should withdraw from Kampuchea and permit the Kampuchean populace, under U.N. supervision, to choose their own government. (Ibid., 19 January.) Malaysia, like other ASEAN states, has sought to press the underground guerrilla Democratic Kampuchea government led by Khieu Samphan and Pol Pot (usually referred to as the Khmer Rouge) to form a working alliance with other anti-Vietnamese Kampuchean factions. In early February, the Malaysian ambassador in Thailand warned the Khmer Rouge that it should not take ASEAN support for granted, even in the United Nations (ibid., 4 February). On 21 June, when the three main anti-Vietnamese Kampuchean factional leaders, Prince Norodom Sihanouk, Democratic Kampuchea's President Khieu Samphan, and former Cambodian Premier Son Sann, met in Kuala Lumpur and agreed to form the Coalition Government of Democratic Kampuchea, the Malaysian government voiced its strong approval (ibid., 14 July).

On 25 July, Vietnamese Foreign Minister Nguyen Co Thach visited Malaysia for three days. The secretary general of the Malaysian Foreign Ministry reported that the impasse between ASEAN and Vietnam over the Vietnamese occupation of Kampuchea still persisted. Thach postponed his planned departure for Bangkok by one day to try to resolve the issue. Complete Vietnamese withdrawal and self-determination for Kampuchea remained Malaysian objectives during the talks, while Thach stressed that as long as the "Chinese threat" remained, the Vietnamese could not completely withdraw. Because of the threat made by Thach during a visit to Singapore a few days earlier that Vietnam would promote subversion in ASEAN countries to retaliate for ASEAN's hostile attitude toward Vietnam, Malaysian Foreign Minister Tan Sri Ghazali Shafie sought "clarification" from Thach. Thach replied that Vietnam did not plan to use subversion, but it reserved the "right to self-defense" if ASEAN continued to be hostile to the Indochinese states (*Straits Times,* 27 July; *FBIS,* 26 July).

Malaysian Premier Datuk Mahathir Mohamed informed Thach that Vietnam did not have the right to invade Kampuchea and establish a government of its own there "in the name of self-defense." The Malaysian premier said that his government would continue to try to find a political solution, so that Kampuchea could have a government selected by self-determination. (*FBIS,* 27 July.) On Thach's departure from Malaysia, Foreign Minister Ghazali suggested another international conference on Kampuchea in the future (ibid., 19 July). Although Malaysian observers generally agreed that the Thach visit had done little to narrow Malaysian-Vietnamese differences over the Kampuchean question (*Straits Times,* 27 July), Kuala Lumpur is still anxious to have a reconciliation with Hanoi. Malaysia fears China's long-term ambitions and appreciates the important role that an independent Vietnam could play as a buffer to block Beijing's expansionism. Hanoi's willingness to confront the Chinese even encouraged "an underlying feeling of admiration" in Malaysian circles for the Vietnamese (Lee Poh Ping, "The Indochinese Situation and the Big Powers in Southeast Asia: The Malaysian View," *Asian Survey,* June, pp. 518–21).

The USSR, observing Kuala Lumpur's more conciliatory posture on the Kampuchean question, has been careful not to antagonize Malaysia. The Soviet press noted Malaysia's desire for developing further trade and economic ties with the socialist countries and cited "Malaysia's peace-loving foreign policy" on the Kampuchean question. During the Thach visit, the Soviet press declared, both countries had affirmed the "possibility" of solving Southeast Asian problems by mutual respect for territorial sovereignty, territorial integrity, and noninterference—a formula frequently advanced by Vietnamese spokesmen in their policy appeals toward ASEAN countries. (*Izvestiia,* 30 August; *FBIS,* 3 September.) In an interview with a visiting Tass correspondent in Kuala Lumpur, Malaysian Premier Mahathir Mohamed reportedly said that there were "no obstacles" to the consolidation of Soviet-Malaysian relations (*FBIS,* 7 October).

University of Bridgeport   Justus M. van der Kroef

Mongolia

Mongolia has the distinction of being the second-oldest communist-ruled state. In 1921, under Sukhe Baton and Choibalsan, Mongolian Communists established the Mongolian People's Party and later that same year proclaimed a people's government. In 1924, the name of the party was changed to Mongolian People's Revolutionary Party. The Mongolian People's Republic (MPR) is a satellite of the Soviet Union and is heavily dependent on the USSR economically and militarily.

Population. 1,759,000 (1982 est.)

Party. Mongolian People's Revolutionary Party (Mongol Ardyn Khuvagalt Nam; MPRP)

Founded. 1921

Membership. 76,240 (June 1981)

General Secretary. Yumjaagyin Tsedenbal

Politburo. 8 full members: Yumjaagyin Tsedenbal (chairman, Presidium of People's Great Hural), Bat-Ochirym Altangerel (chairman, People's Great Hural), Jambyn Batmonkh (premier), Damdinjavyn Maidar (first deputy premier), Tumenbayaryn Ragchaa (first deputy premier), Damdiny Gombojav, Sampilyn Jalan-Aajav, Demchigiyn Molomjamts; 4 candidate members: Bugyn Dejid, Nyamin Jagvaral, Sonomyn Luvsangombo, Choijilsuren

Secretariat. 7 members: Tsedenbal, Gombojav, Jalan-Aajav, Molomjamts, Gelegiyn Adyaa, Paavangiyn, Damdin, Mangaljavyn

Central Committee. 91 full and 71 candidate members

Last Congress. Eighteenth, 26–31 May 1981, in Ulan Bator

Auxiliary Organizations. Mongolian Revolutionary Youth League (over 200,000 members), Lodongiyn

Tudev, first secretary; Central Council of Mongolian Trade Unions (400,000 members), Luvsantseren, chairman; Committee of Mongolian Women, Pagmadula, chairperson

Publications. *Unen* (Truth), MPRP daily organ, published Tuesday–Sunday

Organization and Leadership. Eight major changes occurred in the Ministry of Defense and related military, justice, and public security areas. Minister of Public Security Choijilsuren was promoted to candidate membership on the Politburo. Among those replaced were the minister of defense, minister and first deputy minister of justice, chairman and deputy chairman of the Supreme Court, head of the political administration of the army, and the chairman of the party Central Committee sector responsible for military and public security. A far-reaching purge led to complete reorganization of the Academy of Sciences. The minister and a deputy minister of education and the minister of transportation were also replaced. The State Committee for Higher, Specialized, and Specialized Technical Education was abolished, with the Ministry of Education taking over its jurisdiction. The chairman of the Council of Mongolian Trade Unions and the chairperson of the Committee of Mongolian Women were replaced.

These changes involved the retirement of five longtime major figures from the active political scene: Bata, who had been ambassador to Moscow (1956–1959) and for many years head of the Central Committee sector for military and public security (replaced by Choijilsuren); Lhamsuren, Politburo member (1954–1957, 1962–1973); Ochirbat, ambassador to Beijing (1953–1957, chairman of the Union of Journalists in the 1960s, and chairman of the Trade Union Council since 1976 (replaced by Luvsantseren); Shirendyb, Politburo member (1954–1957), president of the Academy of Sciences (1960–1982) (replaced by Chi Tseren); and Udval, chairperson of the Committee of Mongolian Women since 1964 (replaced by Pagmadula).

Despite these substantial changes, basic overall continuity was maintained with the top team of Tsedenbal as general secretary of the party, Batmonkh as premier, Maidar as principal economic representative in negotiations with the USSR, and Gotov as Mongolian ambassador to the Soviet Union. The new replacements were Soviet-educated and USSR-oriented, with USSR-assisted political careers. They are somewhat younger than their predecessors but are not new to the Mongolian political scene, having risen through the (Soviet-manipulated) system.

Domestic Affairs. The most important development in the Mongolian economy is the steadily increasing amount of copper and molybdenum produced at Erdenet and shipped to the USSR. Now operating at about two-thirds of planned capacity, the Erdenet complex yielded over 70,000 tons of copper and 660 tons of molybdenum in 1981 (total Soviet production of molybdenum is estimated at 10,000 tons). Minerals are rapidly becoming the principal Mongolian export. (*Soviet Geography*, January; *FEER*, November 18.)

Grain yields have been falling in recent years, apparently due to serious soil erosion and mismanagement. The Ministry of State Farms was eliminated, and its operations merged into the Ministry of Agriculture in February. Livestock again totaled under 25 million head, with some 4 million of these privately owned. Barns for the winter now exist for all animals. Drought caused trouble in 1982, and emergency movement of animals was necessary.

International Views and Contacts. Five significant events illustrated Mongolia's intimate role in Sino-Soviet relations: border negotiations, appointment of a new ambassador to Beijing, a Buddhists' conference for peace, a congress of specialists on Mongolia, and a visit by the Dalai Lama. In all of these, Mongolia pursued the line prescribed by the USSR. The MPR, the Inner Mongolian Autonomous Region, Tibet, and Tibet-in-exile (Dalai Lama) engaged in an intricate diplomatic-political minuet inseparable from Sino-Soviet relations, with military, territorial, nationalist, religious, pacifist, and economic dimensions.

The Mongolian army's strength was reported at 31,500, including three infantry brigades, a small air arm including one fighter squadron, and one surface-to-air missile battalion. Regular Soviet forces, in the MPR since 1966, now include two tank and two motorized rifle divisions plus unspecified air force units (*FEER*, 18 November) and various missile emplacements. In China's Inner Mongolian Autonomous Region, a somewhat analogous situation prevails, with a native Mongolian militia and more substantial regular forces from the People's Liberation Army. Tibet follows the same pattern. In March, the MPR accused the Chinese of having set up in Tibet "over 20 military bases, deploying dozens of medium-range missiles and . . . building numerous engineering projects for military purposes." This militarization allegedly has caused "a sharp decrease in the natives' living standards." In May, the MPR accused China of militarizing Inner Mongolia as a "launching pad of struggle against the MPR."

The border commission that met between 18 February and 3 April in Ulan Bator fulfilled provisions of the 1964 protocol to a 1962 border treaty. One of the Mongolian negotiators in December 1962 was P. Shagdarsuren, who was appointed ambassador to China in June. He was received by Ulanfu, another veteran of decades of negotiation and confrontation. The inconclusive border talks dealt with comparatively minor differences, but an article published in Ulan Bator in March complained of "Great Han [Chinese] chauvinists openly encroaching on the territorial integrity and sovereignty of neighboring states." Another published in June claimed that China actually denied sovereignty to the MPR and retained "hegemonistic aspirations."

Despite the renewal of border talks and widespread speculation about improvement in Sino-Soviet relations, the MPR media continued to attack China, particularly its handling of ethnic minorities. They claimed that "mass riots" two years ago in Kuke Khoto were ruthlessly put down, forceful assimilation and cruel suppression continued to be official policy, large numbers of Chinese had moved into minority areas and took over everything, newly established schools were staffed almost solely by Han Chinese who taught only in Chinese, and Sinicization continued unabated despite talk of de-Maoization and reversal of radical policies.

A Westerner's report from the Inner Mongolian side practically confirmed these accusations: Mongols within China resist integration, and many of them dream of union with the MPR. The Han Chinese fear desertion of the Mongols if the Russians ever do invade, and they are all too aware that from the southern border of the MPR, it is but 500 km to Beijing. (*Der Stern*, 21 October.)

Recently Beijing has been paying compensation to Mongols and Tibetans for losses incurred during the Cultural Revolution and has reinstituted a controlled private economy. Privately owned livestock have become fairly common. The PRC's aim is at least partly to compete with MPR policy. The nomads are restless, and they think they see greener grasslands across the border.

The Mongolists' congress (24–31 August) suggests in a far more subtle way the superiority of Russian over Chinese handling of minority peoples and cultures. At the congress, the interconnection of Buryat Mongols, Kalmyks, and Khalkhas was shown, along with old ties to India. Attention was also paid to old ties with Afghanistan. The presentation of nomads of Central Asia, southern Siberia, and the Far East emphasized their long-shared, unique culture. A soft manipulation of scholarship favors the USSR over China. China fights back with its own, less prestigious scholarship. It plans to erect a new monument to Ghengis Khan and has adopted a kind of affirmative action plan exempting non-Han peoples from birth-control regulations and taxes and favoring them for many jobs. The USSR and the MPR project an image of tolerance, of support for the serious study of minorities, of genuine interest in other cultures, unlike the hordes of China, who (it is implied) dominate and assimilate. In 1982, the MPR continued the practice of recent years of accusing local Chinese in Ulan Bator of various kinds of immorality and indecency. Some Mongols have even been heard to talk worriedly of the Yellow Peril.

In late September, the Dalai Lama stated in Ulan Bator that "despite the many changes, there are still traces of that long history of close relations between Mongolia and Tibet, which are very much alive in the Mongolian people's heart . . . Mongols and Tibetans are almost like twin brothers. In daily life there are many similarities. There is much in common racially, culturally, and religiously." The text of his speech was published in the government-controlled Mongolian press. This was the Dalai Lama's second visit to the MPR, the first having been in 1979. Who is most successfully manipulating whom in this sort of situation is difficult to judge.

Beijing is obviously trying to attract the Dalai Lama to return, and the Dalai Lama is just as obviously trying to maximize his leverage and influence. In any case, a certain amount of controlled Buddhism is shrewd politics now, and refurbishing and repair of ruined monasteries goes on under communist auspices all over Central Asia. Another dimension to Buddhist politics concerns the anti-Chinese relations of the MPR with Heng Samrin's Kampuchea and also with Vietnam and Laos. A Buddhist connection helps.

Buddhism and "peace" go well together, and the Communists are exploiting that connection. The

Sixth Conference of Asian Buddhists for Peace (18–20 August) appealed to many countries, including Japan and Sri Lanka. Even the metropolitan of the Russian Orthodox church responded to the call.

Tsedenbal's proposal last year for an Asia and Pacific conference and a neutral zone, which essentially provided a small-country sponsor for the USSR's plan for a "zone of peace" in the Pacific, was pushed again this year. But the MPR uncritically endorsed the USSR's positions and policies and just as uncritically condemned the alleged U.S.-Japan-PRC anti-Soviet alliance.

University of North Carolina at Chapel Hill   Robert A. Rupen

---

Nepal

All political parties have been illegal in Nepal since 1960, but there has been some liberalization in recent years under King Birendra. The leftist movement is quite fragmented, with various Maoist elements commanding much stronger support than the pro-Moscow communist party faction.

Population. 15 million (estimate)

Party. Communist Party of Nepal/pro-Beijing Adhikari faction (CPN/B) (Maoist elements are divided); Communist Party of Nepal/pro-Moscow (CPN/M)

Founded. 1949

Membership. 4,000 (estimate), with pro-Chinese factions probably accounting for all but a few hundred members

Leadership. CPN/B: Secretary General Man Mohan Adhikari; CPN/M: Secretary General Bishnu Bahadur Manandhar, President Keshar Jung Raimajhi

Auxiliary Organizations. CPN/B: All-Nepal National Independent Students' Union; CPN/M:National Student Union

Publications. *Samiksha,* CPN/M weekly

The major communist figures kept a relatively low profile in 1982, although they were undoubtedly encouraged by the surprisingly strong and widespread criticism of Prime Minister Surya Bahadur Thapa. Thapa was harshly attacked throughout the year, even by some cabinet officials and a large number of National Assembly representatives, for government policies that contributed to a food crisis and for increasing corruption. There was at least some justification for the criticism. These as well as other serious problems, such as inflation, continue to provide areas for exploitation by the opposition.

The various democratic and leftist opposition groups are continuing to call for further liberalization, including press freedom, but not through confrontation with the monarchy. This more conciliatory attitude on the part of the politicians may have been one reason why the government allowed Nepal's major political organization (the democratic Nepali Congress) to hold its first national conference in over 25 years. Other party conferences were announced late last year, but the communist parties' plans were not clear. (*FEER,* 17 December.)

Another reason for the government's reluctant acceptance of the Nepali Congress convention may have been the rise in recent years of extreme left-wing elements active in antigovernment activities among students and teachers as well as in infiltration of development programs. Extremist posters in Kathmandu last fall denounced the "unity between the fascist Panchayat (assembly) and the Nepali Congress." Even Adhikari cautioned that the emergence of such extremists threatened national security. (Ibid.)

One of the student confrontations with the government occurred in March. Just before the annual convention of the pro-Chinese All-Nepal National Independent Students' Union was to begin, with 1,200 delegates reportedly expected, police arrested 55 student organizers. Authorities warned that neither this meeting nor the other conventions planned by democratic and extreme Marxist-Leninist student groups would be permitted. (AFP, 27 March; *FBIS,* 30 March.)

On the international scene, the Nepalese government is a staunch advocate of nonalignment. Relations with the United States remain good. Nepal's relationship with the People's Republic of China is a much closer and more cooperative one than that with the Soviet Union.

Earlysville, Virginia   Barbara Reid

New Zealand

Since its formation in 1921, the Communist Party of New Zealand (CPNZ) has splintered into several rival factions. None seems to have more than 200 members, and most of them probably have well under 100 members. The largest is the Moscow-oriented Socialist Unity Party (SUP). Others include two pro-Beijing groups, the Workers Communist League (WCL) and the Preparatory Committee for the Formation of the Communist Party of New Zealand (Marxist-Leninist); and the Trotskyite, Cuban-oriented Socialist Action League (SAL). The communist movement has little popular support in New Zealand, but a number of its leading members also hold posts in labor unions and have had some success in influencing union policies on international issues.

The SUP is by far the most active communist group. It was founded in the mid-1960s by members of the CPNZ who opposed the party leaders' decision to side with the Chinese in the Sino-Soviet ideological debate. The SUP continues to follow Moscow's lead. The New Zealand government expelled the Soviet ambassador in 1980 for providing funds directly to the SUP.

The SUP is governed by a ten-member National Committee elected every three years. The National Committee in turn elects the smaller National Executive, which is responsible for the party's day-to-day affairs. The party has eleven local branches (down from thirteen two years ago), the largest of which is in Auckland. The president of the SUP is Gordon Harold "Bill" Andersen. Andersen, a well-known labor leader, serves as secretary of the Northern Drivers' Union, president of the Auckland Trades Council, and member of the National Executive of the powerful New Zealand Federation of Labor (FOL), the country's principal national union organization (440,000 members). Another SUP leader, George Kenneth Douglas, is the secretary-treasurer of the FOL. Other key SUP leaders are George Edward Jackson, the national secretary, and Ella Ayo, the vice-president. The party publishes a biweekly newspaper, the *New Zealand Tribune,* and a theoretical journal, *Socialist Politics.*

The SUP has contested selected seats in national elections since 1972, but without success. During 1982, the party was on the defensive because of events in Poland. While visiting the Soviet Union,

Andersen issued a statement on Radio Moscow supporting martial law in Poland, a politically embarrassing stance in New Zealand. SUP members generally avoided pressing their views on provocative issues at the FOL conference in May, and Andersen was re-elected to the FOL National Executive.

The remains of New Zealand's original communist party, the CPNZ, continue to expend much energy on self-destructive internal debate. The CPNZ now aligns itself with Albania, having severed ties with China following the purge of the Gang of Four, and now attacks the USSR, China, and the United States in equally harsh terms. It publishes a newspaper, the *People's Voice,* but is otherwise nearly moribund.

The Maoist-oriented WCL is more conspiratorial than the other communist parties. It claims to be an underground organization and does not reveal the names of its leaders or members. It competes with the other parties for influence within the labor movement, but seems to have greater appeal to radical students and intellectuals. It publishes a newsheet, *Unity.*

The SAL also seems to have greater appeal to young radical intellectuals than to trade union members. It differs from the other parties in its heavy emphasis on Latin American issues. It has helped organize a number of seminars designed to build support for pro-Cuban positions on human rights in Chile, revolutionary struggles in Central America, and other issues.

The National Party government of Prime Minister Robert Muldoon, elected in 1981, is staunchly anticommunist and anti-Soviet. Muldoon has urged a stronger Western defense posture to counter the Soviet military buildup. In January, he expressed firm support for the Western stand against the Polish government's crackdown on the Solidarity movement (*FBIS,* 18 January). Muldoon has also been an acerbic critic of communist influence in New Zealand's trade union movement, which has made him a natural antagonist for the communist parties.

During 1982, the communist parties attacked Muldoon's economic policies, including the twelve-month freeze on wages and prices imposed in June. Other issues that attracted communist opposition were tours by South African sports teams and port calls by U.S. nuclear-powered warships. The SUP supported the continuation of the waterfront unions' ban on handling cargo destined to or from Chile, but the ban was lifted nevertheless. The SUP also continued to advocate the nationalization of key banks and industries, greater protection of Maori land rights, and a nuclear-free zone encompassing the Indian Ocean and South Pacific.

Arlington, Virginia   Ralph L. Braibanti

Pakistan

Pakistan has no communist party organization, no communist labor or student fronts, and no communist publications. Communists have played a relatively minor role in the country's politics since the Communist Party of Pakistan (CPP) and its various front groups were banned in 1954. Since then, communist sympathizers have attached themselves to a wide variety of other political parties or established separate, small groups. Whatever limited influence they had was further undermined when demonstrations were prohibited and political parties and labor unions were formally dissolved in 1979 by the martial law government of President Mohammad Zia ul Haq. The leaders of the banned political parties occasionally and openly meet together. The leaders of nine political parties, for example, met in February 1981 to establish the Movement for the Restoration of Democracy (MRD) to press for an elected government. In

March 1982, MRD leaders issued a charter of demands calling for, among other things, the release of political prisoners, a reduction in prices, the abolition of military courts, and the provision of jobs for the unemployed (*Jang*, 12 March).

Pakistan was relatively stable in 1982 in large part because four years of steady economic growth in the country have deprived Zia's opponents of an opportunity to mobilize popular support against the martial law regime. In addition, the opposition remains divided, unable to find a popular issue to arouse open protest, and without a charismatic leader able to coalesce the disparate opposition groups. Zia marked the fifth year of his martial law regime in July, the longest period of military rule since Pakistan's independence in 1947. On 11 January, he convened the Majlis-e-Shoora (federal advisory council), a nominated body with no real power, and also lifted precensorship of the press.

During the year, the president announced that his government was considering ways to give representative institutions an Islamic orientation. According to one press account, he noted that such institutions would not be "conditionally bound" to the principle of majority rule (*Pakistan Times*, 13 September). Zia also hinted at the possibility of elections to local bodies in 1983 (Karachi domestic service, 13 September), although press reports note that candidates for elective office would be screened to ensure "good character" (*Los Angeles Times*, 22 April).

The modest loosening of controls in early 1982 generated a limited reassertion of public criticism of the martial law regime. On 10 February, the government decided to extend the 28-month ban on political activities (*NYT*, 11 February). Later that month, the government arrested a number of people, primarily in Sind, in what it described as a crackdown against "anti-social and subversive elements" (ibid., 1 March). There were scattered demonstrations by teachers in March and by lawyers in October. In July, the government issued an ordinance amending the Pakistan Legal Practitioners and Bar Council Act of 1973 to prohibit the bar councils from engaging in any political activities.

On the foreign policy front, the Soviet occupation of Afghanistan remained a major issue for Pakistan. Islamabad advocates the withdrawal of Soviet troops, the re-establishment of a neutral and nonaligned Afghanistan, and the return of some three million Afghan refugees to their homes. Zia supported a political resolution of the crisis. He backed U.N. efforts to get the interested parties to the negotiating table. Early in 1982, U.N. Secretary General Javier Pérez de Cuellar appointed Diego Cordovez, U.N. undersecretary for special political affairs, as his personal representative for Afghanistan. A U.N. announcement on 21 April reported that Pakistan and representatives from the regime in Kabul had agreed to participate in "indirect talks." Iran would not participate directly, but agreed to be kept informed. The issues to be discussed were withdrawal of foreign troops, international guarantees of noninterference in the internal affairs of states, and the voluntary return of the refugees (U.S. State Department, Special Report no. 106, December). The talks were held 15–24 June at Geneva.

As the Geneva talks approached, the Soviet media stepped up pressure on Pakistan, focusing on themes of Pakistani "military" and "mercenary" interest in Afghanistan. An *Izvestiia* article (19 May), for example, charged that the United States is transforming Pakistan into its gendarme in the region and alleged that Pakistan is allowing the United States to train Afghan insurgents. On 16 May *Sovetskaia Rossiia* denounced U.S.-Chinese and Sino-Pakistani "cooperation" against "India's peace-loving foreign policy." Little forward movement was achieved at the Geneva talks, although the dialogue is important for Pakistan because it keeps international attention focused on a political resolution of the Afghan crisis.

Nonetheless, Pakistan continued to seek an improvement in Pakistani-Soviet bilateral relations. Pakistani Foreign Minister Yaqub Khan met with his Soviet counterpart in New York City in July. The next month, Foreign Secretary Niaz Niak met with the Soviet deputy foreign minister in Moscow. Shortly before these talks, Zia told newsmen that friendly ties with the USSR are "one of the basic objectives" of Pakistani foreign policy (*Muslim*, 19 August). Zia himself met privately with Yuri Andropov on 15 November at the time of Brezhnev's funeral, the first meeting between Pakistani and Soviet heads of state since 1974. Yet the Soviet Union continued to criticize Pakistan both before and during Zia's visit to the United States in December. The November issue of the *USA Institute Journal*, for example, charged that the Zia regime is "repressive," faulting it for limiting political activities, refusing to hold elections, and imposing press censorship.

The large Pakistan Steel project remains the major symbol of Pakistani-Soviet relations. In addition, construction began in early 1982 on the Belarus Tractor Plant, one-third of it funded with credits from the

USSR. This project is unusual in that it is the first time in Pakistan that the USSR has collaborated on a private sector project. There was a marginal increase in bilateral trade. Without communist parties or front groups, the USSR's effort to influence Pakistani public opinion is limited to placing articles in the Pakistani media. Very few Pakistani students study in the USSR; no Soviet book or film exhibits were held in 1982. The USSR operates a Friendship House in Karachi that conducts cultural and informational programs.

Relations with the PRC, Pakistan's closest and most trusted ally, remained extremely good. There were frequent exchanges of high-level visitors, culminating with Zia's trip to China on 17–22 October. The two sides established a joint commission to promote trade and technological cooperation. Several large industrial projects were completed with Chinese assistance, and a new trade protocol was signed. China remains Pakistan's major supplier of imported military equipment.

There are a number of pro-Soviet and, to a lesser extent, pro-Chinese figures who participate in Pakistan's now-banned political parties. *Viewpoint*, a literary journal published in Lahore, occasionally publishes the works of Pakistan's Marxist intellectuals. The orthodox core of the old pro-Soviet CPP are in the National Progressive Party (MPP), led by Azaz Nasir and Afrasiab Khattak. The latter lives in Kabul. The NPP in the past had some limited support in the Northwest Frontier Province (NWFP) and in Karachi. The Kisan Mazdoor Party, once a force in the NWFP, formerly was pro-Chinese, but its leadership is now shifting toward a pro-Soviet orientation. Its leader, Afzal Bangash, is reportedly in Kabul. There are also a few Marxists in the centrist Pakistan People's Party (PPP), although the leadership of Pakistan's strongest political organization remains in moderate hands. There are also some dedicated Marxists in the Baluch Student Organization, perhaps the most popular student group in Baluchistan. In addition, remnant elements of the 1973–1977 Baluchi rebellion are in Afghanistan. According to some press reports, there are between 6,000 and 8,000 former rebels in Afghanistan who receive financial support from the Karmal regime (*Sunday Times*, London, 7 March). Khair Bakhsh Marri, chief of the major Baluchi tribe, is also reportedly in Kabul (*Le Figaro*, Paris, 6 April). Still another group reportedly receiving Soviet and Afghan financial assistance is the Al-Zulfikar group, led by the sons of the late Zulfikar Ali Bhutto, who live in Kabul. The Pakistan government accused Al-Zulfikar of several acts of violence during 1982.

Still other groups that seek a more accommodating posture toward the USSR are the Pakistan Liberation Movement; the Pakistan People's Student Federation (student front of the PPP); the National Democratic Party, led by Sher Baz Mazari and Abdul Wali Khan; the People's National Party, a Baluchi organization led by Ghus Bakhsh Bezenjo and Ataullah Mengal, two Baluchi tribal leaders; and the Jiya Sind Students' Front. The primary objective of many of these organizations is greater autonomy for Pakistan's ethnic groups. However, none of these leftist organizations were able to mobilize significant support against the martial law regime.

The student fronts of the Islamic parties—the Jamiat-e-Tulaba and the Anjuman-e-Tulaba—scored victories in the majority of student union elections conducted during the year. The Islamic parties are generally more sympathetic to Zia than are the other political parties and their student fronts.

Arlington, Virginia   Walter K. Andersen

The Philippines

The Beijing-oriented Communist Party of the Philippines–Marxist-Leninist (CPP-ML) and its guerrilla forces, the New People's Army (NPA), continued to use tactics of selective terror to undermine the Philippine government and its security forces. In 1981 and 1982, the NPA was especially active in the southern provinces trying to provoke a violent government reaction so as to influence the populace to support the CPP-ML.

In mid-December 1981, five NPA commanders were killed in a skirmish in Lopeztown as they led their insurgents in an attack on the town. On 8 January, five guerrillas were slain on the Bataan peninsula, and government troops arrested six NPA insurgents in the south. (*FBIS,* 23 December 1981; *FEER,* 15 January, p. 7.)

Early in 1982, the NPA killed a number of village leaders, and in mid-April, NPA units ambushed two army posts in Camarines Norte province, killing eight and wounding eleven persons. In May, NPA ambushes in Negros Occidental province near Ilo Town resulted in the death of seven noncommissioned officers. (*FEER,* 12 March, p. 11, 23 April, p. 9; *FBIS,* 11 May.) NPA units also tried to disrupt local electons in May, and in Cagayan province NPA troops kidnapped and murdered several local political leaders (*FBIS,* 13 May).

These terrorist attacks misfired in June when public outrage erupted over the killing of a 62-year-old spinster in Lopogandol village in Davao del Sur province for refusing to give contributions to the guerrillas. Local authorities captured the terrorists, who confessed to the killing. (Ibid., 17 June, 14 July.) This tactic of terror has been the pattern of CPP-ML and NPA activities for the past year. While government security forces have managed to limit these actions, they have not completely eliminated the organizational infrastructure of the CPP-ML and NPA forces.

One development the government fears is a united front between the NPA and the Moro National Liberation Front (MNLF). General Delfin Castro of the Southern Military Command asserted in February that NPA and MNLF guerrillas had been training "side by side" in various rural sections of the country (ibid., 23 February). In September, Castro claimed that the MNLF and the NPA had formed an alliance not only with each other but also with other insurgent groups such as the shadowy Sandigan Army of the underground Democratic Socialist Party of the Philippines as well (*Bulletin Today,* Manila, 28 September). But other government spokesmen have pointed out that the MNLF was badly divided and that some MNLF leaders were surrendering.

A new underground Muslim insurgent group called the Islamic Revolutionary Movement of Free Enlightened Muslims was said by the Philippine military to have made its appearance in Mindanao, and reportedly explosives of the kind used both by the NPA and the Islamic guerrillas had been seized as part of the contraband cargo on a interisland vessel docking in Zamboanga City in Mindanao in August (ibid., 26 August). So far, tangible evidence linking the NPA with the MNLF has yet to be found. Armed Forces Vice-Chief of Staff Gen. Fidel Ramos revealed in mid-April that NPA death squads had killed 147 village officials throughout the country and had been especially active in the Samar region. Government troops retaliated later that month in the village of Samuroy, in Samar, by an artillery barrage on a suspected NPA hideout, killing some villagers and wounding others.

The General Political Situation. As the government tried to suppress both communist guerrillas and Muslim insurgents, criticism of the Marcos regime increased in 1982 whenever the government's security forces took vigorous action in the provinces to deal with acts of terrorism and violence. In February, the prestigious Integrated Bar of the Philippines issued a report to Marcos and Defense Minister Juan Ponce Enrile that was severely critical of government torture and human rights violations in the "strategic hamlet" (security resettlement) program being carried out in Davao del Norte province, Mindanao. A few weeks before, Philippine officials had denied that force had been used to resettle some 20,000 farmers away from NPA-infested areas. In early April, however, Enrile ordered the immediate cessation of the strategic hamlet program, claiming that the military involved had never informed him of the program in the first place. (*Asia Record*, March, p. 9, August, p. 14; *FBIS*, 1 March; *FEER*, 12 March, p. 38.)

Although in an Australian interview in April Enrile categorically denied claims made by Amnesty International that at least 2,000 political prisoners were being held in the Philippines and were being abused (*FBIS*, 28 April), public charges of military brutalities have continued. On 30 May, a Concerned Citizens Alliance of Bicol, headed by former senator Tecla San Andres-Ziga, after an investigation, denounced the military atrocities committed in the Bicol area and demanded of Enrile that military action cease in Bicol, that guilty parties be prosecuted, and that their victims be given some indemnity (*Bulletin Today*, 5 August). In early October, Enrile sharply attacked the human rights critics of the Marcos regime, declaring that groups like Amnesty International and the World Council of Churches "have Marxist leanings" (*FBIS*, 5 October).

Whether it is true as CPPML founder José Sison recently stated from his prison cell that the party's mass organizations are located "in the overwhelming majority of the provinces of the country" (*FEER*, 6 November 1981, p. 23) and therefore partly responsible for the increasing public criticism of the Marcos government is very questionable. As the economic recession deepened during 1982, rising unemployment and hard times also contributed to new occurrences of violence during the year.

But the government remains worried that each act of violence will play into the hands of the communist insurgents. In early December 1981, Marcos warned members of the Ulama Council, a group of prominent Muslim leaders, to "guard their flock against communist insurrection" because recent "intelligence reports" had disclosed that Communists were working to infiltrate religious groups. Although Marcos later declared that both the NPA and the MNLF had failed to establish a hold in the Philippines and that the threat posed by these groups had "ceased to be serious" (*FBIS*, 9 December 1981, 4 Jaunary), in February Enrile announced that he would organize a new "elite counterinsurgency force" in order to intensify the political and propaganda offensive against the Communists. Enrile also declared that the Philippine military planned to intensify anti-NPA operations, using new, high-powered Armalite rifles, so that they "will match the Communists bullet for bullet." He also ordered a tightened check on arms smuggling because of what was described as "an upsurge" in guerrilla activities in recent months. (*Straits Times*, Singapore, 8 and 9 February.)

Throughout 1982, the government's anticommunist campaign intensified. On 9 March, Solicitor General Estelito Mendoza announced a new presidential decree authorizing persons involved in rebellion or insurrection to be arrested without a warrant and suspected subversives to be detained "until ordered released by the president" or his authorized representative (*Asia Record*, April, p. 13). On 8 April, Marcos announced that he knew of a plot by subversives to launch a series of strikes, assassinations, and bombings in the coming months, possibly in September when he planned to visit the United States. In this connection, a new list of "subversives" and antigovernment groups was being compiled, the president added, and a "secret, 1,000 strong plainclothes police force" to patrol Manila was being formed. "I understand some of my friends in the political opposition are part of this conspiracy," Marcos said further, though he did not name the alleged conspirators. (*NYT*, 9 April.)

Shortly afterwards, Marcos, speaking at the eighty-fifth anniversary ceremonies of the Philippine army, directed the Philippine armed forces to "pay more attention to guerrilla warfare, counterinsurgency and countersubversion operations," adding that even though the world was concentrating on the problems of nuclear war, during the next several decades "here in Southeast Asia" there would be problems of internal peace "brought about by subversion" (*FBIS*, 4 May).

The frequency of strikes since the lifting of martial law in January 1981 has been particularly disturbing to government economic planners. A 79-year-old longtime labor leader, Felixberto Olalia, Sr., said to be the head of the May First Movement, identified by the government as an "umbrella group" of several workers groups and as a CPP-ML front, was among the most prominent of some fourteen trade union leaders arrested on 13 August in connection with the alleged plot. They were charged with sedition and conspiracy to commit rebellion. Further arrests followed and included some NPA and CPP-ML cadres, such as Central Committee member Isagani Serrano, said to be a leader of party "mass action." The press cited "terrorism," "nationwide violence," and "assassination" as 68 arrests were made. Military lawyers offered affidavits on 4 September to demonstrate that those apprehended had intended to unleash violence and rebellion during Marcos's visit to the United States, planned to begin on 15 September. (*Bulletin Today,* 9 and 19 August; *FBIS,* 16 August, 8 and 18 September; *NYT,* 2 and 5 September.)

Opposition leaders such as former Senator Salvador Laurel argued that the arrests raised the specter of a nationwide anti-Marcos conspiracy and were designed to improve the president's bargaining position during his forthcoming discussions in Washington (*NYT,* 22 August). No details of the alleged plot were ever made available, and even before the president left for the United States, Philippine military spokesmen began to downplay the danger of any new violence. On 10 September, Armed Forces Chief of Staff Gen. Fabian Ver said that "the situation across the country is now under control, and the subversive terror conspiracy has been negated." Special alert orders to the armed forces had been lifted, he added. (*FBIS,* 14 September.) But a military spokesman said that during Marcos's U.S. visit 27 government troops, thirteen civilians, and eleven Communists died in fighting throughout the Philippines (*NYT,* 30 September).

Government authorities continue to point out that certain groups critical of the Marcos regime are linked with the CPP-ML and its NPA forces. A small faction of the Roman Catholic Church called Christians for National Liberation are active on the NPA's behalf (*FEER,* 10 September, pp. 31–32). At the close of September, General Ver ordered the military not to arrest members of the clergy unless they were "caught actually committing subversive acts" (*Bulletin Today,* 28 September). Soon after, the military accused an Australian priest of subversive activities. The charge was denied, and the Association of Superiors of Major Religious Orders in the Philippines said the accusations were "harassments and an attempted frame-up." Continuing reports of extensive cooperation between the clergy and the NPA had soured church-state relations. (*FBIS,* 6 and 7 October.) In mid-October, the Rev. Edgardo Kangleon, head of a social action center on the island of Samar, which has been a suspected area of NPA activity, was arrested. The Philippine military claimed to have found "subversive documents" at the center. At the same time, the military began hunting for four other priests who had reportedly joined the NPA. Defense Minister Enrile subsequently charged that ten priests were active with the NPA and that Marxism-Leninism appeared to have become "fashionable" among some religious elements (*NYT,* 17 and 24 October).

Philippine government and intelligence circles now speak of a radical clergy being a "third force" in rebellion against the Marcos government as well as the church hierarchy (*FBIS,* 3 November). On 28 November, President Marcos declared that "the days when the friars dictated what we should do with respect to our local government and our policies are over." He vowed to crack down on "rebel priests" who assisted antigovernment guerrillas. His remarks came at a time of rising apprehension among religious intellectuals in the Philippines that a conflict between church and state was inevitable. Twelve Roman Catholic bishops in the Philippines urged the Marcos government to be more tolerant of responsible dissent and to seek a solution of the problems of unrest in public life. Defense Minister Enrile replied, however, that the government would not give in to "pressure from dissenting priests" but would continue to exercise its authority to maintain the public order. (*NYT,* 29 and 30 November.)

International Developments. Philippine relations with both the People's Republic of China and the USSR appear to have been strengthened by visits to those countries by Imelda Marcos, the president's wife and minister of human settlements. During Mme. Marcos's visit to Beijing (7–11 June), PRC Premier Zhao Ziyang commented that during the past seven years and since diplomatic recognition, Sino-Philippine relations have been developing "smoothly." On Mme. Marcos's return to Manila, it was announced that Beijing would be purchasing increased quantities of such raw materials as copper, copra, iron ore, and sugar from the Philippines. (*FBIS,* 17 June.)

Prior to Mme. Marcos's visit to the Soviet Union, *Izvestiia* (15 June) carried a feature article by its Manila correspondent on the character and strength of the U.S. military presence in the Philippines. The article noted that air strikes had been staged from U.S.-operated Clark Field in order to suppress "people's uprisings" in China, Korea, and Vietnam (*FBIS,* 22 June). Mme. Marcos's visit to the USSR (3–9 July) was marked by assurances from Vasily V. Kuznetsov, first vice-president of the Presidium of the Supreme

Soviet, that the Soviet Union felt friendship for the Filipino people. Mme. Marcos pledged that her country would do "its modest share" in the quest for world peace. Soviet Minister of Culture Piotr N. Demichev said that Mme. Marcos's visit would further enhance cultural and political relations between the Philippines and the USSR. (Ibid., 8 July.)

A new Soviet-Philippine economic agreement reached during Mme. Marcos's visit called for joint efforts to produce cement in the Philippines and to develop prefabricated housing and oil exploration. The new cement plant will be constructed by the USSR and will have a production capacity of a million metric tons. (Ibid., 14 July.) The plant is to be constructed on Semirara island, Antique province, south of Manila, and its construction replaces a similar project that was to be undertaken by a U.S. firm but never materialized because of alleged Philippine "financial constraints." Considerable political significance is seen in the Soviets' Semirara project, not only because it is the first major Soviet industrial venture in the Philippines, but also because so far none of the members of the Association of Southeast Asian Nations (ASEAN) "has been keen on the idea of streams of Soviet technicians and advisers traipsing around the countryside" (FEER, 3 September, p. 98). During Mme. Marcos's conversations with Soviet Foreign Minister Andrei Gromyko, however, the latter, according to Tass, stressed "the invariability of the Soviet Union's course toward developing all-round mutually beneficial relations" with the Philippine republic (FBIS, 6 July). Coming shortly before President Marcos's visit to the United States, announcement of the Semirara project was also perceived as a Philippine diplomatic attempt to stress Manila's independence and leverage in international relations. On 15 October, in a ceremony in Manila attended by Marcos, his wife, and the Soviet ambassador, Manila and Moscow were declared to be "sister cities" for the purpose of continuing cooperation in trade, cultural affairs, and technology. A Soviet spokesman on this occasion said that Filipino-Soviet relations had steadily improved since the Marcoses' visit to Moscow five years ago (NYT, 16 October).

As for Vietnam, the Philippines attempted to continue to follow a moderate course, while supporting general ASEAN objectives with respect to the Kampuchean problem. During a Manila conference on economic cooperation among developing countries, Marcos took the occasion to assure Vietnamese Deputy Foreign Minister Ha Van Lau that "whatever our disagreements may be in relation to Kampuchea," the "relations between us as friends do not change" (Straits Times, 27 August).

The subsequent Marcos visit to the United States clearly was significant in the context of the Reagan administration's confrontation with perceived Soviet expansionism. The U.S. military installations in the Philippines at Clark Field and Subic Bay were widely considered to be a subject of discussions. Having been refused a state visit to Washington during the Carter administration because of the inadequacies of Philippine human rights policies, the invitation to Marcos by the new Reagan administration was meant as an effort to bolster U.S.-Philippine relations. At the end of March, U.S. Defense Secretary Caspar W. Weinberger visited President Marcos in Manila, amid student protests decrying U.S. involvement in El Salvador and U.S. support for the Marcos regime generally. The protesters included a nascent Filipino antiwar and antinuclear movement, reflecting concern over the proposed construction—with U.S. help—of a nuclear power plant on the Bataan peninsula. According to Philippine sources, Weinberger gave Marcos a personal letter from President Reagan assuring the Philippines of U.S. support "in meeting the challenges of peace and freedom in Southeast Asia" (FBIS, 2 April). On 17 September, President Reagan warmly received Marcos in Washington, at the start of a thirteen-day visit. Reagan described the Philippine president as a "respected voice for reason and moderation in international forums." President Marcos, in turn, strongly reaffirmed the Philippine commitment to the "principles of American democracy." (NYT, 17 September.) Prior to his journey to Washington, Marcos had expressed dissatisfaction both with the state of current U.S. defense arrangements with the Philippines and with the slow pace of negotiations to increase Philippine exports, particularly sugar, to the United States (ibid., 7 September). It has not become apparent, however, that the president's visit resulted in significant changes in these areas of Philippine concern.

In keeping with the Marcos government's policy of undercutting foreign Islamic support for the MNLF, Manila has steadily sought to improve relations with Saudi Arabia, current residence of Nur Misuari, a principal MNLF leader. A visit by Mme. Marcos to Saudi Arabia in mid-June led to assurances by King Fahd that his government valued the friendship of the Philippines (FBIS, 17 June). Although the 42-nation Islamic Conference has repeatedly adopted resolutions urging its members to exert pressure on Manila to grant the MNLF-dominated areas in the Philippines autonomy in accordance with the provisions of the 1976 Tripoli agreement worked out between Mme. Marcos and MNLF supporter Col. Moammar Khadafy of Libya (*YICA*, 1978, p. 308), there has been little implementation. Official MNLF missions have been opened in Libya and Syria, and relations between Malaysia and the Philippines remain cool, partly because of the MNLF issue. Yet the Marcos government believes it has little to fear from the MNLF's foreign diplomatic offensive (*FEER*, 28 May, p. 28; *NYT*, 10 March).

University of Bridgeport   Justus M. van der Kroef

Singapore

The Singapore government under the People's Action Party (PAP) has eradicated communist activity in this island-state, although it is commonly believed that around 200 members of the Communist Party of Malaya (CPM) still operate underground.

On 10 January, the government arrested ten persons who belonged to an organization called the Singapore People's Liberation Organization (SPLO). The government charged them with inflaming racial and religious strife in order to overthrow the government by violence. The government revealed that pamphlets published by the SPLO claimed that Singapore leaders were oppressing Muslims and ethnic Malays in Singapore.

The General Political Situation. Some of the arrested SPLO leaders had been unsuccessful parliamentary candidates on the slate of minor opposition parties, including the Barisan Sosialis, and all were ethnic Muslim Malays or Indian Muslims. According to the governemnt, they had vainly sought support from various foreign sources, including the USSR, the Socialist Republic of Vietnam, Indonesia, and Libya. Propaganda distributed by the SPLO charged that Singapore's Muslim Religious Council, an official body that supervises Islamic affairs, had been "altering the true course of Muslim thinking" and declared that "the PAP fascists have even prohibited students from knowing that Singapore belongs to the Malays" and warned that "if we are complacent, we will end up like the Negroes or Red Indians in America." (*Straits Times*, 11, 22, and 23 January.) Whether the SPLO group represented an outburst of Islamic militancy among ethnic Malay and Indian Muslims or was but the latest CPM attempt to use Islam to stir unrest among Singapore's Muslims has thus far not been ascertained.

Foreign Relations. On 22 February, the Singapore government expelled a Soviet diplomat and a Soviet marine superintendent working at a local shipyard on grounds of espionage. The diplomat, Anatoly A. Larkin, who had been in Singapore since 1979, was the Soviet embassy's second secretary and in charge of press and information. The marine superintendent, A. A. Bondarev, was attached to the semi-government-owned Keppel shipyard in Singapore and was overseeing repairs of Soviet merchant vessels. Larkin was charged with approaching an armed forces technical officer to obtain classified military information. Larkin allegedly offered the officer "monetary incentives," while Bondarev reportedly had been using a Singapore businessman since October 1979 "as part of his intelligence network." (*FBIS*, 22 February.)

The incident doubtlessly reaffirmed the Singapore government's suspicions of Soviet policies in the region. In late 1981, Singapore's second deputy prime minister (foreign affairs), S. Rajaratnam, accused the USSR of "hiding old-fashioned imperialism under its Marxist cloak," in order to dominate not just Asia but the world. He also stated that because "very few Europeans and Americans" now challenged Soviet behavior abroad, such Soviet activities would have to be repulsed "largely by Asians themselves." (*Straits Times,* 22 December 1981.)

From 14 to 16 June, Singapore played host to the fifteenth annual Foreign Ministers Conference of the Association of Southeast Asian Nations (ASEAN), which rejected Vietnam's "unlawful" presence in Kampuchea. Singapore Foreign Minister S. Dhanabalan announced that ASEAN should and would go on applying "all-around" pressure on Vietnam, but would keep the door open to reach a political settlement on the Kampuchean question. He praised internal ASEAN cooperation both over the Kampuchean problem and in intra-ASEAN economic development. (Ibid., 15 June.) After the three major anti-Vietnamese Kampuchean factions met in Kuala Lumpur to form a new coalition government headed by Prince Norodom Sihanouk, the former ruler declared on 22 June that Singapore had offered aid to the Kampuchean anti-Vietnamese resistance movement, but it had not yet decided whether such aid would be military or financial or both (ibid., 28 June).

Relations between Singapore and Vietnam seemed to deteriorate after Vietnamese Foreign Minister Nguyen Co Thach visited Singapore on 19 July to discuss the Kampuchean situation. According to Dhanabalan, Thach mentioned the existence of "Maoist parties in Southeast Asia" while expressing Hanoi's dissatisfaction with ASEAN's hostility toward Vietnam over the Kampuchean question. According to Dhanabalan, Thach threatened that Vietnam either could encourage subversion in Southeast Asia, presumably in the style of local "Maoist parties," or mend its fences with the People's Republic of China. In the latter event, a joint Sino-Vietnamese effort would "deal with Thailand" and then with a "hostile" ASEAN. Thach's various veiled threats, as described by the Singapore foreign minister, provoked such adverse official reaction that Thach called a special press conference in Singapore. Thach denied that he had threatened ASEAN with any retaliation and complained that the press had distorted his general comments. The Vietnamese foreign minister added that his government would react if ASEAN "interference" in Vietnamese (and presumably Kampuchean) affairs continued. He charged that since 1975 ASEAN had engaged in "hostile activities" against the Indochinese states," for example, by supporting the Pol Pot regime against the Kampuchean people. Moreover, ASEAN's support for Sihanouk's new coalition government set "a bad precedent," for it could encourage other countries to interfere in the affairs of others. Thach concluded: "We have warned ASEAN over the last three years about such activity. If they can do such things, we can do the same. We have the right to self-defense." (Ibid., 20 and 21 July.)

Soon afterwards, the Singapore government announced that it would establish a Khmer-language radio service in Singapore as part of its efforts to support the new anti-Vietnamese Sihanouk coalition government. The new service's broadcasts would be aimed at "countering Vietnamese and other Communist propaganda beamed at Kampuchea" by the Hanoi-controlled Heng Samrin government of the People's Republic of Kampuchea now in Phnom Penh (*Asia Record,* September 2). In mid-November, Singapore reportedly sent a secret arms shipment, including assault rifles, to equip some 2,600 troops of the Khmer People's National Liberation Front led by Son Sann, the premier of the new anti-Vietnamese coalition government (*FBIS,* 17 November). Singapore, along with other ASEAN states, played an active role at the United Nations in New York in October in securing recognition of the Sihanouk coalition government as the rightful holder of Kampuchea's seat in the world organization.

University of Bridgeport   Justus M. van der Kroef

Sri Lanka

The conservative United National Party (UNP) government dominated Sri Lankan politics in 1982; the president won re-election, and a popular referendum extended parliament's life. The leftists, still unable to achieve effective cooperation either among themselves or with the noncommunist opposition, are faced with important policy decisions as a result of these defeats.

Population. 15 million (estimate)

Party. Communist Party of Sri Lanka (CPSL)

Founded. 1943

Membership. 6,000 (estimate)

Secretary General. Kattorge P. Silva

Political Bureau. K. P. Silva (secretary general), Pieter Keuneman (president), M. G. Mendis (trade union leader), A. Vaidyalingam (the only Tamil representative), H. G. S. Ratnaweera (former Party Education and Publications Bureau chairman), L. W. Panditha (trade union activist), D. W. Subasinghe, D. E. W. Gunasekara (foreign affairs expert), Jayetilleke de Silva (national organizer), J. A. K. Perera (trade union activist), Sarath Muttetuwegama (member of parliament), Peter Jayesekara (Friendship League coordinator), Leslie Gunawardene (university history professor), A. G. Jayasena

Central Committee. 50 members

Last Congress. Eleventh, 26–30 March 1980, in Colombo

Auxiliary Organizations. Ceylon Federation of Trade Unions, Youth League, Women's Organization

Publications. *Aththa, Mawbima, Deshabimani, Forward* (journal)

The pro-Moscow CPSL was quite active in opposition challenges to the government on several fronts last year. The party continued trying to achieve effective unity with other leftist parties. However, it also decided to work in some cases with the democratic-socialist Sri Lanka Freedom Party (SLFP), Sri Lanka's only viable political alternative to the ruling UNP. The 1980 CPSL Congress had rejected another alliance with former Prime Minister Sirimavo Bandaranaike's SLFP, terming her party "capitalist" (see *YICA*, 1981, p. 198). The impetus for the pro-Moscow party's change of tactics—and, in fact, for the renewed efforts toward unity among a number of opposition parties—was undoubtedly the government's call for early elections.

In January, the Trotskyist Lanka Sama Samaja Party (LSSP) sponsored a meeting of opposition forces aimed at building a united front against the UNP government in the election. Attending was the CPSL, onetime coalition partner with the LSSP in Mrs. Bandaranaike's government, but a major absentee was the former prime minister, whose own SLFP is split and who is herself disenfranchised.

Although Mrs. Bandaranaike and her two former leftist allies later agreed there should be a common candidate to oppose President Junius Richard Jayewardene in the 20 October presidential election, they could not agree on one. Jayewardene defeated five other candidates, receiving about 53 percent of the vote. The SLFP contender ran second and was supported by the CPSL and its newspaper, *Aththa*. (Soon after the election, the government banned *Aththa*.) Separate candidates were put forward by the LSSP, the Marxist-Leninist Janatha Vimukthi Peramuna (JVP), and another Trotskyist faction that had broken away from the LSSP. (*FEER*, 3 September, and 15 October.)

Immediately after his re-election, President Jayewardene charged that a Marxist faction of the SLFP had planned to kill him on election day and "create an Afghanistan-type situation even the U.S. Army could not have saved" (AFP, 30 October; *FBIS*, 1 November). Mrs. Bandaranaike strongly denied the allegation. Reflecting widespread opposition feelings and frustrations, she in turn charged that government claims of a plot and a new proposal to extend the present parliament's term until 1989 without general elections were all part of UNP moves toward dictatorship. The parliamentary extension was approved in a 22 December referendum, with the government winning by a narrower margin than in the October election, according to preliminary information.

Despite these UNP victories, the CPSL's only member of parliament consistently voted against the government's bills enabling the electoral changes. Muttetuwegama also attacked government corruption, alleging that more than 30 percent of foreign assistance was lost through kickbacks, commissions, and waste (*NYT*, 16 May).

In another area of communist activity, the government accused the CPSL earlier in the year of inciting university students to protest proposed educational reforms. Muttetuwegama described the reforms as a subtle attempt to strengthen the socioeconomic position of the privileged classes. (AFP, 23 January; *FBIS*, 26 January.)

Internationally, the pro-Moscow CPSL made no changes in its policies. In January, the party demanded that the government cancel both a proposed agreement to allow a U.S.-affiliated firm to set up an oil facility at Trincomalee port and a Voice of America agreement (*FBIS*, 7 January). Pieter Keuneman also made one of his periodic visits to the USSR in February.

While the leftist movement in general has been suffering major setbacks, the Marxist-Leninist JVP has been growing during the past few years. Originally involved in the 1971 insurgency, some of the young organization's elements and its leader, Rohan Wijeweera, have evolved into a political party that gained official recognition last year. Wijeweera was a presidential candidate, obtaining 4 percent of the vote and ranking third among the six candidates.

The JVP has been actively canvassing support and has been particularly successful among students. Wijeweera, however, denied that the JVP was responsible for any violence during the student protests against the educational reforms. Wijeweera has chosen to avoid direct confrontation with the UNP and has also rejected cooperation with the older leftist parties. He has visited the USSR and Cuba in recent years, but information on the party's foreign orientation is contradictory. Wijeweera is party chairman; the general secretary is Lionel Bopage. (*FEER*, 12 March.)

Earlysville, Virginia   Barbara Reid

Thailand

In 1982, the Thai people celebrated both the 200th anniversary of the founding of the Chakri dynasty and the 50th anniversary of the constitutional monarchy. Occurring simultaneously but not celebrated was the 40th anniversary of the establishment of the Communist Party of Thailand (CPT). The year witnessed the continuing demise of the CPT as a threat to the stability and security of the Thai government.

From the party's beginning, both ethnic Chinese and Chinese communist doctrine have played a leading role. The Third CPT Congress (1961) decided to adopt Maoist guerrilla war tactics and to accept China's view of the Soviets as imperialist-revisionists. Although the ethnic base of the party was widened to include Thais following the establishment in 1965 of the Thai Patriotic Front, the party continued its pro-Chinese policy throughout the mid-1970s. The communist takeover of Indochina and the absorption of ethnic Thai student dissident and activist intellectuals into a United Front after October 1976 caused internal discord between supporters of Hanoi and Beijing. That rift led to the present crisis of the CPT: the virtual collapse of the United Front, the defection of major party leaders, the loss of guerrilla bases, and the reduction of support from China and Indochinese communist parties.

Organization and Strategy. Verifiable information about CPT organization and strategy has been minimal because of the party's clandestine status in Thailand and its state of crisis and flux. Defectors and captured party documents offer contradictory reports of CPT leadership and strategy. Whether the CPT actually held its planned Fourth Congress became a subject of debate and speculation in the absence of hard information. Thai government reports that the congress was held sometime in early 1982 were circulated widely and often with contradictory assessments of leadership changes. Most reports indicated that the Fourth Congress was held in separate regions in March and April 1982. Central Committee members were said to have traveled from place to place and held meetings at the regional level rather than in one central location. Originally the party leadership planned to meet at "Camp 508" in Surat Thani province but the massive government-sponsored military onslaught there in March scuttled those plans. The Thai government reported that about 55 representatives of party branches nationwide met separately in the north, the northeast, and the south.

It is clear that a schism among competing factions existed at the Fourth Congress centering on an analysis of Thai society. The party's Second Congress (1952) had concluded that Thailand was "semi-feudal" and "semi-colonial," whereas more recent CPT leaders have perceived Thailand to be a "rapidly advancing capitalist" country—"semi-colonial" and "semi-capitalist"—and dependent on U.S. imperialism. The latter view was articulated by the Coordinating Committee for Patriotic and Democratic Forces (CCPDF), a front organization staffed originally by student and intellectual activists who had fled to the jungle following the military coup d'etat of October 1976. Many of these activists have defected from the party. The front's chairman, Politburo member Udom Srisuwan, surrendered in September, leaving the CCPDF without leadership or direction.

The three separate party congress meetings concluded their sessions by nominating the new 22-(25-?)member Central Committee in three lists, which were subsequently amalgamated and put forth by the CPT leadership. The Third Congress had elected Charoen Wan-Ngam ("Mitr Samanant") secretary general. According to one Thai government report, his death (either in 1979 or early 1982) led to the Fourth Congress choice of Pracha Tanyapaibul. Thai National Security Council Secretary General Prasong Soonsiri expressed skepticism about the election of Pracha Tanyapaibul, questioning whether such a person existed or whether the CPT leadership wanted a name tag as a cover-up for its irreparable rift and inability to agree on the selection of a leader.

Another report surmised that Pracha Tanyapaibul was the same person as Prasit Tapienthong ("Comrade Sin"), a pro-Chinese but ethnically Thai member of the CPT Politburo. Other observers believe that Pracha Tanyapaibul is in fact the nom de guerre for Politburo member Thong Chaemsi. (*FEER*, 17 September, p. 14.) General Ophat Rattanasin, commander of the Special Branch Police, reported in October that the CPT had appointed three Politburo members as joint secretaries general and that earlier reports that Pracha Tanyapaibul was appointed were wrong. He said the three Politburo members named were Thong Chaemsi, Wirat Angkhathawon ("Chang Yuan"), and Comrade "Khap." General Ophat Rattanasin said that the CPT had leaked the rumor about the appointment of Pracha Tanyapaibul, who did not exist, as a trick to prevent the authorities from knowing the identity of the secretaries general. He said the Thai authorities were investigating the background of Comrade Khap. All that is known about him is that he is a Thai, not more than 40 years old. Thong Chaemsi is a Thai of Vietnamese extraction, and Wirat Angkhathawon, who has lived in Kunming since 1979, is a Thai of Chinese ancestry. (*FBIS*, 3 November.)

In May, the Internal Security Operations Command (ISOC) of the Thai government issued a White Paper on the internal workings of the CPT. The White Paper reported that two major groups have been fighting for dominance within the CPT Politburo, one under Wirat Angkhathawon, a pro-Chinese hard-liner, and the other led by Damri Ruangsutham, under arrest by government authorities since April 1981. Wirat Angkhathawon's faction includes a large number of ethnic Chinese. Damri Ruangsutham's faction, which supports a more moderate post-Mao Chinese policy, includes the Hmong hill people and other minorities living in the north. Thong Chaemsi, a moderate whose base of support is in the northern region, has seen his influence increase markedly, according to the White Paper, although it is not clear which of the two factions he supports. The White Paper concluded by noting that the CPT's leadership core is approaching total collapse. (Ibid., 13 May.)

The collapse was illustrated by the 6 September defection of Udom Srisuwan, a founder and Politburo member of the CPT and chairman of the CCPDF. Udom Srisuwan, 62, also known under the aliases of Uncle Som, Comrade Su, and Comrade Saha, is the highest-ranking CPT member to surrender to the government. (*Bangkok Post*, 8 September.) Udom Srisuwan was named to the Politburo in 1976 and reportedly became acting secretary general of the CPT when the post's previous holder, Charoen Wan-Ngam, died or was incapacitated in Beijing two years ago. Udom Srisuwan may have become disgruntled with the party when he was not named secretary general during the Fourth Congress. Hailing the surrender as a sign of the extent of the rift within the CPT, Army Commander in Chief Gen. Prayut Charumani said he believed Udom Srisuwan was upset after he was not elected party secretary general because of his pro-Hanoi line, which is opposed by the predominantly pro-Beijing faction within the Politburo.

After his surrender, Udom Srisuwan told officials that he had decided to defect because of his disillusionment with the pro-Chinese influence within the party. Documents released by the CPT after the Fourth Congress showed that the party still emphasized its armed struggle based in the rural areas in line with the Maoist strategy of using the rural areas to strangle the urban areas. Udom Srisuwan, on the other hand, favored a shift to an urban struggle.

Another government source said that Udom Srisuwan was not elected to the party's top post partly because of skepticism among the rank and file over his loyalty to the party. Udom was arrested during the Sarit Thannarat administration, and during his detention he allegedly developed friendly relations with senior police officers of the Special Branch Division, including Maj. Gen. Ari Karibut, to whom he surrendered. Some of his opponents even charged him with being a "fifth column" for the government.

National Security Council Secretary General Prasong Soonsiri said that Udom Srisuwan's information showed that the CPT was at its lowest point since the party first announced its policy of armed struggle in 1965. "Only about five percent of the CPT leadership still hangs on to the armed struggle tactic. They are mostly old leaders who were trained in China some 30 years ago." (Ibid., 27 November.)

Udom Srisuwan's defection was followed on 1 December by the surrender of 250 armed insurgents and their 750 dependents and unarmed sympathizers from the mountainous area of the northeast. The surrender represented the total collapse of Zone 444 and undermined the strength of neighboring zones. (*FEER*, 10 December, pp. 15–16.) The secretary of Zone 444, Sawat Mahisaya, explained that the defection arose from widespread dissatisfaction over the outcome of the CPT's Fourth Congress. "The result of the congress did not represent the voice of the Thai people," he said in reference to the failure of the Chinese-dominated leadership to redirect the course of the revolution in conformity with changes in Thai society (ibid., 10 December, p. 16).

This wholesale defection means that the People's Liberation Army of Thailand, the party's armed wing, now has as few as 750 main force guerrillas in the northeast, down from 2,300–2,500 three years earlier (ibid., 10 December, p. 16). Twenty-seven days later, more than 2,000 communist hill people surrendered to government forces in northern Thailand. General Arthit Kamlang-ek, the army's commander in chief presided over the surrender ceremony in Tak province (*NYT*, 28 December).

Udom Srisuwan's surrender led Lt. Gen. Prayoon Bunnag, assistant army chief of staff for operations, to proclaim that the government has scored a "complete victory" over the CPT. He attributed the government's victory to successful implementation of political and military campaigns, starting in 1980. He said that most of the CPT's armed factions had been crushed and a large number of military supplies seized, while major rifts had taken place within the CPT itself. The United Front members have also withdrawn their support for the Communists. He pinpointed major regions where suppression campaigns had been successful. (1) Major CPT bases at Doi Pha Mon, Doi Yao, Doi Phachi, Phu Miang, Phu Khat, Hin Longka, and South Umphang in the north had been destroyed and large amounts of military supplies seized. (2) In the northeast, all major CPT strongholds at Phu Sang and Phu Khiao and the adjoining zonal line of the Second and Third Army Regions had been wiped out in the past year. Pressure was now being exerted on small armed groups. (3) In the central plains, the First Army Region had destroyed bases in Kanchanaburi, Phetchaburi, and Prachin Buri provinces and had been successful in reducing communist influence over the villagers. The First Army had also been successful in thwarting the CPT's united fronts, particularly with its plans to develop urban slum areas. (4) In the south, the Fourth Army Region had seized a major CPT stronghold, Camp 508 in Surat Thani, and the Communist Party of Malaya base at Khao Namkhang. (*Bangkok Post*, 28 September.)

Counterinsurgency. Throughout 1982, the government credited its new anti-insurgency strategy for defections from the CPT. The counterinsurgency campaign puts greater emphasis on political over military operations and on the development of "democracy" as the best means of curtailing the communist movement. The strategy is contained in Order no. 65/2525 issued on 17 May by Prime Minister Prem Tinsulanond. The order calls for the improvement of social conditions and for the purge of corrupt officials. The new order builds on Order no. 66/2523 of 1980, which first emphasized political means for countering insurgency. The prime minister reaffirmed that he will continue the policy of not punishing defectors. The government pledged to guarantee the civil rights and safety of defectors. In 1982, that continued pledge of amnesty appeared to be effective in encouraging defections. Order no. 65/2525 provides the opportunity for all political groupings, including the CPT, to express their political views "within the framework of the country's constitutional law."

The decline in CPT strength in 1982 and the desire of Gen. Arthit Kamlang-ek, army commander in chief, to make the ISOC more efficient have led to the restructuring of the nation's primary anti-insurgency organization. General Arthit Kamlang-ek announced that a number of independent and scattered intelligence agencies will be reduced or consolidated under four centers: the Civic Affairs Center, the Intelligence Coordinating Center, the Operations Center, and the Support Center. The self-defense and development village program, the Thai defense volunteers program, and the hill-tribe project called Center 113 will come under the Civil Affairs Center. The Intelligence Coordinating Center will have under it the Karunyathep Center, the Vietnamese refugee operation called Center 114, and all intelligence work. The Operations Center will coordinate work with the civilian, police, and military center and the Army Operations Center. The Support Center will deal with personnel strength, logistical support, communications, and finance. (*FBIS*, 24 November.)

External Support for Insurgency. In addition to the mass defections and leadership collapse, the CPT suffered in 1982 from a decline in outside support. Chinese Communist Party leader Hu Yaobang announced at the party's congress in September that his country would not back communist insurgencies in Southeast Asia. "The success of the revolution in each country depends on the ripeness of conditions for it and the people's support for the line and policies of the country's communist party. To issue orders or run things for others from outside is absolutely impermissible." (*Asiaweek*, 11 September, p. 11.)

Hu Yaobang's statement corroborated that China was no longer supporting the CPT. The Chinese leadership viewed better relations with the Association of Southeast Asian Nations to be in the best interest of the Four Modernizations program. Moreover, the Chinese desire to retain good relations with the Thai government so that the Chinese can continue to send supplies to Kampuchean rebels through Thai territory. Both Laotian and Vietnamese support for the CPT were negligible in 1982.

The influence of the CPT in the north and northeast, formerly the stronghold of the party, dissipated in 1982 because of defections, reduced support from neighboring nations, internal dissension, and the presence of the Thai military on the border of Kampuchea. The removal of the headquarters of the CPT from Nan province to the southern province of Surat Thani symbolized the declining role of the party. Defections reduced the number of guerrillas in the northeast from 4,000 in 1979 to 1,300 in mid-1982. (*Asia Record*, July, p. 9.)

Following the Fourth Congress, a breakaway pro-Vietnamese faction of the CPT led by Suwit Niamsa ("Commander Yut") is said to have set up headquarters in Udon Thani in the northeast. Suwit is also reported to have offered to surrender if he would not be detained for questioning and if the government would find him a job. Major General Ophat Rattanasin said that the government could not accept the conditions but indicated that if Suwit did surrender, he would be released after interrogation if he had no criminal record. (*Bangkok Post*, 23 October.)

Malaysian chairman of the Regional Border Committee Maj. Gen. Datuk Hashim declared that the Malaysian government is ready to cooperate with Thailand in suppressing Muslim separatist movements that use Malaysian soil as the springboard to carry out subversive activities in Thailand. The senior Malaysian military official made the assurance during a meeting of delegates from the two countries at the Regional Border Committee office in August. Major General Hashim said that his government had not backed any terrorist movements to undermine the stability of the Thai government. Fourth Army Region Commander Lt. Gen. Han Linanon said that certain Muslim separatist movements, financially supported by some Middle Eastern countries, were using Malaysian soil as a springboard to launch armed operations in Thailand. The Thai delegation informed the Malaysian team of its stand against combined military operations between the two countries on Thai soil. General Han accompanied General Hashim and his team in visits to two major strongholds of the Communist Party of Malaya that fell to Thai troops during a large-scale suppression drive in July. (*Nation Review*, 4 August, p. 6.)

Northern Illinois University   Clark D. Neher

Vietnam

The Vietnamese communist movement grew out of the nationalistic anticolonial sentiment that began to develop throughout Indochina after the arrival of the French, about the time of the American Civil War, a sentiment that took on political significance as it began to organize itself at the turn of the century. Initially, this anticolonialism was found chiefly among diffuse bands of Confucian scholars and a scattering of other elements—what the French termed "political tendencies." Gradually these coalesced into two main streams, which later came to be called the Nationalists and the Communists. The latter included Marxist-Leninists *cum* Stalinists, Trotskyites, and, for a period, a youthful brand of indigenous Marxists who followed what today would be called national communism. The struggle between Nationalists and Communists in the 1920s did involve ideology, but primarily it was organizational.

After a brilliant start in 1930, the Indochina Communist Party later in the decade degenerated during a grim period of danger and frustration, and Vietnamese communism came perilously close to extinction. The cause was saved, if that is not too strong a word, by World War II. The momentous and decisive war years provided a needed opportunity for the party and also set a course of history that would serve it well. The war killed colonialism in Asia, a fact that all but the French grasped. It destroyed much of the old social order, including that which had predated the French. Most of all, it engendered the anarchy that only the Communists were prepared to exploit.

The party seized power in the vacuum that Hanoi became at Japan's surrender, but was unable to consolidate its gain. The long, bitter Viet Minh War followed, finally ending at Dien Bien Phu and Geneva in 1954. Vietnamese communist victory should have delivered the country to the Communists, but, they believed, they were cheated out of it by their erstwhile allies, China and the USSR, pursuing their own interests. The goal for Hanoi then became unification of all Vietnam under its banner, which it finally achieved in the spring of 1975.

Population. 52 million (1982 est.)

Party. Vietnamese Communist Party (Dang Cong San Viet Nam; VCP)

Founded. 1930 (as Indochina Communist Party)

Membership. 1,727,784 (1 April)

Chairman. Vacant (since death of Ho Chi Minh)

Secretary General. Le Duan

Politburo. 13 full members: Le Duan, Truong Chinh (president, Council of State), Pham Van Dong (premier), Pham Hung, Le Duc Tho, Van Tien Dung (defense minister), Chu Huy Man (vice-president, Council of State), Vo Chi Cong, Vo Van Kiet, Do Muoi, Le Duc Anh, Nguyen Duc Tam; 2 alternate members: Nguyen Co Thach (foreign minister), Dong Sy Nguyen

Secretariat. 10 members: Le Duan, Le Duc Tho, Vo Chi Cong, Nguyen Duc Tam, Nguyen Lam (chairman, State Planning Commission), Le Quang Dao, Hoang Tung, Nguyen Thanh Binh, Tran Kien, Tran Xuan Bach

Central Committee. 116 full and 36 alternate members

Last Congress. Fifth, 27–31 March, in Hanoi

Auxiliary Organizations. Fatherland Front, Hoang Quoc Viet, president; Ho Chi Minh Communist Youth Union, Dang Quoc Bao, secretary general

Publications. *Nhan Dan* (The people), the VCP daily; *Tap Chi Cong San* (Communist review), VCP theoretical monthly; *Quon Doi Nhan Dan* (The people's army), the army newspaper

Party Internal Affairs. The most important event of the year for the party was the convening of the Fifth Party Congress. It met in Hanoi in Ba Dinh Hall, across from the Ho Chi Minh mausoleum, from 27 through 31 March. It was attended by 1,033 Vietnamese delegates, 32 foreign communist party delegates, and representatives of fifteen other foreign "revolutionary movements." Ranking foreign representative was Soviet Politburo member Mikhail Gorbachev. China was not invited.

Congress Chairman Truong Chinh opened the congress on 27 March with a welcoming address; the afternoon was devoted to Secretary General Le Duan's political report, Prime Minister Pham Van Dong's five-year plan (1981–1985) report, and the party organization report by cadre chief Le Duc Tho. The next two days were devoted to speeches by lesser figures and foreign visitors, a total of about 55 in two days. The final day saw the election of the new party leadership. The theme of the congress—as expressed by its official slogan—was "All for the socialist fatherland and the people's happiness."

The convening of the congress in March came after repeated postponements. Initially, in mid-1980, the expectation was that it would be held in February 1981 (the congresses are to meet every five years, according to party bylaws). The ninth plenum in December 1980 set September 1981 as the date. This was postponed in July 1981 by the Secretariat, acting on Politburo orders. The tenth plenum in late October and early November 1981, dubbed the "marathon plenum" because it lasted a record 25 days, ordered the start of the delegate election process but did not fix a date for the congress itself. The eleventh plenum in early December 1981 announced that the congress would convene in "early 1982." Provincial-level congresses to choose delegates were staged quickly in December and January, apparently in expectation that the congress would convene in February. Finally, in early February 1982, the twelfth plenum set the date for the following month. Thus, four plenums met in advance of the congress and were primarily concerned with it. Three of them appear to have been devoted entirely to drawing up an acceptable list of Central Committee members and drafting coherent policy statements.

The congress officially had an economic orientation and, in fact, was termed by some speakers an "economic congress." About 400 of the delegates chosen (40 percent) were in some way associated with the economic and production sectors, as opposed to 12 percent at the Fourth Congress (1976).

The mood of the Fifth Congress was quite different from that of the Fourth Congress. The assurance, even bravado, that marked the last congress was gone. One high-level official after another addressed his constituency and the party with grim and candidly critical words. Each presented a catalog of complaints, dwelling particularly on organizational shortcomings, cadre and managerial ineptitude, widespread personal misbehavior, and the general decline of quality among party personnel. Blame was levied at all levels of the party, from the basic units to the Central Committee. Only the Politburo was excluded. No less a figure than Pham Van Dong himself told the congress of the dire straits faced by Vietnam. His speech was studded with harsh words such as "country facing acute problems . . . enormous waste of manpower and materials . . . subjectivism and haste . . . failure to define a strategy for socialist industrialization."

Secretary General Le Duan's political report, the most important document at the congress, contained a long litany of complaints, but was much less bombastic than most of his earlier speeches and writings. It was as though he himself were in political trouble. His report announced no significant policy change, but none was expected. A party congress tends to be a ceremonial affair with premium placed on unity and harmony, not a forum for announcing major policy changes. (These usually come in some unlikely setting; the first Hanoi pronouncement agreeing to the Paris talks, for instance, came in the foreign minister's toast to some visiting Outer Mongolians.)

Le Duan singled out China as the chief villain responsible for Vietnam's present plight. Another speaker cited lingering effects of the war: French colonialism; the outside world in general and the United States in particular; counterrevolutionaries; corrupt bureaucrats, "opportunists, exploiters, traffickers, speculators, embezzlers, bribe-takers, bullies, and those with paralyzed revolutionary will." Also, for the first time, the Central Committee admitted its role: "The party Central Committee wishes to criticize itself sternly before this congress." Some of this, of couse, is standard *khiem thao* (self-criticism), although there did seem to be a venom in Le Duan's language not often used in such assemblages.

References to Moscow were effusive. The USSR, said Le Duan, is the "cornerstone" of Vietnamese foreign policy, the country's "strongest and firmest ally." He criticized those party members who failed to understand (or support) this intimate relationship but suggested that the USSR might not be meeting its obligations fully in the present "all-sided cooperation" arrangement.

The major points made by Le Duan in assessing the current Vietnamese position were these: Vietnam is under great threat from China; it is striving to overcome the residue of war, the vestiges of colonialism, and to meet its responsibilities in Kampuchea; many mistakes have been made by party and state alike. The society's two major tasks remain unchanged: to build socialism and to defend the fatherland (stand "combat-ready"). Within these two strategic tasks are four finite ones: to meet the country's basic economic needs and necessities, to develop the economy, to transform the South in socioeconomic terms, and to meet defense requirements. This involves achieving the "correct balance" between agriculture and industry, as in allocation of resources, and the parallel development of national and local economies, that is large- and small-sized economic enterprises. There must be reorganization of the production mechanism. In national defense planning, carefuller attention must be paid to the needs of the civilian economy. A new fiscal and domestic trade system is required and must be established. Planning and managerial work must be improved and the nation's science and technology capacity increased. There must be more capital accumulation and additional redistribution of labor (meaning expanded New Economic Zones). Finally, relations within Indochina (with Laos and Kampuchea) must be expanded and the close association with the USSR maintained. For the most part, these prescriptions were a continuation of previously enunciated policy, with perhaps a slight new tilt toward agriculture in the never ending struggle for resources between agriculture and industry.

Finally, in the psychological dimension, Le Duan called for raising the party's "fighting capacity." The party is beleaguered, he indicated, beset by "enemies of all kinds at home and abroad" who are making a "spearhead attack" on the party in order to wreck it ideologically and organizationally. The party must be strengthened internally, must improve its leadership work at all levels, and, above all, must do a better job of communicating its ideology to the masses.

Pham Van Dong's state plan report was replete with statistics, which, if they are to be believed, indicate that Vietnam's curve of economic decline has flattened out and possibly the economy is beginning to improve.

In the next five-year plan (1981–1985), major production goals per annum include 17 million tons of grain, 5.5 billion kwh of electricity, 8 to 9 million tons of coal, 350,000 to 400,000 tons of phosphate fertilizer, and 2 million tons of cement.

Pham Van Dong notwithstanding, the actual status of Vietnam's current five-year plan is not at all clear. It appears to be in limbo. Despite great attention to it at the Fifth Party Congress, there was no indication that the plan—now approaching the midpoint of its alloted time—actually has been implemented. For the most part, the system seems to operate on annual plans drawn from the five-year plan.

Party personnel chief Le Duc Tho's report, which in official parlance was concerned with "party building," was as usual a technical and somewhat tedious recapitulation of party strengths, weaknesses, and tasks, chiefly involving administrative activity, internal structure, cadre and member behavior, and the general effort by the party to be central to all activity within the society.

The membership of the VCP, as of 1 March, stood at 1,727,784, compared with about 1,553,500 in late 1976. This is broken down into 35,146 basic level (or primary) units (34,545 in 1976); these in turn are broken down into 120,654 chapters or cells (94,846 in 1976). Of the 1.7 million current members, some 200,000 are probationary, meaning they have been admitted to membership in the previous twelve months.

Since the Fourth Party Congress, Le Duc Tho said 86,000 members had been purged (30,000 during 1981 alone). This figure of 86,000 has been generally accepted as the number of party members purged in postwar years and is being used by the Western wire services, *Pravda*, and Radio Beijing. However, statistics published in connection with the Fifth Party Congress indicate the figure is much higher. According to party publications, from 1976 to 1982 a total of 562,500 new members were added. Yet the net increase during this time was only 174,284, meaning that 388,216 were removed from the rolls. Some of these may have been because of death, but the vast majority must have been purge victims.

Le Duc Tho indicated that of the 1.7 million members, 500,000 (29 percent) have high school diplomas; 200,000 (12 percent) were educated beyond high school, either at universities or post-high school vocational schools. Thus, 41 percent of the party have high school educations or above. Some one million members are engaged in educational work at present. About 300 cadres were sent to the USSR for party organizational training during 1981.

Tho's report, beyond the statistical information, was a blunt and wide-ranging document on the internal condition of the party. He employed a long string of socialist expletives: weakness, lack of determination, sluggishness, degraded behavior. Party members guilty of exploitation, "trafficking," speculation, embezzlement, or accepting bribes are to be purged.

The party cadre, the Politburo's favorite whipping boy, was again singled out for special treatment. Tho (as well as Le Duan) found the cadres often "conservative, lazy, backbiting, bureaucratic, irresponsible, dogmatic, undemocratic, high-handed, and paternalistic." Many no longer exemplified revolutionary heroism, while others have lost their militant spirit or neglect their party responsibilities. Still others have become "common criminals."

Tho acknowledged, for the first time in such a forum, the existence of serious factionalism among rank-and-file party members. He made extensive references to disagreement over party policy matters and to the existence of viewpoints involving internal security, ideology, and social problems that "incorrectly reflect the party line." Factionalism is the curse of all Sinic political systems, including Vietnam's, and *bung di* (faction bashing) is the accepted style of political infighting. Hence, Tho's discussion of factionalism is important only to the extent that it indicates the leadership has been "ineffective" in damping it down, which in turn suggests that the party line is on the defensive within the party. Many of the other speeches at the congress were equally critical. In part perhaps, this was beneficial for the leadership, in that the enunciation of complaints acted as a safety valve to relieve some of the pressure within the party.

The most dramatic development to emerge from the congress was the reshuffle of the Central Committee and changes in the Politburo. Most of these, however, had less to do with *bung di* than with age and diminishing capacity.

The Fourth Party Congress Politburo consisted of seventeen members (fourteen regular and three alternates). Six of these were dropped: General Vo Nguyen Giap; economic chief for motivational and emulation activities Le Thanh Nghi; security chief Tran Quoc Hoan; Foreign Minister Nguyen Duy Trinh and the two "city chiefs" (party secretaries), southerner Nguyen Van Linh (Ho Chi Minh City) and Le Van Luu Luong (Hanoi), who was also a major figure in cadre personnel (promotions). Four were added: Col. Gen. Le Duc Anh, Kampuchean command; Nguyen Duc Tam, party personnel officer for economic cadres, who also appears to have some Soviet connections; Maj. Gen. Dong Sy Nguyen, former building czar and apparently a troubleshooter on the state side; and Foreign Minister Nguyen Co thach.

The Politburo's enduring "circle of five" remained: Secretary General Le Duan; chief ideologue Truong Chinh, party ramrod Le Duc Tho, southern czar Pham Hung, and Prime Minister Pham Van Dong.

These five collectively are the unquestioned rulers of Vietnam today. Their average age is 74; hence, government by septuagenarians in Vietnam continues.

All of those Politburo members rated as "front-ranking" following the February 1980 party-state shake-up also remained: Sen. Gen. Van Tien Dung, Sen. Gen. Chu Huy Man, agitprop chief To Huu, and the party's leading economist-theoretician, Do Muoi (moved from alternate to full member).

The three-man "southern mafia" met a mixed fate: Nguyen Van Linh was removed, Vo Van Kiet (internal security) was promoted from alternate to full member, and the durable Vo Chi Cong (the leading southern figure if Pham Hung is considered "national") remained.

The new Politburo is smaller, thirteen regular members plus two alternates. Its average age is lower, about 68, as opposed to 72 for the previous Politburo. Vo Van Kiet at 50 becomes the "baby" of the Politburo. The party chairmanship, vacant since Ho Chi Minh's death in 1969, was again not filled, signaling continuation of the collective leadership at the Politburo level.

Departures from the Politburo should not be viewed as matters of disgrace. Most were without political meaning. Giap probably stepped down of his own volition, although he may have been subjected to new pressure since he has been withdrawing from active duty in stages for several years. He and others may in fact have come privately to believe it was wise to depart if they wished to preserve their image for history; that is, they heeded the advice traditionally ascribed to the Royal Navy: When the water reaches the upper decks, follow the rats. Giap continues to hold a sinecure overseeing development of Vietnam's science and technology sectors. Trinh is in very poor health (he was also dropped from the Central Committee). Hoan is also in bad health, and his age would prevent him from carrying out the vigorous activity required of a security chief in Vietnam today. Nghi clearly was the number-one scapegoat of the congress. He was sacrificed to economic failure, for which he bore some responsibility but hardly major blame. Luong, a Le Duc Tho protégé, appears to be a victim of the factional infighting between the Le Duc Tho and Le Duan factions.

At the Central Committee level, there was considerable change. The Fourth Congress had elected 101 Central Committee members plus 32 alternates. The Fifth Congress raised this to 116 members and 36 alternates. The congress carried over 85 members from the Fourth Congress and dropped 48. Thus, the Fifth Congress added 67 new members.

One characteristic of the new Central Committee, as noted above, is that representation of those from the economic sector increased from 12 percent to 40 percent. Apparently, the average age of the new Central Committee is somewhat lower. Provincial-level party secretaries also gained a presence, a total of fifteen as opposed to two or three in the previous committee. The southern "old guard" was drastically reduced, a process that has been going on for the past seven years. Military representatives increased slightly. Finally there was a slight reduction in those holding both high-level and state positions. Prior to the congress, 25 of the 42 cabinet-level portfolios were held by Central Committee members; that figure has been reduced to 20.

The picture that emerges from this Politburo–Central Committee reshuffle is continued stability at the top (or perhaps more correctly, apparent stability and an effort to portray and assert stability) and considerable instability and turmoil at the middle-level. The upper cadre level, just below the Central Committee, probably is in a condition of great turmoil and uncertainty, although there is no specific evidence to support this.

The most important development in this respect, more significant than changes of individuals, is the loss of certitude by the collective leadership, its faltering sense of its ability to cure the ills of the Vietnamese body politic. This is because of (or perhaps due to) deep divisions over what exactly should be the proper remedial measures. The split is not clearly defined; rather it is a highly amorphous one, constantly shifting. Nor is it ordinary factionalism since there is more doubt and less dogmatism on both sides than is normally the case. This division manifests itself chiefly in the economic sector (see below).

The great danger faced by party leaders, and by Vietnam for that matter, is disunity, which has always been its Achilles' heel. Disunity at the top could trigger a bloody power struggle. It could encourage the rise of the resistance. Possibly it could provoke Chinese involvement. The Politburo and top leadership maintain unity chiefly through appeals utilizing patriotism and fear. In this, the Chinese threat and the war in Kampuchea serve them well. The Fifth Congress was designed in part to enhance and demonstrate that unity. General apathy among party members also serves the cause of unity since it prevents members from becoming excessively aroused over party failures and the need for change. Almost certainly, the present Politburo will remain united. If it does so, Vietnam and its present system will continue to be reasonably invulnerable from catastrophic kinds of change.

Outside observers differed widely on the general meaning of the Fifth Congress. It was variously interpreted as (1) a triumph of realism; (2) a staged party shake-up intended to paper over past failures and throw up a few scapegoats but do nothing that would affect unity or leadership continuity; (3) a simple personnel shuffle at the Central Committee level to eliminate deadwood and invigorate the apparat; (4) a geriatric shuffle that managed to infuse some slightly newer blood; and (5) a struggle between left communism and right communism but of such a nature that it was difficult to determine which was which. A Tass reporter found the congress "businesslike and creative"; China labeled it "Le Duan's gasping lament." There was truth in all of these judgments.

The enduring significance of the congress probably will prove to be that involving the leadership. For the first time, top party officials, many of them original founders still in power, addressed themselves to their own mortality. The movement that resulted was hesitant and limited, but even so was clearly the start of a generational transfer of power. True, the individuals initiated into the ruling circle are not young—most are in their fifties—but since the major Politburo figures are in their seventies, they do represent the next generation. Still in the wings of power is the third generation, the grandchildren of Ho Chi Minh.

Domestic Affairs.   The general condition in which Vietnam found itself during 1982 was a magnified reflection of the party gathering. Indeed, as one observer put it, the Fifth Congress held up a dark mirror of troubles in which the society could view itself.

The year was a grim one: a nation unable to feed itself, surrounded by enemies, bogged down in a war in the west, ever threatened by a new attack from the north, dependent on a distant, never-trusted ally; a society with a failed economic system, lashed by social pathology, its once confident vanguard in disarray, its anachronistic leadership a dwindling band of elders.

For the ordinary Vietnamese, the focus of attention throughout the year was not on the politics of the Politburo, but on mundane economic matters—the scramble for food and other necessities of life that are perennially in short supply and a challenge to obtain even when they are available. Although difficult to measure objectively, it does seem that Vietnamese economic conditions did not worsen during the year and, in some respects—such as agricultural production—may have improved slightly.

Even accepting the most optimistic estimate, however, the Vietnamese economic scene was depressingly grim. The rice ration is now down to about five kilos per month. Food availability, while as equitably distributed as the transportation system can permit, amounts to 2,000 calories per day, just about minimal nutritional need. Grain production this year possibly may reach 16 million metric tons (versus 15 million in 1981 and 14.3 million in 1980). If, as is more likely, the yield is somewhere between 15 and 16 million metric tons, this will mean that production is not much more than in 1970. But the population since 1970 has increased by nearly 15 percent. Each year Vietnam must feed 1.5 million more people than in the previous year.

Inflation is running about 200 percent a year, whereas for years in the North there was none at all. Inflation is due to a heavy internal and external debt, an increased money supply, and one of the world's worst trade imbalances. Vietnam has lost an estimated $4 billion in gold, silver, and jewels since 1976 via the exiting boat people. Remittances to relatives from these same refugees now constitutes the country's chief hard-currency source.

This economy is distorted, particularly in the labor and transportation sectors by the war in Kampuchea. The Chinese claim that Vietnam's military budget is 50 percent of the total state budget, or about $5.6 billion. Soviet economic and military assistance is currently running at $4 to $6 billion (depending on how costs are fixed), but even so the war represents an enormous drain on the Vietnamese economic system.

The system also suffers from high unemployment (or underemployment) because factories operate at only about 15 percent of capacity (the lowest rate in the North during the war was 65 percent) because of a lack of raw materials and spare parts for machinery. Since this is a narrow sector of the economy, it has only limited meaning, although it does affect the all-important agricultural sector.

Per capita income is probably about $160 per year—a kilo of meat costs the average worker two weeks' wages—hence there is low purchasing power. Worker morale, in factory and commune alike, is low, marked by cynicism and disillusionment. The party labels this moral decay a "problem in the quality of socialism," which manifests itself not only in inefficient production but in crime, malfeasance, and what is called "collective corruption," that is, production activities outside the official plan. The party newspaper reported that in the last quarter of 1980 some 2,563 communes and other state enterprises operating in one 15-province sector suffered a total financial loss of $120 million, chiefly due to corruption and mismanagement.

The party pressed forward with its efforts to "break the machine" in the South, as the social reconstruction program there is called. Collectivization of southern agriculture, which Le Duan reported to the Fifth Congress was only 9 percent accomplished, was officially pressed but in actuality apparently was treated only with token gestures. As of late 1982, it appears that the issue of collectivization of southern agriculture is a standoff between the party and southern farmers. The party insists that collectivization will be completed by 1987 but not at the expense of production, which seems an insurmountable task.

The refugee exodus, in the form of the "boat people," continued during the year, but preliminary year-end estimates fixed the total at somewhat below the 1981 outflow of 75,000 and the 1980 outflow of 76,000; the 1982 estimate was from 10 to 15 percent less than these figures.

Foreign Policy. In external affairs, the VCP had two overriding concerns during the year. It wrestled with the war in Kampuchea and its ever greater repercussions throughout the region, and with the changed and changing relations with its principal, and only close ally, the USSR.

The Kampuchean scene in 1982, both militarily and diplomatically, was marked by a great deal of activity both by the Vietnamese and others, although much of this was self-canceling when viewed in terms of decisive outcome. Early in the year, there were several spasms of intense military activity by the Vietnamese army searching for the various resistance elements, but these came to little. Year-end predictions were for a renewed "dry season" offensive in the spring of 1983.

During the year, Hanoi moved to assume a new public position with respect to its relationship to Kampuchea and events there. It was a shift from its posture of several years' standing that Vietnamese activities and events themselves in Kampuchea had created an "irreversible situation." The new posture was that the Kampuchean war was over. By the end of the year, this had become the image projected, the new party line. Since mid-1981, the High Command of the People's Army of Vietnam (PAVN) has acknowledged tacitly that it is involved in a protracted conflict in Kampuchea and has sought to reduce the strain on its military establishment. The 200,000 troops in Kampuchea—now reduced to perhaps 140,000—were redeployed into a more tenable military stance. There were fewer military sweeps into guerrilla lairs, greater use of artillery, more static guard duty, and less road patrolling. Military forces concentrated on keeping open the lines of communication, guarding the towns, and building up the fledgling army of Heng Samrin's People's Republic of Kampuchea. In short, the war is being Khmerized. Withdrawal of troops and other measures were not mere Hanoi legerdemain. They were, at least in part, the Politburo's response to the war's unpopularity within the party.

In June, a much touted withdrawal of PAVN forces began. Official and unofficial figures were bandied about. There were reports of fresh troops being sent to Kampuchea as others departed. However, intelligence reports noted that PAVN forces were being reduced steadily from a high of 200,000 during most of 1981 and throughout 1982. What changed was the publicity attending the withdrawal. The year-end estimate of PAVN strength was about 140,000.

"Welcome home" celebrations for PAVN troops returning from Kampuchea in midyear were widely publicized and created an impression that the war there was ending, as far as the Vietnamese were concerned. Within Vietnam, where information is so closely controlled, this probably became a credible claim. Those families with sons still in Kampuchea might know otherwise, but not the general population.

The new party line was that the Vietnamese-Kampuchean "militant solidarity has entered a new stage of development." Hanoi said it would continue to support and assist Kampuchea, in keeping with the treaty of friendship and cooperation and in the spirit of proletarian internationalism, but the tasks of "reviving the nation, and struggling to defend its independence, sovereignty, and territorial integrity" now belong to the Phnom Penh government.

Vietnamese foreign relations outside of the Indochina peninsula were thrown into a condition of incipient anxiety for Hanoi late in the year when the USSR and China began talks in Moscow on outstanding issues. This was seen in Hanoi as possibly the beginning of a new arrangement between the two communist giants that would have deleterious effects on Vietnam.

The talks served to accelerate what had been under way throughout the year, that is, a changed relationship between Hanoi and Moscow. The USSR during the year involved itself deeply in the reorganizational work within the VCP and probably in the changes at the Politburo and Central Committee levels. It also had a hand in the party purge of ethnic Chinese and Vietnamese with Chinese ties, although party officials apparently did not need much encouragement. The USSR not only funds the war in Kampuchea but is largely responsible for the style of combat there, that is, Western style rather than the kind pioneered by General Giap and others. And, as is discussed below, the USSR is deeply involved in the Vietnamese economy—not only keeping it afloat with massive inputs of aid but also in short-run problem solving and long-range economic development planning.

The Soviet delegate to the Fifth Party Congress noted that joint planning by the two countries calls for a doubling of trade by 1985, which chiefly will mean increased exports by Vietnam. He also indicated there would be an increase of Soviet aid during this same period.

Soviet food deliveries to Vietnam are expected to drop in 1982. Shipments in 1980 totaled 1.2 million metric tons and in 1981, 860,000 metric tons. On the other hand, the USSR in 1981 raised the price it charges the Vietnamese for petroleum to that it charges its allies in Eastern Europe. The increase amounted to 400 percent, although Moscow's price is still below the world level.

Moscow-Hanoi relations continued to drift into new and uncertain waters. The changes were more evolutionary than anything else, but still impressive. It is clear that the postwar relationship that began in 1975 has now ended. The twin pillars of the original relationship—Vietnamese dependence and Soviet opportunism—still remain, but clearly some new configuration is beginning to emerge. Relations have become less ad hoc, more systematized. Chiefly this has involved new mechanisms and devices by which day-to-day relations are conducted. Their advent has institutionalized the association, primarily in the economic and military sectors.

Soviet-Vietnamese economic intercourse involves a formidable bureaucratic process in which, at least theoretically, all planning at the state level in Vietnam is done jointly. Moscow seeks to press on Hanoi the Soviet model for economic development and problem solving. Soviet officials serving in Vietnam seem genuinely convinced that only by embracing Soviet methods can Vietnam solve its many economic problems. Their pressure appears to have triggered something of a doctrinal dispute at the Politburo level. One faction led by Premier Pham Van Dong professes optimism about Soviet methods and argues that the Soviet model does lend itself to the Vietnamese scene, while a second faction led by Truong Chinh opposes this view. In any event, the Politburo is obliged to consider both the practical and the political implications of following Moscow's lead.

The Soviet-Vietnamese military relationship, which has become an alliance in all but name, has taken on some of these same characteristics of integration, although this is more difficult to trace because of the natural secrecy associated with security matters. Clearly, some sort of joint military planning now exists. PAVN preparations and outfitting for conventional war now complement Soviet military preparations on the Asian front, implying some coordinated defense planning.

A second emerging characteristic involves what might be called its serviceability. A redesign effort is under way to make the relationship less of a strain, economically on Moscow and psychologically on Vietnam, and generally more efficient. There is a distinct effort to lighten the Soviet economic burden. Soviet trade officials scour Vietnam looking for any sort of exportable goods. Unfortunately, poverty-ridden Vietnam has little to offer. Moscow also is attempting to gain greater managerial authority within the Vietnamese economic system, a most delicate undertaking. Initially, this involved Soviet insistence on greater controls over Soviet economic aid programs. However, since it is Moscow's opinion that the Vietnamese economic malaise is due to deeper causes, these demands also extend to such matters as state maladministration and party personnel shortcomings. Soviet advisers argue that unless fundamental conditions are corrected, Soviet economic aid is simply being poured into a bottomless rathole.

Soviet advisers now concentrate on the need for cadre development and changes in the personnel structure to improve the general level of quality and effectiveness. The USSR in 1982 offered to underwrite a crash training course to produce large numbers of economic cadres quickly. This was accepted, and such a program is now under way, apparently with considerable day-to-day Soviet involvement. Some 335 Vietnamese currently are studying at the USSR's Academy of National Economy and at other Ministry of Higher and Secondary Specialized Education institutes. Another 300 are taking ideological, political, and theoretical training in Marxism-Leninism, party management, and similar subjects at Soviet party institutes in Moscow. Also, Soviet lecturers are becoming faculty members of the VCP Central Committee Higher Party School in Hanoi.

Biography. *Le Duan.* The pre-eminent Vietnamese communist leader since the death of Ho Chi Minh in 1969 has been Le Duan, a durable sceneshifter with a self-effacing personality and a master of the deadly politics of factionalism that mark the perpetual Vietnamese power struggle. While he is more than simply first among equals, he is not a dominating figure in Hanoi, in part perhaps because he does not have a domineering personality.

Always a party man, one of the original 211 founding members, Le Duan has never held a significant state post and thus lacks experience in government administration. Throughout most of his career, his success in climbing the party ladder was attributed to his close hold on Ho's coattails. Much of this rise was at the expense of Truong Chinh, the party's chief theoretician and Le Duan's longtime political rival, although in recent years his major factional foe has become Le Duc Tho.

Le Duan was born 7 April 1908 in Quang Tri province, the son of a successful farmer in what roughly could be called the gentry class. He received the equivalent of a high school education, a considerable accomplishment for a Vietnamese in those days, and went to work for the Vietnam Railway Company in Hanoi as a clerk. There, in the late 1920s, he became politicized through association with communist and nationalist organizers working among railway employees. He joined the Indochina Communist Party when it was formed in 1930. A year later, the French colonial authorities arrested him and sentenced him to twenty years on Poule Condor (Con Son) Island. He was released in 1936 as part of an amnesty program ordered by the Popular Front government, which had come to power in Paris. He continued his party organizational work until 1940 when he was jailed as part of a general roundup of leftists launched by the French Sûreté at the outbreak of World War II. He was released at the end of the war by the departing Japanese.

Le Duan's contribution to the Viet Minh War was chiefly party work in the South, which was something of a backwater in the struggle against the French. However, this did permit him to establish a political base and a constituency among the Southerners that served him well later.

After the Viet Minh War, Le Duan gained stature by taking on the task of harnessing the party organization in the field of agriculture, with a goal of increased production. Most of his fellow high-level communist leaders were middle- or upper-class urbanites with no experience in farming and not much interest in it. Le Duan picked up the task of social organization work in the countryside after the disastrous initial efforts by Truong Chinh (and Ho) to collectivize agriculture, a task he pushed through to successful conclusion by the late 1950s. He became party secretary general (with Ho as party chairman) at the Third Congress in 1960.

Throughout the Vietnam war, Le Duan was chief policymaker for the struggle in the South. He supervised the formation of the special party unit there called the People's Revolutionary Party as well as the united front organization, the National Liberation Front. Initially, he was identified with what loosely could be called the Chinese strategic approach, which was opposed by General Vo Nguyen Giap and other military figures. This strategy proved unsuccessful, and Le Duan was somewhat discredited but managed to survive, in part because the Giap strategy implemented in the mid-1960s did not prove successful either.

After the war, Le Duan undertook the task of supervising the collectivization of southern agriculture, which is still painfully under way. In the never-ending Vietnamese political infighting, Le Duan in recent years has attempted to emulate his model, Ho Chi Minh, and hold himself aloof from the minutia of day-to-day politics. In this he has been reasonably successful. During 1982, he underwent extensive medical treatment for a liver ailment in Moscow.

University of California at Berkeley   Douglas Pike

EASTERN EUROPE AND THE SOVIET UNION

Introduction

The year 1982 was of signal importance first for the Soviet Union and by inference for Eastern Europe. Any consideration of the meaning of the most significant events of the year should be made with the full realization that no definitive conclusions can be reached without the benefit of hindsight.

Soviet Union. When Leonid Brezhnev died on 10 November at the age of 75, an era of Soviet and world history came to an end. Less than three days later, the Central Committee unanimously elected former KGB chief Yuri Vladimirovich Andropov, 68, member of the party Politburo and Secretariat, the general secretary of the Communist Party of the Soviet Union (CPSU). It was a remarkably swift and for many people unexpected changing of the guard. The "Andropov era" started rather abruptly, reflecting simultaneously the Leninist continuity of party governance and the swift, idiosyncratic changes that the new ruler introduced.

The words "continuity" and "change" require elucidation. Despite everything that distinguished Brezhnev and Andropov in their previous personal lives and careers, they served the Soviet system and never considered changing it fundamentally, going against what the founding father, Lenin, had established in 1917 and the following few years. The nature of this continuity was explained by Henry A. Kissinger in a recent article: "The [Soviet] leaders one in fact encounters are tough, ruthless and persistent. But they have originated no profound initiatives; they have usually avoided great risks. They have expanded into vacuums created by irresolution or weakness." In the second volume of his *Memoirs*, the former secretary of state made the same point more sharply: "Like all Soviet postwar leaders, Brezhnev [one could add here Andropov] *sees the US at once as rival, mortal threat, model, source of assistance and partner in physical survival*. These conflicting impulses make the motivations of Brezhnev's policy toward us ambivalent. On the one hand, he no doubt wants *to go down in history as the leader who brought peace and a better life to Russia*. This *requires conciliatory and cooperative policies* toward us. *Yet, he remains a convinced Communist who sees politics as a struggle with an ultimate winner*; he intends the Soviet Union to *be that winner*. His recurrent efforts to draw us into condominium-type arrangements—most notably his proposal for a nuclear non-aggression pact—are intended both to safeguard peace and to undermine our alliances and other associations." (Kissinger wrote these words in a memorandum to Richard Nixon prior to the 1973 summit; the italics in the text represent the former president's underlinings.)

One particular continuity in Brezhnev's and Andropov's views was the necessity of maintaining the highest level of Soviet military might. Throughout his career, Brezhnev was careful not to alienate the military brass, while Andropov knows how important was the support of the military in his own maneuvering toward supreme political power. There was thus nothing inconsistent or hypocritical in Andropov's encomium to Brezhnev in a speech before the CPSU Central Committee meeting that elected him Brezhnev's successor after he had used every means to discredit Brezhnev's leadership during the last few years of the ailing dictator's life. To Andropov, "Leonid Ilyich Brezhnev will live forever in the memory of thankful mankind as a consistent, ardent and tireless fighter for peace and for removing the threat of world nuclear war looming over mankind." He then immediately added his own concurrence: "We know well that the imperialists will never meet one's pleas for peace. It can only be defended by relying on the invincible might of the Soviet armed forces."

As for the aspect of change, the difference in the personal and political lives of the two men is fundamental. On a strictly personal level, every detail of Brezhnev's life, including his personal bluster and hedonistic proclivities, belonged to the public domain and could be verified by any citizen. In total contrast, and despite a short period of revelations in the Western press about Andropov's personal and social life and interests, remarkably little is known about the present ruler of the Soviet Union. In the words of an American writer, "virtually nothing is known about this man called Andropov: not the names of his parents, not his ethnic background, not his education, not his war service, not his preferences in music and literature, not his linguistic abilities, not his ideas. He stands at the head of Russia, but we don't even know how tall."

In the political realm, the Brezhnev-Andropov contrast does not diminish. In both the domestic and the foreign area, Brezhnev's eighteen-year reign was at first, and for an extended period of time, highly successful, but it ended rather dismally. He offered Soviet citizens the longest period of economic well-being and political stability in the USSR's history. The price of that "normalcy," particularly in his later years and under the impact of his physical infirmities, was economic stagnation, social petrification, and unprecedented corruption. Similar evolution took place in foreign policy. He succeeded in weakening the impact of Khrushchev's denunciations of the crimes of Stalin's era that had shattered the zeal of many Stalinist true believers around the world. His famous "doctrine" remained until the end the symbol of the USSR's readiness to keep the "people's democracies" under Soviet control. He profited from the United States' post-Vietnam malaise to penetrate parts of Africa and the Middle East by using Cuban troops and Eastern European experts to shore up self-styled and inexperienced Marxist-Leninist regimes; he wanted Moscow to remain the center of the world communist movement under the orthodox watchword of "proletarian internationalism"; and he reached a consensus with his Politburo colleagues on the invasion of Afghanistan. To sum up, he left the national economy in shambles but turned the Soviet Union into a military superpower. He expanded directly or by proxy the Soviet Union's territorial domain and political influence on a worldwide basis, beyond the achievements of any of his predecessors.

The list of Brezhnev's foreign political failures is no less impressive. He allowed the conflict with China to escalate to full confrontation, including the prospect of a conventional and/or pre-emptive nuclear war. Moscow's handling of the international communist movement, especially the censorious Eurocommunist parties, was far from successful. Brezhnev was hesitant and unimaginative in wrestling with non-orthodox stirrings in Eastern Europe. The success of Solidarity in Poland became his nightmare because he was at a loss at how to cope with it. The invasion of Afghanistan proved to be anything but a simple operation and emphasized Brezhnev's obvious inability to deal efficiently with the sagging economy and the mounting social, ethnic, intellectual, and religious problems of the progressively restless multinational Soviet empire. All this led to a loss of prestige for the Soviet Union, with Brezhnev no longer a vigorous spokesman at international diplomatic conclaves. Even his earlier, substantive contributions were fading, and at the end he was a clear liability to the Soviet system. The *Washington Post*'s Moscow correspondent, Dusko Doder, wrote a few days before Brezhnev's death that a "crisis of spirit grips the Soviets as promises turn into despair." It was therefore both necessary and urgent that someone else try to rejuvenate the party and "get the country moving again."

Andropov's dazzling success in settling the problem of Brezhnev's succession within days contributed to the interest he elicited everywhere. His political style, a complete contrast to Brezhnev's, fascinated people. Within days he candidly admitted that the national economy was in deep trouble and made radical proposals on combating low labor productivity. He also began eliminating incompetent and corrupt party and state officials—to a large extent the beneficiaries of the Brezhnev regime. To do the job properly, Andropov extended and reinforced the KGB's organization and legal authority. As an illustration of what could be called the "KGBization" of Soviet society during the first 60 days of Andropov's rule, Vitali F. Fedorchuk, a career KGB officer who headed the secret police in his native Ukraine for twelve years and replaced Andropov himself in May 1982 as the KGB chief for the entire country, was appointed minister of internal affairs on 17 December. One of his top deputies, Viktor M. Chebrikov, succeeded him at the KGB.

Andropov justified these and other shifts at lower levels as the expression of the necessity to have "in the decisive sectors politically mature, competent, and resourceful people." Fedorchuk's new assignment was of greatest political and functional importance because he replaced Gen. Nikolai A. Shchelokov, head of the Ministry of Internal Affairs (known as the MVD from its Russian initials) and reputed for years to be a critic of the KGB's methods of operation and its privileged position within Soviet society. Shchelokov was brought to Moscow and assigned to the MVD by Brezhnev in 1968 and since that time was his protégé and personal friend. The fusion of two organizations, or rather the subordination of MVD to KGB, ended a separation that had lasted for nearly 30 years, since the execution of Andropov's longtime predecessor, Lavrenti Beria, who bolstered Stalin's terror by manipulating both police forces. By adding to the KGB's principal role some of the MVD's specific control prerogatives, the new CPSU general secretary forged a unified police apparatus of extraordinary magnitude.

The essential charge against the MVD under Shchelokov was that its personnel were undisciplined and had tolerated widespread corruption for years. It was therefore fitting that the shaking up of the militia epitomized the fight against corruption, the key slogan and target of the new "law and order" campaign. Something similarly innovative happened in the realm of the press. *Pravda* and other newspapers began printing letters from readers criticizing the conditions under which they lived and worked, or the behavior of officials. Likewise the agendas (but not the substance and decisions) of the highest party bodies were made public. In a more subtle and suggestive way, the press had a part to play in the campaign against corruption. The 20 November issue of *Sovietskaia rosiia*, in an article entitled "Reading Lenin Anew," quoted Lenin on the need for a crackdown on corruption and greater concern for ordinary people. Commented a Western weekly: "If the wisdom of Leninist thought is applied as rigorously this time round, half the central committee and two thirds of the government could be candidates for the chop."

Many Western observers believe that Andropov's zeal and speed in consolidating his position derive from the fact that he is a man in a hurry. He is not young (at 68, he is eleven years older than Brezhnev when he came to power in 1964), has a heart condition, and is therefore pushed to move quickly and decisively, especially in view of the high probability that in both domestic and foreign affairs the next few years may be of exceptional importance. Some see him as a populist ("a disciplined Khrushchev"), while for others his inspirational return to Lenin not only confirms the continuity of Soviet rule but justifies the conclusion or anticipation that because of his shrewdness, persistence, and instinct for political maneuvering, he may be the most able Soviet leader since Lenin.

Only the future will give the answer to the question of Andropov's role in Soviet and world history. The evidence offered in 1982 is far from conclusive. His behavior and distinct style suggest a series of hurdles he will have to overcome in the forthcoming years. To begin with, the apparent ease of his victory over his rivals should not lead to the conclusion that the power struggle at the apex of Kremlin's political hierarchy is over. Second, his campaign against corruption and incompetence has already affected a number of people in the middle levels of the Soviet nomenclatura, including government ministers. Up to now one could not speak of a "purge" because those involved have been "transferred to other work"—in other words, demoted. Many of them as well as other Brezhnevites who may expect the ax and who have connections in the Moscow establishment, are at least potential enemies of Andropov's. Third, and most important, Andropov's essential test will be economic reform. The present highly advertised and systematically pursued campaign against the loafers (tolerated by Brezhnev) appears epiphenomenal in comparison to the real problem: the reform of an economic system that has outlived its time and whose generalized crisis has been recognized and described by Andropov himself. It is, however, a field in which he is a novice. In the words of a British Kremlinologist, "Andropov is not an economic manager—he is a KGB man." But since he intends to change conditions within the economy, he will have to depend on the advice of experts and then decide on the economic policy issues. Two key concepts for a genuine and effective reform of the economy (strongly endorsed by many Soviet experts and economists) are decentralization of the system of a command economy based on central planning and the reordering of investment priorities with an emphasis on reducing the huge burden of military defense spending. The problem of options is, however, to a very large extent political because the most rational and promising plans for an effective economic recovery will encounter opposition among top military, entrenched party bureaucrats, and many enterprise managers. They all would be threatened by decentralization and investment shifts. A determined reformer would risk alienating powerful people. But will Andropov's reformist determination be strong enough to risk confrontation with the very same people—especially among the military—who have supported him in his climb to power, and whose support he still politically needs?

In any case, from the moment Andropov assumed the supreme party post, everyone in the Soviet Union and abroad knew or sensed that a totally different kind of political animal was now in control. Doder wrote that after Andropov's first month in the office, the same Muscovites who shortly before had professed to be on the verge of despair, now felt "a new sense of expectation . . . a measure of hazy optimism," anticipating a better future. For the time being, at least, anything seemed preferable to the rot under Brezhnev. Having proved to be a master tactician in internal party infighting during the ten months of 1982 and eager to confront the enormous task of economic recovery at home, Andropov immediately assumed the conduct of affairs in his field of predilection—international relations and confrontation with the United States. His experience was of invaluable help. As the Soviet ambassador to Hungary (1953–1957), he witnessed the disintegration of an established communist regime. He studied the strengths and weaknesses of a spontaneous popular upheaval and had a wealth of data with which to form an opinion on how an efficient communist regime may and should be re-established. Back in Moscow, he was put in charge of liaison with parties in the Soviet bloc and could from this high official position deal with the "fraternal" parties on a broader basis. Finally, as head of the KGB for fifteen years (1967–1982), he became probably one of the best informed men in the world on Soviet domestic, bloc, and international matters.

Two cases are significant here. First, at the time of the invasion of Czechoslovakia in August 1968, Andropov was already at the helm of the KGB. There is no doubt that he supported the decision to attack and that his men participated in the liquidation of the reform-minded Czechoslovak Communists' attempt to establish Socialism with a Human Face. Second, thirteen years later, while Brezhnev was bewildered by the Solidarity phenomenon in Poland and uncertain how to handle it, Andropov did the job in full secrecy. He devised, or at least supervised, the Polish "self-invasion" of 13 December 1981—the military coup by top army officers (all members of the communist party), decisively helped and protected by special units of the security police trained to suppress brutally any attempt at civil disobedience or insurgency. Analyzing what he called the Winter War in Poland, a U.S. historian paid an indirect compliment to Andropov's inventive skill: "If Solidarity had misplayed its hand, it was because, like the West, it was too innocent to imagine the ingenuity that Moscow had displayed in intervening without appearing to do so, thereby safeguarding its antinuclear peace campaign, its Siberian gas deal, and its foreign credits." In full cooperation with top Soviet military officers (who a year later supported him in his accession to Brezhnev's post), Andropov was instrumental in reintegrating Poland into the Soviet bloc and at least temporarily squashing the Solidarity heresy. The martial law ("state of war") in Poland, and its subsequent vibrations elsewhere made Eastern Europe more subservient to the Soviet Union than at any time since Andropov's apprenticeship in Budapest.

Once formally in control, Andropov turned his attention to the essential issue of nuclear weapons and relations with the United States in this connection. The positions of two superpowers seemed irreconcilable on two fundamental points: relative nuclear strength and control of nuclear weapons. According to Ronald Reagan, "In virtually every measure of military power, the Soviet Union enjoys a decided advantage." According to Yuri Andropov: "The allegation [that the Americans] 'lag' behind the USSR is a deliberate untruth." Consequently, the U.S. president was determined at least to neutralize the Soviet military buildup by accelerating U.S. rearmament and then to negotiate arms control and disarmament from a position of strength. His Soviet counterpart was no less determined to thwart these intentions. To do so, he was combining the use of propaganda means of exceptional proportions and military threats of his own.

On 21 December, in Moscow, and in the presence of representatives of 123 foreign communist parties (the Chinese were conspicuously absent) who flocked to the Soviet capital to magnify the celebration of the founding of the Soviet Union in 1922, Andropov made a speech that contained elements of subtle propaganda and brutal threats. He fully endorsed Brezhnev's policies in the nuclear field and used the largest part of his speech to address the problem of medium-range nuclear missiles in Europe and the negotiations about them in Geneva. He made new proposals regarding the reduction of missiles in Europe (for details, see USSR profile) and presented them as Soviet concessions and proof of readiness to achieve a compromise with Washington. He then accused the United States of systematically rejecting all of the Soviet Union's reasonable proposals on arms control and disarmament and stated that U.S. policymakers were interested only in achieving military superiority over the Soviet Union. Andropov's rhetoric was adapted to Western European and U.S. sensitivities on nuclear issues: he occasionally sounded like a pacifist, stressing unilateral Soviet commitments to lessening the dangers of war along with Soviet eagerness "to freeze the strategic arsenals of the two sides." He favored confidence-building measures between the superpowers and endorsed the trend "back to détente." While the commonsense approach prevailed oratorically, his listeners did not miss the other side of Andropov's message. He stated that the Soviet Union could match any U.S. weapons system and that Soviet missiles more powerful than those presently existing were already in the testing stage. Along the same line, he assured his cheering audience that "we will never let our security or the security of our allies be jeopardized."

The negotiations in Geneva had shown no signs of progress by the end of the year. For months Soviet media gloated over disagreements in NATO about a common policy toward the Soviet Union and Eastern Europe. The Soviets also made propaganda points among many people on both sides of the Atlantic (who were not Communists or sympathizers of the Soviet system) who perceived U.S. foreign policy as being in disarray and the Reagan administration as uninterested in serious negotiations with the USSR about arms control. Early in 1983, there were persistent rumors that both sides were becoming more flexible and ready to compromise. Such speculations are beyond the scope of this introduction but indicate that as in the field of domestic economic reform, Yuri Andropov will face hard choices in the international arena.

The conjunction in Andropov's assertions of a rationality intended to pacify the West and the Leninist toughness of his concrete policies, soon emerged as distinguishable traits of his style. His accession to power was greeted in large and influential parts of the Western media, as well as among many reform-hungry Soviet citizens, as the harbinger of a new, authoritarian but progressively liberalizing and enlightened order. Articles presenting Andropov as a "closet liberal" with a predilection for Western clothing, drinks, books, and entertainment and a sympathetic curiosity for dissidents' arguments shouldered aside warnings that Soviet propagandists wanted their new leader to be perceived in the West in such a light. At the same time great hopes were placed in Andropov's willingness to move away from the cold war and military confrontations, toward a more harmonious world and a cooperative international reordering of priorities. It came therefore for many as an unpleasant surprise, and to Western governments as cause of growing concern, that Soviet domestic policies grew more repressive and foreign initiatives more expansionist and threatening. Persecution of dissidents became harder and included hitherto tolerated Marxist historians such as Roy A. Medvedev. Jewish emigration was reduced in 1982 to 2,700 persons, compared with 51,320 in 1979. The Soviet press called unofficial disarmament groups "renegades and criminals." The official amnesty proclaimed on 27 December excluded those convicted of political offenses. As for foreign policy, Western hopes for a shift proved illusory. There was no retreat from Afghanistan. The Kremlin initiated a more active policy in the Middle East, installing new missiles in Syria. A chain of Soviet bases was built in Antarctica, and Japan was threatened with nuclear annihilation if it formed closer military ties with the United States. The mounting evidence of Soviet use of chemical warfare against insurgents in Afghanistan and Southeast Asia was certainly not conducive to building confidence between the superpowers. To a similar category of problems for the West belonged intensified KGB activities abroad, such as a surge in spying and a drive to steal vital Western technology as well as defense secrets on a worldwide scale.

The most intriguing and potentially explosive story of the year came from Rome, where judicial authorities were investigating during the last months of 1982 the background of the so-called Bulgarian connection. The gist of the matter was that the Turkish terrorist who on 13 May 1981 attempted to assassinate Pope John Paul II was an instrument of the Bulgarian secret service, which had acted with the knowledge and approval of the KGB, whose chief at that time was Yuri Andropov. Both *Izvestiia* and *Pravda* (29 December) vehemently denied the "connection," presenting instead the United States as the villain. *Pravda* specifically accused the CIA of inventing the story, denounced the "real terrorism practiced by the United States itself," and explained that the anti-Soviet intrigue fitted into "the Pentagon's rearmament plans aimed at preparing for a nuclear war." The official U.S. reaction to the entire matter was subdued and noncommittal. Many commentators believe that since the material evidence (despite well-founded suspicions) could never be produced, negotiations with Soviet representatives at all levels should proceed. Otherwise the work of diplomacy would be infinitely more difficult.

Eastern Europe. For both general and specific reasons, the states formally belonging to the Soviet bloc (through membership in the Council for Mutual Economic Assistance [CMEA] and the Warsaw Treaty Organization [WTO]) did not fare well in 1982. With considerable variation, they all retrenched economically and were forced to adopt austerity measures. The 1976–1980 five-year plans set the lowest growth rates since the end of the war. Instead of a projected growth rate of 3.5 percent in 1981, the actual figure was 1.9 percent, with no improvement in 1982. The essential reasons for the slump were colossal CMEA indebtedness to Western banks and governments (over $80 billion), an energy crunch made worse by a Soviet decision to decrease exports and to increase the price of oil, and Moscow's decision—caused by the financial difficulties of the Soviet Union itself—to refuse to cover any new credits CMEA members could obtain elsewhere. A CMEA Council meeting, held in Budapest in mid-June, reflected the frustrations of the organization. Without daring to appear as dissenters and in fact disagreeing among themselves on specific issues, the delegates argued in favor of economic decentralization and increased trade with the West. Soviet Prime Minister Nikolai Tikhonov rejected these reformist views and pleaded for greater economic integration and self-reliance.

As for the WTO, the Soviet leaders clearly demonstrated their determination to enhance its role. Between 25 September and 1 October, the WTO held military maneuvers, code-named Shield-82, in Bulgaria. The officers of the Red Army, such as Minister of Defense Dimitri Ustinov and the commander in chief of the WTO, Viktor Kulikov, attended the exercises, made speeches, and offered interviews mixing military and political arguments. Marshal Kulikov was particularly assertive and candid. In an interview given to a Tass correspondent he indicted U.S. imperialism and accused the United States of wanting to dominate the world. He described the global situation as more dangerous than at any time since the end of World War II and contrasted NATO's aggressive nature and the WTO's strategic doctrines based exclusively on defense. He reiterated that the forces of NATO and of the WTO were presently in a state of relative balance and that the United States would never achieve military superiority. He also hailed the unity of communist and workers' parties based on proletarian socialist internationalism.

As stated above, the individual Soviet bloc members showed considerable variation; in some instances these were of paramount importance. Poland is a case in point. Tadeusz Szafar has expressed its peculiarity by writing that 1982 was "the year the communist establishment declared a state of war against the nation and the armed forces carried it out under party guidance." Several elements call for special comments. First, Poland went through an extraordinary variety of political situations, in which violent confrontations between the regime and its opponents would for brief periods of time be replaced by real or rumored attempts at cooperation between the three key factors in the life of the country: the military government of General Jaruzelski; the Catholic church headed by Archbishop Józef Glemp; and the independent trade unions, whose leader, Lech Wałęsa, though interned, enjoyed wide popularity and trust among the workers. Even after the official banning of Solidarity in October and the failure of the general strike in November protesting suppression of the movement, hopes persisted that the suspension of the martial law a year after its introduction would have a liberalizing effect. The opposite happened, for in the words of a *New York Times* correspondent, "the suspension of martial law actually creates a permanent legal system out of what had been a set of emergency measures." Second and more ominous, a process of "purification" took place during the year—a purge of artists, intellectuals, and opposition leaders that, in the view of a prominent U.S. analyst, "may be more dangerous and more far-reaching than anything witnessed in the Soviet bloc since the days of Stalin." This was not a gloomy prediction, for on 20 October *Literaturnaia gazeta* published a long report from its Warsaw correspondent attacking Polish intellectuals in vehement terms. (The Moscow correspondent of the *Los Angeles Times* summarized the attack in an article entitled "Diplomats See Purge of Polish Intellectuals as Latest Soviet Goal.") Striking features of the article include assertions that Polish anticommunist intellectuals are not a minority but "a most significant part" of the Polish intelligentsia, that Catholic priests in churches "pray for arrested criminals," that Poles in general prefer German culture and civilization to Russian, and that "hideous, abominable graffiti [are painted] on monuments to Soviet soldiers." Third, rumblings auguring confrontation between Jaruzelski, with his early promises of economic reforms along Hungarian lines, and Polish communist hard-liners, led by Tadeusz Grabski, obtained credibility by the publication in October of Grabski's four-point program. Presented as an instrument to "save the country from self-destruction," the program advocated final elimination of the anticommunist underground, a revolutionary ideological purge of the party, abandonment of key elements of Poland's economic reform, and a crackdown on the Catholic church. The importance of Grabski's proposals is that they reflect the Kremlin's dissatisfaction with the Polish party, which it finds weak, demoralized, and disoriented. A new leadership was therefore necessary, and there were strong indications that Moscow viewed hard-liners à la Grabski favorably. Fourth, at the 27 October meeting of the Polish Central Committee, a party secretary stated that the breakdown in the economy had reached an "unprecedented scale." At the same time, contrary to the ample financial aid furnished as long as Solidarity was perceived as a danger to communism in Poland and elsewhere, the nature of Soviet aid changed. "A priority now is to repay the Russians something of what they have given us," stated an official close to General Jaruzelski. Fifth, on 29 December, Tass distributed an unprecedentedly harsh and direct attack on the pope, printed in a CPSU political monthly. The attack against the pontiff opened with the statement that unlike his predecessors, he had taken a much more conservative and rigid position vis-à-vis the socialist world. The next two points sounded more ominous. First, "Solidarity was born not in the wave of disorders that swept the country in the summer of 1980 but in the Catholic church." The second point added a wider geographic dimension: Poland "is not the only object for the Vatican's subversive activities." Trained specialists had been sent to other East European countries to "undermine the process of easing of international tensions." Speculations abounded about the motives for such serious charges. Some commentators saw in the article Moscow's rejoinder to the Bulgarian connection. Whatever the motives of the article, Yuri Andropov let Poland and the world know that accommodation with the Catholic church in Poland and Eastern Europe was not on his agenda, at least in the immediate future.

Compared with Poland, the other Soviet-bloc countries went through 1982 more quietly, though without much reason for contentment or optimism for the immediate future. Besides negative economic trends, they all experienced cases of official corruption, deficiencies in capital investments, low labor productivity and morale, worker absenteeism, youth alienation, persistence of nonconformism among intellectuals, and disagreements among experts on economic reform. In some respects Bulgaria fared better than the others; its average annual growth rate was the highest among CMEA members. Results of the highly advertised New Economic Mechanism, inaugurated on 1 January and based on principles of profitability of enterprises and incentives offered to workers, proved to be inconclusive by the year's end. Its terms were too vague, and state intervention legally too permissible. Party officials complained about the mounting problems with youth (consumerism, criminality, alcohol and drug abuse), and the low rate of the population growth. After a period of cultural liberalization that took place under the influence of Lyudmila Zhivkova (who died in 1981), trends toward socialist conformity in the arts were perceptible. Conflict with Yugoslavia over the perennial Macedonian question continued. Nor did the Bulgarian connection case help the country's reputation abroad.

The built-in repressive character of the Gustáv Husák regime in Czechoslovakia did not change in 1982. Dissidents continued to be persecuted, human and civil rights curtailed, and churches under surveillance. Contrary, however, to the post-1968 situation when the regime could offer to the population a fair standard of living, the economy was in deep trouble in 1982. Practically all of the above-mentioned socioeconomic shortcomings affecting the region applied to Czechoslovakia. A significant phenomenon, noted with displeasure by the authorities, was persistent religiosity among younger people.

As for the German Democratic Republic, positive economic results, especially in foreign trade with the Western countries, were counterbalanced by negative ones. Per capita foreign indebtedness (the total ranged between $9.1 and $13.2 billion) was higher than Poland's, and energy needs were far from being covered—in 1983 East Germany's quota of Soviet oil is to be reduced to 17.2 million tons. The most militarized country of the Soviet bloc, East Germany faced a relatively strong and certainly courageous independent peace movement, headed by the Protestant church. Many young East Germans wore sewn-on cloth badges inscribed "Swords into Plowshares." The authorities, whose main line is the identity of socialism and peace, reacted with the official slogan "We need our plowshares and our swords."

Hungary, the usual showcase of communist prosperity, faced serious economic problems, and its future seemed clouded. The country's foreign debt of $8 billion was per capita larger than Poland's. The growth rate was low, and national budget showed a deficit. Tensions over income differentiation complicated social relations, and austerity measures were unpopular. A chronic housing shortage, complicated by decay of existing housing, persisted. Imports of Soviet oil were reduced from 7.5 to 6.4 million tons. Intellectual dissent on a small but qualitatively high level was firmly under the watchful eyes of the police. A Catholic grass-roots movement was noticeable.

Nicolae Ceauşescu's regime in Romania was also experiencing a dire economic slump. A foreign debt of over $10 billion and shortfalls in food and energy characterized the faltering national economy. Although Stalinist-type police control made any type of overt opposition to the regime impossible, Ceauşescu showed signs of nervousness, relying more and more on his numerous family, purging high officials and frequently reshuffling the cabinet. An extremely tough emigration law promulgated in November was badly received in the West and imperiled Romania's trade ties with the United States. The alleged threat of Hungarian "revisionism" in Transylvania was used to divert the populace from the country's economic woes. Romania's foreign policy, known for its maverick character and opposition to Soviet schemes, seemed to mellow in 1982. The process was viewed as a rather desperate attempt by Ceauşescu to obtain from the Soviet Union badly needed economic help. It is questionable whether Andropov will have a sympathetic ear for his mercurial neighbor.

Albania and Yugoslavia, the nonmembers of the Soviet bloc, experienced a particularly eventful year. Bloody settlement of accounts at the top of the Albanian communist party, cabinet reshapings of unprecedented proportions, confusing claims about an aborted invasion from the sea, and maximal tension with Yugoslavia related to the irredentist upheaval of native Albanians in the autonomous Yugoslav province of Kosovo gave Albania a prominent place in the world press. There were indications of an opening to the West, especially in the economic field (West Germany was the preferred partner). At the end of the year, both Moscow and Washington approached Tirana proposing re–establishment of relations. Tirana rejected the offers and reaffirmed its hostility toward China. The prospect of a struggle over the succession to Enver Hoxha enhanced interest in that most isolated and self-professed only orthodox communist country.

The case of Yugoslavia was even more intricate. The London *Economist* called the country's economic crisis the worst since 1945. Its manifestations were a huge foreign hard-currency debt of some $20 billion, a 30 percent inflation rate, and nearly a 15 percent unemployment rate. Industrial production rose by only 0.7 percent instead of the planned 3.5 percent, and the entire 1981–1985 plan had to be revised downward. Strikes were numerous, and shortages of consumer goods extensive. The austerity measures introduced in October were unprecedented in their harshness. Drastic gasoline rationing was ordered, foreign travel sharply curbed, and the use of fuel, electricity, and other energy sources cut back. The main hope for economic improvement in 1983 was a package of credits to be offered by a group of Western countries.

Actual and potential political crises were no less serious. The new federal government formed in May (headed for the first time by a woman, Milka Planinc, 57, a Croatian and protégée of Tito's) proved to be inefficient from the outset. It could not impose central authority on the entrenched localist and autarkic tendencies in the federal republics and autonomous provinces. Malfunctioning of basic institutions, such as the distinctive Yugoslav parliamentary system and even more the highly praised system of workers' self-management have hampered the government's tasks. Violence in Kosovo, caused by separatist elements, had two disruptive manifestations: official and harsh repression by army and militia units, and forced and brutal exile of Serbs by the underground, fanatical militants. The exilings stirred emotions particularly in Belgrade, but state and party leaders disagreed on the causes of the Kosovo insurgency and ways to deal with it. No less threatening were factional struggles within the League of Communists of Yugoslavia, including the state and party collective leaderships. They maintained control over the country, but polemics in the press indicated possibilities of violent settlement of accounts at the very top. Last but not least, a muted but no less perceptible process of de-Titoization capped the events of 1982, the year of generalized Yugoslav discontents.

Hoover Institution   Milorad M. Drachkovitch

Albania

The Albanian Communist Party was established on 8 November 1941 in Tirana on the initiative of Josip Broz Tito, who was implementing Comintern instructions to initiate and control resistance activities against the Germans. Two Yugoslav emissaries, Miladin Popović and Dušan Mugoša, acting on behalf of the Central Committee of the Yugoslav Communist Party, managed to unite the three existing factions of Albanian Communists under one organization and a central leadership headed by Enver Hoxha, who was appointed "provisional secretary" of the party. He has remained party leader for a record 42 years. The first formal congress of the Albanian Communist Party was held on 1 November 1948, after several of its founders were already either imprisoned or executed. The First Congress changed the name of the party to Albanian Party of Labor (APL) and proceeded to purge its ranks of all Titoist elements.

During 1982, the APL, and by extension the state apparatus, was subjected to what may very well be Hoxha's last major purge. All indications are that this process, which commenced with the mysterious death of Premier Mehmet Shehu (18 December 1981), is not over yet. Nevertheless, if placed in historical perspective, recent events in Tirana seem to follow a recognizable pattern in Albanian politics, characterized by the ruthless Stalinist methods used by Hoxha to retain power and, he hopes, to perpetuate his policies after his death.

Three major purges have been conducted in the past by the Hoxha regime (1948, early 1970s, 1975), all under the pretext that "external enemies" did or were about to link up with "domestic collaborators" for the purpose of "liquidating his socialist regime." On 10 November 1982, Hoxha "revealed" to the world that his late prime minister, Mehmet Shehu, has been a "conspirator" simultaneously working for the Soviet, Yugoslav, and U.S. intelligence services. Indications are that under the pretext of threats from external and internal enemies, a large-scale purge of pro-Shehu elements commenced in early January and continued as of late 1982. So far the latest political infighting in Tirana has affected more than two-thirds of the cabinet and several key party figures, military personnel, and technocrats. Hasty promotions of virtual unknowns were announced, along with a promise that Shehu's collaborators would be exposed in the near future (*Zëri i popullit*, 17 November).

Yet, despite the massive changes and turmoil that have taken place since Shehu's death, the APL continues in firm control of all state, military, and security structures as well as mass organizations, labor unions, and professional groups. The pre-eminent role of the party is formally defined in the 1976 constitution, which declares it to be the "sole leading political force" in the country.

Population. 2,752,300

Party. Albanian Party of Labor (Partia e Punës e Shqipërisë; APL)

Founded. 1941

Membership. 122,000 full and 24,363 candidate members; 67.4 percent workers and peasants; 32.6 percent office workers and intellectuals; women, 30 percent of full and 40 percent of candidate members

First Secretary. Enver Hoxha

Politburo. 12 full members: Enver Hoxha (chairman, Democratic Front), Ramiz Alia (president of the republic), Muho Asllani, Adil Çarçani (premier), Hajredin Çeliku (minister of industry and mines), Lenka Çuko, Kadri Hazbiu, Hekuran Isai, Rita Marko (vice-president), Pali Miska, Manush Myftiu (deputy premier), Simon Stefani; 5 alternate members: Besnik Bekteshi (deputy premier), Foto Çami, Llambi Gjegprifti, Qirjako Mihali, Prokop Murra (defense minister)

Secretariat. 5 members: Enver Hoxha, Ramiz Alia, Vangel Çerava, Hekuran Isai, Simon Stefani

Central Committee. 81 full and 39 alternate members (8 November 1981)

Last Congress. Eighth, 1–8 November 1981, in Tirana

Auxiliary Organizations. Trade Union Federation of Albania (UTUA, 610,000 members), Sotir Kocallari, chairman; Union of Labor Youth of Albania (ULYA), Mehmet Elezi, first secretary; Women's Union of Albania (WUA), Lumturi Rexha, chairwoman.

Main State Organs. Council of Ministers (19 members). The People's Assembly (250 members) is constitutionally the leading body in the state, but in reality merely approves decisions made elsewhere.

Parliament and Elections. All candidates run on the ticket of the Democratic Front, an umbrella organization. In elections on 14 November, only one of the 1,627,968 voters voted against the front's nominees.

Publications. *Zëri i popullit*, APL daily; *Rruga e partisë*, APL theoretical monthly; *Bashkimi*, Democratic Front daily; *Zëri i rinisë*, ULYA semiweekly; *Puna*, UTUA semiweekly; the Albanian Telegraphic Agency (ATA) is the official news agency.

Party Internal Affairs. *Purges.* The leadership of the APL has been subjected in 1982 to major purges and changes in personnel. Some of the changes were explained as "natural and necessary" to relieve aging leaders of heavy duties; others were for "failures" in tasks assigned. But the bulk of them seem to be related to the desire of the aging Hoxha to purge the party and the state of followers of Mehmet Shehu, whom he has described as "the most dangerous traitor."

On 19 December 1981, Shehu's death was declared a suicide caused by a nervous breakdown. The Albanian prime minister, for a quarter of a century the number-two man, became a nonperson the day he was buried. Rumors that a gunfight had occurred in a Central Committee meeting circulated in Tirana and were even printed in Yugoslav newspapers (*FBIS*, 11 January). However, Hoxha made a special effort to quash these rumors and to project a sense of normality. A few days after Shehu's death, he appeared at an art exhibition accompanied by Shehu's brother-in-law, Minister of Defense Kadri Hazbiu.

On 14 January, the eighth legislative session of the People's Assembly was called into session to deal with "routine" matters and to elect a new premier. Hoxha nominated as Shehu's successor the first deputy premier and acting premier, Adil Çarçani. Çarçani (see end of profile for a biographical sketch), an economist and a relative latecomer to the upper echelons of power, accepted the nomination and the mandate to form a new cabinet. Proceeding cautiously, Çarçani retained most of the members of the Shehu cabinet, except in posts that mattered. Shehu's nephew, Minister of Interior Feçor Shehu, was removed from his post; he has not been heard of since. Haki Toska, an old Hoxha protégé who had over the years drifted to the Shehu camp, was relieved of his duties as finance minister and was replaced in that post by Qirjako Mihali, who in the shuffle lost his position as deputy premier. The widow of the late prime minister, Central Committee member Figeret Shehu, disappeared from the scene.

Other significant changes occurred during the ninth legislative session of the parliament in July. Veteran Foreign Minister Nesti Nase was "retired" and granted a pension at the relatively early age of 60. He had been appointed foreign minister in 1966 and had held that post longer than any other communist minister except Andrei Gromyko. Nase was immediately replaced by Deputy Foreign Minister Reiz Malile, who is an old hand in foreign affairs and had a career similar to that of his predecessor: both had served as ambassador to China (Nase twice) and to the Soviet Union and as the Albanian representative in international organizations. Nase was identified very closely with Albania's pro-China policy, the high point of his career came when his resolution became the vehicle for Beijing's admission to the United Nations. Nase's removal may signify an opening of Albanian relations to the West and some form of normalization with the Eastern bloc. Nase's tenure as foreign minister coincided with Tirana's strict isolation and xenophobia. Malile is not a member of the Central Committee (possibly an attempt to de-ideologize foreign policy) and has been prominent in contacts with foreign delegations visiting Tirana. He comes from the region of Vlona, which he represented in parliament, and has been a low-key diplomat. His wife and two sons died in a plane crash while he was ambassador to China, and apparently he has not remarried. (*Radio Free Europe–Radio Liberty Background Report*, 12 July.)

In addition, two other changes occurred: Deputy Premier Pali Miska replaced Prokop Murra as minister of energy and the unknown quantity Alli Alushani replaced Llambi Zicishti as minister of health. The latter was fired without explanation. The July changes in the cabinet were followed by changes in party organizations throughout the country. Hoxha announced to the fifth plenum of the Central Committee the elevation of Vangjel Çerava, an obscure candidate-member of the Central Committee, to full membership and immediately appointed him a secretary of that body. At the same meeting, Hoxha "appointed" (the precise word used in Albanian) as alternate members of the Central Committee Gen. Kiço Mustaqi and Simon Ballabani. (*Zëri i popullit*, 15 October.)

Mustaqi, whose past experience was with the Sigurimi (security agency), was elevated to the position of chief of the defense staff, suggesting a need to control more closely the work of that ministry and raising questions about Kadri Hazbiu's future. Although technically Hazbiu retained his portfolio until the new cabinet was recommended by Çarçani following the 14 November elections, one could sense the end of his career as defense minister as early as July. All signs pointed to his eventual political demise. First, he lost ground when Feçor Shehu, his handpicked minister of interior, was replaced soon after Mehmet Shehu's death. Second, throughout the year the deputy minister of defense, Gen. Nazar Berberi, was more visible in military affairs and occasionally pointed to the "lack of discipline" in the armed forces (*Drejtësia popullore*, January–March). Third, Hazbiu was absent from the celebration of Army Day on 10 July. The main address on that occasion was given by Berberi, and most festivities were attended by Prokop Murra, who eventually succeeded Hazbiu. The last major public appearances of Hazbiu were for the celebration of the anniversary of the liberation of Malakaster (18 July), Shehu's birthplace, and the anniversary of the founding of the Democratic Front (16 September) in Peza. It is likely that Hoxha used Hazbiu to calm the population of Malakaster, which is known for its blood feuds and loyalty to Shehu. (*FBIS*, 22 July.) But it is equally likely that Hazbiu visited Malakaster in search of popular support.

Hoxha's purges of major figures occurred in three stages—in January, July, and October—suggesting constant turmoil within the country following Shehu's mysterious "suicide" and a degree of hesitation on the part of the first secretary and careful orchestration of the whole affair.

Throughout the year, the censored Albanian press persistently called for "vigilance" against "internal and external enemies." These calls were often issued by two party leaders: Ramiz Alia and Lenka Çuko. At a gathering of young people in Tirana, they implored the audience to raise their vigilance because of "some internal problems" (ibid., 20 January). On 15 September, Alia gave the major address to the national gathering of the Democratic Front and asked the participants to be vigilant and to "defend the gains of socialism from internal and external enemies" (*Zëri i popullit*, 16 September).

On 25 September, an unusual event buttressed these warnings. A band of self-proclaimed "liberators," said to be connected with the pretender to the Albanian throne, Lekka I, attempted a landing in the coastal area of Sarandes and engaged security forces for approximately six hours (ibid., 28 September; *NYT*, 1 November). The official ATA announcement stated that all "bandits have been liquidated." A week prior to the so-called invasion, Çuko had warned of the dangers of "external enemies linking up with domestic ones to deny the Albanian people their socialist conquests" (*Zëri i popullit*, 5 June).

"Warnings" about enemies reached a high pitch on 10 November, when Enver Hoxha delivered a major "electoral speech" before a selected audience of voters of district 210 of Tirana. In this wide-ranging address (which filled almost the entire 11 November issue of *Zëri i popullit*), Hoxha revealed that Mehmet Shehu had been an agent of the Yugoslavs, the Soviets, and the Americans since the war. Furthermore, he asserted that the Yugoslavs, as in the old days when they had brought King Zogu into Albania "on the back of the remnants of Wrangel's army," were involved in a "conspiracy with the gun and narcotics smuggler and promoter Lekka Zogu." Hoxha's attacks against Shehu and the Yugoslavs made earlier Belgrade assertions that the late premier was either killed during an argument or forced to commit suicide credible. In a manner reminiscent of Stalin's "doctor's plot," Hoxha accused the dead premier of engaging in thirty years of treason. When caught, Shehu had no choice but to commit suicide. Three conclusions are inescapable from reading Hoxha's speech. First, Shehu had "associates" in his "criminal" plans. Second, until they are eliminated, the purges will continue. Third, the late premier was coerced into committing suicide.

Hoxha may currently be conducting his last major purge. There are indications that his health has deteriorated seriously and that he is unable to maintain a heavy work schedule. He gave one of his shortest speeches ever before the gathering of the Democratic Front and delivered his 10 November electoral speech indoors (perhaps for security reasons) and sitting down, flanked by Ramiz Alia and Adil Çarçani (ibid.). Earlier in the summer, he ventured to the mountainous region of Pogradec (instead of going to his usual resort in Vlona) on the advice of comrades who told him to "rest for a while" (*FBIS*, 9 August).

The tumultuous changes that started in January reached their third stage in November following the parliamentary elections. On completion of the electoral process and formal verification of the "winners" (all of whom ran unopposed), the first secretary of the APL appeared again before parliament and nominated Adil Çarçani, on behalf of the Politburo and the Central Committee, to form a new cabinet (*Zëri i popullit*, 23 November). Hoxha's brief speech was intended to affirm before the parliament (which includes almost the entire Central Committee) his personal support of Çarçani. The premier proceeded immediately to announce the composition of his new cabinet, which had eleven new faces, and many surprises.

Prokop Murra, deputy premier, was appointed defense minister, replacing Kadri Hazbiu, who was not even nominated for a seat in parliament. Murra has no experience in military affairs. He is an expert on economic matters, having served as vice-chairman of the State Planning Commission and (in 1980–1981) as minister of industry and mines. When that ministry was split in two, Murra assumed the portfolio of minister of energy and was reappointed to that post in the first Çarçani cabinet (14 January). Given the significance of the defense post, Murra's position was enhanced by the latest changes.

Others did not fare as well. Among those whose fate is unknown are Hazbiu (defense), Rrapo Dervishi (communal services), Victor Nushi (internal trade), and Nesti Nase (foreign affairs). The *New York Times* (19 November) reported that Nase had been arrested following his removal. Several others were demoted. Petro Dode, chairman of the State Planning Commission, became first party secretary of the Vlona district. Rahman Hanku, former minister of construction, is now a member of the Presidium of the parliament. E. Ulginaku was demoted from minister to vice-minister of light and food industries. Pali Miska, a deputy premier, became first party secretary of the Elbasan district. Minister of Foreign Trade Nedim Hoxha and Minister of Mines Llambi Gjegprifti became first party secretary of the Argyrocastron district and director of the Enver Hoxha Combine, respectively.

Not only Murra, but a few other new faces are not matched with the tasks to which they were assigned. Murra's appointment, however, may mean an attempt (actually the first) at civilian control of the military. To this end, Murra may have to depend on his new chief of defense staff, Kiço Mustaqi, for the "dirty" work of cleansing the armed forces of bad influences and for tightening party control. Mustaqi was born in the Sarandes district and is of Greek origin. Unconfirmed reports in Athens place him in the midst of the so-called invasion in Sarandes, and recent escapees interviewed by this writer knew him as a general in the Sigurimi. His elevation to the position of chief of staff sounds like a reward for some achievement in his field.

Among the new faces in the cabinet is Vito Kapo, the widow of the late Hysni Kapo and until then head of the WUA. She assumed the post of minister of light and food industries even though she has no managerial skills or any training in economics. The rest of the new ministers seem to have expertise in their respective fields. Harilla Papagorgji (also of Greek descent), who assumed the high post of chairman of the State Planning Commission, has advanced training in economics. The new minister of foreign trade, Shane Korbeci, served as director of Makinimport and minister of internal trade. Osman Murati, the new minister of domestic trade, served with some distinction as head of the Directorate of Investments in the State Planning Commission. (For a complete list of cabinet members, see *FBIS*, 24 November.)

The sweeping changes in the cabinet, Hoxha's promise to eliminate Shehu's accomplices, and the massive turnover in parliament suggest that the power struggle may intensify in the months ahead. In all probability, 1983 will be a decisive year for Albania for several reasons. First, Hoxha's health is declining, and a successor must be found. Second, if the "Shehu plot" is to be unraveled, as Hoxha promised, it will mean vertical and horizontal purges and probable disruption of the economic and social systems. Shehu was prime minister for 28 years, and it would be safe to assume that he left behind numerous "grateful people" who owe their positions to him. However, if the purges stop (which is unlikely) and if the new cabinet survives the test of time and a troublesome economy, Albania may finally join the world. With few exceptions, the new ministers assigned to economic posts are young technocrats who could very well prepare the country for broader trade and technical exchanges with the West. Changes at the cabinet level reflect previous changes in the party hierarchy. Ramiz Alia and Vangjel Çerava appear to be the winners in the ongoing power struggle.

Alia was in the forefront of those attacking "internal and external enemies" throughout the summer. He is Gheg by origin and has a long record of faithfulness to Hoxha. In the recent changes, Alia assumed the presidency of the republic, replacing Haxhi Lleshi, while he retained his positions on the Secretariat and Politburo. On two occasions, Hoxha indicated that Alia is the number-two man in Albania. On 16 September, Hoxha assigned Alia to deliver the main address at the Democratic Front congress, even though Hoxha is the chairman of the mass organization. Second, Alia was a key speaker at the trade union congress held in Tirana (6–10 June), where he spoke of the need to follow the "correct party line." Third, his nomination to the presidency was made by Simon Stefani, an individual often mentioned as having aspirations for Hoxha's job. In his new position as president of the republic, Alia is expected to gain needed international prominence and experience in foreign affairs. Although in the past the presidency has been an honorific post (the first president, Dr. Omer Nishani, was not even a party member), it is almost certain that this will change with an ideologue like Alia in that post.

Çerava is an unknown quantity who was elevated from alternate membership on the Central Committee to full membership and then made a secretary of that key body. If past history is any guide, Çerava probably owes his rise to power to some special service to Hoxha in recent months. However, Alia may have selected Çerava to relieve himself of some of his duties in the Secretariat when he assumed the presidency.

Three conclusions seem inescapable. First, Enver Hoxha seems determined to dismantle the Shehu state apparatus in order to leave a leadership that will retain his personality cult for at least a decent interval after his death. Second, the elimination of eleven ministers, the 45 percent turnover in the membership of parliament, the virtual eclipse of three major leaders, and the demotion of five members of the upper party and state echelons suggest that the anti-Shehu movement has not run its full course and it would be rather risky to guess the orientation of Albanian politics. Third, the credentials of the top two beneficiaries of the post-Shehu era, Alia and Çarçani, point in opposite directions.

Alia was in the forefront of the anti-Soviet, antirevisionist militancy of the 1960s, and his fortunes rose with the demise of pro-Khrushchevites. Çarçani, on the other hand, has a reputation for being a pragmatic technocrat who is rather uncomfortable with rhetorical excesses. He hails from a well-to-do conservative family of Argyrocastron. To the people who knew him during the war (including this writer's father), the greatest surprise was to find him in the Hoxha camp when the resistance was over and the Communists seized power by default. Çarçani could aptly be described as a "cryptonationalist." If successful in moving fast enough in establishing a degree of personal control over the state apparatus, he might very well bring Albania out of its isolation, closer to the Western world and freer in its domestic politics. To achieve that, he must neutralize Alia or face the prospect of a protracted power struggle for the top position, with Prokop Murra becoming the power broker or even a potential rival for the leadership. Although Hoxha has given every indication that Alia is his choice to lead the party, Alia cannot be considered secure in his status as the front-runner in the politics of succession. In the past, several contenders for the number-one position have been knocked off by relative unknowns.

Albania is entering a peculiar era of nationalist fervor (see below) coupled with Hoxha's old-fashioned Stalinism. This mood can hardly be expressed by a militant Marxist like Alia, with roots outside the country, at a time when the Tirana regime is making determined efforts to marshal support among Albanian émigrés in the United States and Europe, most of whom support the notion of Greater Albania.

Auxiliary and Mass Organizations. All major mass organizations have been galvanized by the intense power struggle that commenced with the death of Mehmet Shehu. The Democratic Front, the ULYA, the UTUA, and even the Pioneers held mass meetings at the regional and national levels to discuss developments in the political and economic spheres and to provide forums for party leaders to explain the year's main events and to demand obedience to the party.

The Democratic Front held its congress on 15 September on the fortieth anniversary of its founding. The proceedings were opened by the chairman of the organization and party first secretary, Enver Hoxha, who used the opportunity to introduce his latest protégé, Ramiz Alia, making it as clear as possible that Alia was his choice for the number-two position. Hoxha gave what must be considered one of his shorter speeches and proceeded to warmly introduce Alia as the keynote speaker and his "distinguished comrade in arms, who led large units of the National Liberation Army for the liberation of Albania and for the liberation of the peoples of Yugoslavia." (*Zëri i popullit*, 16 September.) Alia gave a lengthy speech covering all aspects of domestic and foreign policy, obviously overshadowing Çarçani and his new foreign minister, both of whom were in the audience (for text, see ibid.). Alia is a vice-chairman of the Democratic Front and used the opportunity to urge the organization to select the proper candidates for the 14 November general elections. This year, the Democratic Front congress was converted more openly into a forum to set the party line and to weed unreliable elements out of parliament. Democratic Front leaders undertook the usual task of "preparing" the electorate for the parliamentary elections, thus serving as the party's transmission belt and as the nominal umbrella organization that sponsors candidates for all nonparty elective offices. In its call to the Albanian voters, the Central Committee of the Democratic Front implored them to vote for its "candidates" because by so doing, they "vote for the correct Marxist-Leninist line [and] for the strengthening of the unbreakable union between people and party" (ibid., 19 September).

As has been the case since 1946, the results of the elections were determined the moment the list of candidates was made public. As has also been the practice since 1946, almost all members of the APL Central Committee and Politburo were nominated and elected as deputies to the legislative body. In this year's elections, however, some prominent figures failed to be nominated or even mentioned in the massive propaganda campaign that preceded the actual voting. Prominent among the absentees were Kadri Hazbiu, Figeret Shehu, and Feçor Shehu. However, the turnover went beyond the recognizable names. Out of the total of 250 deputies elected, 113 are new faces, or a 45.2 percent turnover. Sociologically, the deputies are classified as follows: 95 percent of them, both men and women, are "of working class origin, situation, or descent"; 73 deputies are from the "cooperative peasantry," with the rest distributed among the intelligentsia, armed forces, and scientific community. Women represent 30.4 percent of the total, and 24 deputies are "heroes and heroines of Socialist labor." The new parliament is relatively young. Only 6.4 percent of its members are over 60; 128 (or 50 percent) are between 40 and 60; and 98 are 28 to 40. A small percentage (4.4 percent) are 18 to 27. (*FBIS*, 24 November.) The unusually large turnover can only partially be explained as reflecting the "desire" of the party to rejuvenate the system. It would be safer to assume that at this level, too, the anti-Shehu terror that has gripped the country has taken its toll.

The UTUA held its Ninth Congress in Tirana 6–10 June. The congress dealt with numerous issues relating to productivity levels and the quality of export goods. From the tone of speeches delivered by union officials and party representatives, one could surmise that neither productivity nor the quality of work had been satisfactory during the preceding year. The Central Committee and the Politburo of the party were represented at the congress by Lenka Çuko, who used the opportunity to attack Yugoslav revisionists and to warn the mass organization of the existence of internal enemies who "seek to distort the party line" (*Zëri i popullit*, 7 June).

Of importance was the report delivered by the chairman of the organization, Politburo member Rita Marko. Marko's speech was similar in tone to that of Çuko as far as foreign policy issues were concerned. He, too, attacked Yugoslav revisionists and Soviet and U.S. imperialists and issued the traditional warnings about Albania's enemies lurking in the dark, ready to "undo its socialist achievements." But after a few pointed attacks against Solidarity in Poland and those who suppressed it, Marko turned to Albania's endemic economic problems. Specifically, he was less than complimentary about the quality of work, fulfillment of norms, and coordination of planning. Lack of coordination and planning, according to Marko, caused serious disruption in the economy and its "rhythmic fulfillment of plans." More specifically, he underlined the problem of "globalism in the field of commodity distribution." As he defined it, globalism means "nonfulfillment of norms in distribution, although production plans have been fulfilled." This problem, Marko said, "has become an obstacle to the rhythmic fulfillment of plans by other enterprises due to the lack of supplies." Decrying the lag in productivity and eager to be supportive of "the party and its leader," the UTUA passed four major resolutions underscoring the urgent need to be more productive and the "determination" of its members to observe party policies on all issues affecting society and state. These resolutions dealt with problems and promises in the fields of construction, agriculture, communications, communal properties, and mining, giving the impression that there were problems in all major economic fields. (Ibid.)

Two items are worth noting in connection with the UTUA congress. First, the labor federation, apparently on party instructions, made a special effort to invite representatives from similar organizations in the Third World and the West. Fifteen foreign delegations participated in the congress and remained an additional week in the country as guests of the UTUA. Among the key Western countries represented were Great Britain, France, Canada, and Denmark. (*FBIS*, 17 June.) As in the past, however, most delegations represented Marxist-Leninist splinter groups and not legitimate trade unions. Second, the Council of Ministers chose the opportunity of the UTUA congress to announce price reductions ranging from 8 to 30 percent on 135 basic consumer goods. It was the first price reduction on such a mass scale in fifteen years and probably was intended to mobilize mass support for the subsequent leadership changes and the anti-Shehu campaign. (*Zëri i popullit*, 5 June.)

Marko was re-elected president of the UTUA, only to resign his post after the 14 November elections in order to assume new duties as vice-president of the republic. He was replaced in the UTUA by his deputy, Sotir Kocallari.

The ULYA held its Eighth Congress from 4 to 10 October. The congress provided an opportunity for party officials to deliver major addresses dealing with domestic and foreign problems. The opening session of the congress was attended by Enver Hoxha, but he did not make any speeches on that occasion. Two major reports were delivered to the ULYA congress: one by Simon Stefani on behalf of the APL Central Committee and the other by the first secretary of the Central Committee of the youth organization, Lumturi Rexha.

Stefani stressed the need to "struggle against internal and external enemies" (ibid., 5 October). Rexha, on the other hand, aimed her main attacks against Yugoslavia for the "severe oppression that our Kosovar brothers and sisters are experiencing today in Kosovo" (*FBIS*, 5 October). The youth organization also elected a new first secretary, Mehmet Elezi, until then second in command. Rexha assumed the leadership of the WUA, which until 22 November was led by Vito Kapo, who became minister of light and food industries. As a result of these changes, Rexha and Elezi rose in the Albanian leadership. Elezi seems to be a young leader who is rising rapidly. He was named an alternate member of the Central Committee at the Eighth APL Congress and in summer 1982 assumed the editorship of the party organ, *Zëri i popullit*. The ULYA congress was attended by sixteen foreign delegations, including several from Western Europe (Spain, Great Britain, West Germany, France), all of which represented splinter Marxist-Leninist groups (ibid., 1 October).

The Union of Albanian Writers and Artists held a plenary session on 20 March to deal with current problems in Albanian society as they relate to creative work. The surprise of the meeting was a concerted attack by the chairman of the union, Central Committee member Dritero Agoli, against the country's leading author, Ismail Kadare. Agoli's attack was followed by similar criticism by Ramiz Alia. The central point of both criticisms involved Kadare's tendency to become obscure in setting his themes historically, a practice that undermines socialist realism. Agoli, probably reflecting Alia's views, rebuked Kadare for his latest novel, *The Official of the Palace of Dreams*, as well as for "isolationism" and "foreign influences" and demanded to know: "To what period, country, state, and social system do these terms apply?" (*Zëri i popullit*, 20 March.) Western visitors to Tirana found Kadare unremorseful and "educated" by the criticism at the writers' plenum (*JPRS*, no. 8760, CSO 2300/300).

Domestic Affairs. *The Armed Forces.* Problems in the Albanian military have appeared on numerous occasions in the past. In 1982, however, criticism of alien manifestations within the armed forces intensified and may very well have been related to the removal of Kadri Hazbiu from the post of defense minister and his replacement by a nonmilitary party operative, Prokop Murra. In a nutshell, the criticism of the Albanian military was aimed at the emergence of elitism and excessive professionalism. In a major article in *Bashkimi* (4 December 1981), Deputy Defense Minister Veli Lekaj pointed to the problems of a lack of "cooperation between the military commands and staffs, on the one hand and the state and economic organs on the other." Lekaj's criticism was followed by an even sharper one from another deputy defense minister, Simon Ballabani.

Ballabani expressed his concern over misunderstandings in the relationship between defense tasks and the overall economic program of the party and state. Command and staff cadres, Ballabani argued, should "know that without a strong economy, there cannot be strong defense . . . In compliance with this concern they [ought to] coordinate programs so that defense problems and production problems are dealt with without hindering each other." (*Zëri i popullit*, 16 February.) Underscoring the need for a new emphasis on party-military links, the ULYA threw its full support behind the idea of training its members in politico-military schools in order to cement army-to-people links (*Zëri i rinisë*, 3 March). Finally, on the thirty-ninth anniversary of the founding of the People's Army of Albania, Gen. Nazar Berberi, deputy defense minister, reiterated the theme that there was no contradiction between party work in the armed forces and military professionalism (*Zëri i popullit*, 10 July). However, a major article in the review *Drejtësia popullore* (January–March) cited problems in the administration of justice by the prosecutor general's office in the armed forces and sought to define the dividing line between civilian and military authority over violations of law by military personnel.

New Family Law. The new government of Adil Çarçani undertook one massive task during the ninth legislative session: the rewriting of the Albanian Family Code. This massive, legislative piece complements the enactment of the Albanian Civil Code and purportedly seeks to "modernize" the Albanian legal system in order to make it more reflective of the current state of sociopolitical transformation. The new family code assertedly seeks to "strengthen the institution of the family" and to base it on sound law rather than on "anachronistic" traditions, according to Manush Myftiu. In the process of rationalizing the family code, Myftiu offered his view concerning the place of love in society and marriage. The Marxist-Leninist view of "freedom and love," he stated, "has nothing to do with degeneration of relations inside or outside marriage . . . Marriage in our country is based on the unity of ideo-political and cultural views of the partners." (*Zëri i popullit*, 30 June; *Sqiprëria e rë*, April.) Nevertheless, despite efforts to "eradicate" old-fashioned practices and to modernize family life, contradictions persist in Albanian society and, judging from the tone of official criticism, have intensified in some areas.

Nonsocialist Practices. According to several articles in diverse publications, one of the main problems is the persistence of "religious customs disguised in new forms." One manifestation of religious tradition is that the rate of intermarriage between young people of different faiths is not proceeding at the pace expected by the party. This is not a "chance phenomenon," but reflects old beliefs and traditions. Another tradition that persists is the offering of religious masses to the dead. Masses are no longer legal or possible in Albania (all priests were either executed or defrocked), but believers have substituted for that practice the "offering of cookies to all those visiting the bereaved on the anniversary of death." (*Sqiprëria e rë*, April.)

Several other nonsocialist practices plague Albanian society as well. First, the working class does not seem to understand the need to be educated "with the spirit of class struggle" (*Zëri i popullit*, 27 February). Similarly, Albanian youth do not fully realize the need to improve "scientific skills" in order to be "part of a new scientific revolution for the purpose of increased production" (*Rruga e partisë*, February). In the state apparatus, "liberalism," "bureaucratic centralism," "opportunism," and "sectarianism" have not been eradicated (*Bashkimi*, 7 December).

Nationalism. While the state and the party seemed to have occupied themselves with problems of "anachronistic social behavior," they seem also to be fostering a contradictory nationalistic movement. Two major conferences were organized in Tirana with the participation of foreign scholars on the topics of ethnic and linguistic origins of the Albanian nation and the meaning of the seventieth anniversary of Albanian independence. Papers presented by Albanian scholars Aleks Buda (president of the Academy of Sciences) and Androkli Kostallari (director of the Tirana Institute of Linguistics and Literature) at the first conference argued that contemporary Albanians are not only direct descendants of Illyrian tribes, but that Illyrian (and therefore Albanian) influence extended beyond the country's present borders and more or less covered the territories indicated on the Albanian map that made its appearance the preceding year (*Kathimerini*, Athens, 6 June 1981). Characteristic of the new emphasis on nationalism was publication of a series of portraits of patriots spanning the period from 1880 to 1920 (*Zëri i popullit*, 9 May, 23 October, 12, 19, and 25 November). The nationalistic festivities concluded with the opening of a museum honoring the

Albanian hero Gergje Kastriote (Skenderbegj) and the unveiling in the city of Vlona of a life-size statue of Ismail Qemal-Vlora, the father of Albanian independence in 1912. These two major "cultural/scientific" events highlighted other efforts to rekindle Albanian nationalism and indirectly reinforced occasional references to Greater Albanian aspirations. Needless to say, Kosovo was presented as an organic part of the Albanian nation at both conferences. Enver Hoxha, too, stressed nationalist values in his speech to the Tirana electorate and addressed himself to "the entire Albanian nation, within and outside Albania" when he praised the virtues of patriotism and gallantry (ibid., 11 November).

The Economy. The Albanian economy continued to suffer from centralized planning, lack of production incentives, and an apparent difficulty on the part of the Albanian government to find reliable sources of technology and the funds to pay for it. Yet official statistics pretend that everything is going according to plan and that production is growing at a steady pace, following "the period of heroic efforts made by the working masses on all fronts" during the Sixth Five-Year Plan, which was interrupted by the "treachery of the Chinese." Petro Dode, who until 22 November was chairman of the State Planning Commission, presented an ambitious plan for the period 1981–1985, which envisions increases in the "social product" by 34–36 percent over 1980 and in industrial production by 36–38 percent over the net outcome of the Sixth Five-Year Plan. Capital investments proposed for the 1981–1985 period are to reach a level 22–24 percent higher than in the previous five years, national income is to be 35–37 percent higher compared with 1980 levels, and retail trade is to rise by 22–24 percent. Real per capita income, however, is projected to be a mere 8–10 percent higher compared with the level during the Sixth Five-Year Plan. The Seventh Five-Year Plan, the draft proposal of which was approved in early January, also envisions a dramatic growth in foreign trade. The government proposes to increase exports by 58–60 percent over the Sixth Five-Year Plan and to maintain imports at two percentage points below that figure, thus complying with the constitutional requirement prohibiting trade deficits. (Ibid., 16 January.)

The 1982 state budget shows an increase in both revenues and expenditures of approximately one billion leks (3.7 leks equal $1.00). Anticipated income is 8.55 billion leks and expenditures 8.50 billion, leaving a surplus of 50 million. The budget for the district people's councils was increased by approximately 500 million leks to 2.9 billion leks. (Ibid., 17 January.) The defense budget, however, was decreased by approximately 5 million leks to 935 million leks. Despite the rosy picture painted by statistics on fulfillment of the goals of the first year of the Seventh Five-Year Plan, the Albanian economy is experiencing problems. Three areas singled out for indirect criticism during 1982 were inadequate coordination of interlinking enterprises, transportation of goods from one part of the country to the other, and shortages of both skilled and unskilled labor.

The problems in coordination and transportation were discussed at the Ninth UTUA Congress by its chairman, Rita Marko. Inadequate attention to this problem, Marko said, causes the economy to lose its rhythmic growth, "even if quotas assigned to various enterprises were fulfilled." Some enterprises, Marko added, have "manifested tendencies of globalism" and therefore affect the work of other units. (Ibid., 7 June.) Although he did not refer directly to transportation, it appears that it was uppermost in his criticism, judging from the discussion of the Central Committee at its fifth plenum. Pali Miska, deputy premier and minister of energy (until the November changes), submitted a critique of the transportation system and offered proposals for improvements. (Ibid., 17 October.)

The problem of labor shortages is a recurring one in the labor-intensive Albanian economy, and several proposals were floated during the year to deal with it. One proposal was to raise the retirement age in order to recapture approximately 160,000 retirees. In a major article in the theoretical journal *Rruga e partisë* (February), a Central Committee member argued that the party "cannot ignore the activities of 160,000 retirees, whose number will increase by 10,000 to 12,000 every year during the Seventh Five-Year Plan."

In the same issue of the journal, ULYA Vice-Chairman Etemije Zeneli criticized the unenthusiastic responses of Albanian youth to the party's call to participate in a technical and scientific revolution. In her view, "the quality of the assimilation of course work is not satisfactory everywhere."

In foreign economic relations, the Albanian economy followed the patterns of previous years. Trade protocols were signed with most East and West European countries, as well as with countries of the Third World. Notable links during 1982 were with Japan, with which Albania established diplomatic relations, and informally with West Germany (*FBIS*, 9 November). No major commercial links have been announced with Japan thus far. The West German firm of Saltgitter signed a contract with Tirana to supply an industrial plant for nickel-cobalt processing, of approximately 60 million DM (*Radio Free Europe–Radio Liberty Background Report*, 29 November). Albania's annual trade with some 50 trading partners runs at $700–800 million. Ironically, the largest portion ($130 million) is with Yugoslavia, a country with which Albania has serious foreign policy problems (*Swiss Review of World Affairs*, February). Italy is the second largest trade partner, with a trade level of $70 million, followed by Greece with $50 million and Switzerland with $20 million. Albania also signed a transportation agreement with Yugoslavia and commenced work on a rail link between the two countries (*CSM*, 21 May).

Seeking to spark consumption and perhaps to underscore the party's "interest in the working masses," the government announced a reduction in prices in June, amounting to savings of 75 million leks annually for consumers (*Zëri i popullit*, 5 June). However, even with the price reductions, prices remain high for basic goods compared to the average salary.

Foreign Affairs. There were no dramatic changes in the foreign policy of Albania during 1982. The basic principles of the country's external relations as pronounced by Hoxha at the Eighth APL Congress were reaffirmed on several occasions by top leaders. However, there was a "qualitative change" in foreign policy pronouncements and a relative softening of position vis-à-vis Great Britain and West Germany. It cannot be ascertained at this stage whether the search for normalization with these two countries is in any way related to changes in the personnel of the Albanian Foreign Ministry. Albania's new foreign minister, Reiz Malile, is not a member of the Central Committee. There were also some key ambassadorial changes. Socrat Pliaka, until July ambassador to Yugoslavia, was named deputy foreign minister in charge of relations with neighboring countries. The former ambassador to Athens, Lik Seiti, was transferred to Belgrade, and the former ambassador to Rome, Yenophon Nushi, assumed the post in Athens. Albania maintains diplomatic relations with "some 100 states," according to its new foreign minister, and cultural and economic relations with 50 European and Third World countries (*FBIS*, 20 September; *Swiss Review of Foreign Affairs*, February). The new Albanian leadership has shown no inclination to improve relations with the two superpowers. Overtures by the Andropov regime have been rejected as has any notion of establishing relations with the United States (*Zëri i popullit*, 7 December). Prime Minister Adil Çarçani, in announcing the "program of his new government" before the newly elected parliament, stated: "There will never be rapprochement or reconciliation with U.S. imperialism, Soviet socialist imperialism, or any racist regime." The Albanian leadership considers Yuri Andropov a puppet of the Soviet army, "which sooner or later will have its say" (ibid., 24 December).

Yugoslavia. Relations with Yugoslavia followed a schizophrenic pattern during 1982, suggesting no substantive improvement in the near future. The two countries signed agreements linking the two countries by rail via Titograd-Shkodra, as well as an agreement to permit overland traffic between Titograd and Ochrid to transit through Albania, cutting the distance by some 180 miles (ibid., 7 December; *Borba*, Belgrade, 5 April). This development followed signing of a trade protocol setting the volume of trade between the two countries for 1982 at $130 million, making Yugoslavia Albania's number-one trading partner.

At the political level, however, the situation has not changed appreciably. For the second consecutive year, Tirana has maintained an anti-Yugoslav campaign ostensibly aimed against "Great Serbian chauvinism." The Albanian press, following the lead of *Zëri i popullit*, carried several major anti-Yugoslav editorials and on a number of occasions ran compilations of comments from the Western press about the situation in Kosovo. Ramiz Alia used the opportunity of the Democratic Front congress to attack Yugoslavia for its policies on Kosovo and to call on Albanians there to continue their "popular resistance" until their goal of republic status is achieved. (*Zëri i popullit*, 1, 20, and 27 May, 3 June, 4 September, 15 October.) The same attitude and militancy was displayed by Simon Stefani at the ULYA congress and by Lumturi Rexha, then first secretary of the same organization (ibid., 16 September). Hoxha made Yugoslavia his number-one subject in his electoral speech and published two new books (*The Titoites: Historical Reflections* and *The Anglo-American Threat: Memoirs*) identifying Albanian's past and future enemies.

Complicating relations with Yugoslavia and to some extent with Greece is the emergence of a new phenomenon in Albanian foreign policy: historical nationalism with modern implications. At a major conference on ethnicity held in Tirana, the notion of Greater Albania was revived by Professor Aleks Buda (member of the Central Committee), who, among other things, asserted that the Albanian nation is an autochthonous entity and was present in the greater Balkan region long before the Slavs or even the Greeks appeared on the scene.

Despite the denunciations of Belgrade's policies, Albanian leaders state that they did not wish to "destabilize" the Federal Republic of Yugoslavia. But, at the same time, they claim to speak for the "entire Albanian nation" when they boast that any attack on Yugoslavia by the "Bulgaro-Soviet socialist-imperialists" will be resisted by "6,000,000 Albanians, not 3,000,000." (*FBIS*, 4 July; *NYT*, 12 July.) In other words, Tirana claims to speak on behalf of the Kosovo Albanians.

Greece. Greek-Albanian relations proceeded in a satisfactory manner during the year. Enver Hoxha made it a special point to praise the closeness of these relations, but he pointed to two problems. First, he criticized Athens for not "lifting the law on the state of war" still in effect between the two countries. Second, he attacked "northern Epirus chauvinists" for continuing to raise the human rights issue for the Greek minority living in Albania. He denied Western claims that there are "28,000 political prisoners" of Greek descent in Albania and stated that a total of "33 Greeks are in prison, and only four for political crimes." (*Zëri i popullit*, 11 and 24 November.) However, the Central Committee for Northern Epirus Struggle (chaired by the archbishop of Athens and Greece) issued a list of names of 225 political prisoners from one Greek-inhabited region alone, held in nineteen prisons, and a list of 61 prisoners known to have died while incarcerated. Greek parliamentarians (of the New Democracy Party) and foreign press accounts, however, insisted that the figure of 28,000 is on the conservative side (see *Le Soir*, Brussels, 16 May). The current socialist government of Greece expressed its support for the human rights of the Greek minority in Albania (*NYT*, 3 June). Nevertheless, this did not seem to bother Tirana. A new trade agreement signed with Athens involved exchange of light industrial goods and some steel products from Greece in return for petroleum products and "basic minerals" from Albania.

Eastern Europe. Albanian relations with most Eastern European countries in 1982 remained "formally correct," without much evidence that change is in the offing. As Tirana sees matters, these relations cannot improve until these countries free themselves from Soviet hegemony (*Zëri i popullit*, 5 July). However, trade agreements were signed with all East European countries, Vietnam, North Korea, and Cuba. The Albanian leaders took notice of the situation in Poland again, attributing the continuing labor unrest in that country to deviations from "true Marxism-Leninism" not only in Poland but in all of Moscow's "vassals" in Eastern Europe (ibid.).

Western World. During 1982, the Tirana regime softened its position vis-à-vis Great Britain and West Germany and defined the conditions under which relations can be established with the two NATO powers. In his speech before the election, Hoxha praised the development of relations with West Germany in "culture and other areas" and expressed his country's readiness to find a solution to the issue of war reparations, which Tirana sets at $4 billion (ibid., 11 November). Hoxha mentioned no specific figure in his speech. Even though the two countries have no formal relations, Tirana eagerly received West German business delegations. In a gesture of goodwill, the APL Central Committee invited a West German communist delegation (a splinter Marxist-Leninist group) to visit Tirana, and the ULYA Central Committee invited, along with delegations from other West European countries, a delegation from West Germany.

Problems in establishing relations with Great Britain decreased significantly during the past year. In fact, Albania has placed only one condition on establishing relations with London: namely, the return of Albania's gold taken out of the country at the commencement of World War II, plus interest. There have been press stories (not denied by Tirana) that Great Britain, with tacit support from the United States, is exploring ways to solve the problem (*NYT*, 24 December).

Relations with Sweden and Canada continued to improve, even though Albania has no formal links with the latter. Cultural and trade delegations were exchanged between the two countries, and Canada has expressed its readiness to establish formal diplomatic relations with Tirana (ibid., 28 November). The Çarçani government is also considering diplomatic ties with Spain and shows great annoyance and sensitivity to Western press references to Albania as a "hermit" or "isolationist" state (*FBIS*, 6 October).

During the year, Tirana showed a special interest in warming traditional ties with Turkey. Several visits were exchanged between the two countries, and on 11 November the Turkish minister of commerce visited Tirana to sign a trade agreement and received the red-carpet treatment (ibid., 12 November).

China. There were no appreciable changes in relations between Beijing and Tirana. No new contacts have been reported, and for all intents and purposes major APL leaders ignored China in their attacks on the two superpowers. However, Tirana seems to have made a concerted effort to improve relations with communist and noncommunist states on the periphery of China. It established diplomatic relations with Japan and Thailand and had extensive contacts with North Korea and Vietnam (ibid., 2 February, 25 March, 1 October, 22 December).

The Albanian press, however, kept a close watch on developments in Sino-Soviet relations. On two occasions, prior to and after Brezhnev's death, *Zëri i popullit* (30 October) sarcastically remarked that the Chinese were engaging in "cardlaying" as a partner in the triangular maneuvers of Washington-Moscow-Beijing. Referring to the visit by Deputy Soviet Foreign Minister Leonid Ilyichev to Beijing, the APL organ did not find it surprising since "China is capable of becoming an ally of imperialists" (ibid., 21 November).

USSR. Albania maintained its anti-Soviet hostility during the entire year. Çarçani offered no olive branch to the Kremlin on assumption of the premiership. In fact, in his statement to parliament on that occasion, he promised to continue the policy of "no contacts, no relations" with the two imperialist superpowers (*FBIS*, 15 January). The same theme was repeated by Rita Marko at the UTUA congress, by Ramiz Alia in his major speech at the congress of the Democratic Front, and by Hoxha himself in his address to the Tirana electorate (*Zëri i popullit*, 7 June, 16 September, 11 November).

For most of the year, the Albanians seemed to make a concerted effort to link the Soviets with the Yugoslavs and blamed both of them for the "oppression" of their brethren in Kosovo. Enver Hoxha even linked Mehmet Shehu to their secret services and denounced the late prime minister for plotting against him with the help of Moscow and Belgrade. The death of Brezhnev (which was announced in eighteen words in *Zëri i popullit*, 11 November), however, introduced a new element to Moscow-Tirana relations. Specifically, Moscow made a direct offer (in *Pravda*) for the re-establishment of relations between the two countries and linked the initiative to the assumption of the Soviet leadership by Yuri Andropov (*WP*, 10 November; *NYT*, 20 November; *CSM*, 22 December). However, the Albanians had already pre-empted the Andropov offer. Several statements by Albanian leaders dismissed the new Kremlin chief as "a puppet of the Soviet army." The definitive answer to Moscow's overture came in an unsigned article in *Zëri i popullit* (7 December), which stated categorically: "In regard to our country, it has had no links with Khrushchev and Brezhnev, and it will not have them now with Andropov and with whomever will come at the head of the revisionist Soviet Union because it follows an imperialist policy, which aims at enslaving the world, at suppressing and exploiting the people." Such language leaves little room for flexibility and is consistent with the Hoxha line established in 1961. But it is well known, and indirectly admitted, that there was a pro-Soviet group in Albania (linked to Shehu) and the possibility of its making another effort to return to power cannot be excluded.

Consistent with the policies of previous years, Albania continues to oppose the Soviet invasion of Afghanistan and Soviet intervention in the affairs of East European countries (which it continues to call "Soviet vassals") and rejects Soviet pretensions at disarmament in Geneva.

International Party Contacts. Tirana continued throughout 1982 to behave as the "leading" theoretical center for splinter Marxist groups. Representatives of fifteen such groups attended the UTUA congress and fourteen similar delegations participated in the ULYA congress (*FBIS*, 1 and 3 October). A West German communist group was invited by the APL Central Committee to visit Tirana, and Enver Hoxha sent a lengthy message to the Communist Party of Brazil. Relations with ruling communist parties were limited to contacts with Vietnam and North Korea.

Biographies. *Ramiz Alia.* Ramiz Alia, the current number-two man in the Albanian political hierarchy, was born in the city of Shkodra in 1925. He is a Gheg by origin, and his parents allegedly migrated to Albania from Kosovo at the end of World War I.

Although young in age, Alia participated in the resistance, according to official biographies, as a "member of the political section" of the communist-controlled Front Nacionale Clirimtate (National Liberation Front). His first task during the resistance was that of political commissar of the 7th Shock Brigade. Later he served in the same capacity in the 2nd People's Army Division, one of the units that entered the Kosovo-Metohia–Sandjak area in pursuit of retreating German troops. Alia's political fortunes seem to have risen at the expense of other Ghegs from the region of Shkodra. Thus, in the mid-1940s he was elevated to membership on the Central Committee, while some of his compatriots became nonpersons; similarly, he rose even higher in the mid-1950s and early 1960s when the Ghegs Tuk Jakova (defense minister, who escaped to Yugoslavia) and Liri Belishova (a protégée of Nikita Khrushchev's) were denounced (Belishova was executed) as traitors to the socialist cause.

Alia was elected a member of the Central Committe at the First Party Congress (1948) and was assigned the task of liaison with the ULYA. In 1951, he became general secretary of the youth organization, a post he retained until 1955. At the Third Party Congress (1956), he was elected an alternate member of the Poliburo, becoming a full member at the Fourth Congress (1961), the congress that formalized the break with Moscow. On election to full Politburo membership, Alia replaced Liri Belishova in all of her functions in the party and state. Throughout his political career, Alia remained a party functionary and therefore has little experience in other fields. In the mid-1950s, he served briefly as minister of education. In 1961 (Fourth Party Congress), he was also elected a Central Committee secretary and identified very closely with the late theoretician Hysni Kapo, who was reportedly the author of some of the anti-Soviet polemic. Although relatively young and newly elevated to the Politburo membership, Alia made the first major public anti-Soviet speech on Lenin's birthday in April 1963, followed by a more strident, anti-Titoist, anti-Khrushchev tirade on the occasion of the twentieth anniversary of the founding of the party organ, *Zëri i popullit*. Alia has been in parliament since 1950 and is currently vice-chairman of the Democratic Front.

On 22 November, Alia was elected president of the presidium of the parliament (president of the republic). His new post could potentially augment his reputation beyond the national scene and offers an opportunity to gain experience in foreign affairs. On numerous occasions since Shehu's death, Alia served as the point man in warning against domestic and foreign enemies that allegedly threaten Albania. Hoxha used several public appearances to express his confidence in Alia, whom he called his "distinguished comrade in arms." As of the end of 1982, the first secretary has left little doubt that Alia is his choice for the number-two position in the party and, presumably, his successor. However, nothing is certain in Albanian politics, and Alia could not be considered anything more than the front-runner in the ongoing competition. The power struggle is just beginning in Albania, and Alia is a Gheg with foreign roots. Since the assumption of power by the communist regime, most prominent Ghegs have been eliminated by the Tosks, who have dominated postwar politics. Moreover, since 1948, all those considered to be second-in-command have met inglorious ends. (Source: *Radio Free Europe–Radio Liberty Background Report*, no. 201, 30 September.)

Adil Çarçani. The successor of Mehmet Shehu as prime minister was born in the city of Argyrocastron in 1922 and comes from a relatively wealthy family of that city. He is a compatriot of Enver Hoxha (who was also born in the same city) and speaks fluent Italian and Greek.

Assessments of the new premier by Greek refugees from that region vary, but the majority of them suggest that Çarçani was a reluctant communist who joined the movement in the early 1940s when the notion was carefully cultivated in the Balkans that the Western Allies supported only communist groups in Yugoslavia, Greece, and Albania. Çarçani was not present at the founding congress of the Albanian Communist Party, becoming a member almost a year later (July 1942). During the war, he served as the political commissar of the Çerçiz Topulli battalion, which was active in the Argyrocastron-Delvino area. Later he held the same post at the brigade and division levels. It was Hoxha's practice to place Tosks in leadership positions in Gheg territories, and he was appointed party secretary of the Durres and Shkodra regions, thus giving rise to occasional Western misperceptions that he is a Gheg.

Çarçani's rise in the party hierarchy was rather slow in comparison with that of Ramiz Alia. He was elected an alternate member of the Central Committee at the Second Party Congress (1952) and became a full member at the Third Congress (1956). At the Fourth Party Congress, Çarçani was elected a member of the Politburo.

Contrary to Alia's situation, the Albanian premier seems to have extensive administrative experience. He was secretary general of the cabinet in 1948 and deputy minister of commerce. In the 1950s, he served variously as minister of industry, construction, and geology. In 1970, he was given the task of chairman of the Electrification Commission, and under his stewardship total electrification of the country, which is now able to export electricity to Yugoslavia and Greece, was achieved. Çarçani became first deputy premier in 1974 (he had been one of four deputy premiers since 1965), following the purge of Beqir Baluku and Abdyl Kelezi, both deputy premiers.

The Albanian premier lacks broad foreign policy experience. However, he did serve as head of economic delegations to Moscow (1955) and to Beijing (1968 and 1975), where he signed major economic agreements.

In most policy matters, Çarçani seems to follow a moderate path. During his tenure as deputy premier and now as premier, he seems to have initiated a search for broader trade and cultural relations with noncommunist states. At the Eighth APL Congress, Çarçani sought to clarify the Albanian slogan of "self-reliance": "The development of our socialist economy relying on its own forces has always permeated, like a red thread, the economic policy of the party. Self-reliance has nothing to do with an autarkic economy, with a lack of trade with the outside world. Nor does it mean falling back to positions of narrow nationalism as the ideologists of the bourgeoisie and of modern revisionism try to claim." (*Zëri i popullit*, 6 November.)

It cannot be said with certainty whether the views of Çarçani on economic matters and foreign policy issues will prevail over those of Ramiz Alia. One thing is certain, however. Çarçani played no active role in the anti-Soviet polemics of the 1960s, as Alia did. He was too absorbed in economic matters and therefore is much more familiar with the implications of the break in relations with the major patrons of Albania. (Source: *Radio Free Europe–Radio Liberty Background Report*, 25 January.)

Howard University   Nikolaos A. Stavrou

Bulgaria

The Bulgarian Communist Party (BCP) dates its separate existence from 1903 when the Bulgarian Social Democratic Party, founded in 1891, split into "broad" and "narrow" factions. The latter took the name Bulgarian Communist Party and became a charter member of the Comintern in 1919. Outlawed in 1924, the party re-emerged in 1927 as the Workers' Party, changing its name again in 1934 to Bulgarian Workers' Party (Communist). The BCP designation was restored in 1948 after the party was firmly in power. Its founder was Dimitur Blagoev (1856–1924), and its best-known leader was Georgi Dimitrov (1882–1949), secretary general of the Comintern from 1935 to 1943 and premier of Bulgaria from 1946 to his death in 1949.

Although the BCP commanded the support of nearly one-fifth of the Bulgarian electorate in the early 1920s, a combination of inept leadership and government repression reduced its membership to about 15,000 by World War II. The party's resistance efforts during the war, although real, were not decisive in bringing it to power. On 5 September 1944, the Soviet Union declared war on Bulgaria, and three days later the Red Army entered the country unopposed. During the night of 8–9 September, the communist-inspired Fatherland Front coalition carried out a coup d'état, after which the BCP employed tactics that included force and violence to eliminate its rivals and consolidate its hold on the country. The trial and execution of opposition leader Nikola Petkov for treason in 1947 marked the end of organized resistance to communization. Stalinist purges, including the trial and execution of the party's former general secretary, Traycho Kostov, for Titoism in 1949, turned the party into an obedient Soviet tool. During the period of de-Stalinization following Stalin's death, Todor Zhivkov ousted Vulko Chervenkov, Bulgaria's Little Stalin, and since that time has maintained a firm hold on power with obvious Soviet support. Domestically, the Bulgarian communist regime has pursued industrialization, bringing a significant improvement in the material standard of living; in foreign policy it has manifested consistent loyalty to the USSR.

On the whole, 1982 was a quiet year for Bulgaria. There were no major political disturbances or shake-ups, although corruption scandals cost several high-ranking officials their jobs, or worse. The economy continued to perform well, and indebtedness to the West was further reduced. In cultural life there were some signs of a chill, but the more open, varied, and nationalistic policies that marked the cultural regime of the late Lyudmila Zhivkova continued to show vitality. The most dramatic events came on the international scene, with accusations of Bulgaria's involvement in the attempted assassination of Pope John Paul II in 1981 threatening to jeopardize Bulgaria's relations with the West.

Population. 8,903,000 (1 January; *Rabotnichesko delo*, 3 February)

Party. Bulgarian Communist Party (Bulgarska Komunisticheska Partiya; BCP)

Membership. 825,876; 42.7 percent industrial workers

Secretary General. Todor Zhivkov

Politburo. 11 full members: Todor Zhivkov (chairman, State Council), Milko Balev (head of Zhivkov's personal secretariat), Todor Bozhinov (first deputy prime minister, minister of metallurgy and mineral resources), Ognyan Doynov (member, State Council), Tsola Dragoycheva (member, State Council; honorary chairman, Bulgarian-Soviet Friendship Society), Gen. Dobri Dzhurov (minister of national defense), Grisha Filipov (prime minister), Pencho Kubadinski (member, State Council; chairman, Fatherland Front), Alexander Lilov (member, State Council), Petur Mladenov (minister of foreign affairs), Stanko Todorov (chairman, National Assembly); 3 candidate members: Petur Dyulgerov (chairman, Central Council of Trade Unions), Andrey Lukanov (deputy prime minister), Georgi Yordanov (chairman, Committee on Culture)

Secretariat. 10 members: Chudomir Alexandrov (first secretary, Sofia city party committee), Georgi Atanasov (chairman, Committee for State Control), Milko Balev, Ognyan Doynov, Alexander Lilov, Stoyan Mikhailov, Misho Mishev, Dimitur Stanishev, Vasil Tsanov, Kiril Zarev

Central Committee. 194 full and 138 candidate members

Last Congress. Twelfth, 31 March–4 April 1981, in Sofia; next congress scheduled for 1986

Auxiliary Organizations. Central Council of Trade Unions (CCTU, about four million members), led by Petur Dyulgerov; Dimitrov Communist Youth League (Komsomol, 1.5 million members), led by Stanka Shopova; Civil Defense Organization (750,000 members), led by Col. Gen. Tencho Papazov, provides training in paramilitary tactics and disaster relief; Committee on Bulgarian Women (30,000 members), led by Elena Lagadinova, no real significance

Main State Organs. State Council (29 members), Todor Zhivkov, chairman; Council of Ministers, Grisha Filipov, chairman, reports to State Council; National Assembly (400 members), constitutionally superior to State Council and Council of Ministers, but in practice rubberstamps decisions of BCP and State Council

Parliament and Elections. All candidates run on ticket of Fatherland Front, an umbrella organization (4.4 million members) comprising most mass organizations. In last national elections (7 June 1981), Fatherland Front candidates received 99.9 percent of votes cast. Of the National Assembly's 400 members, 271 belong to the BCP and 99 to Agrarian Union; 30 are unaffiliated (some 20 of these are Komsomols). The Bulgarian Agrarian National Union (BANU, 120,000 members) formally shares power with the BCP, has 4 of the 29 State Council seats (justice, public health, communications, forestry) and one-fifth of local people's council seats. BANU leader Petur Tanchev's post as first deputy chairman of the State Council makes him Todor Zhivkov's nominal successor.

Publications. *Rabotnichesko delo* (*RD*; Workers' cause), BCP daily; *Partien zhivot* (Party life), BCP monthly; *Novo vreme* (New time), BCP theoretical journal. *Otechestven front* (Fatherland Front), front daily; *Durzhaven vestnik* (State newspaper), contains texts of laws and decrees; Bulgarska telegrafna agentsiya (BTA) is the official news agency.

Party Internal Affairs. There was no sign of any weakening in Todor Zhivkov's leadership during the year, nor was there any visible challenge to his authority. "I am not in power because of my attractive eyes," he said in a *New York Times* interview (1 September). "I go around visiting the towns and villages, and I know what the people think." He seemed, at age 71, to continue to enjoy good health, and he carried on an active schedule of speeches and travel. On 7 December, however, in an address to youth on the eve of National Students Day, he confessed that he had recently suffered a "grave illness" and that "some viruses even tried to remove me from the ranks." He claimed full recovery, and no further mention of this illness appeared in the press. (Sofia domestic service, 7 December; *FBIS*, 8 December.) When asked during another interview if he planned to retire, he replied that he did not, adding that he had a grandfather who reached the age of 107 and remained hearty until his very last day (Robert Maxwell, ed., *Todor Zhivkov*, Oxford, 1982, p. 352).

Georgi Yordanov, a candidate member of the Politburo and a deputy prime minister since 1979, was elected to head the powerful Committee on Culture at a plenum of that body on 1 February. Although Yordanov, who is 48, had been associated with the late Lyudmila Zhivkova, Todor Zhivkov's daughter and the committee's chairman until her death in 1981 (see *YICA*, 1982, p. 378) and had implemented some of her cultural and educational policies, he is not known to possess any scholarly or cultural credentials in his own right. Zhivkova was a trained historian and had published several books, but of Yordanov it was reported only that he likes to read and to listen to classical music. He was probably selected for his sorely needed administrative skills, demonstrated when he headed the Sliven and later the Sofia district party committee before 1979. (*Radio Free Europe Situation Report*, 11 February, item 1.)

On 2 March, a plenum of the BCP Central Committee announced a number of changes affecting party leadership. Politburo member Grisha Filipov was released from his post as a Central Committee secretary, a move that had been expected since he was appointed prime minister last year (see *YICA*, 1982, p. 378). He was replaced on the Secretariat by Kiril Zarev, 56, a close associate of Filipov, a deputy prime minister, and at the time of his appointment, chairman of the State Planning Committee. Later, on 9 November during the National Assembly session, it was announced that he had left the planning committee. He was replaced by Stanish Bonev, 50, a deputy prime minister and through 1981 the head of the Central Committee's Planning Department. In accepting his new appointment, Bonev gave up the post of deputy prime minister to Georgi Karamanev, who remained minister of internal trade and public services. (*Radio Free Europe Situation Report*, 12 March, item 2; Sofia domestic service, 2 November; *FBIS*, 15 November.)

The 2 March plenum also announced the resignation of Peko Takov from the Politburo "at his own request for reasons of health." Another reason for his resignation became apparent later when it was announced that his son Yancho had been tried along with two others on 1–3 March for "smuggling and currency frauds." One of the other defendants, Atanas Taskov, is the son of Boris Taskov, a former minister and Politburo member. Takov, Taskov, and a third defendant were sentenced to two and a half years' imprisonment and fined 2,500 leva each. Rumors circulated that they had been engaged in drug smuggling. No accusations were leveled at the elder Takov, who retained his membership in the State Council. He was replaced on the Politburo by Milko Balev, 62. Since 1965, Balev has held the post of chief of the Chairman's Office (that is, Zhivkov's principal aide); he has also been a BCP Central Committee secretary since 1977. (*Radio Free Europe Situation Report*, 12 March, item 2, 23 April, item 3.)

Corruption was also involved in the dismissal of Zhivko Popov and Mircho Spasov from the Central Committee. Popov, 52, a candidate member of the Central Committee since 1976, worked as a deputy foreign minister assigned to purchase art works abroad in connection with Lyudmila Zhivkova's plan to construct a major art museum in Sofia. On 4–22 March, he was tried for "embezzlement of especially large size by an official, and representing an especially serious case." He received the maximum sentence of twenty years' imprisonment, confiscation of his entire property, and deprivation of the right to hold responsible office or to reside in Sofia. Three lower-ranking officials were codefendants and received sentences ranging from ten to eighteen years coupled with confiscation of property. Colonel General Mircho Spasov, a full member of the Central Committee since 1962, was dismissed without explanation. Because he had headed the Central Committee department in charge of personnel working or traveling abroad, he may have been involved in the Popov case. At the very least, he was guilty of a lack of vigilance. There was no report of punishment beyond dismissal from the Central Committee, which is not surprising in view of Spasov's age (71), rank, and long record of party service. (Ibid.)

Todor Zhivkov's son-in-law and widower of Lyudmila Zhivkova, Ivan Slavkov, was dismissed as director of Bulgarian Television and relegated to the minor post of chairman of the Bulgarian Olympic Committee. No reasons for this demotion were given, but there were rumors that the handsome Slavkov had brought a good deal of personal unhappiness to his wife before her death and that they had in fact been separated. Todor Zhivkov was said to have taken over supervision of the upbringing of the couple's two children. Other rumors linked Slavkov to the Yancho Takov affair, for the two men were known to travel in the same circles. Still others suggested that he had simply badly mismanaged his job. (Ibid., 12 March, item 3.)

Army General Ivan Mikhailov, a Politburo member from 1954 until his retirement last year, died on 16 May at the age of 85 (*BTA*, 17 May, *FBIS*, 18 May). Death also claimed Dimo Dichev, a Central Committee member since 1945 and the chairman of the Union of Fighters against Fascism and Capitalism, Bulgaria's organization of World War II partisan veterans. Dichev was 80 when he died on 13 July (Sofia domestic service, 14 July; *FBIS*, 15 July). Vladimir Bonev, a member of the Central Committee and the State Council was named the new chairman of the partisan organization on 2 September (Sofia domestic service, 2 September; *FBIS*, 7 September). A second Central Committee member, Dimitur Popov, died on 20 May (Sofia domestic service, 21 May; *FBIS*, 24 May).

Until 1982, Todor Zhivkov's son Vladimir had played no visible role in Bulgarian political life. It was announced, however, at the Komsomol congress in May, that the younger Zhivkov, who is 30, was named to that organization's Central Committee bureau (*Radio Free Europe Situation Report*, 9 June, item 2). Later in the year, he emerged in public view as chairman of the Banner of Peace Children's International Assembly. In this capacity, he made his first national speech on Bulgarian television, appearing quite nervous, but carrying off his duties in a manner that won general approval. In view of the meteoric career of his sister, who, among other things, had initiated the Banner of Peace assemblies, Vladimir Zhivkov will be a closely watched figure in Bulgarian politics.

Mass Organizations. Several of Bulgaria's mass organizations held congresses to discuss and clarify their roles in implementing the decisions of the Twelfth BCP Congress held last year. On 8–10 April, nearly 3,000 delegates convened in Sofia for the Ninth CCTU Congress. In his address, Chairman Petur Dyulgerov called for the unions to assume a more active role in the implementation of the New Economic Mechanism, stating that this would require expanded trade union participation in management and planning. He added that in the past excessive red tape and formalism and failure to protest effectively against abuses of power by management had lowered the unions' prestige. These shortcomings should be overcome, he continued, by greater efforts on the part of trade union officials to learn the concerns and desires of the workers and through greater reliance on elections. At the same time, he stressed the necessity of the unions' operating under the direction of party leadership. Todor Zhivkov, speaking as "one of the delegates," predicted that the need for manual labor in Bulgaria will soon disappear, so that workers must be trained for more complex and intellectually demanding occupations. He also spoke of increasing socialist competition with material incentives, and he called for labor collectives to assume a larger role as "masters of socialist property." Admitting that Bulgaria's housing problem was far from solved, he advocated no increase in construction, but proposed changes in the system of allocating new housing and for expanding trade union recreation and vacation facilities. He also announced that a new labor code was being prepared and would be presented to the country in 1983. (Ibid., 23 April, items 1, 2.) Later in the year a plenum of the BCP Central Committee approved a draft of this code and announced that it would be published for national discussion (Sofia domestic service, 30 November; *FBIS*, 1 December). According to the press, the code will "ensure a job to every man, equal remuneration for equal work, a remuneration according to the quantity and quality of labor, real possibilities for raising the level of education and qualifications, good working conditions" (BTA, 2 December; *FBIS*, 3 December).

At the end of 1981, the Central Committee of the Dimitrov Communist Youth League held a plenum to announce leadership changes. First Secretary Georgi Tanov left the organization to become first secretary of the Kurdzhali district party committee. He was replaced by Stanka Shopova, born in 1954, who is the first woman to hold the Komsomol leadership. (BTA, 24 December 1981; *FBIS*, 7 January.) The Komsomol held its Fourteenth Congress on 25–27 May, at which its new leader delivered a speech criticizing the growth of consumerism, criminality, alcohol and drug abuse, and disinterest in work among Bulgarian youth. She called for the organization to combat these evils, to educate young men and women for healthy family life, and particularly to encourage them to have larger families. She also urged Komsomol functionaries to consider the actual interests of young people when planning agitational work, offering as a concrete suggestion that "current political and cultural information" be presented in discotheques. Todor Zhivkov also addressed the congress, devoting most of his speech to cultural policy (see below). He also told the 2,754 delegates that Bulgaria had not yet created the ideal communist society, and he called for a "frank dialogue" between youth and the party as a means of overcoming weaknesses and achieving progress. (*Radio Free Europe Situation Report*, 9 June, items 1, 2; BCP, Central Committee, *Information Bulletin*, August, pp. 3–13, 79–107.)

The Fatherland Front celebrated its fortieth anniversary this year and held its Ninth Congress on 21–23 June. Chairman Pencho Kubadinski surveyed the front's accomplishments, emphasizing the importance of its voluntary commissions, which performed spot checks on the quality of goods and services in 90 percent of the country's retail establishments. He also boasted of the 49 million workdays contributed by front members during the Seventh Five-Year Plan (1976–1980) to conservation, beautification, and sanitation projects. (*RD*, 22 June.) Todor Zhivkov also addressed the congress, stating that in the future the Fatherland Front would play a major role in improving the quality of local government, studying and shaping public opinion, and providing greater opportunities for direct contacts between the masses and their leaders (ibid., 24 June).

Domestic Affairs. *Economy.* On 11 December 1981, the National Assembly approved the Eighth Five-Year Plan for the 1981-1985 period. The targets for growth in primary economic categories of the economy were national income, 20 percent; labor productivity, 25 percent; industrial production, 28 percent; agricultural production, 18 percent; foreign trade, 40 percent; per capita real income, 15 percent. The plan also called for 37 billion leva to be spent on capital investment (an increase of 19.3 percent) and the construction of 360,000 new housing units. These rates of growth were in most cases lower than those achieved during the Seventh Five-Year Plan and lower still than the targets set for that plan in 1975. The one-year goals for 1982 that were approved at the same time called for the following increases: national income, 3.6 percent; labor productivity, 3.5 percent; industrial production, 4.5 percent; agricultural production, 2.2 percent; per capita real income, 3.0 percent. Again these rates of growth were more modest than those for previous years and were described by the State Planning Committee as "moderate and realistic." (Ibid., 15 January; *Radio Free Europe Situation Report*, 14 January, item 1, 11 February, item 3.) Quarterly reports during 1982 indicated general success in meeting the goals despite occasional setbacks or bottlenecks in particular branches of industry (BTA, 20 April, 20 July, 22 October; *FBIS*, 21 April, 21 July, 25 October). This generally optimistic picture was confirmed in a Wharton Econometrics study that projected an average annual growth in Bulgaria's net material product (gross national product minus services) of 4.1 percent over 1981–1982, putting it in first place among members of the Council for Mutual Economic Assistance (CMEA). The study also reported that over the same period Bulgaria had substantially reduced its indebtedness to the West, from $2.5 billion at the end of 1980 to $1.7 billion at the end of 1982. (*WP*, 13 December.)

As of 1 January, the entire Bulgarian economy became subject to the New Economic Mechanism (NEM), a form of which was introduced in agriculture in 1979 (see *YICA*, 1980, pp. 14–15) and in a few other industries (book publishing, health care) since that time. Although presented as new, the provisions of the NEM seem rather to be a continuation of a tendency toward decentralization that has been under way for some time. Indeed, clear descriptions of the NEM were hard to come by in the press, indicating that the measure was still in a process of definition and testing. In general, the NEM is said to encompass a reduction in the role of central planning and greater reliance on "profitability" as the prime performance indicator at lower levels. It aims at providing incentives for enterprises to raise the quality of their production and to pay greater attention to innovation. Wage and salary funds are supposed to come from "profits," creating the possibility of a sharp drop in income for an enterprise in a bad year. However, the whole reform is hedged with qualifications allowing for various forms of state intervention at all levels. Since Bulgaria has been enjoying relatively good economic performance, it is likely that the government will want to avoid rocking the boat and will proceed with the NEM in a gradual and flexible manner. (*RD*, 30 December 1981, 15 January, 28 February; *Radio Free Europe Background Report*, 26 January, 2 July.)

Following a speech by Zhivkov on 12 March in Burgas dealing with agriculture, a Council on Agricultural Affairs was created, headed by Prime Minister Grisha Filipov. It is intended to coordinate the activities of all ministries and government departments dealing with agriculture. Its first meeting was held on 21 April and included the chairmen of provincial executive committees, the chairmen of the agro-industrial complexes, as well as representatives from the central government. (Sofia domestic service, 5 April, 21 April; *FBIS*, 6 April, 22 April.) In form this body seems to resemble the Bulgarian Industrial Economic Organization set up in 1980 under the direction of Politburo member Ognyan Doynov, whose aim was to share resources and avoid duplication (*Radio Free Europe Situation Report*, 23 July, item 2).

A survey of the 1982 harvest was generally optimistic, although an unusually cold and wet July delayed completion of the grain harvest and resowing of the fields (ibid., 20 August, item 3). A report on long-term agricultural growth stated that between 1965 and 1981 Bulgarians increased their annual per capita consumption of meat from 48 to 61 kilograms, of milk from 148 to 198 liters, and of eggs from 167 to 203 (BTA, 8 September; *FBIS*, 9 September). On the negative side, a survey by the Ministry of Interior's Institute on Criminology reported significant increases in rural theft and embezzlement. Although individual examples were usually on a small scale, they have become such a mass phenomenon that no social stigma attaches to the perpetrator even if caught and convicted. (*Radio Free Europe Situation Report*, 9 June, item 5.)

Foreign Trade Minister Khristo Khristov gave an optimistic picture of Bulgaria's international economic position. In a press interview on 4 May, he stated that Bulgaria has no balance of payments problem and has become one of the world leaders in per capita export of electronic equipment, cigarettes, wine, and processed food (BTA, 4 May; *FBIS*, 5 May). On the other hand, Bulgarian initiatives to promote joint-venture projects with the developed capitalist states have not had much success. Bulgaria organized a symposium on East-West trade, 11–12 May, in Varna attended by about a hundred business representatives from 21 countries. Zhivkov addressed the meeting, calling for expanded economic cooperation, but no concrete results were reported. (*Radio Free Europe Situation Report*, 26 May, item 2.) The European Economic Community has also not responded to Bulgaria's request for preferential tariffs, prompting several Bulgarian complaints that the long delay was not justified (BTA, 4 May; *FBIS*, 5 May).

Demographic Problems. Articles in the press and speeches by important party and government figures indicated that the continued decline in Bulgaria's birthrate was seen as a serious problem. In recent years, the number of births per 1,000 people has fallen steadily, from 17.2 in 1974 to 14.3 in 1980 to 14.1 in 1981. This has caused a corresponding drop in the rate of population increase from 7.4 per 1,000 in 1974 to 3.6 in 1980 to 3.0 in 1981, and some regions—Viden, Lovech, and Mikhailovgrad provinces—have experienced sharply negative rates of growth. Moreover, although Bulgaria no longer publishes population statistics broken down by ethnic group, it is generally assumed that ethnic Bulgarians have the lowest birthrate, while the Turkish, Gypsy, and Muslim Pomak minorities have substantially higher ones, for it is known that population growth has been greatest in regions with the largest concentrations of minorities. On 18 February, Pencho Kubadinski, Politburo member and chairman of the Fatherland Front, presided over a conference organized by the front in Viden devoted to finding measures to reverse the population decline in the province. It adopted the so-called "Bregovo model," based on an earlier experimental program, calling for the state and employers to assume the financial burden for a family's third child by paying the family fifty leva per month until the child reaches the age of eighteen. It also called for providing free food in all provincial daycare centers and schools and for financing the higher education of a larger number of young people. (*Radio Free Europe Situation Report*, 12 March, item 5.) On 1–2 September, Georgi Dzhagarov, deputy chairman of the State Council and a longtime close friend of Zhivkov, published a long article on population problems in the army newspaper, *Narodna armiya*. According to Dzhagarov, Bulgaria's low rate of population growth endangers the country's economic progess and strategic position in the Balkans. He blamed the problem on the availability of contraceptives and abortions (averaging 150,000–160,000 annually compared to about 120,000 live births) and to the material costs of raising larger families. To improve the situation, Dzhagarov proposed imposing a high fee for abortion, increasing the "bachelor's tax" on single people and childless families, and raising the allowance paid to large families. He also suggested that children under sixteen be entitled to rations of free meals, clothes, transportation, etc., so that their gratitude would be properly directed toward the state. As to the lack of adequate housing, which has in the past been frequently cited as the main reason for childless and one-child families, he called for the better distribution of existing housing and better housing design. (Ibid., 7 October, item 2.)

In May, the government also launched a program to promote migration to the more backward and sparsely populated areas of the country. The Strandzha-Sakar region, a very primitive area in the southeastern corner of the country along the Turkish border, was selected as the main target for development. Families volunteering to settle in this region are to receive substantial grants, long-term loans for housing construction, salary bonuses, and free transportation for visits home. It also appears that settlers there in villages and towns without industry will be allowed to engage in handicrafts, trade, and services under conditions approximating private enterprise. At its Fourteenth Congress, the Komsomol pledged to recruit 2,500 settlers for the region and 2,000 more for other backward areas. The Komsomol also designated the Strandzha-Sakar region the Republic of Youth. (Ibid., 9 September, item 1.)

Cultural Affairs. Since the death of Lyudmila Zhivkova in July 1981, there has been considerable curiosity whether the innovative cultural and nationalistic policies she had sponsored as head of the powerful Committee on Culture would be continued. When Georgi Yordanov was selected as Zhivkova's successor to head the committee, Politburo member Alexander Lilov, who is the party's usual spokesman on ideological issues, told the committee plenum that there would be no substantial changes in cultural policy. He added that "dogmatism and sectarian narrow-mindedness" would not be resurrected. (*RD,* 2 February.) There was a substantial turnover of committee personnel at the time of Yordanov's appointment but later developments indicated that this was due to financial mismanagement and misuse of committee funds rather than to policy issues. The first anniversary of Zhivkova's death (21 July) and her fortieth birthday (26 July) evoked a vast outpouring of tributes and pledges to continue what she had begun (*Radio Free Europe Background Report,* 12 October). Yet there were numerous signs during the year that the party was growing apprehensive of some of the directions taken by the cultural intelligentsia under Zhivkova's inspiration. At a discussion of Bulgarian prose published in 1981 organized by the Bulgarian Writers' Union (BWU) on 5–9 April, the principal report attacked alienation and political apathy among contemporary writers, their subjectivism and their interest in "negative characters," and their failure to create convincing communist protagonists. To be sure, several writers objected to this evaluation in the strongest terms, and BWU Chairman Liubomir Levchev, one of Zhivkova's protégés, stated that the report represented the personal views of its author and not the official position of the Union. (Ibid.) Shortly afterward, Todor Zhivkov, in his speech to the Komsomol congress, warned that writers, editors, and critics had shown insufficient ideological vigilance with regard to certain works. He added that Bulgaria has no censorship, but that the party was obligated to struggle against works that "denigrate our reality and deviate from class-party positions." (BCP, Central Committee, *Information Bulletin,* August, pp. 10–12.)

Zhivkov and other critics may have had in mind the new novel *Face* by Blaga Dimitrova, one of Bulgaria's greatest living writers, which paints a dark picture of hypocrisy, corruption, and the degeneration of idealism in Bulgarian life. After a prolonged silence, the press launched a vicious critical attack on the book. The literary journal *Septemvri* spoke of Dimitrova's "deformed, sick subjectivism," and *Puls,* the Komsomol cultural journal, said that it read like pages from the bourgeois press. The work was withdrawn from bookstores and was reportedly selling for astronomical prices on the black market. (*Budeshte/ L'Avenir,* Paris, September, pp. 13–14.)

Party conservatives also criticized the film *Woman at 33* for its theme—an idealistic woman in a coarse, dishonest world sacrifices her values to advance her career and incidentally to achieve party membership—and "lowered ideological and aesthetic criteria" (*Radio Free Europe Situation Report,* 26

May, item 1). Another film, the historical *Measure for Measure*, was attacked for suggesting that Bulgarians as well as Serbs committed atrocities against the inhabitants of Macedonia (*Istoricheski pregled*, no. 1, pp. 81–86).

Foreign Affairs. In recent years, Bulgaria has made considerable efforts to improve relations with the noncommunist world and to overcome the legacy of past isolationist policies. The celebration of the 1,300th anniversary of the Bulgarian state in 1981 was followed by a continuing series of international events and exhibitions devoted to various aspects of the country's cultural heritage. At the second Children's International Assembly, 15–25 August, Bulgaria played host to 1,500 young people from 110 countries (*Narodna kultura*, 20 August). In September, the Slavic Committee was renamed the Committee for Bulgarians Abroad, and it announced an expanded program to develop ties with émigré communities around the world. Most ambitious of all was the project for the creation of the Lyudmila Zhivkova International Foundation. This was first announced in September 1981 at a Rome meeting of the Golden Mercury International Association, an organization that aims to promote international understanding and economic cooperation, with members from 41 nations. On 9 March, an initiative committee with representatives from 19 nations, only 2 of which belong to the communist camp, held its first meeting in Sofia, and elected BWU Chairman Liubomir Levchev as its chairman. Although the functions of the new foundation were not set out in detail, it seems intended to be similar to such institutions as the Alliance Française. Speakers at the 9 March meeting indicated that it would be especially active in contributing to cultural projects in the underdeveloped world. (*Radio Free Europe Situation Report*, 24 March, item 2.)

Without sacrificing its close relationship with the Soviet Union, Bulgaria has tried, through the measures described above and others like them, to project its own identity, particularly in the West. While these efforts have had some success, they were overshadowed by the accusations that Bulgarian agents had planned and organized the attempt on the life of Pope John Paul II in May 1981. These charges first surfaced in a *Reader's Digest* article (September) and were repeated in an NBC television documentary. The supporting evidence, however, was far from conclusive, and the Bulgarian press made a strong case against it (BTA, 7 September; *FBIS*, 8 September). Later in the year, Italian authorities, reportedly relying on information supplied by would-be assassin Mehmet Ali Agca, described a network of Bulgarian intelligence agents and Turkish underworld figures that organized the attempt on the pontiff's life. Serge Ivanov Antonov, head of Bulgaria's Balkan Airline office in Rome and allegedly a State Security agent, was arrested on 25 November, and the Italian prosecutor also sought the arrest of two Bulgarian embassy officials, who had previously returned to Bulgaria. The Italian defense minister accused Bulgaria of committing "an act of war," the Italian ambassador to Sofia was called home, and several Italian politicians called for the complete rupture of diplomatic and economic relations with Bulgaria. Bulgarian authorities denied the charges, but promised to cooperate in the Italian prosecutor's investigation. They also arrested Turkish national Bekir Celenk, one of the figures supposedly involved in the plot. On 17 December, he and the two embassy officials sought by the Italians were made available for questioning by Italian reporters. The Italian prosecutor was also invited to question these men in Sofia, but Bulgaria refused to extradite them. At the same time, Bulgaria put two Italian citizens on trial for espionage. (*WP*, 26 and 27 November, 6 and 12 December; "Transcript of International Press Conference Held in Sofia, December 17, 1982," released by the Bulgarian embassy in Washington; *Newsweek*, 3 January 1983.)

While evidence of Bulgaria's involvement in the assassination attempt remains at this point inconclusive, belief in the charges has been strengthened by alleged Bulgarian connections to past terrorist acts such as the "umbrella murder" of Georgi Markov in 1978, the kidnapping of Brig. Gen. James Dozier by the Red Brigades in Italy in 1981, and the supply of arms to Turkish terrorist groups. If the charges receive further substantiation, they will undoubtedly have a serious effect on Bulgaria's position in Western Europe.

The Soviet Union. As in the past, Bulgarian leaders continued to emphasize their loyalty to the Soviet Union and to support Soviet positions on all major international questions. In his speech to the international conference on Georgi Dimitrov, Todor Zhivkov told the delegates: "It is mankind's supreme happiness that there is the Soviet Union—this giant in the socialist community which, with its high political prestige, inexhaustible economic potential, rich spiritual life, and invincible armed forces, is a reliable shield of the socialist community, of world peace" (BCP, Central Committee, *Information Bulletin*, July, p. 18). Approximately 52 percent of Bulgaria's foreign trade is with the USSR, which provides Bulgaria with 60 percent of its machine imports and 93 percent of its oil (BTA, 9 March; *FBIS*, 10 March). Zhivkov was the guest of Soviet party leaders in the Ukraine on 8–11 June (BTA, 8 June; *FBIS*, 9 June), but he omitted his usual summer visit with Brezhnev in the Crimea, probably because of the Soviet leader's failing health. Brezhnev's death was discussed at an extraordinary meeting of the BCP Politburo on 11 November, which designated 12–15 November as days of mourning (BTA, 12 November; *FBIS*, 12 November). Zhivkov and Grisha Filipov represented Bulgaria at Brezhnev's furneral (Sofia domestic service, 14 November; *FBIS*, 15 November), and Zhivkov returned to Moscow on 20–22 December as head of the Bulgarian delegation to the celebration of the sixtieth anniversary of the formation of the USSR (BTA, 20 December; Sofia domestic service, 22 December; *FBIS*, 20 and 23 December).

Bulgaria has consistently defended the Soviet intervention in Afghanistan. On 16–23 December 1981, Afghan head of state Babrak Karmal met with Zhivkov in Sofia, and the two leaders signed a treaty of friendship and cooperation (*RD*, 24 December 1981). During 1982, it was reported that Bulgaria would build plants in Afghanistan for processing fur and milk, construct water supply systems for several towns, and train some 2,000 Afghan medical students (BTA, 21 April; *FBIS*, 21 April).

Other East European and Balkan Countries. Bulgaria has always stressed its loyal and active participation in the Warsaw Pact and CMEA. On 27–30 September, Bulgaria hosted the Shield–82 Warsaw Pact maneuvers. They were held in the eastern part of the country and avoided operations near the Yugoslav or Greek borders. (*Radio Free Europe Situation Report*, 3 November, item 2.)

Bulgaria welcomed the imposition of martial law in Poland as "necessary, urgent, and lawful" and blamed Poland's economic collapse on sabotage and the unrealistic demands of Solidarity (*RD*, 31 December 1981). In the spring, Politboro member Todor Bozhinov and Polish Deputy Prime Minister Roman Malinowski, who jointly chair the Polish-Bulgarian Commission on Economic Cooperation, announced plans for new forms of cooperation between the two countries. Details were not announced but apparently call for Bulgaria to supply credits and to deliver material and equipment to Poland, while Poland will supply construction workers for various projects on Bulgarian soil. General Wojciech Jaruzelski and a high-level Polish delegation visited Bulgaria on 20 May, probably to clarify these agreements. (*Radio Free Europe Situation Report*, 26 May, item 4.) Bulgaria also made its vacation resorts available to officials from the Polish Interior Ministry, "who showed heroism and selflessness in the struggle against counterrevolution," and to their wives (*Naroden strazh*, 14 July; *FBIS*, 4 August).

Czechoslovak head of state Gustáv Husák visited Bulgaria, 21–23 September, for discussions with Zhivkov on economic issues and to prepare for the CMEA summit meeting in Prague during January 1983. Agreements were announced on long-term cooperation in numerous areas. It was also stated that the two countries would undertake to coordinate their 1986–1990 five-year plans. (*Radio Free Europe Situation Report*, 7 October, item 1.) East German Prime Minister Willi Stoph also discussed long-term economic cooperation with Bulgaria in Sofia on 18–20 October (*RD*, 21 October; *FBIS*, 25 October).

Despite Romania's more independent foreign policy, Romanian-Bulgarian relations continued to be cordial. Zhivkov went to Bucharest on 14–17 January, where he received a Romanian decoration (*RD*, 15 January; *FBIS*, 21 January), and Nicolae Ceauşescu visited Sofia on 12–14 October (Sofia domestic service, 14 October; *FBIS*, 15 October). On these occasions the two leaders reportedly discussed their joint project to develop hydroelectric power along the Danube, where problems have arisen owing to Romania's current economic difficulties. No details were announced, and general agreement was expressed on all major issues. (*Radio Free Europe Situation Report*, 23 July, item 4, 3 November, item 1.)

Relations with Yugoslavia showed some improvement during the year, but disputes over the existence of a Macedonian nationality continued to create conflicts. Bulgaria has offered to guarantee the Yugoslav-Bulgarian border, while leaving to "science" the task of determining whether the inhabitants of Macedonia are Bulgarians or an entirely distinct nationality. In a speech to the Yugoslav assembly, Yugoslav Foreign Minister Josip Vrhovec stated that Bulgarian recognition of frontiers was meaningless without an acceptance of the Macedonian nationality, which would legitimize the existence of the Macedonian republic. He also frankly rejected a role for "scientific inquiry" on the grounds that it might not uphold the Yugoslav position. (Tanjug, 10 February; *FBIS*, 11 February.) Bulgaria, on the other hand, maintains that recognition of a Macedonian nationality is not only historically unjustified but would legitimize Yugoslav claims to the Pirin region, Bulgaria's portion of historic Macedonia. Stanko Todorov, Politburo member and chairman of the National Assembly, led a parliamentary delegation to Belgrade on 10–13 March. On returning to Bulgaria, he reported that both sides had stated their positions on Macedonia but had been unable to reach any agreement. He added, however, that this should not be an obstacle to expanded economic relations between the two countries. (*Radio Free Europe Situation Report*, 24 March, item 4.) In April, a Bulgarian-Yugoslav commission set a goal of reaching $3 billion in trade during the 1981–1985 period, or 2.5 times that of the preceding five-year period (BTA, 12 April; *FBIS*, 13 April). Later in the spring, the Bulgarian press weighed in with questions about a Yugoslav census showing a decrease in Yugoslavia's Bulgarian minority. This triggered a new round of exchanges over the two countries' respective treatment of minorities. (*Radio Free Europe Situation Report*, 9 June, item 4.)

In the disputes with Yugoslavia, Bulgaria has had little to say about Belgrade's problems with its Albanian minority. Bulgaria did, however, take a number of steps to improve its own relations with Albania, signing a trade agreement with Tirana on 14 September and sending an unusually effusive message of congratulations on Albania's national day (*RD*, 28 November; *FBIS*, 3 December).

Bulgaria enjoys good relations with both of the noncommunist Balkan countries. Turkish head of state Kenan Evren visited Sofia on 24–27 February, for meetings with Zhivkov, during which the Bulgarian leader remarked on improvements in bilateral economic cooperation and stated that there are no obstacles to Bulgarian-Turkish friendship (BCP, Central Committee, *Information Bulletin*, April, pp. 3–7). The murder of a Turkish diplomat in Burgas on 9 September was attributed to Armenian terrorists and apparently had no effect on Balkan diplomacy (BTA, 9 September; *FBIS*, 10 September).

Greek Prime Minister Andreas Papandreou also visited Sofia on 24–26 June. Papandreou endorsed Zhivkov's proposal to make the Balkans a nuclear-free zone (see *YICA*, 1982, pp. 386–87) but in general terms and without suggesting specific steps to bring it about. (Sofia domestic service, 24 June; *FBIS*, 25 June.)

The Third World. Todor Zhivkov met with the emir of Kuwait, Sheikh Jabir al-Ahmad al-Sabah, in the Kuwaiti capital on 14–17 March. Five Kuwaiti-Bulgarian agreements were signed, covering economic cooperation, shipping, reciprocal recognition of educational credentials, tourism, and cultural exchanges. It was also announced that the number of Kuwaiti students in Bulgaria would be increased. (BTA, 17 March; *FBIS*, 18 March.) Earlier in the year, Foreign Trade Minister Khristo Khristov signed an agreement establishing direct trade relations between Bulgaria and the United Arab Emirates (BTA, 25 January; *FBIS*, 2 February). Trade agreements were also signed with Libya and Algeria (BTA, 24 March; *FBIS*, 2 March). Stanko Todorov led parliamentary delegations to Iraq, 27 February–2 March (Sofia domestic service, 1 March; *FBIS*, 2 March), Syria, 4–8 May, and Jordan, 8–10 May (BTA, 10 May; *FBIS*, 11 May). In Syria an agreement on cultural cooperation was signed, and in Jordan King Hussein stated that prospects for improvements in trade and cultural relations were very good.

Bulgaria in the past has been neutral in the war between Iraq and Iran, but in June Prime Minister Grisha Filipov signed a trade agreement with Iran and stated that the war had been imposed on Iran by Iraq, which was serving the interests of the United States. He also said that Bulgaria stands ready to help Iran in its work of reconstruction when the war ends. (Sofia domestic service, 19 June; *FBIS*, 23 June.)

Bulgaria has consistently supported and given aid to the Palestine Liberation Organization (PLO) and in January entertained a PLO military delegation seeking to purchase arms (Voice of Palestine, 17 January; *FBIS*, 19 January). Although Foreign Minister Mladenov took a relatively moderate position when interviewed by the Israeli paper *Ma'ariv* (21 April)—he stated that Bulgaria recognizes Israel's right to exist and has a positive attitude toward the Israeli people (*FBIS*, 23 April)—Bulgaria adopted a more strident tone after the Israeli occupation of Lebanon. The Bulgarian press accused Israel of acting as an agent of U.S. imperialism and agreed to provide medical treatment in Bulgaria for PLO wounded (BTA, 7 September; *FBIS*, 8 September). Mladenov accused Israel of trying "to physically exterminate the long-suffering Palestinian people" (*RD*, 9 September; *FBIS*, 13 September).

The prime minister of Malta, Dom Mintoff, met with Zhivkov on 23 July in Sofia to sign an agreement expanding trade and economic cooperation and opening direct air communications (Sofia domestic service, 23 July; *FBIS*, 26 July). Ali Nasir Muhammad al-Hasani of the People's Democratic Republic of Yemen visited Zhivkov in Sofia on 17 September (BTA, 17 September; *FBIS*, 20 September). The press reported only the general remarks of the two leaders in favor of international cooperation and condemning imperialism and Zionism, but it is widely believed that Bulgaria is one of Yemen's major arms suppliers. Libyan head-of-state Moammar Khadafy visited Bulgaria briefly on 23–24 October (Sofia domestic service, 23 October; *FBIS*, 25 October), but nothing of substance was reported about his meeting with Zhivkov.

Nigerian leader Alhaji Shehu Shagari visited Bulgaria on 10–13 September. After his meeting with Zhivkov, the two leaders jointly condemned South Africa and expressed their support for the South-West African People's Organization. They also signed a trade agreement and announced their intention of expanding bilateral contacts. (BTA, 11 and 13 September; *RD*, 14 September; *FBIS*, 13, 14, and 16 September.) During the year, it was reported that Bulgaria has almost 300 specialists in Angola, most of them medical personnel or teachers (BTA, 23 July; *FBIS*, 26 July). Julião Paulo, Angolan minister for state security and Politburo member, met with Zhivkov in Sofia on 10 September (Sofia domestic service, 10 September; *FBIS*, 13 September). Botswana and Bulgaria announced the establishment of diplomatic relations at the ambassadorial level as of 16 August (BTA, 17 August; *FBIS*, 18 August).

Perhaps reflecting the tentative improvement in Soviet-Chinese relations, the usual condemnation of "Beijing hegemonists" became much less common in the Bulgarian press and in statements by leaders. It was announced that trade between Bulgaria and China had increased by 30 percent in 1981. On 26 February, a new trade agreement called for an exchange of goods valued at 177 million Swiss francs. Bulgaria will export to China chemicals, fabrics, cigarettes, and handling equipment. (BTA, 26 February; *FBIS*, 2 March.)

Maurice Bishop, prime minister of Grenada and chairman of the New Jewel Movement's Politburo, met with Zhivkov in Sofia on 14 June. The two leaders expressed concern over the threat of U.S. imperialism in the Caribbean and Central America (Sofia domestic service, 14 June; *FBIS*, 15 June). Zhivkov also expressed Bulgaria's support for the Sandinista government in Nicaragua after a meeting with that country's interior minister in Sofia on 10 September (Sofia domestic service, 10 September; *FBIS*, 13 September).

Western Europe and the United States. Bulgaria's relations with the Western European countries, except at this point for Italy, range from correct to cordial. In recent years, Zhivkov has referred to relations with Austria as a model of cooperation between states with differing social systems. On 3–4 June, he visited Vienna to discuss expanding trade and cultural contacts with Chancellor Bruno Kreisky. After the meeting, Kreisky stated that there were "no problems of any kind" between the two countries. (BTA, 4 June; *FBIS*, 4 June.) Zhivkov later presented the Order of Georgi Dimitrov to Karl Blecha, chairman of the Austro-Bulgarian Friendship Society (Sofia domestic service, 30 July; *FBIS*, 3 August).

West Germany is Bulgaria's largest trading partner in the West. On 27–29 January, Foreign Minister Mladenov visited Bonn to meet with his counterpart Hans-Dietrich Genscher and Chancellor Helmut Schmidt, after which both sides stated they expected continued expansion of trade and tourism (BTA, 28 January; *FBIS*, 29 January).

Bulgaria was visited by the foreign ministers of Spain, 22–23 February (*RD*, 24 February), and France, 6–7 May (BTA, 7 May; *FBIS*, 10 May), both of whom were received by Zhivkov. On each occasion differences of opinion were reported over Poland and Afghanistan, but also hopes for the improvement of bilateral relations. On 6 May, Spain and Bulgaria signed a trade protocol that included provisions for cooperation in North African and Arab markets (BTA, 6 May; *FBIS*, 11 May).

In March Mladenov made goodwill visits to Sweden and Norway, being received by the monarchs of both countries and meeting with other leaders. In both countries he called for expanded economic cooperation, including joint industrial projects. (BTA, 8–12 March; *FBIS*, 9–12 March.) Later in the year, however, the Swedish government protested against Bulgaria's facilitating the transportation of Kurdish refugees from Iraq to Swedish territory. Reportedly, influential Bulgarians were profiting from this traffic in refugees through Bulgaria. (*Radio Free Europe Situation Report*, 20 August, item 4.)

Statements by the press and public figures on the United States continued to reflect the increased hostility in East-West relations. In his address to the trade union congress, Zhivkov accused the United States of accelerating preparations for nuclear war and of trying to bankrupt the socialist camp by forcing it to participate in an unwanted arms race (*RD*, 18 April). At various times during the year, the Bulgarian press accused the United States of backing British colonialism in South America and Israeli imperialism in Lebanon. On the other hand, formal relations between the two countries remained correct. On 19 November, the United States and Bulgaria signed an agreement covering cultural, educational, scientific, and technological exchanges for 1983 and 1984 (BTA, 19 November; *FBIS*, 22 November). On two occasions Zhivkov complained that the United States should pay more attention to Bulgaria, stating that Washington should realize that no crucial Balkan problem can be resolved without Bulgaria (*Afrique-Asie*, 19 July–1 August; *FBIS*, 30 July) and that for the United States Bulgaria is "the last button on the shirt" (*NYT*, 2 September). On 30 June, former president Richard Nixon arrived in Bulgaria for an informal visit. He met with Zhivkov in Varna on the following day for a cordial discussion. (BTA, 1 July; *FBIS*, 2 July.)

International Party Contacts. In connection with the centennial of the birth of Georgi Dimitrov, Bulgaria hosted a major international theoretical conference on 15–17 June devoted to "Georgi Dimitrov's lifework and our time." It was attended by representatives of 148 parties and organizations. In his speech to the delegates, which concluded the conference, Zhivkov surveyed the main accomplishments of Dimitrov's career and argued that the contemporary counterpart of Dimitrov's united front against fascism was the unity of all progressive forces, communist and noncommunist, in an antiwar movement directed against the aggressive and militaristic policies of the United States. He added that it would be a mistake for the antiwar movement to direct its energies against the Soviet Union because its military power, although great, was never used for aggression. (BCP, Central Committee, *Information Bulletin*, July, pp. 5–36.) Bulgarian representatives also participated in events to commemorate Dimitrov's birth in Moscow and Prague.

For several years, Zhivkov has invited communist party leaders to visit Bulgaria's Black Sea resorts for summer vacation. This year his invitation was accepted by the party leaders of Canada, Chile, Denmark, France, Israel, Morocco, Portugal, Switzerland, Tunisia, and Uruguay. At other times during the year, Bulgaria was also visited by the party leaders of Syria and Greece. Zhivkov met personally with all of these leaders, after which the usual statements on peace, solidarity, and cooperation were issued. During the year, high-level Bulgarian delegations represented the BCP at communist party congresses in Yugoslavia, Greece, France, Lebanon, Laos, Cyprus, Vietnam, and Ireland.

This year's recipients of the Order of Georgi Dimitrov included Dolores Ibarruri, president of the Spanish party; Le Duan, secretary general of the Vietnamese party; Erich Honecker, secretary general of the Socialist Unity Party of East Germany; Dinmukhamed Kunaev, member of the Soviet Politburo; Gilberto Vieira, secretary general of the Colombian party; Rodolfo Ghioldi, member of the Executive Committee of the Argentine party; William Kashtan, secretary general of the Canadian party; Niqula al-Shawi, president of the Lebanese party; and Henry Winston, chairman of the U.S. party.

University of Maryland Baltimore County   John D. Bell

Czechoslovakia

The Communist Party of Czechoslovakia (KSČ) was constituted in September 1921 at a merger congress in Prague from several radical socialist and leftist groups among which the left wing of the Czechoslovak Social Democratic Party was the most important. Legal during the First Czechoslovak Republic (1918–1939), it was banned under the German occupation but emerged as the strongest party in the first postwar elections in 1946. In 1948, the KSČ seized all power in a coup d'etat and transformed Czechoslovakia into a communist party-state of the Soviet type. The departure from Stalinist practices started later in Czechoslovakia than in other countries of Central and Eastern Europe, but it led to a daring liberalization experiment known as the Prague Spring in 1968. A Soviet military intervention in August of the same year ended democratization and imposed on Czechoslovakia the policies of so-called normalization—a return to unqualified obedience to the Soviet Union and the emulation of the Soviet example in all areas of life.

Population. 15,344,679 (1 January)

Party. Communist Party of Czechoslovakia (Komunistická Strana Československa; KSČ)

Founded. 1921

Membership. 1,584,011 (26 November); 45.3 percent industrial workers; 5.7 percent cooperative farmers

Secretary General. Gustáv Husák

Presidium. 13 full members: Vasil Bil'ák, Peter Colotka (deputy prime minister), Josef Haman, Karel Hoffman (chairman, Revolutionary Trade Union Movement), Václav Hůla (deputy prime minister; chairman, State Planning Commission), Gustáv Husák (president), Alois Indra (chairman, Federal Assembly), Miloš Jakeš, Antonín Kapek, Josef Kempný, Josef Korčak (deputy prime minister), Jozef Lenárt, Lubomír Štrougal (prime minister); 2 candidate members: Jan Fojtík, Miloslav Hrušković

Secretariat. 9 full members: Gustáv Husák, Mikuláš Beňo, Vasil Bil'ák, Josef Haman, Josef Havlín, Miloš Jakeš, Josef Kempný, František Pitra, Jindřich Poledník; 2 general members: Marie Kabrhelova, Oldrich Svestka

Central Committee. 123 full and 55 candidate members

Last Congress. Sixteenth, 6–10 April 1981, in Prague; next congress scheduled for 1986

Slovak Party. Communist Party of Slovakia (Komunistická Strana Slovenska; KSS); membership, 400,000 full and candidate members; Jozef Lenárt, first secretary; Presidium, 11 members; Central Committee, 91 full and 31 candidate members

Auxiliary Organizations. Revolutionary Trade Union Movement (Tenth Congress, April), Cooperative Farmers' Union, Socialist Youth Union (Third Congress, October), Union for Collaboration with the Army, Czechoslovak Union of Women, Union of Fighters for Peace

Main State Organs. The executive body is the federal government, which is subordinate to the 350-member National Assembly. The assembly, however, merely rubberstamps all decisions made by the KSČ Presidium and Central Committee.

Parliament and Elections. All candidates run on the ticket of the National Front, an umbrella organization comprising the KSČ, four other political parties, and several mass organizations. In the last elections (1981), the front polled over 99 percent of the vote.

Publications. Rudé právo, KSČ daily; Pravda (Bratislava), KSS daily; Tribuna, Czech-language ideological weekly; Predvoj, Slovak-language ideological weekly; Život strany, fortnightly journal devoted to administrative and organizational questions; Práce (Czech) and Práca (Slovak), Trade Union Movement dailies; Mlada fronta (Czech) and Směna (Slovak), Socialist Youth Union dailies; Tvorba, weekly devoted to domestic and international politics; Československá tisková kancelář (ČETEKA) is the official news agency.

Party Internal Affairs. The celebration of the sixty-ninth birthday of Gustáv Husák, at the beginning of the year, was an important event in party life because it underscored the possibility of a change in leadership in the near future. Despite eulogies in the media (Pravda, Bratislava, 9 January), it is known that Husák, for all his loyalty to his Soviet sponsors, does not appear orthodox enough to some conservative hard-liners in the KSČ. It is difficult to predict who has the best chance of replacing Husák in the event of his resignation or retirement. Observers familiar with the KSČ speculate that apparatchiks of long standing, such as Presidium member Miloš Jakeš, could be prospective candidates (interview with former Central Committee secretary Zdeněk Mlynář, *Der Kurier*, Vienna, 17 November).

The most significant party gatherings in 1982 were two plenary sessions of the Central Committee, held in April and in November. The first (sixth according to the official count) met on 20–21 April and dealt with the extension of powers of the national committees (the organs of local self-goverment) and with the unsatisfactory state of consumer services, which could be improved by allowing more room for private initiative in this sector (*Rudé právo*, 21 April). Presidium member Vasil Biľák took this opportunity to deliver a speech on some ideological issues; he charged the United States with the intention of causing civil war in Poland and condemned the doctrine of Eurocommunism, especially as professed by the Italian Communist Party (Radio Prague, 21 April). Concern about the effect of the party's ideological work had been voiced earlier in the year by another Presidium official, Alois Indra, in an article written for the party press. He complained that the party leadership "had lost contact with the masses" and that the influence of some party organizations on noncommunists is nonexistent. He called for "cleansing the party of people incapable of bearing the burden of revolutionary responsibility." (*Nové slovo*, 11 March.) In June, chief party ideologist Jan Fojtík stressed the need for overcoming "pernicious formalism" by hard-hitting propaganda and warned journalists who "want to carry on in a liberalist manner" that they "had no chance here" (speech at the Eighth Congress of the Union of Czechoslovak Journalists, 25 June).

It seemed that the party took these charges seriously; at the November plenum of the Central Committee (the seventh by official records) Fojtík was raised from the Secretariat to candidate membership on the Presidium. Josef Haman was appointed a full Presidium member on the same occasion. (ČETEKA in English, 25 November.) The session also discussed the increasingly urgent problems of the Czechoslovak economy. The closing resolution expressed the hope that "our national economy has the strength and the means to deal with still more demanding tasks," but it admitted "some current problems and shortcomings" (Radio Prague, 25 November).

Domestic Affairs. *The Economy.*   Economic difficulties were the primary concern of the regime during 1982. Czechoslovakia, not unlike its communist neighbors, experienced serious problems in many vital sectors of production and supply. The causes of these difficulties are complex and partly beyond the control of Czechoslovak decision makers, but their political impact has been particularly alarming in the specific Czechoslovak situation, where the post-1968 establishment has been facing a protracted crisis of legitimation. Tolerable economic conditions since the Soviet military intervention have been the only basis of a precarious coexistence between the Soviet-imposed leadership and the population, party and nonparty members alike. Discontent with economic matters may compound the effect of overt political opposition, which the Husák group has more or less kept in check but not stamped out altogether. Significantly, the results of an opinion survey (undertaken at an unspecified time) revealed that "political and social convictions based on the communist Weltanschauung have not yet sufficiently crystallized among the majority of the people." The same report found that "approximately one-fifth of all citizens profess a religious faith of some kind" and that even more people hold views that may be defined as "bourgeois liberalism, abstract humanism, false democracy, and pacifism." (*Sociologický časopis*, no. 3.)

Economic data for 1981, published at the beginning of 1982, indicated the nature and the depth of the current economic crisis. Neither output nor industrial productivity reached planned targets. In comparison with 1980, coal extraction decreased by 2.4 percent, construction by 2 percent, and agricultural production by 3.4 percent. The only improvement took place in the area of foreign trade, where exports grew faster than imports (*Rudé právo*, 2 February). This made 1981 the worst year since 1963, the year that saw the beginnings of the economic reforms eventually leading to the Prague Spring of 1968. Already in 1981, the unsatisfactory state of the economy made necessary a revision of the plan targets for 1982 by the Fifth Plenum of the Central Committee. The planned annual growth was cut from 3.6–4.0 percent to 2.4–3.6; agriculture was affected more strongly by these reductions than industry (ibid., 16 December 1981). Nevertheless, statistics about economic development during the first half of 1982 showed a continuing downward trend. Coal output remained 1.3 percent below the target figure, the food industry lagged 2.7 percent, and no less than 20 percent of all enterprises failed to meet plan quotas (ibid., 28 July). These shortcomings did not improve in any notable way, as the report by Presidium member Miloš Jakeš to the seventh plenum of the Central Committee suggested (*WSJ*, 1 December). The 1982 harvest proved to be only average; in the vital area of cereal grains, yields fell 800,000 tons, or 7.75 percent short of the plan (*Zemědělské noviny*, 7 September). Further plan adjustments had to be envisaged (*Rudé právo*, 19 November).

An important factor in the underperformance of the Czechoslovak economy has been the obsolescence of capital investments—for example, only 25,000 industrial workers are expected to be replaced by robots in this decade—and an inordinately high number of unfinished projects, a problem that only recently has been approached by planners (*Práca*, 19 May; Radio Prague, 25 November). Also, there has been a chronic shortage of qualified labor or, more exactly, mismanagement of the labor reserve. Large numbers of industrial jobs continue to be vacant (about 500,000 in 1982) and more than 60 percent of positions that require college or university education are filled by individuals lacking such qualifications; on the other hand, many workers are redundant in the enterprises that employ them, and many graduates have to accept appointments well below their educational level (*Práca*, 18 March). Over 500,000 employees—or about 7 percent of the work force—"work to no economic effect"; these are found especially in administrative positions (Radio Prague, 8 September). Considerable waste is occasioned by labor turnovers that affect about 500,000 workers a year (ibid., 18 May). Labor morale seems to be very low. Absenteeism is a serious problem, with 4.36 percent of the entire labor force failing to report for work every day (*Plánované hospodářství*, no. 5; *Statistické přehledy*, no. 5). Much concern is caused by the steady rise in the rate of economic crime, from petty larceny to large-scale embezzlement. Every fourth convicted offender is an economic criminal (*Tribuna*, 17 February). According to the party press, "ever new, ever more unusual forms and means of economic crime emerge," and "an ever-growing number of managers and chairmen of institutions face prosecution" (*Nové slovo*, 27 May).

Although reforms appear necessary, it seemed in 1982 that the political obstacles to change were still very strong. Private initiative, especially in retail trade, is tolerated, but the leaders are wary of encouraging individual initiative in industrial management for fear that such reforms might usher in a new political liberalization, something that their Soviet mentors expect them to prevent. Suggestions of the need for reforms, more general than specific, have been made (*Ekonomický časopis*, no. 1). But there has been little response on the part of the power holders, who still appear to set their hopes on the possible effects of an economic reform program introduced in industry in 1981 and in agriculture in 1982 under the rubric Set of Economic Measures. However, complaints were heard that this program, very modest in its ambitions, is not given due attention by enterprises, whose approach to it has been "too administrative" (*Rudé právo*, 15 January, 27 May, 2 November).

Certain measures in response to the deteriorating situation, however unpopular, could not be avoided. In late January, the prices of major consumer items, especially food, were sharply increased. Some, such as rice, doubled; others, such as meat, increased by 41 percent (ibid., 27 January). Wages and salaries, on the other hand, were not raised; only some transfer payments—allowances for widows, children, and disabled workers—were increased by at most 100 Kčs per month (about $10). It is estimated that a family of four now needs 300 Kčs ($30) more to pay for monthly food consumption (*Time*, 10 January 1983). The reduction in the purchasing power of wages is likely to expand the stockpiles of unsold durable consumer goods that accumulated in past years because of prohibitive prices. These stockpiles amounted, at the end of 1980, to 424 billion Kčs ($42.4 billion), almost equal to the total national income of Czechoslovakia (*Finance a úvěr*, no. 1). Czechoslovakia had the slowest growth rate among all members of the Council for Mutual Economic Assistance (CMEA) with the exception of Poland: 0.2 percent in 1981, compared with 6.9 percent in 1970. National income even declined by 4.5 percent (*Politická ekonomie*, no. 9).

Culture, Youth, and Religion. Three congresses were called by the official organizations of Czech and Slovak writers: the Congress of the Union of Slovak Writers in Bratislava, 2 March; the Congress of the Union of Czech Writers in Prague, 3 and 4 March; and the Congress of the Union of Czechoslovak Writers (national organization) in Prague, 9 and 10 March. Party speakers on all three occasions emphasized the need for "a socialist literature as one of the most effective weapons in the continuing ideological struggle," but the writers themselves found that the literary production of recent years was of average quality. Theater and cinema are believed not to have improved, and humor in both Czech and Slovak literature is seen as "almost nonexistent" (*Nové slovo*, 4 March; ČETEKA, 9 March). The dissident Charter '77 group, in an open letter to the writers' congresses, diagnosed these mediocre results as the consequence of cultural censorship reimposed in Czechoslovakia as part of the post-invasion "normalization." The letter listed 200 names of authors whose works have been banned by communist authorities (Reuters, Prague, 8 March).

The conformism and sterility of the cultural scene in Czechoslovakia has been the cause of disillusionment and alienation of a large part of Czech and Slovak youth, who seek other symbols, models, and leaders. One symptom of the conflict between young people and the system has been the so-called Democracy Wall in the Malá strana section of Prague, where slogans definitely not socialist in nature keep appearing in spite of assiduous police efforts to efface them (Svědectví, Paris, no. 66). The fear that the disaffection of youth might generate new foci of domestic opposition was manifest among KSČ leaders. It induced Federal Minister of Interior Jaromír Obzina to write an article for the party's main organizational periodical about the perils to which the youth of Czechoslovakia were exposed. He claimed that the imperialists were out to get Czechoslovakia, not only by disrupting the economy but also by using the younger generation for antisocialist designs. He warned that "new groups to engage in active antistate efforts" were being created and that imperialist security agencies sought to turn the criminal activity of young people into an instrument of anti-Czechoslovak subversion (Život strany, no. 19). He may have meant the activities of groups such as the Plastic People of the Universe, in itself a nonpolitical pop music association. Its activities, however, became highly political and objectionable because it published and distributed literature qualified as "illegal, antisocialist and grossly vulgar." The leader of the group and three codefendants were condemned to prison terms in July. (Reuters, Prague, 10 July.) The official youth organization, the Socialist Youth Union, held its third Congress in October. President Husák and the entire KSČ Presidium were guests of honor at this congress, which, following the statement of Chairman Jaroslav Jenerál, saw its main tasks as strengthening the Czechoslovak economy and contributing to social progress in the world revolutionary struggle (ČETEKA, in English, 1 October).

Persistent religiosity among all age classes of the population appeared to be a challenge to the regime. The brief period of relative tolerance at the end of the 1960s has been succeeded by a new anti-religious drive and the deployment of a whole arsenal of overt and disguised restriction of the exercise of religious activity. It was characteristic of the situation of the Roman Catholic church that although 1982 marked the first time that a delegation of Czech and Slovak bishops, led by the primate of Czechoslovakia, was allowed to travel to Rome, a number of bishops were not permitted to join the delegation (Katolické noviny, Prague, 14 March). That the majority of episcopal seats in Czechoslovakia remain unfilled and an even greater proportion of parishes lack priests—a difficulty shared by all Christian churches—underscores the hardships to which religion has been exposed. Additional problems have been caused by restrictions on admissions to theological seminaries, religious education, and church publications. The delegation informed the pope of these problems, and John Paul II expressed his sympathies for the plight of believers in Czechoslovakia (UPI, Rome, 11 March). A particularly sensitive issue between the church and the state in 1982 was the position of the regime-sponsored organization of Catholic priests, Pacem in Terris, whose right to speak in the name of the church has been challenged by the ecclesiastical hierarchy. Although the pope had stated in December 1981 that participation in this movement was incompatible with the position of a loyal Catholic clergyman and the Vatican Sacred Congregation had issued a declaration to the same effect, the supporters of Pacem in Terris contested these rulings. The publication of a letter from Pacem in Terris spokesmen in the church press (Katolícke noviny, Bratislava, 11 July) moved Czechoslovak primate František Cardinal Tomášek to a written protest (Catholic Press Agency, cited by Radio Vatican, 18 November). The regime responded by denouncing what it considered "the bias of the Catholic church authorities in favor of antisocialist forces," allegedly documented by their "active help to Polish Solidarity" (Tvorba, 11 August). The KSČ's displeasure about the position of the Vatican in this matter may also have been the reason why the chairman of the West German Bishops' Conference, Joseph Cardinal Höffner, who had been invited to Prague with two other senior prelates by Cardinal Tomášek, was refused a ·Czechoslovak visa (Frankfurter Allgemeine Zeitung, 16 June). Another reason may have been the apprehension of the regime's engineers of atheistic propaganda arising from the inefficacy of their efforts. Their own journal had to admit that "religiosity among young people in Czechoslovakia has not been declining at the rate the party had hoped it would" (Ateizmus, no. 3).

Dissidence. The best-known and best-organized opposition group in Czechoslovakia, Charter '77, named after the Helsinki agreement on the protection of civil and human rights, of which Czechoslovakia is a signatory, commemorated the fifth anniversary of its constitution in January. On that occasion, the main spokesman of the group, Ladislav Hejdánek, appealed in a statement handed to Western press correspondents in Prague for continuing support by world public opinion of human rights movements in the Soviet orbit (AFP, 5 January). Three new spokesmen of Charter '77 were then appointed: Ladislav Lis, former KSČ member and an official of long standing; Radim Palouš, former lecturer in chemistry at Charles University in Prague; and Anna Marvanová, a former journalist. They replaced Bedřich Placák, Václav Malý, and Jaroslav Šabata, who had represented the group during 1981. The new spokesmen released a document dealing with the situation in Poland. This document rejected the martial law introduced in Poland in December 1981 and stressed the need for a policy "that would help heal the wounds inflicted on the Polish people in the confrontation between the nation and the communist regime and promote the process of renewal" (*Listy*, Rome, no. 2). Later in the month, the three spokesmen declared 30 January to be Solidarity Day with the Polish people. They stressed that "oppression cannot lead to a real solution of the Polish problems" (AFP, Prague, 27 January). In January, too, the Court of Appeals in Prague confirmed the three-year prison sentence of Jan Litomiský, a Charter '77 supporter, for his activities in the Committee for the Defense of Unjustly Prosecuted (ibid., 7 January). At the end of January, twelve U.S. congressmen, members of the Commission on Security and Cooperation in Europe (CSCE), proposed three East European dissidents, among them Czech playwright Václav Havel, now imprisoned, for the Nobel Peace Prize (CSCE release, Washington, D.C., 29 January). A number of important personalities and initiative groups in the West had been working for the release of Havel, who is serving a four-and-a-half-year prison term imposed in 1979 (*Le Monde*, Paris, 4 August).

During the year, the Charter group issued several statements dealing with the pressing problems of the nation. In February, in a document published by the Palach Press Agency in Paris (named after a student who immolated himself to protest the Soviet military intervention in 1968), Charter '77 took a position on the economic situation in Czechoslovakia. It pointed out that the drop in the living standard was only a symptom of the failure of the centralized planning system forcibly introduced in Czechoslovakia in the course of the Soviet-sponsored "normalization." It called for an open discussion of the economic crisis, but it emphasized that freedom of information and expression would be an indispensable condition of such discussion. (*BBC Current Affairs Research*, 5 March.) Other documents brought to the attention of the public the failure of the regime to implement the agreements of the Madrid CSCE (Charter document no. 8, 3 March), the state of education of children and youth (ibid., no. 20, 1 June), the situation in Czechoslovak prisons (letter to the Federal Assembly, 21 June), and restrictions on scientific research (letter to the federal prime minister, 10 August). Charter '77 also protested, on a number of occasions, against the violation of national and international laws and agreements, unjustified imprisonment of individuals, and religious persecution and expressed sympathy with the protests of Polish workers and the unofficial peace movement in East Germany.

Good grounds for protest were not lacking. The harsh treatment of dissidents and nonconformists betrayed the concern and the seriousness with which the authorities viewed dissident phenomena. It is reported that when the Charter '77 movement began, the federal minister of interior estimated the number of sympathizers and potential signatories at no less than 2 million (*Radio Free Europe–Radio Liberty Situation Report*, 22 January). This may be why in 1982 the Czechoslovak police used physical violence against dissidents either directly during arrests and interrogations or indirectly through hired anonymous thugs. Charter spokesmen protested against these practices in a letter sent to President Gustáv Husák (Charter document no. 9, 3 May). Some Czechoslovak officials seem to have become aware of the injustices perpetrated against individuals who dared express unorthodox views. The Czechoslovak delegate to the June conference of the International Labor Organization in Geneva, Miloš Mašek, openly admitted that certain individuals associated with the human rights groups "had been dismissed from their posts without justification" (*BBC Current Affairs Research*, 17 June).

Foreign Affairs. Czechoslovakia's international contacts in 1982 extended over the countries of the communist bloc as well as the West and the Third World. Contacts with the USSR in the governmental area did not include any first-ranked Soviet officeholders. In May, Deputy Premier Guryi Marchuk arrived for an official visit at the invitation of Federal Premier Lubomír Štrougal (ČETEKA, 10 May). In June, USSR Minister for Machine Tools and Tool Industry Boris Balmont had talks with Czechoslovak Minister of

Engineering Pavol Bahyl and inspected some important engineering plants in Czechoslovakia (*Rudé právo*, 21 June). In May, President Husák received in Prague North Korean Deputy Prime Minister and Foreign Minister Ho Tam, who also paid a visit to his Czechoslovak counterpart, Bohuslav Chňoupek. Further expansion of bilateral relations were discussed on this occasion. (Radio Prague, in English, 27 May.) In September, Bulgarian Premier Grisha Filipov arrived for "a friendly working visit" at the head of a governmental delegation and was welcomed by Premier Lubomír Štrougal and other cabinet members (ibid., 1 September). In the same month, Alois Indra, leading a delegation of the Czechoslovak Federal Assembly, traveled to Central America and discussed bilateral relations with Fidel Castro in Cuba (ibid., 30 September, 5 October). He then proceded to Nicaragua (ČETEKA, 6 October) and Mexico (ibid., in English, 9 October). In Managua, he met with Chairman of the State Council Carlos Muñez, and in Mexico City with both the incumbent president, José López Portillo, and the president-elect, Miguel de la Madrid. Another Latin American country that negotiated cooperation with Czechoslovakia was Brazil. Talks to this effect were held in Prague in September (ibid., 17 September). Mongolian Foreign Minister Mangalyn Dugersuren visited Czechoslovakia 14–17 October (Montsame, Ulan Bator, in English, 18 October). In March, a Romanian military delegation headed by Defense Minister Lt. Gen. Constantin Olteanu held talks in Prague with Gen. Martin Dzúr, minister of national defense (Radio Prague, 5 March). Romanian Prime Minister Constantin Dascalescu came to Prague in September as the guest of Premier Lubomír Štrougal (*Rudé Právo*, 16 September). Although relations with China remained strained in 1982, an agreement on economic exchanges and payments was signed in Beijing by the Czechoslovak deputy foreign minister and his Chinese counterpart (ČETEKA, in English, 18 February). Later in the year, a Chinese governmental delegation led by Deputy Minister of Light Industry Wang Wenzhe participated in a session of the Czechoslovak-Chinese Commission for Scientific and Technical Cooperation (*Rudé právo*, 18 September). In late February, Czechoslovak Deputy Prime Minister Svatopluk Potáč negotiated the details of trade exchanges with Yugoslavia (Tanjug, in English, 26 February). In November, Chairman of the Yugoslav Federal Executive Council Milka Planinc paid an official visit to President Husák and Prime Minister Štrougal. The long tradition of "Slav mutuality" between the two countries was invoked on this occasion (Radio Prague, 11 November). Shortly prior to this event, South Yemen's Minister of Interior Muhammad Abdulah al-Butani came to Prague to "conduct negotiations" with Czechoslovak Interior Minister Jaromír Obzina. The exact object of these negotiations was not revealed. (*Rudé právo*, 27 October.)

On the whole, relations with the West reflected the rather cool climate prevailing in the Soviet-Western relationship, but in some instances they were complicated by specifically Czechoslovak problems or missteps. In May, the Portuguese government withdrew the accreditation of the Czechoslovak ambassador and the third embassy secretary for "inadmissible interference in the internal affairs of the country" (*WP*, 1 May). Prague retaliated by expelling the Portuguese ambassador and charged that "this hostile act was inspired by forces not favoring the development of friendly relations between nations" (Radio Prague, 3 May). In the conflict between Argentina and Great Britain over the Falkland islands, Czechoslovak media took the side of Argentina but laid the blame on the capitalist system to which both rivals adhere (*Rudé právo*, 20 May). At year's end, they attacked British Prime Minister Margaret Thatcher for "not being prepared to react positively" to the arms reduction proposals made to the West by Yuri Andropov (Radio Prague, 17 November). In October, French Foreign Trade Minister Michel Jobert had talks in Prague with Czechoslovak government officials about economic exchanges (which reached 1.4 billion French francs in 1980 [$250 million]). A delegation of the two chambers of the Belgian legislature visited Prague in July and was received by President Husák (ČETEKA, in English, 14 July). Courtesy visits were exchanged also with Czechoslovakia's two Western neighbors, the Federal Republic of Germany and Austria. The visit of the Czechoslovak foreign minister to Bonn in December 1981 was followed in June 1982 by the trip to Prague of Prime Minister of North Rhine–Westphalia Johannes Rau, who was the guest of Czech Prime Minister Josef Korčák (Radio Prague, 13 June). The chairman of the Czech National Council, Josef Kempný, reciprocated by visiting Düsseldorf in September (ČETEKA, Bonn, 24 September). Much attention was paid in the media to official contacts with Austria. Relations had suffered from a number of setbacks, caused chiefly by frequent violations of the norms of international law or human rights by the Czechoslovak regime. Foreign Minister Chňoupek went to Vienna in May for a three-day visit (*Rudé právo*, 8 May), which was followed by visits of several Czechoslovak government officials during the summer and early fall. This goodwill offensive culminated in the state trip of President Husák to Austria in November. Husák met with President

Rudolf Kirchschläger and Chancellor Bruno Kreisky. On this and all previous occasions, similarity of views on important international matters, as well as common interests and cooperation, were emphasized (Radio Prague, 19 November). In October, Federal Premier Štrougal traveled to Helsinki, where he signed a credit agreement with Finland (ibid., 12 October).

Among the developing nations, relations with the Arab states were given considerable coverage by Czechoslovak media. Štrougal signed a protocol on economic cooperation with Tunisia in Tunis (Radio Prague, 22 October). Alois Indra, chairman of the Federal Assembly, led a Czechoslovak parliamentary delegation to Syria in March (ibid., 11 March). A long-term trade agreement with Syria was signed in Prague in April (ČETEKA, 9 April). In June, high officials of the Czechoslovak Ministry of Foreign Affairs met in a special conference in Prague with the envoys of nine Middle Eastern countries and the representatives of the Palestine Liberation Organization to discuss the war in Lebanon (*Pravda*, Bratislava, 12 June). In late May, a protocol on economic and trade cooperation with Libya was renewed (*Práce*, 27 May). Kuwaiti Foreign Minister Sabah-al-Ahmad al-Jahir visited Prague in July (Radio Prague, 2 July). In September, Iranian State Minister for Planning and Budget Muhammad Taqui Banki led a delegation of Iranian economists to Prague to discuss possibilites of enlarging trade and economic cooperation between the two countries (ČETEKA, in English, 23 September). It may be interpreted as a sign of Czechoslovakia's neutrality in the war in the Persian Gulf that in April Chňoupek was received with diplomatic honors in Iraq and that shortly afterwards Iraqi Minister of Interior Sa'dun Shakir arrived in Prague for talks with his Czechoslovak counterpart, Jaromír Obzina; the topics of discussion were not made public (ČETEKA, in English, 23 November). Chňoupek's visit to Iraq was combined with a stopover in Cyprus, where he met with Foreign Minister Nikos Rolandhis (Radio Prague, 22 April). In 1982, Chňoupek also made personal contact with some African political leaders. On the occasion of the U.N. special session on disarmament in New York, he met Angolan Foreign Minister Paolo Jorge (ibid., 12 June). Humphrey Mulemba, general secretary of the Zambian National Independence Party, visited President Husák in Prague in June (ČETEKA, in English, 21 June). At the year's close, diplomatic relations were established between Czechoslovakia and Lesotho (ibid., 22 November).

Foreign Trade and Foreign Debt. It would seem that among the communist countries of Central and Eastern Europe, Czechoslovakia suffers the least from an adverse foreign payments balance. Its present hard-currency indebtedness is $3.51 billion, a fraction of that of Poland—or of some Latin American countries, for that matter (*Neue Zürcher Zeitung*, 23 November). Czechoslovakia has not sought new credits in the West since 1980 (*Financial Times*, London, 12 November). In 1982, the foreign payments situation improved further, and during the first nine months of the year it amounted to 2.15 billion Kčs ($215 million). However, this figure includes a surplus in nonconvertible currencies; the trade deficit with the West in 1981 was $1.89 billion (*Revue průmyslu, obchodu a hospodářství*, no. 4). The positive balance in 1982 was achieved mostly by slowing down or discontinuing investment that requires Western raw materials, equipment, or know-how; nevertheless, the direst consequences have been avoided. A more serious and pressing problem than foreign payments appears to be the gradual loss of Western markets. Exports to the countries of the European Common Market dropped from 16.7 percent of the total export volume in 1975 to 11.9 percent in 1980 (ibid., no. 6). The cause of this unfavorable turn has been the low quality of Czechoslovak products. A similar problem emerged in the trade with developing countries (Radio Prague, 7 August). Even exports to the USSR, thus far the largest and the most receptive market for Czechoslovak goods, were seen by some domestic analysts as threatened. It was pointed out that there have been structural changes in the Soviet economy—the Soviet Union became an exporter of capital goods where until recently it had been an importer—and that Soviet consumers have upgraded their expectations of product quality (*Rudé právo*, 25 January). Exchanges with other CMEA countries do not seem to be exempt from these difficulties (*Život strany*, no. 14).

The integrative plans of the Soviet bloc, favored chiefly by the Soviet Union, did not make much progress in 1982. There has been considerable resistance to the idea of the international socialist division of labor, introduced more than twenty years ago by Nikita Khrushchev. Czechoslovak government and party officials have since the 1968 intervention fully supported the Soviet postion on this issue. Several KSČ officials reiterated the call for an early summit meeting of the CMEA countries that was included in the official communiqué about the talks between President Husák and Leonid Brezhnev in the Crimea in the summer (*Rudé právo*, 6 July).

Relations with the U.S. Czechoslovak relations with the United States, at a low already when the Reagan administration took over in January 1981, chiefly because of the Carter adminstration's emphasis on human rights, remained cool throughout 1982. The issue of nuclear parity tabled by Reagan and U.S. attempts to respond by some concrete measures to the imposition of martial law in Poland did not make things any easier. On the whole, however, the hostility of the Czechoslovak government and media towards the United States was but a faithful replica of the Soviet policy line. Commenting on the resignation of Secretary of State Alexander Haig, Czechoslovak radio said that the "antisocialist and discriminatory stand of the United States" would continue (Radio Prague, 14 July). The press defined the embargo on deliveries for the Siberian pipeline as "a fiasco for the Reagan administration" (ČETEKA, in English, 15 November). The media claimed that the desire to negotiate strategic arms limitation expressed in Reagan's speech of 22 November was "mere smokescreen" and that the Reagan administration had "a ready-made plan for the liquidation of communism" (Radio Prague, 23 November). The declaration by the U.S. ambassador to the United Nations, Jeane Kirkpatrick, that the United States would withdraw from the United Nations if Israel were expelled by a manipulated vote of the General Assembly was labeled "blackmail, so dear to the highest U.S. authorities" (*Pravda*, Bratislava, 19 October). In September, a crowd of several hundred persons, mostly Arab students enrolled at Prague universities, demonstrated outside the U.S. Embassy in Prague, protesting the murders of Palestinian refugees in a Beirut camp. Czechoslovak media reporting on this protest and on the mass murder in Beirut deliberately led readers to believe that the massacre had been perpetrated by the Israeli army (ČETEKA, in English, 22 September). A clearly anti-U.S. position was taken by Federal Assembly Chairman Alois Indra during his trip to Cuba and Central America, especially in his speech to the State Council of Nicaragua (ibid., 6 October) and at a press conference he held after his return to Prague (ibid., 13 October).

Reaction to Polish Events. The imposition of martial law in Poland in December 1981 alleviated the worst fears of Czechoslovak leaders of possible "contamination" by reformist ideas or trade union demands. This was evident from the speeches and documents of the Tenth Trade Union Congress in April. Although the events in Poland were occasionally mentioned, there was less preoccupation with these than during the previous year (Radio Hvězda, 15 April). Contacts with representatives of the Polish military government were made almost immediately. General Wojciech Jaruzelski visited Prague in April at President Husák's invitation. The issues discussed during his visit were mainly economic: possible economic help from Czechoslovakia to Poland in its current plight and corrective measures to counteract the adverse effects on the Czechoslovak economy of the failure of Polish enterprises to deliver goods promised in previous trade agreements. Concrete data about Czechoslovak aid were not released (Radio Warsaw, 4 April). Later in the year, Rudolf Rohlíček, Czechoslovak minister of foreign trade and representative to the CMEA, held talks in Warsaw with his Polish counterpart, Janusz Obodowski, and signed a document specifying further steps in economic cooperation (PAP, 15 April). In May, Polish Politburo member Zbigniew Messner came to Prague and gave an interview to *Rudé právo* (11 May). He stressed the need to carry out economic reform in order to render "the extremists in Solidarity" harmless. In November, Deputy Federal Premier Ladislav Gerle made a "brief working visit" to Poland to discuss the "deepening of cooperation in industry between the two countries" (Radio Prague, 17 November). Western press comment that Brezhnev and Husák made no mention of Poland in the communiqué about their talks reaped a sarcastic comment from Czechoslovak media (Radio Hvězda, 2 August).

The Polish issue was also a bone of contention between the KSČ and the Italian Communist Party (PCI). In a lead article, *Pravda* (Bratislava) condemned the document on Poland published by the PCI and argued that the attitudes adopted by Italian Communists were "grist to the mill of the 'ideosubversive' centers of the imperialist bourgeoisie" (18 January). On 19 October, *Rudé právo* attacked PCI Politburo member and secretary of the communist All-Union Labor Confederation Bruno Trentin, who had declared that after the December 1981 coup d'etat all forms of resistance and protest against the military government in Poland were permissible. The daily claimed that the PCI supports "antisocialist, disruptive plans against People's Poland."

The Soviet Leadership Change. The passing of Leonid Brezhnev in November was observed by flying flags at half-mast throughout the country. A large number of party officials sent condolences to various bodies of the Communist Party of the Soviet Union and Soviet government or to the Soviet embassy in Prague (Radio Prague, 11 November). When Yuri Andropov was elected general secretary of the CPSU, Husák sent a long telegram to the new Soviet party boss and assured him that Czechoslovak Communists would "do their utmost" for the further development of Czechoslovak-Soviet friendship (ibid., 12 November). All subsequent media commentaries on the succession stressed the "continuity" of the present policy line. This was also the tenor of discussion and statements relative to this subject made at the seventh Central Committee plenum. The future will show whether this was a correct analysis of the situation in the Kremlin or only wishful thinking.

International Party Contacts. Relations between the KSČ and other communist parties, especially those outside the Soviet bloc, continued to be complex and delicate. While the legitimacy of the present leadership and of the "normalization" course imposed by the Soviet military intervention of 1968 has not yet been accepted by a number of sister parties, new problems have recently been added to this "unassimilated past." The systematic persecution of various dissident groups by the Husák regime has exacerbated the dispute about the merits and demerits of Socialism with a Human Face. The events in neighboring Poland caused further sharp divisions. The present leadership's hostile position on Polish reform attempts has been dictated partly by the desire to support the Soviet Union. To a large measure it also reflects apprehension that political and social progress in Poland might revive reformist forces in Czechoslovakia. This position, of course, estranged the KSČ from more independent components of the world communist movement. This difficulty was added to earlier problems such as the Sino-Soviet split, conflict with Albania, foreign policy differences with Romania, and disagreement with Yugoslavia over basic questions of socialist theory and practice. In 1982, party diplomacy was in some cases able to paper over these disputes, mainly by avoiding discussion of sensitive issues. Party leaders took great pains to demonstrate absolute unity of views with their sponsors.

In June, a party and state delegation traveled to the Soviet Union, led by Secretary General Husák and Presidium member Štrougal. No concrete subjects were discussed on this occasion; only prestigious decorations and awards were exchanged between the guests and the hosts (*Rudé právo*, 5 June). More important appeared to be the second meeting between Husák and Brezhnev on 30 July during Husák's allegedly "private and recreational" trip to the Crimea. The two party bosses made a *tour d'horizon* of international politics and found complete identity of views on all questions (ČETEKA, in English, 4 August). They also emphasized the significance of a summit meeting on economic issues to be convened in the near future (Tass,in English, 30 July). This "absolute identity" of views between the KSČ and the Soviet party was also established on the occasion of two interparty meetings: the two-day conference of the heads of the ideological departments of the communist parties from the CMEA countries, held in Prague in March (ČETEKA, 25 March), and the international ideological symposium organized in Prague in October and attended by delegates from Marxist-Leninist scientific institutes and central committees of the communist parties (*Rudé právo*, 6 October).

Party spokesmen and media also supported the Soviet stand on China. The Twelfth Congress of the Chinese Communist Party was labeled as both "nothing new" and a "bitter disappointment" (*Pravda*, Bratislava, 24 September). The Chinese party was taken to task for having charged the USSR with "imperialist designs" and "great power chauvinism"; in return, Czechoslovak media accused China of "expansionist policy." This criticism was underscored by the publication in Prague of a Czech translation of a Soviet book, *Asia in Beijing's Plans*, volume one of a planned series titled Maoism—Threat to Mankind (ibid., 17 November). Czechoslovak Communists also accused the Japan Communist Party of anti-Sovietism and of undermining the solidarity of the world communist movement because it had proposed the discontinuation of the journal *World Marxist Review* (Život strany, no. 4). This article was later reprinted in *World Marxist Review* itself (March). The Czechoslovak party also took up arms on behalf of the CPSU against the CPI because of the latter's stands on Poland and Afghanistan. Relations between the KSČ and the CPI have been very bad since 1968, the "normalization" and the harsh repression of dissent by Husák being the main reasons for the hostility on both sides, especially since Italian Communists extended moral and material support to former KSČ members and officials who left the country in protest against the Soviet intervention (ČETEKA, 2 March). Czechoslovak commentators also showed mixed feelings about the League of Communists of Yugoslavia because of what they called "abetting all kinds of Czechoslovak political émigrés and internal spiritual exiles and encouraging them in their provocative acts" (*Pravda*, Bratislava, 17 November). In this vast array of conflicting relationships, there was only one apparent improvement: the French Communist Party, which in the past had questioned the justification for the 1968 Soviet intervention in Czechoslovakia and whose leader, Georges Marchais, as chairman of the French Committee for the Protection of Freedom, used to intercede on behalf of the victims of the persecution, did not in 1982 voice any protest against the repression.

For the rest, contacts with the various chapters of the world communist movement were smooth and uneventful. The visit to Prague by Gus Hall, general secretary of the Communist Party, U.S.A., was an occasion to condemn "the plots of U.S. imperialism," which was blamed for tensions in the world (Radio Prague, 12 July). Among other parties that visited Czechoslovakia in 1982, were the communist parties of East Germany (ČETEKA, in English, 1 October), India (Radio Prague, 17 November), Greece (*Pravda*, Bratislava, 16 January), Luxembourg (Radio Prague, 3 November), Vietnam (ibid., 15 November), Denmark (*Rudé právo*, 10 April), Palestine (Radio Prague, 29 September), Yemen (Radio Aden, 9 September), South Africa (Prague Television, 7 September), Venezuela (Radio Prague, 27 May), Israel (ČETEKA, in English, 9 July), Cyprus (ibid., 11 October), and Afghanistan (*Rudé právo*, 12 October). Czechoslovak party delegations of various levels traveled in 1982 to all parts of the world, either to attend party congresses or to pay courtesy visits to sister parties. In February, Vasil Bil'ák led a group of Central Committee officials to the French party congress (Radio Prague, 2 February). Jozef Lenárt led a delegation to the Cypriot party congress in May (ČETEKA, in English, 11 May). Also in May, Bil'ák led a Central Committee delegation to Africa to visit the ruling parties of Mozambique and Angola (Radio Prague, 19 May). In September, the Trade Union Council sent a special delegation to Afghanistan; it was received by top officials of the Politburo of the People's Democratic Party of Afghanistan (*Pravda*, Bratislava, 7 September).

University of Pittsburgh   Zdeněk Suda

Germany:
German Democratic Republic

The German Communist Party (KPD) developed into one of the world's largest communist parties within a few years of its formation in 1918. The process of bolshevization and Stalinization that the KPD underwent starting in the early 1920s, however, stripped it of all independence. Turned into a pliant tool of Soviet communism, the KPD was repeatedly compelled to pursue policies beneficial to Soviet state interests but inimical to its own viability. Forced to flee Germany when Hitler assumed power, many top KPD functionaries were brought to the Soviet Union, where, working with their Russian counterparts during the 1930s and 1940s, they fashioned plans for a "democratic republic" in postwar Germany. In 1945–1949, they implemented many of these plans, adapted and modified to fit changing circumstances, in the Soviet Zone of Occupation (SBZ). Backed by Soviet occupation authorities, German Communists forced Social

Democrats in the SBZ to "unite" their party with the KPD in 1946. The resulting Socialist Unity Party (SED) has ruled the German Democratic Republic (GDR) ever since.

Population. 16.7 million

Party. Socialist Unity Party of Germany (Sozialistische Einheitspartei Deutschlands; SED)

Founded. 1918 (SED, 1946)

Membership. 2,202,277 (June 1982); workers, 57.7 percent; production workers, 37.5 percent

Secretary General. Erich Honecker

Politburo. 17 full members: Erich Honecker (chairman, State Council), Hermann Axen, Horst Dohlus, Kurt Hager (member, State Council), Joachim Herrmann, Werner Felfe (member, State Council), Heinz Hoffmann (defense minister), Werner Krolikowski (first deputy chairman, Council of Ministers), Erich Mielke (minister of state security), Günter Mittag (member, State Council), Erich Mückenberger (member, Presidium of People's Chamber), Konrad Naumann (first secretary, Berlin regional party executive), Alfred Neumann (deputy chairman, Council of Ministers), Horst Sindermann (member, State Council; member, Presidium of People's Chamber), Willi Stoph (deputy chairman, State Council), Harry Tisch (member, State Council; chairman, Free German Trade Union Federation), Paul Verner (deputy chairman, State Council); 8 candidate members: Werner Jarowinsky, Günther Kleiber (deputy chairman, Council of Ministers), Egon Krenz (member, State Council; chairman, Free German Youth), Ingeborg Lange, Margarete Müller (member, State Council), Günter Schabowski, Gerhard Schürer (chairman, State Planning Commission), Werner Walde (first secretary, Cottbus regional party executive)

Secretariat. 10 members: Erich Honecker, Hermann Axen (international relations), Horst Dohlus (publications), Werner Felfe (agriculture), Kurt Hager (culture and science), Joachim Herrmann (agitprop), Werner Jarowinsky (commerce and welfare), Günter Mittag (economic affairs), Ingeburg Lange (women's affairs), Paul Verner (security)

Central Committee. 156 full and 51 candidate members

Last Congress. Tenth, 11–16 April, in East Berlin; next congress scheduled for 1986

Auxiliary Organizations. Free German Trade Union Federation (FDGB, 9.1 million members), led by Harry Tisch; Free German Youth (FDJ, 2.3 million members), led by Egon Krenz; Democratic Women's League (DFD, 1.4 million members), led by Ilse Thiele; Society for German-Soviet Friendship (DSF, 3.5 million members)

Main State Organs. Council of State, chaired by Erich Honecker; Council of Ministers (45 members, all but 4 belong to SED), chaired by Willi Stoph; both consitutionally answer to People's Chamber

Parliament and Elections. All candidates run on ticket of National Front, an umbrella organization comprising the SED, 4 smaller parties, and other groups. The 500 seats in the People's Chamber are distributed as follows: SED 127, 52 to each of 4 smaller parties, FDGB 68, FDJ 40, DFD 35, Cultural League 22.

Publications. *Neues Deutschland* (*ND*), official SED daily; *Einheit*, SED theoretical monthly; *Neuer Weg*, SED organizational monthly; *Junge Welt*, FDJ daily; *Tribüne*, FDGB daily. The official news agency is Allgemeiner Deutscher Nachrichtendienst (ADN).

Party Internal Affairs. Three major party gatherings highlighted SED activity in 1982. The first, a "consultation of the SED Central Committee Secretariat with the first secretaries of regional [*Kreis*] executives," took place in mid-February. The fourth plenum of the Central Committee convened four months later, followed in late November by the fifth. No new inflections in domestic or foreign policy came to light at any of these sessions although some technical irregularities attracted the attention of outside observers. Honecker's speech to regional first secretaries, for instance, was not carried verbatim in the press (see *ND*, 13/14 February), giving rise to Western speculation that the matters discussed, or the manner in which they were treated, were intended only for the ears of a select audience. In fact, with the exception of 1979 and 1981, Honecker has called these conclaves to order regularly since the Ninth Party Congress in 1976, presumably to initiate a limited circle of party personnel into the arcana of SED policy that the leadership prefers not to comment on at the more open Central Committee plenums or party congresses. In this instance, some commentators surmised that Honecker had on his mind domestic and economic issues that he did not wish aired publicly. (*Deutschland Archiv* [*DA*], no. 4, pp. 392–401; *Frankfurter Allgemeine Zeitung* [*FAZ*], 13 February.)

The SED broke with the tradition of holding two Central Committee plenary meetings annually, one in the spring, the other in the late fall, by postponing the spring session, the fourth plenum, until 23 June. The delay may have been a by-product of the tense international situation and a more complicated internal economic picture (*DA*, no. 8, p. 785). The fifth plenum, on the other hand, met as usual in late November and ran its programmed course with no dramatic announcements, disclosures, or otherwise significant developments.

The SED celebrated Erich Honecker's seventieth birthday in August with elaborate stories in the press commingled with congratulations from Warsaw pact countries and "from around the world." The reports and expressions of best wishes filled the pages of two full issues of *Neues Deutschland* (25 and 26 August) and spilled over into following editions. At the "suggestion" of the Politburo and the Presidium of the Council of Ministers, Honecker was awarded the order Hero of the German Democratic Republic and the Karl Marx medal. The Presidium of the Supreme Soviet also made Honecker a Hero of the Soviet Union and awarded him for good measure the Order of Lenin and the Gold Star medal (ibid.).

Domestic Affairs. *Peace Movement.* The emergence in early 1982 of what leading dissident Robert Havemann called a "free peace movement" (*Soviet Analyst*, 4 August)—one not called to life by the party and therefore less susceptible to manipulation by it—placed the SED on the horns of a dilemma. Because the movement issued a number of implicit and explicit challenges to sacrosanct SED claims that socialism and peace are one and the same, the party had little choice but to the quash the movement with a combination punch of selective repression and heavy-handed coercion calculated to channel backers of the various independent initiatives into the ranks of the official peace campaign. In so doing, however, the SED could not escape embarrassing itself and provided domestic and foreign critics of the regime with powerful arguments against its self-claimed moral and historical right to monopolize all matters bearing on peace. The regime spent the better part of 1982 trying to extricate itself from the predicament.

The first independent peace initiative was the Berlin Appeal (dated 25 January), a document calling on the governments of both Germanies to negotiate the dismantling of all nuclear weapons on East and West German soil and the creation of a nuclear-free zone in Europe. Two other proposals were put forward. The first advocated conclusion of peace treaties between the allies of the World War II and both Germanies, to be followed by the withdrawal of "occupation troops" and a declaration of noninterference in the internal affairs of either Germany. The second proposal enjoined the GDR to reverse the policy of militarization, a demand augmented by the slogan "Create peace without arms" (*Frieden schaffen ohne Waffen*), borrowed from the Western peace movement. The Berlin Appeal bore the signatures of 35 supporters, although at the time it made its appearance in the Western press, 200 persons had reputedly attached their names to the appeal. By May, the number had evidently grown to 700. (*RAD Background Report*, no. 39; *WP*, 17 May.) The GDR's first impulse was to jail Rainer Eppelmann, the Berlin pastor credited with initiating the document, although church intervention secured his release after two days (*World Press Review*, August). A few weeks later, a Peace Forum, sponsored by the Evangelical Lutheran church of Saxony, took place in Dresden. More than 5,000 persons attended the event, originally intended as a commemoration of the Dresden bombing. Following the forum, which state authorities had sanctioned (even though it was not part of the official peace crusade), several thousand of those present made their way to another church, where they lit candles and sang songs. (*RAD Background Report*, no. 47.)

East German secret police agents stayed in the background in Dresden (*Der Spiegel*, 22 February). The appearance throughout the GDR of young people wearing a sewn-on cloth badge reading "Swords into Plowshares," however, soon provoked a sharp response, and many young people have been harassed, detained, and interrogated in the intervening months. Hand in hand with these secret police actions went belligerent pronouncements by state and party spokesmen, who laid down the law clearly and unmistakably. Klaus Gysi, state secretary for church affairs, informed the Lutheran church that the emblem was not to be worn in public because the youth had misused it "as a demonstration of an attitude hostile to the state and participation in an illegal political movement" (*WP*, 1 April). Defense Minister Heinz Hoffman mused in late March that "as much as we would like to scrap our weapons some day, socialism and peace still need our plowshares *and* our swords" (*ND*, 26 March). This riposte became the clarion call of GDR and SED officialdom. Echoing Hoffmann, the chairman of the East German Christian Democratic Union informed his listeners that in order to safeguard socialism in the "current situation," service "with plowshares and with swords" was the order of the day (*FAZ*, 26 April). Speaking at the Twelfth Party Congress of the German National Democratic Party, Heinrich Homann warned that "socialism must keep its powder dry to safeguard peace" (*ND*, 23 April). During the Tenth Congress of the FDGB, an "honor delegation" of the National People's Army (NVA) made its customary appearance to tell the delegates: "The more mastery and control we achieve over our weapons, the more peace is assured. Thus, service in the NVA and in the GDR's border troops is service in the cause of peace." (Ibid.) Egon Krenz, speaking as always in the name of youth in the GDR, referred at the same congress to "actions directed from outside" and offered the audience his firm assurances that the younger generation would not fall for such outside maneuvers to manipulate the peace in order to render socialism defenseless (ibid., 24/25 April). Radio GDR summarized the official attitude toward Swords to Plowshares and the GDR's approach to the question of peace as follows: "Nobody can expect that we, in this situation of all times [as "ever more plowshares are turned into swords" in the NATO countries], will turn our swords into plowshares. Whoever recommends this as a task of the day must be either blind, deaf, or even worse." (*RAD Background Report*, no. 83.)

Later in the year, confrontational public statements tended to give way to claims that underscored the "unity and power of the GDR peace movement." At a meeting of the impotent GDR Peace Council held in July, Werner Rümpel claimed that the desire for peace entertained by GDR citizens was at one with the policy of the state. "The peace movement in our socialist country . . . carries out its activity under the most favorable conditions of complete accord with the policy of our state, which is predicated on peace and prosperity for its citizens." In "our" unified peace movement, Rümpel said, "there is room for everyone." (*ND*, 17/18 July.)

Religion. Two specific issues produced a head-on confrontation between the Protestant church in the GDR and the regime: the church's objections to compulsory military training and studies in the schools and its pleas for some form of alternative military service for conscientious objectors. Authorities have stubbornly ignored these concerns, and the church, in turn, put up a surprising measure of resistance. At the Fourth Federal Synod of evangelical churches in the GDR in late January (to which GDR officials denied Western correspondents access), all state measures that went beyond the authentic "requirement of military security" came up for discussion. The results of talks held with Klaus Gysi, state secretary for church affairs, were also disclosed. According to church representatives, Gysi had repeatedly "underscored, clearly and unmistakably, the state's no to present church proposals, especially the implementation of a social service for peace [in place of military service]." His argument, as it was paraphrased at the synod, ran as follows: "In light of the world political situation and the responsibility of the state for the security of its citizens, neither an interruption of general compulsory military service nor release from the oath of military service could be considered." The present proposals for a social peace service would, he was credited with saying, do away with the principle of general compulsory military service and for that reason would not be countenanced. Although the church offered no direct rebuttal to Gysi, it did rebuke another SED functionary, Werner Walde, who had maintained that the demand for a social peace service was "hostile to peace, to the constitution, and to socialism." (*DA*, no. 3, pp. 230–34.)

In response to the harassment of young people wearing the Swords into Plowshares badge, the Evangelical Lutheran church of Saxony issued this blunt statement and warning read to local parishes on 28 March: "We acknowledge the position of the state authorities with dismay. We decisively reject the insinuations contained therein. Certainly, there are young people for whom the wearing of this symbol is an expression of a broad critical stance. This, however, does not change the fact that young people have recognized this as a public way of showing their responsibility for peace and as a symbol of hope. The prohibition on wearing this symbol will destroy the trust of these young people in a lasting way. It makes it more difficult to talk with those for whom this no is not the first no to peace intitiatives from within their ranks. It is not our task as a church to give advice to young people in this situation. But we must take into account the threatening consequences and say quite clearly: We no longer have any chance to defend the wearers of this emblem." (*RAD Background Report*, no. 83)

The church continued to speak its mind throughout the year. In April, the Greifswald church leadership, for instance, stated that "government measures against the display of the peace symbol must be understood as an attack on the Christian peace movement in our society" (*Rheinischer Merkur,* 2 July). The chief church councillor at youth day festivities in Thuringia went even further: "Whoever attacks the symbol Swords into Plowshares attacks the church itself" (ibid.). In a pastoral letter read in evangelical churches on Easter Sunday in East Berlin and surrounding areas, the church charged that the state's actions against wearers of the badge represented a restriction on freedom of belief and conscience and challenged allegations that such symbols conflicted with official peace efforts or in any way weakened the defense readiness of the GDR. The letter stated bluntly that "the church undertakes its own independent and continual work for peace" and that it did not exist "simply to reinforce the foreign policy of the state" (*RAD Background Report*, no. 94). By the end of the year, although some Western reports spoke misleadingly of an "easing" of church-state tensions in East Germany (*WP*, 4 November), the germ of the conflict was still deeply implanted in East German political life, even if Honecker made a listless attempt to redress the balance in church-state relations by assuming the chairmanship of the state's planning committee for the Luther anniversary. He remarked in *Neues Deutschland* that cooperation between his committee and church planning committees was "an important step of putting into practice the results of my talk with the board of evangelical leaders on 6 March 1978" (ibid.).

Military. The unofficial peace movement in the GDR intensified the regime's natural nervousness about its credibility on the peace issue in the eyes of its citizens. Not that the familiar unreasoned claims about the identity of socialism and peace were advanced in a repackaged form or, for the sake of believability, in any way refurbished; they were just reiterated in 1982 with a greater sense of urgency and used to give the military and its role in "safeguarding peace and the gains of socialism" a new respectability. Erich Honecker told graduates of military academies in late October: "The national holiday celebrated yesterday again emphasized persuasively that the active, passionate struggle for peace is the basic foundation of foreign policy in the GDR" (*ND*, 9/10 October). Colonel General Fritz Streletz, deputy minister of defense, remarked that the GDR and its armed forces, located at the seam separating the capitalist and socialist worlds, represented the "most important guarantee of peace in our time" (*Horizont,* no. 20).

Much time and effort went into disputing Western allegations that the SED had embarked on a policy of militarizing all sectors of East German society. Such West German talk of a "militarization of social life in the GDR," said Honecker, was nothing but a bid to divert attention away from the position of the Federal Republic (FRG) as the second strongest military power in NATO, next to the United States (*ND*, 9/10 October). For something ostensibly so obvious as the GDR's stand on peace and the peacekeeping role of its military, the regime displayed a palpable uneasiness about the young people's grasp of supposedly self-evident facts that "everyone realizes." Streletz said: "We must unmask the aggressive plans of imperialism and its dangerous nature as well as its . . . ideological diversion [the Swords to Plowshares badge], which is designed to lower the defense willingness of young people, to defame the SED's military policy, and the class commission of the NVA and the GDR border troops" (*Horizont*, no. 20). A more elaborate statement of the party's concerns about East German youth and their attitude toward the military appeared in the official SED monthly *Neuer Weg* (no. 3). It was necessary to increase in all citizens, "especially in young people," their conviction of the need to protect "the socialist fatherland." The GDR was facing an enemy led by generals who had sworn full allegiance to the class aims of "monopolistic capitalism"; an enemy being prepared for a "ruthless and brutal way of waging war"; and an enemy, ideologically and psychologically versed in anticommunism, who was at all times willing to obey orders to begin a war against socialism to defend unscrupulously "imperialist class interests." The presence of this enemy demanded an unequivocal response in the GDR. "Systematic ideological work" at the precinct level was imperative to strengthen ideology and class-oriented attitudes that provided the basis for the implementation of decisions reached at the Tenth Party Congress and of military goals "set down in the basic military code." Because some young people manifested deficiencies in military knowledge and physical condition, there had arisen a "true leadership challenge" for the party organizations to carry out an effective "socialist military education" that would develop among young people "class-oriented attitudes toward military service."

There soon followed a full-blown defense of premilitary training of the kind that goes on under the mantle of the Society for Sport and Technology (GST). Printed in *Einheit* (no. 3), the organ of the SED Central Committee, the article said: "As a socialist defense organization in the GDR, the GST is making an important contribution to the protection of socialism and the keeping of peace. At the center of its entire activity is the task set at the Tenth SED Party Congress to continue promoting the GDR citizens' socialist defense readiness and to refine the capabilities of youth through purposefully organized premilitary training and the ongoing shaping of socialist defense motivation." "Most" young people were greatly responsive to such training, and this "healthy attitude of the vast majority" of young people toward the need to defend their "socialist fatherland" was used as the point of departure for political-ideological work in the GST. It was important, however, for young people to deepen their knowledge about the danger of war existing today, caused by imperialism and provoked especially by the United States and NATO. But they should also have an optimistic awareness of the fact "that peace today is not unprotected and not at the mercy of its enemies. Service in the socialist armed forces is service to peace." Defense Minister Hoffmann made the same point a few weeks later in his explanation of the new GDR laws on compulsory military service. "If today the mass media in the FRG fantasizes about a 'growing militarization of GDR society' and disseminates every imaginable suspicion about civil defense training in the FDJ, all this merely serves as ideological diversion against the GDR." Hoffmann added that "service in the NVA and in the border troops of the GDR is the most effective service in the cause of peace." (*ND*, 26 March.) The new military-service law, passed on 25 March at a session of the People's Chamber, supersedes the law in effect since 1962. It is now impossible to defer conscription until completion of an academic course, and women, for the first time, can be called up for military service in the event of mobilization. (In December, a letter to Honecker signed by a number of East German women protesting the new law and demanding the "right to refuse" made its way to the West. Two of the signatories were taken into custody for a time. [*Der Spiegel*, 6 December.]) Although eighteen months of active service remains the norm, most reservists can be called up for a total of two years with up to three months being served in any one year. (*DA*, no. 5, pp. 458–60.) All the mass organizations were enlisted in a crusade of adulation of the armed forces. Egon Krenz, for instance, said at an FDJ Central Council meeting that readiness for armed defense of the socialist fatherland was a particularly consistent form of "service to the cause of peace," for the desire for peace alone "never prevented any of the wars that have darkened the history of mankind." The FDJ hoped in the future to prove itself as an active fighter for peace and do its part "at the line of demarcation between the two opposing world systems and military blocs toward the inviolability of peace and socialism." (*ND*, 17 September.)

Economy. East German economic planners had few grounds for optimism at the end of 1982. For the first time since 1968, the GDR did achieve a modest surplus in trade with Western industrial nations, the FRG, and the developing countries, and SED officials painted this success in gaudy colors, covering over the dim perspectives in virtually every other area. The surplus resulted from the two-pronged policy of rigorously limiting imports from hard-currency countries while urging industry to exert the greatest possible effort in order to produce more goods for export and thus raise the GDR's intake of hard-currency. In 1982, the GDR increased its exports to hard-currency countries by 15.4 percent while holding imports from the same nations to a 6.4 percent increase. This success in foreign trade, however, is tempered by the fact that this economic strategy yields only short-term results and can offer no basis for reasoned long-range planning. (*DA*, no. 8, pp. 794–95.)

Otherwise, a number of nagging problems beset the SED, foremost among them being the country's staggering indebtedness to the West. Western economists set the level of outstanding loans to the GDR at between $9.1 and $13.2 billion, a higher per capita debt figure than in Poland (*WP*, 3 July; *NYT*, 19 July; *WSJ*, 29 September). To make matters worse, 43 percent of East Germany's overall debt came due at the end of 1982 (according to West Germany's Economic Research Institute), and the GDR was expected to ask banks to extend maturities on some of the expiring credits in order to service the debt (*WSJ*, 12 August). The situation deteriorated even further because of East Germany's peculiar trade obligations: more than 80 percent of its exports of machinery and electrical products go eastwards to the members of the Council for Mutual Economic Assistance (CMEA); thus, few commodities are left for export to the West to generate the funds necessary to buy much-needed raw materials to keep the factories producing in the first place (*WP*, 3 July). Added to that is the sinking value of the West German mark against the U.S. dollar. The Economic Research Institute reported that the GDR would cover the approximately $1 billion in interest payments on its debt due in 1982 through its trade with West Germany (which totaled $5.4 billion in 1981, half of the GDR's trade with the West). But in 1982 this portion of East Germany's foreign trade yielded West German marks that had diminished in value compared with the dollar, and the GDR needed to earn dollars on the world market (*WSJ*, 12 August). On the positive side of the ledger, the Helmut Schmidt government did not cut back in any meaningful way on the availability to the GDR of interest-free "swing" credits. Much discussion in the FRG had centered around just such a move as a response to the GDR's increase in obligatory currency exchanges by Western visitors to East Germany. But the outcome of negotiations between the two countries was the announcement that the "swing" would be reduced only incrementally from $345 to $243 million by 1985. This will have no immediate effect on the GDR because the East Germans have never taken full advantage of the available credits. (*WP*, 3 July.)

A chronic problem for the GDR remains its dependence on Soviet oil to run its factories and the necessity of making up for the diminishing supply by purchases on the world market. At the SED's Tenth Party Congress, Honecker had announced a Soviet declaration of intent to provide East Germany with 95 million tons of oil through 1985. This amount was already frozen at the 1980 level of 19 million tons annually, but in November 1981, at the SED's third plenum, a veiled comment by Honecker alluded to Soviet changes in that level: "Socialist intensification [means] . . . that we must make do with even less raw material . . . *than we were counting on at the Tenth Party Congress*" (*ND*, 20 November 1981; italics added). The cut in Soviet oil deliveries to the GDR was announced officially almost a year later: for 1983 the GDR will receive not 19 but 17.2 million tons from the USSR (ibid., 8 September). This shortfall will increase the GDR's outlay of scarce hard currency for purchase of oil at world market prices even more. In 1980, approximately 33 percent of the GDR's export revenues went just to finance oil imports from Western as well as Soviet sources (the latter at prices well below the world market price, but still paid for in transfer rubles). Add to that the expectation of Western observers that this figure will perhaps mount as high as 50 percent by 1985, and a clearer picture of the extent of the problem comes into focus. (See *DA*, no. 3, p. 265.) Nor were the difficulties made any easier to bear by the shortfalls in 1981 and 1982 in coal deliveries from Poland. The GDR had to compensate for the decrease by greater purchases of world oil (ibid., p. 266; *NYT*, 19 July).

In his closing speech to the fifth plenum in November, Honecker disclosed the level of industrial output over the first ten months of 1982. He claimed that production had risen 4.2 percent ("along with a simultaneous 6 percent decrease in raw material usage and energy consumption"), which pointed to a "quite respectable" growth rate (*ND*, 27/28 November).

Dissent and Repression. The text of the infamous "order to shoot" at persons attempting to flee across the border to West Germany had never found its way into Western hands until March, when the West Berlin *Morgenpost* obtained a copy and printed it. The regulation stipulated, among other things, that "units employed for service at the border may take their own decision to make use of firearms if persons fail to heed the warning of the border guard and are obviously attempting to break through the border of the GDR." First aid would be rendered only when the "execution of [other] urgent tasks" allowed, and "fatally injured persons" were to be taken to an area "out of view of the enemy." (*FAZ*, 27 February.) The *Morgenpost* also published another order that took the instructions a step further. Fire should be opened on any fugitive in "close proximity to the frontier fortifications," and warning shots should be fired only if a minimum of 50 meters still separated him from the border (*Die Welt*, 1 March).

In March, the People's Chamber enacted a new border law that contained regulations governing the use of firearms. The only significant difference between the old, unpublished instructions and the new version (see *ND*, 27/28 March) was the understandable absence of any direct reference to attempts to escape from the GDR. Instead, border guards were empowered to take "all necessary measures for the reliable protection of the state border . . . and to assure the territorial integrity of the GDR and the inviolability of its state border, including air and sea space." The law itself was enshrined with a preamble that stressed correctness and legality: "The strict observance of an adherence to generally recognized principles of international law, among them the observance of sovereignty, the inviolability of state borders, territorial integrity, and noninterference in the internal affairs [of other nations], is an essential prerequisite for the development of good-neighborly relations, of security and cooperation between nations, and the decisive foundation of a stable basis for peace." Ushering the new law into effect, Politburo member Alfred Neumann insisted in reference to the use of firearms that "this regulation contains no more and no less than other nations have decided on for their protective organs." The main reason for the law was, needless to say, not to prevent East Germans from trickling out of the country but to "strengthen the character of the GDR state border from the standpoint of international law" and to countervene revanchist outlooks and practices with regard to our Western border." (Ibid., 26 March.) Bonn announced in late December that 2,392 persons had fled the GDR in 1982 (*NYT*, 29 December).

The physicist Robert Havemann, for many years a thorn in the sides of GDR and SED authorities, died in April (ibid., 11 April). He had been under house arrest in recent years for voicing his opposition to the SED on a wide variety of issues.

Culture. The peace issue in general and, more specifically, the existence of unofficial peace actions in the GDR were discussed at three European writers' conferences attended by East and West German literary figures. The first met in East Berlin in mid-December 1981 and, unhappily, coincided with the declaration of martial law in Poland (see *DA*, no. 1, pp. 5–9). The next gathering, the Hague Meeting for the Further Development of the Peace Initiative of European Writers, met on 24 May, followed scarcely a month later in Cologne by Interlit '82, yet another international writers' conference in support of peace. Of course, writers in the GDR, notably pliant or corrupt regime writers, have always been harnessed to organizations, institutions, and public mass actions that provide auxiliary support of state and party policy. Well before the round of writers' meetings held in late 1981 and 1982, GDR writers and cultural-literary organizations were making (East German) news with expressions of agreement with the GDR's peace policy. In 1982, however, they were also pressed into service against members of the unofficial peace movement in the GDR and called to disaffiliate themselves publicly from any such unsanctioned undertakings. The East German dramatist Wolfgang Tilgner illustrated the tack taken in an article subtitled "We Need Our Plowshares and Our Swords." The loftiest truths, those that appeared to have universal validity, could often be turned on their heads. "One can find buttons, for instance, with the well-known saying of forging swords into plowshares," said Tilgner; but today the leaders and spokesmen of ideological warfare sought to use that slogan to "disarm real peace and weaken it." It was imperative to realize that "such a political slogan, rather than reducing the danger of war, will only increase it today." To adopt it in the circumstances of an "altered historical situation" meant "total capitulation to the very real forces of evil, armed to their teeth." Tilgner went on to attack the West German writer Günter Grass, who has been particularly vocal in his criticism of East Germany's double standard in its approach to independent peace initiatives. Tilgner scoffed at Grass: "Recently a famous West German writer a few steps from here [in West Berlin] announced that he was as much afraid of Soviet missiles as of U.S. ones. [This is] a classic stupidity, of which Günter Grass is likely going to be ashamed once he has survived the current dangerous phase of human history thanks to the tough efforts of those he is maligning today . . . That I need not be afraid of Soviet missiles, I know. There is no one in the Soviet Union who would profit from war. But that I need not be afraid of U.S. missiles either is due to the fact that there are Soviet missiles." (*Deutsche Lehrerzeitung*, 2 April).

Similar issues were then debated at the Hague meeting of writers, where Grass called for the establishment of some sort of human rights office to help shield those members of the peace movement harassed in both East and West. The East German writer-functionary Hermann Kant, who would have been the first to back the proposal had it been limited to the protection of those in the West, shied away from any such enterprise; given the absence of repression in the East, the creation of the office would be tantamount to setting up a "phantom," Kant said. He did agree to the publication in the GDR of the following resolution: "We regard it as our duty to help those persons to the best of our ability who are persecuted because of their efforts on behalf of peace." But *Neues Deutschland* promptly deleted the sentence in its printed version. (*DA*, no. 7, pp. 674–76.) Back in the GDR after the Hague conference, Kant grasped at the first opportunity to poke fun at Grass for his quixotic notions. "You can read in the newspaper that the East

German (that's me) said that the peace movement in the GDR is a phantom. But, of course, I did not call the peace movement a figment of the imagination, for I strongly believe in its powerful existence . . . No, I only called a phantasm the description of GDR conditions as depicted by Günter Grass: suffering columns of oppressed young people [supporters of unofficial peace actions], wretched figures as if from the prisoners' chorus of *Fidelio*, only less melodious." (*Sonntag*, 27 June.)

Kant's high-handedness obscured the true nature of Grass's comments and glossed over the concern about the fates of young East German peace supporters that is only too justified. Kant ended his elaborations with his usual type of cynical bon mot. He painted Grass as a ridiculous figure for "even wanting to establish such an office for his invention." However, "we talked him out of it since conditions in the GDR require such an institution [for the protection of harassed members of the peace movement] about as much as Liechtenstein needs a society for rescuing the shipwrecked." (Ibid.)

Foreign Policy. *Relations with the West.* GDR and SED attitudes toward the West in 1982 were, as usual, directly predicated on the current imperatives of Soviet foreign policy. During times of international tension, the USSR and the GDR always fall back on ideologically defined assumptions and hidebound perspectives that have evolved little over the years. Now as before, crises around the world are caused in general terms by the natural aggressiveness of capitalism and, more specifically, by the most recent U.S. policy of confrontation; peace is jeopardized by the Western policy of an arms buildup and defended by a consistent desire and policy for peace that has always been an organic part of domestic and foreign policies pursued by the socialist countries. The Soviet Union, heading a phalanx comprising all peaceloving nations, advocates disarmament and mutual understanding, whereas the United States persists in rejecting all efforts put forward by the USSR to lower tensions and safeguard peace, rationalizing its intransigence with fabricated charges of a supposed "threat from the East." In May, Honecker arranged one of his patterned interviews with a "Western correspondent" and was served up the appropriate strawmen to knock down. In response to the correspondent's statement that attempts were under way to reverse the policy of détente and replace it with one of confrontation and a relentless arms drive, Honecker accounted for the causes of this "dangerous tendency" with this ritualistic explanation: "Evidently the hopes influential imperialist circles pinned on the policy of détente, to which they subscribed only reluctantly at the time, have not materialized. During the seventies the pursuit of peaceful coexistence among states with different social systems made it possible to achieve a great deal that was conducive to the safeguarding of peace and to international cooperation. This was of great benefit to the peoples in both West and East. Those, however, who like to see the world fraught with tensions and with latent and overt conflicts, and with the danger of new wars because they believe they can thus attain their aim of expanding their power, gaining possession of new sources of raw materials and enlarging their sphere of influence, have found their freedom of action curtailed. And they are unwilling to put up with this state of affairs." (*Foreign Affairs Bulletin*, no. 14, 10 May.)

Honecker added the usual accusation that in following a policy of confrontation and arms building, the aggressive quarters of NATO, "most notably of the United States," made no bones about their intention of gaining military superiority over the Soviet Union and the socialist community. Like Soviet ideologues, the East Germans have never regarded Western capitalism as much more than the obverse of fascism, and that identity was clearly alluded to in Honecker's warning: "We know from history that capitalism has on more than one occasion resorted to war in an attempt to find a way out of the crisis in which it finds itself." Honecker also conjured up a vision of a "popular peace movement" that covered a wide spectrum. "Its ranks are made up of representatives of all classes and strata, Marxists, adherents of all the world religions, trade unionists, intellectuals, mayors, parliamentarians, men and women, young and old." Whereas certain quarters demagogically claimed that the arms threat emanated "from East and West alike," there was a growing awareness among the people about the true source of the threat, said Honecker; and "when peace—as is the case in our country—is the official policy and doctrine of the state, it is quite obvious why citizens should closely identify with this state of theirs and its policy." (Ibid.)

The East German press responded to Ronald Reagan's decision to seek congressional approval for the deployment of the MX missile by reprinting editorials and commentaries by Tass and *Pravda* as well as carefully selected commentaries (mostly communist) culled from the Western press and criticism within the United States itself (*ND*, 25 and 26 November). The Tass dispatch disputed claims of Soviet military superiority as a "lie from A to Z" and as a reflection of the persistent U.S. dream of a nuclear monopoly and warned that the socialist countries would not permit the parity between the two military blocs to be disrupted (ibid., 25 November).

U.S. charges that the Soviet Union has introduced chemical weapons into the fighting in Afghanistan were answered in *Neues Deutschland* (2 September), which printed a Tass commentary that turned the matter on its head: not the Soviet Union but the United States had brought chemical weapons into Afghanistan. "Dispatches from Kabul" reported that participants in an "armed band" sent into Afghanistan from abroad had, on encountering "units of the armed forces of the Democratic Republic of Afghanistan," made use of chemical grenades produced in the United States. "Competent Afghan authorities" were currently investigating the application of U.S. chemical weapons in the "undeclared war against Afghanistan." The *GDR Review* (no. 8) carried an East German account about U.S. production and stockpiling of chemical weapons. This story, though obviously a response to U.S. charges lodged against the USSR, ignored these accusations entirely, pointing out only that the Soviet Union and the "other socialist states at the United Nations" had made continued proposals for a complete ban on the manufacture and use of chemical weapons and the destruction of current stocks. The United States, the journal said, had "sabotaged" all such proposals.

Intra-German Relations. The expiration of the agreement governing interest-free West German "swing" credits to East Germany (they provide a savings to the GDR of an estimated $25 million annually) gave rise to hopes that a renewal of the arrangement could be made contingent on an adjustment in the rate of mandatory border exchanges of currency, which the GDR raised in October 1980 (see *YICA*, 1981, p. 251). FRG Minister for Inner-German Affairs Egon Franke warned in March that if the GDR did not revise the exchange rate, it would "reach the end of its rope: then the GDR would have to see to it that it gets along with fewer interest-free credits" (*Der Spiegel*, 5 March). But in the end the West Germans declined to press the issue, and the only meaningful concession wrung from the East Germans was an amnesty of some 38,000 refugees who left the GDR illegally between 1972 and 1 January 1981. Until now, these former East German citizens (barred, of course, from visiting relatives in the East) were still subject to prosecution should they ever fall into the hands of GDR authorities. The amnesty releases them from GDR citizenship, thereby allowing the GDR to recognize their West German citizenship. They can now apply, as West Germans, for visas to visit the GDR without fear of arrest for "fleeing the republic." (*DA*, no. 20, pp. 1017–19.)

The East German press gave broad coverage to the events surrounding the end of the Schmidt era in West German politics, and many articles hinted indirectly at pronounced SED fears that Helmut Kohl's Christian Democrats will prove far less amenable to accommodations favorable to the GDR than Schmidt's Social Democrats had been. This apprehension actually produced in the press some circumspect praise of West Germany, even including talk in *Neues Deutschland* (22 September) of the "by and large positive role" played in recent years by the FRG in international affairs. This was followed by a modest catalogue of past successes subsumed under the rubric of a West German changeover "from cold war to détente" and "from confrontation to East-West cooperation." As for the impending change of goverment, the paper's explanation sounded *mutatis mutandis* like the SED's familiar theory of fascism and its rise to power. "Contradictions" had emerged in the FRG, the story read, so "influential circles determined that it was time to effect a change of government. This would permit [these circles] to draw closer to their objectives, which are at variance with the policy of détente as well as the social security [of West German workers]." The editorial went on to caution that for the twin issues of peace and security in Europe much depended on whether "unpredictability" set up shop in Bonn and embarked on a policy of confrontation or whether politicians who were conscious of their responsibility for the maintenance of peace "at the dividing line of the two social systems and military blocs" and who would adhere to current agreements gained the upper hand. As the Schmidt era neared its end, the press followed an unusual strategy: it covered the sequence of events by quoting lengthy articles from, among others, Polish and Czechoslovak newspapers that analyzed not only developments in Bonn but also the GDR reaction to them. With the situation at its most critical stage, *Neues Deutschland* (1 October) even appeared to side with men like Herbert Wehner, Willy Brandt, and Franz-Josef Strauss, using their names in the titles to stories that quoted their vexed reactions to the maneuverings of the Free Democrats. One short item reported the occurrence of "demonstrations in many

FRG cities" against the change in governments (*ND*, 1 October). After Kohl was named chancellor, the SED voiced its bellicosity toward the Christian Democrats indirectly by reprinting hostile pieces lifted from the Polish party daily, *Trybuna Ludu* (Kohl's first official statement, for instance, represented a "brutal interference in Poland's internal affairs" [ibid., 15 October]; another story noted that Kohl's first actions were "in contradiction to the realities of Europe" [ibid., 19 October]; yet another, from *Zycie Warszawy*, reported on GDR-FRG relations and the "necessity of a continuation of the East-West dialogue" [ibid, 14 December]). Honecker, on the other hand, seemed anxious to avoid aggressive remarks in his response to "a question from ADN" concerning the new Kohl government (ibid., 15 October), and in spite of SED uncertainty about the potential for advantageous deals with a conservative West German party, Honecker was subdued, almost conciliatory, in treating intra-German matters in his address to the fifth plenum in November. Apart from the obligatory slap at "those" in West Germany still dreaming the dangerous dream of an All-German Reich, Honecker shied away from confrontational comments, welcomed Kohl's expression of intent to abide by existing German-German treaties, and interpreted an invitation from Kohl to visit West Germany as an indication of willingness to "develop further" good-neighborly relations between the two countries. He did not say, however, whether he had accepted the invitation. (Ibid., 27/28 November.)

Poland. After the declaration of martial law in Poland and the ensuing stabilization of the situation there, the SED still chose to keep the problem in the public eye. The point of the continuing coverage, in fact, may have been to reinforce the notion among East Germans that any Solidarity-style undertaking in the GDR would be doomed to failure. Certainly the stories about Poland appearing in the press served as graphic evidence of the ease with which the Polish military imposed its authority on the people. The coverage may be broken down into three categories: reports on party and governmental activities, probably designed to suggest to East Germans that the authorities had re-established their control of things; accounts of the various "counterrevolutionary" calls for protests and demonstrations, the sporadic violence connected with them, and the government's response; and incessant accusations that the West was engaging in systematic interference in internal Polish affairs. Reading the reports dealing with unrest (for instance, the demonstrations coinciding with the August agreements), it was hard to escape the feeling that they were supposed to show both opposition to martial law as being restricted to a few unreasonable zealots and the futility of continued resistance. On the other hand, the August demonstration, according to a PAP dispatch printed in *Neues Deutschland* (3 September), resulted in 4,050 arrests. The mention of large numbers of arrests was in this instance likely intended to accentuate in the minds of East Germans the authorities' readiness and ability to deal even with powerful outbreaks of resistance.

The note was struck early on in the GDR that the declaration of martial law was a Polish matter: "Gen. Wojciech Jaruzelski, at the behest of the Polish United Workers' Party [PUWP], the government of People's Poland, and on the strength of a decree promulgated by the State Council of People's Poland, has declared a temporary state of martial law in order to end the chaos in People's Poland caused by the extremists of 'Solidarity' and by Kania [!] and to begin a process of healing. In so doing [Jaruzelski] acted to forestall a nationwide strike scheduled by the Solidarity leadership for 17 December 1981. All of this is an internal affair of People's Poland. The PUWP and the Polish government did not even consult in the matter with the governments of their allies or inform them beforehand. Nor were they under any obligation to do so." (*ND*, 25 January.) Western measures taken in disapproval of this "internal Polish affair" then fell logically into the category of inadmissible interference in Polish matters. The blame for many of the disturbances, in fact, was laid squarely on the West. The August unrest, for instance, was supposedly caused in part by the "external . . . inspiration" of an agency such as Radio Free Europe, which behaved "like a gangster" in calling for action "hostile to the state" and in disseminating "mendacious depictions" of events in Poland (ibid., 3 September). One example of the type of eyewitness reporting carried by the East German press stated: "As I was meeting with a friend in downtown Warsaw on 31 August . . . I observed how a young man, who suddenly appeared at the entrance to the building [of the Council of Ministers], for no apparent reason began insulting two traffic policemen on duty there. The two spoke calmly and reasonably with the rowdy until he finally left, obviously disgruntled. A short time later I heard someone say: 'The fool ought to have mixed it up with a militia patrol and not with those guys from the traffic police.' Not far from the scene of the incident, a man with a TV camera had captured the event on film and another commented on it in

English." (*Horizont*, no. 37.) Reporting of this nature was just a step removed from the coupling of "imperialist intervention" in Poland with the CIA and CIA provocations, a tack already begun prior to 13 December 1981 and continued sporadically thereafter (see, for instance, *ND*, 8 September [a Tass commentary], and *Horizont*, no. 24). Toward the end of the year, stories appeared claiming that the West was actually interested first and foremost in forcing an extension of martial law in order to prevent the restoration of law and order (*ND*, 1 November).

The ban on Solidarity was accompanied in the press by stories calling for a new, "unified" union, one that would "respect the spirit and letter of the August–September agreements of 1980." "Organs of state" supposedly remained commited to such a union (ibid., 5 October). *Neues Deutschland* (13 December) also carried verbatim Jaruzelski's address announcing the official end of martial law.

Israel. The East German press reacted to the Israeli military action in Lebanon by localizing the conflict ideologically within the context of the "extraordinarily tense internal situation" and by asserting that the "aggression against the Palestinians and Lebanese" was possible only because the "Zionist regime" had the backing of "U.S. imperialism" (*ND*, 8 June). Coupling the Israeli action to the univeral U.S. "policy of confrontation," East German commentators charged that the "holocaust" had been planned well in advance to drown the Palestinian resistance movement in blood once and for all. "Do it, but do it quick" was ostensibly Reagan's admonition to the Israelis as they prepared to execute their "'final solution' of the Palestinian question," according to a *Le Monde* report paraphrased in the East German press. (*Horizont*, no. 34.) The use of inverted commas around the phrase "final solution" was meant to press home on East German readers the analogy with Hitler's extermination of the Jews. Later reports on the fighting were no less unambiguous. On 16 August, *Neues Deutschland* carried a Tass commentary entitled "In Hitler's Footsteps." Calling Menachim Begin a "racist and chauvinist arch-terrorist," Tass contended that "the horrible acts of atrocities commited by [Begin's] army on Lebanese soil" reminded the entire civilized world of the "atrocities perpetrated by the Hitler fascists during the World War II years." The Israeli actions brought to mind not only past fascist atrocities but also the Nazis' inhumane ideology, Tass said, and it proceeded to liken the Israeli "expansionist program" to the notion of *Lebensraum*. Begin and his clique were out to press their policy of a Greater Israel by means of the same methods employed "by their ideological relatives—the German fascists," methods redolent of Guernica, Lidice, Coventry, and Minsk. Such insults, given their doctrinal validization on the strength of their source (Tass), supplied East German commentators with a license to engage in drawing similar historical parallels. Following the massacre of Palestinian civilians in Lebanese refugee camps, press reports threw caution to the wind in equating the Israelis with German fascists. Certainly the East Germans never missed a chance to exploit the claims of other communist leaders (Brezhnev's comparison of the Israelis' "bloody slaughter" with Hitler's atrocities, printed in *Neues Deutschland* [21 September]), but other, originally East German news items and editorials expounded freely along the same lines. *Horizont* (no. 39) in a story entitled "Just as in Lidice and Oradour, so now in Chatila and Sabra," eschewed any distinction between indirect Israeli culpability and direct responsibility or involvement in the massacre itself ("By night the Israeli incendiaries fell upon the defenseless living quarters"). "The bloody deeds," *Horizont* wrote, which enjoyed the blessing of Washington, "sprang from the same fascist urge to extermination and contempt for human beings" shown at Babi Yar. "I'll never forget what I heard from survivors of the liquidation of the Warsaw ghetto," said one East German journalist, "'We have to exterminate Jews wherever we find them,' Frank, Hitler's governor-general for occupied Poland, demanded. Has it not been the [Israeli] goal from day one of this war of aggression to render Lebanon 'Palestinian-free'?" The only allusion to the fact that Israeli troops had not carried out the massacre itself was the charge that the Western mass media left no stone unturned in their efforts to whitewash the Israelis of guilt in the matter. This attitude merely spurred the Israeli "mercenaries" (*Soldateska*) to commit further acts of atrocities.

China. Keenly attentive to Soviet signals that the USSR wishes an improvement in Sino-Soviet relations, the East Germans came out for the first time in years with frequent and factual reports from China. The Chinese Communist Party's Twelfth Congress was covered extensively in *Neues Deutschland* (9, 11/12, and 13 September). One account filled an entire page. The comments of the Chinese leaders were by no means reproduced verbatim but rather rendered in indirect speech or paraphrased form. Still, occasional quotes were included, among them: "In the portion of his speech dealing with foreign policy matters, the chairman of the Central Commitee of the Chinese Communist Party declared that China will 'pursue an independent foreign policy course.' He did not exclude the possibility that 'Chinese-Soviet relations' could 'move in the direction of normalization.' As the speaker commented, China had 'noted that Soviet leaders had repeatedly expressed their desire for an improvement in relations with China,' but he stated that 'not words but deeds are important.'" (Ibid., 9 September.) Earlier, *Neues Deutschland* (25 May) gave extensive coverage to a *Pravda* story entitled "Sooner or Later the Unresolved Problems in Sino-Soviet Relations Must Be Clarified," and toward the end of the year, the paper (9 December) carried a report the likes of which had not been seen in the East German press for years ("Impressions from Shanghai").

Third World. The usual round of high-level consultations took place in 1982 betwen SED personnel, usually led by Honecker, and various delegations or heads of state from countries in the Third World with whom good relations and the expansion of political and economic ties mean much to the GDR. In February, Honecker met with Sam Nujoma of the South-West African People's Organization for a "friendly conversation" (ibid., 23 February). Sweeping but equally vague assurances were immediately forthcoming that the GDR "would continue to practice solidarity with the Namibian people and to support it in its struggle" (*Foreign Affairs Bulletin*, no. 7, 3 March). In May, Honecker held talks with the Libyan foreign minister (*ND*, 4 May), followed several weeks later by the arrival in the GDR of Yemen's vice-president. Various accords were signed on economic, industrial, and technical cooperation. (*Foreign Affairs Bulletin*, no. 29/30, 29 October.)

In March, Yassir Arafat headed a Palestine Liberation Organization (PLO) delegation that arrived in East Berlin for discussions with Honecker and other SED officials. The PLO's East Berlin office, in existence since 1973, was elevated to the status of an embassy, but the GDR evidently declined to make available the kind of material assistance that, it was assumed, Arafat had hoped for. (Ibid., no. 9, 22 March; *FAZ*, 10 March.)

During 1982, the East German press continued the practice begun the previous year of publishing lengthy stories on Afghanistan. The reports rarely referred to the presence of Soviet troops in the country, although many mentioned continued fighting. On 27 April, on the fourth anniversary of the "April revolution," *Neues Deutschland* published a dispatch from its correspondent in Afghanistan, who wrote: "This desire [for peace in the country] is entirely understandable, for bandit attacks, pillaging, acts of sabotage, and murders continue; the undeclared war being waged by the forces of internal and external reaction with all the brutality they can muster against the republic and the process of a national democratic revolution begun four years ago goes on." Mention of Soviet military involvement occurred rarely and always contained identical features: "The Soviet Union responded to the request of the Afghan leadership and dispatched, according to the terms of a friendship treaty signed by the two nations in December 1978, a limited contingent of troops to Afghanistan to ward off external aggression, which was threatening the country" (*Horizont*, no. 17). Generally, however, the Soviet invasion has been enveloped in an assortment of doctrinally couched euphemisms, the most commonly employed being "new stage of the April revolution begun in December 1979" (ibid., no. 37), "new, second stage of the revolution," embarked on in December 1979 when "patriotic forces and the current secretary general of the party and chairman of the revolutionary council . . . deposed the group around [Hafizullah] Amin that was hostile to the party" (ibid., no 14), or "second phase of the national democratic revolution" (*ND*, 25 May). Fighting is still categorized ideologically as an "armed counterrevolution" that wages an "undeclared war" through the use of terror, murder, and pillaging to "retard revolutionary development" (ibid., 18 March; *Horizont*, no. 14). Most other reports from Afghanistan fit the description of innocuous travelogues focusing on various "great gains" attained in the face of "internal and external reactions."

In late May, Babrak Karmal arrived in East Berlin to a hero's welcome. Banner headlines heralding the "state and party visit" were plastered across the front pages of East German dailies for three or four days, the normal medals were awarded, the usual declarations of lasting fraternal friendship between the two peoples issued, receptions held, the familiar toasts proposed, solidarity expressed, and the preformulated treaty of friendship and cooperation cosigned. (See *ND*, 20, 21, 22/23 May). But the whole ritual left the impression that the visit was a big show staged for the sake of appearances, to lend much-needed credibility to the current Afghan state and to upgrade the personal prestige of a Soviet marionette.

International Party Contacts. There were the usual meetings between Erich Honecker and other leaders from communist parties around the world in 1982, the most noteworthy in terms of communist protocol being, of course, Honecker's annual appointment with Brezhnev in August in the Crimea. Discussions between Honecker and János Kádár in Budapest took place in June. In November, Honecker led a delegation to Moscow to attend Brezhnev's funeral, and in late December, at festivities held in Moscow in commemoration of the sixtieth anniversary of the formation of the USSR, Honecker spent a morning talking with Yuri Andropov about "a number of pertinent problems of the international situation" (ibid., 21 December). The most important high-level contact this year was probably Wojciech Jaruzelski's visit to East Berlin in late March. The East German press began beating its drums several days before the date, attempting to stir up enthusiasm for the visit. When Jaruzelski arrived (apart from a trip to Moscow, this was only his second visit outside Poland since the declaration of martial law), he was welcomed with full military honors. For the duration of his stay, the press abounded with feature stories about the visit, leading editorials proclaiming unshakable GDR-Polish friendship, and comments from Soviet papers and news agencies concerning the significance of the visit for future cooperation between the two countries. Consequential matters presumably came up for discussion between Honecker and Jaruzelski, most likely the economy and economic relations between the two countries, but the talks were private and few details of any significance were released to the public.

University of North Carolina (Chapel Hill)   David Pike

Hungary

The Hungarian Section of the Russian Communist Party (Bolshevik) was founded in Moscow in March 1918 by Béla Kun (1886–1939) and a few other Hungarian former prisoners of war. The Communist Party of Hungary came into being in Budapest in November 1918. Kun was the dominant figure in the communist–left socialist coalition that proclaimed the Hungarian Soviet Republic on the collapse of Mihály Károlyi's liberal-democratic regime. The red dictatorship lasted from March to August 1919.

During the interwar period, the party functioned as a faction-ridden movement in domestic illegality and in exile. The underground membership numbered in the hundreds. With the Soviet occupation at the end of World War II, the Hungarian Communist Party (HCP) re-emerged as a member of the provisional government. Kun had lost his life in Stalin's purges, and the party was led by Mátyás Rákosi (1892–1971). Although the HCP won no more than 17 percent of the vote in the relatively free 1945 elections, it continued to exercise a disproportionate influence in the coalition government. Thanks largely to Soviet-backed coercive tactics, the HCP gained effective control of the country in 1947. In 1948, it absorbed left-wing social democrats into the newly named Hungarian Workers' Party.

Rákosi's Stalinist zeal was exemplified by the show trial of Jozsef Cardinal Mindszenty and the liquidation of the alleged Titoist László Rajk. The New Course of 1954–1955 offered some relief from economic mismanagement and totalitarian terror; inspired by some of Stalin's successors, it was represented in Hungary by the moderate communist Imre Nagy. De-Stalinization undermined the party's power and unity, and the replacement of Rákosi by Ernö Gerö (1898–1980) could not halt the rising tide of popular opposition. Following the outbreak of revolution on 23 October 1956, Imre Nagy became prime minister for the second time and eventually headed a multiparty government that withdrew Hungary from the Warsaw pact. On 25 October, János Kádár became leader of the renamed Hungarian Socialist Workers' Party (HSWP). The Nagy government was overthrown by the armed intervention of the Soviet Union on 4 November.

Since the end of the revolution, the HSWP has ruled unchallenged as the sole political party, firmly aligned with the Soviet Union. After an initial phase of repression that culminated in the final collectivization of agriculture (1959–1960), Kádár's rule came to be marked by his conciliatory "alliance policy" and by pragmatic reforms, most notably the New Economic Mechanism launched in 1968.

Population. 10.7 million

Party. Hungarian Socialist Workers' Party (Magyar Szocialista Munkáspárt; HSWP)

Founded. 1918 (HSWP, 1956)

Membership. 811,833 (January 1980); workers and farmworkers, 44.6 percent; women, 28.3 percent; average age, 45.5; 74 percent joined after 1956

First Secretary. János Kádár

Politburo. 13 full members: János Kádár, György Aczél, Valéria Benke, Sándor Gáspár (secretary general, National Council of Trade Unions), Ferenc Havasi, Mihály Korom, György Lázár (prime minister), Pál Losonczi (president), László Maróthy (first secretary, Budapest party committee), Lajos Méhes (minister of industry), Károly Németh, Miklós Óvári, István Sarlós

Secretariat. 7 members: János Kádár, György Aczél (culture and ideology), Ference Havasi (economic policy), Mihály Korom (party, mass organizations, and military), Károly Németh (youth and party building), Miklós Óvári (agitprop and cultural policy), Péter Várkonyi (foreign affairs)

Central Committee. 127 full members

Last Congress. Twelfth, 24–27 March 1980, in Budapest; next congress scheduled for 1985

Auxiliary Organizations. National Council of Trade Unions (NCTU, 4.5 million members), led by Sándor Gáspár; Communist Youth League (874,000 nominal members), led by Györgyi Fejti

Main State Organs. Presidential Council; Council of Ministers (18 members); both constitutionally responsible to the National Assembly

Parliament and Elections. Elections are administered by the Patriotic People's Front (PPF), which nominates candidates by presenting them to voters at meetings at which a minimum of one-third of those present may by open vote nominate an additional candidate. At the last general elections there were 15 such double candidacies. PPF candidates received 99.3 percent of the votes. A majority of members of parliament do not belong to the HSWP.

Publications. *Népszabadság* (People's freedom), HSWP daily; *Társadalmi Szemle* (Social review), HSWP theoretical monthly; *Pártélet* (Party life), HSWP organizational monthly; *Magyar Hirlap*, government daily; *Magyar Nemzet*, PPF daily; *Népszava*, NCTU daily. The official news agency is Magyar Távirati Iroda (MTI).

Party Internal Affairs. Periodic reshuffles of personnel in leading party and government positions are characteristic of Kádárism, as is the fact that such shifts seldom denote a fundamental change in policy. At a plenum on 23 June, the Central Committee approved a number of personnel changes.

The most significant was the return of György Aczél to the Secretariat, which he had left in March 1974 to become a deputy prime minister. Aczél is a party veteran who has ruled unchallenged over culture and been an articulate spokesman for Kádárism in both Eastern and Western Europe. András Gyenes, who had been secretary in charge of foreign and interparty affairs since 1975, was appointed chairman of the Central Control Committee. His place in the Secretariat was taken by Péter Várkonyi (born 1931), a former diplomat and head of the government's information office who was elected to the Central Committee in March 1980 and served most recently as editor in chief of *Népszabadság*. That editorship was handed to János Berecz (born 1930), former head of the Central Committee's Foreign Affairs Department. Berecz has experience as a journalist and scholar, has traveled (including a visit to the United States), and enjoys a high profile in Hungary thanks to his frequent appearance in the media as a commentator on international events.

The new head of the Central Committee's Foreign Affairs Department is Mátyas Szürös (born 1933). He was deputy head of that department in 1974, then served as ambassador to East Germany (1975–1978) and to the Soviet Union. Ernö Lakatos, the former director of the official news agency, was named to replace Imre Györi as head of the Central Committee's Agitprop Department. This completes the eclipse of Györi, a man of modest abilities who was a member of the Secretariat between 1974 and 1980.

The Central Committee also approved the nomination of István Sarlós to the post of deputy prime minister. By profession a teacher, Sarlós has been a party member since 1939. Appointed editor in chief of *Népszabadság* in 1970, he was shifted to the post of PPF secretary general in 1974. He has been a member of the Politburo since 1975. The new secretary general of the PPF is Imre Pozsgay (born 1933), a former deputy editor of *Társadalmi Szemle* and minister of education and culture. He was elected to the Central Committee in 1980. A philosophy teacher, sociologist, and an outspoken advocate of economic reform, Pozsgay has reportedly clashed with Aczél over his support for populist intellectual tendencies. A distinguished professor of French, literary historian, and administrator in the Hungarian Academy of Science, Béla Köpeczi (born 1921), was appointed minister of education and culture. Finally, at its 23 June plenum, the Central Committee elected to its membership Sándor Rajnai, ambassador to Romania since 1978.

The role of the party and of individual party members in a modernizing society managed increasingly by technocrats is a question that is periodically re-examined. The problems and proposed remedies seldom change, as was evident in a speech delivered by Károly Németh at a conference of Central Committee secretaries held in Prague to discuss the role and responsibility of basic party organizations (*Pártélet*, June). Németh reported that the HSWP's working methods were being reviewed, from the Central Committee down. One objective is to "rid the party's work of the elements of formality and of excessive administration and unproductive meetings that draw away the party's attention from political work and also place an unnecessary burden on the basic organizations." Németh stressed the importance of free debate in basic organizations, but he noted that the other requirement of democratic centralism, the unanimous acceptance of party policy, is also occasionally flouted. By way of example, he noted that wage differentiation and other economic measures are not fully supported by some basic organizations and members. Once the party has set such policies, party organizations should not interfere with economic management except in case of abuses.

Domestic Affairs. *Economy.* Anxiety over Hungary's economic prospects pervades the entire society and threatens to undermine the pragmatic political consensus that has been the mainstay of Kádárism. In a lecture reported in the press, HSWP Secretary Havasi denounced an unspecified minority that was giving vent to its dissatisfaction and questioning the party's economic policy. However, he acknowledged that in recent years roughly one-third of the population had seen its standard of living decline and another third's standard was stagnant (*Népszabadság*, 14 September). Hungary's positive image abroad is due to a number of perceptions and misperceptions.

Agriculture is the most successful production sector, thanks to heavy investment and incentives for production by collective farms as well as by private farms and household plots. This has assured an adequate domestic food supply as well as substantial exports of foodstuffs, notably some one million tons of grain annually. The supply of consumer goods is varied and ample by East European standards, and queues are uncommon, but the consumption of material goods is lower than in East Germany and Czechoslovakia, while in the period 1976–1980 per capita real income rose at a slower rate than elsewhere in the bloc (excepting Czechoslovakia). The regime's efforts to "reprivatize" presently uneconomical (mainly retail and catering) operations have attracted much attention, but in 1981 only 3.6 percent of the labor force was privately employed (less than half the East German level), and the six percent of retail outlets that were private accounted for less than 1 percent of total retail turnover (*Radio Free Europe Background Report*, 25 May). Finally, at the end of 1981, Hungary's net debt to Western banks and governments approached $8 billion, the highest per capita debt among members of the Council for Mutual Economic Assistance (CMEA). With a growth rate that is among the lowest in the region, Hungary's economy is clearly in trouble.

Already in 1981, the government had resorted to draconian measures to improve the balance of trade, assigning top priority to boosting exports to the West (and certain developing countries, such as Iraq) and curbing imports. The goals, both for the immediate future and for the rest of the current five-year plan (1981–1985), are the restoration of equilibrium in foreign trade, even at the expense of economic growth, and the maintenance of the standard of living. The budget plan for 1982 anticipated a huge deficit (15 billion forints versus 4.5 billion in 1981), an increase of 1.0–1.5 percent in national income, a rise in consumer prices of 4.8–5.2 percent, and a rise in nominal income of 4–5 percent.

At its June session, the Central Committee reiterated the need to increase the profitability of exports, and indeed the government has been concentrating the allocation of state credits on export-oriented, small- and medium-sized development projects. At the same time, a certain structural decentralization of industry is under way, small- and medium-size enterprises having been found to be more profitable. The government is also trying to reduce subsidies to noncompetitive enterprises and to encourage private artisans as well as small-scale, leased private enterprise to concentrate on the needs of the domestic market. The sanctioning of small "private" associations of workers within enterprises is part of an attempt to curtail the underground economy. Such groups are allowed to use, on a contractual basis, the facilities of their enterprise to produce items in local demand and to share the profits. This, one of numerous recent innovations in the sphere of production and distribution, has already engendered some tensions over income differentiation. The early record of another innovation introduced in 1981, the leasing to private management of state-owned retail shops and catering establishments, indicates that profitability generally improved, although many of the shops offered found no takers. A new measure, to be phased in in 1983, aims to improve the efficiency of some 5,000 state-owned retail outlets by giving managers greater autonomy and by greater incentives and differentiation in wages. The objective is to enhance the competitiveness of state retail outlets with respect to private and leased stores.

Several rounds of price increases were announced in 1982 with a view to reducing domestic consumption and subsidies. On 15 April, the price of fuels was raised by an average of 25 percent and of salt by 50 percent; on 8 August, a major hike in the price of foodstuffs and transportation was decreed. The forint was devalued by some 7 percent in June to further dampen demand for imports and promote exports. In September, Hungary notified the administration of the General Agreement on Tariffs and Trade of temporary import quotas on some raw and basic materials and of special import duties on certain industrial components.

This series of austerity measures was designed in part to preserve Hungary's creditworthiness in the wake of martial law in Poland and Western economic sanctions. Hungary had an excellent repayment record, but between January and March its hard-currency reserves plummeted from $1.8 billion to $374 million, and the threat of default loomed. Admittance to membership in the International Monetary Fund (IMF) in May was an encouraging sign, and over the next few months a financial rescue operation unfolded. The Bank for International Settlements advanced $210 million in June and a further $300 million in short-term credits in September. In August, Hungary negotiated a three-year, $260 million loan from a Western bank consortium to finance the purchase of industrial raw materials. Responding to Budapest's request for a standby loan, an IMF delegation visited the country in September, and by December approval had been secured for two loans totaling $596.3 million. As a member of the IMF, Hungary was able to join the World Bank and reaped its first benefit with a $1.5 million contract for cranes in a World Bank development project for the Yugoslav port of Bar.

By the end of 1981, Hungary had managed to accumulate a small surplus in its nonruble trade, and over the first nine months of 1982, the surplus reached $410 million. Exports to the nonruble sector had in fact declined, but the fall in imports was greater. The deficit in the ruble trade sector meanwhile increased. Hungary's economic prospects looked even dimmer when the Soviet Union indicated that it would reduce its annual oil-export quota from 7.5 million to 6.4 million tons (*Népszabadság*, 2 October). In 1981, the

Soviet Union had sold Hungary 9.2 million tons of crude oil. Since imports over the quota must be paid for in convertible currency at world market prices, the regime is planning to moderate the impact by conservation measures and by reducing the proportion of oil in overall energy consumption from 33 percent to 29 percent by 1985. A long-term economic cooperation agreement was signed in Moscow on 9 September. It provides for Soviet assistance in large industrial projects, such as the nuclear power station at Paks and a new coke chemical plant, and for Hungarian contributions, such as construction workers to build a hotel in Chernovtsy. Hungary's involvement with the controversial pipeline that is to bring gas from Urengoi to Western Europe appears to be only tentative; a branch of the pipeline may pass through Hungary, in which case Hungary would supply some equipment in exchange for gas.

Reforms in the Soviet bloc's trading system have been advocated by Hungarian economists for many years, generally in the direction of currency convertibility, multilateral clearing, and export-oriented rather than import-substituting economic policies. Kádár and other Hungarian leaders have endorsed the proposals for a CMEA summit conference to discuss the economic crisis while reaffirming the country's commitment to multilateral trade relations (in contrast to the more autarkic inclination of the Czechs in particular) (*Magyar Hirlap*, 9 September; *Neue Zürcher Zeitung*, 3–4 October).

Tourism is an important source of hard currency, expected to generate over $260 million in 1982. Some three-quarters of Western tourists come from Austria and West Germany. The entry and exit formalities for Western visitors have been eased over the years, and Austria and Hungary no longer require visas for mutual visits by their citizens. Shopping visits by Czechoslovaks (who do not come armed with hard currency) grew so rapidly in number and economic impact that special length-of-visit and currency requirements were imposed in 1982 on tourists from that country.

Regulations governing travel by Hungarians to the West have also been liberalized. They were hitherto entitled to one "tourist" passport every three years and one "visitor" passport (with only a minute currency allowance) every two years. Now Hungarians may travel to the West once a year either as individual tourists or as visitors in group tours. However, exchange controls still limit the scope of such travel.

The chronic shortage of housing and the decay of existing housing stock are issues of ongoing economic and social concern. New regulations were announced in September governing the allocation of state-owned apartments and aiming to discourage "key money" speculation. The regulations also provide for a progressive increase in rents of state-owned housing amounting to an average of 130 percent over the period 1 July 1983–1 July 1988; for pensioners and large families, the impact is to be mitigated by special subsidies. Other provisions tailor state support for private building and home purchases to the size of family.

Dissent. By Soviet bloc standards, the Kádár regime has been remarkably successful in avoiding domestic political strife, thanks to the relative liberalism of its economic and cultural policies. However, over the past two years, the incidence of publicly articulated dissent has increased sharply, inspired in part by the events in Poland. The mass of the population reacted with some ambivalence to the rise of Solidarity, traditional friendship for Poland and sympathy for the political objectives of Solidarity being tempered by fear of the regional consequences of Poland's bankruptcy and possible invasion by the Soviet Union. In a report to the National Assembly's fall session, Interior Minister István Horváth noted the growth in the intensity of imperialist propaganda and in the activity of antisocialist forces in Hungary (*Népszabadság*, 9 October). So far, the regime has reacted with notable prudence and moderation to the rising tide of criticism. The most common punishment of dissidents is loss of employment, and the worst offenders are encouraged to leave the country temporarily or permanently—measures that infringe human rights but fall far short of the neo-Stalinist brutality applied in certain other East European countries.

While the pragmatism of the Kádár regime continues to inspire a wide degree of public confidence, there is widespread alienation from the official ideology and a growing disposition to seek alternative values. Surveys show that adolescents are cynical about high school courses on ideology, deplore the distorted treatment of history, and have a very low opinion of politicians and other public figures. They exhibit a sense of frustrated idealism (the display of religious symbols is one common form of protest), indeed of a certain fatalism regarding the immutability of the political system (*Ifjukommunista*, no. 5). The regime has characteristically responded to some of these feelings by sanctioning a more open treatment of questions and periods of Hungarian history that had been ignored or dealt with in grossly biased fashion since 1948. The matter was discussed at a conference at Eger in June, and some recent publications reflect this more balanced approach, notably a novel by Ferenc Karinthy (*Budapesti ösz*) that paints a realistic picture of the 1956 revolution.

Writers, philosophers, and social scientists are as usual well represented in the small band of active dissidents. The general assembly of the Writers' Union in December 1981 discussed the relation between politics and religion and the role of writers. One participant suggested that official censorship might as well be imposed, an ironic allusion to the existing informal and unlegislated system of controls on publication. In his address to the assembly, party cultural boss György Aczél noted the malaise among certain creative intellectuals and warned that the regime's tolerance must not be answered with provocative intolerance (*Élet es Irodalom*, 23 December 1981). The newly elected president of the Writers' Union, the dramatist Miklós Hubay, is the first incumbent who is not a party functionary. Despite periodic warnings and dismissals, a degree of pluralism prevails in the realm of culture. The more reform-minded young intellectuals are concentrated around the Young Writers' Circle (a branch of the Writers' Union) and such periodicals as *Mozgó Világ* (Moving world) and *Forrás* (Source, published in Kecskemét). "We shouldn't play off the nation's improved economic situation against its spiritual needs," observed the oppositionist writer Sándor Csoóri in an interview (*Mozgó Világ*, no. 1).

The publication in samizdat form of critical opinion and suppressed facts has become a booming cottage industry. A weekly samizdat boutique is operated by László Rajk, 33, an architect and set designer and son of László Rajk, who was the leading Hungarian Communist executed on fabricated charges in 1949. Unauthorized publishing is a criminal offense in Hungary, and on 3 August a young sociologist, Gábor Demszky, was fined for having established illegally the AB Publishing Company. A thousand-page anthology was published in samizdat form in 1981 in honor of the late István Bibó, a liberal and nationalist political scientist whose spiritual legacy has been appropriated and amplified by opposition intellectuals. The Bibó myth was propagated further in a samizdat periodical, *Beszélö* (Speaking hour, as in jails), which first appeared in October 1981 with a circulation of a thousand copies. Its editor, the utopian Marxist philosopher János Kis, later analyzed the impact of Poland's martial law on Hungarian and other East European opposition and called for the development of a new ideology by Hungary's democratic opposition (*Beszélö*, May).

The rise and fall of Solidarity spurred Hungary's dissidents to various forms of supporting activity. In the summer of 1981, two private groups organized holidays in Hungary for 24 children from needy Polish families. After martial law was promulgated, the groups once again made plans to invite Polish children, and over 500 Hungarians volunteered their support. At the last minute, in August, the Polish and Hungarian authorities took administrative measures to abort the operation. On 30 August, a crowd of about a hundred celebrated the second anniversary of the Gdansk agreement in Budapest. Speakers hailed Solidarity, called for the release of Lech Wałęsa, and proclaimed Hungarian-Polish solidarity. Four organizers, the well-known dissidents Miklós Haraszti, Bálint Nagy, László Rajk, and Gábor Demszky, were detained by the police for four hours. Several Hungarian sympathizers have been prevented by the authorities from traveling to Poland and have had their passports confiscated. The most notable case (reported in ibid., January) was that of Tibor Pakh, an intellectual who in 1960 was sentenced to fifteen years' imprisonment for sending to the United Nations the names of minors executed after the revolution. In October 1981, Pakh began a hunger strike in a Budapest church to protest the confiscation of his passport on the occasion of his latest attempt to visit Poland. He was removed to a psychiatric hospital, drugged, and force fed, then released.

An officially sanctioned demonstration that included Western peace marchers took place on 4 August. Police prevented Rajk and Haraszti from handing the marchers leaflets criticizing Hungary's military policies and integration in the Warsaw pact. Of much greater consequence, however, is a rapidly growing Catholic grass-roots movement of the "basic groups." Because of its aggressive pacifism and defense of conscientious objectors, this movement is at odds both with the church hierarchy and with the regime. It is one manifestation of a religious revival among younger people that has oppositionist political undertones.

The causes of mental stress are manifold, but the tensions of life in Hungary seem to be acute, judging by the suicide rate. This, at 44.9 per 100,000 population (1980), is the highest in the world and is arousing professional as well as public debate.

Foreign Affairs.   The official views of the Hungarian party and government on foreign affairs are, as before, scarcely distinguishable from those of the Soviet Union. Nevertheless, the Budapest regime and in particular János Kádár are regarded in the noncommunist world as more liberal and pragmatic than their Warsaw pact partners. The Western powers have shown some readiness to reward such liberalism, and the Hungarians assiduously cultivate this image in the interest of trade and credits. Thus when Deputy Prime Minister József Marjai visited the United States in early May (meeting President Ronald Reagan, Vice-President George Bush, and Secretary of State Alexander Haig as well as lesser officials), he declared that his purpose was to explain "the process of differentiation" among East European countries—that is, the deserving case of Hungary (*NYT*, 12 May). In turn, a delegation of the Senate Appropriations Committee headed by Senator Paul Laxalt visited Budapest in July.

Hungary's comparatively cordial relations with the West were strengthened by two notable visits, that of Kádár to Bonn on 26–28 April and that of President François Mitterrand to Budapest on 7–9 July. Kádár's low-profile working visit was marked by eagerness on both sides to discuss the decline of détente. The relatively trouble-free state of bilateral relations was apparently reaffirmed in Kádár's meetings with Chancellor Helmut Schmidt and Chancellor-to-be Helmut Kohl and with leading businessmen and financiers. The Federal Republic is by far Hungary's most important trading partner in the West.

The French president's arrival capped a flurry of visits, by ministerial and Socialist Party delegations from France and by Hungarian officials, including György Aczél. Mitterrand had met Kádár on two previous occasions (1976 and 1978) and had been positively impressed. Hungary was the first East European country the president chose to visit, and he took the opportunity to expound French policy on détente and disarmament. For Kádár, the visit was above all a diplomatic coup, although it also brought a promise of closer cultural and trade relations.

Other diplomatic activity included visits by Foreign Minister Frigyes Puja to Britain and Iceland (January), Finland and Sweden (April), Cyprus (May), and Canada (June). Austria's share of Hungary's foreign trade has risen from 3 percent in 1965 to 5.1 percent in 1981, and Prime Minister Lázár's visit in September was one in a series of contacts confirming ever-closer commercial relations. Traditionally good relations between Hungary and Finland were reaffirmed on the occasion of President Mauno Koivisto's sojourn in Budapest in early September. Head of state Losonczi's trips to Burma and the Philippines in June, to Portugal in September, and to Kuwait in November were more flag-showing affairs, although all such visits have a trade-expanding purpose as well. A major trade mission took Deputy Prime Minister Lajos Faluvégi to Brazil in March. Finally, a notable foreign visit was that of a Palestine Liberation Organization delegation led by Yassir Arafat in February; it produced the standard declarations of solidarity with the Palestinian people. Hungary subsequently denounced the Israeli invasion of Lebanon.

International Party Contacts.   The Polish crisis continued to predominate in the HSWP's intrabloc relations. The Hungarian Central Committee's periodic communiqués on Polish developments were perhaps a shade more moderate in tone than those of the Soviet and other East European parties, but official relief greeted the declaration of martial law. Media reports on the ensuing stalemate in Poland continued to be fairly factual and objective.

Secretary Gyenes met with his Czech counterpart, Vasil Bil'ák, in Bratislava only hours after the declaration of martial law in Poland, and the two voiced their approval of the steps taken by Gen. Wojciech Jaruzelski. Budapest's general reaction was to approve the restoration of internal order and to offer Poland the benefits of Hungary's experience in achieving economic stability and social peace. The Hungarian Red Cross, the NCTU, and the churches all sent aid to Poland, and a new bilateral agreement, signed in Warsaw in February, provided for expansion of trade. Sándor Gáspár visited Warsaw on 30 January. In a subsequent television interview, Gáspár suggested that the crisis in Poland had been precipitated by the fact that unions in that country did not possess an independent sphere of authority. In contrast, he insisted, the Hungarian unions actively defended the workers' interest in discussions with the government, although this advocacy was for the moment conducted in secrecy (*Radio Free Europe Research,* 4 March). The Hungarian party was also assigned the role of defending Jaruzelski against the criticisms of the Italian Communist Party. To this end, a party delegation was dispatched to Italy in March, led by the deputy director of the Central Committee's Foreign Affairs Department, Gyula Horn. A subsequent article in the HSWP's theoretical journal argued at great length the necessity of martial law to save socialism and warned the Italian comrades against being suborned by bourgeois propaganda and pressure (*Társadalmi Szemle*, March).

Frigyes Puja was the first visitor of foreign-minister rank to arrive in martial law Warsaw (11–12 February). On 21 April, General Jaruzelski paid a twelve-hour visit to Budapest and was praised by Kádár for his "great political courage." On that occasion the delegations discussed mainly economic questions. The visit was followed by a flurry of consultations between the two countries. Deputy Prime Minister Marjai traveled to Poland in June, as did an HSWP delegation to discuss ideological cooperation. In the same month, Polish delegations representing party workers and parliament visited Budapest. Justice Minister Imre Markoja led a delegation to Warsaw in July, and in September an HSWP delegation of economic specialists took the same route. Meanwhile, Polish government spokesman Jerzy Urban came to Budapest for talks on cooperation in "information." In early September, talks were held in Budapest on the coordination of Poland's and Hungary's economic plans for 1983–1985. In order to stimulate the utilization of idle industrial capacity in Poland, Hungary granted the latter hard-currency credits for the purchase of television components, to be repaid with Polish color-television tubes. Cooperation in the manufacture of buses and small agricultural implements was also discussed.

While relations with Poland are cordial and cooperative on both official and popular levels, the unofficial cold war with Romania continues unabated. The publication in April of a polemical work by the Romanian author Ion Lancranjan (*Word on Transylvania*) only exacerbated the historical quarrel over that territory and, implicitly, over the circumstances of the now two-million strong Hungarian minority in Romania. Lancranjan disputed the Hungarian claim to first settlement of the area and the Hungarian (and incidentally Comintern) view that the acquisition by Romania of Transylvania in 1919 was an act of imperialist expansion; he also managed to imply that Kádár was an irredentist. The book was evidently only the latest salvo in an officially managed propaganda campaign designed to affirm both the historical legitimacy of Romanian claims and the current status of Transylvania as an integral part of Romania, an affirmation allegedly necessitated by the manifestations of "neo-revisionism" in contemporary Hungary.

The publication in the HSWP daily of a scarcely veiled satire on Nicolae Ceauşescu's personality cult and historical myth-building was presumably designed to impress the Hungarian public with the party's "correct" sentiments regarding Transylvania (*Népszabadság*, 24 April). Published commentaries indicate widespread dismay at the chauvinism displayed by Lancranjan (*Tiszatáj*, September; *Valóság*, October). Protests were voiced by Transylvanian Hungarians as well, notably in samizdat form (*Ellenpontok*, May). In these circumstances, it is not surprising that Prime Minister Lázár's official visit to Bucharest on 13–14 July, while free of any public show of tensions, did not produce the effusively cordial communiqués customary on such occasions. In November, over 70 intellectuals sent an appeal to Prime Minister Lázár protesting the mistreatment of several intellectuals belonging to the Hungarian minority in Romania.

The election of Yuri Andropov to succeed Brezhnev at the helm of the Soviet party was not entirely unanticipated in HSWP circles and was received with some satisfaction. In his capacity as Soviet ambassador, Andropov had played an essential role in the crushing of the Hungarian revolution of 1956. Subsequently he became a staunch supporter of Kádár's brand of controlled reform, and his elevation is therefore regarded in Hungary as a guarantee of the maintenance of the present system. Andropov was still head of the Soviet secret police when he paid his latest visit to Budapest, on 28–29 December 1981; on that occasion he met with Kádár as well as with Interior Minister Horváth. The latter led a delegation to Moscow in early August at the invitation of the new KGB head, Vitali V. Fedorchuk.

The East German party head and president, Erich Honecker, arrived in Budapest on 2 June on the first such visit in ten years. East Germany is Hungary's second largest and Hungary is its fourth-largest trading partner. On 13 September Czechoslovak leader Gustáv Husák came to Hungary on a "friendly working visit." Kádár and Husák reportedly agreed on the importance of the proposed CMEA summit and of greater economic integration as well as on support for the Polish party's efforts at consolidation. HSWP Secretary Németh visited the Yugoslav party in December 1981.

Babrak Karmal, the Afghan party and state leader, arrived in Budapest on 4 October in quest of moral and material support and received both. Kádár hailed the just struggle of the Afghan people, and the visit produced cooperation agreements at the state and party levels. Hungary is already providing some aid to the beleaguered regime and is financing the education of some one hundred students from Afghanistan. Meanwhile, the revolving door hardly stopped spinning as fraternal party leaders and delegations passed through Budapest: Austrian and Dutch party leaders in January; Salvadoran in February; Jordanian in April; Swedish, French, Mongolian, Portuguese, and Israeli in May; Yugoslav, Haitian, Uruguayan, Tunisian, Venezuelan, and Zambian in June; Palestinian, Belgian, Lebanese, and Peruvian in July; Spanish, Norwegian, and Laotian in August; and Yemeni, Colombian, and Luxembourgeois in September. The more noteworthy visits in the opposite direction include that of a Korom-led delegation to the French Communist Party's congress in February; of Foreign Minister Puja to North Korea, Laos, and Kampuchea in March–April; of Defense Minister Lajos Czinege and a military delegation to Libya and other African points in October; and of a delegation led by Interior Minister Horváth to Nicaragua in November.

Sándor Gáspár attended the congress of the World Federation of Trade Unions (WFTU) in Cuba in February, in his capacity as president of the WFTU. That organization held a working session in Budapest on 5–7 July, and WFTU Secretary General Ibrahim Zakariya met Kádár and presented him with a medal. In April, Warsaw Pact commander Marshal Viktor Kulikov attended Hungarian-Soviet command and staff exercises in Hungary. The CMEA's thirty-sixth session was convened in Budapest in early June, and Kádár met with participating Soviet Prime Minister Nikolai Tikhonov. Frigyes Puja attended the meeting of Warsaw pact foreign ministers held in Moscow on 21–22 October; the resulting communiqué outlined the allies' views on disarmament and the Madrid conference to review compliance with the Helsinki Final Act, which was about to be reconvened.

University of Toronto   Bennett Kovrig

Poland

The year under review, the centennial of what is officially regarded as the foundation of the first revolutionary workers' party in the Polish lands (Social-Revolutionary Party Proletariat, usually referred to as the Great Proletariat, in Warsaw, August 1882), had been intended as a year of celebration of the party's traditions and achievements. The disarray in the Polish United Workers' Party (PUWP) since the mass strikes of July–August 1980, the founding of Independent, Self-Governing Trade Unions Solidarity (Niezalezne Samorządne Związki Zawodowe Solidarność), and in particular the imposition of martial law in December 1981 severely limited the scope of the celebrations. The PUWP considers among its antecedents only one part of the working-class movement in Poland, the one that traces its lineage through the Great Proletariat, the Social Democracy of the Kingdom of Poland and Lithuania (1894–1918), the Polish Socialist Party–Left (1906–1918), the Communist Party of Poland (1918–1938), and the Polish Workers' Party (1942–1948). The PUWP was founded in December 1948, when the Communists forced a merger with the Socialist Party.

Population. 36.2 million (*Trybuna Ludu*, 10 November)

Party. Polish United Workers' Party (Polska Zjednoczona Partia Robotnicza; PUWP)

Founded. 1948

Membership. 2,488,000 (Radio Warsaw, 12 June); 1.7–2.0 million (author's estimate); no class breakdown available, but "intelligentsia" constitutes 36 percent (*Zycie Partii*, 10 October)

First Secretary. General Wojciech Jaruzelski

Politburo. 15 full members: Wojciech Jaruzelski (head, Military Council for National Salvation; prime minister; defense minister), Kazimierz Barcikowski, Tadeusz Czechowicz (first secretary, Lodz voivodship committee), Józef Czyrek, Zofia Grzyb, Stanislaw Kalkus, Hieronim Kubiak, Zbigniew Messner (first secretary, Katowice voivodship committee), Miroslaw Milewski, Stefan Olszowski (foreign minister), Stanislaw Opalko (first secretary, Tarnow voivodship committee), Tadeusz Porębski (first secretary, Wroclaw voivodship committee), Jerzy Romanik, Albin Siwak, Marian Woźniak (first secretary, Warsaw committee); 5 deputy members: Stanislaw Bejger (first secretary, Gdansk voivodship committee), Jan Glówczyk (editor in chief, *Zycie Gospodarcze*), Gen. Czeslaw Kiszczak (minister of internal affairs), Wlodzimierz Mokrzyszczak, Gen. Florian Siwicki (acting defense minister)

Secretariat. 10 members: Wojciech Jaruzelski, Kazimierz Barcikowski (organizational affairs), Józef Czyrek (foreign affairs), Jan Glówczyk (mass media), Manfred Gorywoda (aide to Jaruzelski), Zbigniew Michalek (agriculture and food industry), Gen. Miroslaw Milewski (security forces and state administration), Wlodzimierz Mokrzyszczak (party personnel), Marian Orzechowski (ideology), Waldemar Świrgoń (youth and culture)

Central Committee. 200 full and 70 deputy members (July 1981), some 180 of whom were active in 1982

Last Congress. Extraordinary Ninth, 14–20 July 1981, in Warsaw

Auxiliary Organizations. In a state of flux (see section on front and mass organizations below)

Main State Organs. Council of State (18 members), led by nominal head of state Henryk Jabloński; Council of Ministers (35 members) led by Prime Minister Jaruzelski; both of these constitutional bodies are overshadowed at present by the extra-legal Military Council for National Salvation, also headed by Jaruzelski (see below)

Parliament and Elections. All deputies run on the slate of the Front of National Unity (FJN), which at the time of the last elections in March 1980, included the PUWP, the Democratic Party, and the United Peasant Party, as well as other social and poitical groups. Its candidates received 99.52 percent of the vote. The PUWP received 261 of the 460 seats in the Sejm (parliament), the United Peasant Party 113, and the Democratic Party 37; the remaining 49 seats were filled by representatives of nonparty groups, including 13 from various Catholic groups. Its present makeup cannot be ascertained. Many deputies were excluded or resigned after the imposition of martial law. A consistent core of some twenty deputies voted against or abstained from voting on several bills submitted to the Sejm in late 1982.

Martial Law Regime. The Military Council for National Salvation (Wojskowa Rada Ocalenia Narodowego; WRON) was proclaimed by its chairman, Gen. Wojciech Jaruzelski, on 13 December 1981. It exercised the highest political authority for the duration of the state of war. Besides Jaruzelski, the WRON consisted of three lieutenant generals, one admiral, nine major generals, two generals, three colonels, one lieutenant colonel, and one lieutenant commander. The National Defense Committee, appointed by the Council of Ministers, had overall administrative responsibility for the duration of the emergency. It was headed by Prime Minister Jaruzelski. The powers of the military commissions were deliberately left vague; their responsibility was "to strengthen the country's management." Both the Council of Ministers and the Sejm created several committees to deal with problems arising from the state of war.

Publications. *Trybuna Ludu*, PUWP daily; *Zolnierz Wolności*, army daily; *Rzeczpospolita*, semioffical government daily; *Zycie Partii*, fortnightly PUWP organ; *Nowe Drogi* and *Ideologia i Polityka*, PUWP monthlies. The Polish Press Agency (Polska Agencja Prasowa; PAP) is the official news agency.

The Coup d'Etat. In many respects, the events of 1982 were unique in the history of communist rule. By no means was it the first time that a ruling communist party had recourse to armed force in an attempt to put down popular opposition and to consolidate its rule, whether under the guise of formally imposed martial law ("state of war" in Polish) or not. In some aspects, however, the development in Poland was *sui generis* and has no precedents in other communist-ruled countries.

The so-called coup d'etat of 13 December 1981 (see *YICA*, 1982, pp. 443–45) only superficially resembled military upheavals in various Third World countries. Polish armed forces, arrogating to themselves absolute power in the state for their extra-legal equivalent of a Latin American–style junta, did not deprive the ruling communist party of its powers. Nor did they attempt to change the existing political system. On the contrary, the army, or to be more precise, its officer corps, over 90 percent composed of party members (all general officers belong to the PUWP) and held under the tight control of a special department of the party's Central Committee, called (to deflect attention from its partisan character) the Main Political Directorate of the Armed Forces (GZP), simply responded to an appeal of the party leadership to give succor to a communist system unable, or unwilling, to overcome the crisis by political means. Communists in uniform were asked to do what their comrades in mufti—the party apparatus, the state administration (including internal security forces), the economic management—had obviously failed to achieve: the suppression of a mass movement that realistically refrained from postulating a radical change of the political system, but put forward demands utterly incompatible with continuation of communist rule in its hitherto existing form.

The coup d'etat had been prepared by a union of offices in one person unprecedented in communist countries: during 1981 the minister of national defense and member of the party's Politburo, Gen. Wojciech Jaruzelski, gradually took over the posts of prime minister, first secretary of the PUWP, and finally chairman of the Military Council. This concentration of power was accompanied by the creeping militarization of public life: first the countryside and later towns and cities as well were put under the direct administration of special military task forces led by political officers. Posts vacated by incompetent, discredited, or unreliable members of the ruling establishment, both in the party apparatus and in the state administration, were filled by military men. While both the incumbents and their replacements had been selected through the *nomenklatura* system, the change was by no means a purely formal or cosmetic one, even before this evolution culminated in the proclamation of a state of war and imposition of martial law.

The PUWP, like its predecessors, never fully succeeded in carrying out the Leninist precepts of eradicating differences of opinion among its leading cadres and stamping out factional warfare. The 1980 crisis had naturally exacerbated political conflicts and deepened the split between those who still believed that a certain accommodation with popular demands might save communist rule in Poland and those who were mortally afraid of losing their monopoly of power, who advocated a show of force, and if need be, use of force, to suppress what they regarded as counterrevolution. Predictably, among the latter were security men and officers of the armed forces. After all, they had been meticulously vetted, submitted to a long indoctrination, and, more often than not, kept in isolation from civilian society to protect them against invidious influences.

Charging the armed forces with major and direct responsibility for suppressing the opposition and for running the country in the face of an ever-worsening economic crisis had, from the communist vantage point, some additional advantages. It allowed the party, for instance, to obscure its own culpability and, by playing up the traditional sentimental attachment of Poles to their soldiers, to justify not only the use of force but the suspension or abolition of human and civil rights won by the people in the decades since Stalin. Military rule provided the screen behind which the Communists gained a full year's respite, desperately needed in order to bring their house in order, to suppress opposition and dissent, and to restore the leading role of the party in the political, economic, cultural, and social domain. The state of war and martial law were not suspended until the most active and vociferous opponents of the regime were silenced, and the party retrieved all the instruments—including legal powers—to bring Poland back into line in the Soviet-dominated camp.

Thus, the December 1981 coup and its aftermath, viewed in strictly political terms, meant not a transfer of power from a ruling communist party to the armed forces, but a shift of the center of gravity inside the PUWP leadership—from political proponents of political solutions to those who preferred sheer force. Although the term "normalization" was not widely used in official Polish propaganda, probably because of its association with post-1968 Czechoslovakia, it seems to convey best the essence of 1982—the year the communist establishment declared a state of war against the nation and the armed forces carried it out under party guidelines.

Party Internal Affairs. The proclamation of the state of war and imposition of martial law was preceded by the infliction of a similar state of emergency inside the PUWP. The guidelines (*Instrukcja*) issued by the Politburo, dated 12 December 1981, were never published, and their full text seems to be unknown abroad. They were apparently transmitted to party committees at all levels and read to members of the basic party organizations by representatives of a higher authority. Much later, Kazimierz Barcikowski admitted (*Zycie Partii*, 1 October) that the guidelines suspended many stipulations of the party statutes, in particular most of the amendments approved at the Ninth (Extraordinary) Party Congress in July 1981, which supposedly had increased the democratization of inner-party life. Higher-level party bodies and control commissions were granted wide, in practice arbitrary, powers to dismiss and nominate officials previously elected by the rank and file, to dissolve and replace local and enterprise committees or even entire organizations, and to exclude members from the party.

All the numbers involved have not been published yet. Some big basic organizations in major industrial plants that had been regarded as main strongholds of Solidarity (for instance, in the Katowice Steel Plant in Upper Silesia) were dissolved in their entirety. Their former members were invited to submit individually new membership applications to special ad hoc commissions composed of officials of higher party committees, representatives of control commissions, and officers of the GZP. It· is not clear how new committees in the reconstructed basic organizations, or those which were to replace dissolved committees, were appointed. In the remaining basic organizations, similar bodies proceeded with a "verification" of the membership (the word "purge" was carefully avoided); as a rule, holding elective offices in the suspended trade unions (and in some cases even membership in Solidarity) was considered sufficient grounds for exclusion. According to official figures, in the first two months of martial law, 349 secretaries of rural and urban committees were replaced, as were 307 secretaries of factory committees, 2,091 first secretaries of basic organizations, and about 1,800 members of party committees at the city, commune, and province levels (ibid., 3 March). Many party members, especially industrial workers and intellectuals, left the party of their own will. According to Barcikowski, in the second half of the year, long after the first, most intensive stage of the purge, the number of those renouncing party membership had leveled off at some 20,000 a month (ibid., 1 October).

General confusion was thus caused by the infliction of the state of war and by the purge of party members who had held senior posts in the state and local administration, in economic management, and in all other domains of public life. The replacement of leading cadres in the state and party apparatus by military personnel also resulted in virtual total paralysis of internal party life. Despite claims to the contrary, there was widespread conviction that the party had abdicated its "leading role" to the armed forces. Barcikowski very early warned that "no one can replace the party in fulfilling its mission" and called on the apparatus and party activists to enlarge their number and intensify their activites (*Trybuna Ludu*, 31 December 1981/1 January 1982). This was of no avail: the rank and file and local committees were plunged into the verification campaign and mutual recrimination. The Secretariat tried to check this decomposition by creating another tier of party bureaucracy, not provided for in PUWP statutes: the so-called Regional Centers of Party Activities (ROPP), which, under supervision of provincial (voivodship) committees, were supposed to control the activities of local (rural and urban) organizations. The lower party apparatus and *actif* resented the new centers since they reminded them of the previously disbanded district (*powiat*) level of control (*Zycie Partii*, 23 June).

In order to prepare for a plenary session of the Central Committee, all members and candidates of the Central Committee in good standing, as well as members of the central *actif* (including many officers) were dispatched to the provinces to explain the party's role and function under martial law and to outline its long-term policies. A draft ideological and programmatic declaration prepared by the Politburo and pompously titled "What Are We Fighting For, Where Are We Going?" was to serve as the basis for discussion.

According to the party statutes, the Central Committee should convene in plenary session at least once every three months; the last one had been held in October 1981 to ratify Stanislaw Kania's dismissal and to elect Jaruzelski as first secretary. The first plenum under martial law (the seventh by official count) was convened on 24–25 February. Jaruzelski's address justified the proclamation of the state of war, promised economic reform, and appealed for consolidation of the party, in which there was "no room for factional activity"; the ensuing discussion (60 speakers) closely followed the same pattern, but did not elaborate on the factional struggle although its intensification was an open secret even in nonparty ranks. Personnel changes were minor—three Central Committee members, two workers and a professor, were excluded for their Solidarity sympathies; Minister of Internal Affairs Gen. Czeslaw Kiszczak and an economist turned full-time apparatchik, Marian Woźniak (subsequently appointed first secretary of the Warsaw Committee), were made deputy Poliburo members. The unanimously adopted resolution approved martial law; expressed gratitude to the armed forces, police, and security for having "done their patriotic duty"; and called on party organizations to support the reluctantly formed Citizens' Committees for National Salvation (*Trybuna Ludu*, 25, 26, and 27/28 February). The platform, "What Are We Fighting For," published in the party theoretical monthly *Nowe Drogi* (March), was submitted to an all-party discussion before its announced adoption by the next Central Committee plenum, but apparently has since been forgotten. The plenum brought no perceptible change in intraparty activities, although the purged and reconstructed party committees gradually began to gain, with active military participation, their traditional "leading role" in enterprises and provinces.

Subsequent commentaries in the party press hailed the plenum as the opening of an "ideological offensive" aimed at consolidation of party ranks as well as restoration of the party's credibility and supremacy. It was followed by an ideological conference held in Warsaw on 2–3 April under the effective chairmanship of Stefan Olszowski, then Central Committee secretary in charge of propaganda. The several hundred participants included central leaders, provincial first secretaries and propaganda secretaries, representatives of major industrial plants, as well as leading figures of the so-called ideological front. The conference was officially labeled the "first," and it was widely assumed it would be followed by similar ones at regular intervals. It was, in fact, not repeated. Discussion was held in four groups presided over by Olszowski (scientific and theoretical foundations of the party propaganda), Barcikowski (the leading role of the party in socialist democracy), Orzechowski (main problems of ideological struggle), and Główczyk (general orthodoxy of socialist construction), but dealt mainly with current political problems. The ideological context of the eight lectures delivered did not go beyond general affirmation of Marxism-Leninism and socialist internationalism (loyalty to the Soviet Union). Similar conferences were also organized by provincial party committees; unlike the central one, they were not as carefully prepared and provided a forum for factional controversies. Official dissatisfaction with the results was voiced, even before the central conference, by *Trybuna Ludu* (1 April), which complained that party activists do not "know any more what is in accord with Marxist ideology and what is relevant, or even hostile to it." The paper later ascribed this deplorable state of affairs to the discrepancy "between ideological principles and daily party practice" (20 April). *Polityka* (1 May) printed a discussion among three workers, who were members of the party and unexpectedly critical of the whole discussion and of the programmatic platform "What Are We Fighting For."

Subsequent plenary sessions of the Central Committee steered clear of ideological issues. The Eighth plenum, held on 22–23 April, was devoted to the economic situation: two reports, presented by Marian Woźniak and Deputy Prime Minister Janusz Obodowski (in charge of economic matters in the party and the government, respectively), painted a gloomy picture of falling industrial production and market supply, rising prices, and a resulting fall in living standards without offering hope for a speedy recovery. "We can expect no sudden miracle"—such was the tenor of the reports and of the following discussion. The main subject of the ninth plenum (15–16 July) was the problem of youth. The plenum had been preceded by a lengthy discussion in party-organized meetings all over the country and in the media. Its culmination was a government-approved action program published on the day the session started (*Trybuna Ludu*, 15 July). At the plenum, Jaruzelski said in his opening address that "the party wishes to see in youth an aware and responsible partner in the creation of changes," but the resolution was short on specific measures. It promised instead increased party control over youth organizations and the intensification of political and ideological indoctrination. The establishment of the Committee for Youth by the Council of Ministers seems to have been the only tangible result of year-long deliberations of exceptional urgency (the young generation, openly rebellious against the system, had supported first Solidarity and then the underground movement, providing their most devoted and militant activists).

The ninth plenum brought about the most comprehensive reshuffle in the party leadership since the imposition of martial law. Olszowski, widely regarded as the leader of the hard-line faction, was demoted from the Secretariat and sidetracked to the Ministry of Foreign Affairs (though he retained his membership on the Politburo); Prof. Hieronim Kubiak, a figurehead representing moderate party intellectuals, was also dropped from the Secretariat. Those promoted included two economists (Glówczyk, who took over the Propaganda Department from Olszowski, and Gorywoda, personal aide to Jaruzelski), heads of two major party organizations (Woźniak from Warsaw, Bejger from Gdansk), and another grass-roots representative, Stanislaw Kalkus, a foreman from the Cegielski plant in Poznan who replaced a similar man of straw from the Gdansk shipyard. These changes were generally interpreted as a strengthening of Jaruzelski's personal position and an attempt to clip the factional wings in the party. Of a similar character was the promotion (at the next plenum) of 29-year-old Waldemar Świrgoń, until then leader of the Union of Rural Youth. The youngest member of the PUWP leadership jumped straight from alternate membership on the Central Committee to an influential post in the Secretariat (ibid., 29 October), where he was apparently charged with tightening party supervision over the youth movement and cultural activities.

The next plenum (27–28 October) proceeded on two different planes: ostensibly it dealt once more with the economic situation. The Politburo report was delivered this time by Gorywoda, who tried to find some consolation in statistics showing that the decline in industrial production had halted and, in the last couple of months, even shown a slight increase (over the same period of 1981 when the crisis had reached its height). Even so, he had to admit that the purchasing power of the population had been severely cut (according to different estimates, by 25–40 percent) as a result of price hikes introduced after infliction of the state of war and that not even "modest improvement" could be expected before 1983–1985. The partial abolition of rationing of foodstuffs and industrial goods could not be envisaged earlier than "about the end of the next year" and only if production increased. Further price increases, however, were unavoidable, and there was no improvement in sight in housing since the building industry continued to deteriorate (ibid., 28, 29, and 30 October).

But the most significant event at this session, though never published, was a counteroffensive mounted by the hard-liners. The signal was given by the unauthorized circulation of the text of an "open letter" by leading hard-liner Tadeusz Grabski (see biography at end of profile), but more ominous seemed to be a motion simultaneously submitted to the Sejm by about one hundred PUWP deputies. Their demand for a speedup in the trial and exemplary punishment of former PUWP first secretary Edward Gierek and some of his close collaborators in the party leadership and in the government clearly implied defiant criticism of Jaruzelski and his team, who had promised many times to call to account those held responsible for the policies that had provoked the economic and political crises of 1980 (Le Monde, Paris, 29 October). The motion was sent for further discussion to the parliamentary commission responsible for constitutional matters (Trybuna Ludu, 27 October, 2 November). Many Central Committee members repeatedly raised the same question in the general discussion at the plenum; their remarks were heavily censored in press reports. The practice of publishing more extensive reports on plenary sessions, including texts of discussion, in the next issue of Nowe Drogi, had been discontinued after the February plenum; no reasons were given.

In May, the Politburo had decided to summon, beginning in October, a series of city and provincial conferences devoted to a review of the past performance of PUWP organizations (ibid., 26 May). Usually such conferences are held midway in the term of the party's elected bodies and are preceded by meetings of local and industrial organizations; after discussion, the rank and file elect their committees as well as delegates to higher-level conferences. Under martial law, officials and delegates were appointed from above, and the rank and file was expected to confirm the selection by unanimous, formal vote. The 1982 campaign, therefore, lacked the usual centerpiece, and the meetings were often criticized in the party press for insipid verbosity. Central Committee secretary Mokrzyszczak, for instance, publicly denounced the "shallowness" of the discussion and the "silence" that dominated most of the party meetings. He also admitted that "as yet," new people were showing "no eagerness" to apply for admittance to party membership. (Ibid., 10 December.) In fact, the whole campaign mostly continued the purge under way since the coup. According to Mokrzyszczak, 5,000 additional party members had been excluded and only 1,000 new members admitted.

The campaign, however, also provided a forum for the hard-line faction, critical of Jaruzelski's team and its irresoluteness (to their mind) in suppressing the "counterrevolution" and its alleged supporters inside the party. Although the leadership gradually implemented all the demands of the hard-liners, it had no intention of tolerating their criticism, especially after Grabski's open defiance. Central Committee secretary in charge of ideology Marian Orzechowski made this abundantly clear. Asked about the menace of neo-Stalinist tendencies inside the party, he at first minimized the danger, but then stressed the leadership's determination "to say 'halt' to all those who, from both the right and the left, assail the line [of the Ninth Extraordinary Party Congress in July 1981]. And should the need arise—to get rid of them [and exclude them] from our ranks. I think I have said it clearly enough." (*Glos Szczeciński*, 23 November.)

His words were confirmed soon enough. The new purge in the media in the first half of December was presented as another "clipping of the wings" operation, but its edge was directed mainly against the hard-liners. The Politburo voted a resolution, which contrary to the normal procedure, was not only published in full, but received wide publicity (*Trybuna Ludu*, 18–19 December). It contained a "penetrating analysis of the current internal situation in the party," along with guidelines for "concentrating the efforts of party members in their basic cells," as well as for intensifying their activities in the sociopolitical mass organizations, in particular among the working class, creative intelligentsia, and the youth [in order to] widely reach the nonparty people." The operative part of the resolution provided for immediate dissolution of all PUWP "organizations, associations, and clubs whose activity under the current circumstances causes dissipation of the efforts of the party" and undermines its "ideological, political, and organizational unity." As the "moderate" wing of the party had long ago been deprived of its organizations and, to a large extent, its membership, the resolution, if at all implemented, would mostly harm the hard-line faction.

The resolution left no doubt that the leadership was dissatisfied with the extent of the PUWP's political influence among the population. Such was especially the case among industrial workers. The failure to win them over to the officially sponsored new labor unions was obvious from the very beginning. Even in major plants, party officials and activists had encountered trouble finding the required number of signatures for the "initiative committees," whose only tasks were to draft a statute (or rather copy it from a model text published in *Trybuna Ludu* [23–24 October]) and to apply to the courts for official registration. Nearly three months after the enactment of the trade union law by the Sejm, on the eve of 1 January 1983 when the new unions were supposed to start operations, it was reported that of the 60,000–65,000 enterprises entitled to have a licensed union, only in some 2,000 were the unions duly registered (*Financial Times*, London, 29 December) and that not many more had applied for registration. In Nowa Huta, Poland's largest industrial combine (some 40,000 employees), the union, when registered, claimed 1,300 members—not much more than one-quarter of the number of inscribed PUWP members (*Trybuna Ludu*, 3 December).

Front and Mass Organizations. With the sole exception of the PUWP, the activities of all political, social, cultural, and professional organizations were suspended by the 13 December 1981 proclamation of the state of war; the ban included two minor parties, the United Peasant Party and the Democratic Party, as well as three organizations of secular Catholics, the PAX association, the Christian Social Association, and the Polish Catholic Social Union (popularly known as neo-ZNAK), which had all cooperated with the Communists within the Front of National Unity (FJN). Within several weeks, the military authorities allowed all of them to resume activity, after they had undergone an extensive purge of their central and local committees. The most radical purge was of the PAX leadership; its previous chairman, Ryszard Reiff, who had gradually steered the association away from cooperation with the hard-line faction within the communist party and with the security organs toward a certain independence and support for the Roman Catholic hierarchy (he was rumored to be the only member of the Council of State to vote against the imposition of the state of war), was replaced by Zenon Komender, soon to be rewarded by promotion to deputy prime minister.

The role of the long moribund FJN, chaired by nominal head of state Henryk Jabloński, has never been clearly defined since its appearance in the 1950s. As a coalition of established social and political groups, virtually its sole duty was to present a single slate of candidates for parliamentary and local elections. Under the state of war, the mainly ceremonial functions of the FJN seem to have been taken over by the Citizens' Committees for National Salvation (OKON), which soon after the imposition of martial law sprang up at the provincial, urban, and commune levels. Allegedly, they were set up "spontaneously," but in fact they had been initiated by local PUWP committees. Their self-declared aims were the activization of all patriotic forces; active support for local defense committees, military task forces, and local administration; and intensification of efforts toward stabilization and a return to normal life (ibid., 31 December 1981/1 January 1982.) On 21 July, the Sejm announced the foundation of the Patriotic Movement for National Rebirth (PRON), based on the OKONs and including, along with the communist party, the two minor political parties and the three lay Catholic groupings. The PRON operated at first at the local level only, but on 15 September an initiative commission of 36 members, headed by the Catholic but pro-regime writer Jan Dobraczyński, resolved to constitute, after additional negotiations with unspecified "prominent representatives of social milieus and organizations," an Interim National Council of PRON (ibid., 16 September). The PRON claimed some 160,000 members in 8,000 local OKONs (*Polityka*, 13 November), apparently having failed to turn into a mass movement.

Traditionally, the labor unions have always been considered the most important mass organizations run by the communist party. They played the role of the PUWP's "transmission belt" to the working class. The birth of Solidarity in August–September 1980 deprived the party of its control even over those that had preferred to stay outside the Solidarity movement: the "autonomous" unions would not, and the "branch" unions (see *YICA*, 1982, p. 430) could not, effectively act as the party's auxiliary among the workers. All unions were indiscriminately suspended by martial law and then dissolved and outlawed by the new trade union law, voted by a majority of the Sejm on 8 October (*Trybuna Ludu*, 13 October). The new unions were to start operations on 1 January 1983 and, for a year at least, were to be confined to the enterprise level only.

Mass youth organizations, considered second in importance only to trade unions as instruments for imposing the party's policies, have been treated in a different way, but under martial law did not fare much better than the unions. All were originally suspended. The Independent Students' Association, which was closest to Solidarity and considered the most radical, was disbanded in January. Some of its leaders were interned; many more were expelled from universities and/or drafted for military service. Other youth organizations were gradually reactivated after extensive purges in their ruling bodies and membership. Currently permitted to organize young people are the Polish Socialist Youth Union (ZSMP), which claims, with obvious exaggeration, two million members among young people in all sectors of society (*Walka Mlodych*, 2 May); the Rural Youth Union (ZMW), with an alleged membership of 75,000; the Polish Scouts' Union (ZHP), which despite its 70-year-old tradition was reported to have lost since August 1980 some 40 percent of its members, mainly in high schools; and the Socialist Union of Polish Students (SZSP). The SZSP held its Fourth Congress on 18–19 November and, having admitted its minimal influence in the academic milieu (according to independent estimates, not even every tenth student belongs to the SZSP), decided to recreate a mass organization dissolved in 1973, the Association of Polish Students (ZSP). The new association is supposed to have a trade union–like character, remain apolitical, and represent the material and academic interests of all Polish students irrespective of political opinion, but is committed to promoting a line of "national accord" in the universities and to acknowledging "the leading role of the party" (*Trybuna Ludu*, 20–21 November). The Communist Union of Polish Youth, inspired by the hard-line faction inside the PUWP, at one time claimed a membership of 5,000, but has been ignored by the mass media and never officially recognized. It was officially disbanded in December, together with the Union of Democratic Youth. The four licensed youth organizations (ZSP, ZHP, ZMW, ZSMP) signed a joint Declaration of Principles on Cooperation of Socialist Youth Unions (*Polityka*, 18 December)—a first step towards uniformization of the whole youth movement. All previously registered student organizations were delegalized by the Ministry of Higher Education and Science.

Communist propaganda alternates between verbal wooing of young people with prospects of prosperity and advancement in Socialist Poland and condemning them as juvenile hooligans manipulated by the enemy within and without to provide an overwhelming majority of participants in opposition-inspired street demonstrations. In fact, the authorities have little to offer since jobs for high-school and university graduates are scarce and the waiting time for an apartment has grown to ten or even fifteen years. Decision making on issues young people are most concerned with has been institutionalized in the Youth Department of the party's Central Committee and in the recently created Council of Ministers' Youth Committee; the influence of youth organizations has been *de facto* abolished.

No party-sponsored mass organization managed to replace the independent farmers' movements that had sprung up in the countryside under the influence of workers' Solidarity. On 8 October the Sejm banned all independent peasants' organizations, until then suspended under martial law, and created a single body of rural representation—the National Association of Farmers, Agricultural Circles, and Organizations (*Rzeczpospolita*, 14 October). It is based mainly on party and local administration officials (*Polityka*, 13 November).

No other mass or front organizations play any significant role. Those reactivated after temporary suspension have been severely purged. Some, including the Polish Writers' Union and the organization of filmmakers, have neither been reactivated nor disbanded. The Association of Polish Actors (ZASP) was reactivated during the summer, but since the overwhelming majority of stage, film, and television artists refused, despite pressure and entreaties by Deputy Prime Minister Mieczyslaw Rakowski and the newly appointed minister of culture and arts, Prof. Kazimierz Zygulski, to call off their boycott of the state radio and TV, ZASP was dissolved on 30 November. Other reprisals against artists who refused to take part in official propaganda included the dismissal of two prominent theater directors, the placing of the most representative institutions of creative arts in Warsaw under direct control of the ministry, and preference for provincial actors, less recalcitrant than their colleagues in the capital. Establishment of a new professional association was announced; a widespread purge among artists was generally expected.

The Media. With the proclamation of the state of war, all dailies and periodicals except for the PUWP central organ, *Trybuna Ludu*, and the GZP daily, *Zolnierz Wolności*, were suspended. They re-emerged gradually, as the most stringent purge ("verification") among journalists proceeded, starting with party dailies in the provinces and local army papers. Many journalists and editors involved in the Solidarity press were interned; others, considered supporters of the opposition, were fired or demoted; their number was estimated at 1,200. Almost all those allowed to continue in the media had to sign a declaration of loyalty.

Not all the suspended titles were allowed to reappear: in addition to the Solidarity press, among the best-known casualties has been the weekly *Kultura* (another weekly, *Literatura*, resumed publication in the fall as a monthly of very different profile). A new daily, *Rzeczpospolita* (Republic), was inaugurated in mid-January as a semiofficial organ of the government; several new weeklies were careful to toe the party line.

The purge in the media continued throughout the year, apparently in connection with the infighting between the various factions inside the PUWP. It intensified in particular after Stefan Olszowski was demoted in July as Central Committee secretary in charge of the media and replaced by Jan Główczyk; many of Olszowski's protégés in the propaganda apparatus or those considered as such lost their jobs. In December, a number of editors in chief were dismissed, probably (at least in most cases) for similar reasons.

Virtually all dailies and journals print a considerably smaller number of copies compared with their press runs in 1980 and 1981; the loss of readers is generally attributed not only to much higher prices but above all to the uniformity imposed from above, sharply contrasting with the lively discussions of the preceding period.

A feature unique among all communist-ruled countries is the existence of two weeklies claiming to speak in the name of the PUWP but in fact representing two major factions inside the party. *Polityka*, purged of thirteen members of its editorial board, tries to maintain its traditional image of relative moderation. *Rzeczywistość* (Reality), however, is openly critical of the leadership from the extreme hard-line position. Some Catholic publications, notably *Tygodnik Powszechny* in Cracow, try to maintain a modicum of independence but show in almost every issue visible traces of censorship.

Not the slightest opposition has ever been tolerated in the state-owned broadcasting service, especially the television service. After its militarization in December 1981, it was for some time boycotted by viewers. The news and commentary departments have been vetted with special care, while the actors' prolonged boycott deprived television of its most popular features and forced it to fill the time with reruns of old and worthless propaganda or entertainment films. In December, the chairman of the Committee for Radio and Television, appointed after the imposition of martial law to strengthen party control in broadcasting, and two of his deputies were dismissed; no reasons were given. The state-owned Polish Press Agency was purged at the outset of martial law.

The Association of Polish Journalists (SDP) was one of the first organizations dissolved by the military authorities for being too sympathetic to Solidarity. It was replaced by a new Association of Journalists of the Polish People's Republic, severely purged and now fully controlled by the party. It claims a membership of 4,000 persons (about one-third less than the dissolved SDP), mostly party members and retired journalists whose privileged pensions depend on their affiliation.

Domestic Affairs. *Suppression of Dissent.* On New Year's Day 1982, even the most perspicacious observers of the Polish scene might well have been excused for concluding that the new military government, having crushed the ten million–strong Solidarity movement by a show of force rather than by the use of force, had actually succeeded in clearing the decks and from then on could set about rearranging the whole political, economic, and social life of the nation without having to bother unduly about meeting serious popular resistance or active opposition. The leadership of Solidarity had failed to solve the apparently insoluble dilemma of forcing a meaningful change in the political system without dismantling the existing structure of a communist state supported not only by the local establishment but by the overwhelming might of the adjacent superpower. What is more, it had been obviously unprepared for the coup. Having correctly discounted the immediate threat of Soviet armed intervention, it underestimated the physical strength and the political determination of the ruling party at home, as well as the loyalty of the military officer corps and the security forces to the PUWP leadership. Secure in the belief that nobody inside Poland would dare to confront their movement or challenge the moral authority of the Roman Catholic church, union leaders apparently neglected effective preparations for an armed confrontation. They did not even bother to acquire reliable allies inside the party, prematurely regarded as a spent force and totally discredited in public opinion. Nor did they try to counteract Solidarity's exclusion from influence in the army, in the police and security forces, and among workers in the defense industry.

Consequently, the military perpetrators of the coup found regaining full control over the state easier than expected. Even though spontaneous resistance assumed much larger proportions than has ever been publicly admitted, it did not prove very effective. On the night of the coup and during the next few days, some 5,000 opposition militants, including most Solidarity leaders and advisers, were detained. Almost all industrial plants, including the union's strongholds, were occupied by force, thus thwarting attempts at sit-in strikes that would necessitate prolonged sieges or bloody assaults. The massacre as the Wujek colliery in Katowice, and the sit-in strikes at several other Silesian mines, Huta Katowice, and the Nowa Huta steelworks, the giant Ursus plants near Warsaw, on the Baltic coast, and many other industrial centers all over the country were exceptions rather than the rule. Effective blockade of all centers of passive resistance and the equally effective cutting of all channels of communication prevented the resistance from spreading. By the end of December 1981, the strikes had petered out. The official triumphal pronouncement by the media that 4 January had been the first normal working day was obviously ludicrous, and scattered resistance continued well into January. But generally speaking, the situation was well under control. The specially trained and equipped (with riot control and electronic communication and surveillance gear purchased from the West, thanks to lavish foreign-currency credits and loans) Motorized Reserves of the Citizens' Militia (ZOMO) made superfluous the use of regular army troops or conscripts for armed suppression. Soldiers were confined to watch, guard, and patrol duty. In a few cases, they had to secure the perimeter of ZOMO operations, but their presence had an undoubted psychological impact, deepening the prevalent mood of despair and preventing attempts to organize resistance.

The swift pacification was accompanied by a purge of unprecedented scope. Not only labor organizers, but "unreliable" party officials, civil servants at all levels of central and local administration, economic managers, and others fell victim to the extensive cleansing operation. In the first six weeks of "verification," 760 senior government officials, including six voivods (provincial governors), fourteen deputy voivods, 160 mayors and commune heads, were summarily fired (PAP, 3 February). The purge was particularly severe in the mass media, the judicial administration, and academia. Those spared were obliged to sign a declaration of loyalty to the regime—a source of painful mental conflicts and pangs of conscience despite a kind of general absolution proclaimed by the primate of Poland, Archbishop Józef Glemp, in his Epiphany sermon. Almost immediately military courts, acting under the state-of-war decrees, as well as regular courts dispensing justice under summary procedure (*tryb doraźny*), started meting out long-term sentences on persons found guilty of violation of martial law.

It soon became clear, however, that behind the facade of suppression and repression the party leadership and its military executive arm were trying to conceal almost total helplessness. Apparently, their original idea was that following the proclamation of a state of war, the suspension of the Solidarity unions and of all other more or less independent social organizations, the internment of most radical opposition elements, and the all-embracing purges, the opposition would split and the moderates might be won over to negotiations with the authorities. Under martial law, a kind of "national accord" on terms dictated by the party leadership, seemed at first plausible. Even subsequent reactivation of labor unions—obviously after extensive purification of their leaders and advisers and acknowledgment of the "leading role of the party"—was not ruled out. Thus emasculated, the unions might even be allowed to retain their name; their ultimate *Gleichschaltung* within the Soviet-type state would then become a question of time only. With this in mind Lech Wałęsa, chairman of the democratically elected national leadership of Solidarity, was forcefully brought to Warsaw as a "guest of the government"; a binding order of internment was delivered to him only on 26 January, after all attempts to win him over to negotiating had failed.

This blueprint was quickly proven to be stillborn. Wałęsa consistently refused to engage in talks while in detention and deprived of his advisers. His preliminary conditions for negotiation included immediate release of all internees, lifting of the state of war, and reinstitution of the unions. When Radio Warsaw announced on 5 January that the government had held talks with activists of all labor unions, Solidarity included, leaders of regional Solidarity organizations who had avoided detention and gone into hiding denounced the communiqué as a piece of disinformation. Through quickly restored clandestine channels, they proclaimed that "the union authorities had not authorized, nor would they allow, any of their members remaining at liberty to conduct such talks." The primate met with General Jaruzelski "to exchange views on the current situation and express their intentions in connection with the normalization of life in Poland," but the very vagueness of the joint communiqué emphasized the church hierarchy's intention not to negotiate under the duress created by the state of war. Subsequent pronouncements of Archbishop Glemp and other prelates confirmed this: the church would welcome a dialogue between the authorities and the unions, would try to facilitate it, and even offer its good offices and serve as a go-between, but refused to participate in any talks from which representatives of the society would be excluded.

Thus, very early in the game, it became clear that the PUWP and the government would find no genuine partners in the society; the two minor parties and three groupings of lay Catholics, carefully purged of their more independent-minded elements, certainly could not pretend to such a role. Despite gradual relaxation of some martial law regulations, officially justified by the successful repression and purge, a desperate attempt was made to create the appearance of grass-roots support, in form of the OKONs. This did not change the reality: the military government remained alone, with sole responsibility for solving Poland's deepest political, economic, and social crisis. This was clearly shown at the first session of the Sejm after the imposition of martial law, convened on 25–26 January. Composed entirely of Gierek's nominees, this sham parliamentary body had shown some courage and independence in the fall of 1981 by forcing the party leadership to renounce its plans for introducing a state of emergency by means of Sejm-enacted legislation. For fear of not getting a sufficiently impressive majority (or even no majority at all), the authorities had had recourse to the state of war, inflicted by a simple vote of the Council of State, in blatant violation of the constitution and legality. Martial law had not broken the popular spirit of resistance, but it has proved more than enough to restore the nominated Sejm (with few exceptions) to its traditional rubber-stamp role.

The January session was opened by General Jaruzelski as prime minister. He justified at length the imposition of the state of war and the subsequent measures employed by the military government and demanded that the Sejm *ex post facto* give legal sanction to the December coup. He charged Solidarity "extremists" and the Western powers (in particular their Polish-language radio broadcasts) with sole responsibility for the need to declare a state of war, thus setting the pattern reduplicated by official propaganda throughout 1982. Contrary to some expectations, he did not, however, promise the abolition of martial law or even its relaxation. Nor did he present any coherent plan for alleviating Poland's woes, confining himself to general exhortations for hard work, discipline, and order. According to Jaruzelski, the fight against "all enemies of the state, against the leaders of anarchy and its inspirers" would remain the policy of the party and his government; any "compromises" were ruled out. The overwhelming majority of deputies obediently complied with the demand to legalize the state of war and the subsequent decrees; only one nonparty deputy voted no, and four deputies from the Polish Catholic Social Union and two well-known writers and journalists abstained. The media did not mention the number of deputies who had voted yes or even the number of those present, thus deliberately obscuring the changes in the Sejm's composition imposed since its last session in October 1981 (*Le Monde*, 26 January).

Karol Malcuzyński, one of the two deputies who had the courage to denounce martial law in the debate (the other was Janusz Zablocki, a leader of the Catholic Social Union), warned that continuation of martial law would increase the risk of underground resistance and escalation of ensuing repression, creating a vicious circle to which there would be no peaceful solution. The warning was somewhat belated: while active resistance had been effectively crushed, almost on the morrow of the resumption of work, Solidarity organizers and activists unaffected by the mass internment started to publish underground fliers, leaflets, and newspapers. Some were handwritten or mimeographed, and therefore their impact was limited to one enterprise, or even one workshop. Many others, however, were carefully printed and distributed over whole regions or even beyond it. As the ban on communication was being gradually lifted (it effectively disorganized economic life and in one notorious case caused enormous losses in life and property because it had prevented the timely warning of an approaching flood on the Vistula River), regional leaders in concealment started to rebuild the temporarily disrupted network of Solidarity. The most active among them, Zbigniew Bujak of the Mazowsze (Warsaw) region, managed to grant an interview to a foreign correspondent, warning that passive resistance "would escalate. I see a real possibility of stifling the dictatorship, or at least bringing about its liberalization, and returning their rights to the dissolved and suspended organizations." (*NYT*, 16 January.) In addition to the work slowdown in industry, other manifestations of passive resistance have emerged, such as an ostentatious boycott of television newscasts and (one day a week) the official press, slogans and symbols on walls, denunciations of those regarded as guilty of collaboration, and organized material assistance to internees and their families as well as to workers dismissed from work. Such demonstrations of defiance could not present a serious threat to the military government. Still, the repression went on and even escalated, confirming people, especially young people, in their obstinate rejection of all forms of cooperation with the authorities.

But neither could token resistance bring the people out of their apathy. This was clearly demonstrated by the popular reaction, or rather lack of reaction, to the unprecedented price increases, in particular on foodstuffs and utilities, introduced on 1 February and only partly recompensed to those with below average wages and to the retired. Although for years there had been an economic necessity to set prices of heavily subsidized foodstuffs at a level more closely reflecting their real production costs, former governments had shrunk from alienating the workers, who at least twice (in 1970 and 1980) had toppled the party clique that had dared to raise prices and once more (1976) had come very close to doing the same. Never before, however, were the price hikes so steep and painful; food prices alone were raised an average of 171 percent. Never before had the authorities openly proclaimed the goal of the operation—to reduce the living standard of the population in order to ease pressure on the market and to reduce at least part of the so-called inflationary overhang (that is, the amount of money in private hands without coverage in market goods available). Nonetheless, this time the outrage was accepted with barely a protest, although even before the proclamation of the state of war the number of people living below the established subsistence level was estimated as between nine and ten million, at least a quarter of the entire population (*Slowo Powszechne*, 5–7 March). Even rationed food necessities, whose prices were fixed by the authorities, became too expensive for many working-class families; according to official statistics, only 73 percent of all households could afford to purchase their full meat allocation (*Zycie Warszawy*, 17 November). But after the announcement of price increases, there were only sporadic reports of disturbances in some industrial plants. Nowhere, apparently, did they assume mass character, and such protests as did occur were fairly easily dealt with by the security services and ZOMO.

The population at large had already been conditioned to accept arbitrary economic decisions that would further worsen their situation. The introduction of the economic reform, long postulated by all nongovernmental scholars and in its original form supported by Solidarity, was officially proclaimed on 1 January, under the least propitious circumstances for its implementation. The reform provided for gradual dismantling of the central command economy and for its replacement by autonomy of enterprises and workers' self-management; wages and prices were to be increasingly guided by the market and by laws of demand and supply. Under martial law, however, the central controls were additionally strengthened by adding another tier of military commissars and plenipotentiaries. Sometimes only labels were changed, as lip service to decentralization. All talk of workers' self-management was discarded. In any case, the workers, deprived of their unions, rejected all sham institutions. Economic managers, always opposed to the idea and actively boycotting even the most modest attempts to give the workers any say in running businesses, regarded the state of war as a heaven-sent opportunity to junk self-management once and for all, official demagoguery notwithstanding. The enterprises, allowed to fix prices for their products on a cost-plus basis and enjoying the advantages of a virtual monopoly in their branches (especially since imports were banned), improved their profitability by raising prices at will. The costs not only of consumer products but of supplies to other state-owned plants skyrocketed overnight, making final products more and more expensive. To prevent total anarchy in the economy, the authorities had to resort to fixing prices from above. What was supposed to involve only a few exceptions (called "operative projects"), soon became the rule: the central-level managers gleefully returned to the only mode of direction they were familiar with—a neo-Stalinist command economy. The least protected were, as usual, the consumers. Some necessities, including clothes, shoes, underwear, and medicines, virtually disappeared from the market. Others, like household appliances, were priced out of reach of average people.

The authorities reacted in two ways. They used the police courts against alleged speculators and black marketeers, thus stifling the barely reborn private enterprise, and started distributing articles in short supply not through normal trade outlets but through factories. This solution had an additional advantage: it vastly increased the state grip on the population. Certain categories of consumers, not only security men and party or state officials but also workers in heavy industry whose increased productivity was essential to the functioning of the economy, including miners and others working in export industries, were thus assured of preferential treatment. Loss of employment from then on meant not only loss of nominal wages but also of rationing coupons and preferred supplies as well and could spell total disaster to undisciplined workers and their families. An undernourished population and workers mortally afraid of losing their job obviously make for increased power and job security for the ruling establishment.

For the next couple of months, political developments in Poland proceeded as if on parallel tracks, with no obvious crossing points between them. Inside the PUWP, the hard-line faction was growing critical of the Jaruzelski leadership, accusing it of indecision and lack of a clear conception for the future; rather fainthearted references to the Hungarian experience were scornfully dismissed by reminders that before embarking on the course of reforms and partial liberalization, János Kádár had crushed the counterrevolution and dealt with his adversaries by resorting to the death sentence, long-term imprisonment, and exile to the Soviet Union. The calls for intensified terror were being voiced in private or at party meetings, and the public learned of them mainly from rumors. Discussions at Central Committee plenary sessions or ideological conferences were published as a rule in a bowdlerized version only. The authorities covered up their incapability to solve any of Poland's political, economic, and social problems by blaming all the country's woes on the opposition and its alleged foreign inspirators and by sham feverish legislative activity. The Sejm obediently approved a bevy of new bills and created new bodies of unspecified and largely overlapping competence. In rapid succession the country was made happy by a revised Teachers' Charter, which did nothing to improve the dismal state of national education (26 January), by similar "charters" for longshoremen, miners, and professional groups (27 February), by a new law on cooperatives and their unions, by a series of laws on agriculture and landownership, by creation of a State Tribunal and a Constitutional Tribunal (both of them necessitated constitutional amendments, of dubious validity since they were introduced under martial law), by establishment of a parliamentary Social and Economic Council (26 March), by postponement of elections to local people's councils, by establishment of a National Council for Culture and a Fund for the Development of Culture (4 May), and by the passage of a Higher Education Bill, which effectively curtailed the autonomy of the universities and the rights of students and teachers that had been won in 1981. Most of these legislative acts were not published in full, but in any case the public ignored them, impatiently awaiting some tangible improvement in the economic situation, as well as the lifting of martial law and the restoration of human and civil rights.

In April, the primate's Social Council, set up on the eve of the December 1981 coup and chaired by Prof. Stanislaw Stomma, a well-known Catholic writer and former Sejm deputy, published its first and up till now only White Paper—"Theses in the Matter of Social Conciliation" (*Kultura*, Paris, no. 5/416, May, pp. 3–10). The White Paper, sent for public discussion to all dioceses, condemned martial law and pleaded for an open, serious dialogue between the government and the society, aimed at achieving social agreement. The only precondition was the release of all those interned or imprisoned under martial law. The ten-point draft program suggested that the church would assume the role of a sage and guarded mediator and expressly demanded the reactivation of Solidarity and other independent social organizations and groups. Since the authorities and official mass media passed over it in silence and the opposition was unable to engage in public discussion of its merits, the primate's initiative to promote genuine national accord proved futile.

The same fate befell the fourth report of "Experience and Future," an informal collective of "middle-of-the road" intellectuals, published on 7 April and entitled "Poland in the Face of the State of War," sent to General Jaruzelski and to Archbishop Glemp (ibid., no. 7/418–8/419, July–August). The authorities did not even acknowledge its receipt, and thus another attempt at national reconciliation was thwarted by the instransigence of the party leadership and its hostility to any form of power sharing.

Public opinion, meanwhile, tried to find consolation in the popular slogan "The winter is yours, the spring will belong to us." Although the spring did not bring the expected relaxation, neither did it prove the slogan to be empty or boastful. Having recovered from their initial shock, the regional leaders of suspended labor unions began to set up an underground structure, based mainly on major industrial enterprises. By the end of March, clandestine five-man cells started to call themselves Social Defense Committees. On 12 April, Solidarity's radio program was broadcast in Warsaw and was soon repeated in other major cities. It urged the population to commemorate the coup with symbolic, peaceful protests on the thirteenth of each month.

At the end of April, the establishment of an Interim Coordinating Commission (TKK) was announced. The TKK was originally composed of leaders of the four strongest regional branches of Solidarity: Zbigniew Bujak (Warsaw), Wladyslaw Frasyniuk (Wroclaw), Bogdan Lis (Gdansk), and Wladyslaw Hardek (Cracow) (Le Monde, 29 April). The clandestine meeting apparently took place in Warsaw on 22 April and adopted three declarations. The first one called for resumption of the dialogue between the people and the authorities as the only way to "national accord" and expressed support for the primate's Social Council theses as the basis for negotiations (the only precondition being the release of all those interned or imprisoned under martial law). The second declaration proposed three main fields of clandestine activities (social aid for the victims of repression, discussion groups, and underground press), while the third warned that the outlawing of Solidarity might spark off a general strike and "active defense" of work places. It repeated the call for "a day of protest" on the thirteenth of each month, with a fifteen-minute work stoppage and a one-minute halt in traffic at noon. Thus the "war" declared by the authorities on 13 December 1981 entered its second stage.

The first trial of strength took place on May Day. In Warsaw, parallel to the official, rather modest, parade, a crowd of Solidarity supporters, variously estimated at 10,000 to 50,000, proceeded, after special masses in four Old Town churches, with unfurled banners toward the residence of Primate Glemp. Police roadblocks prevented any clashes between the official and alternative marches, but did not interefere with a mass rally on the banks of the Vistula; the day ended without incident. There were similar peaceful demonstrations in other major centers; in Gdansk some 50,000 people took part in a march past the former union headquarters and the monument to the shipyard workers slain in 1970 to the Walęsa home in the suburbs.

Such leniency must have been unpalatable to the hard-line faction in the PUWP and in the military. The next day the Ministry of Internal Affairs reminded the public that under martial law unauthorized marches, rallies, and demonstrations were illegal and warned that all violations of this ban would be prosecuted. The warning was widely disregarded, and the previously announced celebrations on 3 May (a national holiday, abolished by the Communist regime, but officially observed a year earlier) took place as planned in several localities. The demonstrations were peaceful until the ZOMO brutally attacked with tear gas, flares, water cannon, and rubber truncheons. The number of injured has never been revealed, but according to eyewitnesses was very high. It was officially admitted that 1,372 participants (271 of them in Warsaw) were detained and military courts sent 81 people to jail and fined 355. The cases of 890 others were transferred to civilian courts. In retaliation, the curfew, lifted just a week earlier, was reimposed wherever demonstrations had taken place and intercity telephone links were again cut off.

The first confrontation on a national scale since the December coup proved not only that there still was mass popular support for the suspended Solidarity, but also that the authorities were able and willing to use overwhelming force in the streets and even to provoke clashes and casualties in order to intimidate the population. The contrast between peaceful May Day and bloody 3 May was in this respect particularly instructive. The clandestine TKK decided to forsake street demonstrations for the time being, and to concentrate all efforts on work and traffic stoppages on the thirteenth. Despite a massive show of military and police force in the streets and inside the factories and preventive internment of workers and students, the response all over Poland was even more enthusiastic. The mass media tried to belittle the scope of the protest, and foreign correspondents were prevented from reporting it, but perusal of the provincial press (which could hardly avoid reporting what everybody had seen) confirmed that the fifteen-minute strike was carried out almost everywhere and in some places assumed the character of a general strike. In Warsaw, for instance, between 70 and 80 percent of the industrial workers stopped work at noon. Almost 2,300 arrests were made (the figure, quoted in an official statement of the Council of Ministers, may include those arrested on 3 May). A spokesman for the Ministry of Justice announced on 20 May that 99 strikers had been sentenced for up to three years, 164 got longer sentences, and 211 were interned without charges.

The underground Solidarity leaders were so heartened by this show of national support, and at the same time dismayed by the extent of police repression, that they decided to suspend the earlier methods of protest, including the fifteen-minute warning strikes on the thirteenth of each month. However, they called the clandestine commissions in enterprises to start organizational preparations for a general strike. Its date would be set later, depending on the state of readiness reported from the industrial plants. The TKK emphasized once more its desire for national accord, subject only to one precondition, release of all internees and amnesty for all those arrested and sentenced (*Tygodnik Mazowsze*, Warsaw, 1 June). The authorities, again, showed no tendency toward reconciliation; on the contrary, repression continued unabated, accompanied by increasing attacks against Solidarity in the mass media and in official pronouncements. On 13 June, spontaneous demonstrations took place in several cities, indicating a growing impatience among the rank and file, especially among the younger workers and students. This time, the protests, uncoordinated by the underground leadership, assumed a violent character in Wroclaw, Cracow (Nowa Huta), and Gdansk, where ZOMO attacked the crowds with vicious brutality. Street demonstrations were repeated in Wroclaw on 16 June and occurred again in Poznan on the anniversary of the 1956 revolt (27 June); in Ursus near Warsaw the anniversary of the 1976 strike was commemorated. The vicious circle of protests and repression, although in no way seriously threatening the military government of Poland, assumed proportions that might have brought into question the underground movement's control over spontaneous outbursts and provide the authorities with the long-awaited (at least by some of them) pretext for tightening the screws, perhaps even for a massacre.

It is difficult to say what impact such considerations had on the TKK. At a 26 June clandestine meeting, it ordered—"as a gesture of goodwill and confidence"—a moratorium on organized protest action until the end of July. Obviously an additional reason can be found in its desire to do nothing that might have prevented the pope's second pilgrimage to Poland. John Paul II was expected to take part in the commemoration of the 600th anniversary of the icon of Our Lady of Częstochowa at the Jasna Góra monastery on 26 August. Talks were going on between the authorities and the church, as well as between the Polish bishops and the Vatican. In the second half of June, Archbishop Luigi Poggi, the papal expert on East European affairs, spent two weeks in Poland. On 24 June, a communiqué issued by a joint meeting of government and episcopal representatives announced that the "terms for a papal visit" had been discussed and that further negotiations were scheduled. On 5 July, a senior episcopal delegation, headed by Archbishop Glemp, left for Rome. At the same time, rumors, apparently inspired by the authorities and fed through foreign correspondents to Polish-language radio stations abroad, suggested that at the Sejm session scheduled for the eve of the National Holiday (22 July), a comprehensive amnesty would be proclaimed and martial law suspended or at least significantly curtailed and that the reactivation of Solidarity was still considered a possibility, albeit in a drastically restricted form. Thus, the TKK had good grounds for claiming that the earlier strikes and street demonstrations had convinced the authorities repression was ineffective and made them more sensitive to popular demands. The preparations for a general strike, however, went on: if necessary, it would force the authorities to treat seriously the resumption of the dialogue with the people. The TKK posed only one precondition—the release of all internees and a general amnesty—but dropped its demand for reactivation of Solidarity.

Although the unions scrupulously observed the moratorium, the Sejm session on 21 July and the speeches by General Jaruzelski and Deputy Prime Minister Rakowski (*Trybuna Ludu*, 22 July) quashed all hopes that the authorities might be pushed toward some kind of negotiated settlement and genuine national accord. The partial relaxation of martial law was rather inconsequential. Selective release of some 2,000 internees (including all the women) could not replace the widely expected amnesty. Rakowski shattered the last illusions concerning the future of Solidarity. He categorically rejected a regional structure for unions and demanded, as condition of their rebirth, "explicit acknowledgment of social ownership of means of production as the fundament of the socialist system; unconditional observance of the legal order, and respect for the constitution, as well as acceptance of the leading role of the PUWP in the society and in the state; full acceptance of our alliances." The next day it was announced that the papal visit would not take place in 1982, although Jaruzelski still held out the promise that it might occur the next year, if the opposition would "behave."

The TKK answered almost immediately, thus ringing in the third phase of the state of war. On 28 July, it published, together with programmatic documents on the underground society (see end of this profile for an example), a call for resumption of protest action, this time in a planned and coordinated fashion, throughout the second half of August, to culminate in a peaceful street demonstration on 31 August, the second anniversary of the Gdansk agreement. The strategic goal of the operation was to force the authorities to restore Solidarity and to start negotiations with the unions and with other spokesmen of the society in the spirit of "national accord" postulated by all parties.

As if in reponse to this call, largely spontaneous manifestations took place all over the country on the anniversary of the 1944 Warsaw Uprising (31 July–1 August). They turned into a show of mass support for the opposition. There were no incidents, as the authorities apparently hesitated to use the ZOMO riot police in the cemeteries and thus alienate wide sections of the population not necessarily supportive of Solidarity. But the rulers obviously decided to accept the challenge. Mass media became even more abusive. Insults upon insults were heaped on Solidarity and other opposition activists, who were presented as "counter-revolutionaries" and "agents of imperialism" acting under the inspiration of, and lavishly paid by, "anti-Polish" diversion centers in the West. For the first time, the clandestine unions were openly acccused of "terrorism," even though the only specific case that could conceivably be included in this category was the accidental fatal shooting of a policeman in a Warsaw streetcar when a couple of adolescents tried to get hold of his gun. Although the incident had taken place in February, they were now brought to trial and severely sentenced, together with a parish priest who allegedly had been their accomplice.

Demonstrations organized by the TKK on 13 August were, as a rule, orderly and peaceful—until brutal intervention by ZOMO troops turned them into bloody riots. Similar provocations were repeated throughout the next two weeks; in Warsaw water cannon and tear gas were used to disperse the mostly elderly crowds gathered around a floral cross dedicated to the memory of the late primate, Stefan Cardinal Wyszyński.

Despite repeated warnings by General Jaruzelski and other party leaders (the "next attack must and will be defeated"—Jaruzelski to a gathering of communist officials from major enterprises on 23 August [UPI, 24 August]) and the episcopate's call to preserve calm ("dialogue cannot take place in the streets"—Archbishop Glemp's sermon during the Częstochowa commemoration [*Tygodnik Powszechny*, Cracow, 5 September]), the demonstrations set up for 31 August were the most extensive since the imposition of martial law, in both the numbers of localities involved and of participants. According to information given to the Sejm by Minister of Internal Affairs Kiszczak (*Trybuna Ludu*, 17 September), had demonstrations and clashes with riot police had taken place in 66 urban centers in 34 voivodships (according to government spokesman Jerzy Urban—in 39 voivodships out of 49). For the first time this year, the ZOMO used firearms: three people were fatally shot in the copper-mining center of Lubin and one in Wroclaw, and one man was killed in Gdansk by a concussion grenade. Over 5,100 people were detained or arrested. In summary proceedings, over 4,000 were sentenced or fined, and 228 people were interned. According to incomplete information from underground sources, 50,000 people took part in the demonstrations in Warsaw, a similar number in Cracow–Nowa Huta, and 20,000 in Gdansk.

Retaliation came swiftly. The very next day the WRON met and issued a communiqué ordering local defense committees to step up repression and the police and judiciary to mete out swift punishment, including summary expulsion of workers and students suspected of participation in the demonstrations (even without investigation and retroactively). Judiciary proceedings for "crimes committed against the state and society" were to be started against members of the Committee for the Defense of Workers (KOR) (ibid., 2 September); the latter was a purely political, vindictive measure: KOR had been voluntarily dissolved one year earlier. When the names of those accused of "conspiracy to overthrow the political system by force" were published, it came out that four of them had spent the whole period of martial law in internment and two were abroad. Obviously, it was a crude attempt to find scapegoats for the authorities' failure to end the underground activity of the unions and to drive a wedge between the bulk of the population and the intellectuals. The KOR trial, however, which might have brought the defendants, if convicted, anything from five years in jail to the death sentence, did not take place before the suspension of martial law; it was subsequently delayed at least till January 1983. In the meantime, leaders of another oppositional organization, the Confederacy of Independent Poland, arrested before the infliction of the state of war and on trial for several months, were sentenced in October for up to seven years in jail

Although to avoid additional casualties the TKK desisted from organizing any more mass demonstrations in the streets and concentrated its efforts on preparations inside industrial plants for the expected general strike, calm was not easily restored. Both in September and October, the thirteenth day of the month was spontaneously commemorated. In mid-September, violence on a large scale broke out in four major cities (Wroclaw, Nowa Huta, Szczecin, and Lodz), but in Warsaw, where the ZOMO did not intervene against the crowd assembled at the Wyszyński floral cross, there were no incidents. A month later, after the outlawing of Solidarity, the extent of the spontaneous demonstration was much larger. The general strike at the Lenin shipyards in Gdansk lasted three days and was broken by force only after the militarization of the enterprise; in Nowa Huta a young worker at the steelworks was shot and killed by a secret policeman; thousands of his work comrades came to the funeral, but this time there was no ZOMO intervention and consequently no clashes. Clearly, the violence was deliberately provoked by the authorities, resolved to prove at any cost their mastery of the streets. The recurrent violence showed both the popular support for the underground and its inability to translate this support into an effective weapon, capable of forcing the authorities to engage in a meaningful dialogue. In addition to some prominent leaders of the underground tracked down by the security forces and imprisoned—Zbigniew Romaszewski from Warsaw, the organizer of the Solidarity broadcasting network, was caught in August; Wladyslaw Frasyniuk, head of the Wroclaw unions, was arrested in September and quickly sentenced to six years in jail; his replacement was caught a couple of weeks later and sent to prison for four years—many local organizers gave up clandestine activities, a result, most probably, not only of disappointment and weariness of underground life but also of lack of unanimity in the union leadership.

The circumstances were most propitious for some kind of compromise, but the authorities would accept nothing short of the unconditional surrender of the unions. Attacks against Solidarity were further intensified. Earlier promises that independent unions might be resurrected in some limited form were now categorically disavowed. The church came under concerted attacks for its protests against police violence and appeals for national accord; the bishop of Przemysl, Ignacy Tokarczuk, became the target of especially vitriolic slander for comparing the ZOMO's superfluous brutality with the wartime Nazi terror (*Kultura*, Paris, no.11/422, November). The church as a whole, while assiduously wooed, was accused of giving asylum to demonstrators pursued by police and of paying their fines when caught. At the same time, the Sejm feverishly worked on new acts of legislation calculated to strengthen the repressive role of the state and to prevent any resurgence of opposition if and when martial law were ever lifted. In all, since proclamation of the state of war, the Sejm obediently passed over 50 major bills—more than the number passed in normal times during an entire four-year parliamentary term. Some of these had major social and political repercussions.

In October, a packet of laws dealing with so-called social pathology was enacted: social parasitism, juvenile delinquency, and alcoholism. Especially objectionable was the first one, which in practice allowed administrative authorities to send anyone unemployed for at least three months to forced labor and to jail. It was clearly targeted against recalcitrant labor organizers, fired and blacklisted, and against students expelled from the universities. Despite vocal opposition from scholars (including the official Institute of Law of the Polish Academy of Science), the government-created Social and Economic Council, and the Council of Catholic Bishops (which regarded it as "contrary to the social interest"), the laws, largely patterned after the Soviet model, were rushed through the Sejm with total disregard for regular procedure and despite the protests of a handful of independent deputies.

Even more irregular was the enactment of the bill on trade unions on 9 October, which outlawed all unions suspended by the December 1981 coup and replaced them with uniform unions whose obedience to the party and the state authorities was legally secured. Large categories of employees, including farmers, civil and public servants, and managers, were totally excluded from having unions of their own. Others were permitted to set up, after previous registration of their statutes by the courts, one union in every enterprise. Only after at least one year's probation would they be allowed to unite by branches, but regional structures, which had decisively contributed to Solidarity's strength and independence, were banned forever. The right to strike was recognized in principle, but restrained by so many stipulations, including mandatory, cumbersome arbitration, as to make it virtually inoperative.

The TKK reacted without delay and called for the long-prepared eight-hour general strike on 10 November, the second anniversary of the court registration of Solidarity. But the frustrated public would not wait that long, leading to the spontaneous protest demonstrations and strikes between 11 and 14 October described above. For all its impact, the mid-October outburst could not but weaken the effectiveness of the 10 November general strike; its failure, despite its unprecedented expansion to localities that previously had remained calm, was subsequently admitted by the underground leadership. The Gdansk Regional Coordinating Commission listed among the reasons for the strike's defeat such preventive measures as drafting workers into the army and ZOMO, preventive internment, introduction of military and police patrols within factories, the threatening of workers with harsh prison terms or disciplinary dismissal from work, distribution of fake leaflets calling off the strike, the deployment of police at places designated as rallying points for demonstrations, and the negative attitude of the primate of Poland toward the protest actions called for by the TKK. On 8 November, two days before the date set for the strike, Archbishop Glemp, who four days earlier had returned from an extensive round of consultations with the pope, met with General Jaruzelski (for the third time this year). A joint communiqué announced that the long-awaited pilgrimage of John Paul II to Poland would take place in June 1983; both participants expressed their "common concern" for the preservation of calm and social order, a phrase that could not but be interpreted as a condemnation by the church of the proposed protest action.

The same day it was officially announced that Lech Walęsa's release, after eleven months of solitary confinement, would occur in the next few days. The chairman of Solidarity was indeed set free on 11 November, and arrived home two days later, but the circumstances of his release and deliberately circulated rumors attempted to create the false impression that the most popular leader of the opposition had decided to give up the struggle or had even struck a bargain with the authorities. A few days later, it became clear that the ploy had misfired, but it might well have dampened the enthusiasm of workers, who even without it had had reason enough to be afraid of the consequences of participation in the strike. Thus, amid persistent rumors that martial law would be lifted (or at least suspended) before the end of the year—allegedly following a proposal put forward by PRON and graciously accepted by General Jaruzelski—rumors strengthened by such cosmetic improvements as the release of a number of internees and partial reactivation of the Clubs of Catholic Intellectuals—the fourth stage of the year's political developments in Poland drew to an end.

The last stage consisted mainly of mopping-up operations, conducted by the military government. Although in control, the government was unable to overcome its alienation from the overwhelming majority of the population. If Walęsa's release was calculated to drive a wedge between the widely respected charismatic leader and those of his aides who during his long internment had to bear the brunt of the underground struggle, it misfired—at least in the short term. The TKK not only welcomed his return home but put itself at his disposal and agreed—at his urging—to end its clandestine action, provided only that all internees be released and a general amnesty granted to all those sentenced or arrested for violation of martial law. Forbidden to speak in public, Walęsa, after a month of reflection and consultation with church prelates and his onetime advisers, tried to resume the dialogue with the authorities peacefully. In a letter to General Jaruzelski (4 December), he affirmed that the workers rejected the "currently applied solutions" and took a stand very similar to that of the TKK. He not only reiterated the demands for general amnesty but further demanded reinstatement in previously held (or equivalent) positions of all those fired for union activities. Even the boycott of the officially sponsored unions was echoed in his call for a "return to the principle of pluralism" in the labor movement. Jaruzelski did not deem it necessary to answer a letter from a "former chairman of the former Solidarity" (the expression publicly used by official government spokesman Jerzy Urban, and security forces circulated a falsified version of Walęsa's letter (both the genuine and the false versions of the letter were published in *Le Monde*, 14 December). Walęsa was forcibly prevented from speaking at a commemoration of the Gdansk massacre in 1970, and the ZOMO used tear gas to disperse a demonstration protesting his kidnapping. Along with the exceptionally brutal dissolution of the actors' association and the dismissal of some editors in chief, here was a clear indication that Poland's present rulers would accept nothing short of capitulation of all strata of the population.

Still, the failure to win over the workers can clearly be gauged by the passive resistance offered to the officially sponsored unions. Even more meaningful were statistics quoted by the deputy minister of internal affairs before a parliamentary commission on 9 December: since the imposition of martial law fifteen people had been killed (underground sources claim at least thirty killed) and 991 wounded in street demonstrations; 10,131 people had passed through internment camps, 317 were still held as of 8 December; the official number of those detained for political reasons was 3,616, of which 2,822 had been put on trial. He also gave evidence of the extent of clandestine activity: the security forces had confiscated 730,000 leaflets, 340,000 illegal publications, and 4,000 posters; dismantled 677 clandestine organizations and 360 underground printing facilities; and closed down eleven stations of Radio Solidarity. (*Trybuna Ludu*, 10 December; *Le Monde*, 11 December.) Assuming (very conservatively) that for each seized publication two or three avoided confiscation and circulated freely, each read by several people, one has to conclude that for all its failure to force the authorities to engage in negotiations by means of strikes and street demonstrations, underground Solidarity has achieved a major breakthrough in providing the population with alternative information—to an extent unconceivable in any other totalitarian country.

Nor is there any reason to suppose that the underground would give up its opposition without achieving at least partial satisfaction of its demands. Even before the suspension of martial law, officially announced by General Jaruzelski in a television address on 12 December (excerpts follow this profile), eight top Solidarity leaders held in an internment camp near Warsaw signed a statement (10 December) refusing to accept the outlawing of their union and vowed to fight for its revival: "The state authorities did not organize Solidarity, and the authorities cannot disband the union against the will of the people." The legal basis for Solidarity was the ratification by Poland of "international conventions on human rights, under which the people can organize themselves in labor unions without the permission of the state authorities." (*WP*, 27 December.) The statement was attuned to Wałęsa's call for pluralism in the labor movement, although the Solidarity chairman was, for obvious reasons, a bit less outspoken. But it became obvious that the authorities had abandoned attempts to set union leaders at variance. Of the eight signatories of this statement, for instance, three were subsequently released with the rest of the internees, but five—including all three who had opposed Wałęsa at the Solidarity congress in fall 1981—were immediately rearrested and accused of conspiracy and "antistate" activity. Wałęsa characterized this discrimination as a "dirty trick," directed against his moral authority and credibility. Some of the underground union leaders were viciously slandered in the media (Wałęsa was accused not only of financial irregularities when still leader of Solidarity, but of "pro-German" pronouncements as well). But despite difficulties in coordinating their line, most union organizers have managed to remain united in their views, at least on the most essential points; this, however, might be an indication of how the authorities intend to provoke quarrels among union leaders and their followers in the future.

The Sejm suspended martial law, effective 31 December, and also managed, at three hardworking sessions during the holiday season (13, 18, and 28 December), not only to confirm the budget and the economic plan for 1983 but also to enact a series of laws that made the suspension of martial law a mostly cosmetic operation, which will satisfy neither the active opposition nor public opinion. The new legislation, confirmed (with nine abstentions) by the Sejm, does not provide for a return to normalcy under civilian rule: the WRON stays on, the militarization of key industries continues (albeit restrained), workers are not free to leave their jobs, and the Council of State is empowered "in case of need" to restore martial law in the entire country or in some provinces. Although most of the internees were released before Christmas, seven were immediately rearrested and await trial, while some others have been (according to unconfirmed reports) detained anew by civilian police or drafted for military service (*Le Monde*, 12 December; *NYT*, 1 January 1983).

Instead of a general amnesty, those sentenced for martial law violations were told they may apply individually for clemency. Censorship was upheld, illegal tapes of phone conversations became admissible as evidence in court, and the penal code was amended by introducing punishment up to five years in prison even for possession of single copies of "antistate" leaflets or publications and up to three years for participation in "public disturbances" (*NYT*, 14 December). Thanks to this legislation, aptly described as a "masterpiece of calculated ambiguity" (*Le Monde*, 14 December), the powers of the state, run by the communist party through military and police instruments of power, have been in effect strengthened, not weakened. The Polish people have thus been deprived even of the hope that the most obnoxious measures of repression were temporary and would disappear automatically with the lifting of the state of war; most of the martial law regulations have now assumed permanent character, having received a legal parliamentary sanction.

It was this aspect of the new legislation that drew strong criticisms from the Conference of Polish Bishops. A letter to the Sejm, signed by Primate Glemp and the secretary of the conference, Archbishop Bronislaw Dąbrowski, was a far cry from previous pronouncements of the two prelates and probably reflected the prevailing mood of believers and clergy. The new regulations were denounced as being "of a stricter and more repressive character" than the allegedly suspended martial law, and therefore could lead to " a specific psychological terror." Special condemnation was reserved for the ban on workers terminating employment in militarized enterprises; this was compared to "the tying of the farmers to the land during the period of feudalism" (*Times*, London, 20 December).

The U.S. government and its West European allies also refused to take appearances for reality or to lift the embargo and sanctions under the pretext of suspension of martial law and return to normal civilian rule. If such had been, even in part, the intent of Jaruzelski and the PUWP leadership in introducing the changes, it obviously miscarried, at least for the time being.

Relations with the Church. Policy toward the Roman Catholic church, and by extension toward the Vatican and the Polish-born pope, alternated between fairly consistent and judicious use of carrots and barely veiled threats of the stick. Whatever the incentive applied, it aimed mainly at driving a wedge between the church hierarchy and the unions and other social groups. The moral authority of the church was supposed to neutralize the opposition, to calm down popular dissatisfaction, to induce the population to obey state authority, and to work harder in order to improve the national economy. Had the church accepted such a role, its reward would have been noninterference with its religious and moral mission, especially catechization of the young, as well as many perquisites, such as broadcasting of Sunday mass on radio and television, tolerance for church construction and of charitable activities, and even some preferential treatment in tax policy. But never far below the surface—and in case of need, openly emerging—were various forms of official harassment: detention or even jailing of priests accused of antistate pronouncements and activities, limits on religious publications (in any case severely censored), and removal of crosses and other church symbols. The authorities obviously wanted to impress on the hierarchy how much it could lose by linking its fate with the opposition, how much it could win by supporting the policy of normalization in a way that did not necessarily contradict its principles.

It is much more difficult to characterize in a similar unequivocal manner the policy of the church. There hardly was a consistent line to be deduced from the frequent public pronouncements of John Paul II, Archbishop Glemp, or the Conference of Polish Bishops, as well as from the actual behavior of the parish clergy or even some bishops. Whether those contradictions, possibly more apparent than real, reflected actual divergences of opinion inside the church hierarchy and among the secular Catholic intellectuals or resulted from the unadaptability of earlier agreed tactics to the changed circumstances of the state of war cannot yet be asserted with any degree of certitude. Since the eruption of Solidarity, the church had geared itself to the role of a moral arbiter. It tried to avoid confrontation between the system, which for *raisons d'état* could not be replaced or even meaningfully changed, and the society, whose demands for human civil rights had always enjoyed the church's wholehearted sympathy and now could not be disavowed with impunity. Once it became clear that party, army, and state authorities categorically refused to see in the unions and other oppositional groups a viable partner in a national accord, the church, the only social institution that retained its spiritual independence, could not pretend any more to mediate. At the same time, it could not, and would not, replace Solidarity as a partner, although both the unions and the authorities appeared to push it in that direction. This would practically mean that the church would assume a political function—something no one would accept; hence, the often incomprehensible zigzags and tergiversations in the church's policy—and the fairly widespread (especially recently) erroneous impression that the Vatican and the Polish hierarchy were trying to stay neutral—even though their sympathies were clearly on the side of the oppressed, not the oppressors. Thus, the only constants in the pronouncements of the prelates were the call to avoid direct confrontation, bloodshed, and the resulting menace to the very existence of the Polish nation; defense of human rights and spiritual values; and the safeguarding of the future of the church, even under the least propitious circumstances.

In a sermon given in Warsaw on the day of the proclamation of the state of war, Primate Glemp warned therefore against the shedding of blood and appealed for "utmost prudence." He repeated similar sentiments in his Epiphany sermon, but also denounced the mass internment and arrests and, in particular, the pressure applied in order to force people to sign loyalty pledges under threat of dismissal from work. On 9 January he met with General Jaruzelski and agreed to a communiqué in which the signatories expressed "their intentions in connection with the normalization of life in Poland." The pope, who immediately after the infliction of martial law had sent his representative, Archbishop Poggi, to Warsaw, received the official representative of the military government at the Vatican on 12 January. At the same time, the Polish clergy set up a network of support for people interned or arrested and their families, as well as for workers dismissed from their jobs for being activists or members of Solidarity. They also took on themselves the tremendous task of distributing among the needy a flood of gifts received from abroad. Church representatives, at the first meeting since the coup of the Church-State Commission, expressed concern about the repression and violations of human dignity (Radio Warsaw, 18 January).

After the first visit of Primate Glemp and two other prelates to the Vatican and the clear papal pronouncement (9 February) in support of Solidarity ("The restitution of an effective and complete respect for the [workers'] right to a union, which has already been formed and legalized, is the only way out of this difficult situation"), the Conference of Polish Bishops (25–26 February) not only called for a "social accord" but defined preliminary conditions for talks to begin. These were fully in line with the demands of the unions: an end to martial law, release of internees, amnesty for those condemned for activities related to martial law, immunity for those still in hiding, job security regardless of union affiliation, freedom of religious life, cultural pluralism, and reactivation of youth organizations—all this as restoration of human dignity and safeguards for basic human and civic rights. Similar demands were voiced in the primate's subsequent sermons. He insisted in particular on the need to release Lech Wałęsa but also warned that "social agreement is a compromise, but not with evil; it should fulfill the needs and aspirations of all social groups" (7 March). The previously mentioned White Paper, issued by the Primate's Social Council, summed up the main points of church policy at this early stage.

It was, apparently, the intensification of the opposition to martial law that pushed the hierarchy, or at least some of its prominent members, to greater caution. The specter of bloodshed, followed perhaps by a Soviet armed intervention, seemed to dictate the repeated calls for calm; from then on, the appeals were less frequently addressed to the authorities and more often called on the people to desist from resistance. Even the first anniversary of Primate Wyszyński's death (28 May), and the spontaneous demonstrations around the floral cross laid out in his memory at Victory Square in Warsaw, which had provoked several brutal interventions by police and ZOMO, did not change Archbishop Glemp's restraint. Many devoted Catholics began then to compare the two heads of the Polish church, not necessarily to the incumbent's advantage. Throughout the spring and summer, the episcopate seemed to be concerned mostly with the planned papal pilgrimage and avoided any acts that might put it in jeopardy. Even when the visit was definitely postponed, the pastoral letter of the Bishops' Conference (2–4 August), while obliquely blaming the authorities, appealed above all for calm and assured the faithful that John Paul II on his second trip to Poland would "rise above all social conflicts," thus in advance playing down the possible political impact of his visit.

"Dialogue cannot take place on the streets"—these words from Archbishop Glemp's sermon on 26 August in Częstochowa (*Tygodnik Powszechny*, Cracow, 5 September)—faithfully represented the church's attitude toward the confrontation between the clandestine unions and the authorities that took place in the second half of August and the following months. The courageous sermon delivered by Bishop Tokarczuk and the subsequent vicious media campaign against the church put the hierarchy in a dilemma. The ambivalence can be seen clearly in the communiqué of the Bishops' Conference (15-16 September), in which the episcopate stressed its moral duty to stand up in defense of those who had been "beaten, injured, or morally harmed during the latest incidents," but impartially condemned the use of brutal force on the one side and "pure negation and hatred" on the other. It called, instead, for "reconciliation, forgiveness, and mutual concession."

In several sermons given in October, Archbishop Glemp was more outspoken than ever before in his condemnation of the outlawing of Solidarity, "the chief partner for any real dialogue," and warned the authorities not to "ignore the voice of society as a whole." Nonetheless, the unfortunate timing of his meeting with General Jaruzelski (8 November) and of the announcement of next year's papal visit to Poland gave rise to widespread criticism. These incidents were even cited as factors that contributed to the failure of the general strike proclaimed by the TKK to protest the dissolution of Solidarity. To what extent such criticism, as well as the disillusionment resulting from the failure of the church's far-reaching concessions to bring any substantial relaxation of the repression, influenced the sharpness with which the conference of the Polish bishops denounced the legislation enacted prior to the suspension of martial law is still a matter of conjecture. But it seems that Glemp came under attack even from his own parish clergy. At a meeting on 7 December with some 300 priests from the Archdiocese of Warsaw, a meeting described as "very stormy, difficult and painful," he was censored for being too conciliatory in his relations with the authorities, and not matching the steadfastness of his great predecessor, Primate Wyszyński (*NYT*, 9 December; *WP*, 27 December). As if to answer such criticism, the subsequent letter of the episcopate to the parliament took an exceptionally strong line toward the communist regime.

One aspect of communist policy toward the church has, as yet, brought no tangible success, but efforts in this direction are continuing. The idea of a Catholic or Christian Democratic political party that, with the full blessing of the church hierarchy (and if possible, of the Vatican as well), would play the role of a loyal opposition is not new. It had already emerged in the 1940s, when the PAX association had been cast in this role. Then it was wrecked by intransigent opposition of Primate Wyszyński and of the consecutive popes. A similar ploy was revived in 1980–1981. The PUWP leadership apparently believed that such a party might divide the opposition and serve as a counterbalance to Solidarity. In November 1980, Catholic layman, professor at the Catholic University in Lublin, and prominent member of the Polish Catholic Social Union, Jerzy Ozdowski agreed (apparently with the tacit approval of the hierarchy and of the pope) to join the government as a deputy prime minister. He was later demoted to the much less influential post of deputy speaker of the Sejm and replaced in the government by Zenon Komender, recently instated by Jaruzelski as the leader of PAX.

Glemp at first continued the line of his predecessor and treated the three licensed secular Catholic groups in the same way, carefully refusing to identify the church with any of them. But throughout 1982, rumors about an imminent formation of such a party persisted; it was even said that it would be assigned 25 percent of the seats in the parliament and a proportionate share in the government. Glemp himself, perhaps unwillingly, contributed to these rumors. At the inauguration of the academic year at the Catholic University in Lublin, he asserted forcefully that the church could have no strategy or tactics, could not get involved in any "struggle between [political] parties," or, "become a partner and have enemies." "The church has ambitions larger than political ones" (*Tygodnik Powszechny*, Cracow, 14 November). But shortly afterwards, in a homily delivered on 21 November, after denouncing discrimination against practicing Catholics and believers in public life, he added: "The life of the church also includes the life of Catholics who take part in public life . . . There should be Catholics in communal assemblies, in voivodship national councils, in the ministries, and in the Sejm." (*Le Monde*, 23 November.) Whether, as rumored, the issue had indeed been discussed at the November meeting between Jaruzelski and Glemp, and then at the primate's first encounter with Lech Wałęsa after the chairman of Solidarity had been released from detention, has not been confirmed. The December events—the kidnapping of Wałęsa to prevent him from making a public speech and the bishops' protest against the new legislation—would seem to contradict this, but are not enough by themselves to rule out the possibility altogether. The ambiguity of the attitude assumed by the hierarchy can best be gauged from the primate's stand on the new communist front organization PRON. Playing it safe, he forbade the clergy to participate in its activities in any form, but gave his blessing to secular Catholics and their political groupings who had done so.

The Economy. In one respect, and in one respect only, the ruling PUWP could claim a modest success during 1982; it has prevented—admittedly, at a cost that in the future might prove disastrous—the total disintegration of the national economy and widespread starvation. The military government took over in a situation approaching a debacle. The annual report of the Main Statistical Office (GUS), released at the end of January (*Trybuna Ludu*, 29 January), deliberately contained (unlike previous years) comparisons with 1980 only, the year when the regressive effects of the structural crisis in the national economy had already become fully visible. Even so, it revealed that the net material product had suffered an unprecedented annual drop of nearly 13 percent, net industrial production had fallen by 19 percent, and gross investment by over 25 percent. Some 1,500 major projects had been suspended or abandoned; they alone represented a frozen value of some 880 billion zlotys. The economy as a whole was put back at least ten years.

Even the draconian measures imposed after the proclamation of the state of war, which included the militarization of key economic sectors (mining, heavy industry, transport, part of the light and consumer industries), as well as the gradual reintroduction of the six-day work week and mandatory overtime, at first proved incapable of halting the decline. By mid-1982 overall industrial production was 7.8 percent lower than in the same period of 1981, gross production in the construction industry was down 16.9 percent (in housing down 32.4 percent). As the result of price increases for foodstuffs and consumer goods, imposed under the cover of "economic reform," the cost of living went up nearly 104 percent. The 57 percent rise in nominal income, coupled with the 26 percent decrease in real wages (according to official data; independent estimates suggest a much higher decline, perhaps 40 percent), indicate an inflation rate approaching 100 percent (ibid., 27 July). Except for goods rationed or distributed through enterprises to the work force according to political considerations never revealed to the public, the market virtually ceased to exist. Long lines of would-be buyers before shops and stores, which had been one of the most painful plagues of former years, disappeared since there was nothing for sale. The few goods available were priced at a level that made them inaccessible to the average wage earner.

The resulting deterioration in the relation between wages (and real income in general) and the rising cost of living (according to GUS, of some 26 percent on the average, but 28.7 percent in industry and over 30 percent in transport, communications, and trade) was too obvious to be concealed (*Zycie Gospodarcze*, 15 August). But the authorities also had to admit that the whole price operation had proven ineffective. By the end of 1982, the so-called inflationary overhang—once presented as the main cause of the market disequilibrium, whose elimination had supposedly been the reason for the brutal lowering of living standards—had almost regained its previous size in real terms. That meant that inflation has not been halted. Given the sharp price increases already announced for 1 January 1983 (which, in addition to increases in travel fares, postage, and sundry essential items, provide for a threefold increase in the cost of housing—without, however, promising any meaningful speedup in construction), the next year will bring further pauperization. According to the deputy chairman of the State Planning Commission, from whose interview (*Trybuna Ludu*, 10 December) these data are quoted, "it would be a mistake to claim that the present year ends with a full economic success." To the public this must have sounded like the understatement of the year. The fairly optimistic Three-Year Plan quite unrealistically predicted for 1983 a growth rate in industrial production of 4 percent and an overall 2.5 percent rise in national product—admittedly, in comparison to the rock-bottom level of 1982—and only 7–8 percent inflation (ibid., 29 November; *WP*, 29 December). It was clear that the most painfully afflicted will again be families with the lowest incomes, which already have had to spend up to 60 percent and more of their income on food alone and were openly described as "areas of extreme poverty" (*Zycie Warszawy*, 15 November).

Nonetheless, it is undeniable that industrial production, after three years of decline, had effectively leveled off by mid-1982 and since then (if the monthly GUS reports are to be believed) began, admittedly very slowly and only in relation to 1981, to climb. The improvement, however, was more apparent than real: the rise took place mainly in mineral extraction. There was hardly any progress in manufacturing, which for lack of raw materials, spare parts, and energy, as well as insufficient and inefficient cooperation, was frequently able to use only between 40 and 60 percent of its production capacity. The forced intensification of mining, of coal in particular, justified by the need to increase exports in order to obtain the hard currency needed to pay for imports (without which the economy would grind to a halt), was obtained only in part from increased productivity imposed by the military regime in the mines (striking miners were court-martialed and sent to jail as if guilty of desertion in time of war) and the inflated wages and preferential supply of goods to the miners. Contributing factors included total disregard for safety and health regulations in the mines (in 1982 there were some one hundred fatal casualties from mining accidents in the coal industry alone); concentration on the most productive seams and discontinuation of investment in new collieries; and negligent maintenance of the extracting machinery (see the official report on the 28 November accident at the Dimitrov colliery, where seventeen miners were killed; long ago the mine had been condemned by independent experts as too dangerous for exploitation [*Trybuna Ludu*, 13 December]).

Continuation of such abuses over the next few years must eventually bring a total catastrophe to Poland's coal industry, the main source of foreign currency for its economy.

Similar disregard for the future in the name of immediate or short-term advantages of economic stabilization can be discerned in other fields, but in many cases little information is available. An excellent illustration is provided by what has been recently called "processing service" (*przerób uslugowy*), a neologism coined in 1982. To supplement normal trade relations between Poland and its partners in the Council for Mutual Economic Assistance (CMEA), capacity, made redundant by lack of regular supplies of raw materials, spare parts, and other inputs and/or by loss of market outlets inside the country or abroad, are being leased to the Soviet Union and, to a lesser extent, other communist states. The partners are supposed to supply cooperating Polish enterprises with the components necessary for producing goods made to their order, including, if necessary, some foreign currency needed for purchases unobtainable within the CMEA. In return, they would take away all finished products, minus an agreed part that remains in the domestic market; about 15 percent was at first mentioned as an adequate reward for "services" rendered by the Polish work force on up-to-date Polish machines, often bought with the aid of foreign credits lent by Western banks during the 1970s.

The terms of trade between Poland and its CMEA partners are treated as a state secret. Details of "shared production" deals are difficult to obtain, and the mutual advantages are impossible to assess. Official propaganda profusely praises Soviet "assistance," and the USSR seems to be the only partner that has agreed to a Polish trade deficit not only in 1982 but in 1983 as well (*Financial Times*, London, 3 November). According to official data, Polish indebtedness to the Soviet Union has reached 1.5 billion rubles; it increased in 1982 by 1.2 billion, and next year will rise again by another billion (*Polityka*, 18 December).

"Processing services" might seem, in the short run, rather advantageous for Poland—if they do indeed prevent the shutdown of factories and the firing of their workers. But they seriously increase the dependence of the Polish economy on the Soviet Union and might even prove disastrous: Soviet economic planners and managers do not provide for depreciation of machinery and even less for moral aging. Nor will they invest in Polish industry to compensate for its losses; if and when they decide to modernize, they will do so on their own territory. Once the shared production is over, Polish plants will be left with obsolete or exhausted machines, unable to supply the domestic market or stand up to foreign competition in exports.

The most frequently voiced rationale for this neocolonialist bargain sale of Polish industrial capacities was the necessity to prevent mass unemployment. When the mirage of effective economic reform was still alive, it was estimated that enterprises, once granted autonomy in determining their production, work force, and prices, would have to fire between 1.0 and 1.5 million employees in order to achieve higher productivity and profits. But when martial law put an end to such illusions, the expected surplus of labor did not materialize. By September, the state-owned enterprises had nearly 300,000 vacancies, several times more than the number of unemployed registered as looking for jobs (*Rada Narodowa*, 1 November). Official propaganda tried to explain away this mystery by blaming regulations issued in July 1981 that provided for voluntary early retirement for workers after 25 (for men) or 20 (for women) years of employment. It had been estimated that some 100,000 people would seize the opportunity, thus easing the expected pressure on the labor market; in fact, 616,000 workers opted for this solution, apparently preferring a reduced pension over wages in a situation where higher income could not be redeemed by easily available goods and services (*Rzeczpospolita*, 29 November) or trying to start a new career, if possible, outside the socialized sector of the economy. The latter hopes were soon quashed by new regulations, which once more restricted private enterprise and suspended pensions, wholly or in part, for retirees who continued to work. The number of prospective early pensioners soon leveled off, but the damage done to industry by the departure of highly qualified, experienced workers was beyond repair. Nor was the problem solved: enterprises, still under the same or even tighter control from above, continue to employ a redundant work force, which despite a drastic drop in the industrial production still receives wages instead of unemployment benefits.

Agriculture. Two consecutive years of fairly good harvests (1981 and 1982) created favorable conditions for the reduction of Poland's dependence on agricultural imports and for reaching again a level of farm production that would at least cover domestic consumption. The expected results, however, did not materialize. Having proclaimed in mid-1982 the total suspension of agricultural imports in the name of "food self-sufficiency," in the last quarter of the year the government had to resort to urgent purchases of grain and feed abroad (4.2 million tons, according to latest official data [*Trybuna Ludu*, 23 December]), rendered extremely difficult by acute shortages of foreign exchange and by the unavailability of agricultural surpluses in almost all CMEA countries. Although the level of food rations (which barely covered the minimum needs of the population) were maintained, probable cuts in the allocation of meat and meat products have already been informally announced for 1983.

The main reasons for persistent food shortages are to be found in the inability to supply even the most elementary components farmers need for production and in the practice of arbitrary price fixing. Agricultural machines and tools (including the most primitive ones), fertilizers, insecticides, fodder, seeds, if at all available, are sold exclusively to peasants able to produce documentary proof of having sold their products to state purchasing agencies at fixed prices, much lower (often by half or more) than those paid on the free market or directly by consumers. Consequently, the inflated plan for grain procurement, already reduced from 5.0–5.5 to 3.5–4.0 million tons, has never been fulfilled. Farmers prefer to store their grain, to use it as fodder, to sell meat to consumers (especially since the authorities failed to notice the fall in potato production and to adjust prices correspondingly), or to barter the grain for desired goods. There is no incentive for accepting payment in zlotys, which have lost their value and most of the time cannot be used anyway since the inputs most necessary for farm production have disappeared from the market.

As usual, attempts were made to relieve the crisis not by adjusting prices to the market situation, but by introducing compulsion. During the harvest, military "task forces" were dispatched to the countryside, ostensibly to help the peasants during their most hectic season, but in fact to exert pressure on farmers and to convince them to sell to official buyers at fixed prices. The failure of this method rebounded in the rising demand—in particular on the part of party hard-liners, who had always tended to blame the farmers and to call for forced collectivization of agriculture—to return to the familiar Stalinist pattern of compulsory grain procurement. Their advice has not been followed as yet and might prove much more difficult to implement in the future after the suspension of martial law. The authorities continue to maintain that this year's results in agriculture will not be lower than the fairly successful ones achieved in 1981; the economic plan for 1983, as presented to the Sejm by Deputy Prime Minister Janusz Obodowski, predicted a 2 percent rise in food production, though not in meat (ibid., 4–5 December). Such official optimism is shared neither by independent economists nor by the public.

Foreign Debts and Credits. Poland entered 1982 with a foreign debt estimated at $26–28 billion (the exact amount is difficult to establish since some of the loans had been contracted in various currencies whose exchange rate in dollars fluctuated); about $11.5 billion of this amount was owed to seventeen major Western governments or covered by their guarantees (*NYT*, 15 January). Poland's inability to pay had been recognized early on, and already in April 1981 the Western governments had agreed to postpone repayment of about $2.4 billion of the principal. Shortly before the proclamation of the state of war, private banks did the same, provided Poland promised to pay $500–550 million in interest owed for 1981. At the turn of the year, the military government apparently scraped up part of the interest due; it is still not quite clear whether the repayment was made with the assistance of the Soviet Union, which in an agreement signed on 6 January in Moscow had granted its ally a long-term credit of 2.7 billion rubles. Poland declared, however, its inability to discharge further obligations unless granted additional credits (at least $350 million) by Western banks. Protracted, confidential negotiations then ensued, but Poland's creditors, both private and governmental, refused to declare it in default. The U.S. Department of Agriculture even agreed on 1 February to pay the banks $1.3 million as the settlement of principal and interest on outstanding government-guaranteed debts that Poland had failed to pay by 1 January. Members of NATO and the European Economic Community decided, however, to suspend all additional credits to Poland (except for food aid), as long as martial law remained in force.

By mid-March, Poland had managed to pay the reduced amount of interest for 1981 after the Western banks had rescheduled repayment of 95 percent of the principal (about $2.4 billion) over the next seven and a half years (*WSJ*, 7 April). Negotiations could therefore begin on the rescheduling of payments due in 1982—over $10 billion in principal and interest. Such an amount was considered greatly in excess of Poland's capabilities. A certain amount of blackmail was also involved: the party hard-liners, but never official financial sources, openly threatened to stop all payments, arguing that the lavish credits granted in the 1970s had been nothing but an imperialist ploy to make Poland economically, and therefore politically, dependent on the West and to ruin its national economy; allegedly, the private bankers had already been repaid over and above their due, and anyhow they were nothing but usurers and bloodsuckers, exploiting the toil of Polish workers.

Negotiations were protracted, and the Polish debtor skillfully exploited the lack of unanimity among the Western creditors, bankers and governments alike. In the first half of 1982, Poland successfully negotiated new credits amounting to $893 million (only one-fourth of what had been received in the same period of 1981 but in violation of the agreed embargo on financial assistance), mainly grain credits by Canada and France reportedly committed in 1981 (ibid., 9 November). An agreement signed in Vienna between Poland and over 500 Western banks in early November deferred repayment of 95 percent of Poland's $2.4 billion 1982 commercial debt for eight years (with higher interest); the repayment will begin after four years in seven semiannual installments. The $1.1 billion 1982 interest owed to the banks was to be reimbursed by Poland before the end of March 1983. Half of it, however, was to be "recycled" by the creditors as short-term (three-year) trade credits for Polish purchases of raw materials and industrial goods from the West, ostensibly to promote exports and procurement of hard currency. No debts to Western governments had been rescheduled, in accordance with the NATO resolution of 11 January; nor did Poland make any effort to repay them (ibid., 3 November; *NYT*, 4 November). The Polish authorities' pleasure over these arrangements, according to which in 1983 Poland will pay the Western banks $700 million instead of $3.5 billion and from this sum will receive back half the amount in trade credits, can be concluded from the fact that the mass media, as a rule not allowed to write on the issue of foreign indebtedness, informed the public of the agreement in detail (*Trybuna Ludu*, 4 and 7 November).

A new round of negotiations over payments due in 1983 and 1984 was also announced (ibid., 30 November). The 1983 budget, presented to the Sejm by Deputy Prime Minister Janusz Obodowski on 29 December, anticipated $3 billion in additional credits from Western banks; according to unofficial sources, Poland would apparently seek $800 million in short-term commercial credits, while $2.2 billion in 1983 interest payments would be transferred into the principal owed to the banks. A committee of Western bankers was expected in Warsaw in January 1983 to discuss rescheduling (*NYT*, 30 December). Neither the protests of prominent opposition leaders in Poland against financial assistance that strengthened the military government nor the increased repression directed against the independent unions, obviously unaffected by the suspension of martial law, has proved an insurmountable obstacle to the previous settlement and is unlikely to do so in the future.

Foreign Affairs. The quasi-universal condemnation with which the imposition of the state of war was received by both governments and public opinion all over the world (outside of the Soviet bloc and its allies) unavoidably shaped the foreign orientation of the PUWP and its military executive. There was no room any more for even the modest "opening to the West" attempted, mainly in the economic domain, in the 1970s; far less for the illusionary "equidistance" between East and West that sometimes emerged in Solidarity's theorizing and practice. Although the shrill anti-Western campaign in the media and in official pronouncements did not prevent undercover attempts to drive a wedge between the United States and its Western European allies to neutralize the latter and persuade them to restore a "business as usual" policy in both the economic and political spheres, the official foreign policy of the military government was virtually restricted to the Soviet bloc only.

The first government-level foreign visit was the trip to Moscow on 11 January of then Foreign Minister Józef Czyrek. Economic relations between Poland and the Soviet Union had already been settled in a bilateral trade accord of 6 January, which provided for mutual trade of 8.4 billion rubles in 1982 and for long-term Soviet credits of 2.7 billion rubles. Czyrek apparently dealt mainly with political problems. The most important among them might have been the joint condemnation of the "gross interference" by the West in Polish affairs. The Polish foreign minister was quoted as explaining that martial law had been "prompted by the crucial necessity to prevent bloodshed and civil war" in the face of "the counterrevolutionary threat, encouraged and supported by imperialist circles"—for the entire year the leitmotiv of both Polish and Soviet propaganda. Of particular importance might have also been Czyrek's meeting with Mikhail A. Suslov, the ideologist of the Soviet Politburo; according to unconfirmed reports, among the subjects discussed were the role of the communist party in Poland during the state of war and the prospects for a quick return to Soviet-style "normalcy" (*Financial Times*, 14 January; *NYT*, 16 January).

Predictably, General Jaruzelski began his circuit around the capitals of the Warsaw pact countries from Moscow on 1 March. His arrival at the head of a large party and state delegation was preceded by a hint of Soviet dissatisfaction with results already achieved: the martial law, Politburo spokesman Leonid M. Zamyatin warned on Soviet television, had checked "but not rooted out" counterrevolution (*NYT*, 1 March). The official welcome, however, was rather effusive. Leonid Brezhnev assured his guest that the Soviet leadership "received with full understanding word of the national decision by our Polish friends to defend people's power" by proclaiming the state of war (ibid., 2 January). He also promised increased Soviet economic assistance and accepted an invitation to come to Warsaw; the visit never materialized.

Jaruzelski paid other visits to fraternal capitals presumably in order of their importance to Poland: he was in East Berlin on 29 March, in Prague on 7 April, in Budapest on 21 April, in Sofia on 20 May, and in Bucharest on 4 June. The subjects discussed were similar: "information about the current situation in Poland," calculated to relieve the allies' anxiety about the PUWP's capability to suppress the opposition and to return to normal party rule, and appeals for indulgence for Poland's economic woes, coupled with offers of increased trade and industrial cooperation. The specific results of these travels are difficult to ascertain, but as a rule offical media in the adjacent countries started to play down the threat of conterrevolution in Poland and credited the PUWP rather than the military with successes supposedly achieved in Poland thanks to the policy of normalization.

Before the year was out, Jaruzelski paid several more visits to the Soviet Union. On 16 August, he conferred with Brezhnev and Andrei Gromyko in the Crimea at a time when the underground unions started their second peaceful offensive against the military regime. The wording of the communiqué (*Trybuna Ludu*, 18 August) and in particular the lack of an explicit Soviet endorsement of Jaruzelski's policy and expression of best wishes suggest that opinions on the internal situation in Poland were not necessarily identical. The impression seems confirmed by an article in *Literaturnaia gazeta* (Moscow, 18 August) that blamed the PUWP, asserting that the counterrevolutionary "plot would have been nipped in the bud had the entire PUWP risen to its mission at the correct time"; even eight months later, the party "has not fully re-established the toiling people's trust in it." In mid-November, Jaruzelski attended Brezhnev's funeral and was received by his successor, Yuri Andropov; details of their talks are still unknown. Finally, in the third week of December, Jaruzelski met with Andropov during the festivities marking the sixtieth anniversary of the Soviet Union and invited him to pay a visit to Poland. Shortly before, a Soviet economic delegation, headed by Nikolai Baibakov, deputy prime minister and chairman of the State Planning Commission of the USSR, visited Poland on 6–11 December. The official communiqué, more than usually short on details, mentioned bilateral trade in 1983 and Soviet economic assistance to Poland, cooperation in production, joint investment ventures, and continuation of the processing services rendered by Polish industry to Soviet customers (*Trybuna Ludu*, 13 December). For the first time, "enriching" or "refining" processing was also mentioned in connection with the light, chemical, and metal industries; in this case, half of the final production was supposed to remain on the Polish market (ibid., 10 December), but the financial and other terms of the deal were not revealed.

Poland's relations with the United States went systematically from bad to worse. The economic sanctions announced by the Reagan administration immediately after the imposition of martial law, and since then made even more rigorous by cutting food assistance, abolishing Poland's most-favored-nation status, and blocking its application to the International Monetary Fund, have had an impact on the economic situation, although their effectiveness is still disputed. But they provided the Polish authorities with a handy pretext for making the United States the scapegoat for the crisis, for denouncing alleged U.S. intervention in Polish internal affairs, and for gradually downgrading diplomatic and cultural relations. Two U.S. diplomats and a scholar were expelled. At the end of the year, after measures had been taken to stop all academic and cultural exchanges and to make all activities of the U.S. Information Agency in Poland impossible (ibid., 15 December), bilateral relations were nearing the zero level.

On the other hand, repeated attempts were made to win over, or at least to neutralize, Western Europe. At the turn of the year, Jaruzelski invited all ambassadors of the European Economic Community to Warsaw and followed it up by unofficial missions of his intimate aides to various capitals. Deputy Prime

Minister Rakowski was sent to Bonn and later to Vienna, Czyrek's visit to Paris (ostensibly as a guest of the French Communist Party), was followed by a visit by a prominent economist. In November, Jaruzelski met in Moscow with Greek Prime Minister Andreas Papandreou and apparently convinced him to try and mediate between the European Economic Community and Poland. This was followed by a round of visits by unofficial Polish emissaries to the capitals of Western Europe; they tried to present the already announced suspension of martial law in Poland as a handy opportunity for the West to lift its sanctions and to renew financial and economic cooperation. The results of these efforts are still a matter for speculation, but obviously the West never presented a united front in its reaction to the state of war and the intensified repression in Poland.

Relations with the Third World were mostly restricted to trade, and even in this domain the economic disintegration in Poland acted as a very effective brake. The only exception was Libya, where Polish generals were welcomed guests since Poland was able to barter weapons for oil and had trained an undisclosed but apparently considerable number of Libyan military officers. Colonel Moammar Khadafy's official visit to Warsaw in September, the only visit of a head of state during the state of war, provided a rare opportunity for propagandistic exploitation, and was followed by a working visit to Warsaw by the Libyan chief of staff. Similar publicity surrounded the trip of newly appointed Foreign Minister Stefan Olszowski, who (after an obligatory visit to Moscow) went to India, Kuwait, Greece, and Yugoslavia. This might have been the start of a new diplomatic offensive directed at the nonaligned countries.

International Party Contacts. Under martial law, the PUWP restricted to the bare minimum its official contacts with other communitst parties. There was some exchange of lower-level delegations with other ruling parties in the Soviet bloc, but only a few received any publicity—among them the visits to Warsaw by Konstantin V. Rusakov, secretary of the Soviet Central Committee in charge of relations with other ruling communist parties, who came in May at the height of the first protest campaign organized by the underground unions, and by Vasil Bil'ák, the prominent Czechoslovak party hard-liner.

Among the nonruling communist parties, the French expressed conditional support for martial law, although communist ministers did not publicly dissent from protests and sanctions on the part of the French government. Jósef Czyrek participated in the French party congress in February, but the real reasons for his visit were unofficial contacts with President Mitterrand's aides. The leadership of the Italian Communist Party did not deviate from its initial condemnation of the state of war in Poland and publicly engaged in an acrimonious polemic with the Soviet media over the issue.

Herbert Wehner, chairman of the Social Democratic parliamentary fraction in the West German Bundestag, paid a "private" visit to Poland, but refused to reveal the contents and results (if any) of his talks with the PUWP leaders.

Biography. *Tadeusz Grabski.* Born 1929 in Warsaw into the intelligentsia. Graduate of the Higher School of Economics in Poznan, Ph.D. In the 1950s, for five years career officer in the Polish army's political apparatus; 1956–1970, in industrial management in Poznan voivodship; 1971–1972, economic secretary, PUWP voivodship committee in Poznan; 1972–1975, head of local administration in Poznan; 1975–1979, first secretary, PUWP voivodship committee in Konin; Sejm deputy, 1976–1980. At a 1979 plenary session of the PUWP Central Committee, he openly criticized the economic policy of the Gierek party leadership, in particular the falling living standards of workers; his speech was never published in the official media, but appeared in an underground newspaper. Immediately dismissed, Grabski was sent back to economic management (1979–1980, managing director of MERA automation systems in Poznan). In August 1980, during the wave of mass strikes, appointed deputy prime minister in charge of employment, domestic market, pricing policy, local industry, cooperatives, artisans, and tourism. From September 1980 to July 1981, member of the Politburo, and Central Committee secretary, and member of the Commission for Economic Reform. In September 1980, during a plenary session of the Central Committee, Grabski successfully motioned the expulsion of Gierek's closest associates in the party. In April–July 1981, head of the Commission for the Investigation of the Responsibilities of Former PUWP and Government Leaders.

Along with Stefan Olszowski, but in a much more outspoken way, Grabski is considered a key figure of the hard-line wing of the PUWP, spokesman of that part of the middle and lower levels of the party apparatus, which, defending their monopoly of power and the resulting perquisites, rejected all calls for accommodation with Solidarity. At a plenary session in March 1981, he demanded Kania's dismissal and, together with Olszowski, offered his resignation from the Politburo (not accepted).

Grabski's attempts to gain popularity among manual workers and *apparatchiki* by presenting an alternative platform combining populist egalitarianism with ultra-nationalism and Stalinist party control over all aspects of public life did not meet with success. In June 1981, his candidacy to the PUWP congress was twice rejected at a regional conference of delegates in Poznan. He was elected only after a last-minute telephone intervention by Kania, but at the congress itself failed to be elected to the new Central Committee. Prematurely retired, he tried to organize an oppositional hard-line faction inside the party, based on such structures as the Warsaw '80 Club, Katowice Forum, and others, with a new weekly *Rzeczywistość* (Reality) as its press organ. In December 1981, Grabski was elected chairman of the National Federation of Reality Clubs. After the imposition of martial law, General Jaruzelski reportedly offered him at least two ambassadorial posts and a government ministry, but in fall of 1982, he accepted a minor post as Poland's trade counselor to East Germany.

Before his departure for Berlin, Grabski sent an open letter to his Poznan party organization extremely critical of Jaruzelski's leadership. Martial law, according to him, had not broken the "counterrevolution," and the resulting fall in the standard of living, the growing black market, and privatization policies could become "the source of a much greater explosion than anything the underground can organize." The letter was never published, but its text was widely circulated at a Central Committee plenary session in October 1982, reputedly with the tacit connivance of the party leadership, which, by raising the bogey of hard-line reaction, tried to promote its own centrist image and to justify its repressive policies.

The letter contained a four-point program to "save the country from self-destruction." It provided for (1) final elimination of the anticommunist underground ("all available means" should be used against the "organized counterrevolution . . . it is better to use force and the severity of the law against a group of counterrevolutionaries than to apply means of coercion against the workers"); (2) "a revolutionary ideological purge of the party"; (3) abandonment of key elements of the economic reform (it only started "a process of obvious pauperization of the masses . . . further impoverishment of the poor and enrichment of the rich," "the living conditions of working people have dramatically deteriorated," therefore some elements of the reform should be replaced by "just distribution of the goods that are available"); and (4) a crackdown on the Roman Catholic church, which had assumed "the leadership of the entire social right wing."

Significantly, Kazimierz Barcikowski, the number-two man in the party leadership, replying to questions raised by party members in the Szczecin shipyard, refrained from discussing Grabski's arguments and from accusing him of factional activities inside the party. He admitted only that the open letter had "demonstrated the excessive ambitions of its author" (*Kurier Szczecinski*, 11 November).

While excluded from the party leadership and deprived of his organizational base (Warsaw '80 and similar clubs were dissolved in March 1982, and the weekly *Rzeczywistość* reappeared after its suspension under new editors, less personally indebted to Grabski), the leading hard-liner might well play a major role in the future, for example, in case the failure the Jaruzelski's leadership would necessitate its replacement by a new, less discredited team of proven loyalty to the USSR. (Sources: Joseph Wisniewski, *Who's Who in Poland*, Toronto, 1981, p. 47; *Financial Times*, 29 October; *Times*, London, 30 October; *Le Monde*, 31 October–1 November; *Los Angeles Times*, 30 October.)

Russian Research Center
Harvard University

Tadeusz Szafar

THE UNDERGROUND SOCIETY*

The preliminary theses for the program of the
Interim Coordinating Commission of the Independent Self-Governing Trade Unions Solidarity
The Interim Coordinating Commission is submitting for broad social discussion its preliminary theses in the

---

* Committee in Support of Solidarity Reports, New York, 6 September.

declaration entitled "Underground Society." [The Interim Coordinating Committee was established at the end of April 1982 by the leaders of the four strongest regional branches of Solidarity.]

The experience of eight months under the state of war teaches us that the struggle for our goals requires the universal participation of society, conscious of its inalienable rights and organized for long-term action. The authorities' war on the Polish people continues. Only their tactics change. Today they formally struggle against Solidarity. In fact, however, by questioning the August [1980] agreements they are striking at the fundamental interests of society. Under the guise of the state of war they are liquidating the independence of our organization, won in August, and at the same time the Sejm [parliament], which is at their disposal, is passing laws that take away all that we gained before December [1981]. Society has been deprived of the possibility of independent activity and the active shaping of political life. The authorities aim to create a legal-political order in which any kind of independent social activity will be impossible. All decisions and promises by the authorities seek only to gain time. The authorities expect that society, worn out by struggling for its survival and deprived of hope, will give up its program of reforms and accept treatment as object [instead of being] the subject of policy.

Consequently the Interim Coordinating Commission has consistently assumed the position that only a social contract will make it possible for Poland to emerge from the present crisis. Proposals for such a contract have already been presented by the union, the church, and various social groups. The authorities' response was complete silence. The authorities require only peace, or rather obedience and work under conditions of waste and exploitation.

Our goal is to build an autonomous society—a self-governing republic—in accordance with the program accepted at the First National Congress of Solidarity [in September–October 1981]. In the present situation we can achieve this goal only through an underground society.

The Interim Coordinating Commission is calling for the organization of a universal resistance movement and the creation of an underground society. This movement is a reflection of social attitudes, life, and activities. All groups and localities, the city and the village, constitute the basic conditions of the movement's strength, making it possible for the authorities to create and maintain divisions that antagonize society. The underground movement must lessen the individual's feelings of isolation, must teach collective action, strengthen the awareness that only through organizing ourselves and through self-initiative can we reach our goals. It must show society the strength which flourishes within.

The underground society should above all:
a)   thwart the authorities' attempts to divide society.
b)   develop the capabilities of self-organization and self-defense.
c)   raise the level of political culture and prepare society for life in a democratic Poland.

This underground society movement will be created by organized groups in factories, professional groups, in settlements, and among circles of friends. The character, scope, and form of activities of each group will depend on realistic possibilities.

Special attention should be paid to youth; as the most uncompromising and self-sacrificing group by nature, the weight of organizing various kinds of resistance rests and continues to rest upon them. Mass participation of youth in the underground movement will portend victory.

Every participant should be able to find it possible to act within the framework of the underground society. There is room for everyone who accepts our program. In the underground society movement there is no distinction between small and great matters. What counts is the sum total of attitudes and activities attesting to the independence of thought, a readiness to organize, and the willingness to bring help to those who require it. What counts are consistency, perseverance, and courage in the struggle when it becomes necessary.

We propose the following basic set of activities for the underground movement:
a)   the organization of self-help for victims of repression, for those who have lost their jobs and are living in need, for the sick, and for others requiring material and moral support.
b)   the organization of independent circulation of information, including publishing, distribution, the production of leaflets, and exposing the aims of the authorities' propaganda.
c)   the organization of learning and self-education: independent instruction and an independent

teaching movement; courses in continuing education; workers' universities; discussion clubs; academic publications; the instruction of the movement's organizers and activists; stipends and support for students, teachers, and scholars; the establishment of social foundations, etc.

d) the organization of actions demonstrating society's resistance: anniversary celebrations, posters, leaflets, participation in protests proclaimed by regional decision-making bodies or by the Interim Coordinating Commission.

e) the organization of economic activities (cooperatives, workshops), and influencing economic processes.

The underground society fights against front organizations set up by the authorities, organizes boycotts of official propaganda and of meetings, discussions, and undertakings with a political or propaganda character. It opposes collaboration. The underground society promotes development of national culture, while at the same time it must oppose the authorities' aspiration of one-sided exploitation of national culture and treatment of people as instruments. Special responsibility rests then upon literary, journalistic, and academic centers; their professional codes of ethics should define the dividing line, beyond which collaboration and action contrary to the national interests begin.

The underground society should, by exerting pressure on the authorities, create conditions that draw a social accord nearer, while at the same time gradually expand the scope of its social and political rights.

The underground society movement should be decentralized. All of the elements of the union have the responsibility to undertake actions to inspire and organize the underground society. The underground regional decision-making bodies will fulfill a consultative-coordinative function in each of the various regions. They will give direction to its work, and publish recommendations, instructions, and responses in the underground press. Nationwide coordination is undertaken by the Interim Coordinating Commission.

We anticipate that the underground movement will become an additional factor shaping the international situation and will be in the service of the Polish cause.

The proposed actions will create a movement of a national community united around the idea of Solidarity. The underground society will become the basis for political activity; even if the union is delegalized, it will prevent society from losing faith, exert pressure on the authorities, threaten to isolate them completely, and force them to recognize the fact that only an accord leads toward a solution of the problems presently facing Poland.

The underground society movement establishes the necessary conditions for an effective struggle for our current goals: freeing political prisoners and those interned, ending the state of war, reinstating an independent union movement; and as the long-run goal: the creation of a self-governing Republic.

28 July 1982

Zbigniew Bujak
  Mazowsze Region
Wladyslaw Frasyniuk
  Lower Silesia Region
Wladyslaw Hardek
  Malopolska Region
Bogdan Lis
  Gdansk Region
Eugeniusz Szumiejko
  Member of the Presidium of the National Commission

ADDRESS TO THE POLISH NATION[*]

Citizens of the Polish People's Republic: Difficult years are behind us. Poland has been going through a difficult time. These difficulties have brought internal perplexity. In a dangerous way, this difficult time has weakened the link which united Poles in front of the greatest danger that occurred in centuries. I shall not recall those pre-December days. We all remember them. Nothing can conceal the merciless meaning of the events which took place then. In politics and in the lives of nations, only facts really count. Exactly one year ago, martial law was introduced. Some call it war. Yes, it really has been and is a war for maintaining and continuing the socialist statehood, for saving the withering economy, and for the irreversibility of the line of reforms and renewal. The year which has passed was a great test. We have passed that test.

This test was passed by the party, the people's power, and all citizens who understood the supreme *raison d'etat*. There are many forces in Poland that met with defeat—internal and external forces. However, there is only one victor—the Polish nation. This is the truth about the year that has passed.

The worst is already behind us, but the road ahead for Poland is still not an easy one. One cannot emerge immediately from such a profound crisis. However, we can see brighter horizons. It is with this thought in mind that we stand on the verge of the new year. We were moderate in applying the rigors of martial law. We began to ease them and lift them relatively soon—almost immediately. We counted on the fact that it would be possible to end martial law earlier. The fundamental condition here was public calm. Alas, not infrequently there have been the well-known disruptions. Despite this, the situation in the country was steadily getting better. November and the latest period brought about further tangible progress. The patriotism shown by the public, the wisdom and attitude of the working class, resulted in the fact that the appeals of the enemy fell on deaf ears. Favorable trends began to take root in the economy. Order and observance of the law are getting stronger. This makes it possible to reply in the positive to the appeal of the Patriotic Movement for National Rebirth and to other social initiatives aimed in the same direction.

Citizens: the Military Council for National Salvation is of the opinion that conditions have occurred to suspend martial law. I wish to state this precisely today—on the eve of the first anniversary of the introduction of martial law. The suspension of martial law means that its fundamental rigors will cease to function by the end of 1982. Only such regulations as those which directly protect the fundamental interests of the state, creating a protective shield for the economy and increasing the personal safety of the citizens, should remain in force in total or to a limited extent as a temporary measure.

Not one restriction more than is absolutely essential should be maintained, but at the same time, not one less. Detailed proposals will be put before the Sejm during tomorrow's session. This will be a significant step toward completely lifting martial law. We desire this intention to be fulfilled in the realistically most immediate future. One cannot just jump into complete normalization. One has to make one's way toward it step by step, consistently, with joint efforts because the activities of the opponent have not halted. Hopes still endure for a second stage of the struggle against the socialist state. The national economy which is being regenerated requires certain means of protection. The public is calling for the fight against crime to be stepped up.

Research into public opinion indicates its growing alarm over the possibility of a premature lifting of martial law or of some of its restrictions. Thus, we cannot yet afford to relinquish all the extraordinary means. We did not avail ourselves of martial law in order to ruin today what we have managed to achieve this year through such toil and efforts by millions of Poles.

I make no promises. But I do make one promise: anarchy will not be allowed to enter Poland. Let no one in Poland or abroad cherish illusions for even a moment that the current decisions make a further round possible. I am not wasting words with this warning. Let all those who calculate that they will be able to sow confusion once again consider this well.

Women, men, soldiers: The scope of the presence of the armed forces in the life of the country will change. The Military Council for National Salvation, vacating the function of the administrator of martial law, becomes the guarantor of a secure passage from the suspension of this state to its complete lifting.

There will be a considerable decrease in the number of military commissars. They will remain only in the most important, key sectors of state and economic life. As normalization permits, their activity will be

---

[*] Delivered by Prime Minister Wojciech Jaruzelski; Warsaw domestic service, 12 December; *FBIS,* 13 December.

further limited. The role of the Polish army in this difficult period of our history will be evaluated by the Sejm and by society. The soldiers of the armed forces do their duty not for promotion, decorations, or awards. They have served the homeland well. To benefit the country and society, their responsible, often thankless, duty is carried out by officials of the Citizens' Militia and the security service. They deserve words of sincere recognition.

We are living at a time of increased tensions, of dangers evoked by imperialism. Our Polish affairs are not being played out in an empty arena. The quicker we achieve equilibrium, the greater will be our contribution to the cause of peace in Europe. Poland has ceased to be a potential source of conflict. The point is now for her again to become a permanent factor in international cooperation and stabilization.

We have endured boycott, restrictions, the massed fire of provocative propaganda. The U.S. government and some of its clients have been shown conclusively the bankruptcy of attempts to interfere in Poland's internal affairs. It is not there and not in that way that Poland's fate will be decided. They will be decided only here, on the Vistula and Oder.

The Sejm has not yet made a decision on martial law, and already we have heard the voice of the uninvited foreign commentator. He knows best what Poland needs. We have given enough proof that we will not leave the chosen path. We will act in accordance with one signpost only. It is the good of the nation, of socialist Polish statehood. Those who so bitterly strike at that good will be answered by us with the appropriate decisions.

The past year once again showed the importance of our alliances, the importance of aid extended to us by our Soviet friends. The saying "One for all, all for one" proved to be true. In the mutual interdependence of the national interests of each socialist country with the interests of the socialist community as a whole lies the strength and the power of resistance of all its members.

Citizens: A new period is starting in the life of Poland, the period of suspension of martial law. We want to efficiently utilize it, to consolidate the progress hitherto achieved, to overcome the most acute shortcomings, to draw conclusions from our own errors and weakness, and to consolidate the guarantee that there won't be any more crises in Poland.

What is in store for us during this period? We shall have, above all, a great, common duty of consolidating the socialist state. The state that has been saved from disintegration and is recovering its forces can and must creatively digest and actively utilize the various forms of socialist democracy and self-government that are widely developing. We also expect that this will be a period of revival and development of independent, self-governing trade unions and their acquisition of a proper position. The party, the people's power, will show full understanding and goodwill to them. We must also continue to bring order into the national economy and heal it, to offensively overcome the crisis. Industry must maintain the rhythm of increasing production. Agriculture must overcome the difficulties of the period preceding next year's harvest.

The hitherto applied mechanisms of the economic reform will be corrected in accordance with the experiences of its first, experimental year. The workers' self-management must be finally created and settle down to its work.

People are experiencing difficult times. Efforts aimed at alleviating such difficulties in their everyday lives will be continued; efforts to prevent unbridled inflation and to categorically counteract occurrences of social injustice will be continued. More stringent legal means for combating wastage and bad management will be introduced. Authorities will be using those measures with full resoluteness. A great task of rebuilding the trust and consolidating the link between people's authority with the public is awaiting us— especially with the working class. We are not forgetting social agreements. We all should persist in learning the difficult art of sincere and constructive dialogue, of mutual contact and consultation. Such an atmosphere must be created; such conditions must be created so that every citizen who is aware and hardworking will feel that he is a real comaster in his factory and in his country. An additional, higher level of work, making the apparatus of power more effective and modern, is awaiting us. The past year has brought many beneficial changes as far as this is concerned. However, there is still a lot to be done. The law concerning employees of state offices will soon come into force. Rational principles of cadre policy will be introduced. The comprehensive system of control will be regulated. Institutions of public service should treat the needs and worries of citizens with greater sensitivity.

A decisive and more effective struggle with social evil is awaiting us. New legal instruments will make it possible to combat in a more severe manner crimes that threaten the lives, health, property of citizens: profiteering, bribes, and tax frauds. Laws aimed against the most painful social plagues have come into force or will be introduced shortly—against the plagues that are an insult to morality and justice. In combating demoralization, the cooperation of the entire public is necessary. This can also be one of the broad platforms of cooperation with the church and of activity of milieus that shape opinions. I have presented the key tasks for the period of the suspension of martial law. The better we cope together with those, the quicker full normalization will occur.

Polish men and women: There are unresolved matters amongst us. There is still a lot of doubt and bitterness.

Every day of the week is difficult. The question is often asked: What road are we to take, how are we to emerge from this? We need a certain amount of time to gradually disentangle our Polish affairs and to improve the conditions of life. We also need strenuous work; we need mutual trust.

It is the party and its Ninth Congress that charted the road leading to this goal. There is no turning back from this road, nor will there be. The time has come to construct institutional foundations for national accord. It is not as if we had to speak with one voice, all of us, regarding each individual matter. A new democratic forum, the Patriotic Movement for National Rebirth, is coming into being. Its National Council will soon start its work. Next year the first congress of this movement could take place. One can expect that an original program, one that accords with social expectations, will be worked out.

Only those who wish to be our enemies are the enemy. We will be impatient in the face of evil, but we will be patient in the face of doubts expressed by human beings. I address myself now to those who in the past year did not find a place for themselves. I also speak to those who are still groping their way in the blind alleys of the underground. The suspension of martial law gives another chance. Internment will cease to be applied. Socially justified amnesties are envisaged. If need be, the people's power is severe. When it is possible, it is understanding. Maybe more was expected from today. Maybe there were those who counted on sensational statements.

However, I think it is better that we should go about resolving Polish affairs in a realistic and prudent manner, that we should discuss them calmly, in an ordinary way.

When emotions give way to the desire for peace and normal life, we can speak with greater confidence of our tomorrow. It is on this that we build our hopes, accords, confidence in our own resources.

One year ago, I appealed to you, dear fellow countrymen, to be ready to do without things, to take part in saving the fatherland. You have shown your understanding, for which today I wish to thank you. We have proved ourselves equal to the hour of national trial. We will prove ourselves equal to the tasks of the future.

Romania

The Communist Party of Romania (PCR) was founded on 8 May 1921. Throughout most of the interwar period, the PCR was outlawed. Factionalized and controlled by the Soviet-dominated Comintern, the party had little popular support. The Soviet occupation of Romania in 1944 ensured the emergence of a people's republic headed by the party, which was renamed the Romanian Workers' Party in 1948. Under the leadership of Gheorghe Gheorghiu-Dej, the party gradually initiated, in the 1960s, a more nationalistic internal course and a more autonomous foreign policy. This orientation has been continued by Nicolae Ceauşescu, who succeeded Dej on the latter's death in 1965. In that same year, the party's Ninth Congress proclaimed Romania a socialist republic, and the party reverted to its original name. Since 1948, the PCR . has been the only party in Romania.

By almost any standards except those of the official Romanian press, 1982 was not a good year for the Socialist Republic of Romania, the PCR, or President and General Secretary Nicolae Ceauşescu. The national economy, in serious trouble for some time, sank even deeper into a Poland-like morass of international indebtedness, consumer privation, labor shortages, low productivity, stagnation, and corruption. There were revelations of misconduct and mismanagement among high government and PCR officials. The Ceauşescus' anti-intellectual obscurantism and the crackdown of the secret police took on Stalinist proportions. Romania's international prestige, the source of much, if not all, of Ceauşescu's and the PCR's legitimacy, was severely undermined by Romania's insolvency, violations of human rights, and by the diminished assertiveness of its autonomy from the rest of the Soviet bloc.

Population. 22.5 million

Party. Romanian Communist Party (Partidul Comunist Roman; PCR)

Founded. 1921

Membership. 3,150,812 (31 December 1981); workers, 55.4 percent; peasants and agricultural workers, 22.7 percent; intellectuals, 22 percent

General Secretary. Nicolae Ceauşescu

Political Executive Committee (PEC). 21 full and 19 alternate members; 14 of PEC's 40 members belong to the Permanent Bureau: Nicolae Ceauşescu (president of republic), Stefan Andrei (foreign minister),* Iosif Banc, Emil Bobu (chairman, Council on Problems of Economic and Social Organization), Virgil Cazacu, Elena Ceauşescu (first deputy prime minister), Nicolae Constantin (chairman, General Confederation of Trade Unions), Constantin Dascalescu (prime minister), Paul Niculescu, Gheorghe Oprea (first deputy prime minister), Ion Patan (minister of technical-material supply and control of fixed assets), Dumitru Popescu, Gheorghe Radelescu (vice-president, State Council), Ilie Verdet (chairman, Central Council of Workers' Control of Economic and Social Activities); 8 full members: Lina Ciobanu (minister of machine-building industry), Ion Coman, Ion Dinca (first deputy prime minister), Ludovic Fazekas (deputy prime minister), Alexandrina Gainuse (deputy prime minister), Petru Lupu, Gheorghe Pana, Stefan Voitec (vice-president, State Council); 19 alternate members: Stefan Andrei,* Emilian Dobrescu, Miu Dobrescu, Marin Enache, Petru Enache (vice-president, State Council), Eva Feder, Suzana Gadea (chairwoman, Council of Socialist Culture and Education), Mihai Gere, Nicolae Giosan (chairman, Grand National Assembly), Constantin Leonard, Stefan Mocuta, Ana Muresan (chairwoman, National Council of Women), Elena Nae, Constantin Olteanu (defense minister), Cornel Onescu, Ion Stoian, Iosif Szasz (vice-chairman, Grand National Assembly), Ion Ursu (vice-chairman, National Council of Science and Technology), Richard Winter. (*Andrei is the only Permanent Bureau member who is an alternate rather than a full member of the PEC.)

Secretariat. 8 members: Nicolae Ceauşescu, Iosif Banc, Emil Bobu, Ion Coman, Miu Dobrescu, Petre Enache, Gheorghe Stoica, Ilie Verdet

Central Committee. 251 full and 174 alternate members

Last Congress. Twelfth, 19–23 November 1979, in Bucharest; next congress scheduled for 1984. National Conference meets between congresses to review implementation of party decisions. The last conference occurred 16–18 December 1982.

Auxiliary Organizations. Union of Communist Youth (UTC, 3.2 million members), Pantelimon Gavanescu, first secretary, Nicu Ceauşescu, UTC Central Committee secretary; General Confederation of Trade Unions (7 million members), Nicolae Constantin, chairman; National Council of Women, Ana Muresan, chairwoman; Councils of Working People of Co-inhabiting Nationalities

Main State Organs. State Council (27 members), headed by President Nicolae Ceauşescu; Government (Council of Ministers) consists of Prime Minister Constantin Dascalescu, 3 first deputy prime ministers, 5 deputy prime ministers, 27 ministers, and 22 persons with the rank of minister; state and party bodies include National Defense Council and Supreme Council on Socioeconomic Development, both chaired by Nicolae Ceauşescu.

Parliament and Elections. Grand National Assembly has 369 members. All candidates run on the ticket of Front of Socialist Democracy (FSDU). In the last elections (9 March 1980), front candidates received 98.5 percent of the vote.

Publications. *Scinteia,*PCR daily (except Monday); *Era Socialista,* PCR theoretical and political bi-weekly; *Munca de Partid,* PCR monthly for party activities; *Romania Libera,* FSDU daily (except Sunday); *Lumea,* foreign affairs weekly; *Revista Economica,* economic weekly; Agerpress is the official news agency.

Internal Party Affairs. *Ceauşescu's Tarnished Personality Cult.* Despite the regime's myriad recent problems and the PCR's patent inability to deal with them, Nicolae Ceauşescu and his retinue, including as many as 40 family members, appear to be as firmly entrenched as ever in the foremost positions of party and state authority. And yet, during the spring dramatic leadership shake-ups disturbed Ceauşescu's seventeenth year at the helm of the state and the PCR and left significant marks on him. He continued to reign in the same manner as before, but for a variety of reasons (the dire state of the national economy being the essential one), he seemed to have reached an all-time nadir of popularity by the end of the year (*Economist,* London, 23 October). Everyone at home and abroad was aware of his predicament, and he himself began to behave in uncharacteristic ways that merit close scrutiny.

For a casual observer and reader of the official press, everything seemed on the surface to be as calm and conventional as in past years. As described by the *New York Times'* Bucharest correspondent (20 October), "the Rumanian leader's picture still adorns a wall in every office, signs praising him still stand at 500-yard intervals along country roads, and he still permits not a murmur of dissent." Likewise, the birthdays of Elena and Nicolae Ceauşescu were marked with the usual accolades and the seventeenth anniversary of the Ninth PCR Congress (July 1965), the inception of "the Ceauşescu era," was the occasion for new heights of the personality cult.

The facade of unity and Ceauşescu's rather routine practice of cadre rotation, from which his family and entourage had been exempt in the past, were broken in April and May, and again in November, by party purges and government changes of major proportions. The first cleansing operation was related to the so-called transcendental meditation (TM) scandal (see below) that hit top PCR and government leaders. Dismissals of high-level officials in charge of economic matters occurred simultaneously. On 29 April, Aneta Spornic, minister of education and a member of the PCR's Permanent Bureau, was dismissed along with her two deputy ministers. The most intriguing aspect of her disgrace was that she was a close personal friend and political protégée of Elena Ceauşescu's. Spornic was charged with "lack of vigilance" toward the TM sect. Consequently, the secret police were given a free hand to arrest and interrogate, using typically Stalinist methods, a large number of nonconformist intellectuals. On 21 May, a major government reshuffle took place. Ilie Verdet, prime minister since 1979, and Cornel Burtica, minister of foreign trade and international economic cooperation, both resigned. Their dismissals created a sensation because both men were intimates of the Ceauşescu clan and related to him by marriage. (*Le Matin,* Paris, 22 May; *WP,* 22 May, *NYT,* 30 May.) Verdet, regarded as Ceauşescu's number-two man, was immediately replaced by Constantin Dascalescu, a longtime associate of Ceauşescu's. Dascalescu had no previous experience in government, but had supervised the PCR's organizational section for years. In his inaugural speech, Dascalescu stated that his government would instigate inflexible discipline and take firm action against those who infringed the law (*Scinteia,* 22 May).

The scope of the purges and the personalities of those either eliminated or perceived as candidates for elimination particularly struck foreign observers. An article in the *Washington Post* (22 May) speculated on "the beginnings of a breakup of the extended family dynasty that rules Romania." The London *Times* (24 May) argued along the same lines. *Le Matin* was more dramatic and wondered (22 May) where the present purge would stop: "It is no longer even certain that one should talk about a purge. So many people were removed at such levels of responsibility that it is beginning to resemble a gigantic hara-kiri. People in

Bucharest were already talking about the possible ouster of Elena Ceauşescu, the president's wife. And they add: 'When will Nicolae Ceauşescu be ousted?'"

These and similar alarmist views subsided soon thereafter. Elena Ceauşescu kept all her state and party functions, and Ilie Verdet was rehabilitated, appearing as a member of the PCR's Secretariat later in the year. Cornel Burtica, on the other hand, was permanently purged and sent into oblivion, along with Virgil Trofin, former minister of mines (dismissed after the miners' strike in late 1981), whose "suicide" was officially announced on 21 May, the day of Burtica's downfall. Ceauşescu's entourage was replenished by others, and there were promotions for his own family members. The heir apparent, Nicu Ceauşescu, age 30, was globe-trotting in the Far East, only a year after his highly publicized tour of the Western Hemisphere. In December, the young Ceauşescu was elevated to full membership on the PCR Central Committee. Two other Ceauşescus, brother Ilie, an army historian, and probable brother Nicolae A., a police official, were promoted to the rank of lieutenant general in late December.

A ruthless and skillful politician, Ceauşescu himself used the purges as a means to protect himself and to find among government officials scapegoats for his own wrongheaded economic policies. In the words of one Western European envoy, "there is nothing wrong with Ceauşescu, nothing wrong with his policies and everything wrong with some of his subordinates" (quoted in *NYT*, 20 October). The scandals themselves were of little consequence since corruption and obscurantism pervade the regime. However, Ceauşescu's reaction to them, the fates of the designated scapegoats, and the significant role played by the Securitate reflected the general secretary's growing insecurity in the face of seemingly insurmountable difficulties. His two most important speeches of the year, to the June Central Committee plenum and to the National Conference in December, were defensive in tone. During the first eleven months of 1982, he was seldom, as had been his habit, "among the people," making "working visits" to only eighteen counties and Bucharest, far fewer than in past years. His public appearances seemed even more artificial and staged than usual. Occasionally, he looked his 64 years despite the talents of official photographers. Yet the deduction that such behavior signaled the end of the regime was premature. Nicolae Ceauşescu still firmly controls the only three institutions capable of overthrowing him: the PCR apparat, the military, and the police.

Ceauşescu's tarnished cult at home took on an ominous aspect in the Soviet bloc, which apparently no longer takes him seriously. The *New York Times* correspondent in Bucharest reported in a dispatch (20 October) that "the Hungarian Communist Party newspaper has portrayed him as a charlatan who sneers at 'those who want to speak to me of the standard of living, of the supply of food, of the building of roads.'" And one of the hardest winters since World War II did not enhance Ceauşescu's chances of finding greater understanding and better economic cooperation (on which he was counting) in Yuri Andropov's Moscow.

Strengthening of Party Control. Given the severity of the party and government purges in April and May, further personnel changes were anticipated during the second half of the year. Speculation reached its peak during the period between the announcement of the PCR National Conference at the October Central Committee meeting and the close of the conference on 18 December. In October, the conference's first priority was projected to be "the party's role in the building of socialism," a catchword from both the November 1981 and the June 1982 Central Committee plenums, interpreted to portend personnel changes at the highest level (*Scinteia*, 9 October). The general secretary's allusion to "organizational measures" in his opening speech to the conference (16 December) was anticlimactic in this respect, for the only changes announced were normal Central Committee appointments (*Le Monde*, Paris, 18 and 21 December). However, a large number of new, mostly young, and unheralded county first secretaries were named during the year: 14 of 41 such positions, or a 34 percent turnover, unusually high even for Ceauşescu's policy of cadre rotation. Parallel to such rejuvenation of the middle-echelon cadres were recalls of some RCP veterans. Ion Gheorghe Mauer, who has lived quietly in retirement since he left the Prime Ministry in 1974, was publicly lauded and decorated on his eightieth birthday (*Scinteia*, 31 December). Manea Manescu, who retired as prime minister in 1978 for health reasons, also reappeared, being elected a State Council vice-president in November and delivering the major address at the celebrations marking the thirty-fifth anniversary of the establishment of the republic (ibid.). Both men are highly regarded both at home and abroad and their re-emergence has fueled speculation that Ceauşescu plans to use them to bolster his faltering popularity.

A Central Committee plenum on ideology, announced in 1980 but convened only on 1–2 June, called for intensive political education to narrow, and ultimately to eliminate, the gap between the "material reality" of socialist Romania and the lagging emergence of the new Romanian socialist man, an individual consciously devoted to the norms of socialist morality and behavior (ibid., 2 June; *Era Socialista*, 5 June). This oblique reference to the corruption and inefficiency that have recently characterized the regime was coupled with Ceauşescu's distancing of the PCR, and thus himself, from the country's economic crisis. In his typically long but unusually defensive opening speech to the plenum, Ceauşescu defined the dialectical relationship between the PCR's "leading role in society" and the state's "supreme power in society." While the party devised policies, the state had responsibility for implementing them. The policies, as elucidated at the Twelfth PCR Congress (1979), were faultless. Any failures were, therefore, the responsibility of the state, which required reorganization and strengthening (an esoteric reference to the May governmental shake-up). (*Scinteia*, 2 June.) The general secretary also returned to one of his favorite themes, the identification of the PCR with the Romanian nation. He called for the writing of a unique national history that would include description and analysis of the development of the workers' movement, for the merging of the party and state historical institutes, and for the establishment of a single national history museum (ibid.; *Magazin Istoric*, November).

The plenum's decisions and deliberations were reflected in the Second Congress of Political Education and Socialist Culture (24–25 June), a mere shadow of the First Congress (June 1976), which had been the forum for significant pronouncements on cultural matters. The Second Congress reaffirmed the trend of amateurizing culture, attributed to the initiation of Elena Ceauşescu, epitomized by the insipid annual Hymn to Romania festival. (*Era Socialista*, 5 July.)

Organizationally, PCR membership grew at an annual rate of 3.5 percent in 1981, its 3,150,812 members (as of 31 December 1981) comprising more than 20 percent of the adult population. Membership goals for 1981, elaborated at the Central Committee meeting of 31 March, stipulated that new members should include 55–65 percent skilled workers, 15–25 percent peasants, 50 percent women, and 70 percent from UTC ranks. (*Scinteia*, 28 March, 3 April.)

In March, *Munca de Partid* discussed implementation of the decisions taken at the 8 February PEC meeting. "Public instructors" from the Central Committee were to be sent to subordinate party units to infuse new enthusiasm for achieving party goals. County organizations were instructed to send out similar agitprop specialists to the villages in order to stimulate the peasants to produce more food. In a related move, the periodical announced the shifting of control over the Councils of Workers' Control of Economic and Social Activities from trade unions to party units within enterprises. These measures, coupled with the national campaign for intensifying political education at all levels, appear to have been aimed at strengthening the party's vertical control and presence throughout Romanian society and at mobilizing the entire party and population for the campaign to overcome the country's economic crisis.

In 1982, the greatest part of the PCR's activity was devoted to Romania's economy (see below). However, the party advanced few new ideas, only tinkering with the overly ambitious directives of the Twelfth PCR Congress. Its response to the crisis was classically Stalinist: greater sacrifices from the population, austerity, autarky, repression, and deafening propaganda. The analogy with pre–martial law Poland should not tempt the Western observer because Ceauşescu's regime has never and would never allow the formation of autonomous political forces.

Domestic Affairs. *The Economy.* Romania's faltering economy dominated domestic affairs in 1982. Ceauşescu's response to the worsening situation was to retreat further into the rhetoric and the reality of Stalinist autarky. The 1981 plan's targets, discussed at the 8 February PEC meeting and the Central Committee plenum on the following day, were not fulfilled in a number of areas (*Radio Free Europe–Radio Liberty Background Report* [*RFE BR*], 18 March). Particularly painful for the long-suffering Romanian consumer were shortfalls in food and energy production.

The government's response was to reduce demand and increase supply. In late 1981, draconian measures decreed stiff penalties for hoarding more than a month's supply of basic foods and reintroduced rationing (ibid., 30 October 1981). As had been promised, basic food prices were increased by an average 35 percent in February, but the announcement was coupled with modest wage increases for most Romanian workers and with a compensatory increase in child allowances (*Scinteia*, 15 February). The price increases were particularly onerous for urban workers for whom finding food, at any price, was problematic at best.

Imported food prices were increased the most, the cost of coffee, for example, rising 83 percent. By late spring, coffee had all but disappeared, not only from the markets but also from hotels and restaurants. On weekends large numbers of urban dwellers exited the cities to the country, where fresh vegetables, fruit, dairy products, eggs, and even meat were available from peasant entrepreneurs. Curiously, however, few people appeared to be going hungry. The primary impact of recent agricultural failures and the government's feeble attempts to remedy them seemed to have been the undermining of the official market, where lines were long, goods scarce, and quality uneven, to the benefit of the peasant and other unofficial (black, grey, and brown) markets. The most ludicrous aspect of the government's campaign to reduce food consumption was the July publication of allegedly scientific norms of nutrition that seemed to suggest that Romanians ate too much (*Scinteia*, 14 July).

The 1982 plan, promulgated in November 1981, projected significant increases in investments for agriculture (*RFE BR*, 1 February). Among the measures discussed and implemented to increase food supplies during 1982 were greater deliveries of farm machinery, the dispatch of agricultural specialists to the villages, increased territorial self-sufficiency and unit self-management, greater monetary incentives for peasants to meet and surpass quotas and obligatory deliveries to the state, the building-up of breeding herds, increases in the acreage tilled and irrigated, and a more efficient use of available labor. The 1983 plan, adopted on 9 December, promised more of the same, but stipulated more realistic targets and reduced production costs (*FBIS*, 21 December). Typical of the new realism was the 1983 production target of 669,000 MT of soybeans, as opposed to the 1981 plan's targeted 765,000 MT and harvested 268,000 MT and the 1982 plan's targeted 746,000 MT. Cultivation of soybeans requires comparatively large capital outlays, particularly for petrochemicals, and the target reduction reflects the government's more rational exploitation of existing resources in its drive for food self-sufficiency. Early reports indicated an improved 1982 harvest. In his closing speech to the PCR National Conference, Ceauşescu reiterated the party's determination to overcome the food crisis through the dual strategies of reducing consumption and increasing production, adding ironically, "We do not fear that some peasants will become too rich" (ibid.).

The government's approach to energy shortages was similar. In January, power availability during the early morning and evening hours was reduced, public transportation curtailed, and television programming abbreviated. Gasoline prices were increased in April. And, on 30 June, across-the-board increases in energy prices for individual consumers were enacted. Government efforts to reduce energy consumption were not new, the first set of price increases having gone into effect in 1979, but the 1982 round of consumer restraints had an observably palling effect on the already depressing landscape. City streetlights went unlit, homes and public buildings reduced electric bulb wattages to a somber minimum, and large numbers of workers, unable to find an operating bus or tram, trudged home from factories and offices. (The present writer observed this during a visit to Bucharest in May. Correspondents of major Western dailies and weeklies have described in most evocative terms the plight of urban Romanian citizens and the chilly gloom of Romanian cities. See, for example, *NYT*, 20 October; *Economist*, 23 October.) In anticipation of a cold winter, the government cut prices on ready-to-wear clothing in June.

While reducing energy consumption, the Romanian government overlooked few possibilities in its quest for energy self-sufficiency. During 1982, the feasibility of nuclear, wave, solar, wind, thermal, and biomass energy sources was studied (*Era Socialista*, 20 October). Although long-term autarky might depend on these eccentric and expensive sources, discussions of short-term solutions focused on increased hydrocarbon production and hydroelectricity (ibid., 5 July). Toward the end of the year, however, came revelations of grave deficiencies in these sectors that all but negated any possibility of fulfilling the 1982 plan's targets for generation of electricity and production of coal. Planners tried to offset the reductions in oil and gas production of recent years by implementing programs for secondary and tertiary recoveries from existing fields, including one project for "in-situ combustion" partially funded by the World Bank (*RFE BR*, 14 June). As yet, exploration of the Black Sea shelf, grandiloquently announced by President Ceauşescu in 1979, has not yielded significant results. Similiarly, an ambitious nuclear power program with the goal of making Romania self-sufficient in energy by 1990 has already encountered difficulties. In early September, Canada decided to freeze a credit line of $1 billion for buying reactors. The two nuclear reactors that are being built at present near the Black Sea should be ready in 1985 (*NYT*, 12 September). In a febrile search to increase exports and strengthen domestic productivity and consumption, Romania is pushing in various directions, from producing synthetic diamonds and fostering copper mining to growing rice and cotton (*Radio Free Europe Situation Report* [*RFE SR*], 26 October). Some of these programs seem promising in the long run, while others will face difficulties because of investment shortages, managerial insufficiencies, or natural obstacles.

Unlike the 1982 plan's energy production targets, which reflected a realistic analysis of 1981's shortfalls, the 1983 targets are ambitious and, most likely, unachievable (*RFE BR*, 1 February; *FBIS*, 21 December). In that eventuality, the consumer will again be forced to make up the deficit.

Among the most frequently decried economic problems in 1982 was the continuing lack of labor discipline. Even the most uninitiated visitor to Romania was struck by the number of apparently idle workers on construction sites: workers leaning on their tools, passing the time of day in animated conversation, sleeping, daydreaming, or simply watching the world pass by. One official calculated that interruptions in production, leaves, unpaid vacations, and unauthorized absences cost 155,000,000 man-hours of work in 1981 (*Era Socialista*, 20 June). Student help with harvesting proved to be unsatisfactory; Bucharest admitted that the young volunteers had fulfilled only half of their obligations (*RFE SR*, 26 October). *Revista Economica* (July) connected the need for greater discipline with one of the most curious economic proposals made during the course of the year—selling workers their own property. Under the scheme, approved by the PCR Central Committee in October, workers would be offered bonds in the enterprise in which they worked, which, if plan targets were surpassed, could yield up to an 8 percent annual return (*Scinteia*, 12 October). Rather than increase labor discipline, this unusual offering was more likely aimed at reducing workers' disposable income and increasing investment funds.

It was precisely in the field of investment that the specter of economic realism most haunted Ceauşescu's grandiose plans for multilateral (extensive) development. Not only was there an official admission that investments were poorly utilized (*Era Socialista*, 20 June), but the 1983 plan makes it all but impossible to start new projects, a decision underscored by Prime Minister Dascalescu in his speech to the PCR National Conference (*FBIS*, 21 and 22 December). Furthermore, investment priorities have clearly shifted to benefit agriculture, construction, and transportation at the expense of industry, which, however, still retained the lion's share of planned investments for 1983 (*RFE BR*, 1 February, 18 March; *FBIS*, 21 December). Because of the heavy burden of Romania's hard-currency debt (see below), the PEC decided on 9 April not to seek further Western loans for investment purposes (*Scinteia*, 10 April).

The investment decisions present a paradox. Clearly, the goal of multilateral development has been scaled down, the new emphasis being on increasing the productivity of existing enterprises (the adoption of at least some elements of an intensive development strategy). The short-term success of such policies, as the Polish precedent demonstrates, is largely dependent on the utilization of productivity-increasing technologies available primarily in the West. By abjuring Western credits, however, the Romanian government has foreordained the greater exploitation of domestic sources of investment, already set at the highest level in Europe. Despite the leadership's oft-repeated promises to improve the standard of living, such self-reliance coupled with undiminished goals can only further impoverish the population.

The Spring Scandals. In April and May, major personnel changes were made in the Romanian government as the result of two unrelated scandals, one involving the practice of TM by a large number of Bucharest intellectuals, including some mid-level government officials, and the other involving corruption in the Ministry of Foreign Trade and International Economic Cooperation. The fallout from the scandals was significant because presumed members of the Ceauşescu clique were fired from their high government posts (see above).

One of the most intriguing episodes in recent Romanian politics was the TM scandal. According to Western reports, about 250 officials lost their posts for participating in meditation sessions at the Institute for Educational and Psychological Research of the Ministry of Education. Apparently the ministry had tolerated the holding of TM classes for years. Suddenly, in May, the Romanian political police, the dreaded and omnipresent Securitate, denounced the "sect" as a seditious attempt to pull Romania out of the Warsaw pact. Following the Securitate's interrogation of some 1,500 people, the purge was carried out and—as mentioned before—included Aneta Spornic, minister of education, and two of her deputies. The victims were exclusively intellectuals, and the drastic action may be seen in the light of the Ceauşescus' ongoing anti-intellectual campaign or, more precisely, their realization that Romania's intellectuals have been showing signs of critical independence and could, if left alone, turn into the advance guard of an opposition movement (*Economist*, 22 May).

The corruption in the Ministry of Foreign Trade and International Economic Cooperation, which was gradually revealed in the spring and summer of 1982, was probably no worse than the acknowledged corruption in many other government agencies (*Era Socialista*, 20 July). Ceauşescu, however, had sound political reasons for making an object lesson of the ministry. Despite the silence of the official press, virtually everybody in Romania knew about the foreign debt fiasco (see below). PCR policies were obviously the source of Romania's insolvency, yet if the general secretary could shift the blame to corrupt officials within the ministry nominally responsible for accumulating the debt, he could obscure the party's, and thus his own, culpability. Second, because Burtica was widely believed to be Ceauşescu's nephew by marriage, the general secretary could demonstrate that not even his family was invulnerable to his righteous wrath. Burtica was allegedly dismissed for lack of vigilance whereas three other ministry officials were dismissed for either explicit or implicit corruption. Still apparently unsatisfied with the ministry's perform-ance, which was roundly denounced in August, Ceauşescu replaced Nicolae Constantin, Burtica's suc-cessor, with presidential counsellor and Middle East troubleshooter Vasile Pungan in November (*Scinteia*, 19 August; *Le Monde*, 24 November).

Other Domestic Developments. The TM scandal was not the only manifestation of the Ceauşescus' distrust of Romania's intelligentsia (see, for example, *Romania Libera*, 6 December). Early in the year, *Scinteia Tineretului*, the personal organ of Nicu Ceauşescu, began a concerted campaign to disband artists' unions and replace them with a single union of communist artists. Western analysts interpreted the proposal as a continuation of the attack on the "liberal" opponents of the artistic "dogmatic nationalists," led by Ceauşescu sycophant Eugen Barbu. Although the campaign was cut short, it had a sobering effect on the cultural community, already deprived of the material wherewithal for creative expression. (*RFE SR*, 4 May, 22 September.) What was worse, the PCR leadership, both at the June plenum and the echoing Congress of Political Education and Socialist Culture, reiterated its policy of amateurizing the arts and relegating professionals to advisory roles in preparing troops of workers, peasants, soldiers, and students for participation in the Hymn to Romania festival (ibid., 22 July). The content of what little the artist could produce was ever more strictly prescribed within the confines of "Ceauşescu realism" (see *Era Socialista*, 20 June).

Like culture, religion came under concerted attack during 1982. The campaign proceeded on two tacks. First, alarmed by the large number of young people drawn to the solace of the church, the party press urged greater emphasis on the materialist-atheist content of education (ibid., 24 March, 5 April, 5 August). Second, the most militant of the groups of believers, the neo-Protestants, were condemned as politically subversive and criminal (*Scinteia*, 25 April; *Magazin*, Bucharest, 5 June). When asked about the well-documented cases of persecution of believers, government officials and Romanian Orthodox clergy tended to lapse into embarrassed silence or to parrot the excuse that Bible-smugglers and unauthorized evangelists were, after all, criminals. Still the number of neo-Protestants and other religious dissenters seemed to be increasing, especially among Romania's ethnic minorities. (Based on author's interviews and observations, May 1982.)

At the June plenum, Ceauşescu repeated his contention that socialist Romania had solved the "nationality question" (*Scinteia*, 2 June). An official campaign lauding Romania's interethnic harmony reached its peak in early December, just prior to the PCR National Conference and just after the arrest of a number of dissident Hungarian intellectuals in Transylvania (*FBIS*, 24 November, 8 December). Bucharest's heavy-handed treatment of Hungarian dissidents and its shrill assertion of Romanian historical legitimacy in Transylvania continued to poison Romanian-Hungarian relations (*Economist*, 20 November; *Le Monde*, 11 December).

Foreign Affairs. *Foreign Indebtedness.* As in domestic politics, economics dominated Romania's international relations in 1982. Because of bad planning, a criticism readily accepted by Romanian officials and, in part, the source of Ceauşescu's dissatisfaction with the foreign trade bureaucracy, roughly one-third of Romania's $10 billion (minimum) hard-currency debt fell due in 1981 and 1982. The world economic crisis, high interest rates, Poland's financial problems, and irregular oil deliveries exacerbated the problem. In March, as the result of difficult negotiations with 9 of its some 200 Western creditors, Romania urgently requested the rescheduling of 80 percent of its 1982 payments (*Le Monde*, 4 March). Despite the resistance of some banks, such an agreement was concluded in December. However, the accord did not address the 1983 debt, equal to that of the unrescheduled 1982 debt. As a result, Romania followed Brazil's example and on 3 January 1983 announced a moratorium on payment of the $1.4 billion in principal due in 1983 (*NYT*, 4 January 1983). Romania's inability to pay its debts so troubled the International Monetary Fund (IMF) that it suspended Bucharest's right to draw on a $1.5 billion credit line in November 1981. After lengthy negotiations, the IMF released the remaining $1.1 billion, satisfied that Romania was determined to implement strict austerity measures (*RFE SR*, 1 June).

These measures were reflected in Ceauşescu's policy of economic retrenchment (see above) and in his frequently stated determination to decrease imports and increase exports, a policy that yielded an estimated trade surplus of $1.8 billion in 1982 (*Le Monde*, 18 December). Although such surpluses, planned to be even larger in 1983, will enable Romania to improve its current liquidity problems, rescheduling of the 1983 and 1984 payments is essential to re-establishing Romania's international creditworthiness.

Oil Diplomacy. Much of Ceauşescu's personal diplomacy during 1982 might be related to Romania's debt problems. The Romanian petroleum industry, both a drain on hard-currency reserves and a significant earner of hard currency, did not achieve its 1981 plan targets. With domestic production declining, Romania has had to import increasing amounts of expensive Middle Eastern crude, much of which was exported as refined products to hard-currency markets. Still, Romania's developed oil-processing industry operated at only 65 percent of capacity (*RFE SR*, 15 June; *RFE BR*, 16 July).

In 1982, Ceauşescu undertook diplomatic missions in the Middle East and in Southeast Asia, two regions noted for their oil production. In May, he visited Syria, where Romania has joined in oil exploration projects. In June, he traveled to Iraq and Jordan. The joint communiqué issued in Baghdad specifically mentioned increasing cooperation in the oil and petrochemical industries (*Scinteia*, 18 June). A similar determination was articulated in the Amman communiqué (ibid., 20 June). While Romania roundly condemned the Israeli invasion of Lebanon, in July Ceauşescu dispatched his Middle East troubleshooter, Vasile Pungan, in an attempt to mediate the confrontation in Beirut. Although Philip Habib's mission and ultimate success obviated the Pungan mission, the Romanian proposals, which were remarkably similar to those that eventually allowed the Palestine Liberation Organization and the Israelis to withdraw from the city, were appreciated by all the parties involved. Romania's position on the Middle East was well known. It included guarantees of Israel's security within pre-1967 borders, the establishment of a Palestinian state, and the convening of a peace conference comprising all interested parties, including the United States and the Soviet Union. In the past, Ceauşescu's mediation attempts have won Romania a measure of admiration and respect, and his 1982 activities served to bolster his tarnished international reputation. Of more immediate concern, however, stability in the region might provide Romania's oil-processing industry with a reliable source of crude. Capping off Romania's 1982 Middle Eastern diplomacy were visits to Bucharest of Sudanese President Jafar Numayri in August and Egyptian President Hosni Mubarak in September. In the only other oil-related, high-level diplomacy of 1982, Nigerian President Alhaji Shehu Shagari visited Bucharest in September. The final communiqué specifically mentioned the common desire for greater cooperation in oil production and processing (*Lumea* and *Scinteia*, 16 September).

Asia. In late November, President Ceauşescu visited a number of South and Southeast Asian countries: Pakistan, Singapore, Indonesia, and Malaysia, as well as Kuwait. The latter three are oil exporters. Aside from the transparent economic motives for the tour, the subjects of continuing Soviet and Vietnamese occupations of Afghanistan and Kampuchea as well as Romanian mediation of the long-standing Indonesian-Chinese dispute were broached (*RFE BR*, 16 December). Ceauşescu supported the opposition by members of the Association of Southeast Asian Nations to the Vietnamese presence in Kampuchea. Romania is the only Warsaw pact state that does not recognize the puppet Khieu Samphan regime. In addition, in August Ceauşescu played host to Prince Norodom Sihanouk in a publicly muted visit. Ceauşescu's support for the anti-Vietnamese Sihanouk coalition, voiced during his visit to China (see below) and during his Southeast Asian tour and made manifest during the prince's visit, served to re-establish somewhat the credibility of Romania's autonomy within the Soviet bloc.

The Balkans. The year saw intensive Romanian diplomatic activity in the Balkans. President Ceauşescu visited Greece in May, and Prime Minister Andreas Papandreou returned the visit in November. Ceauşescu met twice with Yugoslav state and party officials: in February in Timisoara and in October in Belgrade. In April, Turkish head of state Gen. Kenan Evren was Ceauşescu's guest in Bucharest. As is their habit, Nicolae Ceauşescu and Todor Zhivkov exchanged visits in 1982. While greater economic cooperation was the keystone of all four sets of talks, two strictly regional political themes recurred. First was Romania's support for Zhivkov's 1981 call for the establishment of a Balkan nuclear-free zone, a suggestion seconded by Greece's leftist government but unappreciated by Turkey. Second was Ceauşescu's call for a Balkan summit meeting to discuss all outstanding issues. The depth of the Cyprus and Macedonian disputes apparently thwarted acceptance of this proposal.

France. Romania's relations with the West reached a nadir during 1982. For many years the West was willing to overlook Romania's poor human rights record because of its compensating foreign policy autonomy and impressive economic growth rate. During the period of Soviet-U.S. détente, Moscow was persuaded to tolerate Romania's budding political and economic cooperation with the West, including particularly close relations with Gaullist France and Nixonian America. Romanian-French and Romanian-U.S. relations deteriorated precipitously in 1982 in part because of the West's delayed realization that international autonomy would not lead to domestic liberalization, in part because of specific Romanian policies.

The traditional Franco-Romanian political affinity was severely tested by intrigue and economic disillusionment in 1982. In May, Virgil Tanase, an émigré critic of the Ceauşescus, was apparently kidnapped on a Paris street. It was rumored the the Securitate had abducted him (*Le Figaro*, 24 May). President François Mitterrand lent credence to the theory by strongly implying the probable involvement of the Securitate and by canceling a state visit to Romania scheduled for September. However, on 31 August Tanase made a spectacular reappearance in Paris in the company of a certain Matei Haiducu, an alleged Securitate operative who had balked when given orders to eliminate Tanase and fellow émigré Paul Goma. With the aid of French counterintelligence and the connivance of President Mitterrand, the fake kidnapping had been staged in order to allow the defecting Haiducu to return to Romania to bring out his family and sensitive documents on East bloc intelligence operations. (*NYT*, 1 September.) The Romanian government, pilloried in the French press, denied any knowledge of the affair. Romania's public image in France was already the object of stinging ridicule, journalists transforming Bucharest into "Ubu-carest" and de-nominating Ceauşescu as "a Danubian Bokassa" (*Le Matin*, Paris, 4 September). Bilateral economic relations complicated by French banks' concerns over Romanian illiquidity, fared little better. A dispute between the French and Romanian partners in the Oltcit automobile joint venture was particularly acrimonious. French Foreign Trade Minister Michel Jobert's July visit to Bucharest solved few, if any, of the bilateral economic problems (*RFE BR*, 2 September).

United States. Romania's relations with the United States suffered setbacks generated by economic problems and human rights concerns. Early in the year, Romania was in technical default on a number of loans made by U.S. institutions. President Reagan responded by refusing to extend the Commodity Credit Corporation credit line a further $66 million. By June, the Export-Import Bank had honored more than $8 million in guarantees on unpaid Romanian loans. (Ibid., 25 March, 22 July.) These problems of liquidity were complicated by Washington's charge that Romania was "dumping" steel on the U.S. market and by a substantial Romanian surplus in bilateral trade, which had been achieved at the expense of U.S. exports. Human rights issues dominated the annual process of renewing the waivers for Romania's most-favored-nation (MFN) status. In a letter to Congress urging a one-year extension, President Reagan decried recent declines in the rate of Jewish emigration and warned that the following year's MFN status would be imperiled by further Romanian foot-dragging. At the same time, 51 senators warned President Ceauşescu that U.S. lawmakers were interested not only in Jewish emigration but also in bureaucratic impediments to family reunions, the alleged persecution of Christians, and the cultural deprivation of Hungarians. A Grand National Assembly delegation, Foreign Minister Andrei, Chief Rabbi Moses Rosen, and newly appointed Romanian Ambassador Mircea Malita were dispatched to assuage the legislators' concerns. (Ibid., 15 June, 22 July, 22 September.) Despite the introduction of disapproval resolutions in both houses of Congress, the MFN extension went into effect on 1 September. The United States, however, remained unconvinced of Romania's good intentions. The head of the U.S. delegation to the Madrid Conference on Security and Cooperation in Europe and the assistant secretary of state for human rights visited Bucharest in September and October and returned deeply troubled by the state of human rights in Romania (ibid., 26 October). The atmosphere was clouded still further by a decree published on 6 November requiring emigrants to pay, in hard currency, for their education before they could be issued exit visas (*Scinteia*, 6 November). The State Department's angry response threatening to end MFN was followed by a warning from President Reagan to President Ceauşescu. The rapid deterioration of Romanian-U.S. relations late in 1982 was coupled with the unexplained retirement of Romania's foremost American specialist, former ambassador Corneliu Bogdan, and the prolonged absence of Ambassador Malita from his post in Washington (*NYT*, 28 December).

Other Western States. The new restrictions on emigration also had unsettling effects on Romania's relations with the Federal Republic of Germany, which welcomes an annual immigration of 12,000 Romanian Germans, many of whom are well educated. As of late 1982, it remained unclear whether Ceauşescu intended to implement the "education tax" vigorously or to use the law as a bargaining chip in his ongoing financial negotiations with the West.

Romania's 1982 official contacts with the noncommunist world represent a significant decline, in both the level and number of contacts, compared with those of recent years. Except for Secretary of State Alexander Haig's February visit and the Canadian governor-general's May visit, no high-ranking Western statesmen traveled to Bucharest to confer with the embattled regime. Among the Third World's recognized leaders, only Pakistan's Mohammad Zia ul Haq and Guinea's Ahmed Sékou Touré paid court in Bucharest. U.N. Secretary General Javier Pérez de Cuellar arrived for a brief stay in July, expressing his appreciation for Romania's active support for and participation in the activities of the world organization. He noted the impact of the petition signed by fifteen million persons supporting Romania's position at the General Assembly's special session on disarmament. (*RFE SR*, 2 September.) The decline in official exchanges at high levels might be explained as indicative of Ceauşescu's preoccupation with the economic crisis. A more likely explanation is that the world no longer perceives Nicolae Ceauşescu and his repressive regime as desirable partners in the largely symbolic and legitimizing exercise of summit diplomacy.

Poland. When martial law was declared in Poland, the sigh of relief in Bucharest was almost audible. Orthodoxy would be reimposed, avoiding regional contagion by Poland's creeping democracy, and it would be reimposed by national, not external (Soviet), forces of order. During Secretary Haig's February visit to Bucharest, Ceauşescu and his guest did not agree on much of anything concerning Poland except that an early end to martial law was desirable. Ceauşescu was especially critical of the West's economic sanctions against the Jaruzelski regime, which, he stated, would only make a bad situation worse (ibid., 25 March). On 23 February, Ceauşescu received Polish Politburo member and Foreign Minister Józef Czyrek, who informed the PCR general secretary about the situation in Poland. Ceauşescu reiterated his party's support for the Polish party's position and urged that steps be taken for national reconciliation (*Scinteia*, 23 February). On 4 June, Gen. Wojciech Jaruzelski paid a twelve-hour visit to Bucharest, the *last* stop in a tour of bloc capitals. That Ceauşescu retained some doubts about the Soviet role in the imposition of martial law was manifest in the content of his public statements. The general secretary reiterated the PCR's well-known principles of interparty relations, foremost among which was noninterference in other parties' internal affairs. General Jaruzelski, on the other hand, seemed to go out of his way to annoy his host by repeating disliked Soviet formulas implying the primacy of the Soviet party (*Lumea*, 10 June; *RFE SR*, 15 June). Later in the year, the sorry state of Romanian-Polish economic relations was discussed in Warsaw. Both sides pledged to overcome recent "difficulties" (*RFE SR*, 16 September).

Soviet Bloc and USSR. Aside from the previously mentioned exchanges of visits with Bulgarian and Yugoslav party leaders, the only other important contacts with Soviet bloc officials were at the prime ministerial and politburo level: the visits of Hungarian Prime Minister György Lázár (July); East German Prime Minister Willi Stoph (November); and Vasil Bil'ák, Czechoslovak Secretariat and Politburo member (April).

Contacts with the Soviet government and the Soviet party were at a ministerial and Central Committee level before the death of Leonid Brezhnev in November. The announcement of Brezhnev's death in the Romanian media was restrained but respectful (see *Scinteia*, 12 November). Brezhnev was remembered in Romania as the author of the doctrine of "limited sovereignty" and as the first secretary of the Moldavian party during the early 1950s when hundreds of thousands of Bessarabians were expelled from their homeland and sent to Central Asia and Siberia. Ceaușescu led the PCR and state delegation to the funeral and used the occasion to meet with Chinese Foreign Minister Huang Hua, President Hafiz al-Asad of Syria, and Sri Lanka's foreign minister. He returned to Moscow in December to participate in the celebrations marking the sixtieth anniversary of the USSR, and he hosted a high-ranking Warsaw pact military delegation earlier in the month.

The succession of Yuri Andropov might not bode well for the Ceaușescu regime. Andropov, who served in the Central Committee Department for Liaison with Ruling Communist Parties before he became chief of the Soviet secret police is not known as a friend of East European autonomy. He is known to have close personal relations with János Kádár, who is not among Ceaușescu's friends. Still, initial contacts have been correct. (*RFE SR*, 8 December.)

China and North Korea. One of the manifestations of PCR autonomy that Andropov may not appreciate is Ceaușescu's continued cultivation of good relations with China. In April, Ceaușescu paid his third state visit to China. Previous visits were in 1971 and 1978. Ceaușescu was received grandly everywhere he went, both hosts and guest stressing the symbolic importance of the trip more than its substantive results. (Ibid., 20 April.) The PCR's and the Chinese Communist Party's positions on party autonomy and Romania's and China's views on international affairs are mutually reinforcing, and both sides emphasized these compatibilities.

From China, Ceaușescu traveled to North Korea, whose political system bears a striking resemblance to that of Romania. If anything, Kim Il-song's personality cult is even more extravagant and his dynastic succession even more assured than Ceaușescu's. Kim's concept of *chuch'e* is similar to Ceaușescu's nationalist political doctrines. The two leaders outdid each other in exchanges of admiration and respect in "a visit of superlatives." (Ibid., 4 May.)

International Party Contacts. Another aspect of the PCR's autonomy that has annoyed Moscow is its cultivation of relations with the Eurocommunist parties. In the dispute between the Soviet and the Italian parties over the Polish crisis, the PCR remained cautiously neutral (ibid., 11 February). Twice during 1982, Ceaușescu received Giancarlo Pajetta, the Italian party's spokesman on international affairs. Ceaușescu also twice received another of the Soviet party's most outspoken Eurocommunist critics, Santiago Carrillo. When Gerardo Iglesias replaced Carrillo as leader of the Spanish party in November, Ceaușescu sent him a warm message of congratulations expressing the PCR's desire for continued close contacts (*FBIS*, 10 November).

The PCR's contacts with other communist parties also saw a marked decline in number and importance during 1982. No French party official of consequence, for example, came to Bucharest, nor did any Cuban dignitary. Preoccupied with Romania's economy and with a wary eye on the succession process in the Soviet Union, General Secretary Nicolae Ceaușescu was not a major player in international communist affairs in 1982.

University of Nebraska at Omaha   Walter M. Bacon, Jr.

Union of Soviet Socialist Republics

The Communist Party of the Soviet Union (CPSU) traces its origins to the founding of the Russian Social Democratic Labor Party in 1898. In March 1919, after the seizure of power, the party was renamed the All-Russian Communist Party (Bolsheviks). When Union of Soviet Socialist Republics was adopted as the name of the country in 1924, the party's designation was changed to All-Union Communist Party (Bolsheviks). The present name was adopted in 1952. The CPSU is the only legal political party in the USSR. As such, it has been assured of a fairly steady growth in membership, rising from 79,000 in April 1917 to nearly 18 million in 1982. The number of party organizations has risen by 87,000 in the past fifteen years. There are now 414,000 primary and 457,000 shop-floor party organizations and more than 618,000 party groups (*Voprosi istorii KPSS*, February; Tass, 23 February).

Population. 269 million (1 January 1982)

Party. Communist Party of the Soviet Union (Kommunisticheskaia Partiia Sovetskogo Souizu; CPSU)

Founded. 1898 (CPSU, 1952)

Membership. 17.8 million (January 1982); workers, 42 percent; peasants, 12.8 percent; remainder consists of white-collar workers, professional personnel, and members of the armed forces. Some 60 percent are Great Russians.

General Secretary. Yuri V. Andropov

Politburo. 12 full members: Yuri V. Andropov, Geidar A. Aliev (first deputy chairman, Council of Ministers), Konstantin U. Chernenko, Mikhail S. Gorbachev, Viktor V. Grishin (first secretary, Moscow city party committee), Andrei A. Gromyko (foreign minister), Dinmukhamed A. Kunaev (first secretary, Kazakh Central Committee), Arvid I. Pelshe (chairman, Party Control Committee), Grigori V. Romanov (first secretary, Lenigrad *oblast* party committee), Vladimir V. Shcherbitsky (first secretary, Ukrainian Central Committee), Nikolai A. Tikhonov (chairman, Council of Ministers), Dimitri F. Ustinov (defense minister); 8 candidate members: Piotr N. Demichev (minister of culture), Vladimir I. Dolgikh, Tikhon Y. Kiselev (first secretary, Belorussian Central Committee), Vasili V. Kuznetsov (first deputy chairman, Presidium of the USSR Supreme Soviet), Boris N. Ponomarev, Sharaf R. Rashidov (first secretary, Uzbek Central Committee), Eduard A. Shevardnadze (first secretary, Georgian Central Committee), Mikhail S. Solomentsev (chairman, RSFSR Council of Ministers)

Secretariat. 9 members: Yuri Andropov (general secretary), Konstantin Chernenko (organizational affairs), Mikhail Gorbachev (agriculture), Boris Ponomarev (international affairs), Vladimir Dolgikh (economy), Ivan V. Kapitonov (cadres), Konstantin V. Rusakov (ruling communist parties), Mikhail V. Zimianin (culture), Nikolai I. Ryzhkov (heavy industry)

Central Committee. 319 full and 151 candidate members

Last Congress. Twenty-Sixth, 23 February–4 March 1981, in Moscow; next congress scheduled for 1986

Auxiliary Organizations. Communist Youth League (Kommunisticheskii Soyuz Molodezhi; Komsomol); 417 million members (claimed), led by Viktor M. Mishin; All-Union Central Council of Trade Unions (AUCCTU; 130 million members), led by Stepan A. Shalayev; Voluntary Society for the

Promotion of the Army, Air Force, and Navy, (about 65 million members); Union of Soviet Societies for Friendship and Cultural Relations with Foreign Countries

Main State Organs. The central government consists of the Council of Ministers, numbering about 115 members. Membership includes the chairman (prime minister), a first deputy chairman, thirteen deputy chairmen, the prime ministers of the republics (who are ex officio members), some ninety ministers, and the heads of important committees and commissions. The Council has a Presidium, which serves as a nominal "cabinet" and meets weekly. The Presidium members include the chairman, first deputy chairman, and the deputy chairmen. The Presidium serves as a coordinating committee for governmental activities but has little policymaking authority. The most powerful heads of ministries and agencies—the minister of defense, the minister of foreign affairs, and the chairman of the Committee for State Security (KGB)—are not included in its membership. Contrary to previous practice, Ivan V. Arkhipov, the first deputy chairman who was appointed in October 1980, was not elected to full or candidate membership on the CPSU Politburo.

Parliamentary Representation and Elections. The USSR Supreme Soviet serves as the country's nominal legislature. It meets twice each year for a few days to rubber-stamp important legislation and to provide an audience for speeches by political leaders. The All-Union Supreme Soviet is divided into two chambers, the Council of the Union, which represents the population via single-member constituencies, and the Council of Nationalities, which represents political subdivisions; each chamber has 750 members. Between the Supreme Soviet's semiannual meetings, a Presidium of 39 members has authority to issue decrees in the name of the broader body. In the last elections for the USSR Supreme Soviet (4 March 1979), 71.7 percent of the candidates elected were members of the CPSU.

Publications. Main CPSU organs are the daily newspaper *Pravda* (circulation more than 11 million), the theoretical and ideological journal *Kommunist* (appearing 18 times a year, with a circulation over 1 million), and the semimonthly *Partiinaia zhizn*, a journal of internal party affairs and organizational matters (circulation more than 1.16 million). *Kommunist vooruzhennikh sil* is the party theoretical journal for the armed forces, and *Agitator* is the same for party propagandists; both appear twice a month. The Komsomol has a newspaper, *Komsomolskaia pravda* (6 days a week); a monthly theoretical journal, *Molodoi kommunist*; and a monthly literary journal, *Molodaia gvardia*. Each USSR republic prints similar party newspapers in local languages and usually also in Russian. Specialized publications issued under supervision of the CPSU Central Committee include the newspapers *Sovetskaia rossiia*, *Selskaia zhizn*, *Sotzialisticheskaia industria*, *Sovetskaia kultura*, and *Ekonomicheskaia gazeta* and the journal *Politicheskoye samoobrazovaniie*. Tass is the official news agency.

Party Internal Affairs. The Brezhnev era ended on 10 November with the death of the 75-year-old Soviet leader, three days after his last public appearance at the sixty-fifth anniversary of the Bolshevik Revolution. Two other senior members of the Kremlin hierarchy, Mikhail Suslov and Andrei Kirilenko, also passed from the scene; Suslov, the 79-year-old party ideological secretary, died in January, and Kirilenko, the 76-year-old party organizational secretary, resigned in November after a long period of declining health. The selection of Yuri Andropov as the new general secretary pointed toward a more vigorous Soviet stance in both domestic and world affairs. The former KGB head was expected to move drastically against internal corruption and to accelerate the upper-level leadership transition that was under way prior to Brezhnev's death.

Between January and November, the political scene featured jockeying for position in the impending succession and hesitant attempts to cope with an array of old and new problems. The death of Suslov in January not only created a major vacuum in the leadership, it triggered a period of instability and uncertainty for the hierarchy, compounded by fresh evidence of General Secretary Brezhnev's physical decline. The elevation of Andropov to Suslov's post in the Secretariat at the May Central Committee plenum appeared to signal a new constellation of power in the Kremlin. This and other events also raised questions about the continued viability of the "stability of cadres" approach and relative "depoliticization" of the Brezhnev years. Awareness of serious problems in the party's contacts with the masses was apparent at trade union and Komsomol congresses, and the May Central Committee plenum was devoted mainly to the deepening crisis in agriculture. The party continued to temporize when faced with the prospect of fundamental reforms, but there were indications of an emerging consensus pointing toward stricter discipline as the preferred solution for many of the society's ills. This impression seemed to be confirmed by the selection of Andropov as general secretary and the new leader's early actions. Meanwhile, on the ideological front, party spokesmen vigorously reaffirmed during the year the "leading role" of the party, the exclusive validity of the Soviet model of social and economic development, and the party's approach to the integration of nationalities.

The Leadership. Mikhail Suslov, the party's chief ideologist and reputed "kingmaker," died on 25 January, after 35 years as a member of the Secretariat (*Pravda*, 27 January). His funeral in Red Square, much publicized by the Soviet media, featured an emotional eulogy by Brezhnev (ibid., 30 January). Given Suslov's position as the de facto number-two man in the Soviet system, his passing necessarily created an enormous void in the Kremlin hierarchy. Perhaps the principal bulwark of the political stability of the party during the Brezhnev years, Suslov was noted as the chief enforcer of the system's "depoliticization," the remarkable reduction of overt conflict over issues and personalities that had characterized the party's operations for at least a decade. The consequences of the loss of Suslov's steadying influence quickly became apparent.

A resurgence of intraparty tensions was linked to the surfacing of the issue of corruption. This issue touched a cornerstone of Brezhnev's leadership, for the apparent rise in official corruption was partially a by-product of the stability of cadres policy and the unprecedented security of upper- and mid-level cadres since 1964. Even more explosive was the personal connection of Brezhnev with participants in a case that assumed the proportions of a major scandal in the aftermath of Suslov's death.

Semyon K. Tsvigun, 64, first deputy head of the KGB and a longtime Brezhnev associate (reportedly also his brother-in-law), died on 19 January, according to an official announcement following a lengthy illness (ibid., 21 January). However, Tsvigun had been actively engaged in a major investigation for several months; reports circulated in Moscow that he had committed suicide. According to these reports, Tsvigun's investigation of a diamond-smuggling case had led to Boris "the Gypsy" Buriatov, a close friend of Brezhnev's daughter, Galina Churbanova; Suslov had violently upbraided Tsvigun for embarrassing Brezhnev and the top leadership and had told the KGB official, "You have nothing left but to shoot yourself." Another version circulating in the Moscow rumor mill had Tsvigun attempting to suppress the investigation to protect the Brezhnev family and friends. Amid the buzz of conflicting rumors, several facts stood out. First, Tsvigun was not accorded the honors normally due one of his eminence in the hierarchy; he had clearly lost the favor of the top leadership. Second, the KGB had taken over the investigation from the regular police in the Ministry of Internal Affairs (MVD), whose first deputy head is Lt. Gen. Yuri M. Churbanov, Galina Brezhnev's husband. Third, there was a delay in prosecution of the case, but events moved rapidly after Suslov's death; Buriatov was arrested on 29 January, and another principal in the case, Anatoly A. Molevatov, head of the Soviet circus organization and a deputy minister of culture, was taken into custody on 17 February, along with a $1.4 million hoard of diamonds and foreign currency (*NYT*, 2 March; *Los Angeles Times*, 26 February, 2 March). Subsequently, another deputy minister of culture, Nikolai I. Mokhov, was forced to retire because of his alleged connection with the case, which had involved the extortion of bribes from circus performers in exchange for permission to travel abroad (*Los Angeles Times*, 11 March).

The Soviet media maintained silence about the scandal, but Western radio broadcasts giving full details of it were not jammed by the Soviets, a most unusual development. When added to the close scrutiny given Brezhnev's emotional performance at the Suslov rites by Soviet television and similar coverage of his tearful breakdown at the funeral of another close friend, it appeared to some Western observers that a faction in the Kremlin, suddenly freed from the restraints of Suslov, was out to undercut Brezhnev's image. This view was lent added credibility by the belated uncovering of one of the most bizarre episodes in the history of the Soviet press.

The December 1981 issue of the literary journal *Avrora*, published in Leningrad, had been entirely dedicated to the celebration of Brezhnev's seventy-fifth birthday. On page 75 of the issue, a 300-word article by Viktor Golavkin entitled "Jubilee" lampooned an aged "exalted writer" who refused to retire or to "believe that he will die" (UPI, 3 March). The parody seemed clearly aimed at Brezhnev, and in late February, copies of the issue began disappearing from libraries in Leningrad and Moscow (*NYT*, 5 March). Reportedly, the editor of *Avrora* was fired, but the appearance of such a story offered strong evidence supporting the view that Brezhnev was losing his grip.

For a time, the chief beneficiary of the newly unstable political situation appeared to be party secretary Konstantin Chernenko, Brezhnev's longtime right-hand man. Chernenko was accorded precedence over all Politburo members except Brezhnev and Tikhonov at Suslov's funeral and, in the following month, was dispatched to Paris to represent the CPSU at the congress of the French Communist Party. In March, he was the most visible political figure at the Trade Union Congress and seemed to be in charge of the conclave's proceedings.

On the eve of the Trade Union Congress, another important step in leadership transition was announced. Aleksei I. Shibayev, 67, head of the trade union organization since 1976, was fired (*WP*, 6 March). His dismissal came as a surprise, particularly in view of his publication three days earlier of an article on union plans in the Central Committee journal for party propagandists (*Agitator*, 2 March). Chernenko was reported to have attended the trade union council meeting at which Shibayev was ousted (AP, 5 March). Shibayev's successor was Stepan A. Shalayev, minister of pulp-, paper-, and wood-processing industries, who had formerly served for several years as a trade union official.

Shibayev's departure fueled speculation about the Kremlin power puzzle. Initially, most Western observers saw it as a setback for Brezhnev; Shibayev had been a firm ally of Brezhnev during the latter's rise to political dominance, especially during the 1960s and 1970s when Shibayev served as Saratov *oblast* first secretary. However, Shibayev had started up the political ladder as a factory manager in Suslov's bailiwick of Rostov and presumably was originally a protégé of the top party ideologue. But the change in trade union leadership was apparently orchestrated by Chernenko, suggesting implications much broader than factional considerations. There was apparently general dissatisfaction with the work of the unions; Brezhnev himself had sharply criticized trade union personnel at the Twenty-Sixth CPSU Congress. The rise of Solidarity in Poland had given some urgency to the task of refurbishing the trade unions' image.

These concerns were reflected in the proceedings of the Seventeenth Congress of Soviet Trade Unions, held in Moscow 16–20 March. In a speech to the congress, Brezhnev urged union officials to "spend more time among the people and less time amid paperwork" (*Pravda*, 17 March). While the party leadership was clearly displeased with the trade unions' performance, no fundamental reforms were envisaged; rather, the session pointed toward the more effective performance by the unions of their role as "transmission belts" for the party. New AUCCTU head Shalayev said that the CPSU leadership is the "source of strength of the trade unions" (ibid., 18 March). The CPSU Central Committee's message to the congress declared that the party highly valued the trade unions "as a reliable support for itself among the masses" (*Izvestiia*, 17 March). The main resolution of the congress concluded that "the main direction of the work of the country's trade unions is to ensure a further upsurge in the political and labor activity of the Soviet people and mobilize their efforts" for fulfillment of the five-year plan (*Pravda*, 21 March).

By the time of Shibayev's dismissal, the atmosphere of political tension in Moscow had become quite obvious. Evidently as a display of solidarity to dispel rumors about infighting among the hierarchs, the leadership staged an unusual public appearance. On 3 March, ten senior officials, including all but three full Politburo members resident in Moscow, attended the play *Thus We Shall Triumph* by Mikhail Shatrov (ibid., 4 March); again, Chernenko was prominently displayed, sitting beside Brezhnev in the leader's box. If the outing was designed to quell doubts about the leadership's unity, it evidently only led to more questions. Two of the missing Politburo members had attended the play earlier in the week; the notable absentee was Andrei Kirilenko. The party organizational secretary had apparently been eclipsed by the rising star of Chernenko. Now he was rumored to have completely fallen from favor or to have suffered an incapacitating illness. In the following months, Kirilenko's lengthy absences from public view and his failure to sign routine Politburo messages intensified this speculation.

Of more interest was the content of the play, which dealt with Lenin's physical decline in 1922–1923 and the intraparty political struggles of that time, a situation perhaps analogous to that of the CPSU in 1982. Lenin was depicted as concerned about the isolation of the party from the masses and the need to "rein in" the general secretary, Stalin. Reportedly, the play's premiere had been delayed for a year due to Suslov's objections to its content (*NYT*, 5 March).

Although Brezhnev's feebleness was evident in his public appearances during February and March, he pursued an arduous round of activities. But a flying visit to Uzbekistan in late March brought the question of his durability dramatically to the fore. Brezhnev made a lengthy speech in Tashkent before a joint session of the Uzbek Central Committee and Supreme Soviet dealing with Uzbekistan's economic development and various international issues and met with leaders of the Uzbek party a day later (*Pravda*, 25 and 26 March). But Brezhnev became ill, either in Tashkent or on the return flight, and was taken from the plane in Moscow to a waiting ambulance. There were unconfirmed reports that Brezhnev had suffered a stroke and had been hospitalized. The authorities obliquely acknowledged Brezhnev's disability with a one-month postponement of a Central Committee plenum scheduled for April. The general secretary was not seen in public for 27 days; he reappeared for the Lenin anniversary celebration on 22 April.

The keynote speech at the Lenin birthday fete in the Kremlin Hall of Congresses was delivered by Yuri Andropov. The KGB chief attacked Western ideas of pluralist democracy, contending that "true democracy" could be found only in a socialist system that guaranteed the workers' interests. Andropov denied that the CPSU sought to impose its model on other parties but maintained that "real existing socialism" had proved its superiority. However, Andropov implicitly conceded that Soviet-style socialism depended on coercion for its cohesion, warning that the struggle against various forms of "defects," or ideological deviations, whether domestic in origin or "inspired from abroad," would continue. Turning to international affairs, Andropov accused the United States of pushing the world toward war and slandering the Soviet Union. American belligerence was contrasted with the USSR's firm commitment to "peace"; Andropov affirmed that there was no alternative to peaceful coexistence (ibid., 23 April).

Kirilenko reappeared in public for the May Day celebration and, in the following week, was the main speaker at the commemoration of Victory Day (ibid., 10 May). However, he continued to be overshadowed by Chernenko, who took precedence over him in the 1 May lineup of the hierarchs on the Mausoleum in Red Square, repeating a similar downgrading of Kirilenko at Suslov's funeral in January. Many Western analysts speculated that Chernenko was being positioned to succeed Suslov, with Brezhnev's support.

However, when the Central Committee met on 24 May, Andropov returned to the Central Committee Secretariat, which he had left in 1967 to assume the chairmanship of the KGB (ibid., 25 May). Two days later, his resignation as KGB chief was announced (*NYT*, 27 May). Andropov took over Suslov's responsibilities for the ideological apparatus and apparently also assumed the supervisory tasks in foreign affairs that Suslov had long performed.

Andropov was generally believed to have sought the Secretariat position as a means of furthering his chances to succeed Brezhnev. Indeed, following the plenum, most Western observers concluded that Andropov had overtaken Chernenko in the succession sweepstakes. If Brezhnev had favored Chernenko as Suslov's successor, then the May plenum represented a major setback for the party leader. Further, in filling the KGB post, the political leadership departed from long-standing practice. Since 1958, the security police had been headed by civilian party figures. Now the KGB was turned over to a career police official, Vitali V. Fedorchuk, 64, head of the Ukrainian KGB since 1970 (AP, 27 April). A hard-line ideologue and ruthless suppressor of dissent, Fedorchuk had no known close connections with Brezhnev or his inner circle. Some observers viewed selection of a career official as a way of neutralizing the KGB in succession politics; presumably, a little-known figure such as Fedorchuk would be unable to maximize police influence in any power struggle. In any case, it was highly unusual that Fedorchuk was advanced over the heads of several more senior KGB officials, including longtime Brezhnev associate Georgi Tsinev, named first deputy head of the security police earlier in the year.

Another significant promotion was announced at the May plenum. Vladimir I. Dolgikh, 57, Central Committee secretary for heavy industry since 1972, was elected a candidate member of the Politburo (*Pravda*, 25 April). Dolgikh's elevation represented something of a break in the stifling personnel immobility associated with the stability of cadres policy. Long regarded as a potential future candidate for prime minister, Dolgikh had in recent years exercised wide authority in energy matters. His projected role after the May plenum seemed to be general direction of industry, for years part of the varied responsibilities assigned to the fading Kirilenko.

Whatever the conflicts simmering behind the scenes, the Politburo had apparently forged a de facto "collective leadership" for the political transition already in progress and was able to present at least a facade of harmony. Brezhnev was reportedly unable to work more than two hours each day, and the real direction of affairs on other than the most basic policy questions had apparently passed to other hands. Following the May plenum, Chernenko and Andropov appeared to have worked out a division of labor for joint supervision of the party organization. They frequently appeared together in public and expressed similar views on issues. Two other Central Committee secretaries with Politburo rank, Gorbachev, in charge of agriculture, and Dolgikh, the industrial overseer, rounded out the emerging collective leadership of the party apparat that had evolved to meet the disruptions produced by Suslov's death, Brezhnev's incapacity, and Kirilenko's decline, which was perhaps as much political as physical.

When pictures of the full Politburo members were set up in downtown Moscow as part of the preparations for celebration of the anniversary of the Bolshevik Revolution, Kirilenko's portrait was missing (*WP*, 5 November). Both Kirilenko and Party Control Committee chairman Arvid I. Pelshe were absent from the anniversary rituals, promoting speculation that both had been dropped from the Politburo ranks. However, Pelshe attended the late November session of the Supreme Soviet, his first public appearance in more than five months (AP, 23 November).

Party leader Brezhnev presided over the anniversary activities in Red Square and the Kremlin. Three days later, he died of heart failure; the public announcement came 26 hours after his death (Tass, 11 November; *Pravda,* 12 November). The Central Committee held an emergency meeting on 12 November and unanimously elected Yuri V. Andropov as Brezhnev's successor in the post of general secretary (*Pravda,* 13 November).

Andropov moved quickly to assert his leadership and gave promise of restoring some degree of vigor and momentum to the Soviet system, lately plagued under gerontocratic rule by stagnation in many areas. In contrast to previous successions, there was little talk of collective leadership, indicating that Andropov had rapidly established his hegemony. However, his accession to power had evidently depended heavily on military support and the depth of his backing at the party's grass roots was questionable. Central Committee and Supreme Soviet sessions in late November left key positions unfilled, and it was clear that Andropov had not consolidated his hold on power to the extent earlier assumed by Western observers.

When the Central Committee met on 22 November, the retirement of Kirilenko was announced and Azerbaijan Communist Party first secretary Geidar A. Aliev was promoted from candidate to full membership on the Politburo. Nikolai I. Ryzhkov (b. 1929), first deputy head of Gosplan (the central economic-planning agency) was named a secretary of the Central Committee (ibid., 23 November). Andropov was expected by most observers to add the head of state portfolio to his party leadership, especially after he was named to the Supreme Soviet Presidium on the first day of the nominal parliament's November meeting; two other potential nominees for the post, Chernenko and Foreign Minister Gromyko, were not elected to the Presidium (*NYT*, 24 November). However, the Supreme Soviet postponed a decision on the question of the presidency and the 81-year-old deputy chairman of the Presidium, Vasili V. Kuznetsov, continued to serve as acting head of state. The Supreme Soviet took one major personnel action, electing new Politburo member Aliev as first deputy chairman of the USSR Council of Ministers (*Izvestiia,* 25 November). When the Supreme Soviet met in December to celebrate the sixtieth anniversary of the USSR, the vacancy in the presidency was again ignored (*NYT*, 22 December). Although the configuration of the upper leadership remained somewhat unsettled at year's end, the winds of change had already begun to sweep the Soviet bureaucracy. In late November, the minister of railways and the minister of rural construction were both fired after their ministries had been sharply criticized by Andropov in his 22 November speech to the Central Committee (ibid., 13 December).

A much more important change was announced in December. After only seven months as head of the KGB, Vitali V. Fedorchuk was shifted to the post of minister of internal affairs, displacing longtime MVD head Nikolai A. Shchelokov, a close associate of Brezhnev's. Viktor M. Chebrikov moved up from the first deputy chairmanship to the chairmanship of the KGB (Tass, 17 December; *Los Angeles Times,* 18 December). This shuffle was widely interpreted as designed to intensify the anticorruption drive and to solidify Andropov's control over the police. However, Fedorchuk's appointment represented at least formally a demotion, and Chebrikov had been a protégé of Brezhnev's, having served as first secretary of the Dnepropetrovsk party *gorkom* in the 1960s and then as one of Brezhnev's "watchdogs" in the KGB.

Organizational Matters. The Nineteenth Congress of the Komsomol was held in Moscow, 18–21 May. More than 5,000 delegates attended, joined as observers by "delegations from youth organizations from 110 countries" (Tass, 19 May; *FBIS*, 22 May). Brezhnev made the keynote speech at the opening session, which was attended by all Moscow-based full Politburo members.

Brezhnev sounded themes that were to dominate Soviet political rhetoric for the remainder of the year: increased discipline as the primary answer to the USSR's domestic problems; support for "peace" movements directed against a Western nuclear buildup and reaffirmation of the USSR's desire to avoid war; and implacable opposition to imperialism, permitting no relaxation in vigilance on the part of the Soviet people.

Brezhnev praised the Komsomol for its work in the 135 "national construction projects under its supervision" and called on Komsomol members to be "pioneers" in eliminating the "misfortune" of carelessness and waste in the utilization of the country's "enormous resources." On the ideological front, Brezhnev bluntly demanded "an uncompromising attitude toward the slightest deviations from our social norms." The Soviet "peace offensive" was furthered by a Brezhnev declaration that the Soviets had "unilaterally discontinued recently a further deployment of medium-range missiles in the European part of the USSR and decided to reduce a certain number of them." (*Pravda*, 19 May.)

The congress received enormous coverage from Soviet media and seemed designed to shore up another vulnerable sector of the USSR's social organization, one that had drawn frequent criticisms from authoritative regime spokesmen over the past decade.

Closely following serious civil disorders in the North Ossetian ASSR in 1981, its party organization head was dismissed in January. Bilar E. Kabaloev, first secretary for North Ossetia since 1961, was fired because of "major shortcomings in the leadership" of the party organization (ibid., 16 January). The October 1981 clashes between Ossetians and Ingush had brought to the fore chronic ethnic tensions in the area and had required the personal intervention of Premier Mikhail S. Solomentsev of the Russian Soviet Federated Soviet Republic (RSFSR). Kabaloev was replaced as first secretary by Vladimir E. Odintsov (*Radio Liberty Research*, 18 January).

Another regional party secretary lost his job in July, apparently a victim of the developing anticorruption campaign. Sergei F. Medunov, 67, a close friend of General Secretary Brezhnev, was fired as first secretary of the Krasnodar *krai* party organization (*Pravda*, 15 July). Medunov had been first secretary in Krasnodar since May 1973 and had been a member of the CPSU Central Committee since 1976. The resort city of Sochi, within Medunov's jurisdiction, had gained national notoriety as a hotbed of bribery.

Dzhabar R. Rasulov, first secretary of the Tadzhikistan Communist Party, died in April (ibid., 6 April) and was succeeded by Rakhman N. Nabiev, 52, who had served as chairman of the Tadzhik SSR Council of Ministers since 1973.

The May plenum of the CPSU Central Committee, which ratified the organizational changes involving Andropov and Dolgikh, was mainly devoted to questions of agriculture. A new "food program" (*Pravda and Izvestiia*, 25–30 May) designed to alleviate the country's chronic agricultural shortfall was adopted (see below). In the following weeks, party organizational meetings at all levels drummed up support for fulfillment of the new plan to cope with what Brezhnev had described in 1981 as the USSR's main economic problem.

Two important party posts changed hands following Andropov's election as general secretary. Yevgeny M. Tyazhelnikov, head of the CPSU Propaganda Department since 1977, was replaced by Boris I. Stukalin, chairman of the USSR State Committee for Publishing Houses, Printing Plants, and the Book Trade. Boris N. Pastukhov, head of the Komsomol since 1978, was succeeded by Viktor M. Mishin, who had served as a secretary of the Komsomol Central Committee since 1978. (*NYT*, 13 December.)

Ideology. CPSU spokesmen had, for more than a decade, periodically acknowledged the existence of a problem of ideological vulnerability under conditions of the "growing importance of the subjective factor" in world affairs. The party's treatment of this problem during 1982 featured a consistent emphasis on orthodoxy, vigorous insistence on the validity of the Soviet model of socialism and the "leading role" of the CPSU in Soviet society, and defense of the Soviet approach to questions of democracy and national integration.

A major and ticklish aspect of the problem of ideological vulnerability has been the phenomenon of

Eurocommunism. In January, the polemical struggle against Eurocommunism escalated sharply, when for the first time a West European Communist Party was classified in effect as being within the imperialist camp. In response to the Italian party's criticisms over Poland, the East-West military confrontation, and Soviet domestic policies, a 500-word *Pravda* editorial (24 January) denounced the Italian Communists for "slander" and accused them of following the line of imperialism: "In today's world, this means direct aid to imperialism, which has been for decades seeking to weaken socialism, to loosen it, and to undermine it ideologically. This means aid to anticommunism and to all forces hostile to the cause of social progress in general." Apparently in response to events in Poland and to the challenge of the Eurocommunists, Konstantin Chernenko vigorously defended the Soviet model of socialism in an article entitled "The Leading Role of the Party of Communists: An Important Condition for Its Growth" in the CPSU theoretical journal, *Kommunist* (April). To seek a model of socialism contrary to "established patterns," Chernenko said, was "harebrained scheming," which could only draw the "revolutionary movement away from socialism." Similar views were offered by Yuri Andropov in his Lenin anniversary speech (*Pravda*, 23 April).

In an earlier article, Chernenko had warned of the need for constant vigilance in maintaining the party's "leading role" and noted (presumably in reference to Poland) that the absence of such leadership could promote "crisis" in the socialist system: "The party must confirm its right to lead society every day and with every decision. Otherwise, as the stern lessons of recent years indisputably show, the political situation can take on a nature of crisis." (*Voprosy istorii KPSS*, February.) The counteroffensive against the Italian party's Eurocommunist stance abated after the verbal barrage of January. In July, a radio broadcast beamed to Italy affirmed that "the essence of socialism is a single one." Historian Lidia Krepitskaya acknowledged the existence of different features of socialist construction in countries of the bloc. But, she said, "in the talk about various models one can see the aspiration of bourgeois ideologists to distort the very essence of socialism and the fundamental traits that distinguish it from capitalism" (Radio Moscow in Italian to Italy, 10 July; *FBIS*, 13 July). After meeting in Rome in late October, the secretary general of the Italian Communist Party, Enrico Berlinguer, and member of the CPSU Central Committee and first deputy chief of the CPSU International Department Vadim Zagladin characterized their talks as "a frank and penetrating exchange of information." It was stressed during the conversation that "cooperation between the [two] parties in the struggle against imperialism, to prevent war and to halt the arms race, is more important than the divergencies that certainly now exist between us . . . [We shall] continue a comradely discussion." (*La Republica*, Rome, 27 October; *FBIS*, 2 November.)

A symposium on the upbringing of youth, reported in the theoretical journal of the Komsomol in July, dramatically emphasized the ideological vulnerability of young people to Western influence. The symposium leader, academician A. I. Gavrikov, said that Soviet youths must be taught to hate their class enemies in the capitalist world: "While raising young people as fighters for peace, we have no right to leave out of their moral makeup an active, irreconcilable, acute hatred toward class enemies." Deploring the subversive influence of Western radio broadcasts, consumer goods, music, and "even toys," Gavrikov added: "We must cultivate in our youth the ability to recognize a class enemy no matter what image it assumes." (*Molodoi kommunist*, July.)

Aside from Gavrikov's concern with toys, the ideological dangers emanating from the West that he scored were identical with those identified by all major speakers, including Brezhnev and Pastukhov, at the Nineteenth Congress of the Komsomol (*Pravda*, 19–21 March). General Aleksei A. Yepishev, head of the Main Political Administration of the Armed Forces, had warned the congress of an even graver threat, the rise of pacifism among young people, repeating an alarm sounded by Army Chief of Staff Marshal Nikolai V. Ogarkov in a pamphlet published in February. According to Yepishev, army recruits displayed "elements of political naiveté, pacifism, and a carefree attitude when assessing the threat posed by our class enemies" (ibid., 20 March).

Two weeks after the appearance of the call for "hatred" among young people, *Pravda* (22 July) added its voice to the demand for intensification of ideological work directed toward Soviet youth. In an editorial entitled "The Force of Ideological Conviction," *Pravda* said that "imperialist circles are systematically organizing ideological campaigns against the USSR and the other fraternal socialist states." In these circumstances, the editorial concluded, "special attention must be devoted to the ideological, political, moral, and labor education of young people."

Two articles published in early May gave oblique support to the *sliianie* (amalgamation) approach to problems of nationality in the USSR. The first discussed the role of the Russian language, "freely accepted by Soviet citizens," as the common language connecting the various national groups (ibid., 5 May). The second, a long article by Piotr N. Fedoseyev, vice-president of the USSR Academy of Sciences and a full member of the CPSU Central Committee, dealt with nationality questions involved in the "homogeniza-tion" of Soviet society, widely heralded by CPSU spokesmen in recent years. Fedoseyev maintained that unification of the Soviet peoples did not mean elimination of national differences but asserted that use of Russian as the common language accords with "the vital needs of the various nations and people." (Ibid., 9 May.)

Although Western observers considered Russian nationalism as one of the main bulwarks of popular support for the regime among the majority Great Russian segment of the population, the authorities have been highly sensitive concerning overt expression of views reflecting support for traditional Russian nationalism. An article by Professor Vasili Kuleshov of Moscow University, prominently featured in *Pravda*, rebuked two prominent literary critics for praising the Slavophile ideas of Fyodor Dostoevsky concerning Russia's "special mission" to lead the world. According to Kuleshov, Dostoevsky saw Russia's "world mission" purely in terms of a supposed moral superiority of the "Russian soul" and ignored the need for concrete social and political change. (BBC, 2 February; *FBIS*, 5 February.)

An article in the armed forces theoretical journal in March attacked Western social-democratic parties and "social-reformist ideology" with "two camps" rhetoric reminiscent of the Comintern's "class against class" campaign in 1928–1934. The article by Col. B. Bogdanov, "The Ideology of Social Reformism at the Service of Capital," acknowledged that social-democratic parties often took positions on international issues that accorded with "common sense" and "realities." But, said Bogdanov, "the anticommunist bias, of which the leaders of the parties of the Socialist International are prisoners as formerly, prevents them from taking a consistently realistic position on the more acute problems of our time." Bogdanov concluded: "Social reformism is the main conductor of bourgeois influence on the working class in the developed capitalist countries and the most important ideological and political support of the bourgeoisie within the worker movement. Therefore, criticism of the ideology of 'democratic socialism' which is striving to halt the process of the revolutionary renewal of peace and inhibit the forward movement of mankind, remains the most urgent task of Marxist-Leninist parties." (*Kommunist vooruzhennikh sil*, no. 6, March; *JPRS*, 6 August.)

Domestic Affairs. The sluggish Soviet economy again attracted most attention among domestic concerns, with agriculture remaining the number-one problem sector. A new "food program" was launched with much fanfare in May, but whatever positive results that might follow this mild reform lie in the future. A fourth consecutive year of severe shortfalls in grain production deepened the gloomy prospects in this sector of the economy; massive importation of food would again be necessary in 1983. The projected natural gas pipeline from Siberia to Western Europe offered hope for an overall improvement in the USSR's trade balance in the late 1980s, and work on the pipeline was pushed, apparently largely unaffected by the Reagan administration's efforts to slow or prevent its completion. Meanwhile, serious social problems supposedly alien to "developed socialism" continued to plague the USSR, with alcoholism at the top of the list. The problem of official corruption, largely masked by media reticence during the Brezhnev era, suddenly erupted as a major political issue; the execution of a former deputy minister highlighted the crackdown on "economic crimes." The KGB's long campaign against dissent appeared to have crushed all major centers of resistance; the only remaining dissident circle in Moscow disbanded. Nevertheless, the KGB continued its relentless campaign for conformity, harassing religious groups and marshaling its forces against the minuscule ranks of those working toward independent trade union or peace movements.

The Economy. The year opened with a number of press commentaries critical of low labor productiv-ity and unsatisfactory performances by planning and management officials. The chronic ills of the economy were exacerbated by the necessity for emergency assistance to Poland (*WP*, 10 January). Economic support for bloc countries and the importation of food and technology have combined to produce the threat of a deficit in the USSR's balance of payments. A study prepared for the U.S. Congress Joint Economic

Committee forecast that the USSR's 1981 trade surplus of $4 billion with the Western industrialized countries may deteriorate to a $7 billion deficit by 1985 (AP, 13 September).

The main hope for maintenance of a trade surplus in the years beyond 1985 lay in the monumental project of a natural gas pipeline from Urengoi in northern Siberia to Western Europe. When completed, the pipeline is expected to earn the Soviets up to U.S. $8 billion a year from deliveries to the West. Early reports indicated that construction was well under way (*NYT*, 21 February). Subsequent efforts by the Reagan administration to curb deliveries of equipment for the pipeline met strong resistance in Western Europe and appeared to present no real obstacles for the project. In late summer, the pipeline construction was reported to be on schedule. Rantik D. Margulov, first deputy minister of the gas industry, said that "only shortsighted people" could seriously hope that "we would be unable to commission the export pipeline without U.S. help" (Radio Moscow domestic service, 11 August; *FBIS*, 12 August).

The pipeline provided virtually the only good economic news. The official economic report for 1981, released in January, indicated weak performance in most sectors. The report contained no figure on the 1981 harvest but acknowledged "extremely unfavorable conditions" in agriculture during the year. Gas production was seven billion cubic meters above target, but the oil industry fell just short of plan projections and coal industry output was reported as 704 million tons, against the goal of 738 million (*Izvestiia*, 24 January). First quarter figures for 1982, released by the Central Statistical Administration in May, claimed a 2.1 percent increase in industrial production and a 2.9 percent increase in agriculture over first quarter 1981. However, output was lower in nearly half of the production categories. (*Pravda*, 24 May.)

Confronted with a wide variety of economic ills, the leadership clearly gave precedence to agriculture. After a year and a half of research and planning, a comprehensive "food program" for the period through 1990 was presented to the Central Committee and approved at the May plenum. The new program called for improvement in management, provided for some reorganization at low and middle levels of the agricultural production-distribution complex, promised great incentives and improved living conditions for farm workers, and set investment targets (ibid., 25, 27, and 28 May; *Izvestiia*, 28 May). However, the program contained only a highly diluted version of the organizational reforms to strengthen incentives that had apparently been successfully tested at the republic level, notably in Georgia and Azerbaijan. The six resolutions constituting the program provided for no fundamental changes and appeared to be a compromise scheme, considerably watered down during its formulation by party and governmental bureaucrats opposed to decentralization.

The relatively mild programmatic changes contrasted starkly with the sense of urgency displayed by officials. A confidential report presented to the top leadership by a special government commission prior to the May plenum depicted extreme disarray in the agricultural sector. According to the report, one-fifth of the grain harvest is lost because it is harvested late or left to rot; losses are even greater for some other crops. The commission noted that Soviet food imports had increased tenfold in a decade, the cost rising from $700 million in 1970 to $7.2 billion in 1980 (*WP*, 23 May). A sense of urgency was fully apparent in announced plans to expand production on the "secret" state farms controlled by the military (*Krasnaia zvezda*, 6, 13, and 15, June, 6 and 10 July; *Radio Liberty Research*, 2 August).

Although prospects for the food program appeared highly dubious to Western observers, it was presented on Soviet television, in major party and government newspapers, and in other journals as a near-panacea for the growing problem. An article by I. Trofimova in *Novoe vremya* (no. 23, 4 June) frankly admitted the purchases of food from abroad and depicted the "food program" as the route to elimination of this dependence.

Whatever its long-range prospects, the "food program" did not change the immediate picture, which was grim. Officials gave early warning of another poor harvest year. On 13 April, *Pravda* noted the late spring affecting most Soviet farmland and roundly scored farm managers for failure to get their machinery in working order, citing one farm where only eight of sixteen tractors were operational. "It is quite urgent that the situation be corrected," the newspaper said. In the same issue, *Pravda* criticized mishandling of railway equipment by the responsible ministry, which resulted in large losses of mineral fertilizer due to defective cars.

Agriculture Minister Valentin K. Mesyats confirmed reports of a poor year at an October meeting of agricultural workers. Mesyats cited bad weather but said that "it would be wrong to blame everything on the 'weather'" (*Pravda*, 8 October). In early October, U.S. President Ronald Reagan offered to sell the Soviets up to 23 million tons of a bumper U.S. grain crop. In late October, a Soviet delegation met with U.S. trade experts to discuss the matter, and the chief USSR bargainer, Boris Gordeyev, indicated that the Soviets would probably buy the entire 23 million tons (UPI, 28 October). However, by mid-November the Soviets had not officially responded to the offer, and their purchases of both wheat and corn were reported down (ibid., 13 November).

Canadian embassy officials in Moscow estimated in early November that the 1982 Soviet grain harvest would total 176 million metric tons (ibid., 1 November). The U.S. Department of Agriculture increased its estimate of the crop from 170 million to 180 million tons (ibid., 13 November). Planned target for the growing season had been 236 million tons. At the Central Committee plenum on 22 November, it was announced that industrial growth for 1982 would amount to 2.8 percent, against the planned target of 4.7 percent (*NYT*, 23 November).

Social Problems. Well along in the phase of "developed socialism," the advent of which had been signaled by the 1977 constitution, the USSR continued to be plagued by social problems that socialism was supposed to have eliminated. Prominent among these was alcoholism, which continued to attract major attention in the Soviet press. In August 1981, *Pravda* had singled out Kostroma as exceptionally afflicted with drunkenness in residences and work places and had blamed the *gorkom* party officials. In a follow-up report, *Pravda* (24 January) noted corrective steps, particularly in the area of preventive work, taken by the Kostroma *gorkom*. On 17 July, the party newspaper carried a 2,200-word article by Deputy MVD Minister B. Shumilin on alcoholism and drunkenness. Shumilin called for a tightening of law enforcement, emphasis on prevention, and reduction in the number of alcohol outlets, especially in the vicinity of work places.

Far more spectacular than alcoholism, at least in political effects, was the rising concern with official corruption. Long recognized by Western observers as a major flaw of the Soviet system, the problem had been largely kept under wraps by the authorities, aside from isolated cases of exemplary punishment, especially in the borderland republics. The stability of cadres policy pursued by the Brezhnev leadership had evidently intensified the problem by assuring greater security for officials and decreasing the risks entailed in corrupt activities. During 1982, despite cautious handling of the problem by the authorities, official corruption emerged as the most explosive domestic political issue for the CPSU.

The year's most celebrated revelation of economic crime, the Boris the Gypsy case (see above), appeared related to political maneuvering among the leadership. But the issue of corruption was not merely a gambit in succession politics; pressures for a crackdown had been building in the party and government for some time, and a vigorous "law and order" campaign seemed to be developing as regime policy.

The head of the Soviet emigration agency, OVIR (Department of Visas and Registration), Konstantin I. Zotov, was reportedly removed from office in early February due to widespread bribery in visa matters (*Los Angeles Times*, 22 February). Notably, Zotov's organization is part of the MVD, which had reportedly been displaced by the KGB on the Boris the Gypsy case due to inept handling of the investigation. Perhaps politically wounded by the two cases, Nikolai A. Shchelokov, head of the MVD and a longtime close associate of Brezhnev, urged an all-union conference of MVD officials in Moscow to intensify the fight against speculation and "parasitism" (Radio Moscow domestic service, 1 February; *FBIS*, 3 February).

Former Deputy Fisheries Minister Vladimir I. Rytov was executed in April for bribery in a caviar-smuggling scheme that had reportedly been broken up in 1980 with the arrest of some 200 people (AP, 27 April). Announcing the execution, *Pravda* (27 April) warned corrupt officials that they would get no leniency. Subsequent media treatment of the case was unusually frank. One journalist quoted Lenin as approving the shooting of "bribe takers and crooks"; a leading Ministry of Justice official called Rytov a "dangerous bribe taker" (*Sotzialisticheskaia industria*, 15 June; *FBIS*, 2 July).

Pointing up the continuing high incidence of economic crimes and other social problems in Georgia, the republic's party chief, Eduard A. Shevardnadze, in an August speech, attributed these conditions to apathy on the part of government and party officials. He called for greater attention to the cause and environmental factors involved in such crimes against the state as "parasitism," domestic disorders, drunkenness, and poor economic discipline. (*Zarya vostoka*, 10 August; *FBIS*, 20 August.)

In view of the reported involvement of the police in political infighting and the drive against corruption, an unusual turnover among police officials attracted considerable attention. At the end of 1981, public announcements of the dismissals of key MVD officials in Lvov and Odessa cited abuses of official positions and "unworthy conduct" (*Pravda*, 26 December 1981). Following the death of KGB First Deputy Chairman Semyon Tsvigun in January, two new first deputy chairmen of the organization were appointed, Georgi K. Tsinev and Viktor M. Chebrikov, both known to be close associates of Brezhnev. This seemed to signal a business-as-usual approach, but other policy appointments during the year appeared on balance to favor a more draconian stance on law and order.

The promotion of career police official Vitali V. Fedorchuk, known for his ruthless suppression of dissent in the Ukraine, as Andropov's successor as head of the KGB certainly promised no liberalization in any area of the security agency's activities. Fedorchuk's successor in Kiev was Stepan N. Mukha, who moved up from the position of first deputy head of the Ukrainian KGB (*Radyanska ukraina*, 5 June). Mukha is evidently a minor member of the "Dnieper mafia"; his career began in the Komsomol organization of Dnepropetrovsk *oblast*, Brezhnev's home base (*Radio Liberty Research*, 28 June). The Ukrainian MVD also changed leadership. Ivan K. Golovchenko, depicted in *samizdat* publications as a relatively liberal figure, retired and was replaced by his deputy, career officer Ivan D. Gladush (ibid.). Estonia, site of student disorders during the winter, also was given a new KGB chieftain. August P. Pork, chairman of the Estonian KGB since 1961, retired and was replaced by Karl E. Kortelaynen (*Sovetskaia estoniia*, 16 June; *FBIS*, 22 July). In Kazakhstan, Vasili T. Shevchenko, who had headed the republic's security apparatus since 1975, was replaced as KGB head by Kazakh Central Committee secretary for ideology Zagash Kamalidenov, 45. Kamalidenov, a rising star in Kazakhstan's politics, has extensive experience in industry, Komsomol, and party organizational work, and is the first non-Slav to head the Kazakhstan KGB since 1963. (*Radio Liberty Research*, 25 March.)

One day after the Fedorchuk-Chebrikov reshuffle in December, the government announced harsh new fines and prison terms, including forced labor, for a wide variety of crimes (*Izvestiia*, 18 December). A week earlier, *Pravda* (11 December) had spotlighted the new "law and order" approach with an unusual front-page report on a Politburo meeting that produced a call for prosecutors and party officials to crack down on social disorder, official corruption, and incompetent managers. *Pravda* noted that questions of law and order "are rising especially sharply in letters from workers and seriously worry them."

Dissent. Having broken the most prominent dissident groups, the authorities concentrated during the year on the fledgling independent trade union and peace movements. Here the main objective was avoidance of spillover effects from events in Poland and the West; this concern was also evident in official policy toward religious groups.

Vsevolod Kuvakin, 40, a member of SMOT, the interprofessional free workers' union set up in 1978, was sentenced in the final week of 1981 to one year of labor camp and five years of internal exile for "anti-Soviet propaganda and agitation" (AFP, 27 December 1981; *FBIS*, 28 December 1981). The KGB arrested twelve dissidents in Moscow in early April; religious materials, icons, and Bibles were reportedly confiscated from four of the men who were members of the Russian Orthodox church (*NYT*, 12 April). In August, Sergei Batovrin, 25, an artist and cofounder of the independent peace movement, the Committee to Establish Trust Between the USSR and the USA, was arrested (*WP*, 7 August).

Members of the peace group had been harassed by police and warned of possible prosecution following formation of the organization in June. While the Soviets were devoting major efforts to encouragement of unofficial peace movements, especially supporters of a nuclear freeze, in the West, they made it clear that they would not tolerate any independent competition to the official Soviet peace movement headed by *Pravda* political commentator Yuri Zhukov. The independent movement had advocated making Moscow a nuclear-free zone and had called for regular exchanges of U.S. and Soviet television programs and cooperative U.S.-Soviet efforts on disarmament, space exploration, and medical research. (*Los Angeles Times*, 13 June.) In July, when 300 Scandinavian women, joined by a thousand Soviet citizens under close police supervision, staged a peace march in Moscow, independent peaceniks were forced by the KGB to leave the capital. On the eve of the Moscow march, two members of the independent peace group, Yuri Medvedkov, 54, and Yuri Khronopulo, 47, were arrested. (*Baltimore Sun*, 19 July.)

The high point of the year for the official Soviet peace movement was the Conference of Religious Workers for Saving the Precious Gift of Life from Nuclear Catastrophe, held in Moscow in May. The conference was attended by a number of Western clergymen, including the Rev. Billy Graham. Graham's address to the conference contained only one brief reference to religious freedom, and several remarks attributed to him by Western newsmen raised a storm of controversy in the West. His quoted remarks implied a high degree of religious freedom in the USSR. Preaching in the Moscow Baptist Church, Graham took no notice of protest signs displayed by believers, including one that read: "We have more than 150 prisoners for the work of the gospel." The service was well attended by KGB plainclothesmen, who confiscated protest signs and reportedly arrested at least one dissident. (UPI, 16 May.) Graham also briefly visited Pentecostals who had taken refuge in the U.S. Embassy and were highly critical of his visit.

Continuing its long drive against Pentecostal groups, the KGB arrested Vasili M. Barats on 9 August at Rovno airport in the Ukraine. Barats, a former army officer, was head of the Committee for Emigration, which supports Pentecostals seeking to leave the USSR. (AFP, 9 August; FBIS, 11 August; AP, 23 August.)

In September, the authorities displayed acute concern over Catholic influence in areas bordering Poland. The Belorussian party newspaper accused church activists and priests of violating Soviet religious laws on instructions from Western religious circles, including Radio Vatican, and called on local authorities to impose harsher sentences on such "extremists" (*Sovetskaia belorussia*, 18 September). In a related development, *Pravda* (20 September) carried a report from Poland criticizing the behavior of Polish bishops.

In September, Yelena Bonner, wife of Andrei Sakharov, announced the disbanding of the Moscow group for monitoring Soviet observance of the Helsinki accords. Sixteen members of the group had been sentenced to labor camps or internal exile; the last member to be jailed had been Ivan S. Kovalyov, 27, sentenced to labor camp in April. When disbanded, the group was down to three members; the authorities were said to be preparing an indictment against one of these, 75-year-old lawyer Sofia Kallistratova. Bonner also reported that Zoya Krakhmalnikova, editor of an underground journal of Christian thought, who had been arrested in August, was being charged in connection with several statements she had signed as a member of the Helsinki monitoring group (*NYT*, 9 September).

Sakharov continued under house arrest in Gorky. In October, Sakharov charged that KGB agents had drugged him and stolen hundreds of pages of memoirs and other documents from his car (AP, 31 October). Anatoly Shcharansky, one of the founders of the Helsinki human rights–monitoring group, began a hunger strike in late September, seeking to obtain permission to correspond with his family. Shcharansky's mother, who announced the hunger strike, said that the family had received no news from her son in the ten months preceding his decision to carry out the only protest available to him. (AFP, 27 September; FBIS, 28 September.) Two months later, the hunger strike was reportedly continuing, causing fears for Shcharansky's life.

For several months prior to the leadership changeover, the KGB stepped up its drive against dissent, with a reported sharp increase in searches, threats, beatings, interrogations, and arrests. Main targets were Jews seeking to emigrate, the few remaining human rights activists, Western-oriented young people, and independent religious sects. Figures from the National Conference on Soviet Jewry showed Jewish emigration declining from 51,320 in 1979 to 9,447 in 1981 to an expected 2,700 in 1982 (*NYT*, 18 November). Telephone links with the West were cut back sharply after midsummer, and censors were reportedly rigidly enforcing a new Central Committee directive ordering tighter ideological control of literature (ibid., 25 October).

Three ethnic Germans from the Volga region who demonstrated in Red Square for permission to emigrate were arrested in September (*Los Angeles Times*, 15 September). Aleksandr Lerner, 69, patriarch of the Jewish emigration movement, agreed to comply with a KGB order to sever all ties with foreigners in the Soviet Union after being told that the alternative was prison or exile (ibid., 19 September).

Foreign Affairs. Major Soviet activities during the year were directed toward prevention of unfavorable changes in the global "correlation of forces," the securing of Western help for the ailing economy, and the shoring up of the Soviet bloc following the events in Poland. The regional correlation in Europe was of most immediate concern; the Soviets encouraged the rise of nuclear freeze movements in Western Europe and the United States that offered hope of undercutting plans for a NATO nuclear buildup. Having created a massive imbalance in nuclear weapons on the continent, the Soviets announced in April a unilateral halt in deployment of the medium-range SS-20 missile. Disarmament talks continued, with little movement, and

Soviet-U.S. relations were mostly tense. Washington's efforts to halt or slow construction of the natural gas pipeline to Western Europe failed, succeeding only in producing tensions within the Western alliance. In October, the Soviets indicated readiness to purchase massive quantities of grain from the United States. Eager to avoid an anti-Soviet stance by the new West German government, the Kremlin dispatched RSFSR Premier Solomentsev to Bonn in October to confer with Chancellor Helmut Kohl. Bogged down in Afghanistan and Poland, the USSR under Brezhnev was unusually passive in critical situations outside Europe, giving mostly rhetorical support to Argentina in the Falklands war and to the Palestine Liberation Organization (PLO) in the fighting in Lebanon. The situation changed under Andropov, who initiated a much more active policy in the Middle East (especially in Syria), showed no inclination to extricate the USSR from Afghanistan, and toughened Soviet attitudes toward Japan. The Soviets sought to move closer to both India and China, but India responded by mending fences with Washington and China declared its neutrality vis-à-vis the superpowers. Apparently worried by reports of inferior performance of Soviet arms against U.S.-made weapons in Lebanon and by the Reagan administration's military program, the Soviet military displayed signs of uneasiness. Brezhnev reassured the generals with a belligerent speech in October, calling for a Soviet arms buildup and promising the military leaders that they would get what they needed (*Pravda*, 28 October). Throughout the year, Soviet spokesmen maintained vehemently that the USSR would never accept military inferiority to the United States. When Yuri Andropov succeeded to the top party post, he reiterated the established position on maintaining Soviet military power.

Arms Control. Soviet-U.S. relations during the year revolved around questions of arms and their reduction, proposals and counterproposals concerning nuclear weapons, and propaganda tilting over issues of nuclear balance and willingness to disarm. In the propaganda arena, the Soviets seemed to be ahead on points. The nuclear freeze movement, which had been triggered by the U.S. initiative to arm NATO with Pershing II missiles to match the European deployment of SS-20s by the USSR, gained thousands of adherents in Western Europe and the United States, notably among clergymen. In November, voters in several states and localities in the United States approved referendums for a bilateral nuclear freeze. The position of the Reagan administration was that a nuclear freeze would perpetuate existing advantages for the USSR and leave the Soviets with no incentive for arms reductions. The Soviets disputed Washington's claims about a nuclear imbalance and maintained that a rough equivalence existed, even in Europe. Nuclear freeze advocates tended to favor the Soviet claims or to argue that a quantitative imbalance made no difference.

In February, Brezhnev proposed a two-thirds cut in medium-range missiles in Europe by 1990 for both NATO and the Warsaw Pact states. According to Soviet figures, NATO had 968 medium-range missiles and the USSR 975; Brezhnev proposed that each side reduce the number to 300 by 1990. (Ibid., 3 February.) The Brezhnev proposal was an elaboration of a plan he had put forward at Bonn in November 1981; the United States had rejected this initiative on grounds that equal cuts would leave the USSR vastly superior in medium-range missiles (*NYT*, 4 February).

The USSR had rejected President Reagan's "zero option" proposal, according to which the United States would refrain from deploying new weapons in Europe if the Soviets destroyed existing stocks of SS-4, SS-5, and SS-20 missiles targeted on Western Europe. The Soviets countered with a tentative proposal for a Soviet moratorium on deployment of the SS-20 coupled with U.S. suspension of deployment of Pershing II and Cruise missiles. Stanislav Menshikov, third-ranking official of the Central Committee's International Department, advanced this idea while in the United States for a conference in Hershey, Pennsylvania. Menshikov suggested that if the two sides could agree on such a proposal, further deployment of weapons would hinge on the success or failure of the Geneva arms limitation talks (*WP*, 1 February). With no agreement in sight, Brezhnev, in his speech to the trade union congress in March, warned that U.S. deployment of new missiles in Western Europe would lead the USSR to take countermeasures to put the United States in an "analogous position" (*Pravda*, 18 March); this was widely interpreted as a scarcely veiled threat to install Soviet missiles in Cuba. Two months later, with the nuclear freeze movement burgeoning in Western Europe and the United States, Brezhnev changed his tack. At the congress of the Komsomol, he declared that the Soviets had "unilaterally discontinued recently a further deployment of medium-range missiles in the European part of the USSR and decided to reduce a certain number of them" (ibid., 19 May). However, Western officials denied that there had been any unilateral freeze by the Soviets. In July, NATO sources said that the USSR was completing work on three more SS-20 bases, two of them west of the Urals, and would finish its deployment program by the fall, bringing the total number of deployed SS-20 missiles up to 342 (*Washington Times*, 15 July).

During the spring and summer, Soviet spokesmen regularly combined statements of lofty Soviet intentions with hard-line attacks on U.S. positions on arms reduction questions. In May, Tass political analyst Yuri Kornilov charged that NATO was seeking "unilateral disarmament" from the USSR, which was "absurd." The two sides were depicted as having irreconcilable positions: "We have more than once proposed the creation of nuclear-free zones, the liquidation in Europe of both medium-range and tactical nuclear weapons. This would be a true 'zero option,' and not the false one which is so often talked about in the West. One notion cannot be replaced with another in this case." (Tass, 3 May; *FBIS*, 3 May.) In late May, a joint U.S.-Soviet statement announced the beginning on 29 June in Geneva of Strategic Arms Reduction Talks (START). General (ret.) Edward Rowny was designated as chief U.S. chief negotiator; career diplomat Viktor Karpov is his Soviet counterpart. In a Memorial Day speech, President Reagan sounded a conciliatory note. "As for existing strategic arms agreements," he said, "we will refrain from actions which undercut them so long as the Soviet Union shows equal restraint" (*NYT*, 1 June).

Reagan's visit to Western Europe in early June apparently succeeded in reducing concerns among West European allies about U.S. military plans. Seeking to regain the momentum of the Soviet peace offensive, USSR Foreign Minister Gromyko delivered a long "carrot and stick" speech to the U.N. General Assembly on 15 June. He read a message from Brezhnev that the USSR would not be the first to use nuclear weapons and stated that the Soviets were willing to agree on elimination of both medium-range and tactical nuclear weapons in Europe, renunciation of medium-range weapons only, or the gradual and "substantial" reduction of medium-range weapons by both sides. Against this Soviet willingness to compromise, Gromyko presented the United States as the principal instigator of the arms race and accused it of barbarism, deceit, and "militaristic intoxication." (Ibid., 16 June.)

On the eve of START, an official Soviet statement promised that the USSR would strive to ensure that "from the very beginning the negotiations be purposeful and constructive." However, the statement also noted that recent U.S. proposals indicated that the United States was aiming to change the existing "correlation of forces" in its favor. (Tass, 28 June; *NYT*, 29 June.) Arriving in Geneva for the talks, Karpov said that the USSR was "ready for a speedy conclusion" of the negotiations and called on the United States to follow Brezhnev's lead in renouncing first use of nuclear weapons. Talks were scheduled to be held twice a week. (AP, 28 June.)

In July, when Reagan called for amendment of two existing treaties in order to provide stricter means of verifying compliance on nuclear testing, an official Soviet commentary dismissed the U.S. concern as a sham and called the proposal a "pretext for sabotaging the talks" on limiting nuclear tests (Tass, 21 July).

Some progress was reported in the Mutual and Balanced Force Reductions (MBFR) talks in Vienna. At midyear, U.S. and Soviet negotiators had reportedly agreed on several concepts, relating to numbers of personnel and verification, essential for an initial MBFR agreement. However, the two sides continued to disagree on the size of Warsaw pact ground forces, with Eastern figures about 150,000 lower than Western estimates (*NYT*, 2 July).

Little palpable progress was recorded in Geneva at the two levels of negotiation. Preceding START, negotiations on the limits on nuclear missiles based in Europe were conducted also in Geneva. They started on 30 November 1981, under the official title of Intermediate-Range Nuclear Forces talks (INF). Paul Nitze, former U.S. secretary of the navy, headed the U.S. delegation, and Yuli Kvitsinsky, a career diplomat, the Soviet. By the end of September 1982, 40 formal bargaining INF sessions had been held. Both sides were continuing to press the proposals advanced earlier by their leaders, and delegation heads, previously reticent, came out with critical public statements. Kvitsinsky said that "the U.S. side should, at long last, make its own contribution to working out an accord consistent with the task of lowering the level of nuclear confrontation and with the principle of equality and equal security." Nitze said that the Soviet Union had continued its nuclear buildup in Europe despite the March announcement of a unilateral moratorium. The U.S. State Department said that deployed SS-20 missiles had increased from 250 at the time the Geneva talks began in late 1981 to 324 in early September. (AP, 28 September.) Meanwhile, in Moscow, Leonid M. Zamyatin, head of the Central Committee's Foreign Information Department, accused the Reagan administration of "sabotaging disarmament talks" and described as "hypocritical rhetoric" White House statements that the United States was seeking arms reductions (Tass, 28 September).

Secret negotiations outside the regular Geneva framework took place in July. Nitze informed Kvitsinsky that the United States was open to a compromise in the sense that instead of an inflexible "zero option" it was ready to talk about numbers. An "informal agreement" was worked out, in which the Soviet Union would reduce the number of its SS-20s and the United States would install fewer Pershing and Cruise missiles. Secretary Andropov spurned the breakthrough in Geneva before President Reagan did. (For the story of the July negotiations, see *New Republic*, 7 February 1983. In early January 1983, Eugene V. Rostow, director of the Arms Control and Disarmament Agency, was dismissed by President Reagan for conducting unauthorized policy by permitting his subordinate, Paul Nitze, to negotiate with Kvitsinsky. Nitze continued to head the U.S. INF delegation.)

The prospects for early arms reductions were not brightened by Yuri Andropov's first speech as Soviet leader. Addressing the CPSU Central Committee following his selection as general secretary, Andropov mentioned neither disarmament nor détente and emphasized the role of the Soviet armed forces: "We know full well that the imperialists will never meet one's pleas for peace. It can be upheld only by resting on the invincible might of the Soviet armed forces." (*Pravda*, 13 November.) On 21 December, in Moscow, on the occasion of the celebration of the founding of the Soviet Union in 1922, Andropov announced a proposal to cut missiles in Europe. It was his first major speech not limited to a party forum, for his audience included representatives from 123 foreign communist parties (there was no delegate from China). Andropov expressed readiness to reduce the number of Soviet missiles targeted on Western Europe to 162, the number of similar missiles maintained by Great Britain and France, as a *quid pro quo* for nondeployment of Pershing II and Cruise missiles in Western Europe (ibid., 22 December). Rhetorically it was a "soft" and accommodating speech attuned to the sensibilities on nuclear matters of large sections of Western European and U.S. public opinion. Andropov favored a "back to détente" international atmosphere and suggested freezing the strategic arsenals of the two sides. He warned the Reagan administration that if it proceeded with new strategic arms systems such as MX weapons, the Soviet Union would deploy analogous missiles together with a long-range Cruise-type missile already being tested. Likewise, to the cheering of his communist listeners, Andropov stated that no one should delude himself: "We will never let our security or the security of our allies be jeopardized." (Excerpts from Andropov's speech, as translated and distributed by Tass, were printed in *NYT*, 22 December.)

The United States (as well as Britain and France) promptly rejected Andropov's proposal on the grounds that it would leave the USSR with 260 SS-20 medium-range missiles "while denying us the means to deter the threat" (AP, 22 December). When President Reagan announced in December adoption of the "dense pack" mode of basing for the MX missile, Moscow denounced the planned deployment as a violation of both SALT I and the unratified SALT II. This issue was temporarily muted by the failure of the U.S. Congress to provide the funds requested for the MX. The United States continued to support Reagan's "zero option," which was adamantly opposed by Moscow. In a statement issued on 26 December, the Soviets said that the "zero option" was not viable and "would disrupt both the regional and the global balance" (*Pravda*, 27 December).

Other Aspects of Soviet-U.S. Relations. At the beginning of the year, two additional sources of tension further strained Soviet-U.S. relations, which had been rather frigid since the USSR's invasion of Afghanistan in December 1979. Washington depicted the imposition of martial law in Poland in late 1981 as orchestrated by Moscow; the Soviets charged Washington with interference in Poland's internal affairs. The Soviets were attempting to finalize arrangements with West European countries on the natural gas pipeline from Siberia while the Reagan administration prepared economic sanctions designed to halt or slow the pipeline's completion.

With these issues poisoning the diplomatic atmosphere, Soviet media launched a double-barreled attack on Washington in the first weekend of the new year. Soviet commentator Georgi Zubkov predicted that Western Europe would not support Reagan's trade sanctions and linked the pipeline issue with the Polish crisis: "The American administration is striving to force its West European allies to support a course of crude interference in the internal affairs of Poland" (Moscow domestic radio and television, 3 January;

AP, 3 January). A *Pravda* commentary (3 January) accused the CIA of supporting a "criminal plot" by Polish counterrevolutionaries, a "violation of the principles of the Helsinki Final Act."

Soviet Premier Tikhonov sent mixed signals of conciliation and threat to Washington in a speech that preceded Foreign Minister Gromyko's departure for Geneva to meet with U.S. Secretary of State Alexander Haig. Tikhonov said that the Soviet Union did not seek confrontation with the United States and called for a "constructive dialogue." However, he accused the Reagan administration of "intensifying the arms race" and "aggravating the international situation." Tikhonov's remarks also reflected the standard Soviet position that the USSR would not accept any significant change in the world correlation of forces: "Those who prefer the language of threats and demonstrations of strength to a peaceful dialogue should understand that we will take all the necessary measures to insure our security and the security of our allies and friends" (*NYT*, 21 January).

The Gromyko-Haig discussions produced no improvement in the diplomatic climate. Soviet-U.S. tensions were further exacerbated by the Falklands war in the spring and the Israeli invasion of Lebanon in late summer. In both cases, Washingtion and Moscow traded sharp verbal blows, but there was little threat of direct confrontation. Mired down in Afghanistan and Poland, the USSR seemed to have lost its much-vaunted capacity for promoting military ventures outside the bloc. The incapacitation of Brezhnev and the muted succession struggle in Moscow further inhibited Soviet policymakers. Brezhnev's deteriorating health provided the backdrop for a nimble diplomatic *pas de deux* executed by the superpowers in April and May. Under pressure from NATO allies to demonstrate willingness to bargain, Reagan proposed a summit meeting with Brezhnev in New York in June. Two days after Brezhnev was hospitalized in Moscow, the Soviets countered with a proposal for a summit meeting in a third country in October (*WP*, 3 May). The United States responded favorably to the Soviet counterproposal, but—as widely expected—no meeting took place. Not only was a summit precluded by Brezhnev's health, neither side was ready for serious bargaining on major issues.

While Soviet world policy seemed to have lost, at least temporarily, some of its characteristic vigor, Moscow was still able to exploit skillfully conflicts of interest among the Western allies. Soviet media constantly played up the "contradictions" afflicting the Western alliance. In a typical commentary in the Soviet army newspaper in late May, Col. M. Ponomarev depicted a breakdown in the "Atlantic discipline" imposed by Washington on its alliance partners. This breakdown was attributed to economic problems, political differences over détente, and "an appreciable change in the correlation of forces in the capitalist world." The meeting of foreign ministers in Luxembourg in May and the scheduled economic and political Western summits at Versailles and Bonn in June were seen as attempts by "U.S. ruling circles" to "tighten the yoke of Atlanticism on the allies and make them obediently follow" Washington's "hegemonist policy." (*Krasnaia zvezda*, 25 May.)

On the eve of Reagan's trip to Bonn, a leading Soviet journal charged that U.S. policy was aimed at "the weakening and exhaustion" of West Germany as a "competitor on the world market" (*Literaturnaia gazeta*, 9 June; *FBIS*, 9 June). The main government daily called the search for a "common denominator" in Bonn a "Sisyphean labor" (*Izvestiia*, 10 June). Press commentaries strongly emphasized the antinuclear demonstrations that accompanied Reagan's tour of West European capitals as indications of Western opposition to Washington-inspired plans for NATO's nuclear modernization (Tass, 8–10 June; *Pravda* and *Izvestiia*, 9 and 10 June).

Although clearly dissatisfied with the Reagan administration's policy toward the USSR, Moscow expressed concern about the departure of Secretary of State Alexander Haig. Leonid Zamyatin, head of the Central Committee's Foreign Information Department, said that Haig's replacement by George Shultz raised the "possibility that the U.S. foreign policy course may become even tougher" (*WP*, 4 July). The U.S. ambassador to Moscow, Arthur Hartman, evidently sought to allay such concerns in his Independence Day address on Soviet television. Hartman said that the United States would like to arrest the decline in "our bilateral relationship." To achieve this, he said, "It will be necessary for both of our countries to act with restraint in the world." (Ibid., 5 July.)

In early August, the USSR expelled a U.S. correspondent, the first such expulsion since the mid-1970s. *Newsweek* correspondent Andrew Nagorski was accused of impersonating a Soviet correspondent during a visit to Vologda in October 1981; Nagorski said the charges were "all bogus" (*CSM*, 3

August). In retaliation, the U.S. State Department revoked the press credentials of *Izvestiia*'s chief Washington correspondent, Melor Sturua (*NYT*, 6 August).

Foreign Minister Gromyko met with Secretary of State Shultz at the United Nations in September and October. They reportedly discussed a number of issues, including Poland, Afghanistan, and arms reduction, but no major problem moved closer to resolution as a result of their talks (AP, 28 September; *NYT*, 5 October). Although Soviet-U.S. relations remained chilly, negotiations over grain sales indicated that the two countries could still cooperate when mutual economic interests dictated it (see above). When Yuri Andropov assumed the post of general secretary in November, Reagan administration officials quickly voiced willingness to work with the new Soviet leadership (*NYT*, 13 November). One early important step was revocation of pipeline sanctions by the United States (ibid., 14 November). However, this move had been planned before the Soviet leadership changeover and mostly reflected U.S. failure to enforce the sanctions and a desire to improve relations with European allies. Lifting of the sanctions had been made possible, according to Reagan, by an agreement among the allies "not to engage in trade arrangements which contribute to the military or strategic advantage of the USSR or serve to preferentially aid the heavily militarized Soviet economy" (AP, 13 November).

Following Brezhnev's funeral, an exchange of signals by U.S. and Soviet officials seemed to add new tensions to the relationship between the superpowers. Washington's basic position was that improvement in relations depended on Soviet behavior. Speaking at a Kremlin luncheon given for participants in the conference of the U.S.-USSR Trade and Economic Council, First Deputy Foreign Minister Georgi M. Kornienko said some people in Washington wanted the Soviets "to remake ourselves" (ibid., 16 November). On the day following Kornienko's blast, U.S. Ambassador Hartman told council members that "it is not realistic—and it has never been realistic—to isolate our economic relationship from our overall political relationship." Georgi A. Arbatov, head of the Institute of the U.S.A. and Canada and a close friend of Andropov's, made an immediate response to Hartman. Arbatov indicated that trade embargoes would not affect Soviet policies and scored the U.S. record on native Americans, Chile, and El Salvador. "Don't think that we owe you something," Arbatov said. "We will not pay for the lifting of sanctions by changing our society." (*NYT*, 18 November.)

Soviet Premier Tikhonov sounded a conciliatory note in his address to the conference, endorsing Reagan's expressed wish for improvements in U.S.-Soviet relations. But, Tikhonov warned, economic cooperation will not be possible if the U.S. continues to apply sanctions and other discriminatory measures against the USSR. (AP, 18 November.)

Shultz, on his return from Moscow, where he and Vice-President George Bush had represented the United States at Brezhnev's funeral, said that Washington will look to changes in the Soviet position at the Geneva arms talks as a sign of a "change in behavior" by the new leadership. The Novosti news agency responded with a statement rejecting the call for a change in Soviet policies, saying that "Soviet-American relations should be a two-way street." Senator Robert Dole, head of a congressional delegation to the Moscow trade conference, said that he saw no signs of any alteration of Soviet positions on Afghanistan, Poland, or human rights (UPI, 19 November).

Western Europe. The most imperative Soviet concern in this area continued to be the projected NATO nuclear buildup. Moscow encouraged Western peace and nuclear freeze movements, and the Soviet media reflected satisfaction over the results of the USSR's latest "peace offensive." Questions of nuclear arms deployment offered some hope of splitting the Western allies; economic issues held an even greater potential. The severe economic problems of the bloc, intensified by the crisis in Poland, generated pressures for the maintenance and improvement of economic ties with Western Europe, and a burgeoning credit crunch added to Moscow's woes. Refusal of major European countries to acquiesce in U.S. sanctions related to the natural gas pipeline constituted a major success for Moscow. Meanwhile, Western governments and banks, caught in a squeeze produced by overextension of credit to the East, were pressured to aid the Soviets in averting a further deterioration of the bloc economy.

West Germany was crucial for both the strategic and the economic objectives of the Soviets. In January, a West German consortium headed by Deutsche Bank failed to agree on a $150 million loan requested by the Soviets; the bankers were worried about the USSR's rapidly dwindling hard-currency reserves (BBC, 22 January). In February, Bonn sent a political signal to Moscow over Poland, barring the opening of new Soviet consulates in West Germany, restricting travel of Soviet diplomats, and halting negotiations on agreements on scientific cooperation and inland shipping. A planned visit of Chancellor Helmut Schmidt to Moscow was postponed, and a government spokesman said that Bonn would not "undermine" sanctions on the pipeline taken by its allies. (UPI, 17 February.)

By midsummer, the hard line of the West Germans had evaporated, as domestic political and economic pressures mounted for the Schmidt government. In July, West German bankers, reluctant in January to grant a small loan, concluded a major credit deal with the USSR. Deutsche Bank announced the availability of credit for export of $1.1 billion worth of pipeline equipment, with up to $1.6 billion to be available by the end of the year. The loans were granted for an eight-year period at an interest rate of 7.8 percent. (Ibid., 13 July.)

Although Schmidt had been a bulwark of German-U.S. cooperation, the fall of his coalition government was not an unmixed blessing for the Soviets. The new coalition had no faction as critical of NATO as the Social Democrats' left wing, and the new chancellor, Helmut Kohl, had long been an advocate of close relations with the United States. The Soviets sought to establish links with the new government via an official visit that had been planned before Schmidt's ouster on 1 October. RSFSR Premier Mikhail S. Solomentsev conferred in Bonn with Kohl six days after the latter's accession to power. Kohl assured Solomentsev that West Germany would remain a "solid, honest, and reliable partner" for the Soviet Union but qualified his wish for continued East-West cooperation by saying he wanted "genuine détente." Kohl expressed concern about Afghanistan and Poland and told Solomentsev that West Germany would go ahead with plans to deploy missiles by 1983 unless agreement on arms reduction was reached earlier. (*WP*, 8 October.)

The Solomentsev trip pointed up the Kremlin's continuing concentration on West Germany as the strategic and economic pivot of the Western alliance, an emphasis reflected in an August visit to Moscow by a top official of Schmidt's party. Horst Ehmke, deputy head of the Social Democrats' Bundestag *fraktion*, met in Moscow in August with several leading CPSU officials, including Leonid Zamyatin, head of the Foreign Information Department, and Vadim Zagladin, first deputy head of the International Department. Ehmke reported that Zagladin had given assurances that the Soviets had suspended deployment of the SS-20 in the European part of the USSR (Moscow domestic service, 18 August; DPA, Hamburg, 18 and 19 August; *FBIS*, 19 August).

Austrian President Rudolf Kirchschläger visited Moscow in May for talks with Brezhnev, Tikhonov, and Gromyko. At the conclusion of the talks, Kirchschläger stated that Austria "highly values the constructive, mutually advantageous relations with the Soviet Union, relations which are in fact a good example of cooperation between states with different social systems" (Tass, 26 May; *FBIS*, 27 May).

Moscow welcomed West European opposition to Reagan's pipeline sanctions, particularly the attitude of France, whose president, François Mitterrand, had been sharply critical of the USSR on Poland. The Soviet media played up French Foreign Minister Claude Cheysson's August statement denouncing the U.S. attempt to impose economic sanctions against the Soviet Union (Moscow domestic service, 10 August; *FBIS*, 11 August). While the pipeline debate raged, the Soviets received a French Foreign Ministry delegation in Moscow for talks with Deputy Foreign Minister Leonid F. Ilyichev on issues before the United Nations (*Izvestiia*, 6 August).

While the Soviets gave priority to Central Europe and to economic and nuclear arms issues, they also expressed alarm over possible changes in the correlation of forces affecting the southwestern part of the continent. Closer U.S.-Portugal military links, particularly the beefing up of the Lajes base in the Azores, were viewed as crucial to U.S. plans for positioning a rapid deployment force. Soviet commentator V. Vinogradov charged that the United States had applied a "carrot" to Portugal by supplying aircraft and a "stick" by threatening to freeze credits and loans (*Sovetskaia rossiia*, 5 June). Even more alarming was Spain's entry into NATO. *Izvestiia* (2 June) condemned the expansion of NATO's "zone of activity" and claimed that Spain's entry would exacerbate its "acute economic crisis." *Izvestiia* also pointed out that in view of the Falklands war, Spain's alignment with NATO would have a "negative effect" on the country's relations with Latin America.

Soviet relations with Britain, never smooth during the four years of Margaret Thatcher's Conservative government, hit bottom with the onset of the Falklands war. The Soviets took a militant pro-Argentine stance, accusing the British of militarism and great-power chauvinism (*Pravda*, 28 April) and even expressing in an official statement the hope that the Thatcher government would fall as a result of the crisis (Tass, 6 April). The Soviets supported the Argentine junta in the United Nations and reportedly used their satellites to track the British fleet for the Argentine forces. The U.S. Defense Department warned Moscow not to interfere in the Falklands conflict (*NYT*, 26 May). When, after the failure of U.S. Secretary of State Alexander Haig's mediation efforts, Washington came down solidly on the side of the British, the Soviets accused the United States and Britain of a joint imperialistic venture and charged that Washington was supporting the British counterinvasion in order to get a base in the South Atlantic (*Pravda*, 30 May).

The Soviets refused to accept the British proclamation of a 200-mile war zone around the Falklands, and for a time, there was some fear in Western circles of a possible naval confrontation between the USSR and Britain in the South Atlantic. However, it soon became clear that Moscow would take no risks in the area. Although backing a loser, the Soviets emerged with some gains from the Falklands episode, strengthening their important connection with the Argentines and identifying themselves with anti-U.S. elements in Latin America, without sacrificing their economic ties with NATO countries.

In southeastern Europe, Moscow moved cautiously to exploit the opportunity offered by the new leftist government in Greece, seeking closer relations with Athens without unduly alienating Turkey. A joint economic commission met in Moscow in June to plan expansion of trade between Greece and the USSR (Tass, 10 June; *FBIS*, 11 June).

Scandinavian countries remained uneasy about Soviet naval activities in the Baltic. In August, there was another scare as Sweden reported "unidentified submarines" in its territorial waters. Moscow denied that Soviet subs were in Swedish waters and angrily denounced charges by the Swedish and Danish defense chiefs that the USSR had operational plans for an attack on Sweden in the event of war (*Krasnaia zvezda*, 5 August). Swedish authorities had concluded that the Soviet Whiskey-class submarine captured in restricted Swedish territorial waters in October 1981 was armed with nuclear-tipped torpedoes. This conclusion was questioned in the November issue of the *U.S. Naval Institute Proceedings*. A U.S. military analyst said that the Whiskey-class submarine was not fast enough to avoid the shock waves associated with nuclear torpedo firings and was probably engaged in laying or servicing nuclear mines (UPI, 6 November). Growing controversy over an alleged conspiracy behind the 1981 attempt on the pope's life shadowed Soviet-Italian relations. When the investigation in Rome yielded charges of involvement by Bulgaria's security service, suspicion pointed to the KGB, generally believed to control the activities of its Bulgarian counterpart. Moscow repeatedly denied any connection between Soviet and Bulgarian security agencies and the attack on the pontiff. *Izvestiia* (29 December) charged that such reports were engineered by "circles of imperialism and special services of the United States and a number of NATO countries" and constituted "a new record of lies, slander, dirty sensation, and political provocation."

Eastern Europe. The main focus of attention in this area continued to be Poland, which remained under martial law until the end of the year. Moscow supported the martial law regime, although its inception had represented the virtual total collapse of the communist party (PUWP) in Poland. The Soviets kept close tabs on events in Poland through frequent travel of officials between Warsaw and Moscow and shored up the military dictatorship with financial aid and shipments of food and other supplies, despite the USSR's own severe economic problems. That situation changed under Andropov's growing influence and will be emphasized as he consolidates his power. In October, Poland was asked to repay part of its debt to the Soviet Union (*CSM*, 27 October).

Polish Premier Józef Czyrek visited Moscow, 10–12 January, for talks with Foreign Minister Gromyko and party secretary Mikhail Suslov (*Pravda*, 11 and 13 January). While the Soviets seemed generally satisfied with the early results of martial law, the Soviet press hinted that further purging of the PUWP was required (ibid., 29 December 1981, 23 January 1982; *Trud*, 13 January). In late February, Polish leader Gen. Wojciech Jaruzelski traveled to Moscow for talks with Brezhnev. At the conclusion of the talks, Jaruzelski blamed U.S. sanctions for aggravating the Polish crisis and called for additional Soviet aid. Jaruzelski described the Soviet-Polish alliance as "lasting and inviolable" and said that Poland will not be a "weak link" in the socialist commonwealth (*Pravda*, 1 and 2 March; AP, 2 March). The latter comment was somewhat pointed since, under the Brezhnev Doctrine, "weak links" provide the justification for military interventions.

The Soviet media expressed no opinions on the outbreak of street violence in Warsaw on 3 May, but Central Committee secretary for bloc affairs Konstantin Rusakov was shortly dispatched to Warsaw for consultations (*CSM*, 3 and 19 May). A continuing source of worry for the Kremlin was the powerful role of the Catholic church in Poland. When it appeared that Pope John Paul II might visit Poland during the summer, a Soviet press release said that the planned trip was a ploy to whip up opposition to martial law and accused the church of providing the climate for "extensive subversive acts" (Tass, 10 July; *FBIS*, 12 July). Apparently stung by Western charges of Soviet domination of Poland, the Soviets responded with vigorous denials. On a visit to Czechoslovakia, Vadim Zagladin described Western talk of "lack of autonomy" and "subordination" of socialist countries to Moscow as a "propagandist fairytale" (*Novoe vremya*, 13 August; *FBIS*, 19 August). In August, Brezhnev received Jaruzelski in the Crimea for a brief meeting on the continuing Polish crisis (Tass, 16 August).

Three days after the Polish parliament outlawed Solidarity, Defense Minister Ustinov sent a message to Jaruzelski pledging Moscow's backing for the intensified crackdown. "The Polish People's Republic," said Ustinov, "as a member of the Warsaw pact, may be absolutely sure of the full support and help of the Soviet Union" (*Krasnaia zvezda*, 12 October). When Solidarity leader Lech Wałęsa was released in November (*NYT*, 14 November), some Western observers saw the move as an indication of liberalizing tendencies on the part of the new Soviet leadership. Other Western analysts interpreted Wałęsa's release as unrelated to the Soviet leadership change; rather it was a sign that Solidarity had been so completely crushed that Wałęsa no longer posed a threat.

Party and government officials in Eastern Europe were reportedly generally pleased with the accession of Yuri Andropov to the first place in Moscow. His purported support for the Hungarian economic reforms during his tenure as secretary for bloc affairs was cited in numerous reports as providing hope to Eastern European leaders for greater flexibility in Moscow's relations with countries of the region.

Two East European countries outside the bloc attracted particular attention during the year. *Izvestiia* (7 June) detailed favorable results of Soviet-Finnish economic cooperation and hailed the USSR's relations with Finland as "evidence of the vitality of the policy of peaceful coexistence of states with different social systems." Moscow was reportedly seeking to take advantage of the new political instability in Albania, which had broken with China in 1978, to restore relations with that country. The U.S. Defense Department reported that the Soviets had expressed interest in obtaining Albanian naval facilities to compensate for the entry of Spain into NATO (*Los Angeles Times*, 2 April).

Afghanistan. The Soviets remained bogged down in Afghanistan, unable to pacify the country or to exit gracefully, and USSR military forces there had risen to some 100,000 troops. At year's end, some Western observers thought the new Soviet leadership would set a high priority on achieving an early negotiated settlement. However, there were some signs during the year that the Soviets might be settling in for a long stay, which, if true, would have serious geopolitical implications for both the West and China. It seemed likely that any Sino-Soviet rapprochement would depend, among other things, on Moscow's willingness to withdraw from the area. Western hopes for greater Soviet flexibility on Afghanistan were squashed by a *Pravda* editorial (16 December) and a Tass statement (31 December) that indicated Moscow's "unyielding stand in the Afghan dispute" (*NYT*, 1 January 1983).

In February, a French newspaper published a photograph of what it claimed was a Soviet missile site in Afghanistan, probably for SS-20s. The newspaper also reported installation by the Soviets of missiles around Kabul. (*Paris-Match*, 5 February.) Against a background of insurgent gains and fierce Soviet retaliations, the Soviets moved to set up a new secret police organization in Afghanistan, with security experts from the USSR and East Germany directing its organization and staffing (*NYT*, 8 March). In July, the Soviets were reported to have begun construction of an airfield at Shindand in western Afghanistan and to have arranged a border adjustment with Kabul designed to strengthen the Soviet position in the northern corridor leading to the frontier with China (ibid., 1 July).

Soviet involvement deepened during the summer, with elite Soviet forces heavily involved in fighting in the Panjshir valley alongside Afghan units, who were increasingly demonstrating an inability to cope with the rebels without strong support and direction from Soviet personnel (ibid., 17 October). In November, a fuel truck explosion in the Salang Tunnel north of Kabul reportedly resulted in the deaths of 2,000 Afghan civilians and 700 Soviet soldiers. Apparently, Soviet officers had assumed that the explosion signaled a rebel attack and had ordered both ends of the tunnel closed, blocking all escape routes for those inside. (AP, 10 November.)

Presumably aiming to dampen speculation prompted by the November meeting between Andropov and Pakistan's Zia, *Pravda* (16 December) reaffirmed the USSR's conditions for troop withdrawal and blamed the United States and Pakistan for the continuing war in Afghanistan. The editorial called the Afghan revolution "irreversible" but did not mention Babrak Karmal or his ruling People's Democratic Party.

Third World. Responding to Western allegations that the USSR's aid to developing countries is low, Yevgenii Makeev, Soviet delegate to the U.N. Economic and Social Council, charged that the West is misrepresenting Soviet aid in an effort to split the "natural alliance between communist and developing countries." Makeev said that the USSR increased economic aid to the Third World from 0.9 percent of its gross national product in 1976 to 1.3 percent in 1980 and that the total aid for 1976 to 1980 amounted to $30 billion. However, Makeev gave no breakdown by country, and it was unclear whether Soviet subsidies to Cuba and Vietnam were included in the figures. (Reuters and UPI, 12 July; *Radio Liberty Research*, 19 July.)

Middle East. The Soviets suffered a major setback in this area when the Israeli invasion of Lebanon forced the evacuation and dispersal of Moscow-backed PLO forces. The prowess of the Soviet military machine was also brought into question by the easy destruction of Syrian-operated MiG fighters and surface-to-air missiles by the U.S.-equipped Israelis.

Government statements condemned the Israeli action as a "massive aggression" and "bandit action" and as "blatant brigandage" (Tass, 6 and 14 June; *FBIS*, 15 June). The Soviets charged the United States with a "policy of connivance and encouragement of the Israeli aggressors" in order to further the "strategic plans and hegemonist aspirations of the present Washington administration regarding the Arab peoples and the whole of the Middle East region" (Tass, 11 June; *FBIS*, 15 June). The Soviets issued a warning to Israel on 14 June that the situation in Lebanon "cannot help but affect the interests of the USSR" and delivered a stern protest following Israeli shelling of the USSR Embassy in Beirut, which caused "material damage" (Tass, 14 and 21 June).

A Soviet military delegation headed by the first deputy commander of the USSR Air Defense Forces arrived in Damascus on 13 June (Damascus domestic service, 13 June; *FBIS*, 16 June). One week later, a "senior official" in Moscow indicated that an escalation of Israel's fighting with Syrian forces or a full-scale Israeli assault on PLO positions inside Beirut might lead to deeper Soviet involvement (*CSM*, 23 June). However, the Soviets limited their overt activity to an airlift of military equipment to Damascus. Visits to Moscow by Jordan's King Hussein and by senior PLO officials (*Pravda*, 26 June, 1 and 5 July) failed to shake the Kremlin's stance of strictly limited involvement. USSR Foreign Minister Gromyko reportedly told Farouk Kaddoumi, foreign affairs spokesman for the PLO, that sending Soviet warships or troops to the region was "out of the question" (*NYT*, 6 July).

Soviet inaction not only aroused bitterness in PLO ranks but also served to diminish the USSR's influence among the countries of the Confrontation Front—Algeria, Syria, Libya, and the People's Democratic Republic of Yemen. Moscow reacted with strong sensitivity to charges that the USSR had rendered "insufficient support to the Arab cause" (Tass, 30 June; *NYT*, 2 July) and repeatedly denied reports concerning the inferiority of Soviet arms used in the conflict (Tass, 30 June, 20 and 27 July; *FBIS*, 21 and 27 July). In August, Brezhnev warned Washington against a U.S. military presence in Lebanon, but the subsequent entry and re-entry of U.S. Marines into the country produced only further denunciations by Moscow. The situation changed at the end of the year when Syria began building sites to handle long-range Soviet antiaircraft missiles (*NYT*, 8 January 1983). A much more active Soviet involvement in the Middle East was expected.

In the Persian Gulf region, Moscow sought to maintain neutrality in the Iraq-Iran war and retain some influence with both sides. The Soviets reiterated their call for a negotiated settlement of the conflict and charged that the war gave the U.S. administration "an excuse to justify its military preparations in the Middle East and the Indian Ocean" (Radio Moscow, 14 July; *FBIS*, 15 July). In February, the USSR and Iran signed an agreement to speed completion of two electric power plants being constructed by the Soviets in Iran (*Izvestiia*, 15 February). Soviet trade with Iran had reportedly increased to $1.2 billion in 1981, a 30 percent increase over 1978, and *Izvestiia* announced that the Soviet Union had purchased 16 million barrels of Iranian oil in 1981 (*WP*, 16 February). A commentary in *Pravda* (9 March) noted the improvement in economic relations and reported that the USSR was engaged in a number of construction projects in Iran. However, *Pravda* warned that certain "right-wing groups" in the Iranian leadership wanted to stop the development of Soviet-Iranian relations "even if this damages the economy of the country and Iran's ability to withstand imperialist pressure." In June, Moscow made one minor move to solidify relations with Iraq. The Iraqi-USSR and USSR-Iraqi friendship societies signed a protocol on cultural, technical, and scientific cooperation (Iraqi News Agency, Baghdad, 7 June; *FBIS*, 9 June).

China. During the year, Moscow sent numerous signals to Beijing indicating a Soviet desire for improved relations. The Chinese responded favorably to some of these signals but also made it clear that the sources of their dissatisfaction with Moscow remained. In November, Beijing issued a ringing declaration of China's neutrality vis-à-vis the superpowers. Chinese leaders seemed determined to maximize their leverage in world politics by themselves playing the "China card" against both Moscow and Washington. The new Soviet leadership appeared desirous of a thaw between Moscow and Beijing, but thorny problems remained; Afghanistan and border issues loomed as major obstacles to an early normalization of relations.

In a February interview, Premier Tikhonov expressed Soviet willingness to deal with the PRC, saying that the USSR would not avoid "concrete steps" to improve relations and expected a reciprocal attitude in Beijing (*WP*, 15 February). Tikhonov's remarks followed delivery, on 1 February, of a Soviet proposal for resumption of border negotiations, which formalized a tentative move in this direction made in October 1981 (AP and UPI, 22 February; Reuters, 23 February). Brezhnev accelerated the Soviet drive for improved relations with his Tashkent speech in March. While Brezhnev criticized China's "alliance with imperialist policies," he asserted that the USSR had never denied "the existence of a socialist system in China" and affirmed Moscow's support for "PRC sovereignty over the island of Taiwan." The USSR was willing to negotiate with the PRC, said Brezhnev, "without any preliminary conditions." (*Pravda*, 25 March.) The immediate Chinese response to Brezhnev's speech was frosty. A PRC Foreign Ministry statement voiced "firm rejection" of the "attacks on China" in Brezhnev's speech. "What we attach importance to," the statement continued, "are actual deeds of the Soviet Union in Sino-Soviet relations and international affairs." (NCNA, 26 March; *Radio Liberty Research*, 6 May.)

Mikhail S. Kapitsa, a top USSR Foreign Ministry expert on China, made a five-day "private trip" to Beijing in May to sound out the Chinese on improving relations (*WP*, 20 May). In a move reminiscent of the Ping-Pong diplomacy between the United States and the PRC in the early 1970s, four Soviet track and field stars competed in a Beijing meet in June (*Pravda*, 16 June); these were the first Soviet athletes to perform in China since 1965. But Beijing continued to avoid any definite steps toward rapprochement, and numerous sharp criticisms of the PRC in the Soviet media during the summer reflected Moscow's growing frustration. However, Soviet press commentaries on the Chinese party's congress in early September were notably restrained, and Brezhnev made another overture in a speech in Baku on 26 September, calling for "normalization" and "a gradual improvement of relations" on the basis of "common sense, mutual respect, and mutual advantage" (ibid., 27 September).

Soviet persistence led in September to a resumption of negotiations, the first high-level formal talks since the invasion of Afghanistan. USSR Deputy Foreign Minister Leonid F. Ilyichev, veteran Soviet negotiator on the border questions, visited Beijing for several days of talks, which were played down by the Chinese side as merely "consultations." The talks evidently produced no positive results; the Soviets reportedly refused to discuss Afghanistan and Vietnam. (AFP, Hong Kong, 16 October; *FBIS*, 18 October.) Meanwhile, the Soviets toned down their press criticism of the PRC. The Chinese press, however, continued to print articles depicting the Soviet Union as expansionistic, and a senior Chinese diplomat was quoted as saying that "Chinese foreign policy will not change because the Soviet Union is still hegemonistic" (*NYT*, 23 October).

An authoritative article in the Chinese party's chief newspaper in early November denounced both the United States and the USSR, condemning them as threats to world peace. Foreign affairs specialist Huan Xiang said that China's policy is never to become attached to any big power or group of powers, never to yield to big-power pressure, and constantly to safeguard Chinese security and interests. The influence of the superpowers on world politics is waning, Huan said, but he warned of the "possibility of regional wars evolving into world wars." He attributed major existing international tensions to the "hegemonism and expansionism" of both superpowers. (AP, 2 November.)

In the following fortnight, the USSR and PRC exchanged positive signals. On the sixty-fifth anniversary of the Bolshevik Revolution, the Chinese held the first reception for Soviet officials in Beijing's Great Hall of the People in twenty years (UPI, 6 November). Soviet media included the PRC delegation to Brezhnev's funeral in listings of guests from friendly communist countries, and the chief Chinese representative, Foreign Minister Huang Hua, met for 90 minutes with Gromyko and was greeted cordially at Brezhnev's funeral by Andropov. However, three days later, Beijing announced Huang's long-expected retirement, which aroused speculation about possible displeasure among the PRC leadership over the Moscow talks. Coincident with Huang's retirement, PRC Premier Zhao Ziyang asserted that improved Sino-Soviet relations depended on specific actions, including removal of Soviet forces away from the Chinese border, withdrawal of Soviet troops from Afghanistan, and an end to support for Vietnam's incursion into Kampuchea (AP, 19 November).

Japan. The desire of the Japanese to recover the Northern Territories lost at the conclusion of World War II continued to be the principal irritant in relations between Moscow and Tokyo. Although there were no indications of a Soviet willingness to yield on this central issue, Brezhnev called, in his March Tashkent speech, for discussions on confidence-building measures between Moscow and Tokyo that would not necessarily require immediate participation by other countries (*Pravda*, 25 March). At the beginning of April, Soviet commentator Stanislas Modenov noted Japan's slowness in responding to Brezhnev's initiative and said that the USSR was not responsible for the absence of a peace treaty between the two countries. He attributed strained relations between Japan and the USSR to "external forces" that sought to propagate the "myth of the Soviet menace" and to inflame passions over the "so-called Northern Territories" (*Sovetskaia rossiia*, 1 April; *FBIS*, 19 April). A June report on a symposium on relations between the USSR and Japan attended by Soviet journalists pictured Japanese public opinion as apathetic on the issue of the Northern Territories and quoted an unnamed Japanese newspaper as blaming the deterioration of relations between Tokyo and Moscow on U.S. influence (*Za rubezhom*, 3 June; *FBIS*, 15 June).

The Japanese government expressed "regret" over President Reagan's decision in June to extend the pipeline sanctions. Officials pointed out that restrictions on equipment sales would delay a Japanese-Soviet oil and natural gas project off the coast of Sakhalin. (*CSM*, 22 June.) While Moscow welcomed any signs of Japanese willingness to cooperate on economic matters, its principal concern appeared to be the regional military correlation of forces. *Izvestiia* (5 July, 9 August) expressed concern over Japanese-Australian military cooperation and viewed with alarm the growing "militarization" of the member-states of the Association of Southeast Asian Nations (ASEAN). In a 9 August commentary, *Izvestiia* charged that the United States had in recent years sold the ASEAN states $2.5 billion in weapons. At the same time, *Izvestiia* claimed that there was growing apprehension in Southeast Asia about the "prospect of Japan's transformation into a powerful military state." The situation turned to the worse at the end of the year, and in early 1983, Japan was warned that its closer military ties with the United States could lead to a Soviet nuclear retaliation.

India. Moscow stepped up attempts to court New Delhi during the year, but on balance, India appeared to have retreated somewhat from its formerly close relationship with the USSR. Worried both by the Soviet presence in Afghanistan and by the flow of U.S. arms to Pakistan, India increased its military budget by 20 percent and continued its recent policy of diversifying arms purchases by concluding in February a $400 million deal for four West German submarines.

The Soviets sought to forge closer links with New Delhi by the March visit of a high-level military delegation headed by Defense Minister Ustinov. Countering Western arms suppliers, Ustinov reportedly offered to sell India MiG-27 combat aircraft, T-82 tanks, and surface-to-air missiles (*Los Angeles Times*, 21 March). When Indian Prime Minister Indira Gandhi's July visit to Washington for talks with President Reagan indicated a warming of U.S.-Indian relations, Moscow emphasized continuing points of disagreement between the United States and India, notably Pakistan and New Delhi's request for a loan from the International Monetary Fund (Tass, 30 July; *FBIS*, 2 August).

In September, the Soviets welcomed Prime Minister Gandhi to Moscow for a state visit and talks with

Brezhnev, Gromyko, and other officials (*Pravda*, 22 and 23 September). Among the subjects discussed were a project for a 1,000-Mw nuclear plant to be built in India with Soviet aid and Brezhnev's call for a "zone of peace" in the Indian Ocean. Gandhi announced India's support for a negotiated political solution to the war in Afghanistan and agreed to a Brezhnev proposal that NATO and the Warsaw pact pledge to refrain from extending their activities to Asia, Africa, and Latin America. (AFP, Paris, 22 September; *FBIS*, 24 September.)

Gandhi returned to Moscow for Brezhnev's funeral in November and talked with Andropov (Tass, 16 November). Andropov also held a private conversation with Pakistani President Mohammad Zia ul Haq, fueling speculation that the new Soviet leader was trying to involve both India and Pakistan in a negotiated settlement of the war in Afghanistan.

Africa. The Soviets confronted new tensions with their principal allies on the African continent during the year. Its resources stretched thin, Moscow was unable to meet the aid demands of the Marxist regimes in Angola and Ethiopia. Angola was reportedly tempted by a Western offer of $80 million in aid in exchange for the departure of 19,000 Cuban troops stationed in that country. However, in July, Angola rejected a U.S. proposal for the simultaneous withdrawal of Cuban troops from Angola and South African occupation forces from Namibia (*Pravda*, 26 July). In June, a detachment of Soviet warships paid an "official friendly visit" to Angola (*Krasnaia zvezda*, 13 June).

The USSR was reported to have established a naval base on Nocra, an island in the Dahlak Archipelago off Ethiopia's Red Sea coast (*WP*, 2 January). The Soviets had given Ethiopia more than $2 billion in military aid, but during the summer, the U.S. State Department reported that there was no evidence of direct Soviet or Cuban involvement in the fresh outbreak of violence in Somalia (*NYT*, 7 July). Despite the heavy influx of Soviet military aid for its conflict with Somalia, the Ethiopian regime was reportedly dissatisfied with the lack of aid for development, famine relief, and other nonmilitary purposes. Moscow had rejected Ethiopia's demand for more economic aid and an extension of the Soviet-Ethiopian oil purchase agreement when Col. Mengistu Haile Mariam visited Moscow in 1981. Ethiopia had responded by initiating economic negotiations with several Western countries. Also in 1981, the Ethiopian government had secured the transfer of the Soviet ambassador in Addis Ababa, Boris Kirnasovsky. On the Soviet side, there was reported dissatisfaction with Mengistu's failure to introduce orthodox Soviet-style party rule in Ethiopia (*Free Press Journal*, New Delhi, 24 March).

In an effort to improve ties with Ethiopia, the Soviets invited Mengistu for another visit to Moscow, where he conferred in October with Brezhnev, Gromyko, and Boris Ponomarev (*Pravda*, 14 October). The official communiqué on the visit indicated agreements on a number of international issues and continuing joint projects, but contained no significant offer of additional Soviet aid (Tass, 16 October; *FBIS*, 18 October).

Latin America. The most dramatic development for the Soviets in this region was the Falklands war. Although emerging on the losing side without taking any unacceptable risks, the Soviets gained additional general influence in Latin America and particularly strengthened their already important ties with Argentina (see above).

The USSR was reportedly helping Cuba build a nuclear power plant and promised to increase its economic aid during the 1981–1985 period by 1.8 percent over the previous five-year period (*WP*, 1 May). The Soviets were also reported to be engaged in a major modernization of Cuban ground, sea, and air forces; the United States claimed that Soviet merchant ships had delivered 66,000 tons of military equipment to Cuba between January 1981 and August 1982. The U.S. State Department said that the military buildup in Cuba "threatens U.S. interests in the Western Hemisphere" (UPI, 22 August).

The growing Soviet interest in the region was pointed up by two official visits during the year. Geidar A. Aliev, first secretary of the Azerbaijan party and then a candidate Politburo member, led a delegation that visited Mexico City in April for discussions with Mexican parliamentarians (*Pravda*, 24 April). A delegation led by Tikhon Y. Kiselev, first secretary of the Belorussian party and a candidate Politburo member, toured Brazil in June at the invitation of the Brazilian Chamber of Deputies (ibid., 30 June, 1 July). Moscow maintained an active interest but a reserved attitude in the potentially explosive situation in

Central America and the Caribbean. It cooperated with the Marxist-Leninist regime in Nicaragua and discreetly supported Cuban activism in El Salvador, Grenada, and Suriname.

International Party Contacts. The most dramatic occasion for contact between the CPSU and other parties during the year was the funeral of Soviet party leader Leonid Brezhnev. Among the leaders of ruling parties who attended the funeral, the greatest media attention was received by Cuba's Fidel Castro, Poland's Gen. Wojciech Jaruzelski, and Afghanistan's Babrak Karmal, all of whom met with Andropov (*NYT*, 15–17 November). For eight months prior to Brezhnev's death, the rapid deterioration of his health had caused him to severely restrict his activities, including meetings with representatives of other communist parties. Some of the slack was taken up by Andropov following his appointment as Central Committee secretary for ideology and foreign affairs in May. Boris Ponomarev, head of the Central Committee's International Department and secretary for nonruling communist parties, also pursued a rigorous schedule. Given the serious problems confronting several communist party-states, Andropov's experience in bloc affairs may have played some role in both of his promotions during the year. Andropov had served as Central Committee secretary for relations with ruling communist parties between 1962 and 1967.

Poland was again the most important area of CPSU concentration within the bloc. The Soviets kept the volatile situation in Poland under close observation through a number of meetings with Polish officials. In January, Stanislaw Gabrielski, chief of a Polish Central Committee section, journeyed to Moscow for talks with Soviet Central Committee cadres secretary Ivan V. Kapitonov on "questions of party political work" (*Pravda*, 23 January). Following new outbreaks of violence in Warsaw, Soviet Central Committee secretary for relations with ruling communist parties Konstantin V. Rusakov visited Poland in May for talks about the crisis with leading Polish officials (ibid., 17 May). In August, Jaruzelski reported to Brezhnev on the situation in Poland at the regular summer meeting with the CPSU leader in the Crimea (ibid., 17 August).

The Polish crisis also figured prominently in Brezhnev's Crimea meetings with East German party chief Erich Honecker and Czechoslovak party head Gustáv Husák (Radio Liberty, 17 August). Earlier, Husák had met Brezhnev in Moscow for talks on Poland (Tass, 3 June). The Polish crisis also formed the backdrop for CPSU Politburo member and USSR Defense Minister Dmitri F. Ustinov's October visit to Prague (Moscow domestic service, 6 October; *FBIS*, 6 October).

A flurry of interparty contacts in June emphasized the close relationship between the USSR and Bulgaria, Moscow's most reliable ally in the bloc and the most vociferous supporter of "proletarian internationalism." The centennial of the birth of Georgi Dimitrov, prominent figure in the Comintern, was marked by an international theoretical conference in Sofia entitled "The Cause of Georgi Dimitrov and the World Today." The CPSU delegation was led by Boris Ponomarev and Mikhail V. Zimianin, Central Committee secretary for culture (BTA, Sofia, 14 June; *FBIS*, 15 June). The Bulgarian party delegation to the Moscow celebration of the Dimitrov centennial was headed by Todor Bozhinov, member of the Bulgarian Politburo and first deputy chairman of the Bulgarian Council of Ministers. Representing the CPSU at the Moscow fete were Moscow city first secretary Viktor V. Grishin, Party Control Committee chairman Arvid I. Pelshe, USSR Minister of Culture Piotr N. Demichev, and Konstantin Rusakov. Rusakov delivered a report entitled "Georgi Dimitrov: Outstanding Fighter for Peace and Socialism" (*Pravda*, 18 June).

A delegation of Bulgarian party workers led by Central Committee secretary Vasil Tsanov visited the USSR, 7–12 June, for an "exchange of experience of work in implementing the Twenty-Sixth CPSU and Twelfth Bulgarian congresses' decisions in the sphere of agriculture and the food industry." The talks were led on the Soviet side by Central Committee secretary for agriculture Mikhail S. Gorbachev. Also participating were Central Committee department heads Vladimir A. Karlov (agriculture), Ivan I. Sakhnyuk (agricultural machine building), and Fedor I. Mochalin (light and food industry) (ibid., 13 June). Grisha Filipov, chairman of the Council of Ministers of the Bulgarian People's Republic and member of the Bulgarian Politburo, was received by Brezhnev two weeks later in Moscow, where he conferred with Soviet Premier Tikhonov (Moscow domestic service, 24 June; *FBIS*, 25 June). Rounding out the heavy schedule of interparty contacts was a visit in June to Moscow by Chudomir Aleksandrov, first secretary of the Sofia city party organization and secretary of the Bulgarian Central Committee (*Pravda*, 27 June).

The close ties between the Soviet and Bulgarian parties were further emphasized by an October visit of

Soviet Central Committee secretary for heavy industry and candidate Politburo member Vladimir I. Dolgikh to Sofia, where he was received by Bulgarian party chief Todor Zhivkov (Moscow domestic service, 5 October; *FBIS*, 6 October).

Chiefs and deputy chiefs of party organizational work sections of the bloc parties met in Moscow in February to prepare for a conference of Central Committee secretaries on party organizational work. The CPSU host delegation was led by N. A. Petrovichev, first deputy head of the Soviet Central Committee's Department of Party Organizational Work, assisted by S. I. Kolesnikov, a senior official in the same department (*Pravda*, 21 February). Also in February, Viktor V. Grishin, Politburo member and Moscow city first secretary, led a delegation to Budapest to take part in the "Moscow Days" (Tass, 26 February; *FBIS*, 1 March). In March, I. P. Dyatlov, deputy chief of the Central Committee's Construction Department, led a delegation to Romania to "familiarize" itself with Romanian experience in capital construction (*Pravda*, 23 March).

A delegation of Mongolian party workers headed by P. Damdin, secretary of the Mongolian Central Committee, visited Moscow, 22 February–2 March, for talks on problems of the light and food industries. The delegation was received by CPSU agriculture secretary Gorbachev and M. I. Polyakov, first deputy head of the Central Committee's Department for Light and Food Industries. (Ibid., 3 March.)

The CPSU dispatched two officials with long experience in Sino-Soviet affairs to the congress of the League of Communists of Yugoslavia, leading to speculation about a possible Soviet bid for Yugoslav mediation in the dispute with the PRC. The CPSU delegation to the congress was led by Soviet vice-president and candidate Politburo member Vasili V. Kuznetsov and included Oleg Rakmanin, first deputy head of the Central Committee's Department for Liaison with the Communist and Workers' Parties of the Socialist Countries (Tass, 25 June; *FBIS*, 25 June).

A Korean Workers' Party delegation headed by Choe Ik-kyu, deputy chief of the Korean propaganda and agitation section, visited Moscow 2–6 July for discussions on party leadership in moviemaking. The delegation was received by Central Committee secretary for culture Mikhail V. Zimianin and Vasili F. Shauro, candidate member of the Central Committee and head of the Culture Department (*Pravda*, 7 July).

Faced with mounting economic troubles at home, the USSR took a tougher stance on aid to countries outside the Soviet inner bloc. Brezhnev met Laotian Prime Minister and Politburo member Kaysone Phomvihan twice during the year, in March and September, to register Soviet complaints about poor economic planning in Laos and waste of Soviet aid. The official communiqué on the September talks in Moscow reported that the leaders had agreed on the need to "raise the efficiency of economic cooperation between the two countries and insure a more rational use of Lao resources" (Tass and Reuters, 29 September).

The war in Lebanon was behind the June visit to Moscow by Nadim 'Abd al-Samad, Central Committee secretary and Politburo member of the Lebanese party. He met with Ponomarev and deputy head of the Central Committee's International Department Karen Brutents (Tass, 25 June; *FBIS*, 28 June).

While the Soviets relied mainly on the Gandhi government in their dealings with India, they also moved to strengthen ties with the Communist Party of India. The CPSU delegation to the Indian party's congress in March was led by Eduard A. Shevardnadze, first secretary of the Georgian party and candidate Politburo member (*Pravda*, 22 March). In June, Rajeswara Rao, general secretary of the Indian party, visited Moscow for talks with Andropov, Ponomarev, and Rostislav A. Ulyanovsky, deputy head of the Central Committee's International Department. Among the topics discussed were disarmament, Lebanon, the proposed "peace zone" in the Indian Ocean, and tensions in Asia (ibid., 27 June).

Soviet activities in the Third World and the accompanying "proletarian internationalism" rhetoric were somewhat curtailed under Brezhnev as the CPSU concentrated on domestic and bloc problems. One notable exception was South Yemen. Several interparty contacts spotlighted the strategic importance of that country for Moscow. General Vasili I. Petrov, Central Committee member and commander in chief of Soviet ground forces, and Gen. Aleksei A. Yepishev, head of the Main Political Administration of the Soviet armed forces, made separate visits to Aden in June (Aden domestic service, 4 June; *FBIS*, 8 June). A delegation headed by F. A. Ahmad, deputy secretary of the Yemen Socialist Party, visited Moscow in the same month (*Pravda*, 10 June). A delegation of the USSR Supreme Soviet was received by Ali Nasir Muhammad al-Hasani, general secretary of the Yemeni party and prime minister of the People's Democratic Republic of Yemen, in August. The Soviet delegation was led by Midkhat Shakirov, first secretary of

Bashkirsky *obkom*, and Richard I. Kosolapov, editor of *Kommunist* (Tass, 13 August; *FBIS*, 16 August). In August, Hasani visited Moscow for talks with Brezhnev, Chernenko, Gromyko, and Ponomarev. Yemen's highest award was presented to Brezhnev (*Pravda*, 17 September), and a credit agreement on construction of a thermopower station in South Yemen was signed (Moscow domestic service, 16 September; *FBIS*, 17 September).

The importance attached to close ties with the French Communist Party was indicated by the designation of ranking Politburo member and Central Committee secretary Chernenko to Paris as chief CPSU delegate to the French party's congress in February (*Pravda*, 4 February). In September, Vadim Zagladin traveled to Paris for "regular consultations" with Maxime Gremetz, secretary of the French Central Committee and member of the French Politburo (ibid., 19 September).

Moscow welcomed the orthodox Alvaro Cunhal, secretary general of the Portuguese party, in June for talks with Brezhnev, Ponomarev, and Zagladin (*Avante*, Lisbon, 24 June; *FBIS*, 2 July).

Relations with the leadership of the Communist Party of Italy (PCI) were strained; the CPSU sought to cultivate links with lower-level PCI activists. In July, a group of PCI members led by Anna-Maria Garloneyi, a secretary of the Bologna city PCI federation, visited Armenia and was welcomed by L. Manaseryan, head of the Armenian party's Information and Foreign Relations Department (*Sovetakan ayastan*, 1 August; *FBIS*, 24 August). A delegation of PCI federation secretaries led by Italian Central Committee member L. Sandirocco, visited the USSR on 22–30 September for talks with Soviet Central Committee and Moscow *gorkom* officials and with personnel of the theoretical journal *Kommunist* (*Pravda*, 2 October). On the other hand, contacts and exchanges of views with top PCI leaders, including Enrico Berlinguer, secretary general of the party, were maintained.

The Soviet "peace offensive" in Western Europe brought two leading West German Communists to Moscow in July. Herbert Mies, chairman of the German party, and Karl Heinz Schröder, member of the Secretariat and Presidium, conferred with Andropov, Ponomarev, and Anatoly Chernayev, deputy head of the Central Committee's International Department (ibid., 27 July).

The CPSU maintained regular contacts with several smaller Western European parties. Ezekias Papaioannou, secretary general of the Progressive Party of the Working People of Cyprus, traveled to Moscow for talks with Ponomarev in July (Tass, 30 July; *FBIS*, 2 August). In June and July, there was an exchange of visits between the CPSU and the Luxembourg party. A group of Luxembourg party activists, led by François Hoffmann, visited Armenia (*Sovetakan ayastan*, 20 June; *FBIS*, 9 July). A CPSU delegation headed by Leonid A. Gorshkov, first secretary of Kemerovsky *obkom*, visited Luxembourg at the invitation of the Luxembourg party (*Pravda*, 2 July). Two groups of Danish Communists visited the USSR. A delegation of party workers led by Poul Emanuel, member of the Executive Committee and secretary of the Danish Central Committee, met with officials of the Soviet Central Committee's International Department, the Belorussian Central Committee, and officials from Gosplan (ibid., 1 June). Danish party chairman Jorgen Jensen and a delegation of the leadership of the Union of Communist Youth of Denmark visited Moscow and Siberia (Moscow domestic service, 30 September; *FBIS*, 1 October). Kharilaos Florakis, general secretary of the Greek party, visited Moscow in August for talks with Andropov and Zagladin (Tass, 27 August; *FBIS*, 30 August).

There were several significant contacts with parties of sub-Saharan Africa. Gennadi V. Kolbin, member of the Soviet Central Committee and second secretary of the Georgian Central Committee, led a delegation to Guinea in January. The delegation was received by Democratic Party of Guinea Politburo members Lansane Diane and Mamady Keita (*Pravda*, 21 January). An agreement was signed in Brazzaville on the plan for 1982–1983 cooperation between the CPSU and the Congolese Labor Party (Radio Moscow, 21 May; *FBIS*, 25 May). General Aleksei A. Yepishev led a delegation of Soviet army and navy political workers on a June visit to Mozambique, where they were received by Gens. Alberto Chipande and Armando Guebuza, members of the Politburo (*Krasnaia zvezda*, 6 June). In September, Jorge Rubelo, member of the Mozambican Politburo and Secretariat, signed an agreement with Ponomarev in Moscow on interparty cooperation for 1983–1984 (*Pravda*, 25 September).

A CPSU delegation led by Yuri N. Khristoradrov, first secretary of Gorky *obkom*, visited Angola in August at the invitation of the Movement for the Popular Liberation of Angola and was received by First Secretary Evaristo Dominges. The official communiqué on the visit pledged solidarity on South African and Lebanese issues (ibid., 11 August). Contacts were also maintained with several key parties in Latin

America. Maurice Bishop, chairman of the Politburo of the New Jewel Movement and prime minister of Grenada, visited Moscow in July and conferred with Tikhonov, Ponomarev, and Gorbachev. Bishop signed economic agreements designed to cut his country's dependence on the West (ibid., 28 July). Ponomarev and New Jewel Politburo member Kendrick Radix concluded an agreement on interparty cooperation (Tass, 27 July; *FBIS*, 28 July).

The CPSU sent greetings to delegates of the Twenty-First Guyanese People's Progressive Party Congress (*Pravda*, 31 July). The CPSU delegation to the congress was led by Piotr Luchinsky, deputy head of the Central Committee's Propaganda Department (Tass, 2 August; *FBIS*, 3 August).

V. N. Ignatenko, deputy head of the Central Committee's International Information Department, represented the CPSU at the Forty-Fourth Conference of the Jamaican People's National Party, an electoral affiliate of the Jamaican Communist Party (*Pravda*, 14 September). Secretary General Guy Daninthe of the Guadeloupe Communist Party visited Moscow in September and conferred with Ponomarev. Daninthe pledged the support of his party on the Lebanese issue and general cooperation against imperialism (ibid., 21 September).

Biographies. *Yuri Vladimirovich Andropov.* Born 15 January 1914, at Nagutskaia village, Stavropol *krai*, Yuri Andropov was the son of a railway worker. After stints as a Volga boatman and a telegraph operator, he graduated from a technical school for water transport and entered Komsomol work at age 22.

Andropov served as secretary, then first secretary, of Yaroslavl *oblast* Komsomol committee, 1936–1940, and as first secretary of the Central Committee of the Karelian Komsomol, 1940–1944. He became a member of the CPSU in 1939 and, during World War II, was a political commissar on the Finnish front. Andropov served as first secretary of the Petrozavodsk party *gorkom,* 1944-1947, and as second secretary of the Central Committee of the Karelian Communist Party, 1947-1951. In 1951, he was transferred to Moscow, where he worked in the CPSU Central Committee apparatus until 1953, when he was appointed ambassador to Hungary. In 1957, he was named head of the CPSU Central Committee's Department for Liaison with the Communist and Workers' Parties of the Socialist Countries, a post he held until 1967; between 1962 and 1967, he was also CPSU secretary for ruling communist parties. Andropov was elected a member of the CPSU Central Committee in 1961. A deputy in the Council of the Union from 1950 to 1954 and from 1962 to the present, he was a member of that body's Foreign Affairs Commission from 1957 to 1967.

Named as head of the Committee for State Security (KGB) in May 1967, Andropov was elected a candidate member of the Politburo in the same year. In May 1973, he was promoted to full membership on the Politburo. On 24 May 1982, the CPSU Central Committee elected Andropov party secretary for ideology to succeed Mikhail Suslov, who had died the previous January. Following the death of Leonid Brezhnev, the Central Committee unanimously elected Andropov CPSU general secretary on 12 November.

Andropov has been awarded two Orders of Lenin and four Orders of the Red Banner of Labor. (Sources: Borys Lewytzkyj and Juliusz Stroynowski, eds., *Who's Who in the Socialist Countries*, Munich, 1978; *Pravda*, 25 May; *NYT*, 13 November.)

Geidar Ali Rza ogly Aliev. Born in Azerbaijan in 1923, Geidar Aliev became a member of the CPSU in 1945 and graduated from Azerbaijan State University in 1957. Recruited for police work in 1941, he served for nearly thirty years in state security organs, mostly in the Azerbaijan Committee for State Security (KGB), rising to the deputy chairmanship of that organization in 1964 and to the chairmanship in 1967. Named first secretary of the Azerbaijan Central Committee in 1969, he was elected full member of the CPSU Central Committee at the Twenty-Fourth Party Congress in 1971. A member of the Council of the Union since 1970, he served on that body's Commission for Youth Affairs, 1970–1974, and was elected deputy chairman of the Council of the Union in 1974.

Aliev was elected a candidate member of the CPSU Politburo following the Twenty-Fifth Party Congress in March 1976. Promoted to full member of the Politburo on 22 November 1982, he was elected first deputy chairman of the USSR Council of Ministers two days later by the Supreme Soviet. Aliev holds the Order of Lenin and the Order of the Red Star. (Sources: Borys Lewytzkyj and Juliusz Stroynowski, eds., *Who's Who in the Socialist Countries*, Munich, 1978; *Pravda*, 6 March 1976; *NYT*, 23 and 25 November.)

Vladimir Ivanovich Dolgikh. Born 5 December 1924 at Ilansky, a town in Siberia, Vladimir Dolgikh became a member of the CPSU in 1942, while serving in the Soviet army. Following graduation from the Irkutsk Mining Institute in 1949, he worked for nine years as an engineer in Krasnoyarsk. In 1958, he was assigned to the northern Siberian city of Norilsk, where he served as chief engineer, 1958–1962, and then director of the metallurgical Zaveniagin Combine.

In 1969, Dolgikh was named first secretary of the CPSU's Krasnoyarsk *obkom*, reportedly as the result of direct intervention by General Secretary Brezhnev. In December 1972, Dolgikh was elected to the CPSU Central Committee Secretariat, with responsibility for heavy industry. In recent years he has reportedly been charged with oversight of the development of West Siberia's oil fields. At the CPSU Central Committee plenum of 24 May 1982, he was elected a candidate member of the Politburo.

Dolgikh has served as a deputy of the USSR Supreme Soviet since 1966 and has been a full member of the CPSU Central Committee since 1971. He has been mentioned recently in Soviet political circles as a possible successor to Prime Minister Nikolai Tikhonov, 77. He is a recipient of the Order of Lenin. (Sources: Borys Lewytzkyj and Juliusz Stroynowski, eds., *Who's Who in the Socialist Countries*, Munich, 1978; *Radio Liberty Research Bulletin*, 30 May; *NYT*, 25 May.)

University of New Orleans   R. Judson Mitchell

Leonid Ilyich Brezhnev. The death of Brezhnev on 11 November 1982 was not unexpected. During the past few years, his public appearances had been infrequent, and observers speculated how much longer a man so obviously suffering from a number of cardiac ailments could survive. The former hard-drinking, chain-smoking gourmand knew that his habits were advancing his arteriosclerosis and tried to curb them, but he also enjoyed many of the other trappings of the ruling class: hunts, swimming, soccer games, the circus, the obligatory kissing of performers and dignitaries. With his wife, Viktoriya, and their three children, he led a fairly quiet, bourgeois life. His son Yuri is first deputy minister of foreign trade; a younger son is still a student at Moscow University. On the other hand, the reputation of his daughter, Galina Churbanova, a journalist for Novosti, whose recent scrape with the law resulted from her "unsavory" acquaintances among artists, added to recent general detraction from Brezhnev's aura of respectability.

Brezhnev was born on 19 December 1906 in Kamenskoye, now called Dneprodzerzhinsk, in the Ukraine, the son of simple working parents. At 15, he went to work in the steel mills like his father, but two years later, he enrolled in and completed night classes at a land survey and reclamation school at Kursk in four years. Already a member of the Young Communist League, he was accepted as a member of the CPSU in 1931, at the age of 25. At the same time, he entered engineering school in Dneprodzerzhinsk, graduating four years later. In 1937, he became mayor of his hometown and the next year party secretary of the Ukraine. Khrushchev was then head of the Ukrainian republican party, and it is assumed that their acquaintance and friendship dated from this period.

World War II saw him as officer and political commissioner for the 18th Army; he met many friends and future political supporters in the military. During the postwar period, he held various civilian party posts, such as supervising reconstruction in the Ukraine. Then in 1950, he was called for further training in Moscow at the Secretariat of the Central Committee. His rise was steady: the same year that he was called to Moscow, he was sent to the Moldavian republic as party chief, elected to membership on the CPSU Central Committee, became a candidate member of the Presidium (now Politburo), and was appointed a Central Committee secretary. This last position he kept until Stalin's death, when he was dropped from the Presidium as well.

After Khrushchev strengthened his grip on the party, he charged Brezhnev with the party leadership of Kazakhstan, where he was to supervise Khrushchev's pet virgin land project. After Brezhnev was able to bring 87 million acres under cultivation in two years, he earned the reputation of a great administrator, of a "man who gets things done," "who can do the impossible."

Between 1960 and 1964, he was president of the Soviet Union; during that time he traveled and did a great deal of public relations work for the USSR. In 1964, he stepped down as president to devote full time to his position as Central Committee secretary in charge of personnel selection to which he had been named the year before. That same year, Khrushchev was forced to retire early, and the leadership was turned over to a troika: Brezhnev, Aleksei Kosygin and Nikolai Podgorny. The then relatively unknown Brezhnev soon made himself the leading figure, altering the power configuration of the Politburo and removing Podgorny from a key Secretariat post to the chairmanship (presidency) of the Supreme Soviet. In 1977, before his age and failing health began to weigh heavily on him, he assumed the leadership of the Soviet state as well, dismissing Podgorny and consolidating his power. In the following years, he leaned more and more on Konstantin Chernenko, his faithful chief of staff for over twenty years, and full Politburo member since 1978, who was evidently Brezhnev's choice as his successor.

The fifteen-year Brezhnev era was one of relative stability. He tried to strengthen party power while modifying radical reforms begun by Khrushchev. He had made some concessions in arms control agreements, permitted many Jews to emigrate, and made conciliatory gestures toward Beijing. However, he faced domestic headaches with the disorderly economy, the growth of corruption, dissidence, and the demands of the military. During his term, the USSR also received worldwide censure for the invasions of Czechoslovakia and Afghanistan and the manipulation of the Polish military government. (Sources: *1982–83 International Who's Who*; Janis Sapiets, "Leonid Brezhnev Obituary," BBC Current Affairs Talks, transcript, 11 November; *NYT*, 12 and 14 November.)

Viktor Mikhailovich Chebrikov. The death of Brezhnev precipitated the second major change in KGB leadership in seven months. On 17 December 1982, Andropov's replacement, Vitali V. Fedorchuk, was in turn replaced by Viktor M. Chebrikov, a career party man like Andropov and a Ukrainian like Fedorchuk.

Chebrikov was born in 1923 in the Ukraine, presumably in Dnepropetrovsk. He entered the army at age eighteen, serving until 1946, and then enrolled in the Metallurgical Institute in Dnepropetrovsk, graduating as a metallurgical engineer in 1950. He now holds the rank of major general. He established his political base in Dnepropetrovsk, where Brezhnev was also party chief. There he joined the communist party in 1944 and was active regionally until 1967. His rise was steady: in 1956 he became a member of the auditing committee of the Ukrainian Communist Party; in 1958 its second secretary; in 1961–1963 its first secretary and head of the Dnepropetrovsk city committee; from 1963 to 1965 its secretary; and in 1965–1967 second secretary of the Dnepropetrovsk oblast committee. Chebrikov was called to Moscow in 1967 to head the cadre (personnel) administration of the KGB, and a year later, Brezhnev named him one of six deputy chairmen of the KGB under Andropov. In 1971, he became a candidate member and in 1981 a full member of the Central Committee of the CPSU.

Chebrikov is regarded as a close supporter and colleague of Andropov, but has also been considered one of the younger generation of Brezhnev supporters, in harmony with the party orientation he expressed in an article in *Molodoi kommunist* (April 1981) warning young people to beware of the bourgeois-inspired generation gap between them and the oldtime party leadership because this kind of internal dissention would delay the perfecting of socialism. (Sources: Boris Lewytzkyi and Juliusz Stroynowski, eds. *Who's Who in the Socialist Countries*, New York, 1978; *NYT*, 18 December 1982; *Los Angeles Times*, 18 December 1982; Alexander G. Rahr, "Chebrikov Replaces Fedorchuk as Head of KGB," *Radio Liberty Research Bulletin*, 12 January 1983.)

Vitali Vasilevich Fedorchuk. The same unsmiling photograph of the stocky, square-jawed Fedorchuk appearing for the first time in Soviet papers on 13 October and subsequently in Western newspapers fits his reputation as the ruthless chief enforcer of the Ukrainian security system for the past twelve years and practically a lifelong associate of the security services. It is difficult to imagine that this stern persecutor of dissidents, of Ukrainians suffering from the "Polish disease" (that is, Solidarity sympathizers among the important Polish minority near the Polish border), started his career as a worker in the district press (*Izvestiia*, 19 December) and supposedly learned English fluently and acquired a reputation as a heavy drinker and womanizer during his assignment in East Germany. He has been variously described as a "real thug," who could quite believably have arranged the rash of kidnappings and accidents that befell expatriates and Western agents in Vienna during his service there at the Soviet embassy, and a ruthless warden of the large, populous Ukraine, which tends to harbor religious (unregistered, illegal Eastern Catholics, Baptists, Jews) and ideological dissidents.

Fedorchuk was born in December 1918 in the Ukraine. Little is known of his early life or his family, except that he graduated from a military school, served in the Soviet army during World War II, and graduated from the KGB Academy with the rank of colonel general. Recently he was promoted to general.

His career as a professional security officer reached its zenith last May, when he was appointed—over other deputies who outranked him—head of the KGB to replace Andropov. Only six month later, on 17 December, a seeming demotion took place when Andropov replaced him with Viktor Chebrikov at the KGB and appointed Fedorchuk head of the Ministry of Internal Affairs (MVD), which operates the *militsia*, the conventional, uniformed police. The MVD is responsible for erasing crime, corruption (rampant even within the ranks of the MVD in connection with the USSR's "second economy," the black market, and for controlling dissent, riots, travel permits, and emigration papers. The functions of the two security agencies overlap somewhat; they were separated only thirty years ago when Beria's excesses and misuses of the agency to continue a reign of terror caused his execution and led to the fragmentation of the security agencies. Andropov, by appointing Fedorchuk, who is considered Andropov's protégé, may have hoped to streamline functions, eliminate waste and inefficiency by bringing in a fellow security officer and a faithful party man (member of CPSU since 1940, member of the Central Committee of the Ukrainian Communist Party though not that of the CPSU Central Committee, deputy of the Supreme Soviet of the USSR, member of the Legislative Proposals Commission of the USSR), and tighten party control over security agencies. It is also true that the security forces are permeating the party. Furthermore, the reorganization will permit the ending of the Brezhnev system of sinecure (the stability of cadres policy). (Sources: BBC, "Current Affairs Talks," 28 May 1982; *NYT*, 28 May, 14 October, 18 December 1982; *Los Angeles Times*, 18 December 1982; *FBIS*, 20 December 1982; *Business Week*, 22 November 1982; Alexander G. Rahr, "Chebrikov Replaces Fedorchuk as Head of KGB," *Radio Liberty Research Bulletin*, 12 January 1983; *Izvestiia*, 12 January 1983.)

Hoover Institution   Margit N. Grigory

Yugoslavia

The Communist Party of Yugoslavia (CPY) was created in June 1920, although Yugoslav Communists date their party to April 1919, when a unification congress in Belgrade established a Socialist Workers' Party of Yugoslavia (Communist), which included both communist and noncommunist elements. This party was disbanded fourteen months later. At the party's Sixth Congress in November 1952, the CPY changed its name to League of Communists of Yugoslavia (LCY). As the only political party in the Socialist Federative Republic of Yugoslavia (SFRY), the LCY exercises power through its leading role in the Socialist Alliance of the Working People of Yugoslavia (SAWPY), a front organization that includes all mass political organizations as well as individuals representing various social groups.

Population.   22.5 million (1 January 1982)
Party.   League of Communists of Yugoslavia (Savez komunista Jugoslavije; LCY)
Founded.   1920

Membership. 2.2 million; white-collar workers, 41.5 percent; blue-collar workers, 29.6 percent; unskilled, 8.8 percent (for a breakdown by nationality, see *YICA*, 1982, p. 495)

President of Presidium. Mitja Ribičič (1-year term)

Secretary of Presidium. Nikola Stojanović (2-year term)

Presidium. 23 members, 3 from each of the 6 republics, 2 from each of the 2 autonomous provinces, and 1 from the army: Slovenia, Mitja Ribičič, Milan Kučan, Andrei Marinc; Croatia, Vladimir Bakarić, Dušan Dragosavac, Jure Bilić; Bosnia-Hercegovina, Nikola Stojanović, Franjo Herljević, Hamdija Pozderac; Montenegro, Veljko Milatović, Miljan Radović, Dobroslav Ćulafić; Serbia, Dragoslav Marković, Dobrivoje Vidić, Dušan Čkrebić; Macedonia, Dimče Belovski, Kiro Hadži-Vasilev, Krste Markovski; Kosovo, Ali Šukrija, Sinan Hasani; Vojvodina, Petar Matić, Marko Djuričin; Army, Dane Ćuić

Central Committee. 165 members

Last Congress. Twelfth, 26–29 June, in Belgrade; next congress scheduled for 1986

Auxiliary Organizations. Confederation of Trade Unions of Yugoslavia (CTUY; 5 million members claimed), League of Socialist Youth of Yugoslavia (LSYY; 3.6 million members, 30 percent of whom are LCY members)

Main State Organs. No member of LCY Presidium may hold executive office in the SFRY, although the Presidium president is ex officio a member of the collective State Presidency and Vice-President Bakarić is on the LCY Presidium. The president and vice-president of the 8-member State Presidency serve 1-year terms, and the positions rotate among the members. The current president is Petar Stambolić (Serbia); the vice-president is Vladimir Bakarić (Croatia). Other members are Sergej Kraigher (Slovenia), Cvijetin Mijatović (Bosnia-Hercegovina), Lazar Koliševski (Macedonia), Vidoje Žarković (Montenegro), Radovan Vlajković (Vojvodina), and Fadil Hodža (Kosovo). The main administrative organ is the 29-member Federal Executive Council (FEC), theoretically chosen by and responsible to the Yugoslav Federal Assembly. FEC members serve 4-year terms. Major figures include Milka Planinc (premier); Zvone Dragan, Borislav Srebrić, Mijat Šuković (vice-premiers); Lazar Mojsov (foreign affairs); Branko Mamula (defense); Stane Dolanc (internal affairs).

Parliament and Elections. All candidates to the 220-seat Federal Chamber and the 88-seat Chamber of Republics and Provinces run on the ticket of the Socialist Alliance of the Working People of Yugoslavia (Socijalistički savez radnog naroda Jugoslavije; SAWPY). All delegates are chosen indirectly through a multilayer process. The people vote freely for delegates only at the local level. At the provincial/republic and federal levels, voters merely confirm delegates nominated by the LCY.

Publications. The main publications of the LCY are *Komunist* (weekly) and *Socijalizam* (monthly). The major daily newspapers are *Borba* (organ of SAWPY, with Belgrade and Zagreb editions), *Politika* (Belgrade), *Vjesnik* (Zagreb), *Delo* (Ljubljana), *Oslobodjenje* (Sarajevo), *Nova Makedonija* (Skoplje). The most important weeklies are *NIN* (*Nedeljne informativne novine*, Belgrade) and *Ekonomska politika* (Belgrade). Tanjug is the official news agency.

Party Internal Affairs. During 1982, LCY leaders at both the national and the local level recognized that their system was in serious trouble. The most obvious outward sign was the sad state of the economy—a foreign debt approaching $20 billion (larger than Poland's on a per capita basis), the highest inflation rate in Europe, unemployment exceeding 15 percent, acute shortages of consumer goods, and debt-ridden, unprofitable enterprises. This state of the economy, the leaders recognized, has its political implications. President of the Presidium Mitja Ribičič spoke in September of a "crisis of confidence" and warned of the "alienation of the party from the working class, a process that was one of the main causes of the catastrophe of the Polish party." He cited "a mounting wave of anticommunism in the world and in our country today, which by and large equates revolution with terrorism, the socialist state with totalitarianism, the dictatorship of the proletariat with arbitrary rule." (*Politika*, 14 September.)

At the same time, LCY leaders seemed caught in a web of contradictions and a no-win situation. They praised Tito's past leadership and yet could not deny that most of the responsibility for Yugoslavia's troubles rested with his closest colleagues whom he had appointed. They paid lip service to the much vaunted self-management system and yet had to admit that it was not producing results. They lauded democracy but were totally intolerant of opposition and condemned all who criticized the Yugoslav system. They emphasized the values and rights of republic and provincial autonomy but at the same time denounced all forms of nationalism. They agreed on much of what was wrong and that remedial action was imperative but seemed helpless to devise and implement concrete solutions.

The LCY Congress. The highlight of party affairs was the holding of the Twelfth Congress (26–29 June), the first since Tito's death. In addition to the delegates, there were representatives from 130 foreign political organizations, notably communist parties. Ruling parties sent high-level representatives, particularly the Soviet and Chinese parties, the latter sending a delegation for the first time to a Yugoslav congress. No mention was made, however, of representatives of Albania, Afghanistan, or Vietnam. Reportedly, as an economy measure, there were some 500 fewer LCY delegates than at the 1978 congress.

The national congress was preceded by congresses in the republics and provinces as well as one of party representatives in the army. Most of these, while pledging loyalty to the LCY, tended to defend the rights of their respective national units, while at the same time condemning nationalism. Because most of the republics perceived Serbia as favoring centralism more than any of them, Serbian Communist leaders went to great lengths to deny such allegations inferentially and to criticize nationalism in the strongest terms.

The main report to the LCY congress was made by Dušan Dragosavac, at that time the president of LCY's Presidium. Besides praising Tito and declaring that Yugoslavia had made much progress since World War II, he stressed the LCY's struggle for "socialist self-management" at home and "nonalignment" in foreign affairs. His more detailed report concentrated on failures, difficulties, and problems, especially in the economy. But he also called attention to the upsurge of nationalism, especially evidenced among the Albanian population of the autonomous province of Kosovo. Though attacking the ousted Kosovo leaders, notably Mahmut Bakalli, Dragosavac was indirectly attacking Tito when he said that past policies "led to the consolidation of Albanian nationalism and irredentism." (*Borba*, 27 June.)

Dragosavac also talked of Yugoslavia's "complex and difficult" relations in foreign affairs. He criticized Bulgaria's leaders for refusing to recognize the Macedonian minority in Bulgaria. He castigated those who would subvert nonalignment and stressed the right of the peoples of Afghanistan and Kampuchea to determine their own social development. With respect to the situation in Poland, he called for constructive public discussion and warned that such crises would arise wherever "socialist forces" failed to open up new roads for social transformation.

The congress was hailed in many circles, especially in the West, as one of "free criticism" and "unprecedented tolerance," but the criticism failed to single out any persons for condemnation. The Slovene daily *Delo* (29 June) commented on the day the congress ended that "all the problems and all the people who caused them" were concentrated at the congress. And the Belgrade weekly *NIN* (4 July) declared that the "congress ended, but the problems have remained," without a single basic change being made.

Delegates argued over "democratic centralism" versus "federalization" of the party, but with inconclusive results. Some delegates argued for more democracy, while others suggested that too many divergent views were already being expressed. A former partisan general and Tito's associate, Peko Dapčević, even urged the party to abandon Leninism as out of date and rejected the concept of the dictatorship of the proletariat as contrary to self-management, which is supposed to be the essence of the Yugoslav brand of socialism. But the party leadership was not ready for such radical changes. Some modifications were made in the party statutes, but even these were said to be provisional and under review until the next LCY congress in 1986.

Party stalwart and respected economic expert Kiro Gligorov was given the job of defending the self-management system. While doing so, he pointed to many shortcomings, adding that "we simply have to stop high living beyond our means" (*CSM*, 13 July). Clearly referring to the Tito years, he declared that the "present difficult situation did not come about overnight but rather as a result of years of tolerating bureaucratic methods" and asserted that changes were imperative, first of all "within the party itself" (*Komunist*, 2 July).

A onetime close associate of Tito's, Svetozar Vukmanović-Tempo, pointed out in a long report to the congress that the main problems in the self-management system stemmed from people "spending what they do not have" (*Borba*, 28 June). Another delegate, Miloslav Vasiljković (from Serbia), went even further; it seemed to him "that our greatest 'successes' have been in having created huge inflation and enormous debts." The "working class is not to blame" for this, he said, while at the same time revealing that Yugoslavs have really worked only five hours a day while receiving full pay. (*Politika*, 29 June.)

On its last day, the congress adopted three lengthy resolutions: (1) on the role and tasks of the LCY in the struggle for the development of socialist self-management and for the country's material and social progress; (2) on the tasks of the LCY in the implementation of economic stabilization; and (3) on the tasks of the LCY in the struggle for peace, equal international cooperation, and socialism in the world. A fourth resolution, seemingly not prepared in advance, condemned Israeli actions in Lebanon and called for the withdrawal of Israeli troops from all occupied Arab territories. (*Borba*, 30 June.) While these resolutions seemed to represent a consensus, the only item on which there was full agreement was that party cards should in the future carry a picture of Tito as one more tribute to the old leader (*Vjesnik*, 30 June).

The congress confirmed the 165 members of the Central Committee, who had been selected by the republic and provincial central committees. Of this number, 90 are "professional functionaries," fifteen are army generals, fifteen are women, eight are workers, and one is a peasant; 95 (58 percent) are serving for the first time (*Komunist*, 9 July). At its first session on 29 June, the Central Committee "elected" (confirmed) the new Presidium. Vladimir Bakarić is the only party leader who is both a member of the Presidium and the State Presidency.

Post-Congress Disunity. Signs of disunity were not slow in appearing in the days and weeks after the congress disbanded. Tito's collective successors seemingly continued to be overcome with a certain degree of immobility. They could repeat his words but lacked the ability or authority to repeat his actions. Nameless "conservative bureaucrats" have been held responsible for all sorts of misdeeds, but no heads have rolled. There is "too much smoke and too little fire," wrote the editor of *Politika* (17 September), adding that the "era when we believed in the power of proclamations and simple solutions is now behind us." Our "problem has been," he noted "that we would like to see 'things changing,' but without endangering the positions and privileges" of certain persons.

The article was written in support of the speech by Presidium President Ribičič noted above where he warned of "Polish-type troubles" if strong measures were not taken to stop further deterioration of the economic and political situation. Speaking at the party school in Tito's birthplace, Kumrovec, he asserted that "during recent times a great deal of what was noncommunist and unprincipled had built up in many party leaderships." "We all swear by stabilization," he said, "but in our social and day-to-day life we behave in a way that is not in keeping with our principled views and positions." He revealed for the first time that "a number of secret sessions of the Central Committee and the party Presidium took place" to discuss "mutual relations within the party and the mounting problems" and declared that "unless we agree unanimously in our assessment of the real causes of our economic crisis, we cannot remove the so-called crisis of confidence in our system." (*Politika*, 14 September.)

Two weeks after his Kumrovec speech, Ribičič warned a meeting of the Central Committee that "the economic crisis has been turning into a political crisis." This political crisis was marked by what he called "ideological disunity" in the party, which in turn led "to indiscipline, disregard for legal regulations, and a wave of violating these regulations." (*Vjesnik*, 25 September.)

At the same meeting, Ribičič's fellow Slovene, France Popit, called for an end to "opportunism" in the LCY and insisted that "party responsibility must be tightened," starting with the Presidium, "which does not dare summon the party leadership of a republic for conferences because it believes that this would be taken as interference in the internal affairs of that particular republic." He concluded by requesting a "full confrontation" with people not willing to obey, adding: "We cannot become beautiful in the eyes of the masses of the people." (Tanjug, 24 September.)

Even before Ribičič's speeches, the Belgrade weekly *NIN* (1 August) had noted: "We all condemn failures, we all have listed disturbing examples, but regardless of all this we have continued to retain our posts." And *Politika* (11 August) had observed that "powerful persons continue in office without impediment . . . taking care not of any responsibility but rather of their own rights and privileges."

In all of these (and other) discussions, it is evident that at issue is the highly sensitive matter of how much autonomy the republic and provincial parties should have. Because conflicting views are strong, some party theorists have argued for radical changes in the LCY. Slobodan Inić, for example, pointed to an "upstairs-downstairs" situation: "An almost invisible mechanism" in the LCY legally produces "a two-story life for the party . . . Everything comes from above and flows downward." Declaring that "party members are no longer willing to engage in empty political maneuvers," he called for a radical reform of the LCY, which "must abandon its practice of 'ruling'[the state] . . . It is difficult to advance the self-management system without the League of Communists, but we cannot make any progress if the League of Communists does not reform by conforming to self-management." (*Danas*, 10 August.) In Inić's opinion, it is not the party but rather "the working class that is capable of taking the destiny of society into its own hands." Ironically, the same dilemma was posed by Milovan Djilas in 1953.

Another party stalwart, Prof. Jovan Marjanović, revived a proposal advanced much earlier by a senior party leader (Milentije Popović, who died ten years ago) for a nonparty system. Autonomy for the parties in the republics and provinces, Marjanović argued, would lead to nationalist parties and hence to the creation of a type of multiparty system. Instead, he advised, "we should develop our political system as a system of nonparty socialist democracy." (*Večernje novosti*, 7 October.)

Kosovo: Test of LCY Nationality Policy. The riots that broke out in 1981 in Yugoslavia's largely Albanian-populated province of Kosovo (see *YICA*, 1982, pp. 498–501) and the continued troubles there have occupied the attention of LCY leaders as well as of the Yugoslav media. In 1981, the tendency was to play down the disturbances, but in 1982, especially with continued antigovernment demonstrations, LCY leaders and the media (especially in Serbia, of which Kosovo is an autonomous province) have been much more open in discussing the question. One reason is that despite 55 trials and the sentencing of some 700 people (*CSM*, 22 July), as well as expulsions from the party and the dismantling of 40 clandestine organizations, disturbances have continued.

Sinan Hasani, president of the LC Kosovo provincial committee, spoke of continued difficulties: "We are dealing here with an organized and planned action of the enemy, an action rooted in indoctrination with Albanian nationalism and irredentism" (interview in *Komunist*; *FBIS*, 1 October). He observed that schoolchildren still write hostile slogans on their desks or paint them on walls. They write leaflets and distribute them. He also spoke of the desecration of graves and of "the raping of women and other brutal actions."

After visiting Kosovo, the president of Serbia, Gen. Nikola Ljubičić (until May Yugoslavia's defense minister), complained that the flight of Serbs and Montenegrins from Kosovo was continuing because of actions by "Albanian chauvinists" (*Večernje novosti*, 18 September). Most estimates suggest that upward of 55,000 left in the past decade, although the Serbian Orthodox church puts the total at over 100,000, presumably the number since World War II. The cradle of the Serbian nation of the middle ages, with many cultural and religious monuments, Kosovo touches the nerves of most Serbs. Their compatriots in Kosovo have been exposed to brutal actions by the Albanians there—hay has been burned, trees cut down, property taken, churches and graves desecrated, women raped—while the ruling Kosovo party, many of whose members are supposedly the guardians of public order, seems helpless to stop the disorders.

LCY leaders in Belgrade have spoken of "gradually limiting the scope for activity of the enemy," but have admitted that the security situation in Kosovo remains unsatisfactory. There are still "a considerable number of hostile leaflets and pamphlets, as well as verbal propaganda, fires, threats to public traffic and attacks on social and personal property." (Tanjug, 30 September; *FBIS*, 1 October.)

The army's representative on the LCY Presidium, Gen. Dane Ćuić, while revealing that "counter-revolutionary groups" composed of soldiers of Albanian origin had been detected in the army, expressed the belief that "we can resolve the problem of Kosovo in an exclusively political way," but, he added, "without abandoning the prerogative of using force if necessary" (*Večernje novosti*, 15 April).

LCY Presidium member and President of the Serbian Central Committee Dušan Čkrebić seemed more bitter when he referred to the Kosovo events as counterrevolutionary: "It is inconceivable that men . . .

who brought a part of the country into that type of political situation would come out only with certain party penalties and with ordinary removal from leading positions" (*NIN*, 19 October).

In May, 21 Serbian Orthodox priests and monks addressed an urgent appeal to the Yugoslav State Presidency, as well as to the State Presidency of Serbia, asking for protection of the Serbian population and its shrines in Kosovo (*Pravoslavlje*, 15 May). Asserting that no "greater shrine, past, present, and future" exists for the Serbs, the appeal stated that "the question of Kosovo is the question of the spiritual, cultural, and historical identity of the Serbian people." What are, the appeal asked, those "infernal and irrational forces" that in a few decades have done what "Turkish enslavement could not do in five centuries"? "It can be said without any exaggeration that a planned genocide is being carried out step by step in Kosovo." In addition, the appeal declared: "Neither we nor you are unaware, nor is our general public unaware, that the forcible emigration of our people from Kosovo has at times been assisted by official authorities in Kosovo."

While there has been no indication of an official response to this appeal, LCY leaders, both nationally and in Serbia, know that what has been happening in Kosovo represents a failure of their nationality policy. The Serbian LC is cognizant of its legal right to intervene in Kosovo—and has done so to a degree by stationing a military presence there—but has demonstrated a reluctance to be forceful with the Kosovo LC authorities, perhaps fearing a worsening of the situation and hoping that the Kosovo Albanians will police themselves.

Late in the year, *Pravoslavlje* (15 November) printed the text of a 1969 letter from the church synod to President Tito complaining of various offenses in Kosovo, as part of a review of what the church has had to endure there "over decades." It also reproduced the text of his answer, promising "to do everything to stop the offenses" and "to secure for all citizens a safe life as well as the safety of their property." The church report then detailed various offenses that had occurred since then. The synod explained that it had decided to publish "one part of the material that deals with the terror in Kosovo" because "our faithful have reproached the church for having taken no measures to have it stopped." (For a vivid description of the situation in Kosovo and the brutality perpetrated against the Serbs that is forcing them into exile, see David Binder's dispatch from Priština, *NYT*, 28 November.)

The LCY Past: De-Titoization? Since Tito's death in May 1980, there have been various signs of "de-Titoization" (see *YICA*, 1982, pp. 495–96), but this seems to be a very sensitive subject. Tito's onetime comrade in arms and official biographer, Vladimir Dedijer, has come in for additional criticism because of the second volume of his projected four-volume biography of Tito, which was a Yugoslav best-seller. Dedijer angered many old partisans by revealing some of Tito's political mistakes, accusing the partisans of excessive harshness in punishing erring comrades, and portraying loose sexual behavior among them (*Economist*, London, 13 February).

While Dedijer's historiographic approach was defended in some Yugoslav circles (*Književna reč*, 10 February) and viewed with a certain benevolence in others (*Politika*, *NIN*, and *Ilustrovana politika*), most joined in a bitter attack. The most prominent personality among the critics was Vladimir Bakarić. Indeed, Dedijer accused Bakarić of inspiring and organizing a campaign of harassment and filed suit against him and some others (*Naša reč*, London, April). Dedijer has been assisted publicly to some degree by a former comrade of Tito's, Svetozar Vukmanović-Tempo, who took issue with Bakarić on a point of party history (*Vjesnik*, 15 February). Related to this controversy was the postponement of the publication (scheduled for 1982) of a long-awaited history of the party, largely because of sharp differences among various authors over the role of the different nationalities in World War II (*Economist*, 3 July).

The Dedijer controversy was perhaps overshadowed by another sign of de-Titoization—revelations about the treatment of Cominformists after Tito's break with Stalin in 1948. Clearly the LCY has not come to terms with this episode in its history. At the center of the controversy is the concentration camp on Goli Otok, a tiny island in the northern Adriatic where thousands (the Yugoslav press says 8,000, and Amnesty International puts the figure at 50,000) of alleged pro-Soviet sympathizers were beaten and otherwise tortured. Two recent books dealing with the subject, Branko Hofman's *Noč do jutra* (Night to morning) and Antonije Isaković's *Tren* (The instant), prompted the LSYY's paper, *Mladost*, to allege that Goli Otok was "in a way worthy of the Nazi concentration camps and Stalin's Gulag" and to request party leaders to investigate the matter (*Borba*, 20 February).

Domestic Affairs. *The New Cabinet.* In May, a new four-year cabinet (officially known as the Federal Executive Council) was formed, headed by the former president of the LC Croatian Central Committee, 57-year old Milka Planinc, the first woman to head the FEC. A Croat born in Dalmatia, she was said by one Yugoslav publication to have "no resemblance whatsoever to the [British] 'iron lady' [Mrs. Margaret Thatcher], although nobody denies that she is a resolute lady" (*NIN*, 2 May). Although she joined the partisans in 1942 and became a party member in 1944, she held mostly local posts until her elevation to the Croatian LC Presidium in 1968. Her party career became really important in December 1971, after Tito purged party leaders in Croatia, followed by her "election" as president of the Croatian LC Central Committee. Of the 29 members of Mrs. Planinc's new government, only 5 were members of the old one.

Among the more important of them was Lazar Mojsov (62), a Macedonian and until his appointment to his cabinet post, a member of the LCY Presidium. He was made minister for foreign affairs, replacing Josip Vrhovec, a Croat. A Serb from Croatia, Adm. Branko Mamula (61) was appointed minister for national defense. He joined the party in 1942 and was elected to the LCY's Central Committee in 1978. He replaced Gen. Nikola Ljubičić, who had held that post since 1967 and has now become Serbia's state president. Slovene Stane Dolanc (57) was appointed minister for internal affairs. He joined both the party and the partisans only in 1944. During most of World War II, he lived in the part of Slovenia annexed by Germany and reportedly belonged to the Hitler youth organization (Dusko Doder, *The Yugoslavs*, p. 74). In the late 1960s and the 1970s, he held important party posts, including the highest at the time, secretary of the Presidium.

The Economy. For at least the past two years, Yugoslav government leaders, as well as the general public, have been aware that their economy was in serious trouble, but no solutions have been forthcoming. The biggest headache has been the servicing of a huge foreign debt, approaching $20 billion. In April, the outgoing head of the cabinet, Veselin Djuranović, told parliament that the nation was in danger of foreign illiquidity (Reuters, 22 April). In May, modest steps were taken toward a partial centralization of hard-currency earnings (*Vjesnik*, 14 May), much to the annoyance of Slovenian and Croatian leaders. Clearly this was not "the solution" and debates within the LCY continued. Several months later, for example, Minister without portfolio Jože Smole (Slovenian) warned that "any rescheduling of Yugoslavia's debts abroad" would mean "total bankruptcy" (*Večernje novosti*, 25 September).

Many factors contributed to Yugoslavia's rising foreign debt. Imports have steadily increased and exports have stagnated. Often plants built with foreign loans produced nothing for export and indeed not infrequently created additional import dependence (*WSJ*, 13 October). Trade barriers between republics and uneconomic duplication (a steel mill in each republic and automobile plants in five of them) added to the country's economic woes (*NYT*, 21 and 27 June). Crude oil was bought on short-term credit at interest rates of 20 to 25 precent (Jure Bilić, a member of LCY Presidium in interview with *NIN*, 10 October). Foreign currency remittances from Yugoslav workers abroad were spent in considerable measure on foreign goods. Although there was some improvement in 1981 in the foreign trade picture (*Ekonomska politika*, 18 January; *Privredni pregled*, 2 February), it was not enough, especially in view of the 1981 inflation rate of 43 percent.

In midyear the government began taking drastic measures. In August, all prices were frozen for six months, with the expectation that the inflation rate would be kept between 25 and 27 percent (*WSJ*, 2 August). On 14 October, the government severely limited the amount of hard currency that could be taken abroad. Even holders of hard-currency accounts can draw only $250 before each trip abroad, and all tourists must deposit the equivalent of $80 for the first trip and $32 for each subsequent journey (ibid., 25 October; *Economist*, 30 October). The deposits are to be returned at the end of the year. Personal importation of consumer goods will be heavily taxed. Private trading of dinars for hard currency is to be punished (*WSJ*, 19 October).

On 17 October, the government introduced gasoline rationing (8.8 gallons per month per motorist) and restrictions on heating and lighting of offices and private homes, and on 22 October, it devalued the dinar by 20 percent (*Economist*, 30 October).

Other austerity measures are designed to reduce investments, especially loans to unprofitable enterprises. The Privredna Banka of Zagreb, once one of the most reputable banks in Yugoslavia, lost its liquidity in large part because of such investments (*FBIS*, 24 August). The bank claimed, however, that it had participated unwillingly in some loans, at the behest of the republic's political leaders (ibid.). The end result may be increased unemployment, which already stands at 15.5 percent (*News World*, 4 October). Real income has fallen by 13 percent in the past two years (*Economist*, 20 February).

Official Yugoslav sources estimated that the country would need $5.3 billion to service the year's payments of interest and principal (Reuters, 2 October); $3.35 billion would need to be borrowed. Loans for about one-third that amount had reportedly been finalized by the end of September (*News World*, 4 October).

At midyear the CTUY heard a report that some 500 strikes take place annually in Yugoslavia, usually lasting from fifteen minutes to five days, and organized by semiskilled and unskilled workers rather than by union leaders (*NIN*, 11 July). Strikes are neither permitted nor forbidden in Yugoslavia, merely tolerated.

It is interesting in this connection to note the comments of Neca Jovanov, perhaps the leading Yugoslav expert on strikes: "I have ceased being occupied with strikes . . . There is something that is more enigmatic, and that is that passive resistance has reached unimagined proportions . . . when translated into the language of politics [it] means passive opposition . . . the explosion of passive resistance always has a social basis against which you cannot employ repression." (*Studenski list*, 12 March; quoted in *Naša reč*, no. 335, May.)

Dissent and Its Suppression. As in the past, the regime has been intolerant of dissent (see *YICA*, 1982, pp. 502–5), although during the year the official press at times resembled a "loyal opposition." Dissidents, such as Milovan Djilas, cannot be published in Yugoslavia, but student papers have been quite bold. For example, they have ridiculed LCY leaders' explanation of the Kosovo events (*Student*, 14 April). The Serbian LC Central Committee, in turn, singled out certain student publications for criticism. The monthly literary journal *Vidici* and the weekly *Student* were accused of becoming a platform for the propagation of "anarchistic, liberal, dogmatic, nationalistic, and other anti-self-management ideas" (*Politika*, 21 January; *Večernje novosti*, 22 January). Subsequently, the Serbian LC Central Committee Presidium criticized another student publication, *Mladost*, as well as the well-known weekly *NIN* (*FBIS*, 17 March).

The focal point of more or less indirect criticism of the regime has been the military regime in Poland. The student literary weekly *Književna reč* (25 July), for example, published the texts of debates among leading Polish dissidents. In an editorial introduction, the journal praised these polemics in Poland as assisting the country in solving the crisis. Some students even brought Solidarity banners to a monthly meeting designed to manifest support for the Palestinian people. The eight young men and women carrying the banners were promptly arrested and sentenced to prison terms of 25 to 50 days (*FBIS*, 21 July). A group of 48 intellectuals, virtually all well known, signed a letter to Gen. Wojciech Jaruzelski criticizing the "state of war" imposed on the Polish people. Understandably, this letter was not reported in the Yugoslav press. Subsequently, at least one of the signers, dismissed philosophy professor Nebojša Popov, was jailed for 30 days (*Los Angeles Times*, 15 August).

During the year, Amnesty International issued a report, *Yugoslavia: Prisoners of Conscience*, severely criticizing the regime for violating the civil rights of its citizens. The report discusses in detail a number of individual cases, as well as the legislation under which they were convicted. The report alleges that there has been a significant increase over the past few years in the number of political prisoners. Milovan Djilas estimated the number of political prisoners to be at least a thousand (*NYT*, 20 June), which on a per capita basis would be more than in the Soviet Union. The Djilas figures included those imprisoned in the past year in connection with the riots in Kosovo.

As if in response to Yugoslavia's critics, a self-styled defender of Marxist orthodoxy, the writer Oskar Davičo, strongly castigated those who have expressed concern for the fate of Yugoslav writers who are in prison (*Vjesnik*, 27 March).

The year witnessed the passing of one of Yugoslavia's most gifted writers, Mehmed (Meša) Selimović, from Bosnia-Hercegovina. At one point the LCY, in line with its policy of seeking the favor of minority nationalities, wanted to classify Selimović as a Muslim, but he was forthright in declaring that he was a Serb of the Islamic faith and that he belonged in the company of Serbian writers and their literature.

Church-State Relations. There is at best a partial and an uneasy truce between the churches in Yugoslavia and the LCY regime. A notable difference in recent years, however, has been the regime's policy of following a "divide and conquer" strategy. Some religious figures in the various denominations have been presented in the official press in a sympathetic manner, as modern, progressive leaders, and honest patriots. In this connection, the pope's encyclical letter, *Laborem Exercens*, was hailed by the Yugoslav press as evidence that the pope was on the side of the working people and not on the side of the capitalist system (see *Borba* and *Vjesnik*, 17 September 1981). The refusal of Zagreb Archbishop Franjo Kuharić to attend the traditional New Year's reception given by the president of the Croatian parliament, on the other hand, was viewed as negative (*Vjesnik*, weekly supplement, 30 January). Moreover, in part because the government feared that Kuharić might be selected as the next cardinal of Yugoslavia (as he indeed was in January 1983), the daily press continued to denounce the religious, national, and political role the late Alojzij Cardinal Stepinac played in Croatia during World War II.

In contrast, for example, the press has presented Croatian Bishop Karmel Zaninović and Slovenian Archbishop Alojzij Sustar as loyal, conciliatory, and responsible prelates (*Vjesnik*, 7 February; *Delo*, 20 February). In early February, Sustar was even allowed to address Slovenian workers in Austria, Switzerland, and Germany from the Ljubljana television studio, an unprecedented event in the history of Yugoslav church-state relations.

Aside from the regime's divide and conquer approach, another notable difference in recent church-state relations has been the increase in responses to press attacks on religion and on church leaders. This has been especially true of the Serbian Orthodox church, which in the past has been extremely timid. One reason has been the burning and desecration of Orthodox churches and monasteries by Albanians in Kosovo. In an interview with *NIN* (16 May), Serbian Patriarch German asserted that he was bound by the precept "render unto Caeser the things that are Caesar's and unto God the things that are God's," adding that the church expected the government to behave on the same basis. In response to a questioner, the patriarch indicated that the government was failing to do this, that promises were not kept, and that there were "unconquerable difficulties" in obtaining permits to build churches.

The Islamic community, about four million strong and the third largest religious denomination in Yugoslavia, has demonstrated great vitality and signs of religious renewal. The regime has evidenced some concern in this respect, especially after the Islamic revolution in Iran. Yet more than a year after Tito's death, the Islamic community in Zagreb obtained a permit to build a mosque there, financed in the main by Libya, Saudi Arabia, and Iraq (*Danas*, 24 August).

Whether engineered by the authorities or not, a fierce debate has developed over the alleged growth of "pan-Islamic nationalism," especially in Bosnia-Hercegovina, where the largest number of Muslims live (ibid., 17 August; *NIN*, 8 August; *Komunist*, 15 January). The president of the Association of Islamic Elders, Ahmed Smajlović, in a speech to the third assembly of the Islamic Community for Bosnia-Hercegovina, Croatia, and Slovenia, charged that there was Islamic agitation from abroad designed to misinform, confuse, and disorient the Islamic faithful in Yugoslavia (*Preporod*, Sarajevo, 15 April).

Foreign Affairs. By and large, Yugoslavia kept a relatively low profile in foreign affairs, in part perhaps because of the overwhelming preoccupation with domestic problems. The Yugoslav Foreign Affairs Ministry indicated that a high level of friendly cooperation had been reached both with the Soviet Union and the United States, on the basis of full equality (*Neue Zürcher Zeitung*, 1 May). Alternatively, the Yugoslavs have blamed the rivalry between the Soviet Union and the United States for the "grave crisis" in international relations (*San Francisco Chronicle*, 11 June).

The Soviet Union. The highpoint in Yugoslav-Soviet relations was the visit of Foreign Minister Andrei Gromyko to Belgrade in early April and the visit to Moscow of Yugoslav Defense Minister Nikola Ljubičić, two weeks later. Gromyko was the first member of the Soviet leadership to visit Yugoslavia since Leonid Brezhnev attended Tito's funeral in May 1980. A joint communiqué at the end of Gromyko's visit said that relations between the two countries were developing positively and that both sides would seek to improve them (*NYT*, 7 April). No mention was made, however, of the Polish crisis or of Afghanistan. General Ljubičić's trip was viewed by most observers as a farewell visit since it had been previously announced that he would be replaced as minister of defense in May.

The improvement in relations did not prevent the Yugoslavs from publishing books and articles on Marxism and the possibility of conflict between socialist countries. Past history was examined, including

Soviet actions, in a critical light, along with inferences concerning possible future ones (for example, see the article by party theorist Miloš Prelević in *Socijalizam*, no. 12, 1981, but distributed only in late February 1982).

Early in the year, a book entitled *Stalinizm: Teorijski pogled na jedan fenomen* (Stalinism: A theoretical view of a phenomenon) portrayed the Soviet system as having become a dictatorship of bueaucrats after Lenin's death. Its author is a well-known Muslim spokesman, Fuad Muhić, a professor in Sarajevo. The author's major purpose appeared to be to show why Yugoslav Communists (as well as many in Western Europe) have been unwilling to accept Moscow as the leading communist center and why they reject the Soviet communist model.

Karlo Štajner (Steiner), a Yugoslav Communist of Austrian origin and Tito's friend in Moscow until he began a twenty-year incarceration in the Soviet gulag (1936–1956), in the course of the year added a chapter to a revision of an earlier book. Included in the most recent edition of *The Return from the Gulag*, the chapter, entitled "Stalinism and Fascism," claims that there was no difference between Stalin and Hitler. The chapter was first published in the new Zagreb weekly, *Danas* (17 August). In a press interview, Štajner, now 80, insisted that conditions in the camps were far worse than anything that Alexander Solzhenitsyn had experienced (*Politika*, 4 September). Even the greatest writer, he said, could not describe the horrible things that the inmates had undergone.

The year brought the death of Veljko Mićunović, twice Yugoslavia's ambassador to Moscow (1956–1958 and 1969–1971), who was a witness to the making of number of Soviet foreign policy decisions and who bore the brunt of many anti-Yugoslav utterances by Soviet rulers. He recorded his experiences in a revealing book, *Moskovske godine, 1956–1958* (a shortened version has been published in the West under the title *Moscow Diary*). At the time of his death, he left a manuscript covering his second tour in Moscow, and *NIN* began serializing it in August.

Eastern Europe. Yugoslavia's relations with East European countries have been mixed. The best relations are with Romania and the worst with Albania and Bulgaria. Although relations with Hungary are rarely mentioned, the Yugoslav press has kept alive the memory of the 1956 Hungarian Revolution. Events in Poland have received a good deal of attention in the Yugoslav press, as has the subject of possible conflicts between communist countries.

Poland. While Yugoslav leaders do not rejoice in the troubles their comrades are having in Poland, they also do not see martial law as an answer. Former member of the LCY Presidium and now a top leader in SAWPY Aleksandar Grličkov has concluded that "socialism cannot be created by martial law" and that martial law "always seeks to perpetuate itself" (Tanjug, 8 October; *Dnevnik*, Ljubljana, 9 October). Moreover, he said, "the majority of Yugoslavia's citizens are convinced that martial law in Poland has trampled democratic relations in society."

Similarly, *Borba*'s foreign editor wrote that martial law had "failed to normalize the situation" and that the ban on Solidarity was "an expression of helplessness" (10 October). And *Politika*'s Warsaw correspondent saw the situation in Poland as "a false truce" and accused the martial law regime of trying "to settle accounts" with the workers rather than starting a dialogue with them (*NIN*, 12 September).

A Slovene journalist, writing in Yugoslavia's equivalent of *Playboy*, declared that Poland has been "turned into a country under siege" and accused the Jaruzelski regime of falsehood when it tried to blame the 31 August demonstrations on outside forces. "Whether anyone likes it or not, the 31 August demonstrations were of such a mass nature that no intelligence service in the world nor any hooligan group could have organized them." The Jaruzelski government, he concluded, "has no positive program capable of giving the people confidence and a desire to cooperate." (*Start*, 11 September.) Earlier *Start* (10 April) published interviews with two Polish publicists who defended the Polish regime and claimed that "Solidarity was used by former Stalinists as an instrument to assume power."

The role played by the army in five major past Polish upheavals (June 1956 riots, August 1968 invasion of Czechoslovakia, the 1970 strikes and riots, the 1976 crisis, and the 1981 crisis) was the subject of an analysis in *Danas* (14 September). The author concluded that in all of these events the army was more or less in the background, with repression being done for the most part by the security forces and the militia because the army was something less than reliable. Moreover, he expressed the view that in any conflict between Moscow and Warsaw, the Polish army would probably accept orders only from Polish commanders.

Albania. Despite Yugoslavia's allegations about Albania's involvement in the Kosovo disturbances, including "territorial aspirations," a series of contacts and agreements made during the year constituted an improvement in state-to-state relations. A trade protocol was signed at the end of December 1981 (*Borba*, 16 January). With 17 percent of Albania's total foreign trade, Yugoslavia remains its top trading partner. In February, Yugoslavia and Albania signed a new agreement on road transport of freight (ibid., 5 April), as well as one providing for a rail link, the first one for Albania outside its borders (*CSM*, 21 May). Albania also agreed to permit transit freight traffic (but no passengers) between Titograd in Montenegro and Ohrid in Macedonia (*Večernje novosti*, 17 September), which would cut the distance to be traveled in half. Nevertheless mutual recriminations in the press have continued (see ibid., 18 September).

Bulgaria. While praising Bulgaria for adopting economic reforms similar to those in Hungary, the Yugoslavs continued to criticize Sofia for its "distortion" of the history of the two countries, particularly on the subject of Macedonia (Tanjug, 29 September). The Yugoslavs noted a "two-faced" Bulgarian policy toward Yugoslavia, charging that Sofia expresses a desire "for fraternal relations" with Belgrade, while continuing "to deny the existence of the Macedonian nation in Bulgaria" (*Vjesnik*, 29 April). The Yugoslavs have also charged that as a member of the Warsaw pact, all of "Bulgaria's initiatives in the international sphere are part of the global policy of that military alliance" (*Radio Zagreb*, 28 February).

Conflict Between Socialist States. Aleksandar Grličkov, at the time still a member of LCY's Presidium, declared that "various roads to socialism" are the only way out of the the impasse in which the international communist movement finds itself (Tanjug, 28 January). Clearly referring to the Soviet Union, Grličkov firmly rejected all attempts "to force upon other people one's own experience" because this could only lead to conflicts. In his opinion, however, "Stalinism has not succeeded in undermining faith in socialism."

In a similar vein, party theorist Mensur Ibrahimpašić wrote: "All the socialist countries that have thus far used armed force in order to resolve their conflicts with other socialist countries have done so by referring to their loyalty to socialist ideas." He believes that this arises because communist leaders have become "the direct holders of economic power in addition to political power," which has led "to contradictions and conflicts, including the employment of armed forces." (*Socijalizm*, November 1981, pp. 1770–72.)

Nonalignment. The Seventh Congress of the nonaligned countries, scheduled to be held in Baghdad in September, was postponed, partly because of the Iraq-Iran war, but mostly because of the disarray in the movement caused by the pro-Soviet actions of such countries as Cuba, Vietnam, Angola, and Libya. Disagreements among several African countries were also a factor. India finally agreed to host the congress in March 1983 (Tanjug, 22 August).

Yugoslavia has continued to reject Cuba's espousal of the idea that the nonaligned movement should become part of the Soviet bloc. Yugoslav publicists Gavro Altman and Ranko Petković argued that the movement must remain a really "bloc free" group. Altman wrote that "it remains completely unclear how one bloc can be supreme without endangering the existence of mankind as a whole." (*Komunist*, 19 February.) In a similar article, Petković sharply rejected Cuba's idea of a "committed nonalignment" (*NIN*, 21 February).

While many nonaligned countries sided with Argentina over the Falkland islands issue, the Yugoslav press limited itself to publishing reports from both Buenos Aires and London.

United States. Defense Secretary Caspar W. Weinberger visited Yugoslavia in December, the first visit by a senior U.S. official since Secretary of State Alexander Haig's in September 1981. Weinberger reiterated U.S. support for Yugoslavia's independence and territorial integrity (*NYT*, 4 and 5 December).

Earlier in the year, the United States sought to assure nervous and apprehensive Western bankers that Yugoslavia, unlike Poland, was a good risk (*WSJ*, 7 May). In December, the Reagan administration was said to be seeking a Western aid package of roughly $1 billion to meet Yugoslavia's cash flow problem (*NYT*, 8 December). Secretary of State George Shultz was understood to feel that help for Yugoslavia was urgently needed to prevent a possible economic and political collapse of that country (ibid.).

International Party Contacts. Aside from Andrei Gromyko's visit to Belgrade, reported above, which involved both state and party affairs, contacts with other communist parties appeared perfunctory. The one exception involved the Italian Communist Party (PCI) and its leaders. Through official visits and through the press, the Yugoslavs utilized Soviet criticism of the PCI to denounce Soviet "hegemonistic policy," but without mentioning the Soviet Union or its leaders by name (*Politika*, 3 March; *Vjesnik*, 25 February, 4 March). In part, Yugoslav press comments and interviews with Yugoslavia's leaders took the form of defending the PCI's stand that the Polish working class alone should resolve Poland's problems and without outside interference (*Politika*, 23 and 26 January). A Zagreb journalist who is considered one of Yugoslavia's leading experts on Soviet-Italian party relations, Davor Šošić, even prophesized that the "ideological war" between the Soviet and Italian Communists would last a long time (*Vjesnik*, 25 and 27 March).

Spokane, Washington   Alex N. Dragnich

Council for
Mutual Economic Assistance

Economic conditions deteriorated further in the member-states of the Council for Mutual Economic Assistance (CMEA) during 1982. New Soviet crop failures and a continuing slowdown in economic growth of CMEA members darkened the outlook for the people of these states. In Poland there was little improvement of the economy under martial law; in Romania the economy went from bad to worse. For several of the member-states, hard-currency foreign debts continued to accumulate, with little prospect for resolution in the short term. Measures introduced by the various CMEA governments to redress the situation did not appear to go far enough. Soviet pressure for integration continued, but progress appeared limited. The death of Leonid Brezhnev in November added another element of uncertainty. Although the Soviet economy and those of most of the member-states were not on the verge of collapse, a sense of drift characterized much of the year's developments.

Background and Functioning. Created in 1949, the CMEA comprises the Soviet Union, Bulgaria, Czechoslovakia, East Germany, Hungary, Poland, Romania, and the non-European states of Cuba, Mongolia, and Vietnam. Structurally, the CMEA rejects the notion of supranationality and appears to conform to the oft-declared principles of national sovereignty and equality of member-states. Unlike the European Economic Community, it does not have an international legal personality. The powers of the CMEA Council, the chief decision-making forum, are strictly circumscribed even though it is composed of the prime ministers of member-states. Its recommendations take effect only if member-governments adopt them. The unanimous vote provision incorporated into the charter continues to determine voting practice. In fact, the CMEA suffers from institutional underdevelopment, and it was only in 1971 that the three major committees were created: the Committee for Planning and Cooperation, the Committee for Scientific and Technical Cooperation, and the Committee for Materials and Technical Supply. These committees were given the right to "influence" the work of other CMEA organs and to assign certain priorities.

Despite the principle of equality, the CMEA was and remains a Soviet-controlled organization. Since World War II, Moscow has sought to impose general conformity in domestic and foreign policies in Eastern Europe. Initially, the motivation was largely political, and Western-style economic integration would not have been compatible with the Soviet and East Central European system of "command economies" revolving around a central plan. Genuine socialist economic integration would involve the creation of a single command economy encompassing all member-states.

The Soviet Union has, however, made significant progress in achieving its goal of greater control over the bloc states and over the newer members outside of Europe. In 1962, Moscow managed to push through the adoption of the "international socialist division of labor," which called for the coordination of member-states' economies and an acceleration of specialization. This attempt failed in large part because of the determined opposition of Romania (with tacit support from some of the other states). Two CMEA banks were also created: in 1964 the International Bank of Economic Cooperation, with the "convertible ruble" as its base currency, and in 1970 the International Investment Bank, as a projected multilateral clearing house. Neither was especially successful, and the ruble continues to have only very limited convertibility. A number of multilateral projects were undertaken, including joint pipelines and joint investment in iron ore extraction. The most significant step toward integration, however, was undertaken in 1971 when the twenty-fifth CMEA Council session adopted the "comprehensive program for economic integration." This program was amplified in 1975 when the twenty-ninth Council session approved a five-year plan for further multilateral economic integration. It envisioned ten large projects, nine of which provided for closer links between the Soviet Union and the bloc states, costing 9 billion transfer rubles (U.S. $12.2 billion) (*Times*, London, 3 January 1976). In 1976, at the thirtieth Council session, further coordination and integration were envisioned. This process has continued. The aim has been to set a "complex target program" for coordinating long-term planning to 1990, involving five "target groups": fuel and energy; machine building; agriculture and food supply; consumer goods; and transport (*Radio Free Europe–Radio Liberty Research*, no. 147, 16 June 1980). To achieve this goal, Soviet Premier Aleksei Kosygin urged members at the thirty-second Council meeting in 1978 to move decisively toward the overall integration of their individual economies (*Scinteia*, 28 June 1978). In 1979, at the thirty-third session, he stressed the need for joint effort in the energy field (see *YICA*, 1980, p. 108).

More than a decade after the CMEA adopted the "comprehensive program," economic integration, defined as the free flow of commodities and harmonization of policies and the creation of a single effective market with unified prices, has been limited. Socialist integration continues to differ from that of market economies and is also subjected to both centrifugal and centripetal forces, both regional and global. Political commitment to socialist integration is vital, especially in the case of the preponderant power and moving force within the grouping. Shortly before his death, Brezhnev noted that "socialist economic integration has become an integral feature of the life of our community, a powerful and stable factor in the all-around progress of the fraternal countries" (*Pravda*, 15 October). He had also singled out two economic tasks that should be tackled more vigorously both domestically and by the CMEA organs: the acceleration of scientific and technical progress and the organization of direct ties between sectors and enterprises (*Izvestiia*, 13 June).

In April, the 103rd session of the CMEA Executive Committee met in Moscow. It studied a draft program for coordinating the national economic plans of CMEA states for 1986–1990. It also examined the fulfillment of the general agreement on cooperation and creation of new capacities for the production of nickel and cobalt in Cuba and the implementation of the agreement on the production of mutual supplies of equipment for nuclear power plants within the organization. The participants also discussed the draft program for cooperation in the development and use organization-wide of microprocessors and new equipment for color television transmission. The Executive Committee approved measures to enhance cooperation in light and woodworking industries. (Tass, 20 and 22 April; *FBIS*, 23 April.)

Thirty-Sixth CMEA Council Session. The most important CMEA meeting of the year took place in Budapest on 8–10 June with all ten member-states in attendance. Yugoslavia, an associate member, sent a delegation led by Zvone Dragan, a deputy premier. Observer delegations attended from Afghanistan, Angola, Ethiopia, Laos, Mozambique, and the People's Democratic Republic of Yemen. At least three basic sets of issues were discussed. The first dealt with an analysis of the social and economic development of the individual member-states as well as the fulfillment of past integration measures. This undoubtedly involved problems of growth, trade within the CMEA, and relations with the West, particularly the economic sanctions imposed by Western nations following the declaration of martial law in Poland, as well as the specific problems of Poland and their impact on the other member-states. The second set of issues covered a series of multilateral agreements to be adopted; the third set involved a discussion of the work of the CMEA Council and the bodies involved in the management of "integration processes" among the member-states. (Prague domestic service, 10 June; *FBIS*, 11 June.)

Specific measures adopted at the session appeared relatively modest in scope, although the participants, as usual, claimed significant achievements. The session adopted four multilateral agreements, concerning (1) robotics, including the design and production of industrial robots; (2) microprocessors; (3) microelectronic components; and (4) a protocol on color television (*Pravda*, 11 June). In the case of robotics, the entire cycle of design and development as well as manufacturing techniques was involved. There was to be a division of labor among the member-states in the manufacture of various components. The same applied to microprocessors and to microelectronic components. The protocol on color television covered studio equipment, transmitters, video recorders, and the entire manufacturing process (including a mutual division of labor among the member-states) in order to bring self-sufficiency in the field to the CMEA states within the next five to ten years.

The session also approved a program for the coordination of national economic plans for 1986–1990 to be supplemented by coordination of economic, scientific, and technical policies. Greater emphasis along these lines will be placed on the international socialist division of labor. Furthermore, plans were made to increase the participation of Vietnam, Cuba, and Mongolia in the international socialist division of labor and (in accordance with the comprehensive program) to continue to provide preferential terms of cooperation to these countries. (Ibid.)

Official statements from the delegations and from the news media in the CMEA states claimed successes that appeared generous in light of what had been accomplished. An *Izvestiia* editorial (10 June) proclaimed that the program for the coordination of national economic plans for 1986–1990 not only was a fundamentally important document but involved a radical change in the cooperation machinery (previously carried out mostly on a bilateral basis). The strengthening of multilaterality, the editorial asserted, was in line with the issues raised by Brezhnev at the 1981 Soviet party congress. The Soviet Politburo and the Soviet government, in approving the activities of the Soviet delegation, contended that the session "confirmed once again the unanimous striving of the fraternal countries to strengthen the cohesion of the socialist community" (Tass, 18 June; *FBIS*, 18 June).

The program to coordinate national economic plans, however, does not appear nearly as impressive on closer examination. It is a timetable agreement that in part resulted from frustration generated by the delay in approving the previous (1981–1985) coordinated plan, which was presented to the thirty-fifth CMEA Council session in July 1981, several months after the commencement of the planning period. There was evidence of friction among the member-states at the Budapest session, and a number of participants, including Czechoslovak representative Lubomír Štrougal, used the code word "frank" to characterize the discussions (Prague domestic service, 10 June; *FBIS*, 11 June). The Czech prime minister cautioned that the coordination of plans had to include economic policy and that there should first be an exchange of views regarding the direction in which each member-state wished to move during the next five- and ten-year periods. Then, in 1983–1984, the group could draw up long-term plans that would take into consideration the questions of division of labor. The cautious approach enunciated by Štrougal seems designed more to avoid the confusions of the previous coordinated plan than to initiate a radical departure from previous practice.

A number of speakers objected that there had been a tendency for countries to adopt multilateral agreements that were subsequently unfulfilled or only partially fulfilled. The Hungarians, Czechs, and East Germans voiced their concerns in this area. (MTI, in English, 8 June; *FBIS*, 9 June.) The expression of some of these concerns constituted rather thinly veiled attacks on the Poles but, in the case of the Hungarians, reflected their frustrations with the process of integration. For some time, the Hungarians have been pressing for fairly radical changes in the CMEA system of cooperation and have emphasized the need for both domestic and intraorganizational reform (*Times*, London, 7 June). Problems of currency convertibility, discrepancies in technological standards, and differences in management systems have been part of the broad range of structural flaws and incompatibilities within the CMEA. The final communiqué and statements issued by the various participants, however, indicate that discussion of substantive reform within the CMEA was deferred until the meeting of party secretaries general, which would most likely take place in 1983. Both the Czechs and the Romanians called for an early meeting, but the death of Brezhnev in November may cause additional delays.

Yet certain signals emanating from the session may provide valuable clues to trends within the CMEA. The Hungarians (perhaps supported by a number of other East European member-states) and the Soviet Union appear to take different approaches to the problems of development and of relations with the West. The Soviet position, as put forth by the chairman of the USSR Council of Ministers, Nikolai Tikhonov, emphasized positive elements of intrabloc cooperation as opposed to the deleterious effects of developing a significant dependence on the West as evidenced in the cases of Poland and Romania. The Soviet approach is one of seeking greater economic integration and self-reliance in the CMEA. Naturally, the Soviet Union, as the largest economic unit and the primary supplier of vital raw materials, would derive significant political benefits from greater CMEA interdependence. Moreover, this would facilitate the Soviet goals of achieving better linkages and a greater identification between the CMEA grouping and the Warsaw Treaty Organization, which, in turn, would help solidify Soviet bloc support for Moscow's foreign policies. On the other hand, the Hungarians have stressed the need for reform. The chairman of the Hungarian Council of Ministers, György Lázár, contended that there was a particularly great need for reform now that economic integration was to be used chiefly for the promotion of intensive development. Trade with the West, which has become extensive, was not harmful, he contended, and the CMEA should pursue and widen economic cooperation with developed states "on the basis of equality and benefits for all sides." (MTI, 9 June; *FBIS*, 10 June.)

Budapest's approach has to be cautious, given the relative political and economic positions of CMEA members. Hungary's position has been made even more difficult by Soviet pressure for integration. Moscow has apparently not viewed reform as a prerequisite for more effective integration. Some Western analysts have suggested that viewed over a long period, Soviet pressure for economic integration in the CMEA has been greatest when momentum for thorough-going economic reform was exhausted (M. Kaser, "COMECON's Commerce," *Problems of Communism*, July/August 1972). In the widest sense, however, integration is inextricably intertwined with growth, reform, and trade within the CMEA and with the West.

Economic Growth and Systemic Problems. Growth rates, one of the main pivots of legitimacy of the socialist states, have been falling dramatically in the 1980s. There has been a major slowdown in industrial growth compared with previous decades, and Soviet agricultural production has continued to flounder. The abysmal performance of the Polish economy has significantly reduced the overall performance of the CMEA. According to one Western source, the 13 percent drop in Poland's net material product (NMP) in 1981 meant that total production among the East European members of the CMEA fell by 1.3 percent instead of increasing by 2.8 percent as planned. Of the other East European states, Bulgaria and East Germany managed to hold their own, and Czechoslovakia registered an NMP increase of only 0.2 percent instead of 2.8 percent as planned, Hungary 1.8 percent instead of 2.0–2.5 percent, and Romania 2 percent rather than the planned 7 percent. (*Economist*, London, 29 May.)

Some improvement in performance in 1982 in Czechoslovakia, Romania, and Bulgaria has not been able to place the CMEA back on its projected growth path. Industrial growth in the Soviet Union in the first four months of 1982 was only 2.1 percent higher than in the previous year, and for the first half the overall year-on-year growth in the CMEA (including the Soviet Union) was only 1.9 percent compared with a planned figure of 4.4 percent. (*Economist*, 29 May; *Keesing's Contemporary Archives*, 19 November, p. 31807.) Inflationary pressures continued to mount in the CMEA states. On 30 January, Czechoslovakia increased meat prices by 41 percent; on 1 February, Poland increased food prices by an average of 241 percent; two weeks later Romania raised the cost of some 200 food items by an average of 35 percent (U.K.

Foreign and Commonwealth Office, *Background Brief*, May, p. 3). Moreover, production inefficiencies and the increased cost of production of raw materials, particularly energy-related products in the Soviet Union, as well as continuing worldwide inflation are all likely to sustain pressure for higher price levels throughout the CMEA.

The most important factors in the grave economic problems faced by the CMEA states are the so-called systemic problems. While central planning has produced impressive growth rates in heavy industry, it has also resulted in significant structural distortions. Growth has been extensive instead of intensive—industry tends to be overcapitalized, and there is generally a lack of competition and of flexibility in the wage and price systems, coupled with risk-avoidance. Not only are CMEA managers finding it increasingly difficult to generate the type of high-technology industry that has been the locomotive driving the economies of the advanced industrialized Western states, but they have also demonstrated a tendency to make poor use of imported high technology from the West. Another factor affecting the CMEA economies in Europe has been a fall in the growth rate of the labor force. These labor inputs are expected to slow down even further as declining birthrates begin to have an effect. Moreover, according to Murray Feshbach, a Georgetown University demographer, the Soviet Union has the dubious distinction of becoming the first industrialized state where life expectancy rates have fallen and infant mortality rates have increased (*Globe and Mail*, Toronto, 27 October). Furthermore, the CMEA labor force has been affected by a very high rate of alcoholism and chronic absenteeism. Perhaps just as important, in several of the CMEA states there have been repeated complaints not only of a labor shortage but also of misassignment of workers because of problems in planning.

This, however, is not to suggest that the economies of the CMEA states are on the verge of collapse. For instance, a study by the U.S. Central Intelligence Agency prepared for the Joint Economic Committee of Congress, released in December, has shown that the Soviet Union's gross national product has grown substantially over the past three decades, although in recent years the rate of increase has dropped to under 3 percent (*NYT*, 26 December). But the economic slowdown and the gravity of the problems in Eastern Europe have led to calls for reform. The Hungarians, whose New Economic Mechanism has yielded impressive results in terms of Soviet bloc development, are the ones who have been pressing for the most radical reforms. Some Hungarian economists have been calling for a "renaissance" ranging from such matters as employing a different approach to the export and use of energy resources to the introduction and application of microprocessors and robots. Furthermore, according to Yugoslav sources, they have contended that cooperation within the CMEA might be placed on a more flexible foundation so that "every country's motivation to give its best efforts might find its full expression" (*Politika*, Belgrade, 28 October; *FBIS*, 5 November). Some Hungarian economists seem convinced that cooperation within the CMEA will continue to be incomplete until all member-states carry out Hungarian-style reforms. These would reduce state interference and allow enterprises to take more independent action. Bulgaria has engaged in some limited decentralization, but most other CMEA states do not appear ready as yet to follow the Hungarian model. The Soviet Union itself recognizes the need for modernization, and *Pravda* (15 October) criticized the CMEA states for excessive delays in introducing new technologies and production methods. In the wake of Brezhnev's death, Soviet economist G. Kulagin, writing in *Pravda*, criticized the Soviet custom of "gigantomania" and suggested that planners should learn from the successes of big Western businesses, such as General Electric, which have switched from enormous production complexes to small, highly automated plants (*Globe and Mail*, 9 December). Yet despite a desire to augment the use of high technology, the Soviet Union, as evidenced by the proceedings of the thirty-sixth CMEA Council session, is not prepared to introduce meaningful reforms, but rather leans toward greater integration as manifested by, among other measures, increased trade and cooperation in energy production.

Trade, Planning, and High Technology. In the case of command economies, however, trade is largely an indicator of results. Still, intra-CMEA exchanges of goods and services are significant variables in the process of economic integration. By the end of 1981, according to the communiqué issued at the end of the thirty-sixth CMEA session, 55 percent of the total trade turnover of the CMEA states was conducted within the organization (MTI, 10 June; *FBIS*, 11 June). Intra-CMEA trade has been growing quite rapidly and in the past decade registered a 3.7-fold increase, to a total of 134 billion rubles (*Pravda*, 15 October). With the exception of Romania, the CMEA members conduct the bulk of their trade within the organization. By the end of 1981, Soviet trade with other CMEA members exceeded 52 billion rubles, with East Germany, Czechoslovakia, Poland, and Bulgaria taking first through fourth places as trading partners (Tass, 29 March; *FBIS*, 2 April).

The economic dominance of the Soviet Union in the CMEA has no parallel in other international economic organizations. As the supplier of a few raw materials, the Soviet Union also enjoys certain advantages. Consequently, Eastern Europe's trade imbalance with the Soviet Union worsened by 6 percent in 1981, and according to Wharton Econometric Forecasting Associates, it was likely to deteriorate by a further 6 to 7 percent in 1982 (*Economist*, 20 May). Soviet trade surpluses with Eastern Europe reached $4 billion in 1981 and, according to Wharton, may rise to $5.9 billion in the current year.

Economic problems, coupled with price increases for fuels and primary commodities provided by the Soviet Union, have resulted, moreover, in a reduction in the growth rate in the customary exchange of surpluses of certain goods and commodities not envisaged in foreign trade agreements and contracts. East European states usually find this secondary trade useful. Whereas in 1981 such trade grew rapidly (by almost 19 percent), projections for 1982 were for an increase of only 6.4 percent (Warsaw domestic service, 22 September; *FBIS*, 24 September). Moscow, however, has shown some flexibility in its conduct of trade. There is evidence to suggest that large preferential sales to Bulgaria enabled that country to improve its hard-currency balance of payments by re-exporting both crude oil and oil products to the West at world prices. Moscow also allowed Hungary to earn a surplus in its "hard-currency trade inside the CMEA" while allowing Budapest to run a large ruble trade deficit (*Economist*, 29 May). These are significant privileges, which, however, also provide Moscow with additional leverage over the CMEA states.

Since trade flows in the CMEA are a function of the central plan, they are a limited catalyst for integration. Therefore, Moscow has been pressing ahead with other measures. Even though Western analysts have often claimed that socialist integration, as opposed to absorption or annexation, is more difficult without the employment of market forces, the East European states and the Soviet Union have contended that planned economies have the advantage. They have argued that the CMEA states are able to determine the main directions of economic development, the supply of raw materials, and technological strategy for many years ahead (*Berliner Zeitung*, East Berlin, 6 October). Economic integration, as noted, is considered vital. Over the past two decades, but particularly since the introduction of the comprehensive program, an entire range of integration measures has been introduced and reinforced. Complementary facilities have been jointly built in the metallurgical and chemical industries. Transportation has been synchronized, and strong efforts have been made to cooperate in a variety of engineering tasks. Joint investments and interlinking efforts have been made in the vital energy field (*YICA*, 1982, pp. 520–22). There have been significant specialization efforts in industrial production among the East European members of the CMEA. Czechoslovakia, for instance, is concentrating on producing refrigerators, equipment for nuclear power stations (as is the Soviet Union), and a variety of other engineering, chemical, and consumer goods. Hungary and the Soviet Union produce about 80 percent of the buses, with Budapest responsible for 80 percent of the large buses. Bulgaria is the largest exporter of electric carts within CMEA, whereas East Germany accounts for 75 percent of the exports of railroad passenger cars. (*Rudé právo*, 22 October; *FBIS*, 1 November.)

In the 1980s, the five integration programs adopted in 1978 and 1979 (dealing with consumer goods and transportation) have been reinforced by measures directed at the rapid growth and application of high technology throughout the organization. As noted, the thirty-sixth Council session placed special emphasis on high technology, particularly robotics and microprocessors. The production and the use of robots (program-controlled automatic manipulators) in industry have been particular concerns throughout the CMEA. There are 5,000 of them in operation in the Soviet Union, and it has been projected that by the end of 1985 tens of thousands of them will be in use, thereby bringing about large savings in expenditures and production and relieving large numbers of workers (*Ekonomicheskaia gazeta*, 30 June; *FBIS*, 16 July). In the first half of 1982, the Soviet Union doubled its output over the previous period in 1981 to 2,200 robots. East Germany was assigned the task of increasing the number of industrial robots of various types in use to 42,000–45,000 by the end of the present five-year-plan period. The CMEA, in fact, plans to have 200,000 robots in operation throughout the member-states by 1990. (*Izvestiia*, 10 August.)

Such extensive introduction of high technology, however, does not necessarily make integration easier. There are indications that the application is likely to be uneven given the significant differences in levels of development of the CMEA member-states. Poland and Romania present special problems in Eastern Europe, and there is a particularly wide gap between the European members as a whole and Vietnam, Cuba, and Mongolia. The Romanians have complained that differences among various CMEA states in the level of economic development attained were growing in both relative and absolute terms (*Radio Free Europe Background Report*, 28 May). CMEA integration under Soviet tutelage may derive its greatest success, however, not from trade or application of high technology but rather from the extensive linkages in the energy sector that are being developed.

Energy. If energy is to function as the key variable in the integration of the socialist bloc, Moscow is likely to continue to incur a substantial, and perhaps growing, opportunity cost. Officials at the U.S. Treasury and State departments have estimated that Soviet oil and raw material subsidies to Eastern Europe have been substantial, averaging $5–6 billion a year between 1975 and 1978 and rising to $10 billion in 1979 and $22 billion in 1980 (*Economist*, 22 May). These figures, however, cover several commodities and may range on the high side. Recently the prices the USSR charges Eastern Europe for fuels and primary commodities have been rising faster than the prices of the machinery and consumer goods sold by the other CMEA states to Moscow (ibid., 29 May). Nevertheless, the CMEA states have been anxious to purchase energy products for which Moscow is the organization's main producer because these (particularly oil) continue to be priced below world market rates. Energy resources thus provide both a bond within the organization and leverage for Moscow. Broadly defined, these resources include oil, gas, and nuclear and electrical power.

Oil is the most visible and, for the time being, the most vital fuel in the CMEA. East European demands for oil have been growing despite some conservation measures at a time when the Soviet Union has found it increasingly more expensive and difficult to produce and ship oil. Consequently, Moscow has not only raised prices but has restricted soft-currency sales. It is true that, as recently as June, the Soviet Union pledged to maintain the 1980 sales level to the CMEA and to provide 400 million tons of oil to the organization during the current five-year plan (Moscow domestic service, 7 June; *FBIS*, 8 June). There is already in place an extensive network of pipelines, and Moscow supplies most of the oil consumed by Czechoslovakia, East Germany, Poland, Hungary, and Bulgaria. Western observers, however, believe that the Soviet Union cut back its supply of subsidized oil to Eastern Europe (with the exception of Poland and Bulgaria) by as much as 10 percent in 1981 and by a similar figure in 1982 (*Economist*, 13 February; U.K. Foreign and Commonwealth Office, *Background Brief*, May). The authoritative *Oil and Gas Journal* (25 January, p. 113) confirmed that Hungary, Czechoslovakia, and East Germany were to receive less oil in 1982 than in 1981. Romania, which has sought to purchase more Soviet oil and has become an adherent of CMEA energy integration, has been unable to acquire additional Soviet supplies (ibid.).

According to U.S. government estimates, the shortfall in the supply of subsidized oil played an important role in the decrease in the growth rate of the East European economies (U.K. Foreign and Commonwealth Office, *Background Brief*, May). But Soviet oil production itself may have reached a plateau and may well begin to decline after 1985. The chief economist for Atlantic Richfield has argued that it is unlikely that the Soviet Union will be able to continue to supply substantial quantities of oil to Eastern Europe beyond 1985, despite large oil reserves, because of the great difficulties in extraction ("Soviet Oil for Eastern Europe May Be Near End," *Oil and Gas Journal*, 16 November 1981, p. 151). He defended the 1977 Central Intelligence Agency report that contended that Soviet energy management suffered from inbred deficiencies that would largely nullify the benefits of potential additional reserves. A study published in May by the Royal Institute for International Affairs in London claimed that by 1985, due to the Soviet Union's inability to supply sufficient quantities of oil, the CMEA states would have to increase net imports of oil from the noncommunist world to 100 million tons per annum, although they would have hard currency to cover only half this amount (*Times*, London, 6 May). Dwindling Soviet sales of oil may decrease Soviet leverage derived from provision of that commodity, although even limited supplies would continue to be much sought after as long as they were sold below world market prices. But the Soviet Union is also an important provider of natural gas.

Moscow has an abundant supply of natural gas and has been augmenting its sales to Eastern Europe. Soviet gas production has been growing. In 1981, for instance, its output of 465 billion m^3 constituted a new record and surpassed the target figure of 458 billion m^3 (*Oil and Gas Journal*, 25 January, p. 113).

According to the Soviet government, over 15 billion m³ was to be delivered to the European members of the CMEA in 1982 (Moscow world service, in English, 4 June; *FBIS*, 8 June). This gas is delivered largely on favorable terms, and East European dependence on the supply is increasing. For instance, natural gas accounted for 24 percent of Hungary's total energy consumption in 1982, and the Soviet Union has contracted to supply Budapest with 55 billion m³ during the next twenty years (*Oil and Gas Journal*, 25 January, p. 114).

Nuclear energy is another variable in the process of energy-stimulated integration. The CMEA has placed a considerable stake on nuclear power and plans a total capacity of 140,000–150,000 Mw by 1990 (See *YICA*, 1982, p. 521). The East European states plan to build power stations with a total output of more than 30,000 Mw in 1986–1990 (*Rudé právo*, 22 October; *FBIS*, 1 November). The reactors are to be produced by the Soviet Union and Czechoslovakia. Progress continues to be made on coordination in production and price mechanisms. In some of the CMEA states, 20–25 percent of the total output is already generated by nuclear power plants (*Ekonomicheskaia gazeta*, 30 June, p. 20; *FBIS*, 16 July). Moscow has claimed that the use of Soviet technical knowhow and the reliability of CMEA cooperation has enabled East Germany and Czechoslovakia to abandon the construction of new thermal power stations in favor of nuclear ones (*Izvestiia*, 10 August). Furthermore, the Soviet Union has persuaded East European states to participate in the construction of very large nuclear power stations on Soviet soil at Khmelnitsky and Konstantinovka, which will start supplying electricity to Hungary, Poland, and Czechoslovakia by 1984 with deliveries of 7.6 billion kwh by 1985 and 20–22 billion kwh by 1990 (*Rudé právo*, 22 October; *FBIS*, 22 October).

Both from an economic and a political point of view, a bloc-wide electrical grid is essential for the Soviet Union to maximize the benefits that it (and the East European states) may receive from the cooperative generation of electrical power. The extensive power grid already in operation is in the process of being significantly enlarged. The construction of a 400 kv power transmission line between Czechoslovakia, East Germany, Poland, and Hungary has already substantially increased the transmission capacity of all participating states. The CMEA countries that have benefited most from Soviet electricity exports have been Bulgaria, East Germany, Poland, Hungary, and Czechoslovakia, which also took part in the construction of the Vinitsa-Albertirsa electricity network. It has saved the importing states millions of tons of standard fuel. By 1980, Soviet exports amounted to 1.6 billion kwh, with Moscow claiming that it could produce the same quantity of electricity for less than it would cost the importing states (*Pravda*, Bratislava, 5 November 1981; *FBIS*, 12 November 1981). The dependence of some of the East European states on electricity imports was clearly illustrated by comments of György Lázár. At the thirty-sixth CMEA Council session, he declared that the smooth operation of the unified energy system of the CMEA was vital for Budapest since 25 percent of the electric energy used by Hungary was imported from the socialist states (MTI, 9 June; *FBIS*, 10 June). Thus, energy continues to afford Moscow a powerful leverage over the East European states.

Western Indebtedness and Trade. Romania's hypothesis that trade with the nonsocialist states would be an important factor in sustaining an autonomous foreign policy has little following in Eastern Europe for a variety of reasons, and even Bucharest has begun to shift more of its trade back to the CMEA. Nevertheless, the East European states and the Soviet Union have increased their trade with the Western nations and in the process incurred huge hard-currency debts. Moreover, the debts have been increasing as their economies encounter greater difficulties. The U.N. Economic Commission for Europe (ECE) reported on 16 March that the collective net hard-currency debt of the CMEA member-states (that is, making allowance for their hard-currency deposits in Western banks) reached $80.7 billion by the end of 1981 as compared with $72.4 billion in 1980 (*Keesing's Contemporary Archives*, 19 November, p. 31807). The executive secretary of the ECE, Janez Stanovnik, reported that the overall CMEA debt to the West would rise to $82 billion by the end of 1981 (*Times*, London, 9 March). Some Western estimates placed the gross debt figures as high as $88 billion for the CMEA, including $27 billion for Poland alone (*Economist*, 30 January). All European members of the CMEA increased their currency debts, with the exception of Bulgaria, and their cash balances fell significantly. According to the CIA's Foreign Assessment Center, the Soviet Union's hard-currency cash balance plunged 75 percent by the end of 1981, to $2 billion (ibid., 13 February).

Western technology and credits have not resolved the CMEA's structural problems, and the hard-currency debts appear to place an additional burden on these economies. According to Stanovnik, the East European states and the Soviet Union spend about one-third of their exports servicing Western debts, and this portion could rise. For all intents and purposes, Poland is bankrupt and Romania nearly so. Yet both need more hard-currency loans to buy Western goods and technology. According to Wharton Econometric Forecasting Associates, net Soviet bloc hard-currency debt to the West could increase to $123–140 billion by 1985 unless the CMEA members take drastic corrective measures (*Times*, London, 14 January). According to a U.S. report presented to the Organization for Economic Cooperation and Development (OECD) in May, the Soviet Union's position itself is likely to deteriorate, with its debt-service ratio (the proportion of exports needed to pay for external debts) rising from 19 percent in 1981 to 25 percent in 1985 and 58 percent in 1990 (*Economist*, 15 May).

In October 1981, the Western participants in the OECD, in an informal agreement setting a floor on interest rates and a ceiling on the maturity of loans, agreed to change the loan status of the Soviet Union from that of an intermediate country with agreed interest rates of 10.5–11.0 percent to the relatively rich category with interest rates of 11.00–11.25 percent. Such a belated step to tighten credit by the West or the CMEA's economic difficulties should not lead to an overestimation of Western leverage. Despite the change in the Soviet Union's categorization, there is still room for subsidized loans since some of the Western nations have rates exceeding those assigned to Moscow and some Western governments are willing to guarantee loans made by private banks. The key problem is in essence the unwillingness of Western nations to risk default or a cutoff in trade. To paraphrase Maynard Keynes, when debts become large enough, leverage shifts to the debtor. Western nations, therefore, have been unwilling to declare Poland or Romania in default and agreed to a rescheduling of Polish repayments in 1982. Still, Western nations have begun to exert more pressure for repayment and have restricted new loans (with the major exception of funding for Soviet gas pipelines).

Consequently, Poland has become an increasing burden to its CMEA partners. The Soviet Union has had to agree to a rescheduling of Polish debt repayments and granted Warsaw credits of 2.7 billion rubles in the first part of the year, an amount representing 73.8 percent of the value of Poland's exports to the Soviet Union for 1982 (Warsaw domestic television, 31 March; *Zolnierz Wolnosci*, 23 March; *FBIS*, 1 and 2 April). Poland has had to shift its trade more to the socialist countries, with the result that total turnover with these countries rose from 54 percent of total trade in 1980 to 64 percent in 1982 (Warsaw domestic service, 13 September; *FBIS*, 27 September). Furthermore, this change has entailed significant difficulties for the other CMEA states. They have repeatedly complained of Polish delays in delivering goods and have blamed some of their own problems on the Poles. But Moscow has been pressuring the East European states to provide more "fraternal assistance" to Poland. This aid has consisted largely of agreements for reductions in contracted deliveries of Polish exports and increased deliveries of Poland's raw materials, semifinished products, and consumer goods. There has been some talk of even "renting" either Polish industrial facilities and of receiving Polish "construction" services as payment for East European goods (*Business Week*, 5 July, p. 44). (See the section on the economy in the profile on Poland for more information on this subject.)

Despite all these difficulties, Moscow's problems should not be overestimated. The Soviet Union still has very significant quantities of desirable commodities to sell on the Western market. The agreement to build the gas pipelines to Western Europe assures Moscow of large sums of hard currency. It could also use large gold sales and oil exports to reduce some of its debts. But, as noted, Moscow has used these difficulties with hard-currency debts with the West and domestic growth problems as proof of a need to turn inward toward a more autarkic development within the socialist bloc and greater socialist integration. Yet, the CMEA states must continue to conduct significant trade with the Western nations. The Soviet Union itself must import large quantities of grain in addition to some high technology. Although the Soviet grain harvest in 1982 is supposed to reach 180 million tons, it still must import 35 million tons, according to the U.S. Department of Agriculture (*Globe and Mail*, 15 December). Czechoslovakia, for instance, is expected to continue to import substantial quantities of modern machine tools in an effort to regain the qualitative edge it once had within the CMEA.

For the East European states, however, it is becoming increasingly more difficult to trade with the West. Only Hungary has an economy diversified enough to provide a reasonably good chance of producing goods consistently acceptable on Western markets, but Budapest's large hard-currency debt (the highest per capita among the CMEA states) has cramped trade expansion plans. Because of difficulties in selling in Western markets, the CMEA states have been pressing the Western nations to accept a different form of exchange—"countertrade." This may be divided into three categories: compensation or buybacks, counter-purchase, and barter. A 1980 Romanian law mandates that all exchanges must be on a countertrade basis, and other East European states have been resorting to it increasingly. There is considerable reluctance on the part of the Western nations to resort to these terms of trade, which they consider retrogressive, but there have been numerous examples of acquiescence. For instance, General Electric has agreed to sell turbines to Romania in return for an equivalent amount of Romanian goods, and McDonnell Douglas of the United States sold Yugoslavia airplanes in return for Yugoslav goods, including canned ham. These companies then become responsible for selling these goods on the U.S. market. McDonnell Douglas apparently ended up serving some of the Yugoslav ham in its own cafeteria. (*WSJ*, 25 October.) Overall, Western reluctance, and the unwieldiness of countertrade itself, is bound to constrain this mode of exchange. The determination of the CMEA states to limit hard-currency imports in order to diminish some of their debt is likely to further restrain trade with the West. Thus, we appear to be witnessing a steady turning inward, as desired by Moscow to enhance socialist integration. Barring any major changes of direction by the new Soviet leadership, Moscow is likely to continue to encourage this trend.

University of Toronto   Aurel Braun

Warsaw Treaty Organization

Greater military and political cohesion remained a primary goal of the Warsaw Treaty Organization (WTO) in 1982. The Soviet Union, as the dominant military force within the organization and the primary provider of external security to the regimes of the member-states, sought to enhance organization-wide support for its policies. It also sought to develop closer linkages between the WTO and the Council for Mutual Economic Assistance (CMEA). The member-states continued to strengthen the effectiveness of their military forces through deployment of more sophisticated weapons and to improve coordination through a series of large-scale military maneuvers. Toward the end of the year, the Soviet Union showed greater interest in the strategically less significant southern tier of the WTO. With the government of Wojciech Jaruzelski apparently firmly in control in Poland, any potential WTO invasion plans appear to have receded or to have been abandoned by Moscow. In the realm of arms control negotiations, the Soviet Union and its supporters in the WTO have sought to reap the maximum propaganda benefits from proposals that presented little that was new but demonstrated how clearly Moscow and its allies were alive to every opportunity presented by Western disarray or indecision. Following Leonid Brezhnev's death, Moscow went to some lengths to stress both Soviet and bloc strength and continuity in foreign policy.

Created on 14 May 1955, the WTO was Moscow's response to the Western decision to include West Germany in NATO. Moscow declared that the WTO's aim was to prevent the remilitarization of West Germany and to help dissolve NATO. Moscow's offer to disband the WTO if NATO is simultaneously liquidated is reiterated every year. In addition to the multilateral WTO, the Soviet Union created a network of bilateral treaties in Eastern Europe after 1955. However, a multilateral treaty provided Moscow with political, military, and juridical benefits that bilateral treaties might not have. Moreover, in certain limited ways, a multilateral forum is useful for conflict resolution among the member-states and as a safety valve for nationalistic frustrations.

Although the disparities between NATO and the WTO regarding the importance and nature of membership make dissolution of the Western alliance such a prize for Moscow that it would be worth the sacrifice of the WTO, this ultimate and often expressed Soviet goal belies the pact's growing importance. The WTO has become a useful forum for articulating policy agreement and support for Soviet proposals. A multilateral alliance is also an important asset to Moscow in its ideological confrontations with the West and the People's Republic of China. Militarily, a multilateral alliance has enhanced the ability of the Soviet Union to create more effective defensive and offensive forces in Europe. Juridically, the WTO provided a partial legal justification for the 1968 invasion of Czechoslovakia. It is little wonder that by 1971 Brezhnev declared that the WTO was "the main center for coordinating the fraternal countries' foreign policies."

Nominally, the WTO is an organization of sovereign states (East Germany, Poland, Czechoslovakia, Hungary, Romania, Bulgaria, and the Soviet Union). Its top governing body is the Political Consultative Committee, composed of the leaders of the communist parties, heads of state, and foreign and defense ministers of the member-states. Day-to-day affairs are handled by the Joint Secretariat, which is chaired by a Soviet official and has a representative from each country. The Permanent Commission (located, as is the Secretariat, in Moscow) makes foreign policy recommendations for the WTO. Supreme military power is supposed to reside in the Committee of Defense Ministers. Created in 1969, it consists of the defense ministers of the six East European states and the Soviet Union. Chaired by the commander in chief of the WTO, it includes, among others, the deputy ministers of defense of the member-states. A second military body, the Joint High Command (JHC), is responsible for strengthening the WTO's defense capabilities, preparing war plans, and deciding the deployment of troops. The Military Council, chaired by the commander in chief of the WTO, advises the JHC on nonoperational matters. The council meets under the chairmanship of the WTO's commander in chief and includes the chief of staff and permanent military representatives from each of the allied armed forces. There is also a Committee of Military Technology. In 1976, a Committee of Foreign Ministers and a Unified Secretariat were added. Both the commander in chief and the chief of staff have always been Soviet generals. Currently, Marshal Viktor G. Kulikov is commander in chief, and Army Gen. Anatoli I. Gribkov is first deputy commander and chief of staff. Air defense, which has a high priority in WTO and Soviet strategic planning, has always been under a Soviet commander. The Soviet Union continues to provide the bulk of WTO air defense, which consists of early radar warning systems, air defense control centers, a manned interceptor force, and surface-to-air missiles and antiaircraft artillery units. These four elements are under the command of Soviet Marshal of Aviation Aleksandr I. Koldunov, who is also a deputy commander in chief of the WTO. The entire air defense system is integrated with that of the Soviet Union. In addition, there are common fuel pipelines, joint arms and ammunition depots, and continuous joint planning. Militarily, then, the WTO appears to be very much a Soviet creature.

Military Developments. In the 1950s, the WTO was largely dormant, with the Soviet Union relying on the geographic benefits of the East European states as a potential defensive or offensive glacis. In the early 1960s, however, Moscow decided to increase the military role of the WTO, and in October 1961 the pact held its first joint maneuvers. Greater roles were assigned to the armed forces of the bloc states, although no WTO military doctrine evolved. Soviet military strategy prevailed, and this helped lead to the evolution of a "tier" system in the bloc. Moscow came to refer to the three countries on the axis of the most likely locus of an East-West conflict—the German Democratic Republic (GDR), Poland, and Czechoslovakia—as the "first strategic echelon" of the WTO. This northern tier continues to receive superior armaments from the Soviet Union and holds Moscow's primary strategic attention.

Effective military integration of the WTO forces is a vital component of Soviet strategic doctrine. The northern tier states with their superior military capabilities and more vital strategic location are especially important to Moscow. Soviet strategy calls for rapid movement of large-scale, integrated battlefield forces able to operate both in conventional and nuclear environments. This emphasis on mobility, quick response, and tremendous firepower requires an effective central command and well-equipped and highly trained forces. Greater military integration and massive modernization of equipment play key roles in shifting the battlefield and theater balance in favor of the WTO, which in turn is important for the implementation of Soviet strategic doctrine.

New equipment was delivered to WTO forces in large quantities in 1982. Soviet forces received more T-64 tanks, additional armored personnel carriers, MiG-23/-27 Flogger aircraft, a large quantity of highly mobile gun systems, and surface-to-air missiles. The other member-states' forces received substantial quantities of T-72 tanks, MiG-23 aircraft (which increase their deep-penetration capabilities), helicopters, and improved air defense systems. (*Air Force Magazine*, December, pp. 70–76.) The Soviet Union has also strengthened its theater and strategic nuclear forces with the addition of new missiles and Backfire bombers.

Soviet and East European military advancement in virtually every major area has been reflected in the steadily tilting balance of power in conventional weapons between East and West. According to a confidential NATO report, the WTO enjoys a wide conventional edge. Worldwide, the WTO has 5.7 million troops compared with 4.4 million for NATO and fields 244 active divisions and 27 brigade equivalents against NATO's 76 active divisions and 113 brigade equivalents. In Europe itself, the WTO deploys 4 million troops against NATO's 2.6 million (including Americans). Furthermore, the WTO's active stock of tanks, artillery, and aircraft vastly outnumbers that of NATO in Europe. (*Times*, London, 15 April.) On 3 May, NATO released a comprehensive comparison between its forces and those of the WTO and concluded that the Soviet and East European forces had the edge in virtually every military area with the exception of helicopters, sea-based combat aircraft, and submarine-tracking aircraft (*Facts on File*, 14 May, pp. 339–40). The shift has not been merely quantitative but qualitative. The level of sophistication of WTO weapons and training of troops has improved significantly. Independent assessments of the balance of conventional forces confirm a significant shift of the balance in favor of the WTO. The International Institute for Strategic Studies' *Military Balance, 1982-83* concluded that the numerical balance over the past twenty years has slowly but steadily moved in favor of the East and that at the same time the West has largely lost the technological edge that it believed could compensate for quantitative inferiority (*Air Force Magazine*, December, p. 143). Moreover, with the Soviet deployment of additional intermediate-range missiles and more sophisticated nuclear-armed aircraft in Europe, the theater nuclear balance has also been shifting in favor of the WTO.

Although these trends are extremely disquieting for NATO, the Western alliance's position is not hopeless. *Military Balance, 1982–83* contended that despite the shift in favor of the WTO, one could not conclude that NATO would necessarily suffer defeat in war. Despite new equipment, better troop training, and standardization of weapons, the WTO suffers from significant shortcomings. Although the East European forces, overall, are important assets for the Soviet Union, their reliability and military effectiveness vary significantly. In the northern tier, the imposition of martial law in Poland would undoubtedly have a deleterious effect on the combat capabilities of Polish forces in an East-West conflict. In the southern tier, where the largest qualitative gap within the WTO exists, Romania has virtually opted out of potential WTO offensive/defensive operation vis-à-vis the West through a reorganization of its forces on the basis of a "people's war" doctrine that is similar to the Yugoslav model of territorial defense. There continues to be resentment throughout Eastern Europe against Soviet military-political domination in the WTO and over Moscow's main weapons design and full-scale production monopoly (John Erickson, "Military Management and Modernization Within the Warsaw Pact," in Robert W. Clawson and Lawrence S. Kaplan, eds., *The Warsaw Pact*, Wilmington, Del., Scholarly Resources, 1982, pp. 213–19). Romania, in fact, is the only WTO state that has been able to design and build its own fighter aircraft (the IAR 93) and military helicopters under Western license (*Aviation Week and Space Technology*, 1 December, pp. 53–62).

On the other hand, WTO weaknesses should not be overstated. Many of the improvements in the WTO military capabilities have been evolutionary, and these often do not easily lend themselves to analyses employing Western-made organizational charts. Recently, however, Moscow has moved from a selective re-equipment of East European forces to an overall modernization (with special emphasis on the northern tier armies). Moreover, Moscow's approach is a comprehensive one designed to overcome all key weaknesses. In an October address, Brezhnev told the commanders of the Soviet armed forces that great emphasis would be placed on raising the level of combat readiness of the army and navy as well as on building and consolidating the material base of the armed forces. Consequently, he contended that important operational, technical, and organizational measures were being implemented in order to increase the effectiveness of the armed forces, particularly through the use of large-scale military maneuvers. (Tass, 27 October; *Facts on File*, 29 October, pp. 793–94.)

Military maneuvers in the WTO have played a key role over the past two decades in improving the military effectiveness of the member-states' forces and also in enhancing the political cohesion of the bloc. The USSR has used "intimidation through maneuver" to convey strong signals to a number of East European states during this period. More recently, the evolution of Soviet strategic and tactical doctrines stressing firepower, mobility, and deep-penetration capabilities have made joint maneuvers an even greater military necessity in the effective integration of WTO forces. The WTO held joint maneuvers in February, March, and September.

In February, 25,000 Hungarian, Soviet, and Czechoslovak troops took part in a six-day set of maneuvers dubbed Operation Friendship '82 in Czechoslovakia's western Bohemia region, not far from the borders of West Germany and the GDR. The joint exercises were supervised by Marshal Kulikov. According to Czechoslovak and GDR news agency reports, the maneuvers included full-scale mock battles, nighttime exercises, and a mock chemical warfare attack. (*Los Angeles Times*, 7 February.) These exercises appear to have been routine. Between 13 and 20 March, another series of WTO maneuvers was conducted in the area of Poland, the GDR, and the western Soviet Union. The maneuvers began in the northwest corner of Poland under the command of Lt. Gen. Tadeusz Molczyk, a Polish deputy minister of defense and a deputy commander in chief of the WTO. The exercises were "tactical-operational," and since they involved fewer than 25,000 men, no official notification was required under the terms of the 1975 Helsinki Final Act. (*Times*, London, 14 March.) In Poland, the maneuvers were held far away from potential trouble spots, but they had particular symbolic importance. As the first WTO maneuvers held inside Poland since the imposition of martial law, they were designed to reflect a certain degree of "normalization" and to indicate both internally and externally that the Polish army was not so stretched by the requirements of martial law that it could not take part in WTO military functions.

The most important WTO maneuvers of the year, code-named Shield-82, took place between 25 September and 1 October in Bulgaria and the adjoining parts of the Black Sea coast (Tass, 1 October; *FBIS*, 1 October). The exercises involved 60,000 troops with representation from all members of the WTO. Bulgarian Army Gen. Dobri Dzhurov, the minister of national defense, was the nominal head of the maneuvers, but Marshal Kulikov and General Gribkov were present both during the preparatory stages and the exercises. Organized under the slogan "United in peace and combat for defending the socialist cause" (*Rabotnichesko delo*, 28 September; *FBIS*, 1 October), Shield-82 presented a number of significant politico-military implications.

Shield-82's very location in Bulgaria is noteworthy. Although Sofia and Moscow were very careful to indicate that these maneuvers were not directed against any of Bulgaria's neighbors and ensured that the participating forces were held at least 100 km east of the Bulgarian-Yugoslav border, the very presence of 60,000 troops (including rear guard services, closer to 80,000) was bound to cause some anxiety in the region. Yugoslavia quickly voiced its concern about the exercises (*Neue Zürcher Zeitung*, 1 October). The location of these large-scale maneuvers in a southern tier state of the WTO may also indicate a new Soviet strategic interest in the area. They increased pressure on NATO's weak southern flank and helped the Soviet Union mark out its presence in the vicinity of the eastern Mediterranean.

There appears to be some confusion about the participation of Romanian forces. The logo of the Shield-82 maneuvers incorporated the Romanian flag, and Soviet and Bulgarian news agencies referred to the participation of "troops from the member-states including Romania" (BTA, 22 September; Tass and BTA, Sofia, 1 October; *FBIS*, 24 September). Yet, it is highly unlikely that Bucharest, which usually sends only staff officers, participated with combat forces. Yugoslav and Western sources claimed that only staff units participated (Belgrade domestic service, 25 September; *FBIS*, 27 September; *Neue Zürcher Zeitung*, 1 October). Romanian media coverage of the maneuvers was much more limited than that of the other states, with the first notice issued only on 1 October (Bucharest domestic service, 1 October; *FBIS*, 4 October). It made no mention of the participation of Romanian combat troops. Furthermore, there are strong indications that Romania did not allow troops to transit its territory. Non-Romanian reports of the maneuvers spoke repeatedly of troops being landed by air and by sea (*Rabotnichesko delo*, 1 October; *FBIS*, 6 October). The Hungarian media, in its coverage of the maneuvers, pointed out that they were a very complicated undertaking since equipment and troops had to be carried over long distances (Budapest domestic service, 2

October; *FBIS*, 4 October). Still, the Romanian delegation was led by Lt. Gen. Constantin Olteanu, the minister of national defense, which may be indicative of Romanian attempts to get closer to the Soviet Union (essentially for economic reasons) and thus willing to participate, at a certain level, in the important affairs of the WTO.

The presence at the maneuvers of the minister of national defense of Mongolia, the first deputy minister of the armed forces of Cuba, and the deputy minister of defense and chief of the general staff of Vietnam (BTA, 26 September; *FBIS*, 28 September), representing the CMEA states that are not members of the WTO, probably represents another attempt by Moscow to link the two organizations more closely.

From a purely military point of view, the maneuvers involved a set of large-scale, thorough-going exercises employing massive land, sea, and air forces. The exercises were to demonstrate the increased organizational capabilities and the enhanced level of preparation of the high command, according to Soviet Minister of Defense Marshal Dimitri Ustinov, who also attended the maneuvers (*Rabotnichesko delo*, 2 October; *FBIS*, 6 October). According to Marshal Kulikov, the exercises also demonstrated the constantly improving level of operational and tactical training of both staffs and troops from all branches of the military (Moscow domestic service, 2 October; *FBIS*, 5 October). They involved large-scale landing of paratroopers, the transportation of heavy equipment, naval landings and exercises by naval ships, including submarines, and the use of sophisticated weapons such as the T-64 and T-72 tanks, MiG-27 aircraft, hovercraft, and electronic countermeasures (*Rabotnichesko delo*, 1 October; *FBIS*, 6 October; *Népszabadság*, 2 October). It was a stark demonstration of Soviet and WTO military strength.

The WTO continued to hold high-level meetings designed to increase the cohesion of the organization. Sessions of the Military Council of the Joint Forces of the WTO in April in East Berlin, in Warsaw 20–22 October, and in Budapest 27–30 October were described by the participants as routine or regular. The WTO members endorsed the Soviet position on negotiations with the West. At the Warsaw meeting, General Jaruzelski praised the role of the WTO in maintaining peace and asserted that Poland remained an important and reliable link in the coalition (Warsaw domestic television service, 22 October; *FBIS*, 25 October). The 21–22 October meeting of the Committee of Foreign Ministers of the WTO in Moscow, however, produced a much more extensive discussion, and the long communiqué at the end of the session dealt with East-West tensions, arms control negotiations, Poland, and the Middle East. The participants, including Romania, endorsed the Soviet Union's proposal of "no first use" of nuclear weapons, declared their opposition to the NATO deployment of medium-range Pershing-II and Cruise missiles in Western Europe, and condemned U.S. "imperialism, threats, and attempts to intensify the arms race." They also condemned the Western stance at the Madrid Conference on Security and Cooperation in Europe and called for the adoption at the next session in the Spanish capital of a decision to convene an all-European conference on confidence- and security-building measures and on disarmament. Furthermore, the participants protested the sanctions against Poland and "interference" in its affairs and called on the West to be more flexible at the Geneva and Vienna talks (Tass, 22 October; *FBIS*, 25 October). Moscow thus showed at this session that it could bring all WTO members into line and had their full support for its position.

Finally, in October there was a meeting of the heads of the civil defense organs of the WTO. Held in the GDR, it was a working meeting, which condemned Western "pressures" (*Neues Deutschland*, 21 October; *FBIS*, 25 October). But the long-awaited WTO summit meeting of party heads, which had been scheduled for 7–9 December in Prague, had to be postponed due to the death of Leonid Brezhnev. The new Soviet leadership was to reschedule this meeting early in 1983.

Political Developments. From its inception, the WTO has incorporated a vital political dimension, entailing a broad definition of security that involves both external and internal security. The late WTO Chief of Staff Sergei Shtemenko contended in an article published posthumously that a key function of the alliance was the "suppression of counterrevolution" in Eastern Europe (*Za rubezhom*, 7 May 1976). Brezhnev himself declared that "the WTO has everything necessary to firmly defend our people's socialist achievements and we will do everything within our power so that this may also be true in the future" (*Rabotnichesko delo*, 2 October; *FBIS*, 6 October). Poland presented a major problem for the Soviet Union and the WTO, and Moscow must have been very relieved that the Jaruzelski regime was managing to hold its own, thereby obviating the need for military intervention. As noted, the foreign ministers' committee at its October meeting condemned Western "interference" in Polish affairs and pledged strong support for the

Polish regime. Marshal Kulikov was rumored to have been in Poland at the time of the imposition of martial law, and he visited Warsaw in mid-March and mid-May (*Keesing's Contemporary Archives*, 8 October, p. 31737). The Soviet government itself openly and strongly supported the imposition of martial law. On 12 October, Soviet Defense Minister Ustinov sent a message to Jaruzelski in which he stated that "the Polish People's Republic as a member-state of the WTO can be certain of the full support and help of the Soviet Union" (*Krasnaia zvezda*, 12 October). And in December, at the sixtieth anniversary celebrations of the founding of the Soviet Union, Jaruzelski was the only East European leader to stay over in Moscow to consult with Yuri Andropov.

Arms control talks between East and West continued at various levels and locations, with the Soviet Union doing its best to use the WTO as a supporting chorus for its policies. The Madrid follow-up talks on the Conference on Security and Cooperation in Europe, the Mutual and Balanced Force Reduction (MBFR) talks in Vienna, and the Intermediate-Range Nuclear Forces (INF) talks and the Strategic Arms Reduction Talks (START) in Geneva yielded few concrete results.

At Madrid, the Polish crisis generated significant repercussions that affected the course of discussions during the February–March sessions. Moscow and its WTO allies, including Romania, had been pressing very hard for an agreement that would have supplemented the Final Act. Part of the agreement would have involved a call for a conference on disarmament in Europe devoted to measures to prevent surprise attack (confidence- and security-building measures). A continued campaign on the issue by the Soviet Union and its allies, however, did have some limited results. The United States, in order to avoid a political rift in the Atlantic Alliance, dropped its refusal to resume negotiations at Madrid in November. Nevertheless, Washington made it clear that it would not be "business as usual" at the session (*NYT*, 7 November). At the MBFR talks in Vienna, disagreements continued over data on the size of WTO forces, on associated measures to verify implementation, and on linkage. A NATO proposal for a draft treaty involving a seven-year program of troop cuts that would leave each side with the same number of troops, brought forth a very cool response from Moscow (CSM, 22 July).

At the INF talks, the Soviet Union continued to reject President Reagan's November 1981 "zero option," which called for the dismantling of Soviet SS-4, SS-5, SS-20 missiles in Europe in exchange for a commitment not to deploy the Pershing-II and Cruise missiles. The talks reopened on 30 September. In December, Andropov offered to reduce Soviet medium-range weapons trained on Western Europe to the total number deployed by France and Britain—162. Presumably this would be in exchange for a decision on the part of the United States not to deploy its new missiles in Europe. The proposal was unacceptable not only to the United States but also to France and Britain. Many Western analysts concluded that the Soviet proposals were largely a propaganda ploy designed to encourage public opposition in Western Europe to the deployment of the new NATO missiles. START, the parallel bilateral negotiations between the superpowers in Geneva made little headway as well. In June, Moscow rejected President Reagan's proposals for substantial reductions in what he has called the most destabilizing offensive strategic weapons—namely, ground-based missiles—as one-sided (*Pravda*, 4 June). Negotiations resumed in October (after the August recess), and chief U.S. negotiator Edward L. Rowny expressed some optimism, but this was not borne out through the remainder of the year. In December, Andropov repeated some previous offers to reduce long-range strategic delivery systems by 25 percent and to renounce "first use" of conventional warfare if the West made the same commitment (*Toronto Star*, 22 December). The United States rejected this offer as no more than a declaratory statement.

Progress in arms control talks at various levels thus may occur only in the new year (if at all) with a consolidation of the new leadership in the Soviet Union and perhaps following the summit of WTO leaders. Within the WTO, Moscow, however, made progress during 1982 both in improving military integration and effectiveness and in strengthening the political cohesion of the organization. The apparently smooth succession following the death of Brezhnev may also have helped minimize dislocation within the WTO.

University of Toronto   Aurel Braun

International Communist Organizations

WORLD MARXIST REVIEW

The *World Marxist Review*, as it is entitled in its English-language editions (other-language editions use the title *Problems of Peace and Socialism*), is an international, Soviet-line ideological monthly that has been headquartered in Prague since 1958. It is in a sense the latter-day successor of the Comintern (1919–1938) and the Cominform (1947–1956), the only formal organization joining the world communist movement under Soviet guidance. As of late 1981, nearly 70 national editions were being printed in 37 languages and distributed in 145 countries. Total claimed circulation was over 500,000. As of late 1982, 65 theoretically equal pro-Soviet and independent communist parties were officially represented on its Editorial Council, again theoretically, the top decision-making body. (The representatives, incidentally, are on average members of their respective central committees.)

In fact, Soviet control of the publication appears pervasive. The magazine's chief editor (currently Yuri A. Sklyarov) has always been a Soviet; so has one of its two executive secretaries (currently Sergei V. Tsukasov). The other executive secretaryship has traditionally been reserved for a Czechoslovak, and the current incumbent (Pavel Auersperg) has been described by an organ of the independent Japan Communist Party as "more Soviet than the Soviets." This same organ described these three officials as "the core of the Editorial Office" and the magazine's Editorial Board as instrumental in maintaining Soviet control of the operation. This latter statement seems plausible. Even according to the magazine's own official account, the board "supervises the work of the editorial staff," and on it are represented only fifteen communist parties, ten of which are strongly pro-Soviet (Argentine, Bulgarian, Czechoslovak, East German, Indian, Iraqi, Mongolian, Polish, Soviet, and U.S.), two of which seem at least mildly so (French and Hungarian), and only three of which appear to be independent (British, Italian, and Romanian). Also, the only time the magazine could ever have been suspected of deviating from the Soviet line came just after the 1968 Czech invasion when the magazine skipped an issue. This was also the occasion for a change of chief editors. Finally, those communist parties that have run completely afoul of the Soviets either never joined in publication (the Yugoslav) or withdrew after relations soured (the Albanian and the Chinese in 1962). The independent parties associated in the effort apparently do so only because they can pick and choose the articles they publish in their own national editions.

There is evidence of direct Soviet control at the working (as opposed to policy) level. Each of the 65 representatives on the Editorial Council apparently also sits on one or more geographical or functional commissions of the magazine, which are responsible for overseeing articles and conferences within their respective spheres of competence. There are ten such commissions: Problems of Socialist Construction (communist-ruled countries), Class Struggle in Capitalist Countries (developed, noncommunist countries), National Liberation Struggle in Asian and African Countries, National Liberation Struggle in Latin America and the Caribbean, General Problems of Theory, Exchanges of Experience of Party Work, Problems of Peace and Democratic Movements (international communist front organizations), Problems of Science and Culture, Communist Press Criticism and Bibliography, and Scientific Information and Documents. From the little evidence that can be gleaned from the pages of the magazine, it appears that each commission has a Soviet secretary who doubles as head of a corresponding department composed entirely of his fellow nationals. The assumption is that the departments were set up to control the commissions (and that this is why the departments were not mentioned in articles describing the work of the magazine in its August and September 1981 issues).

The sponsoring or cosponsoring of thematic conferences is the other major function of the *Review*'s staff. In view of the failure of the Soviets to bring off a new world conference of communist parties (due to the objections of the independent parties) ever since 1973, two of the larger cosponsored meetings (Sofia, December 1978, and East Berlin, October 1980) appeared, because of their scope, to have been intended by the Soviets to be substitutes for a world conference. So also did the last of a series of conferences held to discuss the work of the magazine (Prague, November 1981). It was attended by representatives from 81 communist and 9 "revolutionary democratic" parties. The leader of the Japanese delegation openly criticized Soviet domination of the magazine and later claimed that in so doing he had been explicitly supported by the British, Italian, Belgian, and Spanish delegations and implicitly supported by the Romanian and Swiss ones. At the time of the publication of the November 1982 edition, however, none of these parties had been deleted from the magazine's masthead (even though the Japan Communist Party had called for its dissolution). The *Review* remains an important—indeed, the only—permanent institutional symbol of unity for the world's pro-Soviet and independent communist parties. (The above is a synopsis of an article entitled "New Head, Old 'Problems of Peace and Socialism,'" prepared by the author for the November–December 1982 edition of *Problems of Communism*, pp. 57–63.)

FRONT ORGANIZATIONS

Control and Coordination. The international Soviet-line communist fronts operating since World War II are counterparts of organizations established by the Comintern after World War I. Their function today is the same as that of the interwar organizations: to unite Communists with persons of other political persuasions to support, and thereby lend strength and respectability to, Soviet foreign policy objectives. Moscow's control over the fronts is evidenced by their faithful adherence to the Soviet policy line as well as by the withdrawal patterns of member-organizations (certain pro-Western groups after the cold war began, Yugoslav affiliates following the Stalin-Tito break, and Chinese and Albanian representatives as the Sino-Soviet split developed).

The Communist Party of the Soviet Union is said to control the fronts through its International Department (ID), presumably through the Soviets serving as full-time Secretariat members at front headquarters (U.S. Congress, *The CIA and the Media*, 1981, p. 574). This is the case in eight fronts: the World Peace Council (WPC), the World Federation of Trade Unions (WFTU), the Women's International Democratic Federation (WIDF), the Afro-Asian Peoples' Solidarity Organization (AAPSO), the International Organization of Journalists (IOJ), the Christian Peace Conference (CPC), the International Association of Democratic Lawyers (IADL), and, most recently, the International Union of Students (IUS). Past experience indicates that it may be the Soviet vice-presidents who exercise this function in the two other major front organizations: the World Federation of Democratic Youth (WFDY) and the World Federation of Scientific Workers (WFSW).

In addition to Soviet control of each front through the ID and headquarters personnel, coordination of front activity appears to be effected by the WPC. This makes sense because the Soviets consider the "peace movement" the most important joint action by the "anti-imperialist" forces and the most important of the movements "based on common specific objectives of professional interests"—that is, the front organizations (*Kommunist*, no. 17, November 1972, p. 103, no. 3, February 1974, p. 101; see also J. A. Emerson Fermaat, "Moscow Fronts and the European Peace Movement," *Problems of Communism*, November–December, pp. 43–56). A glance at the nearly 200 positions on the WPC Presidential Committee reveals that they include, in addition to ID Deputy Chief Vitali S. Shaposhnikov, slots for one or two of the top leaders of each of the ten fronts discussed here except for the IADL. The IADL president is, however, one of the 1,500-plus members of the WPC proper. (WPC, *List of Members, 1980–1983*.)

Policies. As in 1981 (see *YICA*, 1982, p. 529), the U.S. "threat" to world peace, most specifically the projected deployment of Pershing II and Cruise missiles in Western Europe and the development of the neutron bomb, appeared to be the major front campaign during the first half of 1982 and again at the end of the year. Such was the emphasis of the WPC Presidential Committee Bureau meeting (Copenhagen, January), the Dialogue for Disarmament and Détente of the International Liaison Forum of Peace Forces (a WPC front) (Vienna, January–February), the IADL's International Lawyers' Peace Conference (Frankfurt, March), and the WPC's meeting of vice-presidents and other leaders (Moscow, April). Apparently certain U.S. delegates were primarily responsible for keeping the roughly 600-delegate World Conference of Religious Workers for Saving the Sacred Gift of Life (Moscow, May) from taking such an unbalanced stand (*Times*, London, 18 May); although sponsored by the Russian Orthodox church and having such anticommunist participants as Billy Graham, this meeting was addressed by leaders of the WPC (including its definitely nonreligious chairman, the communist Romesh Chandra), and it allowed no public mention of East European dissidence on the part of a Dutch church leader who wanted to do so (ibid.). More general efforts to promote the Soviet peace line occurred at the two major front gatherings of the year, the WFTU's Tenth Congress (Havana, February) and the WFDY's Eleventh General Assembly (Prague, June), as well as at a joint meeting of all ten major fronts discussed here except the IADL and WFSW (Prague, March).

This March joint meeting was specifically pointed toward the U.N. General Assembly's June-July Second Special Session on Disarmament (SSOD II). The fronts made a significant input to this meeting but failed to determine its outcome. The WPC's *Peace Courier* (Helsinki) made mention in July of four massive peace rallies in June aimed at influencing SSOD II: in New York ("close to a million participants"), in Bonn ("at least 400,000"), in London ("250,000"), and in Goteborg ("over 100,000"). The implication of the article was that the line taken at these rallies was totally consonant with that of the WPC (and thus of the USSR), but in reality they appeared to have included criticism of Soviet armaments as well (just like the fall 1981 peace demonstrations [see *YICA*, 1982, p. 529]). Again, however, this did not prevent Soviet Peace Committee Chairman Georgi Zhukov from representing the Bonn rally as "several hundred thousand people . . . directed against the deployment of U.S. nuclear missiles in Western Europe" (*Lidova Demokracie*, Prague, 25 October). At the special session itself, leaders of the ten fronts discussed here were among speakers from over 50 nongovernmental organizations who addressed the Ad Hoc Committee of the Whole on 24–25 June. They failed to win the SSOD II over to their way of thinking, however, for the results of that meeting could most charitably be described as "inconclusive" (*U.N. Chronicle*, September, pp. 3–4).

Subsequent emphasis on the denuclearization of Western Europe seemed to have diminished following the Israeli invasion of Lebanon in early June, although the campaign continued with peace marches to and from the USSR (July–August) and even a WFDY-sponsored Baltic cruise for peace (August). The September WFTU Bureau meeting in Prague did, however, yoke opposition to medium-range missiles in Western Europe with "the extermination campaign of Israeli Zionism" as major emphases. By the time of the November Lisbon WPC Presidential Committee meeting, the nuclear issue had returned to its former pre-eminence. In early October, incidentally, a rather unusual Soviet-line peace demonstration involving "over half a million" participants occurred in New Delhi. It was officially sponsored by India's two major communist parties plus four minor leftist parties, and its initiative was attributed to the February WFTU congress. (*New Age*, New Delhi, 10 October.)

The Israeli invasion of Lebanon in June and the September massacre in the Beirut Palestinian refugee camp were, of course, heaven-sent opportunities for Soviet-line propaganda and agitational activities regarding the Middle East. Even before this, however, a Middle Eastern emphasis could be seen in the apparent WPC domination of a February conference in Aden that demanded sanctions against Israel and the de facto abolition of the Sinai multilateral force. In any case, less than a week after Israel had begun its invasion, the WFDY General Assembly elected a Lebanese president for the first time (coincidence?). In late July, all major fronts except the IADL, CPC, and WFSW issued a joint appeal to the U.N. Security Council to condemn the Israeli invasion and find a solution that would place the Palestinians under the leadership of the Palestine Liberation Organization. In mid-August, an International Commission to Investigate Israeli Crimes Against the Lebanese and Palestinian Peoples was noted, with IADL Vice-President John Platts-Mills (U.K.) as chairman and four WPC Presidental Committee members on its seven-member Presidium. In September, the Middle East emphasis appeared to peak with a WPC conference in Vienna devoted to "the struggle against the Israeli occupation of Lebanon" and "the legitimate rights of the Palestinian people," a WFDY fact-finding mission to Lebanon, an IUS Secretariat meeting devoted to "the just struggle of the Palestinian people and the patriotic forces of Lebanon," an apparently similar emphasis by a CPC Secretariat meeting, and the highlighting of the Israeli invasion by the AAPSO's Asian Security Conference in Hanoi.

Continued but secondary emphasis has been placed on nuclear-free "zones of peace," which appear to be so located as to inhibit U.S. approaches to current areas of greatest interest: Western Europe and the Middle East. Pressure for a nuclear-free Scandinavia was especially notable in late 1981, when Soviet diplomats stationed in both Denmark and Norway were discovered to have been funding the active peace movements in those countries (see Fermaat, "Moscow Fronts and the European Peace Movement," p. 55). The WFDY sponsored a Mediterranean Youth Peace Conference (Athens, January), with the theme of making that sea into a "zone of peace," while New Delhi was the site of two conferences with similar aims for the Indian Ocean: a multifront gathering in April and one sponsored by the IADL in September.

Another theme of secondary emphasis during 1982 was support of the Salvadoran revolutionaries, especially just before and after the March elections in that country. Various national Salvadoran "salvation committees" claimed credit for worldwide rallies protesting U.S. policy toward that country on the eve of the elections. In April, in San José, Costa Rica, the theme was continued by the WPC-sponsored Third Conference for Peace and Sovereignty in Central America, Mexico, and the Caribbean. In May, an umbrella organization for the Salvadoran solidarity committees was announced in Mexico City. At least the U.S. committee had input from the national peace committee and the communist party; it is assumed that many of the others did likewise. (See U.S. Congress, *Soviet Active Measures*, pp. 52, 215.)

While the theme of the "depredations" of transnational corporations (the subject of an AAPSO-sponsored conference in Addis Ababa during April–May) might fall into this category of secondary emphasis, other perennials such as "solidarity" with the "peoples" of South Africa, Namibia, Guatemala, Honduras, Puerto Rico, and (Greek) Cyprus and with the "progressive" regimes of Afghanistan, Ethiopia, Grenada, Kampuchea, and Nicaragua, as well as the establishment of "a new international economic order" were definitely tertiary in emphasis. More transitory themes in 1982 were condemnations of "NATO interventionist policy" in Poland and of British activities in the Falkland islands as well as support of leftist trade unionists on trial in Turkey.

Personnel. A possible guide to the relative importance of front leaders within their respective organizations might be a list of those who did and who did not serve as spokesmen at the SSOD II sessions, the most notable example of joint front activity during the year. Among those who spoke were WPC President Romesh Chandra (India), WFTU Secretary General Ibrahim Zakariya (Sudan), WFDY Secretary General Miklós Barabás (Hungary), WIDF Vice-President Valentina Nikolayeva-Tereshkova (USSR), AAPSO Secretary General Nuri Abd-al-Razzaq Husayn (Iraq), IUS President Miroslav Stepan (Czechoslovakia), IOJ President Kaarle Nordenstreng (Finland), CPC President Károly Toth (Hungary), IADL President Joe Nordmann (France), and WFSW President Jean-Marie Legay (France). Top leaders who did not speak included WPC Executive Secretary John Benson (Australia), WFTU President Sándor Gáspár (Hungary), WFDY President Walid Masri (Lebanon), WIDF President Freda Brown (Australia) and Secretary General Mirjam Vire-Tuominen (Finland), AAPSO President Abd-al-Rahman Sharqawi (Egypt), IUS Secretary Srinivasan Kunalan (India), IOJ Secretary General Jiří Kubka (Czechoslovakia), CPC Secretary General Lubomír Mirejovsky (Czechoslovakia), IADL Secretary General Amar Bentoumi (Algeria), and WFSW Secretary General John Dutton (Great Britain).

A few explanations are in order. The WIDF, the only organization not represented by either its president or its secretary general, had earlier protested Washington's refusal to issue visas to "its delegation" to the SSOD II (ADN, East Berlin, 7 June). Brown and Vire-Tuominen might also have been among the seven WPC members refused visas (they are both members of the WPC Presidential Committee) (*Peace Courier*, July, p. 9). All eleven WPC leaders who were admitted were given restricted visas that prohibited them from speaking outside U.N. premises; this applied not only to Chandra but also to ex-president Francisco da Costa Gomes of Portugal, a WPC vice-president (ibid.). The WPC has no secretary general at present (Chandra's former position), and the executive secretaryship held by Benson appears to be definitely lower ranking than the other positions mentioned. While WFTU President Gáspár, as a Soviet bloc national and a leading communist in his own country, would certainly appear to be a safe spokesman from the Soviet standpoint, he did make certain statements at the WFTU congress in Havana that could have been interpreted as soft on Poland (for example, trade unions in "socialist" countries must not become mere instruments of any government or party, they should protect their members against bureaucratic excesses, and "no one can interfere" in Polish events "from abroad") (MTI, Budapest, 11 and 17 February). Masri had just been elected WFDY president earlier in June, while Barabás is a bloc national with longer experience in his position in the organization; there is a similar contrast between Kunalan and Stepan in the case of the IUS. Similarly, in the case of the IADL, Nordmann is a communist and a longtime incumbent; Bentoumi is neither. AAPSO President Sharqawi appears to be largely inactive and is not known to be particularly procommunist; Husayn suffers from neither of these disabilities. The WFSW's Legay moved into his organization's presidency and was succeeded by Dutton as secretary general, apparently during the first half of 1982 (*Scientific World*, no. 2). The choice of Nordenstreng for the IOJ and Toth for the CPC may be due to the prestige afforded by their being a professor and bishop, respectively.

Besides re-electing Gáspár as president and promoting Zakariya from acting to full secretary general, the February WFTU congress expanded the number of vice-presidential slots from three (Czechoslovakia, Benin, and India) to six (Cuba, Cyprus, and Lebanon) (*Flashes from the Trade Unions*, Prague, 20 February). In view of a similar expansion of vice-presidential slots in AAPSO in late 1981 (Afghanistan, South Africa, Sri Lanka, and the USSR in addition to those already held by Cyprus, Guinea-Bissau, and Iraq) and the rather unique meeting of WPC vice-presidents in April, there may be a trend among the international fronts toward developing a smaller decision-making body above the Bureau level.

No such significant expansion took place in the vice-presidency of the WFDY at its 11 June General Assembly, but that body was already a comparatively large one. Still, Portuguese and Angolan vice-presidents were added to those from Argentina, Chile, Cuba, North Korea, India, the Sudan, the USSR, and Vietnam (*World Youth*, Budapest, no. 11/12, pp. 4, 6). A temporary diminution in the number of the twenty-plus WPC vice-presidents has occurred with the failure to fill the slots left open by the deaths of Abe Fineglass (United States) and Albert Norden (East Germany). Georgi A. Zhukov has replaced the deceased E. K. Fedorov as Soviet WPC vice-president, however, and Severo Aguirre del Cristo replaced Elena Gil Izquierdo in the equivalent Cuban position (*New Perspectives*, Helsinki, no. 5, p. 2).

During the year, several minor fronts had major meetings at which their top officers were either re-elected or changed. The regional (Europe/Israel) International Federation of Resistance Fighters re-elected its president, Arialdo Banfi (Italy), and its secretary general, Alix L'Hote (France), at its 9 September congress. Similarly, the WFTU's Trade Union International (TUI) of Metal and Engineering Industries re-elected its president, Reinhard Commer (East Germany), and its secretary general, Alain Stern (France), at its Ninth Conference that same month. Also in September, the WFTU TUI of Textile, Clothing, Leather, and Fur Workers held its Seventh Conference, at which time its president, Gilberto Morales (Colombia), and its secretary general, Jan Kriz (Czechoslovakia), were re-elected. Finally, at the Seventh Congress of the WFTU TUI of Public and Service Workers, Alain Pouchol (France) was newly elected president and Hans Lorenz (East Germany) was re-elected secretary general.

The WFTU and the WFDY issued claims of greatly increased strength during 1982. In Havana at the Tenth Congress of the WFTU, it was announced that since the Ninth Congress (1978), membership had increased from 190 million to 206 million and from 73 to 90 affiliates (*Flashes from the Trade Unions*, 20 February). In mid-1982, the WFDY claimed 270 affiliates in 123 countries; the last noted claim was "over" 250 affiliates in "over" 100 countries (*World Youth*, Budapest, no. 8).

McLean, Virginia   Wallace H. Spaulding

WESTERN EUROPE

Introduction

"Western Europe's Communists are faltering" was the conclusion drawn by an observer of communist affairs in March 1982 (Alberto Jacoviello, *WSJ*, 24 March). In August, another journalist concluded that Western Europe's socialists were taking "a right turn" off the socialist path (Alexander McLeod, *CSM*, 23 August).

Indeed, the most significant development during the year was the unexpected disarray in which Western Europe's communist movement found itself. It was reflected in the significant decline in the popularity accorded François Mitterrand's socialist-communist coalition in France, in Spanish party secretary Santiago Carrillo's loss of control over the Spanish Communist Party, and in the polemics that characterized relations between the Italian Communist Party and the Communist Party of the Soviet Union (CPSU).

In Western Europe as a whole, two general themes characterized communist party domestic and foreign policy positions during the year: unity among leftist parties and support for the "peace movement." But while support for the peace movement increased substantially, "unity of action" was not widely successful. Instead, the major communist parties of Western Europe—in France, Italy, and Spain—became involved in internal and external difficulties that threatened to weaken them seriously in 1983.

Since the mid-1970s, communist party activities have emphasized the importance of "unity of the left" and of the peace movement. The strong support given these two goals—as just and laudatory objectives of domestic and foreign policy—permitted Western Europe's communist parties to assert the common interest of the European left in opposition to NATO, the European Economic Community (EEC), nuclear power, the "arms race," multinational corporations, and "capitalism." At the same time, it allowed these same parties to claim unanimous leftist support for democratic government, socialism in nationalistic colors, disarmament, and world peace. As a consequence, advocacy of these positions continued to be contained in the domestic and foreign policy views and positions of Western Europe's communist parties.

As in 1981, Western Europe's communist parties sought to direct public attention toward Washington's efforts to strengthen the defense capability of NATO. In this area, 1982 brought major demonstrations in a number of West European cities in support of nuclear disarmament and reductions in conventional weapons and forces stationed in Europe. Following the death of Leonid Brezhnev, the new Soviet government continued its support of the peace movement and sought to place President Reagan's administration on the defensive concerning its endorsement of world peace. Major demonstrations in Europe and in the United States involved thousands of participants and received strong support from Western Europe's communist parties. As the year ended, it was clear that the emphasis placed on these demonstrations would be intensified during 1983 and that the peace movement would seek to unify as many Western Europeans as possible in opposition to increased defense expenditures for NATO, whose conventional and nuclear capabilities remained far inferior to those of the Soviet Union.

While the success of the peace movement illustrated both the genuine concern of the public with nuclear war as well as the ability of Western Europe's communist parties to exploit this concern, the communist parties were unable to translate their manipulative success with the movement into electoral victory at the polls. In 1982, poor electoral showings pointed to a significant decline in influence at the municipal, state, and national levels. In 1981, world attention focused on the electoral gains of Western Europe's socialist and communist parties, but in 1982 this attention was directed to their inability to translate the political slogans of the previous year into political reality. The most significant consequences were declining popularity and party strife and factionalism.

In 1982, 15 of Western Europe's 23 parties were represented in their respective parliaments: those of Belgium, Cyprus, Finland, France, Greece, Iceland, Italy, Luxembourg, the Netherlands, Norway, Portugal, San Marino, Spain, Sweden, and Switzerland (the communist party is not represented in the legislatures of Austria, Denmark, Federal Republic of Germany, West Berlin, Great Britain, Ireland, Malta, and Turkey). In 1982, party members held three cabinet posts in both Finland and Iceland and four cabinet positions in France.

National elections were held during the year in four West European countries (nine were held in 1981). In all four countries (Ireland, the Netherlands, Spain, and Sweden), the communist parties proved unusually weak, and in Spain the party lost 19 of the 23 seats it had held previously. Communist party representation continued to be largest in Italy, where the party holds slightly less than one-third of the parliamentary seats (201 of 630). Of the parties with legislative representation, Cyprus had the highest percentage of seats (34.3 percent), followed by Italy (31.9 percent), San Marino (26.7 percent), Iceland (18.3 percent), Finland (17.5 percent), Portugal (16.4 percent), and France (8.96 percent). The remaining parties held between 0.94 percent (Belgium) and 5.73 percent (Sweden) of their respective parliamentary seats.

Declining popularity and party strife produced the conclusion that "the decline of the Communist parties of Western Europe seems irreversible" because of "their incapacity to propose solutions acceptable to the societies in which they operate." Expressed in another way, "Communist parties cannot exist without ideology...ideology is the cement that holds their members together." But ideology cannot solve the practical problems confronting industrialized societies. Indeed, "the guidance of industrially developed societies has become a serious problem even for the ruling classes that led them to the existing results. How, then, could it be easy for the Communists, who have generally opposed the type of development characteristic of industrial societies?" (Jacoviello, *WSJ*, 24 March.)

This dilemma is unlikely to disappear in 1983. On the contrary, it is likely to present an increasingly difficult dilemma in 1983 if Western Europe's communist parties continue to offer ideological panaceas that will not solve problems or alleviate frustrations caused by recession, inflation, unemployment, and an unprecedented Soviet military buildup that frightens particularly the citizens of Western Europe.

Excellent illustrations of this conclusion were provided by the performance and views and positions taken by the communist parties of France, Italy, and Spain. This was particularly clear in France, where the triumph of the left in 1981 produced in 1982 higher inflation, increased unemployment, severe weakening of the French franc, nationalization of major French banks and industries, and changes in tax policy aimed at a small minority for economically unsound and politically punitive reasons.

In 1981, the French national elections established Mitterrand's Socialist Party (PS) as the most powerful political party in the country. As a result of an electoral coalition, the French Communist Party (PCF) was given four ministerial posts in the cabinet, which it continued to hold during 1982: Transport, Civil Service and Administrative Reform, Health, and Professional Training. These appointments were made on the basis of an agreement between both parties that required the PCF to pledge "entire solidarity" at all levels of government (see *YICA*, 1982, pp. 244–45). In 1981, the Soviet Union endorsed this development as "an historic event for France and all Western Europe" (*Guardian*, 5 July 1981). While the results of the French elections, according to French political analyst Jean-François Revel, meant that Marxism had won and that government by ideology had returned to France (*Public Opinion*, August/ September 1981, pp. 2–4), this success did not generate widespread public acclaim for the PCF during 1982.

While the PCF boasted of effective cabinet ministers, the party lacked "the capacity to draw up sufficiently convincing plans to persuade a sizable percentage of the electorate to give it their support" (Jacoviello, *WSJ*, 24 March). This was seen very clearly in declining party membership, a loss of popularity in public opinion polls, and in its decidedly secondary role to the PS. These developments led one political observer to conclude that "the only chance they have in the foreseeable future of changing the basic weakness of their position is a new policy with three new aspects—resignations from the Mitterrand government, combined with dumping Mr. Marchais and an Eurocommunist-style declaration of independence from Moscow" (*Guardian*, 2 February).

When the PCF convened its first party congress in three years in February 1982, it was "divided internally, shattered electorally and holding to a rigidly pro-Soviet line that is rejected by an overwhelming majority of the French" and found itself at "its lowest point since the early 1930's" (Richard Eder, *NYT*, 4 February). In addition, its strongly pro-Soviet position on the military takeover in Poland contrasted sharply with the condemnations voiced by Western Europe's two other major communist parties in Spain and Italy. Thus, while the PCF was supporting the military government in Poland, its four ministers were tacitly forced to subscribe to President Mitterrand's condemnation. This kind of contradiction not only produced internal strain within the party, but was also difficult, if not impossible, to explain to the French voters. Thus, "party leaders and their associates in the labor unions find that their impulse to take advantage of the difficult economic situation by militant actions is circumscribed by the fact that they must either support the Government or be thrown out" (ibid.).

In 1983 the PCF will continue to face the difficulties encountered during 1982, as it simultaneously seeks to demonstrate its responsibility as a junior partner in a left-wing government and to preserve its identity as the revolutionary party of the workers. The first genuine test of the intensity of disaffection in the electorate and within the party itself will be in the crucial municipal elections scheduled for March 1983. The party's direction and possibly the leadership of the PCF will be seriously affected by that electoral outcome. Until then, the PCF will, barring some major unforeseen development, continue its dual role as a "party of struggle/party of government."

As in France, considerable attention will be devoted to the stability of the Italian Communist Party (PCI) during 1983. Unlike the PCF, the PCI is not represented in the Italian government, although the party holds almost one-third of the seats in the Italian parliament (201 of 630).

The PCI, together with the Spanish Communist Party (PCE), took the leading role in the Eurocommunist movement during the 1970s. During 1980 and 1981, the PCI advocated independence from the CPSU as well as the prerogative of openly criticizing Soviet policy. It was joined in this position by many of Western Europe's smaller communist parties, in addition to that of Spain. In 1982, the PCI's relationship with the CPSU continued to deteriorate, but the issue of Poland brought relations between the Italian and Soviet communist parties to the brink of rupture.

There was little change in the position of the PCI on the domestic political level in 1982. The party remained in the opposition at the national level, while holding positions of governmental responsibility in many regions, large cities, and municipalities, most notably in Bologna and Florence. The major focus of attention, however, was the dispute with the CPSU and the internal strife it caused within the party. The effect this rift exerted on the Italian electorate was difficult to measure since national elections are not scheduled until 1984.

The polemical exchange that developed between the PCI and the CPSU was unprecedented, both in terms of the scope of the disagreement and of the language used. In response to the declaration of martial law in Poland, the PCI declared that "democracy and socialism must be considered indivisible" (ANSA, 14 December 1981). The party asserted that a "contradiction" existed in Eastern Europe between "democratic and socialist" forces and that Eastern European governments did not permit "democratic participation in either the production or the political spheres" (ibid.). The central point of this analysis was the conclusion that "the phase in the development of socialism that began with the October Revolution has lost its driving force." The PCI stressed that the role of the Soviet Union "sometimes converges with the interest of the countries and peoples struggling against imperialism . . . but at other times it conflicts with these same interests or even openly violates them, as in the case of the military intervention in Afghanistan." As far as the PCI was concerned, the crisis in Poland was attributable not "to the maneuvers of reactionary forces hostile to socialism" but to "the absence of democratic life in that political system." Finally, the PCI concluded, it intended to maintain ties with "all socialist, revolutionary, and progressive forces" but "on the basis of an absolute autonomy of thought and political action, without ideological, political, and organizational ties." (*L'Unità*, 30 December 1981.)

The response from the CPSU was predictable. The PCI leadership was accused of abandoning the Marxist-Leninist platform, of using the Polish situation as a pretext, of siding with the enemies of peace, of casting doubts on the existence of socialism in the USSR, and of cutting their ties with "the mighty forces of socialism, peace, and freedom" (*Kommunist*, 1982, no. 2).

How this dispute will develop in 1983 is questionable. The future role of the PCI in Italian politics, however, as well as who will lead the party, will undoubtedly be the subjects of debate during the PCI party congress scheduled for 1983. The rift signified, in the view of one Italian observer, that "Marxism itself, has become identified with its practical application: in other words, Soviet society. Today it is becoming increasingly clear that Soviet society presents many serious 'imperfections,' with the result that it has become essential to overhaul its underlying ideology." As far as the PCI is concerned, the party must clearly define in what direction it is to go in the future; for at the present time, "the much-bruited 'third way,' heralded by Mr. Berlinguer, is too vague to win a consensus of the majority." (Jacoviello, *WSJ*, 24 March).

In Spain the communist party (PCE) also experienced major difficulties. At the end of the year the party was weak and in disarray. Legalized in 1977, the PCE emerged as a major advocate of Eurocommunism between 1977 and 1981 under the leadership of Santiago Carrillo. The dissension that plagued the party during 1981 erupted into a major internal dispute during the year. It resulted in Carrillo's resignation as secretary general and his replacement by Gerardo Iglesias (37 years old).

Internal dissension within the party contributed to the creation of a Catalan Communist Party in April by approximately 7,500 pro-Soviet PCE members and to the creation of the pro-Soviet Party for Communist Unification and Recovery in September. The pressure exerted by these parties, as well as the persistent demands of the Eurocommunists for Renewal for a less authoritarian leadership, made it impossible for Carrillo to retain control of the various factions within the PCE. This intraparty strife also contributed to declining support for the PCE among the general electorate. As a consequence, the PCE suffered a major defeat in the October national elections. The party won only 4 percent of the vote and lost 19 of its 23 seats in the Spanish Cortes.

The new PCE leader, Iglesias, endorsed the concept of Eurocommunism, but what this would mean in practice, and what direction the party would choose in the future, remained debatable. It was evident, however, that the PCE would have to undertake a major effort to rebuild and to regain the support of the Spanish electorate at a time when Spain, as the newest member of NATO, is remarkably stable.

To what extent the difficulties encountered by the communist parties of France, Italy, and Spain reflect a "crisis of communist ideology" can only be speculative. But in 1983, the decisions taken by these parties concerning the role they wish to play within their respective countries are unlikely to erase the disarray in which they find themselves. During 1983, their success in re-establishing stability and respect will have a decisive affect on the policies of other communist parties in Western Europe. This is not to suggest that the activities of communist parties elsewhere in Western Europe do not merit careful observation, but the roles they play in their respective countries will not be independent of the directions followed by the communist parties of France, Italy, and Spain.

In Portugal the communist party (PCP) under the leadership of Alvaro Cunhal is strongly pro-Soviet. The party holds 41 of the 250 parliamentary seats, and its influence on Portuguese political life continues to be extensive. The PCP attempted without success during the year to prevent constitutional changes sought by the governing Democratic Alliance, which placed greater power in the hands of the prime minister by dissolving the Council of the Revolution. While Marxist language did remain in the constitution, the party was unable to prevent Prime Minister Francisco Balsemao's decision to encourage the development of private enterprise and to halt further nationalization of industry. Both before and after the constitutional reform, the PCP urged President Ramalho Eanes to dismiss the government, to appoint a caretaker administration, and to call early elections for a new parliament. By the end of the year, sufficient pressure had been placed on the prime minister to force him to resign. While both the socialist and the communist parties considered this development to be positive, it was uncertain what political constellation would result from new elections scheduled in 1983.

In Cyprus, Greece, Turkey, and Malta, communist party activities exerted minimal impact on political life. In Turkey a new constitution was adopted in the autumn, but the communist party remains proscribed, as it has been during most of its 62-year existence. The Communist Party of Malta, established in 1969, is without significant influence. In Cyprus the party (AKEL) draws primary support from the Greek Cypriot majority, which comprises approximately 80 percent of the island's estimated population of 640,000. AKEL membership is claimed to be 12,000, and the party has enjoyed legal status since the establishment of the Republic of Cyprus in 1960. The party is, however, proscribed in the Turkish Federated State of divided Cyprus. During the most recent national elections, held in 1981, AKEL made its strongest showing in history by winning the largest vote share of any political party (32.8 percent) and 12 seats of the 35 seats in the House of Representatives (eight of these seats are held by members of the AKEL Politburo). Despite its strength, the party does not hold cabinet positions; however, in the course of the year AKEL concluded an agreement of "democratic cooperation" with the party of President Spyros Kyprianou (which is consistent with AKEL's past support of Kyprianou's predecessor, Archbishop Makarios). In 1983, the party is expected to support the re-election of President Kyprianou, but it is doubtful that AKEL will emerge as a leading political force based on its performance during 1982 and in view of the complexities of the Cyprus question as a whole.

In Greece the party remains split into pro-Soviet and Eurocommunist factions. In the Greek parliament, the pro-Soviet faction of the party (KKE) holds 13 of 300 seats and maintains positions on domestic and foreign policy issues close to those of the Panhellenic Socialist Movement (PASOK), established by Andreas Papandreou in 1974; the Eurocommunist faction of the KKE failed to win a single seat in the most recent national election in 1981. In that election, the Marxist-oriented PASOK garnered 48 percent of the vote, elected 172 deputies to the Greek legislature, and formed the first socialist government in Greek history. Since the election, Prime Minister Papandreou has softened his pre-election advocacy of Greek withdrawal from NATO and the EEC, and PASOK rejected KKE overtures for participation in the cabinet. As a consequence, KKE became increasingly critical of PASOK during the year. In municipal elections held in October, KKE-supported candidates received almost 20 percent of the vote, giving the party control over several major municipalities. In 1983, the KKE is likely to continue its efforts to appeal to the disenchanted members of PASOK critical of Papandreou's "mild" policies toward the West and "timid" measures in "socializing" the economy. The party will emphasize the slogan "Change cannot be accomplished without the KKE."

In Great Britain and Ireland the communist parties have not played a significant role in many years, and both parties maintained low profiles during 1982. The Communist Party of Great Britain (CPGB) has not been represented in the House of Commons since 1950; however, one member, Lord Milford, sits in the House of Lords. While the party does not enjoy broad support among the British population, it does maintain close ties with the trade union movement. Two members of the party serve on the 38-member General Council of the Trade Union Congress, and the party has successfully encouraged confrontation between the British government and labor unions in recent years. In view of the growing unemployment rate in Great Britain and increased emphasis devoted to the peace movement throughout Europe, the party may be expected to concentrate on these two themes in 1983.

No new developments of major importance were recorded in the activities of the communist parties of Belgium, Denmark, the Netherlands, and Luxembourg. The Luxembourg party was quiescent, and the party apparatus remains under the highly centralized control of the Urbany family. In Belgium the party (PCB) entered the year demoralized from its poor showing in the national elections of November 1981, in which it lost two of its four seats in the 212-member Chamber of Deputies. As a consequence, the party's Twenty-Fourth Congress in March sought to redefine the PCB's direction in terms of "a specific Belgian road to socialism." While the PCB exerts a significant influence in the European "peace movement," its internal party apparatus is decentralized in regional councils in Wallonia, Flanders, and Brussels. This circumstance combined with minimal electoral support in 1981 made party unity a principal issue during the year.

The internal dissension that plagued the Communist Party of Denmark (DKP) during 1981 continued in the new year, and several prominent members resigned. Without seats in the Danish parliament and with little support in the local elections of November 1981, the party was at its weakest point in over a decade. This may account for the emphasis the party devoted to the peace movement and to criticism of NATO and the United States as the principal barrier to disarmament. In the Netherlands longtime party chairman Henk Hoekstra (57 years old) was replaced by Elli Izeboud (33 years old). This change represented a radical shift from the position of orthodox communist party members (CPN), who endorse the ideological principles of Marxism-Leninism and the organizational principle of democratic centralism. The primary aim of the party's new leadership is to form "a new type of communist party" committed to establishing a "parliamentary, democratic-socialist form of government." Whether this attempt will prove successful, however, is open to debate, even though the former CPN chairman was one of the principal architects of the party's new direction. In the national elections held in September, the CPN's vote share declined from 2.05 percent received in 1981 to 1.9 percent, although it retained its three deputies in the Dutch parliament. This lack of support, coupled with the restructuring of the party, gives reason to doubt whether the CPN will emerge as a viable political force in 1983.

In the Nordic countries of Iceland, Norway, Sweden, and Finland, significant developments occurred only in the last country. The Finnish Communist Party (SKP) and the Finnish People's Democratic League (SKDL) have been on the verge of a split since 1969. In the Finnish national elections in 1979, the SKDL won 35 of 200 parliamentary seats. Until 31 December 1982, when the party went into the opposition, it served in the four-party coalition governing Finland, and party members held three cabinet posts (Education, Labor, and Communications). Throughout the year, factional strife occupied the primary attention of both parties, resulted in declining popularity among the electorate according to public opinion polls, and left in serious question how well the SKDL would perform in the national elections scheduled for March 1983. The new chairman of the SKP, Minister of Labor Jouko Kajanoja (replacing Aarne Saarinen), will seek to bring unity to the party.

The communist party of Iceland (AB) held three cabinet posts in the Icelandic government (Social and Health Affairs, Finance, and Industry) and is the third largest of the four parties represented in the Althing, holding 11 of 60 parliamentary seats. In a period of economic recession, the party's participation in the government placed considerable strain on AB efforts to maintain popular support. As a consequence, the AB devoted its primary attention during the year to foreign policy issues, including the peace movement. National elections are scheduled for 1983.

In Sweden the communist party (VPK) received 5.6 percent of the vote in the 1982 national elections and holds 20 of the 349 Riksdag seats. It is represented in all sixteen parliamentary committees except Defense, Taxation, and Justice. During the year, the party concentrated on bringing its support among the electorate above the 4 percent required for parliamentary representation. Following the September elections, the party endorsed the Social Democratic government formed under Prime Minister Olof Palme (defeated in 1976). At the end of the year, however, it was unclear to what extent the VPK would be able to influence Swedish politics in 1983. The Norwegian Communist Party (NKP) remained on the periphery of Norwegian political life in 1982 and has been in a weak position since 1975 when it decided not to merge with several left-socialist parties and factions. This decision split the party and caused its then chairman, Reidar Larsen, to leave the NKP for the new Socialist Left Party. Issues such as the economy, regional development, defense policy, and the "peace movement" remained on the party's agenda, but NKP views did not evoke widespread interest; the party remained staunchly pro-Soviet in its foreign policy views.

The impact of the communist parties of Austria and Switzerland continues to be negligible. While three members of the Swiss party are represented in the Swiss parliament, neither party captured more than 1.5 percent of the vote in the last national elections, held in both countries in 1979. It is doubtful that either party will enjoy increased success in 1983, although the Austrian party is making an attempt to do so following the adoption of a new party program in January 1982, entitled "Socialism in Austrian Colors." The communist party of West Berlin (SEW) is an insignificant factor in the political life of the city. No leadership changes were reported during the year and since the party received less than 1 percent of the vote in elections held in 1981 its popularity has not undergone a positive change. The SEW competes for support with a number of leftist groups in West Berlin and is completely dependent on the East German communist party.

Party officials elected by the Sixth Congress of the German Communist Party (DKP) continued in their positions during the year. The party's organization is highly structured. Numerous communist-led organizations and committees provide the DKP with effective means for its "unity of action" programs, intended to expand its influence, particularly in the peace and ecological movements. In the four state elections during the year, held in Lower Saxony, Hamburg, Hesse, and Bavaria, the DKP received a fractional share of the vote and in no case more than 0.6 percent. Because of the party's relatively insignificant influence on domestic policy, it has devoted major attention to mobilizing massive demonstrations in support of the peace movement and has announced plans to continue these efforts in 1983. Should the German national elections, scheduled for March 1983, produce a conservative government, the DKP's efforts in this regard are almost certain to be intensified significantly.

Hoover Institution   Dennis L. Bark

Austria

The year under review saw the Austrian economy recede, albeit less than most. Unemployment stayed below 4 percent, with inflation hovering around 5 percent; nonetheless, no growth was predicted for 1983 and there was widespread pessimism. The Communist Party of Austria (KPO) did not draw any recorded benefit from the economic situation, nor does it appear to have made an effort to do so.

The year's major organizational event was the unanimous enactment, by 415 delegates, of a new party program at a one-day extraordinary party congress in Vienna on 30 January. The program, "Sozialismus in Österreichs Farben" (Socialism in Austrian Colors), had been discussed for nearly one year.

Population. 7,555,338 (1981 census)

Party. Communist Party of Austria (Kommunistische Partei Österreichs; KPO)

Founded. 3 November 1918 .

Membership. Ca. 15,000 (1982)

Party Chairman. Franz Muhri (b. 1921)

Politburo. 12 members: Michael Graber (editor of *Volksstimme* after 21 September), Franz Hager, Anton Hofer, Hans Kalt (editor of *Volksstimme* until 21 September; secretary of Central Committee after 21 September), Franz Karger, Gustav Loistl, Franz Muhri, Karl Reiter, Erwin Scharf (secretary of Central Committee until 21 September), Irma Schwager, Walter Silbermayr, Ernst Wimmer

Central Committee. 68 members

Last Congress. Twenty-Fourth, 6–8 December 1980 in Vienna; next congress scheduled for 1983

Publications. *Volksstimme* (People's voice), KPO daily organ (Vienna); *Weg und Ziel* (Path and goal), KPO theoretical monthly (Vienna)

Elections. Burgenland (provincial): KPO 0.5 percent (1977: 0.4 percent); Lower Austria (municipal): St. Pölten, KPO 1 seat (1977: 1 seat) and Krems, KPO 1 seat (1977: 1 seat); Vienna (municipal employees): KPO 2.9 percent; railway employees: KPO 4.6 percent, no seat (1977: 5.4 percent, 1 seat) postal employees: KPO 1.48 percent (1978: 2.08 percent)

Party Internal Affairs. *The New Party Program.* The hundred pages of *Socialism in Austrian Colors* contain little that is new, despite Muhri's claim that "for the first time the party's principal document covered . . . important socio-political problems and formulated the main demands and tasks of the party at the present stage" (Tass, 30 January). The program accuses the Socialist Party of Austria (SPO) of not having come any closer to socialism in twelve years of governing. Part of the SPO elite, the program claims, has become "embourgeoised" and part of Austria's state-monopoly system (p. 17). The capital-labor partnership has "de-democratized" the country (p. 22). Austrian capital has succeeded in transforming the SPO, once proud of its radicalism, into its system of privilege (p. 37). The remainder of the program calls for an antimonopolist democracy that eventually will lead to socialism (pp. 43–46). (For a description of the formulation of the program, see *WMR*, April.)

The Party Apparatus. A court case in Vienna in late 1981 revealed some facts about the finances behind the party apparatus of about 200 employees and *Volksstimme,* with its annual deficit of $2 million (*Der Spiegel,* 7 December 1981, pp. 156, 159). To the party's embarrassment, the case revealed that the KPO had acquired some 50 companies, with annual sales of close to $500 million, during the Soviet occupation of northeastern Austria (1945–1955). The companies trade in coal and oil between the Eastern bloc and Central Europe. In order to keep control over Turmoel Company, the party had to produce witnesses to admit under oath that Turmoel was a KPO enterprise.

Additional party activities were a Central Committee plenary meeting in June dealing with the prospects of the communist countries, a forum on family policy in October, and a subscription drive for the party press in December. A Red Youth Week is planned for 18–27 March 1983.

Domestic Affairs. On Austria's national holiday, Muhri issued the following proclamation: "The Austrian Communists have always declared and continue declaring for independent and democratic Austria. They were urging a tireless struggle for that during the years of the Nazi tyranny and in the period after the establishment of the second republic." (Tass, 25 October.)

Foreign Affairs. *Peace Movement and Détente.* At the Central Committee meeting of 22 April, Muhri responded to Brezhnev's proposal for nuclear disarmament. Muhri considered it as proof of the USSR's "sincere striving for détente." He also welcomed Brezhnev's proposal of a Soviet-U.S. summit and "rejected the myth of capitalist propaganda that there is 'the hand of Moscow' behind the large-scale peace movement going on in Europe." (Ibid., 23 April.)

On 10 June, *Volksstimme* announced that the Austrian Students Association had been forced, for financial reasons, to call off the Vienna Peace Festival, which was to be held 6–8 August. Nonetheless, peace marchers did appear in Austria (*Wiener Zeitung,* 31 July). They were to proceed to Vienna, but a *Volksstimme* report of 3 August indicated that the peace festival was held in Linz, the capital of Upper Austria, with about 500 people in attendance.

Other Foreign Matters. On 22 January, *Volksstimme* lamented the U.S. State Department's refusal to grant Austria special funds for Polish refugees. The newspaper also derided the opposition People's Party for its assertion that the Kreisky government had brought the refusal on itself for criticizing the Reagan administration.

President Rudolf Kirchschläger visited the Soviet Union in late May. *Pravda* (31 May) quoted *Volksstimme* on the state visit: "The results of this visit . . . are a success not only for Austria. An important feature . . . is the fact that the president voiced his profound conviction that the Soviet Union is interested in arms limitation and disarmament and that it is possible to hold fruitful talks with the USSR. It is now up to the United States . . . to show in practice that the preservation of peace is for it, too, a most important present-day problem whose resolution must not be made dependent on disagreements over other questions."

On 27 August, *Die Presse* reported that Washington favored equipping the Austrian army with short-range defensive missiles and that this would not impair the State Treaty. *Volksstimme* (28 August) headlined its response "Scandalous New Interference by Washington: Pentagon Wants to Prescribe Missiles for Us." It called the proposal a flagrant violation of the State Treaty. In Muhri's opinion, "The latest U.S. demand constitutes a de facto attempt to integrate neutral Austria more strongly into the Reagan administration's endeavors aimed at using West Europeans as cannon fodder for U.S. interests against the Soviet Union and the other socialist countries" (*Volksstimme,* 29 August).

International Party Contacts. On 12 February, *Volksstimme* reported a visit to Vienna by Enrich Mückenberger, member of the East German Politburo. The communist world movement and interparty relations were discussed. On 26 February, Luís Corvalán, leader of the Communist Party of Chile, visited Vienna (ibid., 27 February). He discussed primarily the "dictatorship" in Chile and U.S. imperialism in Central America. On 14 April, *Volksstimme* reported that Muhri and a member of the Central Committee were visiting Cuba. One month later, *Volksstimme* (19 May) reported the visit to Vienna of Vadim Zagladin, first deputy chief of the Soviet Central Committee's International Department. He held discussions with Muhri, Erwin Scharf, and Johann Steiner, chief of the KPO Central Committee's Foreign Relations Department. In August, a ten-member delegation of Soviet steel engineers, workers, and union officials visited Austria's famous nationalized Voest steel plant in Linz (ibid., 24 August). The Russians came from the Lipetsk plant south of Moscow, which had been built by Voest in 1966. The Soviet delegation used the occasion for discussions with Otto Treml, the KPO's chairman for Upper Austria and Upper Austrian communist trade unionists.

University of Alberta   Frederick C. Engelmann

Belgium

The Belgian Communist Party (PCB/KPB) is a small party in a small country. Therefore, its importance both nationally and internationally is limited, although the PCB/KPB has an influence well beyond its small numbers in the Belgian labor movement nationally and in the European peace movement internationally. The PCB/KPB entered 1982 demoralized from its poor showing in the national elections of 8 November 1981, in which it lost two of its four representatives in the 212-member Chamber of Deputies and won only 2.13 percent of the vote. The Twenty-Fourth Party Congress, held in Brussels on 26–28 March, sought to redefine the party's direction in terms of "a specific Belgian road to socialism."

Population. 9,920,000

Party. Belgian Communist Party (Parti communiste de Belgique; PCB/Kommunistische Partij van Belgie; KPB)

Founded. 1921

Membership. 14,000 (*Europa Year Book, 1982*)

Leadership. President: Louis van Geyt; vice-presidents: Claude Renard (French-speaking wing) and Jef Turf (Dutch-speaking wing)

Politburo. 14 full members; Pierre Beauvois, Marcel Couteau, Jan Debrouwere, Filip Delmotte, Robert Dussart, Roel Jacobs, Ludo Loose, Jacques Moins, Jacques Nagels, Claude Renard, Jef Turf, Louis van Geyt, Jules Vercaigne, Jack Withages

Central Committee. 72 full members: 37 French-speaking wing; 35 Dutch-speaking wing

Last Congress. Twenty-Fourth, 26–28 March 1982 in Brussels; next congress scheduled for end of 1982

Auxiliary Organizations. Communist Youth of Belgium, National Union of Communist Students, and Union of Belgian Pioneers

Publications. *Le Drapeau rouge*, PCB daily organ in French, circulation ca. 15,000; *De Rode Vann*, KPB weekly in Dutch, circulation ca. 12,000; *Les Cahiers communistes*, PCB monthly ideological review in French; *Vlaams Marxistisch Tijdschrift*, KPB ideological quarterly in Dutch

Internal Affairs. The PCB/KPB has remained a unitary party since its founding in 1921, despite the peculiarly divisive language question that has plagued recent Belgian history. The party is, however, characterized by "wings" on three levels. Linguistically, the PCB/KPB has a French-speaking wing, which is numerically stronger and is rooted in the older industrial centers of Wallonia, and a Flemish (Dutch-speaking) wing in the Flanders region. Ideologically, the party has a Stalinist wing and a Eurocommunist wing. Sociologically, the PCB/KPB is marked by a militant trade union wing, strongest in Liége, and an intellectual wing, dominant in Brussels. Organizationally, the PCB/KPB has coped with these divisions by constructing a decentralized system of three regional councils in Wallonia, Flanders, and Brussels. As commentator Guy Duplat of *Le Soir* accurately stated, "This internal decentralization slows down the decision-making process, but has so far prevented the breakup of the party" (*Le Soir*, 3 October 1981).

Party unity was one of the highest priorities of the Twenty-Fourth Party Congress on 26–28 March. As a result, extremists of both ideological wings of the party—Albert Juchmes, the "Stalinist minstrel" from Liège, and Jean Dubosch, the passionate Eurocommunist from Brussels—were not re-elected to the Central Committee. Moreover, in sharp contrast to normal communist practice, the congress's resolutions tended to pass with only two-thirds of the vote rather than with the usual unanimity. Even Louis van Geyt was re-elected president by "a relatively narrow majority of votes" (ibid., 31 March). The fragile unity of the PCB/KPB, so evident at the congress, prompted plans for a Second Twenty-Fourth Congress at the end of the year to effect structural reform of the party. On substantive matters, the congress was most concerned domestically over the economic crisis confronting Belgium, while internationally disarmament received primary emphasis.

Domestic Affairs. The current economic crisis affecting Belgium is perceived by the PCB/KPB to be of such depth as to allow only two possible courses. The present neo-liberal course of Prime Minister Wilfried Martens is seen by Claude Renard, PCB vice-president of the Brussels region, as "a long and painful slide toward underdevelopment and a worsening of all the inequalities." The alternative proposed by the PCB/KPB calls for the "progressive implementation of a new growth model, which can only be the path of self-managing socialism." In practice, this latter course rejects any form of "crisis management." What is required, according to the PCB/KPB, is "a specific Belgian road to socialism." That road is Eurocommunism, defined by Renard as "a drawing nearer of internationalist solidarity, which, without eluding, on the contrary, the necessarily planetary character of the large contemporary confrontations, takes into account with priority the specificity of all problems that proceed from these confrontations in Belgium and in Europe." (Ibid., 15 April.)

The PCB/KPB no longer has its own trade unions. As a result, its militants have generally tended to enter the General Federation of Labor of Belgium (FGTB). These militants, especially in the radical Liège movement, play an important role in trade union activity, leading to fear of communist infiltration of the FGTB on the part of certain Socialist leaders. Guy Duplat further notes that the PCB/KPB "quite often serves the Socialist Party and the trade-union movement as a conscience or guilty conscience" (ibid., 2 and 3 October 1981).

Foreign Affairs. The paramount and proud preoccupation of the PCB/KPB in foreign affairs is its advocacy of disarmament. On the occasion of the Twenty-Fourth Congress, the Soviet party hailed the PCB/KPB for "its clear-cut stand in the vanguard of a broad popular movement for a reduction of senseless military expenditures and for peace and security in Europe" (Tass, 25 March; *FBIS*, 20 March). At the congress, the responsibility of the Reagan administration for the worsening of East-West and North-South tensions was stressed. The PCB/KPB expressed radical opposition to deployment of U.S. missiles in Belgium as well as to Washington's "zero option." Positively, the PCB/KPB, in the words of Renard, called for "foreign policy choices that, through an active contribution of Belgium and, if possible, of the

European Economic Community, going beyond the military blocs, clearly fit into the perspective of nonalignment" (*Le Soir*, 15 April). Such a policy would, according to Renard, inaugurate a new type of international relations and enhance Belgium's influence in the Third World.

International Contacts. The theme of the broadest possible communist support for disarmament dominated the meeting in Paris on 28 April of PCB/KPB President van Geyt and French party leader Georges Marchais (*L'Humanité*, 29 April). The only other major international contact of the Belgian party was van Geyt's meeting with President Mitja Ribičič and other leaders of the League of Communists of Yugoslavia. Reflective of the independent course proposed by the PCB/KPB at its 1982 congress was the shared concern of both parties over the "aggravated international situation" and "the role of the movement of nonaligned countries in the current complex international situation" (Tanjug, 5 October; *FBIS*, 6 October).

Boston College   Francis J. Murphy

Cyprus

The original Communist Party of Cyprus (Kommonistikon Komma Kiprou) was secretly founded in 1922 by Greek Cypriot cadres trained in mainland Greece. Four years later, the party openly held its first congress after the island became a British crown colony. Outlawed in 1933, the party survived underground until 1941, when the party's successor appeared as the Progressive Party of the Working People (Anorthotikon Komma Ergazomenou Laou; AKEL). All political parties were proscribed in 1955 during the insurgency against the British led by the paramilitary group known as EOKA. AKEL leaders chose not to take up arms in that anticolonial campaign and instead "provided a nonviolent alternative to EOKA terrorism in the independence struggle" (*Baltimore Sun*, 18 July 1980). Since the establishment of the Republic of Cyprus in 1960, the AKEL has enjoyed legal status.

The AKEL claims it is "a people's party, a party of Greek and Turkish working people" (*WMR*, September 1979). While the AKEL is officially banned in the Turkish Federated State (TFSC) of divided Cyprus, the Communists have never stopped trying to appeal to the minority population on the island.

Population. 640,000

Party. Progressive Party of the Working People (Anorthotikon Komma Ergazomenou Laou; AKEL)

Founded. 1922 (AKEL, 1941)

Membership. 12,000 est. (*Cyprus Mail*, 26 May 1978); 67 percent industrial workers and employees, 20 percent peasants and middle class, 24 percent women, 30 percent under 30 years old; 80 percent from Greek Cypriot community

General Secretary. Ezekias Papaioannou

Politburo. 13 members: Ezekias Papaioannou, Andreas Fandis, Dinos Konstantinou, G. Katsouridhis, Khambis Mikhailidhis, Andreas Ziartidhis, Khristos Petas, Kiriakos Khristou, Mikhail Poumbouris, G. Khristodoulidhis; A. Mikhailidhis, G. Sophokles, Dhonis Khristofinis

Secretariat. 3 members: Papaioannou, Fandis (deputy general secretary), Konstantinou (organizing secretary)

Last Congress. Fifteenth, 13–15 May

Auxiliary Organizations. Pan-Cypriot Workers' Federation (PEO), 45,000 members, Andreas Ziartidhis, general secretary; United Democratic Youth Organization (EDON), 10,000 members; Confederation of Women's Organizations; Pan-Cyprian Peace Council; Pan-Cyprian Federation of Students and Young Professionals; Union of Greek Cypriots in England, 1,200 members, considered London branch of AKEL

Elections. In May 1981 parliamentary elections, AKEL received 32.8 percent of the vote and 12 of the 35 seats in the House of Representatives to become the largest party in the House

Publications. *Kharavyi* (Dawn), AKEL daily and largest paper in Cyprus; *Demokratia*, AKEL weekly; *Neoi Kairoi* (New times), AKEL magazine; *Ergatiko Vima* (Workers' stride), PEO weekly; *Neolaia* (Youth), EDON weekly

Cyprus, the third largest island in the Mediterranean, became a constitutional republic in 1960, based on the presidential system. It is a member of the British Commonwealth, the Council of Europe, an associate of the European Economic Community (EEC), and the nonaligned group of the United Nations. The president is Spyros Kyprianou, 50-year-old leader of the centrist Democratic Party (DIKO). He was elected for a five-year term in 1978 with the backing of AKEL. DIKO now holds eight seats in the House of Representatives. The center-right party, the Democratic Rally (DISI) headed by Glavkos Kliridhis, shared the lead with AKEL, also winning twelve seats in the House elections of 1981. The socialist party EDEK led by Vassos Lyssaridhis, holds three seats in the House.

Following the Turkish invasion and subsequent occupation of the northern third of the island in July 1974, the sociopolitical setting in the Republic of Cyprus has been a fragile calm. After the first outbreak of intercommunal fighting in 1963, the Cypriot Turks withdrew from the central government and have since held separate elections in their community. Pending a final resolution of constitutional problems in the Republic of Cyprus, the Cypriot Turks formed the TFSC in 1975 and have continued to operate as a quasi-autonomous entity, with help from Turkey. In June 1981, the Cypriot Turks also held elections for president and the 40-member TFSC Federal Assembly, with the party of President Rauf Denktas retaining power. There was no overt communist participation in the Turkish Cypriot elections, but there were numerous unsubstantiated charges by the Denktas forces that "Maoist elements" were in control of his opposition, the Communal Liberation Party, led by Alpay Durduran (*Halkin Sesi*, 13 March 1981).

Party Internal Affairs. The AKEL is reputed to be a tightly controlled apparatus, and few internal disagreements are ever aired in public. In the future, replacement of the gerontocracy that now rules AKEL will be the critical problem to be faced by the younger Communists, as their leaders grow older in their secure party positions.

At the Fifteenth Party Congress in May, some attention was given to the "party and mass movement." The final communiqué hailed the "great success in the organizational sector" and referred to the various steps that had been taken in "the improvement of party work." Cited as specific AKEL accomplishments were "the recruitment of new members, the exercise of regular and constructive control, the promotion in the circulation of party printed matter, the development of its finances and the further strengthening of its international relations with its brother parties abroad." (*Kharavyi*, 30 May.)

The fifth plenum of the AKEL Central Committee and the Central Control Committee in November saw the party as facing "serious duties" because of developments in the Cyprus issue, such as in the "internal policy and economic situation in general, as well as the international arena." The party's response to these duties "demands its multifaceted strengthening." The plenum's resolution closed with this exhortation: "The stronger our party becomes in the political, organizational, ideological, and economic sectors, the more efficiently and satisfactorily it will be able to play its vanguard role and mission and fulfill its duties to the people." (Ibid., 1 November.)

Each September, the AKEL holds "a fund-raising drive to provide money for the party's normal activity" and to demonstrate "a symbolic expression of mass support for the party." Additional operating capital for the AKEL is generated "from activities under the indirect but tight control of the party in . . . branches of . . . production and distribution of goods (cooperatives, retail stores, financing enterprises, tourist agencies, export-import enterprises)." As a result of these activities, the AKEL has "become probably the major employer on the island." (*Andi*, Athens, 16 January 1981.) The two best-known communist-controlled enterprises are the Popular Distiller's Company of Limassol, which produces wines and brandies for the domestic market and export, and the People's Coffee Grinding Company in Nicosia.

Domestic Affairs. The most significant domestic development for the Communists in Cyprus was the announcement on 20 April that a "democratic cooperation" had been reached between AKEL and DIKO (*Kharavyi*, I4 May). In reality, this is a continuation of AKEL's past support for former President Makarios and his successor, Kyprianou. A major difference, however, is that the current accord "is based on a minimum program, which was discussed and decided on jointly, and on measures for the program's implementation." This new cooperation did not give the AKEL its long-sought cabinet seat but does allow the party to express directly "its viewpoint to the president of the republic." DISI party leaders immediately denounced the AKEL-DIKO cooperation as a "popular mini-front." Still, the Communists insisted that their goal at this particular stage of the national struggle was not "to change the social regime, but to make Cyprus truly independent, federated, nonaligned, and demilitarized." Thus, the interests of the "national bourgeois class," as represented by DIKO, and the "working class" of AKEL are now "identical." (Ibid.) The probable result of this cooperation between right and left is that the incumbent president will receive the support of AKEL in the 1983 election.

The new economic policy outlined by the AKEL-DIKO minimum program occupied a special chapter in the Central Committee's report to AKEL's Fifteenth Congress. The sixteen points in the report enumerated the main problems "slowing down the development rhythm," such as the rise in inflation, increase in unemployment, and the deficit in the balance of payments. The AKEL admits that "general ideological differences with regard to the social status" still exist between it and the DIKO, but the implementation of the minimum program "in practice will bring about substantial change for the benefit of the economically weak layers of society" (ibid., 14 and 30 May).

Another resolution passed at the congress repeated the past AKEL position that the proper way to solve the Cyprus problem was for the Cypriots themselves to decide their future through the continuation of substantive intercommunal talks based on U.N. resolutions and other "summit agreements" (ibid., 14 May). Any proposed solution of the problem "must fortify the independence, integrity and freedom of the Republic of Cyprus and offer strong and valid international guarantees through the United Nations." Concerning the "external aspects" of the problem, the congress resolved that the "efforts to internationalize the question do not harm the process of communication." To that end, it emphasized again that an international conference within the framework of the United Nations, which would include the participation of the Soviet Union, be convened.

A seething argument between the AKEL and the church of Cyprus heated up during the year. Archbishop Khrisostomos, the primate of the church, who is pro-Greek and an outspoken opponent of the intercommunal talks, has allied himself with the right wing in an effort to thwart the AKEL-DIKO collaboration for the coming presidential elections. In July, a series of critical questions from the archbishop about the historical role of the AKEL in the island's political life began with the charge that the Communists "believe neither in Christ nor in Greece" (*O Agon*, 21 July). The AKEL has traditionally been reluctant to attack the powerful church of Cyprus, but the party has been on record recently pressing "for State land, Church and monastery land to be given to landless peasants." (*Cyprus Mail*, 8 April 1981.)

Foreign Affairs. The event that played the most important role in the foreign relations of Cyprus in 1982 was the visit of President Kyprianou to the Soviet Union in October. Kyprianou and Soviet President Brezhnev met for an hour and a half during the five-day official visit to discuss the Cyprus problem, bilateral relations, and the international situation in general. The joint communiqué reaffirmed the USSR's "consistent policy of support for the independence, sovereignty and territorial integrity of the Republic of Cyprus and a respect for its policy of nonalignment," as well as its support for "the withdrawal of all foreign troops and the elimination of foreign military bases in Cyprus" (Tass, 2 November). Both sides also reaffirmed their "firm position that international relations should develop on the basis of strict observance of such generally recognized fundamental principles as renunciation of the threat or use of force . . . and noninterference in any form in the internal affairs" of any state. In the field of bilateral relations, an agreement on cooperation in television and broadcasting was signed, as well as another agreement on avoidance of double taxation. (Ibid.) While Brezhnev used the occasion to stress again "the convening of a representative international conference on Cyprus, within the framework of the United Nations," Kyprianou did not endorse that idea in public, but the Cypriot president promised "that cooperation between the two countries will become more profound and broader in the forthcoming period" (*Cyprus Bulletin*, 31 October). The AKEL Central Committee expressed "deep satisfaction" with the results of the Kyprianou visit.

Trade between the Soviet Union and Cyprus in 1982 increased by about 14 percent over that of the previous year, with the total approaching $100 million. (Nicosia domestic service, 6 November.)

The AKEL would like to see Cyprus sever its ties with the EEC and move closer to the Eastern bloc. According to the AKEL, the EEC is an "imperialist gang of robbers" within a "predatory association of multinational monopolies whose primary goal is the disengagement of countries from the socialist community and their incorporation in the EEC countries" (*I Simerini*, 29 November 1981). A Cypriot commercial delegation visited the People's Republic of China, where they were assured by the Chinese that they "will adopt measures to increase the export of Cypriot products to the PRC" (Nicosia domestic service, 28 November).

Despite some tensions with Athens during the year, the AKEL sought to "continue and intensify its efforts for the consolidation and strenghtening of the close, friendly relations between the governments of Cyprus and Greece" (*Kharavyi*, 24 October). The AKEL advocates strengthening the "ties of Cyprus with the socialist, the nonaligned, the neighboring Arab countries, and all the peace-loving countries" that offer the Republic of Cyprus "precious solidarity and support" (ibid., 30 May). It was not surprising to see the AKEL back the Soviet Union's stand on the internal problems in Poland by placing "responsibility for the situation on counterrevolutionary elements which dominated the Solidarity leadership" (Nicosia domestic service, 16 December 1981). The AKEL Central Committee also pledged the "solidarity of the Cypriot people with the Palestinian fighters and the patriotic forces of Lebanon." It claimed that the "tension in the Near and Middle East dangerously deteriorated as a result of the U.S.-inspired aggression of the Zionists in Lebanon." (*Kharavyi*, 24 October.)

International Party Contacts. At the Fifteenth AKEL Congress in May, Papaioannou welcomed "the representatives of the brother parties from abroad who accepted our invitation and are with us today." He requested that the numerous guests invited "convey to the parties and peoples of their countries the warmest militant greetings of our party and people." (Ibid., 14 May.) Among those who spoke at the congress were Moldavian first secretary and head of the Soviet delegation, Semen Grossu; General Secretary Kharilaos Florakis of the Greek Communist Party; a member of the Cuban Central Committee; and General Secretary Ismail Bilen of the outlawed Turkish Communist Party.

The AKEL is known to maintain frequent and extensive relations with both ruling and nonruling communist parties, as well as with all the various international front groups. It is believed that the embassy of the Soviet Union in Nicosia clandestinely transfers operating funds to the AKEL and, in turn, guides and monitors the activities of the Cypriot Communists. Other Eastern bloc embassies also engage in the same practices. For example, DISI leader Glavkos Kleridhis alleged that "AKEL's decision to support Spiros Kyprianou as a presidential candidate was adopted at the East German embassy" (*I Simerini*, 19 May).

Papaioannou paid a one-month visit to Moscow in July, "where he went to rest" at the invitation of the Soviet Central Committee (Nicosia domestic service, 20 August). He had "contacts with political and social officials," including secretary of the Central Committee Boris Ponomarev. The meeting, which covered the Cyprus problem and other international issues, "proceeded in an atmosphere of friendship and complete mutual understanding." (Tass, 30 July.) Papaioannou consistently urges that it is in the national interest of the Cypriot people "to tie even stronger our bonds of friendship and cooperation with that great friendly country, the Soviet Union" (*O Filelevtheros*, 28 April).

A number of Eastern bloc leaders visited Cyprus at the invitation of the AKEL. Dimitur Stanishev, secretary of the Central Committee of the Bulgarian Communist Party, was among those who came to discuss "matters of common interest" (*Kharavyi*, 10 September). In an overture to leftists in the Arab world, the AKEL sent greetings to Syrian Communist Party Secretary General Khalid Bakhdash on the occasion of his seventieth birthday (ibid., 14 November). This was followed by a visit to Cyprus of Palestinian Communist Party Politburo member Naim Ashhab. The AKEL took the occasion to express its wish for the "establishment of a sovereign Palestinian state on the land of their forefathers under the leadership of the Palestine Liberation Organization" (ibid., 17 November).

Washington, D.C.   T. W. Adams

Denmark

Difficulties, both internal and external, continued in 1982 for the Communist Party of Denmark (DKP). The December 1981 parliamentary (Folketing) elections were a disaster for the DKP. With thirteen parties contesting the election, the DKP polled only 34,625 votes (1.1 percent), its worst showing since 1968. The DKP lost all its parliamentary seats in October 1979, when its 1.9 percent vote share fell below the 2 percent minimum required for proportional representation in the Folketing. Internally, the party lost several prominent members, who publicly attacked the party's dogmatism and ideological conservatism.

Population. 5,118,088 (April 1982)

Party. Communist Party of Denmark (Danmarks Kommunistiske Parti; DKP)

Founded. 1919

Chairman. Jorgen Jensen, elected December 1977

Politburo. 15 members: Jorgen Jensen (chairman), Ib Norlund (vice-chairman), Poul Emanuel (party secretary), Ivan Hansen, Dan Lundrup, Freddy Madsen, Ingmar Wagner, Kaj Hansen, and seven others

Central Committee. 49 members, 15 candidate members

Control Commission. 5 members

Last Congress. Twenty-Sixth, 4–6 April 1980; next congress scheduled for 1983

Auxiliary Organizations. Communist Youth of Denmark (Danmarks Kommunistiske Ungdom; DKU), Ole Sorensen (chairman); Communist Students of Denmark (Danmarks Kommunistiske Studenter; KS), Frank Aaen (chairman)

Publications. *Land og Folk* (Nation and people), daily, circulation 10,500 weekdays and 14,000 weekends; *Tiden-Verden Rund* (Times around the world), theoretical monthly; *Fremad* (Forward), monthly

The December 1981 elections reflect the political stalemate and difficulties that have plagued Denmark since the destabilizing election of 1973. Social Democratic minority governments have been the rule, except for the Liberal minority government of 1974 and the unprecedented Social Democratic–Liberal coalition of 1978–1979. Veteran Social Democratic leader Anker Jorgensen has headed these successive governments, and he decided to resign in September when support for his government's economic program evaporated. Jorgensen's fifth government sought parliamentary support from the small Radical Liberal party (Det

Radiakale Venstre; RV), an eclectic left-center party, and the independent Marxist Socialist People's Party (Socialistiske Folkeparti; SF), which had doubled its parliamentary strength in the 1981 elections. This precarious arrangement inevitably collapsed in the face of the serious political and economic problems facing the country.

The DKP is only one of five Marxist groups to the left of the reformist Social Democratic Party (Socialdemokratiet; SDP). In the past ten to fifteen years, these various leftist parties have typically captured an eighth of the parliamentary vote. They appeal to the same voters, and whenever one moves ahead, another leftist party declines. Occasional exceptions have been when the SDP lost popularity (as in 1981), and some of its voters moved to the left. Typically, the SF gains these votes, which is why it was able to double its parliamentary delegation in 1981. The third leftist party with significant support is the Left Socialist Party (Venstresocialisterne; VS), a leftist fragment of the SF that enjoys substantial support from government employees (as does the SF) and students. The VS lost a seat in 1981 and now has five members in parliament.

Less important are two sects: the Communist Workers Party (Kommunistisk Arbejderparti; KAP) and the International Socialist Workers Party (Socialistisk Arbejderparti; SAP). The KAP was formerly known as the League of Marxist-Leninists (Kommunistforbund Marxister-Leninister). It appeared on the ballot for the first time in 1979 and polled 0.4 percent of the vote. In 1981, its share fell to 0.1 percent. Finally there is the SAP, which made its debut in 1979, but received only 2,000 votes. The SAP is the Danish branch of the Trotskyist Fourth International.

Party Internal Affairs. These setbacks inevitably have had repercussions within the DKP. On the surface, the DKP is characterized by continuity. Leadership and Executive Committee membership change very slowly. Jorgen Jensen, who succeeded to the party chairmanship on the death of Knud Jespersen in 1977, is a veteran of more than 30 years of influence in the DKP. Ib Norlund, the party's number-two man and chief theoretician, has been at the top for decades. The same is true for the party's secretary (administrative director) Poul Emanuel. Challengers are forced from the party either by exclusion or resignation. Once again in 1982, several prominent members resigned and attacked the closed leadership. Hanne Reintoft, a popular leftist and former DKP member of parliament, resigned and denounced the party leadership for being "set-in-cement, male dominated, and undemocratic" (*Berlingske Weekendavisen*, 4 June). Part of her disappointment must be connected to the exclusion of her husband, Knud Leihoj, an official in the plumbers' union. Other dissidents joined Reintoft in a denunciation in the mass-circulation, independent tabloid BT of the DKP leadership and its views.

Although Reintoft stated that she believed DKP membership has fallen significantly in recent years, perhaps to under 7,000, DKP officials claim that membership has been stable at about 10,900 (ibid., 11 June). In theory, supreme party authority is the triennial congress, which held its twenty-sixth meeting in April 1980. The Central Committee is elected at the congress, and it, in turn, elects the party's Executive Committee (politburo), chairman, secretary, and other posts. In practice, the DKP functions in the Leninist model of a self-perpetuating elite.

Veteran DKP activist Ingmar Wagner attracted public attention in the spring when he reported the theft of 700,000 kroner about ($80,000) in various foreign currencies from his home. Wagner claimed the funds were for transfer to foreign Communists who needed humanitarian assistance. He was cited by the police for violations of foreign-currency regulations and reprimanded by the DKP Central Committee. (*Nordisk Kontakt*, no. 7; *Berlingske Tidende*, 31 March.)

The party's two main auxiliary organizations, the DKU and KS, attracted less attention. The KS has been effective in capturing control of several student organizations since its formation in 1974. The DKP was not visibly active in the Faeroe Islands or Greenland. There was an attempt to form an autonomous Faeroese Communist Party in 1975 and later years, but it apparently failed to make headway.

Domestic Affairs. In common with many other industrial societies, Denmark felt the full brunt of the international recession in 1982. Unemployment stabilized at about 250,000 (9.4 percent of the labor force), with young and female workers especially hard hit. Despite rising taxes, the national government's deficit soared to over 12 percent of gross national product, and the balance-of-payment deficit remained uncomfortably large. The domestic economic situation was unacceptable across the political spectrum, but a consensus on the proper response was not achieved. Anxious to prevent significant cutbacks in the social sector and to stimulate employment, the SDP government carried on with vague promises of support from parties to its left (SF) and right (RV). It proved nearly impossible to meet the demands of one without alienating the other. The stalemate led to Anker Jorgensen's resignation in September and to the formation of conservative Poul Schluter's minority coalition government.

The DKP could only comment on these events in its press. Without seats in parliament and having lost support in the local elections of November 1981, the party was at its weakest point in over a decade. DKP editorials saw the country moving to disaster as "the propertyless will be punished because they own nothing, and the propertied will be rewarded because they have enough already" (*Land og Folk*, 6 October). Beyond such biblical rhetoric, the DKP would tackle the recession through increased public investment in housing, public transportation, education, and social benefits and, especially, through reduction of the workweek to 35 hours without a reduction in pay. Such policies are similar to proposals of the other leftist parties.

At a large party meeting in September, DKP Chairman Jensen denounced the new government as "the black cabinet." He speculated that leftists would have to turn to the labor movement to protect their economic and social rights. The DKP has long been stronger in the labor movement than in electoral politics, although the national labor federation (Landsorganisationen) is firmly controlled by unionists loyal to, but often critical of, the SDP. Communist strength has been especially visible in the metalworkers', typographers', and seamen's unions. The expulsion of Seamen's Union chief Preben Moller Hansen in 1977 weakened the DKP's hold on this powerful union. Communist and other leftist union activists have made inroads as many union members despair of the SDP's finding a way to revive the industrial sector. A major test for the new, nonsocialist coalition will be the collective bargaining pacts due to expire in March 1983. Wage freezes and unemployment compensation cuts passed in October have already produced massive protests and some strike activity. On several occasions in October, crowds of more than 100,000 demonstrated against the new government's policies. Freed of the responsibility of governing, SDP unionists may regain some lost territory. In opposition, the SDP (already using more radical rhetoric) may be less vulnerable to desertions to the various leftist parties. Thus far, few such desertions have gone to the DKP.

Foreign Affairs. The DKP's foreign and international views are consistent and constant: unswerving support for Soviet foreign policy and unaltered opposition to Denmark's two main links with other Western nations—NATO and the European Economic Community (EEC). In pursuit of both these goals, the DKP works independently and in alliance with noncommunist groups. Reciprocally, the foreign policies of the Soviet Union both toward Denmark and Western Europe have a direct impact on the internal and external politics of the DKP, which was illustrated by the discovery in October 1981 of a Soviet submarine in restricted Swedish waters that may have been armed with nuclear weapons. Despite efforts by the DKP to play down the affair, a Gallup poll a month after the incident indicated that 86 percent of those questioned thought that the Soviet submarine was engaged in espionage (4 percent thought it an accident; 10 percent had no opinion). Even 79 percent of left-wing voters accused the Soviet Union of espionage. (*Berlingske Tidende*, 27 November, 4 December 1981.) A backlash may have contributed to the exceptionally dismal showing of the DKP in the local and parliamentary elections a few weeks later.

East-West relations were prominent again in 1982. The DKP's reaction to events in Poland was predictable. DKP comments stressed that martial law and detention of labor activists were internal Polish affairs. Economic sanctions against Poland or the Soviet Union were attacked. The Danish government itself was not enthused about the efficacy of economic sanctions, and the measures finally adopted in March were mainly symbolic (ibid., 11 March). An important Soviet order for ships from the recession-hit Danish shipyards was "postponed" in apparent retaliation for Western economic measures. The announcement of Soviet measures occurred while DKP Chairman Jorgen Jensen was leading a delegation to Moscow, and the DKP group tried to regain the Soviet order. (*Information*, 15 March.) Ironically, one of the few areas of communist trade union strength has been among shipyard workers.

Despite these issues, once again the peace movement and related issues of East-West relations, particularly in central and northern Europe, dominated Danish foreign policy debate. The arrest of prominent Danish writer Arne Herlov Petersen in November 1981 on charges of espionage and the simultaneous expulsion of a Soviet diplomat dramatized the intrigues surrounding several peace groups. In

April, charges against Petersen were dropped primarily because the government believed there was insufficient evidence of his "willful" violation of Danish law (*Weekendavisen Berlingske Aften*, 23 April).

There was similar concern about the role of several front organizations, not clearly DKP-dominated, but nonetheless capable of covert manipulation. The so-called Cooperative Committee for Peace and Security serves as an umbrella organization of the peace movement. An evenhanded approach to East-West relations was seen by some activists as crucial for maintaining the credibility of the peace movement. Others, like author Erik Knudsen, insisted that "as before, the enemy is on the right" and that the Soviet Union must be protected against aggressive capitalism (*Information*, 6–7 March). A Scandinavian peace march into the Soviet Union during the summer found itself subject to numerous conditions and efforts to direct its message against NATO. To left-wingers, however, that the march had been permitted at all seemed a demonstration of Soviet peace sentiment (*WSJ*, 10 November).

The peace campaign in Denmark has both general and specific themes. In each case, the DKP is able to associate with the movement, always stressing that the West, NATO, or the United States is the principal barrier to disarmament. Danes, like many others, have reacted with alarm to the decline of détente, particularly since the Soviet invasion of Afghanistan in 1979. Specifically, efforts to modernize both the conventional (equipment modernization, F-16 aircraft, pre-positioning supplies) and nuclear forces in NATO (neutron bombs, Cruise missiles, Pershing II's) are seen by many in the peace movement as dangerous, superfluous, and provocative. The further left one goes, the more decidedly anti-Western and anti-American the themes become. Shortly after leaving the government, the SDP surprised many by modifying its security policy positions. It sought to withhold the small Danish financial contribution to the NATO missile modernization program. There had never been any question of placing such missiles on Danish territory, but Denmark was expected to pay a share of the infrastructure costs. Although the new position may reflect the preferences and frustrations of some leading Social Democrats (now freed from governmental responsibility), observers believe the SDP is responding to its left wing and to the loss of significant votes to the pacifist SF in 1981. The DKP applauded the move, despite its suspicions of the SDP leadership (*Land og Folk*, 8 November).

European (EEC) issues bridge foreign and domestic policy and are always prominent in Danish politics. Communists remain active in the Popular Movement Against the EEC with 6 of the 21 seats on the movement's Executive Committee. In the 1979 direct elections to the European Parliament, the movement received 20.7 percent of the vote and one of the four seats (won by Jens Peter Bonde, editor of the anti-EEC weekly *Det Ny Notat* [The new notice]). Anti-EEC sentiment remains strong in Denmark, and the year ended with a confrontation between Denmark and the EEC over fisheries policy.

International Party Contacts. Prominent DKP activists pay regular visits to Eastern Europe and the Soviet Union. Between 9 and 16 March, the DKP leadership paid an especially important visit to the Soviet Union. For the first time in ten years, the DKP delegation was headed by Jorgen Jensen. Meetings were held with Soviet Politburo members Konstantin U. Chernenko and Boris N. Ponomarev. Official communiqués described the talks as "warm and friendly" and covering a wide range of general topics (*Pravda*, 13 March). Danish observers interpreted Soviet press reports as critical of the DKP, especially its relations with the Danish peace movement. Such accusations were vigorously denied by the DKP on the delegation's return to Denmark (*Information*, 8 March). The Soviet press indicated disappointment with the poor showing of the DKP in the last two parliamentary elections and urged greater activism and effort (*Berlingske Tidende*, 10 March). The DKP leadership stressed the party's close ties to foreign communist parties. There were reports of visits from Portuguese and Italian Communists and plans for visits to party congresses in France and Italy. Ties with the East German party were mentioned. (*Land og Folk*, 9 March.)

In April, Jorgen Jensen led a DKP delegation to Czechoslovakia for talks with Gustáv Husák and other Czechoslovak party leaders (*Rudé právo*, 10 April). A DKP delegation headed by Poul Emanuel visited the Soviet Union in June. Talks were held with the Soviet Central Committee's International Department, and the Danes visited Belorussia (*Pravda*, 1 June). Also, DKP activist Ingmar Wagner led a group to Tashkent in July (Tashkent international radio, 7 July).

Other Marxist/Leftist Groups. The DKP is only one of five left-wing parties currently active in Danish politics. The SF is by far the most powerful of these groups, following its strong electoral showing in 1981. The SF splintered from the DKP in 1958, when the Communists expelled the SF's chairman, Aksel Larsen. Ever since it won its first parliamentary representation in 1960, its primary political tactic has been to push the SDP leftward. In 1966–1967 and 1971–1973, SF votes kept the Social Democrats in power. The first experiment in collaboration (the so-called Red Cabinet) ended when the SF's left wing split off to form the VS party. In 1973, several right-wing Social Democrats abandoned their party to form the Center Democrats. Following the SF's advance in December 1981, it appeared that another effort would be made at collaboration. However, the SF and SDP did not have sufficient votes to pass legislation without additional support. The VS rejected any cooperation with the SDP. The Radicals, another traditional support party for the SDP (nudging them rightward), were willing to cooperate on an issue-by-issue basis. Jorgensen's government staggered on for eight more months, through several very close parliamentary divisions, but new economic measures that would win both SF and Radical support could not be framed.

The SF's program is decidedly socialist and based on a Marxist analysis, but it emphasizes its Danish origins and values and rejects foreign socialist models. It is explicitly not Leninist in either internal party politics or its attitudes toward Danish parliamentary democracy. It has had periodic internal feuds and splits, but under the experienced leadership of its veteran chairman, Gert Petersen, the party has become a natural alternative to dissatisfied Social Democrats and other leftist voters. Indeed, internal party democracy may explain the party's erratic positions and performance in recent elections (*Weekendavisen Berlingske Aften*, 4 June).

The SF's foreign policy positions are more rigid and consistent. It is opposed to NATO, U.S. foreign policy, and any Danish defense efforts. It is also critical of Soviet foreign policy, although less vehemently. Although suspicious of DKP dominance in the anti-EEC movement, the SF is opposed to Danish membership and elected one member in 1979 to the European Parliament. Gert Petersen stated in October that even if Denmark were to leave the EEC, it would still participate in a less formal (and obligatory) European political collaboration (*EF-Avisen*, 26 October). The SF has informal but close ties to analogous parties in Norway (Sosialistisk Venstreparti) and Sweden (Vänsterpartiet Kommunisterna) and looser contacts elsewhere. In February, the party was visited by a delegation from the Italian Communist Party, which has frequently been praised by the SF for its independence (*L'Unità*, 20 February).

The SF thus seems to be a permanent and important fixture in Danish politics. For the SDP, the SF is both a competitor for votes and a potential ally in parliamentary coalitions. Although the SF does not have significant strength in the trade union movement, it has gained prominence among white-collar government employees. In 1982, the fruits of the 1981 electoral triumph failed to meet expectations. The party's daily newspaper, *Socialistisk Dagblad* (Socialist daily), ceased publication in May for financial reasons (*Nordisk Kontakt*, no. 11). Hopes of a new collaboration with the SDP collapsed when a nonsocialist government assumed power in September.

The VS is much weaker, but still present in parliament and on several city councils. It is a native party without significant foreign ties, but despite positive references to parliamentary democracy and civil liberties in its program, is ambiguous about their applicability to a revolutionary "situation." The party emphasizes "extraparliamentary" actions: strikes, demonstrations, and occupations. Its congresses are closed, although news still seeps out. Internal power struggles are a regular feature of VS politics. The cumulative effect has been a very small membership, uncertain leadership, and inconsistencies between the party's program and statements by prominent VS politicians. A legacy of the student radicalism of the late 1960s, the VS attracts leftist protest votes as an alternative to the pragmatic SF and the Moscow-oriented DKP. (*Information*, 16 December 1981.) Without influence in daily politics, the VS falls somewhere between a party and a sect.

The remaining fragments of the Danish left can only be characterized as sects. The KAP, headed by Copenhagen University lecturer Benito Scocozza, is presumably still loyal to Maoism, although the party has made fewer references to Beijing in recent years. The Trotskyites in the SAP number about 200 and only drew 2,000 votes in 1981. Through their press (KAP publishes *Arbejderavisen* [Workers' news] and SAP publishes *Klassekampen* [Class struggle]) and liberal access to television time, small Danish factions can apparently survive indefinitely.

University of Massachusetts   Eric S. Einhorn
Amherst

Finland

The Finnish Communist Party (SKP) was founded on 29 August 1918 near Moscow by refugees from the Finnish civil war. It was headquartered in the USSR and operated through various front organizations, until the 1944 armistice with the USSR legalized it. The SKP has lived on the verge of a split since 1969, when the hard-line, Stalinist-wing (sometimes called Taistoite after its leader, Taisto Sinisalo) rebelled against the reformist program adopted by the more moderate majority. Under Moscow's pressure, the party has not formally split, despite the intransigence of the two sides.

Part of the disagreement concerns the role of the SKP's front party, the Finnish People's Democratic League (Suomen Kansan Demokraattinen Litto; SKDL). The Stalinists would like to end what little independence it has. Founded in 1944 as an electoral coalition of the SKP and left-wing socialist associations, it has been one of Finland's four leading parties, attracting from 15 to 25 percent of the vote. The SKDL has developed a nationwide organization of its own and a separate program, more moderate than that of the SKP. Although over 80 percent of its parliamentary representation (29 out of 35) are SKP members, most of its votes come from outside communist ranks. Its chairman has always been a left-wing noncommunist. The current chairman, Kalevi Kivistö, like his predecessor, Ele Alenius, enjoys considerable prestige among noncommunists. The SKDL has served in seven governments, including the cabinet formed in early 1982, until it went into the opposition on 31 December.

Population. 4,800,000 (mid-1981)

Party. Finnish Communist Party (Suomen Kommunistinen Puolue; SKP)

Founded. 1918

Membership. 50,000 (claimed), chiefly lower-paid workers in the industrial centers of the south and in the northern rural areas. Recently, the number of better-paid workers has increased, and the reformist wing has started attracting more intellectuals.

Chairman. Jouko Kajanoja

Politburo. 11 members: (moderates) Jouko Kajanoja, Arvo Aalto (general secretary), Aarne Saarinen, Arvo Kemppainen, Aarne Aitamurto, Heljä Tammisola, Tutta Tallgren; (Stalinists) Veikko Alho (vice-chairman), Taisto Sinisalo, Seppo Toiviainen, Marjatta Stenius-Kaukonen

Central Committee. 50 full and 15 alternate members

Last Congress. Nineteenth, 22–24 May 1981, in Helsinki; next regular congress scheduled for 1984; special congress 14–15 May in Helsinki

Auxiliary Organizations. Finnish Democratic Youth League; Women's Organization

Elections. Received 17.9 percent of the vote in the 1979 parliamentary election and 35 of 200 Eduskunta seats. Held three cabinet ministries (Education, Labor, Communications) until 31 December 1982

Publications. *Kansan Uutiset*, daily; *Tiedonantaja* (Stalinist), daily; *Kommunisti*, monthly; *Folktidningen* (Swedish-language paper), weekly; all published in Helsinki

Factional struggles became severe in 1982, despite the calling of a special SKP congress in an effort to resolve them. Support for the Stalinists from the Communist Party of the Soviet Union (CPSU) angered the majority moderates and worried noncommunist Finns over the potential effects on Finnish-Soviet relations. The surprise election of Jouko Kajanoja as the new SKP chairman, a relatively unknown figure to many Finns or even to CPSU leaders but acceptable to some Stalinists, further complicated CPSU-SKP relations. Replacement of Finland's ailing president, Urho Kekkonen, by Social Democrat Mauno Koivisto ended an era of Finnish history and introduced a note of uncertainty to Finnish-Soviet relations. Koivisto had had little experience with Soviet leaders or with foreign affairs, but by year's end, both party-to-party and government-to-government relations had stabilized and seemed likely to improve. In the last few days of the year, the SKP's majority faction joined the Stalinists to bring down the government coalition over a proposed increase in defense spending, with the March 1983 parliamentary election in view. Prime Minister Kalevi Sorsa reformed the center-left coalition without the SKDL.

Party Internal Affairs. Internal divisions and CPSU intervention led to an open split in 1982, when the Stalinists refused to participate in leadership positions. By the year's end, Aarne Saarinen had resigned as chairman, and new officers had taken over the top party posts.

The two factions, at odds over virtually every issue, divided internally into more extreme and more conciliatory groups. Within the Stalinists, the more extreme hard-liners centered around Urho Jokinen, editor of *Tiedonantaja*, and the more conciliatory elements around Sinisalo. Among the majority moderates, those seeking compromise followed Saarinen's lead, while the larger dissident group, located mainly in northern Finland, insisted on ousting the older leaders and reuniting the party, if necessary by crushing the Stalinists. Arvo Kemppainen, appointed to the Politburo in 1981, became the chief spokesman for the dissident movement. The Stalinists continued to oppose participation in the government coalition under current SKP policies and to seek more militant policies on domestic affairs and closer relations with the CPSU in external policies.

In mid-December 1981, conflict in the SKDL parliamentary delegation led to the exclusion of the Stalinist deputies from the parliamentary group for the remainder of the session after they refused to follow the group's decision on a vote on the government's budget. *Pravda* called the exclusion an attempt "by certain circles" to disrupt the unity of the SKP and to weaken it (Helsinki domestic service, 23 December 1981; *FBIS*, 24 December 1981). During the January presidential election, the Stalinists refused to accept the decision of SKDL Chairman Kivistö, who was the SKDL candidate for the presidency, to throw his support to the Social Democratic candidate, Prime Minister Koivisto, on the first ballot of the electoral college. By early 1982, several party districts, led by those in northern Finland, had voted for an extra congress to force party unity if the Central Committee could not resolve the factional dispute. The Central Committee, meeting on 6–7 February, scheduled the congress for 14–15 May, after the Stalinists threatened to walk out of the committee if the majority took any action against them. (*Nordisk Kontakt*, no. 3.)

Saarinen told the press that during a visit to Moscow in early January, he was encouraged when Vitali Shaposhnikov of the CPSU International Department conveyed CPSU wishes that he stay on as chairman (ibid., no. 1; *Helsingin Sanomat*, 7 January). At the locked-door 6-7 February Central Committee meeting, he put forth a conciliatory program: all Central Committee members would take an oath to follow the party line and statutes, to see that congressional resolutions were carried out by party functionaries and the SKDL parliamentary group, and to make sure that party publications followed Central Committee decisions. Saarinen read a letter from the CPSU Central Committee expressing fear of an SKP split. Sinisalo, who reportedly had cleared Saarinen's proposals in advance, responded that while Saarinen's proposals were a good basis for discussion, there needed to be unity in the party on policies toward participation in the government (*Helsingin Sanomat*, 7 February). The majority of the moderates also were not satisfied with the proposals. General Secretary Aalto sided with the dissidents within the majority moderates. He argued that the time for resolutions was past and that action was now needed to unify the party. He believed that the Stalinist *Tiedonantaja* should be reduced to a weekly and made to adhere to the party line, the number of members of the Politburo should be reduced, and a special congress should be called to replace the entire party leadership. The Stalinists objected to all his suggestions except the last. (*Nordisk Kontakt*, no. 3.) On 23 March, Saarinen announced that he would not stand for re-election at the party congress (ibid., no. 6; *Kansan Uutiset*, 25 March).

As the party congress neared, there were attempts at compromise. Aalto brought together on his staff representatives from both factions, including Leevi Lehto and Juhani Ruotsalo of the Taistoists. Minister of

Labor Jouko Kajanoja chaired the working group that prepared the congress theses. (*Uusi Suomi*, 27 March.) On 21 April, the Stalinist parliamentary deputies unexpectedly announced their willingness to accept the SKDL parliamentary group's terms for re-entry into the group. This move was taken as a sign of possible reconciliation at the congress. (*Hufvudstadsbladet*, 22 April.) At a meeting of the Central Committee on 7–8 May to prepare for the congress, Saarinen again called for Sinisalo to resign as a step toward conciliation (*Kansan Uutiset*, 8 May).

On 9 May, the leaders of the SKP visited Moscow to hold talks with a CPSU delegation. The latter was led by Grigori Romanov and included Arvid Pelshe and Boris Ponomarev. Pelshe read an eleven-page letter to the SKP, which was printed by *Kansan Uutiset* (13 May) when the delegation returned from Moscow. It said that while the CPSU upheld the "principles of independence, mutual respect, and equality" between communist parties, the Soviet Politburo could not refrain from expressing its views on certain trends in the SKP. It stressed that these trends, by jeopardizing the SKP's Marxist-Leninist character and unity, could have "far-reaching negative consequences" for Finland internally and for "the continued development of friendship between the Soviet Union and Finland." Saarinen's recent statements, it claimed, had confirmed the belief that supporters of a different ideology, alien to Marxism-Leninism, were active within the SKP rank and file.

The letter expressed belief that there were some Finnish Communists seeking to introduce a concept of a "Finnish historical compromise." However, the letter did not name Aalto, who had spoken of a "historical compromise" with noncommunist parties on a government program. The letter also criticized those who would abolish party newspapers, a clear reference to the SKP majority's efforts to discipline *Tiedonantaja*, the chief Stalinist publication. Also attacked were those whose "ultimate goal has been to replace the communist party with the SKDL" and those who sought to have the peace movement "directed against both superpowers," thus undermining friendship between the USSR and Finland. Among those named as propounding these views and seeking to "cause rifts in the ranks of the party" were Arvo Kemppainen, Mikko Ekorre, and Aulis Juvela of the SKDL parliamentary group, the staff of *Kansan Uutiset* and its editor, Erkki Kauppila, and the staff of a communist newspaper in northern Finland, *Kansan Tahto*. The letter concluded with support of Aalto's call for party unity, an indication that the CPSU believed Aalto would be elected the new party chairman.

Reaction to the letter was strong, especially in the moderate faction, since it openly sided with the Stalinists. SKDL Deputy Juvela expressed shock at being called "anti-Soviet" and asked for an explanation by the CPSU. He held the Stalinists responsible for the CPSU accusations and charged them with a "ruthless resort" to "despicable and dangerous foreign policy provocations." (*Helsingin Sanomat*, 13 May.) Ekorre accused the Stalinists of having worked out the letter with CPSU leaders and of knowing its contents in advance (*Hufvudstadsbladet*, 14 May). *Uusi Suomi* (13 May) stated that some SKP leaders on their return from Moscow were puzzled and embarrassed by the CPSU interference. *Kansan Uutiset* (13 May) wrote that the CPSU leaders were "gravely concerned" over the prospects of an SKP split and "the good intentions of the statement cannot be questioned." At the same time, the party paper took care to point out that its political line was determined by the SKP leadership.

The special two-day congress met in turmoil. It was made up of the same 522 delegates who had participated in the Nineteenth Congress in 1981 and had the same factional composition—295 majority moderates and 227 Stalinists—and the same disputes. A group of delegates, dubbed the "third line" and led by the "intellectuals" around Aalto, attempted to establish a compromise slate of candidates for leadership positions. But its efforts foundered against the intransigence of the two sides. The dissidents who had fought to replace both Saarinen and Sinisalo at the Nineteenth Congress, sought to oust all Stalinists from leadership positions. Above all, they insisted on Sinisalo's removal as vice-chairman. At first both the Stalinists and the moderates supported Aalto for chairman. As the congress progressed, however, the Stalinists turned against him, blaming him for their loss of influence over the proceedings. (*Hufvudstadsbladet*, 15 May.)

Unable to reach agreement on the makeup of the Central Committee the congress selected a new committee headed by Kajanoja to seek a compromise. Finally, the moderates and the "third line" agreed on a formula that would retain the 29–21 division on the committee between moderates and the Stalinists. Toiviainen would be vice-chairman, and Sinisalo would stay on the Politburo. When the Stalinists refused, insisting that Sinisalo remain vice-chairman, the moderate "third line" slate was pushed through by a vote of 283 to 233. The Stalinists then announced that they would not participate in the Central Committee since they had not been permitted to select their own representatives.

The committee met without them and elected the Politburo and the top leaders. To the surprise of all factions, 39-year-old Minister of Labor Kajanoja, an economist with a legal degree and without a trade union background, was elected chairman, apparently as a gesture toward the Stalinists. But Aalto's continuation as general secretary was recognized by all factions as essential because of Kajanoja's inexperience with party affairs. The new Politburo was reduced from fifteen to ten members and the number of vice-chairmen from two to one. The Stalinists had only three of the ten members: Toiviainen as vice-chairman, Sinisalo, and Marjatta Stenius-Kaukonen. These three refused to take their seats. On the moderate side, Saarinen remained on the Politburo. The moderates counted 21 of the Central Committee members as Stalinists; Stalinist leaders recognized only 15–17 of these as belonging to their faction. Fourteen of these joined the boycott against the committee. One observer in *Helsingin Sanomat* counted 28 Central Committee members as moderates, 4 as "third line," 15 as Stalinists, and 3 as sympathetic to the Stalinists. Those leaders criticized by the CPSU, including Politburo member Arvo Kemppainen, were re-elected. Toiviainen and Sinisalo announced that the Stalinists would not participate in party proceedings until a new special congress had been called and Aalto had been ousted (*Hufvudstadsbladet*, 17 May). That the party did not split altogether was generally attributed to Moscow's pressure on both sides and to the fear of the leaders of both factions that the party would suffer great losses in the upcoming March 1983 general election (ibid., 19 May).

The congress itself supported continued cooperation with the party's coalition partners, but made it clear that the SKP would not enter a government with the conservative National Coalition Party, which had become Finland's second-largest party. The congress did not resolve the problem of *Tiedonantaja*, but authorized the establishment of a party weekly by merging the ideological monthly *Kommunisti* and the international, bimonthly information newsletter *Päivän Posti*. The Central Committee was authorized to lead communist activity in parliament, the government, the trade union movement, and other mass organizations. A resolution was again adopted binding all party officials to obey the party leadership's decisions. Finally, the congress adopted a resolution stating that the SKP was both a national and an international revolutionary party, with special importance given to fraternal relations with the CPSU. It endorsed cooperation with other communist parties as furthering peace, détente, and disarmament goals and as constituting a good basis for closer relations between Finland and the USSR. (Ibid., 17 May.)

In statements following the congress, Aalto and Kajanoja played down the Stalinist boycott and insisted that the first step had been taken in reuniting the party. But both rejected the Stalinist demand for a new congress, and *Kansan Uutiset* observed that those boycotting the party bodies were "the same persons" who had walked out of the SKP congress in 1969 and who had initiated the present split. Their attempts to disrupt party proceedings had failed, the paper concluded, and it was now up to them to decide whether they would assume the positions to which they had been elected. (Ibid.) Following the congress, Kajanoja informed the press he intended to seek negotiations with the Stalinists and convince them to return to their posts as soon as possible (ibid., 18 May). On 19 May, the Politburo, minus the three Stalinists, authorized Kajanoja to negotiate with the minority.

The proceedings and the new situation in the party aroused attention and concern in both the domestic and foreign press because of the potential impact on SKDL actions in the government and parliament and on Finnish-Soviet relations (*Guardian* and *Frankfurter Allgemeine Zeitung*, 17 May). Soviet reaction was limited to a seven-line news item in Tass, which was interpreted, because of its brevity, as an indication of Soviet displeasure. No reference was made to Saarinen's criticisms of the CPSU (*Helsingin Sanomat* and *Hufvudstadsbladet*, 17 May).

Negotiations continued for three months before an agreement was accepted by the Central Committee on 22 August. Stalinist Veikko Alho, a local government official not considered a threat to Sinisalo's leadership of the minority, was named SKP vice-chairman, instead of Toiviainen, who had never occupied the post. Alho was added to the Politburo alongside Toiviainen, bringing the number of Stalinists on that committee to four and the total number to eleven. Sinisalo was made chief of the party's International Department, and *Tiedonantaja* editor Jokinen a member of the Information Section.

While the Central Committee unanimously endorsed the accord and Kajanoja hailed the agreement as reunifying the party, opposition to it remained. Kemppainen maintained that no real settlement had been achieved and that the minority had escaped with its separate institutions intact. Sinisalo announced in September that he would not run for re-election to parliament in the March 1983 election (he had lost his seat in the 1979 election) so that he could devote full time to party affairs (*Helsingin Sanomat*, 9 September).

The CPSU finally blessed the SKP conciliation agreement, but only after creating another problem when it invited an SKDL delegation to Moscow in September and insisted that it be made up only of SKP members. Vadim Zagladin, an official of the CPSU International Department, expressed satisfaction with the new SKP leadership (ibid., 15 September). Because of SKDL disgruntlement with the CPSU invitation and the SKP acceptance of it, Kajanoja made a public declaration at a SKDL Executive Committee meeting that the SKP was not reassessing its relations with the SKDL but, by accepting the CPSU invitation, was trying to improve its cooperation with the CPSU (*Kansan Uutiset*, 24 September).

The infighting at the SKP congress did not carry over to the SKDL's Thirteenth Congress held in Kuopio on 28–30 May, two weeks after the SKP congress. Of the 274 delegates, less than a third were Stalinists. The four top officials were re-elected unanimously: Kalevi Kivistö as chairman, Aarne Saarinen and Ulla-Leena Alppi as vice-chairpersons, and Jorma Hentilä as secretary general. Kivistö is a noncommunist Socialist and the other three are moderate Communists. The Stalinists had opposed Saarinen's re-election and sought to have the new SKP chairman, Kajanoja, replace him, but the argument prevailed that Saarinen's ouster would be interpreted as retaliation for his speech before the SKP congress criticizing the CPSU. Of the 32 members of the new Executive Committee, 12 were noncommunist Socialists, 5 Stalinists, and the remainder moderate Communists.

The congress focused on domestic topics, principally economic problems and peace and disarmament themes. All references to the situation in Poland and to the nuclear powers were eliminated from the foreign policy resolution. However, that resolution charged the United States with chief responsibility for the armaments race and emphasized Moscow's disarmament initiatives, while calling for the dismantling of nuclear weapons in Europe and those directed toward Europe. The European peace movement was endorsed as promoting a nuclear weapons–free Europe. A national referendum on a nuclear weapons–free zone in Scandinavia and a reduction in Finnish defense forces were also recommended.

Domestic Affairs. One of the Stalinists' chief criticisms of moderate policy was that the SKDL was making concessions to its noncommunist partners in the government coalition that compromised Marxist-Leninist principles and did not adequately protect or further worker interests. The Stalinists were particularly incensed over SKDL and SKP acquiescence in government austerity policies that restrained increases in worker income. This dispute came to a head in mid-December 1981 when all the Stalinist parliamentary deputies refused to vote for a portion of the government budget that would decrease taxes on employers for social benefits. The noncommunist and moderate communist deputies then voted to exclude the Stalinists from the SKDL parliamentary group until they agreed to accept the decision of the majority to vote for the budget. (*Helsingin Sanomat*, 11 December 1981.)

Factional controversy carried over into the presidential election of 16-17 January, called to name a successor to the incapacitated President Kekkonen. The Stalinists favored Ahti Karjalainen, a member of Kekkonen's Center Party and Moscow's first choice for the presidency. The SKDL presidential candidate, SKDL Chairman Kalevi Kivistö, who had worked closely with the Social Democratic candidate, Prime Minister Mauno Koivisto, in the cabinet, made clear during the campaign that he preferred Koivisto over Karjalainen. Koivisto swept the election with over 40 percent of the vote and came within eleven seats of winning a majority of the 301 members of the electoral college. Kivistö swung enough votes to Koivisto to secure his election on the first ballot, an unusual development in Finnish history. Koivisto dropped his Social Democratic Party membership during the campaign and tried to rise above partisan strife.

The cabinet formed on 17 February by Social Democratic Party Chairman Kalevi Sorsa was composed of the same coalition parties as before (Social Democratic, Center, SKDL, and Swedish People's). The SKDL again received three seats and, as before, the Stalinists refused to take one of them. Kivistö was retained as first minister of education and Jouko Kajanoja as minister of labor, while Jarmo Wahlström replaced Veikko Saarto as minister of communications. Saarto became the leader of the SKDL parliamentary group. Both Kajanoja and Wahlström are moderate Communists.

The next general election is scheduled for March 1983 (at the latest). SKDL and SKP leaders, worried over opinion poll indications that SKDL electoral support was declining, have tried to devise issues to restore the party's popularity. SKDL and SKP leaders sought to exploit the effects of Finland's deepening recession, especially inflation and rising unemployment, by concentrating on problems of job security, work hours, and tax and social benefits to aid low income groups. They played a difficult and vacillating role in the government, trying on the one hand to take positions in opposition to other government parties while, on the other hand, providing enough cooperation to stay in the coalition.

To keep inflation and interest rates down and to maintain competitiveness in international markets, Prime Minister Sorsa called in early May for a wage and price freeze. Kivistö objected that decreasing real wages was not the appropriate way to fight unemployment and said that instead there should be scaled wage increases that would boost the lowest-paid workers' wages (*Kansan Uutiset*, 7 May). Later in May, the coalition announced a five-point anti-inflation package that took symbolic actions to hold down prices but whose principal purpose seemed to be to prepare the way for early negotiation of nationwide labor-management contracts due to expire in March 1983, at about the time of the parliamentary election.

The new SKP chairman, Labor Minister Jouko Kajanoja, sought to make his imprint on the communist movement in a provocative speech in Oulu in mid-July. He claimed that Finns had become deeply alienated from the present decision-making process and that a new system must be found to give average citizens greater control over their lives and over national policies. He cited the new peace movement as an example of how to raise the level of consciousness and focus attention on important issues. (*Sosialidemokraatti*, 23 July.) Kajanoja's radical terminology, applauded by the Stalinists, aroused considerable attention (*Tiedonantaja*, 27 July). Kajanoja made it clear that he did not seek overthrow of the constitutional system but sought to extend the "democratic process" to "the neighborhoods, the work sites" and to shift the focus away from parliament. He considered the idea of adopting the Soviet system in Finland to be "unrealistic" in view of the "quite different" political backgrounds and traditions of the two countries. (*Uusi Suomi*, 25 July.)

By late fall, plans for the March 1983 parliamentary elections were in full swing and communist leaders were closely watching the trade unions, where communist support was also declining.

At the end of the year, the SKDL parliamentary group, in an attempt to promote an image more independent of the government, announced its opposition to a provision in the government budget to increase defense spending to accommodate purchases of arms from the USSR. Although Prime Minister Sorsa made it clear that he would not tolerate the opposition of the Communists in the group, the entire SKDL delegation voted against the government proposal on 29 December. Kivistö explained to the press that SKDL opposition to the budget measure was "a matter of principle for disarmament," while Sorsa accused the Communists of using the action as part of a campaign strategy "to promote themselves as a disarmament party" prior to the March election. (AP, 29 December.) Sorsa offered the resignation of the cabinet, but President Koivisto accepted only the resignations of the three SKDL representatives and a nonpartisan cabinet member. On 31 December, Sorsa replaced the SKDL members with Social Democrats and the nonpartisan with a representative of the small Liberal Party. The reconstituted coalition had a small but sound majority in parliament.

Foreign Affairs. Finnish foreign policy during 1982 revolved around the question of how the accession of Mauno Koivisto to the presidency would affect Finnish-Soviet relations. During the presidential campaign, the candidates of the major parties reaffirmed their support of the Paasikivi-Kekkonen line and of the 1948 Treaty of Friendship, Cooperation, and Mutual Assistance with the USSR. Immediately after his election, Koivisto sought to reassure Soviet leaders that he would make no change in foreign policy. He insisted that Finland would follow a neutral policy, but said that it was built on the 1948 treaty, which made it possible for Finland to play a greater role in international affairs. (Helsinki international service, 26 January; *FBIS*, 27 January.)

One of Koivisto's first acts as president was to make a "working visit" to Moscow on 8–9 March. His reception indicated that Soviet leaders were as anxious as he to seek accommodation. He was received by President Brezhnev personally at the airport, and he talked with many of the top leaders. At a Kremlin banquet, he pledged to follow Kekkonen's policies, and Brezhnev praised the relations of the two countries as an example of peaceful coexistence between nations with different social systems. Brezhnev's comments that the talks showed "good possibilities" for developing ties was interpreted as indicating cautious confidence in Koivisto. (*NYT*, 10 March.)

While defending themselves against Stalinist and Soviet charges, SKP and SKDL leaders devoted much attention to international issues. Priority was given to improving Finland's relations with the USSR. The Polish issue was carefully handled. In mid-December 1981, for instance, the SKP Politburo expressed hope that a peaceful solution could be found, but also explained that the SKP understood the actions of the Polish military and felt that martial law would help lead Poland out of anarchy and chaos. (*Helsingin Sanomat*, 17 December 1981.) SKP Chairman Saarinen echoed this position (Helsinki radio, 14 December 1981; *FBIS*, 17 December 1981). Kivistö was slightly more critical during the presidential campaign. Democracy had not developed as much in Eastern Europe as in Finland, he asserted, and "we must have the right to criticize the solutions that have been applied in the East European countries" (*Hufvudstadsbladet*, 7 January).

The SKP and the SKDL urged the Finnish government to take the initiative in promoting Kekkonen's Nordic nuclear weapons–free zone plan. Public opinion polls showed that the plan had the support of about 85 percent of the Finnish people. In May, the SKDL proposed that a plebiscite be held in all the Nordic countries, but neither President Koivisto nor Foreign Minister Pär Stenbäck responded to these pressures (*Kansan Uutiset*, 8 May). In mid-September, *Pravda* supported the plan by saying that NATO's preparations to deploy intermediate-range missiles made the plan more relevant; Koivisto stated that while he still favored the idea as the best way to keep nuclear weapons out of Scandinavia, he would move cautiously on the issue (*Helsingin Sanomat*, 14 and 21 September). SKDL and SKP spokesmen encouraged the idea of a "mini-zone" voluntarily established by Finland ·and Sweden alone (*Hufvudstadsbladet*, 18 October).

Communist criticism of the Finnish government for not taking action on the mini-zone issue increased after the new Swedish government took up the issue in early November and began talks with the other Nordic governments, starting with Helsinki. Helsinki held to the Kekkonen plan, while Stockholm presented no clear alternative but spoke of the desirability of including the Baltic Sea area in a Nordic zone because of the suspected presence of nuclear missiles on Soviet submarines in the Baltic. Oslo and Copenhagen had their special considerations as well. In fact, *Kansan Uutiset* (2 November) concluded that the principal problem in establishing a Nordic zone was Norway's and Denmark's membership in NATO.

The SKDL and the SKP were also active in trying to get the government to take initiatives concerning the Israeli-Palestinian conflict in Lebanon. In early August, Sinisalo called for an economic boycott of Israel (*Helsingin Sanomat*, 5 August), and *Kansan Uutiset* (18 August) asked the government to recognize the Palestine Liberation Organization. SKP General Secretary Aalto attacked Foreign Minister Stenbäck as incompetent and said diplomatic relations with Israel should be broken if it did not obey U.N. Security Council decisions (*Helsingin Sanomat*, 2 September).

In the international economic field, trade with the USSR had grown until Finland was, after West Germany, the Soviet Union's most important noncommunist trading partner. In 1981, about 25 percent of Finnish exports went to the USSR, and 24 percent of Finnish imports came from there. The annual trade protocol for 1982, the second under the five-year trade agreement between the two countries, was signed in Helsinki on 1 December 1981. By its terms, trade would increase 24 percent over the 1981 agreement to 31 billion finnmarks ($7.2 billion). But trade had expanded so much over the 1981 agreement that the increase over actual trade was only 8 percent.

While communist leaders universally supported trade expansion with the USSR, in one area they opposed it. In their search for articles Finland could buy from the Soviets, Finnish leaders struck on 300 million finnmarks in weapons. Since such purchases added to defense spending and thus clashed with SKDL and SKP policy of reducing Finnish defense expenditures, the SKP opposed a supplemental approprations bill to authorize such purchases (*Hufvudstadsbladet*, 29 April). In June, SKDL deputies voted against the purchases, despite an appeal by Sorsa that the arms would not mean an increase in defense spending beyond what had been planned (*Helsingin Sanomat*, 24 June). When the budget containing funds for the purchases came to a final vote in parliament at the end of the year, the SKDL and the SKP leaders chose this issue as the one on which to challenge the government.

International Party Contacts. Moscow's siding with the Stalinists and the shaky state of Finnish-

Soviet relations were reflected in party-to-party and government-to-government contacts. There was a large gap in governmental contacts between the last visit of Kekkonen on 12–17 November 1980 and Koivisto's "working visit" to the USSR in March. The success of Koivisto's visit started a greater exchange of contacts between Moscow and Helsinki. Soviet Prime Minister Nikolai Tikhonov scheduled a return visit in November, but President Brezhnev's death forced a postponement. Koivisto led the delegation that attended Brezhnev's funeral on 15 November. Koivisto also headed a delegation to Moscow to celebrate the Soviet Union's sixtieth anniversary on 21–22 December that included Sorsa and representatives of the Social Democratic, Center, and Communist parties. Kajanoja, Aalto, and Sinisalo made up the communist delegation, but no SKDL representatives were invited.

On the party-to-party level, the death of Mikhail Suslov, who had been in charge of relations with the SKP, and the uncertainty of who in the CPSU controlled relations with the SKP in the period before and at the time of Brezhnev's death made SKP leaders apprehensive. Even though the new SKP chairman, Jouko Kajanoja, had been a compromise figure more acceptable to the Stalinists and had worked to bring Stalinists back into leadership positions, it seemed to some SKP members that Moscow was slow in accepting him. He met CPSU representatives for the first time when changing planes in Moscow on a trip to Bulgaria (*Uusi Suomi*, 17 June). In July, he met with Vitali Shaposhnikov of the CPSU International Department on his way to a two-week vacation in the Crimea; afterward, he said that Shaposhnikov had urged the SKP to restore unity (*Helsingin Sanomat*, 13 July). It was not until the end of October that he received an invitation to make a short visit to Moscow on 31 October–1 November for talks with Shaposhnikov and Boris Ponomarev of the Politburo (*Hufvudstadsbladet*, 2 and 3 November). Soviet Prime Minister Tikhonov held brief talks with Kajanoja and other SKP leaders during his visit to Helsinki (ibid., 11 December).

SKDL leaders did not even enjoy Kajanoja's limited success in relations with Soviet leaders. In August, the CPSU issued an invitation to Saarto, chairman of the SKDL parliamentary group, then visiting Moscow, to send representatives of the group to the USSR in September. Kivistö openly welcomed the invitation as a way to raise the "low profile" of relations between the SKDL and the CPSU. The SKDL had not made such a visit since the end of the 1960s. (*Helsingin Sanomat*, 12 August.) But the CPSU made it clear that only Communists were invited. The eight-member delegation consisted of five moderate Communists, including the vice-chairman of the SKDL, Ulla-Leena Alppi, and three Stalinists (*Uusi Suomi*, 13 August). The trip was considered part of the regular exchange program between the CPSU and SKP. At the end of the week-long trip, an SKP official told the press that Vadim Zagladin of the CPSU International Department had expressed to the Finnish delegation the CPSU's satisfaction with the reintegration of the Stalinists into the SKDL parliamentary group in April and into the SKP Politburo and Central Committee in August (*Helsingin Sanomat*, 15 September).

Contacts of government and party officials with Eastern Europe also increased. On the party level, Kajanoja traveled to several East European countries to talk to communist party leaders, including those of Bulgaria and East Germany. Kivistö also traveled to these two countries.

The SKP and SKDL maintained contacts with West European communist parties as well, although these were not as frequent, except in the case of the other Nordic parties. Exchange of information with the neighboring parties was nearly continuous, particularly in the joint effort to foster the Nordic nuclear weapons–free zone. On 29–30 November, the leaders of the four Nordic parties met in Karjalohja to discuss common interests and coordinate activities. Besides concentrating on unemployment, the communiqué called for cooperation of the left, a broad front against "big capital," and joint advocacy of peace and détente. Special emphasis was placed on creating a Nordic nuclear weapons–free zone and on trying to stop the United States and NATO from placing "Euromissiles" in Europe. (Ibid., 9 December.)

Finally, the SKP and the SKDL also played an active role in the Nordic Council, an advisory body to the Nordic parliaments. Ilkka-Christian Björklund was named to head the Council's Secretariat in Stockholm. He had led a joint Nordic communist effort to cut off Nordic arms exports. When he accepted the new office in June, he resigned from the Finnish parliament and from his SKDL posts. He had been influential in the SKDL, but had feuded with Kivistö. On departing, he claimed that he had received no support in the party for his "Eurosocialist" views. (*Nordisk Kontakt*, no. 8.)

Bethesda, Maryland   Finis Herbert Capps

France

The sweeping socialist victory in both the presidential and legislative elections in France in Spring 1981 has significantly altered the traditional role of the French Communist Party (PCF) as the opposition. Following the agreement between the majority Socialist Party (PS) and the PCF on 23 June 1981, President François Mitterrand, in a politically delicate decision, appointed four PCF deputies to minor ministerial positions in his government. Subsequently, the PCF has simultaneously played the double role of "party of struggle/party of government." A year later, PCF Secretary General Georges Marchais could say: "We feel at ease in our position as government member" (*L'Humanité*, 11 June). However, 1982 produced new problems as well as new prospects for the PCF, which is still seeking simultaneously to demonstrate its responsibility as a junior partner in a left-wing government and to preserve its identity as the revolutionary party of the workers.

Population. 54,200,000 (4 March)

Party. French Communist Party (Parti communiste français; PCF)

Founded. 1920

Membership. 710,000 (Report to the Central Committee, 3 February)

Cells. 27,500

Secretary General. Georges Marchais

Politburo. 22 full members: Georges Marchais (secretary general), Gustave Ansart (chairman of Central Commission on Political Control), Mireille Bertrand (health), Jean Colpin (assistance with the advancement of members), Charles Fiterman (minister of transport), Maxime Gremetz (foreign policy), Jean-Claude Gayssot (party activity in businesses), Guy Hermier (editor of *Révolution*), Philippe Herzog (economic section), Pierre Juquin (propaganda), Henri Krasucki (secretary of the General Confederation of Labor), André Lajoinie (chairman of the communist group in the National Assembly), Paul Laurent (party organization), Francette Lazard (director of the Institute of Marxist Studies), René Le Guen (science and technology), Roland Leroy (editor of *L'Humanité* and *L'Humanité dimanche*), Gisèle Moreau (party activity among women), René Piquet (chairman of PCF members in the European Assembly), Gaston Plissonier (coordination of work by the Politburo and Secretariat), Claude Poperen (liaison with party federations), Louis Viannet (Mail Workers Federation), Madeleine Vincent (local communities, elections)

Secretariat. 7 full members: Fiterman, Gremetz, Lajoinie, Laurent, Marchais, Moreau, Plissonier

Central Committee. 145 full members

Central Commission for Financial Control. 5 members

Last Congress. Twenty-Fourth, 3–7 February 1982; next congress planned for 1986

Ministers in the Mitterrand Cabinet. 4 members: Charles Fiterman (transport), Anicet LePors (civil service and administrative reform), Jack Ralite (health), Marcel Rigout (professional training)

Auxiliary Organizations. General Confederation of Labor (CGT, 1,918,583 members), Georges Séguy, secretary general; World Peace Council, Michel Langignon, secretary

Publications. *L'Humanité*, Paris: daily organ, circulation 150,000 (*Europa Year Book, 1982*); and three regional dailies; *L'Humanité dimanche*, Paris: Sunday newspaper, circulation 360,000 (ibid.); *Cahiers du communisme*, official monthly theoretical journal; *Révolution*, weekly, official publication of the Central Committee; Editions Sociales, PCF publishing house, Paris

The Twenty-Fourth Congress of the PCF (3–7 February) sought to address the new position of the party in French politics. The congress, which was the focal point of PCF activity in 1982, additionally attempted to explain the continuing electoral decline of the party and to chart a course for its revitalization. Opposition from militants opposed to collaboration with the reformist PS had to be reconciled with objections from trade unionists distressed by the PCF's continued support of the Polish government against the independent Solidarity union. Beneath the seeming unanimity of the congress, deep, potentially divisive unrest remains. The patience of the French worker is being tested by the government's economic policy of austerity. The unpopularity of the party's continued pro-Soviet policy in support of the regime of Gen. Wojciech Jaruzelski in Poland has not been diminished by the re-establishment of relations with the Chinese Communist Party (CCP). The first genuine test of the intensity of disaffection within the PCF will be in the crucial municipal elections scheduled for March 1983. The direction and possibly the leadership of the PCF will be seriously affected by that electoral outcome. Until then and barring some major unforeseen development, the PCF will continue its dual role as a party of struggle/party of government.

Party Internal Affairs. The dominant event of 1982 for the PCF was its Twenty-Fourth Congress, held in the Paris suburb of Saint-Ouen in February. In addition to the 2,006 delegates, many significant foreign representatives were present, including Konstantin Chernenko, Central Committee secretary and Politburo member of the Communist Party of the Soviet Union, and Józef Czyrek, foreign minister of Poland, whose participation symbolized the two most problematic positions of the PCF: close adherence to the Soviet Union and support of the military regime in Poland.

In general, the Twenty-Fourth Congress reaffirmed directions already dominant in the party. The declining electoral support of the PCF, so evident in its 16.2 percent share of the vote in the first round of the 1981 legislative elections (*YICA*, 1982, p. 278) was explained in terms of "historical lag" dating back to 1956. Only in 1976 did the PCF adopt a correct course toward "socialism in French colors," but as a result electoral support for the PCF continued to decline through 1982 (*L'Humanité*, 4 February). Marchais staunchly affirmed the complete independence of the PCF, but the congress consistently adopted pro-Soviet positions, including renewed support for the Polish government and the principle of democratic centralism.

On the domestic level, Marchais refrained from criticizing the Mitterrand government but warned that "major, serious problems remain." On the European level, PCF fidelity to French treaty commitments, particularly the European Economic Community and the Atlantic Alliance, was assured, while "the simultaneous dissolution of the blocs" was called for. On a global level, the congress espoused "new internationalism," implying the complete autonomy of the PCF, while pledging full cooperation with "all the communist and workers' parties in all socialist countries" and "all revolutionary and progressive parties in Africa, Asia, and Latin America." In sum, no dramatic changes occurred in either the leadership or the direction of the PCF in the wake of the Twenty-Fourth Congress.

Relations between the PCF and French intellectuals remained strained in 1982 due to the party's obdurate position on Poland and continued exclusion of the communist dissidents associated with Henri Fizbin and the Communist Encounters group (*YICA*, 1982, p. 279). The most celebrated PCF loyalist in the literary world, poet Louis Aragon, died on 24 December (*Boston Globe*, 25 December). The Committee for the Defense of Liberties and the Rights of Man, under the personal direction of Georges Marchais, received no major attention in 1982. However, a new mass organization, the National Environmental Struggle Movement, was inaugurated with extensive publicity (*Est & Ouest*, May, pp. 31–32). The PCF took a very active role in the European peace movement, submitting a ten-point proposal to the United Nations' Special Session on Disarmament (*L'Humanité*, 12 May) and organizing a mass disarmament march in Paris on 20 June (*NYT*, 21 June).

Beneath the seeming decline of the PCF in terms of electoral strength, CGT membership, and press readership, renewed efforts can be seen in the revitalization of party cells (*L'Humanité*, 14 May), penetration into the military (*NYT*, 12 September), and insertion of militants into civil service positions made accessible by PCF participation in the government (*Los Angeles Times*, 7 October).

Domestic Affairs. The dual role of the PCF as a party of struggle/party of government requires a continual, delicate balancing act in relations with the dominant PS. Basic relations between the two parties are regulated by the unity agreement of 23 June 1981 in which the PCF pledged "entire solidarity" on all levels of government as well as foreign policy (*YICA*, 1982, p. 280). On the whole, this agreement has worked satisfactorily despite tensions on both sides. PS First Secretary Lionel Jospin evaluated implementation of the agreement as generally "positive," stating that "the communist ministers have respected government solidarity," but noting "a tendency on the part of the communist party leadership to attribute to itself the role of vigilant censor, distributing good and bad words and not always avoiding the temptation to award the good marks to itself and the bad marks to others" (*L'Humanité* 9 January). André Lajoinie, chairman of the PCF parliamentary group, assessed the situation in these terms: "Relations between the PCF and the PS have reached their cruising speed. The union has overcome the ordeal created by Poland, and the relationship can be a lasting one." (*Le Figaro*, 1/2 March.) Twelve months after the entry of the PCF into the government, Marchais cautiously stated: "It is too soon to assess the situation. We are one year into a seven-year term. We feel at ease as a government member. We were portrayed as a party whose vocation was to remain permanently in opposition. The PCF also has a vocation to run the country's affairs, and the communist ministers are demonstrating that." (*L'Humanité*, 11 June.)

In the domestic sphere, tension in 1982 revolved around two main issues: local elections and economic policy. The cantonal elections in March took on added importance because newly implemented decentralization reforms gave local councillors in the 95 departments of France real political and financial powers for the first time in French history (*WP*, 15 March). The local elections produced a hard-hitting campaign, which was the first genuine test of support for the policies of the left-wing government. The success of the opposition was undeniable: control of 58 departmental councils and 51.5 percent of the vote. The PS-PCF coalition won control of only 37 councils and 47.5 percent of the vote. On closer scrutiny, the PCF setback was more marked: a drop from 242 to 194 council seats and 15.9 percent of the popular vote (ibid., 22 March). This figure is below the 16.2 percent vote for the PCF in the May 1981 legislative elections, despite the traditionally stronger performance of the Communists in local elections.

Analysts generally ascribed the diminution in support for the Mitterrand government to dissatisfaction with its economic policy (*NYT*, 23 March). Pierre Juquin, Politburo member in charge of propaganda, attributed the poor PCF performance to the party's Polish policy, which alienated many moderates, and its policy of union of the left, which upset many militants (*Le Matin*, 20 March). The former tended to vote for the opposition; the latter tended not to vote. The paradoxical outcome of the election requires simultaneously that the PS and the PCF work more effectively together to solve the economic distress of France, while each seeks to enhance its standing for the crucial municipal elections scheduled for March 1983. In December, after prolonged dispute, indicating the importance placed on electoral performance in the municipal contests, the PCF and the PS reached accord on procedures for joint candidates of the left (*Le Monde*, 20 December).

Crucial to both the relationship between the PCF and the PS and to the implementation of the government's economic policy is the role of the CGT. While under communist direction with Secretary Henri Krasucki a member of the PCF Politburo, the CGT is nominally autonomous, not officially part of the government, and much more responsive to rank-and-file opinion. The CGT is in a decline, having lost 17.5 percent of its members—2,322,055 in 1977 compared with 1,918,583 in 1980. The CGT was especially damaged in the estimation of workers by its adherence to the PCF policy of opposition to the Solidarity movement in Poland. Moreover, CGT support for the government's economic policy, including the wage freeze imposed in June and the fourteen-month limit placed on wage increases in October, has produced growing dissatisfaction among workers, without solving the problem of unemployment. The reduction of the workweek to 39 hours, without a cut in pay, is the sole tangible benefit for the French worker under the left government (*NYT*, 27 October). The increasing popularity of the rival French Democratic Labor Confederation (CFDT), generally aligned to the PS (*New Statesman*, 8 January), and the more direct strike agitation of the Revolutionary Communist League (*Intercontinental Press*, 14 December 1981) are both responses to the awkward, difficult position of the CGT. More militant action, including strikes, would appease workers and enhance CGT appeal. However, that course of action would jeopardize the government's entire economic policy and dangerously strain relations between the PCF and the PS. Therefore, all three groups—CGT, PCF, and PS—continue to work as cooperatively as possible, hoping that some favorable change in the French economy will develop before it becomes impossible to hold conflicting constituencies together.

Foreign Policy. In the negotiations leading to the agreement between the PCF and the PS on 23 June 1981, foreign policy differences were expected to prove most problematic in future relations between the two parties. The Polish crisis and the PCF's continued support of the Polish regime threatened but did not rupture relations. Events in 1982 have, in fact, brought both parties closer. Despite initial differences, with the PS supporting Great Britain and the PCF backing Argentina, both parties eventually endorsed the resolution of the Falkland islands war (*Le Monde*, 27 May). The reconciliation with the Italian Communist Party (PCI), symbolized by PCI Secretary General Enrico Berlinguer's meeting with Marchais in Paris during May, led to endorsement by the PCF leader of the basic "Euroleft" position espoused by the PCI. Significantly, that position is in general accord with PS policy. Marchais noted, however, that unlike both the PS and the PCI, the PCF was still convinced that the USSR and the East European governments, "despite delays and shortcomings" can find within themselves "the means and strength to overcome their contradictions" (*L'Humanité*, 26 May). The potentially divisive issue of disarmament was handled so as not to challenge the PS in the PCF's policy proposal to the U.N.'s Special Session on Disarmament (ibid., 12 May). In the troubled Middle East, PCF support of the Palestine Liberation Organization, condemnation of Israel for the attack on Lebanon and the subsequent massacre in Beirut, and endorsement of French participation in the multinational U.N. peace force basically coincided with PS policies, despite the harshness of communist invective against Israel. Finally, the general improvement of French-Soviet relations, strained by events in Poland but facilitated by the fall of the Social Democratic government in West Germany, understandably reduces pressure on the PCF (*FBIS*, 21 October).

International Contacts. The reconciliation of the French and Chinese communist parties dominated the international activity of the PCF in 1982. The actual resumption of relations, strained since 1956 and severed since 1965, was effected during Marchais's two-week visit to China in October. The path to reconciliation had been carefully prepared by a preliminary visit to Beijing in March by a PCF delegation headed by Maxime Gremetz, Politburo specialist in foreign relations (*L'Humanité*, 9 March). In announcing the reconciliation at a press conference in Beijing, Marchais acknowledged that differences still existed between the two parties over Afghanistan and Kampuchea, but emphasized the solidarity, independence, shared concern for disarmament, and joint opposition to U.S. imperialism that united them (*FBIS*, 27 October). Resumption of relations with the CCP enhanced the PCF claim of independence from Moscow, while facilitating the re-entry of the CCP into the international socialist community.

The "new internationalism," proclaimed at the Twenty-Fourth Congress, was demonstrated by the PCF not only in renewed relationships with CCP, but in improved rapport with the PCI. Important international visits were made by PCF delegations led by Marchais to Cuba, North Korea, and the Soviet Union. Extensive media coverage and meetings by Marchais with Cuban Premier Fidel Castro (*L'Humanité*, 13 April), North Korean President Kim Il-song (ibid., 29 October), and new Soviet Secretary General Yuri Andropov (*FBIS*, 17 November) further highlighted the new internationalism.

Boston College   Francis J. Murphy

Biography. *Georges Marchais.* Marchais has been PCF secretary general since 1972, when he took over the reins from the ailing Waldeck Rochet. He has been a party member since 1947 and a full member of the Central Committee since 1959. The son of Germaine (née Boscher) and René Marchais, a miner, Marchais was born in La Hoguette, Normandy, on 7 June 1920. He became an aeronautics mechanic. During the war, his skills were coveted by the Germans, and in 1942 he was deported to Germany, escaping a year later. After this compulsory service, he was active in trade union affairs, becoming secretary of the metalworkers' union in 1946 and, a year later, a member of the PCF. He also served as secretary of the Inter-Union Center of the CGT in Issy-les-Molineaux and, from 1953 to 1956, as secretary of the Union of the Metalworkers' Unions of the Seine.

In 1961 after two years' service as a full Central Committee member, he was named to the Politburo and charged with supervising the organizational work of the Central Committee. To forge alliances and widen support, the PCF had sought a coalition with the Socialists during Rochet's stewardship and supported Mitterrand's bid for the presidency in 1965. This tentative joining of forces has continued off and on to the present day. The most recent test of strength, in which Marchais decisively lost to Mitterrand, came in his 1981 candidacy for the presidency.

Marchais's support of Moscow has also begun to waver: he defended Moscow on the issues of Poland and Afghanistan, but lamented the suffering of the people. He, like Carrillo of Spain and Berlinguer of Italy, went to the People's Republic of China in October to repair the break in relations with China and to act on a mandate of the PCF's Twenty-Fourth Congress (*L'Humanité*, 4 February). This new "socialism in French colors," expounded in Marchais's report to the congress (summarized in *IB*, March), is to be democratic, self-managing, and fraternal, but aware and accepting of individual parties' needs and differences (Kevin Devlin, "Marchais in Beijing to Review Relations," *Radio Free Europe–Radio Liberty Background Report*, no. 218).

There have been rumors that Marchais is in ill health (he had a heart attack in 1975), and most of his duties have been delegated to the leader of the Communists in the National Assembly, André Lajoinie (*Economist*, 9 October; *Newsweek*, 11 October). *L'Humanité* (1 October) published an official denial of Marchais's ill health and firmly declared that no change in leadership is contemplated.

Marchais's publications include *Quest-ce que le Parti communiste Français?* (1970); *Les Communistes et les paysans* (1972); *Le Défi démocratique* (1973); *La Politique du Parti communiste français* (1974); *Parlons franchement* (1977); and *L'espoir au présent* (1980. (Sources: *Current Biography*, 1976, pp. 254–57; *1982–83 International Who's Who*; YICA, 1982, pp. 277–82; *Los Angeles Times*, 7 October; *NYT*, 14 October; *FBIS*, 26 and 27 October, 29 November).

Hoover Institution   Margit N. Grigory

Germany: Federal Republic of Germany

The pro-Moscow German Communist Party (Deutsche Kommunistische Partei; DKP) is the successor to the Communist Party of Germany (Kommunistische Partei Deutschlands: KPD), which was founded on 31 December 1918. The KPD was the third largest political party in the Weimar Republic. During the Hitler period, the KPD was outlawed and reduced to an ineffective underground party. Under the Allied occupation following World War II, the KPD was reactivated. In the first national elections in the Federal Republic of Germany (FRG) in 1949, the KPD obtained 5.7 percent of the vote and fifteen seats in the Bundestag. In the next elections in 1953, the communist vote decreased to 2.2 percent, well below the 5 percent required by German electoral law for representation in the federal legislature. In August 1956, the Federal Constitutional Court outlawed the KPD on the basis that the party pursued objectives in violation of the FRG's Basic Law. The KPD went underground and was directed by its leader, Max Reimann, who resided in East Berlin. Membership and influence declined despite substantial financial and operational support from East Germany.

In September 1968, the DKP was founded. The "new" party's leaders had almost all been officials in the underground KPD, which at that time had about 7,000 members. In 1971, the Federal Security Service declared that the DKP, which repeatedly proclaimed that it was part of the international communist movement and the only legitimate heir to the KPD, was the successor of that organization.

Population. 61,560,000 (1980)

Party. German Communist Party (Deutsche Kommunistische Partei; DKP)

Founded. 1968

Membership. 48,856 (claimed by the DKP in May 1981)

Chairman. Herbert Mies

Presidium. 17 members: Herbert Mies, Hermann Gautier, Jupp Angenfort, Kurt Bachmann, Martha Buschmann, Werner Cieslak, Gerd Deumlich, Kurt Fritsch, Willi Gerns, Erich Mayer, Ludwig Müller, Georg Polikeit, Rolf Priemer, Max Schäfer, Karl Heinz Schröder, Werner Stürmann, Ellen Weber

Secretariat. 11 members: Herbert Mies, Hermann Gautier, Vera Achenbach, Jupp Angenfort, Gerd Deumlich, Kurt Fritsch, Willi Gerns, Josef Mayer, Ludwig Müller, Karl Heinz Schröder, Wilhelm Spengler

Executive. 91 members

Last Congress. Sixth, 29–31 May 1981, in Hanover

Auxiliary Organizations. Socialist German Workers Youth (Sozialistische Deutsche Arbeiter Jugend; SDAJ), ca. 16,000 members (SDAJ claim: 35,000), Werner Stürmann, chairman; Marxist Student Union–Spartakus (Marxistischer Studentenbund; MSB-Spartakus), ca. 6,500 members, Uwe Knick-rehm, chairman; Young Pioneer (Junge Pioniere; JP), ca. 4,000 members

Publications. *Unsere Zeit* (Our time). Düsseldorf, DKP daily organ, circulation ca. 50,000 copies; *Elan*, SDAJ monthly organ; *Rote Blätter* (Red leaves), MSB-Spartakus monthly organ

Party Internal Affairs. There were no changes in the leadership of the DKP in 1982. Party officials elected by the Sixth Party Congress retained their positions. The party received about 60 million marks in financial assistance from the German Democratic Republic (GDR) (*Frankfurter Allgemeine Zeitung* [*FAZ*], 10 December). The DKP denies this and claims that all of its income derives from membership fees and donations. Not included in the 60 million marks is the cost of the schooling of DKP functionaries at the Socialist Unity Party (SED) School "Franz Mehring" in Berlin-Biesdorf (East), where about 3,000 DKP cadres have been trained. Participants in this program receive compensation for loss of income and for the support of their families. Also, the expenses of an ambitious delegation program sponsored by the SED are not included in the direct transfer of money to the DKP either via couriers or through the communist-controlled network of firms in the FRG. About 600 delegations with about 10,000 participants visit the GDR annually at the invitation of the SED. (Ibid.)

The organizational structure of the DKP follows the typical communist party model. Emphasis has been on increasing the number of primary party organizations in factories, neighborhoods, and universities. There are more than 1,400 primary party organizations that are subordinated to the 187 county organiza-tions, which in turn are controlled and directed by twelve district organizations.

The SDAJ held its Seventh Federal Congress on 6–7 March in Düsseldorf. It was attended by 768 delegates, among them twelve Bundeswehr soldiers. The importance of the SDAJ to the Soviet Union and the GDR as part of their pro-Soviet and anti-Western propaganda, in spite of the organization's numerical weakness, was demonstrated by the presence at the congress of the Soviet ambassador to the FRG, Vladimir Semenov, East Germany's permanent representative in the FRG, Ewald Moldt, and representa-tives from the embassies of Ethiopia, Afghanistan, Bulgaria, Cuba, Nicaragua, Poland, Romania, Czecho-slovakia, Hungary, and Vietnam (*Deutscher Informationsdienst* [*DI*], 18 March, pp. 2–4). Functionaries from the Komsomol (USSR), Free German Youth (GDR), Communist Youth Cuba, Youth Organization of the Tudeh Party (Iran), and representatives from the Sandinista Youth (Nicaragua) and South-West African

People's Organization were among the 40 delegations from fraternal organizations. Representatives from communist-led organizations in the FRG and from left-wing Social Democratic youth groups were among the guests attending the congress. (Ibid., p. 4.)

Membership figures were not provided; it was reported that the SDAJ was organized in 835 groups (of which 104 were factory groups) and worked with 450 JP groups. Forty-two percent of the 768 delegates were active in peace initiatives, and 37 percent held elected positions in factories or trade unions. The congress elected a nine-member executive and an eight-member secretariat. (Ibid., pp. 2–21.) It also re-elected Chairman Werner Stürmann and Vice-Chairman Hans Kluthe (FAZ, 8 March).

The Fourth Federal Conference of the JP took place in Dortmund on 4–5 December. The DKP regards "youth work" as an important task of "revolutionary politics." Summer camps held in the GDR are designed to produce sympathy for the "youth-loving" communist system and rejection and hate for the "youth-hostile" system in the FRG. In 1981, more than 4,000 children from the FRG attended these camps. (FRG Bundesminister des Innern, Innere Sicherheit, no. 63, 31 August, p. 10.)

A number of communist-led organizations and committees provide the DKP with effective means for its "unity of action" programs, intended to expand its influence particularly in the peace and ecological movements. The Committee for Peace, Disarmament, and Cooperation (KFAZ), founded in 1974, was most successful in organizing numerous demonstrations, meetings, and campaigns for the collection of signatures on peace manifestos that coincided with Soviet peace and disarmament policies. Most of the KFAZ officials are connected with the Soviet-controlled World Peace Council (WPC) or are members of the DKP leadership. Of the 32 German members of the WPC, 6 are members of the KFAZ, 2 are members of the Presidium of the DKP, and 14 belong to various communist front organizations (Information Centre of the World Peace Council, List of Members 1980–83, pp. 43–47).

The German Peace Union (DFU), founded in 1960, is another organization utilized by the DKP to influence the peace movement and to propagate its demand for a reversal of Bonn's support of NATO's December 1979 decision to modernize NATO's medium-range missile systems in Europe. It had been decided to station 572 Pershing II and Cruise missiles on the territory of European NATO members as a counterbalance to the steadily increasing number of Soviet SS-20 missiles in the event that ongoing negotiations in Geneva between the United States and the Soviet Union fail to remove or decrease the number of Soviet intermediate-range ballistic missiles. Key positions in the DFU's Directorate and Federal Presidium are occupied by Communists who ensure that DKP control is maintained in all the actions of the DFU. (YICA, 1982, p. 283.)

The "Krefeld Appeal" specifically demands that the German government rescind its agreement to the NATO decision. By April, the appeal had obtained 2.7 million signatures, and its initiators proposed to make it a genuine people's plebiscite (Unsere Zeit [UZ], 16 April). The DKP and its auxiliary organizations continued to make signature collection for the Krefeld Appeal one of their main activities in 1982. Numerous Social Democrats, Free Democrats, and trade unionists signed the appeal.

Members of the DKP also occupy leading positions in the German Peace Society/United War Service Resisters (DFG/VK), which held its Fourth Federal Congress on 26–28 November (DI, August, p. 3), as well as the Association of Victims of the Nazi Regime/League of Antifascists (VVN/BdA), Association of Democratic Jurists, the Democratic Women's Initiative, and in numerous so-called citizens' initiatives against Berufsverbot (the policy of denying government employment to political extremists), nuclear power plants, extension of airfields, and the alleged denial of civil rights.

The DKP utilizes the increasing number of extremists among foreign workers. The Federal Security Service reported that at the end of 1981, almost 124,000 of the 4.6 million foreigners in the FRG belonged to extremist groups. Pro-Moscow groups account for 68,200. About 24,000 belong to the New Left. (FAZ, 30 September.)

Ideological education of party members continued to be encouraged. The DKP "educational year 1981–82" centered on the role of Communists in the German trade unions and, in particular, on the "alliance policy" of the DKP in the trade unions. The DKP Institute for Marxist Studies and Research organized a number of seminars in Frankfurt/Main, such as the International Scientific Conference on 5–6 June dealing with the economic policies of capitalism in crisis situations. (DI, 15 February, p. 11, 15 May, p. 7.) The DKP also maintains the Karl-Liebknecht School in Leverkusen and the Marx-Engels Foundation as "educational" institutions for party members and sympathizers (FAZ, 10 December).

Domestic Attitudes and Activities. During 1982, elections were held in Lower Saxony, Hamburg, Hesse, and Bavaria. As in past elections, the DKP failed to obtain the support of the voters, polling, at most, only 0.4 percent of the vote in any province (ibid., 23 March, 8 June, 28 September, 12 October). In order to overcome its poor electoral showing, the DKP proposes an "election alliance of democratic and left-wing forces" for the elections in Schleswig-Holstein scheduled for 13 March 1983. The DKP declared itself willing to forgo running its own candidates if the "election alliance" could be formed on the basis of a common election platform. Among the seven points of the proposed platform were the fight against the stationing of U.S. medium-range ballistic missiles, defense of social rights, protection of the environment, opposition to the government's nuclear program, and the fight against *Berufsverbot* and neofascism. (*DI*, 18 June, p. 4.)

As in 1981, the anti-NATO missile campaign, the collection of signatures for the Krefeld Appeal, and the support of various peace demonstrations, such as the demonstration on 10 June during the NATO summit meeting and visit of President Reagan, were among the most successful communist attempts to achieve unity of action among Social Democrats, Free Democrats (and their youth organizations), secular and religious pacifists, ecologists, trade unionists (DGB), and members of the DGB Youth (an organization with about 1.4 million members) (*Österreichische Militärische Zeitschrift*, Vienna, July/August, p. 120).

Another example of successful unity of action with emphasis on cooperation with church-related groups (the Working Group of the Protestant Youth and the League of Catholic Youth) was the so-called peace weeks (7–17 November), organized by the communist-controlled DFG/VK together with Aktion Sühnezeichen/Friedensdienste (Action Sign of Atonement/Peace Services). The DKP and the Krefeld Initiative called on their followers to support the peace weeks and the scheduled protests on 12 December, the third anniversary of the NATO decision. (*DI*, 2 October/1 November, p. 9.) Peace meetings were held in about half of the Protestant churches (*FAZ*, 4 December).

The Communists constitute a minority within the peace movement. However, as a result of their clear objectives, compact organizational structure, and sufficient financial means, their influence goes far beyond their numbers (ibid.). The DKP and the communist-controlled front organizations are directed by the International Department of the Soviet Central Committee. In the FRG, the VVN/BdA and the DFU (the initiator of the Krefeld Appeal) belong to the most important Soviet-front organization, the WPC (report of the Security Service, 1981, quoted in ibid., p. 2). In September, peace talks were held in Moscow, organized by the Soviet Committee for the Protection of Peace and the Martin-Niemöller Foundation of the FRG. The numerous participants from the West covered a wide political spectrum from members of the DKP to the followers of the Green Party (a collection of ecologists, pacifists, anarchists, and left-wing radicals). Soviet representation included the former Soviet ambassador to the FRG and present director of the Department for International Information of the Soviet Central Committee, Valentin Falin, and Georgi A. Arbatov, a member of the Central Committee and director of the Institute of the U.S.A. and Canada. The Martin-Niemöller Foundation was founded in 1977 on the occasion of the eighty-fifth birthday of Lenin Prize–holder Niemöller. The membership of the directorate of the foundation includes the prominent Social Democrat and architect of *Ostpolitik*, Egon Bahr, Communists, and activists of international communist front organizations. (Ibid., p. 5.)

The official DKP organ, *Unsere Zeit* (16 April), openly declared that communist participation in the Easter marches showed that Communists were an active part of the peace movement. The 1982 Easter marches had an entirely different objective from those of the 1960s. The earlier Easter marches were opposed to all nuclear weapons, while in 1982 opposition was limited to "new nuclear weapons," that is, the stationing of new NATO intermediate missiles. (*Radikal*, January–April, p. 3.) The government of the FRG believes that the Easter marches in 1982 were organized and controlled by the DKP, its affiliated organizations, and communist-controlled front organizations (*FAZ*, 24 March).

In spite of the DKP's obvious successes in influencing the peace movement, there have been occasions when unity of action was rejected. For example, at a conference in Bad Godesberg attended by over 800 delegates from 350 organizations, the Greens refused to sign an appeal for the demonstration against the Bonn NATO conference on 10 June. The Greens stated that the appeal was a typical DKP project and that the Communists were organizationally overrepresented (*Der Spiegel*, 12 April, p. 30).

In September, the DFG/VK Land organization of Lower Saxony/Bremen published directives for actions and their objectives. Among them were rescinding the NATO missile decision; blockading future missile locations; establishing symbolic nuclear-free zones in streets, cities, and communities; resisting the military utilization of citizens; creating public awareness by means of nuclear alarm signals; holding hunger strikes; halting ammunition trains; refusing to pay taxes used for armaments; and preventing military instruction in schools (*DI*, 2 October/1 November, pp. 10–11).

After the new government coalition of Christian Democrats and Free Democrats assumed power in October, the DKP called on the peace movement and trade unions to close ranks in the fight against the "coalition of the right." The DKP appeal stated: "Peace weeks, collection of new signatures for the Krefeld Appeal, the support of initiatives of scientists, authors, athletes, and artists for peace, the close cooperation of trade unions and the peace movement, the preparations for the Easter marches of 1983, which should be started now—these will be effective actions for the prevention of stationing nuclear intermediate missiles. We call on all members of our party, all friends and sympathizers of the DKP, to give greater support to the peace movement in order to achieve a decisive success. The NATO missiles decision must fall!" (Ibid., p. 4.) The DKP expects that the change of government will make its "alliance policy" more successful (*FAZ*, 6 October).

Communist infiltration of trade unions remained another main concern of the DKP. Party members are required to participate actively in trade union activities. The implementation of this party order was well illustrated by the 855 delegates attending the Sixth Party Congress, of whom 94.6 percent were active members in one of the seventeen DGB trade unions, 61.1 percent were trade union officials, and 25.3 percent were elected factory stewards. Infiltration of the DGB youth organization remained a special task of the SDAJ. (*Bayernkurier*, 23 October.)

International Views and Party Contacts. Public statements of the DKP on international issues are very much the same as those made by Moscow and East Berlin. At the regular plenum of the DKP Executive in February, DKP Chairman Herbert Mies emphasized the significance of the meetings of West German Chancellor Helmut Schmidt with Leonid Brezhnev and Erich Honecker at the end of 1981. The most important international objectives were revocation of Bonn's consent to the deployment of new U.S. intermediate nuclear missiles on German territory, decreases in military spending, and rejection of all types of sanctions against socialist states and of all measures intended to undermine economic cooperation with them. Mies stated that DKP's main tasks in 1982 were preventing the deployment of U.S. nuclear missiles and collecting signatures for the Krefeld Appeal. (Tass, 7 February; *FBIS*, 8 February.)

The DKP supports the implementation of martial law in Poland as the only way to cope with the "irresponsible and extremist forces" of Solidarity, which drove the country to an economic catastrophe and close to a civil war (*Innere Sicherheit*, no. 62, 27 May, p. 8). DKP Chairman Mies denounced the antisocialist propaganda nurtured by the United States and NATO. The events in Poland have been used by President Reagan and hawks in the FRG as a pretext for launching a slanderous campaign against the Soviet Union and other socialist states. The DKP Executive approved the document "War Should Never Again Come out of German Land: The DKP's Proposals for Alternative Security Policy" (Tass, 7 February; *FBIS*, 8 February).

Before the Bonn NATO summit conference in June, the DKP and the Communist Party, U.S.A. published a common statement calling on the people to stop the armaments race and its supporters in Bonn. The declaration asserted that the course of the reactionary forces of U.S. imperialism constituted a continuous danger for world peace. Both communist parties endorsed the peace demonstrations on 10 June in Bonn and on 12 June in the United States and praised the Soviet disarmament proposals. The "Soviet threat" was disqualified as a "propaganda lie" (*FAZ*, 5 June).

International contacts were maintained throughout 1982 by mutual visits of party leaders. A delegation from the Soviet Union participated in DKP-organized events on International Women's Day on 8 March (*Pravda*, 12 March; *FBIS*, 22 March). Mies and other party officials met with Yuri Andropov, Boris Ponomarev, and Anatoli Chernayev in Moscow on 26 July. Mies also led a party delegation to East Berlin in April. SED Secretary General Erich Honecker and Mies "underlined the alliance between the two parties" (ADN, 26 April; *FBIS*, 28 April). Mies was invited to meet in Prague with representatives of the Communist Party of Czechoslovakia (*Rudé právo*, 1 April; *FBIS*, 7 April), and DKP Deputy Chairman Hermann Gautier paid a visit to Romania at the invitation of the Romanian Central Committee (Agerpress, 14 September; *FBIS*, 17 September). A delegation of the Communist Party of Austria, headed by Chairman

Franz Muhri, visited the FRG on 9–10 September (*Volksstimme*, Vienna, 11 September; *FBIS*, 14 September). SDAJ participation in the Second General Meeting of the World Federation of Democratic Youth in Prague also helped maintain international contacts (*DI*, July, p. 6).

Other Leftist Groups. The New Left includes all groups and parties opposed to the pro-Moscow, orthodox communist organizations. There are ever-changing organizations and splinter groups, each asserting itself to be the only true Marxist-Leninist revolutionary organization. The New Left comprises various Maoist (dogmatic) K-groups and antidogmatist and anarchistic organizations. It appears that the era of the K-groups is ending. Several of these groups have ceased to exist, and their members are searching for different fields for their revolutionary activities.

The decline of the dogmatic New Left began with the dramatic changes in the policies of the People's Republic of China. Countries to which the K-groups looked as models experienced increased difficulties. The chaos of the Chinese Cultural Revolution and the activities of the Pol Pot regime in Kampuchea greatly contributed to their loss of credibility. Even the Maoist-oriented Communist League of West Germany (Kommunistischer Bund Westdeutschlands; KBW), which until recently was able to keep its members committed to the revolutionary cause, has been seriously weakened by the disillusionment of its followers, ideological controversies, and a split in the party. About 600 members left the KBW and founded the League of West German Communists (Bund Westdeutscher Kommunisten; BWK). The KBW has about 1,100 members. For the time being, the KBW has abandoned its objective of establishing the dictatorship of the proletariat and concentrates instead on the infiltration of mass organizations.

The BWK (500 followers) also continues to lose members to the antidogmatic left and admits that it has failed to become a Leninist cadre organization. The BWK is trying to broaden its base in cooperation with other leftist groups (ibid., January, pp. 13–14). The BWK participated in the Land elections in Bavaria and obtained 425 votes (*UZ*, 12 October).

The Communist League (Kommunistischer Bund; KB) has about 450 members and publishes the monthly *Arbeiterkampf*, which reflects the views of the entire New Left. In 1979, about 200 followers split and founded the Center Faction (Zentrumfraktion; Gruppe Z), under the leadership of KB cofounder Jurgen Reents. One of the reasons for the split was the issue of collaboration with the Greens (*DI*, January, p. 14). In Hamburg, the Greens (Green/Alternative List; GAL) consist of two elements. The KB Marxist faction of the left, with a membership in Hamburg of about 50, supports and controls the Alternative List. Group Z dominates the Green. Both groups in the GAL are strongly antiparliamentary and collaborate with militant organizations. (*FAZ*, 16 July.) The success of the GAL in the 6 June elections in Hamburg prevented either of the major political parties from obtaining a majority and forming a functioning government. The Social Democrats attempted to establish a working arrangement with the GAL but failed. New elections on 19 December to try to eliminate the deadlock resulted in a Social Democratic majority; the GAL won 6.8 percent of the vote (DPA, 19 December).

The Communist Party of Germany–Marxist-Leninist (Kommunistische Partei Deutschlands–Marxist-Leninist; KPD-ML), a pro-Albanian splinter group, was also affected by the decline of the dogmatic left, and its membership fell to about 500 (*DI*, January, pp. 14–15). The Rote Hilfe Deutschland (Red Help Germany), a KPD-ML auxiliary, changed its name to Solidarity (ibid., 15 May, p. 11).

The Communist Workers' League of Germany (Kommunistischer Arbeiterbund Deutschlands; KABD) decided at its Fifth Central Delegates' Meeting on 17–20 June in Bochum to found the Marxist-Leninist Party of Germany (Marxistisch-Leninistische Partei Deutschlands; MLPD), "the revolutionary party of the working class." The 133 participants, who met in secrecy, renamed the delegates' meeting the founding congress of the MLPD. On 31 July, six weeks after the congress, *Red Flag*, the KABD central organ, announced that a new communist party had been founded, but did not reveal anything about its elected central and regional leaders. Its classic Marxist-Leninist objective is the violent overthrow of capitalism and the bourgeois state apparatus. Appropriately, the emblem of the party is hammer, sickle, and book. The founding meeting of the MLPD took place on 21 August in Düsseldorf and was attended by about 2,000 people. Stefan Engel is chairman of the party and its Central Committee. He reported that the MLPD has factory cells in the steel industry and publishes factory newspapers in twelve cities. The new party's "spiritual" father is Willi Dickhut, a onetime KPD functionary who believes that he is heir to the party line of Ernst Thälmann, leader of the KPD until 1933 (*Der Spiegel*, 9 August, pp. 31–32).

The groups of the antidogmatic New Left, totaling about 3,000 followers, appear to be the dominant force of the contemporary militant struggle against the democratic state. Among these groups are advocates of social-revolutionary or anarchistic concepts. They all reject Marxist-Leninist dogma and models. The first generation of the antidogmatic left developed in the 1960s when the Socialist German Student League (SDS) dissolved. Some former SDS members are also presently part of the Socialist Buro. The second generation was formed after 1977 by disenchanted followers of the K-groups at various universities. The third generation has emerged since 1980 and developed among militant opponents of nuclear power plants, radicals engaged in house occupations, and adherents of the peace movement.

The borderline between autonomous groups and left-extremist terrorists is difficult to determine. In 1981, 2,241 acts of violence were committed in the FRG. More than 400 incendiary and bombing incidents were among them, with more than 50 of them directed against U.S. military installations. Most of the cases of arson were the work of the Revolutionary Cells (RZ). An RZ leaflet listed 11 incendiary and bombing attacks between 1 and 9 June against U.S. military institutions and U.S.-affiliated enterprises, intended as demonstrations against the visit of President Reagan and the NATO summit conference in Bonn (*DI*, July, pp. 8–9). The terrorists of the RZ are attempting to recruit supporters among left extremists who presently show strong anti-U.S. feelings and are engaged in the struggle against U.S. imperialism (*Innere Sicherheit*, no. 63, 31 August, p. 9).

The Red Army Faction (RAF) has about twenty underground activists and still constitutes a potent danger, especially to NATO military installations (*FAZ*, 27 April). The arrest in November of three RAF leaders who are suspected of participating in several terrorist attacks and murders probably has weakened the RAF for the time being (ibid., 18 November).

The Trotskyite Central Committee of the International Marxist Group, the German section of the Fourth International, has about 300 members (*DI*, 15 August, p. 11).

The Young Socialists (JUSOS), the official youth organization of the Social Democrats, as well as other socialist youth, students, and women's organizations, generally not perceived as left-radical organizations, share many objectives with the extreme left and have participated in numerous unity of actions with Communists and other leftists. Their anti-NATO policy and support of disarmament proposals reflecting Moscow's position provide the basis for cooperation.

WEST BERLIN

West Berlin is still "occupied" by the United States, Britain, and France. The 1971 Quadripartite Agreement concerning Berlin confirms its "special status," based on agreements made in 1944 and 1945 maintaining that the former German capital is not part of the FRG. Even though the 1971 agreement was supposed to cover the area of Greater Berlin, the Soviet-occupied eastern sector of the city has been completely integrated into East Germany and has been declared the capital of the GDR. The Western powers have encouraged the FRG to maintain close ties with West Berlin. The population of West Berlin has declined from 2.3 in 1959 to 1.9 million.

Berlin's special status made it possible for the SED to set up a subsidiary in West Berlin. In 1959, an "independent" organizational structure was devised for the West Berlin part of the SED. In 1962, the party was renamed Socialist Unity Party of Germany–West Berlin; in 1969, the present designation, Socialist Unity Party of West Berlin (Sozialistische Einheitspartei Westberlin; SEW), was introduced in order to create the impression that the party is a genuine, indigenous West Berlin political organization.

The SEW, like the DKP, is a loyal pro-Moscow party, and all its statements parallel the ideological and political views of the East German and Soviet parties. SEW membership remains at about 7,000. In the 1981 elections to the city's House of Representatives, the SEW obtained 8,216 votes, or 0.7 percent, compared with 1.1 percent in 1979. No changes in the SEW leadership were reported in 1982, Horst Schmitt remains SEW chairman, and Dietmar Ahrens deputy chairman. The SEW has a seventeen-member Executive (Buro), a seven-member Secretariat, and a 47-member Presidium.

The party supported many of the numerous demonstrations and house occupations, and West Berlin's Communists have taken a more tolerant view toward the use of violence in the pursuit of their objectives. The Finance Administration of West Berlin paid out 4.8 million marks (almost $2 million) for damages resulting from these violent actions (*FAZ*, 3 September). The SEW also participated in the demonstrations against President Reagan's June visit to West Berlin.

On 26 April, *Die Wahrheit*, the official organ of the SEW, published an unusual critique of actions taken in the GDR against wearers of the emblem Swords into Plowshares, the symbol of the "peace decade" proclaimed by the GDR Lutheran church in 1981 (see GDR profile). Cases have been reported from East Berlin and other GDR localities of police or officials of the State Security Service tearing from wearers' clothing the peace patches, which are said to represent "a derision of the policies of the GDR" (ibid., 27 April).

Contacts with the international communist movement were maintained during 1982. A Soviet party delegation participated in the SEW's May Day events (*Pravda*, 5 May), and a delegation of leading party workers of the SEW, led by Deputy Chairman Dietmar Ahrens, visited the Soviet Union on 15–18 June at the invitation of the Soviet Central Committee (ibid., 26 June). Party Chairman Horst Schmitt headed an SEW delegation visiting the GDR on 25–29 October and met with Paul Verner, Politburo member and secretary of the SED Central Committee (ADN, 29 October). Also, the SEW youth organization, the Socialist Youth League "Karl Liebknecht," kept up its international contacts by participating in communist-sponsored international conferences such as the Second General Meeting of the World Federation of Democratic Youth in Prague (*DI*, July, p. 6).

No major changes were reported in SEW publications and those of the party's auxiliaries. *Die Neue*, a left-wing West Berlin daily newspaper published by the former editor of *Vorwärts* (the official Social Democratic weekly), appeared in the beginning of 1982 each week. At the end of October, it ceased publication because of financial difficulties. (Ibid., 2 October/1 November, p. 6.)

Many of the groups of the New Left and of the left-extremist terrorists find West Berlin a suitable area for their activities. The house occupations offer opportunities to implement their policy of militant resistance. Between December 1980 and April 1982, terrorists together with persons from the "house occupation scene" perpetrated 143 incendiary and bombing attacks following the model set by the RZ (*FAZ*, 18 June).

University of Calgary   Eric Waldman

Great Britain

The Communist Party of Great Britain (CPGB), founded in 1920, is a recognized political party that contests local and national elections. It does not operate in Northern Ireland, which it holds to be within the domain of the Communist Party of Ireland. The party has no members in the House of Commons but has one member, Lord Milford, in the nonelected Upper House. The party has seven local government councillors: four in Wales and three in Scotland. Officially, membership is given at 18,500 out of a British population of 56 million but is now probably below this.

Leadership and Organization. The CPGB is divided into four levels: the National Congress, the Executive Committee and its departments, districts, and local and factory branches. Constitutionally, the biennial National Congress is the supreme authority in the party, but opposition to the leadership is rare. Responsibility for party activities on specific issues rests with the 42-member Executive Committee, which meets every two months. The Executive Committee comprises members of special committees, full-time departmental heads, and the sixteen-member Political Committee, the party's effective controlling body. The leading officers within the Political Committee are Gordon McLennan (general secretary), Mick Costello (industrial organizer), Gerry Pocock (international department), Dave Cook (organization), George Mathews (press), and Jean Styles (women). Mick Costello is McLennan's likely successor as general secretary.

The poor showing of the CPGB at the polls belies its strength in the trade union movement. Although the party does not control any individual union, it is represented on most union executives and has played a major role in government-union confrontations in recent years. The CPGB's success in this field is partly attributable to low turnouts in most union elections, to the fact that it is the only party seeking to control the outcome of those elections, and to its keen critical interest in industrial matters, which ensures it of support from workers who might not support other aspects of the party's program.

There are two members of the CPGB on the 38-member General Council of the Trade Union Congress (TUC): George Guy of the National Union of Sheet Metal Workers and Ken Gill of the Technical and Supervisory Section of the Amalgamated Union of Engineering Workers.

Communist influence in the trade unions extends into the Labour Party. The trade unions dominate the Labour Party by their overwhelming financial support and the system of block voting. In close votes, a handful of trade union executives, who may be under CPGB influence, can decisively affect the vote. Policies originally floated by the CPGB often become official Labour Party policy within two years.

The CPGB controls a small youth wing, the Young Communist League (YCL), which is active in the Campaign for Nuclear Disarmament (CND) and the Campaign Against Youth Unemployment.

Communist activity in industry centers principally on forming work-place branches, of which it has about 200. Their umbrella organization is the Liaison Committee for the Defence of Trade Unions (LCDTU).

Party Internal Affairs. Party membership figures continue to cause great anxiety to the party leadership. The 1981 figure of 18,500 represented a drop of 2,000 since 1979. Although it was hoped that membership would remain at 18,500 in 1983, there were signs that it was more likely to dip below 17,000. YCL membership figures are also now consistently running below 1,000.

The picture of decline is underlined by the state of the party's organ, the *Morning Star*. At the end of 1982, the party was deeply concerned about the future of the paper, which was seriously threatened by closure. Appeals for donations and periodic panics have been a feature of the paper's contents for some time, but by the end of the year, the situation looked worse than usual. An appeal for £100,000 was to be launched while Gerry Cohen was given the special full-time task of winning the paper more readers. The *Morning Star* sells about 30,000 copies a day, of which about half are sold in Eastern Europe. The party has decided to raise domestic circulation in 1983 by at least 3,000 copies by instructing party members to draw up a list of potential readers in likely recruiting areas, such as trades councils, shop stewards committees, women's liberation groups, and antiracist organizations.

Finance is a rather sensitive area for the party, and members are exhorted to pay their membership fees in advance and, if possible, in excess of the obligatory minimum. Despite this discouraging picture, the party retains considerable business interests, including Central Books, Lawrence and Wishart Publishers, Farleigh Press and London Caledonian Printers, Rodell Properties, the Labour Research Department, and the Marx Memorial Library.

Domestic Attitudes and Activities. Communist efforts remained much the same as in 1981, although a greater emphasis on CND activity was discernible. Opposition to the policies of the Conservative Party and right-wing influences within the Labour Party remained the underlying dynamic to most communist work during the year, possibly sharpened by the realization that 1983 was likely to be an election year. By the end of 1982, official figures gave the number of unemployed as over three million, with the real figure possibly over four million. Moreover, the government's monetarist policies were causing sharp reductions in the public sector and encouraging further factory closures, with no end to the rise in unemployment in sight. The government was also anxious to press ahead with its Employment Bill, which, by imposing severe limits on the right to strike, was widely seen as an attack on trade union rights. In this atmosphere, communist propaganda was not without its successes. The CPGB gave enthusiastic support to the TUC's Day of Action strike on 22 September in support of underpaid health workers. Similarly, a strike by the railway engine drivers' union received strong encouragement from the Communists earlier in the year. The CPGB was active in protest demonstrations against the inexorable rise in unemployment, and this was likely to be a still stronger theme in 1983. New eye-catching forms of protest are quite probable.

The CPGB organized two important industrial conferences during the year. In April, its National Industrial Conference was attended by 75 delegates from every district committee, except those in Yorkshire and Kent. The delegates represented a good cross section of manual and clerical workers, but there were only ten females. The emphasis was on the need to develop large-scale working-class action on four issues: unemployment, anti–trade union legislation, maintenance of living standards, and the fight for peace. In December, there was a meeting of the LCDTU, which, although communist run, does include some noncommunist elements. Here the emphasis was on forthcoming actions against the new Employment Bill and unemployment.

International Views and Party Contacts. Internationally, the CPGB retained its customary position of critical support for the Soviet Union. There were two notable areas of controversy with the USSR: Poland and Afghanistan. The CPGB was opposed to the introduction of martial law in Poland, describing the formation of the Military Council for National Salvation as a "serious setback for the process of democratic and socialist renewal." At the same time, however, the CPGB noted that certain statements by Solidarity officials had been provocative and had made the process of dialogue between the party and Solidarity much more difficult. The CPGB had initially opposed the Soviet invasion of Afghanistan but has refrained from calling for the removal of Soviet troops and explicitly favors the Afghan revolution as embodied by the present government.

The main foreign policy issue for Britain in 1982 was the war with Argentina in the South Atlantic over the Falkland islands (Malvinas). Although there was broad, albeit critical, support for the government's decision to send a task force to retrieve the islands after their seizure by Argentina on 2 April, the CPGB was hostile. It dismissed the episode from the beginning as a revival of "gunboat diplomacy" and called for the return of the task force as soon as it was dispatched. Nor did the party have any time for the argument that the Falklanders should enjoy self-determination. On the contrary, it felt that Britain's claim to sovereignty was essentially a hangover from the colonial past and urged immediate negotiations with Argentina. The party did, however, condemn the initial use of force by Argentina.

The party was an enthusiastic supporter of unilateral nuclear disarmament by Britain, opposed the deployment in Britain of new U.S. nuclear weapons, and advocated arms reduction talks with the Soviet Union. The CPGB is critical of Israel and recommends recognition of the Palestine Liberation Organization and is deeply opposed to South Africa's racist apartheid policies, fully backing the black African National Congress. It is also stridently critical of South Africa's continuing occupation of Namibia and periodic military incursions into Angola.

In July, Gordon McLennan visited Bulgaria where he read a speech in honor of the centenary of the birth of the noted Bulgarian Communist, Georgi Dimitrov. In December, the West German Communist Party hosted McLennan and Pocock in Wuppertal.

Publications. The *Morning Star* is the CPGB's daily paper. The party's fortnightly magazine, *Comment*, closed in August because of financial pressure but was partly replaced in November by a new monthly, *Focus. Marxism Today*, the party's theoretical magazine, has undergone a considerable face-lifting and is now aiming at a more popular market, not without some success. *Challenge* is the YCL journal. The party also publishes several journals of more specialized interest: *Link* is a feminist quarterly; *Economic Bulletin* and *Education Today and Tomorrow* are quarterlies; *Our History Journal* deals with party history; while *Medicine in Society* is a discussion forum for health workers.

Other Marxist Groups. In addition to the CPGB, there are several small but zealous groups on the far left. Most active are the Trotskyists, whose brief flowering dates back to the student revolt of 1968.

Membership is small, but most groups have a high turnover rate, which suggests that they may have a higher degree of latent support. The Trotskyist groups are particularly anxious to exploit Britain's economic difficulties. Factory occupations are a favored tactic that they hope to promote.

Several Trotskyist groups practice "entryism"—the tactic of penetrating the larger, more moderate Labour Party. Most important of these is Militant, which derives its name from its paper of the same name. Numbering about 2,000 members, Militant holds all seats on the Executive Council of the Labour Party's Young Socialists and controls about 50 Labour parliamentary constituencies. During 1982, an internal Labour Party inquiry into the activities of the left-wing Militant Tendency was conducted by the Labour Party's secretary and national agent. Published on 19 June, the report concluded that the Militant Tendency was "a well-organized caucus, centrally-controlled, operating within the Labour Party." Moreover, it possessed its own organization with its own distinctive program and propaganda outside the structure of the Labour Party. Since the party constitution expressly forbids the affiliation of groups with their own "programme, principles and policy for distinctive and separate propaganda," the inquiry clearly endangered the future of the grouping within the party. However, by the turn of the year, it seemed unlikely that Militant would be expelled from the Labour Party, although some steps were likely to be taken against it.

The largest Trotskyist organization is probably the Socialist Workers' Party (SWP), which has about 4,000 members. It claims to have small groups of militants in the auto industry, the docks, the railways, the National Union of Mineworkers, the National Union of Teachers, and the National and Local Government Officers' Association. However, despite its efforts, the SWP's base in the working class is probably quite limited.

The SWP's 40-member National Committee, elected at its annual conference, elects the full-time ten-member Executive Committee. Jim Nichol is national secretary, and Steve Jeffery, industrial organizer. The SWP has numerous branches and 70 district committees. It runs "fractions" in the civil service, local government, railways, the postal service, and British Telecom. It claims its greatest support in the north and in Glasgow. SWP chairman is Duncan Hallas, but its best-known personalities are theoretician Tony Cliff and polemical journalist Paul Foot, nephew of the Labour Party leader. The party's organ, *Socialist Worker*, claims a circulation of 20,000, but the real figure is probably much less. Pluto Press, a left-wing publishing house, is closely associated with the SWP.

In 1982, the SWP continued with its strategy of building a grass-roots trade union structure—the Rank and File Movement, which is independent of and often in opposition to the official trade union leadership. The SWP believes that the time for more violent revolutionary action will come when the economy begins to improve and workers are less frightened of losing their jobs.

The other major Trotskyist group is the Workers' Revolutionary Party (WRP), an affiliate of the Fourth International (International Secretariat). Its daily newspaper, *Newsline*, claims sales of 3,000. Its youth wing, the Young Socialists, is comparatively large and enjoys substantial participation by black youths. The WRP is intensely secretive but is known to have militants in the docks and in the engineering, mining, theater, and auto industries. Its best-known personalities are actors Ken Loach, Tony Garnett, and Corin and Vanessa Redgrave.

Other significant Marxist groups are the International Marxist Group (IMG) and the Socialist Organiser Alliance (SOA). The IMG is principally active in entryism in the Labour Party and also in single-issue campaigns. It has a weak industrial base. The SOA was formed as a result of a fusion of the International Communist League, led by Sean Matgamna, and Alan Thornett's Workers Socialist League.

London   Richard Sim

Greece

The Communist Party of Greece (KKE) was founded in 1921. During the 1920s, the party remained small and weak, suffering a series of internal splits. In 1931, it was reorganized under a Comintern-imposed Stalinist group. Five years later, it was forced underground. The party gained extensive influence during the Nazi occupation through its resistance organizations, the National Liberation Front, and its military arm, ELAS. An attempt in December 1944 to seize power by force in newly liberated Greece was put down by the British. A guerrilla campaign (1946–1949), supported mainly by Yugoslavia, was eventually crushed by the Greek army. The party remained outlawed between 1947 and 1974. From 1952 to 1967, the communist left was represented by the United Democratic Left. During the military dictatorship (1967–1974), the party split into two factions, one loyal to Moscow and another (labeled KKE/Interior; KKE-I) espousing a more independent, moderate, Eurocommunist orientation.

Population. 9,740,151 (1981)

Party. Communist Party of Greece (Kommunistikon Komma Ellados; KKE)

Founded. 1921

Membership. KKE: 73,000; 32.8 percent workers, 14.5 percent employers, 18.11 percent farmers, 9.7 percent shopkeepers/artisans, 12.3 percent professionals/intellectuals, 22.6 percent women; KKE-I: 12,000

Secretary General. Kharilaos Florakis (KKE); Yiannis Banias (KKE-I)

KKE Politburo. 9 full members: Kharilaos Florakis, Nikos Kaloudhis, Grigoris Farakos, Kostas Tsolakis, Roula Kourkoulou, Loula Logara, Dimitris Gontikis, Nikos Ambatielos, D. Sarlis; 2 candidate members: Takis Mamatsis, Orestis Kolozov

KKE-I Executive Office. Yiannis Banias, Kostas Gavroglou, Grigoris Yiannaros, Angelos Dhiamantopoulos, Bambis Dhrakopoulos, Nikos Kaimakis, Petros Kounalakis, Takis Benas, Elli Papakonstandinou, Kosta Filinis

Last Congress. KKE: Eleventh, 15–18 December; KKE-I: Third, 17–23 May

Elections. In 18 October 1981 parliamentary elections, KKE won 10.9 percent of the vote and 13 of the 300 seats to become the third largest party; in 17 October 1982 municipal elections, received 19.5 percent of the vote and control of several major municipalities. KKE-I won only 2.7 percent of vote in 1981 parliamentary elections and no seats in parliament; its showing was very poor in 1982 municipal elections.

Publications. KKE: 62-year-old daily *Rizopastis*; monthly theoretical review *Kommunistiki Epitheorisi*; KKE-I: daily *Avgi*

Between 1974 and 1981, the positions advocated by the KKE on domestic and international issues were very similar to those advocated by the Panhellenic Socialist Movement (PASOK), the party established by Andreas Papandreou in 1974. PASOK won a majority in parliament in the 1981 election, and Papandreou became premier. Since that time, Papandreou has toned down his pre-election advocacy of Greek withdrawals from NATO (ousting U.S. bases and nuclear weapons from Greek soil) and the European Economic

Community, the enactment of a socialist constitution, and the socialization of the economy; however, he has not abandoned those objectives entirely. An estimated one-third of PASOK's following has a genuinely Marxist orientation. This section accounts for approximately 16 percent of the total electorate. In the event of a breakup of PASOK, a sizable portion of this Marxist left may join the KKE.

The KKE is influential in several trade unions and university student organizations, where it vies with PASOK for supremacy.

Under the PASOK government, Marxist and pro-Soviet propaganda has been given free reign. Marxist and pro-communist beliefs are no longer a barrier to admission to the country's military officer schools. The continuing occupation of a major part of Cyprus by Turkey and the widespread belief among Greeks that NATO and the United States favor Turkey in Greek-Turkish differences over the Aegean is used by PASOK and the KKE to equate anti-Western positions with patriotism. The deterioration of the economic situation has weakened PASOK's public appeal, and the beneficiary of this disappointment may be the KKE as a consequence of its attraction to many from PASOK's Marxist left.

A major concern for the future is the current exposure of Greek youth to leftist views and the legitimacy accorded Marxist and communist ideological positions.

Party Internal Affairs. Three major developments occurred in 1982. First, relations between the KKE and the governing PASOK party deteriorated. PASOK rejected the KKE's overtures for cabinet positions. When its hopes of participating in the government faded, the KKE launched a campaign criticizing PASOK for "betraying" its promises for a genuine "change" along Marxist-socialist lines. During the October municipal elections, PASOK and KKE candidates fought each other in many municipalities, although there were a few instances of cooperation in localities where the KKE did not run a separate ticket. Second, the success of KKE-sponsored municipal candidates and the numerical increase in the party's electoral support emboldened the party leadership, which intensified its criticism of PASOK. Third, this hardening of positions became even more evident during the KKE's Eleventh Congress. The KKE's obvious objective is to attract PASOK's left wing, which has been showing signs of disenchantment with Papandreou's "mild" policies toward the West and his "timid" measures in "socializing" the economy.

A decision by the PASOK government to allow the unhindered repatriation of persons of Greek origin living in the Soviet Union and Eastern Europe since the collapse of the guerrilla campaign in 1949 may have some effect on increasing the KKE's following. However, many potential repatriates are now elderly, and their children born abroad may not wish to return.

Foreign Affairs. The presentation at the Eleventh Congress of the KKE's views on Greece's international relations brought no surprises. On almost every point, they resembled the positions held by PASOK prior to the 1981 parliamentary election. The KKE's "theses" include: (1) immediate withdrawal from NATO's military wing as the first step in the country's complete disengagement from NATO; (2) immediate removal of nuclear weapons from Greece; (3) removal of U.S. bases from Greek soil; (4) settlement of Greek-Turkish differences outside of the NATO framework; and (5) "internationalization" of the Cypriot problem (*Rizospastis*, 5 September).

International Party Contacts. KKE Politburo member Efstathios Tsambis visited Poland in January. In February, a KKE delegation headed by Secretary General Kharilaos Florakis visited the Soviet Union, Bulgaria, and East Germany. Florakis paid a three-day visit to Syria and Lebanon in March and met with leaders of the Lebanese Communist Party, leaders of the Lebanese nationalist movement, Walid Jumblat of the Progressive Socialist Party, Yassir Arafat, and the command of the Popular Front for the Liberation of Palestine. A KKE delegation under Florakis visited Libya in April and discussed the "coordination of the struggle against U.S. imperialism, conversion of the Mediterranean into a sea of peace, and development of bilateral relations." Leonid M. Zamyatin, Soviet Central Committee member, visited Athens in June at the invitation of the KKE. Florakis met with Libyan and Palestine Liberation Organization representatives in Athens in August. Florakis visited Poland in August at the invitation of Gen. Wojciech Jaruzelski. Also in August, a KKE delegation met the representative of the Iraqi Patriotic Front, which opposes the government of Saddam Husayn. Florakis met on 26 August with Yuri Andropov and Vadim Zagladin in Moscow.

The KKE-I was also fairly active. In April, Kostas Filinis met with Aleksandar Grličkov, member of the Presidium of the League of Communists of Yugoslavia. Petre Lupu, member of the Political Executive Committee of the Romanian Communist Party, represented that party at the Third Congress of KKE-I in Athens. A KKE-I delegation headed by Yiannis Banias met with members of the Romanian Communist Party in September.

While PASOK is not a "communist" party, it maintains close contacts with communist parties and "progressive" organizations in other countries. The PASOK government hosted the Cuban foreign minister in July. A Greek embassy had been established in Havana the previous month. A Bulgarian Fatherland Front delegation visited Greece in February at the invitation of PASOK and met with Papandreou at his home in Kastri. In September, Papandreou met Luís Corvalán, leader of the Communist Party of Chile. Minister of Communications Evangelos Yiannopoulos visited Romania in March. PASOK and Czechoslovak Communist Party delegations met in Athens in September. Soviet Minister of Fruit and Vegetable Farming Nikolai Kozlov visited Athens in April, meeting with government representatives and Florakis. Greece and the Sandinista government in Nicaragua established full diplomatic relations in May. Papandreou visited Bulgaria in June. Oskar Fischer, foreign minister of the German Democratic Republic, visited Athens in July. The PASOK Youth Committee invited representatives of the Soviet Komsomol for a seven-day visit to Greece in July.

Howard University   D. G. Kousoulas

Iceland

The Icelandic Communist Party (Kommunistaflokkur Islands) was formed in 1930 by a left-wing group that had broken from the Labor Party, which was later renamed the Social Democratic Party. In 1938, another left-wing group splintered from the Social Democrats and joined with the Communists to create a new party, the United People's Party–Socialist Party (Sameiningar flokkur althydu–Sosialista flokkurinn; UPP-SP). Patterned on the Norwegian Labor Party, the UPP-SP based its ideology on "scientific socialism-Marxism," but had no organizational ties to Moscow. It was an uncompromising advocate of Iceland's independence from Denmark. By the time independence was achieved in 1944, the other parties had accepted the UPP-SP as a responsible democratic party, participating in coalitions. In 1956, the UPP-SP formed an electoral alliance with still another group of left-wing Social Democrats and the small, isolationist National Preservation Party. This coalition assumed the name People's Alliance (AB). In 1968, the UPP-SP dissolved itself into the AB, which then formed itself into the present national Marxist party. In 1982, it held three cabinet posts: social and health affairs (Svavar Gestsson), finance (Ragnar Arnalds), and industry (Hjörleifur Guttormsson). The prime minister is Gunner Thoroddsen of the Independence Party; the coalition consisted of maverick members of the Independence Party, the Progressive Party, and the AB.

Population. 229,187 (1 December 1980)
Party. The People's Alliance (Althydubandalagid; AB)
Founded. 1968

Membership. 2,200 (est.); mostly workers and intellectuals, located principally in Reykjavik and eastern fjords

Chairman. Svavar Gestsson

Executive Committee. 10 members: Svavar Gestsson, Kjartan Olafsson (vice-chairman), Gudrun Helgadottir (secretary), Tyrggvi Thor Adalesteinsson (treasurer); Adda Barra Sigfusdottir (member of Reykjavik City Council), Alfheidur Ingadottir, Petur Reimarsson (chairman of Organization of Base Opponents), Ludvik Josepsson (former AB chairman), Rannveig Traustadottir (member of Hafnarfjördhur Council), and Ulfar Thormodsson

Central Committee. 42 regular members, plus Executive Committee members and cabinet members as ex officio members; 15 deputy members

Last Congress. 20–23 November 1981, Reykjavik; next congress to meet in 1983

Front Organizations. Organization of Base Opponents (OBO), organizer of peace demonstrations against U.S./NATO bases

Elections. Third largest of four parties represented in Althing; 19.7 percent of vote in 1979 parliamentary elections and 11 of 60 Althing seats

Publications. *Thjodviljinn*, daily (Reykjavik) and at least two weeklies outside capital, *Verkamadhurinn* (Akureyri) and *Mjolnir* (Siglufjordhur)

Continued participation in the government at a time of economic recession placed great strain on the AB. Falling fish catches, the worldwide downturn in economic activity, and continuing high inflation (about 50 percent) forced party leaders to agree to an economic austerity program in late August that entailed an actual decrease in real wages.

In these circumstances, party leaders attempted to appeal to their followers by taking more strident stands on foreign policy issues. Attention focused on the U.S./NATO base at Keflavik. AB cabinet ministers continued to block construction of a new airport to which the United States would contribute funds and opposed attempts to modernize base facilities. Also, they mounted a campaign against foreign investment. Finally, considerable support was given to creation of a "peace" propaganda program directed partly against the USSR but mainly against the United States.

Party Internal Affairs. The AB's traditional secrecy concerning developments and activities within the party could not mask the dislike of the more ardent party militants for the compromises party leaders were making with their coalition partners in the formation of government policy. Indications in public opinion polls that party support was declining sharpened criticism. A poll published in February showed a drop of electoral support from the 19.5 percent the party received in the parliamentary election of May 1981 to 13.4 percent, the lowest support of any of the four major parties (*Morgunbladid*, 20 February). In early March, AB officials angrily denied the claim of a conservative newspaper that 300 members had left the Reykjavik chapter of the AB (ibid., 2 March). But the AB newspaper *Thjodviljinn* (30 April) reported the establishment of a dissident left-wing organization called "Red Labor Unity," which described itself as a "group struggling to establish a new communist party."

The 22 May local elections confirmed the AB's decline in electoral support and disclosed a swing toward the conservative Independence Party. The AB's share of the vote decreased from 25.5 percent in the 1978 local elections to 17.5 percent. In the Reykjavik City Council election, the AB percentage fell from 30 to 19. The conservative press concluded that the AB's loss was due mainly to its participation in both the national government and the outgoing Reykjavik Council (*Morgunbladid* and *Dagbladid-Visir*, 25 May).

Domestic Affairs. Iceland's growing economic problems dominated domestic politics in 1982. Strains in the coalition over economic policies, particularly wage and price controls, began in December 1981 and grew throughout the year (*Morgunbladid*, 12 December 1981). By late April, attention centered on wage negotiations, and the AB tried to make those negotiations the main issue in local government election campaigns (*Thjodviljinn*, 28 April). The AB's May Day activities concentrated on the theme of aiding low-paid workers (ibid., 1 May). Controversy over modernization of Keflavik base facilities, especially the proposed building of new oil tanks at Helguvik, was also an election issue (ibid., 28 April).

The opposition Independence Party's crushing victory in the local elections — it won over 45 percent of the vote nationwide and 12 of 21 seats in the Reykjavik City Council — erased the ruling coalitions in Reykjavik and several other cities. The AB's only consolation was that it emerged with stronger representation than the Social Democrats and in some places gained on the Progressives. Geir Hallgrimsson, chairman of the Independence Party, immediately called for new national elections (ibid., 25 May). To end rumors of a breakup of the coalition, Gestsson pledged that the AB would continue to support the coalition "in accordance with the coalition agreement" and "other basic rules of the coalition," a reference to the AB's insistence that all foreign and defense decisions must have the unanimous support of all three coalition parties (ibid., 26 May; *Morgunbladid*, 27 May). The AB's call for unity of the left to oppose the Independence Party and its criticism of the actions and policies of a fellow coalition partner, the Progressives, aroused a strong reaction from the principal Progressive newspaper, *Timinn* (28 May).

By mid-June, AB Minister of Finance Arnalds was warning that Iceland was suffering its worse recession in 25 years — the gross national product had already dropped by 2 percent — and that strong measures must be taken to counter it (*Thjodviljinn*, 11 July). In August, after hectic negotiations among the government parties, an agreement was reached to (1) devalue the currency by 13 percent, (2) cut wage indexing by one-half for the quarterly calculation in December and negotiate a permanent reduction for 1983, (3) reduce the prices of foodstuffs, (4) limit some imports, and (5) aid ailing industries. The agreement was carried out by provisional decrees, which required later ratification by parliament.

By October, the inflation rate was over 60 percent and still rising, and the trade unions were opposing the proposed reform of wage indexing. International markets for some fish exports were softening and the gross national product had fallen by about 3.5 percent, and the decline was expected to reach at least 4 percent. Unemployment had not yet become a major problem, but many fish-freezing plants had shortened their operating hours.

When parliament resumed in October, the opposition Independence and Social Democratic parties seemed solidly opposed to the ratification of the government's decrees authorizing the economic program. They also opposed the government's budget for 1983 as insufficient to counter inflation. They maintained that the budget merely cut investments and current projects while keeping social and welfare benefits high. (*Morgunbladid*, 13 and 14 October.) Thoroddsen delayed bringing the decrees before parliament and set up a committee of party leaders to try to find compromises on the economic legislation and the budget. Gestsson opposed this procrastination, favoring an immediate vote to see if the coalition would survive. He protested charges that he wanted the coalition to fall, stating that he merely wished to assess the situation, so as to secure a better basis for the government. (Ibid., 15 October.) *Morgunbladid* reported (21 October) that at the request of both the Progressives and the AB, Thoroddsen had agreed to new elections early in 1983.

The 19–20 November AB Party Council meeting was dominated by economic issues. In an appeal to all leftists to unite against right-wing capitalist forces, a council resolution called for limitation on imports, assistance to the fishing industry and agriculture, a step-by-step increase in industry powered by hydro-electricity, reduction in government expenditures, establishment of a fund to raise the wages of low-paid workers, and strengthening of price controls.

On 23 November, a Social Democratic no-confidence motion was defeated by a vote of 31–29 in the combined houses. During the debate, Prime Minister Thoroddsen announced that elections would be held probably in April 1983. Cabinet ministers, led by AB Minister of Finance Arnalds, used the occasion to list the coalition's "accomplishments," particularly the lack of serious unemployment and construction of a new power plant at Blanda.

Foreign Affairs. The ability of the coalition parties to reach agreement on economic policy was not matched in foreign affairs, despite the statement of prime Minister Thoroddsen in October 1981 that foreign policy would not change in 1982. In fact, AB leaders seemed to concentrate on foreign policy issues to offset growing rank-and-file discontent with the party's domestic policies.

Parliamentary group leader Olafur Ragnar Grimsson outlined AB policies during an Althing debate on foreign affairs on 6 April. He pointed out that the party supported the European peace movement and opposed military governments and nuclear weapons. He accused U.S. military authorities of interfering in Iceland's internal affairs in order to further their interests, and the U.S. embassy and Cultural Center in Reykjavik of conniving, with some Icelandic politicians, to further military objectives. Grimsson stressed the danger of U.S. nuclear weapons and military activities for the area around Iceland. Finally, he expressed AB support of aid to developing countries and opposition to the military regimes in Turkey and El Salvador and to the apartheid policies of South Africa. He noted that the Social Democrats had expressed similar attitudes on these latter issues, but he accused the Independence and Progressive parties of supporting the generals in El Salvador and Turkey.

During 1982, AB leaders concentrated on attacking the U.S./NATO base at Keflavik and efforts to modernize base facilities and equipment. In an Althing foreign policy debate early in the year, AB parliamentary group leader Grimsson asserted that Iceland had gradually become integrated into the nuclear arms system of the United States through expansion of base facilities and that the USSR would now conclude that in the first stages of conflict the U.S. bases in Iceland must be destroyed. Foreign Minister Olafur Johannesson responded that Grimsson reminded him of Don Quixote fighting windmills; the danger to Iceland was caused by its location, not by the equipment located on it. (*Morgunbladid*, 11 February.)

Foreign Minister Johannesson, a former chairman of the Progressives who had headed the previous coalition of Progressives, Social Democrats, and the AB, engaged in debate with AB leaders on the question of building a new air terminal at the Keflavik base jointly with the United States. Johannesson, supported by the opposition Independence Party and Social Democrats, sought to start construction in order to commit U.S. funds appropriated by Congress for that purpose.

As the 1 October deadline for the expiration of U.S. funds approached, the dispute heated. The AB opposed accepting U.S. financial support as infringing on Iceland's sovereignty and maintained that if and when an air terminal was needed, it should be small and built with only Icelandic funds. (*Morgunbladid* and *Thjodviljinn*, 12 August.)

On 8 September, AB ministers blocked Johannesson's proposal that the cabinet order immediate construction of the terminal. Independence Party and Social Democratic leaders then proposed that the Althing itself order the construction. Johannesson admitted defeat and said that he would try to get an extension of the U.S. appropriation. He refused to say how he would vote on an opposition proposal in parliament that construction should start. The renegade Independence Party ministers, including Prime Minister Thoroddsen, had their support of Johannesson's proposal written into the minutes of the cabinet meeting. (*Morgunbladid* and *Thjodviljinn*, 9 September.) In an interview on state television, 8 September, Gestsson repeated the AB position that a large terminal should not be built with U.S. financial assistance, and *Thjodviljinn* (10 September) scolded Johannesson for "nagging" the United States to extend its appropriation. When Congess responded to the Icelandic request by authorizing funds for another year, *Thjodviljinn* (28 September) said the action changed nothing and accused Johannesson of preparing for a new government coalition. It said that the action of Congress constituted a "serious interference in our internal affairs" and charged the U.S. ambassador to Iceland of trying to bring down the coalition (ibid., 5 October).

A similar struggle between Johannesson and the AB involved the relocation and rebuilding of oil storage tanks for the Keflavik base in order to reduce environmental danger. Johannesson, citing his authority as foreign minister in charge of defense issues and the Althing's request that the matter be acted on expeditiously, decided that the tanks should be built at Helguvik. Gestsson immediately objected, stating that this would involve new defense force activity and that, as minister of social affairs in charge of planning, he himself should make the decision where the tanks would be built. (Ibid., 27 January.) The AB Executive Committee distributed a resolution to Althing members supporting the AB cabinet minister's position on the Helguvik and air terminal issues and declaring that the basis of the coalition was that all major decisions were to be unanimous. It protested the foreign minister's actions as "jeopardizing the coalition." (Ibid., 17 March.)

The AB revived the Helguvik issue in early September. In a *Thjodviljinn* interview (8 September), a government member of the U.S.-Icelandic Defense Council, which deals with base issues, said that planning of the project was proceeding under the authority of the foreign minister. *Thjodviljinn* also interviewed Gestsson, who repeated his position that such planning authority rested with his Ministry of Social Affairs and that no decision had been made on the Helguvik project. He added that "there is a long way between planning and actually launching a project." (Ibid.)

The AB gave much attention to "peace" themes and support of the "peace movement" in Iceland. AB leaders continued to push for a Nordic nuclear weapons–free zone that would include Iceland. At a meeting of the Nordic Council in Helsinki on 1 March, Gestsson endorsed such a zone, claiming that there were more nuclear weapons in the Atlantic than ever before (ibid., 2 March).

The United States was the principal target of the "peace" effort. An AB Executive Committee resolution demanded that the United States cease "supporting the military governments of El Salvador and other countries in Latin America" (ibid., 5 and 9 February). At its annual fall meeting on 20-21 November, the AB Party Council condemned U.S. support for El Salvador and Guatemala and intervention in the "internal affairs" of Nicaragua. The council called on the Icelandic government to condemn "the acts of violence" of Israel in Lebanon and to support a Palestinian homeland. In parliament, Grimsson proposed that Iceland summon Turkey before the European Human Rights Commission for alleged violations of human rights (ibid., 18 February). The AB and the Social Democrats then presented a joint parliamentary resolution to condemn the abolition of democracy in Turkey (ibid., 15 April).

In late March, the OBO launched a series of meetings throughout Iceland on the peace movement, and nuclear-free zones. The first, directed against the base and NATO, was held at Haskolabio (ibid., 3 March). On 1 April, a meeting was held to protest U.S. nuclear weapons policy in Europe and U.S. actions toward Central America (ibid., 2 April). On 20 April, *Thjodviljinn* announced the formation of a "peace movement" in Akureyri, Iceland's second-largest city, and late in the month, Grimsson attended a meeting of some 50 peace movements in Glasgow, Scotland.

On 6 and 8 August, *Thjodviljinn* proposed that all factions, including those supporting NATO, join in the peace movement. The principal target was nuclear weapons deployment in Europe. The AB Party Council declared its opposition to NATO's decision to deploy "new" intermediate-range nuclear weapons and called on the Icelandic government to work against the deployment. But it also asked the government to protest "plans of the Soviet Union to increase its nuclear missiles in Europe." On 1 December, Gestsson strongly supported the proposal of Mexico and Sweden at the United Nations for a freeze on nuclear armaments. (Ibid., 1 December.)

The USSR and Eastern Europe did not escape criticism. At a demonstration in front of the Polish Embassy in early December 1981, Gestsson, labor leader Asmundur Stefansson, and a representative of the Church of Iceland protested the institution of martial law and restrictions on human rights in Poland (ibid., 11 and 13 December 1981). On 14 December 1981, Grimsson presented a resolution of the AB parliamentary group in the Althing strongly condemning the attempts of "Polish authorities to end the human rights struggle of the Polish nation" and declaring support for the struggle of Solidarity for "human rights and democracy." AB Vice-Chairman Kjartan Olafsson wrote: "It is Soviet power holders who hold responsibility for the terrible situation in Poland now. We declare the Soviet Union to be guilty of the situation in Poland." (Ibid., 15 December 1981.) In the fall of 1982, the AB Party Council's foreign policy resolution stated that "the Soviet Union has exercised military oppression against the countries of Eastern Europe and against Afghanistan" and repeated the party's support for Solidarity. On 21 November, the Central Committee of the Icelandic Federation of Labor passed a resolution strongly condemning Polish authorities for banning Solidarity. (Ibid., 22 November.)

International Party Contacts.   The AB continued its policy of remaining aloof from the international communist movement and seeking to identify itself with nationalistic socialist and labor parties such as that of President François Mitterrand in France and the Labor Party in the United Kingdom. The AB also felt close to the Socialist People's parties in Norway and Denmark. An editorial in *Thjodviljinn* (5 February) developed the theme that leftists in Europe had learned that in order to protect workers' interests and promote real democracy and socialism, neither extreme right-wing nor left-wing policies worked. A "third way" was necessary. He cited the struggle between the Italian Communist Party and the Soviet Union, remarking that this struggle had been most instructive.

The AB sent no representatives to meetings of communist parties abroad. Although critical of Soviet activities in Afghanistan and Poland, its views on many foreign policy topics were similar to those of Moscow. Its failure to speak out against Soviet policies generated criticism by the press and political leaders of the other Icelandic parties.

Exchanges between Icelandic and Soviet authorities were rare. On 1 July, the Soviet deputy minister of foreign trade came to Iceland to sign a new economic cooperation agreement. On 26 July, a seven-member delegation of Soviet parliamentarians and Foreign Ministry officials arrived for five days of talks; it was the fifth such visit in 24 years (Tass, 30 July).

Bethesda, Maryland   Finis Herbert Capps

Ireland

The Communist Party of Ireland (CPI) was founded on 14 October 1921, when the Socialist Party of Ireland expelled right wingers and joined the Comintern. However, the party became irrelevant during the Civil War and disappeared, although small communist cells remained intact. The CPI was refounded in June 1933, which the Communists now consider the date of origin of their party. The organizational structure of the party was disrupted during World War II, largely because of the belligerent status of Northern Ireland and the neutrality of the south. In 1948, the southern Communists founded the Irish Workers' Party and those in the north the Communist Party of Northern Ireland. At a specially convened "unity congress" held in Belfast on 15 March 1970, the two groups reunited.

The CPI is a recognized political party on both sides of the border and contests elections but has no significant support. It has about 500 members and is slightly stronger among northern Protestants than in the Catholic south. However, Irish Marxists tend to join other parties, notably Sinn Fein—The Workers' Party (SFWP) or the Irish Republican Socialist Party (IRSP). The population of the Republic of Ireland is just under 3.5 million and that of Northern Ireland a little over 1.5 million.

Leadership and Organization. The CPI is divided into two geographical branches corresponding to the political division of the country. Theoretically the Congress is the supreme constitutional authority of the party, but in practice it simply endorses the decisions of the national executive. The innermost controlling body is the National Political Committee, which includes Andrew Barr (chairman), Michael O'Riordan (general secretary), Tom Redmond (vice-chairman), and James Stewart (assistant general secretary).

The CPI holds no seats in any significant assembly north or south and has virtually no chance of doing so. It has one councillor in the south, in County Donegal. The Communists do, however, have some influence in the trade union movement and in a Northern Ireland pressure group, the Northern Ireland Civil Rights Association. Andrew Barr is well known in European trade union circles and has held international appointments. The CPI also controls a small youth organization, the Connolly Youth Movement.

Domestic Attitudes and Activities. In May, the CPI held its Eighteenth Congress in Dublin, this time under the motto "For peace, independence and socialism." The congress emphasized the need for unity of action of the progressive, democratic, and patriotic forces that stood for an independent course of development and unification. The creation of a single, united socialist Ireland was held to be the fundamental aim of the working class, small farmers, the progressive intelligentsia, and all Irish working people. The principal obstacle was identified as British imperialism, which was using every means to keep Ireland in subordination. The CPI believed working-class solidarity would achieve the unity of the majority of the population of Northern Ireland, both Catholic and Protestant.

The congress voted in favor of a proposal for writing a neutrality clause into the Irish constitution. A distinctive feature of the congress was concern that pressure was being applied on Ireland to play a supporting role in NATO. The CPI would vigorously oppose any such move. The delegates and guests of the congress strongly applauded a statement by Andrew Barr that Irish Communists were true to proletarian internationalism and to the ideals of friendship with the Soviet party and the USSR. Barr said that Irish communists fully supported the new peace initiatives put forward by Brezhnev. The initiatives confirmed, he said, that the USSR was the main bulwark of peace and freedom of the people.

General elections were held in the Republic of Ireland on 18 February. The CPI ran candidates but failed to come anywhere near scoring any electoral success.

In the north, the CPI denounces the use of force by paramilitaries on both sides of the communal divide. It does, however, seek the eventual withdrawal of the British. The party emphasizes the importance of trade union activity to unite Catholics and Protestants and seeks the implementation of a bill of rights to guarantee fundamental rights. In general, however, policy statements did not differ from previous years.

International Views. The CPI is totally loyal to Moscow and has never voiced any criticisms of Soviet policy. The party, for example, supports the Soviet intervention in Afghanistan and favored the martial law regime in Poland. The Eighteenth Congress voiced agreement with the struggle of the developing nations against imperialism and denounced alleged efforts by Washington and its allies to hinder the final liberation of Afro-Asian and Latin American countries. The congress judged the struggle for peace, détente, and disarmament to be the most pressing issues. It maintained the party's traditional stance of hostility to the European Economic Community, which it sees as a device to draw Ireland into NATO's "militarist" plans.

The congress was attended by a Soviet delegation headed by the secretary of the Central Committee of the Communist Party of Lithuania, who read a message of greetings from the Soviet Central Committee and spoke of the important contribution of the Irish Communists to the people's national liberation movement. In October, the assistant general secretary of the party, James Stewart, visited Great Britain at the request of the Communist Party of Great Britain to participate in a venture aimed at attacking anti-Irish prejudice in Britain.

Publications. The main organ of the CPI is the *Irish Socialist*, published monthly in Dublin. It is supplemented by the *Irish Workers' Voice*, a weekly, and *Unity*, a small monthly published in Northern Ireland.

Other Marxist Groups. There are numerous Marxist groups in Ireland most of them commanding greater support than the minuscule CPI. The most important are the SFWP, the IRSP, and the Provisional Sinn Fein. Of these, the SFWP achieved a brief success in the republic's parliament when together with some independents it briefly held the balance of power. This occurred following the general elections of February 1982.

After its defeat by one vote in the Dail (lower house of Parliament) on 27 January, the governing Fine Gael–Labour Party coalition resigned. A general election was held on 18 February in which no individual party secured a decisive majority. The balance of power was held by four independents and three SFWP representatives. The SFWP representatives together with two independents gave their support to the Fianna Fáil leader, Charles Haughey, who was then duly elected prime minister by a majority of seven.

The Provisional Sinn Fein (the political wing of the Provisional IRA) put up candidates in seven constituencies and fought principally on the demand for a British withdrawal from Northern Ireland. It also called for the establishment of a "democratic socialist republic." Two of the Provisional Sinn Fein candidates were in prison for terrorist offenses at the time of the elections. Prior to the vote, however, the Provisional Sinn Fein announced that it had no intention of assuming any seat it might win. In October, the party scored a noteworthy success in elections to the new Northern Ireland Assembly, by breaking the traditional monopoly of the Catholic vote by the Social Democratic and Labour Party. Several Sinn Fein members were elected but are boycotting the new assembly.

London   Richard Sim

Italy

The Italian Communist Party (PCI) was established in January 1921 when a radical faction of the Italian Socialist Party (PSI), led by Amedeo Bordiga, Antonio Gramsci, and Palmiro Togliatti, seceded from the PSI. Declared illegal under the fascist regime, the PCI went underground and moved the party's headquarters abroad. It reappeared on the Italian political scene in 1944 and participated in governmental coalitions in the early postwar years. Excluded from office in 1947, it has remained in opposition since then, except for a brief period (summer 1976 to January 1979) when it became part of a governmental coalition but without holding cabinet posts.

Population. 57,353,000 est.

Party. Italian Communist Party (Partito Comunista Italiano; PCI)

Founded. 1921

Membership. 1.74 million (*L'Unità*, 30 October), includes members of Communist Youth Federation

Secretary General. Enrico Berlinguer

Secretariat. 7 members: Enrico Berlinguer, Mario Birardi, Gerardo Chiaromante, Adalberto Minucci, Alessandro Natta, Adriana Seroni, Alfredo Reichlin

Directorate. 32 members

Central Control Commission. 55 members

Central Committee. 169 members

Last Congress. Fifteenth, 30 March–3 April 1979; next congress scheduled for March 1983

Auxiliary Organizations. Communist Youth Federation, Marco Fumagalli, secretary general; National League of Cooperatives

Elections. In June 1979 elections, won 30.4 percent of the vote; has 201 members in 630-seat lower house and 109 of 315 seats in the Senate; controls many local governments alone or in coalition with the PSI, especially in Emilia-Romagna, Tuscany, and Umbria

Publications. *L'Unità*, official daily, published in Rome and Milan, Emanuele Macaluso, editor; *Rinascita*, weekly; *Critica Marxista*, theoretical journal; *Studi Storici*, *La Nuova Rivista Internazionale*, *Politica ed Economica*, *Donne e Politica*; Editori Ruiniti, PCI publishing house.

Internal Party Affairs. The bitter polemic that flared up in 1982 between the Italian Communists and the Communist Party of the Soviet Union (CPSU) was bound to have an impact on the internal life of the PCI. As it turned out, these internal repercussions overshadowed other developments and activities in the life of the party. Moreover, the internal affairs of the PCI became the object of much speculation and interest on the part of the political observers and leaders of the other Italian parties.

Ever since the PCI took a strong independent stand vis-à-vis the CPSU, beginning with the speech made by Berlinguer at the Twenty-Fifth Congress (1976) of the CPSU, the question has been raised whether the PCI leadership was speaking for the whole party. A number of observers have suggested that within PCI ranks were groups that did not agree with the leaders on a number of issues — for example, the Soviet intervention in Afghanistan. Renewed PCI criticism of the USSR in December 1981 and January 1982 and the heightening of tension between the two parties made it even more important to ascertain how much of the party supported the secretary general.

As far as the elites and cadres were concerned, it appeared that open dissent with the positions taken by the leadership was quite limited. The January resolution summarizing the official position of the party was overwhelmingly approved by the Central Committee. In answer to reports of internal conflicts among Directorate members circulating at the end of 1981, party leader Emanuele Macaluso said, "Of course there are conflicts. But how far should we publicize them? The issue arose for us back at the time of the Eleventh Congress and the conclusion we reached was as follows: open and public debate in the Central Committee and a frank but confidential debate in the party Directorate . . . I am convinced that the confidential nature of the debate within the Directorate makes us freer." (*La Republica*, 3 and 4 January.)

Five days before Berlinguer's report to the Central Committee, *L'Unità* (6 January) published an article entitled "How I Disagree with the Party Document on Poland," written by Armando Cossutta, a longtime party official and a member of the Directorate. "I express my disagreement," Cossutta wrote, "with the resolution drawn up by the Secretariat . . . because . . . it does not facilitate the necessary unitary conclusions. On some points the document constitutes not only a shift, a turning point, but a rupture with our tradition and our history. In effect, the resolution 'eliminates' all socialist societies hitherto created. Is such a drastic verdict justified? . . . Does this not mean that what the resolution expresses is not a distancing or criticism of the CPSU and other parties but rather a desire for a real rupture?"

Cossutta's position throughout 1982 remained highly critical of the party's stand. In October, he published a book entitled *The Wrench* in which he explained the reasons for his opposition to the positions taken by the party leadership. On 7 October, speaking at a meeting of the Central Committee, he commented on the forthcoming Sixteenth Congress of the PCI. Since the congress represents a significant opportunity to gather support for his dissenting position, Cossutta insisted that it should be an occasion for open and frank debate. Although fairly guarded, his speech hinted at the possibility that the leadership might use unfair methods to select candidates for the congress and thus undermine his efforts to rally a sizable minority. "I believe," he said, "that every congress body must be encouraged to adopt procedures for electing candidates that are most likely to guarantee the faithful representation of the entire congress. This would apply particularly to situations in which the debate provides evidence of specific points of political disagreement." He concluded, "It would also be desirable for section delegates to be chosen from among the members of that same section," hinting that this had not always been the case. (*L'Unità*, 8 October.)

Since Cossutta's chances rest mostly on support for his positions at the mass level, his preoccupation with the composition of the local and national congresses was more than justified. Berlinguer responded that "Cossutta gave the impression of wanting to make some gratuitous distortions, almost with the intention of bringing out in the party all possible sources of unhappiness." As for the selection of delegates, Berlinguer remarked that he did not see how the Central Committee could give instructions to the lower bodies or why "preference should be given to dissenting rather than to consenting comrades. Each congress at the different levels will decide on the compositions of its delegation and how many cadres should be included compared with the number of delegates that are not in the party apparatus." (Ibid., 9 October.)

A different criticism against Berlinguer came from another quarter. Three articles written by Franco Rodano, who until recently had been considered one of Berlinguer's close confidants and advisers, appeared in the daily *Paese Sera*, a newspaper that although formally independent has for a number of years been close to the PCI. Rodano, who belongs to a group of Catholic intellectuals affiliated with the PCI, branded the idea that the October Revolution had lost its creative power in the USSR a "politically infantile and unequivocally unhistorical, ignorant assertion." As for Berlinguer's notion of a "third way" between "real socialism" and social democracy, Rodano called it a "helpless slipping on the inclined plane of error and misperception into the nebulous region of simpleminded social democracy." For Rodano, "despite occasional detours, the Soviet Union is and remains the most important, historically proven driving force for humanity's development toward socialism; without it, this process is unthinkable." (*Die Weltwoche*, 24 February.)

Observers disagree on the extent of dissent among the rank and file. Asked to comment on a study showing that approximately 30 percent of PCI supporters approved the Soviet invasion of Afghanistan and thus disagreed with the strong condemnation issued by their leaders, a PCI official said, "No, that figure seems exaggerated to me . . . it would be superficial to cite figures on this phenomenon . . . I can tell you, however, that from Czechoslovakia through Afghanistan, and now Poland, I have gradually found a substantial broadening of the sections of cadres and workers who sincerely share the positions of the leadership." (*La Republica*, 3 and 4 January.)

A poll of PCI members in February showed that about 25 percent held views in conflict with the official party position. About 67 percent of those interviewed gave their unconditional approval to the break between the PCI and the CPSU. At the same time, 66 percent of the sample expressed the opinion that Cossutta should not be expelled from the party. (*L'Espresso*, 21 March.) There were other reports indicating that there was a considerable amount of confusion, anxiety, and bewilderment over the conflict with the CPSU. Said a dissenting PCI official and member of the PCI regional committee of Lombardy, "The climate for those who do not agree with the line recently taken by the party . . . is certainly not ideal for expressing dissent . . . I believe that party members are not taking this well." (Ibid.)

Some rank-and-file dissenters from the party's position chose to express their feelings by writing letters to the Soviet *New Times*. "Our magazine's editorial office has recently received a particularly large number of letters from Italian readers. Their letters attest to their authors' critical attitude toward statements made by the PCI leadership on the policies of the CPSU and on the experience of building socialism in the USSR and other communist countries." (*Novoe vremya*, 14 November.) The letters expressed dissatisfaction with the position of the PCI, confirmed the readers' solidarity with the CPSU, and blamed the Italian communist leaders for the break. Some of the letters were hostile to the party leadership. One dissenter stated: "I cannot reconcile myself with the way in which politicians in the PCI leadership equate the CPSU and the USSR with the imperialist bandits headed by Reagan. This is an unforgettable mistake . . . We will not be deceived . . . the masses are on the right track, and it is the leadership that should reconsider its positions." (Ibid., 14 April.)

Another source of tension was the growing generation gap between the older militants and the younger cohorts. Several aspects of this gap were evident in an interview given by Marco Fumagalli, secretary of the Communist Youth Federation, which in the past had been closely aligned with the party. Noting that at the federation's last congress a motion critical of the party daily had been approved with a standing ovation, Fumagalli explained that the communist youth of today have doubts "on many aspects of communist culture, of the culture of the workers, of the PCI itself . . . There are new issues, such as a different relationship with politics, a different conception of sexuality, of music, and of the environment . . . and we ask that these issues be discussed. The party is having considerable difficulties in quickly taking hold of these new ideas. The society in which we live is much more complex than many of our older comrades perceive it to be. Perhaps more important than a job to us young Communists today is the guarantee of a satisfying quality of life. But try to tell this to an old worker who has spent his entire life on the job . . . We are the first generation without myths. We grew up in the era of Vietnam, Cambodia, Afghanistan, and Poland. The experiences of those governments have nothing whatsoever to do with the socialism in which young people believe. In fact, from our viewpoint, there are no models for our socialism, not even that of the 'third way.'" (*L'Espresso*, 27 June.)

Speculation about a possible change at the top was fueled by an apparently casual remark made by Berlinguer in a televised interview: "Whether I still have the strength, the energy to continue with my present duties, this is a question that exists and that the party organs will certainly discuss and about which I will have something to say myself"(ibid., 25 July). Some observers believe that there is a possibility that Berlinguer could be replaced by a collective leadership, for example, a committee including all major party leaders. This question will also contribute to making the Sixteenth Congress important in PCI history.

Domestic Affairs. There was little change in the domestic position of the PCI in 1982. The party remained in opposition at the national level while sharing governmental responsibility in many regions, large cities, and municipalities. The PCI continued to press for the "democratic alternative" line, a stand inaugurated in late 1980 that represented a shift from the "historic compromise" strategy pursued earlier. The central component of the democratic alternative is a future alliance between the Socialists and the Communists with help from other left-wing groups. During 1982, the alliance of the PCI and PSI became part "of a broader formula comprising other democratic forces, including groups within the Catholic camp" (*L'Unità*, 8 July). While continuing to criticize the incumbent cabinet headed by Prime Minister Giovanni Spadolini and pressing for a change in coalition formulas, the PCI leadership made it clear that it might support a government without participating in the cabinet if the new government represented a "change of direction" (ibid.).

Since the democratic alternative presupposes a policy change by the Socialists, the PCI continued to pressure the PSI to leave the governing coalition. "If the PSI really wants to bring about a convergence among the forces of reform and of the left, it must change course and come to terms with the PCI" (ibid., 28 August). In November during the crisis involving the second cabinet headed by Spadolini, the PCI depicted the Socialists as being "still entangled in contradictions between the substance of the program and the logic of the old alliances . . . The danger is that everything will be reduced to a grim dispute over the duration of the new government and a quarrel about the date of early general elections. The recourse to temporary governments dependent on agreements on early elections is now intolerable." (Ibid., 19 November.) The Socialists' decision at the end of 1982 to enter a new four party coalition headed by Christian Democrat Amintore Fanfani represented a setback for the PCI, and the party voted against the new government in parliament.

In the spring, the PCI became the protagonist in an incident that caused the party considerable embarrassment and eventually led to the replacement of Claudio Petruccioli as editor of the party's daily. In mid-March, *L'Unità* published a document purporting to show that two Christian Democratic members of the cabinet had had contacts with a gangster serving a term in a maximum security prison. According to the document, attributed to the Ministry of the Interior, the two politicians had asked the gangster to act as a middleman in contacts directed to freeing a Christian Democratic politician kidnapped by the Red Brigades. (*NYT*, 19 March.) The author of the article refused to disclose the source and was arrested. Petruccioli took full responsibility and wrote an editorial stating, "The line of the party is not involved here . . . the decision to publish the article was made by the newspaper and by the newspaper alone" (*France Presse*, 18 March). In the meantime, the document had been exposed as a fake, and *L'Unità* had to admit that the materials published "do not correspond in whole or in part to the truth" (ANSA, 22 March). The resignations tendered by the editor and his deputy were accepted. But the PCI also mentioned the possibility that it might have been the victim of a maneuver to embarrass the party.

Several times during the year, PCI leaders opposed holding parliamentary elections ahead of schedule, siding with the Christian Democrats against the Socialists. The PCI justified its position on the grounds that the serious social and economic situation of the country would be made even more serious by an anticipated election and that a dangerous political vacuum might result (ibid., 7 January; *L'Unità*, 28 August). However, many observers speculated that the PCI leadership was worried about a possible decrease of mass support resulting from the delicate internal situation of the party. These losses might be contained if the elections were to be held as scheduled in 1984. In this case, the party would have a chance to regroup its forces after the forthcoming national congress of 1983 and might be able to wage a more effective electoral campaign a year later.

Foreign Affairs. The tension between the PCI and the CPSU, which had been building for some time, exploded in open conflict with the declaration of martial law in Poland in mid-December 1981. In past years, the PCI had increasingly distanced itself from the position of the CPSU and from other communist parties of Eastern Europe and had asserted its right to full autonomy. It had voiced criticism of communist regimes and expressed sympathy for dissent movements against these regimes, had sought to normalize relations with the Chinese Communist Party, had condemned the Soviet invasion of Afghanistan, and had strongly objected to the handling of the situation in Poland. But the polemics in late 1981 and early 1982 were unprecedented in the history of the relationship between the two parties, both in scope and language.

On news of the declaration of martial law in Poland, the PCI reacted with strong words of condemnation and called for an immediate restitution of civil liberties and union rights. A document by party leaders stated that "democracy and socialism must be considered indivisible" (ANSA, 14 December 1981) and urged that the Polish crisis be resolved through open discussion "in order to ensure the rights of freedom for the Polish people and the independence of the nation without acts of violence" (*Frankfurter Allgemeine Zeitung*, 15 December 1981).

Two weeks later, after a long and intense debate, the party Secretariat issued a resolution prepared at the instruction of the Directorate. Referring to the repressive measures taken in Poland, the document stated: "These measures, which are incompatible with our democratic and socialist ideals, cannot resolve . . . the profound crisis. Nor can they be justified by the need to salvage the substance of a socialist type regime because when one can no longer deal with the protest of the working class and the people by political means and one resorts to military strength, this constitutes a blow to the very cause of socialism." The document argued that in Eastern European countries there was a "contradiction between democratic and socialist factors and a system that does not permit real democratic participation in either the production or the political spheres. This nullifies freedom and creative energies . . . nurturing a continuous conflict between reformist thrusts and authoritarian constraints." The central point of the analysis was the realization that "the phase in the development of socialism that began with the October Revolution has lost its driving force."

The document continued with an explanation of what had gone wrong in the development of communist regimes: "The Twentieth CPSU Congress [1956] was an exceptionally important event and inspired great hopes . . . But after some years, this regeneration gradually came to a standstill . . . partly because . . . by concentrating on the 'cult of personality,' the congress failed to carry out a thorough analysis of the structure of the political system of the USSR." After recognizing that the October Revolution was the major revolutionary event of this era, the PCI leadership added: "The PCI does not underestimate the role played by the USSR at the world level. This role sometimes converges with the interest of the countries and peoples struggling against imperialism . . . but at other times it conflicts with these same interests or even openly violates them, as in the case of the military intervention in Afghanistan."

This logic extended to the events in Poland: "The USSR and other Warsaw pact countries exerted a great negative influence on this crisis . . . There were heavy pressures, illicit forms of interference, and an incessant political and ideological campaign against the renewal effort to which a major section of the Polish party, of Solidarity, and of the church were committed." For Italian communist leaders, the crucial element in the dispute was the nature of the developments in Poland. The crisis in Poland was "a very acute social and political crisis . . . which cannot be attributed to the maneuvers of reactionary forces hostile to socialism . . . the dissatisfaction and revolt were directed against the absence of democratic life in that political system . . . against the trade unions' inability to defend the interests of the workers and also against the positions of privilege and the cases of corruption within the party itself." Realizing the implications that such statements would have for relationships with other communist parties, the PCI document stated that the Italian party "intends to maintain normal relations" with all communist parties, but added "as it does with all other socialist, revolutionary, and progressive forces, without any special privilege with anyone and on the basis of an absolute autonomy of thought and political action, without ideological, political, and organizational ties." (*L'Unità*, 30 December 1981.)

Two weeks later, a meeting of the Central Committee and the Central Control Commission was called to debate the stance taken by the leadership. In a long report Secretary General Berlinguer confirmed the conclusions reached earlier. Berlinguer's report was approved by an overwhelming majority of the Central Committee; only two members abstained and one voted against (ANSA, 15 January).

Under such attacks, the CPSU and other communist parties of Eastern Europe could not remain silent. Even before Berlinguer's report to the Central Committee, the Italian position was described as follows: "In both bourgeois Italy and other capitalist countries, the PCI has been applauded for taking a stand against the Polish people's efforts to restore order and tranquility . . . This is fresh evidence of how very misleading the illusions about Eurocommunism can be. The PCI leadership has slid down the slippery path of Eurocommunism to the other side, into the camp of the enemies of our common cause." (*Rudé právo*, 8 January.)

The CPSU response came first in a long editorial published in *Pravda* on 24 January and then in a number of other articles. The PCI leadership was accused of abandoning the Marxist-Leninist platform, of using the Polish situation as a pretext, of siding with the enemies of peace, of casting doubts on the existence of socialism in the USSR, and of cutting its ties with "the mighty forces of socialism, peace, and freedom" (*Kommunist*, no. 2.)

The response of the CPSU was soon supported by statements of other aligned parties. The East Germans charged that the PCI had formulated the "monstrous thesis" that "the policy of the USSR and other Warsaw Treaty states does not differ from the foreign policy of the United States and of NATO" (*Neues Deutschland*, 26 January). The Hungarians argued that the PCI leaders had misdirected their reproaches and asked: "How does it happen that the PCI leaders do not draw a distinction between the mistakes of the former [Polish] leaders and the constructive efforts of the new ones? How did it happen that the PCI leaders attacked the Polish party just as the party entered into a selfless struggle to defend socialist Poland and peace in Europe?" (*Népszabadság*, 6 February.) The Communist Party, U.S.A. spoke of "impermissible, irresponsible and slanderous statements by some leading circles of the communist parties of Italy [and] Spain" (*Information Bulletin–CPUSA*, March). The (West) German Communist Party said that the Italian position "added grist to the mill of reaction" (*Unsere Zeit*, 1 February).

A response by the PCI provoked a series of rejoinders, and the debate continued during the first few months of 1982. Each side accused the other of misrepresenting its positions. The PCI, having published in full the articles that had appeared in *Pravda* and *Kommunist*, remarked that the CPSU had not printed the response by the Italian Communists (*L'Unità*, 26 January). Regarding the Soviet claim that political democracy already existed in the USSR, the Italian daily asked: "In which party assembly, union, and production assembly, and in which soviet . . . can the Communist or citizen who dissents on general political matters express his dissent, and where and how is the public informed of the issues of dissent?" (Ibid.)

In the months that followed, the polemic between the two parties abated somewhat, but the relationship between the PCI and the CPSU remained tense. The documents prepared by the Italian party leadership for the 1983 national congress confirmed the positions elaborated at the beginning of the year. Whether they will change in the immediate future will depend largely on the outcome of the Sixteenth Congress.

International Contacts. As in previous years, the PCI maintained a large number of contacts with political parties of other countries, mostly with communist parties. These contacts were conditioned by the position of the PCI in the communist movement. Thus in February, an Italian delegation attended the congress of the French Communist Party, but it was not headed by PCI leader Berlinguer. Berlinguer's absence was interpreted in some quarters as a reflection of the strained relations between the two parties.

Berlinguer did go to France at the end of March for a meeting with Lionel Jospin, first secretary of the French Socialist Party, as well as with President François Mitterrand. Berlinguer and Jospin made similar analyses of the international situation, and condemned bloc politics, and agreed that the CPSU could no longer play a positive role in the development of world socialism. There did appear to be, however, disagreement over the balance of military power in Europe. "On this point," said Berlinguer, "our party considers itself closer to the views of the West German Social Democrats," (ANSA, 1 April).

A meeting between Berlinguer and Georges Marchais, secretary general of the French Communist Party, took place in late May. The concluding statement indicated that differences over Soviet policies remained. The joint communiqué stated that the two parties would continue their cooperation but "without masking differences of opinion and certain divergent views" (*NYT*, 26 May).

In late October, Vadim Zagladin, member of the CPSU Central Committee and first deputy chief of the CPSU International Department, visited Rome. The visit triggered speculations about the relationship between the two parties, which had been severely strained by the reciprocal attacks earlier in the year. Zagladin met with several PCI leaders prior to a final meeting with Berlinguer. At the end of the week's visit, it was apparent that little progress had been made toward normalizing relations. "The discussion had continued in the most frank atmosphere" and, in the words of one PCI leader, "To sum up in a few words such a complex issue, I would talk in terms of a new and clear recognition of the assertion of each party's full autonomy and of its right to defend it firmly . . . We said that in matters concerning the internal life of the PCI only the Communists of this country have a say." (*L'Unità*, 26 and 28 October.) For his part,

Zagladin said that "the talks had been a frank and penetrating exchange of information . . . it was stressed that cooperation between the parties in the struggle against imperialism, to prevent war, and to halt the arms race is more important than the divergences that certainly exist now between us . . . such cooperation implies the opportunity to continue a comradely discussion, without abandoning the respective principles but in an attempt to bring our stances closer together." (*La Republica*, 27 October.)

There were other international contacts by the PCI. In February, the PCI sent a message to the Polisario Front expressing solidarity with the Saharan Democratic Arab Republic (SDAR) in its fight against Morocco. The PCI pledged its commitment to push for recognition of the SDAR in Europe (*L'Unità*, 27 February). In the same period, Berlinguer held talks in Rome with the Salvadoran Democratic Revolutionary Front (FDR) representative in Italy. Berlinguer affirmed the solidarity of the Italian Communists with the FDR's struggle in El Salvador (ibid., 28 February). In March, Giancarlo Pajetta, the head of the PCI International Section, met with the foreign minister of Romania (ibid., 3 March). Shortly afterwards, Paolo Bufalini of the PCI Directorate and Angelo Oliva of the Central Committee went to Lisbon for a meeting with Alvaro Cunhal, secretary general of the Portuguese Communist Party. "Although major differences of opinion emerged, the two delegations expressed the desire to develop relationships and to continue a frank examination of all issues" (ibid., 24 April). A similarly cold tone was used by the PCI daily in reporting on a visit to Sofia of the Foreign Section chief, Antonio Rubbi (ibid., 30 April).

In April, Sergio Segre, chief of the European Economic Community Section, met with a representative of the Danish Socialist People's Party (ibid., 28 April). A month later, Pajetta received Robert Mugabe, prime minister of Zimbabwe, and confirmed the PCI commitment to "step up solidarity action in support of all the patriotic and progressive forces of the countries of southern Africa" (ibid., 24 May). A "different assessment of the current situation" emerged from talks between PCI officials and the Israeli United Workers' Party (ibid., 29 May). There were also talks between Berlinguer and representatives of the Dutch Labor Party and the Lebanese National Movement (ibid., 7 May, and 4 July). Finally, in June, a PCI delegation headed by Pajetta went to Tunis for talks with the Tunisian Communist Party, and a delegation of the Iranian Tudeh Party held talks in Rome with a group of PCI officials (ibid., 4 and 29 July).

Other Communist Groups. The Party of Proletarian Unity for Communism (PDUP) and Proletarian Democracy (DP) compete with the PCI on the left wing of the political spectrum. In the 1979 election, the PDUP obtained six seats in parliament. The DP, though unrepresented in Italian assemblies, does hold a seat in the European Parliament.

A number of self-styled real communist groups have been operating underground for over a decade and have claimed responsibility for acts of political violence against policemen, members of the judiciary, business executives, politicians, prison guards, and journalists. Although a large number of terrorists have been arrested and convicted, the activities of groups such as the Red Brigades continued in 1982. Information provided by arrested terrorists who have chosen to collaborate with authorities indicate that some of the Italian groups have extensive international contacts and support and that a number of nations (Yemen, Libya, Cuba, and some Eastern European countries) have provided financial assistance, training facilities, weapons, and false documents.

Ohio State University   Giacomo Sani

Biography. *Enrico Berlinguer.* Berlinguer was born into a well-to-do landowning family on 25 May 1922 in Sassari, Sardinia, of Catalonian ancestors. His father, Mario, was a lawyer, a Socialist cabinet minister, an antifascist, and an acquaintance of Antonio Gramsci, a PCI founder, who was also a Sardinian. Berlinguer's intellect was honed by political controversy, questioning of authority, and a brief stint as a criminal lawyer. He joined the PCI in 1943 to focus his struggles against Mussolini. Palmiro Togliatti, the liberal PCI leader, who also spent his childhood in Sardinia, became his mentor and guided Berlinguer's rise in the party (at 23 he became a Central Committee member). It was also Togliatti's idea of national communist party independence, as well as an informal consensus among the French, Spanish, and Italian Communists, that resulted in Berlinguer's support of Eurocommunism.

Since the 1960s, Berlinguer has been critical of Moscow-directed party actions, beginning in 1964 with his trip to Moscow to demand an explanation for Khrushchev's ouster and his support of Togliatti's will, a document deploring the Soviets' desire to run Western European communist parties and their lack of concern for human rights. When he was elected deputy secretary general at the Twelfth Congress in 1969, he denounced the Soviet invasion of Czechoslovakia, as he did a decade later that of Afghanistan. He has consistently supported dissident groups, including Solidarity, and has been highly critical of East European governments for their lack of resistance to Soviet pressures. In response, *Pravda* (24 January) and *Kommunist* (no. 2) took the PCI to task for diverging from the Soviet line but never mentioned Berlinguer by name, referring only to the "PCI leadership."

At the Thirteenth Congress in 1972, Berlinguer succeeded Luigi Longo as general secretary, but the PCI made little gain in national politics. In late 1973, he called for a "historic compromise," a possible coalition with the Christian Democrats and Socialists. Although these parties rejected the proposals, the PCI made substantial gains, which may be attributed to its efficient administration of city governments where it was in power (Naples, Florence), and its consequent popular support. Furthermore, to allay the economic disaster threatening Italy, Berlinguer, in 1974, endorsed participation in the European Economic Community. To show his independence from Moscow, he supported NATO membership in 1975 and traveled to Yugoslavia to meet with Tito. Tensions with Moscow escalated to the point that Berlinguer did not attend the Twenty-Sixth Congress of the CPSU in 1981 but sent his deputy Giancarlo Pajetta, who was instrumental in establishing contact with the Chinese Communist Party. There are rumors that Berlinguer is getting old, weary of confrontations with committees and the Secretariat, acting more and more without consultation, and not permitting dissenting views to be published in *L'Unità*. (Sources: *Current Biography*, 1976, pp. 30–32; *World Press Review*, April; *YICA*, 1982, pp. 306–12; *NYT*, 19 and 25 August; *FBIS* 19 and 23 August, 23 September, 23 November; *NYT Biographical Service*, January–June 1978.)

Hoover Institution   Margit N. Grigory

Luxembourg

The pro-Soviet Communist Party of Luxembourg (CPL) played a minor role in Luxembourg's politics prior to World War II. After 1945, the CPL's position improved. Communists were elected to serve in parliament and in several communities. From 1945 to 1947, Luxembourg's cabinet included one communist minister. The best election results were achieved in 1968. The communist vote declined in the elections of 1974 and 1979. In the June 1979 elections, the CPL received 5 percent of the vote. In the first elections to the European Parliament on 10 June 1979, the CPL obtained 5.1 percent. In municipal elections on 12 October 1981, the CPL received 7.2 percent compared with 16 percent in 1975.

Population. 365,000 (1980)
Party. Communist Party of Luxembourg (Parti communiste luxembourgeois; CPL)
Founded. 1921
Membership. 600 members (est.)
Chairman. René Urbany

Executive Committee. 10 members: Aloyse Bisdorff, Joseph Grandgenet, François Hoffmann, Jacques Hoffmann, Fernand Hübsch, Marianne Passeri, Marcel Pütz, Dominique Urbany, René Urbany, Jean Wesquet

Central Committee. 28 full, 6 candidate, and 7 honorary members

Secretariat. 2 members: René Urbany, Dominique Urbany

Last Congress. Twenty-Third, 31 May–1 June 1980

Auxiliary Organizations. Communist Youth Organization (Jeunesse communiste luxembourgeoise); League of Luxembourg Women (Union des femmes luxembourgeoises); several "friendship" organizations

Publications. *Zeitung vum Lëtzeburger Vollek*, official daily, circulation 1,000–5,000 copies

The party leadership is dominated by the Urbany family. Party chairman René Urbany succeeded his father, Dominique, at the first meeting of the Central Committee after the Twenty-Second Party Congress in 1977. Members of the Urbany family hold many key positions in the party and its auxiliaries. René Urbany is also director of the party press. His brother-in-law, Central Committee member François Frisch, heads the organization of former resistance fighters and is also secretary of the Luxembourg Committee for European Security and Cooperation. René Urbany's sister, Yvonne Frisch-Urbany, leads the Soviet-sponsored Pushkin Cultural Center. His father-in-law, Executive Committee member Jacques Hoffmann, serves on the executive board of the communist printing company Cooperative ouvrière de press et d'édition (COPE).

The usefulness of the CPL for the Soviet Union is primarily its propaganda value. For example, a Soviet-produced letter allegedly written by Gen. Alexander Haig when he left the NATO command in June 1979 and addressed to NATO Secretary General Joseph Luns, was published on 10 May 1982 in *Zeitung vum Lëtzeburger Vollek*. This "letter" dealt with a possible nuclear first strike. The publication of this falsification was timed to give support to the anti–nuclear weapons demonstrations in the West. (International Communication Agency, *Amerikadienst*, 28 July, pp. 5–6.)

Contacts with fraternal parties were maintained during 1982. A Soviet party delegation headed by Leonid A. Gorshkov, first secretary of a district committee, visited Luxembourg at the end of June following an invitation from the "leadership of the CPL" (*Pravda*, 2 July; *FBIS*, 14 July). In February, CPL chairman René Urbany "exchanged views" in East Berlin with East German Politburo member and secretary of the Central Committee Hermann Axen. They came to the conclusion "that the large scale anti-communist and anti-Soviet incitement campaign conducted by imperialism calls for the continued consolidation of the unity of action of the communist government." (ADN, 26 February; *FBIS*, 1 March.) In June a group of CPL activists, headed by François Hoffmann, visited the Central Committee of the Armenian Communist Party (*Sovetakan ayastan*, 20 June; *FBIS*, 9 July). On 27–30 September, René Urbany paid a visit to Hungary and conferred with János Kádár, head of the Hungarian party (MTI, 30 September; *FBIS*, 1 October).

COPE, the CPL's publishing company, prints the French edition of the *World Marxist Review*. COPE's new and modern technical equipment and production facilities, exceeding by far local requirements, serve communist parties and organizations in several other countries.

University of Calgary   Eric Waldman

Malta

The Communist Party of Malta (CPM) was founded in 1969, four years after the island gained its independence from the United Kingdom. The founders were former members of the Malta Labor Party (MLP), who had united for the country's independence struggle, even though many openly espoused communist principles during the colonial period. From its initial secret congress in the island town of Gwardamangia, the CPM's leading figure has been Anthony Vassallo, the party's first and only secretary general. Legal since its inception, the CPM describes itself as a "voluntary organization made up of the most politically conscious members of the workers' class, together with others who are exploited by the capitalist system, who are determined to found a Socialist Malta" (*Proletarjat*, no. 1). The current strength of the CPM is estimated to be some 150 members, not including members of the various communist front organizations. According to the official census of 1981, the population of the Republic of Malta is 330,262, with a density of 2,600 persons per square mile.

Leadership and Organization. The CPM is headed by a Central Committee, elected at a party congress held about every three years. The Central Committee elected at the Second Congress in February 1979 consisted of Chairman Anthony Baldacchino, who is a shipwright and a General Workers' Union shop steward at the Malta Drydocks; Secretary General Anthony Vassallo, who is a careerist in the CPM; International Secretary Paul Agius, who is vice-president of the Malta-USSR Friendship Society and general secretary of the Malta Peace Committee; Education and Propaganda Secretary Mario Vella Macina, who is former head of the Communist Youth League (CYL) and an economist at the government-operated Malta Development Corporation; Documentation Secretary Lilian Sciberras, who is former international secretary of the CYL and assistant librarian at the University of Malta; and John Agius, Philip Bugeja, Renald Galea, Mario Mifsud, John Muscat, and Paul Muscat.

The CPM has close contact with some disgruntled members of the ruling MLP. That party rests its philosophy on a social democratic basis, which the Communists openly oppose. It is believed that a substantial number of Communists are also members of the MLP, despite that party's policy of prohibiting such dual memberships. In addition, CPM operatives have infiltrated the government-controlled General Workers' Union, which is the island's largest, comprising more than 50 percent of organized workers in the country. In the early 1970s, the CPM also established the League for Social Justice, in a largely unsuccessful effort to appeal to students at the island's two universities, who tend to be more socialist- than communist-oriented. Under the auspices of the Malta-USSR Friendship and Cultural Society, a number of Maltese students have been sent to Soviet or Eastern bloc universities. Guzeppi Schembri, the first graduate from a Russian university (in 1981), is now employed in the Foreign Office of the republic.

The ceremonial head of state for the Republic of Malta is the president, Agatha Barbara, a 59-year-old former teacher and cabinet minister, who was elected by the parliament for a five-year term in 1982. Malta's government is led by Bulgarian-born Prime Minister Dominic Mintoff, leader of the MLP, who has held this office since 1971. The MLP regained control of the 65-member parliament in the December 1981 elections, with the full support of the CPM, over the church-dominated Nationalist Party and the conservative Christian Democratic Party. While the CPM has often declared its intent to field its own candidates in parliamentary elections, no CPM members ran under the party's banner in the 1981 contests.

Party Internal Affairs. The leadership of the CPM is stable, and party members are loyal and obedient. The CPM exercises its influence through the MLP government "primarily toward improving the working and living conditions of the working people" (*Népszabadság*, Budapest, 14 July). In order "to prevent a division of the democratic forces," the CPM chooses not to "take away votes" from the ruling MLP. Thus, a major problem of the CPM is to keep its identity while ostensibly being an operational adjunct of Prime Minister Mintoff's government. Apparently, the CPM leadership has decided to work behind the scenes for the time being rather than to engage in polemics with the other political parties. There was public acknowledgment of the CPM role, for example, in the spate of agreements signed between the USSR and Malta in 1981. Also, in 1981, the CPM was successful in its efforts to establish a Soviet embassy in Malta. If there have been any disagreements or purges within the CPM in the past thirteen years, little publicity has been made of them.

Domestic Affairs. A major goal of the CPM is "to oppose the concessions being made to domestic and foreign capital and to resolve the country's social problems on the basis of socialist concepts" (ibid.). Despite substantial economic progress, unemployment remains one of Malta's principal problems. The CPM was successful in helping to eliminate the British military presence when the base agreement expired in 1979. But with that accomplishment came the gradual loss of 11,000 Maltese jobs at the military bases. Even though Soviet ships gained the use of former NATO oil facilities in 1981, the benefit to indigenous employment was slight. As a consequence of that nagging problem, the CPM claims that the MLP "lost voters among the workers and small artisans, as well as working people employed in the service sectors," to the Nationalist Party in the 1981 elections (ibid.). Although the CPM continues to criticize the government on certain domestic political issues, the only positive suggestion that the island's Communists seem to offer is for Malta to continue to seek economic assistance from the Eastern bloc countries. To that end, a trade protocol was signed between Bulgaria and Malta in July to "start joint production of electric motors, pumps and light industry products." Also, an agreement was reached on inaugurating freighter service between Bulgaria and Malta, "which will contribute to making the economic relations brisker" (BTA, Sofia, 1 July).

Foreign Affairs. In contrast to domestic policy, the CPM generally supports the government's foreign policy and concurs with "the policy of nonalignment, which is most consistent with the country's interests." The CPM believes that relations with the European countries are very important to solving the problems that ensued in Malta "following the departure of the British, the economic transformation . . . [and] the crises besetting the world economy." However, nothing is more important to Maltese Communists "than preserving peace and security." As for tensions in the Mediterranean area and the Middle East, the CPM supports "the struggle of the people of Cyprus against military bases, as well as that of the Italian working people against the establishment of missile bases in Sicily . . . [and] the struggle of the Palestinian people for their own homeland and human rights." Moreover, the CPM condemns "Israel's Lebanon aggression" and renounces "a military solution of disputed issues." (*Népszabadság*, 14 July.)

International Party Contacts. According to the CPM's own estimation, its "international relations are extensive . . . with regular bilateral meetings taking place." However, the CPM hopes for "additional opportunities to develop further relations with the communist parties of the socialist countries." Regarding disputes among communist parties, the CPM leadership feels that these "must be constructive, avoiding any intervention in other parties' internal affairs." Furthermore, "the unity and collaboration of the communist and workers' parties constitute an indispensable prerequisite for preserving the security of mankind and world peace." (Ibid.)

On the occasion of the fifteenth anniversary of the establishment of diplomatic relations between the Soviet Union and Malta, the former sent greetings, noting that "the ties between our country and the small Mediterranean Republic of Malta have developed particularly fruitfully in recent years." The report also mentioned the visit in January of Maltese Foreign Minister Alex Sceberras Trigona to Moscow, which resulted in a communiqué devoted to the Mediterranean area, "where it is the concern of all involved states to turn the region into a zone of stable peace and international cooperation." (Moscow domestic service, 26 July.) Following that visit, an agreement was signed between the USSR and Malta "on cooperation in culture, education and science" (Tass, 18 March).

Prime Minister Dom Mintoff paid an official visit to Bulgaria in July where he was "greeted with military honors." In June, the prime minister made an official seven-day visit to the People's Republic of China, where he expressed confidence "that the dialogue started ten years ago between our two countries will continue for many years to come in a spirit of friendship, trust and mutual respect" (NCNA, Beijing, 28 June). The CPM did not comment officially about the visit to China, but it is believed that the Maltese Communists support the USSR in the Sino-Soviet dispute.

Publications. *Proletarjat*, begun in October 1977 and suspended with issue number 13 in April 1979, was an early bilingual publication of the CPM. It was replaced in May 1980 by a monthly newspaper in Maltese, *Zminijietna* (Our times), aimed at factory workers rather than the party faithful. The CYL published a mimeographed bilingual journal, *Spartakus*, issued three times during 1977-1978. Another CYL mimeographed journal, *Il Bandiera l-Hamra* (Red flag), began publishing in 1981. Communist publications are available at the offices of the Progressive Bookshop and Progressive Tours, Ltd., which is owned by Paul Agius. These profitable enterprises represent Eastern bloc commercial interests and constitute the main source of CPM operating funds.

Washington, D.C.   T.W. Adams

Netherlands

The Communist Party of the Netherlands (CPN) was founded in 1909 as the Social Democratic Party (Sociaal-Democratische Partij) by radical Marxists; it assumed the name Communist Party of Holland (Communistische Partij Holland) in 1919 when the party affiliated with the Comintern. The present name dates from 1935. The party has always been legal except during World War II.

Population. 14,288,901 (1 January)

Party. Communist Party of the Netherlands (Communistische Partij van Nederland; CPN)

Founded. 1909

Membership. 15,000; older component of industrial workers (coal, textile, shipbuilding), younger group of intellectuals, women, social workers

Chairperson. Elli Izeboud

Executive Committee. 10 members: Elli Izeboud, Ina Brouwer, Joop Wolff, John Geelen, Karel Hoogkamp, Boe Thio, Simone Walvisch, Barth Schmidt, Frank Biesboer, Ton van Hoek

Secretariat. 3 members. John Geelen (secretary)

Central Committee. 55 members

Last Congress. Twenty-Eighth, 26–28 November; next congress scheduled for late 1983

Auxiliary Organizations. General Netherlands Youth Organization; Netherlands Women's Movement; also active and heavily represented in peace movement's umbrella organization, Stop the Neutron Bomb—Stop the Nuclear Arms Race Committee

Elections. Won 1.9 percent of the vote in September general election (down from 2.05 percent in 1981), elected 3 delegates (Ina Brouwer, Gijs Schreuders, Evelien Eshuis) to 150-member parliament; won 1.95 percent of vote in March provincial elections

Publications. *De Waarheid* (Truth), official daily, circulation 20,000–25,000; *CPN leden-krant*, new publication for CPN members, appears 10 times a year; *Politick en Cultuur*, CPN theoretical journal, appears 10 times a year; *Komma*, quarterly issued by CPN's Institute for Political and Social Research; CPN owns Pegasus Publishers and operates 2 printing plants.

The CPN's "new coalition policy," adopted at the Twenty-Sixth Party Congress in 1978, underwent a radical change in 1982. This change was more psychological than political. Increased cooperation with the small leftist parties brought about by the new coalition policy in the national elections in September did not affect the size of CPN representation in the lower chamber of the Dutch parliament, nor did it lead to further cooperation with the Labor Party, which, with 30.4 percent of the vote, became the largest party in the Netherlands.

Insofar as the new coalition policy was intended to make the CPN appear more democratic and open, it encouraged those within the party who believed in more party democratization. This group, about 80 percent of the CPN, composed of women, intellectuals, social workers, and students, was able to capture the leadership of the party at the Twenty-Eighth Congress and to affect wide-ranging changes in overall CPN strategy. The radical nature of these changes was demonstrated by the demand of orthodox CPN members for a return to the ideological principles of Marxism-Leninism and to the organizational principle of democratic centralism and by the development of significant opposition among traditional CPN members to the new leadership. Furthermore, the Labor Party, while distancing itself from the attempt of the CPN to pool their voting lists in both the March provincial and the September general elections, is responding positively to the new situation within the CPN.

The CPN's first priority—the effort to influence the government on the stationing of intermediate-range nuclear missiles in the Netherlands—has not significantly changed, although its emphasis on eliminating military blocs and its critical views on Soviet armament policies have led to sharp debate within the party. While in 1981 orthodoxy prevailed within the CPN, the Twenty-Eighth Congress demonstrated that this is no longer the case. The consequences of this change cannot be predicted with any certainty. But since the traditional source of CPN rank-and-file membership has largely disappeared due to structural changes in the Dutch economy, it is questionable whether the CPN can remain a viable political party.

Party Internal Affairs. The new Central Committee elected at the Twenty-Eighth Congress consists of 55 members or 18 less than the previous committee. According to *CPN leden-krant* (no.9), 24 were new members and female membership increased from 14 (19 percent) to 19 (34 percent). On 11 December, the Central Committee chose Elli Izeboud, age 33 to replace Henk Hoekstra, 57, as chairperson of the party. Izeboud is a corporation sociologist and has been active in the student and feminist movements. She was chosen as a member of the Central Committee in 1978 and has functioned as deputy chairman for two years.

The Twenty-Eighth Congress of the CPN confirmed the policy of renewal as set forth in a new draft party program published in December 1981 under the authority of former chairman Henk Hoekstra. The new program replaces the old program dating from 1946. The resolution adopted at the congress supports the call from within the party for further democratization. The principal features of this new policy of renewal are to integrate the women's movement into the CPN program, to grant the party's newspaper, *De Waarheid*, editorial independence, to push forward with the new coalition policy, and to break relations with the communist parties of Poland and Czechoslovakia.

The resolution also called for a change of internal organization. It recommended the creation of a party council, the creation of a special foreign affairs commission to determine foreign policy, the direct election of the Executive Committee by the Central Committee, and a change in election procedures whereby election to the party congress will be from party sections instead of districts.

The purpose of the new draft party program, according to Hoekstra, is to form "a new type of communist party" committed to bringing about a "parliamentary, democratic-socialist form of government." The question arises whether this attempt to affect changes in the party, which the CPN hopes will be acceptable to other leftist parties, can be taken seriously. If the CPN's new coalition policy is to be successful, the CPN must give up the ideological doctrine of Marxism-Leninism. Thus far, no clear denial of the doctrine has been made by the leadership of the party. Also, the draft program rejects the "outmoded dogmatic notion of democratic centralism," yet no assurances have been given that socialism and democracy are inseparable. If that is true, as has been suggested by the CPN, then the CPN must deny that the Soviet Union is a socialist country. In late 1983, the CPN is to hold an extraordinary congress to decide on adopting the new program.

These ambiguities in the draft party program have caused considerable disquiet among old CPN members who were expelled from the party in the late 1950s and 1960s and among those "real Communists" in the party who accept that change is necessary, but must proceed at a slower pace. The latter have organized the Horizontal Consultation of Communists outside the party in order to challenge the new policy. They claim the new draft party program dilutes the class struggle and threatens the identity of the party when operating in the new coalition.

This debate has been complicated by the successful attempt of the new party leadership, led by Chairperson Elli Izeboud and Ina Brouwer with the tacit support of Hoekstra, to de-Stalinize the party. The Twenty-Eighth Congress withdrew party support from a report issued by the CPN in 1958 entitled "The CPN in the War." The report was written by Marcus Bakker under instructions from the party chairman Paul de Groot. It resulted in the expulsion of several members of the party. While accused of working against party interests through espionage activities on behalf of the British, they were in fact expelled for attempting to de-Stalinize the party following Khrushchev's revelations. Since this period, no attempt has been made by the party leadership to reveal these facts. The party, for this reason, has been suspect to the other leftist parties in the Netherlands.

Domestic Affairs. The main objective of the CPN in 1982 was to prevent the election of a new center-right coalition cabinet in the September general election. The strategy adopted by the CPN was to pool election lists with small leftist parties and progressive parties. The pooling of election lists is a technical arrangement to help increase the possibility of capturing parliamentary seats under the proportional representation system. Such a coalition policy was accepted in some sections of the Socialist Pacifist Party and the Political Radical Party in the March and the September elections. The poor overall performance of the CPN in these elections was due to the reluctance of many to accept such a coalition policy with the CPN due to their "revolutionary élan" and to the usurpation of the nuclear missile issue by the Labor Party. The Labor Party resisted all efforts to implement a coalition policy with the CPN and thus frustrated the attempts of the CPN to pool voting lists.

A second objective of the CPN was to continue its attempts to influence nonparliamentary organizations by placing its members in the leadership of these organizations. One particular example of the effectiveness of this policy is CPN influence over some sections of the Netherlands' Federation of Trade Unions (FNV) in proportion to its membership in the union, which is less than 1 percent. The CPN has been successful in placing several members on the FNV sections dealing with research and education and the contact group dealing with youth. Hanneke Jagersman became the first CPN mayor in the Netherlands with her appointment in Beerta in the province of Groningen.

In support of this policy, the CPN, together with trade union members and members of other leftist parties, formed the Dialogue of Driebergen in November 1981. Although the initial conferences of this group attracted few participants, mostly CPN members, the group did adopt a draft action plan in early 1982 and will hold a special congress in January 1983 on the problem of a "progressive" response to the current parliamentary situation.

The CPN's activities in the peace campaign were kept under cover in 1982. The CPN had managed to gain an international reputation due to its Stop the Neutron Bomb campaign, but the Polish situation and allegations of Soviet financial assistance for the peace campaign have forced the CPN to play down the issue. The CPN still considers peace and security its number-one priority. In this context, a conference took place in Amsterdam on 13–14 February with 30 peace groups from 25 countries in attendance. Most of the participants had close relations with the Soviet-front World Peace Council. The conference dealt with questions of strategy in connection with the development of the peace campaign in 1982. The conference took place after discussions in Amsterdam between a Soviet delegation led by A. P. Popov of the foreign affairs section of the Soviet Central Committee and Nico Schouten, a CPN member who heads the umbrella peace organization, Stop the Neutron Bomb–Stop the Arms Race Committee. Present at the conference was a delegation from the Czechoslovak Peace Committee.

Foreign Affairs and International Party Contacts. The imposition of martial law on 13 December 1981 in Poland has played an important role in CPN foreign activities. On 14 December 1981, the CPN became the first Dutch political party to condemn martial law. The resolution adopted by the Twenty-Eighth Congress formally broke ties with the Polish party and supported Solidarity. The Twenty-Eighth Congress also broke off relations with the Communist Party of Czechoslovakia in favor of Charter '77. With respect to the Soviet Union, the CPN declared that the Soviet party was no longer the "automatic and natural partner in the struggle against the buildup of arms and the danger of war."

These views, which have been well known since the publication of the new draft party program in late December 1981, did not prevent a large Soviet delegation from visiting the Netherlands in January 1982. The purpose of the visit was to determine if the CPN would support the international peace campaign and show solidarity with the socialist countries. The peace issue was no doubt also discussed in a meeting in September 1982 in the Netherlands between Hoekstra and Vadim V. Zagladin, the first deputy chief of the Soviet Central Committee's International Department. Nevertheless, CPN relations with the USSR and other East European countries are undergoing scrutiny because of the party's stand on Poland and Czechoslovakia. Moscow did not issue invitations to the CPN to attend Brezhnev's funeral nor was the CPN formally notified of his death. *Rudé právo*, the organ of the Czechoslovak party, severely attacked the CPN in December for supporting "underworld movements" both in Czechoslovakia and in Poland. The newspaper also strongly objected to CPN opposition to an international conference of communist parties.

The high priority given to the peace campaign by the CPN and its solidarity with the international communist movement on the peace issue probably prevented agreement with the Chinese Communist Party on the extension of relations between the two parties during a visit to China in early June by Hoekstra.

Because the CPN gives highest priority to peace and security, it does participate in actions with the international communist movement. For example, it helped the Italian Communist Party set up a campaign against the deployment of intermediate-range nuclear missiles in Sicily. The Comiso Committee created in the Netherlands to support action against nuclear missile deployment in Sicily consists of groups in the Netherlands including the umbrella peace organization, Stop the Neutron Bomb–Stop the Nuclear Arms Race Committee.

International Documentation and Information Centre   C. C. van den Heuvel
The Hague

Norway

The Norwegian Communist Party (NKP) remained on the periphery of Norwegian politics in 1982. The September 1981 parliamentary elections, in which the NKP received only 7,025 votes (0.3 percent), confirmed it as the country's least popular party, Marxist or otherwise. The NKP has been very weak since its decision in 1975 not to merge with several left socialist parties and factions. This decision split the party and caused its chairman, Reidar T. Larsen, and several other leaders to leave the NKP for the new Socialist Left Party (Sosialistisk Venstreparti; SV). The SV has since been the strongest of several parties to the left of the Norwegian Labor Party (Det Norske Arbeiderparti; DNA), which is a reformist social-democratic movement and the main governing party since 1945. Gains by the conservatives in the 1981 elections forced Labor into opposition as Kaare Willoch formed a conservative government resting on parliamentary support from several other nonsocialist parties. Labor remains, however, the country's strongest political party. The third active Marxist party is the Maoist Workers' Communist Party (Arbeidernes Kommunistiske Parti; AKP), which has run in the last three parliamentary elections as the Red Electoral Alliance (Rod Valgallians; RV).

Collectively, the three Marxist parties have captured less than 6 percent of the vote in recent elections. Nowhere in the Nordic region is the Marxist left weaker electorially. Even the SV, which doubled its parliamentary seats (from 2 to 4 in the 155-seat Storting), gained principally at the expense of the DNA. Norwegian politics has operated under special conditions for the past decade, as rich domestic petroleum resources have shielded the country from the economic recession plaguing most of the world. The Norwegian economy faltered somewhat in 1982. Falling oil prices and oil demand stopped economic expansion. The Norwegian gross national product is expected to decline marginally in 1982 (− 0.1 percent), but slow growth is expected to resume in 1983. With unemployment generally below 3 percent, Norway is the envy of nearly every other industrial economy. (*Nordisk Kontakt*, no. 13.)

Norwegian Communists faced another year of political insignificance. Issues such as the economy, regional development, defense policy, and global concerns remained important on the NKP agenda, but the Communists' views were rarely of interest and never of significance to their fellow citizens.

Population. 4,100,000 (1982 est.)

Party. Norwegian Communist Party (Norges Kommunistiske Parti; NKP)

Founded. 1923

Chairman. Hans I. Kleven (elected December 1981)

Central Committee. 15 full members: Hans I. Kleven (chairman), Arne Jorgensen (vice-chairman and editor of *Friheten*), Trygve Horgen (deputy vice-chairman), Odd S. Karlsen (organizing secretary), Martin Gunnar Knutsen (past chairman), Asmund Langsether, Rolf Dahl, Gunnar Wahl, Rolf Galgerud, Bjarne Baltzersen, Grete Johansen, Kare Andre Nilsen, Berit Frederiksen, Bjorn Kjenong, Arvid Borglund. 8 substitute members: Bjorn Naustvik, Harald Holm, Henning Solhaug, Ornulf Godager, Unni Kinn, Egil Andersen, Kirsti Kristiansen, Alf Ingum

National Executive Committee. 35 members and 47 substitute members

Last Congress. Seventeenth, 4–6 December 1981, in Oslo; next congress scheduled for 1985

Auxiliary Organizations. Norwegian Communist Youth League (Kommunistisk Ungdom; NKU)

Publications. *Friheten* (Freedom), semi-weekly, published in Oslo

Party Internal Affairs. Two events dominated the NKP's internal affairs during 1982: the party's Seventeenth Congress held in Oslo in early December 1981, and the election of Hans I. Kleven to the party chairmanship at a National Executive Committee meeting in late January 1982. Kleven, a 55-year-old lawyer and civil servant and a party member since 1945, had been vice-chairman. He replaced Martin Gunnar Knutsen, a 63-year-old primary school principal, who had been chairman since the 1975 split.

Eighteen of the 35 Executive Committee votes were cast for Kleven. Seventeen went to Arne Jorgensen, editor of *Friheten*. Jorgensen was unanimously elected vice-chairman, and Trygve Horgen was elected deputy vice-chairman. Horgen is new to the party leadership and is deputy chairman of the Bergen branch of the Iron and Metal Workers Union.

Knutsen claimed his resignation stemmed from conflicts between his work and the time demands of the party chairmanship. Hans Kleven indicated that he intends to take a leave of absence from his government job to serve as a full-time salaried party chairman. (*Friheten*, 26 January.)

The issue of the party chairmanship had arisen at the party congress, but had been postponed eight weeks to prevent the competition from spilling over into public debate. NKP congresses are closed to the press, unlike those of other Norwegian parties (except the AKP). Although Knutsen's statement about resigning because of work pressures is credible, some noted that the party had made no progress under his leadership (*Arbeiderbladet*, 31 December 1981).

Arne Jorgensen's unanimous re-election as editor of *Friheten*, his election as vice-chairman, and Knutsen's election to the National Executive after his resignation indicate that there are no serious party feuds (*Aftenposten*, 25 January). Upon his election, Kleven reiterated the party's program adopted at the recent congress. There was no objection, for example, to the imposition of martial law in Poland, which had occurred since the NKP congress. Commentators outside the party stressed the party's isolation and decline. Although exact figures are not made public, current NKP membership is considerably reduced from the 2,000 to 5,000 estimated before the 1975 schism. Disillusionment on the Norwegian left with Soviet policies toward Afghanistan and Poland have hurt the NKP, which never criticizes Soviet actions. A generational crisis is another internal threat to the NKP. Most of its remaining members stem from the World War II generation, whose attachment to the Communists' role in the resistance movement has been unshakable. Such attitudes have held a loyal core but produced few new members in recent years.

Non-NKP journalists suggest that there may be more dissatisfaction within the NKP. The party's youth affiliate, the NKU, has been critical of the party's indifference to events in Poland. NKU Chairman Henning Solhaug obejcted to the declaration of martial law in Poland and the arrest of Solidarity trade union officials. Solhaug would not specifically blame the Soviet Union for events in Poland, however. (*Klassekampen*, 22 December 1981.)

Domestic Affairs. The NKP's minimal electoral support precludes even a protest role in national, regional, or local politics. Only through its semiweekly newspaper and occasional notice by the noncommunist press do its views receive national circulation. The 1981 congress did not alter the domestic program issued several months earlier in connection with the parliamentary elections. That program too is unchanged since 1973, before the party schism. Among the main points were increased state subsidies for collective housing construction, price controls, higher social security payments, longer paid vacations, shorter working hours, and additional employee control over management. Tax reform is stressed, with heavier taxes on higher incomes to replace taxes on low incomes and advocacy of a value-added tax. These proposals do not differ significantly from either the SV's or RV's, and they highlight the NKP's problem in projecting a distinctive profile.

The effects of the world recession and petroleum glut on Norway were felt in stagnating incomes and rapidly rising unemployment levels. Various public opinion polls during 1982 showed modest gains for the opposition Labor Party, stability for the SV, while neither the NKP nor the AKP had enough support to be registered. County and municipal councils will hold elections in 1983.

The larger trade unions, as well as the Norwegian Trade Union Confederation, are firmly controlled by Laborites. The NKP has traditionally been stronger in the trade union movement than in electoral politics, and a large proportion of its members are industrial workers than is the case with the SV or AKP. The NKP's new deputy vice-chairman, Trygve Horgen, is a union official from Bergen. Radical groups are most common in the Construction Workers Union, where unemployment has been high in recent years. They are also visible in the metal, wood, and electrochemical fields, particularly in the older industrial cities of the eastern and north-central parts of the country.

Foreign Affairs. The international views of the NKP remain constant. Those members who seek more nuanced positions or object to events in Afghanistan and Poland either leave the party (and many have done so) or remain silent. Thus, the NKP remains unswervingly loyal to the principles of "proletarian internationalism" and Soviet foreign policy. The Seventeenth Congress confirmed this position and stressed that the two main foreign policy issues currently of concern to the NKP were the campaign against new nuclear weapons in Europe (presumably new NATO weapons) and the establishment of a nuclear-free zone in the Nordic region (*Friheten*, 8 December 1981). This is consistent with the party's traditional anti-NATO stance, and its special concern with NATO plans involving Norway. In recent years, the NKP has joined with other far-left groups to oppose NATO theater nuclear forces, development of the neutron bomb, and the pre-positioning of NATO supplies in Norway. On some of these issues, there is consensus on the political left, including elements of the Labor Party and nonsocialist parties. Thus, the NKP role is neither distinctive nor influential.

What does distinguish the NKP from other socialist parties is its refusal to criticize any aspect of current Soviet foreign policy. Although elements of the NKU have questioned events in Afghanistan and

Poland, the NKP leadership remains silent. Soviet-Norwegian relations have been strained in a number of areas in recent years, including the demarcation of territorial limits in the Barents Sea, Soviet activities on Svalbard, and occasional Soviet violations of Norwegian waters and airspace. In November, a Soviet icebreaker refused to leave Norwegian waters until Norwegian patrol craft threatened to open fire (*Los Angeles Times*, 11 November). From the mid-1960s until the schism of 1975, the NKP had adopted a nonaligned policy and had criticized the Soviet intervention in Czechoslovakia. Those who remain in the NKP are now among the most consistently pro-Soviet of the West European communist parties. The new party chairman, Hans Kleven, wrote in support of Soviet military intervention in Eastern Europe several years ago.

International Party Contacts. The NKP foreign policy position assures it of close ties to the Soviet party and other pro-Soviet movements. The Soviet party sent both fraternal greetings and a delegation to the NKP Seventeenth Congress. The latter was headed by Karl G. Vaino, Central Committee member and first secretary of the Estonian party. NKP support for Soviet foreign policy, especially in Europe, was noted in the congress's declaration (*Pravda*, 4 December 1981).

In April, Kleven led a party delegation to Prague. A meeting was held with Czechoslovak party chief Gustáv Husák in which the two party leaders exchanged information and views. On foreign policy matters, the two leaders were in complete agreement. (Prague domestic radio, 14 April.)

In late September, Trygve Horgen led a delegation to the Soviet Union. Moscow and Minsk were the two main points on the itinerary, and talks were held with the Soviet Central Committee's International Department (*Pravda*, 29 September). Such visits are important to the orientation and morale of the younger NKP activists since older members have occasionally maintained very close personal ties with the USSR. Ex-chairman Martin Knutsen lived in Moscow from 1952 to 1955 while studying education. He also worked for the Soviet radio service (*Ny Tid*, 18 November 1981).

Other Marxist/Left-Socialist Groups. The SV absorbed many Communists when it was formed in 1975 out of the Socialist Electoral Alliance (Socialistisk Valgallians), which captured sixteen parliamentary seats in the 1973 elections. The AKP/RV has maintained an independent position since it was organized in 1972. Its lineage, like that of the SV, can be traced back to the Socialist People's Party (Sosialistisk Folkeparti; SF),which was formed in 1961 by dissident Laborites including Finn Gustavsen.

In a small country, personalities are crucial in the small parties. Internal SV affairs are discussed quite openly both in the general press and in the party's own newspaper, *Ny Tid* (New times). Unlike the NKP and AKP, SV congresses are open to outside observers. Few commentators doubt that the SV members are committed to democratic procedures within the party and in the country at large. They are, in brief, pragmatic Marxists, who do not find the Leninist tradition relevant to modern Norway. They are willing, however, to support foreign Marxist movements less committed to Western parliamentary and constitutional traditions.

The SV leadership has remained stable during the past few years. This will change in 1983 because the current party chairman, Tromso University lecturer Berge Furre, has announced that he will not seek re-election at the SV congress scheduled for March 1983. The SV's youth affiliate, Socialist Youth (Sosialistisk Unodom; SU), has not been as harmonious. At the SU congress in Oslo in November 1981, there was a bitter clash between the Oslo branch, generally more radical,and the provincial branches. The organization managed to expel dissidents through reconstitution (a legal maneuver), and Oystein Gudim emerged again as chairman of the new SU. The "purified" (of more radical elements) SU will be able to support the SV's domestic and foreign policy line more consistently, the chairman explained (*Klassekampen*, 16 November 1981).

The third Marxist faction in Norway more closely resembles the NKP in ideology and internal procedures. Its meetings are closed, and there is little public discussion among party members. The AKP evolved in the early 1970s from radical student and youth movements. Originally very much attracted to Maoism, it is now less attached to foreign models such as China and Albania. Paal Steigan has been the party's only chairman. The AKP uses an electoral front, the RV, to attract a wider range of leftist votes. Although the RV has gained votes in recent elections, it is still a very small movement. Reports during the year indicate that despite representations to the contrary, the RV is fully subservient to the AKP Central Committee (*Arbeiderbladet*, 4 January).

The two leftist alternatives to the NKP differ in both program and procedure on Norwegian domestic politics. With its four parliamentary seats, the SV is able to make its views known. Parliamentary questioning, committees, and other tactics allow the SV to affect the public debate. Although the SV doubled its small parliamentary delegation in 1981, the movement of the Labor Party into opposition weakened the SV's political clout. Between 1975 and 1981, the Labor government occasionally had to rely on the SV's two votes to prevail. The SV and its predecessor of the 1960s, the SF, have had some influence, chiefly in domestic politics, through this small but crucial margin of support. Loss of influence with the nonsocialist government has not modified the SV's domestic political goals. The 1981 electoral program called for a six-hour workday and stressed greater support for local social programs. Norwegian oil and its utilization have produced several inconsistencies in the SV position. On the one hand, the SV is very much concerned about environmental, regional developmental, and occupational safety issues. On the other hand, the country's large petroleum revenues have become the fiscal *deus ex machina* for implementing the SV's expensive domestic program

The AKP's most recent statement of domestic political goals is contained in the RV electoral program for 1981. The RV no longer bases its plans for a socialist Norway on any foreign models, and its domestic program differs little from either the NKP's or SV's.

Foreign and international affairs are the major concern of the SV. The SV's political and ideological precursor, the SF, was formed in 1961 by Laborites who objected mainly to the Labor Party's pro-NATO and pro-Western policies. The 1972 campaign over Norwegian membership in the European Economic Community revived and established the SV. Hence, the party vigorously pursues foreign and security policy questions. These loomed large in Norwegian politics in 1982. As the international situation remained tense, the SV ceased to be the only mouthpiece for neutralist Norwegians. Fears about East-West relations brought out anti-NATO and, in some cases, pacifist elements in most political parties, socialist and nonsocialist alike. Ironically, international developments have strengthened the attachment of the Norwegian public to NATO, but they have also made opposition groups more active and militant. The SV, AKP, and NKP are all opposed to the so-called dual track NATO policy of preparing for a modernization of NATO nuclear forces if negotiations with the Soviet Union fail to reduce or eliminate new Soviet nuclear weapons intended for use against West European targets. An important development in 1982 was the shift by the leadership of the Labor Party into opposition to Norwegian financial support (small but symbolic) for the NATO nuclear modernization (Radio Norway, 5 October). The new position generated enormous tension within the Labor Party and between the party and the nonsocialist parties. Since 1949, Labor and the nonsocialists, with the Liberals occasionally wavering, have consistently supported NATO. In June, 21 Laborites joined the SV and seven nonsocialists in voting against NATO's nuclear policies. With a decision in October by the Labor Executive Committee to oppose these policies more strongly unless there is progress in the U.S.-Soviet negotiations, the conservative government's defense policies may be in jeopardy (*Nordisk Kontakt*, no. 11; *NYT*, 3 October). This is a substantial boost for the SV's foreign policy line.

A second element in the far left's foreign policies is the concept of a Nordic nuclear weapons–free zone embracing Finland, Sweden, Denmark, Norway, and Iceland. The Soviet Union has obviously encouraged this movement without committing the Warsaw Pact or Soviet territory or the international waters of the Baltic. Soviet credibility was substantially weakened by the U-137 submarine affair in Swedish coastal waters in the autumn of 1981. The SV was critical of Soviet behavior but felt the incident stressed the importance of creating a nuclear-free zone (*Ny Tid*, 11 November 1981). The SV also presented a detailed, nonaligned, nonnuclear alternative defense plan for Norway in November 1981. In brief, the SV plans call for four-month universal military service with annual exercises and decentralized, local defense effort, devoid of high-technology weapons (including apparently aircraft and any naval craft larger than a patrol boat) (ibid., 2 December 1981). With the new socialist government in Stockholm committed to negotiation on the Nordic nuclear-free zone, the issue is likely to remain prominent in Norway and the other Scandinavian states. The issue is puzzling to some outside observers because no Scandinavian country has either nuclear weapons or foreign forces on its territory. These national positions are not limited by treaty, except for nuclear weapons. (*Orbis*, Summer, pp. 451–76.)

University of Massachusetts
Amherst

Eric S. Einhorn

Portugal

The communist movement had the tightest and most influential organization of all opposition groups in Portugal during 47 years of underground operation. During the first two years following the 1974 overthrow of the dictatorship, Communists significantly infiltrated and extended their control over key areas of national life—labor, the armed forces, farmworkers' collectives in southern Portugal, students, news media, and national and local government. After a frustrated 1976 coup attempt, Communists have been excluded from the cabinet, and their impact has been much diminished—except in the labor movement. The party remains the most Stalinist, pro-Soviet group in Western Europe. Numerous radical-left groups, principally Maoist and Trotskyist splinterings who in the 1960s rejected the more moderate policies of the "revisionist" pro-Moscow Communists, flourished after 1974 but have languished in recent years.

Population. 9,964,540

Party. Portuguese Communist Party (Partido Comunista Português; PCP)

Founded. 1921

Membership. 187,000 in early 1982 (1980 figures still cited by party [PAP, Warsaw, 9 April]), compared with 100,000 in 1975, 15,000 in 1974. The PCP announced 5,699 new members recruited in first half of 1982 (*Militante*, August) and claims more card-carrying members than any other political party in Portugal.

Secretary General. Alvaro Cunhal, since 1961; in every cabinet for almost two years following 1974 revolution, but has since been excluded from government

Secretariat. 7 members: Jorge Araújo, Carlos Costa, Alvaro Cunhal, Joaquim Gomes, Octávio Pato, Blanqui Teixeira, Sérgio Vilarigues

Central Committee. 72 members

Last Congress. Ninth, 1–3 June 1979, next congress in 1983

National Elections. 1980: 17 percent of vote and 41 of the 250 seats in parliament; controls 50 of the 305 town councils

Auxiliary Organizations. Popular Democratic Movement (Movimento Democrático Popular), a communist-front "satellite" coalition of opposition parties during final years of Caetano dictatorship, transformed into political party in 1974; General Confederation of Portuguese Workers (Confederacão Geral de Trabalhadores Portugueses—Intersindical Nacional; OGTP-IN), Portugal's largest labor grouping, comprising 201 trade unions with 1.5 million workers and claiming to represent 85 percent of the labor force through affiliated unions and others that cooperate with it and an increase in number of strikes from 145 in 1977 to 315 in 1981 (*WMR*, February)

Publications. *Avante!*, weekly newspaper; *O Militante*, theoretical journal; and *O Diário*, semiofficial daily newspaper (all published in Lisbon)

Domestic Affairs. The PCP struggled vainly during 1982 to prevent constitutional changes sought by the governing Democratic Alliance (Aliança Democrática; AD). Communists denounced the proposed "constitutional coup d'etat" that would "pave the way for a right-wing takeover" and undermine the "socialist conquests" of the 1976 constitution—the Western world's "most progressive" (*CSM*, 22 February, 13 August; Lisbon domestic radio, 10 July; *FBIS*, 13 July).

The new document, approved by parliament in August and in force on 30 October, put more power in the hands of the prime minister by dissolving the Council of the Revolution and sharply curtailing the powers of the president. A follow-up November law totally subordinating the armed forces to the government was cited by Cunhal as "open proof" of the AD's plans for a coup. (*WP*, 15 August; *NYT*, 22 August, 31 October, 21 November.) The Communists had insisted during the debate over the Council of the Revolution and presidential prerogatives that it was essential to maintain a balance of power among the leading organs of sovereignty. Power concentrated in the government, they asserted, would permit it to manipulate the law, the armed forces, and police and eventually to destroy democracy. (*CSM*, 22 February; *O Jornal*, 5 May.)

Marxist language in the constitution, the PCP's second main concern, was not totally excised since the AD had to compromise with the Socialist Party in order to secure the two-thirds majority needed for reform. Nationalization of key sectors of the economy was to remain irreversible, but the pledge to continue nationalization was eliminated. To the dismay of the Communists, Prime Minister Francisco Pinto Balsemão then detailed a plan to trim the large deficit-ridden public sector and to allow private enterprise to compete with it (*WP*, 15 August; *NYT*, 22 August; *CSM*, 29 September).

Socialist leader Mário Soares's "capitulation" to the "reactionary" forces in agreeing to a common platform on constitutional revision prompted open communist efforts to divide the Socialist Party and to "step up relations" with social democrats (MTI, Budapest, 17 May; Lisbon domestic radio, 7 September; *FBIS*, 18 May, 8 September). An indignant Soares "suspended" his party's relations with the Communists in June because of their "clear interference" in the internal life of his party; the PCP Central Committee had urged Socialist deputies to vote against their party's line on reform. Soares's action was simply seen as "further proof" of his collaboration with the AD. Cunhal did not despair that "opportunistic Soarism" might yet be eliminated from the socialist leadership. (*O Jornal*, 5 March; *Avante!*, 9 June; *FBIS*, 22 June.)

Before and after the constitutional reform, the Communists continually urged President Antonio Ramalho Eanes to dismiss the government, appoint a caretaker administration and call early elections for a new parliament. They felt this was essential in order to thwart the AD's "putschist" offensive against the main achievements of the 1974 revolution. (*CSM*, 26 January; *O Militante*, February; Lisbon domestic radio, 7 September; *FBIS*, 8 September.) To reinforce its appeals, the PCP sponsored numerous antigovernment demonstrations and work stoppages. A one-day general strike by communist-controlled labor unions on 12 February was said to involve some 1.5 million workers, although the government claimed it really failed to rally many workers or to disrupt essential services (Lisbon domestic radio, 13 February; *FBIS*, 16 February). Socialist leader Soares, whose party did not back the strike, condemned the PCP's "adventurist" radicalizing policies aimed at frustrating constitutional revision; he accused the Soviet Union of giving the PCP the task of spreading chaos in Portugal (*O Jornal*, 15 January; *CSM*, 10 February).

On May Day, two workers were shot when riot police sought to break up fighting between members of rival PCP and Socialist labor unions. The PCP characterized the "savage behavior" of the police as a deliberate "provocation" by the Balsemão government. A 24-hour strike called by the CGTP-IN to protest the deaths shut down most of Portugal's heavy industry. (*NYT*, 2 and 12 May; Lisbon domestic radio, 2 May; *FBIS*, 3 and 4 May.)

Communists continued to insist that with an honest cabinet to oversee elections, the AD would suffer a crushing defeat. Cunhal did not give much credence to reports that President Eanes, facing new constitutional restrictions on his power, might support the formation of a party of his own; this was therefore a compelling reason, Cunhal said, for the president to use his constitutional power to dissolve the parliament (*O Jornal*, 23 April, 9 July; *L'Unità*, Rome, 16 June). By the end of the year, Balsemão was under growing pressure from both Socialists and Communists to resign, especially after the AD suffered a setback in key municipal elections on 12 December. The Socialists' share of the vote rose, at the expense of the AD, from 26 to 30 percent, while the Communists held steady at almost 20 percent. The AD continued to dominate local government, but bitter infighting within the alliance prompted the prime minister to resign a week after the elections. By year's end, he had not yet been replaced. (*NYT*, 16, 20, and 28 December; *CSM*, 24 December.)

Foreign Affairs. The PCP denounced the "fanatical" anti-Polish campaign unleashed in Portugal by reactionaries who "hypocritically" defend the workers of Poland while themselves "exploiting, oppressing and repressing" Portuguese workers (*Avante!*, 18 March; *FBIS*, 2 April). The AD government was charged with turning provocation against the socialist countries into a "shameful foreign policy habit" (Lisbon domestic radio, 4 July; *FBIS*, 7 July). This campaign was to be explained, according to Cunhal, by frustration over the "collapse like a house of cards" of counterrevolutionary forces in Poland and by the need to divert the Portuguese people's attention from their own extremely grave problems (*Avante!*, 30 December 1981; *FBIS*, 8 January). An April visit to Poland convinced Cunhal that the country had been spared economic and social chaos and civil war. He decried "alarmist" reports by the media about the military presence in Warsaw; he saw "only an occasional tank and a few patrols scattered around the city." (Lisbon domestic radio, 10 April; Tass, 8 May; *FBIS*, 12 April, 10 May.)

The Communists smarted at socialist and AD "slander" that the PCP, in defending Soviet intervention in Poland and elsewhere, was serving foreign interests and took its orders from Moscow. Cunhal insisted that autonomy and independence were a reality within the international communist movement. Taking a swipe at Eurocommunism, he said his party would not become communist in name and social democratic in ideology.(*IB*, May.)

During 1982, PCE delegations, usually headed by Cunhal, visited Bulgaria, Czechoslovakia, Cape Verde, East Germany, Hungary, Poland, and the Soviet Union. East German, Bulgarian, and Finnish Communists attended "friendship rallies" in Portugal.

Other Far-Left Organizations. Prime Minister Balsemão announced in February that the government had uncovered a plot to subvert the country's democratic institutions on the night of the 12 February general strike. Reportedly, however, no clear evidence was actually produced that a left-wing guerrilla group formed in 1980, the Popular Forces of 25 April, had planned to jam a state radio frequency with an inflammatory broadcast on the night of the strike. (*NYT*, 16 February; *CSM*, 22 February.)

A schism in the PCP (Reconstituted) developed as the party prepared for its Fourth Congress. Resentful that their position papers were not distributed to members, 41 leaders withdrew and announced plans to organize a "broad, unitary, democratic and revolutionary" political group (*Diário de Notícias*, Lisbon, 10 August; *FBIS*, 16 August).

Government Foreign Policy Toward Communism. In January, the Portuguese government protested Soviet involvement in the Polish crisis by expelling two Soviet diplomats and refusing visas to a high-ranking Soviet delegation invited to a rally by the PCP. Portugal also reportedly offered at a special NATO meeting to cut the Soviet diplomatic mission by a third as well as to impose restrictions on its freedom to travel in Portugal. *Pravda* noted that Portugal had gone further than its NATO partners in the campaign to aggravate international tensions over Poland. The Soviet embassy in Lisbon warned of "serious consequences" for Soviet-Portuguese relations, an allusion to Portuguese dependence on Soviet oil and to the growing importance of trade between the two countries; but by June, the two governments were negotiating a further trade expansion. (*FBIS*, 18 January, 3 June; *CSM*, 26 January; *Radio Free Europe–Radio Liberty*, 27 January; Tass, 2 June.)

The Balsemão government also strengthened trade ties with China and with Portugal's Marxist-led former colonies of Angola and Mozambique. It agreed to supply the latter country with small arms to fight the rebel Mozambique National Resistance. Portugal was expected to become that nation's second largest military supplier after the Soviet Union. Lisbon was said to feel that Portugal and NATO stood to gain from any reduction in the dependence of Mozambique and Angola on the Soviet bloc. (Lisbon domestic radio, 19 May; *FBIS*, 24 May, 28 June, 4 October; *NYT*, 13 and 29 November; *CSM*, 17 November.) The PCP characterized the government's initiatives in Africa as "the Trojan horse of neocolonialism, ready to stab in the back the countries for whom it professes friendship" (Lisbon domestic radio, 4 July; *FBIS*, 7 July).

Portugal also cultivated ties of friendship with Yugoslavia, welcoming visiting President Sergej Kraigher in April. President Eanes rejoiced that the two countries, though differing in ideology, could have close relations and be in accord in refusing to accept decisions imposed from abroad (Tanjug, Belgrade, 1 April; *FBIS*, 2 April).

Elbert Covell College
University of the Pacific   H. Leslie Robinson

San Marino

The world's smallest republic, with 20,000 inhabitants, San Marino is entirely surrounded by Italy, which provides it with connections to the world. Politics in San Marino are an extension of politics in Italy. Although treated by the world's communist parties as an independent entity, the Communist Party of San Marino (Partito Communista di San Marino; PCS) is a branch of the Italian Communist Party. Membership is estimated at about 300.

A profile on the activities of the PCS does not appear in this edition of the *Yearbook on International Communist Affairs*. Should the activities of the PCS so warrant, a profile on it will be included in the next edition.

Spain

The communist movement in Spain is currently weak and in disarray. Very strong during the civil war and the most influential of the repressed political groups during the Franco dictatorship, it emerged in the years immediately after Franco's death as a major potential force. Since then it has fragmented into numerous dissident groups, and its national impact has been significantly reduced. The main communist party's loss of members as well as of votes in regional and national elections finally forced the resignation of the secretary general in 1982. Marxist Basque terrorists, said to have the backing of foreign communist groups, and a few other minor left-wing extremists have been weakened, but they continue to be active.

Population. 39 million

Party. Spanish Communist Party (Partido Comunista de España; PCE)

Founded. 1920

Membership. Estimated at less than 100,000 (*NYT*, 20 June); sharp decline from 200,000 in 1977, though still exceeding the 1976 total of 15,000; pre–civil war membership, 300,000

Secretary General. Gerardo Iglesias

President. Dolores Ibarruri (legendary La Pasionaria of civil war days)

Secretariat. 11 members: Leopoldo Alcaraz, Jaime Ballesteros, Santiago Carrillo Solares, Enrique Curiel, Anselmo Hoyos, Ingacio Latierro, Juan Francisco Pla, Adolfo Pinedo, Francisco Romero Marín, Simón Sánchez Montero, and Nicolás Sartorius

Executive Committee. 24 members

Central Committee. 104 members

Last Congress. Tenth, 28–31 July 1981; notable for its dissension among the majority pro-Carrillo Eurocommunists, the anti-Carrillo Eurocommunists for Renewal, and the pro-Moscow hard-liners

National elections. Won 3.8 percent of the vote on 28 October and four seats in the 350-member parliament, a decline from 10 percent and 23 seats in 1979

Auxiliary Organizations. Workers' Commissions (Comisiones Obreros; CC OO)—Marcelino Camacho, CC OO chairman and member of PCE Central Committee until June resignation from the latter; represents almost one-third of Spain's labor union delegates, but losing members and influence to the Socialist unions

Publications. *Mundo Obrero* (Labor World), weekly; *Nuestra Bandera* (Our flag), bimonthly ideological journal; both published in Madrid

Party Internal Affairs. The demoralized PCE was shaken with new purges, resignations and secessions, and, finally, the replacement of its secretary general. Having survived growing challenges to his leadership in the Ninth and Tenth congresses, Carrillo gave up trying to answer protests about his "insensitivity" to the needs of the party (*CSM*, 3 February; *NYT*, 7 November).

In April, the party lost some 7,500 pro-Moscow dissidents who broke away to form the Catalan Communist Party so that they could remain faithful to Marxist-Leninist orthodoxy (*Le Monde*, Paris, 14 April; *Pravda*, 17 April; *FBIS*, 22 April). In September, the newly founded pro-Soviet Party for Communist Unification and Recovery (Partido por la Recuperación y la Unificación Comunista) claimed 5,000 members, 60 percent of whom were said to have come from the PCE (*FBIS*, 14 September). Graver repercussions evolved from the persistent demands of the Eurocommunists for Renewal in Madrid and in regional communist parties for a less authoritarian leadership (see *YICA*, 1982, p. 331). The disgruntled Basque Communist Party (EPK) defied Carrillo by merging with the larger left-wing Basque nationalist Party of the Basque Revolution, the principal member of the regional alliance, Euzkadiko Ezkerra (Basque Left). The PCE retaliated by ousting the ringleaders from the communist party, although they considered they had seceded, and by appointing a rival EPK "provisional" leadership. (*Radio Free Europe Research*, 2 November 1981; *Economist*, 1 May.)

Some 56 prominent PCE "renewalists," who supported the Basque dissidents in a public rally in Madrid, were disciplined by the party for their "factionalism"; six who were members of the Central Committee were expelled from that governing body. Among them was 45-year-veteran Manuel Azcárate, who had been the party's foreign affairs spokesman. When the Central Committee dissolved various local party committees that rejected the disciplinary action, a number of Communists in public office bolted from the party. Shockwaves reached the Galician Communist Party, which was reportedly considering a merger of its own with a leftist regional group. (*Radio Free Europe Research*, 2, 11, and 20 November 1981; *Neue Zürcher Zeitung*, 10 November 1981; *WP*, 13 November 1981; *Der Spiegel*, Hamburg, 21 June; *FBIS*, 24 June.) In March, the Association for the Renewal of the Left (Asociación por la Renovación de la Izquierda) was organized in Madrid, not as a political party but as a catalyst to revive the Spanish left with some fresh ideas. Manuel Azcárate was one of the thousand supporters, most of whom were allegedly present or expelled Communists. (*El País*, Madrid, 4 March.)

Carrillo's draconian tactics were said by close associates to be based on a preference for operating with a smaller, utterly loyal party that could go underground in case of a military coup (*CSM*, 3 February). Most observers considered the party seriously weakened by the defection of its more prestigious militants. Even Marcelino Camacho, veteran CC OO leader and former ally of Carrillo, resigned in June from the Central

Committee so he could devote all his time to "strengthening the independence of the CC OO." Also in June, an estranged Nicolás Sartorius, the presumed eventual successor to the top post, resigned as deputy secretary general to protest Carrillo's methods. (*NYT*, 11 June; Madrid domestic radio, 13 June; *FBIS*, 14 and 18 June; *Actualidad Económica*, 24 June.) Sartorius said there was no doubt that the PCE was "more democratic than any other Spanish party," but he insisted it must open up still further to differing opinions; he concluded that there was no future in Spain for a "dogmatic, sectarian and old communist party" (*O Jornal*, Lisbon, 5 March; *El País*, 18 June; *FBIS*, 2 July).

A defensive Carrillo instructed his critics that the PCE, "like any democratic community, has rules of the game which must be respected"; otherwise, it "would become a zoo" (*FBIS*, 25 January). He said the "renewalists" did not really want discussion, but sought to impose their own minority position (*Radio Free Europe Research*, 20 November 1981). He also charged Sartorius and Camacho with attempting to position themselves to seize control of the party when they blamed him for the PCE's poor showing in the Andalusian elections in May. Carrillo then resigned but acceded to the Central Committee's appeal to return to his post. (*NYT*, 11 and 14 June.)

The secretary general resigned again in November when his tactics and personal behavior were more openly impugned following the Communists' severe setback in the October national elections. When he designated a little-known but faithful protégé as his successor, it was widely assumed he had no intention of relinquishing actual control of the party; he thereby headed off demands for an extraordinary party congress that many believed would have led to the election of Sartorius. The new party leader, Gerardo Iglesias, a former coal miner from Asturias, received 64 of 104 Central Committee votes. He pledged to support Eurocommunism, but Manuel Azcárate lamented that the Eurocommunist idea had by now been destroyed. This was one of Carrillo's "greatest services to the Soviet Union in a very long time," he said. (Ibid., 7 and 11 November; *Los Angeles Times*, 8 November.) Carrillo remains a deputy in parliament.

Domestic Affairs. Siphoning off electoral support from a disintegrating government coalition as well as from the fractious communist party, Felipe González's Socialists swept to an overwhelming victory in the October parliamentary elections. Attracting 46 percent of the vote, the Spanish Socialist Workers' Party (Partido Socialista Obrero Español; PSOE) won a decisive majority in the lower chamber—202 of 350 seats. The PCE lost 19 of its 23 seats, pulling only 4 percent of the vote. Carrillo was one of the winners, but his was expected to be a lonely voice in a parliamentary sea of Socialists and conservatives of the second-place Popular Alliance (Alianza Popular; AP), which won 106 seats and 25 percent of the vote. The biggest loser was the Union of the Democratic Center (Unión del Centro Democrático; UCD), which had controlled the government since the death of Franco and which dropped from 168 to 12 seats. (*NYT*, 30 October.)

The PCE was vehemently opposed to holding elections five months ahead of the constitutionally scheduled time. Prime Minister Leopoldo Calvo Sotelo explained that the early dissolution of parliament was unavoidable because defections from the UCD had made it impossible to govern. Communists asserted that his real aim was to facilitate the bipolarization of Spanish politics—an objective for which the right wing had been "working for year." Polls and the results of May regional elections in Andalusia had clearly pointed to the likelihood of a national sweep by the PSOE and the AP. Conservatives expected a Socialist government to founder, thus setting the stage for a "very tough right-wing offensive." (*Nuestra Bandera*, July; *Mundo Obrero*, 9-15 July, 17-23 September; *FBIS*, 24 September; *CSM*, 1 September.) The threat of a rightist coalition centering around the AP's Manuel Fraga Iribarne, said the Communists, had become "truly disquieting" (*El País*, 4 July).

Communists were equally critical of the Socialists. Early in the year when it was not yet clear that the PSOE would win so handily, the PCE continued to press the theme that only agreement with the Communists would permit the PSOE to govern; instead, the latter was seen as "preferring" to cooperate with the right. Carrillo accused the Socialists of moving toward a "Soares-type line, only worse"—a reference to the Portuguese socialist leader—by dissociating themselves from "revolution by democratic means" and declaring themselves "social democrats." (*Mundo Obrero*, 12–18 February, 16–22 April; *FBIS*, 22 June; *El País*, 4 July.)

Felipe Gonzáles, who was elected prime minister by the new legislature, did indeed project a moderate image throughout the campaign not only by insisting that there would not be a coalition with the PCE but also by opposing excessive regionalism and by downplaying socialism. After he was installed in office, he reiterated a promise that there would be no sweeping nationalizations (except in the energy sector), no major tax changes, and no broad new programs of social welfare. Dismissing this program as scarcely socialist, Carrillo countered with a pledge that the PCE would call for the nationalization of the firms that finance the AP and the UCD and of the banks that financed the aborted coup of February 1981. (Madrid domestic radio, 21 February; *FBIS*, 22 February; *Visión*, New York, 29 September; *NYT*, 13 and 28 October.)

Communists joined most politicians in expressing outrage at the "smear campaign" that sought to implicate King Juan Carlos in the 1981 coup attempt (see *YICA*, 1982, p. 332). The PCE proposed a parliamentary commission to defend the king against slander (*CSM*, 5 April). The party also insisted that the mild sentences passed in May on most of the indicted plotters should be appealed (Madrid domestic radio, 3 June; *FBIS*, 8 June). One of the coup ringleaders declared from prison that he saw no distinction between Communists and the victorious Socialists. Socialists were "better prepared and better disguised these days," he said, but they were "Marxists, Marxists, Marxists." (*CSM*, 12 October.)

A partial private survey early in the year concluded that CC OO was most influential in 41 percent of the work places studied and the Socialist General Union of Spanish Workers (UGT) in 28 percent. However, UGT shop stewards were regarded as having the most influence through their ability to bargain with employers under the officially sanctioned collective bargaining agreements. Most labor unrest in 1981 took place in the Basque area, Navarre, and the Canary Islands. (*Actualidad Económica*, 14 January.)

Foreign Affairs and International Party Contacts. During the campaign for the October elections, Carrillo seemed to soft-pedal his criticism of Moscow (*NYT*, 11 November). Earlier in the year, however, he spoke harshly of a fundamental split between the PCE and a "no longer communist" Soviet Union. He also proposed a new international alignment of socialists, communists, and liberation movements to supersede the Soviet model, which had "clearly failed," as shown by events in Poland. An easily identifiable "hand" had orchestrated the Polish crisis with a military crackdown that was "unimaginable for a Marxist." (*La Vanguardia*, Barcelona, 12 January; *FBIS*, 12 and 25 January, 8 February; *France-Soir*, Paris, 4 February.) The PCE issued statements, including a two-page advertisement in a Madrid newspaper, citing the "gravest" danger that millions, disillusioned by this behavior, might cease to believe in the liberating nature of communism and be beguiled by solutions offered by social democrats or the bourgeoisie. These official PCE denunciations were viewed as "merely acceptable" by the "renewalist" Eurocommunist sector of the party, which wanted to sever relations with the Polish party. (*El País*, 13 January; *FBIS*, 29 January; *CSM*, 3 February.)

The similar reactions of the PCE and of the Italian Communist Party to the Polish situation were reportedly agreed at a December 1981 meeting between Carrillo and Enrico Berlinguer. However, the Spanish Communists were not denounced by the Kremlin for their attacks as fiercely as were the Italians, presumably because they were less influential and perhaps because the Kremlin did not wish to alienate Carrillo's numerous opponents in the PCE (*El País*, 13 January; *FBIS*, 29 January).

The PCE said it was not unaware of the "pharisaism" and anticommunist manipulations of "imperialism," which exaggerated events in Poland while concealing its own atrocities. Such abuses included U.S. "backing" of terrorist dictatorships in Turkey and Latin America and "complicity" in the Israeli aggression against Lebanon and the genocide of Palestinians. President Reagan's attempt to lead the Europeans into a trade war against the Soviet Union was also seen as a grave threat to peace. Under these conditions, the Calvo Sotelo government's decision to move Spain into NATO "appeared even more inappropriate and dangerous," putting Spain "in the eye of the hurricane without any advantage." The PCE warned that the move was actually prompted by the domestic need of the "right-wing sociopolitical bloc" to be reinforced by a guarantee from U.S. imperialism. (*Mundo Obrero*, 8–14 January, 12–18 February, 9–15 July; *FBIS*, 1 February, 20 July; *WMR*, February; *El País*, 8 July.)

During the year, Carrillo and other key officials visited Romania, Hungary, and Yugoslavia.

Other Far-Left Groups. Although Basque terrorism reached an all-time low at the close of 1981, the provocative killings and bombings intensified in 1982. The main offensives were timed to coincide with the court martial of officers involved in the aborted coup of February 1981 and with the parliamentary election campaign later in the year. The principal terrorist organization continued to be the military wing of Basque

Homeland and Liberty (ETA-M), while the less violent "political-military" faction (ETA-PM) announced in February that it was ending its almost yearlong abstention from armed struggle. This followed the police discovery of over five tons of arms belonging to the group and the rescue of a kidnap victim. (*CSM*, 3 December 1981, 22 January, 19 February, 20 April, 27 October; *NYT*, 20 February.) Euskadiko Eskerra, a legal Basque political coalition, then renounced its close ties with ETA-PM, describing the kidnapping and armed struggle as "gravely destabilizing" (*CSM*, 22 January; *La Vanguardia*, 23 March; *FBIS*, 15 April).

A utility company suspended work in February on a nearly completed nuclear power plant outside Bilbao because of repeated ETA terrorist attacks. The terrorists, unappeased by the decision to give the Basque government managing control of the plant in May, murdered the plant's general project director. When intimidated employees refused to go back to work, it was decided to replace them with foreign technicians. (*NYT*, 18 February; *CSM*, 7, 20 May.)

Most of Spain's other far-left groups, formed when Franco died, have reportedly become defunct. The principal survivor, though a fitful one, is the October First Antifascist Resistance Group (Grupo de Resistencia Antifascista Primero de Octubre; GRAPO). It is a mysterious terrorist group that has repeatedly managed to reorganize for fresh attacks just when police thought it had been dismantled. After a number of bank robberies in 1982, GRAPO announced a continuation of its armed struggle with a wave of bomb attacks in Madrid in September. Shortly after the elections, it promised to dissolve itself if the Socialist government heeded certain demands; in December, the group's leader was killed by police. (*Economist*, 1 May; Madrid domestic radio, 6 September; *FBIS*, 8 September; EFE, Madrid, 6 November; *NYT*, 6 December.)

Biography. *Gerardo Iglesias.* The PCE's new secretary general is an obscure 37-year-old from Asturias who first joined the party as a 15-year-old coal miner. As a child, he helped communist guerrillas in Spain and later became a regular party organizer in the mines. He served a five-year prison term during the Franco dictatorship. Intensely loyal to Santiago Carrillo and Eurocommunism, Inglesias actively supported Carrillo's authoritarian control over the party. When elected to succeed the latter, he insisted he was not going to allow anyone "to exercise the secretary generalship from the shadows." (Sources: *NYT*, 7 and 11 November; *WP*, 7 November.)

Elbert Covell College
University of the Pacific   H. Leslie Robinson

Santiago Carrillo. Born 18 January 1915 in Gijon, Asturias, to a working-class father active in socialist politics, Carrillo spent 22 of his 45 politically active years as the leader of the communist movement of Spain. Since 1976, at least two Soviet-inspired attempts have been made to dislodge him because of his independent Eurocommunist stance.

His independence was further resented because of his conversion in Moscow in 1936 from socialism to communism. He denounced his socialist father publicly and remained unreconciled with him until 1956, when they were both political refugees in France. Moreover, he avidly supported Moscow's program of weeding out Trotskyites from among the Spaniards freed from Nazi camps (*NYT Magazine*, 19 November 1978, p. 154). In Prague in 1959, he was elected secretary general of the exiled PCE, which he led and expanded until 1977, when it became a legal political party in Spain.

Carrillo's leadership was challenged by the secession of the Catalan party, the PCE's largest regional branch, and by his poor showing in the July 1981 election for secretary general. In June, Deputy Secretary General Nicolás Sartorius resigned in protest over Carrillo's authoritarian leadership, and labor leader Marcelino Camacho resigned from the Central Committee.

Despite various threats to his leadership, Carrillo managed to retain control of the PCE until his resignation on 6 November. He first recommended Adolfo Piñedo, secretary general of the Madrid communist party, to succeed him. When the Executive Committee rejected Piñedo, he proposed Gerardo Iglesias as the new secretary general of the PCE.

Hoover Institution   Margit N. Grigory

Sweden

The Party of the Left—the Communists (Vänsterpartiet Kommunisterna; VPK), originally formed in 1921 as Sweden's Communist Party (Sveriges Kommunistiska Partiet), took its present name in 1967 in an effort to form a more moderate, nationalistic policy independent of Moscow. The party has a history of factionalism and splits. It gained its widest popular support at the end of World War II, winning 11.2 percent of the vote in the 1946 local government elections. Since 1950, the party has held 3–6 percent of the vote; since 1970, it has at times barely cleared the 4 percent barrier necessary for parliamentary representation. Historically supported mainly by blue-collar workers, since 1967 it has attracted greater numbers of white-collar workers and intellectuals. It has recently appealed especially to young people; in 1979, 50 percent of the VPK electorate was under 30 years of age.

Despite its attempt to dissociate itself from Moscow, the VPK suffered a severe setback in the parliamentary election of 1968, held in the wake of the Warsaw Pact suppression of the Czechoslovak reform movement. A revolt against the party leadership unseated former party chairman C. H. Hermansson and partially halted the move away from the international communist movement. The party program states that the party's foundation is scientific socialism, "the revolutionary theory of Marx and Lenin," and that "the party's goal is to have the struggle of the working class and of the people, guided by the ideas of revolutionary socialism, lead to victory over capitalism and to a classless society." Four factions seeking more orthodox doctrines or closer association with either China or the USSR have formed splinter parties since 1967, mainly from VPK defectors.

The VPK has often played a key parliamentary role despite its small size. Because of the almost even balance between the Social Democrats and the three center-right parties—Moderates, Liberal, and Center—VPK support kept the Social Democrats in power in the first half of the 1970s. Since the 1982 election, it again finds itself in a similar situation, able to unseat the Social Democrats who returned to power after a six-year hiatus. Although the Social Democrats, under moderate leadership, refuse to make any arrangement with the VPK, the latter has traditionally followed a policy of refraining from actions that would bring the center-right parties to power. Only in rare cases has the VPK forced the Social Democrats to retract proposals it opposes; the Social Democrats have usually found support from the parties to its right in such cases.

During 1982, the VPK spent most of its energies in an attempt to bring its support among the electorate above the 4 percent needed for parliamentary representation. It at first concentrated on dissociating itself from the USSR over Poland and incidents involving Soviet submarines off Sweden's coast. Toward the end of the campaign, it found a winning formula in exploitation of growing worker concern with the worsening economic situation and rising unemployment. In the 19 September election, it held the 20 seats it had previously won in the 349-seat Riksdag. The VPK applauded most of the policies of the Social Democratic minority government formed under Prime Minister Olof Palme after the election. But Lars Werner used the VPK's leverage in parliament to confront the government and force it to change its emergency economic program and lower food prices. Also, throughout the year, the VPK encouraged and exploited the burgeoning peace movement in Sweden.

Population. 8,323,000 (31 December 1981)

Party. The Party of the Left—the Communists (Vänsterpartiet Kommunisterna; VPK)

Founded. 1921 (VPK, 1967)

Membership. 17,800 (*Ny Dag*, 21 December 1981), mainly in Stockholm, Göteborg, and far north

Chairman. Lars Werner

Executive Committee. 9 members: Lars Werner, Eivor Marklund (vice-chairman), Bo Hammar (secretary), Bror Engström, Viola Claesson, Lennart Beijer, Margó Ingvardsson, Kenneth Kvist, Bertil Mábrink

Party Board. 35 members

Last Congress. Twenty-Sixth, 20–24 November 1981, in Stockholm; next congress scheduled for 1985

Auxiliary Organizations. Communist Youth (KU); Communist Women's Organization

Elections. Won 5.6 percent of vote and 20 of 349 Riksdag seats in 19 September elections; represented on all parliamentary committees except defense, taxation, and justice

Publications. *Ny Dag* (New day), semiweekly; *Socialistisk Debatt* (Socialist debate), monthly; both published in Stockholm

Party Internal Affairs. In its fight for survival as a political force in the September elections, the VPK papered over its factional strife and gave unusual support to its leaders. Preparations for the campaign began at the Twenty-Sixth Congress in late November 1981. A declaration of party principles, "For Democracy and Socialism," long in preparation and adopted unanimously by the congress, was an attempt to broaden the party's appeal to the Swedish electorate and erase some criticism of the VPK's support of socialist regimes in Eastern Europe. The declaration stressed the need for "democratic freedoms and rights," especially the rights to assemble, strike, and form organizations, but said "the battle for democracy must go further." It declared that "only socialism creates the possibility for complete development of democracy" and deplored "restrictions on democratic freedoms and rights in socialist countries" as "foreign and inhibiting elements" for socialism. (*Ny Dag*, 5 November 1981.)

Werner's opening speech to the congress was along the same lines. He described Sweden's Communists as adherents of proletarian internationalism who demanded respect for the self-determination and sovereignty of individual nations, a clear reference to the Polish situation. "We are disappointed when violations occur in the name of socialism, but U.S. imperialism is the enemy of the people and the biggest threat to world peace," he said. (*Dagens Nyheter*, 23 November 1981.)

Doctrinal differences and relations with the USSR and Eastern Europe nevertheless surfaced during debate on the declaration. A group whose principal spokesman was Per Kageson took a more critical attitude toward the Soviet and East European regimes. Kageson had been a member of the working group that had drafted the declaration. He sought unsuccessfully to get the congress to establish a working group to undertake a "scientific analysis" of the situation in those countries, with the object of discovering why such "great shortages of democratic freedoms and rights" existed there. Kageson also asked the congress unsuccessfully to break relations with the Soviet party except on topics where there were clear agreements. (*Ny Dag*, 27 November 1981.) "I want the VPK to express its support for the battle for democracy and freedom of expression in the socialist countries of Eastern Europe," he declared (*Dagens Nyheter*, 24 November 1981).

Concern over the Polish issue mounted as repressive actions against Solidarity took place in Poland. In an interview with the conservative *Svenska Dagbladet* (5 January), Werner, while speaking of the attempts of the Swedish and other West European communist parties to disassociate themselves from Polish government actions, said that the VPK had no formal ties with the Communist Party of the Soviet Union (CPSU) to break. He cited the Italian Communist Party as following the line the VPK could fully agree with. He asserted that "we had already chosen our position in the mid-1960s, when we decided to follow the path of pluralism, a multiparty system . . . It is the 'third path' as the Italians call it. And we say the same thing—a third path between the dictatorships in Eastern Europe and social democracy."

VPK leaders took extraordinary measures to counter the effects of the Polish issue, including the naming of a working group headed by Werner to study the Polish situation, an action interpreted as a further step away from Moscow (*Neue Zürcher Zeitung*, 5 January). But these developments and the pressure of the campaign were not enough to end dissension in the party. At the end of March, Per Kageson announced his intention to leave the party because of its failure to adopt a strong enough position against Soviet behavior toward Poland (*Svenska Dagbladet*, 31 March).

According to opinion polls and political observers, the VPK's appeal to the electorate was being undermined by the Swedish public's reaction not only to the Polish developments but also to the continued disclosures of foreign submarines in Swedish territorial waters. These submarines were believed to be Soviet, recalling the stranding of a Soviet submarine off a Swedish naval base in the fall of 1981. Until the very end of the campaign, reliable polls showed VPK support among the electorate hovering around the 4 percent mark, at times dropping as low as 3 percent, touching off speculation that a VPK decline could throw the election to the center-right parties. Domestic issues took the limelight in the latter days of the campaign, however, as unemployment grew, and VPK leaders, particularly Werner, were able to make their attacks on government policies heard. Thus, under these circumstances, the party's ability to maintain its 1979 level in votes and parliamentary seats was taken as a victory in the party and among political observers generally.

On 14 November, the Party Board re-elected the Executive Committee. Bo Hammar was formally named party secretary, replacing the ailing Tore Forsberg. Hammar had acted as secretary throughout the election campaign. The number of members of the Executive Committee was increased from eight to nine.

Domestic Affairs. Building on the resolutions of the Twenty-Sixth Congress, VPK leaders started organizing the party's electoral campaign at the beginning of the year. As early as 9 January, the themes that later dominated the party's campaign efforts were made at an open meeting in Stockholm to prepare for the election: reduction of unemployment, the right of youth to jobs, and decreases in high prices and high rents (*Ny Dag*, 12 January). By 25 January, the VPK had prepared a twelve-point program to address the worsening economic situation. It called for creation of 100,000 new jobs, more housing, increased child-care programs, more job training for youth, and a six-hour workday (ibid., 26 January).

In February, the VPK delegation proposed to parliament an environmental program to protect lakes, rivers, and beaches (ibid., 16 February). Party leaders were concerned about the rise of a new party, the Environmental Party (Miljöpartiet), although polls showed that it was drawing support mainly from center-right groups; only some 7 percent of the new party's followers had formerly supported the VPK (ibid., 25 April).

At the beginning of April, the Party Board added to the list of important goals for the election (1) removing indirect taxes on food, (2) guaranteeing existing social welfare benefits against inflation, (3) dismantling Sweden's nuclear power plants, (4) increasing women's rights, aiding the Third World, and fostering disarmament, and (5) extending democracy to the work place (ibid., 6 April).

By May, the election campaign had begun in earnest, and on 27 May the party unveiled a twelve-point electoral program built around the issues in the Party Board's statement of April. The preamble called on the Social Democrats not to deal with the bourgeois parties but to join with the VPK during the first 100 days of a leftist government to change Sweden's policy course radically. The list of actions to be taken was headed by the party's proposal to create 100,000 new jobs, guarantee work and training to all youth, and severely restrict foreign investment. Other important proposals were calls to reduce the workday to six hours, institute a freeze on rent increases, remove the value-added tax on food, reinstate insurance payments for the first three days of sick leave under the national health system (the Center Party–Liberal government had taken away these payments as an economy measure), and increase national government payments to local governments until they again were as large as they had been before the then governing coalition took office. At the bottom of the list were proposals to reduce the number of nuclear power plants, to turn down the request of the military for development of a high-technology aircraft (the JAS) and put the money into civil defense, and to create a Nordic nuclear weapons–free zone. (Ibid., 27 May.) The VPK initiative drew no response from Social Democratic leaders.

Foreign policy played a minor role in the twelve-point program, but a five-point election declaration of 29 July led off with a call for a "peace" campaign to prevent war. It declared that Scandinavia should contribute to peace by reducing its production and export of war materials and stressed VPK opposition to the construction of more nuclear power plants and support for the dismantling of those in operation. (Ibid., 29 July.)

As the campaign progressed, the VPK, like the Social Democrats, increasingly emphasized economic issues. Sweden was in the trough of a recession, with inflation still high and unemployment increasing. An inflation rate of 12 percent in 1981 had outstripped the average rise in wages by about 3 percentage points, and in 1982, despite a falling inflation rate, real wages dropped still further, by about 4 percent.

The VPK gave primary attention to unemployment, particularly to the relatively high rate among youth. Arguments that the tax system was unjust and that there should be a freeze on rents also became important issues in the VPK campaign and were usually put forward along with the theme of unemployment. VPK spokesmen attacked the three-year agreement that the Social Democrats had made in April 1982 with the two government parties to reform and lower taxes after the 1982 election.

The swing to the parties on the left in the election was so great that the Social Democrats alone won more seats than the three center-right parties combined (166 to 163), making the new Social Democratic government under Palme less dependent on the VPK than had been expected. The Social Democrats had neither responded to VPK exhortations for cooperation nor reacted aginst VPK electoral initiatives, and Palme made no concessions to the VPK in determining the new government's policies and statements. Only in one area did the VPK improve its parliamentary position; the other parties agreed to adopt a proportional representation system for assigning committee seats in parliament, which meant that the Social Democrats gave up one seat to the VPK on most committees. As a result, the VPK, which had formerly had no representation on committees, gained a seat on thirteen of the sixteen standing committees, including the Foreign Affairs Committee. It still had no representation on the Defense, Justice, and Taxation committees, except for an alternate on the Taxation Committee. (*Norrskensflamman*, *Ny Dag*, and *Dagens Nyheter*,7 October.)

There was little change in the distribution of VPK strength. Support went up slightly in Bohuslän and Örebro and down slightly in Värmland, Halland, Gotland, and Jönköping. The strongest support, about 10 percent of the vote, continued to be in the city of Stockholm, Göteborg, and Norrbotten in the far north. The party received some 6 percent in Uppsala, Stockholm, and Gävleborg provinces. In Stockholm province, despite a decline in VPK support in the provincial election (local elections were held concurrently with the national), the Social Democrats won such a plurality that the provincial government, which had consisted of the three center-right parties for sixteen years, was ousted.

Foreign Affairs. The principal effort of the VPK in 1982 was an attempt to disassociate itself from the Polish military regime and Soviet policy toward Poland. The issue of what attitude the VPK should take toward Eastern Europe had arisen at the Twenty-Sixth Congress, when a faction led by Eurocommunist Per Kageson argued that repressive socialist regimes such as those in Eastern Europe should be condemned in Marxist terms. Another group argued that Swedish Communists should not get bogged down in debating the rights and wrongs of actions in socialist states but should instead concentrate on the Swedish path to socialism. (*Ny Dag*, 27 November 1981.)

The military takeover and repressive actions against Solidarity heightened the party's embarrassment and were generally believed to have caused a loss in its popular support. Party leaders then launched a propaganda campaign to make clear their distaste for the Polish regime, but in terms that would not cause another defection of more doctrinaire Communists. On 4 January, the Executive Committee named Werner to head a four-man "working group" to foster discussion with foreign communist and socialist parties on the Polish situation. Werner stressed "great agreement in our party on condemnation of military rule in Poland." As for the question of breaking relations with the CPSU over the issue, pressed by some party members such as Kageson, Werner said that "we have no agreements or treaties to break." He cited the Italian Communist Party's position of a third way between the CPSU and the traditional social-democratic model as similar to that of the VPK. (Ibid., 7 January.)

Three weeks before the election, the VPK Executive Committee issued a statement on Poland. It said that the Polish military takeover had "brutally broken" Poland's development toward "democracy and social renewal." It expressed solidarity with those in Poland working for such renewal and said that the VPK joined international efforts to seek removal of the government's emergency powers, the freeing of union leaders, a free union movement, and democratic freedoms and rights in Poland. (Ibid., 26 August.)

VPK leaders attempted to counter the effects of the Polish issue by concentrating on the "peace" theme. The Swedes were receptive to the peace movement that was gaining momentum on the continent as fear of nuclear war grew. VPK spokesmen directed their attacks mainly at the U.S. administration and its policies on nuclear weapons and warfare. At the same time that the Party Board issued its statement on Poland in early February, it released another statement, entitled "Stop Reagan Imperialism." That statement charged Washington with intervening over the whole world, urging NATO countries to undertake actions risking war, increasing nuclear arms in Europe, and upholding racist, fascist, and military dictators in South Africa, Chile, and Turkey. Washington was also accused of extending military and economic aid to El Salvador and Guatemala that was being used to kill people. The VPK called on the Swedish government to protest directly and through the United Nations as well as to extend aid to the rebel El Salvadorans and to liberation movements everywhere. (Ibid., 9 February.) American "imperialism" in the Third World was a favorite topic; *Ny Dag* (11 March) claimed, for instance, that the Turks had no chance to solve their class and ethnic conflicts because the United States backed the military junta to serve its own interests (U.S. bases in Turkey) and the interests of "stability."

Chief attention was given the nuclear weapons confrontation in Europe. On 13 May, *Ny Dag* deplored Washington's and Moscow's "tendencies" to dismiss each other's proposals on nuclear weapons. But it added that it was clear that President Brezhnev wanted to start with intermediate-range missiles because of their direct threat to the Soviet heartland, but less clear why President Reagan would not approach talks except from a strategic viewpoint. The paper expressed belief that there probably would not be disarmament unless it took place under the present strategic balance and that Reagan must therefore be forced to compromise; "only an international mass movement" could supply the necessary pressure.

The VPK made every effort to associate with and exploit the peace movement. At the Twenty-Sixth Congress, it had defended itself and the peace movement against charges that the movement was being directed by Moscow. But when a motion was put forward that the VPK should leave the Swedish Peace Committee because of the committee's alleged connections with the USSR, it was voted down. Those who advocated continued affiliation argued that the peace movement connected with the committee was the only one that stood on anti-imperialistic grounds and that had broad international connections, particularly with Third World countries. (Ibid., 27 November 1981.)

In late January, a three-day, mass "Parliament for Peace," supported by a wide variety of forces, including all political parties except for the conservative Moderates, was held in Stockholm. Made up of 475 representatives of youth, women's, labor, and religious organizations, its chief purpose was to mobilize opinion behind the U.N. special session on disarmament. Its chief organizers were the respected Swedish U.N. Association and the Swedish Peace Council, both umbrella organizations with many member associations. It was the second such disarmament "parliament" in Sweden—the first one was held in 1978 before another U.N. session on disarmament—and the number of people it attracted and the attention it received in the press disclosed wide popular support for the peace movement.

The call of the Parliament for Peace for a Nordic nuclear weapons–free zone rekindled popular support for that proposal, which had declined after the stranding just off a Swedish naval base in the fall of 1981 of a Soviet submarine carrying nuclear weapons. The VPK made the issue the chief theme of its May Day activities and sentiment for a Nordic zone remained strong among Swedes throughout the year, despite the continued disclosures of foreign submarines in Swedish territorial waters, assumed to be Soviet.

The VPK downplayed military reports of foreign submarine activity off Sweden's coasts, but feelings ran so high in late September and early October (when the Swedish government thought a submarine had again been trapped) that Werner called for stronger military measures to force submarines violating territorial waters to the surface (ibid., 7 October).

Much of the VPK's attention was given to U.S. policies and actions in Latin America, particularly in El Salvador. On 18 June, *Ny Dag* took the position that while U.S. policy toward Latin America had been formed before President Reagan took office, he had gone the furthest in trying to realize the "old U.S. ambition" of creating a counterpart of NATO in the South Atlantic, particularly by using the Argentine junta as a proxy in several countries. The U.S. administration was using the danger of Soviet influence in Latin America as a pretext for its policies, the paper declared, and had unsuccessfully sought to prove that Salvadoran guerrillas received materials from Nicaragua, Cuba, and the USSR.

In the summer and fall, the VPK also focused on the Lebanese crisis, as the Swedish public became aroused over the bloodshed. Party Secretary Bo Hammar told the press that the VPK condemned Israel's "terror war" and declared its "solidarity with the Palestinian people's battle for their national and democratic rights" (ibid., 8 June). Pictures of bombings and shellings by Israeli forces were highlighted in

Ny Dag and brochures in a sustained propaganda campaign. *Ny Dag* (16 June) called on its readers to collect funds and send them to the office of the Palestine Liberation Organization (PLO) in Stockholm, to a special Palestinian group connected with the Red Cross, or to a special VPK "solidarity" fund. The VPK also supported pressure on the government to recognize the PLO (ibid., 10 June, 28 September).

International Party Contacts. As a result of forces within and without the party, the VPK further reduced its contacts with the CPSU and the East European communist parties. Werner did not accept an invitation to the Soviet National Day celebration in 1981 and did not invite the CPSU to send representatives to the VPK's Twenty-Sixth Congress. But the Party Board did decide to send Bo Hammar to attend Brezhnev's funeral.

On the other hand, the VPK increased its contacts with other West European communist parties on such issues as Poland and the Nordic nuclear weapons–free zone, but continued to try to identify itself with such leftist, noncommunist parties as the Socialist Left in Norway and the Socialist People's Party in Denmark. Representatives of these two parties and of the communist parties of Norway and Denmark attended the Twenty-Sixth Congress (ibid., 2 December 1981). On 20–23 May, the VPK hosted a "Marxist people's university" at Stockholm. The principal guests were Gert Petersen, leader of the Danish Socialist People's Party; Berge Furre, leader of the Norwegian Socialist Left; and Gunnar Asplund, member of the Central Committee of the Finnish Communist Party. While the participants admitted economic and social differences among the Scandinavian countries, they agreed that there should be more cooperation among the forces on the left. (Ibid., 27 May.) On 29–30 November, the leaders of the communist parties of Sweden, Norway, Denmark, and Finland met in Finland to discuss common interests and coordinate their activities, particularly in the domestic economic area. Besides concentrating on the unemployment problem, the communiqué called for cooperation of the left, a broad front against "big capital," and a common fight for peace and détente. Special emphasis was placed on creating a Nordic nuclear weapons–free zone and on trying to stop the United States and NATO from placing "Euromissiles" in Europe (ibid., 9 December).

Although the VPK kept its distance from the CPSU, some Soviet officials of fairly high rank visited Stockholm as the guests of other groups. Georgi Arbatov, member of the Soviet Central Committee and an adviser to President Brezhnev, was hosted by the Executive Club of the conservative newspaper *Svenska Dagbladet* in early September. Arbatov charged that the Reagan administration was a danger to peace, in contrast to the Soviet leadership, and that the Swedish government failed to maintain an "active neutrality," such as that followed by Austria and Finland (*Svenska Dagbladet*, 8 and 9 September).

As part of the VPK's efforts to foster relations with other West European communist parties and to take common stands particularly on the Polish issue, Werner hosted a Spanish party delegation led by Santiago Carrillo that visited Stockholm on 1–4 June. Their communiqué underscored "the neutrality movement's great importance for national independence" (*Ny Dag*, 8 June). Both supported the peace movement and "broad leftist cooperation in the West European countries." Their communiqué underscored "the neutrality movement's great importance for national independence" (*Ny Dag*, 8 June). Typical of other exchanges with West European communist parties was a visit of two top Italian party officials to Sweden, Finland, and Denmark in February. The two Italians, in addition to discussions with VPK leaders, also talked with Olof Palme and other Social Democrats in efforts to explain PCI policies and stir interest in cooperation on the left.

At the invitation of the Chinese Communist Party, a VPK delegation visited China in mid-June. It was headed by Bo Hammar, who later expressed satisfaction with his reception and with the fact that the two parties were resuming contacts with each other. The Chinese Central Committee extended an invitation to VPK Chairman Werner to visit China. (Ibid., 22 June.)

Rival Communist Groups. The pro-Soviet Communist Workers' Party (Arbetarpartiet Kommunisterna) was founded in 1977. Its chairman is Rolf Hagel. Its daily, *Norrskensflamman* (Northern lights), is the traditional communist spokesman in the far north. In 1982, it won 0.1 percent of the vote and twelve local government seats, mainly in northern Sweden.

The pro-Chinese Sweden's Communist Party (Sveriges Kommunistiska Partiet) was founded in 1967 as the Communist League of Marxists-Leninists. It took its present name in 1969. Its chairman is Roland

Pettersson, and its publication is the weekly *M-L Gnistan* (The spark). It ran no national candidates in 1982, but won nine seats in local governments.

The pro-Albanian Marxist-Leninist Communist Party, Revolutionary (Kommunistiska Partiet Marxist-Leninisterna, Revolutionärerna) was founded in 1970 and is led by Frank Baude. It publishes the weekly *Proletären*. It won three seats in the 1982 local government elections.

The Socialist Party (Socialistiska Partiet) was founded in the early 1970s as the Communist Workers' League and assumed its present name in 1982. It is the Swedish section of the Trotskyist Fourth International and is directed by the Executive Committee of the International. It publishes *Internationalen*. In the 1982 elections, it received about 3,900 votes, but won no seats.

Bethesda, Maryland   Finis Herbert Capps

Switzerland

The Swiss Labor Party (Partei der Arbeit/Parti du travail/Partito del Lavoro; PdA) is the oldest communist party in Switzerland. It was founded on 5 March 1921 as the Swiss Communist Party. It was outlawed in 1940 and re-established under its present name on 14 October 1944. The PdA is pro-Soviet. Current membership is estimated at 5,000. Switzerland has a population of 6,343,000 (1979).

The Progressive Organizations Switzerland (Progressive Organisationen Schweiz; POCH) was founded in 1972 by student dissidents of the PdA who considered themselves no longer part of the world communist movement, but rather as "newly emerging forces." POCH, with a membership of less than a thousand, describes itself as communist and pro-Soviet.

The Autonomous Socialist Party (Autonome Sozialistiche Partei/Parti socialiste autonome/Partito Socialista Autonomo; PSA) was organized in 1969 by Socialists (Second International) and is more militant than the PdA. Its membership is about 700.

The PdA, POCH, and PSA cooperated in the 1979 national elections. Three PdA and four POCH/PSA elected representatives form a fraction of seven in the 200-member lower house (Nationalrat). In the 46-member upper house (Standerat), the coalition has no seats.

The Socialist Workers' Party (Sozialistische Arbeiter partei/Parti ouvrière socialiste; SAP) is the new name adopted in October 1980 by the Marxist Revolutionary League (LMR), which goes back to 1969. The LMR was founded by about a hundred young intellectuals who left the PdA. The LMR joined the Fourth International (Trotskyist). The party emphasizes revolutionary cadre work and is not represented in any legislative bodies at the cantonal or federal level. Membership is estimated at about 500.

The Communist Party, Switzerland (Kommunistische Partei, Schweiz), with about 100 members, claims to be Marxist but not Leninist. The Communist Party, Switzerland, Marxist/Leninist (KPS/ML), with a membership of about 200, is pro-Chinese. Both parties are the product of the left-extremist movement that made its appearance in Switzerland in 1980. Their followers, who are also known as "chaoists," reject bourgeois parliamentarianism and advocate direct actions against the state and its institutions. They organized street demonstrations that frequently turned into violence as a result of leadership by well-organized assault units. Members of these groups hide their identity by wearing masks. Many of the participants of the violent demonstrations are foreigners. The Swiss chaoists are linked with the West European squatter movement and with the Greens, the coalition of environmentalists and antinuclear activists. In addition to these organizations, there are about 50, mostly unstructured left-extremist groups holding views from radical socialism to anarchism.

The PdA's secretary general is Armand Magnin. The central committee has 50 members, representing all linguistic regions of Switzerland. It was elected by the Twelfth Party Congress, which met 26–27 May 1979. The congress also approved the fourteen members of the Politburo and the five-member Secretariat.

In spite of its official pro-Soviet position, the PdA opposed the imposition of martial law in Poland but parroted the communist version of the cause for Poland's military rule, asserting that Solidarity extremists "encouraged by an irresponsible international campaign" were striving to seize power and thereby cause the intervention of the Polish army. However, the Politburo stated, "a true solution of the crisis is possible only by restoring democratic freedoms and the rights of the unions." Magnin declared that his party "assigns first place to the defense and expansion of democratic freedoms and rights. It is, therefore, normal that the party opposes any violations of these basic rights in socialist countries as well as anywhere in the world." (*Die Weltwoche*, 17 February.)

The World Peace Council (WPC) is most active among the groups and organizations connected with the Swiss peace movement. The ten Swiss members of the WPC are representative of the organizations in the Soviet-sponsored front organzation.

The official organs of the PdA are the daily *Voix ouvrière*, (Geneva), with a circulation of about 7,000 copies; the weekly *Vorwärts* (Bael), 6,000 copies; *Emanzipation*, a women's weekly; the weekly *Tribune ouvrière*; and the monthly *Positionen*. The SAP's publications include the bimonthly *Bresche* (German) and *La Brèche* (French). The KPS/ML publishes, at irregular intervals, *Offensive* and the monthly *Oktober* (French and German).

University of Calgary   Eric Waldman

Turkey

The Communist Party of Turkey (Türkiye Komunist Parti; TKP) remains illegal, as it has been throughout most of its 62-year existence. Its secretary general is Ismail Bilen, and it appears to be based in Moscow. Its most prominent activity has been radio broadcasts (Voice of the Turkish Communist Party and Our Radio) beamed both at Turkey and at Turkish *Gastarbeiter* in Europe, particularly in West Germany. Reliable information concerning leading personnel and activities of the party is difficult to obtain, particularly after the current Turkish regime carried out a massive sweep that one newspaper labeled "1981 Operation Sledgehammer." The detailed information published by this newspaper (the Instanbul daily *Tercüman*) concerning the activities of the TKP between 1973 and 1981 seemed to be based exclusively on confessions of those arrested. Since there have been widespread accusations of torture of prisoners, this testimony must be regarded with skepticism, particularly since it implicates relatives and others associated with formerly prominent Turkish politicians as well as noncommunist organizations allegedly infiltrated by the TKP, whose real record thus remains murky.

The year under review was dominated by two major developments: (1) a continued crackdown on terrorists and others suspected of dissidence or opposition to the regime and (2) the adoption of a new constitution.

The crackdown took the form of continuing investigation and arrest of those accused of plotting or committing acts of political violence, sedition, or such crimes as defaming the Turkish state, as well as trial and conviction of those arrested previously. Although the government had claimed early in 1981 that all extremist and terrorist organizations had been smashed, arrests of new groups were reported from time to time during 1982, especially in the Kurdish areas of the east and southeast. The main groups identified were the extreme leftist Dev Yol (Revolutionary Way) and Dev Sol (Revolutionary Left) and the TKP. On the extreme right, the so-called Idealists or Gray Wolves associated with Alparslan Türkeş's Nationalist Action Party were major targets of investigation and prosecution, as was Türkeş himself.

Late in 1981, the government announced that more than 43,000 people had been detained since the military coup of September 1980. As of mid-1982, the regime reported that more than 23,000 people had been sentenced, while an additional 20,000 were being detained pending indictment. Some detainees had apparently spent well over a year in prison awaiting trial. The government demanded literally hundreds of death sentences, although only 21 were reportedly carried out. The regime also moved against those who fled prosecution by leaving the country by depriving them of Turkish citizenship.

Perhaps not surprisingly, the government found it necessary to respond to increasingly widespread charges of violations of the human rights of prisoners, including allegations of torture. Amnesty International adopted several "prisoners of conscience," including former professor Ismail Beşikçi, a sociologist who had published extensively on the treatment of Kurds in eastern Turkey. Although he had been harassed by the authorities since 1972, it was reported that he was arrested by the military regime barely three months after his release in 1981 from an earlier prison term. He was charged with having "sullied the good reputation of the Turkish state." Later, it was reported that Beşikçi had been convicted and sentenced to a new term of ten years. There were also reports that he had been tortured. (*New York Review of Books*, 21 August.)

The Turkish government responded to such charges late in 1981 by noting that it had received 342 complaints in the fifteen months since the coup, of which 104 were found to lack substance while 89 were substantial enough to warrant further investigation. Three policemen were sentenced to a year's imprisonment for the torture and death of a prisoner in their custody. No information was available concerning the remaining 149 complaints. In May, the government issued another report acknowledging charges against 112 security officers. It also said that there were 45 trials on such charges, of which 37 were then in progress, while 8 others had resulted in convictions. The government also denounced such accusations as anti-Turkish propaganda. (*Keesing's Contemporary Archives*, 27 August, p. 31675.)

The handling of the Confederation of Revolutionary Trade Unions (DISK), often thought of as pro-communist if not fully infiltrated, also aroused foreign interest. The confederation was banned immediately after the coup. By the end of 1980, the regime reported that it had initiated legal action against approximately 2,000 members, charging them with attempting to overthrow the constitutional order and establish a communist state (ibid., 22 January). A year later, it was reported that the government had finally prepared an indictment that included a demand for the death penalty against 52 DISK leaders, among them Chairman Abdullah Baştürk and General Secretary Fehmi Işiklar. Several others associated with DISK were arrested in 1981, and one former member of its executive board was reported shot to death by police. (Ibid.) As of late 1982, the cases of those indicted had not yet been disposed of, although trials had begun. They had now languished in jail for some 27 months. Both the Brussels-based International Confederation of Free Trade Unions and the West German Trade Union Federation protested the handling of these cases, the former charging "completely unacceptable repression of human and trade union rights" (ibid.). The European Parliament suspended Turkish membership partly as the result of this case (ibid., 27 August).

Another prominent case was that of former prime minister Bülent Ecevit, leader of the moderate social-democratic Republican People's Party, which was banned by the junta along with other parties in 1981. Ecevit was tried, sentenced, and jailed late in 1981 for violating a decree prohibiting political statements by former political leaders. That alone was sufficient for the European Economic Community to suspend a $650 million economic aid package. The suspension held throughout 1982. On 1 July, five members of the Council of Europe (France, Denmark, Norway, Sweden, the Netherlands) filed a petition with the European Commission on Human Rights charging that the Turkish regime had violated several articles of the European Convention on Human Rights, that Turkish claims of an emergency threatening national security could no longer be sustained, and that measures adopted by the authorities were repressive. (Ibid.) In short, the behavior of the Turkish government had become a major source of friction between Turkey and Europe.

The Turkish government reacted sharply to these complaints. Prime Minister Bülent Ulusu warned on

26 June that Europeans should not indulge in a "historical error which would inevitably affect their relations with Turkey even after the restoration of democracy" (*Facts on File*, 6 August). Head of state Kenan Evren also indicated that foreign intervention in essentially domestic concerns of Turkey would not be tolerated. He was especially articulate on this point during the campaign preceding the popular referendum on the new constitution during the fall. He repeatedly reminded the public of the anarchic conditions preceding the coup of 1980 and pointedly suggested that those who now complained of excessive authoritarianism were threatening to bring back the "bad old days." Notably, the U.S. government publicly dissociated itself from European criticism of the regime.

Supporters of the junta have argued that the extremist groups engaged in violence prior to the coup of 1980 were inspired and supported by external forces. Apparent confirmation for this claim surfaced late in 1982 with the arrest in Italy of a Bulgarian official on charges of complicity in the 13 May 1981 attempt to assassinate the pope. A Turk named Mehmet Ali Agca had been tried, convicted, and sentenced for the attempt. Italian authorities suggested that during the period between Agca's escape from a Turkish jail in 1979 and the assassination attempt on the pope, he was financed and armed by the Bulgarian secret service. A detailed report on Agca (*Reader's Digest*, September) suggests that he was supported by a mysterious source (presumably Soviet) even before he was arrested in 1979 for the murder of the prominent, politically moderate newspaper editor Abdi Ipekçi. Agca is said to have admitted that he was a member of several extremist organizations of both right and left and was trained in guerrilla tactics by leftists associated with the Palestine Liberation Organization in Lebanon. If he was indeed an extreme rightist, as he maintained when first incarcerated, it would not be the first time that the Soviets made common cause with their ideological opposites against the democratic center.

These issues were intertwined with the adoption of a new Turkish constitution. It represented an important milestone on the path to restoration of democratic government, which might help mend relations between Turkey and Europe. Publication of the preliminary draft of the constitution in July, however, gave rise to grave disappointment in Europe and evoked strong criticism in Turkey. Among the most vocal critics were labor unions, who objected to the ban on cooperation between themselves and political parties; leaders of defunct political parties, who were barred from political activity for a period of ten years; journalists, who were alarmed at provisions permitting prior restraint of publication and distribution; lawyers, who worried about restrictions on individual rights and threats to the independence of the judiciary; and finally those who were apprehensive about the extensive powers granted the president of the republic, as well as the provision (added later) that automatically made General Evren president upon approval of the constitution in the popular referendum held on 7 November.

The constitution was approved by an overwhelming 91.5 percent of the voters in the referendum. This vote of confidence, ardently sought by General Evren and his colleagues, was sullied by the manner in which it was elicited. First, all public discussion of the constitution was banned, save for the general's "explanations." Second, the ballots were color-coded (white for affirmative; blue for negative) and deposited in translucent envelopes in full public view. Moreover, although there was hope that the normalization of politics foreshadowed by the referendum might soften the harsher aspects of military rule, there was every indication that the junta intended to retain significant political power even after full implementation of the constitution. In addition to the elevation of General Evren to the presidency and the transformation of the junta into a consultative council attached to his office, there were indications that Prime Minister Ulusu, also a retired military officer, might form a new centrist political party.

These events continued to stir European skepticism. The European Parliament called the document "undemocratic" and asked for revisions (*FBIS*, 6 October). A prominent leftist professor of constitutional law in Ankara put the matter more pungently during the summer: "The members of the Constitutional Commission seem to have forgotten that they have been appointed to their positions to protect the oppressed people of Turkey within the framework of a legal system supported by a constitution and not to realize the wishes of the most cruel employer circles in Turkey . . . [T]he draft is full of clauses which may create crises rather than resolve them."

As for the TKP, the tough-fisted policy of the military regime presented it with many opportunities for propaganda but little leeway for action. It denounced the junta as a tool of U.S. imperialism and Turkish monopoly capitalism. It engaged in a sharp and detailed criticism of the new constitution, echoing many of the points outlined above, but with particular emphasis on alleged violations of the rights of Kurds in eastern Turkey. An unusual note was sounded during the fall campaign on the constitution when General Evren devoted one of his speeches to an extensive response to these communist broadcasts. The tenor of his remarks made it clear that he wished to discredit critics by identifying them with the TKP.

At the end of 1982, it was unclear whether the attitudes and measures adopted by the military junta would serve to suppress leftism once and for all, or whether it would only drive it underground where it could continue to prey on feelings of deprivation and oppression. The Turkish record of 1982 also raises the question of whether democracy is feasible in the face of the forces of rapid social and political change unleashed by the process of economic development.

University of Illinois at Chicago   Frank Tachau

Select Bibliography, 1981–82

GENERAL ON COMMUNISM

Bains, Hardial. *The Necessity for Revolution*. Toronto: People's Canada Publishing House, 1982.

Barbaria, Frank A. *Modern "Asiatic" Despotism Masquerading in Communist Workers' Ideology*. La Mesa, Calif.: IDEAS, 1981. 400 pp.

Bertsch, Gary K. *Power and Policy in Communist Systems*. Rev. ed. New York: Wiley, 1982. 192 pp.

Besançon, Alain. *Anatomie d'un spectre: L'Economie politique du socialism réel*. Paris: Calman-Lévy, 1981. 169 pp.

Bobbio, Norberto. *Le ideologie e il potere in crisi: Pluralismo, democrazia, socialismo, comunismo, terza via e terza forza*. Florence: Felice le Monnier, 1981. 229 pp.

Boggs, Carl. *The Impasse of European Communism*. Boulder, Colo.: Westview Press, 1981. 225 pp.

Buchanan, Allen E. *Marx and Justice: The Radical Critique of Liberalism*. Totowa, N.J.: Rowman and Littlefield, 1982. 206 pp.

Burke, John P.; Lawrence Crocker; and Lyman H. Legters. *Marxism and the Good Society*. Colloquium in Social Theory, University of Washington. New York: Cambridge University Press, 1981. 225 pp.

Callinicos, Alex. *Is There a Future for Marxism?* Atlantic Highlands, N.J.: Humanities Press, 1982. 263 pp.

Dörrer, Hans, et al. *Der Internationalismus der Arbeiterklasse*. East Berlin: Dietz Verlag, 1981. 184 pp.

Feenberg, Andrew. *Lukacs, Marx, and the Sources of Critical Theory*. Totowa, N.J.: Rowman and Littlefield, 1981. 286 pp.

Fougeyrollas, Pierre. *Ciencias sociales y marxismo*. Mexico City: Fondo de Cultura Económica, 1981. 253 pp.

Gilbert, Alan. *Marx's Politics: Communists and Citizens*. New Brunswick, N.J.: Rutgers University Press, 1981. 326 pp.

Gorman, Robert A. *Neo-Marxism: The Meaning of Modern Radicalism*. Westport, Conn.: Silkwood Press, 1982. 306 pp.

Hobsbawm, Eric J., ed. *The History of Marxism*, vol. 1, *Marxism in Marx's Day*. Bloomington: Indiana University Press, 1982. 376 pp.

Holmes, Leslie, ed. *The Withering Away of the State: Party and State Under Communism*. Beverly Hills, Calif.: Sage Publications, 1981. 294 pp.

Hook, Sidney. *Marxism and Beyond*. Totowa, N.J.: Rowman and Littlefield, 1982. 225 pp.

Horak, Stephan M. *Russia, the USSR and Eastern Europe: A Bibliographic Guide to English Language Publications*. Littleton, Colo.: Libraries Unlimited, 1982. 279 pp.

Horvat, Branko. *The Political Economy of Socialism: A Marxist Social Theory*. Armonk, N.Y.: M. E. Sharpe, 1982. 671 pp.

Isa Conde, Narciso. *Comunismo vs. socialdemocracia*. Santo Domingo: Taller Republicana Dominicana, 1981.

Jacoby, Russell. *Dialectics of Defeat: Contours of Western Marxism*. New York: Cambridge University Press, 1981. 202 pp.

Kaeselitz, Hella. *Kommunistische Parteien in den Hauptländern des Kapitals*. East Berlin: Verlag der Wissenschaften, 1982.

Kolkowicz, Roman, and Andrzej Korbonski, eds. *Soldiers, Peasants, and Bureaucrats: Civil-Military Relations in Communist and Modernizing Societies*. Boston: G. Allen & Unwin, 1982. 340 pp.

Lane, David. *Leninism: A Sociological Interpretation*. New York: Cambridge University Press, 1981. 150 pp.

Lendvai, Paul. *The Bureaucracy of Truth: How Communist Governments Manage the News*. Boulder, Colo.: Westview Press, 1981. 285 pp.

Lerner, Warren. *A History of Socialism and Communism in Modern Times: Theorists, Activists, and Humanists*. Englewood Cliffs, N.J.: Prentice-Hall, 1982. 253 pp.

McLellen, David, ed. *Karl Marx: Interviews and Recollections*. London: Macmillan, 1981. 186 pp.

Molyneux, John. *Leo Trotsky's Theory of Revolution*. New York: St. Martin's Press, 1981. 252 pp.

Narkiewicz, Olga A. *Marxism and the Reality of Power, 1919–1980*. London: Croom Helm, 1981. 337 pp.

Nelson, Daniel N. *Communism and the Politics of Inequalities*. Lexington: University of Kentucky Press, 1982.

Nelson, Daniel N., and S. White, eds. *Communist Legislatures in Comparative Perspective*. Albany: State University of New York Press, 1982. 201 pp.

Rigby, T. H., and Ferenc Fehér, eds. *Political Legitimation in Communist States*. New York: St. Martin's Press, 1982. 177 pp.

Rockmore, Tom, et al. *Marxism and Alternatives: Towards the Conceptual Interaction Among Soviet Philosophy, Neo-Thomism, Pragmatism, and Phenomenology*. Boston: D. Reidel, 1981. 311 pp.

Roemer, John E. *Analytical Foundations of Marxian Economic Theory*. New York: Cambridge University Press, 1981. 230 pp.

Rubel, Maximilien. *Rubel on Karl Marx*. New York: Cambridge University Press, 1981. 309 pp.

Ryan, Michael. *Marxism and Reconstruction: A Critical Reconstruction*. Baltimore, Md.: Johns Hopkins University Press, 1982. 232 pp.

Schaff, Adam. *Die kommunistische Bewegung am Scheideweg*. Vienna: Europaverlag, 1982. 223 pp.

Silva Santisteban, Luís. *Karl Marx: Ideas fundamentales y ensayos sobre praxis y alienación*. Lima: Centro de Investigación y Capacitación, 1981. 157 pp.

Szajkowski, Bogdan, ed. *Documents in Communist Affairs, 1981*. London: Butterworth Scientific, 1982. 347 pp.

Weigel, George. *The Peace Bishops and the Arms Race: Can Religious Leadership Help in Preventing War?* Chicago: World Without War Publications, 1982. 54 pp.

White, Stephen, et al. *Communist Political Systems: An Introduction*. London: Macmillan, 1982. 293 pp.

Wiles, Peter, ed. *The New Communist Third World: An Essay in Political Economy*. New York: St. Martin's Press, 1981. 392 pp.

Wolfson, Murray. *Marx, Economist, Philospoher, Jew: Steps in the Development of a Doctrine*. New York: St. Martin's Press, 1982. 279 pp.

Wood, Allen W. *Karl Marx*. Boston: Routledge & Kegan Paul, 1981. 282 pp.

Zinoviev, Aleksandr. *Le Communisme comme réalité*. Paris: Juillard, 1981. 332 pp.

AFRICA AND THE MIDDLE EAST

Baker, Donald G. *Zimbabwe: Development Problems and Prospects*. New York: Praeger, 1982. 235 pp.

Der bewaffnete Kampf der Völker Afrikas für Freiheit und Unabhängigkeit. East Berlin: Militärverlag der Deutschen Demokratischen Republik, 1981. 523 pp.

Callaghy, Thomas M., ed. *South Africa in Southern Africa*. New York: Praeger, 1982. Ca. 288 pp.

Cornevin, Robert. *La République populaire du Bénin: Des Origines dahoméennes à nos jours*. Paris: Maisonneuve & Larose, 1981. 584 pp.

Davidson, Basil. *No Fist Is Big Enough to Hide the Sky: The Liberation of Guinea Bissau and Cape Verde*. London: Zed Press, 1981. 187 pp.

_____. *The People's Cause: A History of Guerrillas in Africa*. Burnt Hill, Eng.: Longman, 1981. 210 pp.

Dehqani-Tafti, H. B. *The Hard Awakening*. New York: Seabury, 1981. 116 pp.

Gavshon, Arthur. *Crisis in Africa: Battleground of East and West*. New York: Penguin, 1981. 320 pp.

Gitelman, Zvi. *Becoming Israelis: Political Resocialization of Soviet and American Immigrants*. New York: Praeger, 1982. 362 pp.

Halliday, Fred, and Maxine Molyneux. *The Ethiopian Revolution*. London: NLB, 1981. 304 pp.

Heikal, Mohamed. *The Return of the Ayatollah: The Iranian Revolution from Mossadeq to Khomeini*. London: André Deutsch, 1981. 217 pp.

Jabbari, Ahmad, and Robert Olson, eds. *Iran: Essays on a Revolution in the Making*. Lexington, Ky.: Mazda, 1981. 214 pp.

Keddie, Nikki R. *Roots of Revolution: An Interpretive History of Modern Iran*. New Haven, Conn.: Yale University Press, 1981. 321 pp.

Khalidi, Rashid. *The Soviet Union and the Middle East in the 1980's*. Beirut, Lebanon: Institute for Palestine Studies, 1980. 40 pp.

Kotze, D. J. *Communism and South Africa*. Rev. ed. Cape Town: Tafelberg, 1982. 260 pp.

Marr, Pheobe, ed. *Revolutionary Regimes in the Middle East: A Comparative Study*. New York: Praeger, 1982. 185 pp.

Mittleman, James H. *Underdevelopment and the Transition to Socialism: Mozambique and Tanzania*. New York: Academic Press, 1981. 277 pp.

Ottaway, Marina S. *Soviet and American Influence in the Horn of Africa*. New York: Praeger, 1982. 187 pp.

Red Locusts: Soviet Support for Terrorism in Southern Africa. Alexandria, Va.: Western Goals Foundation, 1981. 82 pp.

South African Communists Speak: Documents from the History of the South African Communist Party, 1915–1980. London: Inkululeko Publications, 1981. 469 pp.

Stempel, John D. *Inside the Iranian Revolution*. Bloomington: Indiana University Press, 1981. 336 pp.

Stone, Russell A. *Social Change in Israel: Attitudes and Events, 1967–1979*. New York: Praeger, 1982. 336 pp.

Stookey, Robert. *South Yemen: A Marxist Republic in Arabia*. Boulder, Colo.: Westview Press, 1982. 124 pp.

Ya-Otto, John. *Battlefront Namibia*. Westport, Conn.: Lawrence Hill, 1981. 151 pp.

Zabarah, Mohammed Ahmad. *Yemen: Traditionalism vs. Modernity*. New York: Praeger, 1982. 154 pp.

THE AMERICAS

Alexander, Robert J. *Bolivia: The Past, Present and Future of Its Politics*. New York: Praeger, 1982. 176 pp.

_____. *The Right Opposition: The Lovestoneites and the International Communist Opposition of the 1930's*. Westport, Conn.: Greenwood Press, 1981. 342 pp.

Anderson, Thomas P. *Politics in Central America*. New York: Praeger, 1982. 240 pp.

Armstrong, Robert, and Janet Shenk. *El Salvador: The Face of Revolution*. Boston: South End Press, 1982. 283 pp.

Arnson, Cynthia. *El Salvador: A Revolution Confronts the United States*. Washington, D.C.: Institute for Policy Studies, 1982. 118 pp.

Booth, John A. *The End and the Beginning: The Nicaraguan Revolution*. Boulder, Colo.: Westview Press, 1982. 279 pp.

Brandt, Joseph, ed. *Gus Hall Bibliography. The Communist Party, USA: Philosophy, History, Program, Activities*. New York: New Outlook Publishers & Distributors, 1981. 181 pp.

Bunster, Ximena, and Elsa M. Chaney. *Sellers and Servants: Working Women in Lima, Peru*. New York: Praeger, 1982. 200 pp.

Canada's Party of Socialism: History of the Communist Party of Canada, 1921–1976. Toronto: Progress Books, 1982. 319 pp.

Castro, Fidel. *Fidel Castro Speeches: Cuba's Internationalist Foreign Policy, 1975–1980*. New York: Pathfinder Press, 1981. 391 pp.

Cole, Lester. *Hollywood Red: The Autobiography of Lester Cole*. Palo Alto, Calif.: Ramparts Press, 1981. 448 pp.

Cuba. Partido Comunista de Cuba. *Política cultural del la Revolución cubana documentos presentados al Segundo Congreso del Partido Comunista de Cuba*. Havana: Editorial de Ciencias Sociales, 1981.

Dahlin, Therrin C. *The Catholic Left in Latin America: A Comprehensive Bibliography*. Boston: G. K. Hall, 1981. 410 pp.

Di Giovanni, Cleto, and Mose L. Harvey. *Crisis in Central America*. Washington, D.C.: Advanced International Studies Institute, 1982. 116 pp.

Dyson, Lowell. *Red Harvest: The Communist Party and American Farmers*. Lincoln: University of Nebraska Press, 1982. 259 pp.

Franklin, Woodman B. *Guatemala*. Santa Barbara, Calif.: ABC-Clio, 1981. 109 pp.

Galindo, Alberto Flores. *El pensamiento comunista, 1917–1945*. Lima: Mosca Azul Editores, 1982. 228 pp.

Isserman, Maurice. *Which Side Were You On? The American Communist Party During the Second World War*. Middletown, Conn.: Wesleyan University Press, 1982. 305 pp.

Mercado, Rogger. *El Partido Comunista del Perú: Sendero Luminoso*. Lima: Ediciones Cultura Popular, 1982. 81 pp.

Montgomery, Tommie Sue. *Revolution in El Salvador*. Boulder, Colo.: Westview Press, 1982. 224 pp.

Neymet, Marcela de. *Cronología del Partido Comunista Mexicano*. Vol. 1. Mexico City: Ediciones de Cultura Popular, 1981.

Peru. Partido Comunista Revolucionario. Conferencia Nacional. *Tercera Conferencia Nacional del Partido Comunista Revolucionario: Persisten en el Mariateguismo, via peruana al socialismo*. Lima: Partido Comunista Revolucionario, 1981. 207 pp.

Revolutionary Communist Party, USA. *New Programme and New Constitution of the Revolutionary Communist Party, USA*. Chicago: RCP Publications, 1981. 122 pp.

Stanford Central America Action Network, ed. *Revolution in Central America*. Boulder, Colo.: Westview Press, 1982. 525 pp.

Tyson, James L. *Target America: The Influence of Communist Propaganda on U.S. Media*. Chicago: Regnery Gateway, 1981. 284 pp.

Walker, Thomas W., ed. *Nicaragua in Revolution*. New York: Praeger, 1981. 416 pp.

Wesson, Robert, ed. *Communism in Central America and the Caribbean*. Stanford: Hoover Institution Press, 1982. 177 pp.

Whelan, James. *Allende, Death of a Marxist Dream*. Westport, Conn.: Arlington House, 1981. 230 pp.

ASIA AND THE PACIFIC

Averill, Stephen Carl. *"Revolution in the Highlands: The Rise of the Communist Movement in Jiangxi Province."* Ph.D. dissertation, Cornell University, 1982. 421 leaves.

Aley, Roderic, ed. *New Zealand and the Pacific*. Boulder, Colo.: Westview Press, 1982. 300 pp.

Brown, Harrison, ed. *China Among the Nations of the Pacific*. Boulder, Colo.: Westview Press, 1982. 136 pp.

Burchett, Wilfred. *The China-Cambodia-Vietnam Triangle*. Chicago: Vanguard Books, 1981. 235 pp.

Bush, Richard, ed. *China Briefing, 1982*. The Asia Society. Boulder, Colo.: Westview Press, 1982. 125 pp.

Buss, Claude A. *The United States and the Republic of Korea: Background for Policy*. Stanford: Hoover Institution Press, 1982. 184 pp.

Chan, F. Gilbert, and Harlan W. Jencks, eds. *Chinese Communist Politics: Selected Studies*. Hong Kong: Asian Research Service, 1982. 197 pp.

Chen Po-wen. *The Crumbling Chinese Communist People's Commune*. Taipei: Asian Peoples' Anti-Communist League, Republic of China, 1981. 58 pp.

China Under the Four Modernizations, part 1, *Selected Papers Submitted to the Joint Economic Committee of the United States Congress*. Washington, D.C.: Government Printing Office, 1982. 610 pp.

Chiu, Hungda. *Agreements in the People's Republic of China: A Calendar of Events, 1966–1980*. New York: Praeger, 1981. 331 pp.

Choudhury, G. W. *China in World Affairs: The Foreign Policy of the PRC Since 1970*. Boulder, Colo.: Westview Press, 1982. 310 pp.

Ellison, Herbert J. *The Sino-Soviet Conflict: A Global Perspective*. Seattle: University of Washington Press, 1982. 408 pp.

Fairbank, John King. *Chinabound: A Fifty Year Memoir*. New York: Harper & Row, 1982. 480 pp.

Garver, John W. *China's Decision for Rapprochement with the United States, 1968–1971*. Boulder, Colo.: Westview Press, 1982. 174 pp.

Gupta, Bhabani Sen. *The Afghan Syndrome: How to Live with Soviet Power*. New Delhi: Vikas, 1982. 296 pp.

Harding, Harry. *Organizing China: The Problem of Bureaucracy, 1949–1976*. Stanford: Stanford University Press, 1981. 418 pp.

Hook, Brian, ed. *The Cambridge Encyclopedia of China*. New York: Cambridge University Press, 1982. 500 pp.

Huynh, Kim-Khanh. *Vietnamese Communism, 1925–1945*. Ithaca, N.Y.: Cornell University Press, 1982. 379 pp.

Institute of North Korean Studies. *The Red Dynasty*. Seoul, 1982. 151 pp.

Kapur, Harish. *The Awakening Giant: China's Ascension in World Politics*. Alphen aan den Rijn, Netherlands: Sijthoff and Noordhoff, 1981. 314 pp.

Kautsky, John H. *Moscow and the Communist Party of India: A Study in the Postwar Evolution of International Communist Strategy*. Westport, Conn.: Greenwood Press, 1982.

Kushnik, Hubert. *Afghanistan Through the Eyes of a Witness*. Moscow: Progress Publishers, 1982. 181 pp.

Lindsay, Michael. *The Influence of Marxist Leninist Ideology on the Chinese Party*. Conference on the History of the Republic of China, no. 27. Taipei, 1981. 28 pp.

Marr, David G. *Vietnamese Tradition on Trial, 1920–1945*. Berkeley: University of California Press, 1981. 468 pp.

Misra, K. P., ed. *Afghanistan in Crisis*. New Delhi: Vikas, 1981. 150 pp.

Nguyen Long. *After Saigon Fell: Daily Life Under the Vietnamese Communists*. With Harry H. Kendall. Berkeley: University of California, Institute of East Asian Studies, 1981. 164 pp.

Pye, Lucian W. *The Dynamics of Chinese Politics*. Cambridge, Mass.: Oegelschlager, Gunn & Hain, 1981. 307 pp.

_____. *Guerrilla Communism in Malaya: Its Social and Political Meaning*. Westport, Conn.: Greenwood Press, 1981. 369 pp.

Richer, Philippe. *L'Asie du Sud-est: Indépendances et communismes*. Paris: Nationale, 1981. 430 pp.

Romich, Manfred F. *Chinas Volkskommunen: Revolutionäres Erbe oder Aufbruch in eine kommunistische Zukunft*. Frankfurt/Main: R. G. Fischer, 1981. 190 pp.

Rosenberg, William G., and Marilyn B. Young. *Transforming Russia and China*. New York: Oxford University Press, 1982. 397 pp.

Segal, Gerald, ed. *The China Factor*. New York: Holmes and Meier, 1982. 210 pp.

Short, Philip. *The Dragon and the Bear: Inside China and Russia Today*. London: Hodder and Staughton, 1982. 519 pp.

Song Chol-min, ed. *Kimilsongchuui Taeui* [The outline of Kim Il-song–ism]. Pyongyang: Samhak-sa, 1982.

Steinberg, David Joel. *The Philippines: A Singular and a Plural Place*. Boulder, Colo.: Westview Press, 1982. 160 pp.

Stuart, Douglas T., and William T. Tow, eds. *China, The Soviet Union and the West*. Boulder, Colo.: Westview Press, 1981. 310 pp.

Suh, Dae-Sook. *Korean Communism, 1945–1980: A Reference Guide to the Political System*. Honolulu: University Press of Hawaii, 1981. 592 pp.

Sung Chul Yang. *Korea and Two Regimes: Kim Il Sung and Park Chung Hee*. Cambridge, Mass.: Schenkman Publishing Co., 1981. 438 pp.

Terrill, Ross. *Mao: A Biography*. New York: Harper & Row, Colophon Books, 1982. 481 pp.

Thion, Serge, and Ben Kiernan. *Khmers rouges! Matériaux pour l'histoire du communisme au Cambodge*. Paris: J. E. Hallier–Albin Michel, 1981. 396 pp.

Unger, Jonathan. *Education Under Mao: Class and Competition in Canton Schools, 1960–1980*. New York: Columbia University Press, 1982. 308 pp.

Waller, Derek J. *The Government and Politics of the People's Republic of China*. 3rd ed. New York: New York University Press, 1981. 228 pp.

Wilson, Dick. *The Long March, 1935: The Epic of Chinese Communism's Survival*. New York: Penguin, 1982. 228 pp.

World Anti-Communist League. *Bitter Lessons and a Solemn Mission: Responses by Chinese at Home and Abroad to Chinese Communist Peace Overtures*. Taipei: World Anti-Communist League, China Chapter, 1981. 75 pp.

EASTERN EUROPE

Adelman, Jonathan R. *Communist Armies in Politics*. Boulder, Colo.: Westview Press, 1982. 225 pp.

Ascherson, Neal. *The Polish August: The Self-Limiting Revolution*. New York and London: Allen Lane, 1981. 316 pp.

Böhme, Irene. *Die da drüben: Sieben Kapitel DDR*. West Berlin: Rotbuch Verlag, 1982. 125 pp.

Bromke, Adam. *Poland: The Last Decade*. Oakville, Ont.: Mosaic, 1981. 189 pp.

Bruns, Wilhelm. *Deutsch-deutsche Beziehungen: Prämissen—Probleme—Perspektiven*. Opladen, West Germany: Leske & Budrich, 1982. 167 pp.

Carter, April. *Democratic Reform in Yugoslavia: The Changing Role of the Party*. Princeton, N.J.: Princeton University Press, 1982. 288 pp.

Charpentier, Jean Marie. *Solidarnosc: Un An de luttes sociales en Pologne*. Paris: Montholon-Services, 1981. 160 pp.

Checinski, Michael. *Poland: Communism, Nationalism, Anti-Semitism*. New York: Karz-Cohl, 1982. 289 pp.

Dähn, Horst. *Konfrontation oder Cooperation: Das Verhältnis von Staat und Kirche in der SBZ/DDR, 1945–1980*. Cologne: Westdeutscher Verlag, 1982. 295 pp.

Davis, Norman. *God's Playground: A History of Poland*. New York: Clarendon Press, 1982. 2 vols.

Davisha, Karen, and Philip Hanson, eds. *Soviet–East European Dilemmas: Coercion, Competition, and Consent*. New York: Holmes and Meier, 1981. 226 pp.

Dedijer, Vladimir. *Novi prilozi za biograpfiju Josipa Broza Tita*. Zagreb: Mladost, 1980–1981. 2 vols.

Docheff, Ivan. *Half Century Struggle Against Communism for the Freedom of Bulgaria*. New York: Bulgarian National Front, 1982. 188 pp.

Documents on the Policy of the GDR (March 1982): Report by the Central Statistical Office of the GDR on the Fulfillment of the National Plan in the First Half of 1982. East Berlin: Panorama DDR, 1982. 39 pp.

Documents on the Policy of the GDR, no. 6, 1981, *Extracts from the Report to the Third Plenary Session of the SED Central Committee, 19 November 1981*. East Berlin: Panorama DDR, 1981. 13 pp.

Drachkovitch, Milorad M., ed. *East Central Europe: Yesterday–Today–Tomorrow*. Stanford: Hoover Institution Press, 1982. 417 pp.

Drewnowski, Jan. *Crisis in the East European Economy: The Spread of the Polish Disease*. London: Croom Helm, 1982.

Dunn, Dennis, ed. *Religion and Communist Society: Selected Papers from the Second World Congress for Soviet and East European Studies*. Berkeley, Calif.: Berkeley Slavic Specialties, 1982.

Eckhardt, Karl-Heinz. *Demokratie und Planung im Industriebetrieb der DDR: Theorie und Praxis*. Opladen, West Germany: Leske & Budrich, 1981. 279 pp.

Esprit, Paris. Special Number on Poland, March 1982.

Finn, Gerhard. *Politischer Strafvollzug in der DDR*. Cologne: Verlag Wissenschaft und Politik, 1981. 166 pp.

Fricke, Karl Wilhelm. *Die DDR-Staatssicherheit: Entwicklung, Strukturen, Aktionsfelder*. Cologne: Verlag Wissenschaft und Politik, 1982. 280 pp.

Giertych, Jedrzej. *In Defence of My Country*. London: The author, 1981. 748 pp.

Glässner, Gert-Joachim. *Sozialistische Systeme: Einführung in die Kommunismus und DDR-Forschung*. Opladen, West Germany: Westdeutscher Verlag, 1982. 315 pp.

Grube, Frank, and Gerhard Richter, eds. *Der Freiheitskampf der Polen: Geschichte, Dokumentation, Analyse*. Hamburg: Hoffman und Campe, 1981. 288 pp.

Gudorf, Odilo. *Sprache als Politik: Untersuchung zur öffentlichen Sprache und Kommunikationsstruktur in der DDR*. Cologne: Verlag Wissenschaft und Politik, 1981. 289 pp.

Heinrich, Wolfgang. *Das unverzichtbare Feindbild: Hasserziehung in der DDR*. Bonn: Howacht, 1981. 111 pp.

Henkys, Reinhard, ed. *Die evangelischen Kirchen in der DDR: Beiträge zu einer Bestandsaufnahme*. Munich: Kaiser, 1982. 500 pp.

History of the Party of Labour of Albania, 1966–1980 (chapters 7–9). 2d ed. Tirana: The "8 Nëntori" Publishing House, 1981. 327 pp.

Honecker, Erich. *From My Life*. New York: Pergamon Press, 1981. 515 pp.

_____. *Reden und Aufsätze*. Vol. 7. East Berlin: Dietz Verlag, 1982. 631 pp.

Hoxha, Enver. *The Anglo-American Threat to Albania: Memoirs of the National Liberation War*. Tirana: The "8 Nëntori" Publishing House, 1982. 446 pp.

_____. *The Titoites: Memoirs*. Tirana: The "8 Nëntori" Publishing House, 1982.

Jaeger, Manfred. *Kultur und Politik in der DDR: Ein historischer Abriss*. Cologne: Edition Deutschland Archiv im Verlag Wissenschaft und Politik, 1982. 204 pp.

Janos, Andrew C. *The Politics of Backwardness in Hungary, 1825–1945*. Princeton, N.J.: Princeton University Press, 1982.

Jaroslawski, Jan. *Die Intellektuellen und der Sozialismus*. Baden-Baden: Nomos Verlag, 1981.

Johnson, A. Ross. *Poland in Crisis*. Santa Monica, Calif.: Rand Corporation, 1982.

Johnson, A. Ross; Robert W. Dean; and Alexander Alexiev. *East European Military Establishments: The Warsaw Pact Northern Tier*. New York: Crane, Russak & Co., 1982. 200 pp.

Kanturkova, Eva. *Douze femmes à Prague*. Paris: Maspero, 1981. 267 pp.

Karpinski, Jakub. *Countdown: The Polish Upheavals of 1956, 1968, 1970, 1980 . . .* New York: Karz Publishers, 1982. 214 pp.

Kindersley, Richard, ed. *In Search of Eurocommunism*. New York: St. Martin's Press, 1981. 218 pp.

Koch, H., ed. *Zur Theorie der sozialistischen Kultur*. East Berlin: Dietz Verlag, 1982. 459 pp.

Kolkowicz, Roman, and Andrzej Korbonski, eds. *Soldiers, Peasants, and Bureaucrats: Civil-Military Relations in Communist and Modernizing Societies*. Boston: G. Allen & Unwin, 1982. 340 pp.

Kriwanek, Gerd. *Polen: Solidarität als Hoffnung*. Zurich: Orell Füssli, 1981. 200 pp.

Kwiatkowska-Viatteau, Alexandra. *Katyn, l'armée polonaise assassinée*. Brussels: Editions "Complex," 1982.

Leskovesek, Valentin. *Yugoslavia: A Bibliography*. New York: Studia Slovenica, 1974–1982. 4 vols.

Liber, George. *Polish Dissident Publications: An Annotated Bibliography*. New York: Praeger, 1982. 208 pp.

Lieser-Triebnigg, Erika. *Die DDR in der osteuropäischen Wirtschaftsintegration*. Cologne: Verlag Wissenschaft und Politik, 1982. 167 pp.

Luchterhandt, Otto. *Die Gegenwartslage der evangelischen Kirche in der DDR*. Tubingen: Mohr, 1982. 120 pp.

MacShane, D. *Solidarity: Poland's Independent Trade Union*. Nottingham, Eng.: Spokesman, 1981. 172 pp.

Mampel, Siegfried. *Die sozialistische Verfassung der Deutschen Demokratischen Republik: Text und Kommentar*. Frankfurt/Main: Metzner, 1982. 1364 pp.

Markov, Georgi. *Zadochni reportazhi za Bulgariya*. Zurich: Izdanie na Fond "Georgi Markov," 1979, 1981. 2 vols.

Maxwell, Robert, ed., *Todor Zhivkov; Statesman and Builder of New Bulgaria*. Oxford: Pergamon Press, 1982.

Michel, Patrick. *L'Eglise de Pologne et l'avenir de la nation*. Paris: Centurion, 1981. 193 pp.

Morawski, D. *Chrétienne Pologne*. Paris: France-Empire, 1981. 253 pp.

Myant, Martin. *Socialism and Democracy in Czechoslovakia, 1945–1948*. New York: Cambridge University Press, 1981. 302 pp.

Die nationale Front der DDR: Ihre Rolle und Funktion. Bonn: Forschungsinstitut Friedrich-Ebert-Stiftung, 1981. 41 pp.

Noll, Fritz. *Über Schwerter und Pflugschare: Der DDR-Friedensbewegung*. Neuss, West Germany: Plambeck & Co., 1982. 141 pp.

Nowak, Jan. *Courier from Warsaw*. Detroit: Wayne State University, 1982. 480 pp.

Offredo, Jean. *Lech Walesa, ou, l'été polonais*. Paris: CANA, 1981. 181 pp.

Okey, Robin. *Eastern Europe, 1740–1980: Feudalism to Communism*. Minneapolis: University of Minnesota Press, 1982. 264 pp.

Oschlies, Wolf. *Kinder der Solidarität*. Cologne: Bundesinstitut für Ostwissenschaftliche und Internationale Studien, 1982. 36 pp.

Pécsí, Kálmán. *The Future of Socialist Economic Integration*. Armonk, N.Y.: M. E. Sharpe, 1981. 189 pp.

Plevza, Viliam. *Slovakia in Socialist Czechoslovakia*. Prague: Orbis Press Agency, 1981. 220 pp.

Pol'sha' 1980. "Solidarnost'": God pervy. London: Overseas Publications Interchange, 1981. 239 pp.

Pomian, Krzysztof. *Pologne: Défi à l'impossible? De la révolte de Poznan à "Solidarité."* Paris: Editions Ouvrières, 1982. 235 pp.

Popov, Liubomir K. *Die Rechtsstellung des Ausländers in Bulgarien*. Baden-Baden: Nomos Verlag, 1981. 245 pp.

Potel, Jean-Yves. *Gdansk, la mémoire ouvrière, 1970–1980*. Paris: Maspero, 1982. 249 pp.

_____. *Strike Scenes in Poland*. New York: Praeger, 1982. 320 pp.

Problemy upravleniia v sotsialisticheskoi respublike Rumynii. Moscow: Nauka, 1981. 160 pp.

Pusylewitsch, Teresa. *Rechtsquellen zur gegenwärtigen Situation in Polen*. Kiel, West Germany: Institut für Recht, Politik und Gesellschaft der Sozialistischen Staaten der Universität Kiel, 1981. 218 pp.

Radio Free Europe–Radio Liberty. *Czechoslovak, Hungarian and Polish Attitudes Toward the Communist Party Leader and Toward the President of the United States: Effectiveness and Validation*. Munich, 1982. 17 leaves.

_____. Audience and Public Opinion Research Department *Czechoslovak, Hungarian and Polish Attitudes Toward "Serious Conflict" Between the United States and the Soviet Union*. Munich, 1981. 226 pp.

Raina, Peter K. *Independent Social Movements in Poland*. London: London School of Economics and Political Science, 1981. 632 pp.

Schaufele, William E. *Polish Paradox: Communism and National Renewal*. New York: Foreign Policy Association, 1981. 72 pp.

Shoup, Paul. *The East European and Soviet Data Handbook: Political, Social, and Developmental Indicators*. New York: Columbia University Press, 1981. 481 pp.

Slavov, Atanas. *The "Thaw" in Bulgarian Literature*. Boulder, Colo.: East European Monographs, 1981. 191 pp.

Spanger, Hans-Joachim. *Die SED und der Sozialdemokratismus: Ideologische Abgrenzung in der DDR*. Cologne: Verlag Wissenschaft und Politik, 1982. 255 pp.

Sozialistische Einheitspartei Deutschlands. *Direktive des X. Parteitages der SED zum Fünfjahrplan für die Entwicklung der Volkswirtschaft der DDR in den Jahren 1981 bis 1985*. East Berlin: Dietz Verlag, 1981. 45 pp.

_____. *Dritte Tagung der ZK der SED, 19./20. November 1981. Aus dem Bericht des Politbüros an die SED*. East Berlin: Dietz Verlag, 1982. 126 pp.

_____. *Zehnter Parteitage der SED im Palast der Republik in Berlin, 11–16, April 1981*. East Berlin: Dietz Verlag, 1982. 2 vols.

Staar, Richard F. *Communist Regimes in Eastern Europe*. 4th ed. Stanford: Hoover Institution Press, 1982. 375 pp.

Stanković, Slobodan. *The End of the Tito Era: Yugoslavia's Dilemmas*. Stanford: Hoover Institution Press, 1981. 154 pp.

Starrels, John. *East Germany: Marxist Mission in Africa*. Washington, D.C.: Heritage Foundation, 1981. 54 pp.

The Strike in Gdansk, August 14–31, 1980. New Haven, Conn.: Don't Hold Back, 1981. 50 pp.

Suckut, Siegfried. *Die Betriebsrätebewegung in der sowjetische besetzten Zone Deutschlands, 1945–1948*. Frankfurt/Main: Haag & Herchen, 1982. 764 pp.

Summerscale, Peter. *The East European Predicament*. New York: St. Martin's Press (for the Royal Institute of International Affairs), 1982. 147 pp.

Szymanski, Leszek. *Candle for Poland: 469 Days of Solidarity*. San Bernadino, Calif.: Borgo Press, 1982. 128 pp.

Treffen des Generalsekretärs der ZK des SED und Vorsitzenden des Staatsrates der DDR, Erich Honecker, mit dem Bundeskanzler der BRD, Helmut Schmidt, in der DDR, 11–13. Dezember 1981. East Berlin: Panorama DDR, 1981. 62 pp.

U.S. Central Intelligence Agency. National Foreign Assessment Center. *Directory of Officials of the Hungarian People's Republic*. Washington, D.C., 1982. 145 pp.

U.S. Congress. House. Committee on the Budget. *The United States and Poland: A Report on the Current Situation in Poland After the Declaration of Martial Law*. Washington, D.C., April 1982, 24 pp.

Vrsau, E. *La Jugoslavia economica dopo Tito: Regime dell'autogestione, sistema dei rapporti economici con l'estero, accordi economici Jugoslavia, Italia, CEE*. Trieste: Edizioni Rivista "Mladika," 1981. 223 pp.

Weber, Hermann. *DDR: Grundriss der Geschichte, 1945–1981*. Hannover: Fackelträger, 1982. 242 pp.

_____. ed. *Parteiensystem zwischen Demokratie und Volksdemokratie: Dokumente und Materialien zum Funktionswandel der Parteien in der SBZ/DDR, 1945–1950*. Cologne: Verlag Wissenschaft und Politik, 1982. 600 pp.

Weschler, Lawrence. *Solidarity: Poland in the Season of Its Passion*. New York: Simon & Schuster, 1982. 221 pp.

Who's Who, What's What in Solidarność: Leksykon Zwiakowy. Gdansk: BIPS, 1981. 112 pp.

Zagajewski, Adam. *Polen, Staat in Schatten des Sowjetunion*. Reinbeck bei Hamburg, West Germany: Rowohlt, 1981. 207 pp.

Zhivkov, Todor. *Report of the Central Committee of the Bulgarian Communist Party to the Twelfth Congress and the Forthcoming Tasks of the Party, March 31, 1981*. Sofia: Sofia Press, 1981. 124 pp.

Zoubed, Jan. *Poland: The Current Crisis and Outlook*. Brussels: East-West (Research & Advisory), 1981. 153 pp.

SOVIET UNION

Adomeit, Hannes. *Soviet Risk-Taking and Crisis Behavior*. Winchester, Mass.: Allen & Unwin, 1982. 377 pp.

Amann, Ronald, and Julian Cooper, eds. *Industrial Innovation in the Soviet Union*. New Haven, Conn.: Yale University Press, 1982. 526 pp.

Barry, Donald D., and Carol Barner-Barry. *Contemporary Soviet Politics: An Introduction*. 2d ed. Englewood Cliffs, N.J.: Prentice-Hall, 1982. 420 pp.

Bernshtam, M. S., ed. *Nezavisimoe rabochee dvizhenie v 1918 godu: Dokumenty i materialy*. Paris: YMCA Press, 1981. 329 pp.

Besançon, Alain. *The Rise of Gulag: Intellectual Origins of Leninism*. New York: Continuum, 1981. 329 pp.

Bialer, Seweryn, and Thane Gustafson. *Russia at the Crossroads: The 26th Congress of the CPSU*. Winchester, Mass.: Allen & Unwin, 1982. 223 pp.

Brown, Archie, et al., eds. *The Cambridge Encyclopedia of Russia and the Soviet Union*. New York: Cambridge University Press, 1982. 492 pp.

Chernenko, Konstantin V. *The Development of the Working Class in Socialist Society*. Moscow: Nauka, 1982. 526 pp.

Dawisha, Adeed, and Karen Dawisha, eds. *The Soviet Union in the Middle East*. London: Heinemann (for the Royal Institute of International Affairs), 1982. 172 pp.

De Boer, S. P.; E. J. Driessen; and H. L. Verhaar; eds. *Biographical Dictionary of Dissidents in the Soviet Union, 1956–1975*. Amsterdam: University of Amsterdam, Institute of East European Studies, 1982. 680 pp.

Dziak, John J. *Soviet Perceptions of Military Power: The Interaction of Theory and Practice*. New York: National Strategy Information Center, 1981. 72 pp.

Frankel, E. R. *"Novy mir": A Case Study in the Politics of Literature, 1952–1958*. New York: Cambridge University Press, 1981. 206 pp.

Gelman, Harry. *The Politburo's Management of Its American Problem*. Prepared for the Office of the Secretary of Defense, Director of Net Assessment. Santa Monica, Calif.: Rand Corporation, 1981. 70 pp.

Grieg, Ian. *They Mean What They Say: A Compilation of Soviet Statements on Ideology, Foreign Policy and the Use of Military Force*. London: Foreign Affairs Research Institute, 1981. 118 pp.

Gustafson, Thane. *Reform in Soviet Politics: Lessons of Recent Policies on Land and Water*. New York: Cambridge University Press, 1981. 218 pp.

Hammond, Thomas T. *Witness to the Origins of the Cold War*. Seattle: University of Washington Press, 1982. 318 pp.

Heller, Michel. *L'utopie au pouvoir: Histoire de l'U.R.S.S. de 1917 à nos jours*. Paris: Calmann-Lévy, 1982. 658 pp.

Horn, Robert C. *Soviet-Indian Relations: Issues and Influence*. New York: Praeger, 1982. 231 pp.

Jain, R. K. *The USSR and Japan, 1945–1980*. Brighton, Eng.: Harvester, 1981. 397 pp.

Kanet, Roger E., ed. *Soviet Foreign Policy in the 1980's*. New York: Praeger, 1982. 364 pp.

Katz, Mark N. *The Third World in Soviet Military Thought*. Baltimore, Md.: Johns Hopkins University Press, 1982. 188 pp.

Kennan, George F. *The Nuclear Delusion: Soviet-American Relations in the Atomic Age*. New York: Pantheon, 1982. 208 pp.

Khrushchev, Nikita S. *Vospominiia: Izbrannye otryvki*. New York: Chalidze Publications, 1979–1981. 2 vols.

Kopylova, L. P., ed. *KPSS o profusoiuzakh* [sostavitel' sbornika i avtor vstupitel'noi stat'i L. P. Kopylova]. Moscow: Profizdat, 1982. 494 pp.

KPSS o vooruzhennykh silakh Sovetskogo Soiuza: Dokumenty, 1917–1981. Moscow: Voen. izd-vo, 1981. 621 pp.

Kvasha, A. IA. *Demograficheskaia politika v SSSR*. Moscow: Finansy i statistika, 1981. 198 pp.

Lazaris, Vladimir. *Dissidenty i evrei-kto porval zheleznyi zanaves?* Tel Aviv: Effect, 1981. 179 pp.

Leites, Nathan. *Soviet Style in War*. New York: Crane, Russak & Co., 1982. 400 pp.

Lenczowski, John. *Soviet Perceptions of U.S. Foreign Policy*. Ithaca, N.Y.: Cornell University Press, 1982. 312 pp.

Lendvai, P. *The Bureaucracy of Truth: How Communist Governments Manage the News*. Boulder, Colo.: Westview Press, 1981. 285 pp.

Lenin, V. I. *The CPSU on the Party Statutes*. Moscow: Politizdat and Progress Publishers, 1981. 181 pp.

Liska, George. *Russia and the Road to Appeasement: Cycles of East-West Conflict in War and Peace*. Baltimore, Md.: Johns Hopkins University Press, 1982. 261 pp.

Litvinova, G. I. *Pravo i demograficheskie protsessy v SSR*. Moscow: Nauka, 1981. 198 pp.

Löwenhardt, John. *Decision Making in Soviet Politics*. London: Macmillan, 1981. 238 pp.

_____. *Soviet Politburo*. New York: St. Martin's Press, 1982. 151 pp.

Mitchell, R. Judson. *Ideology of a Superpower: Contemporary Soviet Doctrine on International Relations*. Stanford: Hoover Institution Press, 1982. 159 pp.

Pipes, Richard. *U.S. Soviet Relations in the Era of Détente*. Boulder, Colo.: Westview Press, 1981. 227 pp.

Pond, Elizabeth. *From the Yaroslavsky Station: Russia Perceived*. New York: Universe Books, 1981. 296 pp.

Ponomarev, Boris N., ed. *The Constitution of the USSR: A Political-Legal Commentary*. Moscow: Politizdat, 1982. 398 pp.

Problemy istorii sovetskogo krest'ianstva: Sbornik statei. Adademiia nauk SSSR, Institut istorii SSSR. Moscow: Nauka, 1981. 348 pp.

Robinson, Logan. *An American in Leningrad*. New York: W. W. Norton, 1982. 320 pp.

Rockett, Rocky L. *Ethnic Nationalities in the Soviet Union: Sociological Perspectives on a Historical Problem*. New York: Praeger, 1981. 171 pp.

Rosenberg, D., comp. *Swords into Plowshares: Soviet Initiatives for Peace, Security and Disarmament, 1917–1982*. New York: National Council of Soviet-American Friendship. 1982. 35 pp.

Rubinstein, Alvin Z. *Soviet Policy Toward Turkey, Iran, and Afghanistan*. New York: Praeger, 1982. 200 pp.

Ruble, Blair A. *Soviet Trade Unions: Their Development in the 1970s*. New York: Cambridge University Press, 1981. 432 pp.

Simis, Konstantine *USSR: The Corrupt Society*. New York: Simon & Schuster, 1982. 316 pp.

Somerville, John, ed. *Soviet Marxism and Nuclear War: An International Debate from the Proceedings of the Special Colloquium of the XVth World Congress of Philosophy*. Westport, Conn.: Greenwood Press, 1981. 166 pp.

Spechler, Dina R. *Permitted Dissent in the USSR: "Novy mir" and the Soviet Regime*. New York: Praeger, 1982. 293 pp.

Sullivan, David S. *The Bitter Fruit of SALT: A Record of Soviet Duplicity*. Houston: Texas Policy Institute, 1982. 105 pp.

Tikhonov, Nikolai A. *Osnovnye napravleniia ekonomicheskogo i sotsial'nogo razvitiia SSSR na 1981–1985 gody i na period do 1990 goda: Doklad XXVI s'ezdu KPSS 27 fevralia 1981 goda*. Moscow: Izd-vo polit. lit-ry, 1981. 46 pp.

Whiting, A. S. *Siberian Development and East Asia: Threat or Promise?* Stanford: Stanford University Press, 1981. 276 pp.

Zeldes, I. *The Problems of Crime in the USSR*. Springfield, Ill: C. C. Thomas, 1981. 140 pp.

Zinoviev, A. *My i Zapad: Stat'i interv'iu, vystupleniia, 1979–1980 gg*. Lausanne: Editions l'Age d'Homme, 1981. 154 pp.

WESTERN EUROPE

Ahola, David John. *Finnish-Americans and International Communism: A Study of Finnish-American Communism from Bolshevization to the Demise of the Third International*. Washington, D.C.: University Press of America, 1981. 346 pp.

Almanacco PCI. Vol. 1982 and Supplemento all'Almanacco 1982: Voci della nostra storia. Rome: Partido Comunista Italiano, 1982. 79 pp. and 2 records.

Amyot, C. Grant. *The Italian Communist Party: The Crisis of the Popular Front Strategy*. New York: St. Martin's Press, 1981. 252 pp.

Ardagh, John. *France in the 1980's*. London: Secker & Warburg and Penguin, 1982. 672 pp.

Arrabal, Fernando. *Carta a los comunistas españoles y otras cartas*. Murcia: Editorial Godoy, 1981. 232 pp.

Atlas eleitoral; Compilação dos resultados eleitorais dos quatro maiores partidos (CDS, PCP, PS e PSD) em todas as eleições presidenciais em 1976 e 1980. Lisbon: Edições Progresso Social e Democracia, 1981. 222 pp.

Azcárate, Manuel. *Crisis del Eurocomunismo*. Barcelona: Argos Vergara, 1982. 345 pp.

Baker, Blake. *The Far Left: An Exposé of the Extreme Left in Britain*. London: Weidenfeld and Nicolson, 1981. 182 pp.

Berlinguer, Enrico. *After Poland*. London: Spokesman, 1982. 114 pp.

Botti, Alfonso. *Religione, questione catolica e DC nella politica comunista (1944–45)*. Rimini: Maggioli, 1981. 120 pp.

Bourderon, Roger, et al. *Le PFC: etapes et problèmes, 1920–1972*. Paris: Editiones Sociales, 1982. 639 pp.

Brown, Bernard E. *Socialism of a Different Kind: Reshaping the Left in France*. Westport, Conn.: Greenwood Press, 1982. 201 pp.

Buffin, Didier, and Dominique Gerbaud. *Les Communistes*. Paris: Albin Michel, 1981. 283 pp.

Burles, Jean; Roger Martelli; and Serge Wolikow. *Les Communistes et leur stratégie*. Paris: Editions Sociales, 1981. 254 pp.

Butler, David. *European Elections and British Politics*. New York: Longman, 1981. 193 pp.

Critchley, Julian. *The North Atlantic Alliance and the Soviet Union in the 1980s*. London: Macmillan, 1982. 210 pp.

Cunhal, Alvaro. *Avanço e derrota do plano subversivo "AD" 1980*. Lisbon: Avante, 1982. 2 vols.

Current Left and Labour Press, 1978–1981: General Register, International Association of Labour History Institutions. Bochum, West Germany: Institut zur Geschichte der Arbeiterbewegung, 1981. 347 pp.

Davidson, Alastair. *The Theory and Practice of Italian Communism*. London: Merlin Press, 1982.

Diener, Ingolf. *Ils vivent autrement: L'Allemagne alternative*. Paris: Editions Stock, 1982. 299 pp.

Duhamel, Alain. *La République de M. Mitterrand*. Paris: Grasset, 1982. 257 pp.

Esche, Matthias. *Die Kommunistische Partei Griechenlands: Ein Beitrag zur Politik der KKK vom Beginn der Resistanz bis zum Ende des Bürgerkriegs*. Munich: R. Oldenbourg Verlag, 1982. 397 pp.

Fontaine, André. *Un Seul Lit pour deux rêves: Histoire de la "détente," 1962–1981*. Paris: Fayard, 1981. 538 pp.

France. Congrès du Parti Communiste Français (24th, 1982). *Cahiers du communism: 24ᵉ Congrès du Parti communiste français, février 1982*. Paris, 1982. 495 pp.

Galleni, Mauro. *Rapporto sul terrorismo*. Rome: Rizzoli, 1981. 552 pp.

Ghirelli, Antonio. *L'effetto Craxi*. Milan: Rizzole Editore, 1982. 232 pp.

Giovagnoli, Giorgio. *Storia del partito comunista nel riminese, 1921–1940: Origini, lotte e iniziative politiche*. Rimini: Maggioli, 1981. 406 pp.

Goldring, Maurice, and Yvonne Quiles. *Sous le marteau, la plume: La Presse communiste en crise*. Paris: Megrelis, 1982. 378 pp.

Harmsen, Ger. *Nederlands kommunisme: Gebundelde opstellen*. Nijmegen: Socialistiese Uitgeverij Nijmegen, 1982. 388 pp.

Hincker, François. *Le Parti communiste au carrefour: Essai sur quinze ans de son histoire, 1965–1981*. Paris: Albin Michel, 1981. 262 pp.

Holmberg, Hakan. *Folkmakt, folkfront, folkdemokrati: De svenska kommunisterna och demokratifragan, 1943–1977*. Uppsala: Almqvist & Wiksell, 1982.

Ilardi, Massimo, and Aris Accornero, eds. *Il Partito Comunista Italiano: Struttura e storia dell'organizzazione, 1921–1979*. Milan: Feltrinelli Editore, 1982. 1212 pp.

Jupp, James. *The Radical Left in Britain, 1931–1941*. London: Frank Cass & Co., 1982. 261 pp.

Kekkonen, Urho. *Gedanken eines Präsidenten: Finnlands Standort in der Welt*. Dusseldorf: Econ Verlag, 1981. 142 pp.

Kommunisticheskaia partiia Finliandii: Dokumenty i materialy, 1970–1981. Moscow: Politizdat, 1982. 229 pp.

Lupi, Giancarlo. *Il crollo della grande coalizione: La strategia delle élites die partiti, 1976–1979*. Milan: Sugarco, 1982. 133 pp.

Marengo, F. D. *Rules of the Italian Political Game*. London: Gower, 1981. 134 pp.

Margiocco, Mario. *Stati Uniti e PCI, 1943–1980*. Rome: Laterza, 1981. 327 pp.

Markovits, Andrei Steven, ed. *Political Economy of West Germany: Modell Deutschland*. New York: Praeger, 1982. 238 pp.

Meissner, Boris. *Weltmacht Sowjetunion: Die Doppelstrategie von Entspannung und Revolution*. Munich: Bayerische Landeszentrale für politische Bildungsarbeit, 1982. 52 pp.

Meliá, Josep. *Asi cayo Adolfo Súarez*. Barcelona: Editorial Planeta, 1981. 201 pp.

Morán, Gregorio. *Los españoles que dejaron de serlo: Euskadi, 1937–1981*. Barcelona: Editorial Planeta, 1982.

Mujal-León, Eusebio. *Communism and Political Change in Spain*. Bloomington: Indiana University Press, 1982.

Northcutt, Wayne. *The French Socialist and Communist Party Under the Fifth Republic, 1958–1981: From Opposition to Power*. New York: Irvington Publishers, 1982.

Northedge, F. S. *Britain and Soviet Communism: The Impact of a Revolution*. London: Macmillan, 1982. 280 pp.

Nugent, Neill. *The Left in France*. New York: St. Martin's Press, 1982. 275 pp.

Pecorari, Paoilo. *Giuseppe Toniolo e il socialismo*. Bologna: Pàtron Editore, 1981. 322 pp.

Pickles, Dorothy. *Problems of Contemporary French Politics*. London: Methuen, 1982. 160 pp.

Pieretti, A. *Il marxismo italiano degli anni settanta: Bilancio di un decennio*. Perugia: Perugia University, 1981. 239 pp.

Reinares-Nestares, Fernando, comp. *Terrorismo y sociedad democrática*. Madrid: Akal, 1982. 185 pp.

Ross, George. *Workers and Communists: From Popular Front to Eurocommunism*. Berkeley: University of California Press, 1982. 357 pp.

Ruscoe, James. *On the Threshold of Government: The Italian Communist Party, 1976–1980*. New York: St. Martin's Press, 1982. 305 pp.

Sassoon, Don. *The Strategy of the Italian Communist Party: From the Resistance to the Historic Compromise*. New York: St. Martin's Press, 1981. 259 pp.

Schain, Martin. *French Communism and Local Power: Urban Politics and Political Change*. New York: St. Martin's Press, 1982.

Schuster, Friedmann. *Alternativ sein, Kommunist sein: Ansichten jünger DKP-Mitglieder*. Frankfurt/Main: Marxistische Blätter, 1981. 108 pp.

Shaffer, Harry G. *Women in the Two Germanies: A Comparative Study of a Socialist and Non-socialist Society*. London: Pergamon, 1981. 235 pp.

Tartakowsky, Danielle. *Une Histoire du P.C.F* Paris: Editions des Presses Universitaires, 1982. 126 pp.

Timmermann, Heinz. *Der Konflikt zwischen den italienischen und den sowjetischen Kommunisten: Anlass, Hintergrund und Perspektiven*. Cologne: Bundesinstitut für Ostwissenschaftliche und Internationale Studien, 1982. 46 pp.

Vega, Pedro, and Peru Erroteta. *Los herejes del PCE*. Barcelona: Editorial Planeta, 1982. 335 pp.

Vilmar, Fritz, et al. *Was heisst hier kommunistische Unterwanderung? Eine notwendige Analyse, und wie die Linke darauf reagiert*. Frankfurt/Main: Ullstein, 1981. 206 pp.

Whetten, Lawrence L. *New International Communism: The Foreign and Defense Policies of the Latin European Political Parties*. Lexington, Mass.: Lexington Books, 1982. 262 pp.

Willis, F. Roy. *The French Paradox: Understanding Contemporary France*. Stanford: Hoover Institution Press, 1982. 151 pp.

Index of Biographies

Index of Names

Index of Subjects

Discussions that can be readily located under the subheadings within each profile are not indexed here. A reader interested in Soviet foreign relations, for example, should first consult the "Foreign Affairs" section of the USSR profile. Listed here under "USSR, foreign relations" is information on this subject that occurs in other profiles.